THE ECONOMICS OF STRATEGY

David Besanko / *Northwestern University*

David Dranove / *Northwestern University*

Mark Shanley / *Northwestern University*

JOHN WILEY & SONS, INC.
NEW YORK / CHICHESTER / BRISBANE / TORONTO / SINGAPORE

Dedicated to our children for their energy and inspiration, and to our wives Maureen, Debbie, and Kathleen, for their love and support.

ACQUISITIONS EDITOR   Whitney Blake
MARKETING MANAGER   Leslie Hines
SENIOR PRODUCTION EDITOR   Jeanine Furino
COVER AND TEXT DESIGNER   Karin Gerdes Kincheloe
ASSISTANT MANUFACTURING MANAGER   Mark Cirillo
ASSISTANT EDITOR   Ellen Ford
DEVELOPMENTAL EDITOR   Gerald Lombardi
PHOTO ASSOCIATE   Michelle Orlans
ILLUSTRATION COORDINATOR   Gene Aiello, Jr.

Cover Photo: Giraudon/Art Resource

Fig. 17.2a and b: Courtesy AT&T Archives.

This book was set in 10/12 Janson Text by General Graphic Services and printed and bound by Courier Companies. The cover was printed by Phoenix Color.

ISBN 0-471-59849-6

Printed in the United States of America

10 9 8

PREFACE

In the preface to his classic work, *Competitive Strategy*, Michael Porter argued that the field of business strategy lacked an analytical base and contained few generalizable or robust insights. He also noted that economists, whose work on industries and competition might serve as the basis for the development of such insights, were by and large insensitive to the needs of practicing managers. Porter's book provides an important illustration of how economic reasoning can inform and develop useful insights for practicing managers, particularly with regard to strategies for dealing with a firm's external environment. Since the publication of Porter's work researchers in economics and strategic management have made significant strides in developing an understanding of both the external market environment of firms and their internal organization. The objective of this book is to organize this learning in a way that is accessible to MBA students, advanced undergraduate students, students in executive programs, and practicing managers. The book adopts a comprehensive economic point of view, based on our belief that insights from economics can provide a coherent basis for the formulation and evaluation of the external and internal strategies of the firm. However, readers of this book need not have taken a course in microeconomics in order to understand and benefit from its contents. The basic economics required of the reader is developed in an Economics Primer, and we have attempted to illustrate key propositions and arguments with examples involving real companies and industries.

This book represents the results of a partnership that developed four years ago when each of us joined the Department of Management and Strategy of the J.L. Kellogg Graduate School of Management at Northwestern University. The department then offered and continues to offer a first-year, Fall quarter course titled the Management of Organizations. For years the course had been taught as a traditional case-based business policy course that emphasized the integration of the functional areas of business (marketing, finance, production, and so forth) and the development of a "general management perspective." Though once very popular and skillfully taught, by 1991 the course had fallen on hard times, and it had become nearly impossible for discipline-trained faculty members to teach.

The three of us were given the responsibility to redesign this course. The challenges we faced were substantial. The school's policy was (and still is) not to allow students to waive from this course. While many students who come to Kellogg have undergraduate training in business and economics, many do not. In addition, in the Kellogg curriculum, students take this course before taking courses in microeconomics, finance, and marketing. Finally, once the Winter quarter begins, first-year students at Kellogg who seek internships with consulting firms begin the process of going through case interviews with the consulting firms, so they need to learn material in the Fall quarter that will help them get up to speed and perform well in these interviews.

As we looked at the Kellogg curriculum, it seemed natural that the course we were asked to redesign should attempt to give students a solid foundation in the tools and concepts of strategic analysis. Given our research and teaching backgrounds in applied economics and strategic management, we believed that in order for the course to be teachable, it would need to have a coherent intellectual core drawing from work in industrial economics, transactions cost economics, economics of organization, and the modern strategy literature. We also felt that the course should have a strong managerial, empirical, and historical perspective. Unfortunately, as we looked around we were unable to find a satisfying textbook to go along with the teaching perspective we were developing for the course. Most of the available standard texts in strategic management lacked disciplinary grounding, and few contained discussions of the new knowledge generated in the 1980s and 1990s by researchers in economics and strategy (e.g., few had discussions of transactions cost economics or of the resource-based view of the firm). Moreover, most of these books were targeted at more general audiences than the students one finds at a business school such as Kellogg. Discussions with colleagues around the country led us to conclude that we were not the only ones struggling to find an appropriate text for teaching business strategy. Indeed the choice of a text for the core strategy course appears to be problematic at many business schools. We concluded that there was a void in the market, and we wrote this book to fill that void.

Organization of the Book

This book is organized in four parts. Part One focuses on the boundaries of the firm. Major topics include the economics of the make-versus-buy decision (vertical boundaries), the transactions costs of market exchange, economies of scale and scope, and diversification. Part Two covers competitive strategy from the perspective of industrial organization (IO) economies. It includes "traditional IO" topics such as market structure and "modern IO" topics such as dynamic pricing rivalry. It also contains a discussion of commitment, a topic which has received much attention in both the economics and strategy literatures in recent years. Part Three of the book covers strategic positioning and dynamics. The chapters in this section provide an economic foundation for understanding what competitive advantage is, how it might be diagnosed, the conditions under which it might be sustained, and how it might be acquired in the first place. This portion of the book draws from modern literature in both economics and strategy. For example, Chapter 14 in this section contains an extensive discussion of the resource-based view of the firm. Part Four covers topics associated with internal organization, including the economics of agency relationships, the economics of organizational design, and politics, power, and culture. A key innovation in this section of the book is the attempt to integrate insights from economics with those from organization theory.

The book is liberally interspersed with real world examples that bring the economic models to life. Every chapter has at least three "example boxes" that discuss a wide variety of organizations in detail. The business world is ever changing, and by the time this book hits the market, many of our references to organizations and individuals will be obsolete. It is our hope that the lessons learned from them will endure.

We believe that this book can either be used as a text in a core strategy course or in a business economics course that focuses on the economics of industry and the economics of the firm. For a strategy or strategic management course for MBA students, we recommend use of the chapters in Parts One, Three, and Four. In our 10 week Fall quarter strategy course for first-year MBA students at Kellogg, we typically assign the following chapters:

Chapter 1   The Evolution of the Modern Firm

Chapter 2   The Vertical Boundaries of the Firm

Chapter 3   The Transactions Costs of Market Exchange

Chapter 4   Organizing the Vertical Chain: The Economics of Vertical Integration

Chapter 5   The Horizontal Boundaries of the Firm: Economies of Scale and Scope

Chapter 7   Industry Analysis

Chapter 12   Strategic Positioning for Competitive Advantage

Chapter 13   Analyzing Cost and Differentiation Advantage

Chapter 14   Sustaining Competitive Advantage

Chapter 17   Strategy and Structure

Chapter 19   The Role of the General Manager

We exclude Chapter 6 on diversification in teaching our course because that topic is covered in depth in a later course. If diversification is covered in a basic strategy course, then that chapter should be included in the above list. If we had an entire semester for our strategy course, we would add Chapters 8 (Market Structure and Competition), Chapter 15 (Origins of Competitive Advantage: Innovation, Evolution, and the Environment), Chapter 16 (Incentives and Agency), and Chapter 18 (Power and Culture).

Our placement of the boundaries of the firm chapters before the strategy chapters (7 and 12-15) may strike some as atypical. However, it is not essential that the instructors follow this ordering. As long as students understand the material in the Economics Primer and the material on economies of scale and scope in Chapter 5, the strategy chapters (12-15) can be taught before the chapters on the boundaries of the firm (2-4 and 6).

The set of chapters 9-11 relating to commitment, dynamic competition, and entry/exit are the ones that are most closely tied to modern industrial organization economics and are thus the most "game theoretic" of the chapters in the book (though the introduction to game theory in the primer coupled with material in Chapter 8 should be sufficient for students to understand this material.) This set of chapters is the most demanding one for students with weaker economic backgrounds. Because students in our basic strategy course at Kellogg have not yet taken economics, we do not cover these chapters. The material in Chapters 12 and beyond does not depend on the material in the Chapters 9-11, so these chapters can be easily skipped without any loss in continuity.

The book can also be used in a strategy or managerial economics course that emphasizes competitive strategy and modern industrial organization. For a one-quarter, we recommend use of these chapters:

Chapter 5   The Horizontal Boundaries of the Firm
Chapter 7   Industry Analysis
Chapter 8   Market Structure and Competition
Chapter 9   Strategic Commitment and Competition
Chapter 10   The Dynamics of Pricing Rivalry
Chapter 11   Entry and Exit
Chapter 12   Strategic Positioning for Competitive Advantage
Chapter 13   Analyzing Cost and Differentiation Advantage
Chapter 14   Sustaining Competitive Advantage
Chapter 15   The Origins of Competitive Advantage: Innovation, Evolution, and the Environment

For a one-semester course, one could add Chapter 6 to the above list and supplement the material from all the chapters with advanced readings on competitive strategy, industrial organization, and game theory.

Acknowledgments

We owe debts of gratitude to many individuals. We want to thank Jim Keefe for encouraging us to embark on this project. We are especially grateful to Whitney Blake of Wiley for the substantial work she did in developing this book. Among other things she arranged for the copy editing, found reviewers, and coordinated the marketing of the book. In addition, besides sustaining our enthusiasm for this undertaking, she was unfailingly helpful in dealing with the questions and concerns that came up during the writing of this book. We want to thank Frederick Courtright for the work that he did in securing copyright permissions for the various figures, tables, and quotations taken from other sources and we want to thank Jeanine Furino of Wiley for so ably keeping the production of this book on track. We are deeply grateful to Gerald Lombardi who painstakingly copyedited the initial drafts of each chapter. He had excellent suggestions for enhancing the readability and teachability of the book, and his careful editing clarified our prose and sharpened the exposition of difficult ideas.

The book benefited from classroom testing by an number of our colleagues and friends at Kellogg and elsewhere. In this regard, we want especially to thank Rebecca

Henderson at the Sloan School of MIT, Rob Gertner of the Graduate School of Business of the University of Chicago, and our colleague Jim Dana at Kellogg. Rebecca and Rob provided excellent comments about how to position and elaborate on topics throughout the book. Jim also provided outstanding and extremely useful feedback on the content of the book and in addition, called our attention to many typographical errors and silly mistakes that we had failed to catch during our copyediting. The book has also benefited from discussions with our colleagues at the Kellogg School including Daniel Spulber, Kathryn Spier, Kate Rockett, Pierre Regibeau, Margaret Peteraf, Ed Zajac, and Ranjay Gulati. We especially want to thank Steve Postrel, whose insights about positioning and dynamics greatly influenced the ultimate content of Chapters 12, 13, and 14. Considerable gratitude also goes to Dean Donald Jacobs and to Associate Dean Mark Satterthwaite of the Kellogg School for giving us the opportunity to develop Kellogg's basic strategy course and for the enthusiasm and support they showed for us in writing in this book.

We are also grateful for the comments we received from those who reviewed the book. Their advice on which topics to include, which to emphasize and how best to order the topics has clearly strengthened the book. Besides Rebecca Henderson and Rob Gertner, thanks go to Gary Bolton, Glen Carroll, Kalyan Chatterjee, Herman Daems, Carl Enomoto, Trey Fleisher, Charles Gray, William Gunther, Bruce Jaffee, Tom Lyons, Ashish Lall, Rick Miller, Darwin Neher, Charles Snow, Pablo Spiller, and Mark Zupan.

A number of Kellogg Masters of Management students provided valuable assistance for specific parts of the book. We want to thank John Aeillo for proofreading and copyediting Chapters 1-8. William Furniss also proofread many chapters for us and also provided useful substantive comments on many chapters. Ana Dutra helped research and write Example 6.2 in Chapter 6 on the merger between Continental Bank and Bank of America. Susan Ivelich wrote the section of Chapter 7 on the photocopier industry. Diane Kityama, Jon Passman, Craig Safir, Todd Reichman, and Philip Yau contributed material for Example 10.3 in Chapter 10 on the cigarette industry. Joseph Baumann helped research and write Example 16.3 in Chapter 16 on the Illinois Department of Children and Family Services. Michael Lounsbury helped research and write Example 17.6 in Chapter 17 on Samsung.

Finally, we want to thank all of the Kellogg students during the 1993-94 and 1994-95 academic years who took Management and Strategy D31 (Management of Organizations) or Managerial Economics D41 (Competitive Strategy) with one of us or with Jim Dana and who thus read the early drafts of this book. Their criticisms, comments, and suggestions have helped to improve the book's teachability. We are especially grateful for the numerous real world examples that our students suggested as illustrations of conceptual points throughout the book. We also appreciate the tolerance and good cheer that our students showed when we asked them to read some fairly rough early drafts of this manuscript. The origin of this book lay in our desire to develop a challenging, principle-based strategy course for students at Kellogg. We are pleased to say that our students have had a significant impact on the final product.

David Besanko
David Dranove
Mark Shanley

Evanston, Illinois   *August 1995*

CONTENTS

PART FOUR: INTERNAL ORGANIZATION

INTRODUCTION: STRATEGY AND ECONOMICS

WHY STUDY STRATEGY? ◆ ◆ ◆ ◆ ◆

To answer this question, we first have to understand what strategy is. Consider how three leading contributors to the field define the concept of strategy:

> . . . the determination of the basic long-term goals and objectives of an enterprise, and the adoption of courses of action and the allocation of resources necessary for carrying out these goals.—Alfred Chandler.[1]

> . . . the pattern of objectives, purposes or goals, and the major policies and plans for achieving these goals, stated in such a way as to define what business the company is in or should be in and the kind of company it is or should be.—Kenneth Andrews.[2]

> . . . what determines the framework of a firm's business activities and provides guide-lines for coordinating activities so that the firm can cope with and influence the changing environment. Strategy articulates the firm's preferred environment and the type of organization it is striving to become.—Hiroyuki Itami.[3]

These definitions have much in common. Phrases such as "long-term goals" and "major policies" suggest that strategy has to do with the "big" decisions a business organization faces, the decisions that ultimately determine its success or failure.

---

[1]Chandler, A, *Strategy and Structure: Chapters in the History of the American Industrial Enterprise*, Cambridge, MA: MIT Press, 1962, p. 13.

[2]Andrews, K., *The Concept of Corporate Strategy*, Homewood, IL: Irwin, 1971.

[3]Itami, H., *Mobilizing Invisible Assets*, Cambridge, MA: Harvard University Press, 1987.

The emphasis on "patterns of objectives" and "the framework of a firm's business" suggests that strategy is revealed in terms of consistent behavior, which in turn implies that strategy, once set, is not easy to reverse. Finally, the idea that strategy "defines . . . what kind of company it is or should be" suggests that strategic decisions shape the firm's competitive persona, its collective understanding of how it is going to succeed within its competitive environment.

Strategy is, in short, fundamental to an organization's success, which is why the study of strategy can be both profitable and intellectually engaging. The objective of this book is to study and analyze strategy primarily (though not exclusively) from the perspective of economics. Our central theme is that much can be learned by uncovering durable principles that are applicable to many different strategic situations. This value shows up in two fundamental ways: one, by gaining a better understanding of how firms compete and organize themselves (knowledge that we think is virtuous in its own right), and two, by developing a more secure foundation for making good strategic decisions. Having said this, we need to add that this is not intended to be a book of "strategic recipes." The situational complexity of real industries and real firms makes memorizing buzzwords or following fads risky business indeed. The successful application of the concepts and principles that are discussed in this book depends on the institutional, organizational, and economic complexity that occurs when a particular company faces a particular situation. We cannot promise you that this book will guarantee that you will become a more skillful strategic decision maker. What studying this book can help you do is make much better sense of messy and ambiguous strategic situations, and that is an essential step toward skillful strategic decision making.

◆ ◆ ◆ ◆ ◆ WHY ECONOMICS?

One can approach the study of strategy in many ways. One could study strategy from the perspective of mathematical game theory, seeking to discover the logic of choice in situations that involve rivalry. Strategy could also be studied from the perspective of psychology, focusing on how the motivations and behaviors of individual decision makers shape the direction and the performance of their organizations and on how competitive or strategic decisions can be understood as reflecting the biases of individual decision makers. One could study strategy-related questions from an organizational perspective, drawing from either the discipline of sociology, which stresses the role of social structures, peer networks, and organizational routines in determining the decisions made by complex organizations, or political science, which emphasizes the importance of governance structures and coalitions.

There is much to be said for viewing strategy from the perspective of multiple models and multiple disciplinary lenses. But depth of strategic knowledge is as important as breadth of strategic knowledge. In other words, there is much to be gained from detailed application of economics. Deep knowledge of economics permits the formulation of more subtle and powerful hypotheses and the development of richer strategies. Borrowing from concepts to be introduced in this book, we believe that there are deep "product-specific economies of scale" that justify a "focus" on economics.

An advantage of economics, and one reason for its widespread use for analyzing individual and institutional decision making, is that it requires the analyst to be explicit about the key elements of the process under consideration. Economic models must carefully identify each of the following:

* *Decision makers.* Who are the active players? Whose decisions are taken as "fixed" in the situation at hand?

* *Goals.* What are the decision makers trying to accomplish? Are they profit maximizing? Do they have nonpecuniary interests? How do decision makers trade off these conflicting goals?

* *Choices.* What actions are under consideration? What are the strategic variables? (For example, can manufacturers select different levels of quality or is quality fixed?) What is the time horizon over which decisions can be made?

* *Relationship between choices and outcomes.* What is the mechanism by which specific decisions translate into specific outcomes? Is there a functional relationship between certain choices, such as price, and certain outcomes, such as market share? Is the relationship complicated by uncertainty regarding such factors as taste, technology, or the choices of other decision makers?

While political scientists, sociologists, and psychologists sometimes have to ask the same questions, economic theory is distinctive, we think, in that the answers to these questions are nearly always specified explicitly as part of the development of the theory. The advantage to this is that there is clear linkage between the conclusions one draws from the application of economic reasoning and the assumptions that the scholar is making in studying the situation at hand. This leaves what Garth Saloner has called an "audit trail" that allows one to be able to distinguish between unsupported conjectures or claims and logically derived propositions.[4]

The explicit nature of economic models permits the application of economics to a wide variety of problems. Economics has been used to study Supreme Court decisions, divorce, and drug addiction, for example. Moreover, economics offers a wide range of perspectives, from an almost exclusive focus on the interaction of firms within an industry to views of individual interactions within the context of an organization. We believe that this book demonstrates that economics provides significant insights into the major themes of strategy that we describe below.

On the other hand, economic modeling, by its very nature, abstracts from the situational complexity that individuals and firms face. Thus, the application of economic insights to specific situations to gain insight often requires creativity and a deft touch. It also often requires explicit recognition of the constraints imposed on

---

[4]Saloner, G., "Modeling, Game Theory, and Strategic Management," *Strategic Management Journal*, 12, Winter 1991, pp. 119–136.

firms by mistakes, history, and organizational and political factors. Nor does economics fully address the *process* by which choices are made and translated into actions and outcomes. The process of managing the implementation of a competitive strategy decision or a change in the nature of internal organization is often fundamental to their success. Our emphasis on economics in this book is not intended to downgrade the importance of process; it is simply beyond the scope of our expertise to say much about it.

◆ ◆ ◆ ◆ ◆ THE NEED FOR PRINCIPLES

There is a keen interest among serious observers of business to understand the reasons for profitability and market success. This is understandable, since profit is the fundamental motive for business activity. However, observers of business often uncritically leap to the conclusion that the keys to success can be identified by watching and imitating the behaviors of successful firms. A host of management prescriptions by consultants and in the popular business press is buttressed by allusions to the practices of high-performing firms. These recommendations carry all the more weight if the firms in question, and their industries, are new. The examples of biotechnology firms, such as Genentech, and semiconductor firms, such as Intel, easily come to mind.

However, uncritically using currently successful firms as a standard for action assumes that successful outcomes are associated with identifiable key success factors, and by imitating these factors, other firms can achieve similar successful results. While we do not believe that firms succeed randomly, we are convinced that using a given firm's experiences to understand what would make all firms successful is extremely difficult.

There are several dangers in jumping too quickly to the conclusion that the observable practices of successful firms provide lessons that observers can apply to their own firms. The reasons for success are often unclear, even to the executives of the successful firms, and also are likely to be complex. Many factors may contribute to a firm's performance, including some that are not apparent to observers. For example, the internal management systems of a firm may spur product innovation particularly well and not be apparent to individuals who are unfamiliar with how the firm operates.

The industry and market conditions in which successful firms operate may differ greatly from the conditions faced by would-be imitators. In past merger waves, for example, many firms sought to expand to gain the advantages of scale and market power. Many of these firms found out, to their dismay, that the technological conditions in their industries had to be just right before large firms can gain such advantages. Success may also be due in part to a host of idiosyncratic factors, including luck, that will be difficult to identify and impossible to imitate.

Finally, there may be a bias resulting from trying to understand success solely by examining the strategies of successful firms. Strategies associated with many successful firms may have been tried by an equally large number of unsuccessful firms. For example, one may find that among a sample of 100 successful firms, 65 utilize "flat" organizational structures (organizational structures with few levels of hierarchy between the top and bottom of the organization), and from this one might be tempted to conclude that lack of hierarchy is a hallmark of successful firms. However, without studying unsuccessful firms, this conclusion would be invalid. For example, if a well-matched sample of 100 unsuccessful firms revealed that 68 of them had a flat organizational structure, the correct (and possibly uninteresting) conclusion is that a flat organizational structure is a general characteristic of the 200 firms studied and not a particularly strong factor of success.

We do believe that it is useful to study the behaviors of firms. The value of this study, however, lies in helping us identify the general principles behind why firms behave as they do, not in trying to develop lists of characteristics that lead to automatic success. Success or failure will be the result of firms pursuing their goals in a specific way and in a specific business context. The results of a firm's activities will be determined by the principles guiding its actions and how those principles match the conditions the firm faces. A strategy textbook can provide the general principles that underlie strategic decisions. It is not an exhaustive cookbook of uniformly effective recipes for business success. Success depends on the manager who must match principles with conditions.

To see this point, consider the variety that a serious observer of business in the 1990s who attempted to identify success strategies would face. He or she would first of all encounter a broad range of management practices among firms. Take, for example, three highly regarded and successful firms: Nike, Motorola, and Wal-Mart. Each of them has a different organizational structure and corporate strategy. Nike performs few of the functions traditionally associated with large industrial firms and instead uses independent contractors for much of its initial production work and to distribute its products. Nike's success is built largely on marketing campaigns involving well-known athletes. Motorola emphasizes quality and relies on tightly monitored in-house design and production. Unlike the first two, Wal-Mart is a distributor and retailer. It relies on the initiative of its local store managers, combined with sophisticated purchasing and inventory management, to keep its retailing costs below those of its rivals. Making sense of this variety of successful management practices can be frustrating, especially because other companies are much less successful using the same practices. For every Nike, there is an L.A. Gear. For every Motorola, there is a Texas Instruments. For every Wal-Mart, there is a Zayres.

If we find this variety of management practices bewildering, imagine the reactions of a manager from 1910, or even 1950, who was transported ahead in time. The large hierarchical firm that dominated the corporate landscape until the 1970s seems out of place today. General Motors received its share of criticism in the wake of the oil shortages and Japanese invasion of the 1970s, but its structure and strategy were models for manufacturing from the 1920s through the 1960s. United States Steel (now USX), the first firm in the world to achieve annual sales of one billion dollars at the time of its inception in 1901, has greatly declined in relative size and now must rely on selling oil to remain one of the 25 largest U.S. industrial firms. The list of once-admired firms that today are struggling to survive is a long one.

There are two ways to interpret this bewildering variety and evolution of management practice. The first is to believe that the development of successful strategies is so complicated as to be essentially a matter of luck. If this is true, then a manager does not need to systematically study strategy except to track current trends and absorb the advice of management "gurus."

The second interpretation presumes that successful firms succeeded because the strategies their managers chose best allowed them to exploit the potential profit opportunities that existed at the time or to adapt to changing circumstances. We believe in this second interpretation. We believe that success is no accident, coming at random to those who follow strategy fashions. Instead, it can be understood by basic principles of strategic action that are applied under varying conditions by managers making choices. Throughout this book we identify what we believe are general principles of firm behavior, industry structure, and market performance that are as applicable today as they were at any other time in business history. While these principles do not uniquely explain why firms succeed, they should be the basis for any systematic examination of strategy.

Note that this interpretation does not necessarily imply that the managers of successful firms were conscious of the link between their choices and the profit opportunities that existed. Nor, conversely, does it imply that the failure of a particular strategy or management practice means that the decision to undertake it was inconsistent with rational, principled decision making. What it does imply, it seems to us, is that it should be possible to identify underlying principles of strategy that reveal for us the conditions under which some practices are likely to be more successful than others. If this is so, then the study of strategy is indispensable to the manager who must confront change and uncertainty.

◆ ◆ ◆ ◆ ◆ A FRAMEWORK FOR STRATEGY

In our opening discussion of what strategy is, we asserted that strategy is concerned with the "big" issues that firms face. But what specifically does this mean? What are these "big" issues? Put another way, to formulate and implement a successful strategy, what does the firm have to pay attention to? We would argue that to successfully formulate and implement strategy, a firm must confront four broad classes of issues:

- *Boundaries of the firm*—What should the firm do, how large should it be, and what businesses should it be in?

- *Market and competitive analysis*—What is the nature of the markets in which the firm competes and the nature of competitive interactions between firms in those markets?

- *Position and dynamics*—How should the firm position itself to compete, what should be the basis of its competitive advantage, and how should it adjust over time?

- *Internal organization*—How should the firm organize its structure and systems internally?

Boundaries of the Firm

The firm's boundaries define what the firm does. Boundaries can extend in three different directions: vertical, horizontal, and corporate. The firm's vertical boundaries refer to the set of activities that the firm performs itself and those that it purchases from market specialty firms. The firm's horizontal boundaries refer to how much of the product market the firm serves, or essentially how big it is. The firm's corporate boundaries refer to the set of distinct businesses the firm competes in. All three boundaries have received differing amounts of emphasis at different times in the strategy literature. The Boston Consulting Group's emphasis on the learning curve and market growth in the 1960s gave prominence to the firm's horizontal boundaries. Formal planning models organized around tools, such as growth-share matrices, gave prominence to the firm's corporate boundaries. More recently, such concepts as "network organizations" and the "virtual corporation" have given prominence to the firm's vertical boundaries. Our view is that all are important and can be fruitfully analyzed through the perspectives offered by economics.

Market and Competitive Analysis

To formulate and execute successful strategies, firms must understand the nature of the markets in which they compete. As Michael Porter points out in his classic work *Competitive Strategy*, performance across industries is not a matter of chance or accident.[5] There are reasons why, for example, even mediocre firms in an industry such as pharmaceuticals have, by economywide standards, impressive profitability performance, while the top firms in the airline industry seem to achieve low rates of profitability even in the best of times. While the relative importance of industry- versus firm-specific effects is still under debate, the nature of industry structure cannot be ignored either in attempting to understand why firms follow the strategies they do or in attempting to formulate strategies for competing in an industry.

Position and Dynamics

Position and dynamics are shorthand for how and on what basis a firm competes. Position is a static concept. At a given moment in time, is the firm competing on the basis of low costs or because it is differentiated in key dimensions and can thus charge a premium over the prices charged by the other firms with which it competes? Position, as we discuss it, also concerns the resources and capabilities that

---

[5]Porter, M., *Competitive Strategy*, New York: Free Press, 1980.

underlie any cost or differentiation advantages that a firm might have. Dynamics refers to how the firm accumulates resources and capabilities, as well as to how it adjusts over time to changing circumstances. Fundamentally, dynamics has to do with the process emphasized so eloquently by the economist Joseph Schumpeter, who argued that "the impulse of alluring profit," even though inherently temporary, will induce firms and entrepreneurs to create new bases of competitive advantage that redefine industries and undermine the ways of achieving advantage.

Internal Organization

Given that the firm has chosen what to do and has figured out the nature of its market, so that it can decide how and on what basis it should compete, it still needs to organize itself internally to carry out its strategies. Organization sets the terms by which resources will be deployed and information will flow through the firm. It will also determine how well aligned the goals of individual actors within the firm are with the overall goals of the firm. How the firm organizes itself—for example, how it structures its organization, the extent to which it relies on formal incentive systems as opposed to informal influences, such as culture—embodies a key set of strategic decisions in their own right.

The remainder of this book is organized along the lines of this framework. Chapters 1 through 6 have to do with the firm's boundaries. Chapters 7 through 11 deal with industry structure and market analysis. Chapters 12 through 15 address position and dynamics. Chapters 16 through 19 deal with internal organization.

PRIMER: ECONOMIC CONCEPTS FOR STRATEGY

◆ ◆

In 1931 conditions at the Pepsi-Cola Company were desperate.[1] The company had entered bankruptcy for the second time in 12 years, and in the words of a Delaware court, was "a mere shell of a corporation." The president of Pepsi, Charles G. Guth, even attempted to sell Pepsi to its rival Coca-Cola, but Coke wanted no part of a seemingly doomed enterprise. During this period, Pepsi and Coke sold cola in 6-ounce bottles. Attempting to reduce costs, Guth purchased a large supply of recycled 12-ounce beer bottles. Initially, Pepsi priced the 12-ounce bottles at 10 cents, twice the price of 6-ounce Cokes. However, this strategy did little to boost sales. But, then, Guth had an idea: why not sell 12-ounce Pepsis for the same price as 6-ounce Cokes? In the midst of the Depression, this was a brilliant marketing ploy. Pepsi's sales shot upward. By 1934 Pepsi was out of bankruptcy. Its profit rose to $2.1 million by 1936, and by 1938 profit had doubled to $4.2 million. Guth's decision to halve Pepsi's price and undercut Coca-Cola saved the company.

This example illustrates a simple but important point. Clearly, in 1931 Pepsi's chief objective was to increase profits so it could survive. But merely deciding to pursue this objective could not make it happen. Charles Guth could not just order his subordinates to increase Pepsi's profits. Like any company, Pepsi's management had no *direct* control over its profit, market share, or any of the other markers of

---

[1]This example is drawn from Richard Tedlow's excellent history of the soft drink industry in his book, *New and Improved: The Story of Mass Marketing in America*, New York: Basic Books, 1990.

1

business success. What Pepsi's management did control were marketing, production, and administrative decisions that shaped its competitive position and determined its ultimate profitability.

The link between the decisions managers control and a firm's profitability is mediated by a host of economic relationships. The success of any strategy depends on whether the firm's decisions are compatible with these relationships. For Pepsi in the 1930s, the success of its strategy can be understood in terms of a few key economic relationships. The most basic of these is the law of demand. The law of demand says that, all other things being the same, the lower the price of a product, the more of it consumers will purchase. Whether the increase in the number of units sold translates into higher sales revenues depends on the strength of the relationship between price and the quantity purchased. This is measured by the price elasticity of demand. As long as Coke did not respond to Pepsi's price cut with one of its own, we would expect that the demand for Pepsi would have been relatively sensitive to price, or in the language of economics, price elastic. As we shall see later in this chapter, price-elastic demand implies that a price cut not only translates into higher unit sales, but also into higher sales revenue. Whether Coke is better off responding to Pepsi's price cut depends on another relationship, that between the size of a competitor and the profitability of price matching. Because Coke had such a large fraction of the market, it was more profitable to keep its price high (letting Pepsi steal some of its market) than to respond with a price cut of its own.[2] Finally, whether Pepsi's higher sales revenue translates into higher profit depends on the economic relationship between the additional sales revenue that Pepsi's price cut generated and the additional cost of producing the higher volume of Pepsi-Cola. That profits rose rapidly after the price reduction suggests that the additional sales revenue far exceeded the additional costs of production.

The importance of economic relationships for strategy is a central theme of this book. Most of the important contributions to the literature on strategy in the past 20 years, such as Michael Porter's "Five Forces" framework or C.K. Prahalad and Gary Hamel's concept of "core competences," are based on well-developed ideas from economics. As we argue throughout this book, an understanding of robust economic relationships can help us understand why some strategies are well suited to one set of conditions but not others. The judicious application of economic principles to a firm's particular circumstances can increase the odds of successful formulation and execution of business strategy.

This chapter lays out the basic economic tools that we shall use to develop the principles you will study in this book. We focus here on those parts of intermediate microeconomics that are relevant for understanding business strategy. Most of the elements that contributed to Pepsi's successful price-cutting strategy in the 1930s will be on display here. An understanding of the language and concepts in this chapter will, we believe, "level the playing field," so that students with little or no background in microeconomics can navigate the main body of this book just as well as students with extensive economics training.

---

[2]We will discuss this relationship in Chapter 10.

This chapter has five main parts: (1) costs; (2) demand, prices, and revenues; (3) the theory of price and output determination by a profit-maximizing firm; (4) the theory of perfectly competitive markets; and (5) game theory. An appendix provides a brief introduction to present value analysis.[3]

COSTS

◆ ◆ ◆ ◆ ◆

A firm's profit equals its sales revenues minus its costs. We begin our economics primer by focusing on the cost side of this equation. We discuss four specific concepts in this section: cost functions; economic versus accounting costs; long-run versus short-run costs; and sunk costs.

Cost Functions

Total Cost Functions

Managers are most familiar with costs when they are presented as in Tables P.1 and P.2, which show an income statement and a statement of costs of goods manufactured for a hypothetical producer during the year 1995.[4] The information

TABLE P.1
INCOME STATEMENT: 1995

(1) Sales Revenue		$35,600
(2) Cost of Goods Sold:		
Cost of Goods Manufactured	$13,740	
Add: Finished Goods Inventory 12/31/94	$3,300	
Deduct: Finished Goods Inventory 12/31/95	$2,950	
		$14,090
(3) Gross Profit: (1)-(2)		$21,510
(4) Selling and General Administrative Expenses		$8,540
(5) Income From Operations: (3)-(4)		$12,970
Interest Expenses		$1,210
Net Income Before Taxes		$11,760
Income Taxes		$4,100
Net Income		$7,660

(all amounts in thousands)

[3]The third, fourth, and fifth sections are the most "technical." Instructors not planning to cover Chapters 8-11 can skip this material.

[4]The first part of this section closely follows the presentation of cost functions on pp. 42-45 of Dorfman, R., *Prices and Markets*, 2nd ed., Englewood Cliffs, NJ: Prentice–Hall, 1972.

TABLE P.2
STATEMENT OF COSTS OF GOODS MANUFACTURED: 1995

Materials:		
Materials Purchases	$8,700	
Add: Materials Inventory 12/31/94	$1,400	
Deduct: Materials Inventory 12/31/95	$1,200	
(1) Cost of Materials Used		$8,900
(2) Direct Labor		$2,300
Manufacturing Overhead:		
Indirect Labor	$700	
Heat, Light, and Power	$400	
Repairs and Maintenance	$200	
Depreciation	$1,100	
Insurance Expense	$50	
Property Taxes	$80	
Miscellaneous Factory Expenses	$140	
(3) Total Manufacturing Overhead		$2,670
Total Cost of Manufacturing: (1)+(2)+(3)		$13,870
Add: Work-in-Process Inventory 12/31/94		$2,100
Deduct: Work-in-Process Inventory 12/31/95		$2,230
Cost of Goods Manufactured		$13,740

(all amounts in thousands)

in these tables is essentially retrospective. It tells managers what happened during the past year. But what if management is interested in determining whether a price reduction will increase profits, as with Pepsi? The price drop will probably stimulate additional sales, so a firm needs to know how its total costs would change if it increased production above the previous year's level.

This is what a *total cost function* tells us. It represents the relationship between a firm's total costs, denoted by TC, and the total amount of output it produces in a given period of time, denoted by Q. Figure P.1 shows a graph of a total cost function.[5] For each level of output the firm might produce, the graph associates a unique level of total cost. Why is the association between output and total cost unique? A firm may currently be producing 100 units of output per year at a total cost of $5,000,000, but if it were to streamline its operations, it might be able to lower costs, so that those 100 units can be produced for only $4,500,000. We resolve this ambiguity by defining the total cost function as an efficiency relationship. It represents the relationship between total cost and output, *assuming that the firm*

---

[5]The reader may wonder where the total cost function "comes from." In Chapter 12, we discuss techniques that could be used to statistically estimate total cost functions. Even if managers do not have precise estimates of the total cost function, the concept is still useful for thinking about the broad effects of managerial decisions, such as pricing, that affect how much a firm will produce.

FIGURE P.1
TOTAL COST FUNCTION.

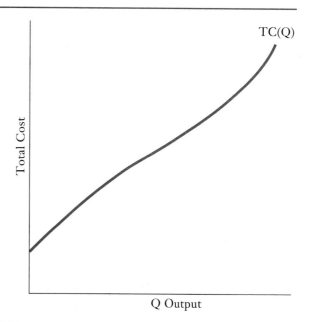

TC(Q)

Total Cost

Q Output

The total cost function *TC(Q)* shows the total costs that the firm would incur for a level of output *Q*. The total cost function is an efficiency relationship in that it shows the lowest possible total cost the firm would incur to produce a level of output, given the firm's technological capabilities and the prices of factors of production, such as labor and capital.

produces in the most efficient manner possible given its current technological capabilities. Of course, firms do not always produce as efficiently as they theoretically could. The substantial literature on Total Quality Management and re-engineering attests to the attention managers give to improving efficiency. This is why we stress that the total cost function reflects the current capabilities of the firm. If the firm is producing as efficiently as it knows how, then the total cost function must slope upward: The only way to achieve more output is to use more *factors of production* (labor, machinery, materials), which will raise total costs.[6]

Fixed and Variable Costs

The information contained in the accounting statements in Tables P.1 and P.2 allows us to identify the total cost for one particular level of annual output. To more completely map out the total cost function, it is necessary to distinguish between *fixed costs and variable costs.* Variable costs, such as direct labor and commissions to salespeople, increase as output increases. Fixed costs, such as general and administrative expenses and property taxes, remain constant as output increases.

---

[6]Students sometimes confuse total costs with average (i.e., per unit) costs, and note that for many real-world firms "costs" seem to go down as output goes up. As we will see presently, average costs could indeed go down as output goes up. The total cost function, however, always increases with output.

Three important points should be stressed when discussing fixed and variable costs. First, the line dividing fixed and variable costs is often fuzzy. Some costs, such as maintenance or advertising and promotional expenses, may have both fixed and variable components. Other costs may be *semifixed:* fixed over certain ranges of output but variable over other ranges.[7] To illustrate, a beer distributor may be able to deliver up to 5,000 barrels of beer a week using a single truck. But when it must deliver between 5,000 and 10,000 barrels it needs two trucks, between 10,000 and 15,000, three trucks, and so forth. The cost of trucks is fixed within the intervals (0,5000), (5000, 10,000), (10,000, 15,0000), and so forth, but is variable between these intervals. Second, when we say that a cost is fixed, we mean that it is invariant to the firm's output. It does not mean that it cannot be affected by other dimensions of the firm's operations or decisions the firm might make. For example, for an electric utility, the cost of stringing wires to hook up houses to the local grid depends primarily on the number of subscribers to the system, and not on the total amount of kilowatt-hours of electricity the utility generates. Other fixed costs, such as the money spent on marketing promotions or advertising campaigns, arise from management decisions and can be eliminated should management so desire.[8] Third, whether costs are fixed or variable depends on the time period in which decisions regarding output are contemplated. Consider, for example, an airline that is contemplating a one-week-long fare cut. Its workers have already been hired, its schedule has been set, and its fleet has been purchased. Within a one-week period, none of these decisions can be reversed. For this particular decision, then, the airline should regard a significant fraction of its costs as fixed. By contrast, if the airline contemplates committing to a year-long reduction in fares, with the expectation that ticket sales will increase accordingly, schedules can be altered, planes can be leased or purchased, and workers can be hired. In this case, the airline should regard most of its expenses as variable. Whether the firm has the freedom to alter its physical capital or other elements of its operations has important implications for its cost structure and the nature of its decision making. This will be covered in more detail below when we analyze the distinction between long-run and short-run costs.

Average and Marginal Cost Functions

Associated with the total cost function are two other cost functions: the *average cost function*, $AC(Q)$, and the *marginal cost function*, $MC(Q)$. The average cost function describes how the firm's average or per-unit costs vary with the amount of output it produces. It is given by the formula:

$$AC(Q) = TC(Q)/(Q)$$

---

[7]This term was coined by Thomas Nagle in *The Strategy and Tactics of Pricing*, Englewood Cliffs, NJ: Prentice-Hall, 1987.

[8]Some authors call these *programmed costs.* See, for example, Rados, D.L., *Pushing the Numbers in Marketing: A Real-world Guide to Essential Financial Analysis* (Quorum Books: Westport, CT), 1992.

If total costs were directly proportional to output–for example, if they were given by a formula, such as $TC(Q) = 5Q$ or $TC(Q) = 37,000Q$, or more generally, by $TC(Q) = cQ$, where c is a constant – then average cost would be a constant. This is because:

$$AC(Q) = \frac{cQ}{Q} = c$$

Often, however, average cost will vary with output. As Figure P.2 shows, average cost may rise, fall, or remain constant as output goes up. When average cost decreases as output increases, there are *economies of scale*. When average cost increases as output increases, there are *diseconomies of scale*. When average cost remains unchanged with respect to output, we have *constant returns to scale*. A production process may exhibit economies of scale over one range of output and diseconomies of scale over another. Figure P.3 shows an average cost function that exhibits economies of scale, diseconomies of scale, and constant returns to scale. Output level Q' is the smallest level of output at which economies of scale are exhausted and is thus known as the *minimum efficient scale*. The concepts of economies of scale and minimum efficient scale are extremely important for understanding the size and scope of firms and the structure of industries. We devote all of Chapter 5 to an analysis of economies of scale.

Marginal cost refers to the rate of change of total cost with respect to output. Marginal cost may be thought of as the incremental cost of producing exactly

FIGURE P.2
AVERAGE COST FUNCTION.

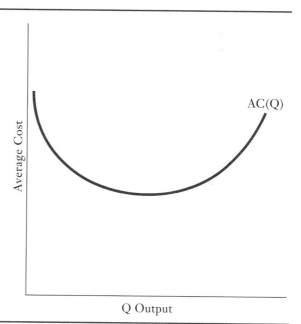

AC(Q)

Average Cost

Q Output

The average cost function $AC(Q)$ shows the firm's average, or per-unit, cost for any level of output Q. Average costs are not necessarily the same at each level of output.

FIGURE P.3
ECONOMIES OF SCALE AND MINIMUM EFFICIENT SCALE.

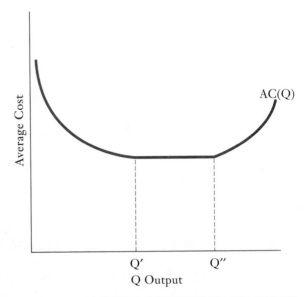

This average cost function exhibits economies of scale at output levels up to Q'. It exhibits constant returns to scale between Q' and Q''. It exhibits diseconomies of scale at output levels above Q''. The smallest output level at which economies of scale are exhausted is Q'. It is thus known as the minimum efficient scale.

one more unit of output. When output is initially Q and changes by ΔQ units and one knows the total cost at each output level, marginal cost may be calculated as follows:

$$MC(Q) = \frac{TC(Q + \Delta Q) - TC(Q)}{\Delta Q}.$$

For example, suppose when $Q = 100$ units, $TC = \$400,000$, and when $Q = 150$ units, $TC = \$500,000$. Then $\Delta Q = 50$, and $MC = \frac{(\$500,000 - \$400,000)}{50} = \$2,000$. Thus, total cost increases at a rate of \$2,000 per unit of output when output increases over the range 100 to 150 units.

Marginal cost often depends on the total volume of output. Figure P.4 shows the marginal cost function associated with a particular total cost function. At low levels of output, such as Q', increasing output by 1 unit does not change total cost much, as reflected by the low marginal cost. At higher levels of output, such as Q'', a 1-unit increase in output has a greater impact on total cost, and the corresponding marginal cost is higher.

Businesses often use information about average cost to estimate the marginal cost of a change in output. But average cost and marginal cost are generally different. The exception is when total costs vary in direct proportion to output, $TC(Q) = c \times Q$. In that case:

$$MC(Q) = \frac{c(Q + \Delta Q) - cQ}{\Delta Q}$$

$$= c$$

FIGURE P.4
RELATIONSHIP BETWEEN TOTAL COST AND MARGINAL COST.

The marginal cost function $MC(Q)$ on the bottom graph is based on the total cost function $TC(Q)$ shown in the upper graph. At output level Q', a one-unit increase in output changes costs by $TC(Q' + 1) - TC(Q')$, which equals the marginal cost at Q', $MC(Q')$. Since this change is not large, the marginal cost is small (i.e., the height of the marginal cost curve from the horizontal axis is small). At output level Q'', a one-unit increase in output changes costs by $TC(Q'' + 1) - TC(Q'')$, which equals the marginal cost at Q''. This change is larger than the one-unit change from Q', so $MC(Q'') > MC(Q')$. Because the total cost function becomes steeper as Q gets larger, the marginal cost curve must increase in output.

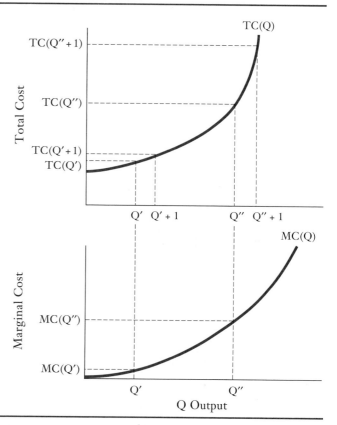

which, of course, is also average cost. This result reflects a more general relationship between marginal and average cost (illustrated in Figure P.5):

- When average cost is a decreasing function of output, marginal cost is less than average cost.

- When average cost neither increases nor decreases in output—either because it is constant (independent of output) or is at a minimum point—marginal cost is equal to average cost.

- When average cost is an increasing function of output, marginal cost is greater than average cost.

These relationships follow from the mathematical properties of average and marginal cost, but they are also intuitive. If the average of a group of things (costs, test scores, or whatever) increases when one more thing is added to the group, then it can only be because the value of the most recently added thing—the "marginal"—is greater than the average. Conversely, if the average falls, it can only be because the marginal is less than the average.

FIGURE P.5
RELATIONSHIP BETWEEN MARGINAL COST AND AVERAGE COST.

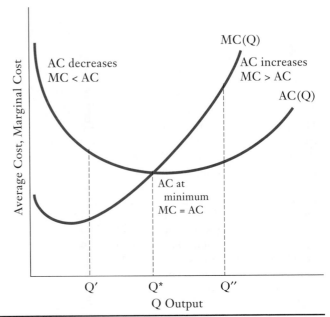

When average cost is decreasing (e.g., at output Q'), $AC > MC$, that is, the average cost curve lies above the marginal cost curve. When average cost is increasing (e.g., at output Q''), $AC < MC$, (i.e., the average cost curve lies below the marginal cost curve). When average cost is at a minimum, $AC = MC$, so the two curves must intersect.

Economic versus Accounting Costs

The costs in Tables P.1 and P.2 reflect the accountant's concept of costs. This concept is grounded in the principles of accrual accounting, which emphasize historical costs. Accounting statements—in particular, income statements and balance sheets—are designed to serve an audience outside the firm—for example, lenders and equity investors. The accounting numbers must thus be objective and verifiable, principles that are well served by historical costs.

However, the costs that appear in accounting statements are not necessarily appropriate for decision making inside a firm. Business decisions require the measurement of economic costs, which are based on the concept of *opportunity cost*. This concept says that the economic cost of deploying resources in a particular activity is the value of the best forgone alternative use of those resources. Economic cost may or may not correspond to the historical costs represented in Tables P.1 and P.2. Suppose, for example, that the firm purchased its raw materials at a price below their current market price. Would the costs of goods manufactured in Table P.2 represent the economic cost to the firm of using these resources? The answer is no. When the firm uses them to produce finished goods, it forsakes the alternative of reselling the materials at the market price. The economic cost of the firm's production activities reflects this forgone opportunity.

At a broader level, consider the resources (plant, equipment, land, and so forth) that have been purchased with funds that stockholders provide to the firm. To attract these funds, the firm must offer the stockholders a return on their investment that is at least as large as the return that they could have received from investing in activities of comparable risk. To illustrate, suppose that at the beginning of 1996, a firm's assets could have been liquidated for $100 million. By having their funds tied up in the firm, investors lose the opportunity to invest the $100 million in an activity providing an 8 percent return. Moreover, suppose because of wear and tear and creeping obsolescence of plant and equipment, the value of the assets declines by 1 percent over the year 1996. The annualized cost of the firm's assets for 1996 is then (.08 + .01) × $100 million or $9 million. This is an economic cost, but it would not appear in the firm's income statement.

In the study of strategy, we are interested in analyzing why firms make the decisions that they do and what distinguishes good decisions from poor ones, given the opportunities and the constraints firms face. In our formal theories of firm behavior, we thus emphasize economic costs rather than historical accounting costs. This is not to say that accounting costs have no place in the study of business strategy. Quite the contrary: In assessing the past performance of the firm, in comparing one firm in an industry to another, or in evaluating the financial strength of a firm, the informed use of accounting statements and accounting ratio analysis can be illuminating. However, the concept of opportunity cost provides the best basis for good economic decisions when the firm must choose among competing alternatives. A firm that consistently deviated from this idea of cost would miss opportunities for earning higher profits. In the end, it might be driven out of business by firms that are better at seizing profit-enhancing opportunities or it may find itself starved for capital as investors bid down its stock price. Whenever we depict a cost function or discuss cost throughout this primer and the remainder of the book, we have in mind the idea of costs as including all relevant opportunity costs.

$\mathcal{E}$XAMPLE P.1

ECONOMIC VALUE ADDED

G. Bennett Stewart, co-founder of the financial consulting firm of Stern-Stewart, is an articulate proponent of using opportunity costs in business decision making.[9] Stewart has developed a comprehensive approach to financial planning built around the concept of *economic value added* (EVA). In its simplest form, EVA is given by

$$EVA = \text{operating profit} - \text{cost of capital} \times \text{capital}$$

---

[9]This example is based on Stewart's book, *The Quest for Value: A Guide for Senior Managers,* New York: Harper Business, 1991.

EVA is a method of measuring a firm's true profitability, taking into account the opportunity cost investors incur by having their capital tied up inside the firm. Stern-Stewart keeps track of EVAs for hundreds of companies. For example, in 1992 IBM had a negative EVA of over $6 billion. By contrast, Wal-Mart had a positive EVA of close to $1 billion.

Stewart likens a company with a high operating profit but a negative EVA to a basketball player who scores a lot of baskets (i.e., has high accounting earnings) only because he takes lots of shots (i.e., invests lots of capital). Just as the team might do better if the player passed the ball to other teammates whose scoring efficiency is higher, a negative EVA company would make its investors better off by forgoing investments in marginal projects and returning funds to shareholders whose alternative investment opportunities are better than the company's.

The concept of EVA has been embraced by both investors and senior managers. Eugene Vesell, a senior vice president of Oppenheimer Capital, which manages $26 billion in funds, has stated "We like to invest in companies that use EVA and similar measures. Making higher returns than the cost of capital is how we look at the world." Coca-Cola's CEO Roberto Goizueta, an enthusiastic believer in EVA, says: "When I played golf regularly, my average score was 90, so every hole was a par 5. I look at EVA like I look at breaking par. At Coca-Cola we are way under par and adding a lot of value."[10] In the late 1980s, Coca-Cola adopted EVA techniques for financial planning throughout the company and has been using EVA as a basis for managerial compensation and bonuses.

The Importance of the Time Period: Long-Run and Short-Run Cost Functions

We emphasized the importance of the time horizon when discussing fixed versus variable costs. In this section, we develop this point further and consider some of its implications.

Figure P.6 illustrates the case of a firm whose production can take place in a facility that comes in three different sizes: small, medium, and large. Once the firm commits to a production facility of a particular size, it can vary output only by varying the quantities of inputs other than the plant size (e.g., by hiring another shift of workers). The period of time in which the firm cannot adjust the size of its production facilities is known as the *short run*. For each plant size, there is an associated short-run average cost function, denoted by *SAC*. These average cost functions include the annual costs of all relevant variable inputs (labor, materials) as well as the fixed cost (appropriately annualized) of the plant itself.

If the firm knows how much output it plans to produce prior to building a plant, then to minimize its costs, it should choose the plant size that results in the lowest short-run average cost for that desired output level. For example, for output Q_1, the optimal plant is a small one; for output Q_2 the optimal plant is a medium one;

---

[10]Both quotes come from "The Real Key to Creating Wealth," *Fortune*, September 23, 1993: pp. 38–50.

FIGURE P.6
SHORT-RUN AND LONG-RUN AVERAGE COST FUNCTIONS.

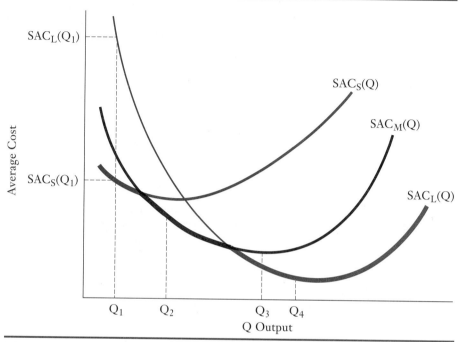

The curves labeled $SAC_S(Q)$, $SAC_M(Q)$, and $SAC_L(Q)$ are the short-run average cost functions associated with small, medium, and large plants, respectively. For any level of output, the optimal plant size is the one with the lowest average cost. For example, at output Q_1, the small plant is best. At output Q_2, the medium plant is best. At output Q_3, the large plant is best. The long-run average cost function is the "lower envelope" of the short-run average cost functions, represented by the bold line. This curve shows the lowest attainable average cost for any output when the firm is free to adjust its plant size optimally.

for output Q_3, the optimal plant is a large one. Figure P.6 illustrates that for larger outputs, the larger plant is best; for medium output levels, the medium plant is best; and for small output levels, the small plant is best. For example, when output is Q_1, the reduction in average cost by switching from a large plant to a small plant is $SAC_L(Q_1) - SAC_S(Q_1)$. This saving not only arises from reductions in the fixed costs of the plant, but also because the firm can more efficiently tailor the rest of its operations to its plant size. When the firm produces Q_1 in the large plant, it may need to utilize more labor to assure steady materials flows within the large facility. The small plant may allow flows to be streamlined, making such labor unnecessary.

The *long-run average cost function* is the lower envelope of the short-run average cost functions, and is depicted by the bold line in Figure P.6. It shows the lowest attainable average cost for any particular level of output when the firm can adjust its plant size optimally. This is the average cost function the firm faces before it has committed to a particular plant size.

In this example, the long-run average cost function exhibits economies of scale. By operating with larger plant sizes, the firm can lower its average costs. This raises a deceptively simple but extremely significant point. To realize the lower average costs, the firm must not only build a large plant but must also achieve sufficient output, so that the large plant is indeed the optimal one. It would be disastrous for the firm to build a large plant if it only achieved an output of, say, Q_1. The firm would be saddled with an expensive underutilized facility. If we were to observe a firm in this situation, we might be tempted to conclude that the scale economies inherent in the production process were limited or nonexistent. This would be incorrect. Scale economies exist, but the firm is not selling the output needed to exploit them.

It is often useful to express short-run average costs as the sum of *average fixed costs* (AFC) and *average variable costs* (AVC):

$$SAC(Q) = AFC(Q) + AVC(Q)$$

Average fixed costs are the firm's fixed costs (i.e., the annualized cost of the firm's plant plus expenses, such as insurance and property taxes, that do not vary with the volume of output) expressed on a per-unit-of-output basis. Average variable costs are the firm's variable costs (e.g., labor and materials) expressed on a per-unit-of-output basis. For example, suppose the firm's plant has an annualized cost of $9 million and other annual fixed expenses total $1 million. Moreover, suppose the firm's variable costs vary with output according to the formula $4Q^2$. Then we would have:

$$AFC(Q) = \frac{10}{Q}$$

$$AVC(Q) = 4Q$$

$$SAC(Q) = \frac{10}{Q} + 4Q$$

Note that as the volume of output increases, average fixed costs become smaller, which is a force that works to pull down SAC. Average fixed costs decline because total fixed costs are being spread over an ever larger production volume. Offsetting this (in this example) is the fact that average variable costs rise with output, which pulls SAC upward. The net effect of these offsetting forces creates the U-shaped SAC curves in Figure P.6.

Sunk Costs

When assessing the costs of a decision, the manager should consider only those costs that the decision actually affects. Some costs must be incurred no matter what the decision is. They are costs that have already been incurred and cannot be recovered. These are called *sunk costs*. The opposite of sunk costs are *avoidable costs*. These are costs that can be avoided if certain choices are made. When weighing the costs of a decision, the decision maker should ignore sunk costs and consider only avoidable costs.

To illustrate the concept of sunk costs, consider the case of a mail order merchandiser of laser printers. The merchandiser traditionally purchased large quantities of printers from the manufacturer, so that it could satisfy rush orders. Increasingly, though, the merchandiser was carrying extremely high inventories, including some lines that the manufacturer no longer produced and would not repurchase. A natural response to this problem would be to run a sale to reduce the inventory of the discontinued lines. However, the firm's managers were reluctant to do this. They felt that even in the best of times the margins on their products barely covered their overhead, and by cutting the price, they would be unable to cover their cost of goods sold.

This argument is clearly wrong. The cost incurred to purchase the laser printers is a sunk cost as far as the pricing decision is concerned. Whether the merchandiser cuts price or not, it cannot avoid these costs. If it succumbs to the argument that a seller should never price below average cost, the merchandiser will end up with large losses. Instead, it should accept the fact that it cannot undo past decisions (and their associated sunk costs) and should strive to minimize its losses.

It is important to emphasize that whether a cost is sunk depends on the decision being made and the options at hand. In the example above, the cost of the discontinued lines of printers is a sunk cost with respect to the pricing decision today. But before the printers were ordered their cost would not have been sunk. If the merchandiser decided not to order them, it would have avoided the purchase and storage costs.

Students often confuse sunk costs with fixed costs. The two concepts are not the same. In particular, some fixed costs need not be sunk. For example, a railroad serving Chicago to Cleveland needs a locomotive and a crew no matter whether it hauls a single carload of freight or 20 carloads of freight. The cost of the locomotive is thus a fixed cost. However, it is not necessarily sunk. If the railroad abandons its Chicago-to-Cleveland line, it can sell the locomotive to another railroad, or perhaps redeploy it to another one of its routes.

Sunk costs are important for the study of strategy, particularly in analyzing rivalry among firms, entry and exit decisions from markets, and decisions to adopt new technologies. For example, the concept of sunk costs helps explain why an established American steel firm would be unwilling to invest in a new technology, such as continuous casting, while a new Japanese firm building a "greenfield" facility from scratch would adopt the new technology. The new technology has higher fixed costs, but lower variable operating costs. For the established American firm, the fixed cost of its old technology is *sunk*. This firm will adopt the new technology only if the savings in operating costs exceed the fixed cost of the new technology. For the Japanese firm starting from scratch, the fixed cost of the old technology is *avoidable* if it adopts the new technology. Thus, this firm will adopt the new technology if the savings in operating costs exceeds the *difference* between the fixed costs of the new and old technologies. This is a weaker threshold.

We will return to the concept of sunk costs in our discussions of commitment in Chapter 9, entry and exit in Chapter 11, sustainable advantage in Chapter 14, and innovation in Chapter 15.

◆ ◆ ◆ ◆ ◆ DEMAND AND REVENUES

The second component of profit is sales revenue, which is intimately related to the firm's pricing decision. To understand how a firm's sales revenue depends on its pricing decision, we will explore the concept of a demand function and the price elasticity of demand.

Demand Function

The *demand function* describes the relationship between the quantity of product that the firm is able to sell and all the variables that influence that quantity. These variables include: the price of the product, the prices of related products, the incomes and tastes of consumers, the quality of the product, advertising, product promotion, and many other variables commonly thought to make up the firm's marketing mix.

Of special interest is the relationship between quantity and price. To focus on this important relationship, imagine that all the other variables that influence the quantity demanded remain fixed, and consider how the quantity demanded would change as the price changes. We would expect this to be an inverse relationship, as shown in Figure P.7: the lower the price, the greater the quantity demanded; the higher the price, the smaller the quantity demanded. This inverse relationship is called the *law of demand*.

FIGURE P.7
DEMAND CURVE.

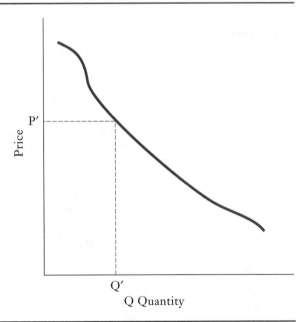

The demand curve shows the quantity of a product that consumers will purchase at different prices. For example, at price *P'* consumers purchase *Q'* units of the product. We would expect an inverse relationship between quantity and price, so this curve is downward sloping.

The law of demand may not hold if high prices confer prestige or enhance a product's image. If a seller of fine scotch or crystal lowered its price, it might attenuate its prestige value, and thus sell less rather than more. A related phenomenon would occur when consumers cannot objectively assess the potential performance of a product and use price to infer quality. A lower price might signal low quality, reducing rather than increasing sales. Both prestige and signaling effects could result in demand curves that slope upward for some range of prices. Even so, personal experience and countless studies from economics and marketing confirm that the law of demand applies to most products.

As Figure P.7 shows, the demand curve is typically drawn with price on the vertical axis and quantity on the horizontal axis. This may seem strange because we think of the quantity demanded as being determined by price, not the other way around. However, this representation emphasizes a useful alternative interpretation for a demand curve. Not only does the demand curve tell us the quantity consumers will purchase at any given price, it also tells us the highest possible price that the market will bear for a given quantity or supply of output. Thus, in Figure P.7, if the firm sets a target of selling output level Q' (which might be what it can produce by running at full capacity), the demand curve tells us that the highest price the firm can charge is P'.

The Price Elasticity of Demand

Consider a firm that is considering a price increase. The firm understands that according to the law of demand, the increase in price will result in the loss of some sales. This may be acceptable to the firm if the loss in sales is not "too large." If sales do not suffer much, the firm may actually increase its *sales revenue* when it raises its price. If sales drop substantially, however, sales revenues may decline, and the firm could be worse off.

Figure P.8 illustrates the implications of the firm's pricing decision when its demand curve has one of two alternative shapes, D_A and D_B. Suppose the firm is currently charging P_0 and selling Q_0, and is considering an increase in price to P_1. If the firm's demand curve is D_A, the price increase would cause only a small drop in sales. In this case, the quantity demanded is not very sensitive to price. We would suspect that the increase in price would *increase* sales revenue because the price increase swamps the quantity decrease. By contrast, if the firm's demand curve is D_B, the increase in price would cause a large drop in sales. Here, the quantity demanded is very sensitive to price. We would expect that the price increase would decrease sales revenues.

As this analysis shows, the shape of the demand curve can strongly affect the success of the firm's pricing strategy. The concept of the *price elasticity of demand* summarizes this effect by measuring the sensitivity of quantity demanded to price. The price elasticity, commonly denoted by η, is the percentage change in quantity brought about by a 1 percent change in price. Letting subscript "0" represent the initial situation and "1" represent the situation after the price changes, the formula for elasticity is:

$$\eta = -\frac{\frac{\Delta Q}{Q_0}}{\frac{\Delta P}{P_0}}$$

FIGURE P.8
PRICE SENSITIVITY AND THE SHAPE OF THE DEMAND CURVE.

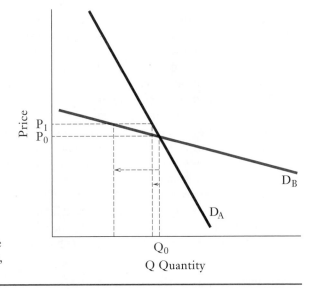

When the demand curve is D_A, a change in price from P_0 to P_1 has only a small effect on the quantity demanded. However, when the demand curve is D_B, the same change in price results in a large drop in quantity demanded. When D_A is the demand curve, we would conjecture that the increase in price would increase sales revenues but when D_B is the demand curve, the price increase would reduce sales revenues.

where $\Delta P = P_1 - P_0$ is the change in price, and $\Delta Q = Q_1 - Q_0$ is the resulting change in quantity.[11] To illustrate this formula, suppose price is initially $5, and the corresponding quantity demanded is 1,000 units. If the price rises to $5.75, though, the quantity demanded would fall to 800 units. Then

$$\eta = -\frac{\frac{-200}{1000}}{\frac{.75}{5}} = \frac{.20}{.15} = 1.33$$

Thus over the range of prices between $5.00 and $5.75, quantity demanded falls at a rate of 1.33 percent for every 1 percent increase in price. The price elasticity η may be less than 1 or greater than 1. If η is less than 1, we say that demand is *inelastic*, which is the situation along demand curve D_A for the price change being considered. If η is greater than 1, we say that demand is *elastic*, which is the situation along demand curve D_B for the price change being considered.

Given an estimate of the price elasticity of demand, a manager could calculate the expected percentage change in quantity demanded resulting from a given change in price by multiplying the percentage change in price by the estimated elasticity. To illustrate, suppose management believed $\eta = .75$. If it contemplated a 3 percent increase in price, then it should expect a $3 \times .75 = 2.25$ percent drop in the quantity demanded as a result of the price increase. One complication should

---

[11]It is customary to put the minus sign in front, so that we convert what would ordinarily be a negative number (because ΔQ and ΔP have opposite signs) into a positive one.

be noted: A given product's price elasticity of demand is not the same at all price levels.[12] This means that an elasticity that is estimated at a price level of, say, $10 would be useful in predicting the impact of an increase in price to $11, but would not be very accurate in predicting the impact of an increase to $20.

Price elasticities can be estimated using statistical techniques, and economists and marketers have generated estimates of price elasticities for many products. But in most practical situations managers will not have the benefit of a precise numerical estimate of elasticity based on statistical techniques. Consequently, the manager must rely on his or her knowledge of the product and the nature of the market to be able to make educated conjectures about price sensitivity. Among the factors that tend to make demand for the firm's product *more sensitive* to price are:

- The product has few unique features that differentiate it from rival products, and buyers are aware of the prices and features of rival products. Airline service is a good example of a product that is hard to differentiate and where consumers can easily inform themselves of the range of prices that exist in a particular market.

- Buyers' expenditures on the product are a large fraction of their total expenditures. In this case, the savings from finding a comparable item at a lower price are large, so consumers tend to shop more than when making small purchases. Refrigerators and washing machines are good examples of products whose demand is fairly price sensitive because consumers are motivated to shop around before making purchases.

- The product is an input that buyers use to produce a final good whose demand is itself sensitive to price. In this case, if buyers tried to pass through to their customers even small changes in the price of the input, demand for the finished good could decrease dramatically. The input buyers will thus be very sensitive to price. For example, a personal computer manufacturer's demand for components and materials is likely to be highly price elastic because consumer demand for personal computers is highly price elastic.

Among the factors that tend to make demand *less sensitive* to price are the following:

- Comparisons among substitute products are difficult. This could be because the product is complex and has many performance dimensions; because consumers have little or no experience with substitute products and thus would face a risk if they purchased them; or because comparison shopping is costly. Items sold door-to-door, such as Avon cosmetics, have traditionally been price inelastic because, at the time of sale, most consumers lack good information about the prices of alternatives.

- Because of tax deductions or insurance, buyers pay only a fraction of the full price of the product. Health care is an excellent example.

---

[12]This is due to the properties of percentages, which require dividing by base amounts. If the price is so high that the quantity demanded is close to zero, even small absolute increases in quantity can translate into huge percentage increases.

- A buyer would incur significant costs if it switched to a substitute product. Switching costs could arise if the use of a product requires specialized training or expertise that is not fully transferable across different varieties of the product. For example, to the extent that a consumer develops expertise in using a particular word processing package that is incompatible with available alternatives, switching costs will be high and price sensitivity for upgrades will be low.

- The product is used in conjunction with another product that buyers have committed themselves to. For example, an owner of a copying machine is likely to be fairly insensitive to the price of toner, because the toner is an essential input in running the copier.

Brand-Level versus Industry-Level Elasticities

A common mistake made by students is to suppose that just because the demand for a product is inelastic, the demand facing each seller of that product is also inelastic. Consider, for example, cigarettes. Numerous studies have documented that the demand for cigarettes is price inelastic, with elasticities well below 1. This suggests that a general increase in the price of all brands of cigarettes would only modestly affect overall cigarette demand. However, if the price of only one brand of cigarettes increases, the demand for that brand would probably drop substantially because consumers would switch to the now lower-priced brands. Thus, while demand can be inelastic at the industry level, it can be highly elastic at the brand level. Research by Frank Irvine nicely illustrates this difference for the automobile industry.[13] While estimates of the industry-level price elasticity for automobiles are on the order of 1 to 1.5, Irvine found that the average price elasticity for individual makes of automobiles ranged from 6 to 10.

Brand-level elasticities are higher than industry-level elasticities because consumers have greater substitution possibilities when only one brand raises its price. Brand-level elasticities should also increase as more firms enter the market and more brands are offered. A recent study of the personal computer industry by Joanna Stavins illustrates this point.[14] She finds that the average brand-level elasticity rose over time from 5.0 in 1977 to 12.4 in 1988 as new firms entered the market. These elasticity estimates highlight an important reason for the increasing price competitiveness in that industry.

What determines whether a firm should use an industry-level elasticity or a brand-level elasticity in assessing the impact of a price change? The answer depends on what the firm expects its rivals to do. If a firm expects that rivals will quickly match its price change, then the industry-level elasticity is appropriate. If, by con-

---

[13]Irvine, F.O., "Demand Equations for Individual New Car Models Estimated Using Transactions Prices with Implications for Regulatory Issues," *Southern Economic Journal*, 49, January 1983: pp. 764–982.

[14]Stavins, J., "Estimating Demand Elasticities in a Differentiated Product Industry: The Personal Computer Market," Harvard University, working paper, October 1992.

trast, a firm expects that rivals will not match its price change (or will do so only after a long lag), then the brand-level elasticity is appropriate. In the example in the introduction, Pepsi's price cut succeeded because Coke did not cut its price in retaliation. Had Coke cut its price, the outcome of Pepsi's strategy would have been different. Making educated conjectures about how rivals will respond to various kinds of pricing moves is a fascinating subject. We will encounter it again in Chapter 8, and we will study it in detail in Chapter 10.

Total Revenue and Marginal Revenue Functions

A firm's *total revenue function*, denoted by $TR(Q)$, indicates how the firm's sales revenues vary as a function of how much product it sells. Recalling our interpretation of the demand curve as showing the highest price $P(Q)$ that the firm can charge and sell exactly Q units of output, we can express total revenue as

$$TR(Q) = P(Q)Q$$

Just as a firm is interested in the impact of a change in output on its costs, it is also interested in how a change in output will affect its revenues. A firm's marginal revenue, $MR(Q)$, is analogous to its marginal cost. It represents the rate of change in total revenue that results from the sale of ΔQ additional units of output:

$$MR(Q) = \frac{TR(Q + \Delta Q) - TR(Q)}{\Delta Q}$$

It seems plausible that total revenue would go up as the firm sells more output, and thus MR would always be positive. But with a downward-sloping demand curve, this is not necessarily true. To sell more, the firm must lower its price. Thus, while it generates revenue on the extra units of output it sells at the lower price, it loses revenue on all the units it *would have sold* at the higher price. For example, a compact disc store may sell 110 compact discs per day at a price of $11 per disc, and 120 discs at $9 per disc. It gains additional revenue of $90 per day on the extra 10 discs sold at the lower price of $9, but it sacrifices $220 per day on the 110 discs that it could have sold for $2 more. The marginal revenue in this case would equal $-\$130 \div 10$ or $-\$13$; the store loses sales revenue at a rate of $13 for each additional disc it sells when it drops its price from $11 to $9.

In general, whether marginal revenue is positive or negative depends on the price elasticity of demand. The formal relationship (whose derivation is not important for our purposes) is

$$MR = P\left(1 - \frac{1}{\eta}\right)$$

For example, if $\eta = .75$, and the current price $P = \$15$, then marginal revenue $MR = 15(1 - \frac{1}{.75}) = -\$5$. More generally, when demand is price elastic, so that $\eta > 1$, it follows that $MR > 0$. In this case, the increase in output brought about by a reduction in price will raise total sales revenues. When demand is price inelastic, so that $\eta < 1$, it follows that $MR < 0$. Here, the increase in output brought about by a reduction in price will lower total sales revenue.

Note that this formula implies that $MR < P$. This makes sense in light of what we just discussed. The price P is the additional revenue the firm gets on each additional unit it sells, but the overall change in revenues from selling an additional unit must factor in the reduction in revenue earned on all of the units that would have sold at the higher price, but are now being sold at a lower price.

Figure P.9 shows the graph of a demand function and its associated marginal revenue function. Because $MR < P$, the marginal revenue curve must lie everywhere below the demand curve, except at a quantity of zero. For most demand curves, the marginal revenue curve is everywhere downward sloping and at some point will shift from being positive to negative. (This occurs at output Q' in the figure.)

◆ ◆ ◆ ◆ ◆ THEORY OF THE FIRM: PRICING AND OUTPUT DECISIONS

Part II of this book studies the structure of markets and competitive rivalry within industries. To set the stage for this analysis, it is useful to explore the *theory of the firm*, a theory of how firms choose their prices and quantities. This theory has both explanatory power and prescriptive usefulness. That is, it sheds light on how prices are established in markets, and it also provides tools to aid managers in making pricing decisions.

FIGURE P.9
THE MARGINAL REVENUE CURVE AND THE DEMAND CURVE.

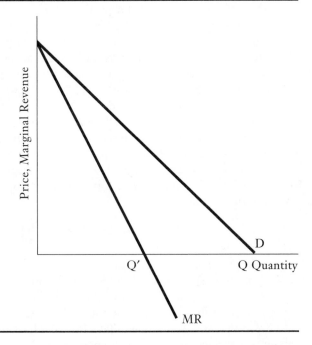

MR represents the marginal revenue curve associated with the demand curve *D*. Because $MR < P$, the marginal revenue curve must lie everywhere below the demand curve except at a quantity of 0. Marginal revenue is negative for quantities in excess of Q'.

The theory of the firm assumes that the firm's ultimate objective is to make as large a profit as possible. The theory is therefore appropriate to managers whose goal is to maximize profits. Some analysts argue that not all managers seek to maximize profits, so that the theory of the firm is less useful for describing actual firm behavior. An extensive discussion of the descriptive validity of the profit-maximization hypothesis would take us well beyond the scope of this primer. Suffice it to say that a powerful "evolutionary" argument supports the profit-maximization hypothesis: If, over the long haul, a firm's managers did not strive to achieve the largest amount of profit consistent with industry economics and its own particular resources, the firm would either disappear or its management would be replaced by one that better served the owners' interests.

Ideally, for any given amount of output the firm might want to sell, it would prefer to set price as high as it could. As we have seen, though, the firm's demand curve limits what that price can be. Thus, when determining the amount it wants to sell, the firm simultaneously determines the price it can charge from its demand curve.

How, then, is the optimal output determined? This is where the concepts of marginal revenue and marginal cost become useful. Recalling that "marginals" are rates of change (change in cost or revenue per one-unit change in output), the change in revenue, cost, and profit from changing output by ΔQ units (where ΔQ can either represent an increase in output, in which case it is a positive amount, or a decrease in output, in which case it is a negative amount) is:

$$\text{Change in Total Revenue} = MR \times \Delta Q$$
$$\text{Change in Total Cost} = MC \times \Delta Q$$
$$\text{Change in Profit} = (MR - MC) \times \Delta Q$$

The firm clearly would like to increase profit. Here's how:

- If $MR > MC$, the firm can increase profit by selling more ($\Delta Q > 0$), and to do so, it should *lower its price*.

- If $MR < MC$, the firm can increase profit by selling less ($\Delta Q < 0$), and to do so, it should *raise its price*.

- If $MR = MC$, the firm cannot increase profits either by increasing output or decreasing it. It follows that output and price must be at their optimal levels.

Figure P.10 shows the situation of a firm whose output and price are at their optimal levels. The curve D is the firm's demand curve, MR is the marginal revenue curve, and MC is the marginal cost curve. The optimal output occurs where $MR = MC$, that is, where the MR and MC curves intersect. This is output Q^* in the diagram. The optimal price P^* is the associated price on the demand curve.

An alternative and perhaps more managerially relevant way of thinking about these principles is to express MR in terms of the price elasticity of demand. Then the term $MR = MC$ can be written as:

$$P\left(1 - \frac{1}{\eta}\right) = MC$$

FIGURE P.10
OPTIMAL QUANTITY AND PRICE FOR A PROFIT-MAXIMIZING FIRM.

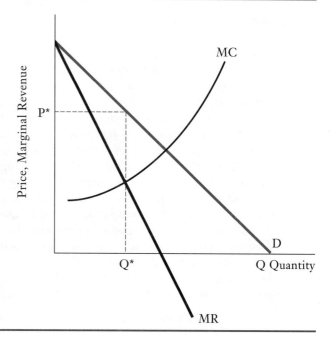

The firm's optimal quantity occurs at Q^*, where $MR = MC$. The optimal price P^* is the price the firm must charge to sell Q^* units. It is found from the demand curve.

Let us now suppose, that as a first approximation, the firm's total variable costs are directly proportional to output, so that $MC = c$, where c is the firm's average variable cost. The *percentage contribution margin* or *PCM* on additional units sold is the ratio of profit per unit to revenue per unit, or $\frac{P-c}{P}$. Straightforward algebra establishes that:

$$MR - MC > 0 \ \text{ as } \eta > \frac{1}{PCM}$$

$$MR - MC < 0 \ \text{ as } \eta < \frac{1}{PCM}$$

This implies:

- A firm should lower its price whenever the price elasticity of demand exceeds the reciprocal of the percentage contribution margin on the additional units it would sell.

- A firm should raise its price when the price elasticity of demand is less than the reciprocal of the percentage contribution margin of the units it would not sell by raising its price.

These principles can guide pricing decisions even though managers do not know the firm's demand curve or marginal cost function. All that is required is that managers make educated conjectures about the relative magnitude of elasticities and contribution margins.[15] An example may help cement these concepts. Suppose $P = \$10$ and $c = \$5$, so $PCM = .5$. Then the firm can increase profits by lowering its price if its price elasticity of demand η exceeds $1 \div .5$ or 2. If, instead, $P = \$10$, and $c = \$8$, so that $PCM = .2$, the firm should cut its price if $\eta > 5$. As this example shows, the lower a firm's PCM (e.g., because its marginal cost is high), the greater its price elasticity of demand must be for a price-cutting strategy to raise profits.

PERFECT COMPETITION   ◆ ◆ ◆ ◆ ◆

A special case of the theory of the firm is the theory of perfect competition. This theory highlights how market forces shape and constrain a firm's behavior and interact with the firm's decisions to determine profitability. The theory deals with a stark competitive environment: an industry with many firms producing identical products (so that consumers choose among firms solely on the basis of price) and where firms can enter or exit the industry at will. Admittedly this is a caricature of any real market, but it does approximate an industry, such as personal computers, in which numerous firms produce nearly identical products and compete primarily on the basis of price.

Because firms in a perfectly competitive industry produce identical products, each firm must charge the same price. For any individual firm, this market price is beyond its control; it must take the market price as given. For a firm to offer to sell at a price above the market price would be folly because it would make no sales. Offering to sell below the market price would also be folly because the firm would needlessly sacrifice revenue. As shown in Figure P.11, then, a perfectly competitive firm's demand curve is perfectly horizontal at the market price, even though the industry demand curve is downward sloping. Put another way, the firm-level price elasticity of demand facing a perfect competitor is infinite, even though the industry-level price elasticity is finite.

Given any particular market price, the decision facing each firm is how much to produce. Applying the insights from the theory of the firm, the firm should produce at the point where marginal revenue equals marginal cost. When the firm's demand curve is horizontal, each additional unit it sells adds sales revenue equal to the market price. Thus, the firm's marginal revenue equals the market price, and the optimal output, shown in Figure P.11, is where marginal cost equals the market price. If we were to trace out a graph that showed how a firm's optimal output changed as the market price changed, we would trace out a curve that is identical to the firm's marginal cost function. This is known as the *firm's supply curve*. It shows the amount of output the perfectly competitive firm would sell at various market prices. What we have just seen is that the supply curve of a perfectly competitive firm is identical to its marginal cost function.

---

[15]The use of this formula is subject to the caveat expressed earlier about the use of elasticities. It is useful for contemplating the effects of "incremental" price changes rather than dramatic price changes.

FIGURE P.11
DEMAND AND SUPPLY CURVES FOR A PERFECTLY COMPETITIVE FIRM.

A perfectly competitive firm takes the market price as given and thus faces a horizontal demand curve at the market price. This horizontal line also represents the firm's marginal revenue curve *MR*. The firm's optimal output occurs where its marginal revenue equals marginal cost. When the market price is P_0, the optimal output is Q_0. If the market price were to change, the firm's optimal quantity would also change. At price P_1, the optimal output is Q_1. At price P_2, the optimal output is Q_2. The firm's supply curve traces out the relationship between the market price and the firm's optimal quantity of output. This curve is identical to the firm's marginal cost curve.

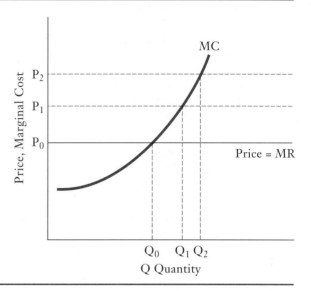

If we aggregate over the firm supply curves of all active producers in the industry, we get the *industry supply curve*, depicted in Figure P.12 as *SS*. This figure shows an industry with 1,000 identical active firms. At any price, the industry supply is 1,000 times the supply of an individual firm. Given the industry supply curve, we can now see how the market price is determined. For the market to be in *equilibrium*, the market price must be such that the quantity demanded equals the quantity supplied by firms in the industry. This situation is depicted in Figure P.13, where P^* denotes the price that "clears" the market. If the market price was higher than P^*, then there would be a greater quantity of the product offered for sale than consumers would like to buy. The excess supply would then place downward pressure on the market price. If the market price was lower than P^*, then there would be a smaller quantity of the product offered for sale than consumers would like to buy. Here, the excess demand would exert upward pressure on the market price. Only when the quantities demanded and supplied are equal—when price equals P^*—is there no pressure on price to change.

The situation shown in Figure P.13 would be the end of the story if additional firms could not enter the industry. However, in a perfectly competitive industry, firms can enter and exit at will. The situation in Figure P.13 is thus unstable because firms in the industry are making a profit (price exceeds average cost at the quantity q^* that each firm supplies). Thus, it will be attractive for additional firms to enter and begin selling. Figure P.14 shows the adjustment that occurs. As more firms enter, the supply curve *SS* shifts outward to *SS'*. As this happens, the quan-

FIGURE P.12
FIRM AND INDUSTRY SUPPLY CURVES UNDER PERFECT COMPETITION.

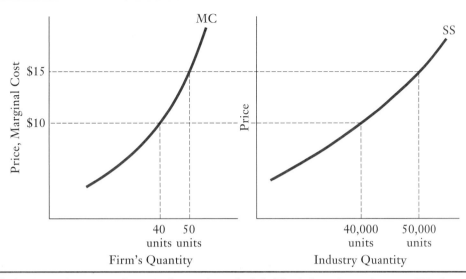

A single firm's supply curve is shown in the graph on the left. The industry's supply curve *SS* is shown in the graph on the right. These graphs depict an industry of 1,000 identical firms. Thus, at any price the industry supply is 1,000 times the amount that a single firm would supply.

FIGURE P.13
PERFECTLY COMPETITIVE INDUSTRY PRIOR TO NEW ENTRY.

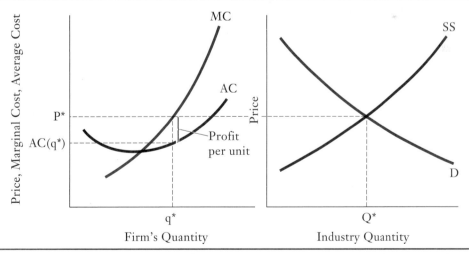

At the price P^*, each firm is producing its optimal amount of output q^*. Moreover, the quantity demanded equals the quantity Q^* supplied by all firms in the industry. However, each firm is earning a positive profit because at q^*, the price P^* exceeds average cost $AC(q^*)$, resulting in a profit on every unit sold. New firms would thus want to enter this industry.

FIGURE P.14
PERFECTLY COMPETITIVE INDUSTRY AT LONG-RUN EQUILIBRIUM.

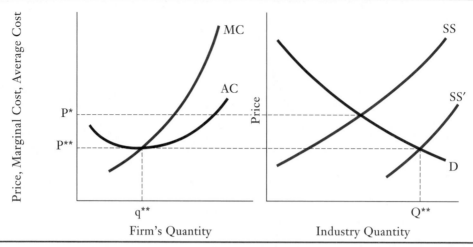

At price P^*, new entrants are attracted to the industry. As they come in, the industry's supply curve shifts to the right, from SS to SS', resulting in a reduction in market price. Entry ceases to occur when firms are earning as much inside the industry as they can earn outside it. Each firm thus earns zero economic profit, or equivalently, price equals average cost. Firms are choosing the optimal output and earning zero economic profit when they produce at the point at which market price equals both marginal cost and average cost. This occurs when the price is P^{**} and firms produce q^{**}. Firms are thus at the minimum point on their average cost function.

FIGURE P.15
EFFECT OF A REDUCTION IN DEMAND ON THE LONG-RUN PERFECTLY COMPETITIVE EQUILIBRIUM.

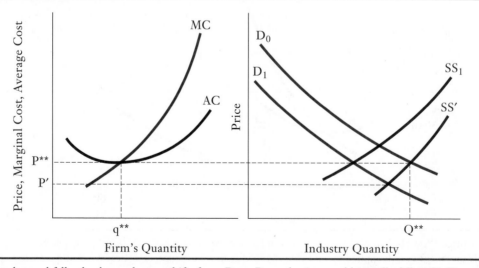

When demand falls, the demand curve shifts from D_0 to D_1, and price would initially fall to P'. Firms would earn less than they could elsewhere and would eventually begin to leave the industry. As this happens, the supply curve shifts to the left from SS' to SS_1. The industry shakeout ends when price is again P^{**}.

tity supplied exceeds the quantity demanded, and there is pressure on price to fall. It will continue to fall until no additional entry occurs. This is when the market price just equals a typical firm's average cost. As we have seen, to optimize on output, firms produce where market price equals marginal cost. Thus, in the *long-run equilibrium* depicted in Figure P.14, firms are producing at minimum efficient scale (recall, this is the quantity corresponding to the minimum point on the average cost curve), and the equilibrium market price P^{**} equals the minimum level of average cost.

Suppose, now, that market demand suddenly falls. Figure P.15 shows what happens. The fall in market demand is represented by a shift from demand curve D_0 to D_1. Initially, market price would fall to P', and firms' revenues would not cover their costs. The industry "shakeout" then begins. Firms begin to exit the industry. As this occurs, the industry supply curve shifts to the left, and price begins to rise. Once the "shakeout" fully unfolds, the industry supply curve will have shifted to SS_1, and the market price will once again reach P^{**}. Firms are then again optimizing on output and earning zero profit. Thus, no matter what the level of industry demand is, the industry will eventually supply output at the price P^{**}.[16]

A key implication of this theory is that the free entry exhausts all opportunities for making profit. This implication sometimes troubles management students because it seems to suggest that firms in perfectly competitive industries would then earn zero net income. But keep in mind the distinction between economic costs and accounting costs. Economic costs reflect the relevant opportunity costs of the financial capital that the owners have provided to the firm. Zero profits thus means zero *economic* profit, not zero *accounting* profit. Zero economic profit simply means that investors are earning returns on their investments that are commensurate with what they could earn from their next best opportunity.[17]

That free entry dissipates economic profit is one of the most powerful insights in economics, and it has profound implications for strategy. Firms that base their strategies on products that can be easily imitated or skills and resources that can be easily acquired put themselves at risk to the forces that are highlighted by the theory of perfect competition. To attain a competitive advantage, a firm must secure a position in the market that protects itself from imitation and entry. How firms might do this is the subject of Chapters 11, 12, 13, 14, and 15.

---

[16]This result is subject to the following qualification. If certain key inputs are scarce, the entry of additional firms results in the prices of these inputs being bid up. The firm's average and marginal cost functions then shift upward, and in the long run, the market price will settle down at a higher level. An industry in which this happens is known as an *increasing-cost industry*. The case we focus on in the text is known as a *constant-cost industry*.

[17]See the appendix on page 35 for a discussion of the relationship between economic profit and the concept of net present value from finance.

◆ ◆ ◆ ◆ ◆ GAME THEORY

The perfectly competitive firm faces many competitors, but in making its output decision, it does not consider the likely reactions of its rivals. This is because the decisions of any single firm have a negligible impact on market price. The key strategic challenge of a perfectly competitive firm is to anticipate the future path of prices in the industry and maximize against it.

In many strategic situations, however, there are few players. For example, there are only three producers of commercial airframes: Boeing, Airbus, and McDonnell-Douglas. In the market for aspartame, the artificial sweetener used in Diet Coke and Diet Pepsi, there are only two competitors: NutraSweet and Holland Sweetener Company. In these "small numbers" situations, a key part of making strategic decisions—pricing, investment in new facilities, and so forth—is anticipating the likely reactions of rivals.

A natural way to incorporate the reactions of rivals into your analysis of strategic options is to assign probabilities to their likely actions or reactions and then choose the decision that maximizes the expected value of your profit, given this probability distribution. But this approach has an important drawback: How do you assign probabilities to the range of choices your rivals might make? You may end up assigning positive probabilities to decisions that, from the perspective of your competitors, would be foolish. If so, then the quality of your "decision analysis" would be seriously compromised.

A more penetrating approach would be to attempt to "get inside the minds" of your competitors, figure out what is in their self-interest, and then maximize accordingly. However, your rivals' optimal choices will often depend on their expectations of what you intend to do, which, in turn, depend on their assessments of your assessments about them. How can one sensibly analyze decision making with this circularity?

It is precisely in such contexts that *game theory* is most valuable. Game theory is the branch of economics concerned with the analysis of optimal decision making when all decision makers are presumed to be rational, and each is attempting to anticipate the likely actions and reactions of its competitors. Much of the material we present in Section II on industry analysis and competitive strategy draws on basic ideas of game theory. In this section, we introduce these basic ideas. In particular, we discuss games in matrix and game tree form, and the concepts of a Nash equilibrium and subgame perfection.

Games in Matrix Form and the Concept of Nash Equilibrium

The easiest way to introduce the basic elements of game theory is through a simple example. Consider an industry that consists of two firms, Alpha and Beta, that produce identical products. Each must decide whether to increase its production capacity in the upcoming year. We shall assume that each firm always produces at full capacity. Thus, expansion of capacity entails a tradeoff. The firm may achieve

TABLE P.3
CAPACITY GAME BETWEEN ALPHA AND BETA

		Beta	
		DO NOT EXPAND	EXPAND
	DO NOT EXPAND	$18, $18	$15, $20
Alpha			
	EXPAND	$20, $15	$16, $16

All amounts are in millions per year. Alpha's profit is first; Beta's is second.

a larger share of the market, but it may also put downward pressure on the market price. The consequences of each firms' choices are described in Table P.3. The first entry is Alpha's annual economic profit; the second entry is Beta's annual economic profit.

Each firm will make its capacity decision simultaneously and independently of the other firm. To identify the "likely outcome" of games like the one shown in Table P.3, game theorists use the concept of a *Nash equilibrium*. At a Nash equilibrium outcome, each player is doing the best it can, given the strategies of the other players. In the context of the capacity expansion game, the Nash equilibrium is that pair of strategies (one for Alpha, one for Beta) such that

- Alpha's strategy maximizes its profit, given Beta's strategy.
- Beta's strategy maximizes its profit, given Alpha's strategy.

In the capacity expansion game, the Nash Equilibrium is (EXPAND, EXPAND), that is, each firm expands its capacity. Given that Alpha expands its capacity, Beta's best choice is to expand its capacity (yielding profit of 16 rather than 15). Given that Beta expands its capacity, Alpha's best choice is to expand its capacity.

In this example, the determination of the Nash equilibrium is fairly easy because for each firm, the strategy EXPAND maximizes profit *no matter what decision its competitor makes*. In this situation, we say that EXPAND is a *dominant strategy*. When a player has a dominant strategy, it follows (from the definition of the Nash equilibrium) that that strategy must also be the player's Nash equilibrium strategy. However, dominant strategies are not inevitable; in many games players do not possess dominant strategies (for example, the game in Table P.4).

Why does the Nash equilibrium represent a plausible outcome of a game? Probably its most compelling property is that it is a self-enforcing focal point: If each party expects the other party to choose its Nash equilibrium strategy, then both parties will, in fact, choose their Nash equilibrium strategies. At the Nash equilibrium, then, expectation equals outcome—expected behavior and actual behavior converge. This would not be true at non-Nash equilibrium outcomes, as the game in Table P.3 illustrates. Suppose Alpha (perhaps foolishly) expects Beta not to expand capacity and refrains from expanding its own capacity to prevent a drop in the industry price level. Beta—pursuing its own self-interest—would confound Alpha's expectations, expand its capacity, and make Alpha worse off than it expected to be.

The "capacity expansion" game illustrates a noteworthy aspect of a Nash equilibrium. *The Nash equilibrium does not necessarily correspond to the outcome that maximizes the aggregate profit of the players.* Alpha and Beta would be collectively better off by refraining from the expansion of their capacities. However, the rational pursuit of self-interest leads each party to take an action that is ultimately detrimental to their collective interest.

This conflict between the collective interest and self-interest is often referred to as the *prisoners' dilemma.* The prisoners' dilemma arises because in pursuing its self-interest, each party imposes a cost on the other that it does not take into account. In the capacity expansion game, Alpha's addition of extra capacity hurts Beta because it drives down the market price. As we will see in Chapters 8 and 10, the prisoners' dilemma is a key feature of equilibrium pricing and output decisions in oligopolistic industries.

◆◆◆

*E*XAMPLE P.2

THE PRISONERS' DILEMMA AND THE LAW

Modern American society has been criticized for being excessively litigious. Individuals and firms seem increasingly willing to turn to lawyers to resolve their disputes. But if, as is commonly argued, this dependence on litigation has significant social costs, why would a free market system generate so much business for lawyers?

The research of two economists, Orley Ashenfelter and David Bloom, suggests a possible answer.[18] The decision to hire a lawyer to resolve a dispute, they argue, may be the result of a prisoners' dilemma. Their argument is simple. Two parties to a dispute are collectively better off when they settle the dispute between themselves or hire a neutral arbitrator to resolve their differences. But if a party believes that by hiring a lawyer it will increase the odds of winning by a sufficiently large amount to make hiring a lawyer worthwhile, it will be a dominant strategy to hire a lawyer. But when both parties do this, the dispute is resolved no differently than if neither hired a lawyer, and each party is worse off by the amount it pays its attorney.

To test this theory, Ashenfelter and Bloom analyzed public employee wage disputes from 1981 to 1984 in New Jersey. They also studied union grievance proceedings involving the rights of discharged workers in Pennsylvania. In both cases, they found strong evidence that hiring a lawyer is a dominant strategy and that the decision to hire a lawyer leads to a prisoners' dilemma. Based on the New Jersey data, for example, they found that when one party hired a lawyer, the chances of

---

[18]Ashenfelter, O. and D. Bloom, "Lawyers as Agents of the Devil," Princeton University, working paper, 1994.

successfully persuading the arbitrator to accept its wage proposal went up from roughly 50 percent to 75 percent. When both sides hired lawyers, though, the odds of winning remained roughly 50 percent, indicating that the benefit of hiring a lawyer is canceled out when the other party also hires a lawyer.

The possibility that hiring a lawyer is a prisoners' dilemma suggests that making society less litigious is likely to prove quite difficult. Lawyers clearly have no interest in curbing the demand for their services. And the grim logic of the prisoners' dilemma suggests that a party in a dispute has a strong individual incentive to hire a lawyer, even though society as a whole would be better off if it did not.

Game Trees and Subgame Perfection

The matrix form is particularly convenient for representing games in which each party moves simultaneously. In many situations, however, decision making is sequential rather than simultaneous, and it is often more convenient to represent the game with a *game tree* instead of a game matrix.

To illustrate such a situation, let us modify the capacity expansion game to allow for the firm to choose among three options: no expansion of current capacity, a small expansion, or a large expansion of current capacity. To serve as a point of contrast, let us first examine what happens when both firms decide simultaneously. This game is represented by the 3 × 3 matrix in Table P.4. We leave it to the reader to verify that the Nash equilibrium in this game is (SMALL,SMALL).

But now suppose that Alpha seeks to preempt Beta by making its capacity decision a year before Beta's. Thus, by the time Beta makes its decision, it will have observed Alpha's choice and must adjust its decision making accordingly.[19] We can represent the dynamics of this decision-making process by the *game tree* in Figure P.16.

In analyzing this game tree, we seek what is known as a *subgame perfect Nash equilibrium* (SPNE). In an SPNE, each player chooses an optimal action at each stage in the game that it might conceivably reach and believes that all other players will behave in the same way.

TABLE P.4
MODIFIED CAPACITY EXPANSION GAME BETWEEN ALPHA AND BETA

		Beta		
		DO NOT EXPAND	SMALL	LARGE
	DO NOT EXPAND	$18, $18	$15, $20	$9, $18
Alpha	SMALL	$20, $15	$16, $16	$8, $12
	LARGE	$18, $9	$12, $8	$0, $0

All amounts are in millions per year. Alpha's profit is first; Beta's is second.

[19]To keep the example as simple as possible, we shall assume only two stages of decision making: Alpha makes its choice first, and then Beta responds. We do not consider the possibility that Alpha might respond to the capacity decision that Beta makes.

FIGURE P.16
GAME TREE FOR SEQUENTIAL CAPACITY EXPANSION GAME.

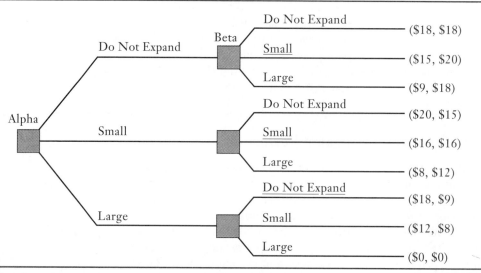

Alpha has three choices: DO NOT EXPAND, SMALL, and LARGE. Given Alpha's choice, Beta must then choose among DO NOT EXPAND, SMALL, LARGE. For whatever choice Alpha makes, Beta will make the choice that maximizes its profit. (These are underlined.) Given Beta's expected choices, Alpha's optimal choice is LARGE.

To derive the SPNE, we use the so-called *fold-back method:* We start at the end of the tree, and for each decision "node" (represented by squares), we find the optimal decision for the firm situated at that node. In this example, we must find Beta's optimal decision for each of the three choices Alpha might make: DO NOT EXPAND, SMALL, and LARGE:

- If Alpha chooses DO NOT EXPAND, Beta's optimal choice is SMALL.
- If Alpha chooses SMALL, Beta's optimal choice is SMALL.
- If Alpha chooses LARGE, Beta's optimal choice is DO NOT EXPAND.

(Beta's optimal choices are underlined.)

By folding back the tree in this fashion, we are assuming that Alpha anticipates that Beta will choose a profit-maximizing response to any strategic move Alpha might make. Given these expectations, we can then determine Alpha's optimal strategy. We do so by mapping out the profit that Alpha gets as a result of each option it might choose, *given that Beta responds optimally*. The fold-back analysis tells us:

- If Alpha chooses DO NOT EXPAND, then given Beta's optimal reaction, Alpha's profit will be $15 million.
- If Alpha chooses SMALL, then given Beta's optimal reaction, Alpha's profit will be $16 million.

- If Alpha chooses LARGE, then given Beta's optimal reaction, Alpha's profit will be $18 million.

The SPNE is thus for Alpha to choose LARGE. Beta responds by choosing DO NOT EXPAND.

Note that the outcome of the sequential-move game differs significantly from the outcome of the simultaneous-move game. Indeed, the outcome involves a strategy for Alpha (LARGE) that would be dominated if Alpha and Beta made their capacity choices simultaneously. Why is Alpha's behavior so different when it can move first? Because in the sequential game, the firm's decision problems are linked through time: Beta can see what Alpha has done, and Alpha can thus count on a rational response by Beta to whatever action it chooses. In the sequential-move game, Alpha's capacity choice has *commitment value*; it allows Alpha to force Beta into a corner. By committing to a large capacity expansion, Alpha forces Beta into a position where Beta's best response yields the outcome that is most favorable to Alpha. By contrast, in the simultaneous-move game, Beta cannot observe Alpha's decision, so the capacity decision no longer has commitment value for Alpha. Because of this, the choice of LARGE by Alpha is not nearly as compelling as it is in the sequential game. Commitment is discussed in detail in Chapter 9.

APPENDIX: ECONOMIC PROFIT AND NET PRESENT VALUE ◆ ◆ ◆ ◆ ◆

Economic profit is closely related to the concept of net present value from finance. We will use an example to illustrate this relationship. Consider a perfectly competitive industry in which a minimum efficient scale plant has a capacity of 100,000 units per year. The firm's production expenses when it produces at minimum efficient scale are $5 per unit of output. The cost of building the plant is $15 million. To make the example as simple as possible, we assume that the plant has an infinitely long life, (i.e., it does not depreciate). Suppose, finally, that the firm's cost of capital is 10 percent. This rate reflects what the firm's investors could make from alternative investments of comparable risk and thus also the appropriate opportunity cost for evaluating the investment in the plant.

Now suppose that the market price is currently $25 per unit and is expected to remain at that level for the foreseeable future. Is it worthwhile for the firm to enter the industry by building a minimum efficient scale plant and producing up to the plant's capacity? We can look at this decision in two seemingly different, but (as it turns out) equivalent, ways. First, we could calculate economic profit in the manner we discussed in the text. Total revenues would be $2.5 million per year. The total production costs that would show up on the firm's profit and loss statement would be $500,000 per year. In addition, though, the annualized opportunity cost of the plant would be the 10 percent cost of funds times the investment of $15 million, or $1.5 million per year. Total costs thus equals $2 million per year. Since this is less than total revenue, the investment in the plant yields a positive economic profit, so the firm should build it. Put another way, by investing in the plant, the firm delivers $500,000 per year above and beyond what its investors would receive in alternative investments of comparable risk.

The second way to analyze this decision is to use net present value analysis. To explain this approach, we must first introduce the concept of present value. The *present value* of a cash flow C received in t years at an interest rate i is equal to the amount of money that must be invested today at the interest rate i so that in t years the principal plus interest equals C.[20] Mathematically, present value would be given by

$$PV = \frac{C}{(1 + i)^t}$$

The present value of a stream of cash flows received over a period of years is the sum of the present values of the individual sums. Thus, the present value of cash flows C_1, C_2, ... C_T received one year from now, two years from now, ..., T years from now, is

$$PV = \frac{C_1}{(1 + i)} + \frac{C_2}{(1 + i)^2} + \ldots + \frac{C_T}{(1 + i)^T}$$

which can be written more compactly as

$$PV = \sum_{t=1}^{T} \frac{C_t}{(1 + i)^t}$$

The *net present value* (*NPV*) of an investment is simply the present value of the cash flows the investment generates minus the cost of the investment.

Given the assumptions that the investment has an infinite life and that the price and revenues are expected to remain the same over the foreseeable future, the *NPV* of the investment in the plant is given by

$$NPV = \sum_{t=1}^{\infty} \frac{2,000,000}{(1.10)^t} - 15,000,000$$

This looks intimidating, but fortunately the term in the summation is the present value of a *perpetuity*. A perpetuity is a level cash flow C received each year forever. The present value of a perpetuity has a convenient formula: It is equal to the cash flow divided by the interest rate, $\frac{C}{i}$. With this formula, we can rewrite *NPV* as

$$NPV = \frac{2,000,000}{.10} - 15,000,000 = \$5,000,000$$

Since the net present value is positive, the firm should undertake the investment.

---

[20]For a good introduction to the basic concepts of present value, see Brealey, R.A. and S.C. Myers, *Principles of Corporate Finance*, 3rd ed., New York: McGraw-Hill, 1988.

Note that the calculations of *NPV* and economic profit are similar. Indeed, with a constant annual cash flow and an infinitely lived investment, economic profit is simply equal to the *NPV* times the cost of capital. When cash flows are not constant and/or when the investment has a finite life, the relationship between *NPV* and economic profit is more complicated. However, a fundamental property still holds: *A firm's economic profit is positive if and only if the present value of its future cash flows exceeds the cost of the investments needed to achieve those cash flows.* Economic profit can thus be thought of as an annualized *NPV* calculation. The concept of zero economic profit thus begins to make more sense. It does not mean that the firm's net cash flows are zero, but that the present value of these cash flows just covers the cost of the firm's investments.

PART ONE

FIRM BOUNDARIES

THE EVOLUTION OF
THE MODERN FIRM

1

*T*his book identifies what we believe are general economic principles of strategy. Because these are general principles, they should be useful to managers facing a wide range of business conditions. This is of obvious benefit to any manager trying to make sense of an existing business that is less successful than desired. Immediate improvements can be made just by matching the firm's strategy to its particular business environment. This is also of benefit to the managers of the most successful firms. As any manager recognizes, conditions change over time, so that strategies that are appropriate to today's business environment may be inappropriate in the future. Sometimes conditions that influence the business environment change gradually, as with growth of the suburbs during the last half of the 20th century. Sometimes changes are more fast paced, as with the rapid improvements in information processing technology during the 1980s. Some changes seem to occur overnight, as with the fall of Communism in 1989. Armed with a set of principles, the manager can successfully adjust his or her firm's business strategy to its ever-changing environment.

To demonstrate the general applicability of principles to widely disparate business conditions, we will undertake a brief historical analysis. This chapter examines the evolution of the modern business firm by focusing on economic activity and business organization at three points in time: 1840, 1910, and today. For each period, we will discuss the infrastructure of business and market conditions that firms faced, how those conditions affected the size and scope of the activities of the firm, and how business organizations responded to changes.

These dates were not chosen randomly. The period before 1840 was one in which firms were constrained by conditions to operate in small localized markets. Changes in infrastructure between 1840 and 1910 encouraged the growth of corporate giants, such as Standard Oil, U.S. Steel, and DuPont. Even the largest and best-managed firms of that time were still constrained by the problem of control—how to gain sufficient information on a timely basis to adapt to change. Since 1910, and particularly in the past 30 years, changes in telecommunication and data processing have enhanced the information processing and control capabilities of the firms. As a result, an increasing diversity of organizations are able to respond effectively to their business environments.

◆ ◆ ◆ ◆ ◆ THE WORLD IN 1840

Doing Business in 1840

Before 1840, businessmen[1] largely managed their own firms and did so in ways that their counterparts today would find unfamiliar. The experience of John Burrows provides an example.[2] Burrows was an Iowa merchant who bought potatoes from nearby farmers, cleaned them, and packaged them. Hearing that potatoes were fetching $2 a bushel in New Orleans, he loaded an Illinois River flatboat and floated downstream. On the trip, he was offered 50 cents a bushel but rejected it in hope of getting a better price. While floating south, he was joined by other potato merchants seeking high New Orleans prices. Soon, the New Orleans market was glutted with potatoes. Simple supply and demand dictated that potato prices would plummet. When Burrows' six-week journey ended, he sold his potatoes to a Bermuda ship captain for eight cents a bushel.

Burrows was the kind of a merchant known as a "factor." Farmers in the United States sold their output to factors like Burrows, who brought the goods to major markets, such as New Orleans or New York, in search of buyers. Some buyers were local merchants, looking to stock their grocery stores. Most buyers were "agents," representing out-of-town merchants, including some from Europe. Factors and agents rarely transacted directly with each other. Instead, they enlisted the help of "brokers." Brokers served as matchmakers between factors and agents. They possessed specialized knowledge of market conditions (knowledge that individual factors and agents lacked), including the names of factors and agents, the availability of supplies, and the magnitude of demands.

Selling was informal. Factors and agents sought out brokers with whom they had done business before. Selling arrangements were rarely set in advance or specified in a contract. Instead, the brokers tried to arrange a price that best balanced supply and demand. This was how most business was transacted in 1840. The brokerage arrangement no longer dominates the American business landscape, but it does survive in various forms, such as in real estate. An important modern-day example of the broker is the "market maker" in securities transactions. Market makers in the New York Stock

---

[1] We use the term *businessmen* literally. Few, if any, women were involved in business in 1840. This had not changed much by 1910.

[2] This example comes from William Cronon's excellent history of the city of Chicago, *Nature's Metropolis*, New York: Norton, 1991.

Exchange (NYSE) match the buy and sell orders of parties who do not know each other, facilitating transactions that would otherwise be difficult to conduct.

Buy and sell orders for shares traded on the NYSE are filled almost immediately, so that both parties to a given transaction can be reasonably certain about the price at which the exchange will occur. John Burrows' experience shows us that this was not the case in 1840. Factors and agents faced considerable price risk—that is, the price that they received when the transaction took place may have been quite different from what they expected when they began doing business (e.g., when John Burrows started floating downstream). This risk obviously increased with the distance between the site of production and its final destination. Thus, European merchants trading with the United States ran even larger risks than those Mr. Burrows faced.

The lack of knowledge about prices, buyers and sellers, and the associated risks, dramatically shaped the nature of business. Farmers faced the most risk, and they relied on factors like Burrows to assume at least some of it, by selling different farm products at different times of the year, and by having the opportunity to sell specific products at various times on the way to market. Presumably, Burrows was more willing to bear risk than most farmers, and this may have been why he chose to be a factor rather than a farmer. Once Burrows reached the market, he relied on brokers to find buyers for his goods, a task that he could not easily perform himself.

The nature of information and risk had other implications for the size and structure of business. With few exceptions, such as in the textiles, clockmaking, and firearms industries, goods were produced by small, family-operated "firms." This stands in stark contrast to today, where a firm employing 100 workers is considered small, and there is often a clear distinction between owners (shareholders) and managers. Given the tremendous uncertainty about the market value of output, it is not surprising that individuals were reluctant to use their own resources to expand the productive capabilities of their businesses. For similar reasons, banks were also unwilling to extend loans for such a purpose. Given problems with transportation and communication, which we describe below, family-operated firms could not justify investments in raw materials acquisition, or final product distribution, even though such investments might have allowed them to better coordinate the production process and become more efficient. Production and distribution proceeded through many individual firms, simply because the market conditions were not right for anything else.

Conditions of Business in 1840: Life Without a Modern Infrastructure

The dominance of the family-run small business in 1840 was a direct consequence of the *infrastructure* that was then in place. Infrastructure includes those assets that assist in the production or distribution of goods and services that the firm itself cannot easily provide. Infrastructure facilitates transportation, communication, and financing. It includes basic research, which can enable firms to find better production techniques. The government also has a key role, both because government affects the conditions under which firms do business (e.g., by regulating telecommunications), and because the government is a direct supplier of infrastructure (e.g., the interstate highways).

By modern standards, the infrastructure of 1840 in Europe and America was poorly developed. Limitations in transportation, communications, and finance created the business environment with which John Burrows and others of his time had to cope. While we discuss the situation in America, European businessmen were faced with similar general limitations, which were often confounded by political factors.[3] Given these limitations, which we detail below, it should be apparent that the ways in which business was conducted in 1840, though alien to us today, were appropriate for the time.

Transportation: Transportation was undergoing a revolution in the first half of the 19th century, due to the harnessing of steam power. Although the Romans had made attempts to develop road beds by means of rails of different sorts, the modern railroad did not begin to develop and begin adding value to commerce until the introduction of the steam engine and the use of iron and steel rails. By 1840, the railroads had finished their "demonstration decade" of the 1830s and had begun to replace the horse and wagon for the shipment of raw materials and consumer goods.[4] The development of rails in the United States took time, however. As late as 1836, only 175 miles of railroad track were laid in one year.[5] As late as 1850, U.S. railway systems were still too fragmented to foster the growth of national markets.[6] There were few rails running west of the Appalachian Mountains, "connecting" lines often had different gauges, and schedules were seldom coordinated. The development of an integrated transportation infrastructure through railroads in the United States would not be complete until after 1870.[7]

---

[3]For comparisons of Europe and America on these issues see Chandler, A.D. and H. Daems (eds.), *Managerial Hierarchies: Comparative Perspectives on the Rise of the Modern Industrial Enterprise,* Cambridge, MA: Harvard University Press, 1980. For issues concerning industrialization within Europe, see Pollard, S., "Industrialization and the European Economy," *Economic History Review,* 26, November 1973: pp. 636–648.

[4]Chandler, A.D. and R.S. Tedlow, *The Coming of Managerial Capitalism,* Homewood, IL: Irwin, 1985, p. 179.

[5]Cochran, T.C. and W. Miller, *The Age of Enterprise: A Social History of Industrial America,* New York: Harper and Row, 1961, p. 45.

[6]Chandler, A.D. *The Visible Hand,* Cambridge, MA: Belknap, 1977; *Scale and Scope: The Dynamics of Industrial Capitalism,* Cambridge, MA: Belknap, 1990.

[7]Completed railroad mileage in the United States grew from 2,808 in 1840 to 52,922 in 1870 to 163,597 in 1890, with a peak of 254,000 miles in 1916 (Beniger, J.R. *The Control Revolution,* Cambridge, MA: Harvard University Press, 1986, p. 213). Railroad development in Germany paralleled developments in the United States (Chandler, *Scale and Scope,* 1990, p. 411). In France, the government played a major role in construction through the railroad laws of 1842 and 1857. The French rail system expanded from 3,627 kilometers in 1851 to 16,207 kilometers in 1858. The rail system in Italy developed later and to a lesser degree than in France (1,758 kilometers in 1860 to 7,438 kilometers in 1876). Railroads developed at a similar pace in Canada and Australia (Langer, W.L., *An Encyclopedia of World History,* Boston: Houghton Mifflin, 1980; pp. 684, 708, 835, 929).

Until the railroads developed, manufacturers used the waterways to transport goods over long distances, though transportation by water often left much to be desired. For example, while the new steamships plied major American rivers and the Great Lakes as early as 1813, there was no direct route connecting the major cities in the east to the Great Lakes until the completion of the Erie Canal in 1825, and steamships could not unload in Chicago until the 1840s. The trip from New York to Chicago was both lengthy and risky, especially during bad weather. Possible routes for waterways were limited and the construction and maintenance of canals was expensive.[8] Even with such limitations, however, the growth spurred by the opening of the Erie Canal was startling. For example, between 1830 and 1840, the population of Illinois tripled, from 157,000 to 476,000, and the population of Chicago grew eight times, from 500 to over 4,000.[9]

While canals and railroads spurred growth, in 1840 they were still in their initial stages of development. Without safe and reliable means of transporting large volumes of goods, producers were reluctant to make the investments necessary to expand their production capabilities, or to expand into raw materials acquisition. The emergence of an industrial economy centered around large industrial firms would have to wait for the completion of the railroad system and the development of effective communications capabilities.

Communications: The primary mode of long distance communication in 1840 was the public mail. Postal service predated the Industrial Revolution. The United States Federal Postal Service was chartered in 1791. As is often still claimed today, however, the postal service may have served everyone, but it was very slow. As late as 1840, it depended almost exclusively on the horse, and had difficulty adjusting to the expanded volume of communication that followed the western expansion of the United States and the gradual development of a mass-production economy.

The first modern form of communications was the telegraph, which required laying wires between points of service. In 1830, Samuel Morse linked Baltimore and Washington by telegraph. Telegraph lines soon flourished. By 1852 virtually every train line was paralleled by a telegraph line. By 1870, Western Union was one of the largest firms in the United States, and the telegraph provided the communication infrastructure for the growth of an industrial economy.[10]

The local scale of business activities in 1840 was partially attributable to the lack of a modern communication infrastructure. A businessman transacting with distant trading partners needed to be able to respond if market conditions changed.

---

[8]Chandler and Tedlow, *The Coming of Managerial Capitalism*, p. 176.

[9]Cochran and Miller, *The Age of Enterprise*, p. 42.

[10]Beniger, J.R., *The Control Revolution*, Boston: Harvard University Press, 1986; Chandler, A.D., *The Visible Hand.*

Without adequate communication, businessmen preferred to delegate responsibility for the transaction to agents or factors, such as Mr. Burrows, rather than assume the risk themselves. If a businessman did establish geographically separate facilities, he would wish to be able to communicate with each facility and coordinate their activities. Again, inadequate communication made this impossible. Similarly, railroads could not schedule trains reliably and safely. This interfered with the flow of goods over long distances and increased the risks associated with large-scale production.

Finance: Few individuals could afford to build and operate a complex firm themselves. Financial markets bring providers and users of capital together. Financial markets also enable buyers and sellers to smooth out cash flows and reduce the risk of price fluctuation. Most businesses in the first half of the 19th century were partnerships and found it difficult to obtain long-term debt. Stocks were not easily traded, thereby diluting their value and increasing the cost of equity capital. The lack of a developed financial infrastructure inhibited firms from raising capital for the larger projects that a mass-production economy required. It also limited the extent to which investors could protect themselves against the increased risks of larger capital projects.

The major role of private banks at this time was the issuance of credit. By 1820, there were over 300 banks in the United States. By 1837, the number had grown to 788. By offering short-term credit, banks smoothed the cash flows of buyers and sellers and facilitated reliable transactions, although there remained considerable risk from speculation and inflation throughout the 19th century. There was a recurring pattern of boom and bust, with periodic depressions, such as the "Panic of 1837."[11]

The availability of credit was far from uniform for smaller firms, however, and if it was available at all, credit was often granted informally on the basis of personal relationships. This limited the scope of possible activities for smaller firms. Larger projects, such as the Erie Canal, were primarily funded by government or private consortia—groups of private individuals brought together around a specific project. As the scale of capital projects greatly increased after 1840, government support or larger public debt or equity offerings by investment banks increasingly replaced financings by private individuals and small groups of investors.

Financial institutions also reduce business risks. The mechanism for reducing the risk of price fluctuation is the futures market, in which individuals purchase the right to buy and/or sell goods on a specified date for a predetermined price. Futures markets require verification of the characteristics of the product being transacted. They also require that one party to the transaction is willing to bear the risk that the "spot" (i.e., current) price on the date the futures transaction is completed differs from the transacted price. In 1840, there were no institutional mechanisms for reducing the risk of price fluctuation. The first futures market was created by the Chicago Board of Trade in 1848, and was to profoundly affect the farming industry, as we discuss in Example 1.1.

---

[11]Cochran and Miller, *The Age of Enterprise*, pp. 43–49.

Production Technology: Production technology refers to the application of scientific or technical knowledge to production processes. Firms often direct resources toward internal innovation and toward spurring the demand for new products from the market, both of which help spur technological development. However, the ability of any single firm or group of firms to change general levels of production technology is limited, and the expansion of business activity is inevitably constrained by the current state of technology. Technological constraints were substantial in 1840.

Technology was relatively undeveloped in 1840, compared with what it would become in the next half century. Most factories produced goods the same way they had been produced in the previous century, and even the most advanced factories were not equipped to produce standardized goods at high volume to an extent that would become common by 1910. Even though the mechanization of textile plants had begun before 1820 and standardization was common in the manufacture of clocks and firearms, the "American System" of manufacturing through the use of interchangeable parts was only just beginning. Until the 1870s, factories continued to operate on the basis of internal contracting, in which their facilities were leased to a supervisor who in turn hired workers and produced goods. Even within those factories that produced more standardized items with interchangeable parts, there was still a small scale of production and little use of inanimate sources of power, which would have increased the pace of production and required new forms of factory organization and coordination.[12]

Government: Government resolves disputes and sets the rules under which business operates. It becomes even more important when it participates more directly in economic activity through the provision or purchase of goods and services, through tax policies, or through regulation. Historically, most infrastructure investments are left to the public sector. Private investors are reluctant to invest in infrastructure because while they would bear the cost of this investment, their competitors would share in the benefits. Government agencies do not compete with private firms, so they are better suited to support the development of infrastructure resources, such as canals and railroads, that serve the common good. For example, from 1820 until 1838, 18 states authorized advances of credit of $60 million for canals, $43 million for railroads, and $4.5 million for turnpikes.[13] Apart from the development of these large, fixed-cost resources, direct government involvement in the U.S. economy in 1840 was relatively low, especially when compared with the levels of government spending that would be common by the 1930s. Given the limited state of local markets at the time, this lack of involvement probably inhibited economic expansion.

---

[12]Best, M., *The New Competition: Institutions of Industrial Restructuring*, Cambridge, MA: Harvard University Press, 1990, chap. 1; Robinson, R.V. and C.M. Briggs, "The Rise of Factories in Nineteenth-Century Indianapolis," *American Journal of Sociology*, 97, November 1991: pp. 622–656.

[13]Cochran and Miller, *The Age of Enterprise*, p. 42.

Summary

The lack of a modern infrastructure generally limited economic activity in 1840. Firms in 1840 were small and informally organized, which was a direct result of conditions that made modern business institutions impractical. Production technology was not sufficiently developed to permit a significant expansion of production over traditional levels. Even if such a technology had been available, the limited transportation infrastructure, coupled with difficulties in obtaining accurate and timely information, would have made investments in large production and distribution capabilities too risky to be reasonable to businessmen in 1840. There were no professional managers as we think of them today: Owners ran their own enterprises. Levels of market demand and technological development would need to increase before high-speed and high-volume production and distribution could develop. This required an expanded economic infrastructure.

There were forces in play, however, that would change the conditions in which business activity took place and greatly increase its scale of operations. The full effect of these changes could not be felt until a transportation and communications infrastructure had developed to control increased volumes of activity over a broader geographic domain. The growth of large projects would also await the development of techniques for assuring management control and reducing the organizing costs for owners associated with large capital projects and the larger firms that developed to manage them.

$\mathcal{E}$XAMPLE 1.1

THE EMERGENCE OF THE CITY OF CHICAGO[14]

The emergence of Chicago as a major commercial center in the 1800s illustrates the core concepts that we have discussed, albeit for a city rather than a business. In the 1840s, a number of growing cities in the American Midwest, including Cincinnati, Toledo, Peoria, St. Louis, and Chicago, were all competing, as vigorously as firms in any other markets might compete, to become the region's center of commerce. Their success would ultimately be decided by the same conditions that determined the horizontal and vertical boundaries of business firms. Significant changes in *infrastructure* and *technology* enabled Chicago's business organizations, and with them the city's financial fortunes, to rise well above those of other cities. For example, by 1860, the Chicago Board of Trade bought and sold nearly all of the grain produced in the Midwest. Similarly, by 1890, the nation's meat-packing industry was dominated by two Chicago meat packers, Armour and Swift.

---

[14] This example draws from Cronon, *Nature's Metropolis*.

Chicago prospered because it conducted business in new and different ways from those that characterized other competing commercial centers. Chicago was the first to take advantage of new technologies that reduced the costs and risks of doing business. For example, Swift and Armour simultaneously adopted the refrigerated train car, which had been put in limited use by Illinois fruit growers. (The refrigerator car was produced by lining a standard freight car with ice carved from Lake Michigan.) This allowed cattle and hogs to be butchered in Chicago, before they lost weight (and value) on the way to market. Cyrus McCormick and others took advantage of the recently invented grain elevator to inexpensively sort, store, and ship grain bought from Midwest farmers. They reduced the riskiness of dealing with large quantities of grain by buying and selling grain futures at the Chicago Board of Trade.

The businesses run by Swift, Armour, McCormick, and other Chicago business leaders required substantial investments in rail lines, icing facilities, grain elevators, the futures market, and so forth. These businessmen recognized that they could not recoup their investments unless they had sufficiently high volumes of business. This would require *throughput:* the movement of inputs and outputs through a production process. The meat-packing and grain businesses of Chicago required large supplies of ice, large assured movements of grain and livestock from the farmlands, and large assured movements of grain and butchered meat to the eastern markets. The need for throughput explains why Chicago, rather than any other city, was to emerge as the business center of the Midwest. Only Chicago, with its unique location as the terminus of rail and water routes from the East and West, had the transportation infrastructure necessary to assure throughput. Chicago thus emerged during the mid-1800s and remains today the "market leader" among Midwest cities.

Figure 1.1 shows the extent of the American railroad system in 1840, 1870, and 1890. As the figure shows, Chicago became the hub of significant East/West and North/South rail lines. This was in part due to the efforts of local business leaders to promote the city's growth. Once Chicago started to appear as a hub, however, it was increasingly reasonable to have further railroad lines pass through the city, making it an even larger transportation center. Of its major "competitors," only St. Louis could have competed in terms of rail throughput. But St. Louis lacked quick access to the Great Lakes—the preferred shipping route for grain during summer and fall and the principal source of ice for meat packers.

THE WORLD IN 1910 ◆ ◆ ◆ ◆ ◆

Doing Business in 1910

Business in many sectors of the economy changed greatly from 1840 to 1910, and the business practices and organizations of 1910 would seem much more familiar to the modern businessperson than those of 1840. In some sectors, such as farming

FIGURE 1.1
GROWTH OF AMERICAN RAILROADS FROM 1840 TO 1890.

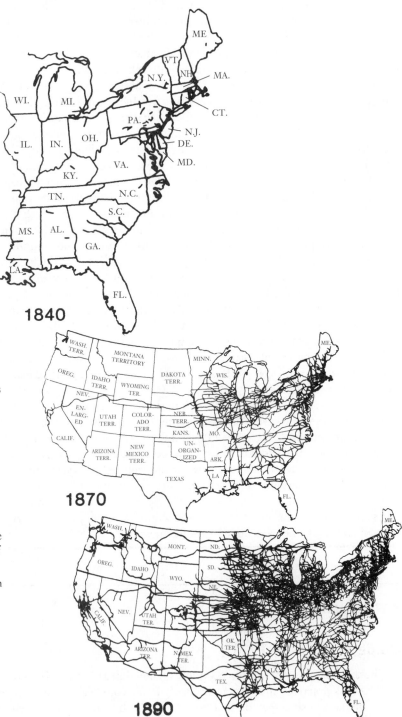

1840

1870

1890

By 1870, Chicago had become a major rail hub. This was due in part to its location on Lake Michigan and in part to efforts by local business leaders to promote the city's growth. Once the hub was established, it made sense for more rail lines to connect through the city. By 1890, Chicago had clearly become the transportation center of the Midwest.

Source: Association of American Railroads. Reprinted from Beniger, J.R., *The Control Revolution*, p. 212.

and textiles, small firms still predominated, but were faced with a well-developed set of buyers and suppliers and of service providers to facilitate commerce and circulate information. In other sectors, such as chemicals, steel, and transportation, business was increasingly dominated by large firms that not only produced finished goods, but were heavily involved in raw materials acquisition and end-product distribution. These firms were too large for their owners to be involved in everyday decision making, so a new class of "professional" managers emerged with no ownership interest in the firms they guided. These firms had internal hierarchies in which lower-level managers supervised day-to-day activities and reported to upper management, who attempted to shape the various departments and divisions into a cohesive whole.

The evolution of the hierarchical firm was the direct consequence of changes that were taking place in infrastructure and technology. No change was more important than the development of mass production technologies, such as the Bessemer process for making steel, or the continuous-process tank furnace that facilitated mass production of many products, such as plate glass. These new technologies made it possible to produce goods at costs far below anything that could be achieved by firms using older technologies. To fully exploit these production opportunities, firms needed reliable supplies of inputs, as well as access to widespread distribution and retail outlets. The large fixed investments required to develop these outlets were justified only when large volumes of goods flowed through these outlets. In short, firms needed to assure a sufficiently large throughput to make the expansion of productive capacity economical. Achieving the needed throughput was assured by the development of the infrastructure: railroads for shipping inputs and finished goods; telegraph and telephone for comunication, control, and coordination of materials over expanded areas; and banking and accounting practices to allow acquisition of the investment capital needed to finance the construction of production and distribution facilities.

The potential benefits of reorganizing production to reach many customers at lower costs per customer were not lost on businessmen. Historian Alfred Chandler has noted how businessmen reorganized their firms to take advantage of new production technologies.[15] The owner-operator who invested in a new technology found that he needed to substantially increase production to recoup his investment. This required a tremendous increase in throughput. This increased the owner-operator's responsibilities in functional areas of business, such as purchasing, sales, distribution, and finance. These all needed to be coordinated by a central office to assure that production runs went smoothly and finished goods found their way to market. This growth in size and enhancement of functional responsibilities in a business area is an example of what we refer to as *horizontal integration*.

Product line and volume expansion altered relationships among manufacturers, their suppliers, and their distributors. Manufacturing firms increasingly chose to

---

[15]Chandler, *Scale and Scope.*

vertically integrate, that is, they chose to produce raw materials and/or distribute finished goods themselves, rather than rely on independent suppliers, factors, and agents. Chapters 2 through 4 discuss at length the benefits of vertical integration, but briefly, manufacturing firms in 1910 found it desirable to vertically integrate because the high volume of production made the firm more vulnerable to gaps in the chain of supply and distribution. This explains why vertical integration occurred in some industries, such as steel, chemicals, and machinery, but not in others, such as textiles and furniture. Vertical integration only made sense when firms could exploit new technologies to achieve cost savings from high-volume production. In industries like furniture and textiles, few technological breakthroughs occurred. High-volume firms in these industries had no advantages over low-volume firms, so vertical integration to assure throughput did not occur in them.

New production technologies also allowed firms to produce a wider range of products at lower costs than if they were produced separately. In the years immediately following 1910, many firms, such as DuPont, General Motors, and Alcoa, expanded their product lines well beyond their original boundaries. They found that the increased size and complexity of multiproduct operations necessitated a further reorganization into semiautonomous divisions, each of which in turn would be vertically and horizontally integrated in various degrees. Each division in these firms made the principal operating decisions for their own businesses, while a separate corporate office made decisions that affected the entire corporation. For example, the divisions of General Motors made operating decisions for each car line, while corporate management would make decisions regarding corporate finance, research and development, and new model development. This organizational form, known as the multidivisional or *M-form*, became characteristic of the largest industrial firms until the 1960s.

The growth of vertically and horizontally integrated firms often reduced the number of firms in an industry and increased the potential for collusion to restrict competition and increase profits. This was especially true in industries where rapid expansion of high fixed cost production had resulted in overcapacity, which led to destructive price rivalry as firms tried to build volume and spread their fixed costs. Mergers and informal associations of firms to restrict competition were common in such industries as tobacco, steel, aluminum, and oil. During the period around 1910, the U.S. government directed antitrust activities toward breaking up firms that appeared to be national monopolies. Among the major cases during this time were those involving Standard Oil (1911); American Tobacco (1911); DuPont (1912); International Harvester (1918); and Eastman Kodak (1920).[16]

Besides vertical and horizontal integration, large firms needed to develop managerial hierarchies. As Alfred Chandler describes, the role of the managerial hierarchy was to substitute the *visible* hand of management for the *invisible* hand of the market.[17] That is, it provided administrative coordination across the variety of

---

[16]Fligstein, N., *The Transformation of Corporate Control*, Cambridge, MA: Harvard University Press, 1990, chaps. 2 and 3.

[17]Chandler, *The Visible Hand*.

functions that had been brought inside the firm. The growth of managerial hierarchies brought with it the emergence of a class of professional managers, many of whom owned little or no share of the business. The manager worked on behalf of the owners, however, and the problem of ensuring that managers worked in the best interests of owners grew along with the importance of general managers.

Business Conditions in 1910: A "Modern" Infrastructure

A substantially new infrastructure for the conduct of business had emerged by 1910, most notably in transportation and communications. These developments fostered the growth of national markets by enabling firms to count on the fast and reliable movements of goods, along with instantaneous and accurate communication over vast geographic areas.

Production Technology: Production technology developed greatly between 1840 and 1910, which promoted the growth of mass production. Mass production processes had become much more common, permitting high-volume, low-cost manufacturing of many products, including steel, aluminum, automobiles, and chemicals, to name only a few.

Transportation: For mass production to be viable, producers needed assured throughput. This was made possible by the continued growth of the railroads. By 1910, railroads dominated passenger and freight transportation. Travel became faster, safer, and more reliable. Manufacturers could obtain raw materials from distant sources, and swiftly ship their product to customers hundreds or even thousands of miles away. In many cases, smaller manufacturers sold to the newly created mass distribution firms, such as Sears, who could efficiently distribute via the rails vast arrays of consumer goods to widely scattered customers.[18] The development of the railroads helped the emerging industrial economy in other ways. For example, the enormous quantities of steel required to build the railroads fueled the initial growth of the steel industry. The railroads also had to solve problems of organization and accounting that set the example for the later development of these business practices in other industries.[19]

Communications: The communications infrastructure in 1910 enabled businesses to communicate more accurately and quickly than ever before and allowed managers of growing firms to feel more confident in expanding their volume of transactions well beyond traditional levels. The principal components of the communications infrastructure in 1840—the postal system and the telegraph—were

---

[18]The automobile was emerging as a competitor for passenger transport. Trucks, however, did not seriously compete with rails for freight transport until the 1950s.

[19]Chandler, A.D., "The Railroads: Pioneers in Modern Corporate Management," *Business History Review*, 39, Spring 1965: pp. 16–40.

still important in 1910. During this time, however, the telephone was growing in importance, relative to other means of communications. A few phone calls made directly to suppliers and distributors instantly assured managers that large production runs were feasible, and that there were markets for their output.

While the development of the telephone was important for the growth of the communications infrastructure, the growth of the largest telephone firm, American Telephone and Telegraph (AT&T), illustrates how the development of large firms during this period depended on the appropriateness of market and technological conditions. When the telephone was invented in 1876, its technological potential (and hence its profitability) was uncertain because some related devices essential for telephone service as we know it, such as the switchboard, had not yet been developed. The market conditions facing the telephone were also uncertain because major patent conflicts were unresolved, and as a result, there was competition to provide local telephone service. By the 1880s, patent conflicts had been resolved, and new technology made consolidation possible. In 1883, AT&T adopted a strategy of consolidating local telephone companies into a national system. The resulting network greatly reduced the costs of interconnecting large numbers of users, and the telephone quickly replaced the telegraph as the communications technology of choice.[20]

Finance: In 1910, active security markets publicly traded the shares of the largest industrial firms. Since the 1860s, the large investment banking houses had been underwriting most stock transactions that were essential for meeting the financing needs of large firms. Investment bankers like J.P. Morgan were among the most powerful businessmen in the world in 1910.[21] The development of a financial infrastructure was further aided during this period by the systematization and circulation of information about credit (credit bureaus), the increased availability of installment financing, and the further development of the communications infrastructure.

Between 1840 and 1910, owners, managers, and investors also increasingly realized that the growing scope of business activity required new ways of keeping track of a firm's activity and reporting its results to interested parties. During this period, new accounting techniques were developed, and mandatory reporting standards for public firms became law. The newly grown large firms developed these techniques to solve record-keeping problems occasioned by the size and scope of their activities. For example, the railroads produced major innovations in cost accounting to manage their requirements of operating efficiencies. The newly

---

[20]For details, see Garnet, R.W., *The Telephone Enterprise: The Evolution of the Bell System's Horizontal Structure, 1876–1909*, Baltimore, MD: Johns Hopkins University Press, 1985. Also see, Smith, G.D., *The Anatomy of a Business Strategy: Bell, Western Electric, and the Origins of the American Telephone Industry*, Baltimore, MD: Johns Hopkins University Press, 1985.

[21]Chernow, R., *The House of Morgan: An American Dynasty and the Rise of Modern Finance*, New York: Simon & Schuster, 1990.

formed mass marketing firms, such as Sears, developed new accounting concepts, such as inventory turnover, to link profits to fluctuations in sales volume. As large multidivisional firms developed, techniques were developed to track the productivity of investments to guide corporate resource allocation decisions.[22]

Accounting developments also focused around the idea of public accounting—the public disclosure of details of a firm's operations to insure that investors were not being cheated by managers and that capital was being maintained. In England, for example, laws enacted between 1844 and 1900 required: the presentation of a "full and fair" balance sheet at shareholders meetings; the payment of dividends out of profits; the maintenance of a firm's capital stock; and the conduct of compulsory and uniform audits of all registered firms. Similar developments occurred in the United States. For example, by the 1860s, the railroads employed more accountants than the U.S. government. The American Association of Public Accountants was formed in 1897.[23]

Government: Government interactions with the economy were becoming more important during this period. The role of government in regulating the conditions under which business was conducted, in such areas as antitrust, provisions for disability insurance and worker safety, and insurance for widows and children also increased. (Securities markets were not regulated until the 1930s.) Near-universal, mandatory secondary-school education also became the norm for industrialized nations in the first half of the 20th century. This produced a workforce able to meet the specialized needs of large integrated and bureaucratically organized firms.

Summary

The expanded business infrastructure in 1910 made it reasonable and cost effective for firms to expand their markets, product lines, and production quantities. It is thus not surprising that the capital stock of the United States grew at a faster rate than the gross national product in the second half of the 19th century as businessmen made the investments necessary to capture the benefits of new technologies.[24] New technologies permitted the higher volume of standardized production, while the growth of the rail system permitted the reliable distribution of manufactured goods

---

[22]Chandler, A.D. and H. Daems, "Administrative Coordination, Allocation, and Monitoring: Concepts and Comparisons," in Horn, N. and J. Locka (eds.), *Law and the Formation of the Big Enterprises in the 19th and Early 20th Centuries: Studies in the History of Industrialization in Germany, France, Great Britain, and the United States,* Gottingen: Vandenhoeck & Ruprecht, 1979, pp. 28–54.

[23]Carruthers, B.G. and W.N. Espeland, "Double Entry Bookkeeping and the Rhetoric of Economic Rationality," *American Journal of Sociology,* 97, July 1991, 31–70; Chandler, *The Visible Hand,* p. 464.

[24]See Gallman, R.E., "The United States Capital Stock in the Nineteenth Century," chap. 4 in Engerman, S.L. and R.E. Gallman (eds.), *Long-Term Factors in American Economic Growth,* Chicago: University of Chicago Press, 1986, pp. 165–214.

to a national market. The telegraph enabled large firms to monitor and control geographically separate suppliers, factories, and distributors. The growth of futures markets, capital markets, insurance companies, investment banks, and other financial institutions enabled business to be transacted on a scale that would have been impossible in 1840. By one estimate, the "transaction-processing sector," which included transportation, communication, and financial institutions, grew to be one-third of the U.S. economy by 1910.[25]

To best take advantage of the cost savings afforded by mass production, many firms chose to reorganize. This growth of vertically and horizontally integrated firms is a defining characteristic of the period between 1840 and 1910. Increasingly, critical decisions for firms were made not by the traditional owner-operator or by the marketplace but by managers, a new class of professional workers that had developed during this period. These managers became expert in functions that had not previously been handled by individual owners and entrepreneurs, and their new skills became a source of competitive advantage for M-form firms and a key to success in industries with the potential for scale and scope economies.

◆ ◆

$\mathcal{E}$XAMPLE 1.2

RESPONDING TO THE BUSINESS ENVIRONMENT: THE CASE OF AMERICAN WHALING

Historical accounts, such as Chandler's, have featured large manufacturing and distribution firms to emphasize how these firms developed into their modern forms as technological and market conditions permitted. However, firms also had to respond to changing conditions when scale and scope economies were not available and when growth into a multidivisional structure did not offer a competitive advantage. The American whaling industry in the 19th century provides an example.[26]

In the middle of the 19th century, whaling was a competitive industry that consisted of many relatively small firms. There were no appreciable cost advantages to large firms, because whales had to be caught one at a time, and the whaling ships had to go to the whaling grounds to make their catches. The technology for catch-

[25]Wallis, J.J. and D.C. North, "Measuring the Transaction Sector in the American Economy, 187–1970," chap. 3 in Engerman, S.L. and R.E. Gallman (eds.), *Long-Term Factors in American Economic Growth*, Chicago: University of Chicago Press, 1986, pp. 95–161.

[26]This discussion is based on Davis, L.E., R.E. Gallman, and T.D. Hutchins, "Productivity in American Whaling: The New Bedford Fleet in the Nineteenth Century," chap. 3 in Galenson, D.W. (ed.), *Markets in History: Economic Studies of the Past*, Cambridge: Cambridge University Press, 1989.

ing whales did improve productivity during the century, with such innovations as whale guns and more effective lances, but these developments did not change the basic processes by which whales were caught, and they certainly did not improve productivity to the same degree that the introduction of mass production and distribution techniques did for other industries. Whaling ships at this time also did not make use of the advances in steam power that were becoming common in passenger and freight transport, due to particular requirements for navigation and storage during whaling voyages. The only innovations were in new types of sailing vessels specifically designed for the needs of whalers, and these were largely incremental in their effects on productivity.

The principal whaling products at the time, spermaceti, sperm oil, and whale oil, were used as illuminants and lubricants. By 1850, whale oils were facing increasing competition from other illuminants, such as coal, oil, coal gas, and kerosene. Demand for lubricants was also increasing at this time, as new manufacturing facilities, such as the textile mills, needed to lubricate their machines. The growth in demand offset the increases in competition, so that the real price of sperm oil (i.e., the price after adjusting for inflation) doubled between 1820 and 1850, while the real value of the industry's output rose tenfold.

Whalers responded to the rapid increase in demand by searching out whaling grounds in the Pacific, Indian, and Arctic Oceans. Exploiting these grounds required longer voyages, often lasting up to four years, which in turn led to the use of larger ships and increased the logistical problems of provisioning them. The longer voyages to new grounds made whaling riskier and increased the chance of losing the entire ship to one in ten. When these problems became sufficiently large and distant whaling grounds became sufficiently desirable, the geographic center of the American whaling industry shifted from New Bedford, Massachusetts, to San Francisco, California. These changes in the whaling business, along with the incremental technological adjustments mentioned above, were the only reasonable responses available to an industry that could not adopt high-volume production and distribution techniques.

These changes in the whaling industry also had negative consequences for the industry's performance. On the whole, they made whaling less desirable for qualified seamen, a serious problem in a labor-intensive industry. This problem was especially severe after 1850, when opportunities in commercial shipping or on land were rapidly increasing, due to industrialization. To respond to this problem, whalers either had to pay experienced seamen increased rewards, which were based on the size of the catch, or attract less experienced hands, who could be paid less and who were less aware of the rigors of the longer voyages. As the 19th century progressed, whalers chose the latter course, that of hiring inexperienced seamen, which reduced the productivity of whaling voyages.

The American whaling industry declined after 1870 and had all but disappeared by 1914, due to product obsolescence. The industry that remains today focuses on different products (whale meat and cooking oil) and uses modern techniques in shipping and whalecraft that were pioneered by the Norwegians.

◆ ◆ ◆ ◆ ◆ The World Today

Doing Business Today

Since 1910, and particularly in the past 30 years, the ways of doing business have changed profoundly. Many strategies that were effective when American firms competed mostly with each other no longer seem to work in an era of global competition. In many industries, firms that relied on cost advantages associated with high volumes of production have been slow to adapt to changes that allow specialized niche firms to offer tailor-made products at low cost. Business practices that evolved in an era of political stability can no longer be taken for granted in conditions of rapid and unpredictable change, and business–government relations now fundamentally affect a firm's strategy and operations.

Compared with 1910, the scope of product market activities carried out within firms today has changed. While some firms had begun to diversify beyond traditional product lines as early as 1890, the pace of diversification increased significantly after World War II. Some of this diversification was the result of antitrust pressures that prevented large firms from growing even larger by acquiring rivals in the same industry. It also occurred because new opportunities opened in related markets and distribution channels. For example, consumer products companies like Philip Morris and Quaker Oats realized that they could distribute a much wider range of products through their distribution channels than they had previously considered. Technology-oriented companies, such as United Technologies, realized that they could take skills mastered in an underlying technology, such as jet engines, and apply them to a group of business units.

Other firms acquired portfolios of unrelated businesses. The commonly expressed rationale for this "unrelated diversification" was to reduce risks that are idiosyncratic to specific business units, leaving investors only with the risks to which all business units are exposed.[27] These so-called conglomerate firms, such as ITT and Textron, differed from firms like Philip Morris that pursued "related diversification" in that their corporate managers took much less interest in making decisions regarding research and development, advertising, and major capital projects. Instead, these managers ran their firms as holding companies, in which nearly all strategic and operating decisions were delegated to the individual business units. The job of the corporate headquarters was monitoring the returns of the businesses in the corporate portfolio and buying and selling businesses based on their returns.

---

[27]This rationale raises interesting questions, though, about the efficiency of securities markets. In well-functioning securities markets, risk-averse investors could presumably construct their own personal portfolios to optimally diversify risk. Thus, it is not clear why corporate managers need to provide this "risk diversification" service for their shareholders, unless shareholders cannot somehow achieve the right level of diversification for themselves. This issue is taken up in detail in Chapter 6, which discusses corporate diversification.

Industry structure has also changed significantly since 1910, with many industries becoming far more competitive than they once were. This has occurred for several different reasons. In some industries, such as automobiles and machine tools, foreign entry has increased competition in what had been stable oligopolies throughout much of the post–World War II era.[28] In other industries, such as mass retailing and air express, new organizational approaches toward purchasing, warehousing, and logistics have fundamentally transformed the way firms compete. In still other industries, for example, soft drinks and cigarettes, brand proliferation and "niche" marketing have greatly increased competition. In a host of industries, ranging from airlines and trucking to financial services and health care, the deregulation of prices and entry restrictions has increased competition in prices and services, as firms struggle to gain market share.

Changes in the scope of modern enterprises and the nature of product market competition have been accompanied by changes in how firms develop their strategies. The increased diversification of large firms has required new concepts of how corporate strategic planning adds value. Strategic planning in diversified firms needs to combine detailed information about the industry situations of particular business units with overall corporate goals in a process that informs corporate managers, achieves agreement and commitment to plans from division managers, and provides a basis for strategy implementation. Planning tools developed by the Boston Consulting Group, McKinsey, and General Electric, among others, served as the basis for strategic planning in many diversified firms.

Not only have firms reevaluated strategy formulation in the current environment, but they have also reconsidered the structures they use to carry out those strategies. Until the 1960s, most large diversified firms followed the General Motors model and employed the M-form. But as these firms diversified into less-related businesses, the role of corporate management changed, necessitating changes in the role of the corporate headquarters. Highly diversified conglomerates increasingly utilize "flat" hierarchies and small corporate staffs. Even within firms with related product lines, the M-form has sometimes become increasingly outdated as the nature of competition in product markets has changed. Some firms, such as Dow Corning, Amoco, and Citibank, have had particularly difficult problems in coordinating complicated production processes across different customer groups and market areas using traditional multidivisional structures. These firms have enhanced the extent of control and the complexity of the internal hierarchy through matrix structures, in which two or more overlapping hierarchies are used at one time to coordinate people in the firm. Other firms, including Benetton, Nike, Rollerblades, and Harley-Davidson, have gone in the opposite direction and have organized with simple internal hierarchies. These firms control product design and brand image but leave most other key organizational functions, including manufacturing, distribution, and retailing to independent market specialists.

---

[28]An oligopoly is a market structure dominated by a few large firms.

Just as the new position of manager in 1910 incorporated administrative functions within the firm that had been left to the market, in the 1990s, many administrative functions are increasingly returned to the market through downsizing, as firms with large administrative components attempt to reduce costs and increase flexibility. Aggressive market specialists, such as EDS and Servicemaster, are increasingly assuming management functions that were done in-house in the large hierarchical firm. In many industries, the balance of costs between using the firm and using market specialists appears to have shifted back toward the market. Those managerial functions that are not returning to the market are being increasingly automated, so that those managers who remain now focus on a mix of highly technical, specialized, coordinative tasks and broader, general management duties.[29]

Changes in the nature of industry conditions, organizational structure, and the balance of activities done inside the firm have fundamentally changed the job of the general manager. In the large hierarchical firm that dominated the industrial landscape through the 1970s, a manager's source of power came from the vertical chain of command. The manager's career path was usually within a particular functional department, and evaluations were based on the manager's contribution to departmental objectives. Control in the organization was achieved through highly structured administrative systems, highly circumscribed job descriptions, and hierarchical relationships involving "bosses" and "subordinates." In many firms today, however, traditional hierarchies are weakening. Increased competition in many industries has placed a premium on skills at anticipating shifts in market demand and quickly transforming new ideas into marketable products.[30] Such skills typically necessitate much more coordination across functional departments than existed in the traditional hierarchical firm, resulting in changes in the locus of power in the organization, changes in the nature of career paths, and changes in the bases of performance evaluations.

The traditional hierarchy has also been changed by the increased use of outside independent contractors to perform many of the firm's traditional administrative functions. With this increased "outsourcing" comes greater opportunity for novel organizational arrangements, such as joint ventures and strategic partnerships with suppliers, that cut across the organizational chart and ignore the chain of command. Rosabeth Moss Kanter, writing about the emerging role of the modern manager, recounts the experience of a purchasing manager who found that her job changed radically following the initiation of joint ventures between her company and several of its suppliers.[31] The purchasing department became an important center of action in the company, and this manager found herself setting procurement strategy and interacting on a regular basis with the top management of both

---

[29]Kotter, J.P., *The General Managers*, New York: Free Press, 1982.

[30]See Stalk, G., P. Evans, and L. Shulman, "Competing on Capabilities: The New Rules for Corporate Strategy," *Harvard Business Review*, March–April 1992: pp. 57–69.

[31]Kanter, R.M., "The New Managerial Work," *Harvard Business Review*, November–December 1989: pp. 85–92.

the supplier and her own company. Moreover, suppliers began contributing to this manager's performance appraisals, and these appraisals were tied not only to her own performance, but also to the performance of the team of managers she led.

The Infrastructure Today

Infrastructure today is marked by sophisticated communications, transportation, and computing technologies that make effective coordination of extensive activities on a global scale increasingly commonplace. This, in turn, increases the interdependence of what had been separate geographic markets and has magnified the costs of infrastructure failure. The financial markets in New York and Chicago, for example, are thoroughly linked with those in Tokyo, Hong Kong, and London, such that businesspeople today increasingly need to consider more information from a wider geographic area in making even routine decisions.

Transportation: Automobile and air travel have been the areas of greatest change in the transportation infrastructure since 1910. The enormous increase in the number of motor vehicles, greatly aided by national highway systems, also created a major industry in its own right. Interstate trucking has become a major competitor to the railroads. Air transportation, of both passengers and freight, also changed the nature of business in terms of the volume of traffic carried, the speed at which it was carried, and the predictability of air travel.

Air, rail, and ground travel have also become better coordinated. Increasing demands from shippers of large volumes of goods for efficient and reliable transportation over long distances, coupled with increased sophistication in communications and data processing technology, allowed intermodal approaches to transportation to develop, in which goods are shipped by containers that move from ships to railroads to trucks. Because of the increased importance of air travel for both freight and passengers, geographic proximity to railroads and waterways is not as important as it once was for cities and firms.

Communications: The extensive development of telecommunications technologies, such as the fax or the modem, have made possible the nearly instantaneous transmission and reception of large volumes of information over long distances, making global markets possible for a wide range of products and services. This technology, coupled with data processing technology, has also drastically changed the abilities of individuals to do their work and of firms to coordinate workers in a variety of situations and circumstances. In particular, communications and computing advances greatly facilitate the ability of independent firms to coordinate their activities, reducing the benefits of vertical integration. Although fundamental developments in computer technology occurred before World War II, many observers have argued that the growth of data processing technology, especially when combined with telecommunications and production technology, has been the defining characteristic of changes in economic infrastructure in the second half of the 20th century.

Finance: The failure of financial markets in 1929, linked to worldwide recession in the 1930s, led to the restructuring of the financial infrastructure into its modern form, through the separation of commercial and investment banking, the enhanced role of the central banks, and the increased regulation of securities markets. The result through the 1970s was a stable financial services sector that supplied firms with equity and debt funding that the firms themselves could not provide through their retained earnings.[32]

Deregulation of financial services in the 1970s and 1980s led to major changes in the role of the financial sector as part of the economic infrastructure. Since 1980, capital market actors have been more active in evaluating firm performance. The ready availability of large amounts of funds through so-called "junk" bonds allowed mergers and acquisitions to multiply in number and dollar amount per deal. This increased takeover activity has in turn stimulated responses by managers to restructure their firms in order to raise their stock price and protect against takeover. Some observers characterized this activity as the workings of a "market for corporate control" that could discipline errant management teams.[33] The increased activity of capital markets, coupled with the diversification of firms out of single business areas, has made finance not just a support service, but increasingly the central functional focus of large firms.

Financial accounting further developed to adjust to the increased complexity of multidivisional firms, a process that began with the consolidation of General Motors in the 1920s and has continued with accounting procedures for mergers and acquisitions, restructuring, and hostile takeovers. In addition, cost or managerial accounting developed after 1910 has become important in providing managers with timely and accurate information on which to base their decisions. These developments were often made in conjunction with developments in data processing technology and statistical quality control techniques.

Production Technology: Production technology has become much more sophisticated since World War II, due to technological innovations and advances in computerization and quality management. These changes have led to production capabilities becoming a part of a firm's strategy and to the firm's research and development (R&D) program becoming a major part of a firm's capital investment. This issue is often made in comparisons of U.S. and Japanese firms, in which American firms are noted for their lack of investment in R&D and manufacturing.[34]

---

[32]Donaldson, G. and J. Lorsch, *Decision Making at the Top*, New York: Harper, 1983.

[33]See Manne, H., "Mergers and the Market for Corporate Control," *Journal of Political Economy*, 73, 1965: pp. 110–120; Jensen, M.C., "Takeovers: Folklore and Science," *Harvard Business Review*, November–December 1984: pp. 109–121; or Useem, M., *Executive Defense: Shareholder Power & Corporate Reorganization*, Cambridge, MA: Harvard University Press, 1993.

[34]For more detail on these issues, see Kantrow, A. (ed.), *Survival Strategies for American Industry*, New York: Wiley, 1983. Also see Hayes, R. and S. Wheelwright, *Restoring Our Competitive Edge: Competing Through Manufacturing*, New York: Wiley, 1984.

The economic implications of the new technology for firms are complex. Changes in production technology, such as the development of computer-aided design and manufacturing (CAD/CAM), have changed traditional ideas of price/quality tradeoffs and allowed the production of high quality, tailor-made goods at low cost. The adoption of these technologies is not a simple tradeoff of capital for labor. On the contrary, as changes in production technologies influence corporate strategies, they create whole classes of highly skilled positions—to operate the machines and coordinate the more complex organizational structures that result from these technologies. In using new technologies, managers in the 1990s must make a strategic choice between reorganizing around new information/production technologies or using these technologies incrementally, in order to reinforce traditional modes of production and organization. These are some of the issues behind the debate on corporate "reengineering."[35]

Government: Between 1910 and today, the role of government in the economic infrastructure became very complex. Government bureaucracy and the scope of government regulation of economic activities greatly increased in the first half of the 20th century, in response to two world wars and to the Great Depression of the 1930s.[36] Direct government expenditures on the military and public works become major aspects of the economy. Government manpower requirements during World War II alone greatly increased the diffusion of bureaucratic and differentiated personnel practices across many industries.[37] Federal antitrust developed after World War II to include the regulation of potential competition through the control of horizontal mergers.[38] Industry-specific regulations became highly developed in several sectors (telephones, railroads, airlines, communications, financial services).

Since the 1960s, many of the traditional regulations on industries have been reduced, while others have grown. The breakup of the Bell System, the deregulation of the airline, trucking, and financial service industries, and the weakening of bank regulations have been major factors in the economy since 1980. Regulations on health care, on the safety of conditions in the workplace, and on the relationships of the firm to the environment became common in the 1960s and 1970s. These included equal opportunity employment, occupational safety and health, and environmental protection.

---

[35]Hammer, M., "Reengineering Work: Don't Automate, Obliterate," *Harvard Business Review*, 1990, 69: pp. 104–113.

[36]Higgs, R., *Crisis and Leviathan: Critical Episodes in the Growth of American Government*, Oxford: Oxford University Press, 1987.

[37]Baron, J.N., F.R. Dobbin, and P.D. Jennings, "War and Peace: The Evolution of Modern Personnel Administration in U.S. Industry," *American Journal of Sociology*, 92, September 1986: pp. 350–383.

[38]Fligstein, N., *The Transformation of Corporate Control*, Cambridge, MA: Harvard University Press, 1990, chaps. 5 and 6.

Summary

While the first half of the 20th century was the era of the large hierarchical firm, changes in market conditions and infrastructure in the past 30 years have made smaller and flatter business organizations the preferred way of structuring business activities in many industries. This has come about for many reasons. The globalization of markets, facilitated by improvements in the transportation, communications, and financial infrastructure, has increased the intensity of competition in many industries, which in turn has placed a premium on quickness and flexibility in responding to shifts in market demand. Changes in technology have taken the advantages of large-scale production out of many production processes. Advances in communications and computing have made it possible for independent market specialists to coordinate complex activities at great distances, thus reducing the need for vertical integration. These changes have already begun to alter the role of the business manager and will continue to do so in the future.

The changes in the market conditions, infrastructure, and the ways of doing business in the past 30 years have created both opportunities and constraints. For example, the growth of global markets has greatly increased the potential sales of key products, but has also introduced powerful foreign competitors into the world and domestic markets. Similarly, changes in capital markets have made huge pools of resources available to firms that could not have previously obtained them, but they have also made large industrial firms potential targets of hostile takeovers. Technological innovation and computerization have given firms more control over production processes than ever before, but have also given smaller firms the ability to compete on even or better terms with larger firms, who had previously been the primary beneficiaries of production improvements. Finally, at a time when management skills are becoming more important for firms, competitive pressures to outsource and downsize are thinning management ranks.

◆ ◆

$\mathcal{E}$XAMPLE 1.3

EVOLUTION OF THE STEEL INDUSTRY

Nowhere has the changing nature of business had a greater effect than in the American steel industry. Given the market conditions and infrastructure in the first half of the 20th century, success in the steel industry required both horizontal and vertical integration. Traditionally, the leading firms, such as U.S. Steel, Bethlehem Steel, and Republic Steel, produced a wide array of high-volume steel products and controlled all of the key stages of the production process, from the mining of ore through the production of the finished steel products to marketing and distribution. But beginning in the early 1950s, changes in the nature of market demand and the technology of steel production began to transform the industry.

The most significant change in market demand was driven by shifts in the economy at large: Beginning in the 1950s, "lighter" products, such as strips and sheets used to produce appliances, automobiles, and computers, became relatively more important than "heavier" products, such as rails and plates used for railroad and ship building. But the large steel producers, particularly U.S. Steel, were committed to the "heavy" products. In addition, much of the steel makers' capacity was poorly located to serve the new demands for lighter products. These factors created opportunities for foreign producers to penetrate American markets.

The most notable technological advances were the basic oxygen furnace, the continuous casting process, and scrap metal processing with the electric arc furnace. The basic oxygen furnace, which was commercialized in 1950 by an Austrian firm, Linz-Donawitz, replaced the open-hearth process as the fastest way to convert iron into raw steel. The continuous casting process, a German invention that was perfected in the early 1960s by a small American company, Roanoke Electric, allowed steel producers to bypass the costly process of pouring molten steel into ingots and then reheating them for milling and finishing. Unlike the basic oxygen furnace and continuous casting, the electric arc furnace was available before World War II, but it was little used before 1960. However, the increasing availability of scrap steel due to breakthroughs in the shredding of discarded automobile bodies changed that, and by 1970, the electric arc furnace had become a viable way of producing nonalloy steel.

These technological advances had two profound effects on the industry. First, in postwar Japan and Germany, and later in Brazil and South Korea, startup steel firms were not hesitant to adopt the basic oxygen furnace and continuous casting. By contrast, in the United States, the established integrated mills had made nonrecoverable investments in the older technologies, both in terms of physical capital and expertise in producing with the older processes. These firms were therefore reluctant to shift to the new technologies. As late as 1988, 93 percent of all Japanese firms and 88 percent of South Korean steel firms had adopted continuous casting, while only 60 percent of American firms had done so, and nearly half of this adoption had occurred in the 1980s.[39] U.S. Steel (now called USX) still does not have continuous casting at two of its major steel producing plants.[40] This allowed foreign producers to quickly become significant competitive threats to the large integrated American producers. Second, the electric arc furnace and advances in continuous casting spurred the development of *minimills*, small nonintegrated producers that convert scrap metal into finished steel products. The success of minimill producers, such as Nucor, Chapparal, and North Star, is emblematic of the significance of this new way of producing steel. Minimills have eliminated the advantages of high-volume manufacturing in product lines, such as steel bars, structural

---

[39]Adams, W. and H. Mueller, "The Steel Industry," in W. Adams (ed.), *The Structure of American Industry*, 8th ed., New York: MacMillan, 1988, p. 90.

[40]Barnett, D.F., and R.W. Crandall, "Steel: Decline and Renewal," in L.L. Duetsch (ed.), *Industry Studies*, Englewood Cliffs, NJ: Prentice-Hall, 1993.

shapes, and wire rods, and with Nucor's recent breakthrough in thin-slab casting, they may also take away the advantages of scale in the production of hot- and cold-rolled sheet. While the large integrated producers have not disappeared, their importance has clearly diminished. From 1970 to 1990, American integrated producers retired nearly 40 percent of their capacity (55 million tons), while in the same period minimills increased their capacity sixfold, from 4.5 million tons to 29 million tons.[41]

Faced with strong competition from abroad and competition at home from low-cost minimills, the older, integrated steel makers have been forced to become more efficient, but they are still barely profitable. Not surprisingly, they have turned to government trade regulations for relief.

◆ ◆ ◆ ◆ ◆ THREE DIFFERENT WORLDS: CONSISTENT PRINCIPLES, CHANGING CONDITIONS, AND ADAPTIVE STRATEGIES

The enormous differences in business practices and infrastructure among the three periods we surveyed illustrate a key premise of this book: *Successful strategy results from the application of consistent principles to constantly changing business conditions.* Strategies are—and should be—the adaptive, but principled, responses of firms to their surroundings. The infrastructure and market conditions of business do not uniquely determine the strategies that firms choose. In all three of our periods, there was considerable experimentation by firms, as well as variation in the characteristics of firms that were successful and those that failed. But market conditions and infrastructure do significantly constrain how business can be conducted and the strategic choices that managers can make. For example, the development of the railroad, telegraph, and telephone by 1910 doomed most of the factors, agents, and brokers who facilitated trade in the 1840s.

Because circumstances change, one might be tempted to conclude that nothing endures in business strategy. Whatever one learns is bound to be obsolete as markets change or infrastructure evolves. This is true if one is looking for a set of recipes or checklists that will make a firm successful under *any* conditions. If the historical survey in this chapter suggests nothing else, it is that recipes that purport to work under any market conditions or within any infrastructure (e.g., "divest any business that does not have the largest or second largest share in its market") are bound to fail eventually. Principles, however, are different from recipes. Principles are economic and behavioral relationships that are general enough to be applicable to wide classes of circumstances. Because principles are robust, organizing the study of business strategy around principles will allow us to understand why certain

[41]Barnett and Crandall, p. 143.

strategies, business practices, and organizational arrangements are appropriate under one set of conditions but not others. To illustrate, consider a simple, yet important principle that has had direct relevance throughout business history for a common decision that firms make regarding whether they should produce some good or service themselves or purchase it from another firm (the so-called "make-or-buy" decision):

> A production technology that involves a large upfront investment in facilities and equipment will have a cost advantage over a technology that involves a small upfront investment only if the firm can achieve a sufficiently large level of throughput.

This principle is robust. It is as valid today as it was in 1840 or 1910. Applying this principle to the different conditions that existed in 1840, 1910, and today goes a long way toward explaining why large, vertically integrated firms were appropriate in 1910 but not in 1840 or, perhaps, today. In 1910, firms in industries such as steel, farm machinery, chemicals, and cigarettes could make their investments in new capital-intensive production techniques pay only if they could achieve sufficiently large throughput. These firms could have relied on independent market specialists to produce key inputs and components and bring their finished products to market. But the rudimentary conditions of communications and transportation, although vastly more developed than those that had existed in the 1840s, would have made it difficult for independent firms to coordinate the procurement, production, distribution, and marketing functions to achieve the needed throughput. In many industries, it was better to bring all of these critical functions inside a single vertically integrated firm and build a managerial hierarchy to coordinate them.

Vertical integration was not needed in 1840, because many of the technologies offering efficiencies from mass production did not exist. Even if they had existed, the undeveloped transportation and communications infrastructure would have limited the size of markets, constraining firms from achieving the throughput needed to take advantage of the new technologies. Vertical integration is less beneficial in today's business environment for a different reason. As stressed earlier, modern communications and computing technologies have significantly reduced the costs of coordinating complex transactions in the market. Independent suppliers and purchasers can work together to plan production runs and set delivery schedules more easily than they could have in 1910. As a result, transactions that in 1910 were most efficiently guided by the "visible hand" of internal hierarchy can be carried out in the marketplace between independent specialists.

This book is about principles, not recipes. In the remaining chapters of this book, we develop principles that pertain to the boundaries of the firm, the nature of industry structure and competition, the firm's strategic positions within an industry, and the internal organization and management of the firm. Through the study of these principles, we believe that students of management can better understand why firms and industries are organized the way they are and operate the way they do. We also believe that by judiciously applying these principles, managers can enhance the odds of successfully adapting their firms' strategies to the environment in which they compete.

CHAPTER SUMMARY

◆ A historical perspective demonstrates that while the nature of business has changed dramatically since 1840, successful businesses at all points in time have applied consistent principles to their business conditions.

◆ In 1840, communications and transportation infrastructures were poor. This increased the riskiness of business enterprise and mitigated against large-scale production. Business in 1840 was dominated by small, family-operated firms that relied on specialists in distribution as well as market makers who matched the needs of buyers and sellers.

◆ By 1910, innovations in production technology made it possible to greatly reduce unit costs through large-scale production.

◆ Businessmen in 1910 who invested in these new technologies needed assurance that there was a sufficient flow of throughput to keep production levels high. As a result, manufacturing firms vertically integrated into raw materials acquisition, distribution, and retailing.

◆ Manufacturing firms also expanded their product offerings, creating new divisions that were managed within an "M-form" organization.

◆ These large hierarchical organizations required a professional managerial class. Unlike managers in 1840, professional managers in 1910 generally had little or no ownership interest in their firm.

◆ Continued improvements in communications and transportation have made the modern marketplace a global one. At the same time, new technologies have reduced the advantages of large-scale production and vertical integration.

◆ In many industries, small manufacturers find that they can meet the changing needs of their clients better than can large hierarchical firms. In other industries, market specialists use computers, facsimile machines, and modems to coordinate activities that used to require a single integrated firm.

QUESTIONS

1. In light of recent downsizing and restructuring of Corporate America, was Chandler's explanation of benefits of size incorrect?

2. Many analysts say that the infrastructure of Eastern Europe today resembles that of the United States at the start of the twentieth century. If this is true, then what patterns of industrial growth might you expect in the next decade in the context of contemporary competitive forces?

3. In the past half-century, several cities have been identified with specific industries: Akron/tires; Macon/carpets; Sunnyvale/computer chips; Orlando/tourism. Why do such centers emerge? Given evolving technology, what is their future?

4. How might U.S. industry have evolved differently if strong antitrust laws had been in place as of 1900?

THE VERTICAL
BOUNDARIES
OF THE FIRM

2

*T*he production of any good or service usually requires a fairly wide range of activities. The process that begins with the acquisition of raw materials and ends with the distribution and sale of finished goods is known as the *vertical chain*. A central issue in business strategy is how to organize the vertical chain. In Chapter 1 we saw that in the 1840s, the vertical chain featured many intermediaries. By 1910, production was dominated by large *vertically integrated firms*, that is, hierarchical firms that performed many of the steps in the vertical chain themselves. The 1990s business landscape still features many vertically integrated firms, such as Scott Paper, which cuts its own timber, mills it, makes paper products, and distributes them to the market. Other well known firms, such as Nike and Benetton, are vertically "disintegrated": They perform few tasks in the vertical chain themselves. The *vertical boundaries* of a firm define the activities that the firm performs itself as opposed to purchasing from independent firms in the market. The next three chapters examine a firm's choice of its vertical boundaries and how they affect the efficiency of production.

MAKE VERSUS BUY ◆◆◆◆◆

The vertical chain within the modern industrial enterprise involves a large variety of specialized support activities, ranging from product design and materials procurement to distribution and sales. As described in Chapter 1, large hierarchical enterprises began to perform these activities in order to coordinate the flow of production through the vertical chain. This coordination was essential for achieving the sufficiently large throughput that was needed to make investments in mass production facilities economically viable. Over time, the specialized activities that support production have become more prominent. Today, many manufacturing firms are well known for their expertise in tasks not directly related to the production of consumer goods and services: Baxter and General Electric in strategic planning, Pepsi and Philip Morris in marketing, EG+G and Dow Corning in financial planning, United Technologies in human resource management, and Inland Steel in logistics. In entire industries, such as soft drinks and athletic shoes, supportive activities are the lifeblood of the major players.

While many firms have succeeded by producing their own supportive activities, others prefer to obtain these activities from specialized providers in the market, or what we call *market firms*. (When a firm buys activities or inputs from market firms, we say that it is *using the market*; when a firm provides the activity or makes the input itself, we say that it is *vertically integrated* in that activity or input.) Former Hewlett-Packard CEO John Young described the downsizing of his firm in the early 1990s as follows: "We used to bend all the sheet metal, mold every plastic part that went into our products. We don't do those things anymore, but somebody else is doing it for us."[1] When industrial firms, such as Hewlett-Packard, increasingly use the market to obtain inputs, they shrink their vertical boundaries, that is, become less vertically integrated. As John Young points out, the vertical boundaries of firms may shrink even as their industry is growing.

It is no wonder that many firms prefer to use the market for many of the activities that support their production, distribution, and sales. The firms specializing in supporting functions include many recognized leaders in their fields, and they perform these activities as well or better than the firms they supply them to could. Examples of leading specialists in supporting functions include: Leo Burnett, which provides market research and creates and shows advertisements for large industrial enterprises; Servicemaster, which supervises janitorial personnel for hospitals, schools, and industrial concerns; and United Parcel Service, which distributes products to customers of many manufacturers and retailers. Because of firms such as these, a manufacturer can obtain a superior marketing program, improve the efficiency of its housekeeping, and secure rapid, low-cost distribution without having to perform any of these tasks itself.

It is not always desirable to use the market, however. A firm must address certain issues before it can determine how best to coordinate the activities of its suppliers and distributors. These issues are associated with how firms deal with their *upstream* and *downstream* trading partners.

Upstream, Downstream

Economists often refer to one firm's relationship to another as being upstream or downstream. The terms are relative—a firm may be upstream from some firms and downstream from others. In general, goods in an economy "flow" along the

---

[1] From *Chicago Tribune*, February 21, 1993: Sec. 1, p. 15.

vertical chain from raw materials and component parts to manufacturing, through distribution and retailing. Economists say that early steps in the vertical chain are upstream in the production process, and later steps are downstream, much as lumber flows from upstream timber forests to downstream mills. Thus, Ford Motor Company is downstream from U.S. Steel but upstream from local Ford dealerships.

Figure 2.1 depicts a vertical chain for the production and sale of furniture. The vertical chain includes activities directly associated with the processing and handling of materials from raw inputs (e.g., wood) through the finished product. Processing activities include raw materials acquisition, goods processing, and assembly. Handling activities include all associated transportation and warehousing. When we discuss activities that are upstream or downstream in a production

FIGURE 2.1
THE VERTICAL CHAIN OF PRODUCTION FOR FURNITURE.

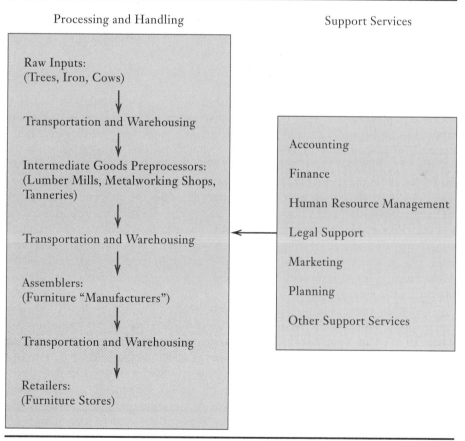

The materials necessary to make furniture are processed and handled through each step of the vertical chain. Professional support services are provided all along the chain.

process, we are usually referring to these processing and handling activities. Each processing and handling step may also require an array of professional support services, such as accounting, finance, human resources management, and strategic planning. We place these services outside the vertical chain to indicate that they support each step along the chain.

The decision of a firm to perform an upstream, downstream, or professional supporting activity itself or purchase it from an independent firm is called a *make-or-buy* decision. Typical make-or-buy decisions for a manufacturing firm include whether to develop its own source of raw materials, provide its own shipping services, or operate its own warehouses and retail stores, rather than rely on outside suppliers and merchants. Firms at other points in the vertical chain must also come to grips with make-or-buy decisions. Raw materials suppliers can integrate forward (downstream) into production, as when Alcoa began manufacturing aluminum foil in the 1920s. Retailers can integrate backward (upstream) into distribution, as when WalMart developed a sophisticated warehouse and integration network in the 1960s. Distributors can also integrate backward, as when Vestron, a video distributor, produced its own movie, *Dirty Dancing*, in 1987, or forward, as when John Rockefeller, who owned oil pipelines, bought oil refineries in the 1870s.

The Value Chain

As goods and services move along the vertical chain from raw materials to final output, and as professionals lend their supportive expertise, value is created. For example, raw timber is of relatively little value to most consumers, but they may value finished furniture highly. The value of finished furniture, in turn, depends on whether it is sitting on a warehouse floor or is on display in a retail showroom. One may think about the vertical chain, therefore, as a series of activities that adds value. The *value chain*, developed by Michael Porter, describes the activities within firms and across firms that add value along the way to the ultimate transacted good or service.[2] Porter divides value-creating activities into five primary activities (inbound logistics, manufacturing operations, outbound logistics, marketing and sales, and customer service) and four support activities (procurement, technology development, human resources management, and infrastructure activities, such as finance and accounting).

While the concept of the value chain has received much attention as an alternative to the notion of the vertical chain, the two ideas are, in fact, quite similar. The vertical chain is a series of activities that must be performed to produce a good or service, whereas the value chain is a series of activities that add value. Porter's list of value-creating activities corresponds closely to the list of activities in the vertical chain of furniture making depicted in Figure 2.1. In general, any activity on the value chain must lay on the vertical chain. At the same time, any activity on the vertical chain should be on the value chain. If not, then by definition it adds no value and should not be included in the vertical chain.

---

[2]Porter, M., *Competitive Advantage*, New York: Free Press, 1985.

TABLE 2.1
BENEFITS AND COSTS OF USING THE MARKET

Benefits

- Market firms can achieve economies of scale that in-house departments producing only for their own needs cannot.
- Market firms are subject to the discipline of the market and must be efficient and innovative to survive. Overall corporate success may hide the inefficiencies and lack of innovativeness of in-house departments.

Costs

- Coordination of production flows through the vertical chain may be compromised when an activity is purchased from an independent market firm rather than performed in-house.
- Private information may be leaked when an activity is performed by an independent market firm.
- There may be costs of transacting with independent market firms that can be avoided by performing the activity in-house.

Defining Boundaries

Regardless of a firm's position along the vertical chain, it needs to define its boundaries. To resolve the associated make-or-buy decisions, the firm must compare the benefits and costs of using the market as opposed to performing the activity in-house. Sometimes firms must use the market because they lack the capacity to perform a task in-house. In the long run, if the costs of using the market exceed the benefits, the firm will have to find a way to increase its in-house capabilities or bear the inefficiency of using independent firms. In the rest of the chapter, we assume that firms are solving long-run make-or-buy problems, so that capacity is not constraining. Table 2.1 summarizes the key benefits and costs of using independent firms. These are discussed in detail in the remainder of this chapter.

◆ ◆

XAMPLE 2.1

MAKE VERSUS BUY: PEPSI-COLA AND ITS BOTTLERS

When the cola industry began, the two major suppliers were Coca-Cola and Pepsi-Cola. Coke and Pepsi were primarily syrup manufacturers. They obtained raw materials, such as caramel and sugar, from independent suppliers and relied on independent bottlers to distribute and market their products. This allowed Coke and Pepsi to protect the source of their advantage in the market—their syrup formulas—while using independent firms to perform all other tasks. This division of labor made sense. Upstream inputs like caramel and sugar can be obtained from competitive markets at prices at or near minimum average cost. Downstream bottlers knew their local consumers better than did the Pepsi and Coke corporate offices, and could better judge the need for price discounts and other marketing ploys.

As the market for cola has grown, Coke and Pepsi have continued to obtain raw inputs from the market. However, both of them, especially Pepsi, have increasingly consolidated distribution and marketing. Whereas Pepsi at one time relied exclusively on independent bottlers, it now owns over 60 percent of its bottling operations.[3]

Timothy Muris, David Scheffman, and Pablo Spiller have identified several important reasons for the consolidation of ownership of cola bottlers.[4] Changes in the technology of bottling have created economies of scale that have reduced the number of bottling plants by 85 percent. Roughly 5 percent of existing bottling plants continue to close each year, their output taken up by expanding existing facilities. The remaining independent bottlers are larger and more strongly committed to their own marketing philosophies. This became a large problem for cola makers, who found that in the 1980s they needed to substantially increase the coordination of their retailing activities across the different regions served by bottlers.

The need for increased coordination of retailing activities can be traced to several changes in marketing. First, the 1970s and 1980s saw the emergence of regional and national purchasers of cola products, including major grocery chains, discount general merchandise retailers, and fast-food outlets. Retailers, such as WalMart, purchase soft drinks through a national office and use sophisticated sales information to design their own marketing plans. Coke and Pepsi need to be equally centralized and sophisticated to service these customers. Second, Coke and Pepsi increasingly use sophisticated advertising and promotions—the "Pepsi Challenge" is a good example—as a major competitive weapon. These require a strong national marketing campaign and the cooperation of bottlers in implementing the promotions across different territories.

Coke and Pepsi must determine how to coordinate the marketing and distribution functions when there are important national and local components. Pepsi found that its national marketing themes and campaigns often conflicted with those of local bottlers. In one instance, Pepsi distributors promoted a "real fruit" display for Pepsi Slice while Pepsi's national marketing division was pushing an end-of-aisle display by offering VCRs to store managers. Neither promotion was fully implemented, and Pepsi was left with a surplus of VCRs.[5] The solution to the coordination problem has been simple—Pepsi has bought out many of its bottlers and centralized its marketing activities.

---

[3] Coke is the largest shareholder of Coca-Cola Enterprises, its largest bottler, and is part owner of many other "independent" bottlers.

[4] Muris, T., D. Scheffman and P. Spiller, "Strategy and Transaction Costs: The Organization of Distribution in the Carbonated Soft Drink Industry," *Journal of Economics and Management Strategy*, 1, Summer 1992: pp. 83–128.

[5] See "Pepsi-Cola U.S. Beverages (A)" Case #9-390-034, Harvard Business School, 1990.

Some Make-or-Buy Fallacies

Before detailing the critical determinants of make-or-buy decisions, it is necessary to dispense with three common, but *incorrect* arguments:

1. Firms should generally buy, rather than make, to avoid paying the costs necessary to make the product.
2. Firms should generally make, rather than buy, to avoid paying a profit margin to independent firms.
3. Firms should make, rather than buy, because a vertically integrated producer will be able to avoid paying high market prices for the input during periods of peak demand or scarce supply.

The first argument is easy to reject. Consider an activity on the vertical chain, say, the distribution of finished goods from a manufacturer to retailers. The manufacturer could distribute the goods itself, or use an independent distributor. While it is true that if it uses an independent distributor, the manufacturer will not have to purchase trucks, hire drivers, and so forth, this does not imply that it is less costly to use the independent distributor. The simple reason is that the independent distributor will have to purchase the trucks and hire the drivers and will then charge the manufacturer a price sufficient to cover the associated expenses. Choosing to buy, rather than make, does not eliminate the expenses of the associated activity. Make-or-buy choices can, however, affect the efficiency with which the activity is carried out, which is the central argument of this chapter.

The basic flaw in the second argument can be illuminated by again considering the case of distribution. Suppose that a distributor pays $200,000 for a truck and charges a fee that is comparable to its competitors, and for which it expects to generate $220,000 in net revenues in excess of operating expenses. It appears that the distributor is realizing a "profit margin" of 10 percent that the manufacturer could avoid if it bought the truck itself. But the expected margin of 10 percent may mask a substantial amount of variation in profit margins per truck. Some trucks may be fully utilized, while others may go idle. The 10 percent "profit margin" may be necessary to entice banks to lend to distributors the funds necessary to purchase trucks. (If the 10 percent margin exceeded the amount needed to mollify lenders, we would expect additional truck purchases as would-be distributors attempt to cash in on this opportunity to make money. This could be expected to drive down net revenues per truck, reducing the profit margin.)

Now suppose the manufacturer purchases the truck itself. In effect, the manufacturer is investing $200,000 of its own funds. The return on this investment depends on whether it uses the truck often enough, so that it proves cheaper to own the truck rather than to use independent distributors. Thus, the manufacturer faces a risk on its $200,000 investment, just as a bank lending to an independent trucker faces a risk. If the firm can reliably predict its trucking needs, this should reduce the risk to independent truckers that contract with the firm, reduce the margin needed to attract investment in them, and reduce the fee that the independent trucker would be willing to charge. Unless the manufacturer has a greater tolerance for risk than banks, which seems unlikely (banks have diversified holdings that allow them to bear the risks of individual investments), there is no inherent reason why it should be more willing to put up the $200,000 investment than would a bank.

This example points out the critical difference between *accounting profit* and *economic profit*. Accounting profit is the simple difference between revenues and expenses. In this case, the independent distributor earns an accounting profit of $20,000. Economic profit represents the difference between the profits earned by investing resources in a particular activity, and the profits that could have been earned by investing the same resources in the most lucrative alternative activity. Because economic profit speaks to the relative profitability of different investment decisions, it is more useful than accounting profit when making business decisions.

In the trucking example, if the distributor could invest the $200,000 in an equally risky activity (say, warehousing) and also expect to generate $220,000 in net revenues, then it earns zero economic profit from the decision to invest in a truck. Similarly, if the manufacturer could invest $200,000 in some other equally risky venture and generate $220,000 in expected net revenues, then it too generates zero economic profits should it choose to purchase a truck. The manufacturer has nothing to gain by tying up $200,000 in a truck instead of letting an independent distributor make the purchase.

A different example will illustrate the flaw of the third argument. Consider an orange juice producer that has integrated backward into orange growing. The third argument holds that a vertically integrated orange producer would have a tremendous competitive advantage over nonintegrated producers during periods of peak demand or scarce supply of oranges because the nonintegrated producers are buying oranges at a high market price, while the vertically integrated producer acquires its oranges "at cost." To be concrete, suppose a quart of juice requires five oranges, and each orange costs $.05 to grow but sells for $.20 in the open market. Suppose, too, that a quart of juice sells for $1.30 and requires $.12 worth of processing costs (direct labor and manufacturing overhead). The vertically integrated producer thus seemingly earns a higher profit margin on juice production ($1.30 - .12 - 5 \times .05$ or $.93 per quart) than the nonvertically integrated producer ($1.30 - .12 - 5 \times .20$ or $.18 per quart). However, this comparison is incomplete. When the integrated firm produces juice using its own oranges, it forgoes a profit of $.15 per orange from outside sales. Because each quart of juice requires five oranges, the juice produced in the integrated firm involves an additional opportunity cost of $.75 per quart.

The way for the vertically integrated producer to correctly account for the cost of the oranges used in juice production would be through *transfer pricing*. A transfer price is an internal price between divisions of a vertically integrated firm. A key principle in transfer pricing is that when there is a highly competitive outside

---

[6]See, for example, Kaplan, R.S. and A.A. Atkinson, *Advanced Managerial Accounting*, 2nd ed., Englewood Cliffs, NJ: Prentice-Hall, 1989, pp. 597–599.

market for the internally produced activity or input, the transfer price should be equal to this outside market price.[6] This gives the vertically integrated firm the correct "signal" about the opportunity cost of the internally produced input. In our example, with a transfer price of $.20 per orange, the profit margin from juice production in the vertically integrated firm is $1.30 - .12 - 5 \times .20$ or $.18 per quart, the same as a nonintegrated juice producer. The profit margin from the integrated firm's orange production is $.15 per orange, the same as a nonintegrated grower's profit margin. In this example, then, the vertically integrated enterprise creates no economic benefits that could not also be achieved in the nonintegrated market relationship between an independent juice producer and orange grower. It follows, then, that there is no economic benefit to vertical integration.

BENEFITS OF USING THE MARKET   ◆ ◆ ◆ ◆ ◆

Firms that use the market can better exploit efficiencies that they cannot themselves achieve, and can take advantage of the hard-edged incentives that only the market can offer. We discuss these advantages in turn.

Market Firms Can Achieve Economies of Scale

When *economies of scale* are present, firms that produce more of a good or service do so at lower average (per unit) cost. Increased volume can benefit firms in ways other than lower costs, however. Repetition frequently improves the quality of the output of labor-intensive processes. For example, lawyers who have handled many product liability suits generally obtain verdicts superior to those of lawyers who handle only a few. Chapter 5 discusses in detail the variety of ways in which firms can benefit from increased volume. To keep things simple here, we will concentrate on cost reductions.

Market firms—firms that specialize in the production of an input—can often achieve greater scale, and thus lower unit costs, than can the downstream firms that use the input. The reason for this is that a market firm can aggregate the demands of many potential buyers, whereas a vertically integrated firm would typically produce only for its own needs. To illustrate this point, consider automobile production. An automobile manufacturer requires a vast variety of upstream inputs: steel, tires, anti-lock brakes, stereos, computer equipment, and so forth. A manufacturer, such as Ford, could integrate upstream and produce inputs, such as anti-lock brakes, itself, or it could obtain them from an independent supplier, such as Kelsey-Hayes.

Figure 2.2 illustrates an average cost function for anti-lock brakes. The production of anti-lock brakes displays declining and then constant average costs, indicating that there are economies of scale in production. The *minimum efficient scale* of production is the smallest output at which average cost is minimized. In this example, the minimum efficient scale of production is output level A^*, with resulting average cost C^*.

FIGURE 2.2
PRODUCTION COSTS AND THE MAKE-OR-BUY DECISION.

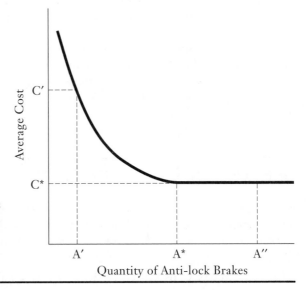

Firms need to produce quantity A^* to reach minimum efficient scale and achieve average costs of C^*. A firm that requires only A' units to meet its own needs will incur average costs of C', well above C^*. A firm that requires output in excess of A^*, such as A'', will have costs equal to C^* and will not be at a competitive disadvantage.

Suppose that Ford expects to sell A'' automobiles with anti-lock brakes, where $A'' > A^*$. Thus, Ford expects to sell enough automobiles so that it can achieve minimum efficient scale in the production of anti-lock brakes by producing for its own needs alone. This is seen in Figure 2.2, where the average cost of output A'' roughly equals C^*. From a cost perspective, Ford gets no advantage by using the market.

Suppose instead that Ford expects to sell A' automobiles with anti-lock brakes, where $A' < A^*$. In that case Ford cannot achieve minimum efficient scale by producing only for its own needs. This is seen in Figure 2.2, where the average cost associated with output A', denoted C', exceeds the minimum average cost C^*. Ford could try to expand anti-lock brake output to A^*. If it did, Ford would be able to fully exploit the available scale economies in anti-lock brake production, and in-house production of anti-lock brakes would not entail a cost disadvantage. However, to profitably increase production beyond its own needs, Ford would need to find buyers for its anti-lock brakes.

Other car makers might be reluctant to buy their anti-lock brakes from Ford when alternative sources of supply exist. (Although competitors sometimes do buy inputs from each other. For example, the Taiwanese firm Giant makes frames for its own bicycles, as well as for competitors, such as Trek.) They might fear that Ford would use its power in the anti-lock brake market to put them at a disadvantage, either by charging higher prices (a tactic known as the "vertical price squeeze") or by withholding supplies during periods of peak demand. At the same time, Ford may feel that a major expansion into anti-lock brake manufacturing may detract from its focus on automotive design and assembly. As we discuss in Chapter 6, many firms are reluctant to diversify in this manner.

Alternatively, Ford could purchase anti-lock brakes from an independent manufacturer, such as Kelsey-Hayes. Kelsey-Hayes reaches production of A' in Figure 2.2 just from its sales to Ford. It could also sell its anti-lock brakes to other car makers, thus expanding output and lowering costs. If it passes some of these cost savings along to Ford, then Ford will prefer to buy rather than make anti-lock brakes.

Under what circumstances will an independent firm pass along its cost savings to the downstream buyer? A basic tenet in microeconomics is that if markets are perfectly competitive, prices in those markets will approach average cost.[7] Thus, if the upstream supplier is in a perfectly competitive market, market forces will drive its price down toward average cost. If the upstream market is not perfectly competitive, then the upstream supplier may charge a price well in excess of its average cost. It cannot charge too high a price, however, for this might encourage the downstream buyer to produce the input itself. In the previous example (Figure 2.2), if Ford requires A' anti-lock brakes and the anti-lock brake manufacturer charges a price above C', Ford should produce the anti-lock brakes itself.

The production of automobiles is largely organized along the lines suggested by the above discussion. The largest auto maker, General Motors, produces its own anti-lock brakes, whereas other car makers, including Ford, buy them from specialized producers. The same is true for other specialized inputs, such as car stereos. In some cases, such as tires, even General Motors buys from independent manufacturers. A similar phenomenon occurs in the distribution of breakfast cereals. Large firms, such as General Mills, use in-house distribution. Smaller firms, such as Ralcorp (a spinoff from Ralston Purina), use cereal "brokers" who achieve scale economies by distributing several firms' cereal products.

Figure 2.2 illustrates a case in which a market firm produces input more cheaply than a vertically integrated firm because the market firm achieves a larger volume of output in every year of production. Similar logic applies when the market specialist achieves economies of scale by aggregating the demands of buyers over many years. Suppose, for example, an oil refiner is choosing between producing its own valves or purchasing them from a small specialized valve manufacturer. If it produces its own valves, the oil refiner would have to incur various up-front costs, such as the costs of design, tooling, and setting up a production facility. The valve producer is likely to be able to satisfy the oil refiner's needs more cheaply than the refiner itself can because of an important scale economy: The outside manufacturer does not have to incur these setup costs each time it takes on a new buyer. One exception to this would be if the valves demanded by the oil refiner are so specialized that they require the valve producer to develop an entirely new design and invest in new tooling and equipment. In this case, the valve producer would face the same setup costs as the oil refiner and thus would not have a cost advantage.

---

[7]See the Economics Primer for a discussion of perfectly competitive markets.

◆◆

ℰXAMPLE 2.2

ORGANIZATIONAL CAPABILITIES

In the process of producing and selling one output, firms often develop capabilities that may be applied to other outputs. For example, Philip Morris developed expertise in the marketing and distribution of cigarettes, and exploited these skills after acquiring Miller Beer. Another example is General Electric Finance, which originated as a vehicle for financing the purchases of big ticket General Electric products, and then expanded to become a self-contained financial services firm. By expanding outside their original markets, firms that have developed specific capabilities in the performance of one activity can apply that expertise to perform other activities. These *organizational capabilities* form the basis of an economy of scale that allows market specialists to perform activities at a lower average cost than their downstream customers could. The economy of scale arises because the market specialist's investment in the development of its capabilities is, in effect, a fixed setup cost. The specialist does not have to reinvest in developing the capabilities each time it takes on a new customer. However, for a downstream firm to perform the activity as well as the market specialist can, it too would have to incur this fixed investment cost. Because it sells to many customers, the market specialist can spread this fixed investment cost over a larger quantity of output than the downstream firm producing only for its own needs, and the specialist can thus achieve lower average costs than the downstream firm.

An example that has attracted much attention recently is American Airline's exploitation of its skills in yield management.[8] American Airline's SABRE computerized reservation and scheduling system is the world's most successful, used in over 60 countries and by about 50 airlines. As a result of the SABRE system, American has developed considerable expertise in related activities. American consults with telemarketing firms on handling switchboards. It customizes data processing operations for the health care industry. And it sells yield management systems to railways and even Club Med, which operates resort hotels in exotic locations. These spinoff activities are proving far more profitable than the parent company's airline operations. Of course, the former would not be possible without the latter.

The point of these examples is that the source of a firm's profitability is not necessarily the specific products that it sells, but the specific capabilities that it has developed while learning how to manufacture and market the products. Such scholars as David Teece, Richard Nelson, and Sidney Winter have argued that the exploitation of these capabilities is the key to the firm's strategic success.[9] As Teece

---

[8]This example is taken from "Managing the Future," *The Economist*, December 19, 1992: pp. 68–69.

[9]Nelson, R. and S. Winter, *An Evolutionary Theory of Economic Change*, Cambridge, MA: Belknap Press of the Harvard University Press, 1982.

put it, the firm has "a variety of end products that it can produce with its organizational technology."[10] We will discuss these ideas in detail in Chapter 15.

"The Division of Labor IS Limited by the Extent of the Market"

The preceding analysis presumes that there are economies of scale in production of the upstream input. The upstream firm exploits these economies by making the necessary fixed investments and producing a large volume. Obviously, upstream firms will not make large fixed investments unless demand justifies it. This is the logic underlying Adam Smith's famous theorem, "The division of labor is limited by the extent of the market." (Adam Smith is the father of laissez-faire economics. His famous book, *Wealth of Nations*, was published in 1776.) The *division of labor* refers to the specialization of production activities that results when firms or individuals make fixed investments in productive assets. The *extent of the market* refers to the magnitude of demand for these activities.

Implicit in Smith's theorem is the idea that an individual must make up-front investments of time and/or money to develop special skills. For example, an accountant may spend a year learning tax law or a baseball player may spend several months improving his bunting skills. These investments may also involve fixed capital, such as when a jeweler purchases a high-temperature furnace necessary to work with platinum, or a graphics designer purchases a computer work station. These investments cannot be scaled down if market demand is low. For example, the accountant must spend a full year learning tax law to obtain certification in the area whether he or she subsequently serves one client or 100 clients. Thus, by their nature, these investments cannot be recouped unless subsequent demand is large enough. Hence the division of labor is limited by the extent of the market.

An implication of Smith's theorem is that the growth in the demand for activities (e.g., due to population growth or higher income) ought to be accompanied by increasing specialization in the provision of those activities. Much casual evidence supports this implication. Full-service automobile service stations have been replaced by self-service gasoline retailers, specialty muffler shops, and 10-minute oil change shops. Internal forecasting and planning departments in hierarchical firms have yielded to specialty firms in marketing and consulting. Pet stores have given way to dog grooming salons and aquarium shops. Smith's theorem applies cross-sectionally as well as over time. Larger markets ought to support a more specialized array of activities than smaller markets. This, too, is consistent with what we observe. For example, while one of the finest restaurants in Ann Arbor, Michigan offers Italian *and* French cooking, restaurants in Chicago are highly specialized. There is even a Chicago restaurant that focuses exclusively on the cooking of Alsace, a region of eastern France. Although specialization is no guarantee of quality, the associated investments of time and resources frequently do pay off—the Alsatian restaurant is regarded as one of the finest restaurants in the nation.

---

[10]Teece, D., "Towards an Economic Theory of the Multiproduct Firm," *Journal of Economic Behavior and Organization*, 3, 1982: pp. 39–63.

Smith's theorem also sheds light on the growth of the hierarchical firm. In a small market, the entrepreneur must perform all of the tasks in the vertical chain because the market cannot support specialists. Specialists emerge in larger markets, and the growing firm can use them for many activities. When the market gets even larger, the demand for the firm's product may become so big that the firm can produce enough of its inputs in-house to fully exploit the available economies of scale. The firm makes the necessary investments to develop human and physical capital, thereby adding to its corporate hierarchy. For example, the volume of demand for processing the paperwork created by its Discover Card was so great that Sears could not find a market firm large enough to handle the job. Sears handled payment processing, statement mailing, and even statement embossing itself. Perhaps this is one reason why the venture was spun off from Sears.

◆ ◆

$\mathcal{E}$XAMPLE 2.3

THE DIVISION OF LABOR IN MEDICAL MARKETS

An interesting application of Smith's theorem involves the specialization of medical care. In the United States, physicians may practice general medicine or specialty medicine. "Generalists" and "specialists" differ in both the amount of training they receive and the skill with which they practice. Take the specific case of surgery. To become general surgeons in the United States, medical school graduates spend three to four years in a surgical residency. They are then qualified to perform a wide variety of surgical procedures. Because their training is broad, general surgeons do all kinds of surgery with good, but not necessarily great, skill.

Contrast this with the training and skills of a thoracic surgeon. Thoracic surgeons specialize in surgery in the thoracic region, between the neck and the abdomen. To become a thoracic surgeon in the United States, a medical school graduate must complete a residency in general surgery, and then an additional three-year residency in thoracic surgery.

Figure 2.3 depicts average "cost" curves for thoracic surgery performed by a general surgeon and a thoracic surgeon. We use "cost" in quotes because it represents the full cost of care, which is lower if a more effective cure is achieved. The average cost curves are downward sloping to reflect the spreading out of the initial investments in training. The cost curve for the thoracic surgeon starts off much higher than the cost curve for the general surgeon because of the greater investment in time. However, the thoracic surgeon's cost curve eventually falls below the cost curve of a general surgeon because the thoracic surgeon will perform thoracic surgery more effectively than will the general surgeon. The result could be fewer complications, shorter hospital stays, and a greater probability of overall success.

According to Smith's theorem, when the demand for thoracic surgery in a market is low, then the market will not be able to support a thoracic surgeon.

FIGURE 2.3
COST CURVES FOR GENERAL AND THORACIC SURGEONS.

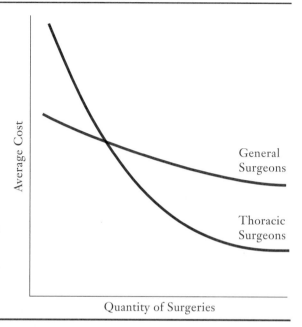

General surgeons incur lower training costs than do thoracic surgeons, but usually are less efficient in performing thoracic surgery. Thus, the general surgeon's average cost curve is below the thoracic surgeon's for low volumes (reflecting lower average fixed costs) but above the thoracic surgeon's for high volumes (reflecting higher average variable costs).

Instead, thoracic surgery will be performed by a general surgeon, who may also perform other kinds of surgery. This may be seen in Figure 2.4, which superimposes demand curves over cost curves. For low levels of demand, such as at D_1, the market can support a general surgeon. As long as the general surgeon charges a price for thoracic surgery above P_1, he or she can more than cover average costs. When demand is D_1, the market cannot support a thoracic surgeon. There is no price high enough to enable thoracic surgeons to recoup their initial investment in time.

When demand increases to D_2, the market can support a thoracic surgeon. As long as the thoracic surgeon charges a price above P_3, he or she can cover average costs. Moreover, at prices between P_2 and P_3, the thoracic surgeon can make a profit, but the general surgeon cannot. Thus, at this high level of demand, the thoracic surgeon can drive the general surgeon from the market for thoracic surgery. At the same time that the demand for thoracic surgery has increased sufficiently to support a thoracic surgeon, we might expect the demand for other specialized surgeons to increase also. Thus, in large markets, we may expect to see a range of specialized surgeons, and few or no general surgeons.

Researchers at the RAND Corporation have documented this pattern of the division of labor in medical markets.[11] They found that general practitioners are

[11]Newhouse, J. et al., "Does the Geographic Distribution of Physicians Reflect Market Failure?" *Bell Journal of Economics*, 13, 2, 1982: pp. 493–505.

FIGURE 2.4
COST AND DEMAND FOR THORACIC SURGERY.

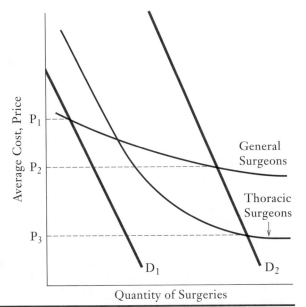

At low demands (D_1) general surgeons may be able to cover their average costs but thoracic surgeons may not. At high demands (D_2) thoracic surgeons may be able to offer lower effective prices than can general surgeons (where the effective price to the consumer includes the costs associated with ineffective surgery).

disproportionately located in smaller towns—they do not appear to fare well in larger markets, which have a wider assortment of specialists. James Baumgardner also found that physicians who practice in small towns treat a wider range of illnesses than their big city counterparts do.[12]

Market Firms Are Subject to the Discipline of the Market

A second advantage that "buying" has over "making" is that a market firm will typically have stronger incentives to hold down costs and to innovate than a division performing the same activity within a vertically integrated firm. If a market firm fails to produce efficiently or innovate, it will lose business to more efficient and innovative rivals. But a division within a vertically integrated firm does not face such pressure. It usually has a captive market for its output. In addition, when there are common overhead or joint costs that are allocated across divisions, it is tough to measure an individual division's contribution to overall corporate profitability. The absence of market competition, coupled with difficulties in measuring divisional performance, make it hard for top management to know just how well an internal division is doing relative to its best achievable performance. This, in turn, gives

---

[12]Baumgardner, J., "What Is a Specialist Anyway?" Duke University, working paper, 1991.

division managers the latitude to engage in behavior that is inconsistent with corporate profit maximization: cutting corners on product quality or cost control, padding expenses, or even shirking on the job. Such latitude leads to two important classes of costs: *agency costs* and *influence costs*. While these costs may also be present inside a market firm, they are often more severe when an activity is internalized within a division of a vertically integrated firm. We discuss each of these costs in turn.

Agency Costs

Agency costs are the costs associated with slack effort by employees and the costs of administrative controls designed to deter slack effort. A vivid example of agency costs is provided by the case of Crown, Cork and Seal. When John Connelly became an outside director of Crown, Cork and Seal in 1956, he found an organization full of slack. According to one story, Connelly was escorted through a Crown manufacturing plant by a foreman who sang as they walked. The singing served as an early warning to workers, who were all hard at work when Connelly greeted them. Connelly asked the foreman to stop singing and continued the tour alone. He found some workers asleep; those who were not, were playing cards. The next year Connelly took over the presidency of Crown, Cork and Seal, and promptly laid off nearly a fourth of the workers.[13]

Agency costs may be as simple as overstaffing or using express mail when regular mail will do. Agency costs can affect the firm's bottom line, but within divisions of a large vertically integrated firm, they may go unnoticed by top management. This is particularly likely if the vertically integrated firm possesses some inherent advantages in the market that insulates it from competition. The famous economist Frederick von Hayek pointed out, "How easy it is for an inefficient manager to dissipate the differentials on which profitability rests."[14] Even when agency costs are noticed, however, management may find it less costly to ignore them than to eliminate them. For example, many firms are unwilling to endure the ill-will generated by firing a nonproductive worker who is near retirement age. The unwillingness of top management to eliminate agency costs further down in the organization is a potential obstacle to efficiency.

Agency Costs and Innovation

Some agency costs can be severe. For example, departments within a large hierarchical firm may be under little pressure to innovate, and may actually prefer the status quo as a way of protecting established jobs and business relationships. As a result, small entrepreneurial firms may innovate more rapidly and can overtake the large industrial "dinosaurs." Paul Tiffany argues that U.S. Steel's decline in the 1960s was a direct result of its failure to develop and adopt new technologies, such as the basic oxygen furnace and continuous casting.[15] (See Example 1.3 for a detailed dis-

---

[13]"The Unoriginal Ideas that Rebuilt Crown Cork," *Fortune*, October 1962: pp. 118–164.

[14]"The Use of Knowledge in Society," *American Economic Review*, 35, September 1945: pp. 519–530.

[15]Tiffany, P., *The Decline of American Steel*, Oxford: Oxford University Press, 1988.

cussion of the evolution of the American steel industry.) Texas Instruments (TI) and Fairchild, the leading developers of the integrated circuit provide a similar example. When the metal oxide semiconductor (MOS) was being developed, TI and Fairchild did not research this slower but less costly alternative to the integrated circuit. By the time that TI and Fairchild had learned the value of MOS technology, smaller firms had made substantial progress in process technology that they could not match.[16]

It should not be surprising that a department within a large firm may be at a disadvantage relative to an independent firm in promoting innovation. If an independent input supplier develops an improved version of the input, the supplier has clear title to the stream of profits from the innovation, which in turn creates strong pressure to innovate. The owner/entrepreneur can therefore aspire to be like Ben Segal and Jerry Greenfield of Ben and Jerry's or Microsoft's Bill Gates and reap huge rewards from innovation. By contrast, untangling responsibility for the same innovation inside the firm may be more difficult. Many divisions may participate in discussions that lead to innovations. Given this ambiguity, the supplying division may not get full credit for the innovation, which works to undermine the incentives to innovate.

In principle, a large firm could replicate internally the innovative incentives of market firms by judiciously designing incentive contracts that tie employees' pay and/or department budgets to specific measures of innovative performance or effort. Such companies as 3M, Merck, and Cray Research have had mixed success doing this. For example, Cray provided the seed money for Circuit Tools, a firm developed by a Cray Research employee who developed an application of the Cray supercomputer for testing other high-tech equipment. On the other hand, Cray could not come to terms with Stephen Chen, the developer of the first parallel processing supercomputer, when Chen requested millions in development funds for a new generation of supercomputers. Ironically, Chen was lured away by IBM, which provided over $100 million in funding, yet was never able to develop a marketable product for them.

Internal mechanisms for promoting innovation can break down for a number of reasons. As IBM's experience with Chen demonstrates, it can be difficult to determine the merits of proposals to do innovative work. One reason is that it is difficult to predict whether an innovative idea will be *scientifically successful*, that is, whether it will achieve its scientific objectives. Chen's proposal to use vector processors to increase computation speed is an example of a project that has not been scientifically successful. The best judge of whether a project will be scientifically successful is probably the researcher who proposes it. However, would-be innovators may be reluctant to fully reveal their plans to big companies for fear that they will be appropriated. For these reasons, many investors believe that the best

---

[16]Brittain, J.W. and J.H. Freeman, "Organizational Proliferation and Density Dependent Selection," in Kimberly, J., Miles, R. and Associates, *The Organizational Life Cycle*, San Francisco: Jossey Bass, 1980, p. 308.

way to spur innovation is to encourage innovators to start up their own R&D firms. The investor provides seed money, but the innovator also provides time and money. Cray's support of Circuit Tools is an example. This model serves two purposes. First, it discourages individuals from seeking funding for projects that lack scientific merit. Second, it provides strong incentives to the innovator to continue working hard.

Without special mechanisms to reward innovation, such as seed money, firms may choose to raise the salaries of innovative employees to spur innovation. For example, research universities normally pay higher salaries to the most productive research faculty. It may be difficult, however, to implement salary schedules that fully reflect differences in productivity. It has been estimated that researchers within the same scientific discipline can differ in their productivity, as measured by the number of publications, by a factor of 50 or more.[17] Salary schedules within most organizations, especially in the public sector, are unlikely to reflect such differences, whether for political or social reasons. Indeed, one study found that to win a 10 percent raise, research workers must increase their publications by 30 to 50 percent. This compression of the salary structure is a disincentive to the most innovative workers to continue working their hardest.

Another challenge when assessing innovative ideas is that scientifically successful projects must also prove to be *commercially successful*. Firms often have a particularly difficult time assessing commercial viability. During the 1930s, IBM believed that the market for computers consisted of fewer than a dozen users. Radios, lasers, and video cassette recorders were all thought to have limited markets. In all of these cases, innovations from outside firms were necessary to make the products viable. Buried within large firms, these products might have never sold well without these additional innovations. Even so, they might have lived up to management expectations, with no repercussions for the divisions that handled them.

Influence Costs

In addition to agency costs, another class of costs that arise when transactions are organized internally are what Paul Milgrom and John Roberts have called *influence costs*.[18] Influence costs are the costs of activities aimed at influencing the distribution of benefits inside an organization. Influence costs not only include the direct costs of influence activities (e.g., the time consumed by a division manager lobbying central management to overturn a decision that is unfavorable to his or her division). They also include the costs of bad decisions that arise from influence activities (e.g., resources that are misallocated because an inefficient division knows how to lobby for scarce resources).

---

[17]Shockley, W., "Variations of Individual Productivity in Research Laboratories," *IEEE*, December 1957: pp. 279–280.

[18]Milgrom, P. and J. Roberts, "Bargaining Costs, Influence Costs, and the Organization of Economic Activity," in Alt, J. and K. Shepsle (eds.), *Perspectives on Positive Political Economy*, Cambridge: Cambridge University Press, 1990.

Influence costs imply that vertical integration may be a more "forgiving" mode of organizing transactions than market exchange. Even when internal divisions are nominally subject to a hard-edged incentive system, an internal supplier that delivers a low-quality input or incurs inefficiently high costs may lobby headquarters to override the incentive system and give it a second chance. As the following excerpt shows, supply relationships within U.S. automobile firms nicely illustrate the effects of influence activity on the power of market incentives within a vertically integrated firm:

> Let's take the example of one of GM's in-house suppliers. We'll imagine the program manager for a new GM product is unhappy with the in-house supplier's bid—it's too high and in the past the supplier had quality and delivery problems. However, no sooner does the manager identify an alternative bidder outside the company than the in-house supplier goes to corporate headquarters and explains the loss of business on this part will require an increase in the costs of similar parts already being supplied by other GM products. Why? Because economies of scale will be lost and the in-house supplier will have excess capacity.
>
> Headquarters, always respectful of scale-economy and capacity-utilization justifications in a mass-production firm such as GM, then has a talk with the program manager. The in-house supplier makes solemn promises to try harder to reduce costs in the future while improving quality and delivery reliability—and gets the business. In this way, the internal market, which supposedly keeps the in-house supply divisions honest, is gradually diluted. This process explains how GM managed to have both the world's highest production volume and the world's highest costs in many of its components supply divisions through much of the last decade.[19]

Exposing Internal Divisions to Market Forces

The notion that the market disciplines performance better than internal controls underlies recent moves by large vertically integrated firms, such as General Motors and IBM, to either shed in-house divisions entirely or subject them to market forces. In the mid-1980s, when General Motors sought to develop a new line of automobiles to compete head to head with the highly reliable Honda Civic and Toyota Corolla, it established its first new nameplate division in several decades, the Saturn Division. Saturn was given far more autonomy than other GM divisions. For example, it does its own design and shares no chassis with other divisions. Saturn has quickly earned a reputation for reliability and value. Similarly, in the late 1980s, IBM concluded that to measure divisional performance relative to best attainable performance, its divisions had to be more exposed to the pressures of the marketplace. This was the rationale behind the December 1991 reorganization in which IBM was broken up into 13 semiautonomous units, each of which keeps its own set of books. Firms can expose divisions or departments to the discipline of the market without granting them complete autonomy. For example, upstream

---

[19]Womack, J., D. Jones, and D. Roos, *The Machine that Changed the World: The Story of Lean Production*, New York: HarperCollins, 1990, p. 143.

divisions are often explicitly required to offer downstream divisions a price that is at least as favorable as the downstream division could get from an independent vendor. Such policies compel the upstream divisions to stay abreast of the latest technologies while holding the line on cost.

COSTS OF USING THE MARKET ◆◆◆◆◆

The three major costs associated with using the market include the costs of poor coordination between steps in the vertical chain, the reluctance of trading partners to develop valuable information that might be appropriated, and transactions costs. We discuss each in turn.

Coordination of Production Flows Through the Vertical Chain

A key to successful exploitation of economies of scale is the coordination of production flows throughout the vertical chain, from raw materials acquisition, through production, to finished goods distribution. For coordination to be successful, a number of players must make decisions that depend, in part, on the decisions of others. Suppliers must plan for and produce adequate supplies of the right quality and design. Distributors must be able to transport and warehouse the goods. Retailers must have appropriate space and the right marketing concept. Without good coordination, bottlenecks may arise. The failure of one supplier to deliver parts on schedule can shut down a factory. A failure to coordinate advertising images across local markets can undermine a brand's image and dampen sales.

While coordination problems can arise between in-house departments of vertically integrated firms, they are often more serious when independent firms contract with each other in the market. The reason is that when an activity is carried out within a vertically integrated firm, coordination can be achieved through centralized administrative control. Such control is absent when independent firms contract with each other in the market.

Paul Milgrom and John Roberts explain that coordination is especially important in problems with "design attributes," that is, attributes that need to relate to each other in a precise fashion to maximize their value.[20] Examples of design attributes include a sequence of courses in an MBA curriculum (e.g., you must take financial accounting before you take corporate finance) or the various components of an automobile (e.g., the sunroof glass must precisely fit the opening in the car roof or it will not operate properly). With design attributes, the downstream firm often understands how the various inputs and outputs should relate to each other, but the various input suppliers may not adequately coordinate with each other. The failure

---

[20]Milgrom, P. and J. Roberts, *Economics, Organization and Management*, Englewood Cliffs, NJ: Prentice-Hall, 1992.

to achieve the right relationship among inputs can be very costly. As a result, it often makes sense to integrate all critical upstream and downstream activities and rely on administrative control to achieve the appropriate coordination, rather than rely on independent firms and hope that coordination emerges automatically through the market mechanism.

Many firms encounter coordination problems in the production of photocopies. Copies often must arrive before a certain time, such as before an important meeting. Business education provides a good example where the timing of the delivery of copies is critical. Weeks before the beginning of classes, dozens of professors at each major business school assemble reading packets for their courses. Each packet may contain dozens of articles, each of which must be photocopied for every student in the class. All told, a single business school may require millions of pages to be photocopied, collated, and assembled into reading packets.

Business schools often outsource the production of reading packets to independent photocopying services. One advantage of doing this is that the independent services can achieve the scale economies needed to support high-volume copiers. Another advantage is that the school can play one service against another, obtaining competitive prices. Relying on the market can create a severe coordination problem, however, because the reading packets must be available when classes begin. If packets are late, students and professors may not have necessary materials for lectures and case discussions.

The coordination problem is represented by Figure 2.5. The curve labeled MC^1 represents the marginal cost to the school of each additional day of delay in reading packet production. This is initially zero—as long as copies are available well before the start of classes, there is no cost of an additional day's delay. As the start of school approaches, marginal cost rises rapidly. For example, if the reading packets have not arrived by the day that classes start, the cost of an additional day's delay is MC^a. Eventually, the school will begin copying itself, limiting further costs. The curve labeled MB^1 represents the marginal benefit to the copying service of delaying the completion of reading packets. The copying service benefits from delays for two reasons. First, a rapid completion would require the service to hire additional workers and operate equipment beyond their designed capacity. Second, the copying service would like to squeeze in additional jobs, rather than devote its copiers exclusively to the reading packets. MB^1 is downward sloping, indicating that the benefits of delay fall as the copying service has additional time to juggle its schedule. Eventually MB^1 is negative, as the copying service wastes time and energy responding to irate students and faculty.

An efficient contract would equate the marginal cost of delay to the school and the marginal benefit of delay to the copying service. This occurs at time T^* in Figure 2.5. Although the school bears some cost of delay, it prefers this time to earlier times because the copying service enjoys the benefits of delay, and can pass those benefits on to the school in the form of a lower rate. But how can the school assure that the copies will be ready by time T^*? If the school offered a fixed fee for completing the job, the copying service would not finish the job until T^{**}, the time at which MB^1 equals zero. The school could set a stiff fine for any delivery after

FIGURE 2.5
THE COORDINATION PROBLEM IN THE PRODUCTION OF READING PACKETS.

The curve labeled MC^1 represents the marginal cost to the school of delaying case packet production by an additional day. It is initially 0 well before the start of classes, but it rises rapidly as the start of school approaches. For example, if the readings packets have not yet arrived by the start of classes, the cost of an additional day of delay is MC^a. The curve labeled MB^1 is the marginal benefit to the copying service of delaying production. The optimal time of delivery occurs at date T^*, where MC^1 equals MB^1. If the school offers the copy service a flat fee for copy services, independent of the delivery date, the copy service will maximize profits by setting MB^1 equal to zero, and delivering the readings packets on date T^{**}. If the school offers the copy service a contract that imposes a late fee of MC^* for each day of delay, but the actual marginal benefit curve for the copy service is MB^2, then the copy service would deliver the packets by date T^{**} as well.

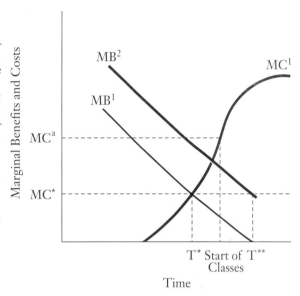

time T^*. But this would punish the copying service even if the late delivery were not its fault. For example, a dispute over permission to copy a copyrighted article might delay reproduction through no fault of the copying service. The copying service may be unwilling to assume such risk, and the service and the school may be unwilling to bear the legal costs needed to resolve disputes.

Another solution is to impose a fixed per diem late fee. If the late fee is set equal to the marginal cost of delay at time T^*, or MC^* in Figure 2.5, then the copying service will find it optimal to aim for completion by that time. The penalty for additional delay would exceed the marginal benefit. Many delivery contracts, including contracts for highway construction, and library borrowing privileges have such late fees. The late fee may not be very effective for the business school, however. To see why not, suppose that the business school miscalculates the MB curve for the copying service. Instead of MB^1, the actual marginal benefit curve is MB^2. If the late penalty is MC^*, then the copying service will aim for completion by time T^{**}. But this is too late for the school, whose students and faculty will suffer substantially from the short delay. Note that there is a critical difference between highway construction and library borrowing on the one hand, and reading packet preparation on the other. In the first two, each additional day of delay is about as costly as the previous day's delay. This is not the case in reading packet preparation, where delays around the start of class are much more costly than delays just a week or two prior. Thus, small errors in pricing the copying contract can lead to very costly delays.

The decision to make or buy copying services is a balancing act. On the one hand, independent copying centers can exploit economies of scale and must be efficient to survive. On the other hand, the coordination costs of using an independent service can be high. If the school believes that by producing packets internally it can do a better job of assuring completion by T^*, then it might prefer to "make" packets. Some schools, such as the University of Chicago Graduate School of Business, handle reading packet preparation internally, whereas others, such as the Kellogg Graduate School of Management, use the market. Interestingly, both schools obtain copyright permissions internally. This necessary task for reading packet production also presents coordination problems, but does not involve significant scale economies. Hence, it makes sense to perform it internally.

A steep marginal cost curve, which indicates that total costs rise rapidly as performance deviates from desired levels, is the hallmark of a potential coordination problem. As in the photocopying example, the marginal cost curve may describe the marginal cost associated with delayed delivery of an input. Another example is the development of applications software for CareMark, which provides home intravenous drug infusion therapy for patients with AIDS, cancer, and other illnesses. Software development time is often the critical determinant of time-to-market for new drug therapies, and delays in development can lead to costly delays in therapy. The marginal cost curve may describe other critical determinants of success. For example, it may describe the cost of failing to achieve a precise fit of a component in a technically sophisticated product, or it might describe the cost of failing to achieve a desired style. This could be extremely costly for matching the desired colors for fabrics used by Benetton, for example. When small errors in a component or task can lead to large costs, it often makes sense for the manufacturer to abandon the market price system and make the component or perform the task itself. In each of the above examples, the firms make the critical inputs or perform the critical tasks themselves.

Timing and coordination problems become extreme when no one is willing to carry out a productive task. Once again, if the cost curve to the buyer is steep, the consequences can be disastrous. This may happen, for example, if farmers deliver their perishable products to a port, but no boat is available to take their products to market. Shippers recognize the consequences of timeliness, and when a shipper has the only boat available to transport perishables, it may raise its fee considerably. At the opposite extreme, problems may arise when more than one seller attempts to sell a product for which demand is limited. At one time New York City used a simple price system to dispatch ambulance services to an accident—the first to arrive could transport the patient and receive the fee. On a few occasions, two ambulances would reach a patient simultaneously and then have their personnel come to blows over who would transport the injured party. Newspaper accounts of these events eventually led to an overhaul of the ambulance dispatch system.

Leakage of Private Information

A firm's *private information* is information that no one else knows. Private information often gives a firm an advantage in the market. It may pertain to production know-how, product design, or consumer information. When firms use the market to obtain supplies or distribute products, they risk losing control of valuable private information. Speaking about relying on outside Japanese suppliers, a vice president of technology and market development for Xerox stated, "It's not a game for the naive player. It demands careful study. If you bungle a relationship with the Japanese, you can lose your technology, your business."[21]

The disastrous consequences of information leakage can be seen in the example of IBM's development of its OS-2-based personal computer. IBM wished to develop a new operating system that would feature the operational convenience of Macintosh. It entered a partnership with Microsoft, which had developed software called Windows to emulate the Macintosh environment. Armed with the information that IBM was planning a new product that might make its Windows obsolete, Microsoft redoubled its efforts to improve Windows. By the time the IBM OS-2 system was unveiled, Windows had become so popular that few personal computer users switched to OS-2.

Benetton and Hewlett-Packard (HP) are two firms that have used the market very judiciously because of their concern over leakage of valuable private information. While Benetton contracts out many production and distribution activities, it selects dyes and designs and does the actual dyeing of fabrics in-house. These activities are generally regarded as the source of its advantage in the market. By keeping them in-house, Benetton has limited competitors' ability to discover and master its secrets. Until 1995, HP relied on Canon to produce the engines that go into its laser printers. When HP and Canon reached this agreement, HP was careful to deny Canon access to the software that differentiates HP printers from those of competitors. Without this access, Canon has been unable to clone HP's laser printers and has a relatively small presence in the laser printer market.

Transactions Costs

The concept of *transactions costs* was first described by Ronald Coase in his famous paper, "The Nature of the Firm."[22] Coase raised the following question: In light of the efficiencies of the competitive market mechanism emphasized in economic theory, why does so much economic activity take place outside the price system, that is within firms in which market transactions are replaced by centralized direction? Coase concluded that there must be costs to using the market that can be eliminated by using the firm. These costs have come to be known as transactions costs.

Transactions costs include the time and expense of negotiating, writing, and enforcing contracts. Transactions costs arise when one or more parties to a transaction have a chance to act opportunistically—to seek private gain at the expense of the greater good. Transactions costs include the adverse consequences of opportunistic behavior, as well as the costs of trying to prevent it. Contracting costs are certainly one component of transactions costs. After all, a key purpose of contracts (and of the lawyers paid to ensure their enforcement) is to protect each

---

[21]Excerpted from the *Wall Street Journal*, July 29, 1992: A5.
[22]Coase, R., "The Nature of the Firm," *Economica*, 4, 1937: 386–405.

party's interests in an exchange relationship. But transactions costs can take more subtle forms. To fully understand these subtleties, we explore *transactions costs economics* in greater depth in the next chapter.

◆◆◆

Example 2.4

"Downsizing"—A Buzz Word for the Nineties

The recession that took place during the early 1990s was characterized by an unusually large number of permanent layoffs at some of America's largest companies. Tens of thousands of positions were permanently cut at General Motors, General Electric, Sears, Westinghouse, and other giants. While many bemoaned the apparent decline of these firms, others saw these moves as sensible responses to changes in technology that have reduced the advantages of in-house production and reduced the advantages of scale in the product market.

The 1980s saw the emergence of the computer and telecommunications as both management and production tools. Thanks to the fax and modem, independent firms can communicate their intentions and coordinate their production activities far more easily than ever before. These new technologies have thus reduced the advantages of "make" decisions. At the same time, new technology has also reduced the advantages of scale in the product market. For example, computer-aided design and manufacturing (CAD-CAM) minimizes setup costs associated with frequent changes in product designs and manufacturing runs. This reduces the cost advantages of large production runs, making smaller firms more competitive with industrial giants. Computer and telecommunication advances also facilitated innovations in inventory management that further reduced the advantages that used to accrue only to the largest firms.

It is important to note that downsizing does not imply that the level of economic activity or overall level of employment will decline. In fact, while the years 1992 and 1993 were notable for a series of layoffs at large firms, overall employment in the United States rose considerably. Hewlett-Packard's John Young put it this way: "The Fortune 500 is not growing, but what nobody looks at is how much they have rationalized and created a whole bunch of new jobs in other places."[23] The popular and business press has been slow to recognize Young's insight that downsizing is not synonymous with a decline in overall employment. For example, in a recent article entitled "What Happened to the Jobs?," *Fortune* magazine's top explanation for the decline in employment during the recession of the early 1990s was that firms were electing to buy rather than make.[24]

---

[23]*Chicago Tribune*, February 21, 1993: Sec. 1, p. 15.
[24]Fierman, J., "What Happened to the Jobs?," *Fortune*, July 12, 1993: pp. 40–43.

EXAMPLE 2.5

AN APPLICATION OF THE MAKE-OR-BUY FRAMEWORK TO CHILDREN'S MEMORIAL HOSPITAL

Although the trend in most industries is to "buy" rather than "make," there is an unprecedented amount of vertical integration currently under way in the health care industry. Integrated health care systems, such as the Henry Ford system in Michigan and the Sutter system in California, have consolidated the vertical chain, placing hospitals, physician offices, home health care, pharmacies, health insurance, and diagnostic imaging facilities in a single corporate entity. Increasingly, however, health care systems are recognizing that full vertical integration is not always optimal, and many are evaluating each link in the vertical chain to determine which activities to "make" and which to "buy." An interesting example of a make-or-buy decision occurred in 1993 when the Children's Memorial Hospital in Chicago chose to retain ownership of its pediatric home care subsidiary. The framework developed in this chapter can be used to analyze the economics of this decision.

Home health care includes nursing, therapy, homemaker, and other services delivered to patients in their homes. Industry experts believe that home health care is a cost-effective alternative to care in more costly institutional settings. The Chicago area contained dozens of home care agencies in 1993, including CM Health Care Resources (CMHR), which was wholly owned by Children's Memorial Medical Center, the owner of Children's Memorial Hospital (CMH). The vast majority of CMH patients who received home care got it from CMHR. On the other hand, CMHR received more than half of its patients from hospitals other than CMH. An important strategic question faced by CMH's owners in 1993 was whether to spin off CMHR to make it a fully independent firm or to keep CMHR as a wholly owned subsidiary. By spinning off CMHR, CMH would have more flexibility to contract with other independent home care agencies. This would, in effect, be a decision to "buy" or "use the market." By retaining ownership of CMHR, CMH would continue to rely almost exclusively on CMHR for home care services. This, in effect, would be a decision to "make."

What are the potential benefits to CMH from using the market? Because home care is labor intensive, economies of scale in the provision of home care services themselves are probably minimal. The only potentially significant source of scale economies stems from transportation costs. As a tertiary care children's hospital, CMH gets patients from throughout the Chicago area. The labor costs of a home care agency increase when nurses must travel great distances between patients. Thus, it might make sense for CMH to use independent home care agencies rather than CMHR to service distant communities. These agencies could combine patients from hospitals in their local areas with CMH patients to reduce transportation costs. CMHR could then redeploy its nurses more efficiently to serve nearby communities with an adequate patient density.

Using the market would also be attractive if the market provides discipline and sharp incentives for efficiency that CMH cannot instill in an integrated CMHR. CMHR was at best an average cost supplier in the market, as indicated by the fact that several health insurers directed CMH to discharge patients to less costly home care agencies. This suggests that CMHR either was less efficient than other home care agencies in the Chicago area, or at the very least, that CMHR had selected a cost/quality position that was not suited to all consumers. CMHR did have reason to feel complacent: Many CMH physicians felt loyal to CMHR and referred to them without considering alternatives. Thus, CMHR had some guaranteed sales regardless of how efficiently it operated.

Still, CMHR was probably not grossly inefficient. The majority of CMHR business came from other hospitals. This could not occur if CMHR did not provide a reasonable cost/quality mix. CMH encouraged CMHR to continue to compete for non-CMH patients, and CMHR's continued success at doing so is powerful evidence that CMHR's efficiency was not terribly out of line with competing independent home care agencies.

Despite the potential for scale economies based on transportation cost savings and concerns over operating efficiency, CMHR probably did not suffer too much in comparison to market firms. The advantages to CMH from using the market were most likely not overwhelming. Still, unless there were offsetting advantages to keeping CMH and CMHR vertically integrated, perhaps a case could be made to spin CMHR off. What, then, were the advantages to "making" rather than "buying" in this case?

One benefit to "make" comes from enhanced coordination in the vertical chain of health care delivery for home care patients. Decisions about nurse training, drug use, and therapy regimens all must be coordinated between the hospital and home care agency. CMHR works with CMH to develop protocols to improve these areas of care. Families that use CMH and CMHR benefit from using the same supplies and equipment in the inpatient and home settings. There are also critical timing decisions involved in discharging a patient home. Poor coordination between CMH and an independent home care agency in arranging nursing care for a patient in his or her home can delay a patient's discharge from the hospital and drive up costs. Close coordination between CMHR and CMH prevents these bottlenecks.

The fact that CMH and CMHR are under common ownership also helps to align their incentives. A critical factor here is the relatively low payments made by Medicaid to CMH. CMH would like to discharge Medicaid patients as soon as it is safe to do so. This will allow CMH to treat more patients, and get more revenues. Many independent home care agencies are reluctant to accept Medicaid patients, because payments are so low. But CMHR accepts them from CMH. This reduces CMHR's profits but increases CMH's. We estimated that CMHR's policy of accepting Medicaid patients from CMH boosts the overall financial performance of CMH's owner, Children's Memorial Medical Center, by more than $1,000 per patient.

One might wonder whether vertical integration really has an advantage here.

Why couldn't CMH and an independent home care agency similarly resolve the Medicaid problem through an arm's-length contract? For example, CMH might pay an independent agency $500 to accept Medicaid patients so as to free up hospital beds for more remunerative patients. The problem with a contract like this is that it risks violating federal anti-kickback statutes. In particular, if the home care agency ever recommended that one of its patients receive hospital care at CMH, the $500 fee could be considered a fee to generate future referrals, and could therefore be illegal. Joint ownership eliminates concerns about the anti-kickback laws.

Joint ownership of CMH and CMHR may also encourage investments in *relationship-specific assets*, a concept that will be discussed at length in Chapter 3. Relationship-specific assets are investments in physical capital or know-how that are made in support of a specific transaction. A key characteristic of a relationship-specific asset is that its value is greatest when it is deployed in the transaction for which it was created; it is less valuable when it is redeployed to another transaction or put to another use. A key relationship-specific investment in this case is nurses' training: CMHR trains nurses who work full-time at CMH. This training improves the discharge process and the training of home caregivers. However, the profitability of this training depends on the fact that CMHR receives most of the patients that CMH discharges to home care. CMHR would be reluctant to make these investments if it could not count on receiving the bulk of CMH's business.

To summarize, vertical integration of CMH and CMHR reduced CMH's flexibility to use other home care agencies, which may raise the costs of delivering home care due to sacrificed scale economies. It may also have partially shielded CMHR from market forces, making CMHR somewhat less efficient than competing home care agencies. However, the fact that CMHR competes for non-CMH patients minimizes this latter concern. CMH and CMHR probably gained significant benefits from being vertically integrated. These gains are attributable to the benefits from coordinated discharge and treatment protocols and from CMHR's willingness to accept Medicaid patients. Vertical integration has probably also created stronger incentives for CMHR to train nurses at CMH. On balance, we conclude that it makes sense for CMH and CMHR to remain vertically integrated. If Medicaid payment rules change, however, so that many other agencies are willing to accept CMH discharges, then integration becomes less attractive, and Children's Memorial Medical Center perhaps should revisit the issue of spinning off CMHR.

CHAPTER SUMMARY

◆ The production of any good or service usually requires a wide range of activities organized in a vertical chain. Production activities are said to flow from upstream suppliers of raw inputs to downstream manufacturers, distributors, and retailers.

◆ Activities in the vertical chain include processing and handling activities, associated directly with the processing and distribution of inputs and outputs, and professional support activities, such as accounting and planning.

◆ A fundamental question for any firm is which activities in the vertical chain it should perform itself, and which it should leave to independent firms in the market. This is known as the "make-or-buy" problem.

◆ A fallacious make-or-buy argument is that firms should buy to avoid incurring the associated costs. The firm it buys from will have to incur these costs, and will charge accordingly. A second fallacy is that firms should make, rather than buy, to keep for themselves the profits earned by independent firms. These profits usually represent the returns necessary to attract investment, and would be required of the firm that "makes" just as they are required of independent firms. A third fallacy is that vertically integrated firms can produce an input at cost and thus have an advantage over nonintegrated firms that must buy inputs at market prices. This argument ignores a hidden opportunity cost to the vertically integrated firm: By using the input to produce its final output, it forgoes outside sales in the open market.

◆ The solution to the make-or-buy decision depends on which decision leads to the most efficient production. This is determined by assessing the benefits and costs of using the market.

◆ Market firms are often able to achieve economies of scale in production of an input that are unattainable to firms that choose to make the input themselves.

◆ Market firms offer other advantages. While a division within a hierarchical firm may hide its inefficiencies behind complex monitoring and reward systems, independent firms must survive the discipline of market competition. This encourages productive efficiency and innovation.

◆ Vertically integrated firms can try to replicate market incentives but may encounter problems associated with motivation (agency costs) and internal lobbying for resources (influence costs).

◆ Use of market firms often presents coordination problems. This is especially problematic for inputs with design attributes that require a careful fit between different components.

◆ Firms may be reluctant to use the market when they risk losing control of valuable private information.

◆ Use of market firms may entail transactions costs.

QUESTIONS

1. In each of the following situations, why are firms likely to benefit from vertical integration?

a. A *grain elevator* is located at the terminus of a *rail line*.

b. A *manufacturer* of a product with a national brand name reputation uses *distributors* that arrange for advertising and promotional activities in local markets.

c. A *biotech firm* develops a new product that will be produced, tested, and distributed by an established *pharmaceutical company*.

2. Universities tend to be highly integrated—many departments all belong to the same organization. There is no technical reason why a university could not consist of freestanding departments linked together by contract, much in the same way that a network organization links freestanding businesses. Why do you suppose that universities are not organized in this way?

3. Consider the following pairs of situations. In each pair, which situation is more likely to be susceptible to *coordination* problems?

a. Maintenance of a *homeowner's lawn* by a gardening company versus maintenance of a *football or soccer stadium's grass turf* by a gardening company.

b. Design of a *toolbox* to hold *tools* versus design of a *wafer* to hold the wires of a microscopic *silicon chip*.

4. A manufacturer of pencils contemplates backward integration into the production of rape seed oil, a key ingredient in manufacturing the rubberlike material (called factice) that forms the eraser. Rape seed oil is traded in world commodity markets and its price fluctuates as supply and demand conditions change. The argument that has been made in favor of vertical integration is this: "Pencil production is very utilization-sensitive—i.e., a plant that operates at full capacity can produce pencils at much lower cost per unit than a plant that operates at less than full capacity. Owning our own source of supply of rape seed oil insulates us from short-run supply–demand imbalances and therefore will give us a competitive advantage over rival producers." Explain why this argument is wrong.

THE TRANSACTIONS COSTS OF MARKET EXCHANGE

3

*I*n the standard textbook model of microeconomics, market exchange is simple and powerful. Large numbers of buyers and sellers engage in straightforward transactions. Each possesses perfect information about market prices and exchange opportunities. Market prices emerge to clear the market, that is, equate supply with demand. In this context, market exchange has many desirable features. Buyers and sellers exhaust all mutually beneficial trading opportunities without having to communicate their preferences or technologies to each other or to a central authority. Sellers face strong pressures to improve production processes and innovate new products. And since the dynamic of market competition tends to drive inefficient agents from the market, market exchange generates valuable information that allows buyers and sellers to measure their actual performance against optimal performance.

In some real-life markets, this representation of market exchange is extremely accurate. Markets for fuels, agricultural commodities, and financial instruments usually operate smoothly and efficiently. In many other settings, however, market exchange can entail significant costs. Consider the following examples in which market transactions proved to be costly:

- The production of aluminum requires several stages.[1] The first two of these are mining bauxite ore and refining the ore into alumina, the chief chemical ingredient of semifinished aluminum. The mineralogical properties of bauxite vary considerably across deposits, and the refinery for a particular deposit cannot accept

---

[1]The following discussion draws heavily from John Stuckey's *Vertical Integration and Joint Ventures in the Aluminum Industry*, Cambridge: Harvard University Press, 1983.

ore from another deposit without incurring substantial expense to reengineer the plant. As a result, a particular bauxite supplier and its designated alumina refiner are strongly dependent on each other. They agree to a contract that guarantees exclusivity and specifies that the refiner pay the market price for bauxite.

This dependency can create problems. Suppose the supplier and refiner are surprised by an unexpected surge in the demand for finished aluminum. The refiner would like to process more bauxite to reap additional profits. The bauxite supplier recognizes the tremendous profit that the refiner stands to reap, and tries to force it to pay more than the market price in exchange for accelerated production. The two sides hire lawyers, and the negotiations consume the time of top management. Eventually production is increased, but only after costly delays and legal expenses.

- When the New York crime syndicate headed by "Lucky" Luciano decided to open the first gambling casino in a barren section of Nevada that was eventually to become Las Vegas, it initially assigned all responsibility to "Bugsy" Siegal, who, with his girlfriend, had responsibility for a vast array of entrepreneurial tasks, such as site selection and marketing campaigns. Siegal repeatedly requested additional funding from Luciano, who had no alternative but to continue supporting Siegal or stop construction. After sinking over $50 million into the Flamingo casino, Luciano discovered that Siegal's girlfriend had embezzled most of the funds for her own purposes.

- In 1970 IBM needed to obtain a family of specialized integrated circuits for a new product that it was planning to market two years later.[2] While similar circuits were available commercially, none had ever been produced with the tight quality tolerances IBM required. IBM turned to a small electronics firm, International Systems, who agreed to build a production line dedicated to the IBM circuits. All went well initially, but in mid-1974, IBM began to detect serious quality problems with one specific circuit, the BR1. Reports from the field indicated that the BR1 was experiencing abnormally high failure rates, with extremely serious consequences for the performance of the new product. IBM managers suspected that International Systems had not done a careful job managing the dedicated line, for example, inappropriately rotating labor on the line, and not keeping the air in the facility clean enough. International Systems countered by challenging the validity of IBM's quality testing procedures and claiming that the defects were not its fault. In spite of time-consuming negotiations involving top managers on both sides, nothing was resolved. IBM managers had to admit that because the process of making these circuits involved a considerable dose of "black magic," they could not rule out the possibility that the problem was due to circumstances beyond International System's control.

All three examples illustrate the difficulties that can arise in market transactions. At the heart of each example is the absence of a sufficiently powerful contract

---

[2]This example comes from Corey, R.E., *Procurement Management: Strategy, Organization, and Decision-Making*, Boston: CBI Publishing, 1978.

to assure efficient performance. In the first example, the bauxite miner and alumina refiner failed to account for a possible sharp and sustained increase in the demand for aluminum. Given their complete reliance on each other, they ended up in a costly battle over how to divide resulting profits. The firms might be advised to do what nearly all alumina refiners and bauxite miners have done—merge into a single firm. In the second example, the New York crime syndicate could have asked Siegal to sign a contract that specified performance criteria and penalties in the event of cost overruns. Of course, the syndicate would not want to enforce such a contract in court. After implementing its own form of enforcement—Siegal was murdered—the New York syndicate took more direct responsibility for its Las Vegas actions. In the third example, IBM could not directly observe how careful International Systems had been in producing the BR1, so a contract that penalized International Systems for sloppy operation of its production facility was impossible. IBM and International Systems did agree on quality standards, but when those standards were not met, IBM could not tell whether International Systems had been careless or not. Because no other outside vendor knew how to produce this important component, IBM simply had to accept International System's word and hope that quality would improve. Quality did improve for a while, but in 1975, after its own engineers had figured out how to produce the circuit, IBM terminated its contract with International Systems and produced the BR1 itself.

The transactions in these examples share key similarities: a strong mutual reliance by each party on the other once the deal had been struck; efforts by one or both parties to sweeten its end of the deal; and an inability to write enforceable contracts that cover important contingencies and penalize shirking. Each transaction also gave rise to significant costs. These included extra negotiations; delays and disruptions in production; and efforts by both parties to safeguard their positions once they entered into the contract (e.g., Bugsy Siegal took elaborate precautions to protect himself against a mob hit; IBM had to develop internal production capabilities to avoid dependence on a sole supplier). Costs like these occur in many market transactions. Economists refer to the costs of organizing and transacting exchanges as *transactions costs*. These costs are considered so important that an entire branch of economics—transactions costs economics—is devoted to their study.

Chapter 2 provided an overview of the benefits and costs of using independent market firms to perform activities in the vertical chain but only briefly discussed transactions costs. This chapter develops the concept of transactions costs in much greater detail and discusses how they work to determine the vertical boundaries of the firm.[3] The main emphasis in this chapter is on the costs of *arm's-length market*

---

[3]The chapter draws heavily on the work of Ronald Coase, Oliver Williamson, and others who have made pivotal contributions to transactions cost economics. Seminal works include Coase's article, "The Nature of the Firm," *Economica*, 4, 1937, pp. 386–405; Oliver Williamson's books *Markets and Hierarchies: Analysis and Antitrust Implications*, New York: Free Press, 1975 and *The Economic Institutions of Capitalism*, New York: Free Press, 1985; and Klein, B., R. Crawford, and A. Alchian, "Vertical Integration, Appropriable Rents and the Competitive Contracting Process," *Journal of Law and Economics*, 21, 1978, pp. 297–326.

transactions. An arm's-length market transaction is one in which autonomous parties exchange goods or services with no formal agreement that the relationship will continue into the future. Purchases of computer equipment, office supplies, or construction of an office building are examples of exchanges typically carried out through arm's-length transactions. Arm's-length transactions are governed by contract law, and serious disputes about whether one party has fulfilled its obligations are often resolved through litigation. Of course, arm's-length transactions are not the only way that a firm might "use the market." A firm might enter into a long-term relationship with an input supplier, through a long-term (e.g., 20-year) contract or through a strategic alliance. But the nature of these arrangements is likely to be quite different than an arm's-length transaction. Each party's obligation to the other would be less precisely defined, and disputes are less likely to be resolved through litigation. We defer discussion of these alternative modes of organizing exchange to Chapter 4.

This chapter is organized in three main sections. The first section discusses the role of contracts and contract law in market exchange and introduces the important concept of an *incomplete contract*. The second section develops three important concepts that are needed to understand why market exchange can entail transactions costs: *relationship-specific assets*, *quasi-rents*, and the *holdup problem*. The third section discusses why vertical integration might be a good alternative to market contracting when the exchange involves incomplete contracting and relationship-specific assets.

◆ ◆ ◆ ◆ ◆ CONTRACTS AND MARKET EXCHANGE

The Economic Foundations of Contracts

Any analysis of the costs of arm's-length market exchange must begin with a discussion of *contracts*. A contract is an agreement that defines the conditions of exchange. Contracts may take standardized forms, such as the "Conditions of Contract" on the back of an airline ticket or the terms and conditions of purchase printed on the back of a company's purchase order. Or they may be lengthy and complicated because they are carefully tailored to a specific transaction. For example, the contract for the sale of the Empire State Building in the 1960s involved more than 100 attorneys and was over 400 pages long.[4]

Contracts are a key element of a private-ownership economy. Their philosophical foundations include important social values, such as the sanctity of promises, the right of individuals to enter into autonomous transactions, and economic efficiency. Our focus is on economic efficiency.

To understand how contracts promote economic efficiency, it is useful to highlight an obvious but nevertheless significant characteristic of market transac-

---

[4]Macauley, S., "Non-Contractual Relations in Business: A Preliminary Study," *American Sociological Review*, 28, 1963, pp. 55–67.

tions: In most exchanges, parties perform their obligations sequentially rather than simultaneously. For example, a steel firm might ship steel to a customer, who pays for it after taking delivery. But in an economy without contracts, the sequential nature of many exchanges leads to the possibility that one party will take advantage of weaknesses in another party's bargaining position that arise as the transaction unfolds. For example, without enforceable contracts, once it delivered steel to a customer, a steel firm would be vulnerable because the customer could refuse to pay.

Without contracts, exchange activities would be biased toward those in which performance occurs simultaneously with payment. For instance, the steel firm would refuse to sell steel unless customers paid cash immediately, and customers would refuse to pay cash unless the firm could fill the order immediately. An insistence on simultaneous performance would clearly raise the costs of transacting business. In our example, the customer would have to carry enough cash to complete all its transactions, and the steel firm would have to have enough steel on hand to fill all its orders as they arise. In addition, in an economy without contracts, parties would invest in private safeguards to prevent themselves from being exploited. In the extreme case, a seller might purchase a gun and threaten to shoot its customers if they do not pay for delivery of a good. This is what often happens in illegal transactions, such as drugs or smuggling. This mode of transacting exchange would not only be costly, but it would also have an insidious effect on the legitimacy of private ownership and government institutions that are built around it.

Contracts, then, protect parties to a transaction from opportunistic behavior. By so doing, they allow transactions to be organized in more economical ways. However, contracts are not equally effective in all circumstances. Their ability to facilitate exchange depends on (1) the "completeness" of the contract, and (2) the available body of contract law. We discuss each of these factors in turn.

Complete versus Incomplete Contracting

A *complete contract* eliminates opportunistic behavior. A complete contract stipulates each party's responsibilities and rights for each and every contingency that could conceivably arise during the transaction. A complete contract would bind the parties to particular courses of action as the transaction unfolded. Neither party would be free to exploit weaknesses in the other's position while the transaction was in progress.

The requirements of complete contracting are severe. Parties to the contract must be able to contemplate all relevant contingencies and agree on a "mapping" that specifies for each possible contingency a set of actions that each party must take. The parties must also be able to stipulate what constitutes satisfactory performance and must be able to measure performance. Finally, the contract must be enforceable. This means that parties do not have the freedom to unilaterally renege on the contract. It also implies that an outside party, such as a judge or an arbitrator, must be able to observe which contingencies occurred and whether each party took the actions that were required for those contingencies. For example, a contract in which the price of an item is tied to the seller's production costs might not be enforceable without an independent auditing mechanism that could verify those costs.

An *incomplete contract* is one in which the "mapping" from possible contingencies to rights, responsibilities, and actions is not fully specified. This might be because some of the relevant contingencies cannot be contemplated, or in those that can be contemplated, performance obligations cannot be articulated. As might be imagined, virtually all real-world contracts are incomplete to some degree. Incomplete contracts involve some degree of open-endedness or ambiguity; there are circumstances under which neither party's rights and responsibilities are clearly spelled out. Consider, for example, the case, *Cook v. Deltona Corp.*[5] In 1971 Deltona Corporation, a land developer, sold Cook a piece of property in Marco Shores, Florida. The land was under water at the time of the sale. The title to the land was to be delivered in 1980, by which time Deltona was to have dredged and filled the land. However, during the 1970s changes in federal policy toward wetlands made it increasingly difficult for developers to obtain dredge and fill permits from the Army Corps of Engineers. In 1976, after failing to obtain permits on nearby land, Deltona gave up trying to obtain a permit for Marco Shores. The sale contract did not specify the buyer's rights and the developer's responsibilities under these circumstances, so the contract was incomplete. Because the contract was silent on this unanticipated turn of events, it was not clear whether Deltona had breached the contract by not delivering the land in the condition promised. The outcome was a lawsuit that took nine years to resolve. (Cook won the suit.)

Three factors prevent complete contracting:

- Bounded rationality
- Difficulties specifying or measuring performance
- Asymmetric information

We will discuss each in turn.

Bounded Rationality   Bounded rationality refers to limits on the capacity of individuals to process information, deal with complexity, and pursue rational aims. Boundedly rational parties cannot contemplate or enumerate every contingency that might arise during a transaction. As a result, they cannot write complete contracts. In the example of *Cook v. Deltona Corp.* above, Deltona essentially offered a defense based on bounded rationality. It argued that changes in regulatory requirements by the Army Corps of Engineers seemed so unlikely when the contract was written as to be essentially unforeseeable. The court acknowledged that, in principle, this could be a valid defense, but held that evidence that the Army Corps of Engineers had begun to toughen its policy meant that Deltona should have accounted for this risk in the contract.

Difficulties Specifying or Measuring Performance   When performance under a contract is complex or subtle, not even the most accomplished wordsmiths may be able to clearly elaborate each party's rights and responsibilities. Language in

---

[5]*Cook v. Deltona Corp.*, 753 F2d 1552 (1985) United States Court of Appeals, Eleventh Circuit.

contracts is thus often left so vague and open-ended that it may not be clear what constitutes fulfillment of the contract. For example, a standard clause in lease contracts for new cars allows the company to bill the lessee for "excess wear and tear." However, the contract does not specify what "wear and tear" or "excess" mean. Some leasing companies have used this clause to charge customers who return the car in less than showroom condition.

A related problem is that dimensions of performance may be ambiguous or hard to measure. For example, in relationships between airframe manufacturers and engine suppliers, engine thrust is the subject of much contention. Thrust cannot be measured exactly, and each engine supplier uses a different measurement methodology. John Newhouse, in *The Sporty Game*, writes of Boeing engineers who "speak astringently about a Hartford pound of thrust [Pratt & Whitney], a Cincinnati pound of thrust [GE], and a Derby pound of thrust [Rolls-Royce]."[6]

Asymmetric Information   Even if the parties can foresee the contingencies and the relevant performance dimensions can be specified and measured, a contract may still be incomplete because the parties do not have equal access to all contract-relevant information, that is, a condition of *asymmetric information* exists. If one party knows something that the other does not, that party may distort or misrepresent that information. For example, suppose a contract stipulates that a manufacturer is to receive a bonus if it produces an item below budget, but because the manufacturer controls its internal accounting system, it is the only one that can verify with certainty that the budget has been met. The manufacturer would want to claim that it has produced the item under budget even when it has not. Understanding the manufacturer's self-interest, the buyer would protest the manufacturer's claims. To enforce this contract, a court would have to look at evidence (e.g., an independent audit or testimony from each party) to ascertain whether the contract was fulfilled. But if the item being produced is complex or unique, this evidence may well be inconclusive, and the court would have little basis on which to resolve the dispute. Under these circumstances, contracting for "coming in under budget" would not be attractive to the two parties.

Asymmetric information takes two generic forms: *hidden information* and *hidden action*.

Hidden Information

A party possesses hidden information when it has knowledge about the conditions of demand, technology, or cost that other parties do not have and cannot learn.[7] In

---

[6]Newhouse, J., *The Sporty Game*, New York: Knopf, 1982, pp. 53–54.

[7]Economists often refer to hidden information as the *adverse selection problem*. The term is borrowed from the insurance literature, where it refers to the effects of offering uniform policy terms to diverse consumers with private information about their risk characteristics. The term has since come to refer to any circumstance in which one party has private information about any *intrinsic* characteristic (e.g., preferences, technology, risk) that might be relevant to performance in a contracting situation.

any transaction, one or more parties may possess different hidden information. When this happens, the contract governing the exchange must often be left incomplete. In some cases, the contract will be silent about key performance parameters; in other cases, the contract will be silent about key contingencies.

A contract cannot be made contingent on performance parameters unless those parameters are measurable. Often, the hidden information that a firm possesses is directly related to its performance. Under these circumstances, performance-based contracts can be fraught with problems because, as just discussed, the firm possessing the hidden information may misrepresent it or disclose it selectively.

If one party to a contract has hidden information about key contingencies, it may prefer to omit those contingencies from the contract. The reason is that if the party suggests including a provision in the contract to cover that contingency, it may signal adverse information to the other party that it would prefer to keep hidden.[8] To illustrate, consider a hypothetical twist on the *Cook v. Deltona* case discussed above. Suppose Deltona had insisted on a clause absolving it of any responsibility if changes in federal policy make it impossible for the developer to obtain permits to dredge and fill the land. The buyer, Cook, who had not even considered this possibility, would not become suspicious that Deltona has hidden information about changes in the policy on granting permits. To protect itself against what it would now see as an increased risk that the government would change its policy, Cook would either insist on a lower price or refuse to purchase the land altogether. Anticipating this, Deltona might be better off negotiating an incomplete contract that was silent on what would happen if changes in policy made it impossible for the seller to get the needed permits.

Hidden Action

Contracts are also incomplete because a party can take hidden actions. A hidden action affects contract performance but cannot be observed or verified.[9] For example, to ensure that it receives merchandise that performs as promised, a buyer might want to write a contract that stipulates requirements for quality control in the manufacturer's plant. However, what goes on in the manufacturer's plant is the manufacturer's business. It would probably be very difficult to monitor or verify the manufacturer's level of "care" in producing and inspecting the products, and so care is a hidden action. A contract that required the manufacturer to take a specified level of care would undoubtedly be contentious and very costly to enforce.

---

[8]This is an example of what Roger Myerson has called the "informed principal" problem. See Chapter 10 of Myerson, R., *Game Theory: An Analysis of Conflict*, Cambridge: Harvard University Press, 1991.

[9]Economists refer to hidden action as the *moral hazard problem*. This term is also borrowed from the insurance literature, where it refers to the problem that an insurance company faces when policyholders can take actions that the insurance company could not monitor or prevent that raise the risk of the insured event actually occurring. Moral hazard has since come to refer to a wide class of circumstances in which parties in a contractual relationship can take actions that cannot be verified and thus cannot be contracted upon.

If the performance of the merchandise can be measured, a contract could be written directly on the basis of the performance of the delivered goods. If there is a one-to-one correspondence between care and performance, then contracting on performance will induce the desired level of care. More typically, though, the relationship between care and performance is complicated by factors outside the manufacturer's control. Higher care will sometimes increase performance, but sometimes it may not. When the correspondence between performance and care is not perfect, contracting on performance would not be as effective as contracting directly on care.

To see this, suppose that the performance of a machine depends on (i) the manufacturer's care; (ii) how well the buyer follows the manufacturer's instructions when installing the machine; and (iii) "random" conditions beyond both the manufacturer's and buyer's control. A contract that penalized the manufacturer for a machine that performed poorly might create an incentive for good care in manufacturing, but it could also make the buyer careless about following instructions when it installs the machine. Moreover, the contract would introduce randomness into the manufacturer's compensation, and the manufacturer might demand compensation for bearing this risk, raising the overall cost to the buyer.[10] The point is that while a contract based on performance might induce the manufacturer to increase its level of care, it is likely to be more costly than one based directly on care *in an ideal world in which the level of care is verifiable.*

The Role of Contract Law

A well-developed body of contract law makes it possible for transactions to occur smoothly when contracts are incomplete. In the United States, contract law is embodied in both common law and the *Uniform Commercial Code* (UCC), the law governing contracts in all states except Louisiana. The doctrines of contract law specify a set of "standard" provisions applicable to wide classes of transactions. These doctrines eliminate the need for parties to specify these provisions in every single transaction.

For example, the UCC contains a number of general rules known as *gap fillers* that the courts must apply in setting specific terms of exchange (e.g., delivery time, location, price, or quantity) when the contract is silent on them. Section 2-309(1) of the UCC, for instance, provides that, unless otherwise specified in the contract, delivery must occur within a "reasonable time," with "reasonable" being determined by factors such as the nature and uses of the goods purchased and transportation conditions. As another example, Section 2-305 of the UCC directs the courts to determine a "reasonable price" when the contract is silent on the price or contains a price-setting formula that cannot be applied because of a change in circumstances. In the case *North Central Airlines, Inc. v. Continental Oil Co.*, the parties

---

[10]The effect of hidden action and hidden information on the optimal design of contracts is studied in detail in Chapter 16.

agreed to a contract for aviation fuel in which the price would be determined by a formula based on the market price of crude oil produced in the United States.[11] But this formula became inapplicable when the U.S. government instituted a complex system of price controls on crude oil in 1973. The court resorted to the "reasonable price" standard in the UCC to complete this contract.

However, contract law is not a perfect substitute for complete contracting for two important reasons. First, the doctrines of contract law are phrased in broad language ("reasonable time," "reasonable price") that is open to differing interpretations when applied to specific transactions. For complicated or novel exchanges, the relevant law may be unclear. Ambiguities in doctrines and uncertainty about how particular doctrines will be applied raise the costs of transacting the exchange relative to an ideal world in which complete contracting is possible.

Second, litigation can be a costly way of "completing" contracts. A vivid illustration of this occurred in the mid-1970s when Westinghouse invoked the doctrine of *commercial impracticability* to justify reneging on contracts to deliver 70 million pounds of uranium.[12] This doctrine excuses a seller from performing its obligations under a sales contract if "performance has been made impracticable by the occurrence of a contingency the nonoccurrence of which was a basic assumption on which the contract was made" (UCC 2-504). In the early 1970s Westinghouse had agreed to sell uranium at $10 per pound to a group of electric utilities. Soon after signing the contracts, the price of uranium increased dramatically, to $26 per pound in 1975. Westinghouse argued that the price increase was the result of unforeseeable events (the Arab oil embargo and the subsequent runup of oil prices), and that it would be impossible to deliver the uranium without incurring serious financial harm—losses of over $1 billion on the contracts. The subsequent breach-of-contract litigation took over three years to resolve. Eventually, most of the cases were settled out of court, but the utilities accepted payments that were smaller than the value of the uranium they would have received under the original contracts.

Litigation is also costly because it can weaken or destroy business relationships. As Stewart Macauley writes, "A breach of contract suit may settle a particular dispute, but such action often results in 'divorce,' ending the 'marriage' between two businesses, since a contract action is likely to carry charges with at least overtones of bad faith."[13] The termination of longstanding business relationships as a result of a breach of contract suit can be especially costly if the parties have made investments in the relationship over the years that have made them mutually dependent on one another. Establishing new relationships that are equally beneficial to both parties may be difficult or even impossible.

---

[11]*North Central Airlines, Inc. v. Continental Oil Co.*, 574 F2d 582 (1978), D.C. Circuit.

[12]Joskow, P, "Commercial Impossibility, the Uranium Market, and the Westinghouse Case," *Journal of Legal Studies*, 6, 1977, pp. 119–176.

[13]Macauley, S., "Non-contractual Relations in Business: A Preliminary Study," *American Sociological Review*, 28, 1963, pp. 55–67.

TRANSACTIONS WITH RELATIONSHIP-SPECIFIC ASSETS

◆ ◆ ◆ ◆ ◆

Contract law might ameliorate problems of opportunism that can arise under incomplete contracting, but it is unlikely to eliminate them. Thus, incomplete contracting will inevitably entail some transactions costs. To help explain more precisely the nature of these transactions costs and how they might bias economic decision making, this section introduces three important theoretical concepts from transactions-cost economics: *relationship-specific assets*, *quasi-rents*, and *the holdup problem*. The following subsections define these concepts and explain their significance.

Relationship-Specific Assets

A relationship-specific asset is an investment made to support a given transaction. A relationship-specific asset cannot be redeployed to another transaction without some sacrifice in the productivity of the asset or some cost in adapting the asset to the new transaction. When a transaction involves relationship-specific assets, parties to the transaction cannot costlessly switch trading partners. This is because the assets involved in the original exchange would have to be reconfigured to be valuable in the new relationship or the investments would have to be made all over again in the new relationship. This implies that investments in relationship-specific assets lock the parties into the relationship to a certain degree.

Each of the examples in the introduction to this chapter involved relationship-specific assets:

- An alumina refiner makes a relationship-specific investment when it builds a refinery to accommodate a particular grade of bauxite ore. After it is set up, the refinery cannot be reconfigured to handle other grades of bauxite without significant expenditures to redesign the facility. This investment makes both parties in the transaction strongly dependent on one another. The alumina refiner would not be able to replace the bauxite supplier without incurring significant costs in reconfiguring its plant. The bauxite miner may have no other possible customers because no other refinery is set up to process its particular grade of bauxite.

- The New York crime syndicate made a relationship-specific investment when it hired Bugsy Siegal to develop Las Vegas. Once the syndicate had committed funds to Siegal, he was able to develop transaction-specific knowledge and skills that made him, for a time, indispensable. Replacing Siegal with another mobster would have delayed the development of their gambling empire and thus entailed significant costs.

- International Systems made relationship-specific investments in production facilities and the development of production know-how in its contract with IBM for delivery of integrated circuits. These investments bound International Systems and IBM together in a mutually dependent relationship. International

Systems was strongly dependent on IBM because its dedicated facilities could not be easily adapted to produce other products, and the know-how it developed in producing the specialized integrated circuits for IBM had limited usefulness in producing other products. IBM was strongly dependent on International Systems because no other suppliers had the facilities or the know-how to produce integrated circuits with the tolerances IBM required.

The Fundamental Transformation

The need to create relationship-specific assets creates an important transformation in the nature of the relationship as the transaction unfolds. Before the relationship-specific investments are made, a party may have many alternative trading partners, for example, a buyer may be able to choose among many possible sellers. This allows competitive bidding. But after the relationship-specific investments have been sunk, the parties to a transaction have few, if any, alternative trading partners. Competitive bidding is no longer possible. Instead, the terms of the exchange are determined by bilateral bargaining between the parties to the transaction. In short, once the parties make investments in relationship-specific assets, the relationship changes from a "large numbers" bidding situation to a "small numbers" bargaining situation. Oliver Williamson refers to this change as the *fundamental transformation*.[14]

◆ ◆

ᴇXAMPLE 3.1

THE FUNDAMENTAL TRANSFORMATION IN THE U.S. AUTOMOBILE INDUSTRY[15]

A real-life example of the fundamental transformation is the relationship between U.S. automobile assemblers and their component suppliers. Assemblers usually use competitive bidding for outside suppliers. The assembler solicits bids for short-term (usually one-year) supply contracts. These contracts specify price, quality (e.g., no fewer than two bad parts per thousand), and a delivery schedule. Before the contract, there are many potential bidders. Once the contract is let, however, specific investments on both sides bind the assembler and supplier together in a mutually dependent relationship. For some components, the assembler must make large specific investments in production tooling. The supplier must invest in equipment that is tailored to the assembler's component specifications. Because of asset specificity, suppliers and assemblers understand that suppliers are bidding not just for a one-year contract, but for a business relationship that could extend for many years.

---

[14]Chapter 2 of Williamson, O., *The Economic Institutions of Capitalism*, New York: Free Press, 1985.

[15]This discussion draws from Chapter 6 of Womack, J., D. Jones, and D. Roos, *The Machine that Changes the World: The Story of Lean Production*, Cambridge: MIT Press, 1991.

The fundamental transformation makes the relationship between assemblers and suppliers contentious. Because suppliers see themselves entering a long-term relationship rather than a short-term contract, they will sometimes bid below cost to win the contract, a strategy known as "buy-in." A supplier knows from experience that it may be able to renegotiate with the assembler based on claims that unanticipated events (e.g., poorer than expected qualities of key materials) have raised costs. Because changing suppliers at this stage is costly, the assembler may acquiesce. On the other hand, the assembler's procurement managers are under tremendous pressure to hold costs down. At the competitive bidding stage, assemblers will routinely share production drawings with several potential suppliers. Thus, while it may be costly for an assembler to replace a supplier once the component goes into production, it can still do so. Assemblers do threaten to replace suppliers to hold component prices down. Because a supplier makes investments that are specific to its relationship with an assembler, termination of a supply contract can harm it severely. The supplier thus cannot take these threats lightly. The upshot is that once the fundamental transformation occurs, the relationship between the assembler and its suppliers often becomes one of distrust and noncooperation. Suppliers are reluctant to share information on their production operations or their production costs with the assembler for fear that the assembler will use this information to bargain down the contract price in subsequent negotiations. As Womack, Jones, and Roos express it, a supplier's attitude is "what goes on in my factory is my own business."[16] This greatly impedes the ability of the assembler and a supplier to work together to enhance production efficiencies and develop new production technologies.

Forms of Asset Specificity

Asset specificity can take at least four different forms:

- Site specificity
- Physical asset specificity
- Dedicated assets
- Human asset specificity

Site Specificity Site specificity refers to assets that are located side-by-side to economize on transportation or inventory costs or to take advantage of processing efficiencies. Traditional steel manufacturing offers a good example of site specificity. Side-by-side location of blast furnaces, steelmaking furnaces, casting units, and mills permits significant savings in fuel costs. The pig iron, molten steel, and semifinished steel do not have to be reheated before being moved to the next process in the production chain. In the beverage industry, a standard arrangement is to locate can-producing plants next to can-filling plants to economize on inventory and transportation costs that arise from the bulkiness of metal cans.

---

[16]Womack, J., D. Jones, and D. Roos, *op cit.*, p. 144.

Physical Asset Specificity   Physical asset specificity refers to assets whose physical or engineering properties are specifically tailored to a particular transaction. For example, glass container production requires the use of molds that are custom tailored to particular container shapes and glass-making machines. Physical asset specificity inhibits customers of glass containers from switching suppliers.

Dedicated Assets   A dedicated asset is an investment in plant and equipment made on behalf of a particular buyer. Without the promise of that particular buyer's business, the investment would not be profitable. International Systems' investment in an assembly line to manufacture integrated circuits for IBM is an example of a dedicated asset.

Human Asset Specificity   Human asset specificity refers to cases in which a worker, or group of workers, has acquired skills, know-how, and information that are more valuable inside a particular relationship than outside it. Human asset specificity not only includes tangible skills, such as expertise with a company-specific computer operating system, but it also encompasses intangible assets. For example, every organization has unwritten "routines" and "standard operating procedures." A manager who has become a skillful administrator within the context of one organization's routines may be less effective in an organization with completely different routines. Consider also a defense contractor that is attempting to convert its production to commercial markets. Human asset specificity makes conversion difficult. Successful marketing in defense contracting requires managers who have specialized expertise in the intricacies of government budgetary and procurement processes and are skilled at lobbying Congress and the executive branch. These skills are nearly worthless in the commercial market. To successfully market a commercial product, managers must be able to anticipate customer needs and craft quick responses to shifts in market demand. Rockwell's unsuccessful experience in electronic calculators and digital watches illustrates the difficulty of transferring skills from defense contracting to commercial ventures.[17] Rockwell did not lack the technological expertise to compete; benefiting from its experience in miniaturization for the space program, its watches and calculators were at the cutting edge of technology. However, its managers apparently did not understand these commercial markets very well. Its products were overpriced and were not responsive to consumer fashions.

Rents and Quasi-Rents

The fundamental transformation that occurs because of asset specificity has significant consequences for the economics of the bargaining between buyer and seller, which in turn affects the costs of arm's-length market exchange. To set the stage for our discussion of these costs, below, this section develops two important concepts: rent and quasi-rent.

---

[17]This example is drawn from Lundquist, J., "The False Promise of Defense Conversion," *Wall Street Journal*, March 18, 1993, p. A12.

A simple numerical example, summarized in Table 3.1, illustrates these concepts. We imagine a seller that is going to manufacture a good for a buyer. Given the buyer's requirements, the total variable production cost is estimated to be $3,000,000 per year. To produce the item, the seller must build a plant that requires an up-front investment of $40,000,000. Given the alternative investment opportunities for the seller's funds, the minimum acceptable annual rate of return on the investment in the plant is 5 percent. Thus, on an annualized basis, the *ex ante* opportunity cost of the investment is $2,000,000.[18] The sum of the total variable production cost and the investment cost, which is $5,000,000, is the minimum amount of revenue the seller requires to enter the relationship with the buyer. A seller's *rent* is equal to the difference between the revenue it *actually* receives and the minimum amount of revenue it *must receive* to make it worthwhile for it to enter the relationship.[19] A seller can command a positive rent if the item it sells is in limited supply. However, we would expect that when there are many potential suppliers, *ex ante* competitive bidding would drive a seller's rent to zero. Let us assume that this is the case, so the seller's annual revenue is $5,000,000, and its rent is thus zero.

Suppose that the plant has been specifically dedicated to the buyer's requirements. Thus, once the plant has been built, the seller has few alternative uses for the facility. In particular, suppose that in its "next best" use, the plant would generate annual earnings of $500,000. The minimum revenue the seller must receive to find it worthwhile to remain in the relationship with the buyer is $3,500,000 per year, which is the sum of the annual production costs of $3,000,000 and the *ex post* opportunity cost of $500,000. To see why, suppose it received a revenue of

TABLE 3.1
RENTS AND QUASI-RENTS

(1) Total variable costs	$3,000,000/year
(2) *Ex ante* opportunity costs of the investment in the plant	$2,000,000/year
(3) Minimum revenue seller requires to enter relationship = (1) + (2)	$5,000,000/year
(4) Actual revenue	$5,000,000/year
(5) Seller's rent = (4) − (3)	$0/year
(6) *Ex post* opportunity cost of the plant	$500,000/year
(7) Minimum revenue seller requires to prevent exit = (1) + (6)	$3,500,000/year
(8) Seller's quasi-rent = (4) − (7)	$1,500,000/year

[18]The term *ex ante* means "before the fact." In this example, it refers to the period before the funds have been committed to the construction of the plant. The term *ex post* means "after the fact." In this example, it refers to the period after the plant has been built.

[19]Equivalently, rent is equal to the difference between the seller's accounting profit and the $2,000,000 annual return on the investment it requires in order to be induced to make the investment. This alternative definition makes it clear that the concept of rent is synonymous with the concept of *economic profit* discussed in the Economics Primer.

$3,250,000. Its earnings would be $3,250,000 − $3,000,000 = $250,000. But this is less than what the seller could earn by redeploying the plant to its next best use. Under these conditions, the seller would discontinue the relationship with the buyer. The seller's *quasi-rent* is the difference between (a) the revenue the seller would *actually* receive if the deal were consummated according to the original terms of the implicit or explicit contract; and (b) the revenue it *must* receive to be induced *not to exit* the relationship after it has made its relationship-specific investments. In this case, the seller's *quasi-rent* is the difference between its annual revenue of $5,000,000 and the annual revenue of $3,500,000 that it must receive to prevent it from exiting the relationship.

The example illustrates that while *ex ante* competitive bidding will drive rents to zero, it will not eliminate quasi-rents when there are relationship-specific assets. To make this point more generally, let

p = price per unit

Q = quantity produced

TVC = seller's total variable costs

I = *ex ante* opportunity cost of the investment

S = *ex post* opportunity cost of the investment

Then,

$$Seller's\ Rent = pQ - TVC - I$$
$$Seller's\ Quasi\text{-}rent = pQ - TVC - S$$

If *ex ante* competitive bidding drives the seller's rent to zero, then $p=(TVC+I)/Q$, and the seller's quasi-rent is $I - S$. Positive quasi-rents arise in an *ex ante* competitive bidding setting only if there is asset specificity, $S < I$.

The difference between the concepts of rent and quasi-rent is that rent refers to the *ex ante* situation and quasi-rent refers to the *ex post* situation. In an environment without asset specificity—where $S = I$—the minimum revenue needed to induce the seller to enter the relationship would equal the minimum revenue needed to prevent exit. Thus, if the contract resulted in zero rents, it would also result in zero quasi-rents. However, with asset specificity, there is an asymmetry between the *ex ante* situation and the *ex post* situation, that is, $S < I$. Then, the minimum revenue that prevents exit, $TVC + S$, would be lower than the minimum price that elicits entry, $TVC + I$. In the example above, $TVC + S = $3,500,000$, while $TVC + I = $5,000,000$. In this case, there are zero rents, but positive quasi-rents.

The Holdup Problem and Transactions Costs

Even when the *ex ante* contracting environment is competitive, the existence of quasi-rents creates an *ex post* "pie" that the buyer and the seller can negotiate over. For example, a seller might attempt to exploit a buyer who is dependent on the seller by claiming that production costs have risen and demanding that the price be renegotiated upward. The seller may threaten a unilateral termination of the relationship if the buyer does not agree to renegotiate. This sort of opportunistic behavior is an example of the *holdup problem* that arises when a party in a contractual relationship exploits the other party's vulnerability due to relationship-specific assets.[20] The holdup problem is manifested in the redistribution of quasi-rents either through contract renegotiation or unilateral actions that benefit one party at the expense of another.

$\mathcal{E}$XAMPLE 3.2

TACO BELL AND THE HOLDUP PROBLEM[21]

In the late 1980s and early 1990s, Taco Bell pursued a growth strategy to make its market presence comparable to McDonald's. Taco Bell significantly increased the number of its outlets all over the U.S. It also introduced Taco Bell Express, concession stands that offer a limited menu of its food. Existing Taco Bell franchisees strongly opposed this strategy fearing that new outlets would cut into their business.[22]

At first glance, it is not immediately clear why a policy that harms its franchisees would be beneficial to Taco Bell. If Taco Bell sold franchises through an up-front franchise fee, its optimal policy would be to give each franchisee an exclusive territory (essentially making each franchise a local monopoly) and sell the franchises through a competitive auction. A potential franchisee's *reservation price*—the most it would be willing to pay to obtain a franchise—would be the present value of the monopoly profits it expects to earn from the exclusive territory. In a competitive auction, the price of a franchise would be bid up to this reservation price.[23] But Taco Bell does not employ this policy. Its franchisees pay a royalty based on a percentage of their sales revenues. This drives a wedge between the *ex post* interests of Taco Bell and its franchisees. Adding outlets in a local market creates additional competition that most likely hurts existing franchisees. But by

---

[20]The expression "hold up problem" was coined by Victor Goldberg in his article, "Regulation and Administered Contracts," *Bell Journal of Economics*, 7, Autumn 1976, pp. 426–448.

[21]This example draws from "Indigestion at Taco Bell," *Business Week*, December 14, 1992, pp. 66–67.

[22]The president of the Taco Bell franchise organization claims to have documented 70 instances in which new franchises have stolen business from existing outlets. See "Indigestion at Taco Bell," p. 67.

[23]The result that exclusive territories and up-front franchise fees constitute an optimal franchising contract is proven in Mathewson, G.F. and R.A. Winter. "An Economic Theory of Vertical Restraints," *RAND Journal of Economics*, 15, Spring 1984, pp. 27–38.

giving Taco Bell greater visibility or creating locational convenience for some consumers, the additional outlets could stimulate total market demand and increase total market revenues, which makes Taco Bell better off.[24]

Taco Bell franchisees are caught in a classic holdup situation. Their contracts give them exclusive rights to their own restaurants but not to their territories. Taco Bell is free to open other outlets in the same local market. It is not even required to study the market impact of new outlets on existing franchisees. Of course, in principle, a franchisee could terminate its relationship with Taco Bell. But many franchisees have undoubtedly built up relationship-specific human capital. For many, the "next best" outside opportunity is probably less attractive than running a Taco Bell franchise, even taking into account the reduction in profits due to the opening of new outlets in their market. In short, franchisees have quasi-rents in their relationship with Taco Bell, and Taco Bell's growth strategy has probably redistributed a portion of those quasi-rents from the franchisees to itself.

The holdup problem raises the cost of transacting arm's-length market exchanges in four ways. It can lead to:

- More difficult contract negotiations and more frequent renegotiations
- Investments to improve *ex post* bargaining positions
- Distrust
- Reduced investment in relationship-specific investments

Contract Negotiation and Renegotiation The most obvious way in which the holdup problem raises the costs of market transactions is by increasing the difficulty of contract negotiations and the frequency of contract renegotiations. When each side anticipates the possibility of holdup, the initial contract negotiations are likely to be time consuming and costly as each party attempts to protect itself against being held up later on. But if the relationship is sufficiently complex, the ability to write complete contracts that safeguard each party is limited, and as circumstances change in unanticipated ways, the temptation for a party to hold up its trading partner is likely to lead to frequent renegotiations of contracts. This, too, raises the direct costs of carrying out the transaction. In addition, more frequent renegotiations are likely to be associated with more frequent delays or disruptions in the exchange, raising production costs and impeding delivery of products to customers. This problem can be particularly serious when the exchange is part of a sequential production process in which precise synchronization among different stages of production is key. For example, in traditional steel production, heating economies make it desirable to locate the stages of production next to each other.

---

[24]Total revenues could also go up if additional competition within a local market intensifies pricing rivalry and market demand is elastic. (See the Economics Primer for a review of the concept of demand elasticity.) In that case, the lower prices due to greater competition would result in greater overall revenues.

In principle, each stage could be independently owned and operated, and exchanges between separate processes (e.g., production of pig iron) could be mediated by arm's-length contracts. However, given the significant site-specific investments involved and the inefficiencies that would result from the interruptions in product flows that would arise from contractual holdup, arm's-length contracting is inferior to other arrangements, such as common ownership of the site-specific facilities.

Investments to Improve *Ex Post* Bargaining Positions The possibility of holdup may also lead parties to make investments that improve their postcontractual bargaining positions. This can take several forms. For example, a manufacturer may acquire a standby production facility for a key input as a hedge against contractual holdup by the input supplier. A firm might also seek a second source for an input in order to reduce the risk of holdup by a sole supplier. For example, in the early 1980s, its customers (including IBM) pressured Intel to provide second sources for its 8088 and 80286 microprocessors. While holding standby facilities and contracting with second sources can reduce the possibility of holdup, they are not without cost. A standby facility that duplicates the production facility of the input supplier may stand idle much of the time, thus representing costly excess capacity. Diverting volume to a second source will reduce the primary source's scale of production, and when there are economies of scale, this will raise production costs.

Distrust A less tangible, but real, cost of holdup is the distrust that can arise between parties in the relationship. Lack of trust raises the costs of contracting in two ways. First, it raises the direct costs of contract negotiation as parties insist that more formal safeguards be written into the contract. For instance, some communities have begun writing detailed contracts with any business that receives tax breaks and specific infrastructure improvements.[25] When the village of Hoffman Estates, Illinois provided tax incentives to support Sears' new corporate headquarters, its officials negotiated an extensive agreement with Sears that, among other things, obligates Sears to pay $70 million in village expenses for 20 years, support a public transportation project, and refrain from protesting real estate taxes or assessed valuations.[26] While formal contracting of this sort creates stronger safeguards than handshake agreements, it is also costly. Sear's negotiations with Hoffman Estates took 18 months and involved executives at the highest levels.

Second, distrust impedes opportunities for sharing information or ideas to achieve production efficiencies or quality improvements. As discussed in Example 3.1, distrust characterizes the relationship between U.S. auto assemblers and their suppliers. Industry experts cite it as a reason for high production costs and the less-than-satisfactory quality of components.[27]

---

[25]See "Firms Finding it More Difficult to Leave Town," *Wall Street Journal*, March 3, 1993, p. B8.

[26]"It's All in Writing in the Sears Move" (letter to the editor), *Chicago Tribune*, April 10, 1993.

[27]Womack, J., D. Jones, and D. Roos, *op cit.*

Reduced Investment   Finally, and perhaps worst of all, the possibility of holdup can reduce incentives for investment in specific assets. This might occur in several ways. A firm might reduce the scale of its investment in relationship-specific assets (e.g., an alumina producer might build a small refinery rather than a large one), or it might substitute general-purpose assets for more specific ones (e.g., an alumina producer might build a refinery that can process many different grades of bauxite, instead of just one grade). Incentives for investment are reduced because when holdup is possible, a party may not fully capture the potential profits from its investment. If so, it might not pay to make an investment that would otherwise be made in the absence of the holdup problem. In the appendix to this chapter, we develop a numerical example that illustrates this point in a simple contracting setting.

The tendency to underinvest in relationship-specific assets is problematic because relationship-specific investments usually allow firms to achieve efficiencies that they cannot achieve with general-purpose investments. For example, an alumina refinery that is set up to accommodate more than one grade of bauxite is generally more costly to operate than one that is designed to accommodate a particular type of bauxite. When the holdup problem leads to underinvestment in relationship-specific assets, the result is likely to be lower productivity and higher production costs.

In a recent study of small subcontractors in Great Britain, Bruce Lyons found evidence that firms avoid relationship-specific investments when faced with the possibility of contractual holdup.[28] Half of the firms in Lyons' sample indicated that an ideal relationship-specific production technology was available, but only 40 percent of them said they were using it or planning to do so. The firms that were most likely to avoid investing in the relationship-specific technology saw themselves as vulnerable to opportunistic behavior by their customer, and their transactions were characterized by a high degree of distrust. These are exactly the circumstances under which the threat of holdup problem is greatest.

◆ ◆

EXAMPLE 3.3

HOSTILE TAKEOVERS AND RELATIONSHIP-SPECIFIC INVESTMENTS AT TRANS UNION

Andre Shleifer and Lawrence Summers use the concepts of transactions-cost economics to explore some of the possible adverse consequences of hostile takeovers.[29]

---

[28]Lyons, B., "Contracts and Specific Investment: An Empirical Test of Transaction Cost Theory," *Journal of Economics and Management Strategy*, 3, Summer 1994, pp. 257–278.

[29]Shleifer, A. and L. Summers, "Breach of Trust in Hostile Takeovers," in Auerbach, A., (ed.), *Corporate Takeovers: Causes and Consequences*, Chicago: University of Chicago Press, 1988.

They suggest that hostile takeovers are often motivated by shareholders' desire to renege on *implicit contracts* (i.e., unwritten but mutually understood agreements) with employees who have made relationship-specific investments in the firms they work for. A serious consequence of this—and a key reason why, according to Shleifer and Summers, hostile takeovers hurt the economy—is that in a climate of hostile takeovers, employees will refrain from making investments in relationship-specific skills in their firms. This will reduce productivity and raise production costs. To support their argument, Shleifer and Summers quote from William Owen's book, *Autopsy of a Merger*, about the merger between Trans Union and the Pritzker family's Marmon Group.[30] Most of the employees at Trans Union's corporate headquarters lost their jobs after the merger, in violation of what many of them felt was an implicit promise of guaranteed employment by the management of Trans Union. Owens asked many of these former employees what they had learned from the experience. One said that in the future he would be much less willing to make specific investments in his relationship with his employer:

> I learned that I should cover my butt the next time around . . . and have my foot out the door immediately the next time it happens. . . . All of a sudden, you find the rug pulled out from under you—and there is nothing you can do about it. . . . You've worked hard for many, many years, tried to do the best job you could for the company—I loved that company—but what do you have to show for it? How can you go to another company and give 100% of your effort?[31]

TRANSACTIONS COSTS AND VERTICAL INTEGRATION

◆ ◆ ◆ ◆ ◆

The previous arguments suggest that the possibility of contractual holdup can raise the costs of negotiating and writing contracts and might also increase production costs. To avoid these inefficiencies, a natural alternative to market exchange is vertical integration.[32] But this immediately raises the question: What difference would vertical integration make? If there is a strong likelihood that an independent input-supply firm can hold up the firm that buys the input, why would there not be an equally strong likelihood of holdup when the independent input supplier now becomes the selling division in a vertically integrated firm? In short, why can internal organization better resolve the holdup problem than arm's-length market contracting?

---

[30]Owens, W., *Autopsy of a Merger*, Deerfield, IL: William Owen, 1986.

[31]*Ibid.*, p. 251.

[32]Chapter 4 discusses alternatives to both arm's-length market exchange and vertical integration.

In this section, we argue that vertical integration might dominate market exchange for three reasons:

- *Differences in governance*: Vertical integration gives the parties access to more powerful governance structures than those available with arm's-length market contracting.

- *Repeated relationship*: Vertical integration places the transacting parties in a repeated relationship.

- *Organizational influences*: By placing the parties in the same organization, vertical integration may temper opportunistic behavior.

We will discuss each of these reasons in turn.

Differences in Governance   *Governance mechanisms* permit the adaptation of the terms of a transaction when circumstances change or when disputes arise. The governance of inside-the-firm transactions is fundamentally different from the governance of arm's-length market transactions. This difference is frequently described in terms of an employment or authority relationship, in which the employee, in exchange for a longer term of employment, predictable compensation, or other arrangements, agrees to work at the direction and discretion of a superior within general bounds (or as Chester Barnard called it, a "zone of indifference") rather than according to a thoroughly defined employment contract.[33]

Use of an authority/employment relationship, in effect, moves the dispute resolution mechanism for a variety of conflicts from the courts to administrative mechanisms inside the firm, such as managerial fiat, recourse to general rules, or informal mediation between parties. There is more flexibility for management in the choice of these mechanisms, and this flexibility will presumably lead to more efficient dispute resolution in situations where continued recourse to the courts would be costly, both in time lost and production disrupted.

To illustrate this point, suppose that a seller refuses to honor an arm's-length supply contract with a customer because the seller's costs have unexpectedly increased. The buyer and the seller could, in principle, renegotiate a new contract. Failing that, though, the buyer's main recourse would be a breach-of-contract lawsuit. As discussed above, breach-of-contract litigation is usually a costly way of resolving disputes, sometimes resulting in the termination of business relationships. It is also fairly inflexible in that the court's focus would be on assessing damages that are consistent with each party's obligations under the initial agreement. The court would not attempt to fashion an adjustment that would allow the parties to resume their relationship under the changed conditions.

By contrast, if the conflicting parties are separate divisions within a vertically integrated firm, more powerful and flexible administrative mechanisms are available. For example, top management could resolve the conflict directly by working out the issues that were caused by the differences between the initial agreements and changed conditions. This resolution can then be imposed on the parties.

---

[33]Barnard, C., *The Function of the Executive*, Cambridge: Harvard University Press, 1938.

Management can also mediate a compromise solution to the conflict. Management can act unilaterally in these situations because the courts give wide latitude to internal governance mechanisms. If, for example, top management imposed a solution that forced a division to accept a higher transfer price, the division would not be able to appeal to the courts to rescind the increase.

Why internal governance mechanisms can be superior to external ones in certain situations is an interesting question. In some sense, the calculations made by parties in agreeing to such arrangements are of the same kind as those made in choosing market mechanisms. The bases of influence of management in internal governance arrangements are also similar to those in use in market mechanisms—withdrawal from future business and/or reductions in compensation. Furthermore, recourse to the courts would not be totally excluded from internal governance arrangements if extreme conflicts arise. Parties may also exit internal arrangements if their benefits are no longer comparable to those obtainable from the marketplace.

But one key difference between the employment/authority relationship of internal governance mechanisms and arm's-length market contracting is in the accommodation of the internal governance mechanisms to the bounded rationality of the parties and the complexity of contracting conditions—in other words, the sorts of factors that give rise to incomplete contracting in a market setting. For example, management can require the submission of detailed and standardized information from subsidiaries that would be much more costly to obtain from parties in an arm's-length relationship. This allows better information to be brought to bear in resolving disputes than would be available in a court-mediated resolution of the dispute, where such information would have to be obtained through discovery procedures. Access to such information would allow for higher-quality decisions to be made to resolve the disputes. It would also make the behavior of actors in the firm more observable to management and thus reduce the chances for opportunistic hidden actions.

Repeated Relationship   A second reason why vertical integration could resolve the holdup problem better than market contracting is that vertical integration binds the parties in a repeated relationship over time. Of course, vertical integration is not the only way to bind the parties together this way—for example, they could sign a long-term contract—but it can be a powerful way of doing so. Two divisions bound together within a given firm may have more incentive to make relationship-specific investments aimed at lowering costs than they would if they were separate firms, since the benefits of such investments can be calculated with relative certainty and the costs of the other party leaving the relationship are much higher. Both divisions know that their relationship is likely to persist and both recognize that they are more likely to recoup the fruits of their investment than if contractual holdup and termination of the relationship were likely. Moreover, the fact that both divisions are in a long-term relationship without a definite end period reduces the likelihood that one or both of the divisions will engage in opportunistic activities around the end period, after which no retaliation by the other division would be possible.

Organizational Influences   The fact that two parties are in the same organization may by itself temper opportunistic behavior. Two divisions within the same organization may be more likely to behave cooperatively (e.g., in making relationship-specific investments to lower costs) because they see themselves as bound together in a common purpose to maximize the organization's welfare, rather than as adversaries in a market-mediated transaction. This raises the issue of why parties to an arm's-length transaction are less likely to take advantage of gains from cooperative behavior than parties who are participating in an identical exchange inside a common organization. Put another way, why do "organizations" create opportunities for promoting "good" behaviors that arm's-length market contracting settings do not?

One reason is that firm members may be bound by ties of family or social similarity, so that they value their association with the firm, with its subunits, or with other workers in the firm in addition to monetary compensation. The commitment of the individual to the organization would thus supplement the more formal governance mechanisms inside the firm, and would thus make internal governance more effective than market governance of transactions. In small businesses, conflict resolution is often a matter of working things out among family members.

Corporate culture may provide an analogous condition for larger firms. Organizations have histories, folklore, and other cultural elements that can powerfully influence individual behavior. For example, a culture that stresses teamwork may make the opportunities for mutual gains from cooperative behavior much more salient than they would be in an arm's-length market setting. The presence of cultural influences indicates the importance for workers of work-group acceptance, adherence to group norms, and status within the organization, and these factors can often determine the degree of cooperation within the organization. A nonpecuniary penalty, such as a loss in status within an organization for noncooperative behavior (e.g., refusing to be a "team player"), might be just as powerful for workers as would be termination of a formal contract in a market setting. In these situations, culture can complement the formal governance mechanism in the firm and make internal organization a more effective mode for organizing the transaction than the market would be. Examples of these situations are often found in Japanese firms.

Of course, nothing guarantees that two parties on the same "team" will relate to each other as "teammates." There are many examples of adversarial relationships between divisions within a single firm (e.g., the U.S. automobile assemblers relationships with their in-house suppliers). Indeed, capital budgeting and profit center systems within firms often presume competitive rather than cooperative systems between divisions. Moreover, fashioning highly desirable career paths and highly competitive tournaments among management prospects is how firms can use individually oriented incentives, in addition to any market incentives, to promote greater efficiency.

Gary Miller argues that exercising the "political leadership" to balance incentives for competitive and cooperative behaviors among autonomous units within the firm is the single most important task of top management.[34] Our point is that

---

[34]Miller, G., "Managerial Dilemmas: Political Leadership in Hierarchies," in Cook, K. S. and M. Levi, (eds.), *The Limits of Rationality*, Chicago: University of Chicago Press, 1990.

the sociology of organizations opens up potential avenues for discouraging opportunistic behavior and achieving cooperative outcomes that are not available in a market contracting setting.

The preceding discussion leaves us with an important issue. While vertical integration undoubtedly has advantages over market contracting in terms of economizing on transaction costs, we have also seen from Chapter 2 that vertical integration has important drawbacks. How do the factors discussed in Chapter 2 interact with the transactions-cost considerations to determine how the vertical chain is actually organized? This is the subject of the next chapter.

◆ ◆

XAMPLE 3.4

ASSET SPECIFICITY IN AUTOMOBILE MANUFACTURING

This chapter emphasizes the importance of relationship-specific investments in the vertical chain. These investments in dedicated physical and human capital can greatly improve productivity. But they come at a cost. Firms that make specific investments are subject to holdup. The associated transactions costs can discourage independent firms from making these efficiency-enhancing investments. Jeffrey Dyer has recently documented how automakers in Japan are far more willing to make relationship-specific investments than their American counterparts, and shows how these investments yield dramatic improvements in productivity.[35]

Dyer examined the relationship between two Japanese automakers, Nissan and Toyota, and 96 of their direct suppliers. He compared these with the relationships between Ford, Chrysler, and General Motors and 125 of their suppliers. Perhaps the most striking of Dyer's findings is that Japanese suppliers make site-specific investments with the auto makers. For example, Toyota's affiliated supplier plants are, on average, only 30 miles away from assembly plants, and Toyota's independent suppliers are, on average, only 87 miles away. In contrast, the distance between U.S. suppliers and assemblers is 350 to 400 miles. Not only does proximity reduce shipping costs, it provides assurance to assemblers that necessary parts can be provided in a timely manner. As a result, inventory costs at Japanese assembly plants are 50 percent or less than those at U.S. plants.

Dyer also documents human asset specificity in auto production. Suppliers must often work from blueprints provided by the auto makers. These blueprints are often incomplete, and omitted details can frustrate well-intentioned suppliers. Suppliers with a long history of experience and communication with an auto maker can usually figure out how to meet its needs without costly detailed written explanations for each aspect of the blueprint. This reduces product development times

[35]Dyer, J., "Dedicated Assets: Japan's Manufacturing Edge," *Harvard Business Review*, November–December 1994, pp. 174–178.

and product reliability. Dyer also finds that Japanese suppliers are far more likely to customize the engineering of parts to meet the needs of a particular supplier, whereas U.S. suppliers tend to make generic parts that can be used by several manufacturers. Customized parts add to product integrity and quality.

Dyer's findings raise several issues. First, why are U.S. firms unable to obtain the same dedicated investments from their suppliers as do their Japanese counterparts? The answer appears to lie in the differing traditions of vertical relationships in the two nations. Japanese firms in a vertical chain tend to remain business partners indefinitely. This is partly the result of the formal and informal linkages in Keiretsu—a network of vertically related firms described in Chapter 4. In contrast, U.S. firms will readily switch partners to get a better deal. This volatility discourages relationship-specific investments. Second, are U.S. firms as short-sighted as Dyer suggests? We think not. Although long-term relationships of the sort documented by Dyer do facilitate specific investments, they create many of the same problems as "make" decisions. Trading partners face less pressure to be efficient and innovative, because they are assured of continued business. Innovative new suppliers may be unable to break into the market because of the reluctance of manufacturers to end longstanding relationships with established suppliers. If Dyer is correct, then the balance of these factors favors long-term commitments over flexibility in auto making at this point in time. This does not imply that this balance will remain unchanged, or that similar conclusions would apply in other industries. The dominance of U.S. firms in silicon chip technology and biomedical research suggests that the flexibility of the free-wheeling U.S. production system offers significant advantages in many cases.

CHAPTER SUMMARY

◆ This chapter has examined the costs of using arm's-length market exchange to carry out exchanges of goods and services, costs that we referred to as transactions costs. In many circumstances, transactions costs can be significant, and help explain why organizations carry out transactions internally rather than relying on market specialists.

◆ A starting point for analyzing the costs of market exchange is an analysis of contracts. Contracts are needed because all but the simplest transactions will expose a party to the risk of opportunistic behavior by its trading partner. A complete contract—one that provides a complete and thorough specification of the responsibilities and rights of each party in the relationship—would completely protect parties from opportunistic behavior. However, the requirements of complete contracting are extremely rigorous, and therefore most real-world contracts are incomplete to some degree. An incomplete contract involves some ambiguity or open-endedness about what each party to the contract is required to do and what rights each has in the relationship. Often, this ambiguity or open-endedness is not apparent until the relationship begins to unfold.

◆ Contracts are incomplete for a variety of reasons. These include bounded rationality, difficulties in specifying or measuring performance, and asymmetric information: hidden knowledge about contract-relevant parameters or contingencies and hidden actions that parties can take to influence contractual outcomes.

◆ Contract law reduces the costs of relying on contracts in a world of incomplete contracting. Doctrines of contract law relieve parties of the necessity of writing down low-probability contingencies in each and every transaction. But litigation is costly, so contract law is not, in general, a perfect substitute for complete contingent contracting.

◆ The problem of opportunistic behavior is particularly serious when the transaction involves relationship-specific assets. When a transaction involves relationship-specific assets, parties to the transaction cannot costlessly switch trading partners. Transacting with relationship-specific assets involves a fundamental transformation in the nature of contracting possibilities. Before the relationship-specific investment is made, the firm may face a competitive bidding situation with many potential trading partners. After the investment is made, however, the firm has few, if any, alternatives to its current trading partner. Asset specificity takes several forms including physical asset specificity, site specificity, dedicated assets, and human asset specificity.

◆ Relationship-specific assets give rise to quasi-rents, which in turn create opportunities for one party in the relationship to capture the quasi-rents of the other party. This could happen through contract renegotiations that directly benefit one party at the expense of the other or actions by one party that the other cannot stop because of a combination of incomplete contracts and being locked into the relationship. A renegotiation or action that redistributes quasi-rents from one party to the other is referred to as the holdup problem.

◆ The holdup problem raises the costs of exchange in a variety of ways. It increases the amount of time and money parties spend in contract negotiations. The possibility of holdup often leads to distrust, resulting in lost opportunities for achieving production efficiencies. Holdup induces parties to safeguard their bargaining positions through investments in standby facilities or development of second sources. These strategies can give rise to production cost inefficiencies. Finally, parties threatened with holdup may refrain from investing in relationship-specific assets. When this occurs, production costs will generally be higher than they would be otherwise.

◆ Organizing the transaction inside a firm—vertical integration—may avoid the transactions costs of market exchange. Vertical integration may lower the transactions costs that stem from the incomplete contracting and the holdup problem for three reasons. First, organizing the transaction inside the firm opens up opportunities for distinctive governance arrangements that allow more flexible and more powerful forms of dispute resolution and greater adaptability of the transaction to unforeseen changes in circumstances. Second, parties that transact inside the firm deal with each other in a repeated relationship that reduces uncertainty and thus makes investments in relationship-specific assets more profitable. Third, sociological influences, such as organizational culture, enhance the willingness and ability of parties to transact in a cooperative, as opposed to adversarial, mode.

QUESTIONS

1. Some contracts, such as those between municipalities and highway construction firms, are extremely long with terms spelled out in minute detail. Others, such as between consulting firms and their clients, are short and fairly vague about the division of responsibilities. What factors might determine such differences in contract length and detail?

2. As developing countries begin to prosper, what do you expect will happen to their demand for specific assets? How will this affect the boundaries of firms doing business in these countries?

3. Noted fashion expert Sid Sims has been asked by New World Movie Studios to design the wardrobe for the forthcoming film "Bananas and Fog." The wardrobe will test Sims' abilities—the fashions are to be made entirely of old newspapers, dead leaves, and scrap iron. The studio offers Sims the following contract: It will pay $500,000 upon acceptance of the wardrobe by the movie studio. Sims estimates that he can get the newspapers and leaves for free, must pay $50,000 for the scrap iron, and must commit an additional $350,000 in labor to produce the wardrobe. Full of excitement, Sims signs the contract.

    a. What is the rent that Sims hopes to realize prior to signing the contract?

    b. After the wardrobe is complete, what is the quasi-rent? What assumptions, if any, did you make to obtain this figure?

    c. Offer a scenario whereby the studio holds up Sims.

    d. Can Sims hold up the studio? Explain.

4. Consider two different sorts of transactions between a buyer and a seller. In both transactions, the buyer can potentially choose between many vendors at the initial contracting stage. Both transactions involve relationship-specific assets. In the first sort of transaction, the relationship-specific assets are *physical assets* (e.g., specialized presses and dies). In the second sort of transaction, the relationship-specific assets are *human assets*, such as expertise and know-how about the production process. Without knowing anything further about these two different sorts of transactions, why would we expect that vertical integration is more likely to be chosen for the transaction involving human assets than for the transaction involving physical assets?

APPENDIX: THE HOLDUP PROBLEM AND INCENTIVES FOR INVESTMENT IN RELATIONSHIP-SPECIFIC ASSETS

◆ ◆ ◆ ◆ ◆

$\mathcal{T}$o emphasize the point that the holdup problem can lead to underinvestment in relationship-specific assets, this appendix presents a numerical example of a simple contracting situation in which the threat of holdup may cause a firm to avoid making a cost-reducing investment.[36] The example shows that a firm is more likely to avoid making the investment, the more relationship-specific the investment is.

Consider a setting in which a buyer and a seller have contracted for the delivery of a specialized item. The seller will manufacture the item; the buyer will purchase it from the seller and market it to final buyers. We imagine the action evolving in three stages.

Stage 1: The buyer and seller sign an initial supply contract. At this stage, the buyer is uncertain about demand from final buyers and thus does not know the revenues it will get from marketing the item. To keep things simple, suppose that if the buyer pays a price p for the item, there is a .5 probability that it will make $1,000,000 $- p$ from marketing the item and a .5 probability that it will make $2,000,000 $- p$. Although the outcome of this demand uncertainty will eventually be known to both the buyer and seller, it cannot be independently verified by third parties. Thus, the buyer and seller cannot contract on it.

Stage 2: The seller decides how it will configure its production process. The seller can invest $150,000 in a process improvement that will lower the cost of producing the item. Without this investment, the item costs $600,000 to produce. With the investment, the item costs $400,000.

We assume that the investment has three special properties. First, it is a hidden action; third-parties, such as courts or arbitrators, cannot verify that it has been made. Thus, the seller and the buyer cannot write an enforceable contract in which payments are contingent on the seller making this investment. Second, although third parties cannot verify the investment, the buyer is savvy enough to know whether the seller has made the investment. This implies that the investment decision can affect subsequent renegotiations between the buyer and seller. Third, a portion of this investment is relationship specific. In particular, once the seller makes the investment, its value in its "next best" use outside the relationship is $150,000k$, where $0 \le k \le 1$ is a parameter that indicates the degree of asset specificity. If $k = 1$, the asset is nonspecific. If the relationship between the seller and buyer terminates before production takes place, the seller can "get its money back" on the investment. By contrast, if $k = 0$, the investment is fully specific to the

---

[36]This example is based on the models of opportunism in Grout, P. "Investment and Wages in the Absence of Binding Contracts," *Econometrica*, 52, 1984: 449–460, and Besanko, D. and D. Spulber, "Sequential Equilibrium Investment by a Regulated Firm," *RAND Journal of Economics*, Summer 1992: 153–170.

relationship. If the relationship terminates after the seller makes the investment but before production takes place, the seller cannot recoup anything from the investment. As k moves from 1 to 0, the degree of asset specificity increases.

Stage 3: The buyer learns whether the seller has made the investment. The buyer and seller receive information that fully resolves the uncertainty about the market potential of the item. At this stage, the buyer and seller may seek to renegotiate the original contract.

We assume that in the initial contracting stage, the buyer and seller agreed upon a price of $950,000 for the item. Suppose the third stage has now rolled around, and the buyer and seller learn that the item has low market potential, that is, the revenues will be $1,000,000. In this case, we assume that the buyer becomes dissatisfied with the initial contract and demands renegotiation. Because the seller is locked into the relationship, it agrees to renegotiate. The outcome of the renegotiation depends on whether it has made the investment. Table A3.1 describes the situation, where p denotes the renegotiated price.

The table shows the quasi-rents for the buyer and seller as a function of p. Note that if the seller makes the investment, the calculation of the quasi-rent includes the *ex post opportunity cost* of the investment—its value ($150,000k$) in the next-best alternative. The seller must receive profits that are at least as large as this opportunity cost, or it will exit the relationship. The total *ex post* gain from exchange is the sum of the buyer's and seller's quasi-rents. The *ex post* gain from exchange is positive whether the seller makes the investment or not. We assume that the buyer and seller make the efficient decision to go ahead with production.[37] The only issue in the renegotiation is the price. We assume both parties are equally effective negotiators, so the result of the renegotiation is a price that splits the gains from exchange equally, that is, equalizes the quasi-rents of the buyer and seller. The bottom row of the table shows the price that equalizes the quasi-rents. It is calculated by equating the buyer's and seller's quasi-rents and solving for p. Thus, for example, when the seller makes the investment, the price is the solution for p to the equation $1,000,000 - p = p - 400,000 - 150,000k$, which works out to $p = 700,000 + 75,000k$.

TABLE A3.1
QUASI-RENTS, GAINS FROM EXCHANGE, AND RENEGOTIATED PRICE WHEN MARKET POTENTIAL IS LOW

LOW POTENTIAL	No Investment	Investment
Buyer's quasi-rent	$1,000,000 - p$	$1,000,000 - p$
Seller's quasi-rent	$p - 600,000$	$p - 400,000 - 150,000k$
Gain from exchange	$400,000$	$600,000 - 150,000k$
p	$800,000$	$700,000 + 75,000k$

[37] In effect, we are ruling out the possibility that the contract renegotiation delays or disrupts the exchange. Including this possibility would not change our main point.

TABLE A3.2
QUASI-RENTS, GAINS FROM EXCHANGE, AND RENEGOTIATED PRICE WHEN
MARKET POTENTIAL IS HIGH

HIGH POTENTIAL	No Investment	Investment
Buyer's quasi-rent	$2,000,000 - p$	$2,000,000 - p$
Seller's quasi-rent	$p - 600,000$	$p - 400,000 - 150,000k$
Gain from exchange	$1,400,000$	$1,600,000 - 150,000k$
p	$1,300,000$	$1,200,000 + 75,000k$

Suppose that in the third stage, the seller and the buyer discover that the market potential for the item is high. Realizing that the buyer may reap a windfall, the seller demands that the contract be renegotiated. Because the item is important, the buyer agrees to go along. As before, the outcome depends on whether the seller has made the investment. Table A3.2 shows the renegotiation situation the buyer and seller face. We use the same logic to derive the numbers in Table A3.2 that we used in Table A3.1.

Will the seller make the investment? Suppose it is forward looking and anticipates the subsequent contract renegotiation described in Tables A3.1 and A3.2. Table A3.3 shows the choice it then faces. The expected price in Table A3.3 is the expected value of the price that emerges from the contract renegotiation stage, that is, the last rows of the two previous tables.[38]

The seller will not invest if the net profit from not investing is higher than the net profit from investing, or

$$400,000 + 75,000k < 450,000$$

which is equivalent to $k < 2/3$.

TABLE A3.3
EXPECTED PRICE AND PROFITS WITH AND WITHOUT INVESTMENT IN THE
PROCESS IMPROVEMENT.

	No Investment	Investment
(1) Expected price	$1,050,000$	$950,000 + 75,000k$
(2) Production cost	$600,000$	$400,000$
(3) Investment cost	0	$150,000$
(4) Net profit = (1) − (2) − (3)	$450,000$	$400,000 + 75,000k$

---

[38]The "expected value" of a random amount (price, profit, or whatever) is found by multiplying each possible realization of the amount by its associated probability and then summing up over all possible realizations. For example, if the seller does not make the investment, the expected price is $.5(1,300,000) + .5(800,000) = 1,050,000$.

Recall that k indicates the degree of asset specificity, where $k = 1$ is no specificity, and $k = 0$ is complete specificity. Our result says that the seller will avoid making the investment if it is sufficiently relationship specific. Note that from an efficiency perspective, the investment is desirable. An expenditure of $150,000 "buys" a cost reduction of $200,000. But our analysis implies that there are circumstances, that is, $k < 2/3$, in which the seller does not make the cost-reducing investment even though it is efficient to do so.

This result occurs because of the conjunction of incomplete contracts and asset specificity. The buyer and seller cannot bind themselves not to renegotiate, so the seller anticipates that the final price of the item will depend on its investment decision. *Because the buyer can capture some of the seller's quasi-rents in the ex post renegotiation, the seller cannot reap the full benefits of its investment decision.*

The parties could achieve the efficient outcome if they could bind themselves not to renegotiate the price. If the seller knows that the price will remain at the initial level of $950,000, the profit from investing is $950,000 − $400,000 − $150,000 = $450,000, while the profit from not investing is $950,000 − $600,000 = $350,000. The seller would thus invest. More generally, whatever the initial contract price, if the seller regards it as fixed, it would invest whenever the investment is efficient. This is because with the price fixed, the seller would evaluate the investment by comparing the cost of the investment with the resulting reduction in production costs. Alternatively, the parties could achieve the efficient outcome if they could contract on the investment. The contract would stipulate that the seller must make the investment, or otherwise the seller must pay a large penalty. The buyer would make an up-front payment to cover the seller's investment cost, and the parties could negotiate a final delivery price once they learn the state of demand.

ORGANIZING VERTICAL BOUNDARIES: THE ECONOMICS OF VERTICAL INTEGRATION

4

*I*n Chapters 2 and 3, we argued that the organization of the vertical chain is a matter of choice. Firms can organize exchange around arm's-length market transactions, or they can organize exchange internally, that is, they can vertically integrate. Although we discussed different factors that affect the relative efficiency of market exchanges versus vertical integration—scale economies, leakages of private information, incentives, and the transactions costs of market exchange—we have not yet systematically studied how these factors tradeoff against one another in particular circumstances. This is essential if we are to understand why vertical integration differs across industries (e.g., firms in the aluminum industry are generally more vertically integrated than firms in the tin industry), across firms within the same industry (e.g., GM is more vertically integrated than Ford), and across different transactions within the same firm (e.g., Heinz makes its own metal cans but outsources the production of bottles). The first part of this chapter assesses the merits of vertical integration as a function of the industry, firm, and transactions characteristics. It then presents evidence on vertical integration from studies of a number of specific industries including automobiles, aerospace, and electric utilities.

This chapter also examines whether there might be other factors apart from those discussed in Chapters 2 and 3 that might drive a firm's decision to vertically integrate. We focus on two alternative classes of explanation. First, we consider a theory offered by Sanford Grossman and Oliver Hart that stresses the role of asset ownership and its effect on investments in relationship-specific assets as a key determinant of vertical integration. As we will see, while this theory is deeply rooted in the tradition of transactions-cost economics explored in Chapter 3, it goes beyond the transactions cost framework because of its emphasis on the rights of control over key assets in the production processes. A second class of explanations we focus on might loosely be labeled "market imperfections" motivations for vertical integration. These motivations arise because the structure of the product markets of the upstream or downstream firms is imperfectly competitive or because of imperfections in information flows.[1]

The final purpose of this chapter is to explore other ways of organizing exchange besides arm's-length market contracting and vertical integration. We focus on four important alternatives: (1) tapered integration (i.e., making and buying); (2) joint ventures and strategic alliances; (3) Japanese *keiretsu* (tightly knit networks of independent firms); and (4) implicit contracts supported by reputational considerations.

◆ ◆ ◆ ◆ ◆ TECHNICAL VERSUS AGENCY EFFICIENCY

The Notion of Economizing

The costs and benefits of relying on the market can be usefully classified as relating either to *technical efficiency* or *agency efficiency*. Technical efficiency has several interpretations in economics. A narrow interpretation is that it represents the degree to which a firm produces as much as it can from a given combination of inputs.[2] Recalling John Connelly's experiences with Crown, Cork, and Seal (see Chapter 2), a firm whose employees spend time asleep or playing cards at work, likely falls short of full technical efficiency. A broader interpretation—the one used throughout this chapter—is that technical efficiency indicates whether the firm is using the least-cost production process. For example, if production of a particular good displays economies of scale, but the firm has failed to make the investments necessary to realize those economies, then it has failed to achieve full technical efficiency. The firm could achieve technical efficiency by purchasing the good in question from a market firm that is realizing scale economies, or by investing in the necessary equipment to achieve economies of scale itself.

Agency efficiency refers to the extent to which the exchange of goods and services in the vertical chain has been organized to minimize the coordination, agency, and transactions costs discussed in Chapters 2 and 3. If the exchange does not minimize

---

[1]There is a third class of alternative explanations for vertical integration which we do not study in this chapter that we might loosely label as "pecuniary." These include examples of vertical integration that are driven by regulatory or tax incentives. For example, a regulated utility might integrate backward into coal production and charge itself a high transfer price in order to increase the amount of revenue the regulator permits it to collect from final consumers of electricity.

[2]Caves, R. and D. Barton, *Efficiency in US Manufacturing Industries*, Cambridge: MIT Press, 1990.

these costs, then the firm has failed to achieve full agency efficiency. Agency efficiency has to do with the process of *exchange* while technical efficiency has to do with the process of *production*. To the extent that the process of exchange raises the costs of production (e.g., when the threat of holdup leads to reductions in relationship-specific investments and consequent increases in production costs), we would classify this as an agency inefficiency rather than a technical inefficiency.

The resolution of a make-or-buy decision often has conflicting implications for agency and technical efficiency. For example, when a computer maker obtains memory chips from the market, it may improve technical efficiency by taking advantage of specialized chip manufacturers. But this arrangement may reduce agency efficiency by necessitating detailed contracts specifying performance and rewards. The appropriate vertical organization of production must balance technical and agency efficiencies. Oliver Williamson uses the term *economizing* to describe this balancing act.[3] Williamson argues that the optimal vertical organization minimizes the sum of technical and agency inefficiencies; the firm economizes by minimizing the sum of production costs and transactions costs. To the extent that the market is superior for minimizing production costs but vertical integration is superior for minimizing transactions costs, tradeoffs between the two costs are inevitable. Even the best organized firms confront the footprints of this tradeoff, in the form of higher production costs, bureaucracy, breakdowns in exchange, and litigation.

The Technical Efficiency/Agency Efficiency Tradeoff and Vertical Integration

Figure 4.1 provides a useful way to think about the interplay of agency efficiency and technical efficiency.[4] The figure describes a situation in which the quantity of the good being exchanged is fixed at a particular level. The vertical axis measures cost differences (costs resulting from internal organization minus costs resulting from market transaction). Positive values indicate that costs from internal organization exceed costs from market transactions. The horizontal axis measures asset specificity, denoted by k. Higher values of k imply greater asset specificity.

The curve ΔT measures the differences in *minimum production costs* when the item is produced in a vertically integrated firm and when it is exchanged through an arm's-length market transaction. By "minimum production cost," we mean to exclude from this difference any increases in production costs that result from differences in incentives to control costs or to invest in cost-reducing process improvements across the two modes of organization. ΔT thus reflects differences in technical efficiency when the item is produced internally and when it is produced

---

[3]See Williamson, O., "Strategizing, Economizing and Economic Organization," *Strategic Management Journal*, 12, Winter 1991: 75–94, for a complete explanation of this concept along with a brief discussion of its intellectual history.

[4]This figure has been adapted from Oliver Williamson's discussion of vertical integration in *The Economic Institutions of Capitalism*, New York: Free Press, 1985, chap. 4.

FIGURE 4.1
TRADEOFF BETWEEN AGENCY EFFICIENCY AND TECHNICAL EFFICIENCY.

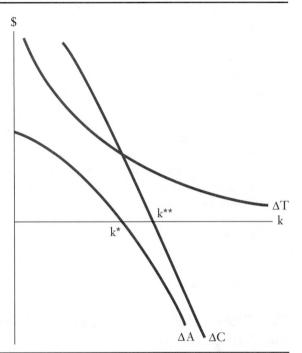

The curve ΔT represents the minimum cost of production under vertical integration minus the minimum cost of production under arm's-length market exchange, that is, it reflects differences in technical efficiency. The curve ΔA represents the transactions costs when production is vertically integrated minus the transactions costs when it is organized through an arm's-length market exchange. (This difference includes any increases in production costs over their minimum level that are due to poor incentives or investments that are not made because of the holdup problem). This curve reflects differences in agency efficiency. The curve ΔC is the vertical sum of ΔT and ΔA and represents the overall cost difference between vertical integration and market exchange. When this cost difference is negative, which occurs when asset specificity is sufficiently high, vertical integration is preferred to market exchange.

by an outside supplier. This difference is positive for any level of asset specificity because outside suppliers can aggregate demands from other buyers and thus can take better advantage of economies of scale and scope to lower production costs than in-house input producers can. The cost difference declines with asset specificity because greater asset specificity is likely to imply more specialized uses for the input and thus fewer outlets for the outside supplier. As a result, with greater asset specificity, the scale- and scope-based advantages of outside suppliers are likely to be weaker.

The curve ΔA reflects differences in *exchange costs* when the item is produced internally and when the item is purchased from an outside supplier in an arm's-length transaction. When the item is purchased from an outside supplier, these costs comprise the direct costs of negotiating the exchange, the costs of writing and enforcing contracts, and the costs associated with holdup and underinvestments in relationship-specific assets discussed in Chapter 3. They also include the costs of breakdowns in coordination and leakage of private information discussed in Chapter 2. When the item is produced internally, these costs include the agency and influence costs discussed in Chapter 2. In short, the ΔA curve reflects differences in agency efficiency between the two modes of organizing transactions.

The ΔA curve is positive for low levels of asset specificity ($k < k^*$) and negative for high levels of asset specificity. When asset specificity is low, holdup is not a significant problem. In the absence of significant holdup problems, market exchange is likely to be more agency efficient than vertical integration because, as discussed in Chapter 2, independent firms often face stronger incentives to innovate and to control production costs than divisions of a vertically integrated firm. As asset specificity increases, the transactions costs of market exchange increase, and beyond a critical level, k^*, these costs are so large that vertical integration is more agency efficient than market exchange.

The curve ΔC is the vertical summation of the ΔA and ΔT curves. It represents production and exchange costs under vertical integration minus production and exchange costs under market exchange. If this curve is positive, then arm's-length market exchange is preferred to vertical integration. If the curve is negative, the exchange costs of using the market more than offset the production costs savings, and vertical integration is preferred. As shown in Figure 4.1, market exchange is preferred when asset specificity is sufficiently low ($k < k^{**}$). When asset specificity is greater than k^{**}, vertical integration is the preferred mode of organizing the transaction.

Vertical integration becomes increasingly attractive as the economies of scale in production become less pronounced. To see this, recall that the height of the ΔT curve reflects the ability of an independent producer to achieve scale economies in production by selling to other firms. Weaker economies of scale would correspond to a downward shift in ΔT, which in turn results in a smaller range in which vertical integration dominates arm's-length market contracting increases. In the limit, as economies of scale disappear, the ΔT curve coincides with the horizontal axis, and the choice between vertical integration and market procurement is determined entirely by agency efficiency, that is, the ΔA curve.

Figure 4.2 shows what happens to the choice between market contracting and vertical integration as the scale of the transaction increases. There are two effects. First, the vertically integrated firm would now be able to take fuller advantage of scale economies because it produces a higher output. This reduces the production-cost disadvantage of internal organization and shifts the ΔT curve downward. Second, increasing the scale of the transaction would accentuate the advantage of the mode whose exchange costs are lower. Thus, the ΔA curve would "twist" clockwise through the point k^*. The overall effect of these two shifts is to move the intersection point of the ΔC curve to the left, from k^{**} to k^{***}. (The solid lines are the shifted curves; the dashed lines are the original curves.) This widens the range in which vertical integration is the preferred mode of organization. Put another way, as the scale of the transaction goes up, vertical integration is more likely to be the preferred mode of organizing the transaction for any given level of asset specificity.

Figures 4.1 and 4.2 yield three powerful conclusions about the relationship between the attractiveness of vertical integration and the conditions of input production and the product market scale of the firm:

FIGURE 4.2
THE EFFECT OF INCREASED SCALE ON TRADEOFF BETWEEN
AGENCY EFFICIENCY AND TECHNICAL EFFICIENCY.

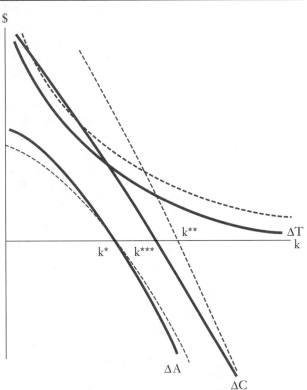

As the scale of the transaction increases, the firm's demand for the input goes up, and a vertically integrated firm can better exploit economies of scale and scope in production. As a result, its production cost disadvantage relative to a market specialist firm will go down, so the curve ΔT will shift downward. (The dashed lines represent the curves at the original scale of the transaction; the solid lines represent the curves when the scale of the transaction increases.) At the same time, increased scale accentuates the advantage of the organizational mode with the lowest exchange costs. Thus, curve ΔA twists clockwise through point k^*. As a result, the intersection of the ΔC curve with the horizontal axis moves leftward, from k^{**} to k^{***}, expanding the range in which vertical integration is the least-cost organizational mode.

1. *Scale and scope economies*: A firm gains *less* from vertical integration the greater the ability is of outside market specialists to take advantage of economies of scale and scope relative to the firm itself. As we will discuss at length in the next chapter, a key source of economies of scale and scope is "indivisible," up-front "setup" costs, such as investments in physical capital or in the development of production know-how. From this, it follows that when production of the input involves significant, up-front setup costs *and* there is likely to be a large market outside the firm for the input, vertical integration is likely to be inferior to market exchange, and the firm should rely on outside market specialists for the input. This will often be the case for routine products and services that are capital intensive or cost less to manufacture as the producer acquires experience and know-how.

2. *Product market scale and growth*: A firm gains *more* from vertical integration the larger is the scale of its product market activities. This is because the more the firm produces, the greater its demand for the input and the more likely that in-house input production can take advantage of economies of scale and scope

to the same extent that an outside market specialist can. This implies that a firm with a larger share of the product market will benefit more from vertical integration than a firm with a smaller share of the product market. It also implies that in a firm with multiple product lines, the firm will benefit more from being vertically integrated in the production of components for those products in which it can achieve significant market scale. It will benefit less from being vertically integrated in the production of components for "boutique" or "niche" items that it produces on a small scale.

3. *Asset specificity*: A firm gains *more* from vertical integration when production of inputs involves investments in relationship-specific assets. If asset specificity is significant enough, vertical integration will be more profitable than arm's-length market purchases, even when production of the input is characterized by strong scale economies or when the firm's product market scale is small.

Evidence from the Real World

Do real-world firms behave according to this theory? Much evidence suggests that they do. Let us look first at evidence from business history. The evolution of the hierarchical firm discussed in Chapter 1 is certainly consistent with the product market scale and the asset-specificity effects. Recall that a key step in the growth of the modern firm was forward integration by manufacturers into marketing and distribution.[5] Between 1875 and 1900, technological breakthroughs led to the potential for unprecedented economies of scale in a number of manufacturing industries. This, coupled with improvements in transportation and communication that expanded the scope of markets, led to vast increases in the size of firms in capital-intensive industries, such as steel, chemicals, food processing, and light machinery.

As these firms grew, they vertically integrated. Before 1875, most manufacturers relied on independent commercial intermediaries to distribute their products. Because an intermediary could aggregate the demands of many manufacturers, it could sell and distribute at a lower cost per unit than any individual manufacturer could. However, there were limits to the economies of scale and scope in selling and distribution. As the scale of the manufacturers in the capital-intensive industries grew, independent wholesaling and marketing agents lost much of their scale- and scope-based cost advantages. As this happened, manufacturers forward integrated into marketing and distribution, a result consistent with the firm-size hypothesis. As predicted by the asset-specificity hypothesis, forward integration was most likely to occur for products that required specialized investments in human capital (e.g., George Eastman's marketing of cameras and film) or in equipment and facilities (e.g., Gustavus Swift's refrigerated warehouses and boxcars). For those industries in which manufacturers remained small (e.g., furniture or textiles) and/or marketing and distribution did not rely on specialized assets (e.g., candy),

---

[5]Chandler, A.D., Jr., *Scale and Scope: The Dynamics of Industrial Capitalism*, Cambridge, MA: Belknap, 1990.

manufacturers continued to rely on independent commercial intermediaries to distribute and sell their products.

Statistical evidence on vertical integration from a variety of different industries is also consistent with the theory developed above. Consider a number of specific examples.

Automobile Industry   Kirk Monteverde and David Teece studied the choice between vertical integration and market procurement of components by General Motors and Ford.[6] Monteverde and Teece surveyed design engineers to determine the importance of applications engineering effort in the design of 133 different components. Greater applications engineering effort is likely to involve greater human asset specificity, so Monteverde and Teece hypothesized that car makers would be more likely to produce components that required significant amounts of applications engineering effort and more likely to buy components that required small amounts of applications engineering effort. Their analysis of the data confirmed this hypothesis. Monteverde and Teece also found that GM is more vertically integrated than Ford on components with the same asset specificity. This is consistent with the firm-size hypothesis.

Aerospace Industry   Scott Masten studied the make-or-buy decision for nearly 2,000 components in a large aerospace system.[7] He asked procurement managers to rate the design specificity of the components, that is, the extent to which the component was used exclusively by the company or could be easily adapted for use by other aerospace firms or firms in other industries. A transistor or resistor would be an example of a nonspecific item; a circuit board designed to individual specifications would be an example of a component with a high degree of design specificity. Consistent with the asset-specificity hypothesis, Masten found that greater design specificity increased the likelihood that production of the component was vertically integrated. He also studied the effect of the complexity of the component, that is, the number of relevant performance dimensions and the difficulty in assessing satisfactory performance. He found that more complex components were more likely to be manufactured internally. This is consistent with the discussion in Chapter 3 about the hazards of incomplete contracting: When the item being purchased is complex or performance measurement is difficult, it is difficult for parties in an arm's-length market transaction to protect themselves with contracts, which increases the risk of holdup.

Electric Utility Industry   Paul Joskow studied the extent of backward integration by electric utilities into coal mining.[8] Coal-burning electricity-generating plants

---

[6]Monteverde, K. and D. Teece, "Supplier Switching Costs and Vertical Integration in the Automobile Industry," *Bell Journal of Economics*, 13, Spring 1982, pp. 206–213.

[7]Masten, S., "The Organization of Production: Evidence from the Aerospace Industry," *Journal of Law and Economics*, 27, October 1984, pp. 403–417.

[8]Joskow, P., "Vertical Integration and Long-Term Contracts: The Case of Coal-Burning Electric Generating Plants," *Journal of Law, Economics, and Organization*, 33, Fall 1985, pp. 32–80.

are sometimes located next to coal mines. This is done to minimize the costs of shipping coal and to maximize the operating efficiency of the generating plant. A utility that makes a "mine-mouth" investment will typically design its boilers with tight tolerances to specially accommodate the quality of coal from that particular mine. In addition, the utility may make large investments in rail lines and transmission capacity, and the mine will often expand its capacity in anticipation of the utility locating its plant on-site. The relationship between the utility and the mine thus involves both site specificity and physical-asset specificity. Joskow found that mine-mouth plants are much more likely to be vertically integrated than other plants. Where mine-mouth plants were not vertically integrated, Joskow found that coal suppliers relied on long-term supply contracts containing numerous safeguards to prevent holdup. Mine-mouth plants rarely relied on short-term arm's-length contracts with the coal mine.

Electronic Components Industry   Erin Anderson and David Schmittlein studied the decision by firms in the electronic components industry to forward integrate into marketing and distribution and use an in-house sales force or to rely on independent manufacturers' representatives.[9] Manufacturers' reps offer selling services to manufacturers in exchange for a sales commission. Manufacturers' reps operate like the sales department of a firm except that they usually represent more than one manufacturer. (Sometimes a rep will carry complementary products, for example, computers and modems, but often a manufacturers' reps will carry products of competing manufacturers). Anderson and Schmittlein surveyed territory sales managers in 16 major electronics component manufacturers to determine the extent to which the manufacturers relied on manufacturers' reps or on their own sales forces in a given sales territory for a given product. The survey measured the amount of asset specificity in the selling function and the degree of difficulty in evaluating a salesperson's performance. The measure of asset specificity embraced factors such as the amount of time a salesperson would have to spend learning about the company's product; the extent to which selling the product would necessitate extra training even for a person experienced with the product class; and the importance of the personal relationship between the salesperson and the customer. Consistent with the asset-specificity hypothesis, Anderson and Schmittlein found that greater asset specificity in the selling function was associated with a greater likelihood that firms rely on their own sales forces rather than manufacturers' reps. They also found that holding asset specificity constant, larger manufacturers were more likely to use a direct sales force than smaller firms, a result consistent with the firm-size hypothesis. Finally, they found that the more difficult it was to measure performance, the more likely it was that manufacturers would rely on direct sales forces rather than manufacturers' reps. This is consistent with the notion that when the transaction environment is less amenable to contractual safeguards (e.g., because contracting on performance is more difficult), arm's-length market contracting becomes a relatively more costly form of organizing an exchange.

---

[9]Anderson, E. and D.C., Schmittlein, "Integration of the Sales Force: An Empirical Examination," *RAND Journal of Economics*, 15, Autumn 1984, pp. 385–395.

◆◆

ᴇXAMPLE 4.1

ᴛʜᴇ ᴠɪʀᴛᴜᴀʟ ᴄᴏʀᴘᴏʀᴀᴛɪᴏɴ

One of the best selling management books of the early 1990s was *The Virtual Corporation*, by William Davidow and Michael Malone.[10] The book's basic premise is that because technological and competitive conditions are changing more rapidly than in previous decades, business organizations need to be far more flexible in responding to changing circumstances than they have traditionally been. Davidow and Malone argue that to enhance flexibility, firms must abandon their traditional reliance on internal hierarchy, and instead continually fashion relationships with independent vendors in the marketplace. In terms of the traditional make-or-buy problem, Davidow and Malone argue that each element in the vertical chain must remain independent; that is, buy should dominate. Indeed, the virtual corporation is even less rigidly structured than the "network organization" advocated by Tom Peters and other management gurus because the network organization presumes long-lasting relationships in the vertical chain.[11]

Given our discussion of vertical integration, it is tempting to dismiss Davidow and Malone's arguments as incomplete. They seem to ignore the costs of coordination and the transactions costs of market exchange, assuming that independent market experts can come together to achieve efficient production without any problems with coordination or holdup. What makes their arguments plausible, however, is the recognition that advances in data processing, telecommunications, and computer-assisted manufacturing have minimized coordination costs, while also reducing the degree of asset specificity in many production relationships. In terms of Figure 4.1, the ΔA curve has flattened, so that agency efficiency differences between internal and market organization have diminished. As a result, technical efficiencies achievable by using market experts have come to dominate vertical integration decisions.

Whether Davidow and Malone's recommendations make sense for a particular organization depend, of course, on the relevant technological and agency conditions. While the virtual corporation will be an inappropriate structure for many firms, and no manager should adopt the model without seriously considering the consequences for agency efficiency, it may be increasingly appropriate for some firms. Just as changes in communication and production technology between 1840 and 1910 rendered organizational structures obsolete with the passage of time, further changes in the decades ahead could permit the virtual corporation to replace the variety of structures that dominate business today.

---

[10]Davidow, W.H. and M.S. Malone, *The Virtual Corporation*, New York: HarperBusiness, 1992.

[11]See Peters, T., *Liberation Management: Necessary Disorganization for the Nanosecond Nineties*, New York: Knopf, 1992.

VERTICAL INTEGRATION AND ASSET OWNERSHIP ◆ ◆ ◆ ◆ ◆

The basic argument of the preceding section is that the interplay of technical and agency efficiency (which is influenced by the factors discussed in Chapters 2 and 3) determines the relative desirability of vertical integration versus arm's-length market contracting.

Sanford Grossman and Oliver Hart, however, develop a different theory for comparing vertical integration with market exchange.[12] Their theory focuses on the importance of asset ownership and control. The resolution of the make-or-buy decision determines ownership rights. The owner of an asset may grant another party the right to use the asset, but the owner retains all rights of control that are not explicitly stipulated in the contract. These are known as *residual rights of control*. When ownership is transferred—when these residual rights are purchased—they are lost by the selling party, which fundamentally changes the legal rights of that party.

To illustrate, consider the relationship between PepsiCo and its bottlers. PepsiCo has two types of bottlers: independent bottlers and company-owned bottlers.[13] An independent bottler owns the physical assets of the bottling operation and the exclusive rights to the franchise territory. It can thus determine how these assets are used, for example, how frequently to restock particular stores. PepsiCo has no direct authority over how the independent bottler manages the operations within its territory. If, for example, a bottler refuses to participate in a national campaign like the Pepsi Challenge, PepsiCo has little choice other than to attempt to persuade the bottler to cooperate. Suppose, however, PepsiCo acquires one of its independent bottlers. The bottler is now a subsidiary of PepsiCo, so PepsiCo can specify what actions the bottler must take. PepsiCo could cede to the bottler specific forms of authority over the assets; for example, PepsiCo could delegate responsibility for local advertising and product promotion to the bottler. However, PepsiCo, not the bottler, has the ultimate authority over how the bottling assets are deployed and how the bottler's territory is managed. If the management of the bottling subsidiary refused to participate in a national advertising campaign, PepsiCo could dismiss them and replace them with a more cooperative management team.

Grossman and Hart begin their analysis by pointing out that if contracts were complete (specified every action under every contingency) it would not matter who owned the assets. The contract would spell out exactly what actions should be taken at all times, as well as fully specify the compensation for all parties. In other words, in a world of complete contracts, the resolution of make-or-buy decisions would be inconsequential.[14] As discussed in Chapter 3, though, for several funda-

---

[12]Grossman, S. and O. Hart, "The Costs and Benefits of Ownership: A Theory of Vertical and Lateral Integration," *Journal of Political Economy*, 94, 1986, pp. 691–719.

[13]See Chapter 2 for additional discussion of vertical integration in soft drink bottling.

[14]Grossman and Hart point out the need to be able to enforce the contracts in a court of law. This includes the ability to collect penalties for contract breach.

mental reasons, contracts may be incomplete (e.g., individuals cannot contemplate all possible contingencies, performance cannot be precisely measured, or hidden action or information make it difficult to verify that appropriate actions were taken for a given contingency). Taking incomplete contracting as a starting point, Grossman and Hart then analyze the importance of asset ownership.

Their theory involves two units that can enter into an exchange relationship. For simplicity, imagine unit 1 as being upstream of unit 2 in the vertical chain. The theory distinguishes between two types of decisions: noncontractible and contractible. The noncontractible decisions are a pair of unverifiable up-front *investments* in relationship-specific assets. The contractibles are a pair of verifiable *operating decisions*. The parties negotiate over these decisions, but if the negotiations break down, control over an *operating decision* reverts to the party with the residual right of control over the assets that are relevant to the decision. Grossman and Hart analyze three different organizational arrangements:

1. *Nonintegration*: The units are independent firms, each with control over its own assets, and thus each makes its own operating decision in the absence of a negotiated contract on these decisions.

2. *Forward integration*: Unit 1 owns the assets of unit 2 (i.e., unit 1 forward integrates into the function performed by unit 2 by purchasing control over unit 2's assets), and unit 1 thus has control over both operating decisions.

3. *Backward integration*: Unit 2 owns the assets of unit 1 (i.e., unit 2 backward integrates into the function performed by unit 1 by purchasing control over unit 1's assets), and thus unit 2 has control over both operating decisions.

Grossman and Hart establish that the form of integration affects the power of each unit during the negotiations over the operating decisions. This affects the distribution of quasi-rents emerging from the negotiation.[15] This, in turn, affects each unit's incentives to invest in the unverifiable relationship-specific assets, which then determines the total profit from the venture. Figure 4.3 illustrates this chain of causation. It then follows that the costs and benefits of each form of integration depend on the sensitivity of total profits to each unit's investment in the relationship-specific investments. Grossman and Hart argue that the greater the scope of a unit's control in the vertical organization, the stronger are its incentives to make unverifiable investments. They conclude that ownership should be given to the unit whose investments have the strongest impact on the total profits of the venture. For example, if unit 1's investment in specific assets has a much greater impact on the total profits of the venture than unit 2's investment does, then forward integration is optimal—unit 1 should control unit 2. If both units' investments have about the same impact on the overall profitability of the venture, then nonintegration is the optimal form. Example 4.2 presents a real-world illustration of where Grossman and Hart's theory might apply. The Appendix to this chapter

---

[15]Recall from Chapter 3 that quasi-rents are the profit that a party makes over and above what the party could get if it redeployed its relationship-specific asset to its next best use.

FIGURE 4.3
GROSSMAN AND HART'S THEORY OF ASSET OWNERSHIP.

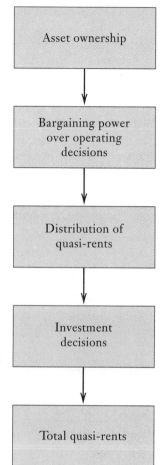

Asset ownership determines control over the assets when the parties cannot reach an agreement. Ownership thus shapes the parties' bargaining power over the operating decisions, which in turn determines the distribution of quasi-rents that emerges from the bargaining. Forward-looking parties anticipate the results of this bargaining, which thus shapes their investment decisions. These decisions then determine the total quasi-rents available for the parties to bargain over.

presents an algebraic illustration of their theory for more mathematically inclined readers.

By emphasizing the importance of asset ownership, Grossman and Hart's theory clarifies what exactly is meant by vertical integration and suggests that there are degrees of vertical integration depending on the extent to which specialized assets are controlled by one party or the other. This clarification helps us better understand certain real-world arrangements that seem to fall in the cracks between vertical integration and arm's-length market contracting. For example, in the automobile industry, General Motors and Ford will often own their own specialized tooling and dies even though the production of body parts and components is carried out in an independent firm. This is especially likely to be the case for components, such as radiators and starters, that require specialized physical assets, but that do not require much specialized engineering or operational know-how.[16] Similarly, in the glass bottle industry, large buyers will often retain ownership of specialized molds even though an independent manufacturer produces the jars and bottles. Grossman and Hart's theory implies that this is a form of vertical integration and is distinct from the situation in which the independent supplier carries out production and owns the physical asset.

Their emphasis on asset ownership also suggests that physical-asset specificity and human-asset specificity can have different implications for the degree of vertical integration. Ownership of specialized physical assets can be transferred, but ownership of specialized human capital often cannot be. Thus, we might expect that the degree of vertical integration is likely to be affected not only by the degree of asset specificity, but also by its form. Benjamin Klein, who studied the 1925 vertical merger between General Motors and Fisher Body, notes that if the only relationship-specific investments had been in physical assets (dies and stamping machines), the potential for Fisher to hold up General Motors would have been removed if General Motors had simply retained ownership of the specialized physical assets and contracted with Fisher to produce auto bodies using GM's capital.[17] That would have preserved the advantages of having Fisher Body as an independent supplier. This arrangement was not chosen because much of the asset specificity in this case came from investments in relationship-specific know-how by Fisher workers, which would have made it difficult for General Motors to find another supplier if Fisher had tried to engage in holdup.

◆ ◆

$\mathcal{E}$XAMPLE 4.2

VERTICAL INTEGRATION OF THE SALES FORCE IN THE INSURANCE INDUSTRY

In the insurance industry, some insurance products (e.g., whole life insurance) are usually sold through in-house sales forces, while other products (e.g., fire and casualty insurance) are often sold through independent brokers. Grossman and Hart's theory can shed light on this pattern. Relying on independent agents versus in-house sales employees is essentially a choice by the insurance firm for nonintegration versus forward integration into the selling function. This choice determines

---

[16]See Masten, S., J.W. Meehan, and E.A. Snyder, "Vertical Integration in the U.S. Auto Industry: A Note on the Influence of Transactions Specific Assets," *Journal of Economic Behavior and Organization*, 12, 1989, pp. 265–273.

[17]Klein, B., "Vertical Integration as Organizational Ownership," *Journal of Law, Economics, and Organization*, 1988, pp. 199–213.

the ownership of an extremely important asset in the selling process of insurance: the list of clients. Under nonintegration the agent controls this key asset; under forward integration, the insurance firm controls it.

If the agent owns the client list, the agent controls access to its clients; they cannot be solicited without the agent's permission. A key role of an insurance agent is to search out and deliver persistent clients to the insurance company, clients who are likely to renew their insurance policies in the future. To induce an agent to undertake these activities, the commission structure must be "backloaded," for example, through a renewal commission that exceeds the costs of servicing and resigning the client. When the insurance company owns the client list, however, this commission structure creates incentives for the company to hold up the agent. It could do so by threatening to reduce the likelihood of renewal (e.g., by raising premiums or restricting coverage) unless the agent accepts a reduction of his or her renewal commission. Faced with the possibility of this holdup problem, the agent would presumably underinvest in searching out and selling insurance to persistent clients. By contrast, if the agent owned the client list, the potential for holdup by the insurance company would be much weaker. If the company actually did raise premiums or restrict coverage, the agent could invite its client to switch companies. Threats by the company to jeopardize the agent's renewal premium would thus have considerably less force, and underinvestment in the search for persistent clients would not be a problem.

There are also circumstances in which the holdup problem could work the other way. Suppose the insurance company can engage in such list-building activities as new product development. The agent could threaten not to offer the new product to the customer unless the insurance company paid the agent a higher commission. Faced with the prospect of this holdup, the company is likely to underinvest in the development of new products. By contrast, if the insurance company owned the list, this type of holdup could not occur, and the insurance company's incentive to invest in new product development would be much stronger.

This suggests that there are tradeoffs in alternative ownership structures that are similar to those discussed above. According to Grossman and Hart's theory, the choice between an in-house sales force versus independent agents should turn on the relative importance of investments in developing persistent clients by the agent versus list-building activities by the insurance firm. Given the nature of the product, a purchaser of whole life insurance is much less likely to switch insurance companies than, say, a customer of fire and casualty insurance. Thus, the insurance agent's effort in searching out persistent clients is less important for whole life insurance than it is for fire and casualty insurance. For whole life insurance, then, backloading the commission structure is not particularly critical, which diminishes the possibility of contractual holdup when the insurance company owns the client list. The Grossman and Hart theory implies that whole life insurance would typically be sold through an insurance company's in-house sales force. This implication is consistent with industry practice: Most companies that offer whole life insurance have their own sales forces. By contrast, for products such as term life insurance or substandard insurance, the agent's selling and renewal-generation efforts are relatively more important. Consistent with Grossman and Hart's theory, many insurance companies rely on independent agents who own the client list to sell these products.

♦ ♦ ♦ ♦ ♦ PROCESS ISSUES IN VERTICAL MERGERS

The principles presented in this chapter so far are often taken as a basis for assessing the desirability of vertical mergers.[18] If the net balance of technical efficiencies and agency inefficiencies is more favorable following a merger between a buyer and a supplier than before the merger, then the merger is appropriate. If the net balance of expected efficiencies following the merger is negative, however, the merger is not appropriate. The decision of whether or not to vertically merge is not so simple, however. Merging on the vertical chain is not a clear make-or-buy decision, but more a matter of "buying" an opportunity to "make." Whether or not that opportunity will be productive will depend on how governance arrangements between the two merging firms develop.

Assessing whether a merger on the vertical chain will enhance efficiency must take into account the fact that the governance arrangements between the acquired and acquiring firms need further adjustment after the combination has been formally completed. After the merger, the acquired firm, while now a unit of the acquirer, will have governance arrangements based on being an independent firm. Its managers will be used to exercising the discretion in decision making and dispute resolution that will accrue to the managers in the acquiring firm. These managers will now have decision-making authority over the unit and will expect to be able to exercise that authority.

The Grossman-Hart theory discussed in the previous section suggests a criteria for judging which governance arrangements will be efficient. It addresses situations in which the specialized human capital of acquired firm managers and employees may be important for the success of a merger. Ownership rights over such assets cannot be transferred even if ownership over the physical assets associated with that capital can be transferred. If the specialized assets of these managers are not employed in the interests of the firm, the profitability of the merged firm will suffer. A governance arrangement that does not grant acquired managers decision-making rights commensurate with their control over specialized resources thus runs the risk of being inefficient. This suggests that decision-making rights for an activity should be given to those managers whose decisions will have the greatest impact on the performance of the activity and ultimately on the profitability of the firm. For example, if the success of a merger depends largely on synergies associated with the combined physical assets of two firms, such as through the resolution of coordination problems between a buyer and a supplier, then decision-making

---

[18]See Williamson, O.E., *Antitrust Economics*, Oxford, UK: Basil Blackwell, 1987, chaps. 1 through 4, for a discussion of the role of transactions cost considerations in antitrust policy.

authority should be centralized. If, however, success depends on the specialized knowledge of acquired managers, such as their knowledge of key contacts in local markets, then decision authority should be decentralized.

Who will actually exercise decision-making authority in the combined firm? What governance arrangements will develop between formerly independent firms? It is not clear in advance which of several possible governance arrangements will develop after a merger. On the one hand, managers at the acquiring firm may significantly delegate decision-making authority to unit managers and grant them an autonomy that parallels their prior independent state. On the other hand, managers at the acquiring firm may assume authority for most decisions themselves. In between are numerous arrangements in which authority is delegated on some decisions and not on others. The actual arrangements that develop may or may not be efficient, in that they will not necessarily reflect the transactions-cost requirements suggested by Grossman and Hart. The process by which governance develops will also exhibit *path dependence*, in that certain arrangements may be excluded by earlier decisions. An efficient governance structure could actually be precluded, for example, if the period following a merger was marked by conflict, while an efficient governance structure requires cooperation between acquired and acquiring firm managers.

These same considerations will also apply to vertical disintegration. At first glance, a vertically related unit of a firm that was spun off to the market as an independent firm would appear to be a market actor. Initially, however, managers in that unit will not be used to making decisions as an autonomous market actor and may instead rely on prior associations with managers in the former parent firm. This would make the relationship between the two firms following a spinoff not a market transaction, but rather a long-term informal association, which is somewhere between being part of an integrated firm on the one hand and a specialized market actor on the other.

The path-dependent nature of the processes by which firms develop can also affect vertical relationships by affecting the capacity of the firm to sell the products of a unit to other downstream buyers besides itself. In Chapter 2, we suggested that market specialists could be more efficient sources of an input for a firm than self-manufacture, since specialists could gain economies of scale, by selling to multiple downstream buyers, that were not available to a firm that self-manufactured. Firms manufacturing for internal uses would typically not sell excess output to other firms. Our assumption in making this claim is that, for firms that built their abilities to self-manufacture in order to supply their internal needs, the sale to outside firms of excess product would be both a distraction and an activity for which the firm lacked the requisite skills. If a firm acquired rather than built its supply capacity, however, the situation would be different. The acquired firm would have had experience and skills at selling to multiple buyers. This marketing capacity would presumably be one of the resources acquired by the parent at the time of the merger. In such a situation, selling product produced primarily for internal uses to outside firms would be neither a distraction nor a matter for which the firm lacked resources. The firm's opportunities for selling to other users of the product could be limited by competitive conditions, however.

◆ ◆ ◆ ◆ ◆ MOTIVES FOR VERTICAL INTEGRATION BASED ON MARKET IMPERFECTIONS

Up to now, we have emphasized the theme that vertical integration results from an efficiency-driven balancing act—minimization of technical and agency inefficiencies. This theme stresses that vertical integration emerges from the interplay between production technology (economies of scale and scope) and the process of exchange (need for coordination, incentives, and transactions costs). Nowhere in this analysis does the nature of market structure or competition play a significant role. Put another way, our explanations for vertical integration apply as well to fragmented industries as they do to industries with few competitors and weak rivalry. But vertical integration may also depend on the nature of market structure and the degree to which firms can exploit market power. In particular, firms may vertically integrate to:

- Undo the effects of imperfect competition
- Achieve price discrimination
- Foreclose entry or avoid foreclosure
- Acquire information, when markets for information are incomplete

We bundle this set of determinants of vertical integration under the broad banner of market imperfections.

Vertical Integration to Undo the Effects of Imperfect Competition

Vertical integration may be desirable when one or more stages in the vertical chain are imperfectly competitive.[19] We will illustrate this point with an example. Imagine a small local brewery that distributes its beer through a large firm that monopolizes distribution within the brewery's market territory and thus possesses significant market muscle over the brewery. Suppose that the *trade price* (the price a brewery or a distributor gets when it sells beer to the "trade"—liquor stores, bars, etc.) is $50 per barrel, while the marginal cost of distribution is $10 per barrel. If distribution were perfectly competitive, distributors competing for the brewery's business would bid the wholesale price (the price the brewery gets when it sells to a distributor) up to $40, the difference between the "trade" price and the marginal cost of distribution. However, because the distributor has market power, it can negotiate a wholesale price of, say, $25. Thus, the wholesale price reflects a $15-per-barrel "markdown" below the perfectly competitive wholesale price.

---

[19]See, for example, Spengler, J.J., "Vertical Integration and Antitrust Policy," *Journal of Political Economy*, 53, 1950, pp. 347–352, McKenzie, L.W., "Ideal Output and the Interdependence of Firms," *Economic Journal*, 61, 1951, pp. 785–803, and Machlup, F. and M. Taber, "Bilateral Monopoly, Successive Monopoly, and Vertical Integration," *Economica*, 27, 1950, pp. 101–119.

If the brewery could distribute its beer at the same marginal cost as the large distributor, it would clearly be better off distributing its beer itself and avoiding the distributor's markdown. But self-distribution would be feasible only if the brewery could afford to invest in its own distribution capacity, and it would be profitable only if the brewery could achieve marginal-distribution costs less than the difference between the trade price and the wholesale price offered by the distributor. If the distributor benefits from economies of scale that the brewery could not achieve carrying only its own brand, self-distribution may not be profitable.

But even if self-distribution is not feasible or profitable for the small brewery, the distributor's market power still creates a motive for vertical integration. Specifically, the brewery and the distributor have a collective incentive to merge and eliminate the markdown below the perfectly competitive price. Figure 4.4 illustrates why. In the figure, MC denotes the brewery's marginal cost of producing beer. As discussed in the Economics Primer, the marginal cost function shows the rate at which total cost increases as output increases. In this case, the marginal cost curve indicates that production costs increase at a rate of $20 dollars per barrel at volumes less than 10,000 barrels per month, $30 dollars per barrel at volumes between 10,000 and 20,000 barrels per month, and $60 per barrel at volumes in excess of 20,000 barrels per month. Facing a wholesale price of $25 per barrel, the brewery's optimal production volume (the volume at which the wholesale price intersects the marginal cost schedule) is 10,000 barrels per month. This occurs when the brewery sells 10,000 barrels of beer a month to the distributor. At this volume, the distributor's monthly profit is $(50 - 10 - 25) \times 10,000 = \$150,000$, and the

FIGURE 4.4
PRODUCTION VOLUME OF AN INDEPENDENT AND A VERTICALLY INTEGRATED BREWERY.

The brewery's marginal production cost is given by *MC*. When the brewery and the distributor are independent and the wholesale price offered by the distributor is $25, the brewery produces 10,000 barrels of beer a month. When the brewery and distributor are vertically integrated, the effective price per barrel of beer (trade price less marginal distribution cost) is $40, and the optimal production volume is $20,000 barrels per month.

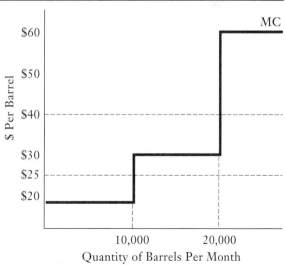

brewery's monthly profit is $(25 - 20) \times 10,000 = \$50,000$. If the distributor and the brewery merged together, the optimal production volume occurs where the trade price net of the marginal distribution cost ($\$50 - \$10 = \$40$) intersects the marginal cost schedule. (Recall that the marginal cost of distribution is $10.) From Figure 4.4, this occurs at a volume of 20,000 barrels a month. At this volume, total production costs are $20 \times 10,000 + 30 \times 10,000 = \$500,000$, and monthly profits are thus $40 \times 20,000 - 500,000 = \$300,000$, twice as much as the combined profit in the premerger situation.

What is going on here is that an independent brewery produces only 10,000 barrels a month to maximize its profits in the face of the distributor's market power. But producing 10,000 rather than 20,000 barrels a month hurts the brewery more than it benefits the distributor, so at a volume of 10,000 barrels per month, combined profits in the vertical chain are not maximized. This inefficiency is sometimes called *double marginalization*, because in the absence of vertical integration, each firm independently equates its marginal revenue to marginal cost. In so doing, each firm fails to internalize the effect that its production and pricing decision has on the other party. By vertically integrating, the brewery and the distributor can undo the harmful effect of the distributor's market power on the volume of beer production and achieve the volume of production that maximizes profit in the vertical chain. The fact that combined profits would go up following a merger is crucial to whether it should take place. Because combined profits go up, it follows that there must be a "bargaining range" of acquisition prices such that if the distributor bought the brewery at a price in that range, both the distributor and the brewery owners would be better off than they were before.

Note that vertical integration is not the only way to maximize profits within the vertical chain. One could imagine the distributor and the brewer signing a contract whereby, in exchange for a fixed annual payment from the brewery, the distributor agrees to purchase the brewery's output at $40 per barrel. The brewery would then produce 20,000 rather than 10,000 barrels per month. The fixed fee can be set so that the distributor earns at least as much profit as it would at a wholesale price of $25. This shows that if vertical integration did occur in this situation, it would, in a sense, be due not only to imperfect competition, but also to incomplete contracting, that is, constraints that make any other forms of vertical contracting except simple wholesale pricing infeasible.

Vertical Integration to Achieve Price Discrimination

Vertical integration can also be used to achieve price discrimination.[20] To illustrate this incentive, consider a large chemical producer who has a monopoly over a particular coating compound that is used as an input by producers of floppy diskettes

---

[20]This incentive for vertical integration was first discussed in Wallace, D.H., *Market Control in the Aluminum Industry*, Cambridge: Harvard University Press, 1937. Perry, M., "Price Discrimination by Forward Integration," *Bell Journal of Economics*, 9, 1978, pp. 209–217, presents the most general analysis of this incentive.

for computers as well as by producers of magnetic recording tape. The producers of recording tape can substitute another chemical compound for it, but computer diskette producers cannot. As a consequence, the demand for this coating compound by floppy-disk producers is less price elastic than is the demand by magnetic-tape producers. From the logic of optimal pricing discussed in the Economics Primer, the chemical manufacturer would maximize its profits by charging a higher price to diskette producers than to magnetic-tape producers. However, this arrangement may not be viable. The price discrimination could be thwarted by clever tape producers who buy large quantities of the compound and resell them to diskette manufacturers at a price that undercuts the chemical manufacturer's. If so, then the chemical manufacturer may be forced to sell the compound at the same price to all customers, suffering a reduction in profits relative to what it could have achieved if it had been able to price discriminate.

But suppose the chemical firm forward integrated into the production of magnetic tape. By lowering the final price of magnetic tape, it could expand production of coating compound for tape production to a level that matched what it would have sold under the optimal price discrimination scheme, and it could raise the price for the compound to diskette producers to the profit-maximizing discriminatory price. In effect, by forward integrating into the relatively more price-elastic stage, the monopolist can replicate the outcome it would have achieved under optimal price discrimination. This strategy results in what has been called the "vertical price squeeze." The squeeze occurs because by lowering the final price of magnetic recording tape, while also raising the price of the coating compound, the vertically integrated chemical manufacturer puts independent magnetic-tape manufacturers at a disadvantage. It is important to note that a reversal of this strategy—forward integration by the chemical manufacturer into diskette production, the more inelastic stage—would not work. To replicate the optimal price discrimination outcome, the monopolist would have to lower the price of the coating compound to tape producers, while reducing the amount of coating compound used in diskette production by raising the final price of floppy diskettes. But this would be extremely counterproductive. It would invite additional entrants into the floppy diskette market who could obtain the coating compound at the lower price from the chemical manufacturer (assuming the manufacturer could not refuse to sell to the new entrants) or from magnetic-tape producers who buy in large quantities from the manufacturer in order to resell it to entrants.

$\mathcal{E}$XAMPLE 4.3

FORWARD INTEGRATION BY ALCOA: 1888–1930

The theory in this section sheds light on Alcoa's forward integration into markets for finished aluminum goods from 1888 through 1930.[21] During this period, Alcoa

---

[21]This example draws directly from Perry, M.K., "Forward Integration by Alcoa: 1888–1930," *Journal of Industrial Economics*, 29, 1980, pp. 37–53.

was the only U.S. producer of aluminum. Unlike its backward integration into bauxite mining and alumina refining, which can be explained largely on grounds of transactions-cost considerations (see Chapter 3), Alcoa's forward integration into the production of finished goods (e.g., cooking utensils) is more puzzling. One possible explanation is that Alcoa forward integrated into finished goods to persuade independent fabricators to use aluminum. This is somewhat unpersuasive, however, because independent firms in many of the finished goods industries complained that they were subject to a vertical price squeeze by Alcoa and convinced the Federal Trade Commission to investigate Alcoa throughout the 1920s.

The theory in this section suggests a different explanation. During this period, there were four major users for aluminum: cookware, aluminum cable, auto parts, and aircraft parts. Of these, the demand for aluminum was very elastic in cooking utensils, where good substitute materials existed, and very inelastic in aircraft parts. Cable and automobile parts exhibited intermediate degrees of price elasticity. The pattern of vertical integration exhibited by Alcoa during this period was roughly consistent with these elasticities and the theory above. Alcoa heavily integrated into the production of aluminum cable, selectively integrated into the production of cooking utensils and automobile parts, and integrated only slightly into the production of aircraft parts.

Vertical Integration to Foreclose the Market or Avoid Foreclosure

Vertical integration may also be motivated by a desire to foreclose competitors from entering a market or growing larger. An established firm may integrate backward to lock up the supply of a scarce input. An interesting example of this that was the subject of an early antitrust case was the Terminal Railroad Association of St. Louis. This organization, which was jointly owned by a group of railroads, monopolized all of the ferries and bridges across the Mississippi River at St. Louis. A railroad seeking access to St. Louis from the east would be forced to bear the substantial cost of building its own bridge across the Mississippi.

Even if the established firm does not control 100 percent of the input market, vertical integration may still foreclose entry. If there are few remaining suppliers of the key input, new entrants may not be able to come in or existing competitors may be unable to expand without significantly driving up the price of the input. Of course, if firms anticipate the possibility of being foreclosed, they may seek to lock up their own sources of supply. This may explain the rapid backward integration in the steel industry during the last four years of the 19th century. Before 1896, the iron ore that came from the Lake Superior region was largely owned by small, independent firms. By 1900, eight steel producers owned 75 percent of the Lake Superior ore. Many of these steel firms subsequently merged to form U.S. Steel, which continued to acquire ore properties in the region. Control over iron ore deposits was most likely an important barrier that sustained U.S. Steel's dominance in the early 20th century.

Foreclosure, or fear of foreclosure, might also explain forward integration. If there are barriers to entry into wholesale and retail markets, a manufacturer may integrate forward into wholesale and retail distribution in order to foreclose market access by rivals or new entrants or prevent foreclosure by firms that have already forward integrated. This explains Pennzoil's purchase of the Jiffy Lube chain in 1989. Pennzoil feared that Quaker State and Valvoline, each of whom had their own retail subsidiaries, would lock up access to the growing quick lube market.

Vertical Integration to Acquire Information

Kenneth Arrow has argued that vertical integration might also be motivated by a desire to acquire information.[22] To illustrate, consider the refining of bauxite into alumina. To efficiently make capacity and production decisions, an alumina refiner would like to be able to forecast the price of bauxite. While the price of bauxite from a particular location depends in part on unpredictable factors, such as the discovery of new deposits, it also depends on local conditions, such as the size and composition of the deposit. Much of this is likely to be closely guarded by the firm that owns the mine, and it seems unlikely that this information could be bought and sold in anything approaching a competitive market. Given all of this, a potentially effective way for the refiner to acquire the information it would need to efficiently plan its capacity and production decisions would be to integrate backward into the production of bauxite. John Stuckey has argued that information acquisition has been a motive for vertical integration in the aluminum industry:

> . . . the owner of a bauxite deposit has an incentive to produce falsely optimistic information about his deposit to attract as many refiners as possible to commit themselves to him as a supplier. . . . As a result, his arm's length customers may build capacities in excess of his capacity, and thus he has superior bargaining position when commodity trading begins. To avoid outcomes like this, refiners have an incentive to integrate across the information market, and they do this by undertaking their own exploration programs and by owning their own inventory of mine leases.[23]

ALTERNATIVES TO VERTICAL INTEGRATION ◆ ◆ ◆ ◆ ◆

This chapter poses the problem of the firm's vertical boundaries rather starkly—the firm must either make an input or purchase it from an independent firm through an arm's-length market transaction. A variety of in-between alternatives may capture the best of both worlds. In this section we consider four "hybrid" ways

---

[22]Arrow, K., "Vertical Integration and Communication," *Bell Journal of Economics*, 6, Spring 1975, pp. 173–182.

[23]Stuckey, John A., *Vertical Integration and Joint Ventures in the Aluminum Industry*, Cambridge: Harvard University Press, 1983, p.75.

of organizing exchange: (1) *tapered integration*, in which the firm both makes and buys a given input; (2) *joint ventures*; (3) closeknit semiformal relationships among buyers and suppliers, best embodied by the Japanese *keiretsu*; and (4) *long-term implicit contracts* that are supported by reputations for honesty, cooperativeness, and trust.

Tapered Integration: Make and Buy

Tapered integration represents a mixture of vertical integration and market exchange. A manufacturer might produce some quantity of an input itself and purchase the remaining portion from independent firms. It might sell some of its product through an in-house sales force and rely on an independent manufacturers' representative to sell the rest. Examples of tapered integration include such retailers as Blockbuster Video and Wendy's, who own some of their retail outlets but award franchises for others; Coca-Cola and Pepsi, who have their own bottling subsidiaries, but also rely on independently owned bottlers to produce and distribute their soft drinks in some markets, and General Motors, which has its own market research division but also purchases market research from independent marketing firms.

Tapered integration offers several benefits. First, it expands the firm's input and/or output channels without requiring substantial capital outlays. This is helpful to growing firms, such as fledgling retail chains. Second, the firm can use information about the cost and profitability of its internal channels to help negotiate contracts with independent channels. The firm can also use the threat to further use the market to motivate the performance of its internal channels. Third, the firm may also develop internal input supply capabilities to protect itself against holdup by independent input suppliers.

Oil refiners provide a classic example of tapered integration. The largest refiners, such as Exxon and Shell, are active in exploration and production of crude oil. Because they can refine twice as much oil as they internally produce, they make substantial purchases in the open market. This forces their internal production divisions to stay competitive with independent oil producers. Oil refiners also own small fleets of oil transport vessels to complement shipping services provided by independent fleets. This allows refiners to keep shipping costs down by ensuring that their own fleets can access critical ports when the local supply of independent shippers is low.

However, if tapered integration offers the best of both the make-and-buy worlds, it may also offer the worst. Forced to share production, both the internal and external channels may not achieve sufficient scale to produce efficiently. Shared production may lead to coordination problems because the two production units must reach agreement on product specifications and timing of delivery. Moreover, a firm's monitoring problems may be exacerbated. Not only must it duplicate contracting and monitoring efforts, it cannot be certain that any of its production units are producing efficiently. For example, the firm may mistakenly establish the performance of an inefficient internal supplier as the standard to be met by external suppliers.

◆ ◆

*E*XAMPLE 4.4

TAPERED INTEGRATION IN GASOLINE RETAILING

Gasoline retailing offers an interesting example of tapered integration.[24] The major oil refining companies (e.g., Exxon, Mobil) own and operate their own service stations. The refiner determines the hours of business and the retail prices at the stations it operates, and station personnel are employees of the refiner. Refiners also sell their gasoline through service stations that carry their brand name, but are operated by independent dealers who either own the service station outright or lease it from the refiner.[25] At independent stations, the dealer, not the refiner, sets the retail price of gasoline and the hours of business. Roughly 16 percent of U.S. retail sales of gasoline occurs through company-operated stations.

Tapered integration did not always exist. In the 1920s and 1930s, most large oil companies were fully integrated at the retail level: They owned almost all the stations that sold their gasoline. In the mid-1930s, the possibility that Iowa might impose a "chain-store" tax led the major refiners to begin experimenting with sales through independent franchised dealers. The oil companies soon found that this arrangement had significant advantages. Selling gasoline through independent dealers gave the major refiners access to many local markets without having to make substantial capital investments. Independent operation also relieves the refiner of having to monitor and evaluate the activities of the service station and instead subjects dealers to the discipline of the market forces. But sales through independent dealers also has a significant disadvantage. The refiners cannot set retail prices, and imperfect competition in downstream markets often leads independent dealers to impose high markups over the wholesale price of gasoline. The resulting decrease in volume hurts the refiner by reducing the profit from its markup over the unit cost of production. This is an example of the double marginalization effect discussed above.

Because vertical integration has advantages as well as disadvantages, it is not surprising that the major oil companies continue to own and operate their own stations. What is interesting is that changes in the way in which gasoline is sold at the retail level has changed the balance between the costs and benefits in a way that seems to favor vertical integration. Traditionally, most gasoline stations not only

---

[24]This example draws heavily from Borenstein, S. and R. Gilbert, "Uncle Sam at the Gas Pump: Causes and Consequences of Regulating Gasoline Distribution," *Regulation*, 1993, pp. 63–75.

[25]Independent operators who lease from the refiner receive the profits (or bear the losses) from running the station. Oil companies often lease stations as a way to generate the capital to finance its construction. A local investor will put up money for the construction of a service station on the promise that the oil company will lease the station from the investor on a long-term basis. The oil company then leases the station to the dealer on a shorter-term basis (e.g., 3 years).

sold gasoline, but also automobile maintenance and repair services, such as oil changes or brake replacement. For these stations, the cost of monitoring salaried employees was likely to be substantial because many repair tasks were nonroutine and the quality of a worker's output was difficult to measure. Thus, in most cases the optimal arrangement for these stations was likely to be independent operation. However, since 1980, the traditional service station has given way to large "pumper" stations—gasoline stations with ten or twelve self-service pumps staffed by a single cashier—and maintenance and repair business is increasingly being done by specialized outlets such as Jiffy Lube and Midas Muffler.[26] The result has been a shift in the relative proportion of independently operated and company-operated gasoline stations. Between 1980 and 1990, the number of major-brand, independently-operated stations declined from about 180,000 to 110,000, while the number of company-operated stations grew from about 8,000 to 11,000.

Strategic Alliances and Joint Ventures

In the late 1980s and early 1990s, firms increasingly turned to *strategic alliances* as a way to organize complex business transactions collectively without sacrificing autonomy. In a strategic alliance, two or more firms agree to collaborate on a project or to share information or productive resources. Alliances may be *horizontal*, involving collaboration between two firms in the same industry, as when United Technologies and Daimler Benz teamed up to cooperate on a range of engine development activities. They may be *vertical*, involving collaboration between a supplier and a buyer, as when Texas Instruments (TI) and ACER (in the late 1980s, the largest computer company in Taiwan) jointly built a plant in Taiwan to manufacture DRAM chips. Or they may involve firms that are neither in the same industry, nor related through the vertical chain, as when Toys "R" Us and McDonald's of Japan entered an agreement to build six toy stores in Japan that would each include a McDonald's restaurant on site.

A *joint venture* is a particular type of strategic alliance in which two or more firms create, and jointly own, a new independent organization. The new organization may be staffed and operated by employees of one or more parent firms, or it may be staffed independently of either. Examples of joint ventures include Coca-Cola's and Cadbury Schweppes' agreement to bottle and distribute Coca-Cola in Great Britain; Merck's and Johnson and Johnson's venture to market over-the-counter medicines such as Pepcid, an anti-ulcer treatment; and Genetics Institute's (one of the largest U.S. biotech companies) and Wellcome's (the largest British pharmaceuticals company) agreement to manufacturer products based on recombinant DNA.

---

[26]Another increasingly common arrangement are convenience stores that sell gasoline on a self-service basis. However, the gasoline sold at these outlets is usually not produced by the major brand name refiners.

Alliances and joint ventures fall somewhere between arm's-length market transactions and full vertical integration. As in arm's-length market transactions, the parties to the alliance remain independent business organizations. But a strategic alliance involves much more coordination, cooperation, and information sharing than an arm's-length transaction. Kenichi Ohmae has likened a strategic alliance to a marriage: "There may be no formal contract. There is no buying or selling of equity. There are few, if any, rigidly binding provisions. It is a loose, evolving kind of relationship."[27]

A joint venture or strategic alliance is desirable when three conditions are met:

1. The development, production, or marketing of a product requires expertise in a number of functional areas.

2. It is excessively costly for any one firm to develop all the necessary expertise itself. This is usually due to indivisibilities (developing the expertise to operate on even a small scale requires significant up-front investments in information acquisition and training) and the presence of an experience curve (the cost of developing incremental expertise becomes less costly the more that expertise has been acquired).

3. Successful development, production, or marketing requires close coordination among different areas of expertise.

To illustrate these points, consider the joint venture between McDonald's and Toys "R" Us, mentioned earlier. In a market in which shopping malls are rare and most retailing is through small "mom-and-pop" stores, success in the proposed venture requires substantial expertise in selecting sites, an expertise that McDonald's of Japan can offer to Toys "R" Us at a cost that is much less than Toys "R" Us would incur if it entered the Japanese market on its own, even at a small scale. Success also requires capabilities in marketing toys and operating a fast-food restaurant, skills that are probably not closely related to each other.

More generally, joint ventures are appealing because they can combine the scale and scope advantages achieved by independent firms and the coordination of design attributes normally associated with a vertically integrated firm. In addition, the partners can create strong incentives for the joint venture by giving it its own set of financial records and autonomy to face market discipline.

Collaborative Relationships: Japanese Subcontracting Networks and *Keiretsu*

Japanese industrial firms are less vertically integrated than their American and European counterparts. They tend to be smaller and more specialized to their

---

[27]Ohmae, K., "The Global Logic of Strategic Alliances," *Harvard Business Review*, March–April 1989, pp. 143–154.

particular place in the vertical chain.[28] For example, the ten largest Japanese auto-mobile firms outsource about 75 percent of their components; in the United States only Chrysler has approached this degree of outsourcing. But Japanese firms do not organize the vertical chain through arm's-length contracts. Instead, they rely on a labyrinth of long-term, semiformal relationships between firms up and down the vertical chain. We consider two closely related types of relationships: subcontractor networks and *keiretsu*.

Subcontractor Networks

Many Japanese manufacturers make extensive use of networks of independent sub-contractors with whom they maintain very close long-term relationships. These relationships are different from the relationships many American and European firms have with their subcontractors in that they typically involve a much higher degree of collaboration between the manufacturer and the subcontractors and delegation of a more sophisticated set of responsibilities to the subcontractor. Toshihiro Nishiguchi's study of Japanese and British subcontracting in the electronics industry illustrates these differences.[29] In Great Britain, electronics manufacturers typically rely on sub-contractors for specific, narrowly defined jobs. Their relationship is mediated by con-tractual agreements on price and performance and often does not persist beyond a small number of clearly defined transactions. Subcontractors are much less dedicated to the needs of particular buyers, and the customer base of a particular supplier is usu-ally much larger than a Japanese subcontractor of comparable size. By contrast, the re-lationship between a Japanese electronics manufacturer and its suppliers often persists over long periods of time, sometimes even for decades. Subcontractors generally per-form more sophisticated and comprehensive tasks than their British counterparts. For example, rather than just fabricating a component, a subcontractor might also be in-volved in its design and the testing of prototypes. In addition, subcontractors typically see their role as not just to fill the buyer's orders, but more generally, to closely inte-grate its operations with the buyer's, for example, by dedicating assembly lines to the buyer's product, by developing special-purpose machines that can produce to the buyer's specifications more efficiently, or by working closely with the customer to im-prove the production process. Nishiguchi concludes that the relationship between electronics manufacturers and subcontractors in Japan involves significantly greater amounts of asset specificity than the corresponding relationship in Great Britain.

Keiretsu

Keiretsu are closely related to subcontractor networks, but they involve a somewhat more formalized set of institutional linkages. The six largest *keiretsu*—Mitsubishi, Sumitomo, DKB, Mitsui, Fuso, and Sanwa—each have over 80 members, with a

---

[28]See Clark, R., *The Japanese Company*, New Haven: Yale University Press, 1979, or Nishiguchi, T., *Strategic Industrial Sourcing: The Japanese Advantage*, New York: Oxford University Press, 1994.

[29]Nishiguchi, T., *Strategic Industrial Sourcing: The Japanese Advantage*, New York: Oxford University Press, 1994.

core bank that facilitates relationships between members. Figure 4.5 depicts the complex nature of these linkages. Most of the key elements in the vertical chain are

FIGURE 4.5
DEBT, EQUITY, AND TRADE LINKAGES IN JAPANESE *KEIRETSU*.

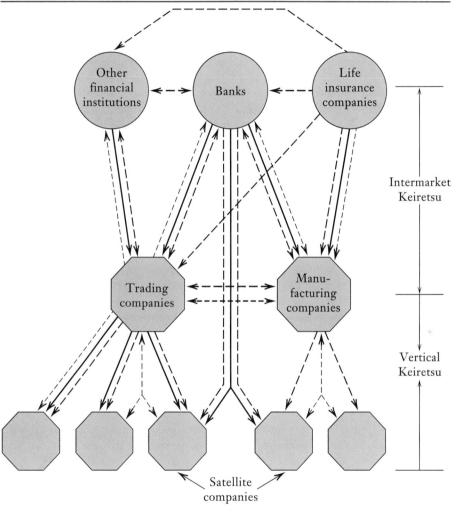

--- ➤ Equity shareholdings
——➤ Loans
- - - ➤ Trade (supplies, finished goods, bank deposits, life insurance policies)

Source: Gerlach, M.L. and J. Lincoln, "The Organization of Business Networks in the United States and Japan," in *Networks and Organizations: Structure, Form, and Action*, Nigria, N. and R.G. Eccles (eds.), Boston: Harvard Business School Press, p. 494.

The dashed lines show equity holdings within a typical *keiretsu*; the solid lines show loans, and the small dashed lines show the patterns of exchange within the *keiretsu*.

represented in a *keiretsu*, from banks to production facilities to distribution channels. The firms in a *keiretsu* exchange equity shares, and place individuals on each other's boards of directors.[30] For example, the core banks of the Mitsubishi and Mitsui *keiretsu* place nearly 200 bank representatives on the boards of other *keiretsu* members and effectively choose the CEOs of about 20 percent of the member firms.

In addition to these formal linkages, firms in a *keiretsu* are linked by informal personal relationships. Top executives belong to the same clubs and frequently socialize together. An executive who retires from say, Toyota, may then go to work for one of the component suppliers in the Toyota *keiretsu*. Each member of a *keiretsu* believes that it will be the first choice of another *keiretsu* member in future business dealings. As a result, each has invested in learning each of the others' businesses, inventory needs, marketing practices, and so forth. When a *keiretsu* member involved in production experiences a sharp upsurge in demand, it is understood that suppliers in the *keiretsu* will increase their production without raising supply prices. If one *keiretsu* member requires a product change, it is understood that its suppliers will participate in the design discussions. These activities eliminate many of the coordination problems discussed in Chapter 2. They also reduce the chances for holdup, including the possibility that one firm will take advantage of another firm for short-term gains.

Implicit Contracts and Long-term Relationships

An *implicit contract* is an unstated understanding between parties in a business relationship. The understandings that exist among members of the *keiretsu* are examples of implicit contracts. But implicit contracts are generally not enforceable in a court of law, so parties to an implicit contract must rely on alternative mechanisms to make the understanding viable. A powerful mechanism that makes implicit contracts viable is the threat of losing future business if one party breaks the implicit contract for its own gain.[31]

To see why the threat to withdraw future business can be so powerful, imagine two firms in the vertical chain who routinely transact business with each other. Their longstanding relationship has enabled them to better coordinate their activities through formal planning and monitoring of product quality, and as a result, both firms have profited significantly. In particular, suppose that the upstream firm sells inputs to the downstream firm for a $1 million profit every year, and the downstream firm processes the inputs and sells a finished product to consumers for a $1 million profit of its own. Each firm has an alternative trading partner, but each would only reap profits of $900,000 per year if forced to switch.

---

[30]This is known as an "interlocking directorate," and is prohibited under many circumstances in the United States under antitrust laws.

[31]The idea that future profit flows provide firms with incentives to maintain ongoing relationships was initially developed by Benjamin Klein and Keith Leffler in the article "The Role of Market Forces in Assuring Contractual Performance," *Journal of Political Economy*, 89, 1981, pp. 615–641.

While it seems as if each firm has no reason to switch, in fact the relationship has a potential complication. Each firm could increase its profit at the expense of the other by performing less of the planning and monitoring that make the relationship successful. Specifically, suppose that the upstream firm estimates that by breaking its implied commitments to the downstream firm, it could boost its annual profits to $1.2 million. If it does this, however, the downstream firm will learn that it has broken its commitments, and the relationship will end. Each firm would then be forced to do business with another trading partner.

How much does the upstream firm benefit by honoring its implicit contract indefinitely? In one year, it makes $100,000 more by transacting with the downstream firm than with its alternative trading partner. If the firm's discount rate is 5 percent, the net present value of honoring the implicit contract indefinitely would be $2 million.[32] This far exceeds the short-term (i.e., one-year) increase in profit of $200,000 from breaking the contract. Indeed, to make breaking the implicit contract worthwhile, the discount rate would have to be 50 percent! This high hurdle for switching helps sustain the implicit contract.

Thomas Palay's study of rail freight contracting provides a nice example of the power of long-term relationships in sustaining cooperative behavior.[33] He discusses a railroad that purchased specially designed autorack railcars to move a particular make of automobile for a major auto manufacturer. Soon after the railroad made the investment, however, the manufacturer changed the design of the car, making the auto-racks obsolete. Even though it was not contractually obligated to do so, the manufacturer compensated the railroad for over $1 million to cover the unamortized portion of the investment. The director of shipping at the automobile manufacturer alluded to the importance of maintaining a long-term relationship as the basis for this action. "We've got to keep them healthy, viable, and happy to guarantee that we'll get the equipment we need, when we need it."

CHAPTER SUMMARY

◆   The advantages and disadvantages of relying on the market versus relying on internal organization can be expressed in terms of a tradeoff between technical efficiency and agency efficiency. Technical efficiency occurs if the firm is using least-cost production techniques. Agency efficiency refers to the extent to which the firm's production and/or administrative costs are raised by the transactions and coordination costs of arm's-length market exchanges or the agency and influence costs of internal organization.

---

[32]If the discount rate is r, then an infinite-lived stream of X dollars per year is worth X/r in today's dollars.

[33]Palay, T., "Comparative Institutional Economics: The Governance of Rail Freight Contracting," *Journal of Legal Studies*, 13, 1984, pp. 265–287.

◆ Vertical integration is preferred to arm's-length market exchange when it is less costly to organize activities internally than it is to organize them through arm's-length market exchange. This cost difference will reflect differences in both technical efficiency and agency efficiency across the two modes of organization.

◆ Vertical integration is relatively more attractive (a) when the ability of outside market specialists relative to the firm itself to achieve scale or scope economies is limited; (b) the greater the scale of the firm's product market activities; (c) the greater the extent to which the assets involved in production are relationship specific.

◆ Vertical integration changes the pattern of asset ownership and control, and thus alters the bargaining power between parties in a vertical relationship. This, in turn, affects incentives to invest in relationship-specific asset. Vertical integration will be attractive when there are large asymmetries in the importance of relationship-specific investments in achieving the full efficiencies from the exchange, and where it is important for one party to control the use of those assets.

◆ Vertical integration may also be driven by imperfect competition. Firms may vertically integrate to undo the effects of market power, to achieve price discrimination, to foreclose access to product or input markets or to avoid such foreclosure, and to acquire information that cannot be bought and sold in the market.

◆ Vertical integration and arm's-length market exchange are not the only ways to organize transactions. A firm may pursue tapered integration, in which it supplies part of its input requirement itself and relies on market exchanges for the remainder. Firms may undertake strategic alliances or joint ventures. Although the transacting parties remain legally separate under these modes of organization, they typically entail much closer cooperation and coordination than an arm's-length exchange between two independent firms. Firms may also be bound together in cooperative relationships in long-lasting networks, such as the Japanese *keiretsu*. Finally, long-term, arm's-length market relationships can provide strong incentives for cooperative behavior and can thus achieve the advantages of vertical integration (e.g., avoidance of transactions costs, flexibility in governance) without incurring the disadvantages (e.g., softening incentives for innovation).

QUESTIONS

1. Explain why the following patterns seem to hold in many industries:

    a. Small firms are more likely to outsource production of inputs than are large firms.

    b. "Standard" inputs (such as a simple transistor that could be used by several electronics manufacturers) are more likely to be outsourced than "tailor-made" inputs (such as a circuit board designed for a single manufacturer's specific needs).

2. The following is an excerpt from an actual strategic plan (the company and product names have been changed to protect the innocent):

Acme's primary raw material is PVC sheet that is produced by three major vendors within the United States. Acme, a small consumer products manufacturer, is consolidating down to a single vendor. Continued growth by this vendor assures Acme that it will be able to meet its needs in the future.

Assume that Acme's chosen vendor will grow as forecast. Offer a scenario to Acme management that might convince them that they should rethink their decision to rely on a single vendor. What do you recommend Acme do to minimize the risk(s) that you have identified? Are there any drawbacks with your recommendation?

3. Shaefer Electronics is a medium-size producer (about $18 million in sales in 1993) of electronic products for the oil industry. It makes two main products—capacitors and integrated circuits. Capacitors are standardized items. Integrated circuits are more complex, highly customized items made to individual customer specifications. They are designed and made to order, they require installation, and sometimes require postsale servicing. Shaefer's annual sales are shown in the table below.

Shaefer relies entirely on manufacturers' representatives (MRs) located throughout the United States to sell its products. MRs are independent contractors who sell Shaefer's products in exchange for a sales commission. The company's representatives are not exclusive—they represent manufacturers of related but noncompeting products, such as circuit breakers, small switches, or semiconductors. Often a customer will buy some of these related products along with integrated circuits or an order of capacitors. MRs have long experience within local markets, close ties to the engineers within the firms that buy control systems, and deep knowledge of their needs. In the markets in which they operate, MRs develop their own client lists and call schedules. They are fully responsible for the expenses they incur in selling their products.

Once an order for one of Shaefer's products is taken by the MR, Shaefer is then responsible for any installation or postsale servicing that is needed.

Shaefer recently hired two different marketing consultants to study its sales force strategy. Their reports contained the conclusions reported below. Please comment on the soundness of each conclusion.

a. "Shaefer should continue to sell through MRs. Whether it uses MRs or an in-house sales force, it has to pay sales commissions. By relying on MRs, it avoids the variable selling expenses (e.g., travel expenses for salespeople) it would incur if it had its own sales force. As a result, Shaefer's selling expenses are lower than they would be with an in-house sales force of comparable size, talent, and know-how."

b. "Selling through MRs made sense for Shaefer when it was first getting started and specialized in capacitors. However, given its current product mix, it would not want to set itself up the way it is now if it were designing its sales force strategy from scratch. But with what it has got, Shaefer should be extremely cautious about changing."

SHAEFER ANNUAL SALES ($ 000)

	1980	*1985*	*1989*	*1990*	*1991*	*1992*	*1993*
Capacitors	$5,568	$6,488	$7,131	$7,052	$7,043	$7,360	$8,109
Integrated Circuits	$ 678	$1,679	$4,651	$6,245	$7,363	$8,589	$9,508
Total	$6,246	$8,167	$11,782	$13,297	$14,406	$15,959	$17,617

◆ ◆ ◆ ◆ ◆ APPENDIX: AN ALGEBRAIC ILLUSTRATION OF THE GROSSMAN-HART THEORY

*A*n algebraic example is an effective way to illustrate the specific insights of Grossman and Hart's theory. Consider a production unit that consists of a factory, production equipment, and production managers. The production unit relies on a marketing unit that consists of a sales force, distribution assets, and marketing managers to sell and distribute its output to final consumers. As indicated above, there are three different modes of organization: (1) *nonintegration*—the production unit and the marketing unit are independent firms; (2) *forward integration*—the production unit forward integrates and owns the marketing unit; the production unit has the right to control the assets of the marketing unit; and (3) *backward integration*—the marketing unit backward integrates and owns the production unit; the marketing unit has the right to control the assets of the production unit.

The interaction between the units occurs in two stages. At stage one, each unit makes an up-front investment in skills development. Let x denote the amount of skills development investment by the production unit, and y denote the amount of skills development investment by the marketing unit. For simplicity, we assume that x and y each take on one of two values, 1 or 2. These investments determine the subsequent profitability of the units in a manner to be described below. We also assume that third parties, such as a court or an arbitrator, cannot verify the levels of the investments in skills development by the two units. Thus, the two units cannot contract on the investments x and y. At stage one, each unit makes its investment decision independently, without involving the other unit.

At stage two, the units negotiate over a pair of operating decisions. The marketing unit's operating decision is marketing effort; the production unit's operating decision is cost-reduction effort. In contrast to the investment decisions, these decisions are verifiable, so the units can contract on them. Each unit can choose a "HIGH" or "LOW" level of effort. The consequences of these effort decisions are shown in Table A4.1.

The entries in Table A4.1 are the quasi-rents of the production unit and marketing unit, respectively. For example, if the stage one investments are $x = 1$ and $y = 2$, the marketing effort is LOW, and the cost-reduction effort is HIGH; then the production unit's quasi-rent is $0, and the marketing unit's quasi-rent is $8. (See Chapter 3 for a definition and discussion of quasi-rent.) Several points should be made about the payoffs in the table. First, a unit's quasi-rent is higher if it has

TABLE A4.1
QUASI-RENTS FOR THE PRODUCTION AND MARKETING UNITS

		Marketing Effort	
Cost		LOW	HIGH
Reduction	LOW	2x, 2y	4x, 0
Effort	HIGH	0, 4y	3x, 3y

chosen a higher level of skill development investment in stage one. Thus, skill development investments make a unit more effective in its operating decision, and thus raise the profitability of those investments. Second, the payoffs in Table A4.1 reflect a complementarity in efforts. No matter what the investments in skill development are, each unit is better off when the other unit has chosen the HIGH effort. HIGH cost-reduction effort benefits the marketing unit because it can sell the goods at a lower price to final consumers. HIGH marketing effort benefits the production unit because more of the item is sold to final consumers.[34] Third, each unit prefers that its own operating decision be LOW. This reflects the notion that supplying effort is costly to each unit. Fourth, despite the costliness of effort to each unit, the jointly optimal decisions—the decisions that maximize the sum of the payoffs—are (HIGH, HIGH). (The reader should verify that this is true no matter what the values of x and y are.)

In thinking about the interaction of the two units, it is convenient to work backwards, first focusing on the stage-two contract negotiations over the operating decisions and then on the stage-one investment decisions. How will the negotiations in stage two proceed? We assume that the units not only negotiate a pair of decisions but also a "side payment" that will be denoted by p. When p is positive, it represents a payment from the production unit to the marketing unit; when it is negative, it represents a payment from the marketing unit to the production unit. When the units are independent firms, one can think of the side payment p as an arm's-length payment for marketing or production effort. When the units are vertically integrated, one can think of p as an internal transfer price for marketing or production effort. In effect, then, the units are negotiating over the size of the pie, which is determined by the operating decisions, and on how the pie is divided up, which is determined by the side payment p.

---

[34]To be more specific, the payoffs in the table are based on the following "story." The production unit sells the item to the marketing unit at a transfer price equal to a fixed markup above the production unit's variable costs. When the production unit exerts high cost-reduction effort, production costs are lower, and the transfer price is lower, and the marketing unit can charge consumers a lower final price and sell more items. Thus, the marketing unit prefers it when the production unit chooses HIGH cost-reduction effort. The production unit prefers the marketing unit to exert HIGH marketing effort because the production unit sells more of the item at the cost-plus transfer price to the marketing unit, thereby making a higher profit.

Let us assume that the negotiations over the operating decisions reach the efficient outcome, (HIGH, HIGH), that is, the two units agree on the decision that makes the size of the pie as large as possible. The real contention comes from the side payment because that determines how the pie is to be divided up. A natural assumption is that bargaining over the side payment depends on what would happen if an agreement over operating decisions is *not* reached. If a unit can do well without an agreement, then one would expect it to command a larger slice of the pie. What happens without an agreement depends on the mode of organization:

- Under nonintegration, each unit makes its operating decision independently. From Table A4.1 above, it is clear that each unit is better off with a lower level of effort. The outcome would be (LOW, LOW) with payoffs $(2x, 2y)$. (Remember the production unit's payoff is always listed first.)

- Under forward integration, the production unit owns the marketing unit, which means that the production unit not only controls its own effort decision but can also choose the operating decision for the marketing unit. From the production unit's perspective (as opposed to the collective perspective) the best pair of decisions is LOW cost-reduction effort and HIGH marketing effort. The payoffs are thus $(4x, 0)$.

- Under backward integration, the marketing unit owns the production unit, which means that the marketing unit not only controls its own effort decision but can also choose the operating decision for the production unit. From the marketing unit's perspective, the best pair of decisions is HIGH cost-reduction effort and LOW marketing effort. The payoffs are thus $(0, 4y)$.

Note that in all cases, not reaching an agreement results in a set of operating decisions that does not maximize the size of the pie. Thus, there are gains from coordination between the divisions that are not realized if the units do not negotiate an agreement.

To reflect the influence of a unit's "no-agreement" position on its ability to cut a good bargain with the other unit, we assume that negotiation between units results in a side payment that gives each unit an equal gain relative to its no-agreement payoff. Thus, a unit would fare better in the negotiation the more favorable its no-agreement payoff is. In general terms, the following equation thus determines p:

$$3x - p - (\text{production unit's payoff without agreement}) =$$
$$p + 3y - (\text{marketing unit's payoff without agreement})$$

Solving this equation for p in each of the three cases and then plugging back to determine the payoff of each unit yields the outcomes shown in Table A4.2.

To illustrate how the expressions in the table are derived, consider the case of nonintegration. Using the expression above and the expressions in Table A4.1, the side payment p is given by $3x - p - 2x = p + 3y - 2y$, or $p = .5x - .5y$. The production unit's profit when there is an agreement is $3x - p$, and plugging in the expression for p that we just derived yields $3x - (.5x - .5y) = 2.5x + .5y$, the entry in the table. Similarly, the marketing unit's payoff when there is an agreement is $3y + p$, and substituting in the expression for p yields $3y + (.5x - .5y) = .5x + 2.5y$.

TABLE A4.2
PRODUCTION AND MARKETING UNIT'S PAYOFF UNDER EACH ORGANIZATIONAL FORM

	Side payment	Production unit's payoff	Marketing unit's payoff
Nonintegration	.5x − .5y	2.5x + .5y	.5x + 2.5y
Forward integration	−.5x − 1.5y	3.5x + 1.5y	−.5x + 1.5y
Backward integration	1.5x + .5y	1.5x − .5y	1.5x + 3.5y

Note that each of the unit's payoffs is higher the higher its stage-one investment in skills development is. This reflects the beneficial impact of skills development investment discussed earlier. Note, too, that no matter what the organizational mode, the last two columns always add up to $3x + 3y$, the total payoff from the operating decisions (HIGH, HIGH). Thus, in stage two, the organizational mode affects the division of the pie but not its size.[35]

Now we are ready to investigate the stage-one investment decisions. Let us suppose that for each unit the incremental cost of a higher level of investment is $2, that is, increasing x from 1 to 2 costs the production unit $2; increasing y from 1 to 2 costs the marketing unit $2.[36] What will the units do at stage one? If they are forward looking, they will anticipate the effects of their investment decisions on the stage-two negotiations, which, as we have seen, depend on the mode of organization, as summarized in Table A4.2. For example, consider the nonintegration case. The production unit, having figured out the entry in Table A4.2, reasons that increasing x from 1 to 2 increases its stage-two payoff by $2.5. Since this exceeds the incremental cost $2 of increasing the investment, the best choice for the production unit is $x = 2$. Similarly, the marketing unit reasons that under nonintegration an increase of y from 1 to 2 increases its payoff by $2.5 (see Table A4.2). This, too, exceeds the incremental cost of the investment, so the marketing unit sets $y = 2$.

Table A4.3 summarizes the outcome of the first-stage investment decisions for each of the organizational modes. It also displays the total surplus (payoff for production unit plus payoff for marketing unit minus total investment costs for each unit). Note that under backward integration, the production unit invests less in skills development than under nonintegration or forward integration. Why is this? Recall that under backward integration, the marketing unit owns the production assets, so it has the right to control the cost-reduction effort decision without a stage-two agreement. This puts the production unit at a disadvantage in stage-two bargaining relative to the marketing unit, and as a result, the production unit commands less of the pie than it would under nonintegration or forward integration. Anticipating this in stage one, the production unit invests less in skills development

---

[35]The example has been rigged to achieve this outcome. We could have rigged the example so that the organizational mode affected the size of the stage-two pie, but this would have made the example more complicated than it already is.

[36]Suppose setting $x = 1$ or $y = 1$ is costless for each unit. Thus total investment costs are $2(x−1)$ and $2(y−1)$, respectively.

TABLE A4.3
PRODUCTION AND MARKETING UNITS' FIRST-STAGE INVESTMENTS UNDER EACH ORGANIZATIONAL FORM

	Production unit's investment	Marketing unit's investment	Total surplus
	x	y	$3x + 3y - 2(x - 1) - 2(y - 1)$
Nonintegration	2	2	8
Forward integration	2	1	7
Backward integration	1	2	7

because it knows it will receive a fairly low return on this investment as a consequence of its negotiations with the marketing unit.

In this example, nonintegration dominates both types of vertical integration, because it promotes the best incentives for investment in skills development. But this is obviously special to this example. What determines which mode is best? To answer this question, we alter the example slightly. Suppose that the production unit's investment choice is between $x = 1$ and $x = 1.25$, and the marketing unit's investment choice is between $y = 1$ and $y = 1.75$. Keep everything else in the example the same (including the incremental cost of going from the lower to the higher investment level, which is still $2). The marketing unit's investment is now relatively more important than the production unit's investment in the sense that an increase in marketing investment has a bigger impact on total surplus than an increase in manufacturing investment. Redoing Table A4.3 with the new investment choices gives Table A4.4.

To illustrate the derivation of the numbers in the table, consider nonintegration. Here, neither unit finds it optimal to increase its investment. Again using the payoff formulas in Table A4.2, the marketing unit's gain from increasing investment from $y = 1$ to $y = 1.75$ is $2.5(1.75) - 2.5(1) = \$1.875$, which is less than the incremental cost of the investment, $2. Similarly, the production unit's gain from increasing its investment from $x = 1$ to $x = 1.25$ is $2.5(1.25) - 2.5(1) = \$.625$, which is also less than the incremental cost of the investment, $2. Similar logic indicates that neither unit will increase its investment under forward integration. The

TABLE A4.4
PRODUCTION AND MARKETING UNITS' FIRST-STAGE INVESTMENTS WHEN MARKETING UNIT'S INVESTMENT IS MORE IMPORTANT

	Production unit's investment	Marketing unit's investment	Total surplus
	x	y	$3x + 3y - 2(x-1) - 2(y-1)$
Nonintegration	1	1	6
Forward integration	1	1	6
Backward integration	1	1.75	6.75

marketing unit finds it worthwhile to increase its investment under backward integration. This is because its control over the production unit's assets gives it a favorable stage-two bargaining position, which implies that it will reap a good return on its increased investment. Because backward integration provides the best overall incentives for investment, backward integration results in the highest level of total surplus.

The main implication of Grossman and Hart's theory follows the story line of the example. When there are two units, unit 1 should own unit 2 when unit 1's investment is much more important than unit 2's. In this case, inducing investment by unit 1 is crucial. When unit 1 controls unit 2's assets, unit 1 has a strong bargaining position and can command a large share of the quasi-rents in the relationship. As a result, unit 1 will achieve a large return on its initial investment. Unit 2 should own unit 1 when unit 2's investment is much more important than unit 1's. Here, inducing investment by unit 2 is key. When unit 2 controls unit 1's assets, unit 2 has a strong bargaining position and will claim a large share of the quasi-rents in the relationship, thus strengthening its investment incentives. Nonintegration is desirable when both parties must make investments of roughly equal importance. Nonintegration gives each party a more equal share of the quasi-rents, and thus reasonably good incentives to invest in relationship-specific assets.

HORIZONTAL BOUNDARIES: ECONOMIES OF SCALE AND SCOPE

5

$\mathcal{T}$he *horizontal boundaries* of the firm are the quantities and varieties of products and services that the firm produces. Examination of even a few industries reveals enormous differences in how the horizontal boundaries of firms can be drawn. In some industries, such as frozen foods, aluminum production, and airframe manufacturing, a few large firms (e.g., General Foods, Alcoa, and Boeing) account for an extremely large share of industry sales, and there are virtually no viable small firms. In other industries, such as advertising and management consulting, small firms predominate. Even the largest firms in these industries (e.g., Young and Rubicam, Andersen Consulting) are small by most conventional measures of business size, such as sales revenue and number of employees. In still other industries, such as beer and computer software, small firms (Boston Brewing Company, Broderbund) and corporate giants (Anheuser-Busch, Microsoft) coexist successfully. Why do giants dominate some industries and not others? In this chapter we argue that the horizontal boundaries of firms depend critically on economies of scale and scope.

Economies of scale and scope are present whenever large-scale production, distribution, or retail processes have a cost advantage over small processes. Economies of scale and scope often dictate the success and failure of firms. According to Alfred Chandler, it was the ability of giant firms, such as DuPont and General Motors, to exploit economies of scale and scope that allowed them to drive out their smaller rivals.[1] Economies of scale and scope are not always available,

---

[1]Chandler, A., *Scale and Scope: The Dynamics of Industrial Capitalism*, Cambridge, MA: Belknap, 1990.

however. Many activities, such as farming, tailoring, management consulting, and the preparation of gourmet food, do not appear to enjoy substantial scale economies. These activities are typically performed by individuals or relatively small firms.

By offering cost advantages to large-scale producers, economies of scale and scope not only affect the sizes of firms and the structures of markets, but they also shape critical business strategy decisions, such as whether independent firms should merge, and whether a firm can achieve a long-term cost advantage in its market through expansion. Thus, an understanding of the sources of economies of scale and scope is not only important for making sense of the enormous variety of firm sizes and industry structures in the economy, but it is also critical for formulating competitive strategy.

◆ ◆ ◆ ◆ ◆ FORMAL DEFINITIONS OF ECONOMIES OF SCALE AND SCOPE

We begin with formal definitions of economies of scale and scope without dwelling on why they might arise, which we take up in the next section.

Definition of Economies of Scale

The production process for a specific good or service exhibits *economies of scale* over a range of output when average cost—cost per unit of output—declines over that range. For average cost (AC) to decline as output increases, the marginal cost (MC)—the cost of the last unit produced—must be less than the overall average cost.[2] If average cost is constant, then marginal cost must equal average cost, and we say that production exhibits *constant returns to scale*. If average cost is increasing, then marginal cost must exceed average cost, and we say that production exhibits *diseconomies of scale*. To summarize, there are economies of scale whenever $MC < AC$, constant returns to scale whenever $MC = AC$, and diseconomies of scale whenever $MC > AC$.

Economies of scale can be visualized by examining a production process and its corresponding cost curves. Figure 5.1 depicts a hypothetical average cost curve for the production of the opera, *The Merger of Figaro*. The production of the opera displays a U-*shaped average cost curve*—average costs decline with the first performances, and increase as the opera is performed again and again. The region of the

---

[2]If you do not understand why this must be so, consider this numerical example. Suppose that the total cost of producing five bicycles is $500. The AC is therefore $100. If the MC of the sixth bicycle is $70, then total cost for six bicycles is $570 and AC is $95. If the MC of the sixth bicycle is $130, then total cost is $630 and AC is $105. In this example (and as a general rule), when $MC < AC$, AC falls as production increases, and when $MC > AC$, AC rises as production increases.

FIGURE 5.1

AVERAGE COST CURVE FOR THE *MERGER OF FIGARO*.

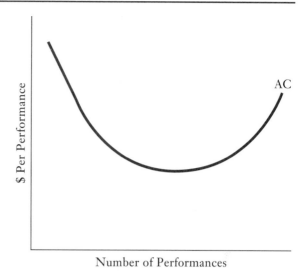

Average costs decline initially as fixed costs are spread over additional performances. Average costs eventually rise as production runs up against capacity constraints.

curve in which average costs are declining corresponds to the range of economies of scale. The region in which the average costs are increasing corresponds to the range of diseconomies of scale.

Economists argue that a combination of factors causes most cost curves to be U-shaped. A common explanation for the initial decline in average costs is the spreading of fixed costs over increasing output. *Fixed costs* are costs that must be expended regardless of the total output, such as expenses for property, plant, and equipment. As output increases, these costs are averaged over greater volumes, tending to drive down average costs. A common explanation for the eventual upturn in average costs is the rise in variable costs as output increases. *Variable costs* are costs that increase as output increases, and include expenses for labor and materials. As output increases, capacity constraints may result in bottlenecks, and there may be bureaucratic and agency problems. These can drive up average variable costs, which tends to drive up average costs overall. We will develop these ideas more fully in this chapter.

The factors that cause cost curves to be U-shaped, including the spreading of fixed costs over increased output, capacity constraints, and agency problems, have their real-world counterparts in most production processes, including the production of operas. Even before the first performance of *Figaro*, the opera company must incur substantial fixed costs, including time and money for rehearsals, costume design, and set construction. During the run of *Figaro*, there are substantial variable costs associated with rehearsal time, set maintenance, and performances. Table 5.1 reports values for fixed, variable, and total (i.e., fixed plus variable) costs for various numbers of performances of *Figaro*. These are the values from which the average cost curve in Figure 5.1 was generated.

TABLE 5.1
EXPENSES TO PRODUCE *THE MERGER OF FIGARO*

No. of Performances	Fixed Costs	Average Fixed Costs	Variable Costs	Average Variable Costs	Total Costs	Average Total Costs
1	300,000	300,000	100,000	100,000	400,000	400,000
2	300,000	150,000	200,000	100,000	500,000	250,000
3	300,000	100,000	300,000	100,000	600,000	200,000
4	300,000	75,000	420,000	105,000	720,000	180,000
5	300,000	60,000	550,000	110,000	850,000	170,000
6	300,000	50,000	690,000	115,000	990,000	165,000
7	300,000	42,857	876,000	125,143	1,176,000	168,000
8	300,000	37,500	1,100,000	137,500	1,400,000	175,000
9	300,000	33,333	1,410,000	156,667	1,710,000	190,000
10	300,000	30,000	1,800,000	180,000	2,100,000	210,000

In this example, fixed costs equal $300,000. If *Figaro* is performed just once, the average fixed cost is $300,000; if the number of performances increases to five, average fixed costs decrease to $60,000 (e.g., $300,000 divided by the number of performances, which is 5). Note that as the number of performances increases, average fixed costs continue to decline, but at a slower rate. Thus, the advantages of spreading fixed costs decline as the production run increases.

The costs of rehearsals, performances, and maintenance during the production run represent variable costs to the opera producers because these costs increase as the production run lengthens. As long as these variable costs remain about the same for each performance, average costs will continue to decline due to declining average fixed costs. This is the case for the first few performances of *Figaro*, where the sharp decline in average fixed costs contributes to a steeply declining average cost curve.

One can imagine, however, that as the opera season wears on, singers may weary of their parts, costumes may wear out, and sets may fall apart. In other words, the opera company may begin to bump up against its "capacity constraint." Variable costs associated with finding and rehearsing new singers and repairing costumes and sets may start to mount. In this example, the variable cost for each of the first three performances is $100,000, but it begins to increase as the number of performances increases. The balance of these two forces is a U-shaped average cost curve. In this particular case, average costs are minimized at six performances. In general, the point on the average cost curve at which average costs are minimized is known as the *minimum efficient scale* (MES).

The standard textbook presentation usually depicts average cost curves as U-shaped, with diseconomies of scale beyond *capacity* that are roughly as significant as the economies of scale up to capacity. (Capacity is defined to be the output at which average total costs begin to rise sharply.) Economists disagree about the severity of diseconomies of scale. Some argue that firms can easily increase capacity, especially if given a long planning horizon. If correct, this argument implies that diseconomies of scale may be minimal. The noted econometrician John Johnston once examined production costs for a number of industries and determined that the corresponding cost curves were closer to L-shaped than U-shaped. Figure 5.2 depicts an L-shaped cost curve. When average costs are L-shaped, diseconomies of scale are either minimal or nonexistent. This implies that once a firm has reached MES, it may continue to grow without experiencing increases in average costs.

The next section describes many of the technological factors that determine the shape of average cost curves. It is important to note that in addition to technology, the shape of the cost curve also depends on the time horizon for which decisions are being made. Capacity constraints that contribute to rising marginal costs, and eventually to rising average costs, can be avoided if the firm can replicate its activities as it grows larger. For example, although a bottling plant may have a capacity constraint that limits production to a certain number of bottles, it can expand beyond that level by opening another plant. In the short run, the bottler may face rising marginal costs as it tries to squeeze additional production out of its one plant. This would imply that the bottler's short-run average variable cost curve would begin to increase as it nears it capacity constraint. But in the long run, the bottler can build its new plant, expand its capacity, and experience lower production costs. Thus, the bottler's long-run average cost curve may be flatter than the short-run average cost curve.

While we will generally discuss economies of scale with reference to average cost curves, the concept can also be developed mathematically. To do so, we begin by defining the following terms:

FIGURE 5.2
AN L-SHAPED AVERAGE COST CURVE.

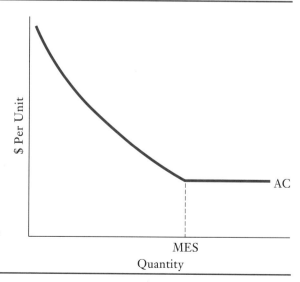

When capacity does not prove to be constraining, average costs may not rise as they do in a "U-shaped" cost curve. Output equal to or exceeding minimum efficient scale (MES) is efficient from a cost perspective.

Q_x = the quantity of good X

$TC(Q_x)$ = the total cost of producing quantity Q_x

$AC(Q_x)$ = average cost of producing $Q_x = TC(Q_x)/Q_x$

We say economies of scale are present whenever $AC(Q_x)$ decreases as Q_x increases. For example, if $TC(Q_x) = 576 + 4Q_x^2$, then $AC(Q_x) = 576/Q_x + 4Q_x$ and production exhibits economies of scale over the range of Q_x from 0 to 12. (This is easily checked by calculating $AC(Q_x)$ for different values of Q_x.) If $AC(Q_x)$ increases as Q_x increases, the production exhibits diseconomies of scale. Continuing the example, this particular production process exhibits diseconomies of scale whenever $Q_x > 12$.

Definition of Economies of Scope

Economies of scale are related to economies of scope, and the two terms are sometimes used interchangeably. Economies of scale exist if the firm achieves unit-cost savings as it increases its level of a given activity, such as the production of a given good. *Economies of scope* exist if the firm achieves savings as it increases the variety of activities it performs, such as the variety of goods it produces. Whereas economies of scale are usually defined in terms of declining average cost functions, economies of scope are usually defined in terms of the relative total cost of producing a variety of goods together in one firm versus separately in two or more firms.

Formally, let $TC(Q_x, Q_y)$ denote the total cost to a single firm producing Q_x units of good X and Q_y units of good Y. Then a production process exhibits scope economies if

$$TC(Q_x, Q_y) < TC(Q_x, 0) + TC(0, Q_y)$$

This formula captures the idea that it is cheaper for a single firm to produce both goods X and Y than for one firm to produce X and another to produce Y. To provide another interpretation of the definition, note that a firm's total costs are zero if it produces zero quantities of both products, so $TC(0, 0) = 0$. Then, rearrange the above formula to read:

$$TC(Q_x, Q_y) - TC(0, Q_y) < TC(Q_x, 0) - TC(0, 0)$$

This says that the incremental cost of producing Q_x units of good X, as opposed to none at all, is lower when the firm is producing a positive quantity Q_y of good Y.

The cost implications of economies of scope are shown in Table 5.2, which shows the production costs of a hypothetical manufacturer of adhesive message notes (good X) and tape (good Y). To produce tape, the firm must spend $100 million to perfect the process of working with chemical adhesives, attaching these adhesives to cellophane, and manufacturing and packaging tape. Once this setup cost is incurred, each role of tape can be produced at a cost of $.20 each. Thus, we can write $TC(0, Q_y) = \$100m + .20Q_y$. For example, if $Q_y = 600$ million roles of tape, total cost is $220 million.

Table 5.2
Costs to Print Message Notes and Tape

Q_x	Q_y	$TC(Q_x, Q_y)$
100m	0	$55m
0	600m	$220m
100m	600m	$245m
200m	0	$60m
0	1200m	$340m
200m	1200m	$370m

Now, given that the firm has made the investment in developing the know-how for manufacturing tape, much of that know-how can be applied to producing related products, such as adhesive message notes. Suppose that the additional investment needed to ramp up production of message notes, given that the up-front setup costs in tape production have already been incurred, is $20m. Suppose also that the cost per ream of message notes is $.05. Then $TC(Q_x, Q_y) = \$120m + .05Q_x + .20Q_y$. For example, if $Q_y = 600$ million and $Q_x = 100$ million, then total cost is $245m. The additional cost to the firm of adding message notes to its product line is only $245m − $220m = $25m.

By contrast, if the firm did not produce tape, much of the up-front investment in developing the know-how for working with chemical adhesives would have to be made just to get the expertise needed to make message notes. If the development of this know-how requires an investment of $50m, then with a per-ream cost of $.05, $TC(Q_x, 0) = \$50m + .05Q_x$. Thus, if $Q_x = 100m$, total cost would equal $55m. This more than doubles the additional cost to the tape manufacturer to add message notes to its production line.

This example illustrates the economic logic of exploiting economies of scope. This logic has received much attention in the business press, and is often known as "leveraging core competences," "competing on capabilities," or "mobilizing invisible assets."[3] In this example it makes much more sense for the tape manufacturer to diversify into the production of message notes than it would for a firm producing unrelated products, such as a prepared-food manufacturer. Economies of scope may arise at any point in the production process, from acquisition and use of raw inputs to distribution and retailing. Many of the sources of scope economies are detailed in the next section.

---

[3]Prahalad, C.K. and G. Hamel, "The Core Competence of the Corporation," *Harvard Business Review*, May–June, 1990, pp. 79–91; Stalk, G., P. Evans, and L. Shulman, "Competing on Capabilities: The New Rules of Corporate Strategy," *Harvard Business Review*, March–April, 1992, pp. 57–69; Itami, H., *Mobilizing Invisible Assets*, Cambridge, MA: Harvard University Press, 1987.

◆ ◆ ◆ ◆ ◆ WHERE DO ECONOMIES OF SCALE AND SCOPE COME FROM?

It is tempting to assume that scale and scope economies are always present. But bigger is not always better. Failure to identify a source of scale and scope economies suggests that the economies may be illusory. This section identifies four major sources of scale and scope economies:

- Indivisibilities and the spreading of fixed costs
- Increased productivity of variable inputs (mainly having to do with specialization)
- Inventories
- The cube-square rule

If bigger really is better, then one or more of these sources of scale and scope economies should be present. We discuss each in detail.

Indivisibilities and the Spreading of Fixed Costs

The most common source of economies of scale is the spreading of fixed costs over an ever-greater volume of output. Fixed costs arise because the quantities of certain inputs cannot be adjusted as output is varied. This fixity may occur simply because it takes time to adjust certain inputs (e.g., it may take time to replace a larger jet with a smaller jet when an airline experiences a long-term drop in traffic over a particular route). Fixed costs also arise when there are *indivisibilities* in the production process. Indivisibilities are a paramount source of economies of scale and scope.

Indivisibility simply means that an input cannot be scaled down below a certain minimum size, even when the level of output is very, very small. For example, imagine that a railroad is shipping a boxcar full of merchandise from Chicago to New York. Among the required inputs are 840 miles of railroad track, a locomotive and boxcar, and an engineer. Shipping half the amount would require the same inputs. Thus, the track, cars, and engineer are indivisible, and the railroad must bear the associated costs no matter how little is shipped. By the same token, these are costs that do not increase as output increases. Shipping twice the amount of freight does not require additional track or a second engineer. Indivisibilities may give rise to fixed costs, and hence scale and scope economies, at several different levels: the product level, the plant level, and the multiplant level. The next few subsections discuss the link between fixed costs and economies of scale at each of these levels.

Spreading of Fixed Costs at the Product Level

The production of a specific product usually involves fixed costs. Product-specific fixed costs may include the costs of special equipment, such as tools and dies—for example, the cost to manufacture special dies used to make an aircraft fuselage. Fixed costs may also include research and development expenses—for example, the estimated $150 million to $300 million required to develop a new pharmaceutical product. Fixed costs include training expenses—for example, the three years necessary to become a lawyer. Fixed costs may also include the costs necessary to set up a production process—for example, the time and expense required to set up a newspaper before printing it.

Even a simple production process, such as that for an aluminum can, requires a substantial fixed investment. The production of an aluminum can involves only a few steps. Aluminum sheets are cut to size, formed into a rounded shape, and then punched into the familiar cylindrical can shape. A lid with an opener is then soldered on top. Though the process is simple, a single line for producing aluminum cans costs about $50 million. If the opportunity cost of tying up funds is 7.5 percent, then if we amortize this cost over an expected 20-year life span, fixed costs expressed on an annualized basis would amount to about $5 million per year.[4]

It is obvious that the average fixed costs of producing aluminum cans will fall as output increases. But just how important is it for a firm to keep its can line operating at full capacity? To answer this question, it is helpful to know how average fixed costs vary with output. Suppose that the peak capacity of an aluminum can plant is 500 million cans annually, or about 1 percent of the total U.S. market. The average fixed cost of operating a fully automated plant operating at full capacity for one year is determined by dividing the annual cost ($5,000,000) by total output (500,000,000). This works out to one cent per can. On the other hand, if the plant operates at 25 percent of capacity, for total annual production of 125 million cans, then average fixed costs equal four cents per can. The underutilized plant is operating at a three-cent cost differential per can. In a price-competitive industry, such as aluminum can manufacturing, such a cost differential is likely to make the difference between profit and loss.

Suppose a firm is considering entering the can manufacturing business, but does not anticipate being able to sell more than 125 million cans annually. Is it doomed to a three-cent cost differential and eventual bankruptcy? The answer depends on the nature of the alternative production technologies. The fully automated technology described above may yield the greatest cost savings when used to capacity, but it may not be the best choice at lower production levels because there may be an alternative to the fully automated plant that requires less initial investment, albeit with a greater reliance on ongoing expenses. A firm choosing this "partially automated" technology may be able to enjoy fairly low average costs even if it produces less than 500 million cans annually.

Suppose the fixed costs of setting up a partially automated plant are $12.5 million, annualized to $1.25 million per year. The shortcoming of this plant is that it requires additional labor costs of one cent per can, compared with the fully automated plant. To simplify matters, assume that the fully automated plant has zero labor costs and that material costs are three cents per can at both plants. With these assumptions, the cost comparison between the two plants is shown in Table 5.3.

---

[4]The opportunity cost is the best return that the investor could obtain if he or she invested a comparable amount of money in some other similarly risky investment. See the Economics Primer for further discussion.

TABLE 5.3
COSTS OF PRODUCING ALUMINUM CANS

	500 million cans per year	*125 million cans per year*
Fully Automated	Average fixed costs = .01 Average labor costs = .00 Average materials costs = .03 Average total costs = .04	Average fixed costs = .04 Average labor costs = .00 Average materials costs = .03 Average total costs = .07
Partially Automated	Average fixed costs = .0025 Average labor costs = .01 Average materials costs = .03 Average total costs = .0425	Average fixed costs = .01 Average labor costs = .01 Average materials costs = .03 Average total costs = .05

Table 5.3 shows that while the fully automated technology is superior for high production levels, it is markedly inferior at lower production levels. This is seen in Figure 5.3, which depicts average cost curves for both the fully and partly automated technologies. The curve labeled SAC_1 is the average cost curve for a plant that has adopted the fully automated technology; the curve labeled SAC_2 is the average cost curve for a plant that has adopted the partially automated technology. At output levels above 375 million cans, the fully automated technology has lower average total costs. At lower output levels, the partially automated technology is cheaper.

FIGURE 5.3
AVERAGE COST CURVES FOR CAN PRODUCTION.

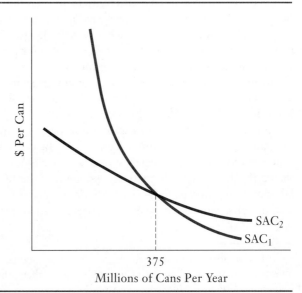

SAC_1 represents a high fixed/low variable cost technology. SAC_2 represents a low fixed cost/high variable cost technology. At low levels of output, it is cheaper to use the latter technology. At high outputs, it is cheaper to use the former.

The aluminum can example illustrates the distinction between economies of scale that arise because of fuller or more efficient capacity utilization, and economies of scale that arise because of tradeoffs between technologies with low fixed costs and higher variable costs on the one hand, and high fixed costs and lower variable costs on the other. Reductions in average costs due to increases in capacity utilization within a plant of a given size are *short-run* economies of scale. Reductions due to adoption of a technology or larger plant size that have high fixed costs but lower variable costs are *long-run* economies of scale.

Figure 5.4 illustrates the distinction between short-run and long-run economies of scale. SAC_1 and SAC_2, which duplicate the cost curves in Figure 5.3, are the short-run average cost curves for the partially automated and fully automated plants respectively. Each decreases because as output within each plant grows, fixed costs are spread over more and more units. If we trace out the lower regions of each curve, the so-called "lower envelope" of the curves, we see the long-run average cost curve. The long-run average cost curve is everywhere on or below each short-run average cost curve. This reflects the flexibility that firms have to adopt the technology that is most appropriate for their forecasted output.

Capital-Intensive versus Labor-Intensive Production

When fixed capital costs are a significant percentage of total costs, we say that production is *capital intensive*. Much productive capital, such as factories and assembly lines, is indivisible. Thus, when production is capital intensive, the average total cost of production contains a substantial fixed component. Increases in output may

FIGURE 5.4
SHORT-RUN VERSUS LONG-RUN AVERAGE COST.

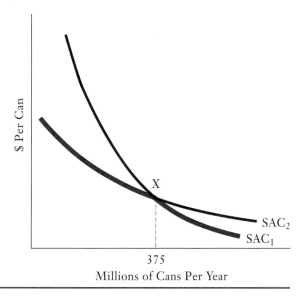

In the long run, firms may choose their production technology as well as their output. Firms planning to produce beyond point X will choose the technology represented by SAC_1. Firms planning to produce less than point X will choose the technology represented by SAC_2. The heavy "lower envelope" of the two cost curves represents the lowest possible cost for each level of production, and is called the *long-run average cost curve*.

be achieved by increasing the utilization of existing production facilities, often at little additional expense. As a result, average cost falls. Conversely, cutbacks in production may not reduce total costs by very much. As a result, average costs rise. When most production expenses go to raw materials or labor, we say that production is *materials* or *labor intensive*. In such a production process, the average total cost of production depends mainly on the amount of materials and labor that goes into each unit of output. Because materials and labor are divisible, they can change in proportion to changes in output, with the result that average costs do not vary with output. It follows that substantial product-specific economies of scale are more likely when production is capital intensive, and minimal product-specific economies of scale are more likely when production is labor intensive.

Spreading of Fixed Costs at the Plant and Multiplant Levels

Economies of scope that arise when a firm diversifies into several products at one or more plants are known as plant and multiplant economies of scope. These economies arise because of inputs that can be shared to produce several products. Plant-level economies of scope arise when a firm is able to utilize more fully the facility and the machinery devoted to its main product line by manufacturing additional product lines. This could happen because certain processing units are indivisible. For example, in cereal factories, the minimum efficient size of a packaging line is often much greater than the market for any one brand of cereal.

Economies of scope at the plant level often occur in retailing. Few, if any, retail stores sell a single product. Having borne the fixed expense of leasing store space, hiring and training store personnel, and so forth, the store manager economizes by spreading these costs across several products. The consumer also benefits from scope economies by enjoying the convenience of being able to purchase several products at one store. Having borne the fixed expenses of driving to the store, finding parking, and so forth, the consumer spreads these costs across several purchases. Shopping malls afford consumers even greater economies, by enabling them to spread fixed travel costs across many stores.

Multiplant economies of scope arise when there are shared inputs that can be applied to products that are produced in different plants. Intangible organizational capabilities that have been acquired in the production of the firm's core business are a good example of this.[5] As discussed above, a cellophane tape manufacturer that has developed capabilities in working with the technology of adhesives may be able to exploit that capability by producing adhesive message notes. The firm may have to build a specialized factory and acquire new machines to produce the message notes, but it does not have to invest in the discovery of the know-how that it acquired over the years in the process of making cellophane tape.

Economies of scope at both the plant and multiplant levels may be related to make-or-buy decisions. By offering a broad product line, the plant manager may achieve sufficient scope of operations to justify "making" instead of "buying" cer-

---

[5]See Chapter 2 for additional discussion of the logic of exploiting organizational capabilities.

tain specialized inputs, such as accounting, marketing, legal counsel, and finance. This is an example of the division of labor being limited by the extent of the market. When the firm is small, it hires outside accountants and selling agents who may be knowledgeable about the firm's industry but lack detailed firm-specific knowledge. When the firm grows, it may employ its own accountants and salespeople who may make the investments necessary to develop firm-specific knowledge. Of course, the decision to "make" accounting and selling services in-house is subject to the same concerns described in Chapter 2.

❖ ❖

XAMPLE 5.1

HUB-AND-SPOKE NETWORKS AND ECONOMIES OF SCOPE IN THE AIRLINE INDUSTRY

An important example of multiplant economies of scope arises in a number of industries in which goods and services are routed to and from several markets. In these industries, which include airlines, railroads, and telecommunications, distribution is organized around "hub-and-spoke" networks. In an airline hub-and-spoke network, an airline flies passengers from a set of "spoke" cities through a central "hub," where passengers then change planes and fly from the hub to their outbound destinations. Thus, a passenger flying from, say, Omaha to Louisville on American Airlines would board an American flight from Omaha to Chicago, change planes, and then fly from Chicago to Louisville.

Recall that economies of scope occur when a multiproduct firm can produce given quantities of products at a lower total cost than the total cost of producing these quantities in separate firms. This is equivalent to saying that a firm producing many products will have a lower average cost than a firm producing just a few products. In the airline industry, it makes economic sense to think about individual origin–destination pairs (e.g., St. Louis to New Orleans, St. Louis to Houston, etc.) as distinct products. Viewed in this way, economies of scope would exist if an airline's average cost is lower the more origin–destination pairs it serves.

To understand how hub-and-spoke networks give rise to economies of *scope*, it is first necessary to explain *economies of density*. Economies of density are essentially economies of scale along a given route, that is, reductions in average cost as traffic volume on the route increases. (In the airline industry, traffic volume is measured as revenue-passenger miles [RPM], which is the number of passengers on the route multiplied by the number of miles, and average cost is the cost per revenue passenger mile.) Economies of density occur because of spreading flight-specific fixed costs (e.g., costs of the flight and cabin crew, fuel, aircraft servicing) and because of the economies of aircraft size. In the airline industry, traffic-sensitive costs (e.g., food, ticket handling) are small in relation to flight-specific fixed costs. Thus, as its traffic volume increases, an airline can fill a larger fraction of its seats on a given type of aircraft (in airline industry lingo, it increases its *load factor*—the ratio of passengers to available seats), and because the airline's total costs increase only slightly, its cost per RPM falls as it spreads the flight-specific costs over more traffic volume. As traffic volume on the route gets even larger, it becomes worthwhile to substitute larger aircraft (e.g., 300-seat Boeing 767s) for smaller aircraft (e.g., 150-seat Boeing 737s). A key aspect of this substitution is that the 300-seat aircraft flown a given distance at a given load factor is less than twice as costly as the 150-seat aircraft flown the same distance at the same load factor. The reason for this is that doubling the number of seats and passengers on a plane does not require doubling the sizes of flight and cabin crews or the amount of fuel used, and that the 300-seat aircraft is less than twice as costly to build as the 150-seat aircraft, owing to engineering properties related to the cube-square rule, which will be discussed below.

Economies of scope emerge from the interplay of economies of density and the properties of a hub-and-spoke network. To see how, consider an origin–destination pair—say, Indianapolis to Chicago—with a modest amount of daily traffic. An airline serving only this route would use small planes, and even then, would probably operate with a relatively low load factor. But now consider an airline serving a hub-and-spoke network, with the hub at Chicago. If this airline offered daily flights between Indianapolis and Chicago, it would not only draw passengers who want to travel from Indianapolis to Chicago, but it would also draw passengers traveling from Indianapolis to all other points accessible from Chicago in the network (e.g., Los Angeles or San Francisco). An airline that includes the Indianapolis–Chicago route as part of a larger hub-and-spoke network can operate larger aircraft at higher load factors than can an airline serving only Indianapolis–Chicago and, as a result, can benefit from economies of density to achieve a lower cost per RPM along this route. (It can also justify offering more frequent service, making it more convenient for Indianapolis travelers.) Moreover, because there will now be passengers traveling between Chicago and other spoke cities in this network, the airline's load factors on these other spokes will increase somewhat, thereby lowering the costs per RPM on these routes as well. The overall effect is that an airline that serves Indianapolis–Chicago as part of a larger hub-and-spoke network will have a lower average cost overall than an airline that only serves Indianapolis–Chicago. This is precisely what is meant by economies of scope.

Increased Productivity of Variable Inputs

Economies of scale can also arise because of increases in the productivity of variable inputs as the firm becomes larger. Recall Adam Smith's dictum from Chapter 2, "The division of labor is limited by the extent of the market." We discussed the division of labor in the context of the emergence of market specialists. But the division of labor also occurs within firms, by way of increasing task specialization. As the scale of a firm's operations increases, workers can be assigned to increasingly specialized tasks. In a variety of manufacturing contexts, workers are more productive when repeating a single operation over and over again, than when performing a wide set of tasks. When this is so, a firm's labor costs per unit of output will fall as the firm's volume of output increases.

Economies of scale can also be due to efficiencies in energy usage. Doubling the size or the capacity of a machine often does not double the energy needed to operate it. When this is so, the firm may find it optimal to substitute larger machines for smaller machines as its volume of production goes up, and energy costs per unit of output go down.

Inventories

Economies of scale may arise when firms must carry inventories. Firms carry inventories to minimize the chances of a "stock-out" (i.e., running out of stock). Inventories are important whenever the cost of a stock-out exceeds the costs of carrying inventory. The cost of a stock-out may be high. It can cost a retailer lost sales, and drive away potential customers who seek more reliable sources of supply. For a manufacturer, a stock-out for a single part may delay an entire production process. Of course, there are costs to carrying inventory, including interest on the expenses borne in producing the inventory and the risk that it will depreciate in value while waiting to be used or sold, perhaps due to changes in fashion or technological obsolescence.

Inventory costs drive up the average costs of goods that are actually sold. Suppose, for example, that a firm needs to hold inventories equal to 10 percent of its sales to maintain a tolerable level of expected stock-outs. This will increase its average cost of goods sold by as much as 10 percent. (The increase will be smaller if, at the end of the selling season, the firm can sell its inventories at some fraction of original cost.) In general, the greater the percentage of sales held in inventory, the higher the average cost of goods sold. Management of inventory is cited as a key determinant of success of many firms, such as WalMart. The need to carry inventories creates economies of scale because firms doing a high volume of business usually need to carry proportionately less stock in inventory than do firms doing a small volume of business to achieve the same level of stock-outs. This has the effect of reducing the average cost of goods sold for larger firms.

Queuing theory explains why large firms can carry smaller inventories as a percentage of sales than can small firms. Queuing theory takes information about *arrival rates* (the rate at which people enter the queue) and *service rates* (the rate at which people leave the queue because they have obtained the desired good or service) to determine the statistical properties of the queue. Variables may include the average waiting time for people in the queue and the average inventory. Inventories include goods that are available for arriving consumers but not yet sold, or personnel who are available to help consumers but are idle because not enough consumers are arriving. Either way, inventories entail costs.

A key result of queuing theory is that as the arrival rate increases, the seller is able to carry a smaller excess inventory in percentage terms to maintain a fixed rate of stock outages. The corollary of this result is that if one fixes excess inventory in percentage terms, then higher arrival rates are associated with lower rates of stock outages. These results are illustrated in Table 5.4, which shows the excess inventory as a percentage of expected demand needed to maintain a constant rate of stock outage. The first column gives varying levels of expected demand, from 100

TABLE 5.4
INVENTORIES AND SALES

Expected Demand (units per month)	Monthly Inventory	Excess Inventory (% of monthly inventory)
100	117	17.0%
150	170	13.3
200	224	12.0
250	276	10.4
300	329	9.7
350	381	8.9
400	433	8.3

to 400 units per month. The second column gives the monthly inventory needed to maintain a stock outage of 5 percent. The third column reports inventory in excess of expected demand expressed as a percentage of monthly demand.

An experience of one of the authors in trying to park his car in a crowded city neighborhood provides a more tangible illustration of these results. The particular building in which he lived ("Building A") has a parking alcove with room for two cars. When the author wished to park his car for a few minutes, he would use the alcove. Directly across the street was another building with its own alcove ("Building B"), also with room for two cars. Occasionally, the alcove in front of Building A was full, that is, Building A had a "stock outage." The author once tried to use Building B's alcove, but was chased away by a doorman with a baseball bat. The author was not surprised, since his doorman did the same to residents of Building B when their alcove was full! By enforcing their "occupants-only" parking policies, the two buildings failed to make full use of their inventory of alcoves. To see why, it is helpful to make the example more concrete. Suppose that the number of residents of Building A desiring a parking spot ranged from 0 to 4, according to the probabilities given in Table 5.5. The number of residents of Building B desiring parking also ranged from 0 to 4. Assume that cars arrive in front of the two buildings independently, so that a change in demand from the residents of one building does not predict a change in demand from the residents of the other building.

TABLE 5.5
DEMAND FOR PARKING IN FRONT OF TWO HIGH RISES

Parkers at Bldg A	Probability	Parkers at Bldg B	Probability
0	.6	0	.6
1	.1	1	.1
2	.1	2	.1
3	.1	3	.1
4	.1	4	.1

We can see from Table 5.5 that the probability that at any one time there were three or more individuals desiring the two spots in front of Building A was .20. Building B had the same rate of "stock outage." Had the two buildings permitted their residents to use each other's spaces, the frequency of stock outages would have fallen. Stock outages would occur if five or more people from both buildings wanted to park at the same time. This would occur with probability .10.[6] The underlying intuition for the economical use of parking spaces is simple. When the buildings merge, on those occasions when one alcove is full and the other is not, the residents of the building with the full alcove need not be turned away.

These principles have many other practical implications. In health care, for example, larger hospitals can keep fewer empty beds, in percentage terms, and still be able to accommodate emergency patients. This helps explain why large hospitals have higher bed occupancy rates than small hospitals. Another example is provided by grocery stores, which long ago switched from maintaining separate sales clerks in each department to a single bank of clerks by the store exit. This reduces each clerk's idle time and the number of customer transactions.

The Cube-Square Rule and the Physical Properties of Production

Economies of scale also arise because of the physical properties of processing units. An excellent example of this is the *cube-square rule*, well-known to engineers. It states that the volume of a structure increases with the cube of its linear dimension, whereas the surface area increases with the square of its linear dimension. Table 5.6 gives the surface area, volume, and ratio of surface area to volume for boxes with dimensions $A \times A \times 2A$, as A increases from 1 to 5.

What does the cube-square rule have to do with economies of scale? In many production processes, production capacity is proportional to the *volume* of the production vessel, whereas the total cost of producing at capacity is proportional to the *surface area* of the vessel. This implies that as capacity increases, the average cost of producing at capacity decreases because the ratio of surface area to volume decreases. More generally, the physical properties of production often allow firms to expand capacity without comparable increases in cost.

Oil piplines are excellent examples of this phenomenon. The cost of transporting oil is an increasing function of the friction between the oil and the inner surface of the pipe. The amount of friction increases with growth in the pipe's surface area, hence transportation costs increase in proportion to the pipe's surface area. By contrast, the amount of oil that can be pumped through the pipe depends

---

[6]This is calculated as follows. Stock outages for Buildings A and B combined occur whenever the following combinations of parkers occur: 4 at Building A, 1, 2, 3 or 4 at Building B; 3 at Building A, 2, 3, or 4 at Building B; 2 at Building A, 3 or 4 at Building B; 1 at Building A, 4 at Building B. There are a total of ten different combinations, each with a probability of .01. Thus, the total probability is .10.

TABLE 5.6
THE CUBE-SQUARE RULE

Dimensions	Surface Area	Volume	Surface Area/Volume
$1 \times 1 \times 2$	10	2	5
$2 \times 2 \times 4$	40	16	2.5
$3 \times 3 \times 6$	90	54	1.67
$4 \times 4 \times 8$	160	128	1.25
$5 \times 5 \times 10$	250	250	1.0

on its volume.[7] Thus, as seen in Table 5.7, the average cost of an optimally configured pipeline declines as desired throughput increases. Other processes that exhibit scale economies owing to the cube-square rule or related properties include the old Bessemer process for making steel (the size of the vessel used to melt the steel determined the productive capacity), warehousing (the cost of making the warehouse is largely determined by its surface area), and brewing (the volume of the brewing tanks determines output).

◆ ◆ ◆ ◆ ◆ SPECIAL SOURCES OF SCALE AND SCOPE ECONOMIES

The sources of economies of scale described above are related mainly to the engineering properties of production. This section describes three special sources of economies of scale having to do with areas other than production:

TABLE 5.7
HYPOTHETICAL COSTS OF OPTIMALLY CONFIGURED OIL PIPELINE[a]

Rate of Throughput (thousands of barrels per day, MBCD)	Optimal Pipeline Diameter	Total Cost ($millions per year)	Average Cost ($millions per MBCD per year)
100	14	9.54	.0954
200	20	13.49	.0675
300	24	16.52	.0550
400	28	19.08	.0477
500	31	21.33	.0427

[a]Assumes a pipeline of 2,000 miles over level terrain; a before-tax cost of capital of 7 percent; electricity costs of $.01 per KWH; average labor costs of $25 per hour; and a pipeline with a 40-year life.

---

[7]See Cockenboo, L., "Production Functions and Cost Functions: A Case Study," in Mansfield, E. (ed.), *Managerial Economics and Operations Research*, 5th ed. New York: Norton, 1987.

- Marketing economies
- Purchasing economies
- Research and development

Marketing Economies

The costs of marketing a product are often calculated to equal the cost per message received by a potential purchaser of the product. Economies of scale exist in marketing whenever the costs of marketing are lower for firms with higher volumes of output. Such economies may exist for two reasons:

- Spreading advertising costs over larger markets
- Reputation effects

Spreading Advertising Costs over Larger Markets

Firms that sell a wide variety of products or that sell in many markets may enjoy scope economies in purchasing advertising. To understand why, it is important to recognize that the cost of an advertisement is measured in terms of the cost per effective message received, where a message is effective only if its recipient can buy the advertised product.

Contrast the cost per effective message for a firm with a national presence, say Budweiser Beer, and a firm with a local presence, say Henry Weinhardt's Private Reserve (owned by G. Heileman but available mainly on the West Coast). Suppose both firms wish to advertise on television. The cost per viewer of placing a national ad with a major network during a prime time broadcast is approximately half the cost of placing the same ad with a single local affiliate.[8] Budweiser would clearly desire to place a national ad. Henry Weinhardt must settle for local ads, since viewers throughout most of the United States could not buy its beer even if they wanted to. Assuming that the ads themselves are equally persuasive, Budweiser enjoys a much lower cost per effective message.

Another reason why national television ads are cheaper than local ads is because there are fixed costs for negotiating and scheduling any ad. Contrast the simplicity of placing an advertisement with NBC with the complexity of placing the same ad with each local NBC affiliate. Large advertisers may also enjoy purchasing power that enables them to obtain discounts from television stations.

When two firms have national presences, the larger one may still enjoy an advantage. Suppose that Wendy's and McDonald's both place advertisements on rival television networks to air at the same time. The ads are seen by audiences of equal sizes and cost the same to place. Suppose also that both ads are equally persuasive—20,000 viewers of the McDonald's ad have an urge to visit McDonald's;

---

[8]The cost of a network ad was obtained from "New "Late Night" Might Be an Ad Bargain," *Atlanta Constitution*, April 30, 1993, Sec. D, p. 5. The cost of a local ad was obtained from "WDIV, WXYZ Battle to Be No. 1 New Station," *Crains Detroit Business*, September 17, 1990, Sec. 1, p. 3.

20,000 viewers of the Wendy's ad are motivated to visit Wendy's. Despite these similarities, the cost per effective message is much lower for McDonald's. The reason is that there are about 10,000 McDonald's in the United States, so that almost all of the 20,000 viewers craving McDonald's can find one nearby. However, there are only about 3,000 Wendy's, so that many of the 20,000 who crave Wendy's will not find one nearby, and will either eat elsewhere or go unsatisfied.

Reputation Effects and Umbrella Branding

The cost of advertising a given product may be reduced for a firm that has an established reputation in the marketplace based on the sale of other products. For example, an advertisement for a particular model of Bang and Olafson speakers may encourage customers to consider other products by Bang and Olafson. This is known as *umbrella branding*. Umbrella branding is effective when consumers use the information in an advertisement about one product to make inferences about other products with the same brand name, thereby reducing advertising costs per effective image. Umbrella branding may also reduce the riskiness of new product introductions. Consumers are often reluctant to try new products because they are unsure about their quality. If consumers infer product quality from the brand name, firms may leverage the reputation of an existing brand name to help launch a new product. Umbrella branding explains why Diet Coke and Cherry Coke are more successful than the products Coke introduced at earlier times, Tab and Mr. Pibb, which did not share the Coke image and reputation for flavor.

Umbrella branding has some risks. Some conglomerates have been unable to create a corporate brand identity despite extensive advertising. One example is Beatrice, which attempted but failed during the 1980s to create a corporate brand identity for an array of products that included Levelor blinds, Danskin exercise clothes, and Butterball turkeys. Sometimes firms prefer to keep brand identities separate, such as when Kraft Foods acquired the Seven Seas brand name, so that it could use it to introduce a line of zestier salad dressings rather than do so under the Kraft name. Some firms fail to recognize potential diseconomies of scope associated with conflicting brand images. This occurred when British conglomerate EMI initially signed and then bought out of its recording contract with punk pioneers the Sex Pistols in the mid-1970s. EMI feared that the band's violent and anarchic reputation might harm the company's image, particularly among hospitals and physicians considering the purchase of EMI's new CT scanner medical diagnostic equipment. Although EMI salvaged its CT sales, it suffered in the music market. It was unable to sign any significant "new wave" performers for several years thereafter.

Research and Development

Manufacturers must often make substantial investments in R&D to develop new products, or to improve existing products or production processes. R&D expenditures exceed 5 percent of total sales revenues at many companies in a variety of industries, including Dow Chemical, Cray Research, Merck, and Eastman Kodak. R&D involves significant indivisibilities. The nature of engineering and scientific research implies that there is a minimum feasible size to an R&D department. As a result, R&D can create significant economies of scale, with R&D cost per unit of output falling with sales volume.

Economies of scope may result from R&D spillovers. Spillovers result when ideas that arise in one research project are of help in another project. A firm with a diversified research portfolio may be better positioned to determine the general applicability of new ideas than a firm with a narrower portfolio of projects. Using detailed R&D data obtained from several pharmaceutical companies, Rebecca Henderson and Iain Cockburn documented the magnitude of spillovers for that industry.[9] They measured productivity as the number of patents per dollar of R&D. They found that for an average firm with 19 research programs, the addition of two research programs increased the productivity of existing programs by 4.5 percent. There would also be an increase in the productivity of programs at *other firms* of about 2 to 3 percent.

Economies of scale and scope in R&D are important enough to materially affect market structure in some industries. Following the logic of Alfred Chandler (discussed in Chapter 1), firms in research-intensive industries require throughput to achieve the sales volumes necessary to defray fixed R&D costs. Thus, we would expect large firms to dominate R&D-intensive industries.

One such industry may be pharmaceuticals. Henderson and Cockburn's research documents scope economies due to spillovers. There may be significant scale economies as well. Researchers at Tufts University have carefully measured the costs of developing new pharmaceutical products for the U.S. market.[10] They found that drug companies spend approximately $200 million on R&D for each drug the Food and Drug Administration approved for marketing in the United States. Since many drugs have lifetime sales of only a few million prescriptions, average fixed costs can easily exceed $1 per prescription.

Lacy Glenn Thomas argues that high R&D costs have favored large pharmaceutical firms.[11] Thomas feels that larger companies may be able to better manage the complexities of the FDA approval process by virtue of their experience. They also have the production and sales organizations to assure the throughput and high sales volumes necessary to expand output and drive down average fixed costs. Thomas may be right. A glimpse of the leading pharmaceutical manufacturers in the 1990s reveals few newcomers since the 1960s and several significant mergers in the industry have contributed to consolidation. Providing the "exceptions that prove the rule," when smaller pharmaceutical firms successfully innovate, they frequently sell their innovations to larger drug houses that then shepherd the drugs through the regulatory process and market them.

---

[9]Henderson, R. and I. Cockburn, "Scale, Scope, and Spillovers: Research Strategy and Research Productivity in the Pharmaceutical Industry," Massachusetts Institute of Technology, working paper, 1994.

[10]DiMasi, J. et al., "Cost of Innovation in the Pharmaceutical Industry," *Journal of Health Economics*, 10(2), 1991, pp. 107–142.

[11]Thomas, L. G., "Regulation and Firm Size: FDA Impacts on Innovation," *RAND Journal of Economics*, 21, Winter 1990, pp. 497–517.

The dominance of large drug houses in pharmaceuticals is just one piece of evidence on an old and interesting question: Are large firms more innovative than small firms? We have already seen in this and earlier chapters some theoretical reasons to suspect that the answer is far from straightforward. On the one hand, large firms can reduce the average costs of innovation by providing throughput. On the other hand, small firms may be better able to motivate workers and may have greater flexibility in their use of resources. On efficiency grounds, it seems as if there is no clear answer.

Efficiency is not the only determinant of innovativeness, however. Firms need incentives to innovate. In his famous book, *Capitalism, Socialism, and Democracy*, Joseph Schumpeter advanced the hypothesis that larger firms have greater incentive to innovate than small firms.[12] This is due, in part, to the infrastructure within large firms that allows them to mass produce and distribute their innovations. Thus, large firms may gain more from successful innovation. But it is also due to the possibility that if a large firm has a dominant share of its market, it will face less competition and therefore justify greater R&D expense. This argument is not universally accepted. Indeed, a competitive firm may gain more from innovation because it stands to gain monopoly profit. We elaborate on this view in Chapter 15. Suffice it to say that economic theory and empirical evidence is ambiguous about whether big firms may be more innovative than small firms.

Purchasing Economies

Most of us have experienced the benefits of purchasing in bulk. Whether we are buying gallon containers of milk or six packs of soda, the price per unit of many items falls as the number of items we purchase increases. Purchasers all along the vertical chain may be able to realize discounts for volume purchasing, giving large purchasers an inherent cost advantage over small purchasers.

Why do firms offer discounts for volume purchasers? After all, why should a firm care whether its sales of X units come from a single buyer or from X different buyers? One reason is that it may be less costly for a firm to sell to a single buyer. If each sale requires some fixed cost, say in writing a contract, setting up a production run, or delivering the product, then it truly is less costly to sell in bulk. Another reason is that the bulk purchaser may be more price sensitive. For example, someone making weekly grocery purchases is more likely to consider the price of soda than someone purchasing a can of soda at the beach. And finally, unit-price differences mean more to purchasers when they buy more units. This may encourage large purchasers to shop more aggressively for the best prices.

It is not necessary for independent firms to merge to obtain the benefits of bulk purchasing. Independent firms may form purchasing alliances that buy in bulk to obtain quantity discounts, but otherwise remain independent. Example 5.2 describes one retail industry that is largely organized around purchasing groups—hardware.

---

[12]Schumpeter, J., *Capitalism, Socialism, and Democracy*, New York: Harper Collins, 1950.

EXAMPLE 5.1

THE ACE HARDWARE CORPORATION

With the recent growth of national hardware "superstore" chains such as Home Depot and Builder's Square, it might seem that "neighborhood" hardware stores will be unable to stay in business. After all, the chains enjoy significant purchasing and marketing economies of scale. In fact, thousands of independently owned hardware stores do enjoy many of the same scale economies realized by national giants, by virtue of membership in hardware purchasing groups. Thanks to these groups, independent hardware stores continue to thrive.

One of the two largest purchasing groups is the Ace Hardware Corporation. Ace began as a hardware wholesaler and distributor based in the Midwest. A dealer buyout in 1974 led to a national expansion. Today, the Ace cooperative is jointly owned by its 5,200 member stores. (The members of the other large cooperative, Cotter and Co., operate under the True Value name.) Ace purchases in bulk from over 4,000 suppliers, including Stanley Tools, Toro (lawnmowers), and Weber (grills). This gives individual store owners access to the distribution channels comparable to Home Depot and Builder's Square. Ace employs its own buyers, who obtain quantity discounts that are then passed on to individual stores. Ace provides its members with other benefits as well. It places national advertising and coordinates national marketing campaigns. It provides information about local marketing practices and new products. It developed and supervised the installation of electronic systems for store owners, allowing them to rapidly check on inventories and prices (this is especially helpful for products such as lumber, which experience volatile price movements), place special orders, and communicate by e-mail with other stores. Furthermore, Ace used its clout to push suppliers to adopt bar codes to facilitate pricing and inventory maintenance.

Individual Ace hardware stores can match the purchasing and marketing economies of national chains. At the same time, they enjoy the benefits of independence. Store owners face hard-edged market incentives that limit their ability to shirk in areas such as customer service. (Market analysts often comment about how Home Depot and Builder's Square employees are working hard to develop the same "small town" friendliness that is often the norm at Ace and True Value.) Stores can tailor their prices and supplies to local needs, and the typical Ace store obtains only half its merchandise from the purchasing group. Indeed, whereas some Ace stores resemble indoor flea markets, others look more like department stores *sans* clothing, stocked with appliances, televisions, cutlery, bicycles, bedding, and the occasional hammer.

The cooperative concept has disadvantages, though. Absent direction from a central office, individual stores may cannibalize each other through aggressive pricing and marketing practices. Store locations are not chosen with a mind toward inventory management. Key decisions regarding inventories, purchasing, and marketing can be delayed due to the democratic nature of the cooperative. And Ace lacks the standardization that assures a Home Depot customer of consistent selection and service at all stores.

◆ ◆ ◆ ◆ ◆ THE LEARNING CURVE

Medical students are encouraged to learn by the axiom "See one, do one, teach one." This axiom belies the importance of experience in producing skilled physicians. Experience is an important determinant of ability in many professions, and strategists have discovered in the past three decades the signficance of experience for firms. The importance of experience to firms is conveyed by the idea of the learning curve.

The Concept of the Learning Curve

Economies of scale refer to the cost advantages that flow from producing a larger output at a given point in time. The *learning curve* (or experience curve) refers to cost advantages that flow from accumulating experience and know-how. While practice may not always make perfect, it generally moves one in the desired direction. Hence, individuals generally improve their performance of specific tasks as they gain experience. Organizations can also learn. A manufacturer can learn the appropriate tolerances for design attributes. A retailer can learn about community tastes. An accounting firm can learn the idiosyncracies of its clients' inventory management. The benefits of learning manifest themselves in lower costs, higher quality, and more effective pricing and marketing.

The magnitude of learning benefits is often expressed in terms of a *progress ratio*. The progress ratio for a given production process is calculated by examining how far average costs decline as the cumulative production output increases. It is important to use cumulative output rather than output during a given time period to distinguish between learning effects and other scale effects. Following Figure 5.5, suppose that a firm has cumulative output of Q_X. Currently, its average cost of production is AC_1. Suppose next that the firm's cumulative output doubles to $2Q_X$, and the average cost is AC_2. Then the progress ratio equals AC_2/AC_1.[13] Any progress ratio less than 1 suggests that learning is taking place.

Progress ratios have been estimated for thousands of products.[14] The median progress ratio appears to be about .80, implying that for the typical firm, doubling cumulative output reduces unit costs by about 20 percent. Progress ratios vary from

---

[13]This is sometimes referred to as the slope of the learning curve.

[14]See, for example, *Perspectives on Experience*, Boston: Boston Consulting Group, 1970, for estimates of progress ratios for over 20 industries. See Lieberman, M., "The Learning Curve and Pricing in the Chemical Processing Industries," *RAND Journal of Economics*, 15, Summer 1984, pp. 213–28, for learning curve estimates for 37 chemical products.

FIGURE 5.5
THE LEARNING CURVE.

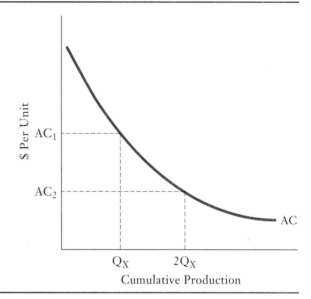

When there is learning, average costs fall with cumulative production. Here, as cumulative production increases from Q_X to $2Q_X$, the average cost of a batch of output falls from AC_1 to AC_2.

firm to firm and industry to industry, however, so that the actual progress ratio enjoyed by any one firm for any given production process generally falls between .70 and .90 and may be as low as .6 or as high as 1.0 (e.g., no learning). Note that while learning curve analysts may announce that an industry has a progress ratio of, say, .75, this does not imply that continual doubling of output inexorably leads to further and further cost reductions. Estimated progress ratios usually represent averages over a range of outputs and do not indicate if and when learning economies may be fully exploited.

While the progress ratio concept has been applied mainly to cost measurement, it applies equally well to quality. For example, Harold Luft, John Bunker, and Alain Enthoven found that more experienced medical providers enjoyed significantly lower surgical mortality rates for a number of common surgical procedures.[15] These authors use this evidence to promote the development of regional referral centers for the provision of highly specialized medical care. These regional centers would perform many specific surgical procedures (e.g., heart surgery), replacing local facilities with lower volumes and presumably higher mortality rates.

---

[15]Luft, H., J. Bunker, and A. Enthoven, "Should Operations Be Regionalized? The Empirical Relation Between Surgical Volume and Mortality," *New England Journal of Medicine*, 301, 1979, pp. 1364–1369.

Exploiting Learning to Obtain a Cost Advantage

The substantial evidence that learning reduces costs raises a number of questions. Can firms exploit learning to obtain a cost advantage in the market? Why does learning vary across products and firms? Can firms take steps to maximize learning effects (or minimize "forgetting")?

The presence of learning effects suggests that firms may wish to lower prices in the short run to increase output and reduce costs in the long run. The reason is that the expectation of reduced future costs effectively reduces the cost of current production. To see why this is so, consider the following example.

Suppose that a manufacturer of silicon chips has cumulative production of 10,000 chips. It currently costs $2.50 to manufacture one additional chip. Based on experience, the firm believes that once it has produced 20,000 chips its unit costs will fall to $2.00, with no further learning benefits. The chipmaker has orders to produce an additional 200,000 chips when it unexpectedly receives an offer to bid on an order for 10,000 chips to be filled immediately. What price would it be willing to bid to get the order?

Assuming that filling the new order does not create delays that jeopardize other business, the chipmaker must compare the price that the new buyer is willing to pay against the cost of producing additional chips. A myopic chipmaker might examine its current production costs and, ignoring learning effects, conclude that it must receive a price of at least $2.50 per chip to justify the new business. This would be a mistake, as shown by an analysis that takes learning into account.

To determine a reasonable price for the new order, the chipmaker must consider how the accumulated knowledge will affect future costs. Before it received the new order, the chipmaker had planned to produce 200,000 chips. The first 10,000 chips would cost $2.50 per chip, and the remaining 190,000 would cost $2.00 per chip, for a total of $405,000 for 200,000 chips. The new order enables the chipmaker to fully exploit available learning economies before producing the previously ordered 200,000 chips. Once the new order is filled, the cost of producing the next 200,000 chips is only $400,000.

By filling the new order, the chipmaker reduces its future production costs by $5,000. In effect, the full cost of filling the additional order is only $20,000 (current costs of $25,000 less the $5,000 future cost savings), or $2.00 per chip. The firm should be willing to bid any price over this amount, even though a price between $2.00 and $2.50 per chip does not appear to cover current production costs.

Learning and Organization

The variation in progress ratios across firms and products merely gives hard evidence of the obvious point that learning occurs at different rates for different organizations and different processes. There has been little systematic study of the determinants of learning, so that managers have little more than common sense to help them identify situations in which learning is likely to be important.

Complex tasks offer greater opportunities for learning. If tasks are too complex, however, learning done by individuals may be difficult to transmit across the firm. Examples include many professional services, in which individual knowledge of how to combine skills in functional areas with specific and detailed knowledge of particular clients or markets may give individuals advantages that they cannot easily pass along to others.

Learning rests within the employees of the firm. The firm can facilitate the adoption and use of newly learned ideas by encouraging the sharing of information, establishing work rules that include the new ideas, and reducing turnover. Unfortunately, these practices often stifle creativity and prevent new learning by codifying particular production practices and insulating the firm from new ideas. Unless the firm is blessed with workers who continually strive to improve their own performance and share their ideas with their coworkers, the tradeoff between institutionalizing existing knowledge and encouraging new knowledge is inevitable.

The Learning Curve versus Economies of Scale

It is important to distinguish economies due to the learning curve from economies of scale. Economies of scale refer to the ability to perform activities at a lower unit cost when those activities are performed on a larger scale. Learning economies refer to reductions in unit costs due to accumulating experience. Economies of scale may be substantial even when learning economies are minimal. This is likely to be the case in simple capital-intensive activities, such as two-piece aluminum can manufacturing. Likewise, learning economies may be substantial even when economies of scale are minimal. This is likely to be the case in complex labor-intensive activities, such as computer software development.

Figure 5.6 illustrates how one can have learning economies without economies of scale. The left side of the figure shows a typical learning curve, with average costs declining with cumulative experience. The right side shows two average cost curves, for different experience levels. Both average cost curves are perfectly flat, indicating that there are no economies of scale. Suppose the firm under consideration enters a given year of production with cumulative experience of Q_1. According to the learning curve, this gives an average cost level of AC_1. This remains constant regardless of current output because of constant returns to scale. Entering the next year of production the firm has cumulative output of Q_2. Its experiences in the previous year enable the firm to revamp its production techniques. In thus moving down the learning curve, it can enjoy an average cost level of AC_2 in the next year of production.

Managers who do not correctly distinguish between economies of scale and learning may draw incorrect inferences about the benefits of size in a market. For example, if a large firm has lower costs because of economies of scale, then any cutbacks in production will raise costs. If the lower costs are the result of learning, the firm may be able to cut back without necessarily raising its costs. To take another example, if a firm enjoys a cost advantage due to a capital-intensive production process and resultant scale economies, then it may be less concerned about labor turnover than a competitor that enjoys low costs due to learning a complex labor-intensive production process.

FIGURE 5.6
LEARNING ECONOMIES WHEN SCALE ECONOMIES ARE ABSENT.

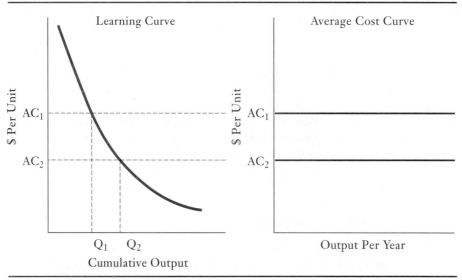

It is not necessary to have economies of scale to realize learning economies. The production process depicted here shows constant returns to scale, as evidenced by the flat average cost curves, which show output *within a given year*. The level of average cost falls with cumulative experience *across several years*, however, as shown by the learning curve.

XAMPLE 5.3

THE BOSTON CONSULTING GROUP GROWTH/SHARE PARADIGM

The Boston Consulting Group (BCG) had a major impact on corporate strategy beginning in the 1970s when it introduced the *growth/share matrix*, an outgrowth of its success advocating learning curve strategies.[16] Figure 5.7 depicts a typical BCG matrix. The matrix allows firms to distinguish their product lines on two dimensions: growth of the market in which the product is situated, and the product's market share relative to the share of its next largest competitors. A product line was classified into one of four categories. A rising star is a product in a growing market with a high relative share. A cash cow is a product in a stable or declining market with a high relative share. A problem child is a product in a growing market with a low relative share. A dog is a product in a stable or declining market with a low relative share.

---

[16]For a discussion of their treatment of the learning curve, see Boston Consulting Group, *Perspectives on Experience*, Boston: Boston Consulting Group, 1970.

FIGURE 5.7
THE BCG GROWTH/SHARE MATRIX.

The Growth/Share Matrix divides products into four categories according to their potential for growth and relative market share. Some strategists recommend that firms use the profits earned from "Cash Cows" to ramp up production of "Rising Stars" and "Problem Children". As the latter products move down their learning curves, they become "Cash Cows" in the next investment cycle.

		Relative Market Share	
		High	Low
Relative Market Growth	High	Rising Star	Problem Child
	Low	Cash Cow	Dog

The BCG strategy for successfully managing a portfolio of products was based on taking advantage of learning curves and the *product life cycle*. BCG had observed that learning curves offered significant cost advantages in many markets. They also felt that most products had a characteristic life cycle, as shown in Figure 5.8.[17] According to this product life cycle model, demand for the product is initially low just after it is introduced. The product then enters a phase in which demand grows rapidly. As demand becomes increasingly driven by replacement sales rather than sales to new customers, demand growth levels off, and the product reaches its maturity stage. Finally, as superior substitute products eventually emerge, demand for the product will begin to decline.

BCG felt that its clients could secure long-term cost advantages in each of their markets by increasing production in the early stages of the product's life cycle to secure learning economies. BCG recommended that firms use the profits from cash cow products to fund increased production of problem child and rising star products. In other words, the firm served as a "banker," using retained earnings to fund new ventures. Learning economies would cement the advantages of rising stars while enabling some problem children to become more competitive. As their markets matured and demand slackened, these products would then become cash cows to support learning strategies in new emerging markets.

BCG deserves credit for recognizing the strategic importance of learning curves, and many firms have prospered by utilizing the growth/share matrix framework. BCG also deserves credit for offering a rationale for maintaining a portfolio of products within a single diversified firm. However, it would be a mistake to apply the BCG framework without considering its underlying principles. As we have discussed, learning curves are by no means ubiquitous or uniform where they do occur. Increasing production runs will not by itself necessarily generate learning

---

[17]The product life cycle model has its origins in the marketing literature. See, for example, Levitt, T., "Exploit the Product Life Cycle," *Harvard Business Review*, November–December 1965, pp. 81–94.

FIGURE 5.8
THE PRODUCT LIFE CYCLE.

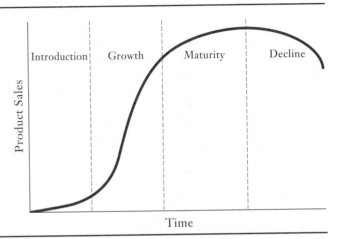

Product demand is thought to move through four stages. When the product is first introduced, sales and growth are low. Product demand then grows rapidly, but sales level off, and the industry enters a maturity phase. Eventually, demand declines as other superior products or technologies supplant it. It can be difficult to predict when each stage will begin.

economies, and knowledge gained from learning may rapidly depreciate. At the same time, product life cycles are easier to identify after they have been completed than during the planning process. Many products ranging from nylon to dedicated word processors that were forecast to have tremendous potential for growth did not meet expectations. Firms that invested heavily in them to secure learning advantages were losers. We conclude that one needs to do careful research about the learning curves and markets for the specific products in question before applying a learning curve strategy. Finally, the role of the firm as banker is questionable. As we discuss in Chapter 6, diversified firms have not demonstrated consistent success across diversified business lines. Moreover, the emergence of venture capitalists has enabled independent firms with potential stars of their own to obtain financing without being dependent on corporate authority.

◆ ◆ ◆ ◆ ◆ SOURCES OF DISECONOMIES OF SCALE

Given that there are so many potential sources of scale and scope economies, it may be surprising that there is not some colossal "mega-firm" dominating production across all industries. Perhaps no firm has tried. More likely, though, firms understand that there are limits to economies of scale, so that beyond a certain size, bigger is no longer better. Firms may even experience diseconomies of scale, so that bigger is worse. Diseconomies of scale can arise for a number of reasons that we discuss in this section:

- Rising labor costs
- Incentive and bureaucracy effects
- Spreading of specialized resources

Labor Costs and Firm Size

Larger firms generally pay higher wages. Evidence from as early as the 1890s pointed to the wage premium paid to workers in large manufacturing firms compared with smaller firms.[18] The wage premium persists. Data from the U.S. Current Population Survey reveal that companies with 500 or more employees pay their workers 35 percent more, on average, than do smaller firms. The wage gap cuts across all manufacturing and service industries. Even if one controls for other determinants of wages, such as work experience and job type, a wage gap of 10 percent or more still persists.

One reason for the wage gap is that large firms are more likely to be unionized than small firms. H. Gregg Lewis summarized 40 studies of wage differentials between unionized and nonunionized firms.[19] After controlling for a variety of other possible sources of wage differentials (such as sex, race, and experience) he found that unionized workers earn around 10 to 18 percent more than comparable nonunionized workers.

Offsetting the wage gap is that worker turnover at larger firms is generally lower than at small firms. Since it can cost thousands of dollars to recruit and train new employees, this may offset some of the added costs due to higher wages.

Incentive and Bureaucracy Effects

Is it difficult for large firms to motivate workers?[20] In smaller firms, worker pay is much more likely to be tied to firm performance (for an entrepreneur, pay is completely tied to firm performance). Whether a worker is on an assembly line or is part of a large team, it is difficult to tie worker and firm performance when firms are large. Larger firms may also have a more difficult time monitoring and communicating with workers, further leading to difficulties in promoting effective performance. On the other hand, large firms may provide incentives to their workers by offering opportunities for advancement up the corporate ladder. One solution adopted by many large firms is the adoption of work rules to ensure that workers do not slack off. While these rules may lead workers to perform specific tasks as desired, they may also stifle creativity and lead workers to feel detached from the organization. These issues are addressed in more detail in Chapters 16 and 17.

---

[18]For a comprehensive discussion of size effects on workers, see Brown, C., J. Hamilton, and J. Medoff, *Employers Large and Small*, Cambridge, MA: Harvard University Press, 1990.

[19]See *Handbook of Labor Economics*, Ashenfelter, O. and R. Layard (eds.), New York, North Holland, 1986.

[20]For example, see Jennergren, L. "Decentralization in Organizations," in Nystrom, P. and W. Starbuck (eds.), *Handbook of Organizational Design*, New York: Oxford University Press, 1981.

Spreading Specialized Resources Too Thin

Many talented individuals believe that having achieved success in one venture, they can duplicate it elsewhere. Some succeed. But others fail because they lack the skills necessary to translate their success to a new situation or they spread themselves too thin. A good example is provided by chefs, such as Chicago's Michael Foley. Foley achieved acclaim for his first restaurant, Printer's Row. He opened two other restaurants while continuing to operate Printer's Row. Not only did the new restaurants fail, the reviews for Printer's Row became negative as well. The reviews improved and business at Printer's Row picked up only after Foley returned to its kitchen. Michael Foley could not replicate himself. Thus, he could not easily replicate the success of his first restaurant. Other professionals share the same difficulties. When the key to a professional's success is the dedication of many hours to a single activity, performance may suffer across the board if he or she tries to devote time to several activities. The same lessons also apply to specialized capital inputs, such as computers, tools and dies, or assembly lines. If a specialized input is a source of advantage for a firm, and that firm attempts to expand its operations without duplicating the input, the expansion may overburden the specialized input.

◆ ◆ ◆ ◆ ◆ THE IMPORTANCE OF SCALE AND SCOPE ECONOMIES: FIRM SIZE, PROFITABILITY, AND MARKET STRUCTURE

Economies of scale and scope provide large firms with an inherent cost advantage. Not only does this encourage small firms to explore ways to grow in order to take advantage of scale economies themselves, it also limits the number of firms that can successfully compete in the market. This section explores these ideas.

Scale, Scope, and Firm Size

Scale and scope economies give large firms a cost advantage over small firms. In markets where consumers are price sensitive, large firms can pass along some of their cost advantage to consumers. This will drive small firms out of business or into niches not served by the large firms. If small firms are to match the production costs achieved by large firms, they must grow. A recent study by Timothy Dunne, Mark Roberts, and Larry Samuelson demonstrates the link between survival and growth.[21] They examined the growth of U.S. manufacturing plants from 1963 to 1982 and found that most plants opened during this time had closed within ten years. However, of those that remained open, most had grown significantly.

---

[21]Dunne, T., M. Roberts, and L. Samuelson, "Patterns of Firm Entry and Exit in U.S. Manufacturing Industries," *RAND Journal of Economics*, 19, Winter 1988, pp. 495–515.

While new plants tended to be only about one-third the size of existing plants at the time they opened, they roughly doubled in size within five years and tripled in size within ten years.

Firms can expand output in a number of ways. Expansion strategies may be internal, relying on retained earnings, equity, and debt, or external, relying on formalizing relationships with other firms. Internal expansion strategies include product portfolio management, such as the Boston Consulting Group Growth/Share Matrix strategy discussed earlier in this chapter, new product development, or geographic diversification. External strategies for growth typically involve mergers. Announcements about corporate mergers frequently refer to "synergies" that exist between the merging firms. Synergies are economies of scale waiting to be exploited. The efficiencies can be so large that the Department of Justice and the Federal Trade Commission, which enforce U.S. antitrust laws, will permit a merger between large firms that may create some monopoly power if the merger allows the firms to achieve substantial efficiencies through economies of scale. Mergers in the airlines (Republic/Northwest) and soft drink (Seven-Up/Dr Pepper) industries have been approved on these grounds.

The Relationship Between Market Share and Profitability

When economies of scale or scope exist, but only some firms have been able to exploit them, one would expect to find a positive correlation between a firm's market share and profitability. This relationship seems to be borne out in certain industries. For example, Figures 5.9 and 5.10 show a generally positive relationship between market share and profitability in two specific industries: automobiles and cigarettes.

Does the correlation exhibited in Figures 5.9 and 5.10 show up more generally across many industries? The answer seems to be yes. For example, D. Hall and Leonard Weiss found that among U.S. manufacturing firms, firm size is positively correlated with profitability, even after controlling for differences in industry conditions.[22] Robert Buzzell, Bradley Gale, and Ralph Sultan analyzed the PIMS (Profit Impact of Market Strategies) data collected by the Marketing Science Institute and found that among the firms in that sample, market share and profitability are positively correlated.[23] (This finding is summarized in Table 5.8.) Robert Jacobson and David Aaker also found a positive relationship between market share and profitability, though the correlation they estimated was weaker than that found by Buzzell, Gale, and Sultan.[24]

---

[22]Hall, D. and L. W. Weiss, "Firm Size and Profitability," *Review of Economics and Statistics*, 49, 1967, pp. 319–331.

[23]Buzzell, R. D., B. T. Gale, and R. G. M. Sultan, "Market Share: A Key to Profitability," *Harvard Business Review*, January–February 1975, pp. 97–106.

[24]Jacobson, R. and D. Aaker, "Is Market Share All That It's Cracked Up to Be?" *Journal of Marketing*, 49, Fall 1985, pp. 11–22.

FIGURE 5.9

DOMESTIC MARKET SHARES AND CORPORATE RETURNS ON EQUITY,
U.S. AUTOMOBILE INDUSTRY, 1971–75.

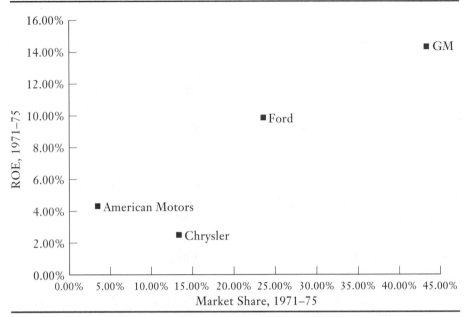

The horizontal axis shows a firm's average market share over the period 1971–75, while the vertical axis shows a firm's average return on equity (ROE) over the same period.

Source: Table 1-1 in Thomas, L. G., "The Economics of Strategic Planning: A Survey of the Issues," in Thomas, L. G. (ed.), *The Economics of Strategic Planning: Essays in Honor of Joel Dean*, Lexington, MA: Lexington Books, pp. 1–21.

In the 1970s, evidence such as that presented in Table 5.8 was used by management consultants and some academics to support the recommendation that raising market share should be the primary strategic objective of any business. This view has now been widely discredited. The observed correlation between market share and profitability should not be taken to imply that any strategy designed to boost market share will increase a firm's profitability. For one thing, the existence of positive correlation between market share and profitability does not mean that a large market share "causes" profits to be high. The economic mechanism underlying the correlation is likely to be more subtle. For example, it may be that a firm was able to succeed in capturing a high market share over time because its product created superior benefits for customers. This in turn, might have propelled the firm down a learning curve or allowed it to exploit scale economies in production, further increasing profits. A competitor that attempts to "buy" market share (e.g., by cutting its price or increasing advertising) may find that it is unable to achieve the same profitability as the market leader, either because its products do not offer a comparable level of quality to consumers or because it is unable to catch up to the initial advantage of the leader.[25]

FIGURE 5.10
DOMESTIC MARKET SHARES AND LINE OF BUSINESS RETURN
ON SALES, U.S. TOBACCO INDUSTRY, 1980.

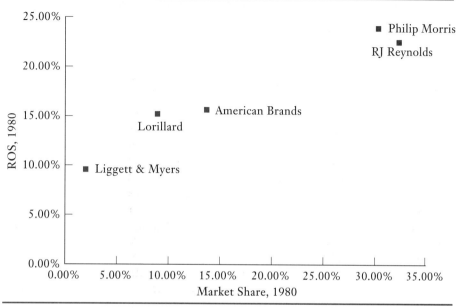

The horizontal axis shows a firm's market share in 1980, while the vertical axis shows a firm's return on sales (ROS) in 1980.

Source: Table 1-2 in Thomas, L. G., "The Economics of Strategic Planning: A Survey of the Issues," in Thomas, L. G. (ed.), *The Economics of Strategic Planning: Essays in Honor of Joel Dean*, Lexington, MA: Lexington Books, pp. 1–21.

TABLE 5.8
RELATIONSHIP BETWEEN MARKET SHARE AND PRE-TAX PROFIT AS
PERCENT OF SALE (ROS): OVERALL PIMS SAMPLE OF BUSINESSES

Market Share	ROS
< 10%	−0.16%
10%–20%	3.42%
20%–30%	4.84%
30%–40%	7.60%
> 40%	13.16%

Source: Exhibit 2 in Buzzell, R. D., B. T. Gale, and R. G. M. Sultan, "Market Share: A Key to Profitability," *Harvard Business Review*, January–February 1975, pp. 97–106.

---

[25]Chapter 14 discusses the dynamics of early mover advantages.

In addition, market shares in an industry must, by definition, add up to 100 percent. Thus, it would be impossible for all firms in an industry to increase market share simultaneously. If firms attempted to do so, either through cutting prices, raising advertising levels, or even enhancing the quality of their products, the result would most likely be diminished, rather than increased, profitability for all firms. The key point is that a strategy designed to exploit the positive relationship between market share and profitability has no hope of succeeding unless the linkage between market share and profitability is imperfectly understood by participants in an industry. But this undermines the general value of advice that *all* firms should "go for share."

Scale, Scope, and Market Structure

Economies of scale also help to determine the structure of the market that individual firms will compete in. *Market structure* refers to the number and size distribution of the firms in a market. A key determinant of market structure is the magnitude of demand relative to the minimum efficient scale of production. Figure 5.11 illustrates a demand curve in a market where the minimum efficient scale is large relative to overall demand. A single firm selling to the whole market can set any price above AC^* and make a profit. If another firm entered the market, it could not drive its costs down as low as the first firm unless it stole away some of its customers. Indeed, the most efficient configuration in this industry is for one firm to

FIGURE 5.11
DEMAND AND COST UNDER "NATURAL MONOPOLY".

In this situation, there is just enough demand in the market to exhaust the output of a single firm producing up to minimum efficient scale Q^*. Any firm that entered the market would have to sell less than Q^*, and would therefore have higher costs than the firm producing Q^*. A firm that tried to sell Q', for example, would have to set a price of AC' to break even, and therefore could not take business away from the incumbent firm charging a price around AC^*. This situation is described as a "natural monopoly" because it is most efficient to have a single firm selling to the whole market.

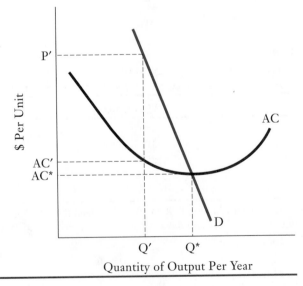

satisfy all market demand. If two firms split the market at a given price, they would have higher costs than if a single firm sold to the entire market at that price. For example, if two firms shared the market by selling output Q' at price P', average cost would exceed AC'.

When there is insufficient demand in a market for more than one firm to reach minimum efficient scale, the market is described as a *natural monopoly*. Many public utilities are thought to be natural monopolies. Governments frequently protect the status of these utilities as sole providers to allow them to fully exploit scale economies. In exchange, the utilities agree to allow the government to control their prices.

Figure 5.12 illustrates a demand curve in a market in which the minimum efficient scale (Q^*) is small relative to overall demand at the corresponding average cost (AC^*). Several firms can "fit" into this market and produce efficiently. It is possible to derive a general rule of thumb regarding the number of firms that can fit into a market. Let AC^* denote the average cost of production when firms achieve minimum efficient scale and Q^* denote the corresponding quantity. If D^* denotes the quantity of goods that will be purchased if price is set equal to AC^*, then the market can fit D^*/Q^* firms each producing at minimum efficient scale and setting price equal to average cost. As the market grows in size (D^* increases), more firms can fit into it. On the other hand, if the minimum efficient scale (Q^*) increases, fewer efficient firms will fit into it.

This analysis implies that industries with substantial economies of scale—industries with capital-intensive technologies—may come to be dominated by a few

FIGURE 5.12
DEMAND AND COST WHEN THERE IS ROOM FOR MANY FIRMS.

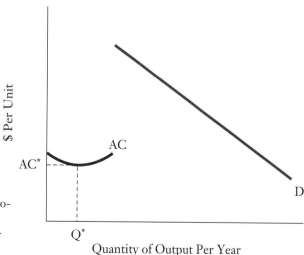

Unlike the natural monopoly, a single firm producing at minimum efficient scale Q^* cannot crowd out competitors. There is sufficient demand for additional entrants.

large firms.[26] Table 5.9 gives the market shares controlled by the three largest firms in 12 different industries in six nations. The higher the market shares of the largest firms, the more *concentrated* the industry. (Naturally, the largest firms in one nation need not be identical to the largest firms in another nation.) The figures are for 1970 but similar patterns would probably emerge today.

Three features of Table 5.9 are striking. First, concentration can vary substantially by industry. Second, concentration levels for a given industry appear to be comparable across nations. Cigarettes, glass bottles, and refrigerators are highly concentrated in most nations, and shoes, paints, and fabric weaving show low concentrations in most nations. The fact that concentration levels are comparable across nations suggests that the technology of production, that is, economies of scale, rather than regulatory and competitive environments, or sheer luck, is the major determinant of market concentration. The industries with the highest concentration tend to have capital-intensive technologies whereas the industries with low concentration generally do not.

TABLE 5.9
THREE-FIRM CONCENTRATION RATIO FOR TWELVE IDENTICALLY DEFINED INDUSTRIES IN SIX NATIONS

Industry	United States	Canada	United Kingdom	Sweden	France	West Germany
Brewing	39	89	47	70	63	17
Cigarettes	68	90	94	100	100	94
Fabric weaving	30	67	28	50	23	16
Paints	26	40	40	92	14	32
Petroleum refining	25	64	79	100	60	47
Shoes (except rubber)	17	18	17	37	13	20
Glass bottles	65	100	73	100	84	93
Portland cement	20	65	86	100	81	54
Ordinary steel	42	80	39[a]	63	84	56
Antifriction bearings	43	89	82	100	80	90
Refrigerators	64	75	65	89	100	72
Storage batteries	54	73	75	100	94	82
Simple average	41	71	60	83	66	56

[a]Prenationalization value.

Source: Scherer, F. M., A. Beckenstein, E. Kaufer, and R. D. Murphy, *The Economics of Multi-Plant Operations: An International Comparison Study,* Cambridge: Harvard University Press, 1975, pp. 218–219 and 426–428.

---

[26]Economies of scale is an example of an *entry barrier.* The importance of entry barriers in explaining market structure is explored in Chapter 11.

The third striking feature is that markets in the United States tend to be less concentrated than in other nations, and markets in Sweden and Canada tend to be more concentrated. This makes sense. Recall from Figure 5.12 that as demand grows, more firms can "fit" into a market. Because the United States has more people and greater aggregate wealth, demand is likely to be greater in the United States. This allows more firms to enter, so that the largest firms have a smaller share of the total market. This is a key insight that sheds light on why U.S. markets that were once dominated by a few large firms (e.g., automobiles and steel) have seen a tremendous influx of significant new competitors during the last 30 years. Growing populations and incomes in Japan and Western Europe enabled manufacturers in these countries to achieve scale economies domestically. This has allowed them to compete on the basis of cost with older U.S. firms. At the same time, reductions in transportation and communication costs and in trade barriers have greatly lowered the costs of international trade. This enables manufacturers to obtain access to global markets, further increasing their ability to achieve scale economies. The number of firms in a given market in a given country increasingly depends on how many firms can fit in the worldwide market.

$\mathcal{E}$XAMPLE 5.4

HUB AND SPOKE NETWORKS AND THE STRUCTURE OF THE U.S. AIRLINE INDUSTRY

Nowhere is the role of scale and scope economies in shaping market structure more evident than in the U.S. airline industry. Prior to 1978, the industry was heavily regulated by the Federal Aviation Administration (FAA). Through its power to allocate interstate routes, the FAA was the prime determinant of market structure. The market was dominated by several major "trunk" carriers. For example, United Airlines controlled East–West interstate travel through the northern third of the nation, TWA the middle third, and American the lower third. The dominant presence of these airlines in the 1980s in Chicago, St. Louis, and Dallas-Ft. Worth, respectively, may be traced in part to the legacy of FAA regulation. Similarly, Eastern, Republic, and Western Airlines controlled North–South interstate routes and continued their strong positions in the early postderegulation period. Following deregulation of the industry in 1978, fierce price competition spurred on by newcomers such as People's Express and Midway Airlines forced all carriers to find ways to reduce costs. In short order, all of the major carriers emphasized hub-and-spoke networks. The growth of hubs such as United's hub at O'Hare Airport and American's hub at Dallas-Fort Worth has dramatically changed the way in which U.S. air passengers fly, with consequences for convenience and pricing.

Nowadays, individuals originating in a hub city often have little choice as to which airline they will choose. In some cities, a single airline accounts for over 60 percent of all departures. This has generally been the case for Pittsburgh (USAir's hub), Minneapolis (Northwest Airlines), Washington Dulles (United), and Dallas/Ft. Worth (American). These dominant airlines face little serious competition and often are able to raise prices (for routes of a given distance) over prices charged when there are two or more carriers flying the same route.

While residents of some hubs have seen a reduction in price competition, residents of smaller towns have actually seen an increase in competition. Recall from Example 5.1 the hypothetical traveler flying from Omaha to Louisville. Prior to deregulation, there may have been one carrier authorized by the FAA to fly that route. Nowadays, the traveler has several choices. He or she may fly direct on United (through O'Hare), American (through O'Hare or Dallas/Ft. Worth), or Delta (through Atlanta). Other carriers such as Southwest and USAir may also offer direct flights through their hubs. The result is that the Omaha to Louisville route is very competitve, and fares for two-leg journeys are likely to be lower than fares for non-stop flights of comparable distance originating from a hub.

"Exogenous" versus "Endogenous" Fixed Costs and Market Structure

Ordinarily, one thinks of the source of fixed setup costs as being technological; for example, a steel firm must incur the cost of blast furnaces and ingot casters before it can efficiently produce steel on a large scale, or an airline must invest millions in airport hub operations before it can efficiently transport passengers between many cities. Such fixed costs may be thought of as *exogenous*—any firm wishing to produce a large amount of output at low costs must incur these expenses. Traditionally, when economists emphasize the importance of fixed costs for determining market structure, they are usually referring to exogenous fixed costs. However, John Sutton points out that many fixed expenditures are not necessitated by production considerations.[27] Good examples are research and development aimed at product improvement, and advertising expenses aimed at increasing consumer awareness of one's product. These may be thought of as *endogenous* fixed costs because the firm can continue to produce any level of output it chooses without incurring them. The firm will choose to make these expenditures as long as the additional benefits in terms of increased sales revenue exceed the additional costs.

Sutton points out that endogenous fixed costs can be as important a determinant of market structure as exogenous fixed costs. Sutton finds supporting evidence by examining market structure for over 20 categories of food products, including bread, margarine, soft drinks, pet foods, and beer. Sutton estimates the fixed setup costs of production by estimating the cost of establishing a minimum efficient scale production plant in each of these industries. He then estimates the ratio of market

---

[27]Sutton, J., *Sunk Costs and Market Structure*, Cambridge, MA.: MIT Press, 1992.

size to these fixed setup costs to determine how many firms could "fit" into the market if the only fixed costs were those associated with production. He finds that in the United States and other countries, one might expect several dozen to several hundred firms in each food market.

Of course, most food categories in most nations are dominated by a few large firms. The U.S. frozen-food industry provides a good example. From a technological standpoint, the minimum efficient scale of production of frozen foods is small; according to Sutton, it is less than 1 percent of total U.S. industry size. Even so, each frozen-food submarket (e.g., frozen juices, frozen vegetables, etc.) appears to be dominated by a small number of brands. What accounts for this domination when scale economies appear to be minimal? The explanation is that each brand must make a substantial investment in developing an identity in its submarket (e.g., Minute Maid, Birds Eye). Sutton finds very little success for small to midsize firms in these segments because of the substantial cost required to establish comparable brand-name recognition. Interestingly, he finds that brand-name recognition in one segment does not spill over into other segments. He notes failed efforts in the 1970s by Sara Lee to enter the frozen entree market and by Stouffer to enter the frozen baked goods market. He does not offer an explanation for why reputation benefits of a brand name do not seem to carry over across markets.

Sutton contrasts the U.S. experience with that of the United Kingdom. There, a few grocery retailers (Sainsbury's, Marks and Spencer, and Tesco) dominate the industry. They have their own brand-name reputations that cut across food categories. (This is analogous to the broad brand-name reputation that Sears enjoys in appliances and Neiman-Marcus enjoys in apparel.) With an established and broad-based reputation, these retailers had relatively low costs of establishing name brand credibility in the frozen-food market, and have successfully introduced frozen-food products in competition with Minute Maid in juices and Birds Eye in vegetables.

The Survivor Principle

Writing about economies of scale, Nobel Prize recipient George Stigler said, "competition of different sizes of firms sifts out the more efficient enterprises. . . . An efficient size firm is one that meets any and all problems an entrepreneur actually faces."[28] These ideas have come to be known as the *survivor principle*. The allusion to ecology is intentional. Just as the fittest species survive in their natural environments, the fittest firms survive in their market environments. According to the survivor principle, industries with significant economies of scale should be dominated by large firms. Stigler constructed a simple test for the importance of economies of scale in a specific industry. The survivor technique identifies the optimal firm size as follows: Classify the firms in an industry by size, and calculate the share of industry output coming from each size class over time. If the share of a given class falls, it is relatively inefficient, and in general is more inefficient the more rapidly the share falls.

---

[28]Stigler, G., *The Organization of Industry*, Chicago: University of Chicago Press, 1968.

TABLE 5.10
SURVIVORSHIP TEST FOR U.S. BEER INDUSTRY

Listed Capacity Barrels (Thousands)	1959	1963	1967	1971	1975	1979	1983
10–100	68	54	36	21	10	10	15
101–500	91	72	44	33	19	13	12
501–1000	30	33	35	32	13	8	2
1001–2000	18	17	18	21	13	11	13
2001–4000	8	10	10	12	12	13	9
4001+	2	3	4	7	15	20	23

This test has been applied to many industries, including automobiles and hospitals. Table 5.10 illustrates the test for the brewing industry.[29] The table shows the distribution of brewery sizes (in terms of annual brewing capacity) during 1959–1986. (Microbreweries, which have capacities of less than 10,000 barrels annually, are excluded.) There has clearly been a shift away from breweries with capacities below 1 million barrels and toward larger breweries, especially those with capacities of 4 million barrels or more.

We conclude from Table 5.10 that economies of scale have increased in significance since 1959. A number of factors have contributed to this trend. Improvements in refrigeration make it possible to transport beer over longer distances, thus facilitating large-scale, centralized brewing. The most cost-effective bottling lines can fill 1,000 bottles per minute while modern canning lines can fill 2,000 cans per minute.[30] A brewery must have an enormous capacity to utilize this equipment economically. Finally, the importance of advertising in helping to create a nationwide, premium brand image has driven many regional brewers from the market.

While Stigler wrote about efficient-size firms, survival in competitive markets also requires that firms choose efficient methods of production, compensation systems, and product characteristics. It should be possible to identify a range of successful management practices by studying successful firms. The technique of scanning one's environment for keys to success underlies many popular management books, such as Tom Peters and Robert Waterman's *In Search of Excellence*.[31]

But when scanning an industry, it would be a mistake to restrict attention only to successful firms. As in the brewery example, it is necessary to examine all firms. Suppose, for example, that a firm observes that it advertised less than the *most*

[29]*Source:* Elzinga, K. J., "The Beer Industry," in Adams, W. (ed.), *The Structure of American Industry*, 8th ed., New York: MacMillan, 1990.

[30]Elzinga, K. J., "The Beer Industry," in Adams, W. (ed.), *The Structure of American Industry*, 8th ed., New York: MacMillan, 1990.

[31]Peters, T. and R. Waterman, *In Search of Excellence*, New York: Warner Books, 1982.

successful firms in its industry. The firm might increase its advertising budget. But what if the firm learned that it also advertised less than the *least* successful firms? The firm might instead conclude that advertising is not critical for its success or failure.

To summarize, the survivor principle may be used to assess the importance of a variety of firm characteristics, including firm size. The steps to survivor analysis are:

1. Classify the firms according to the characteristic in question.
2. Measure performance (e.g., market share, profits) of firms over time.
3. Identify classes of characteristics that show improving performance.

The survivor principle is reactive, rather than proactive. The firm may use it to identify important trends in management practices that it has missed, but cannot rely on it to identify new ways to beat its competitors.

CHAPTER SUMMARY

◆ A production process exhibits economies of scale if the average cost per unit of output falls as the volume of output increases. A production process exhibits economies of scope if the total cost of producing two different products or services is lower when they are produced by a single firm instead of two separate firms.

◆ An important source of economies of scale and scope is the spreading of indivisible fixed costs. Fixed costs do not vary as the level of production varies.

◆ In general, capital-intensive production processes are more likely to display economies of scale and scope than are labor or materials intensive processes.

◆ There are economies of scale in inventory management, so that processes with large volumes need to carry less inventory on a percentage-of-output basis than similar processes with small volumes.

◆ The physical property known as the cube-square rule confers scale economies on processes, such as warehousing, where costs are related to the geometric volume of the production "vessel."

◆ There are often economies of scale associated with marketing expense, research and development, and purchasing. Large-scale marketing efforts often have lower costs per message received than do smaller-scale efforts. The costs of large research ventures may be spread over greater output, although big size may be inimical to innovation. Small firms may obtain purchasing discounts comparable to those obtained by large firms by forming purchasing groups.

◆ Individuals and firms often improve their production processes with experience. This is known as learning. In processes with substantial learning benefits, firms that can accumulate and protect the knowledge gained by experience can achieve superior cost and quality positions in the market.

◆ Sometimes, large size can create inefficiencies. These may result from higher labor costs, bureaucracy, or dilution of specialized resources.

◆ A manager needs to know about the potential for economies of scale and scope to assess growth strategies as well as to predict and understand the structure of the market.

◆ In some industries, such as food retailing, firms may make expenditures to create scale economies that previously did not exist, such as expenditures to create and reinforce brand image.

◆ By studying the history of an industry, and examining the characteristics of successful firms, managers can assess the importance of size and other firm characteristics. The survivor principle states that the most efficient firms will gain market share at the expense of less efficient firms.

QUESTIONS

1. During the 1980s, firms in the Silicon Valley of Northern California experienced high rates of turnover as top employees moved from one firm to another. What effect do you think this turnover had on learning-by-doing at individual firms? What effect do you think it had on learning by the industry as a whole?

2. Historically, product markets were dominated by large firms and service markets by small firms. This seems to have reversed itself somewhat in recent years. What factors might be at work?

3. Trade barriers between European nations continue to fall. Many experts believe that this will allow businesses in different parts of Europe to merge. What effect, if any, will this have on competition with U.S. and Japanese firms in Europe and elsewhere? Does your answer depend on the industry under consideration?

DIVERSIFICATION

6

$\mathcal{B}$ecause firms may be able to reduce costs and improve marketing effectiveness by exploiting economies of scale and scope, most well-known firms are *diversified*—they produce in more than one output market. For example, McDonnell Douglas is a diversified manufacturer of aerospace equipment, and Sears is diversified both in its product line and in the locations its stores serve.

Since about 1950, many large and important firms have expanded well beyond the boundaries of any particular business area. Careful readers of Chapter 5 will be left scratching their heads trying to determine the economies of scope to be derived from combining the production of toasters and turbine generators (General Electric), salt and aerospace equipment (Morton Thiokol), electronics and cement (Martin Marietta), and seat belts and credit rating services (TRW). In analyzing these broadly diversified firms, which are sometimes called *conglomerates*, it is often difficult to specify what business the firm is in, what its key resources are, and what contribution is to be expected from corporate management of the individual business units.

This chapter examines corporate diversification. After describing its history in the U.S. economy, we explore the degree to which diversification can be explained by the pursuit of scale and scope economies. Most strategists agree that, in fact, a substantial percentage of diversifications are pursued for other goals. We explore what these goals may be, and then review the performance of diversified firms. The result is clear—the most successful diversifications combine businesses that can exploit scope economies. Diversification for other reasons tends to be less successful.[1]

◆ ◆ ◆ ◆ ◆ THE EXTENT OF DIVERSIFICATION

We begin our exploration of diversification by exploring how diversification has changed over the past century. Diversification activity seems to ebb and flow, and each new wave seems to have a different character, with different implications for efficiency.

A Brief History

Firms can diversify in a variety of ways, including internal development of new business areas, joint ventures with other firms, and acquisition of firms in unrelated lines of business. One can see the variety and extent of diversification by looking at periods during which the number of mergers was unusually high—the so-called "merger waves." There have been four such waves in the United States within the past century.

The first merger wave began after the worldwide depression of 1883, which left many capital-intensive industries with considerable overcapacity. The wave peaked around 1900 and ended shortly afterward. This wave involved roughly one-sixth of all U.S. manufacturing firms. It began with the "trust" movement of the 1880s, in which firms combined under the control of a trustee, who made decisions for the collective good of the trust. It continued in the 1890s, as firms combined using the new "holding company" structure and as the trust form became subject to increasing regulatory attack and was outlawed by the Sherman Antitrust Act of 1890. Some combinations, such as Standard Oil and United States Steel, were able to monopolize their industries.

A second, smaller merger wave occurred after World War I in the early 1920s. By that time, new antitrust laws, such as the Sherman Act and the Federal Trade Commission Act, discouraged grabs for monopoly power that failed to promote increased efficiency. As a result, many combinations stopped short of achieving 50 percent market share, and their industries resembled oligopolies instead of monopolies. Many other combinations in this wave involved vertical, rather than horizontal, integration. The formation and growth of General Motors had elements of both types of integration. In 1908, William Durant combined several independent auto makers, including Oldsmobile, Cadillac, and Pontiac, to form a potent competitor to Henry Ford. In 1919, Durant acquired Fisher Body to facilitate coordination of the vertical chain.

---

[1]There are several aspects to diversification, such as the structuring of diversified firms, the conduct of strategic planning, and the integration of parent and acquired firms, that are beyond the scope of this chapter. Some of these topics are considered in other chapters. For a comprehensive review of issues related to corporate diversification, see Ramanujam, V. and P. Varadarajan, "Research on Corporate Diversification: A Synthesis," *Strategic Management Journal*, 10, November–December 1989, pp. 523–553.

The reasons for the first two merger waves are easy to understand. Firms in the same market combined to reduce competition and achieve scale economies. The emergence of manufacturing giants tilted the calculus of the make-or-buy decision in favor of vertical integration. The Great Depression, which began in 1929, and American participation in World War II (1941–45) put a damper on merger activity until 1950. Antitrust laws, especially the Celler-Kefauver Act, were then toughened, further hindering both horizontal and vertical merger activity. By the late 1950s and early 1960s, managers understood that diversified combinations were legal, while horizontal and vertical mergers were more likely to encounter antitrust problems.[2]

By 1960, the pace of merger activity had again quickened. Unlike the previous waves, this third merger wave was characterized by increased levels of corporate diversification and produced large conglomerates selling extensive product lines in diverse markets. In addition, the generally prosperous state of the economy and the rising stock prices of large firms made the purchase of firms through merger less costly than diversification via internal growth. Mergers in the 1960s resulted in firms such as American Can, which sold cans, clothing, and financial services, and ITT, whose portfolio of businesses included life insurance, car rental, hotels, and vending machines.

There was scarcely a lull between the merger wave that created many of the conglomerates that we see today, and the fourth merger wave of the 1980s. The mergers of the 1980s were much different from their predecessors, however. Many cash-rich firms saw in a slumping stock market the opportunity to expand by buying up other firms at "bargain" prices. There is no better example than Philip Morris, which, flush with cash from its successful tobacco business, bought General Foods in 1985 and Kraft in 1988.

These bargain-seeking mergers were accompanied by a new type of acquisition, the "hostile takeover."[3] The 1980s was a time of great innovation in financial markets, exemplified by the development of so-called "junk bonds," that allowed individuals with little capital to make billion-dollar acquisitions by promising large returns to investors willing to take on unprecedented risks. Corporate raiders such as Boone Pickens, Irwin Jacobs, Henry Kravis, and Sir James Goldsmith, offered to pay owners of companies as much as twice the going market price for their shares. Despite the protests of management (whereby the takeover would be labeled "hostile"), shareholders frequently agreed to sell their shares to the raiders. Economists, such as Randall Morck and Robert Vishny, have argued that the fourth merger

---

[2]For an extensive discussion of these waves, see Fligstein, N., *The Transformation of Corporate Control*, Cambridge, MA: Harvard University Press, 1990, and also Attack, J. and P. Passell, *A New Economic View of American History*, 2nd ed., New York: W.W. Norton & Company, 1994, pp. 481–489.

[3]A hostile takeover (or hostile tender offer) involves two parts. The first is the *tender offer*, which is a direct offer to shareholders to purchase a quantity of shares at a given price. This offer succeeds or fails independently of the approval of a firm's managers. The second part, whether the offer is hostile or not, refers to whether top management of the acquired firm approves of the offer. If top management disapproves of the initial offer, the takeover attempt is hostile, regardless of whether approval is obtained for subsequent offers.

wave was a reaction to the wave of conglomerations that preceded it. Many acquisitions, including Goldsmith's hostile takeover of Crown Zellerbach and Jacobs' hostile takeover of AMF, were made expressly to break up conglomerates that had been formed earlier.[4]

"Relatedness" Over Time

Over the past century, firms seem to have become less focused in their traditional business activities. To document and evaluate this trend more carefully, Richard Rumelt developed the idea of *relatedness* to measure the degree of similarity across the portfolio of a firm's products, technologies, and markets. Rumelt measured relatedness according to how much of a firm's revenues were attributable to product market activities that had shared, or related, technological characteristics, production characteristics, or distribution channels. In measuring differences in diversification, he focused on three firm characteristics: the proportion of a firm's revenues (1) from its largest business; (2) from its largest group of related businesses; and (3) from the stages of a vertically integrated production process.[5]

Rumelt classified firms into four major categories according to the relatedness of their business activities. Rumelt's classification scheme is somewhat hard to follow, owing to the lack of a precise definition of relatedness. In some cases, it is easy to identify related activities, for example, when two lines of business have the same four-digit Standard Industrial Classification (SIC) code.[6] In other cases, Rumelt's classification seems more subjective, such as his decision to classify auto parts and industrial machine parts as related. Even so, Rumelt's work provides a unique view of the evolution of diversification in the United States.

Rumelt defines a *single business* firm as one with more than 95 percent of its business in a single activity or line of business. Examples of this type are Wrigley's Gum and Ashland Oil. A *dominant business* firm has between 70 percent and 95 percent of its annual revenues in a principal activity. Examples include Alcoa, the *New York Times*, and Philip Morris. A *related business* firm derives less than 70 percent of

---

[4]See Davidson, K.M., *Megamergers*, Cambridge, MA: Ballinger, 1985; Galambos, L. and J. Pratt, *The Rise of the Corporate Commonwealth*, New York: Basic Books, 1988; Shleifer, A. and R. W. Vishny, "Takeovers in the '60s and the '80s: Evidence and Implications," *Strategic Management Journal*, 12, Special Issue, 1991, pp. 51–60.

[5]This discussion of Rumelt's work is based on Rumelt, R., *Strategy, Structure, and Economic Performance*, Boston: Division of Research, Harvard Business School, 1974. For a review of research building on Rumelt's work, see Galbraith, J.R. and R.K. Kazanjian, *Strategy Implementation*, 2nd ed., St. Paul, MN: West Publishing, 1986.

[6]SIC codes were developed by the Bureau of the Census to classify industries. The SIC system identifies different products and services with a seven-digit identifier, with each digit representing a finer degree of classification. The four-digit SIC classification is the one most commonly used in scholarly research on industries. An example of a four-digit SIC industry is 2043, "Cereal Breakfast Foods," which includes both ready-to-eat cereals and prepared cereals, such as oatmeal.

its revenue from a primary area, but has other lines of business tangibly related to the primary area. Examples include Borg-Warner, Dow Chemical, and General Mills. Finally, an *unrelated business* firm derives less than 70 percent of its business from a primary area and does not have a substantial number of related lines of business. Examples include GAF, Martin Marietta, and TRW. These are commonly called "conglomerates."[7] Rumelt further subdivided the general categories of dominant, related, and unrelated diversification so that eventually his analysis had nine categories.[8]

Rumelt examined major corporations in 1949, 1959, and 1969. His findings, summarized in Table 6.1, confirm the increase in corporate diversification that occurred through the 1960s, and in particular, the emergence of the conglomerate. In 1949, 70 percent of all firms had a single-business or dominant-business focus. By 1969, only about 35 percent were similarly focused. In contrast, the proportion of firms with unrelated business portfolios increased from 3.4 percent of all firms in 1949 to 19.4 percent in 1969. Although Rumelt has not repeated his analysis for more recent years, there is general agreement that the trend toward unrelated diversification ended in the mid-1970s, and has been reversed as a result of the fourth merger wave.[9]

TABLE 6.1
GENERAL TRENDS IN CORPORATE DIVERSIFICATION: 1949–1969

Type of Business	1949	1959	1969
Single Business	34.5%	16.2%	6.2%
Dominant Business	35.5%	37.3%	29.2%
Related Business	26.7%	40.0%	45.2%
Unrelated Business	3.4%	6.5%	19.4%

Source: Rumelt, R., *Strategy, Structure, and Economic Performance*, Boston: Division of Research, Harvard Business School, 1974.

---

[7] This is the meaning we attach to conglomeration. In other lines of research, to be a conglomerate can simply mean to be diversified or it can be to diversify via merger and acquisition. We choose this particular meaning because it is most common in both the popular business press and in research on corporate diversification.

[8] Dominant business firms were subdivided into dominant-vertical, dominant-constrained, dominant-linked, and dominant-unrelated categories. Related business firms were subdivided into related-constrained and related-linked categories. Unrelated firms were subdivided into unrelated-passive and acquisitive conglomerate categories. For classification details, see Rumelt, R., *Strategy, Structure, and Economic Performance*, Boston: Division of Research, Harvard Business School, 1974, pp. 29–32.

[9] For an application of diversification ideas to service firms, see Nayyar, P., "On the Measurement of Corporate Diversification Strategy: Evidence from Large U.S. Service Firms," *Strategic Management Journal*, 13, 1992, pp. 219–236.

Gerald Davis, Kristina Dieckman, and Catherine Tinsley updated Rumelt's findings through 1990.[10] To measure diversification, they use an "entropy" measure. Entropy equals 0 for a firm that derives all of its sales from a single four-digit SIC category, and increases as the firm's sales are spread across more and more categories. For example, for a firm that derives 5 percent of its sales from each of 20 different lines of business, entropy ≈ 2.996. They find for Fortune 500 firms, entropy fell from an average of 1.00 in 1980 to an average of .67 in 1990; that is, these firms had become less diversified.

EXAMPLE 6.1

CHANGES IN DIVERSIFICATION FROM AMERICAN CAN TO PRIMERICA

American business history is filled with examples of firms that have reinvented themselves, sometimes more than once. The managers of many firms, when confronted with changes in technological and market conditions, refocused their businesses into areas less subject to environmental threats or else entered new businesses that forced them to acquire new organizational capabilities to enable their firms to better compete under changed conditions.[11]

Among contemporary businesses, American Can provides one of the most interesting examples of adjustment and refocusing. American had long been a manufacturer of tin cans and other metal containers for a variety of buyers, including major food and beverage companies. In Rumelt's typology, it was a single-product firm. The can industry, however, became increasingly unfavorable during the 1950s and 1960s for several reasons. First, can manufacturing technology was simple, so that American Can had many close competitors. Second, forward integration by aluminum producers and backward integration by food companies eroded American's market share and limited its ability to raise prices. Finally, the advent of plastic containers threatened the marketability of cans because plastics could be used in ways that cans could not.

Beginning in the 1950s, American Can diversified into businesses unrelated to can manufacturing, including paper products and printing. In 1977, the company

---

[10]Davis, G.F., K.A. Dieckman, and C.H. Tinsley, "The Decline and Fall of the Conglomerate Firm in the 1980s: A Study in the De-Institutionalization of an Organizational Form," Unpublished manuscript, Northwestern University, September 1993. For another example of a study using this type of entropy measure, see Amit, R. and J. Livnat, "Diversification, Business Cycles, and Performance," *Strategic Management Journal*, 9, March–April 1988, pp. 99–110.

[11]Best, M., *The New Competition: Institutions of Industrial Restructuring*, Cambridge, MA: Harvard University Press, 1990, chap. 1.

acquired Pickwick International, a record distributor, and its retail subsidiary Musicland. In 1978, it purchased the direct mail marketer Fingerhut. By 1980, American Can was an unrelated business firm.

In 1980 American Can began to refocus its entire portfolio of businesses. The first move was to acquire Associated Madison, a life insurance company. American proceeded during the 1980s to acquire several other financial services businesses, including Barclays Bank and Smith Barney. In 1986, American Can sold off its can business, and has since sold off other businesses. The restructuring of American Can was crowned in 1987 when the firm changed its name to Primerica. Today, Primerica is largely a financial services firm. In 1993, it merged with Travelers, adopting its partner's well-known name and umbrella logo.

American Can is not the only firm to diversify away from the business around which it was built to refocus on another business. USX, formally US Steel, today derives most of its revenue from oil, and remains in steel largely because of labor considerations. International Harvester (IH), once focused on farm equipment, diversified in the 1930s and 1940s into trucks and construction equipment. Facing bankruptcy in the 1980s, IH sold its farm equipment business (and the rights to the "International Harvester" name) to Tenneco and sold its construction equipment business to Dresser Industries. The firm that remained is called Navistar and is a world leader in medium and heavy truck production.

RATIONALES FOR DIVERSIFICATION ◆ ◆ ◆ ◆ ◆

Rationales for diversification range from traditional efficiency enhancement, such as the exploitation of economies of scope and the disciplining of bad managers, to more troubling explanations, stemming from the use (some would say abuse) of power by top management.

Economies of Scope

Clearly, many major firms have engaged in extensive diversification of their business portfolios over the past century. In Chapter 5 we suggested one motive: achieving economies of scope. To illustrate this motive, suppose there are economies of scope in the production of electronic calculators and digital watches. The definitions in Chapter 5 imply that it is less costly for a digital watch producer to move into the production of electronic calculators than it would be for a new firm or a firm producing products that are unrelated to digital watches or calculators to enter the market. Is the evidence consistent with the idea that diversification is driven by scope economies? The answer is that much diversification does not appear to be well explained by the pursuit of scope economies.

In analyzing diversified firms, Daniel Nathanson and James Cassano sought to determine whether most diversifications involved related businesses.[12] They reasoned that for diversification to achieve economies of scale and scope, businesses would have to be related in one of two ways: firms could derive economies either by selling *similar products* (i.e., similarity of production technology) or by selling to *similar markets* (i.e., similarity of consumers of the firm's products). In their research, Nathanson and Cassano were interested in assessing the degree to which diversified firms exploited economies along these two dimensions. They classified over 180 large multiproduct firms according to the degree of their "product diversity" and "market diversity." Firms with low levels of product and market diversity, they argued, would be better able to spread their capabilities and exploit scope economies than would firms with high levels of product and market diversity. If diversification is driven by a desire to exploit economies of scope, we should expect to see many more multiproduct firms with low levels of diversity than with high levels of diversity.

Table 6.2 presents Nathanson and Cassano's findings. Some firms, such as Schlitz, Maytag, and Zenith, are relatively undiversified on both dimensions. These firms produce multiple products, but their products are essentially in one line of business. These firms may be seen as pursuing economies of scale and scope in narrow markets with a common technology. At least as many firms, however, are highly diversified on both dimensions. Firms such as Union Carbide, Allis-Chalmers, and Gulf and Western, produce products that shared little technology and are sold to consumer groups that had little in common.

If we take the perspective that diversification is driven mainly by economies of scope, a possible explanation of the findings in Table 6.2 is that economies of scope can come from sources other than the sharing of a common technology or a common market of consumers. C. K. Prahalad and Richard Bettis argue that managers of diversified firms may see themselves as deriving economies of scope through their proficiency in spreading scarce top management skills across nominally unrelated business areas. They call this a *dominant general management logic*, which comprises "the way in which managers conceptualize the business and make critical resource allocations—be it in technologies, product development, distribution, advertising, or in human resource management." According to this view, corporate managers develop synergies for their firm by becoming skilled in the logic appropriate to their business mix. This is akin to the idea developed by Michael Goold, Alexander Campbell, and Marcus Alexander of the corporate "parenting" style.[13]

---

[12]Nathanson, D.A. and J. Cassano, "What Happens to Profits When a Company Diversifies?" *Wharton Magazine*, Summer 1982, pp. 19–26. Table 6.2 is adapted from Cassano, J., "The Links Between Corporate Strategy, Organization, and Performance," chap. 7 in Babian, H. and H. Glass, eds., *Handbook of Business Strategy: 1987/88 Yearbook*, Boston: Warren, Gorham, and Lamont, 1987.

[13]Prahalad, C.K. and R.A. Bettis, "The Dominant Logic: A New Linkage Between Diversity and Performance," *Strategic Management Journal*, 7, 1986: 485–501. Goold, M., A. Campbell, and M. Alexander, *Corporate-Level Strategy: Creating Value in the Multibusiness Company*, New York: John Wiley, 1994, p. 58.

TABLE 6.2
PRODUCT DIVERSITY AND MARKET DIVERSITY FOR SELECTED FIRMS

Low ← ——————————————————————— → Product

Market Diversity		SN	HRN	HRVN
Low	SBG	Wrigley, Schlitz, UARCO, Int'l Packings, Freeport Minerals, Southland Royalty / Deluxe Check Print, Copeland Corp, Nat'l Spinning, Consol. Packaging, United Refining	Signode, Florida Steel, General Shale, Danly Machine, Standard Register	Hormel, Marion Corp.
	HRBG	Hanes, Maytag, Valmont, Modine Mfg., Western Publishing, Leggett & Platt, Dan River, Debron	Arcata National, Houghton Mifflin, Zenith Radio, Tonn Corp., Pitney-Bowes, Xerox, Stand. Pres. Steel, Dunron Co., Clow Corp. / G.E. Bus. Equip., Owens Corning Fiberglass, Mine Safety Appl., Johnson Controls, Frantz Mfg., Loral Corp., Amer. Ship Build., AEL Industries	Exxon, Amerada-Hess, Stand. Oil (Ind.), Stand. Oil (Ohio), Sun Co. / Kerr-McGee, Bethlehem Steel, U.S. Steel, Armco Steel, Nat'l Steel
	RBG	R.R. Donnelly & Sons, Anderson Clayton	Wyman-Gordon, Merck & Co., Caterpillar Tractor, Clark Equipment, MPB, Optical Coat Labs., ARO, Pako, Recognition Equip.	Firestone Tire & Rubber, Central Soya, Kennecott Copper
	DBG		Albany Int'l., Pittsburgh-Des Moines Steel, Amer. Biltrite	Con Agra, Staley
	HDBG	Crouse-Hinds, Economics Labs	McGraw-Hill, Inmont	Mead, Great Northern Nekoosa
High	UBG			B.F. Goodrich, Uniroyal, Reynolds Metals, Alcoa, Alcan Aluminum, Scott Paper, Kimberly Clark

TABLE 6.2
PRODUCT DIVERSITY AND MARKET DIVERSITY FOR SELECTED FIRMS
(*Continued*)

Diversity ———————————————————————————————— High

	RN	DN	UN
SBG	Atlantic Steel / Franklin Mint Royster / U.S. Gypsum Nat'l Gypsum / Pentec Computer Flintkote / Technicon	Philips Ind. A.B. Dick	
HRBG	Tonka Corp. Nat'l Can NCR Cameron Iron Works Timken Stone Container	Gifford-Hill	Dentsply Int'l
RBG	Ashland Oil / Belden Kellogg / Norton H.J. Heinz / Barry Wright Green Giant / Memorex General Foods / Libbey-Owens-Ford Quaker Oats / Buttes Oil & Gas Sherrill Gordan / North Natural Gas Alex & Baldwin / Hazeline Peavey / AM R.J. Reynolds Ind. / Joy Mfg. Abbott Labs. / Ceco Upjohn / Lipe-Rollway	Brown & Sharpe Salem Owens-Illinois Armstrong Cork Amer. Hospital Supply	PET
DBG	Pillsbury Int'l Multifoods Anchor Hocking Narco Scientific Moog Inc. Int'l Harvester Gardner-Denver Cyclops	Nashua / MacMillan Union Pacific / Dynatectron Miles Labs / Air Products & Cooper Ind. / Chemicals East Gas & Fuel / Connelly Container Assoc. / Crane Co. Chesebrough-Pond's	Victor Comptometer
HDBG	General Mills / Pullman Leeds & Northrup / PPG Industries Carner Corp. / Ingersoll Rand McQuay-Perfex / Buckeye Int'l Kennametal, Inc. / Rogers Corp. Nalco Chemical / Dennison Mfg.	Robbins & Meyers / Ex-Cell-O Illinois Tool Works / Diamond Shamrock Pepsico, Inc. / Tenneco Rexnord, Inc. / American Can	McGraw-Edison Sperry Rand
UBG	Commercial Shearing Texas Instruments Dravo Kent-Moore Celanese DuPont Dow Chemical Pennwalt Dexter	Cutter-Hammer Honeywell General Signal Perkin-Elmer	AMF / North Amer. Union Carbide / Philips Corp. Olin / Eltra Amer. Standard / Westinghouse Studebaker-Worth / Vernitron Allis-Chalmers / IC Industries Borg Warner / SCM Rockwell Int'l / Northwest Ind. GE / Gulf & Western

TABLE 6.2
PRODUCT DIVERSITY AND MARKET DIVERSITY FOR SELECTED FIRMS
(*Continued*)

Product Diversity Categories	*Market Diversity Categories*
SN Essentially one product or product line *Examples*: Wrigley, Schlitz, Maytag	*SBG* Essentially one business market *Examples:* Wrigley, Schlitz
HRN Majority of business in one product or product line *Examples:* Caterpillar Tractor, Merck, McGraw-Hill, Xerox	*HRBG* Majority of business ($\geq$ 70%) in one business market *Examples:* Tonka, Valmont, oil, steel
HRVN Vertically integrated companies *Examples:* Oil, steel, rubber, paper	*RBG* Majority of business ($\geq$ 60%) in one business market or general industry *Examples:* Clark, General Foods, Memorex
RN Majority of business related by either raw materials, engineering, or technology *Examples:* Gardner Denver, McQuay Perfex, International Harvester	*DBG* Two to four unrelated business markets *Examples:* Moog, Nashua, Air Products
DN Majority of business accounted for by unrelated products but engaged in no more than seven unrelated areas *Examples:* Air Products, Tenneco	*HDBG* Five to six unrelated business markets *Examples:* Ingersoll-Rand, Excello, Illinois Tool Works
UN Majority of business accounted for by unrelated products with at least eight unrelated areas *Examples:* Gulf & Western, Northwest Industries, Rockwell International	*UBG* Seven or more unrelated business markets *Examples:* Dow, General Electric, Gulf & Western, Olin

This logic applies most directly when managers develop specific skills, say in information systems, and seemingly unrelated businesses rely on these skills for success. This logic is sometimes mistakenly applied by managers who develop particular skills but diversify into businesses that do not require them. For example, a large chemical company developed considerable expertise in the manufacture of capital-intensive products. It diversified into a product line that appeared to be related to the first line on the basis of consumer characteristics, but which in fact was much more labor intensive in its manufacturing process. The result was a troubled merger integration.

The dominant general management logic is also sometimes mistakenly applied by managers who perceive themselves as possessing above-average general management skills with which they can justify any diversification. Without detailed knowledge about the particular businesses involved in a diversification initiative, it is impossible to know at the time of the diversification whether the new business fits the "dominant logic" or whether the general manager involved is above average or not. In the absence of obvious relationships between businesses, such as those identified by Nathanson and Cassano, claims that economies of scope derive from the dominant general management logic are difficult to defend.

If we rule out the dominant general management logic, then Table 6.2 tells us that many diversified firms are not positioned to exploit scope economies. If this is true, then why do they diversify? In addition to economies of scope, three broad rationales for diversification are frequently offered:

- Financial synergies
- Economizing on transactions costs
- Pursuit of managerial (rather than firm) objectives

We discuss each of these rationales in turn.

$\mathcal{E}$XAMPLE 6.2

ACQUIRING FOR SYNERGY: BANKAMERICA BUYS CONTINENTAL

A recent example of strategic diversification in the banking industry is the acquisition of the Continental Bank by BankAmerica (BAC), which was announced in January of 1994. Although both corporations are commercial banks, this acquisition represents a diversification strategy, since it enables the Bank of America to build a significant presence and a strong portfolio of corporate banking clients in the Midwest. When the deal is completed, the BankAmerica/Continental merger will constitute one of the largest banking mergers ever, with BankAmerica paying approximately $1.9 billion. A premise of this chapter has been that, in order to create economies of scale and scope, businesses have to be related in one of two ways—products or markets. The BAC/Continental combination fits into both rationales for diversification very well.

BAC is a San Francisco bank that has always invested heavily in its corporate banking business. It has maintained a high credit rating since its founding in 1904 and is today the second largest American bank in terms of total assets (Citibank is first). The geographic concentration of BAC activities on the West Coast, however, has limited the bank's potential for expansion into the large commercial centers of the Midwest and East. BAC officers have frequently mentioned their intention to build a presence in the Midwest, and through its acquisition of Continental, BAC appears to have found a way to enter the Midwest corporate banking business.

Continental Bank, based in Chicago, is the second largest financial institution in the Midwest, with assets totaling $22.6 billion. Continental does business with most of the large firms headquartered in the Chicago area and generates more than a third of its revenues in Illinois. After almost going out of business in 1984, during which time the Federal Deposit Insurance Corporation (FDIC) temporarily took control of the bank's holding company, Continental has returned to modest prosperity and is admired by its competitors for smart marketing and innovative deal making. Continental recovered from near death by focusing on the commercial side of its business, which has given the bank strong profits in recent years. Continental has never fully recovered its credit rating, however, which has limited the bank in the services that it can provide to corporate clients.

In considering the synergies that each bank brings to this transaction, most observers believe that BAC's principal strength is its strong credit rating, which is critical to winning clients in high-margin corporate financial transactions. In addition to its credit rating, BAC brings billions of dollars of low-cost deposits, gathered through its multistate branch network, to fund commercial loans. Continental brings a strong client portfolio to the deal. Continental has a wide and strong client network in the Midwest, but has been unable to fully service these clients alone because of its poor credit rating, the consequence of its brush with failure in 1984. Continental has a stable and loyal customer base of over 2,000 long-term corporate clients. BAC, in turn, hopes to capitalize upon Continental's client relationships and use them as a channel through which additional products can be sold. BankAmerica Chairman Richard Rosenberg says that, counting on Continental's client base, the merger will boost BAC from second to first in U.S. corporate business in terms of the number of corporations that rely on BAC as their main bank. BankAmerica's commitment to investments in corporate banking business is shown in its plans to move the bank's corporate business headquarters to Chicago in early 1995.

How BankAmerica will implement the merger is an issue that has been raised by observers. In its past mergers, BAC has emphasized the consolidation of similar businesses to realize economies of scale. For example, in a 1991 deal totaling $4.7 billion, BAC acquired Security Pacific Corporation, creating a giant West Coast bank. The lessons BAC may have taken from this deal concern the high price paid, the high levels of employee turnover, and the loss of some corporate customers due to postmerger disturbances. The fundamental difference between the Security Pacific and Continental deals is that the Continental acquisition involves both geographic expansion and product diversification into corporate business. The Security Pacific deal was neither. This suggests an effort to avoid the difficulties associated with large business consolidations.

Both banks are already thought to have efficient operations. This, when combined with the synergistic goals of the merger, suggests that job loss due to the combination will be minimal. In terms of culture, however, there is a sharp contrast between BankAmerica's bureaucratic and hierarchical culture and Continental's freewheeling and entrepreneurial culture. Meshing these cultures may prove difficult and will be a major challenge in combining the banks.

Industry and financial analysts view the merger as an excellent strategic fit. Continental's strong customer relationships will benefit from BAC's network, product line, and credit rating. More than that, the deal brings financial efficiencies and an infusion of new talent to BAC. It is for these reasons that we see this combination as an example of productive diversification, based on plausible opportunities for scale and scope economies.

Financial Synergies

One argument for diversification is that the long-term success of a growing firm requires it to develop a portfolio of businesses that assures an adequate and stable cash flow with which to finance its activities. Such a portfolio strategy underlies the BCG growth/share matrix that we described in Chapter 5. In addition to boosting and stabilizing cash flows, the parent firm can use profits from one business to subsidize another. While portfolio strategies may smooth cash flows and prop up expanding or troubled businesses, they do not necessarily create additional value for the owners of the firms. This is so for several reasons.

First, shareholders of firms can diversify their own personal portfolios. They do not need corporate managers to smooth earnings flows for them. For example, shareholders of Philip Morris could have purchased shares of Kraft Foods to diversify their portfolios. By purchasing Kraft, Philip Morris failed to reduce shareholder risk any more than shareholders could have reduced it themselves. Indeed, many shareholders may have preferred not to be diversified in this particular way, which implies that the acquisition of Kraft may have made them worse off, absent any other efficiency gains from the purchase. One might argue that a corporation can diversify more extensively or more cheaply than shareholders themselves can. But this is highly questionable. It is usually less expensive for shareholders to diversify their personal portfolios through the purchase of stocks and bonds than it is for one large firm to purchase and integrate another firm. The one possible exception to this is that investors with large ownership blocks in a firm may be unable to fully diversify their holdings themselves and thus may value a firm's risk reduction efforts.[14]

The notion that the diversified firm can create value by serving as a source of investment funds for internal divisions is also questionable. Unless the parent firm is a bank or other financial institution, it presumably performs its financial functions as a byproduct of doing business in another area. While some firms are large enough and conduct enough transactions to develop a skill in banking (for example, GE Capital Corporation), a diversification strategy based on the "firm-as-banker" rationale can succeed only if the firm can outperform bankers in evaluating and servicing its investment opportunities. In other words, the firm-as-banker rationale can succeed if the diversifying firm is skillful at identifying firms that are undervalued by the rest of the market. This may be possible if the firm possesses special knowledge of the business being evaluated. But this is likely to be true only if the two firms are related, and therefore is not a good reason for unrelated diversification. Moreover, many firms that appear to use the firm-as-banker strategy contract out financial evaluation activities to independent firms, such as the Alcar

---

[14]See Shleifer, A. and R.W. Vishny, "Large Shareholders and Corporate Control," *Journal of Political Economy*, 1986, pp. 461–468.

Group. By relying on independent firms to perform the essential banking activity of financial evaluation, the firm-as-banker cannot possibly outperform the independent firms in this area.

Other adherents of the firm-as-banker strategy may believe that they are well above average at identifying undervalued firms. Firms that are being scrutinized for possible purchase by diversifying firms are known as *target* firms. A target firm is often being considered by several firms at once. The firm that acquires the target is generally the one that perceives it to be of the highest value, and is therefore willing to bid the most to acquire it. The managers of the acquiring firm may congratulate themselves for finding a "bargain," but they might also ask why other potential acquirers bid less than they did. Perhaps the target was less valuable than the acquirer's management thought.

This is an example of the more general phenomenon known as the *winner's curse*, in which the winning bidders in auctions and similar sales arrangements tend to be overly optimistic in their appraisal of the value of the item being sold. As Max Bazerman and William Samuelson point out in their article "I Won the Auction But Don't Want the Prize," unless the diversifying firm knows much more about the target than other bidders do, it will probably pay too much to "win" the bidding.[15] In addition, by bidding on the target, the diversifying firm signals the possibility of unexploited profits to other potential bidders. This may drive up the bidding, and further dissipate potential gains.

Even if financial synergies arguments are plausible (and we do not believe they are), they fail to justify a merger. Combinations that can exploit economies of scope can also get financial synergies. Thus, combinations for financial synergies alone will always be outperformed in the market by combinations that achieve both types of synergies.

Economizing on Transactions Costs

Even if economies of scope form the principal rationale for corporate diversification, the issue of transactions costs is also relevant if diversification occurs through merger or acquisition. A merger or acquisition is only a legal basis for combining firms. If the firms involved can exploit economies after the legal change in ownership, why couldn't they do so before the change? This question was asked in a seminal article on multiproduct firms by David Teece. He asked why scope economies cannot be achieved by coordinating several independent firms; why must business units be brought into the firm for economies to be realized?[16]

Teece argues that the multiproduct firm is an efficient choice when coordination among independent firms is complicated by transactions costs and the associated holdup problems. Recall from Chapters 3 and 4 that transactions costs are more likely to arise in relationships with independent firms when the production

---

[15]Bazerman, M. and W. Samuelson, "I Won the Auction But Don't Want the Prize," *Journal of Conflict Resolution*, 1983, pp. 618–34.

[16]Teece, D., "Toward an Economic Theory of the Multiproduct Firm," *Journal of Economic Behavior and Organization*, 3, 1982, pp. 39–63.

process involves specialized assets, such as human capital, organizational routines, or other forms of proprietary organizational know-how. In the absence of specialized assets, transactions costs are not likely to be a problem. In this case, market coordination may provide superior incentives and flexibility.

Many decisions regarding whether to diversify or operate as independent firms follow the logic of minimizing transactions costs. Consider the way higher education is organized. Undergraduate universities represent the "merger" of separate schools and departments, each of which could, in principle, offer educational programs located contiguously but operated completely independent of each other. Undergraduate students tend to take courses in many departments, however, creating economies of scale in locating the departments near each other, and near common dormitory, library, athletic, and other facilities. The common location of these facilities means that any investments by any department are, in part, relationship specific. In other words, the value of one department's investments depends on the actions taken by other departments. For example, even if the Northwestern University Department of Economics recruits several prize-winning teachers, their value in the classroom will not be fully realized if the university cannot attract high-quality students. This might happen if, say, the other departments were of low quality or refused to support actions aimed at enhancing the educational experience, such as funding for the library, student computer labs, and residence halls. Common "ownership" of Northwestern's various departments allows for a single policy regarding hiring and promotion, and investment in libraries, computer labs, and residence facilities.

Contrast the organization of undergraduate education into "diversified" firms with the way many paraprofessional training schools, such as schools for legal assistants or medical technicians, are organized. Students interested in paraprofessional training generally do not require courses in other areas, so there is no need to assure access to them. The paraprofessional school reaps the full benefits of its investments in plant and labor, and does not have to fear holdup by other schools that share in the student population. Given the absence of transactions costs facing paraprofessional schools, it is not surprising that many of them are freestanding; they offer training in only one area and do not invest in facilities that are shared by other schools.

A transactions-cost explanation for horizontal diversification is analogous to the explanation for vertical integration presented in Chapters 3 and 4. Both vertical and horizontal relationships often involve relationship-specific investments. When the self-interested behavior of independent firms jeopardizes the value of these investments, integration is a solution.

Influence Costs and Incentive Effects

Influence costs are another problem associated with vertically integrated firms that can also adversely affect diversified firms. Corporate management must evaluate each division to determine where to allocate resources. This evaluation is generally done during the course of the firm's strategic planning and capital budgeting processes. The success of these processes depends on the quality of information received from division heads, and the ability of corporate management to evaluate that information objectively, rather than let personal feelings affect resource allocation decision. To the extent that these decisions are affected by internal lobbying, resource allocations may be inefficient.

Resource allocation for independent firms is performed by the capital market. Capital market observers regularly monitor how the firm acquires and uses its funds. The firm's share price and bond ratings are constantly reevaluated on the basis of monitoring results. Poor judgment in the use of investment funds by managers will decrease stock prices and diminish access to additional capital. We do not expect fund managers to fall prey to influence costs, especially those associated with personal lobbying. Thus, capital markets are probably more efficient allocators of resources than corporate managers. This effect is attenuated for large firms that compete in stable product markets through the opportunities of the managers of these firms to control the use of retained earnings.

Corporate management of diversified firms must also use control systems that reward division managers on the basis of division profits, and discipline managers by tying their careers to the attainment of business unit objectives. Capital markets also provide incentives for managers to act in the best interests of shareholders, for example, to provide large financial rewards for superior returns and penalties for inferior returns. Shareholders are usually reluctant to replace poor performing managers, however, so that the manager of an independent firm may have greater job security than the division manager in a diversified firm. This might promote greater efficiency within the diversified firm. Of course, this argument presupposes that corporate management has the proper incentives to work in behalf of shareholders. If inefficient managers of small independent firms are hard to replace, then managers of large diversified firms must be even harder to replace, especially if a takeover is required to bring about the change.

Diversification Mode

The issue of *how* to diversify—that is, *diversification mode*—is separate from the questions of whether and to what extent to diversify. Our concern is largely with the latter two issues. However, if one grants that diversification has to do jointly with the potential for scope economies and the transactions costs of market versus nonmarket options for obtaining those economies, then a variety of nonmarket options are feasible for attaining diversification objectives. Alternatives to traditional mergers and acquisitions include internal development, joint ventures, and different types of informal or formal strategic alliances and minority participation.[17] These alternatives may achieve the sought-after scope economies without suffering from diseconomies of scope that limit the optimal breadth of the organization. Despite recent widespread attention in the popular business press given to alterna-

---

[17]Chapter 4 defines and discusses joint ventures and strategic alliances.

tive modes of diversification, there has been little systematic research to date to show the conditions under which one mode is preferable to others.[18]

A related set of issues that we cannot consider in detail concerns changes in the levels of diversification in a firm's business portfolio. Since the combination of business units in a diversified firm depends in part on transactions-cost considerations, then changes in the conditions faced by diversified firms will change the severity of transactions-cost problems and possibly make reduced levels of diversification more desirable. Reducing levels or changing patterns of diversification are reasonable strategic options for diversified firms facing changing environments. For example, in the past decade, a variety of conglomerates have refocused their strategic positions and restructured their portfolios of businesses. Jack Welch's change in strategic focus at General Electric after 1980 is an example. Kodak's decision to divest its chemical, pharmaceutical, household products, and medical-testing device businesses in 1993 and 1994 is another. American Can's metamorphosis out of the metal can business altogether and into specialty financial services discussed in Example 6.1 is still another. The possibilities for realizing additional returns from refocusing a firm's diversification profile make divestitures and spin-offs viable components of a firm's strategy. Michael Useem makes the general case that the restructuring of large corporations in the 1980s was a response to changes in the activities and influence of capital market actors that allowed for much greater stockholder control over professional managers.[19]

Managerial Reasons for Diversification

The rationales discussed above presume some efficiency-enhancing objective for diversification, whether it is exploiting economies of scope or achieving transactions-cost economies. A third reason for diversification is what we call managerial. Managerial reasons for diversification are oriented toward maintaining or enhancing the position of executives making diversification decisions, rather than efficiency or enhancing shareholder wealth. Diversification based on managerial reasons is

---

[18]For a review of research on internal diversification, see Simmonds, P.G., "The Combined Diversification Breadth and Mode Dimensions and the Performance of Large Diversified Firms," *Strategic Management Journal*, 11, September 1990, pp. 399–410, and Kazanjian, R. and R. Drazin, "Implementing Internal Diversification: Contingency Factors for Organization Design Choices," *Academy of Management Review*, 12, 1987, pp. 343–354. For examples of research on joint ventures, see Kent, D., "Joint Ventures vs. Non-Joint Ventures: An Empirical Investigation," *Strategic Management Journal*, 12, July 1991, pp. 387–393; Harrigan, K., "Joint Ventures and Competitive Strategy," *Strategic Management Journal*, 9, March–April 1988, pp. 141–158; and Kogut, B., "Joint Ventures: Theoretical and Empirical Perspectives," *Strategic Management Journal*, 9, July–August 1988, pp. 319–332.

[19]Useem, M., *Executive Defense: Shareholder Power and Corporate Reorganization*, Cambridge, MA: Harvard University Press, 1993. For an overview of research on corporate restructuring, see Bowman, E. and H. Singh, "Corporate Restructuring: Reconfiguring the Firm," *Strategic Management Journal*, 14, Special Issue, Summer 1993, pp. 5–14.

efficient for managers, but not for shareholders. That executives would make such decisions is not surprising. Indeed, much of the literature on organizations takes management's proclivity toward self-serving behavior as the basis for the corporate governance problem. If shareholders are unable to judge the effectiveness of managers, then managers need not always act in their best interest. As we discuss in Chapter 16, the potential for divergence between management action and shareholder interest is greatest in an environment of incomplete and imperfect information. For an example of how managers can make strategic decisions to pursue their own self-interest rather than the interest of shareholders, consider the situation faced by top managers in a firm targeted for a hostile takeover. These managers realize that if the hostile acquisition goes through, they are likely to lose their jobs. They may be able to elude takeover by agreeing to be acquired by a third firm. In such a "friendly" deal, incumbent managers may be able to retain their positions and perquisites for a longer time than they could under a takeover. Shareholders stand to lose, however, because management will promote the tender offer of the friendly acquirer, regardless of which offer is higher. As long as shareholders are not fully informed about the value of the competing tender offers, managers have a chance to succeed with this plot to retain their jobs.

Another common managerial rationale for diversification is the pursuit of growth, which argues that managers diversify when it is easier to acquire new sales than to develop them internally. As Dennis Mueller has pointed out, diversification buys growth that cannot be achieved through internal development.[20] Growth is pursued because the pecuniary and nonpecuniary advantages to managing large growing firms are appealing to managers, although not necessarily to shareholders. For example, growth may provide increased career development opportunities for managers and employees, even if it reduces profitability for shareholders. Growth is not necessarily unprofitable or inefficient, although it can be. Again, as long as shareholders are not fully informed about the benefits to them of growth through diversification, managers can pursue their own objectives at shareholder expense.

If diversification is a strategy for growth, then we may expect to see greater unrelated diversification by firms with fewer opportunities for internal growth or related diversification. This is consistent with the increase in diversification that followed passage and enforcement of the Celler-Kefauver Act in 1950, which made related acquisitions more difficult. During this time conglomerate mergers increased in frequency, while horizontal mergers decreased.

Yakov Amihud and Baruch Lev suggest another reason why managers pursue unrelated acquisitions: to avoid getting fired.[21] They observe that shareholders are unlikely to replace top management unless the firm performs poorly relative to the overall economy. To reduce the risk of job loss, managers must therefore reduce

---

[20]For the principal statement of this rationale, see Mueller, D., "A Theory of Conglomerate Mergers," *Quarterly Journal of Economics*, 82, November 1969, pp. 643–659.

[21]Amihud, Y. and B. Lev, "Risk Reduction as a Managerial Motive for Conglomerate Mergers," *Bell Journal of Economics*, 12, 1981, pp. 605-617.

the risk of poor performance. One way to do this is through unrelated acquisitions. Simple statistics tell us that the performance of a highly diversified firm is likely to mirror the performance of the overall economy, and is therefore less likely to lead shareholders to fire management. To support their point, Amihud and Lev show that manager-controlled firms engage in more conglomerate acquisitions than owner-controlled firms. While these acquisitions reduce the risk of job loss for top management, they may not benefit shareholders, who may reduce their own financial risk by managing their portfolio of investments, for example, by purchasing mutual funds.

A Positive View of Managerial Motives

Thus far, it appears as if unrelated diversification may fulfill managerial objectives at the expense of shareholders. Several authors have offered rationales for unrelated diversifications that support both managerial and shareholder goals. Debra Aron points out that unrelated diversification can improve incentives by reducing the cost of motivating managers under pay-for-performance schemes.[22] Gordon Donaldson and Jay Lorsch argue that managers will be reluctant to make firm-specific investments if they do not see the prospects for advancement within the firm. They view diversification as a substitute for a steeply rising wage structure as a means for promoting managerial motivation. Donaldson and Lorsch also argue that diversification offers managers opportunities for lateral movement.[23] Of course, if the divisions are unrelated, it is not clear if there is any value to lateral movement, apart from the dominant general management logic that we have already discussed.

The persistence of diversification despite vigorous antitrust enforcement, coupled with the poor performance of conglomerates (described in the next section of this chapter) and the weak rationales for unrelated diversification, suggest that managerial rationales help us explain diversification activity. The possibility that managers may protect and expand their personal empires at the possible expense of shareholders is both troubling and intriguing. We believe, of course, that managers should work to enhance shareholder wealth, but we recognize that circumstances have historically permitted managers to do otherwise.

If managers do entrench themselves at shareholder expense, then profit opportunities will arise for shareholders to more vigorously monitor management performance, and for outsiders to replace self-aggrandizing managers and offer shareholders a better value. One principle of economics is that when profit opportunities exist, individuals will take advantage of them. The fourth wave of corporate acquisitions that began in the mid-1970s is a testament to this principle.

---

[22]For a detailed presentation of this point, see Aron, D.J., "Ability, Moral Hazard, Firm Size, and Diversification," *RAND Journal of Economics*, 19, Spring 1988, pp. 72–87. The use of pay-for-performance to motivate managers is discussed in detail in Chapter 16.

[23]Donaldson, G. and J. Lorsch, *Decision Making at the Top*, New York: Harper Collins, 1983.

The Fourth Acquisition Wave and the Market for Corporate Control

What limits the ability of managers to use corporate resources for their own benefit and neglect the interests of shareholders? Put a little differently, if managerial reasons for diversification are plausible, what keeps the attention of managers on the goals of owners and on improving efficiency within the firm? While boards of directors may provide some control, the discretion of top managers in slating boards, controlling elections, and providing board members with information can often limit the ability of boards to act independently. If top managers stray too far from the interests of owners, then shareholders, or actors external to the firm, must step in to replace them.

This is the rationale expressed by the architects of hostile takeovers, including Goldsmith, Pickens, Icahn, and Jacobs. These corporate "raiders" publicly claimed that they were replacing entrenched, inefficient management to benefit shareholders. While their claims were hotly contested by those who thought the raiders were little more than speculators, the idea of disciplining errant managers by corporate takeover has a long history and has come to inform many studies of corporate control changes.

The classic statement of this rationale for takeovers is provided by Henry Manne, who argued for the existence of a "market for corporate control" (MCC).[24] According to this idea, control of corporations is a valuable asset that exists independently of economies of scale or scope. If this is so, then a market for this control exists and operates such that the main purpose of a merger is to replace one management team with another. The management team in charge of a firm must continually generate maximal value for shareholders. If a team fails to generate sufficient value, this poor performance will be noticed by observers of the firm, and competing management teams can displace the incumbents via takeover. This threat of takeover will discipline management and thus attenuate the governance problems in firms in ways that improve on what is possible through boards of directors, which incumbent teams can control. In addition, the potential for competitive bidding once a tender offer has been made will ensure the highest valuation for firms and the largest returns to shareholders.

A corporate raider may need specialized knowledge and/or resources to bring to a combination, however, or else the expected benefits from the takeover may not be achieved due to poor implementation or may even be bid away in the auction that follows the initial tender offer. In addition, if the poor performance of the target is due to industrywide factors, the attempts of a raider without specialized resources to realize value from a takeover may actually signal new sources of value to industry rivals.[25] These considerations imply that the market for corporate control

---

[24]Manne, H., "Mergers and the Market for Corporate Control," *Journal of Political Economy*, 73, 1965, pp. 110–120.

[25]Chatterjee, S., "Sources of Value in Takeovers: Synergy or Restructuring—Implications for Target and Bidder Firms," *Strategic Management Journal*, 13, 1992, pp. 267–286.

argument needs to be supplemented by a scope argument. It further implies that, without a specialized resource to bring to a combination, the winner of the auction in the market for corporate control will have overpaid and be subject to the "winner's curse."[26]

The MCC Perspective, Hostile Takeovers, and Managerial Opportunism

The MCC perspective has proved appealing to individuals involved in merger activity and to academics who study mergers. It has significantly altered the rules, and even the language, of mergers and acquisition activity in the 1980s and 1990s, giving terms such as "white knights" and "shark repellents" whole new meanings.[27] It has also motivated important research focusing on stock price valuations of corporate control transactions. The threat of takeover provides a plausible limit on opportunistic managerial behavior, and the idea of a corporate control market is especially convincing for "bustup" hostile takeovers, in which the takeover is paid for by selling off the constituent business units of the acquired firm, in effect undoing the conglomerate. A good example of this is the takeover of the AMF corporation by Irwin Jacobs.

Several studies have found characteristics of hostile takeovers that are consistent with the predictions of the MCC perspective. For example, Randy Morck, Andrei Shleifer, and Robert Vishny found that targets of hostile takeovers tend to be in declining or rapidly changing industries where managers have failed to properly adjust the scale and scope of operations.[28] They argue that managers may be protecting their domain of control. Michael Jensen found that prior to takeovers, managers of oil industry firms continued costly explorations despite declining oil prices.[29] Shleifer and Vishny report that prior to takeovers, managers of airlines were unwilling to cut union wages from unrealistically high levels that had been reached under regulation. Lastly, in a paper titled "Do Bad Bidders Make Good Targets?" Mark Mitchell and Kenneth Lehn find that corporate raiders profit by acquiring and busting up firms that had previously pursued unprofitable diversification strategies.[30]

---

[26]Shleifer, A. and R.W. Vishny, "Takeovers in the 60's and the 80's: Evidence and Implications," *Strategic Management Journal*, 12, Special Issue, 1991, pp. 51–60.

[27]A white knight is a friendly acquirer sought by a firm under threat of hostile takeover as an alternative to the hostile acquirer. A shark repellent is a measure, such as the amendment of corporate bylaws, that firms can take to make takeover less attractive. The lexicon of takeovers is too broad to repeat in detail here. Useful summaries can be found in Davidson, K.M., *Megamergers*, Cambridge, MA: Ballinger, 1985 and Commons, D.L., *Tender Offer*, Berkeley, CA: University of California Press, 1985.

[28]Morck, R., A. Shleifer, and R.W. Vishny, "Characteristics of Targets of Hostile and Friendly Takeovers," in Auerbach, A. (ed.), *Takeovers: Causes and Consequences*, Chicago: University of Chicago Press, 1989.

[29]Jensen, M.C. and R.S. Ruback, "The Market for Corporate Control: The Scientific Evidence," *Journal of Financial Economics*, 1983, pp. 5–50.

[30]Mitchell, M. and K. Lehn, "Do Bad Bidders Make Good Targets?" *Journal of Political Economy*, 98, 1990, pp. 372–92.

To the extent that the MCC perspective helps explain diversification behaviors, its implications for managers of both acquired and acquiring firms are clear. Scrutiny by the external environment limits the abilities of managers to entrench themselves and profit from their control of large firms at the expense of shareholders—the market can help mitigate the problems that have been issues for corporate governance ever since the inception of the modern corporation and have been especially difficult for those individuals who run these large firms and are thus outside the purview of the firm's bureaucratic controls. This market-based limit on opportunistic managerial behavior does not mean that managers will not try to enrich themselves. It suggests that the most effective way for managers to do so is to pursue strategies that enrich shareholders and managers.

It is unclear whether this role of disciplining poorly performing managers accounts for more than a small number of mergers. Even so, the threat posed by the MCC may deter many managers from blatant pursuit of self-interest. Recent research strongly confirms that managers who fight off hostile takeovers do not serve their shareholders' interests. Hostile acquirers usually offer shareholders of the target firm a substantial premium above the pre-tender offer market value of the firm. Several studies conclude that when management of a target firm successfully fights off a hostile takeover, the target's market value quickly falls back to the pre-tender offer level.[31] These findings belie the oft-heard claim by target management that hostile acquirers actually undervalue the firms' assets, and that their bids should be rejected in the name of increasing shareholder value. In spite of such findings as these, management at many firms have fought to change corporate control laws, for example, by including "poison pill" provisions, to frustrate the workings of the corporate control market. Perhaps in response to such changes, shareholders at some firms have sued boards of directors for failing to properly monitor management. The concentration of shareholders into large ownership blocks controlled by mutual funds has provided another check on management abuse.

Diversification, Wealth Redistribution, and Long-Run Efficiency

The MCC argument hinges on the ability of capital market observers to identify and replace inefficient management teams so that new managers can realize efficiency gains. But the MCC argument fails to clarify who benefits and loses from efficiency gains. If the gains from the replacement of management teams come from improvements in operating economics, then shareholders, employees, and others with a stake in the firm (called *stakeholders*) can win. The firm will be more profitable and less risky, which makes it possible for multiple stakeholders to benefit with minimal losses. If takeovers occur without a basis in operating synergies, however, gains may accrue largely to new owners at the expense of workers, buyers, suppliers, or local communities. This happens because, since no new wealth is

---

[31]See Jarrell, G., J. Brickley, and J. Nutter, "The Market for Corporate Control: The Empirical Evidence Since 1980," *Journal of Economic Perspectives*, 2, 1988, pp. 49–68.

being created, gains to some parties must come at the expense of others. If this is the case, then takeovers redistribute rather than create wealth. This raises obvious concerns about equity, and, as Andrei Shleifer and Lawrence Summers point out, may also raise concerns about long-run economic efficiency.[32]

Shleifer and Summers argue that wealth redistribution may adversely affect economic efficiency when the acquired wealth is in the form of quasi-rents extracted from stakeholders who have relationship-specific investments in the target firm. Recall from Chapters 3 and 4 that after an individual makes a relationship-specific investment, he or she expects to receive quasi-rents that exceed the amount of the investment. These quasi-rents may take the form of wages in excess of what the worker could earn elsewhere, promotion opportunities, or perquisites such as a company car. Once the investments are sunk, however, he or she will proceed with the deal if quasi-rents are positive. Firms facilitate relationship-specific investments. A relative benefit of firms over markets is the ability of workers and managers to rely on implicit versus explicit contracts in settling disputes within the firm. Indeed, it is precisely the inability to efficiently forge sufficiently complete contracts that makes firms necessary in the first place.

Employees (or providers of other factors) who develop firm-specific assets become vulnerable to having quasi-rents taken by new owners, who are not bound to honor the implicit contracts made with old owners. This can occur because employees cannot readily sell firm-specific assets to other employers at a comparable price to that which they currently receive. New owners can reduce that price substantially before the market value of the firm-specific asset is reached and the employees consider leaving the firm.

Two examples may be useful. First, employees who work for a long time with a single firm develop assets that are valuable chiefly to their firm, such as knowledge of how to operate the firm's specialized equipment or how best to make use of the firm's administrative procedures. These resources are not readily saleable on the job market, since other firms have their own specialized equipment and practices with which new employees must become familiar. A new owner could break longstanding assurances of job security and reduce wages significantly before the employee would find it worthwhile to look for a new job.

Second, consider the relationship between a city or town and a major production facility located there that is part of a much larger concern. (The negotiations between Anaheim, California and Walt Disney over the expansion of the original Disneyland come to mind.) In this situation, municipal administrators could easily be tempted to provide infrastructure improvements, such as new sewers and roads, as incentives to keep the plant in the area or induce the owner of the plant to locate new facilities there. Once those improvements are made, however, they cannot be easily unmade. Roads and sewers cannot be moved elsewhere. The firm, however, could move elsewhere, such as United Technologies did when it moved

---

[32]Shleifer, A. and L.H. Summers, "Breach of Trust in Hostile Takeovers," in Auerbach, A.J. (ed.), *Corporate Takeovers: Causes and Consequences*, Chicago: University of Chicago Press, 1988, chap. 3, pp. 33–68.

its American Bosch manufacturing plant from Springfield, Massachusetts to Columbia, South Carolina. Firms may threaten to move to seek tax abatements and other changes in the conditions under which they do business, thereby reducing the pay that the town receives as a provider of infrastructure.

While takeovers motivated by redistribution may be rational for an acquirer in the short term, they may have adverse consequences for firms in the long term. In the short term, the raider obtains gains from redistribution. In the long term, employees of the firm, as well as other parties who do business with the firm, will be aware of the firm's past behavior and may be unlikely to invest in firm-specific assets in the future, unless they are adequately compensated for their risk of future redistribution. If the raider had foresight, it would anticipate such problems and view them as acceptable costs of doing the deal.

Shleifer and Summers are more concerned about the effects of hostile takeovers on the stakeholders of firms other than the target. These stakeholders may observe the upheaval in other firms and conclude that their own jobs are in jeopardy and that it no longer pays to make firm-specific investments.[33] If this were to happen, the productivity of these workers would decline and the economy as a whole would be worse off because of hostile takeovers. Even if the raider had foresight, it would not count these as costs of the deal because they are largely borne by firms other than the target.

Two concerns have been raised about the Shleifer and Summers argument. The first is that firms do not have to be acquired to extract quasi-rents from stakeholders. As long as wages, promotions, and so forth are not dictated by contract, a firm can always renege on implicit agreements when it believes that its wages have gotten out of hand. Shleifer and Summers counter that firms that have honored commitments for many years often find it difficult to break them. For example, the firm's middle managers may have risen through the ranks and have friendships with other workers. These friendships cause middle managers to act in their staff's best interests, even when the firm could profit by slashing wages. This assures workers that their investments in firm-specific knowledge will be rewarded. Similarly, managers of firms located in a community for many years may live there and might oppose moving the firm for personal reasons, even if it makes good business sense. This assures the community that their investments in infrastructure are secure. An outside acquirer does not have such ties to workers and community, and will be less reluctant to break implicit agreements. Absent such trust, workers and firms must rely on contracts to assure that they will not be held up. For example, communities that make investments in infrastructure to attract new businesses frequently specify penalties for firms that leave before a specified length of time.

The second concern is that the argument is difficult to test and as a result, its practical implications are unclear. The claim that the activities of an acquirer are redistributing rather than creating wealth can easily be countered by the response that the actions taken (firing employees; salary reductions) improved the efficiency

---

[33]Example 3.3 from Chapter 3 provides a vivid illustration of this point in the context of the acquisition of the Trans Union Corporation by the Marmon Group in 1981.

of the firm and that the employees affected were overpaid or even redundant. Such a dispute is, in principle, resolvable. One could identify the standards for efficient behavior for the employees and determine if the actual employees met these standards. However, if the productivity of workers was easily ascertainable and their performance was easily monitored, the transactions-cost issues at the heart of the Shleifer and Summers argument probably would not exist.

◆ ◆ ◆ ◆ ◆ EVIDENCE ON THE PERFORMANCE OF DIVERSIFIED FIRMS

We have discussed several reasons why diversification is potentially profitable. Even so, there are many who are skeptical of the ability of diversification strategies to add value. Perhaps Michael Goold and Kathleen Luchs, in their review of 40 years of diversification activity, sum up the skeptic's viewpoint:

> Ultimately, diversity can only be worthwhile if corporate management adds value in some way and the test of a corporate strategy must be that the businesses in the portfolio are worth more than they would be under any other ownership.[34]

Studies of the performance of diversified firms, undertaken from a variety of disciplines and using different research methods, have consistently found that while diversification up to a point can be efficient, the sources of performance gains for diversified firms are unclear. Realizing efficiencies from diversification can also be difficult. Extensive diversification is often associated with poorer performance.

In this section we review some of the research that led Goold and Luchs and others to question the value of diversification.

Studies of Diversified Firm Performance Using Accounting Data

A first group of researchers has studied performance in terms of some measure of capital productivity, such as return on invested capital, by comparing the performance of firms in different diversification categories. These studies found the relationship between performance and corporate diversity to be unclear. Profits were more likely to be determined by industry profitability, coupled with how the firm related new businesses to old ones, rather than by diversification *per se*.[35] These results have persisted in spite of a variety of methodological issues, including the

---

[34]Goold, M. and K. Luchs, "Why Diversify? Four Decades of Management Thinking," *Academy of Management Executive*, 7, 1993, pp. 7–25.

[35]The classic study on this point is Christensen, H.K. and C.A. Montgomery, "Corporate Economic Performance: Diversification Strategy versus Market Structure," *Strategic Management Journal*, 2, 1981, pp. 327–343. Also see Bettis, R.A., "Performance Differences in Related and Unrelated Diversifiers," *Strategic Management Journal*, 2, 1981, pp. 379–383.

measurement of both diversification and performance, as well as the appropriate time frame to use in assessing changes in performance.

Some examples of these studies may be helpful. Richard Rumelt found several systematic relationships between diversification and firm performance. In particular, moderately diversified firms had higher capital productivity. Firms with moderate to high levels of unrelated diversification, however, had moderate or poor productivity. Cynthia Montgomery reconfirmed Rumelt's results for more recent years, using different measures of diversification.[36] Daniel Nathanson found that diversification is associated with deteriorating performance. In many cases, corporate performance never surpassed the levels obtained prior to the initiation of a diversification strategy. Noel Capon and his colleagues found that firms that restricted their diversification to narrow markets performed better than did broadly specialized firms, presumably due to their learning particular market demands.[37] Donald Hopkins examined unrelated diversifications, as well as diversifications based on shared markets or technologies. He found that market-based diversifications performed the best of the three groups, but did not outperform undiversified firms.[38]

Stock Price Studies of Diversified Firms

A second group of diversification studies has considered the reaction of the stock market to the announcement of diversification activities, such as mergers, acquisitions, divestments, and hostile takeovers. This research sought to assess the extent to which stock prices reflected gains upon the announcement of an action that were abnormally above or below those that would have been predicted in the absence of the announcement. These studies presume some degree of market efficiency in the assimilation of information about firms into share prices. Thus, the market value of a firm at any point in time is assumed to reflect the best estimate of the firm's future stream of profits. If a firm's stock price increases when it announces that it intends to acquire another firm, this is assumed to reflect the strategic value created by the acquisition. A decrease in share value would indicate that the market believes the acquirer is probably overpaying for the target.

These stock price studies, many of which are summarized in Michael Jensen and Richard Ruback, considered the reactions of the stock market to announcements of corporate control changes.[39] Three important results emerge:

---

[36]Montgomery, C.A., "The Measurement of Firm Diversification: Some New Empirical Evidence," *Academy of Management Journal*, 25, 1982, pp. 299–307.

[37]Capon, N., J.M. Hulbert, J.U. Farley, and L.E. Martin, "Corporate Diversity and Economic Performance: The Impact of Market Specialization," *Strategic Management Journal*, 9, January–February 1988, pp. 61–74.

[38]Hopkins, H.D., "Acquisition Strategy and the Market Position of Acquiring Firms," *Strategic Management Journal*, 8, November–December 1987, pp. 535–548.

[39]Jensen, M.C. and R.S. Ruback, "The Market for Corporate Control: The Scientific Evidence," *Journal of Financial Economics*, 11, 1983, pp. 5–50.

- The combined value of parent and target firms tended to rise following the announcement of a combination, leading to the claim that mergers were efficient.

- A preponderance of abnormal returns accrue to target firm shareholders (as high as 30 percent, on average).

- Acquiring firm shareholders receive small and statistically insignificant returns (4 percent or less).

These results suggest that acquisitions do have the potential to create value to acquirers—either by exploiting synergies, removing ineffective managers, or redistributing wealth—but that the wealth is bid away as several firms bid for control.

These results generated a second set of studies to more precisely identify the how different types of diversification might lead to different allocations of wealth among acquirer and target. Harbir Singh and Cynthia Montgomery found that acquirers had greater returns when they targeted related firms than they did from unrelated acquisitions.[40] Indeed, the gains to unrelated acquirers appeared to be completely bid away during the auction for the target.

As with the research based on Rumelt's work, stock price studies of diversification have found that diversifying mergers and acquisitions can be associated with performance gains. Mergers can create value for parent firms, both in terms of increased stock returns and reduced risk. If performance gains are to be realized, however, diversification must involve related business areas—diversification must make use of specialized and intangible resources that the parent brings to a combination. Firms that fail to diversify this way have poorer results, consistent with an inefficient and/or managerially motivated strategy. In one of the most comprehensive stock price studies of diversification, Sayan Chatterjee and Birger Wernerfelt find that firms with highly specialized resources engage in more related diversification strategies and achieve superior results over firms that diversify making use of nonspecialized resources, such as cash.[41]

Long-Term Performance of Diversified Firms

A third set of studies concerned with the performance of diversified firms has compared results of the mergers of the 1960s with those of the 1980s. The intuition of this work is that the true time horizon for assessing the results of diversification is longer than is commonly taken in research and that the longer-term performance of diversified firms has been poor.

---

[40]Singh, H. and C.A. Montgomery, "Corporate Acquisitions and Economic Performance," *Strategic Management Journal*, 8, July–August 1987, pp. 377–386.

[41]Chatterjee, S. and B. Wernerfelt, "The Link Between Resources and Type of Diversification," *Strategic Management Journal*, 12, January 1991, pp. 33–48.

Michael Porter considered the corporate portfolios of 33 major diversified firms and found that over one-third of all acquisitions between 1950 and 1986 are eventually divested.[42] Over half of acquisitions into new businesses are eventually divested. Since divestiture is nearly always for poor performance, this result indicates the failure of acquisition policies. Porter suggests basing diversification strategies on three factors: (1) industry attractiveness; (2) cost-effective entry; and (3) acquirer ability to make a combined firm more valuable, based on identifiable corporate resources that can create value when spread over new divisions—he suggests that diversification decisions be grounded on clearly defined and focused strategic analysis.

Andrei Shleifer and Robert Vishny summarize and compare the evidence on the merger waves of the 1960s and 1980s.[43] They conclude that the merger wave of the 1980s, which is characterized by more related acquisitions and by corporate refocusing, can be best understood as a broad correction to the conglomerate mergers of the 1960s. This implies some capital market imperfections in how conglomerate mergers were evaluated in the 1960s, and highlights the importance of government antitrust policy in merger activity, since the mergers of the 1980s coincided with a period of relaxed antitrust enforcement, which permitted a degree of horizontal and vertical combination that had not been possible in the 1960s. In a related study, Constantinos Markides looked at mergers in the 1980s and identified overdiversified firms. The returns to these firms from refocusing were significant and positive, consistent with Shleifer and Vishny's conclusion that the mergers of the 1980s corrected the mistakes of the 1960s and refocused overdiversified firms.[44] Robert Hoskisson and Michael Hitt echo this idea of refocusing by arguing that diversified firms need to reduce their scope of activities to reach a point where profitable diversification is possible.[45]

Larry Lang and Rene Stultz provide further evidence that overdiversification is inefficient. They use "Tobin's q" to measure how well firms deployed their assets. (Tobin's q is the ratio of the market value of a firm to the replacement cost of its tangible assets.) They found that Tobin's q of specialized firms was 10 percent higher than for diversified firms in the same industries.[46]

---

[42]Porter, M.E., "From Competitive Advantage to Corporate Strategy," *Harvard Business Review*, May–June 1987, pp. 43–59. See Ravenscraft, D.J. and F.M. Scherer, *Mergers, Sell-Offs, and Economic Efficiency*, Washington, D.C.: Brookings Institution, 1987, for a large-scale study with similar results.

[43]Shleifer, A. and R.W. Vishny, "Takeovers in the '60s and the '80s: Evidence and Implications," *Strategic Management Journal*, 12, Special Issue, 1991, pp. 51–60.

[44]Markides, C.C., "Consequences of Corporate Refocusing: *Ex Ante* Evidence," *Academy of Management Journal*, 35, 1992, pp. 398–412.

[45]Hoskisson, R.E. and M.A. Hitt, *Downscoping: How to Tame the Diversified Firm*, New York: Oxford University Press, 1994.

[46]Lang, L. and R. Stultz, "Tobin's q, Corporate Diversification, and Firm Performance,"

The poor long-term performance of diversified firms is often attributed to their lack of investment in research and development. The failure to make and manage these investments leads diversifying firms to be unresponsive and noninnovative in the face of environmental changes and foreign competition. While there is some evidence of differences between diversifying and nondiversifying firms regarding R&D expenditures, whether diversification is harmful to corporate innovation has not been established.[47]

In summary, three different lines of research on the performance of diversified firms have led to similar overall conclusions. Diversification can create value, although its benefits *per se* relative to nondiversification are unclear, due to industry effects and other factors. Among diversifying firms, there is no clear association between simple measures of diversity within a business portfolio and overall corporate performance. However, firms that diversify according to a core set of resources and with an eye toward integrating old and new businesses tend to outperform those firms that do not work toward building interrelationships among their units. This is consistent with the generally accepted idea that defensible diversification will combine some basis in scope economies with transactions-cost conditions that make organization of diverse businesses within a single firm efficient, relative to joint ventures, contracts, alliances, or other governance mechanisms.

◆ ◆

EXAMPLE 6.3

DIVERSIFICATION AND CORPORATE PERFORMANCE FOR PHILIP MORRIS

Performance issues for diversified firms can be made clearer by considering how they arise for specific firms. Philip Morris has engaged in a large and widely followed diversification program since the mid-1960s.[48] It has always highlighted innovation. Not a part of the tobacco cartel at the turn of the century, by 1950 it was last among major firms in the industry in terms of relative market share. It thus had little to lose and much to gain from going about its business differently. It pioneered the use of discount cigarette brands in the 1930s. It was the first to introduce filter tip cigarettes with a brand initially targeted at women and named

---

[47]See Hall, B.H., "The Effect of Takeover Activity on Corporate Research and Development," in Auerbach, A.J. (ed.), *Corporate Takeovers: Causes and Consequences*, Chicago: University of Chicago Press, 1988, pp. 69–100. Also see Hitt, M.A., R.E. Hoskisson, R.D. Ireland, and J.S. Harrison, "Effects of Acquisitions on R&D Inputs and Outputs," *Academy of Management Journal*, 34, 1991, pp. 693–706.

[48]The discussion that follows is based on several public sources of information, but also draws heavily on the superb case study of the tobacco industry by Robert Miles and Kim Cameron, *Coffin Nails and Corporate Strategies*, Englewood Cliffs, NJ: Prentice-Hall, 1982.

Marlboro. Philip Morris was also a pioneer in the marketing of low-tar cigarette brands, such as Merit and Marlboro Light.

A period of significant environmental turbulence for the cigarette industry began in 1950, with the publication of the initial report linking smoking and lung cancer. This was followed in 1953 by the report from the Sloan-Kettering Institute on smoking and cancer in laboratory animals and in 1954 by a key article in *Reader's Digest* that put the link between smoking and lung cancer before the public. Considerable further research and several reports of the U.S. Surgeon General on smoking and health have built upon these initial reports.

In their industry history, *Coffin Nails and Corporate Strategies*, Robert Miles and Kim Cameron detail the response of tobacco firms to this environmental threat, both in terms of product-market diversification, lobbying to prevent government restrictions on smoking, and research support for alternative positions on the cigarette-cancer linkage. Philip Morris began diversifying in the 1950s and initially focused on small companies in a mixed set of unrelated businesses, ranging from paper products and shaving products to hospital supply, chewing gum, and real estate development.

A major change in the Philip Morris diversification took place in 1969, when the Miller Brewing Company was acquired for more than $200 million. This acquisition signaled an effort to buy firms that were large enough to become leaders in their industries and that could benefit from Philip Morris applying its marketing and distribution skills. Miller had traditionally occupied a small high-quality niche in the beer market (it advertised itself as the "champagne of bottled beers"). In seven years (and after early losses), Miller had been turned around in a campaign highlighted by increased marketing efforts that transformed industry practice and made Miller second in the industry. In 1978, Philip Morris acquired Seven-Up in an apparent attempt to repeat the success obtained with Miller. This deal was followed by the acquisitions of General Foods in 1985 and Kraft in 1988.

How does one assess the performance of Philip Morris in light of this diversification program? Has it been successful or not? On the surface, Philip Morris would appear to be a success. Its stock price has been consistently strong during this period: Philip Morris is now included in the Dow-Jones index of 30 leading industrial firms. Its sales growth has also been strong. Ranked 218th on the *Fortune* 500 in 1955, by 1980 it had climbed to 49th. Its nontobacco group alone would rank 111th. Philip Morris also ranked 32nd in net earnings in 1979.

The effectiveness of this diversification strategy, however, is different from the effectiveness of the firm as a whole. The Seven-Up acquisition failed, and the business was sold (the international portion to Pepsico and the domestic portion spun off to join with Dr Pepper). The food businesses have grown slowly. Even the success of Miller has to be qualified, since it took seven years to produce and has not been sustained in recent years.

Perhaps the most interesting issue about the Philip Morris diversification, however, arises when one considers that before the Kraft deal in 1988, nearly 80 percent of its earnings came from a single cigarette brand, Marlboro (long the world's most profitable brand). Even today, around 60 percent of corporate profits arise from cigarettes. In what ways can the noncigarette businesses of Philip Morris be seen as contributing to its performance? They do not contribute to profits in any way near what one would expect, given the billion-dollar size of these deals. They have not been high-growth businesses. They do not appear to benefit from association with Philip Morris. Indeed, the Kraft-General Foods group within Philip Morris does not actively utilize its link with Philip Morris in major corporate promotions.

An alternative explanation for diversification is that it involves stable businesses that produce predictable cash flows. As such, these businesses are desirable vehicles for reinvesting the substantial profits of the tobacco business of Philip Morris in an environment in which reinvestment in tobacco is unlikely to affect market share. The plausibility of this alternative story was borne out recently when Philip Morris announced significant price reductions in its cigarette brands, in response to the increasing market share of generic and discount brands. This signal of vulnerability in its base business caused a substantial drop in the Philip Morris share price. Even after more than two decades of major diversification, the key factors affecting the firm still concern its core tobacco business.

CHAPTER SUMMARY

◆ A firm is *diversified* if it produces in more than one output market. Most large and well-known firms are diversified to some extent. Broadly diversified firms (*conglomerates*) have portfolios of businesses that go beyond conventional ideas of scope economies. In these firms, it is often difficult to identify the core skills of the corporation.

◆ Firms can diversify in several ways, ranging from internal growth, to strategic alliances, to joint ventures, to formal combinations via merger or acquisition. Merger and acquisition have been the principal modes of diversification, although alternative modes, such as alliances and joint ventures, have become increasingly popular in the 1980s and 1990s.

◆ The extent of diversification has increased dramatically since 1950, largely in two merger waves—the first in the 1960s highlighting the growth of conglomerates and the second in the 1980s highlighting more focused diversification and the deconglomeration of broadly diversified firms.

◆ It has been difficult to measure the extent of diversification. Most approaches have considered the similarity of businesses in a firm's portfolio according to some measure of technological or market relatedness—that is, according to how similar the businesses are in terms of the products sold or the customers served.

◆ Scope economies provide the principal rationale for why firms diversify. These economies can be based on market and technological factors, as well as on managerial synergies, due to a "dominant general management logic." Financial synergies, such as risk reduction or increased debt capacity, comprise a related rationale that emphasizes corporate management's role as a banker and financial advisor to its business units.

◆ Transactions-cost economizing is another important part of a diversification rationale. This is because the diversifier must consider the costs of a particular mode of diversification in addition to the benefits that are obtained. Common ownership, for example, is justified only when transactions-cost problems make less formal combinations, such as strategic alliances, infeasible.

◆ Diversification may also occur for managerial reasons, such as the smoothing of firm performance to reduce the risk of job loss. The "market for corporate control" limits the extent to which firms can diversify for primarily managerial motives. Firms that do not pursue the interests of shareholders can become vulnerable to hostile takeover. Hostile takeovers may not be efficiency-enhancing, however, if they redistribute rather than create value for shareholders.

◆ Research on the performance of diversified firms has shown mixed results. Where diversification has been effective, it has been based on economies of scope among businesses that are related in terms of technologies or markets. More broadly diversified firms have not performed well, and many conglomerates refocused their business portfolios during the 1980s. While mergers have led to increases in shareholder value, these increases have largely gone to acquired firm shareholders. Over a longer time frame, active diversifiers have divested many of their acquisitions.

QUESTIONS

1. Many managers justify diversification as a way to diversify risk. Use the ideas in Chapters 2 through 4 to explain why diversification may diversify the manager's job risk. Shareholders can, of course, diversify risk themselves, for example, by holding a diversified portfolio of stocks and bonds. Under what conditions can a diversified firm spread the risk to its shareholders to a greater extent than the shareholders can themselves?

2. With the growing number of firms that specialize in corporate acquisitions (e.g., Berkshire Hathaway, KKR), there appears to be a very active market for corporate control. As the number of specialist firms expands, will control arguments be sufficient to justify acquisitions? Do you think that relatedness will become more or less important as competition in the market for corporate control intensifies?

3. Suppose you observed an acquisition by a diversifying firm and that the aftermath of the deal included plant closings, layoffs, and reduced compensation for some remaining workers in the acquired firm. What would you need to know about this acquisition to determine whether it would be best characterized by value creation or value redistribution?

4. How is expansion into new and geographically distinct markets similar to diversification? How is it different?

5. There is a large literature assessing the performance of diversified firms. Consider the following recent diversifications:

   a. Seagram's (a major distiller) sale of its holdings in DuPont and subsequent acquisition of entertainment giant MCI.

   b. Viacom's (a major cable TV company) merger with Blockbuster Video.

How would you assess the success or failure of these deals? To what extent would you rely on the same indicators of performance? To what extent would you use different measures?

6. How might a firm's diversification strategy affect how it chooses to resolve make-or-buy decisions? How can you tell whether the businesses owned by a firm are better off than they would be under different forms of ownership?

PART TWO

MARKET AND
COMPETITIVE ANALYSIS

INDUSTRY ANALYSIS

7

$\mathcal{C}$hapters 7 through 11 are concerned with the economics of industries and market competition. Although the roots of these fields can be traced to the 1930s or earlier, they had little impact on business strategy until Michael Porter published a series of articles in the 1970s that culminated in his pathbreaking *Competitive Strategy*.[1] In this book, Porter presented a convenient framework for exploring the economic factors that affect the profits of an industry. Porter's main innovation is the classification of these factors into five major forces. A *five-forces* analysis systematically and comprehensively applies economic tools to analyze an industry in depth. Nearly two decades old today, the five-forces approach is flexible enough to accommodate new economic concepts as they emerge. This chapter reviews the five-forces approach in the context of the economics of firms and industries. Although a rigorous five-forces analysis requires the application of principles to be developed in Chapters 8 through 11, we illustrate its usefulness here, by examining four industries: Hospitals, Photocopiers, Tobacco, and Banking.

The five forces, as represented in Figure 7.1, include:

- Internal rivalry
- Entry
- Substitute products
- Supplier power
- Buyer power

Internal rivalry is in the center because it may be affected by each of the other forces.

---

[1]Porter, M., *Competitive Strategy*, New York: Free Press, 1980.

FIGURE 7.1
THE FIVE-FORCES FRAMEWORK.

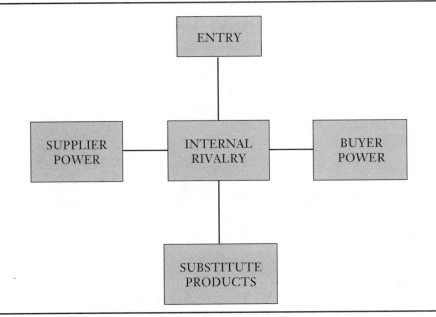

One assesses each force by asking "Is it sufficiently strong to reduce or eliminate industry profits?" Because the framework is comprehensive, the process of working through each of the five forces requires the systematic evaluation of all the significant economic factors affecting an industry. This process is often its own reward, because while doing it one develops a deeper understanding of these factors, independent of the ultimate conclusions of the five-forces analysis.

The five-forces framework has several limitations. First, it is not especially concerned with the magnitude or growth of demand. The framework assumes that demand is sufficiently large for firms to be profitable under the most favorable competitive conditions. Second, it focuses on a whole industry, rather than on that industry's individual firms. Before using the framework it is necessary to define the industry—the discussion of market identification in Chapter 8 will be helpful here. The framework is useful for assessing the likely profitability of an *average* firm in an industry. Chapters 12 through 15 of this text provide some tools that firms may use to outperform their industry norm. Third, the framework does not explicitly account for the role of the government, except when the government is a supplier or buyer. The government as a regulator can profoundly affect industry profitability, and could be considered a sixth force. Fourth, the five-forces analysis is qualitative. For example, an analysis of industry structure may suggest that the threat of entry is high, but the framework provides little guidance about how to estimate the probability of entry. Because it is qualitative, the framework is especially useful for assessing trends—that is, for determining whether industry profitability is likely to increase or decrease.

THE ECONOMICS OF THE FIVE FORCES ◆ ◆ ◆ ◆ ◆

Some of the economic principles that underlie the five-forces framework have already been developed in Chapters 2 through 6. Others will be developed in greater detail in Chapters 8 through 11. This section provides an overview of several key concepts as they apply to the five forces.

Internal Rivalry

Internal rivalry refers to the jockeying for share by firms within a market. As will be discussed in detail in Chapters 8 through 10, firms may compete on a number of price and nonprice dimensions. Price competition erodes profits by driving down price-cost margins. Nonprice competition erodes profits by driving up fixed costs (e.g., new product development) and marginal costs (e.g., improvements in product quality). To the extent that firms can pass cost increases along to consumers in the form of higher prices, nonprice competition is less likely to erode profits than is price competition.

Price competition is likely to be especially fierce when:

- There are many sellers in the market.
- Consumers regard products as homogeneous.
- Switching costs are low.
- Terms of sales transactions by firms are secret or only imperfectly observed by other firms.
- Sales orders are large and are received infrequently at irregular intervals.
- The industry has excess capacity.

An assessment of internal rivalry requires an analysis of market structure, product differentiation, the nature of the sales process, and capacity utilization. The role of the consumer is important. Internal rivalry heats up when consumers are *motivated* to shop around because they perceive that the potential savings may be great, and are *capable* of shopping around in the sense that they can readily evaluate different alternatives.

Theories of competition can be complex, so firms without many apparent competitors may be constrained to set competitive prices. History may offer some guide about how to resolve ambiguities. Firms that have a history of coexistence without price rivalry (e.g., because of "facilitating practices" such as price leadership, or signaling, as we will discuss in Chapter 10) are likely to fare better than firms that have undergone repeated price wars. When firms do manage to avoid fierce price competition, such as in the competition between anti-ulcer medications Zantac and Tagamet, substantial profits are possible.

Entry

Profits are a siren call to investors, and often lead to entry. Entry erodes incumbents' profits in two ways. First, entrants steal their business, essentially dividing up market demand among more sellers. Second, entrants decrease market concentration, thereby heating up internal rivalry and reducing price-cost margins. As will be discussed in detail in Chapter 11, entry barriers may be structural, such as:

- Economies of scale and scope
- Limited access to essential resources or channels of distribution
- Patents
- The need to establish brand identity or overcome established identities of incumbents
- Other cost disadvantages, for example, an incumbent's learning economies

Entry barrier may also be strategic, for example, when incumbents maintain excess capacity or threaten to slash prices. Exit barriers may also serve as entry barriers, because they raise the financial stakes for newcomers who ultimately fail.

A historical perspective is useful for assessing entry. An industry with a higher-than-average rate of entry in the past may have structural features that facilitate future entry. A historical analysis of entry can be misleading, however. Technological change may reduce entry costs in industries with historically high structural barriers. In some cases, there has historically been little entry because the other economic forces are fierce and industry profitability is low. Were these other economic forces to subside and profits return, entry could well eliminate them.

Substitutes

Substitutes erode profits in the same way as entrants by stealing business and intensifying internal rivalry. A unique consideration is that *new* substitutes frequently represent new technologies, whose costs are likely to decline over time because of the learning curve. Thus, new substitutes may pose large threats to established products and incumbent firms in the near future, even if they seem harmless now.

Determining whether a product is in the same market as existing products (and therefore contributes to internal rivalry), a new entrant, or a substitute depends on how one defines the market. Different analysts may use different definitions. This may require the use of different economic tools. For example, recall from the Economics Primer that the degree of competition among firms within an industry is captured by the firm-level price elasticity of demand. In contrast, the threat posed by substitutes is captured by the industry-level price elasticity of demand. As long as analysts comprehensively examine all three forces, using the appropriate data for each one, they will arrive at the same conclusions about the threats to industry profits, although they may attribute them to different forces.

Supplier Power and Buyer Power

Supplier power refers to the ability of input suppliers to negotiate prices that extract profits from their customers. The extreme case where suppliers have *no* power occurs when the input supply industry is perfectly competitive. Input suppliers must then act as price takers and prices are set by the interaction of supply and demand. Recall from Chapters 2 through 4 that upstream suppliers have power to erode industry profits if (a) they are concentrated, or (b) their customers are locked into relationships with them because of relationship-specific investments.

An input supplier with monopoly power can raise prices when its target industrial market is faring well, thereby extracting a share of the industry's profits. The converse also applies—a supplier may lower prices when its target market is doing poorly. Consistent application of both pricing strategies will permit the supplier to extract much of its target market's profits without driving that market to extinction. Historically, unions have used this strategy to increase workers' wages. Similarly, an input supplier with a relationship-specific investment in an industry can squeeze profits from a successful industry and ease the burden on an industry in trouble.

Supplier power should not be taken as synonymous with the "importance" of an input to a firm or an industry. For example, jet fuel is an important input in the airline industry, constituting about 20 percent of the operating costs of a typical airline. However, jet fuel is purchased in a competitive market in which suppliers act much like price takers. If the fortunes of the airline industry were to soar, jet fuel suppliers could not renegotiate contracts to raise the price of jet fuel and extract airline profits, except to the extent dictated by the forces of supply and demand.

Buyer power is analogous to supplier power. It refers to the ability of individual customers to negotiate purchase prices that extract profits from sellers. Buyer power is obviously related to internal rivalry, but the two competitive forces are conceptually distinct. In many markets, individual buyers have little power to negotiate with sellers, but the markets are nevertheless price competitive. This is true of many retail markets and commodities spot markets. Price-cost margins are low in these markets because sellers compete for the business of price-sensitive consumers. The willingness of consumers to shop for the best price is a source of internal rivalry, not buyer power.

On the other hand, in many industrial markets, fierce internal rivalry and buyer power can go hand-in-hand. In these markets, each transaction is the result of a bargain struck between a sales agent and a purchasing agent, and the contract price for identical products may differ significantly from one customer to another. Buyers may be powerful in this context if (a) there are few of them, and (b) a seller is locked into a relationship with the buyer because of relationship-specific investments.

Strategies for Coping with the Five Forces

A five-forces analysis identifies the threats to industry profits that all firms in the industry must cope with. Firms may pursue several strategies to do this. First, firms may *position* themselves to outperform their rivals, by developing a cost or differentiation advantage that somewhat insulates them from the five forces. Chapter 12 discusses positioning strategies in detail. Second, firms may *identify an industry segment* in which the five forces are less severe. For example, in the 1970s, Crown Cork and Seal served manufacturers of "hard-to-hold" liquids, a niche market that was far less competitive than the metal can segments served by industry leaders American Can and Continental Can. As a result of this and similar strategies, Crown earned significantly higher rates of return. Third, a firm may try to *change the five forces*. Firms may try to reduce internal rivalry by creating switching costs, such as when a manufacturer requires consumers to use its parts to keep its warranty in force. This creates a cost—in the form of a voided warranty—to consumers who purchase parts from another supplier. Firms may reduce the threat of entry by pursuing entry-deterring strategies. Firms may try to reduce buyer or supplier power by tapered integration. In the examples that follow, we will see how firms in a variety of industries have attempted to cope, with varying degrees of success, with the five forces.

◆ ◆ ◆ ◆ ◆ APPLYING THE FIVE FORCES: SOME INDUSTRY ANALYSES

The best way to illustrate the five-forces framework is by example. In this section we perform four detailed industry analyses.

Hospital Markets Then and Now

Hospitals have experienced great financial difficulties in recent years. Hospital bankruptcies were once rare. Since the mid-1980s, however, an average of 80 hospitals a year have gone bankrupt (about 1.5 percent of the nation's total each year). Many community hospitals struggle to stay solvent, and average operating margins are at or near all-time lows. Hospitals are examining new and risky strategies to compete. A comparison of the five forces at two points in time, 1980 and today, readily demonstrates the problems that hospitals have grown accustomed to.

Hospital Markets: Internal Rivalry

We begin our assessment of internal rivalry by defining the hospital's market. We consider the *product market* to be acute medical services. These services include maternity and surgical care, and complex diagnostic services. While other sellers offer many of these services—outpatient surgery centers are a good example—we will treat offerings of other sellers as substitutes in this analysis. This decision is not essential to our conclusions, and illustrates the flexibility of the five-forces framework. (We would be remiss, of course, if we did not consider outpatient surgery at all.) Some consideration of the *geographic market* is essential. Hospital services are largely sold in local markets, and it would be a mistake to assume that internal rivalry is the same everywhere. The courts in recent antitrust cases have concluded that some cities, such as Rockford, Illinois and Roanoke, Virginia, are fairly well-defined geographic markets in the sense that few patients come from outside these areas, and few local residents go to outside hospitals. We will assess internal rivalry in the Chicago metropolitan area. This area also has few patient inflows and outflows. If anything, the area has several distinct submarkets, but these are difficult to identify with certainty.

There are about 70 community hospitals in the Chicago market.[2] One typically associates such a large number of competitors with fierce internal rivalry. But several factors mitigated against fierce rivalry among Chicago hospitals in 1980. At that time, hospitals were selected by patients and their admitting physicians. Most patients had insurance that paid for the bulk of the hospital bill, so that price was not important. Moreover, hospital pricing was arcane. Hospitals set prices for each individual service, from the bed day to the X-ray. This made it difficult for consumers to comparison shop, for they had to compare many different prices, and did not know how many of each item they would need to purchase. Physicians were equally unconcerned about prices. Finally, insurers usually paid whatever the hospital charged, or some margin above costs, without regard to price or cost differences across sellers. We conclude that consumers were neither motivated nor able to shop around for the best prices in 1980, so that price competition was virtually nonexistent.

Patients and physicians might have been sensitive to differences in hospital quality, for example, differences in mortality rates. In 1980, it was difficult for patients to compare quality at different hospitals, except for such relatively unimportant things as the quality of the food. Physicians may have been sensitive to quality differences, but they too had little information about important dimensions like mortality. Policy makers have argued that physicians sought to admit their patients to hospitals that had the latest medical technology. However, generous insurance payment rules allowed hospitals to raise prices to cover the costs of this gadgetry. Thus, quality competition also did not represent a threat to profits. In sum, internal rivalry in the Chicago hospital market in 1980 was *low*.

Driven by low internal rivalry, hospital prices soared throughout the 1970s and early 1980s. Facing a threat to their own profitability, health insurers attempted to impose market discipline on hospitals. Hospitals in Chicago today cannot admit privately insured patients unless they have contracts with their insurers (who have come to be known as "managed care payers"). Unlike patients and physicians, insurers are motivated to shop around to get the best prices because they keep any savings. They are also capable shoppers, taking advantage of sophisticated price and outcomes data to compare hospitals on the basis of prices and costs (which are determined by prices per service and the number of services used). They are increasingly using information on nonprice dimensions, such as mortality, and resist efforts by hospitals to pass on cost increases associated with new but unnecessary technology. Insurers increasingly view most hospitals as commodities, and will ex-

---

[2]Community hospitals treat a variety of patients on a short-term basis. Another type of hospital not considered here is the psychiatric hospital.

clude all but the leading teaching hospitals from contracts if their prices are too high. Finally, the market has substantial excess capacity—over 30 percent of hospital beds go unfilled on a typical day. These factors all intensify price rivalry, and evidence from other markets that have gone through similar changes suggests that price-cost margins have probably eroded significantly since the mid-1980s.

In response, hospitals have consolidated into local "systems"—horizontally integrated firms—but there are at least a half dozen systems along with many hospitals that are still independent. We can conclude that internal rivalry in the Chicago hospital market today is high.

Entry

Few hospitals have been built in Chicago in the past two decades. One reason is severe state regulatory restrictions on new hospital construction. Another reason is that the market has become too unprofitable to attract much new investment, although several outside investors have acquired existing facilities. To assess the threat of entry, it is useful to assess the magnitude of entry barriers in an unregulated, surging market. There are several barriers to opening a new hospital. Hospitals are capital intensive. A new 500-bed hospital can easily cost $500 million to build. A new hospital would have to attract new medical staff, and find a location where it did not draw too many patients from any existing hospital, thereby risking a price war. The combination of regulatory and structural entry barriers suggests that the threat of entry was low in 1980. Although regulatory barriers are lower today, structural barriers remain, and a new hospital might face a price war if it did not choose its location wisely. This suggests that the threat of entry is slightly higher today. It is perhaps best characterized as medium.

Substitutes

In 1980, few inpatient services could be performed outside the hospital. Thus, the threat from substitutes was low. Since then, hospitals have faced a growing number of substitutes. Thanks to improvements in surgical technique, anesthetics, and antibiotics, many types of surgery can nowadays be performed outside the hospital. Other substitutes for hospital services include outpatient diagnostic facilities, which provide state-of-the-art technologies, such as magnetic resonance imaging, and home health care, which enables nurses and physicians to monitor patient well-being and provide some treatments at home rather than in the hospital. While many services must still be provided in the hospital—transplants are a good example—the rapid growth of substitutes that represent evolving technologies implies that the threat to hospitals is high.

Supplier Power

The main suppliers to hospitals include labor (nurses, technicians, etc.), medical equipment companies, and drug houses. We consider admitting physicians to be buyers because they often determine which hospitals patients will purchase services from. Hospital-based physicians, such as radiologists, anesthesiologists, and pathologists (RAP physicians) are better regarded as suppliers. Nurses and technicians represent powerful suppliers. Traditionally, these positions were filled by women. But as women have enjoyed increasing opportunities in the workplace, both in and out of medicine, the supply of nurses and technicians to hospitals has fallen relative to demand. Because women may now sell their services to a much broader market, hospitals have been forced to raise their wages. Between 1985 and 1990, it was not uncommon for nurses to realize real annual wage increases of 5 percent. Medical equipment suppliers and drug houses have varying amounts of power. For commodity products, such as surgical gloves, their power is probably weak. There are many suppliers, and there is no asset specificity. For more complex supplies or equipment where the number of suppliers is limited because of patent protection or a single firm's specialized technical know-how, supplier power can be substantial.

Hospitals and their suppliers make few relationship-specific investments. Personnel learn to work in teams, but seem to be able to adjust rapidly to new settings. Hospitals can usually replace them at the market wage, and some hospitals routinely use "nursing pools" to handle short-term needs. A national recruiting market usually makes RAP physicians easy to replace, although hospital bylaws and staffing policies can occasionally create exit barriers. Medical suppliers without monopoly power cannot credibly threaten to hold up hospitals to obtain higher prices.

The magnitude of supplier power has not changed very much over time. While no consistent picture emerges from this analysis, we can tentatively conclude that supplier power was medium in 1980 and remains medium today.

Buyer Power

Buyers include patients, physicians, and insurers, who decide which hospitals will get business and how they will be paid. Patients and their physicians did not wield purchasing power in 1980, and generally do not wield it today. Insurers in 1980 were also passive. Most of them reimbursed whatever the hospital charged, and did not shop around for the best value. Indeed, state regulations generally prevented such price shopping by insurers. The two major government insurers, Medicaid and Medicare, also had generous reimbursement rules. Buyer power in 1980 was low. Today, insurers wield substantial power. The largest insurers in Chicago, Blue Cross in the private sector and Medicare in the public sector, use their size to negotiate significant price discounts. Medicare, which insures the elderly and disabled, has forced all hospitals to accept fixed price contracts, so that hospitals must bear the risks of excessive treatment costs. Medicaid is the toughest payer of all. Medicaid negotiates a separate price with every hospital willing to accept its patients. These prices are often 25 to 50 percent less than those paid by other insurers for comparable services. Medicaid knows each hospital's cost-and-profit position, and can use this information to minimize what it offers to pay each hospital. Physicians may also wield significant power, especially those charismatic and highly skilled physicians who can attract patients regardless of where they practice. A classic example is the local physician who pioneered the use of the "neural knife" surgical technique. He switched hospitals after a bidding war drove up his wages, and thereby extracted from the winning hospital a significant percentage of the profits that his services generate. To the extent that managed care payers are less likely to demonstrate loyalty to individual physicians, this power has diminished somewhat since 1980. While there are no relationship-specific investments to speak of, buyer power in the Chicago market is high.

Hospitals have attempted to combat buyer power. Some have sought to differentiate their services by developing "centers of excellence" in clinical areas, such as cancer care and heart surgery. They hope that insurers will tolerate higher prices to obtain superior quality. Thus far, there is no systematic evidence that this strategy has been successful. Others have forward integrated by offering an insurance-like product such as a "physician-hospital organization" or a "managed care system." These new structures must keep the internal payments to hospitals low to stay competitive with other insurance products, and so do not really solve the problem of buyer power.

Table 7.1 summarizes the five-forces analysis of the Chicago hospital market in 1980 and today. Virtually every factor that affects industry profitability has changed for the worse since 1980. Hospital managers face a number of dilemmas, and it is no wonder that so many hospitals are in financial disarray.

Tobacco

Tobacco firms include some of the largest and most profitable companies in the world. For 1980–1990, *Fortune* reported that the tobacco industry had the fifth highest total return to investors (out of 24 groups), even though this group excludes the industry leaders Philip Morris and RJR Nabisco. Philip Morris and RJR Nabisco rank in the top 75 firms in the *Fortune* Global 500. Though highly diversified, these giants earn a disproportionate amount of their income from tobacco. Philip Morris, for example, owns Kraft, General Foods, Miller Beer, and Oscar Mayer Foods. Even so, through the early 1990s it obtained 40 percent of its sales and 60 percent of its profits from tobacco. RJR Nabisco is also highly diversified, selling products such as Nabisco cookies, Life Savers candy, A1 sauce, and Milk-Bone dog biscuits. Yet it received 55 percent of its sales and 75 percent of its profits from tobacco. Tobacco sales are so critical to these firms that when a cigarette price war erupted in 1993, tobacco stocks lost 20 to 30 percent of their value. A five-forces analysis helps explain why the tobacco industry has been so profitable, and why it has recently struggled.

TABLE 7.1
FIVE-FORCES ANALYSIS OF THE CHICAGO HOSPITAL MARKET.

Force	Threat to Profits: 1980	Threat to Profits: Today
Internal Rivalry	Low	High
Entry	Low	Medium
Substitutes	Medium	High
Supplier Power	Medium	Medium
Buyer Power	Low	High

Internal Rivalry

The cigarette is a technically simple product that can be made in large quantities at low cost. Smokers often disagree about whether there are discernible differences in the way that cigarettes taste. In the early days of the industry, enough smokers were willing to switch brands that price wars were common. In fact, Philip Morris, originally a British brand, first became prominent in the United States by selling discount brands, while the established firms were raising prices. Price competition has significantly diminished since the 1930s, however. Elie Applebaum estimated that before the most recent price wars, the price-cost margin for the industry was .65, extremely high when compared with other industries.[3]

Several factors contribute to the historically low internal rivalry. The major producers grew out of the Tobacco Trust, which was the target of two famous antitrust cases. The first was *U.S. v. American Tobacco Co.* (1911), which resulted in the breakup of the famous Tobacco Trust into 16 smaller firms, including American Tobacco, Liggett and Myers, and Lorillard. In the second case, *American Tobacco Co. v. U.S.* (1946), the U.S. Supreme Court found that the three major tobacco firms that existed during the Great Depression of the 1930s—American Tobacco, Liggett and Myers, and Lorillard, had violated antitrust laws by conspiring to lower prices to drive discount cigarette brands out of business. Thus, there is a history of cooperative pricing that facilitates "friendly" price competition.[4] The major players continue to dominate the industry—the industry four-firm concentration ratio has exceeded 80 percent since 1950.[5]

Beginning in the 1950s, the industry introduced marketing practices that attached an image to specific brands. One of the first efforts, and by far the most successful, was Philip Morris' promotion of Marlboro as a rugged "man's" cigarette. (Ironically, Philip Morris initially test-marketed Marlboro as a "woman's" cigarette.) Image-conscious smokers became reluctant to switch brands. As Americans grew wealthier after the Second World War, tobacco became a less significant part of their budgets, again reducing the desire to shop around.

Without price competition, firms have sought to increase their share by new product introductions, innovations (e.g., the 100-millimeter cigarette), and new brand identities. These activities are relatively inexpensive, and costs have historically been passed along to consumers. Hence, we rate internal rivalry as being historically low.

Entry

Tobacco has been an industry with traditionally high entry and exit barriers. All of the major U.S. firms today had been established in the industry by 1932. Cigarette production is characterized by significant economies of scale in both production

---

[3]Miles, R.H., *Coffin Nails and Corporate Strategies*, Englewood Cliffs, NJ: Prentice-Hall, 1982, pp. 33–34; 102–103.

[4]Example 10.3 in Chapter 10 contains a detailed discussion of pricing rivalry in the tobacco industry.

[5]Miles, R.H., *Coffin Nails and Corporate Strategies*, pp. 33–34.

and marketing. This makes entry into the branded cigarette market a risky proposition. Established manufacturers may also have favorable access to distribution and
retail channels, such as vending machines, bars, and gas stations. Exit from the industry is difficult. Antitrust concerns would probably prevent an established firm
from selling its assets to a competitor. This further raises the potential costs of entry, since a newcomer that failed might not be able to sell its assets. All of these factors suggest that the threat of entry is low.

Substitutes

Any discussion of substitutes in the cigarette business must consider that cigarette
smoking is generally habitual (to the point of being addictive). While economists,
such as Gary Becker and George Stigler, may challenge whether smoking is addictive or not, the habitual nature of smoking has become one of the critical aspects
of the debate about the dangers of smoking that colors consideration of advertising
policies, promotional programs, and governmental regulation.[6] It also turns the
search for substitutes into a choice for the consumer of whether to change brands
of cigarette or else quit smoking altogether.

There are two types of plausible economic substitutes for tobacco products, especially cigarettes. Neither of these has been sufficiently strong to challenge the
high profitability of the industry. The first is some other type of product that satisfies the addiction to nicotine, such as a low-tar cigarette, chewing tobacco, or a
nicotine patch. The proliferation of new brands suggests that smokers might switch
to an alternative, such as a low-tar cigarette, rather than quit. The second type of
substitute is some nontobacco product that is consumed in place of cigarettes, such
as snack food or gum. The extensive diversification by such firms as Philip Morris,
RJR, and Grand Metropolitan shows the relationship between cigarettes and the
food business. Substitutes clearly pose a negligible threat to the industry.

Buyer and Supplier Power

Supplier power is nonexistent. The principal suppliers are unorganized tobacco
farmers who sell at below competitive prices, thanks to the 1985 Food Security Act
income support program. Other inputs, including labor and paper, are obtained
from competitive markets. Buyer power is also low. Distributors and retailers are
largely fragmented. Vending machines represent one of the only relationship-specific investments, and manufacturers are in a better position to exploit the relationship than are the vendors, owing to their wide choice of retail outlets.

Table 7.2 summarizes the five forces of the tobacco industry.

It is no wonder that the major tobacco firms have been so profitable. This
analysis raises one remaining question: Why has price competition intensified in
the 1990s? Several reasons come to mind. First and foremost, the demographics
of the cigarette consumer have changed dramatically. The average consumer is

---

[6]Becker, G. and G. Stigler, "Degustibus Non Est Disputandum," *American Economic
Review*, 67, 1977, pp. 76–90.

TABLE 7.2
FIVE-FORCES ANALYSIS OF THE TOBACCO INDUSTRY.

Force	Threat to Profits
Internal Rivalry	Low
Entry	Low
Substitutes	Low
Supplier Power	Low
Buyer Power	Low

younger and has less income than in the past. Younger consumers have developed less brand loyalty, and lower-income consumers are more willing to switch brands to save money. Recent tax increases further motivate low-income smokers to shop around to save money. This intensifies internal rivalry. Second, retail outlets, such as Wal-Mart stores have opened up new channels for off-price and "generic" cigarettes. This has increased the threat of entry.

It is important to put these threats in perspective. While price competition has intensified, before-tax prices in the United States in 1994 were about where they were in 1989. The industry raised prices precipitously in the early 1990s, and finally met consumer resistance. Even at the lower prices, the industry remains highly profitable.

The major threat to the industry, government regulation, is not captured by the five forces. Health concerns and resulting regulations have changed smoking habits, significantly reducing cigarette consumption in the United States. Cigarette markets continue to expand overseas, where the forces affecting profitability remain favorable. Unless demand in the United States completely goes up in smoke, tobacco companies should continue to enjoy high returns.

Photocopiers

The technology for mechanical reproduction of printed matter is fairly new. Mimeograph machines were common through the 1960s, but the copying industry really began in 1959, when Xerox introduced the first machine to use the xerography technique invented by Chester Carlson in 1941. The first plain paper copier, the Xerox 914, weighed 648 pounds and produced seven copies per minute. The market began to flourish in the 1970s when photocopy technology advanced enough to allow for faster, more legible copies and surpassed the standard set by the then existing norm for document reproduction: carbon copies. Today, the product for this industry includes any copier either "standing alone" or networked, analog or digital, color or black and white, that can reproduce documents. Copiers range from simple desktop models reproducing copies at a rate of 15 copies per minute to high-speed machines that generate 135 copies per minute. Competition is global. Xerox, Canon, Sharp, and Mita have held 75 percent of the copier market since 1991 and compete fiercely among themselves and with eight other players that comprise the remaining 25 percent of the market.

Internal Rivalry

Consumers evaluate copiers according to four dimensions: price, speed, reliability, and service. In the early 1970s Xerox, Eastman Kodak, and IBM dominated the market by establishing branch networks that covered the country. This permitted them to establish high standards for service quality, albeit at high prices. In the mid-1970s, three Japanese manufacturers, Canon, Minolta, and Ricoh, entered the U.S. market, eschewed branches in favor of dealer networks, and set out to carve their own niche within the market. The Japanese competitors offered a product line that was less expensive but somewhat less reliable.

At first, the U.S. giants ignored their Japanese competitors, perceiving them to be too small to go against head-to-head. Canon, Ricoh, and Minolta quickly gained a foothold within the American market and used their experience to improve their product and chip away at the market share of the American players. At the same time, niche players entered the growing market, serving specifically targeted segments such as color copiers. Today, Canon is the largest player in the $6 billion U.S. market, with a roughly 28 percent market share in 1993. Xerox and Sharp control another 34 percent. Roughly 20 other firms account for the remaining 38 percent. Less than one percent of copiers sold in 1993 were color copiers. Of those, Canon had a 75 percent market share, and Kodak and Xerox had 14 percent between them.

Nowadays, the copy machine market is largely a replacement market. Consumers are knowledgeable, often make large purchases, and occasionally have sophisticated and unusual needs. Consumers view the basic offerings of most manufacturers as very close substitutes. They also gripe that the biggest problem with copiers is downtime, and are sensitive to reliability and service. Consumers of basic machines will shop on the basis of price, but will remain loyal in the replacement market to those manufacturers whose machines remained up and running. In the past three years, demand for technologically advanced high-volume and color copiers has grown. The introduction of digital copiers in the early 1990s created an enormous new market as well. Some customers also demand "value-added services," such as managing document storage and networking systems.

Margins on basic machines are low. The industry often refers to the analogy of "giving away the razor to assure the sale of the blades." Margins on supplies, such as toner, paper, and so on, can run as high as 60 percent. These high margins allow sellers in effect to charge higher prices to consumers who use machines more often. Occasional users can obtain machines at prices below average total costs, and pay little extra for supplies because of their infrequent use. Heavy users, who value the machines the most, pay more than average total costs through their purchases.

High margins in the digital and color markets, combined with the expensive toners and the variety of photographic paper, make them the most lucrative segments to pursue. Margins on the "box" are high in these segments for two reasons. First, there are fewer sellers, due to the high cost of R&D and the steep technological learning curve. Second, buyers are less likely to shop on the basis of price because service and reliability are critical in these complex machines.

Service competition is as critical as price competition, and exists in all market segments. Today's copiers average less than 1 percent downtime: on-site service response is guaranteed within four hours, and prices have not risen more than 5 percent over the previous three years. Dealers and sales representatives compete fiercely to lock clients into exclusive sales and service relationships that often take months or years of strategic planning to negotiate. Ironically, although service calls are highly profitable, sales in the long run go to those manufacturers whose products require the least service.

Internal rivalry is difficult to summarize. The threat to profits from rivalry is high at the low end of the market, where there are many sellers, and consumers view the products as commodities and base their decisions about which model to buy on price and the ability of the local service representative. At the high end of the market, such as in color copiers, rivalry is much weaker. There are only a few sellers, and price is secondary to quality and service.

Entry

High research and development costs, economies of scale in manufacturing, and established sales networks represent formidable barriers to entry. Color and digital technology require extensive R&D expenditures. Incumbent sellers have a huge edge over newcomers, having made the necessary initial R&D investments and moved down the design and manufacturing learning curves. As long as there are no significant changes in copier technology that cause a rapid devaluation of accumulated knowledge, incumbent sellers should retain their learning advantage. Large research expenditures, combined with close contacts with academic scientists, assure incumbents that they will be the first to adopt any new technologies that are developed, such as digital copying. Large production capabilities, and the associated scale economies, also protect incumbents from entry.

Just as important as R&D is an efficient sales and service network, either direct or through outside dealers. Service representatives must be highly skilled in computer systems and must continually update their knowledge of new product technology to meet client needs. Manufacturers rely on the skill and reputation of their service representatives to maintain customer loyalty. A new player within this market would have to come in with very deep pockets or look to team up with an already existing player to achieve both nationwide distribution and servicing of copiers. While this may be facilitated by the recent growth of dealer networks that we describe below, it is still a challenge. We conclude that the threat of entry is relatively low.

Substitutes

The desktop printer is the most threatening substitute to the copy machine. Workers would rather print multiple copies on a desktop printer than go to a copy center in the office and wait for copies to be printed. Copiers have approached this challenge by networking copiers directly to PCs within the office and offering such services as two-sided copies, collation, and color enhancement. There may eventually be a shakeout between the two industries, but for the present, low-volume copying has been taken over by the desktop printer while high-volume reproduction is still the domain of the copy machine. Although some people use their fax machine as a default copier, the per page expense and lack of flexibility does not allow us to consider the fax machine as a serious threat to the copier. It is more likely that, in the future, the PC or copier will incorporate the fax machine as one of its regular features. Owing to the rapid pace of technological development in personal computing and desktop printing, the threat of substitutes is medium and could potentially increase.

Buyer Power

Historically, the largest buyer of copying machines in the United States has been the federal government. It has commanded low prices, virtually buying the machines at marginal cost. Sellers have recouped fixed costs, however, by maintaining high margins on service. Sales to corporate and personal users are traditionally handled through local, independent dealerships. Dealers usually obtain exclusive rights to distribute one or two brands in an area. Exclusivity is necessary because dealers must make relationship-specific investments to learn about a particular manufacturer's products and stocking parts. Dealer territories are usually no larger than a state or metropolitan area, and there are over a thousand dealers in the United States alone. Individual dealers are small and relatively powerless. Those dealers with outstanding reputations for service may be a great asset to their suppliers, but cannot exploit their value because they face high switching costs. To see why, suppose that a highly regarded Canon dealer tried to get a better deal from Canon. It probably could not threaten to switch to some other brand, such as Ricoh, because there probably already is a Ricoh dealer in its market. Nor could it credibly threaten to stop selling Canon copiers, due to its high relationship-specific investments. Thus, even the best dealers cannot squeeze higher profits from manufacturers.

Relationships between dealers and manufacturers are rapidly changing. In the past three years, the Alco Office Products division of Alco Standard Corporation has formed the largest copier dealership network in the world, with sales topping $2 billion in fiscal year 1994. Alco started as a purchasing group for independent dealers, but began to acquire dealers in 1993, and is now acquiring 20 dealers per year. Danka Business Systems is pursuing a similar growth strategy, and had sales of $550 million in fiscal year 1994. These consolidated dealerships have an edge selling to national and international accounts like Citibank and McDonald's and can be expected to grow. As they continue to acquire independent dealers, they will obtain the clout needed to negotiate favorable deals with manufacturers. They will then be able to threaten to change brands and can avoid the asset specificity problem in any given dealership by shifting inventories to other dealers. The rapid rise of Alco and Danka suggests that historically low buyer power is now moderate and rising.

Supplier Power

Supplier power is low within the copier industry. Supplies are readily available, and manufacturers may buy parts from many suppliers. Although many copiers are manufactured overseas where labor costs are lower than within the United States,

TABLE 7.3
FIVE-FORCES ANALYSIS OF THE PHOTOCOPYING INDUSTRY.

Force	Threat to Profits
Internal Rivalry	Medium to High
Entry/Exit	Low
Substitutes	Low
Buyer Power	Medium (growing)
Supplier Power	Low

assembly of high-end copiers still takes place within this country. For some more sophisticated machines, the parts are wholly developed and manufactured within the company itself.

Summary

The major threats to profitability are fierce price competition at the low end of the market and the growth of powerful dealership networks. As in any other high-tech industry, technological innovators may affect entry and substitutes. Table 7.3 summarizes the five forces in the copier industry.

Commercial Banking

Commercial banks perform many services, including issuing credit cards, cashing checks, and operating ATMs. The historical distinction between commercial banks and other financial institutions has two principal aspects: (1) commercial banks hold (and pay interest on) the funds of their depositors, and (2) banks lend funds out to customers and receive interest on those loans. This means, of course, that ordinary individuals are both the banks' suppliers and buyers—they supply money as depositors and buy money as borrowers. The difference between the interest paid to banks by borrowers and the interest paid out by banks to depositors (called the *spread*) is the principal source of the bank's earnings. Banks also charge for the other services they provide, and some, such as Bank of America, make billions of dollars annually in the credit card market.

The commercial banking industry is one of the largest in the United States, with twice the assets of the insurance industry ($3.5 trillion versus $1.7 trillion) and more employees than the auto, steel, and oil industries combined (1.7 million). Regulations stemming from the stock market crash of 1929 and the Great Depression of the 1930s narrowly limited both the geographic and product markets in which commercial banks could operate. Until recently, for example, commercial banks could do business only in a single state. Financial services in general, and banks in particular, were affected by the deregulation wave of the late 1970s and 1980s, and the industry now faces far fewer regulatory obstacles. While the industry still features thousands of regional banks that provide limited services in local markets, there are several national giants, including Citicorp and Bank of America, as well as "super-regional" banks, such as Ohio-based Banc One. The giants continue to press Congress for further deregulation, hoping to enter related businesses, such as the buying and selling of stocks and bonds.

Internal Rivalry

As anyone who has shopped for a loan can attest, the banking industry is generally competitive. Consider, for example, the market for home loans (mortgages). Consumers (mortgagees) are generally price sensitive. One reason for this is that the mortgage represents a significant expenditure, which motivates shopping. Mortgagees also perceive the product to be homogeneous and can easily compare prices. Indeed, many newspapers report comparative interest rates on a daily or weekly basis. In addition, switching costs for mortgagees are low, as evidenced by the fact that many mortgagees do not even know the name of their lender (mortgages are bought and sold, so that a mortgagee may not know who the seller of the mortgage is). Finally, mortgagees can usually choose from dozens of competing sellers. These factors contribute to intense consumer search for the best price—a mortgagee will often select a bank on the basis of a price difference of just .125 percentage points. The market for commercial loans is equally competitive. Banks rarely maintain price differentials for very long. The prime rate, which is the interest rate charged to the best commercial risks, is usually the same at all banks.

Deregulation has increased competition. Before deregulation, competition was restricted to local markets, and many markets had only a few competitors. Normally, this would tend to decrease competitive pressures. On the other hand, the inherent homogeneity of the product can promote fierce price competition even when only two firms are in the market. In reviewing the evidence on the relationship between price and concentration in banking, Leonard Weiss concludes that before deregulation, banks in concentrated markets charged higher interest rates for mortgages and commercial loans.[7] In a typical study reviewed by Weiss, a 10% increase in the market share held by the three largest firms in the market was associated with between a 0.3 and 1 percent increase in the commercial and mortgage interest rate.

Until the early 1990s, one major product line of commercial banks appeared immune to price pressures—the interest rate charged for outstanding balances on credit cards. In the late 1980s, when inflation was below 5 percent annually, many credit card holders paid annual interest rates of 18 to 21 percent. A few low-interest-rate cards were available at that time—some banks charged annual rates of around 10 percent. But consumers have only recently shopped aggressively for lower interest rates. Part of the reason has to do with entry from unexpected players, whom we describe below.

---

[7]Weiss, L., *Concentration and Price*, Cambridge, MA: MIT Press, 1989.

Entry

Regulation has both facilitated and hindered entry in banking. The most significant potential barrier to entry is the need for a bank to assure depositors that their money is safe. In the United States, the Federal Deposit Insurance Corporation (FDIC) provides that assurance. Any bank that meets regulations regarding its investment portfolio and maintenance of reserves can use the FDIC program to guarantee the security of deposits. Borrowers may also worry about the integrity of their bank, but this seems to be less of a problem, as many lenders in the mortgage and commercial loan markets remain anonymous. Lenders may use well-known local and national banks as conduits for their funds (much as fashion designers use well-known retailers as conduits for their clothing). Well-known banks may still profit from their brand name in this way, but entry by mortgage brokers suggests that the value of a brand name is limited.

Until the 1980s, federal and state regulation strictly limited entry into banking. For example, interstate banking was prohibited and investment banks, such as Morgan Stanley (which arrange for equity capital for business), could not provide commercial banking services. These restrictions have begun to fall, due to the weakening of the Glass-Steagal Act that had regulated banking since 1933 and the increasing use of reciprocal agreements between states permitting interstate banking. These changes have promoted entry in two significant ways. First, there has been significant entry of national banks into local markets. Examples include Bank of America's expansion east from its California base. Besides setting up new branches, national banks are acquiring small banks in their entirety, enabling them to quickly become formidable competitors in local markets.

Entry into the credit card business has become widespread. Such companies as General Motors, American Airlines, and Apple are teaming up with banks large and small to use credit cards as a new marketing tool. Armed with data about purchasing habits and credit histories, these joint ventures are targeting heavy credit card users and, by offering discounts on products and services, capturing the large profits to be had by servicing their credit cards. These innovations, combined with entry into the credit card market by nonbanks, such as General Electric and Sears, has heightened consumer awareness. The result is that interest rates on cards that do not offer product tie-ins have fallen considerably in the past three years.

Taken together, entry by national firms, mortgage brokers, and nontraditional credit card sellers poses a major threat to industry profitability.

Substitutes

Deregulation has also increased the threat of substitutes. For example, the deregulation of insurance companies and savings and loan institutions (direct competitors in the output market for home mortgages) has allowed them to better compete with banks for the deposits of businesses and the financing of real estate developments. Banks are also pressured by nonbank actors in a process known as *disintermediation*. Large firms can increasingly handle their own financing and cash management needs internally. Nonbank firms can also help satisfy their employees', buyers', and suppliers' financial needs, through such products and services as credit unions and commercial paper. Nonbank financial service firms, such as investment banks and brokerage firms, can offer services that are similar to those of banks (such as money market accounts), but which are not covered by banking regulations and reserve requirements. The threat from substitutes is already high and is still growing.

Supplier Power and Buyer Power

The most significant supplier in the banking industry is the federal government. The government "supplies" regulation. The Federal Reserve supplies the funds that banks need to maintain reserves, and the price that the Fed charges for those funds, called the *federal funds rate*, largely determines interest rates. The FDIC supplies insurance that protects depositors and facilitates entry. Historically, the federal government has used its power to assure the stability of the banking industry, rather than to extract excess profits from it.

Large depositors and borrowers may use purchasing power to obtain favorable interest rates. Leonard Weiss cites studies that show that without competitive pressures, banks still offered higher deposit rates to larger customers. Even so, suppliers and buyers exercise their clout largely by being aggressive consumers who add to the intensity of internal rivalry, rather than by using the threat of holdup to renegotiate contracts. Overall, the direct threat of supplier and buyer power through such negotiations is small.

Summary

Money is inherently a homogeneous good that any number of firms can supply and for which consumers will shop around extensively. Suppliers, whether banks, savings and loans, or other companies, may have to rely on brand name identity to obtain funds, but this has not seemed to restrict entry. Even in the highly lucrative credit card market, profits have suffered as new entrants and intensified internal rivalry bring down interest rates. Table 7.4 summarizes the five forces in the commercial banking industry.

TABLE 7.4
FIVE-FORCES ANALYSIS OF THE COMMERCIAL BANKING INDUSTRY.

Force	Threat to Profits
Internal Rivalry	High
Entry	Medium to High
Substitutes	High
Buyer Power	Low
Supplier Power	

CHAPTER SUMMARY

◆ An industry analysis provides an overview of the potential profitability of the average firm in an industry.

◆ A comprehensive analysis examines the five forces: internal rivalry, entry, substitutes, buyer power, and supplier power. The latter four operate independently and may also intensify internal rivalry.

◆ Internal rivalry is fierce if competition drives prices toward costs. This is more likely when there are many firms, products are perceived to be homogeneous, consumers are motivated and able to shop around, prices may be set secretly, sales orders are large and received infrequently, and the industry has excess capacity.

◆ The threat of entry is high if firms can easily enter an industry and capture market share from profitable incumbents while intensifying price competition.

◆ Substitutes also capture sales and intensify price rivalry.

◆ Buyers and suppliers exert power directly by renegotiating the terms of contracts to extract profits from profitable industries, and indirectly by shopping around for the best prices.

◆ The government can affect profitability, and should be considered either as part of the five forces or as a separate force.

◆ Profits may be threatened by any or all of the five forces. While it is useful to construct a "five-forces scorecard" on which the forces can be rated, the exercise of assessing the five forces is more important than the actual scores. Through this exercise the analyst develops deep knowledge of key strategic issues affecting the industry in question.

◆ A sound five-forces analysis should be based on economic principles. The tools for analyzing internal rivalry, entry, and substitutes are derived from industrial organization and game theory, which are discussed in Chapters 8 through 11. The tools for analyzing buyer and supplier power are derived from the economics of vertical relationships, which were discussed in Chapters 2 through 4.

QUESTIONS

1. How does the magnitude of scale economies affect the intensity of each of the five forces?

2. How does the magnitude of consumer switching costs affect the intensity of internal rivalry? Of entry?

3. Advances in computer-aided design have allowed small manufacturing plants to nearly match the cost advantages of larger plants. How will this affect the supplier power of the aforementioned firms in the downstream industries that they supply?

4. Comment on the following: All of Porter's wisdom regarding the five forces is reflected in the economic identity:

$$\text{Profit} = (\text{Price} - \text{Average Cost}) \times \text{Quantity}.$$

5. It has been said that Porter's five-forces analysis turns antitrust law—law intended to protect consumers from monopolies—on its head. What do you think this means?

MARKET STRUCTURE AND COMPETITION

8

$\mathcal{U}$ ntil the early 1960s, the two leading manufacturers of large turbine generators in the United States, General Electric and Westinghouse, enjoyed substantial profit margins in this line of business.[1] Following an unexpected decline in demand, both companies had excess capacity. A vicious price war followed, in which prices barely covered marginal costs and fell well short of average total costs. Neither firm could sustain such pricing for very long. Eventually, General Electric raised its prices and intimated that it would not reduce them again, so long as Westinghouse raised its prices to match. Stability and profitability quickly returned to the turbine generator market.

This episode illustrates the interplay between market structure and competition. The large turbine generator market was a highly concentrated oligopoly in which General Electric and Westinghouse accounted for over 90 percent of industry sales. While neither firm historically lowered prices to attract new business, both were willing to slash prices to protect their market shares when faced with excess capacity. Price wars resulted in low prices and low profits for GE and Westinghouse. Prices and profits improved when the price wars ended.

The *structure* of a market refers to the number and characteristics of the firms in it. Many markets, including those for soft drinks, airframe manufacturing, and large turbine generators, are dominated by a few firms. Other markets, such as those for fresh-cut roses and personal computers, contain many sellers. In some markets such as metals and chemicals, products are homogeneous because sellers

---

[1]Large turbine generators are used by utility companies to generate electric power.

can meet the needs of consumers equally well. In other markets, such as soft drinks and personal computers, products are heterogeneous. As a result, different customers may have preferences for different sellers.

As discussed in Chapter 7, market structure can have a significant impact on how firms compete and the level of profitability they achieve. The purpose of this chapter is to develop the link between market structure and competition in greater detail. The chapter begins with a discussion of how to define markets and measure market structure. It then considers competition within four broad classes of market structures: perfectly competitive markets; monopolistically competitive markets; oligopolistic markets; and monopoly markets. The chapter concludes with a discussion of evidence on the relationship of market structure and firm and industry performance.

◆ ◆ ◆ ◆ ◆ MARKET STRUCTURE

The structure of a market describes the number and characteristics of the firms that compete within it. A given firm may compete in several input and output markets at the same time. It may face differing degrees of competition in each of its markets because their structures may differ. For example, a coal mining operation in a small town in West Virginia may have little or no competition in the market for labor, but may face many competitors in the market for coal.

Market Definition

The process of identifying the market or markets in which a firm competes is known as *market definition*. George Stigler and Robert Sherwin have described a market as "that set of suppliers and demanders whose trading establishes the price of a good."[2] Thus, two sellers are in the same market if one seller's production and pricing decisions materially affect the price that the other seller may charge. For example, if General Motors were to lower the price and increase the production of its Saturn line of family sedans, then Honda might have to adjust the price it charges for its family sedans. However, Honda's pricing of its motorcycles would probably not be affected. This is because Saturn family sedans and Honda family sedans are in the same market, but Honda motorcycles are not.

Qualitative Approaches to Market Definition

There are several approaches to defining markets. The qualitative approach is based on the idea that two products are in the same market if they are close *substitutes*. Honda and Saturn family sedans are good examples of close substitutes. In general, two products X and Y are substitutes if, when the price of X increases and

---

[2]Stigler, G. and R. Sherwin, "The Extent of the Market," *Journal of Law and Economics*, 28, 1985, pp. 555–585.

the price of Y stays the same, purchases of X go down and purchases of Y go up. We can think of good X as being Hondas, and good Y as being Saturns. During 1992–1993, a strong yen forced Honda to raise the price of its sedans relative to the price of Saturn and other U.S.-made sedans. This is one of the principal reasons why Honda sales fell while the sales of Saturn and other U.S.-made sedans increased.

Products tend to be close substitutes when three conditions hold:

- They have the same or similar *product performance characteristics*.
- They have the same or similar *occasions for use*.
- They are sold in the same *geographic market*.

A product's performance characteristics describe what it does for consumers. Though highly subjective, listing product performance characteristics often clarifies whether products are substitutes. Honda and Saturn sedans have the following product performance characteristics in common:

a. Seat four comfortably

b. Good fuel economy

c. Reliability

d. Acceptable acceleration and handling

Based on this short list, we can assume that the products are in the same market.

A product's occasion for use describes when, where, and how it is used. Both orange juice and cola are drinks that quench thirst, but because they are used in different ways (orange juice is primarily a breakfast drink and cola is consumed with lunch, dinner, or between meals), they are probably in different markets.

Products with similar characteristics and occasions for use may not be in the same market if they are in different geographic markets. In general, two products are in different geographic markets if: (a) they are sold in different locations; (b) it is costly to transport the goods; and (c) it is costly for consumers to travel to buy the goods. For example, a company that mixes and sells cement in Cleveland is not in the same geographic market as a similar company located in Phoenix. The cost of transporting cement over long distances is so large relative to its price that it would not be economical for the Cleveland cement seller to ship its product to Phoenix, even if cement prices in Phoenix were higher.

Efforts to identify competitors and define markets are often limited to the type of qualitative analysis that we have described above. While potentially informative, it has several shortcomings. First, identifying substitutes based on product performance characteristics is subjective and imprecise (e.g., is a Lexus sedan in the same market as Honda and Saturn?). As a result, market definitions are often a matter of much debate. Second, it is difficult to calibrate the degree to which products substitute for each other (e.g., airport limo service is undoubtedly a substitute for taxi service, but how *close* a substitute is it?). Finally, it is often difficult to assess the importance of transportation costs (e.g., how important are transportation costs in a consumer's choice of a doctor or dentist?). For these reasons, quantitative approaches to defining markets and identifying competitors can be useful supplements or alternatives to qualitative analysis.

◆ ◆

XAMPLE 8.1

SUBSTITUTES AND COMPETITION IN THE POSTAL SERVICE[3]

One of the few constants about international business is that the postal service is a government-regulated or government-owned monopolist. Among the developed countries, only Holland has fully privatized its postal service. Advocates of maintaining government monopoly control of the postal service claim that it is in their nation's best interest to assure that all residents, regardless of location, have equal access to communication by post. Considering the growth of advertising ("junk") mail on the one hand, and the growth of telephones, televisions, modems, and facsimile machines on the other, it is hard to maintain this argument. Postal communications seem less than vital, and access to other sources of communication continues to grow. Another justification for government-sponsored monopoly is that it is unnecessarily costly for two or more people to deliver mail to the same addresses. Some arguments for government control, such as some Britishers' concern that a private post office may not wish to depict the Queen on stamps, seem less compelling.

Guaranteed their monopoly status, postal services have operated with legendary inefficiency. News reports from Chicago, for example, routinely report bags of undelivered mail found abandoned in unlikely places (e.g., under highway overpasses, in workers' garages). But changes in technology and global competition are beginning to catch up with postal services, and their protected status is at risk.

Government regulations do not limit all forms of competitive postal delivery. Parcel and express mail delivery are often open to competition. On the local level, most big cities have private courier services that deliver mail between downtown office buildings in a matter of hours or less. In the past two years, competition for postal service has intensified. A British company has offered to provide universal postal service in direct competition with the British postal service. Thus far, the British postal service has kept its monopoly status. Greater success has been realized by the now privatized Dutch postal service, and a private postal firm from Australia, TNT. These private competitors are contacting businesses throughout Europe and offering to deliver their mail worldwide. Holland's postal service will pick up mail in England, for example, bring it back to Holland, and then post it

---

[3]This example draws on information in "Hitting the Mail on the Head," *The Economist*, April 30, 1994, pp. 69–70.

back to England—for a lower price than is charged by the British postal service! TNT is working with several European postal services to create a consortium that will pick up mail from large firms and distribute it throughout Europe, without resorting to the cumbersome rerouting employed by the Dutch.

Competition also comes from products that are close substitutes to postal service. Postal services are not protected from communications technologies such as fax, electronic mail, and interactive television. Individuals can now pay bills and file taxes electronically. One European post office estimates that the growing use of fax and e-mail could cost it $750 million annually by 1997.

Some national post offices are responding to these competitive threats. In addition to Holland's privatization, Sweden, Canada, and New Zealand have liberalized restrictions on their postal services' commercial activities. New Zealand's post office responded by cutting 40 percent of its work force. Other postal services are contemplating entering the courier service market. While cost cutting may be necessary for survival, it is doubtful that product line expansion will offer postal services the same protection that they enjoyed before the growth of substitutes. Overnight mail and courier service are fiercely competitive markets, and e-mail appears to be expanding independent of government, or postal service, intervention. As postal services struggle to stave off competition, it will be interesting to see how long their governments continue to protect them, or whether they will go the way of Holland's and New Zealand's postal services.

Quantitative Approaches to Defining Markets and Identifying Competitors

We consider four quantitative approaches to defining markets and identifying competitors:

- Demand elasticities
- Residual demand curves
- Price correlations
- Trade flows

We discuss each in turn.

Own-Price Elasticity of Demand and Cross-Price Elasticity of Demand If a firm raises price and, as a result, loses most of its customers to other firms, we may conclude that it has many competitors. If it keeps most or all of its customers, we may conclude that it faces little competition. The magnitude of consumer responses to changes in price is measured by the *own-price elasticity of demand*, which equals the percentage change in a firm's sales that results from a 1 percent change in price. If η_x denotes the own-price elasticity of demand facing firm X, Q_x denotes the quantity sold by firm X, and P_x the price, then

$$\eta_x = - (\Delta Q_x/Q_x) / (\Delta P_x/P_x)$$

We use the negative sign so as to make η_x a positive number, since ΔQ and ΔP will generally have the opposite sign.

The larger η_x, the greater the demand response to a change in price. It is tempting to conclude that if a firm faces a large η_x, it faces many close substitutes. This may not be true, however. Remember from the Economics Primer that η_x depends on the price level that the firm selects. A firm with no apparent competitors would raise price until $\eta_x > 1$, since if $\eta_x < 1$, the firm can increase revenue and reduce cost (thereby increasing profits) by raising price. Eventually, price increases will choke off sales, and η_x will exceed 1, even if consumers do not switch to any close substitute.

Although knowledge of η_x may not allow the firm to identify substitutes, knowledge of substitutes may allow firms to assess whether η_x is changing. This, in turn, may help the firm adjust price as market conditions change. For example, a firm may find from experience that a 10 percent price increase leads to a 20 percent decrease in sales, that is, $\eta_x = 2$. If the firm has constant marginal costs of 10, then it will maximize profits by setting $P = 20$. (Recall from the Economics Primer that if P is chosen optimally, then $(P-MC)/P = 1/\eta_x$.)[4] If a new entrant appears, and the firm finds that its customers view it as a substitute, then η_x will probably have increased. The firm should lower its price to mitigate any reduction in profits. If the firm determines that the new $\eta_x = 3$, then it should set $P = 15$. This kind of analysis helped Philip Morris conclude that it needed to reduce the price of its Marlboro brand in 1993 in response to entry by private-label sellers and to the growing price sensitivity of cigarette purchasers.

A group of sellers considering a concerted price change can also benefit from knowledge of the price elasticity of demand. In this case, they need to know about the elasticity facing the group as a whole, rather than the elasticity facing an individual seller. Consider the market for cement in the Chicago area. There are dozens of competitors, and if one seller raises price, it can expect to lose a lot of business to its competitors, that is, η is large. If all cement sellers in the Chicago area raise price together, however, consumers are unlikely to buy cement from somewhere else because the transportation costs would be prohibitive. The value of η facing all the cement sellers collectively—known as the price elasticity of market demand—is very small.

If the cement sellers discover that the market price elasticity is small, say .10, then a concerted increase in price by all cement sellers would substantially increase their profits. The cement sellers may wish to coordinate their pricing, or even to merge into a single firm to establish one price. Of course, pricing coordination would harm consumers, who would have to pay the higher price, since there is no good substitute product.

The antitrust laws are designed to protect consumers from such restraints of trade. In recent years, the U.S. Department of Justice and the Federal Trade

---

[4]This follows because, in general, marginal revenue (MR) can be expressed as $MR = P(1 - 1/\eta_x)$. (See the Economics Primer.) Thus, $MR = MC$ implies $P(1 - 1/\eta_x) = MC$, or $(P - MC)/P = 1/\eta_x$.

Commission—the top antitrust enforcers—have argued in court (not always suc-cessfully) that many organizations, including elite universities, airlines, and hospi-tals, have engaged in activities designed to illegally reduce the amount of price competition in their markets.

Measuring the own-price elasticity of demand tells us whether a seller or prod-uct faces close substitutes, but it does not identify what those substitutes might be. One may identify substitutes by measuring the *cross-price elasticity of demand* be-tween two products. If the products in question are X and Y, then the cross-price elasticity measures the percentage change in demand for good Y that results from a 1 percent change in the price of good X. Formally, if η_{yx} denotes the cross-price elasticity of demand of product Y with respect to product X, Q_y the quantity of Y sold, and P_x the price of product X, then

$$\eta_{yx} = (\Delta Q_y/Q_y) / (\Delta P_x/P_x)$$

When η_{yx} is positive, it indicates that consumers increase their purchases of good Y as the price of good X increases. Goods X and Y would thus be substitutes.

Given data on the price and sales of two goods at different points in time, it is possible to measure cross-price elasticities. For example, it has been estimated that a 10 percent rise in the price of natural gas would lead to a 1.5 percent increase in the demand for a substitute product, electricity.[5]

Residual Demand Analysis If a market is well defined, then the pricing deci-sions of sellers in the market should not be constrained by the possibility that con-sumers will switch to sellers outside the market. If pricing is constrained, then the market definition should be expanded to include these "outside" sellers. This is the basis of the *residual demand curve* approach to market definition. Under this ap-proach, a market is defined as a group of products and a geographic area such that if the firms in the group acted collectively as a profit-maximizing monopolist, they could raise price above a certain threshold, even after taking into account the sup-ply responses of firms outside the group. For example, to assess whether the Chicago metropolitan area constitutes a well-defined market for cement, the resid-ual demand curve approach would attempt to assess how much Chicago producers could raise price if they collectively acted as a profit-maximizing monopolist. If, on careful analysis, it becomes clear that Chicago producers could raise the price of ce-ment by only 1 percent (e.g., because at higher prices cement producers from Milwaukee would enter the market and compete away business from Chicago firms), then residual demand curve analysis would imply that the Chicago metro-politan area is not a well-defined geographic market. If, by contrast, Chicago pro-ducers could profitably raise price by 15 percent, then it is plausible to conclude that the Chicago metropolitan area does constitute a well-defined market.

The difficulty with this approach is in assessing by how much a group of firms acting in unison could profitably raise price. Unless the firms have already been

[5]Chapman, D., T. Tyrreoo, and T. Mount, "Electricity Demand Growth and The Energy Crisis," *Science*, 178, November 17, 1972, p. 705.

setting price in unison, there may be no record to determine what happens to their sales when they do. The firms may have raised price at the same time in the past, but this might have been in response to an increase in demand and would not fore-shadow their ability to raise price if demand were held constant.

One approach to determining whether a group of firms can profitably raise price is to identify a period when the firms in the group, and only those firms, were forced to raise price for a reason that has nothing to do with a surge in demand, such as an increase in input costs that affected only those firms. If their sales revenue increased after the price hike, then it is fair to say that the firms face few substitutes and that a coordinated price hike could, in fact, lead to an increase in profits. This idea underlies the approach used by Jonathan Baker and Timothy Bresnahan to assess the degree of competition faced by breweries.[6] Using sophisticated empirical techniques, they found that after 1975, Miller constrained the ability of Anheuser-Busch to raise its prices, and therefore these firms competed in the same market. By contrast, Coors' ability to raise price was not constrained by Anheuser-Busch or Miller, and therefore it competed in a distinct market.

Price Correlations   George Stigler and Robert Sherwin argue that if two sellers are in the same market, then they should be subject to the same demand forces.[7] Thus, if demand increases for one seller, it should also increase for another, and both should increase their prices. They conclude that if two sellers are close substitutes, their price changes should be highly correlated. Stigler and Sherwin analyze price movements for a variety of products, including flour and silver. For flour, they find a high correlation between prices in Buffalo and Minneapolis, but a smaller correlation between Buffalo and Portland, Oregon. They conclude that flour in Minneapolis is a closer substitute for Buffalo flour than it is for Portland flour.

Although conceptually simple, price correlations are difficult to interpret. There is no standard for what constitutes a high correlation. Without further analysis, it may be difficult to determine whether the goods with high price correlations are competitors in input or output markets, or both. Price correlations have had limited use in antitrust cases, suggesting that the results are not always convincing.

Trade Flows

As discussed above, otherwise identical products will not be good substitutes if they are sold in different geographic areas, and the cost of transporting the product (or the consumer) from one area to another is prohibitive. To identify a geographic market, one might use census-defined areas, such as cities or states, classifying all firms within the same area as competitors. Without knowledge of actual product or consumer flows, however, this can lead to gross errors in market identification. For example, it is unlikely that all ice cream parlors in Cook County, Illinois are in the

---

[6]Baker, J. and T. Bresnahan, "The Gains from Merger or Collusion in Product-Differentiated Industries," *Journal of Industrial Economics*, 33, 1988, pp. 427–444.

[7]Stigler, G. and R. Sherwin, "The Extent of the Market," *Journal of Law and Economics*, 28, 1985, pp. 555–585.

same geographic market. Those in northern Cook County can probably raise their prices without losing business to those in the rest of the county.

An alternative to this *ad hoc* approach to geographic market definition is to directly examine flows of goods and services across geographic regions to identify possible competitors. To illustrate this approach, consider how a hypothetical sporting goods store in the Sunset section of San Francisco, "Bay City Sports," might try to identify its competitors. Bay City Sports could simply assume that its market includes all of San Francisco, but no other cities. This is mere guesswork and is probably wrong. Bay City Sports might instead survey its customers to find out where else they shop. The results of such a survey could be misleading, however, because it ignores customers who live near Bay City but always shop elsewhere.

Bay City Sports would be better off adopting a two-stage approach to defining its market. First, it should ask its customers which neighborhoods and suburbs they come from. The store can then identify the contiguous area from which it draws most of its customers, sometimes called the *catchment area*. Bay City Sports could reasonably assume that people prefer to buy their sporting goods close to home, so that other sporting goods stores in the catchment area are potential competitors to Bay City. Some residents of the catchment area, especially those who live on its fringes, may prefer to travel outside the area to buy their sporting goods. To identify these fringe competitors, Bay City Sports should perform a second survey of all residents of its catchment area to determine if they shop at stores outside the area. If many do, then competition from outside the market area must be also reckoned with.

Kenneth Elzinga and Thomas Hogarty used these concepts to recommend an approach for identifying geographic competitors that has been frequently used in antitrust cases.[8] Elzinga and Hogarty claim that a geographic market, and the competitors within it, are properly identified if two conditions are satisfied: (1) The firms in that market must draw most of their customers from that area; and (2) the customers residing in that area must make most of their purchases from sellers in that market. Using their approach, if it turns out that (1) sporting goods stores in the Sunset section of San Francisco draw 80 to 90 percent of their business from residents of Sunset, and (2) residents of Sunset buy 80 to 90 percent of their sporting goods from stores in Sunset, then Sunset is a well-defined market. Bay City Sports could therefore restrict its competitor analysis to other stores in Sunset.

Other Approaches to Defining Markets

Absent data needed to estimate elasticities, price correlations, or trade flows, one must turn to other methods to define markets. A simple and commonly used approach is to define markets according to the Standard Industry Classification (SIC). The SIC system is used by the U.S. Bureau of the Census to analyze and report on U.S. business activity. It identifies different products and services by a seven-digit identifier, with each digit representing a finer degree of classification. For example,

---

[8]Elzinga, K. and T. Hogarty, "The Problem of Geographic Market Definition Revisited: The Case of Coal," *Antitrust Bulletin*, 23, 1978, pp. 1–18.

within the two-digit category 35 (Industrial and Commercial Machinery and Computer Equipment) are four-digit categories 3523 (Farm Machinery and Equipment) and 3534 (Elevators and Moving Stairways). Within 3534 are six-digit categories for automobile lifts, dumbwaiters, escalators, and so forth. One should use caution, however, in using SIC codes to define markets. Although products with the same SIC code often share the same product performance characteristics and may correctly be considered competitors, this is not always so. For example, all pharmaceuticals share the same four-digit SIC code (2834), but not all drugs substitute for each other. In this case, the four-digit SIC code is too aggregated for a meaningful identification of competitors. In other cases, firms that probably compete with each other may have different SIC codes. An example is variety stores (5331), department stores (5311), and general merchandise stores (5399). These SICs are too disaggregated for a meaningful identification of competitors.

EXAMPLE 8.2

DEFINING COCA-COLA'S MARKET

In 1986, the Coca-Cola Company sought to acquire the Dr Pepper Company. At the time, Coca-Cola was the nation's largest seller of carbonated soft drinks, and Dr Pepper was the fourth largest. The Federal Trade Commission (FTC) went before federal judge Gerhard Gesell seeking an injunction to block the merger on the grounds that it violated Section 7 of the Clayton Act, which prohibits any acquisition of stock or assets of a company that may substantially lessen competition. Coca-Cola apparently sought the deal to acquire, and more fully exploit, the Dr Pepper trademark. Coca-Cola's marketing skills and research ability were cited as two factors that would allow it to increase the sales of Dr Pepper. Judge Gesell also noted that Coca-Cola was motivated, in part, by a desire to match the expansion of Pepsi-Cola, which had simultaneously been seeking to acquire Seven-Up. Although the threat of FTC action caused Pepsi to abandon the Seven-Up acquisition, Coca-Cola elected to press on.

Judge Gesell supported the FTC's motion for an injunction, and the Coca-Cola/ Dr Pepper deal was never consummated. In his decision, Judge Gesell devoted considerable attention to the question of market definition. In his opinion, Judge Gesell wrote: "Proper market analysis directs attention to the nature of the products that the acquirer and the acquired company principally sell, the channels of distribution they primarily use, the outlets they employ to distribute their products to the ultimate consumer, and the geographic areas they mutually serve." He was concerned not only with the end-user market, but also intermediate markets for distribution and retailing. Reduction of competition in any of these markets could harm consumers.

Depending on how one defined the market in which Coca-Cola and Dr Pepper competed, one might conclude that the merger would either have no effect on competition or a significant effect. The FTC argued that the appropriate "line of commerce" was carbonated soft drinks. It presented data to show that under this definition, the merger of Coca-Cola and Dr Pepper would increase Coca-Cola's market share by 4.6 percent nationwide, and by 10 to 20 percent in many geographic submarkets. (Geographic submarkets were considered because of the special characteristics of soft drink distribution channels.) Given Coca-Cola's already high market share of 40 to 50 percent in many of these markets, the merger would significantly reduce competition.

In defending the merger, Coca-Cola attempted to define the relevant market as "all . . . beverages including tap water." Under this definition, the proposed merger would have a negligible effect on competition. Judge Gesell ruled: "Although other beverages could be viewed as within 'the outer boundaries' of a product market . . . determined by the reasonable interchangeability of use or the cross-elasticity of demand between carbonated soft drinks and substitutes for them, carbonated soft drinks . . . constitute a product market for antitrust purposes." In reaching this decision, Gesell relied on factors such as the product's distinctive characteristics and uses, distinct consumers, distinct prices, and sensitivity to price changes. Judge Gesell found such indicia to be present in this case, stating that the rival firms "make pricing and marketing decisions based primarily on comparisons with rival carbonated soft drink products, with little if any concern about possible competition from other beverages." In other words, carbonated soft drink makers constrain each others' pricing decisions, but are unconstrained by other beverages. Thus, carbonated soft drinks constitute a well-defined market.

Measuring Market Structure

Markets are often described as being *concentrated* (having just a few sellers) or unconcentrated. As we will see, such characterizations often permit a quick and accurate assessment of the likely nature of competition in a market. These characterizations are aided by having measures of market structure.

Recall that market structure refers to the number and distribution of firms in a market. Most theories of competition suggest that the performance of a market depends more on the characteristics of its largest firms, than of its smallest, or *fringe* firms. Thus, the most commonly used measures of market structure are far more sensitive to the makeup of the largest firms.

A commonly used and easy-to-calculate measure of market structure is the *N-firm concentration ratio*. This gives the combined market share of the *N* largest firms in the market. For example, the four-firm concentration ratio in the soft drink industry is about .90, which indicates that the combined market shares of the four largest soft drink manufacturers is about 90 percent. When calculating market share, one usually uses sales revenue, although concentration ratios based on other measures, such as production capacity, may also be used. Table 8.1 shows four-firm and eight-firm concentration ratios for selected U.S. manufacturing industries in 1987.

TABLE 8.1
CONCENTRATION STATISTICS FOR SELECTED U.S. MANUFACTURING INDUSTRIES, 1987.

SIC code	Industry description	Number of firms	4-firm CR	8-firm CR	Herfindahl index	Numbers-equivalent of firms
2024	Ice cream and frozen desserts	469	25	39	.028	36
2033	Canned fruits and vegetables	462	29	40	.030	33
2037	Frozen fruits and vegetables	194	31	45	.034	29
2041	Flour and other grain mill products	237	44	63	.065	16
2043	Cereal breakfast foods	33	87	99	.221	5
2046	Wet corn milling	31	74	94	.164	6
2047	Dog and cat food	130	61	78	.151	7
2067	Chewing gum	8	96	100	***	***
2111	Cigarettes	9	92	***	***	***
2273	Carpets and rugs	419	34	49	.042	24
2411	Logging	11,852	18	24	.015	67
2448	Wood pallets and skids	1,678	4	7	.001	769
2511	Wood household furniture	2,771	20	29	.015	67
2731	Book publishing	2,182	24	38	.026	39
2771	Greeting cards	147	85	89	.283	4
2812	Alkalies and chlorines	27	72	93	.233	4
2841	Soap and other detergents	683	65	76	.170	6
2911	Petroleum refining	200	32	52	.044	23
3221	Glass containers	35	78	89	.213	5
3274	Lime	56	43	59	.064	16
3312	Blast furnaces and steel mills	271	44	63	.061	16
3334	Primary aluminum	34	74	95	.193	5
3411	Metal cans	161	54	70	.108	9
3491	Industrial valves	310	20	30	.020	51
3511	Turbines and turbine generators	68	80	95	.216	5
3562	Ball and roller bearings	113	58	68	.097	10
3565	Packaging machinery	415	19	29	.017	60
3571	Electronic computers	914	43	58	.069	14
3581	Automatic vending machines	97	52	76	.100	10
3632	Household refrigerators and freezers	40	85	98	.226	4
3633	Household laundry equipment	11	93	***	.286	4
3711	Motor vehicles and car bodies	352	90	95	***	***
3823	Process control instruments	707	24	34	.022	47
3931	Musical instruments	402	31	46	.038	26
3995	Burial caskets	213	59	66	.182	5

Source: "Concentration Ratios in Manufacturing," *1987 Census of Manufacturing*, MC 87-S-6, Washington, DC: U.S. Department of Commerce, Economics and Statistics Administration, Bureau of the Census, 1992.

Another commonly used measure that is slightly more difficult to calculate is the *Herfindahl index*.[9] The Herfindahl index equals the sum of the squared market shares of all the firms in the market, that is, letting S_i represent the market share of

---

[9]The index is named for Orris Herfindahl who developed it while writing a Ph.D. dissertation at Columbia University on concentration in the steel industry. The index is sometimes referred to as the Herfindahl-Hirschman index and is often abbreviated HHI.

firm i, Herfindahl = $\Sigma_i(S_i)^2$. Thus, in a market with two firms each with 50 percent market share, the Herfindahl index equals $.5^2 + .5^2 = .5$. In general, the Herfindahl index in a market with N equal-size firms is $1/N$. Because of this property, the reciprocal of the Herfindahl index is referred to as the *numbers-equivalent of firms*. Thus, a market whose Herfindahl is .125 has a numbers-equivalent of 8. When calculating a Herfindahl, it is usually sufficient to restrict attention to firms with market shares of .01 or larger, since the squared shares of smaller firms are too small to affect the total Herfindahl.

Given the relative complexity of the Herfindahl, it is worth asking whether it conveys any more information than does the N-firm concentration ratio. One problem with the N-firm ratio is that it is invariant to changes in the sizes of the largest firms in the market. For example, a four-firm ratio does not change value if the largest firm gains 10 percent share at the expense of the second largest firm. The Herfindahl index does increase under such circumstances. If one believes that the *relative size* of the largest firms is an important determinant of conduct and performance, then the Herfindahl is likely to be more informative.

LINKING MARKET STRUCTURE AND COMPETITION

◆ ◆ ◆ ◆ ◆

Many economic models link the structure of a market to the conduct and financial performance of its firms. The Economics Primer discussed models of price determination, showing that as a firm faces more elastic demand, the desired margin between price and marginal cost narrows. In the extreme case of a perfectly competitive market, firms face infinitely elastic demand, so that price is equated to marginal cost. With free entry and exit, all profit opportunities are eroded, so that price is also driven to minimum average cost. In contrast, the price set by a monopoly exceeds marginal cost, often by a substantial amount.

This discussion suggests that a firm may face a continuum of pricing possibilities, depending on the nature of the competition it faces. Economists have divided this continuum into four broad categories, which are identified in Table 8.2. Associated with each category is a range of Herfindahls that is common for each

TABLE 8.2
FOUR CLASSES OF MARKET STRUCTURE AND THE INTENSITY OF PRICE COMPETITION

Nature of Competition	Range of Herfindahls	Intensity of Price Competition
Perfect competition	Usually below .2	Fierce
Monopolistic competition	Usually below .2	May be fierce or light, depending on product differentiation
Oligopoly	.2 to .6	May be fierce or light, depending on interfirm rivalry
Monopoly	.6 and above	Usually light, unless threatened by entry

kind of competition. These ranges are only suggestive and should not be taken as gospel, however. For example, later on in this chapter, we describe circumstances in which a market with only two firms would be characterized by fierce price competition. Additionally, as we shall see in Chapter 11, some economists believe that some conditions produce competitive pricing even when there is only one firm in the market.[10] For these reasons, it is essential to assess the circumstances surrounding the competitive interaction of firms to make conclusions about the intensity of price competition, rather than rely solely on the Herfindahl or other measures of concentration.

We have introduced perfect competition and monopoly in the Economics Primer. The ensuing discussion of these competitive conditions highlights some relevant issues for firm conduct. We have not yet discussed monopolistic competition or oligopoly. We will introduce these concepts informally in this chapter. But because the theory of oligopoly is especially rich, we will elaborate on it in Chapters 9 and 10.

Perfect Competition

In the theory of perfect competition, there are many sellers of a homogeneous good and well-informed consumers who can costlessly shop around for the best price. Under these conditions, there is a single market price that is determined by the interaction of all sellers and buyers, but is beyond the control of any one of them. This implies that each firm faces infinitely elastic demand. If a firm charges even one penny more than the market price it sells nothing, and if it sets a price below the market price, it needlessly sacrifices revenue. Its only decision, then, is how much output to produce and sell.

Recall from the Economics Primer that a firm maximizes profit by producing a volume of output at which marginal revenue equals marginal cost. Recall, too, that the *percentage contribution margin* (PCM) equals $(P-MC)/P$, where P = price and MC = marginal cost. The condition for profit maximization can then be written $PCM = 1/\eta$.[11] In perfect competition, $\eta = \infty$, so the optimal PCM is 0. Many markets approximate perfect competition, including markets for many metals and agricultural commodities. As the model predicts, price competition in these markets is fierce. Sellers set identical prices, and prices are generally driven down to marginal costs.

Many other markets, including those for most consumer goods and professional services, do not fit the literal conditions of the model of perfect competition. Even so, some of these markets may experience fierce price competition, in which prices are driven down toward marginal costs. Market conditions will tend to drive down prices when two or more of the following conditions are met:

---

[10]This is called a *contestable market*. See Baumol, W., J. Panzar, and R. Willig, *Contestable Markets and the Theory of Industry Structure*, New York: Harcourt Brace Jovanavich, 1982, for a definition of contestable markets and an extensive analysis of the conditions that might give rise to contestability.

[11]See the Economics Primer.

- There are many sellers.
- Consumers perceive the product to be homogeneous.
- Excess capacity exists.

We discuss how each of these features may contribute to fierce pressure to reduce prices.

Many Sellers

A top airline executive once said that "the industry is led by its dumbest competitor."[12] He made this statement in conjunction with a round of price cutting by two competitors. He probably meant that the airlines could increase their profits if they would stop cutting prices in vain attempts to increase market share. Of course, if the members of an industry could successfully collude to maintain high prices, consumers would suffer. To prevent this from occurring, the DOJ and FTC rigorously enforce antitrust laws designed to prevent collusive pricing. In enforcing these laws, the DOJ and FTC are seldom concerned about markets with more than a few sellers. Experience coupled with economic theory has taught them that it is unusual for more than a handful of sellers to raise prices much above costs for a sustained period. This is so for a number of reasons.

First, a large number of sellers will find it difficult to agree to raise prices. A price increase will result in fewer purchases by consumers, so some sellers will have to reduce production to support the elevated prices. But the more sellers there are, the more difficult it is to agree on who should cut production.

Second, even if sellers reach an agreement, some firms may be tempted to cheat on the agreement by increasing production. A firm that undercuts the collusive price may trigger a price war among the erstwhile colluders. Among the firms most tempted to lower prices are those with small market shares, of which there will be many when the market is relatively unconcentrated. A small firm may view the collusive bargain among bigger rivals as an opportunity to increase market share. Recall from Chapter 5 that along with increased market share may come learning benefits and economies of scale that will enhance a firm's competitive position in the future. A small firm may also feel that its larger rivals will be unable to detect its price reductions. Even if they did, they may find it hard to agree on an appropriate "punishment." The most effective punishment that a large firm can impose on a small firm is to further reduce its own prices. But the large firm may not wish to do this, since it stands to lose more (in absolute terms) from a price war than does the small firm.

A third reason why markets with many sellers tend to have lower prices is that in an industry with many sellers, there is likely to be a diversity of pricing preferences. A seller may actually prefer a low price, for example, if it has low costs. Even facing the threat of retaliation, the firm may cut its price if it feels that it will enjoy short-term benefits that exceed the long-term costs of industrywide price instability. For example, the major airlines have complained bitterly about carriers that are

---

[12]*Fortune*, October 20, 1980, p. 27.

allowed to fly while under bankruptcy protection, arguing that bankrupt airlines will be willing to slash prices to get short-term gains in market share. Often, the major airlines match these price cuts to keep the struggling carriers from getting off the ground—literally and financially.

EXAMPLE 8.3

THE OPEC CARTEL

Sellers who agree not to cut prices are said to be in a *cartel*. Perhaps the best known cartel is the Organization of Petroleum Exporting Countries (OPEC). OPEC was formed in 1960 by Saudi Arabia, Venezuela, Kuwait, Iraq, and Iran in response to efforts by U.S. oil refiners, led by Standard Oil of New Jersey, to reduce the price they were paying for imported oil. (Indeed, OPEC, a cartel of oil producers desiring to raise oil prices, was a response to an effort by a cartel of oil buyers to suppress prices!) Until the 1972 oil boycott, OPEC had little impact on world markets. It was not until the early 1980s, however, that OPEC attempted to explicitly raise the price of oil. (The U.S. antitrust laws do not apply to OPEC, which consists of government-controlled businesses.)

To maintain high prices, the OPEC members must restrict their output, or else they will produce more oil than the world will demand. Each member nation must therefore agree to an output quota. In 1982, OPEC set an overall output limit of 18 million barrels per day, down from 31 million barrels per day in 1979. Prices were to be maintained at $34 per barrel. Each member nation had an individual production quota, except for Saudi Arabia, which adjusted its output as necessary to maintain prices.

Maintaining the cartel has proven difficult. Sometimes, such as during the Iran-Iraq War, member nations sought to produce more than their allotment. This glutted the world market with OPEC oil. Despite Saudi Arabia's efforts to reduce output, prices plunged. Further pressure on prices came from companies that elected not to participate in OPEC, such as the British National Oil Company. When this company cut the price of its North Sea oil by $3 per barrel in 1983, the Nigerian oil minister was prompted to say "We are ready for a price war." Before long, OPEC had slashed its price by 15 percent and reduced its output by 3 percent. Today, OPEC accounts for less than 50 percent of world oil production, and with world oil prices hovering at $20 per barrel, OPEC appears to have a negligible effect on prices.

There have been efforts to cartelize many other international commodities industries, including copper, tin, coffee, tea, and cocoa. A few cartels have had short-term success, such as bauxite and uranium, and one or two, such as the DeBeers diamond cartel, appear to have enjoyed long-term success. In general, however, most international cartels are unable to substantially affect pricing for very long.

Homogeneous Product

When a firm lowers its price, it expects to increase its sales. The sales increase may come from three different courses:

1. Increased sales to existing customers
2. First-time sales to customers who previously did not buy the product at all
3. Sales to new customers who previously shopped elsewhere but switch to take advantage of the lower price

We say that a product is *homogeneous* if the characteristics of the product do not vary from one seller to another. When products are homogeneous, customers are very willing to switch from one seller to another to obtain a better price. This tends to intensify price competition.

Some products are clearly homogeneous. A share of IBM stock sold by one trader provides the same financial rights as a share of IBM stock sold by another. One ounce of 24 karat gold is completely interchangeable with another. On the other hand, some products that we commonly perceive as homogeneous really are not. Wheat is graded into four classes; compact disk players have distinctive sounds.

Some apparent product differences do not markedly reduce price competition. Consider two sellers of light bulbs. A sells bulbs individually, while B sells identical bulbs in packs of two. Obviously, competition will force the sellers to maintain price ratios of roughly 1:2. Or suppose that A sells a 60 watt light bulb that produces 1,000 lumens of light output and has an expected duration of 1,000 hours. Seller B's bulb is identical, except that it is expected to last 2,000 hours. Once again, the price ratio between the two sellers, products will be forced to be roughly 1:2. In both examples, nearly all consumers can agree that a given product offers a proprortionately higher or lower value than another product. In such cases, the threat of consumer switching will force prices to keep in that fixed proportion.

Excess Capacity

The rule of capacity in pricing problems may be understood by recalling the distinction between average costs and marginal costs that was made in the Economics Primer and in Chapter 5. For production processes that entail high fixed costs, marginal cost can be well below average cost over a wide range of output. Only when production nears capacity—the point at which average cost begins to sharply rise—does marginal cost begin to exceed average cost.

The numerical example in Table 8.3 illustrates the implications of excess capacity for a firm's pricing incentives. The table depicts the situation facing a diesel engine manufacturer whose plant has a capacity of 50,000 engines per year. Because of depressed conditions, the manufacturer has firm orders for only 10,000 engines during the upcoming year. It is confident, however, that it can increase sales by another 10,000 engines by stealing a major customer from one of its competitors. To do so requires that it offer this customer a price of $300 per engine.[13] Should the manufacturer offer this price?

TABLE 8.3
CAPACITY UTILIZATION AND COSTS

Annual Output	Total Variable Cost ($millions/year)	Total Fixed Cost ($millions/year)	Total Cost ($millions/year)	Average Cost per Engine
10,000	$1	$12	$13	$1300
20,000	2	12	14	700
30,000	3	12	15	500
40,000	4	12	16	400
50,000	8	12	20	400

The manufacturer is better off offering this price and stealing the business from its rival even though this price is well below the average cost of $700 that would result if it filled the order. To see this, note that the increase in the manufacturer's revenue is $3,000,000 while the increase in its total cost is only $1,000,000. It is better off selling the extra engines at $300 apiece because in so doing it increases its contribution to fixed costs. Of course, the firm's rival may not stand by and let the firm steal its business, so the result may be a pricing battle that drives the price for this order below $300. But as long as the order carries a price greater than the *average variable cost* of $100, the manufacturer would be better off filling the order than not filling it.

In the long run, competition like this can drive price below average cost. Firms may choose to exit the industry rather than sustain long-run economic losses. But if firm capacity is industry-specific—that is, it cannot be used for anything other than production in this industry—firms will have no choice but to remain in the industry until the plant reaches the end of its useful life or until demand picks up again. If demand does not pick up, the industry may experience a protracted period of excess capacity, with prices below average costs.

◆ ◆

XAMPLE 8.4

PRICING IN THE AIRLINE INDUSTRY

The airline industry has been plagued in recent years by frequent price wars and large financial losses. These losses may be directly tied to industry cost structure and the nature of competition among carriers. Airline costs fall into three broad categories:

---

[13]We will assume that this offer does not require the manufacturer to adjust the price at which it sells engines to its other customers.

- *Flight-sensitive costs*, which vary with the number of flights the airline offers. These include the costs associated with crews, aircraft servicing, and fuel. Once the airline sets its schedule, these costs are fixed.

- *Traffic-sensitive costs*, which vary with the number of passengers. These include the costs associated with items such as ticketing agents and food. Airlines plan their expenditures on these items in anticipation of the level of traffic, but in the short run, these costs are also fixed.

- *Fixed overhead costs*, which include general and administrative expenses, costs associated with advertising and marketing, and interest expenses.

Once an airline has set its schedule, flight-sensitive and overhead costs are fixed. Traffic-sensitive costs, which make up only a small percentage of total costs, are the only variable costs. This means that the airline is better off selling a seat at a low price—near marginal cost but well below average total cost—than not selling the seat at all. In addition, from the point of view of airline passengers, airline service is nearly homogeneous—if prices are similar, then most passengers are roughly indifferent about which airline delivers them to their destination. Thus, airlines face tremendous pressure to reduce prices to fill their planes. Airlines are willing to fly passengers at prices far below average costs—close to marginal costs. The tendency to set prices near marginal costs is greater during periods of low demand, such as the recession of the early 1990s, since airlines are even less likely to be flying at capacity.

The problem with such pricing practices in the airline industry is that because marginal costs are so far below average costs, airlines can lose staggering amounts of money during price wars. The airlines may cover their marginal costs, but will fail to make any contributions toward fixed costs. Many in the industry, including American Airlines' CEO Robert Crandall, expect that eventually there will be less capacity in the system, so that marginal costs will equal or exceed average costs, and prices and profits will increase accordingly.

Monopolistic Competition

The term *monopolistic competition* was introduced by Edward Chamberlin in 1933 to characterize markets with two main features:[14]

1. *There are many sellers.* When there are many sellers, it is reasonable to suppose that no one seller can take an action that will materially affect other sellers. For example, consider the retail women's clothing market in Chicago. There are many sellers in this market (there are three pages of listings in the Chicago *Yellow Pages*). If any one seller were to lower its prices, it is doubtful that

---

[14]Chamberlin, E. H., *The Theory of Monopolistic Competition*, Cambridge, MA: Harvard University Press, 1933.

other sellers would react. Most sellers would probably be oblivious to the price reduction. There are simply too many retailers to keep track of. Even if some sellers did notice a small drop-off in sales, they would probably not alter their prices just to respond to a single competitor.

2. *Each seller is slightly differentiated from the rest.* Recall that when products are homogeneous, consumers willingly switch from one seller to another just to obtain a small price savings. Consumers will not all be eager to switch, however, if they do not agree on which product is best. Products A and B are *differentiated* if there is some price for each product at which some consumers prefer to purchase A and others prefer to purchase B. The notion of product differentiation captures the idea that consumers make choices among competing products on the basis of factors other than just price.

Economists distinguish between *vertical differentiation* and *horizontal differentiation*. The distinction corresponds roughly to the distinction between making a product *better than* the products of competitors (vertical differentiation) versus making the product *distinctive* from those of competitors (horizontal differentiation), which may involve making it better, more appealing, or more suitable for one class of potential customers, but making it worse, less appealing, or less suitable for other potential customers. A producer of a household cleaner engages in vertical differentiation when it enhances the cleaning effectiveness of its product (e.g., by altering the formula so that less cleaner needs to be mixed with water to clean a given surface). This enhances the product for all prospective consumers. It engages in horizontal differentiation when it adds a pine scent to the cleaner. This makes the cleaner more attractive to some consumers (e.g., those who associate a clean house with the aroma of a pine forest) but perhaps less attractive to others (e.g., those who are sensitive to smells or associate other scents with cleanliness). Sellers of vertically differentiated products may charge different prices, since some customers may be more willing than others to pay for additional quality. If they charge the same price, however, everyone can agree on which product is preferred, and all will buy that one product. On the other hand, if sellers of horizontally differentiated products charge the same prices, consumers will disagree about which product is preferred, and each seller will capture a share of the market. In much of the analysis that follows, the exact nature of differentiation is not important. What matters is that the purchases of a product do not fall off to zero when its price is raised above that of other products.

An important source of differentiation is geography, because consumers prefer stores offering convenient access. For example, consumers living in Brooklyn will tend to frequent stores in Brooklyn, and consumers in Manhattan will tend to frequent stores in Manhattan. Figure 8.1 depicts a market in which products are differentiated based on location. The figure shows the town of Linesville. The only road in Linesville—Straight Street—is depicted by the straight line in the figure, and is exactly ten miles long. There is a video rental store at each end of Straight Street. Store L is at the left end of town; store R is at the right end. Each store carries identical inventory. There are 100 video rental customers in Linesville, and

FIGURE 8.1
VIDEO RETAILERS IN LINESVILLE

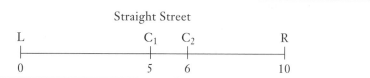

If store L and store R both charge $3 per video, then all consumers living to the left of C_1 shop at store L and all consumers living to the right of C_1 shop at store R. If store L lowers its price to $2 per video, then some customers living to the right of C_1 may wish to travel the extra distance to buy from store L. If travel costs $.50 per mile, then all customers living between C_1 and C_2 will travel the extra distance to save a dollar on the rental.

their homes are equally spaced along Straight Street. Thus, 50 consumers live closer to store L, and 50 live closer to store R.

When consumers decide which store to visit, they take two factors into account: the prices that each store charges and the cost of traveling to each store. Transportation costs can include direct costs, such as gasoline, as well as indirect costs, such as the cost of the time required to get to the store. Let the cost of traveling one mile equal $.50, which we assume to be identical for all consumers. Given this information, we can determine the degree to which consumers will switch from one store to another as they vary their prices.

Suppose first that both stores charge $3 per video rental. In this case, the two stores will split the market—each store will have 50 customers. Now suppose that store L lowers its price per video from $3 to $2, while store R keeps its price at $3. How will this affect the sales of both stores? To answer this question, we need to identify the location on Straight Street at which a consumer would be indifferent between purchasing from R and L. All customers living to the left of that location will visit store L and all customers living to the right will visit store R.

A customer will be indifferent between the two stores if he or she faces identical costs of purchase, where costs include both video rental and transportation costs. Consider a customer living M miles from store L (and therefore living $10-M$ miles from store R) who is planning to rent just one video. For this customer, the total cost of visiting store L is $2 + .50M$. The total cost of visiting store R is $3 + .50(10-M)$. These costs are equal if $M = 6$. A consumer located at $M = 6$ will have total purchase costs of $5, regardless of which store he or she visits. Thus 60 consumers will visit store L, and 40 will visit store R.

In this market, the video stores are horizontally differentiated because their locations differ and consumers bear positive transportation costs. Store R's location makes it a particularly attractive source of purchase for consumers located at the right end of Straight Street, even when R's price is higher than L's. As a consequence of transportation costs, store L gains only 10 customers from store R even though it charges $1 less per rental. One would intuitively expect that as product differentiation declines in importance—that is, as the transportation cost decreases—store L would gain even more from its price decrease. This is borne out by the model. If the transportation cost were only $.20 per mile rather than $.50, the indifferent consumer lives at $M = 7.5$, so that store L has 75 customers. As transportation costs diminish further, stores L and R become homogeneous—consumers have no strong preference for either store. Indeed, if the transportation cost is $.01, then store L need only lower its price by 10 cents to gain all the business.

The idea that differentiated products can be represented by distinct "locations" can be applied to a variety of settings. The straight line in Figure 8.1 could represent the sportiness of automobiles, the sweetness of colas, or the cut of business suits. Individuals with strong preferences for, say, conservative suits, would be "located" at one end of the line, whereas individuals who preferred more stylish suits would be at the other end. "Transportation costs" would be high if individuals were unwilling to purchase a suit that was not to their liking just to save some money.

Under what conditions might individuals be reluctant to switch sellers to save money? This might occur if preferences were highly *idiosyncratic*, that is, if tastes differ markedly from one person to the next. In this case, different sellers could keep loyal followings even if they raise prices. Switching may also be mitigated if consumers lack information about alternatives. If, in the above example, video store L did not publicize its price decrease, customers who frequented store R may not have found out about it, and would therefore have no reason to switch. On the other hand, if preferences are not highly idiosyncratic, and consumers are well informed about alternatives, switching is more likely.

A Graphical Depiction of the Theory of Monopolistic Competition

The theory of monopolistic competition emphasizes the importance of consumer switching as a determinant of the demand facing individual sellers. This may be illustrated by comparing demand curves with and without switching. First, imagine a market consisting of many differentiated sellers, say, the market for furniture. To understand the role of switching in such a market, suppose initially that each seller sets exactly the same prices at all times, and that consumers are well informed about prices. Consumers would evaluate the style, color, materials, and location of each seller, but not the price, and would choose the seller that provided the best idiosyncratic match. If there are M customers and N sellers in the market, a typical seller would have M/N customers. Call these the sellers' "regular customers."

The demand curve facing an individual seller when each seller sets the same price at all times is depicted by the curve labeled DD in Figure 8.2. The DD curve is obtained by dividing the total demand for furniture from the M customers in the population, by the number of sellers N. It is downward sloping because as all sellers lower price in unison, total demand for furniture increases. For example, if all sellers lower price from, say, P_0 to P_1, each seller sells a bit more furniture to its regular customers. The amount by which regular customers increase their purchases is easily read off the demand curve to be $Q_1 - Q_0$.

The DD curve does not reflect consumer switching. Since all prices change together, there is no reason for consumers to switch. However, the assumption that

FIGURE 8.2
DEMAND CURVE FACING AN INDIVIDUAL SELLER WHEN ALL FIRMS CHANGE PRICE IN LOCKSTEP.

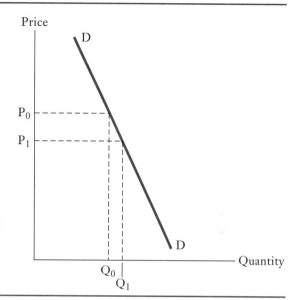

At price P_0, the firm's demand is Q_0, which is equal to the total market demand at P_0 divided by the number of firms. When all firms lower the price to P_1, the firm moves along curve DD, and its demand increases to Q_1.

all prices move in lockstep seems unreasonable in a market like furniture that has many sellers. It is hard to imagine that all sellers would be able or willing to coordinate their pricing so carefully. Consider, instead, what happens when only one seller changes its price, with the other sellers keeping their prices unchanged. For example, suppose initially that all sellers set a price P_0. If one seller lowers its price to P_1, and the other sellers do not match the price reduction, the seller will gain sales for two reasons. First, its regular customers may increase their purchases, because the price is lower. Second, some customers who were previously loyal to another seller will now *switch* to this seller to take advantage of the lower price.

The demand curve facing a seller who independently changes price is depicted by the curve labeled *dd* in Figure 8.3. This curve is flatter than the *DD* curve due to consumer switching. As the seller lowers its price from P_0 to P_1 its sales increase from Q_0 to Q_{11}. This can be broken down into two components: $Q_{11} - Q_0 = (Q_{11} - Q_1) + (Q_1 - Q_0)$. The first component represents the increase in demand due to consumers who switch from other stores. The second component is the increase in demand from loyal customers.

The greater the willingness of consumers to switch among sellers when one seller changes its price, the flatter will be the *dd* curve. Put another way, when *dd* is relatively flat, the price elasticity of demand facing an individual seller is large in magnitude. When demand is elastic, sellers have much to gain by lowering prices, and the PCMs that arise from profit-maximizing behavior will be fairly small. In

FIGURE 8.3

DEMAND CURVE FACING AN INDIVIDUAL SELLER WHEN IT INDEPENDENTLY
CHANGES PRICE.

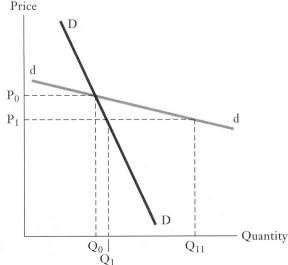

When the seller unilaterally reduces its price from P_0 to P_1 (with all other sellers holding their prices at P_0), it moves along demand curve dd, and its sales increase to Q_{11}. Part of the increase, $Q_1 - Q_0$, is increased demand from loyal customers. The remainder, $Q_{11} - Q_1$, is from customers who have switched from other firms.

contrast, if there is little switching, the dd is relatively steep, and the price elasticity of demand is small in magnitude. In this case, sellers have little to gain by undercutting their competitors. Thus, we expect PCMs to be lower in markets with more switching.

Entry into Monopolistically Competitive Markets

In differentiated product markets, each firm faces a demand curve with less than infinite elasticity; that is, $\eta < \infty$. The theory of optimal pricing implies that firms will set prices in excess of marginal costs. The resulting PCMs help to defray the fixed costs of doing business. If prices are high enough to exceed average costs, firms will earn positive economic profits. These profits will be attractive to investors and entrepreneurs seeking profits of their own and will therefore invite entry. Entry will reduce prices and erode market shares, until economic profits equal zero.

These forces can be understood with a numerical example. Suppose that there are currently 10 firms in a market, called *incumbents*. Each of the 10 incumbents has a constant marginal cost of $10 per unit and a fixed cost of $120. Each incumbent sells a horizontally differentiated product and faces a price elasticity of demand η equal to 2. With this elasticity, the profit-maximizing price for each incumbent firm is $20.[15] Suppose that at this price, the total market demand is 240, which is divided evenly among all sellers in the market. Thus, each incumbent sells 24 units.

---

[15]Recall that the optimal PCM $= 1/\eta$. Thus, in this case, $(P-10)/P = .5$. Solving for P yields $P = \$20$.

It is straightforward to calculate each incumbent's profits. Each one has revenues of $480 and total costs of $360, so profits equal $120. These facts are summarized in Table 8.4 in the column labeled "Before Entry."

Profits attract entry by other firms. Suppose that entrants' and incumbents' costs are identical, and that each entrant can differentiate its product so that all sellers have the same market share. Suppose further that differentiation is such that the price elasticity of demand η facing each seller remains constant at 2. Then each entrant will set a price of $20. If enough entrants are interested in pursuing profit opportunities, entry will continue until there are no more profits to be earned. This occurs when there are 20 firms in the market, each with sales of 12. The last column of Table 8.4 summarizes these results.

This example shows that even when product differentiation enables sellers to set prices well above marginal costs, new entrants will erode the resulting profits. Entrants usually steal some market share from incumbents, thereby reducing each incumbent's revenue and making it increasingly difficult for incumbents to cover fixed costs. In our example, entry did not intensify price competition. If that happens (e.g., because entrant's products are not highly differentiated from incumbent's), entry will erode profits even faster.

Oligopoly

In perfectly competitive and monopolistically competitive markets, sellers do not believe that their pricing or production strategies will affect the overall market price or volume of production. This makes sense in a market with many sellers. In a market with only a few sellers, however, it seems more reasonable to expect that the pricing and production strategies of any one firm will affect overall industry price and production levels. A market in which the actions of individual firms materially affect the industry price level is called an *oligopoly*.

The economics literature has produced many models of how firms should and do behave in oligopolistic markets. A central element of many models is the careful consideration of how firms respond to each other and to opportunities in the market. This is illustrated by considering two of the oldest and most important oligopoly models—*Cournot quantity competition*, and *Bertrand price competition*. We investigate these models below, and will elaborate on oligopoly models in the next two chapters.

TABLE 8.4
PROFITS AND NUMBER OF FIRMS UNDER MONOPOLISTIC COMPETITION

	Before Entry	After Entry
Number of Firms	10	20
Fixed Costs per Firm	$120	$120
Marginal Cost	$10	$10
Price	$20	$20
Market Demand	240 units	240 units
Sales per Firm	24 units	12 units
Profit per Firm	$120	0

Cournot Quantity Competition

One of the first models of oligopoly markets was developed by Augustin Cournot in 1835.[16] Cournot initially considered a market in which there were only two firms, which we call firm 1 and firm 2. These firms produce identical goods, so that they are forced to charge identical prices. In Cournot's model, the sole strategic choice of each firm is the amount they choose to produce, Q_1 and Q_2. Once the firms are committed to production, they set whatever price is necessary to "clear the market." This is the price at which consumers are willing to buy the total production, $Q_1 + Q_2$.

We will analyze the output decisions of firms facing specific demand and cost functions. Suppose that each firm has the following total costs of production:

$$TC_1 = 10Q_1$$
$$TC_2 = 10Q_2$$

In other words, both firms have constant marginal costs of $10 per unit. Thus, if $Q_1 = Q_2 = 10$, then $TC_1 = TC_2 = 100$. Let market demand be given by $P = 100 - Q_1 - Q_2$. With this demand curve, the market price falls if either or both firms try to increase the amount that they sell. For example, if $Q_1 = Q_2 = 10$, then $P = \$80$. If $Q_1 = Q_2 = 20$, then $P = \$60$.

How much will each firm produce? The answer to this question depends on how much each firm expects the other firm to produce. Cournot investigated production under a very simple set of expectations: Each firm makes a "guess" about how much the other firm will produce. A firm believes that its rival will stick to this level of output no matter how much the firm chooses to produce. Each firm's optimal level of production is the *best response* to the level it expects its rival to choose. In other words, each firm chooses the level of production that maximizes its own profits, given the level of production it conjectures the other firm will choose.

A *Cournot equilibrium* is a pair of outputs Q_1^* and Q_2^* and a market price P^* that satisfy three conditions:

(C1) P^* is the price that clears the market given the firms' production levels, that is $P^* = 100 - Q_1^* - Q_2^*$.

(C2) Q_1^* is firm 1's profit-maximizing output given that it conjectures firm 2 will choose Q_2^*.

(C3) Q_2^* is firm 2's profit-maximizing output given that it conjectures firm 1 will choose Q_1^*.

Thus, in a Cournot equilibrium each firm's conjecture about its rival's production level is "correct," that is, it corresponds to the output its rival actually chooses.

---

[16]Cournot, A., "On the Competition of Producers," chap. 7 in *Researchers into The Mathematical Principles of the Theory of Wealth*, translated by N.T. Bacon, New York: Macmillan, 1897. For an excellent review of the Cournot model and other theories of oligopoly behavior, see Shapiro, C., "Theories of Oligopoly Behavior," chap. 6 in Willig, R. and R. Schmalensee (eds.), *Handbook of Industrial Organization*, Amsterdam: North Holland, 1989.

To find the market equilibrium choices of Q_1 and Q_2, consider first firm 1's choice of Q_1. According to condition (C2), for Q_1 to be an equilibrium choice, it must maximize firm 1's profits, given firm 2's choice of Q_2. Suppose that firm 1 thinks that firm 2 is going to produce output Q_{2g}, where the g subscript reminds us that this is a guess, rather than the actual value. Then firm 1 estimates that if it produces Q_1 units of output, its profits, denoted by π_1 will be:

$$\pi_1 = \text{Revenue} - \text{Total cost} = P_1 Q_1 - TC_1 = (100 - Q_1 - Q_{2g}) Q_1 - 10Q_1.$$

Firm 1 needs to solve for the value of Q_1 that maximizes its profits. We can use calculus to determine that the profit-maximizing value of Q_1 satisfies:[17]

$$\text{Profit-maximizing value of } Q_1 = 45 - .5Q_{2g}.$$

The profit-maximizing value of Q_1 is called firm 1's *best response* to firm 2. According to this equation, firm 1's best response is a decreasing function of Q_{2g}. This implies that if firm 1 expects firm 2 to increase output, it will reduce its own output. This makes sense. If firm 2 increases output, then condition (C1) states that the market price must decrease. Facing a lower price, firm 1 prefers to produce less itself. The line labeled R_1 in Figure 8.4 depicts firm 1's choice of Q_1 as a function of its conjecture about Q_2. Economists call this line firm 1's *reaction function*.

In a similar manner, we can use condition (C3) to solve for firm 2's best response to firm 1's choice of Q_1:

$$\text{Profit maximizing value of } Q_2 = 45 - .5Q_{1g}$$

Firm 2's choice of Q_2 as a function of firm 1's choice of Q_1 is shown as reaction function R_2 in Figure 8.4.

We need one more step before we can solve for the equilibrium choices of Q_1 and Q_2. Recall that in equilibrium, each firm's guess about its rival's output must be correct. If a firm guesses incorrectly, then it would have an incentive to change its output, thereby violating condition (C2) or C3). For example, suppose that firm 1 expects firm 2 to choose $Q_2 = 50$ and, as a result, firm 1 selects $Q_1 = 20$. If it turns out, though, that firm 2 chooses $Q_2 = 30$, then firm 1's choice would not be optimal, and firm 1 would want to adjust its output.

Only one pair of outputs is simultaneously the best response to each other. These outputs, which we denote by Q_1^* and Q_2^*, are found by solving both firms' reaction functions simultaneously. This solution turns out to be $Q_1^* = Q_2^* = 30$. Graphically, this corresponds to the point in Figure 8.4 where the two reaction functions intersect. We can also solve for the equilibrium market price P^* and the profits each firm earns. Recall that the $P = 100 - Q_1 - Q_2$. In this case, $P^* = \$40$.

---

[17]Profit π_1 can be written as: $90Q_1 - Q_1^2 - Q_{2g}Q_1$. If we treat Q_{2g} as a constant and take the derivative of π_1 with respect to Q_1 we get

$$\frac{d\pi_1}{dQ_1} = 90 - 2Q_1 - Q_{2g}$$

Setting this derivative equal to 0 and solving the resulting equation for Q_1, yields the profit-maximizing value of Q_1.

FIGURE 8.4
COURNOT REACTION FUNCTIONS.

The curve R_1 is firm 1's reaction function. It shows firm 1's profit-maximizing output for any level of output Q_2 produced by firm 2. The curve R_2 is firm 2's reaction function. It shows firm 2's profit-maximizing output for any level of output Q_1 produced by firm 1. The Cournot equilibrium outputs, denoted by Q_1^* and Q_2^*, occur at the point where the two reaction functions cross. In this case, the equilibrium output of each firm is 30. At the Cournot equilibrium, each firm is choosing its profit-maximizing output, given the output produced by the other firm.

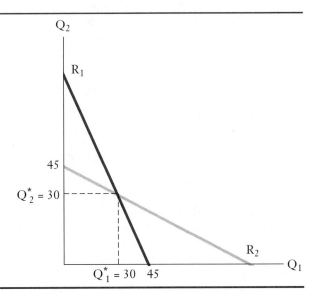

Substituting price and quantity into the equation for each firm's profits reveals that each firm makes $900 in profit in equilibrium.

Cournot's assumption that firms will simultaneously select the best response to each others' choices is often hard to accept as an accurate depiction of how real firms behave. It seems to impose an unrealistic measure of omniscience on each firm. Each firm somehow expects that its rival will choose its Cournot equilibrium output, and in response, each firm actually chooses its Cournot equilibrium output.[18]

However, in a Cournot model, the firms need not be omniscient for the equilibrium quantities to emerge. Suppose that the two firms are "out of equilibrium," in the sense that at least one firm has chosen to produce a quantity other than 30. For example, suppose that $Q_1 = Q_2 = 40$. Neither firm will be happy with its choice of quantity—each is producing more than it would like given its rival's production. As a result, we would expect each firm to adjust to the other firm's choices.

Table 8.5 shows an example of the adjustment process. Suppose that firm 1 makes the first adjustment. It examines its profit-maximization equation and determines that if $Q_2 = 40$, it should choose $Q_1 = 25$. Suppose now that firm 1 re-

---

[18]Cournot's assumption is actually a special case of a modeling assumption known as the *Nash equilibrium*, which is used to identify likely strategies in a variety of contexts. The concept of a Nash equilibrium is discussed in the Economics Primer. We will rely heavily on it in Chapters 9 and 10.

TABLE 8.5
THE COURNOT ADJUSTMENT PROCESS

Starting Q_1	Starting Q_2	Firm That Is Adjusting	Ending Q_1	Ending Q_2
40	40	Firm 1	25	40
25	40	Firm 2	25	32.5
25	32.5	Firm 1	28.75	32.5
28.75	32.5	Firm 2	28.75	30.63
28.75	30.63	Firm 1	29.69	30.63

duces its output to 25. Firm 2 will examine its own profit-maximization equation and determine that if firm 1 chooses $Q_1 = 25$, then it should choose $Q_2 = 32.5$. Now it is firm 1's turn to adjust its output. If $Q_2 = 32.5$, then firm 1 will prefer $Q_1 = 28.75$. Table 8.5 shows that Q_1 and Q_2 continue to converge toward the equilibrium values of $Q_1 = Q_2 = 30$.

An important implication of the Cournot model is that the equilibrium industry output does not maximize industry profit. Industry profit is maximized at a total output of 45 and a market price of $55.[19] By independently maximizing their own profits, firms produce more output than they would if they collusively maximized industry profits. This is characteristic of oligopolistic industries: The pursuit of individual self-interest does not maximize the well-being of the group as a whole. This occurs under Cournot competition for the following reason. When a firm expands its output, it reduces the market price and thus lowers the sales revenues of its rivals. The firm does not care about this *revenue destruction effect* because it is maximizing its own profit, not total industry profit. Thus, each firm expands its production volume more aggressively than it would if its objective had been the maximization of industry profit.

The smaller is a firm's share of industry sales, the greater the divergence between its private gain and the revenue destruction effect from output expansion. This suggests that as the number of firms in an industry exhibiting Cournot competition increases, the greater is the divergence between the Cournot equilibrium and the collusive outcome. Table 8.6 illustrates this point by showing equilibrium prices, profits, and outputs in a Cournot industry with the same demand curve and cost function as in the above example. The equilibrium price and profit per firm decline as the number of firms increases. More generally, it can be shown that the average PCM of a firm in a Cournot equilibrium is given by the formula $PCM = H/\eta$, where H denotes the Herfindahl and η is the price elasticity of market demand. Thus, the less concentrated the industry (the lower the industry's H), the smaller will be PCMs in equilibrium.

---

[19]Derivation of the profit-maximizing industry output is discussed below in the section on monopoly.

TABLE 8.6
COURNOT EQUILIBRIA AS THE NUMBER OF FIRMS INCREASES

Number of firms	Market Price	Market Quantity	Per-Firm Profits	Total Profits
2	$40	60	$900	$1800
3	$32.5	67.5	$506.25	$1518.75
5	$25	75	$225	$1125
10	$18.2	81.8	$66.94	$669.40
100	$10.9	89.1	$0.79	$79

$\mathcal{E}$XAMPLE 8.5

COURNOT EQUILIBRIUM IN THE CORN WET MILLING INDUSTRY

Michael Porter and Michael Spence's case study of the corn wet milling industry provides an interesting real-world illustration of the Cournot model.[20] Firms in the corn wet milling industry convert corn into corn starch and corn syrup. The corn syrup industry had been a fairly stable oligopoly until the 1960s, when several new entrants came into the market, including Archer-Daniels-Midland and Cargill. The addition of new competitors and new capacity to the market disrupted the old equilibrium and drove prices downward. By the early 1970s, however, competitive stability returned to the industry, as capacity utilization rates and prices rose.

In 1972, a major development hit the industry: the production of high fructose corn syrup (HFCS) became commercially viable. HFCS is a highly sweetened form of corn syrup that can be used instead of sugar to sweeten products, such as soft drinks. With sugar prices expected to rise, a fairly significant market for HFCS was expected to develop. Firms in the corn wet milling industry were faced with the decision of whether and how to add capacity to accommodate the expected demand.

Porter and Spence studied this capacity expansion process. They did so through a detailed simulation of competitive behavior based on an in-depth study of the 11 major competitors in the industry. Porter and Spence postulated that each firm's expansion decision was based on a conjecture about the overall expansion of industry capacity, as well as expectations about demand and sugar prices. Their model also took into account that capacity choices coupled with demand conditions determined industry prices of corn starch, corn syrup, and HFCS. The notion that a firm's capacity choice is based on conjectures about the capacity choices of other firms is directly analogous to the idea in the Cournot model that each firm bases

---

[20]Porter, M. and A.M. Spence, "The Capacity Expansion Decision in a Growing Oligopoly: The Case of Corn Wet Milling," in McCall, J.J. (ed.), *The Economics of Information and Uncertainty*, Chicago, IL: University of Chicago Press, 1982, pp. 259–316.

its output choice on conjectures of the output choices of other firms. The notion that capacity decisions then determine a market price is also analogous to the Cournot model.

Porter and Spence's simulation of the industry attempted to find an "equilibrium": an industry capacity expansion path that, when each firm made its optimal capacity decision based on the conjecture that that path would prevail, resulted in an actual pattern of capacity expansion that matched the assumed pattern. This is directly analogous to the notion of a Cournot equilibrium, in which each firm's expectations about the behavior of its competitors is confirmed by their actual behavior. Based on their simulation of industry decision making, Porter and Spence determined that an industry equilibrium would result in a moderate amount of additional capacity added to the industry as a result of the commercialization of HFCS. The specific predictions of their model compared with the actual pattern of capacity expansion are shown below.

	1973	1974	1975	1976	post-1976	Total
Actual industry capacity (billions of lbs)	0.6	1.0	1.4	2.2	4	9.2
Predicted equilibrium capacity	0.6	1.5	3.5	3.5	0	9.1

Though not perfect, Porter and Spence's calculated equilibrium comes quite close to the actual pattern of capacity expansion in the industry, particularly in 1973 and 1974. The discrepancies in 1975 and 1976 are mainly a reflection of timing. Porter and Spence's equilibrium model did not consider capacity additions in the years beyond 1976. However, in 1976, the industry had over 4 billion pounds of HFCS capacity under construction, and that capacity did not come on line until after 1976. Including this capacity, the total HFCS capacity expansion was 9.2 billion pounds, as compared with the 9.1 billion pounds of predicted equilibrium capacity. Porter and Spence's research suggests that a Cournot-like model, when adapted to the specific conditions of the corn wet milling industry, provided predictions that came remarkably close to the actual pattern of capacity expansion decisions.

Bertrand Price Competition

In Cournot's model, each firm selects a quantity to produce, and the resulting total output determines the market price. Alternatively, one might imagine a market in which each firm selects a price and stands ready to meet all the demand for its product at that price. This model of competition was first analyzed by Joseph Bertrand in 1883.[21] In Bertrand's model, each firm selects a price to maximize its

---

[21]Bertrand, J., "Book Review of *Recherche sur Les Principes Mathématiques de la Théorie des Richesses*," *Journal des Savants*, 67, 1883, pp. 499–508.

own profits, given the price that it believes the other firm will select. Each firm also believes that its pricing practices will not affect the pricing of its rival; each firm views its rival's price as fixed.

We can use the cost and demand conditions from the Cournot model to explore the Bertrand market equilibrium. Recall that when $MC_1 = MC_2 = \$10$ and demand is given by $P = 100 - (Q_1 + Q_2)$, then the Cournot equilibrium is $Q_1 = Q_2 = 30$ and $P_1 = P_2 = \$40$. This is not, however, a Bertrand equilibrium. Consider, for example, the pricing decision of firm 1. If firm 1 believes that firm 2 will charge a price of \$40, then it will not wish to also charge a price of \$40. Firm 1 would figure that if it were to slightly undercut firm 2's price, say by charging a price of \$39, it would get all of firm 2's business. Thus, firm 1 believes that if $P_1 = \$39$ and $P_2 = \$40$, then $Q_1 = 61$, and $Q_2 = 0$. In this case firm 1 expects to earn profits of \$1,769, well above the profits of \$900 it would earn if it charged a price of \$40.

Of course, $P_1 = \$39$ and $P_2 = \$40$ cannot be an equilibrium, because at these prices, firm 2 will wish to undercut firm 1's price. As long as both firms set prices that exceed marginal costs, one firm will always have an incentive to corner the market by slightly undercutting its competitor. This implies that the only possible equilibrium is $P_1 = P_2 = $ marginal cost $ = \$10$. At these prices, neither firm can do better by changing its price. If either firm lowers price, it will lose money on each unit sold. If either firm raises price, it would have no sales at all.

In Bertrand's model, rivalry between two firms is enough to achieve the perfectly competitive outcome. Price competition is particularly fierce in this setting because the firms' products are perfect substitutes. When firms' products are differentiated (as in the case of monopolistic competition), price competition is less intense. (Later in this chapter, we will examine Bertrand price competition when firms produce differentiated products.)

Bertrand competition can be very unstable in markets where firms must make up-front investments in plant and equipment to enter. As firms cut prices to gain market share, they may fail to cover long-run costs. If one firm should exit the market, the remaining firm could try to raise its price. But this might simply attract a new entrant that will wrest away some of its business. Fierce price competition may also end if one or both firms run up against capacity constraints (so that the ability to steal market share is limited), or learn to stop competing on the basis of price. These ideas are covered in greater depth in Chapter 10.

Why Are Cournot and Bertrand Different?

The Cournot and Bertrand models make dramatically different predictions about the quantities, prices, and profits that will arise under oligopolistic competition. How can one reconcile these dramatic differences?

One way to reconcile the two models is to recognize that Cournot and Bertrand competition may take place over different time frames. Cournot competitors can be thought of as choosing *capacities* and then competing as price setters given the capacities chosen earlier. The result of this "two-stage" competition (first choose capacities and then choose prices) can be shown to be identical to the Cournot equilibrium in quantities.[22]

Another way to understand the difference between the Cournot and Bertrand models is to recognize that they make different assumptions about the expectations each firm has about its rivals' reactions to its competitive moves. The Cournot model applies most naturally to markets in which firms must make production decisions in advance and face high costs of holding inventories. In such settings, prices will adjust more quickly than quantities, and each firm will set a price so that it can sell all that it produces. Under these circumstances, it is natural for each firm to expect that its competitors will instantaneously match any price change that the firm might make so that competitors can keep their sales equal to their planned production volumes. Consider, now, what a Cournot firm expects to happen if it attempts to increase its volume through a cut in price. The firm expects that the price decrease may increase the amount it will be able to sell to its existing customers. It may also induce purchases from new customers who have not heretofore purchased the good. It does not expect that the price decrease will steal away business from its rivals, however, because it expects that its competitors will instantaneously match any price cut in order to preserve their volumes at their currently planned levels. Because "business stealing" is not an option, Cournot competitors set prices less aggressively than Bertrand competitors. For this reason, the Cournot equilibrium outcome, while not the monopoly one, nevertheless results in positive profits and a price that exceeds marginal and average cost.

The Bertrand model can be thought of as pertaining to markets in which capacity is sufficiently flexible that firms are able to meet all of the demand that arises at the prices they announce. In the Bertrand model, a firm makes a conjecture about the prices that its competitors will charge, and chooses an optimal price, given these conjectures. When firms' products are perfect substitutes, each Bertrand competitor believes that it can steal business from its competitors through a small cut in price. In contrast to the Cournot model, where a price cut generated increased volume to a firm by, in effect, moving the firm down the industry demand curve, in the Bertrand model a price cut increases volume largely by stealing business from competitors. Of course, all competitors think this way, so each firm in the market attempts to steal market share from competitors through price cutting. In equilibrium, price-cost margins and profits are driven to zero.

There are many other issues to consider when assessing the likely conduct and performance of firms in an oligopoly. Competition may be based on a variety of product parameters, including quality, availability, and advertising. Firms may not know the strategic choices of their competitors. The timing of decision making can profoundly influence profits. We take up all of these issues in Chapters 9 and 10.

---

[22]The idea that the Cournot equilibrium can (under some circumstances) emerge as the outcome of a "two-stage game" in which firms first choose capacities and then choose prices is due to Kreps, D. and J. Scheinkman, "Quantity Precommitment and Bertrand Competition Yield Cournot Outcomes," *Bell Journal of Economics*, 14, 1983, pp. 326–37.

Bertrand Price Competition When Products Are Horizontally Differentiated

In many oligopolistic markets, firms produce products that are close, but not perfect, substitutes. The Bertrand model of price competition described above does not fully capture the nature of price competition in these settings. Fortunately, it is straightforward to adapt the logic of the Bertrand model to deal with the case of horizontally differentiated products.

When firms' products are horizontally differentiated, a firm will not lose all of its business to rival firms that undercut its price. As in the theory of monopolistic competition, this implies that a firm's demand will decrease "smoothly," rather than discontinuously, with a decrease in rivals' prices. To illustrate, consider an industry with two firms whose demand functions are given by

$$Q_1 = 160 - 2P_1 + P_2$$
$$Q_2 = 80 - 2P_2 + P_1$$

With these demand functions, as firm 1 raises its price above that of firm 2, firm 1's demand falls gradually.

Suppose each firm has an identical cost structure with a constant marginal cost equal to $10. What price will each firm charge? As in the models above, an equilibrium occurs when neither firm has an incentive to change its price, given the price set by the other firm. The logic of finding this equilibrium is very similar to the logic of the Cournot model. We begin by deriving each firm's reaction function, that is, the firm's optimal price as a function of its conjecture about its rival's price. Firm 1's optimal price maximizes its profit, which can be written as its price-cost margin times the quantity it sells, which is given by its demand function:

$$\pi_1 = (P_1 - 10)(160 - 2P_1 + P_{2g})$$

(We again use the subscript g to emphasize that firm 1 is making a guess about firm 2's price.) Using calculus to solve this maximization problem yields a reaction function[23]

$$P_1 = 45 + .25P_{2g}$$

Firm 2's optimal price is derived similarly. It maximizes

$$\pi_2 = (P_2 - 10)(80 - 2P_2 + P_{1g})$$

---

[23]Differentiating total profit π_1 with respect to P_1 (treating P_{2g} as a constant)

$$\frac{d\pi_1}{dP_1} = 180 - 4P_1 + P_{2g}.$$

Setting this expression equal to 0 and solving the resulting equation for P_1 yields firm 1's reaction function.

which yields a reaction function

$$P_2 = 25 + .25P_{1g}$$

Note that these reaction functions, displayed in Figure 8.5, are upward sloping. Thus, the lower the price the firm expects its rival to charge, the lower the price it should charge. In this sense, "aggressive" behavior by one firm (price cutting) is met by "aggressive" behavior by rivals. Note the contrast with the Cournot model, where "aggressive" behavior by one firm (output expansion) was met by "passive" behavior by rivals (output reduction).

Solving the two reaction functions simultaneously yields the Bertrand equilibrium in prices:

$$P_1 = \$54.67$$
$$P_2 = \$38.67$$

Both equilibrium prices are well in excess of marginal production cost. This illustrates that product differentiation softens price competition. This is because when products are differentiated, price cutting is a less effective weapon for stealing a rival's business than when products are perfect substitutes.

FIGURE 8.5

BERTRAND EQUILIBRIUM WITH HORIZONTALLY DIFFERENTIATED PRODUCTS.

Firm 1's reaction function shows its profit-maximizing price for any price charged by firm 2. Firm 2's reaction function shows its profit-maximizing price for any price charged by firm 1. The Bertrand equilibrium prices occur at the intersection of these reaction functions. In this example, this is at $P_1 = \$54.67$ and $P_2 = \$38.67$. At this point, each firm is choosing a profit-maximizing price, given the price charged by the other firm.

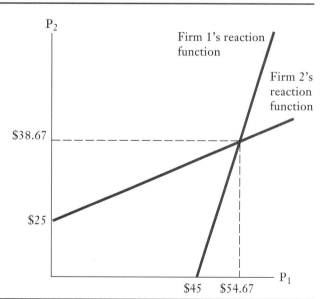

Monopoly

The noted antitrust economist Frank Fisher describes *monopoly* power as "the ability to act in an unconstrained way."[24] Examples of unconstrained actions include increasing prices and reducing product quality without losing customers. A firm can take such actions if its customers cannot take their business elsewhere. In other words, a firm has monopoly power if it faces little or no competition in its output market. Competition, if it exists at all, comes from *fringe* firms—small firms that collectively account for no more than around 30 to 40 percent market share and do not threaten to erode the monopolist's market share.

A firm is a *monopsonist* if it faces little or no competition in one of its *input* markets. Analysis of monopoly and monopsony is closely related. We will discuss issues concerning monopolists, but all of these issues are equally important to monopsonists. Whereas a discussion of monopoly focuses on the ability of the firm to raise output prices, a discussion of monopsony would focus on its ability to reduce input prices.

A monopolist usually ignores fringe firms when setting its own price, since it does not believe that the decisions of the fringe firms can materially affect its profits. Instead, it considers the entire market demand for its product, and selects price, so that the marginal revenue from the last unit sold equals the marginal cost of producing it. For example, suppose that the market demand for a product was given by $P = 100 - Q$, and the total cost of production was $TC = 10Q$. These are exactly the demand and cost conditions in the Cournot and Bertrand examples. It is straightforward to calculate the monopolist's price, quantity, and profits.

The monopolist's total revenue is price times quantity, or $100Q - Q^2$. The corresponding marginal revenue is $100 - 2Q$ (see the Economics Primer for further discussion of marginal revenue), while marginal cost equals \$10 per unit. Hence, marginal revenue and marginal cost are equal when $Q = 45$. It follows that $P = \$55$, and profits (total revenues minus total costs) equal \$2,025. As noted above, this far exceeds the combined profits of Cournot competitors.

Compared with Cournot and Bertrand equilibria, most of the monopolist's profits come at the expense of consumers. The monopolist produces less than do Cournot or Bertrand competitors and can raise price as a result. Some consumers are therefore unable to obtain the product even though they value it at more than the marginal cost. A concern over the detrimental effects of monopoly pricing on consumer welfare lies at the heart of antitrust policies in the United States and the European Community aimed at deterring the creation and exercise of monopoly power. However, the economist Harold Demsetz notes that high prices and profits do not necessarily justify government efforts to bust up monopolies and prevent new ones from forming.[25] Demsetz argues that most monopolies arise when a firm

---

[24]Fisher, F., *Industrial Organization, Antitrust, and the Law*, Cambridge, MA: MIT Press, 1991.

[25]Demsetz, H., "Two Systems of Belief About Monopoly," in Goldschmidt, H. et al (eds.), *Industrial Concentration: The New Learning*, Boston: Little Brown, 1974.

discovers a more efficient way of manufacturing a product, or creates a new product that fulfills unmet consumer needs. Consumers benefit from such innovations. But innovation is risky, and firms will continue to innovate only if they can expect high profits when successful. If Demsetz is correct, then restrictions on monopoly profits may hurt consumers in the long run, by choking off innovation.

There are many examples of firms that have reaped substantial market power and profits through innovation. Wal-Mart dominates retailing in many small markets, but it achieved this status through its low cost structure. Wal-Mart could monopolize markets only by passing some of its efficiencies to consumers, in the form of lower prices. Another example is Xerox, which discovered the eponymous technique known as Xerography and dominated the plain paper copier market until the expiration of its patents. Most countries recognize that the benefits usually offset the problems of monopoly, and award patents to protect innovators from competition. While the patentee receives high profits, consumers reap the benefits of the innovative new product. Without patents, firms might be unwilling to make the investments necessary to innovate, for fear that others would steal their products without making similar investments themselves.

EVIDENCE ON MARKET STRUCTURE AND PERFORMANCE ◆ ◆ ◆ ◆ ◆

The theories examined in the previous sections suggest that market structure should be related to the level of prices and profitability that prevail in a market. Many economists have tested whether the predicted link between structure and performance actually exists. Some of this research focuses directly on the relationship between price and seller concentration. The literature on structure and performance is much broader than this, however. For example, there is substantial research on the relationship between economies of scale, advertising, and profits. In this section we discuss some of the most important findings of this literature.

Price and Concentration

The relationship between price and concentration could be studied by comparing differences in prices and concentration levels across different industries. But comparing price differences across markets and attempting to infer the extent to which market structure is responsible for these differences is very difficult. For example, price differences between the concentrated airframe manufacturing industry and the unconcentrated gasoline retailing industry are due not only to differences in market structure, but also to the fact that firms in these two industries have vastly different cost structures. One way to get around this difficulty is to compare price-cost margins across different industries. As discussed above, economic theory suggests that price-cost margins should be higher in more concentrated markets (e.g., recall the discussion of the Cournot model). But price-cost margins may vary across markets for other reasons, such as regulation, product differentiation, the nature of sales transactions, and the concentration of buyers. The researcher needs to control for these before confidently relating variation in the margins to variation in concentration.

An important source of variation in price-cost margins across industries that is difficult to control is the way in which they are calculated. Since the predictions of economic theory pertain to the margin between price and *marginal cost*, price-cost margins should be computed using marginal cost. However, accounting cost data usually allow the researcher to infer average costs rather than marginal costs. The difference between average and marginal cost may vary by industry in ways that are not obvious to the researcher. Depending on how these issues are resolved, researchers may overestimate marginal costs in some industries and underestimate them in others. The researcher may then find differences in the price-cost margin that appear to be due to variations in the degree of competition, but unknown to the researcher, are really due to differences in accounting practices.

For these reasons, most economists focus on industry-specific studies to assess the relationship between concentration and price.[26] In these studies researchers compare prices for the same products in geographically separate markets that have different numbers of competitors. By comparing the same products across distinct markets, researchers can be more confident that variations in price are due to variations in competition, rather than variations in accounting, or other factors.

Leonard Weiss summarizes the results of price and concentration studies in over 20 industries, including cement, railroad freight, supermarkets, and gasoline retailing. He finds that with few exceptions, prices tend to be higher in concentrated markets. The magnitude of the relationship can be substantial. For example, one study found that gasoline prices in local markets in which the top three gasoline retailers had a 60 percent market share were, on average, about 5 percent higher than in markets in which the top three retailers had a 50 percent market share. Given the historically low margins in gasoline retailing, this 5 percent price differential can translate into substantially higher profits.

Studies of the effects of advertising on price provide further evidence of the relationship between competition and price. Many states ban price advertisements for certain products, especially those related to professional services. In the absence of price advertising, consumers have a more difficult time shopping around for good deals. This could allow sellers to raise their prices without losing too many customers. Two studies find evidence that this, in fact, does occur. Lee Benham compared eyeglass prices in states that banned eyeglass price advertising with those that did not; John Cady did a similar comparison of retail pharmacy prices.[27] Both found that prices were higher in the states that banned price advertising.

---

[26]Two excellent surveys are provided by Weiss, L. (ed.), *Concentration and Price*, Cambridge, MA: MIT Press, 1989, and Schmalensee, R., "Studies of Structure and Performance," in Schmalensee R. and R. Willig (eds.), *The Handbook of Industrial Organization*, Amsterdam: North-Holland, 1989.

[27]Benham, L., "The Effect of Advertising on the Price of Eyeglasses," *Journal of Law and Economics*, 15, 1972, pp. 421–77. Cady, J., *Drugs on the Market*, Lexington, MA: Lexington, 1975.

Timothy Bresnahan and Peter Reiss used a novel methodology to study the relationship between concentration and prices. They asked the following question: "How many firms must be in a market for price to approach competitive levels?"[28] They examined locally provided services such as doctors, tire dealers, and plumbers. For each service, they calculate "entry thresholds," defined as the minimum population necessary to support a given number of sellers. Let E_n denote the entry threshold for n sellers. For all services, they find that E_2 was about four times E_1. This could make sense only if prices are lower when there are two sellers than when there is one. When this happens, demand must more than double to make up for the intensified competition. They also find that $E_3 - E_2 > E_2 - E_1$, suggesting further intensification of price competition as the number of sellers increases from two to three. Lastly, they find $E_4 - E_3 \approx E_3 - E_2$, suggesting once there are three sellers in a market, price competition is as intense as it can get.

$\mathcal{E}$XAMPLE 8.6

PRICE AND CONCENTRATION IN LOCAL HOSPITAL MARKETS

There has been growing debate about whether competition in health care markets leads to lower or higher prices. The answer to this question is of vital importance to the larger debate about how, if at all, the U.S. health care system should be reformed. Advocates of a centralized health care delivery system, such as the system in place in Canada, often argue that health care is unlike other goods and services, so that competitive forces do not work to benefit consumers. Advocates of market-based reforms argue that competition can contain prices.

Health economists have measured the relationship between the degree of competition and the levels of costs and prices in health care markets. Early studies tended to confirm the argument that competition does not affect health care prices in the same way that it affects prices of other goods and services. Researchers reported that during the 1970s and early 1980s, prices and cost levels appeared to be the same or higher in markets in which there were more hospitals. Studies in recent years, however, find just the opposite to be true—competition appears to reduce hospital prices and costs.

What changed in the health care industry to reverse the relationship between structure and performance? Before the mid-1980s, the choice of a hospital in the United States was left entirely up to individual patients and their referring physicians. Patients and their physicians do not necessarily make for good shoppers. They have a difficult time comparing the prices of different hospitals. Moreover, patients with health insurance may not care about price. Faced with such unmoti-

---

[28]Bresnahan, T. and P. Reiss, "Entry and Competition in Concentrated Markets," *Journal of Political Economy*, 99, 1989, pp. 997–1009.

vated and unskilled shoppers, hospitals during the 1970s and early 1980s did not need to maintain low prices to attract their share of patients. Competitive pressures were not a major factor in pricing decisions.

Today, the locus of purchasing power in hospital markets has shifted away from individual patients and physicians toward large purchasers of hospital services, such as employers and Health Maintenance Organizations. These large purchasers steer patients to hospitals perceived as offering the best value. They are motivated shoppers because they keep any cost savings they may realize by shopping around. They are also skillful shoppers, collecting large amounts of data that enable them to evaluate and compare the costs of different hospitals. Hospitals increasingly find that if they do not offer low prices, they will lose substantial market share. As researchers, such as David Dranove, Mark Shanley, and Will White, have shown, this has held down the rate of growth of hospitals' prices and costs, especially in markets in which there are many sellers with excess capacity.[29] It is precisely in these markets that economic theory says that employers and insurers are able to shop around most effectively.

Other Studies of the Determinants of Profitability

Chapter 5 discussed the theoretical link between economies of scale and market structure, while this chapter has discussed the theoretical link between market structure, competition, and profitability. Together, these theories suggest a link between economies of scale and profits. Researchers have used a number of approaches to validate these ideas. One is to separately validate the individual links in the chain. Another is to directly relate the determinants of economies of scale to market structure. The evidence from both approaches confirms the theories.

Studies by dozens of researchers in several countries verify the link between economies of scale and market structure. One consistent finding is that the same industries tend to be highly concentrated in all countries. This supports the idea that some underlying factor—for example, economies of scale—determines market structure in all markets. Studies in which researchers have attempted to measure the magnitude of scale economies are also consistent with this conclusion. Industries in which the minimum efficient scale of production is large relative to the size of the market tend to be more concentrated than industries with minimal scale economies.

Researchers have had a more difficult time demonstrating the link between concentration and profitability. Richard Schmalensee has summarized this work as follows: "The relation, if any, between seller concentration and profitability is weak statistically, and the estimated concentration effect is usually small."[30] One problem

---

[29]Dranove, D., M. Shanley, and W. White, "Price and Concentration in Local Hospital Markets: The Switch from Patient-Driven to Payor-Driven Competition," *Journal of Law and Economics*, 36, 1993, pp. 179–204.

[30]Schmalensee, R., "Interindustry Studies of Structure and Performance," in Schmalensee, R. and R. Willig (eds.), *The Handbook of Industrial Organization*, Amsterdam: North-Holland, 1989.

may be the difficulty in comparing accounting profits across industries, where different conventions for depreciating overhead, paying taxes, and so on, may hide underlying differences in profitability. Another problem may be that if an industry was truly profitable, we would expect to observe entry. The fact that an industry has only a few firms may simply indicate that it is inherently unprofitable for reasons that the researcher cannot identify. To more fully test the link between concentration and profits, researchers need to identify industries that are concentrated because entry is difficult even when profits are available.

A second line of research copes with this problem by examining the relationship between profits and economies of scale that might limit entry. Some researchers have examined economies of scale in production processes as reflected in large capital-to-sales ratios. Others have examined economies of scale in marketing as reflected in large advertising-to-sales ratios. In most cases, industry profits are higher when production and/or marketing displays economies of scale. This is consistent with the idea that when industries are concentrated because entry is difficult, profits are high.

CHAPTER SUMMARY

◆ The structure of the market describes the number and size of firms that compete within it. Firms may compete simultaneously in several input and output markets. Each market that the firm competes in may have a different structure.

◆ To describe the structure of a market, it is first necessary to define the market. A market consists of the buyers and sellers whose interactions determine the price and quantity of the transacted good.

◆ Generally, two sellers will be in the same market if their products are close substitutes, that is, have similar product-performance characteristics. Price elasticities are useful for determining if a product has close substitutes.

◆ Economists have developed other techniques for identifying close competitors in product markets and in geographic markets. These include residual demand curve estimation, examination of price correlations, and inflow/outflow analysis.

◆ Once a market is well defined, its structure may be measured using an *N*-firm concentration ratio or a Herfindahl index.

◆ The structure of a market is often related to the conduct of the firms within it. The spectrum of competitive interaction ranges from perfect competition and monopolistic competition to oligopoly and monopoly.

◆ In competitive markets, consumers are extremely price sensitive, forcing sellers to set prices close to marginal costs. Markets with homogeneous products and many sellers are more likely to feature competitive pricing. Excess capacity exacerbates pricing pressures, often driving prices below average costs.

◆ Monopolistically competitive markets have many sellers, each with some loyal customers. Prices are set according to the willingness of consumers to switch from one seller to another—if consumers are disloyal, sellers may lower prices to steal business from their competitors. Profits may be eroded further by entrants establishing market niches—and finding loyal customers—of their own.

◆   In oligopolies, there are so few firms that each firm's production and pricing strategy appreciably affects the market price. Market prices can be well above marginal costs, or driven down to marginal costs, depending on the nature of the interaction between oligopolists and the degree of product differentiation between them.

◆   Monopolists have such a substantial share of their market that they ignore the pricing and production decisions of fringe firms. They may set price well above marginal cost without losing appreciable amounts of business. Firms that compete to achieve the monopoly position may dissipate monopoly profits.

◆   Studies of many industries confirm that prices are strongly related to industry structure. Price-cost margins tend to be much lower in more competitive markets.

◆   Factors that may deter entry, such as economies of scale and advertising, are associated with higher profits, This is consistent with the theoretical link between market structure and firm profits.

QUESTIONS

1.   Consider two industries with comparable consumer demands. In industry 1, production involves substantial fixed costs. In industry 2, production involves minimal fixed costs. Which industry is more likely to see price rivalry during its growth? How would price rivalry in each industry change if demand declines unexpectedly?

2.   Why is it that a firm in one geographic market that has achieved minimum efficient scale may be highly profitable, yet a firm in the same product market but a different geographic market, that has also achieved minimum efficient scale, may not be profitable at all? (Assume that both firms have achieved the same level of agency efficiency.)

3.   In a recent antitrust case, it was necessary to determine whether certain "elite" schools (mainly the Ivy League schools and MIT) constituted a separate market. How would you go about identifying the market served by these schools?

4.   How would you characterize the nature of competition in the restaurant industry? Are there submarkets with distinct competitive pressures? Are there important substitutes that constrain pricing? How can a restaurant be profitable?

5.   How does the calculation of demand responsiveness in Linesville change if customers rent two videos at a time? What intuition can you draw from this about the magnitude of price competition in various types of markets?

6.   What role does industry-level price elasticity of demand play in shaping the opportunities for making profit in an industry? What role does firm-level price elasticity of demand play in shaping the opportunities for making profit in an industry?

7. Wal-Mart has just built a new store in Martinsville, IN. Given the current population and spending habits in the local market, Wal-Mart is earning a profit that just barely covers its cost of capital. In the next five years, market demand is expected to double in size. Is it likely that a second discounter will enter the market when this happens?

STRATEGIC
COMMITMENT AND
COMPETITION

9

*I*n 1982, the management of Philips, N.V. of the Netherlands faced a critical choice: Should Philips build a disk-pressing plant to supply compact disks (CDs) to the American market, or should it delay its decision a year or so, until the commercial appeal of the compact disk market became more certain?[1] Philips' prototype had emerged as the industry standard for CDs, and within the next year, Philips was preparing to introduce CDs in the American market. By investing in a substantial amount of capacity in the American market in 1982, Philips might be able to discourage other firms—including its erstwhile partner Sony, who had allied itself with Philips in 1979 to promote the Philips CD standard—from making investments of their own in disk-pressing capacity in the United States, an outcome that might avert overcapacity and brutal price competition. Yet in 1982, the commercial viability of the CD was very much in question. With a cost of $25 million, a minimum efficient scale CD plant was an expensive proposition. If Philips' bet on the commercial success of the CD proved to be wrong, it would be stuck with a costly facility with practically no alternative uses.

Decisions such as investments in new capacity or introductions of new products are examples of *strategic commitments*. Strategic commitments are decisions that have long-term impacts and are difficult to reverse. Strategic commitments should be distinguished from *tactical decisions*—decisions that are easily reversed

---

[1]This discussion is based on McGahan, A.M., "The Incentive Not to Invest: Capacity Commitments in Compact Disc Introduction," *Research on Technological Innovation, Management and Policy,* 5, 1993, pp. 177–197.

and whose impact persists only in the short run. Decisions about what price to charge or how much output to produce in a given quarter are examples of decisions that can be easily altered or reversed. Unlike strategic commitments, tactical decisions can be adapted to the current situation the firm faces.

Strategic commitments can have an important influence on the nature of competition in an industry. A decision by a firm to expand capacity, for example, might deter new firms from entering the market, but it also could intensify pricing rivalry among existing firms. If firms are farsighted when they make their commitments, however, they will anticipate the effect their decisions have on market competition later on. This, then, implies that the details of market rivalry can have an important influence on the kinds of commitments firms make and the levels of commitment they choose.

Philips' dilemma illustrates the tensions associated with strategic commitments: When they work they can often shape competitors' expectations and change their behavior in ways that benefit the firm making the commitment. But because they are hard to reverse, commitments are inherently risky. Firms facing commitments of the sort Philips faced must balance the benefits that come from preempting or altering competitors' behavior with the loss in flexibility that comes from making competitive moves that may be hard to undo once they have been committed to. This chapter discusses economic considerations that underlie this balancing act.

◆ ◆ ◆ ◆ ◆ WHY COMMITMENT IS IMPORTANT

We illustrate the importance of commitment with a simple example. Two firms are competing in an oligopolistic industry. Firm 1, the dominant firm, is contemplating its capacity strategy and is considering two options, which we will broadly characterize as "aggressive" and "soft." One should think of the "aggressive" strategy as involving a large and rapid increase in capacity aimed at increasing its market share, while the "soft" strategy involves no change in the firm's capacity. Firm 2, a smaller competitor, is also contemplating its capacity expansion strategy; it will also choose between an "aggressive" strategy or a "soft" strategy. Table 9.1 shows the net present value of profit associated with each pair of options the two firms choose.

TABLE 9.1
PAYOFFS IN THE SIMPLE STRATEGY SELECTION GAME

| | | Firm 2 | |
		Aggressive	Soft
Firm 1	Aggressive	12.5, 4.5	16.5, 5
	Soft	15, 6.5	18,6

Net present values are in millions of dollars. First payoff listed is Firm 1's; second is Firm 2's.

If we imagine that they choose their strategies simultaneously, there is a unique Nash equilibrium in this game: Firm 1 chooses "soft," and Firm 2 chooses "aggressive," yielding a net present value of 15 for Firm 1.[2] From Firm 1's perspective, this is not the best outcome. For example, Firm 1 is always better off if Firm 2 chooses "soft," and it most prefers the outcome in which both firms choose "soft." Yet, without the cooperation of Firm 2, Firm 1 could probably not achieve this outcome. Can Firm 1 improve on the equilibrium that is actually reached?

It turns out that Firm 1 can improve upon the equilibrium outcome by a commitment to choose the aggressive strategy no matter what Firm 2 does. One way to pull this off would be for Firm 1 to make a *preemptive move:* accelerating its decision process and aggressively expanding its capacity before Firm 2 decides what to do. Such a move would transform a *simultaneous move* game into a *sequential game* in which Firm 2 would choose its capacity strategy after it has seen what Firm 1 has done. Another way would be for Firm 1 to announce to the industry that it planned to "go for share" and that to motivate its managers to achieve this goal, it would reward them on the basis of market share rather than profit. That way, it would be in the interest of Firm 1's managers to select the aggressive strategy even though it is seemingly less profitable than the soft strategy.

It may seem odd that Firm 1 would want to tie its hands so that it forces itself into the aggressive strategy no matter what. After all, for Firm 1 the profit from soft is greater than the profit from aggressive, *no matter what strategy Firm 2 chooses.* Yet, look what happens when Firm 1 commits itself to aggressive. Firm 2, realizing that Firm 1 has bound itself in this way, finds that it is better off choosing soft rather than aggressive. The resulting equilibrium (Firm 1 chooses aggressive, Firm 2 chooses soft) gives Firm 1 a higher profit (16.5 versus 15) than it would have gotten in the equilibrium that would have resulted if it had not committed itself to aggressive.

This simple example illustrates a profound point. Strategic commitments that seemingly limit options can actually make a firm better off. *Inflexibility can have value.* This is so because a firm's commitments can alter its competitors' expectations about how it will compete, and this, in turn, will lead competitors to make decisions that benefit the committed firm. In our simple example, by committing itself to choose what seems to be an inferior strategy (aggressive), Firm 1 alters Firm 2's expectations about what it will do. Had Firm 1 not made the commitment, Firm 2 would understand that it would have been in Firm 1's interest to "capitulate" and play soft. This would have led Firm 2 to choose aggressive. Firm 1's commitment makes aggressive an undesirable strategy for Firm 2. With Firm 1 committed to play aggressive, Firm 2 chooses soft, moving the industry to an equilibrium that makes Firm 1 better off.

Generals throughout history have understood the value of inflexibility, as the famous example of Hernań Cortes' conquest of Montezuma's Aztec empire in Mexico illustrates. When he landed in Mexico, Cortes ordered his men to burn all

---

[2]See the Economics Primer for a formal definition and discussion of the concept of a Nash equilibrium.

but one of his ships. Rather than an act of lunacy, Cortes' move was purposeful and calculated: By eliminating their only method of retreat, Cortes' men had no choice but to fight hard to win. According to Bernal Diaz del Castillo, who chronicled Cortes' conquest of the Aztecs, "Cortes said that we could look for no help or assistance except from God for we now had no ships in which to return to Cuba. Therefore we must rely on our own good swords and stout hearts."[3]

Of course, commitments must be visible and understandable if they are to work. In our example, Firm 2 must understand that Firm 1 has made the commitment to the aggressive strategy. Thus, whatever tangible form the commitment takes, whether it be through preemptive capacity expansion or a change in compensation structure for Firm 1's managers, Firm 2 must observe and understand it. Otherwise, it will not affect Firm 2's decision making. But visibility and understandability are not enough; the commitment must also be *credible*. Firm 2 must believe that Firm 1 intends to limit its options the way it claims it will. This is important because in our simple example, Firm 1's ideal course of action is to *bluff* Firm 2 into believing that it intends to choose aggressive, thereby causing Firm 2 to choose soft, but then to actually choose soft. For example, Firm 1 might *announce* that it intends to expand its capacity in the hope that Firm 2 will then abandon its decision to expand. Once this happens, Firm 1 would then abandon its own decision to expand.[4] If Firm 1 bluffs and forces the outcome (soft, soft), Firm 1 enjoys a profit of 18, as opposed to the 16.5 it would get if it carried out the aggressive strategy. Of course, Firm 2 should understand this, and discount as bluster any claims that Firm 1 makes regarding its intention to choose the aggressive strategy unless those claims can be backed up with credible actions.

A key to credibility is *irreversibility*. To be a true commitment, a competitive move must be hard or costly to stop once it is set in motion. For Firm 1 to make a public statement, for example, that it intends to expand its capacity may not be enough. "Talk is cheap," and press releases can be repudiated. It may instead have to begin constructing a new plant, which is far more irrevocable than a press release.

The degree to which real firms see competitive moves as irreversible commitments or reversible tactics is an interesting question.[5] Competitive moves, such as capacity expansion, that require significant up-front expenditures and result in the creation of relationship-specific assets, have a high commitment value. This is because once the assets have been created, the firm's ability to redeploy them

---

[3]This quote comes from Luecke, R., *Scuttle Your Ships Before Advancing and Other Lessons from History on Leadership and Change for Today's Managers*, Oxford: Oxford University Press, 1994, p. 23.

[4]One might wonder whether Firm 2's decision to abandon a capacity expansion decision is irreversible. Why couldn't Firm 2 reverse its decision not to build once its sees that Firm 1 has called off its plans? However, in some circumstances, this may be difficult to do. For example, Firm 2 may have an option on the land where the plant is to be built that it may not be able to exercise later if it does not act now. If other sites are distinctly inferior, Firm 2's choice may essentially be "now or never."

[5]Avinash Dixit and Barry Nalebuff's excellent book *Thinking Strategically: The Competitive Edge in Business, Politics and Everyday Life*, New York: Norton, 1991 contains a thorough discussion of credibility and the commitment value of various competitive moves.

outside their intended use is limited. For example, a CD pressing plant of the sort contemplated by Philips had virtually no alternative uses. Once it was built, Philips would have few options other than to run it full out.

Contracts can also facilitate commitment. One example of this that will be discussed in greater detail in Chapter 10 is a contract provision known as a *most favored customer clause* (MFCC). If a seller includes such a clause in a sales contract with a buyer, the seller is required to extend the same price terms to the buyer that it extends to its other customers. For example, if the seller discounts below its list price to steal a customer from a competitor, the buyer with an MFCC in its contract is entitled to the same discount. The MFCC makes discounting "expensive," and for this reason it can be thought of as a tool that creates a credible commitment not to compete on price.

Sometimes even public statements of intentions to take actions ("We plan to introduce a new and improved version of our existing product six months from now") can have commitment value. For this to be true, however, the firm's competitors and its customers must understand that the firm or its management are putting something at risk if it fails to match words with actions; otherwise, they will recognize that talk is cheap and discount the claims, promises, or threats the firm is making. The credibility of public announcements is enhanced when it is clear that the reputation of the firm or its senior management suffers when the firm fails to carry out what it has said it will do. In the computer software industry, it is more common for established firms, such as Microsoft, to make promises about new product performance and introduction dates than it is for smaller firms or industry newcomers to do so. This may, in part, be related to the fact that a newcomer has far more to lose in terms of credibility with consumers and opinion setters in the various personal computer magazines (an important forum for product reviews) than an established firm has. For this reason, smaller firms may be more reluctant to make exaggerated claims than established firms who have had a past track record of success. Failure to match actions to words will result in a significant loss of face or diminution of reputation for the firm and its senior management.

Example 9.1

COMMITMENT AND IRREVERSIBILITY IN THE AIRLINE INDUSTRY

In a recent study, Ming-Jer Chen and Ian MacMillan surveyed senior airline executives and industry analysts (e.g., financial analysts and academic experts) to study the degree of irreversibility in various competitive moves in the airline business.[6]

---

[6]Chen, M.-J. and I.C. MacMillan, "Nonresponse and Delayed Response to Competitive Moves: The Roles of Competitor Dependence and Action Irreversibility," *Academy of Management Journal*, 35, 1992, pp. 539–570.

Mergers and acquisition, investment in the creation of hubs, and feeder alliances with commuter airlines had the highest perceived irreversibility. Hubs required the creation of transaction-specific assets (e.g., maintenance facilities) that could not be redeployed if the hub was abandoned. Mergers and acquisitions required cooperation with the management of other airlines and third parties, such as investment bankers and regulatory authorities. Not only does the negotiation of the merger or acquisition entail significant nonrecoverable negotiation costs, it may also entail significant transaction-specific changes in operating procedures or systems. In addition, the reputation of a firm's management would suffer greatly (e.g., the firm would be seen as capricious or frivolous) if, after all the work involved in negotiating the merger or acquisition, it backed out at the last minute or tried to undo it once it was consummated. Feeder alliances with commuter airlines were seen as hard to reverse because employees and unions would oppose reversing the move.

Promotions, decisions to abandon a route, and increases in commission rates for travel agents were seen as being the easiest moves to reverse. Price cuts, while seen as having a below-average degree of irreversibility, were not viewed as the competitive move that was the easiest to reverse. Evidently, airline executives and industry analysts believe that once an airline cuts its prices, the inescapable cost of advertising the change is significant enough to make the airline maintain the new prices for some time. However, because price cuts are visible and clearly and immediately affect competing airlines' profitability, they are more provocative than other moves, such as temporary ad campaigns, that might be considered more reversible. Indeed, as we show in the next section, a firm's profit-maximizing response to a price cut by a competitor is generally to cut its own price as well. In addition, as we point out in Example 10.2 in Chapter 10, in the airline business, prices are instantaneously observable through a computerized clearinghouse, so competitors learn them right away and can quickly match them.

Chen and MacMillan hypothesized that competitors are less likely to match an airline's competitive move when the original move is hard to reverse. Their logic is akin to the simple example we discussed above. The more credible a firm's commitment to play aggressive, the more likely it is that its competitors will respond by playing soft. This logic would suggest that a preemptive move by one airline to expand its route system by acquiring another airline is less likely to provoke a matching response than a decision to engage in a short-term promotional or advertising campaign. Chen and MacMillan test this hypothesis through an exhaustive study of competitive moves and countermoves reported over a seven-year period (1979–1986) in the leading daily trade publication of the airline industry, *Aviation Daily*. In general, their findings support their hypothesis: harder-to-reverse moves are less frequently matched than easier-to-reverse moves. The study also supports the notion that price cuts are especially provocative and thus likely to be matched frequently and quickly. MacMillan and Chen find that rival airlines responded to price cuts more frequently than other moves they saw as having a similar, or even higher, degree of irreversibility.

STRATEGIC COMMITMENT AND COMPETITION ◆ ◆ ◆ ◆ ◆

In the simple game described by Table 9.1, the link between strategic commitments and tactical decisions was not spelled out explicitly. In the next two sections, we develop this connection more clearly, so that we can better understand how strategic commitments alter competition between firms.

Strategic Complements and Strategic Substitutes

The concepts of strategic complements and substitutes are important pieces in developing this understanding. To introduce these concepts, we return to the two models of product market competition introduced in Chapter 8: the Cournot model of quantity setting and the Bertrand model of price setting. Recall that in the Cournot model it was convenient to represent the equilibrium using reaction functions. In a two-firm Cournot industry, a firm's reaction function shows its profit-maximizing quantity as a function of the quantity chosen by its competitor. In the Cournot model, reaction functions are downward sloping, as Figure 9.1a shows. Reaction functions in the Bertrand model with horizontally differentiated products are defined analogously.[7] However, in this case, the reaction functions are upward sloping, as shown in Figure 9.1b.

In general, when reaction functions are *upward sloping*, we say that the firm's actions (e.g., prices) are *strategic complements*. When reaction functions are *downward sloping*, the actions are *strategic substitutes*.[8] When actions are strategic complements, the more of the action one firm chooses, the more of the action the other firm will also optimally choose. In the Bertrand model, prices are strategic complements because a reduction in price is the profit-maximizing response to a competitor's price cut. When actions are strategic substitutes, the more of the action one firm takes, the less of the action the other firm optimally chooses. In the Cournot model, quantities are strategic substitutes because a quantity increase is the profit-maximizing response to a competitor's quantity reduction. Determining whether actions are strategic complements or substitutes involves careful consideration of the competitive interdependence among the firms. One general rule of thumb is that prices are nearly always likely to be strategic complements, whereas quantity and capacity decisions are nearly always likely to be strategic substitutes.

---

[7]Reaction functions in the Bertrand model with undifferentiated products are not interesting because a firm always wants to slightly undercut its rival's price. Hence, throughout this section, we confine our attention to Bertrand industries where firms' products exhibit some degree of horizontal differentiation.

[8]The terms *strategic complements* and *strategic substitutes* are due to Bulow, J., J. Geanakopolos, and P. Klemperer, "Multimarket Oligopoly: Strategic Substitutes and Complements," *Journal of Political Economy,*" 93, 1985, pp. 488–511.

FIGURE 9.1
STRATEGIC SUBSTITUTES AND COMPLEMENTS.

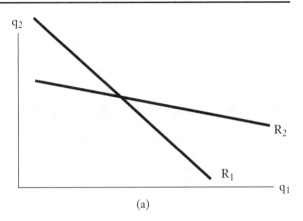

(a)

Panel (a) shows the reaction functions in a Cournot market. The reaction functions R_1 and R_2 slope downward, indicating that quantities are strategic substitutes. Panel (b) shows the reaction functions in a Bertrand market with differentiated products. The reaction functions slope upward, indicating that prices are strategic complements.

(b)

We will employ these concepts later in our discussion. But to preview why they are important, note that these concepts tell us something about how a firm expects its rival to react to its tactical maneuvers. When actions are strategic complements, one firm's aggressive behavior leads its competitors to behave more aggressively as well. For example, if a firm lowers its price (an aggressive move), its rival will also lower its price (an aggressive response), since its price reaction function is upward sloping. When actions are strategic substitutes, aggressive behavior by a firm leads its rival to behave less aggressively. For example, if a firm increases its output (an aggressive move), its rival will decrease its output (a soft response), since its output reaction function is downward sloping.

XAMPLE 9.2

STRATEGIC SUBSTITUTES IN THE WORLD MARKET FOR MEMORY CHIPS

As discussed in Chapter 8, the Cournot model of quantity setting can be thought of as pertaining to a market in which firms first choose capacities and then compete on price. This interpretation would then suggest that capacities are strategic substitutes and that a reduction in capacity by one firm would be expected to induce its competitors to increase their capacities. The $22 billion world market for memory chips provides an interesting illustration of this dynamic.[9]

The demand for memory chips, wafers of silicon smaller than a thumb nail, has exploded in recent years, driven by increased demand for personal computers and cellular phones as well as by the growing electronic sophistication of products, such as stereos and automobiles, that increasingly rely on memory chips. The timing of new investments is a critical part of doing business in this industry. New chip factories cost over $1 billion, but they become obsolete quickly, in some cases within three years.

In the early 1980s, the memory chip industry was dominated by American semiconductor firms. But in 1984, a drop in prices caused leading American chip makers, such as Intel and Texas Instruments, to postpone plans to build new chip factories. Japanese firms, such as Toshiba, NEC, and Oki Electric, responded by increasing their investments in new capacity. By the late 1980s, the Japanese had captured 80 percent of the world market, while the Americans held but 15 percent. Some American firms, such as Intel, abandoned the memory chip industry altogether.

A replay of this dynamic is occurring in the 1990s, but this time the firms that are aggressively expanding capacity are South Korean. Around 1990, in the midst of an industry downturn, major Japanese firms scaled back chip production. Then, as the Japanese economy entered a recession, Japanese chip makers began delaying investments in new chip factories, and those that did not delay found it increasingly difficult to finance new plants due to a weak Japanese stock market. By contrast, South Korean firms, such as Hyundai, Samsung, and Goldstar Electron, invested heavily in new chip-making capacity. By 1994, the South Koreans had 36 percent of the memory chip market, and Samsung had become the world's largest producer of memory chips.

Some industry observers are skeptical about whether Japanese firms will survive the fight. Japanese executives worry that memory chips could go the way of the Japanese steel and shipbuilding, once strong industries that fell victim to aggressive

---

[9]This example draws from "Silicon Duel: Koreans Move to Grab Memory-Chip Market From the Japanese," *Wall Street Journal*, March 14, 1995, pp. A1, A8.

South Korean competition. The head of Oki Electric's memory chip operation, Tetsuzo Taniguichi, states "Korean manufacturers have already replaced Japanese makers as the main producers of memory chips. . . . From now on, that kind of competition is over for Japan."

Strategic Incentives to Make Commitments

Let us again consider a market in which only two firms compete with each other. Firm 1 (but not Firm 2) is contemplating making a strategic commitment.[10] For example, the commitment might be the decision to adopt a process innovation that lowers variable production costs, such as Nucor's decision in 1987 to pioneer the thin-slab casting process in the steel industry. Or it might be a decision about how to position a new product, such as Quaker's recent decision to begin selling bagged, as opposed to boxed, cereals to appeal to the more price-elastic segment of the cold cereal market. Whatever its nature, the decision has two key properties. First, the rival firm must be aware of it. Second, it cannot be reversed once the firm makes it. The commitment is thus credible.

The timing of decision making in this market is as follows. Firm 1 first decides whether to make the commitment. Then, the two firms compete with each other. This two-stage game corresponds roughly to the distinction between strategy and tactics: Firm 1 first makes a strategic commitment in stage 1, then both firms maneuver tactically in stage 2. We will focus on two competitive scenarios in stage 2: Cournot quantity competition and Bertrand price competition. In the Cournot model, once Firm 1 decides whether to make the commitment, both firms then simultaneously choose quantities. In the Bertrand model, once Firm 1 decides whether to make the commitment, both firms then simultaneously choose prices.

Direct Effects and Strategic Effects

In analyzing the commitment decision, we want to distinguish between its *direct* and its *strategic effect.* The direct effect of the commitment is its impact on the present value of the firm's profits, *assuming that the firm adjusts its own tactical decisions in light of this commitment, but that its competitor's behavior does not change.* For example, if the commitment is an investment in a process improvement that reduces average variable costs, the direct effect of the investment is the present value of the increase in the firm's profit due to the reduction in its average variable costs, less the up-front cost of the investment. The increase in profit would come not only

---

[10]The case in which both firms make strategic commitments is similar to the one where only one firm makes a commitment. However, the economics of this case are more difficult to describe, so we concentrate on the simpler case of a one-firm commitment to keep the discussion compact.

from cost savings on existing units produced but also from any benefits the firm gets from lowering its price or increasing its output.[11]

The strategic effect takes into account the competitive side effects of the commitment: How does the commitment alter the tactical decisions of the rival and, ultimately, the Cournot (or Bertrand) equilibrium? The resulting change in the equilibrium also affects the firm's profits. Implicit in our consideration of the strategic effect is that Firm 1 takes the "long view" when making its commitment decision; that is, it takes into account how the commitment alters the nature of the equilibrium between the firms. In the simplest case to analyze, Firm 1 makes a key assumption: that the market will quickly reach the relevant equilibrium once it has made the commitment. In the quantity-setting market, Firm 1 believes that the market will immediately reach a new Cournot equilibrium after it has made its commitment. In the price-setting market, Firm 1 believes that the market will quickly reach a new Bertrand equilibrium. The assumption that Firm 1 is forward looking and anticipates how its commitment will alter the market equilibrium means that we are searching for a subgame perfect Nash equilibrium (SPNE) in a two-stage game in which, at stage 1, Firm 1 makes its commitment decision, and then at stage 2, both firms simultaneously choose quantities (or prices).[12]

Stage 2 Competition Is Cournot

Should Firm 1 make the commitment and if so, at what level? To answer this question, it must consider not just the direct effects of the commitment, but also the strategic effect. That is, Firm 1 should anticipate how the commitment might alter the Cournot equilibrium between it and Firm 2. As a starting point, we consider two alternative outcomes:

- The commitment makes Firm 1 tough. This means that if it makes the commitment, then no matter what output level Firm 2 produces, Firm 1 will produce *more* output than it would have done if it had not made the commitment. This corresponds to an outward shift in Firm 1's reaction curve R_1, from R_1^{before} to R_1^{after}, as shown in Figure 9.2. For example, Firm 1 would be making a tough commitment if it adopted a process innovation that reduced its marginal cost of production.[13]

---

[11]If changes in cost are small, this latter benefit is also likely to be small. This stems from the application of a principle known as the *envelope theorem:* If a firm is optimizing on one dimension (e.g., price or quantity) and selects a new level for a second dimension (in this case, average variable cost), then the incremental profits from refining the level of the first dimension in light of the change in the second dimension are relatively small and can be ignored when evaluating small changes in the second dimension.

[12]The Economics Primer contains a full discussion of the SPNE.

[13]Strategic incentives for investments of this kind have been analyzed by Brander, J. and B. Spencer, "Strategic Commitment with R & D: The Symmetric Case," *Bell Journal of Economics*, 14, Spring 1983, pp. 225–235.

FIGURE 9.2
COMMITMENT MAKES FIRM 1 "TOUGH" IN A COURNOT MARKET.

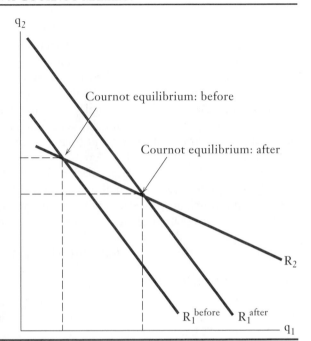

For any output produced by Firm 2, Firm 1 wants to produce more output than it would have before it made the commitment. This is represented by an outward shift in its reaction function from R_1^{before} to R_1^{after}. As a result, the Cournot equilibrium moves to the southeast and involves a higher quantity for Firm 1 and a lower quantity for Firm 2.

- The commitment makes Firm 1 soft. This means that if it makes the commitment, then no matter what output level Firm 2 produces, Firm 1 will produce *less* output than it would have done if it had not made the commitment. This corresponds to an inward shift in Firm 1's reaction curve R_1, as shown in Figure 9.3. To illustrate a soft commitment under Cournot competition, suppose that Firm 1, in addition to producing the good it produces in the Cournot market, has the opportunity to sell the same good as a monopolist in a second, geographically distinct, market. Suppose, further, that the marginal cost of production is an increasing function of the total amount of the good the firm produces in both markets combined; that is, the firm's technology is characterized by what economists call diminishing marginal returns. This might occur because the firm would use the same factory to produce both products, and as a greater volume of output is produced, the managerial resources of the firm become increasingly strained and production efficiency suffers. The decision to enter the monopoly market would be a soft commitment: By making that decision, Firm 1 would cause its marginal cost in the Cournot market to go up, and as a result, it would reduce its profit-maximizing output level for any given output expected from Firm 2. This would shift Firm 1's reaction function inward, as shown in Figure 9.3.

FIGURE 9.3
COMMITMENT MAKES FIRM 1 "SOFT" IN A COURNOT MARKET.

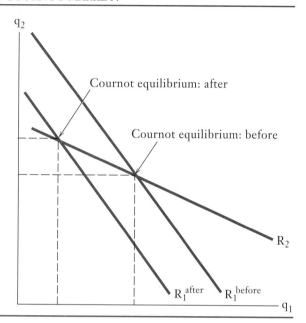

For any output produced by Firm 2, Firm 1 wants to produce less output than it would have before it made the commitment. This is represented by an inward shift in its reaction function from R_1^{before} to R_1^{after}. As a result, the Cournot equilibrium moves to the northwest and involves a lower quantity for Firm 1 and a higher quantity for Firm 2.

Figure 9.2 reveals that Firm 1 gets a beneficial competitive side effect from making the tough commitment: R_1 shifts outward, which results in a Cournot equilibrium in which Firm 2 produces less output. Because, in the Cournot model, Firm 1 is better off the less output its rival produces (since the market price will be higher), the Cournot equilibrium in which Firm 1 makes the commitment is better than the Cournot equilibrium in which Firm 1 does not make the commitment.

Taking this beneficial side effect into account can significantly impact how Firm 1 evaluates the commitment. In particular, the commitment might be valuable in this case, even though its direct effect is unfavorable. For example, suppose the commitment is an investment in a new process innovation for which the direct effect is negative (i.e., the present value of the investment assuming no competitive reactions is less than the up-front investment cost). It is possible that the beneficial strategic effect could outweigh the negative direct effect, and if so, the firm should make the investment for strategic purposes, even though its direct effect is negative. Drew Fudenberg and Jean Tirole call this the "top-dog strategy": Be big or strong to become tough or aggressive.[14] The market for memory chips discussed in Example 9.2 provides a possible example of the top-dog strategy. South Korean

---

[14]Fudenberg, D. and J. Tirole, "The Fat-Cat Effect, The Puppy-Dog Ploy, and the Lean and Hungry Look," *American Economic Review*, 74, May 1984, pp. 361–366.

companies, such as Samsung and Hyundai, collectively lost billions of dollars on their initial investments in memory chip production. But to the extent that these investments by Korean firms preempted the Japanese and caused them to scale back their plans, these investments may have had positive strategic effects, even though their direct effect may have been negative.

By contrast, as shown in Figure 9.3, when the commitment makes Firm 1 soft, it has a negative strategic effect. Firm 1's reaction curve R_1 shifts inward, resulting in a Cournot equilibrium in which Firm 2 produces more output than it would have produced had Firm 1 not made the commitment. If the direct effect of the commitment is negative, zero, or even slightly positive, Firm 1 should not make it. This analysis would suggest, for example, that entry into a new market in which the firm would be a monopolist may be undesirable if, due to diminishing marginal returns or diseconomies of scope, the firm's marginal cost in its first market goes up. Fudenberg and Tirole use the term "lean and hungry look" to characterize cases in which a firm refrains from making strategic commitments that make it soft or weak.[15] Refusing to make such commitments keeps the firm lean and hungry so that it looks tough or aggressive.

Stage 2 Competition Is Bertrand

Incentives for strategic commitment are different when stage 2 competition is Bertrand. As before, we distinguish between two cases:

- The commitment makes Firm 1 tough. This means that if Firm 1 makes the commitment, then no matter what price Firm 2 charges, Firm 1 will charge a *lower* price than it would have if it had not made the commitment. This corresponds to an inward shift in Firm 1's reaction curve R_1, as shown in Figure 9.4. As before, an example of a commitment that makes Firm 1 tough would be an investment in a process improvement that reduces its average variable and marginal cost of production.

- The commitment makes Firm 1 soft. This means that if Firm 1 makes the commitment, then no matter what price Firm 2 charges, Firm 1 will charge a *higher* price than it would have if it had not made the commitment. This corresponds to an outward shift in Firm 1's reaction curve R_1, as shown in Figure 9.5. For example, a soft commitment in the Bertrand context would be for Firm 1 to horizontally differentiate its product, for example, to reposition it so that it is better suited to the tastes in a niche of the market that is not well served by Firm 2. Expressed in terms of the model of spatial competition discussed in Chapter 8 (i.e., the "Linesville" example), this would involve moving Firm 1's product further away from Firm 2's product in geographic or product attribute space.

Consider, now, the competitive side effects of the commitment when it makes Firm 1 tough. As shown in Figure 9.4, Firm 1's reaction curve R_1 shifts inward,

---

[15] *Ibid.*

FIGURE 9.4
COMMITMENT MAKES FIRM 1 "TOUGH" IN A BERTRAND MARKET.

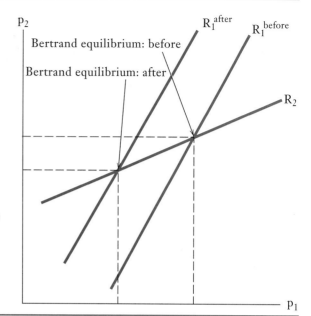

For any price charged by Firm 2, Firm 1 wants to charge a lower price than it would have before it made the commitment. This is represented by an inward shift in its reaction function from R_1^{before} to R_1^{after}. As a result, the Bertrand equilibrium moves to the southwest and involves a lower price for Firm 1 and a lower price for Firm 2.

FIGURE 9.5
COMMITMENT MAKES FIRM 1 "SOFT" IN A BERTRAND MARKET.

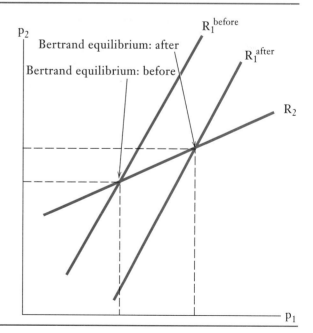

For any price charged by Firm 2, Firm 1 wants to charge a higher price than it would have before it made the commitment. This is represented by an outward shift in its reaction function from R_1^{before} to R_1^{after}. As a result, the Bertrand equilibrium moves to the northeast and involves a higher price for Firm 1 and a higher price for Firm 2.

moving the Bertrand equilibrium down to the southwest.[16] Firm 1 charges a lower price in equilibrium, but so does Firm 2, although its drop in price is not as large as Firm 1's. Firm 2's drop in price hurts Firm 1; the strategic effect is negative from Firm 1's perspective. If, for example, the strategic commitment is investment in a process innovation, and the direct effect is somewhat positive (i.e., the present value of the investment assuming no competitive reactions exceeds the up-front investment cost), it might be optimal for Firm 1 to refrain from this investment if the strategic effect is sufficiently negative. Fudenberg and Tirole call this strategy the "puppy-dog ploy": the firm stays small or weak to look soft or nonaggressive. Under the puppy-dog ploy, a firm either scales back the level of commitment, or refrains from making it altogether, so as to avoid heating up pricing rivalry with its competitors.

If the net present value of a cost-reducing commitment is positive, why wouldn't Firm 1 make the investment, but keep its price constant afterwards? It would then enjoy the benefits of its commitment (the cost reduction) without the negative competitive side effects. However, it is not clear that Firm 1 would be able to implement this strategy because even though this strategy is appealing *before* the commitment is made, it runs counter to Firm 1's self-interest *after* the commitment is made. After Firm 1 makes the commitment, its profit-maximizing price is lower than it was before; its reaction function shifts inward (see Figure 9.4). Thus, once the commitment has been made, Firm 1 wants to behave more aggressively in the second-stage pricing game. Since Firm 2 observes the commitment, it anticipates that Firm 1 will behave more aggressively, and it does so too. The result is the Bertrand equilibrium in which both firms charge lower prices than they would have before Firm 1 made its commitment. Firm 1 could attempt to short circuit this dynamic by announcing in advance that it planned to cut its costs, but not its price. But such an announcement would not be credible because both parties would understand that it would require Firm 1 to go against its self-interest once the commitment is made.

Finally, let us consider the incentives to make the commitment when it makes Firm 1 soft. In that case, shown in Figure 9.5, the commitment shifts Firm 1's reaction function outward. This, in turn, moves the Bertrand equilibrium to the northeast. The result is a higher price for both Firm 1 and Firm 2. This competitive side effect benefits Firm 1 and may make the commitment worthwhile, even if its direct effect is negative.

Consider, for example, the direct and strategic effects of repositioning Firm 1's product so that it appeals to a narrower segment of the market in which consumers

---

[16]It is also conceivable that Firm 1's commitment could result in a shift in Firm 2's reaction function. For example, if Firm 1 made its product less differentiated from Firm 2's, Firm 2's demand function would change, which would alter its profit-maximizing pricing decisions and thus shift its reaction function. However, taking this shift into account would reinforce the effect on the Bertrand equilibrium: It would move it even further down to the southwest in Figure 9.4.

have more specialized tastes. Holding prices of both firms fixed, the direct effect of this move is probably negative because Firm 1's product now appeals to fewer consumers than before, effectively shifting its demand curve inward. However, the strategic effect may be positive. The more horizontally differentiated the products of Firms 1 and 2 are, the less incentive each firm has to cut price to capture each other's customer base. Taking into full account the competitive implications, the commitment by Firm 1 to reposition its product might well be positive. Fudenberg and Tirole use the term "fat-cat effect" to refer to this case: A firm makes a strategic commitment to make itself soft—to become a fat cat that does not compete very hard—which has the beneficial side effect of softening price competition in the market.

A Taxonomy of Commitment Strategies

Figure 9.6 summarizes the discussion in the previous section. Whether a firm should make a strategic investment depends on whether the commitment makes the firm tough or soft and on whether the tactical variables in the stage 2 competition are strategic substitutes or complements.

FIGURE 9.6
A TAXONOMY OF STRATEGIC COMMITMENTS.

Commitment makes the Firm ...

Stage 2 tactical variables are...	Tough	Soft
Strategic Complements (e.g., prices)	"Puppy-Dog Ploy" Strategic effect is negative: commitment causes rival to behave more aggressively.	"Fat-Cat Effect" Strategic effect is positive: commitment causes rival to behave less aggressively.
Strategic Substitutes (e.g., quantities)	"Top-Dog Strategy" Strategic effect is positive: commitment causes rival to behave less aggressively.	"Lean and Hungry Look" Strategic effect is negative: commitment causes rival to behave more aggressively.

The impact of strategic commitments on the market equilibrium depends on whether the Stage 2 tactical variables are strategic complements or strategic substitutes and on whether the commitment makes the firm tough or soft. This yields the four different possibilities.

If the stage 2 tactical variables are strategic complements—that is, the reaction curves slope upward—and the commitment makes the firm tough, then the commitment alters the stage 2 equilibrium, so that rival firms behave more aggressively (e.g., set lower prices in the Bertrand model). In this case, the commitment has a harmful strategic effect, and the firm has an incentive either to forgo the commitment altogether or to underinvest in it—to make the commitment at a lower level (e.g., spend less on an investment in a process innovation) than it would have had it not considered the strategic side effects. This is the puppy-dog ploy. By contrast, when the commitment makes the firm soft, it results in an equilibrium in which rivals behave less aggressively (e.g., set higher prices). The commitment thus has a beneficial strategic effect, and the firm has an incentive to overinvest in it—to make the commitment at a higher level than it would have had it not considered the competitive side effects. This is the fat-cat effect.

If the stage 2 tactical variables are strategic substitutes—that is, the reaction curves slope downward—and the commitment makes the firm tough, then in the second-stage equilibrium, rival firms become less aggressive (e.g., choose lower quantities). The commitment has a beneficial strategic effect, and the firm has an incentive to overinvest in the commitment. This is the top-dog strategy of investing to become a more aggressive competitor. The other possibility is that the commitment makes the firm soft, which has a negative strategic effect because rival firms respond by behaving more aggressively. Here the firm has an incentive to underinvest in the commitment. This is the lean and hungry look.

The analysis summarized in Figure 9.6 has two important implications for strategic decision making and market analysis. First, and most basic, it suggests that when making hard-to-reverse investment decisions, managers ought not to look only at the effects of the investment on their own firm. They should also try to anticipate how the decision to invest or not invest will affect the evolution of market competition in the future. A recent management fad that is intended to promote this way of thinking is known as "war gaming": Elaborate computer simulations allow managers to track the likely competitive implications of pricing and investment decisions over many years.[17] For example, the consulting firm Coopers & Lybrand commissioned the creation of a war game known as TeleSim for Pacific Telesis. TeleSim allows Pacific Telesis's managers to analyze the competitive effects of changes in regional toll rates and investments in new plant and equipment. RJR managers used a war game created by the consulting firm Booz Allen to help plot competitive reactions to Philip Morris' decision to cut the price of its Marlboro brand of cigarettes in April 1993.

Second, the details of market rivalry can profoundly influence the willingness of firms to make commitments. For example, the theory developed above tells us that an investment in a process innovation that reduces marginal costs has

---

[17]See "Business War Games Attract Big Warriors," *Wall Street Journal*," December 22, 1994, pp. B1, B4.

a beneficial strategic effect in a Cournot industry, but has a negative strategic effect in a Bertrand industry. At one level, this implication may not seem to be terribly useful. In practice, it is often very difficult to distinguish which model applies in any particular situation. Indeed, as will be argued in Chapter 10, neither the Cournot nor the Bertrand model may do an especially good job of capturing the richness of repeated interactions among firms. However, one should not take the models of product market competition so literally that they obscure the robust point that comes out of the theoretical discussion above: A commitment that induces competitors or potential entrants to behave less aggressively—for example, to refrain from price cutting, to postpone or abandon capacity expansion plans, or to cut back on the amount of advertising or promotional activity that they engage in—is likely to have a beneficial strategic effect on the firm making the commitment. By contrast, a commitment that induces competitors or potential entrants to behave more aggressively is likely to have a harmful strategic effect.

The assessment of how a commitment will affect the evolution of market competition will depend on industry conditions and the characteristics of the firm's competitors. Sometimes the effect of the strategic commitment on a competitor may depend on whether the competitor is currently in the industry or has not yet entered. For example, if a firm adopts a process innovation, it may price more aggressively, disrupting the industry equilibrium and leading to more aggressive pricing by existing competitors as they attempt to preserve their market shares. Yet the expectation of intensified pricing rivalry may deter potential competitors from entering the market in the first place.

The strategic effects of the commitment might also depend on capacity utilization rates in the industry. For example, when industry capacity utilization rates are low, a firm's commitment to a new process innovation that lowers its marginal cost may be met by an aggressive price response from rivals who fear further losses in capacity utilization and who have the ability to take on new business that comes their way if they cut price. In this case, the strategic effect of the commitment is likely to be negative. By contrast, when capacity utilization rates are high, competitors are less well positioned to respond aggressively unless they expand their capacities. But the expectation of more aggressive behavior by the firm making the commitment may deter its competitors from going forward with their plans to expand capacity. If so, the strategic effect is likely to be positive.

The strategic effects of the commitment may also depend on the degree of horizontal differentiation among the firm making the commitment and its competitors. For example, Figure 9.7a shows that in a Bertrand market the magnitude of the strategic effect depends on the degree of horizontal differentiation. When the firms' products are highly differentiated, as in panel (a), the strategic effect from an investment in cost reduction is likely to be relatively unimportant. However, when products are relatively less differentiated, as in panel (b), the strategic effect is relatively larger.

FIGURE 9.7
STRATEGIC EFFECTS AND PRODUCT DIFFERENTIATION.

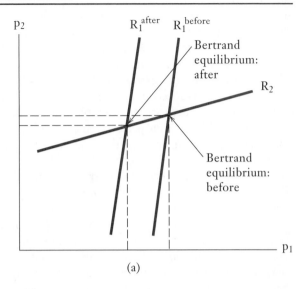

(a)

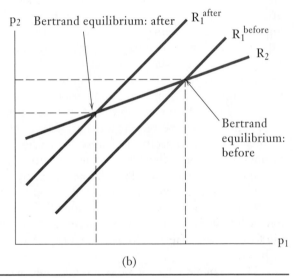

Panel (a) shows a market in which the two firms' products are highly differentiated. Firm 1's commitment to a cost-reducing investment hardly affects Firm 2's pricing decision, so the strategic effect in this case is negligible. Panel (b) shows a market in which the two firms' products are less differentiated. Firm 2's commitment to a cost-reducing investment has a relatively bigger impact on Firm 2's pricing decision, so the strategic effect is more significant than it is in the market in panel (a).

(b)

EXAMPLE 9.3

COMMITMENT AT NUCOR AND USX: THE CASE OF THIN SLAB CASTING[18]

Pankaj Ghemawat's case study of the adoption of thin slab casting by Nucor and the nonadoption by USX provides an excellent illustration of the relationship between commitment and product market competition and how previous commitments by a firm can limit its ability to take advantage of new commitment opportunities.

The modern production of steel relies on a process called continuous casting. Under this process hot molten steel is cast into a long continuous slab, about 8 to 10 inches in thickness. The long slab is then cut into smaller slabs of about 20 to 40 feet, which are then sent on for further processing for conversion into finished products, such as sheet steel. Continuous casting, which was commercialized in the 1950s, was a major technological breakthrough in the steel industry. However, the efficiency of continuous casting for the production of sheet steel was limited by the need to reheat the slabs prior to rolling them into thin sheets. Major cost savings would result if the molten steel could be cast directly into thin sheets. Development of such a process, known as thin slab casting, proved elusive until the mid-1980s, when a West German company, SMS Schloemann-Siemag, developed a commercially viable thin slab casting process.

In 1987, Nucor Corporation became the first American firm to adopt thin slab casting. At that time, Nucor was looking for a way to enter the flat-rolled sheet segment of the steel business, a segment that had heretofore been unavailable to the so-called minimills, of which Nucor was the largest. Adoption of this technology was a major commitment for Nucor. All told, the up-front investment in developing the process and building a facility was expected to be $340 million, close to 90 percent of Nucor's net worth at the time. The commitment appears to have been a successful one for Nucor. By 1992, Nucor's thin slab casting mill in Crawfordsville, Indiana had become profitable, and Nucor currently is building a second thin slab casting plant in Arkansas.

USX, the largest American integrated steel producer and a company 60 times as large as Nucor, also showed an early interest in thin slab casting, spending over $30 million to perfect a thin slab casting technology known as the Hazelett process. Yet, USX eventually decided not to adopt thin slab casting. Ghemawat argues that this decision is anomalous in light of extant economic theory on process innovations. This theory suggests that if (i) an innovation is nondrastic (i.e., it will not lower the first-adopter's costs so much as to make all other firms in the industry noncompetitive);

---

[18]This example is based on Ghemawat, P., "Commitment to a Process Innovation: Nucor, USX, and Thin Slab Casting," *Journal of Economics and Management Strategy*, 2, Spring 1993, pp. 133–161.

(ii) the innovation is likely to make the adopter tough as opposed to soft in postadoption competition; and (iii) the returns from the process involve relatively low amounts of uncertainty as compared to returns from the existing technology, then a large incumbent firm (i.e., USX) will have a stronger incentive to adopt the technology than a new entrant (i.e., Nucor). (This is a complicated example of the top-dog strategy discussed earlier.) Ghemawat makes the case that all of these conditions held in the case of thin slab casting: It was a nondrastic innovation; capacity utilization rates in the industry were well below 100 percent, which suggested that firms in the industry competed as Bertrand price setters, which in turn would suggest that a process innovation like thin slab casting that lowered average variable costs would make the adopter tough, rather than soft. And the returns from thin slab casting were probably fairly predictable since the process Nucor adopted was, from the perspective of 1986–87, considered to be incremental as opposed to pathbreaking.

So why did USX not adopt? One way of explaining USX's nonadoption is to modify the theory just described to include scale constraints. If the entrant adopts the new technology and the efficient size of a new plant is relatively small, then the incumbent's incentive to adopt first is weakened. In effect, the entrant becomes a puppy dog, which reduces the incumbent's incentive to adopt the technology preemptively. Still, as Ghemawat notes, this explanation is not entirely persuasive. Even though the efficient scale of a thin slab casting plant is relatively small, Nucor had announced its intentions to construct several more thin slab casting plants if the new process worked as planned at its Crawfordsville facility.

A more compelling explanation of USX's nonadoption, argues Ghemawat, involves a recognition of various prior organizational and strategic commitments that constrained USX's opportunity to profit from thin-slab casting. For example, in the mid-1980s, USX had already modernized four of its five integrated steel mills. The fifth plant, located in the Monongahela River Valley in Pennsylvania, was a vast complex in which the steel making facility and the rolling mill were 10 miles apart. Moreover, the labor cost savings that would accrue to a nonunionized firm like Nucor would not be nearly as significant to unionized USX, which was bound by restrictive work rules. Finally, there was doubt as to whether appliance manufacturers, who were major customers of the sheet steel produced in the Monongahela Valley plant, would purchase sheet steel produced via continuous casting due to the potential adulteration in the surface quality of the steel from the new process.

Ghemawat argues that the prior commitment by USX to modernize existing facilities—in particular the one at Monongahela Valley—as opposed to building "greenfield" plants, locked USX into a posture in which nonadoption of thin slab casting was a natural outcome. This conclusion highlights an important strategic point: In forecasting the likely reactions of competitors to major strategic commitments, a firm should recognize that prior commitments made by its competitors can constrain their potential responses. In this case, USX's behavior was anticipated by Nucor's management, who made the decision to enter the flat-rolled sheet steel business based on the expectation that integrated producers, such as USX, would decline to adopt thin slab casting.

EXAMPLE 9.4

FINANCIAL STRUCTURE AND PRODUCT MARKET COMPETITION

James Brander and Tracy Lewis have applied the theory of strategic commitment to study the effects of the firm's financial structure on product market competition.[19] In the first stage of the setting they study, firms choose how much debt to issue to finance their investment. In the second stage, the firms compete as Cournot quantity setters in a market in which demand is uncertain. Because demand is uncertain, a firm that issues debt faces the possibility of bankruptcy; it will be unable to make its required payments to creditors.

The more debt the firm uses, the more aggressive it will be. (Recall, in the Cournot context, "more aggressive" means that the firm will want to produce more output, for any given amount of output produced by its competitors.) Why is this so? To explain this linkage between financial structure and product market behavior, we need to take a short detour into finance theory to explore stockholders' preference for the riskiness of debt. Because the liability of corporate stockholders is limited, whenever the stockholders issue risky debt, they are, in effect, purchasing a "call option" on the earnings of the firm.[20] Shareholders exercise this option when they repay the debt.[21] Basic option theory tells us that the value of an option increases the greater the volatility of the underlying asset.[22] Viewing the firm's earnings as the underlying asset, this then implies that the greater the firm's financial leverage is, the more its shareholders prefer earnings volatility. The intuition is that shareholders prefer higher profits to lower profits, but once the firm has been pushed into bankruptcy, they are indifferent to whether its losses are large or small.

By tying these insights back into the Cournot model of product market competition, we can see why more debt makes the firm behave more aggressively. In the Cournot model, demand uncertainty leads to fluctuations in the market price. The more output the firm produces, the more susceptible it will be to these fluctuations, and thus the more volatile its earnings will be.[23] If the firm's management chooses output in the second stage to maximize shareholder wealth, its incentive to expand output in the second stage will be greater the more debt the firm has issued in the first stage.

---

[19]Brander, J.A. and T.R. Lewis, "Oligopoly and Financial Structure: The Limited Liability Effect," *American Economic Review*, 76, 1986, pp. 956–970.

[20]A call option gives the holder the right to purchase a share of a stock at a prespecified price (called an *exercise price*) on or before a specific date.

[21]The insight that debt is analogous to a call option was first recognized by Black, F. and M. Scholes, "The Pricing Options and Corporate Liabilities," *Journal of Political Economy*, 81, May–June 1973, pp. 637–654.

[22]See, for example, Brealey, R.A. and S.C. Myers, *Principles of Corporate Finance*, 3rd ed., New York: McGraw Hill, 1988.

Because debt makes a firm more aggressive, the logic of the top-dog strategy applies. Brander and Lewis show that each firm in the Cournot market has an incentive to take on more debt than it otherwise would have had it ignored the strategic effect of debt. This is because the issuance of debt is a strategic commitment to behave more aggressively in its interactions with rivals in the product market, which, as we have seen, is valuable in the Cournot model. Indeed, even when the existence of bankruptcy costs and the absence of tax benefits from debt would lead a firm to choose all-equity financing, the strategic effect of debt can lead to an optimal debt–equity ratio that is positive.

Of course, as we have stressed, the details of product market competition matter. Thus, Brander and Lewis's theory only provides a suggestion about what *might* happen, rather than offering a definitive prediction about what *will* happen. For example, if the firms competed as Bertrand price competitors in a market with horizontal differentiation, the puppy-dog ploy, not the top-dog strategy, would apply. The strategic effect of debt would then be unfavorable, since by committing to a high level of debt a firm would anticipate that it would ultimately elicit a more aggressive response from its competitors.

In the Brander and Lewis model, debt influences the firm's product market behavior because it provides an incentive for the firm's management to alter output or pricing decisions in order to increase earnings volatility. But financial structure decisions could also influence product market decisions in other ways. Suppose, for example, that a firm has the opportunity to make future investments in capacity expansion or in process improvements that lower marginal cost. If increased debt reduces the firm's future borrowing capacity, increasing its debt–equity ratio (e.g., through a stock repurchase financed by borrowed funds) would be a way for the firm to credibly commit *not* to expand capacity or invest in cost-reducing process improvements. Whether such a commitment is desirable would again depend on the details of product market competition. Since this is a commitment that makes the firm soft, then with Cournot quantity competition, the lean and hungry look would apply, and the firm would want to refrain from increasing its debt in this manner. On the other hand, with Bertrand price competition, the fat-cat effect would apply, and firms should increase leverage to soften price competition.

Is there evidence that financial structure decisions affect the intensity of product market competition? Recently, Gordon Phillips studied this question using data from four industries: fiberglass roofing and insulation, tractor trailer manufacturing, polyethylene chemicals, and gypsum wallboard manufacturing.[24] Each of

---

[23]Technically speaking, the impact of the demand uncertainty on the volatility of the firm's earnings also depends on the marginal impact of the demand uncertainty on the slope of the market demand curve (since by expanding output, a firm in the Cournot model reduces market price). Taking this effect into account, for plausible specifications of demand uncertainty, it can be shown that increases in output increase the volatility of the firm's earnings.

[24]Phillips, G.M., "Capital Structure, Firm Performance, and Competition," unpublished Ph.D. dissertation, Harvard University.

these industries is a concentrated oligopoly, and in the 1980s one or more of the dominant firms in each industry underwent a major leveraged recapitalization that substantially increased the proportion of debt in its capital structure. For example, Owens-Corning Fiberglass, the largest firm in the fiberglass insulation market, used a leveraged recapitalization to increase its debt–equity ratio by over 50 percent in 1986. Using statistical techniques designed to estimate the intensity of price competition over time, Phillips found that increased leveraged significantly altered product market competition in all four industries. In the gypsum wallboard industry, the intensity of price competition increased. In the fiberglass insulation, tractor trailer, and polyethylene chemicals businesses, price competition decreased, a result consistent with the hypothesis that debt restricted the firms from investing free cash flow in process improvements or capacity expansion that would lower marginal costs.

FLEXIBILITY AND OPTION VALUE   ◆ ◆ ◆ ◆ ◆

The strategic effect of a commitment is positive when the commitment alters competitors' behavior in ways that are advantageous to the firm making the commitment. These beneficial strategic effects are often rooted in inflexibility. For example, by preemptively investing in capacity expansion, a firm may leave itself little choice but to price aggressively in order to maintain capacity utilization rates. In doing so, however, it may foreclose growth opportunities for rival firms, forcing them to scale back their plans to expand capacity.[25]

However, strategic commitments are almost always made under conditions of uncertainty about market conditions, costs, or competitors' goals and resources. For example, in deciding whether to build a CD plant in the United States, Philips had to confront the risk that the CD would have little appeal to all but the most dedicated audiophiles. When competitive moves are hard to reverse and the outcomes of those moves are shrouded in uncertainty, the value of preserving flexibility, of keeping one's future options open, must be factored into the process of evaluating the benefits of the commitment.

Flexibility is important because it gives the firm *option value*.[26] A simple example of option value occurs when the firm has the opportunity to delay an investment and await the revelation of new information that bears on its profitability. To illustrate the option value of delay, consider a firm that can spend $100 million on an investment in a plant to enter a new market. Given the uncertainties about the level of market acceptance of the new product, the firm forecasts two scenarios: a "high-acceptance" scenario in which the investment will have a present value of

---

[25]This is an example of the top-dog strategy.

[26]See Dixit, A.K. and R.S. Pindyck, *Investment Under Uncertainty*, Princeton, NJ: Princeton University Press, 1994, for pioneering work on the option value of real investments.

$300 million, and a "low-acceptance" scenario in which the present value of the investment will be $50 million. The firm believes that each scenario is equally likely. If the firm invests today, the expected net present value (NPV) of the investment is .5(300) + .5(50) − 100 = $75 million. But suppose, by waiting a year, it can learn for certain which scenario will arise (perhaps by observing the demand for the product in another geographically distinct market). If the firm waits, and it turns out that the product has a high level of market acceptance investment, the firm should invest and get a net present value of $200 million. But if the investment has a present value of $50 million, the firm is better off not investing in this project and putting its money in the next best alternative, which we shall assume is a zero NPV investment. Assuming a 10 percent annual discount rate, if the firm waits, its expected NPV is [.5(200) + .5(0)]/(1.1) = $91 million, which exceeds the $75 million NPV from investing right away.[27] The option value of delay is the difference between the expected net present value if the firm invests today and the expected net present value if the firm waits until the uncertainty resolves itself. In this case, the option value of delay is $91 − $75 = $16 million.

More generally, option value arises when the firm leaves itself with options that allow it to better tailor its decision making to the underlying circumstances it faces. In the above example, by waiting, the firm avoids the possibility of making a big mistake: investing in a bad project (i.e., one with a present value of $50 million). Of course, there are factors that limit option values. For instance, our example did not take into account the fact that by waiting the firm risks having the investment opportunity preempted by competitors. A complete analysis of the option value of delaying investments should attempt to factor in such considerations.

$\mathcal{E}$XAMPLE 9.5

COMMITMENT VERSUS FLEXIBILITY IN THE CD MARKET

In the introduction to this chapter and again in this section, we have referred to Philips' decision in 1983 whether to invest in a new CD pressing plant in the United States. That decision highlights the tension between the strategic effects of commitment and the option value of waiting. By building a plant in 1983, Philips might preempt Sony and other potential competitors from building their own CD plants, an example of the top-dog strategy. But because the investment in a CD plant involved a large irreversible commitment, there was an option value for Philips to waiting and seeing whether market acceptance of CDs would be strong enough to make an investment in a U.S. plant worthwhile.

---

[27]We divide by 1.1 to reflect the fact that if the firm waits, all cash flows from the investment are delayed by one year. Alternatively, we could have adjusted the present values of the investment to reflect the time value costs of delay.

Anita McGahan studied Philips' decision in detail and derived thresholds on what the probability of market acceptance would have to have been for it to have been worthwhile for Philips to delay investment.[28] To isolate the pure option effect, McGahan first analyzed what Philips' decision would have been if it had faced no competition in the CD market. She concludes that Philips would have been better off waiting and retaining flexibility if the probability that the popular market would accept the CD was .38 or lower, indicating a nontrivial, albeit not overwhelmingly large, option effect. By contrast, if Philips faced competitors who would learn about market demand at the same time it did, Philips would have been better off delaying investment only if the probability of market acceptance was .006 or lower. This substantially lower threshold indicates that had Philips faced competitors who would be as well informed as it would be about market demand, Philips should have almost certainly built a plant right away despite the demand uncertainty. This indicates that Philips' incentive to be a top dog was very strong, even taking into account the option value of flexibility. But, as McGahan points out, Philips' information about demand was likely to be obtained through proprietary experience gained through its CD operations in Europe. Thus, it would know before the competition whether market acceptance was likely to be high enough to make a CD plant in the United States worthwhile. This informational advantage raises the option value of flexibility; McGahan estimates that Philips would have been better off waiting if the probability of market acceptance was .13 or lower.

Philips ultimately decided not to build the U.S. plant in 1983, suggesting that it was fairly pessimistic about the prospects of CDs in the American market. In 1984, Sony became the first CD manufacturer to produce in the United States, opening a plant in Terre Haute, Indiana. Philips initially chose to increase capacity at its pressing plant in Hanover, Germany. It decided to invest in a U.S. plant only after Sony's plant was fully operational.

A FRAMEWORK FOR ANALYZING COMMITMENTS ◆ ◆ ◆ ◆ ◆

Pankaj Ghemawat argues that major strategic decisions nearly always involve investments in "sticky factors": physical assets, resources, and capabilities that are *durable*, *specialized* to the particular strategy that the firm follows, and *untradeable* (i.e., they cannot be sold on the open market).[29] Once investments in such assets have been made, they cannot easily be transformed or redeployed elsewhere. For example, once Wang Laboratories staked its future on dedicated word processing, it would have been extremely difficult to alter its strategy and move into personal computer manufacturing, which required capabilities that Wang did not have and

---

[28]McGahan, A.M., "The Incentive Not to Invest: Capacity Commitment in the Compact Disc Introduction," *Research on Technological Innovation, Management and Policy*, 5, 1993, pp. 177–197.

[29]Ghemawat, P., *Commitment: The Dynamic of Strategy*, New York: Free Press, 1991.

could not quickly acquire. Because strategic investments are durable, specialized, and untradeable, after a firm has made them, it is stuck. The firm must continue with its chosen strategy for a considerable time. In this sense, according to Ghemawat, the choice of a strategy is manifested in a few commitment-intensive decisions. The essence of strategy, in his view, is getting these commitments right.

But getting these decisions right is difficult. Commitment-intensive decisions are fraught with risk and require that managers take a deep look into the future to evaluate the benefits and costs of alternative strategic actions. To aid managers in making such choices, Ghemawat sets forth a four-step framework for analyzing commitment-intensive choices:

- Positioning analysis
- Sustainability analysis
- Flexibility analysis
- Judgment analysis

Positioning analysis can be likened to the determination of the direct effects of the commitment. It involves the analysis of whether the firm's commitment is likely to result in a product market position in which the firm delivers superior consumer benefits or operates with lower costs than competitors. Chapters 12 and 13 develop a set of concepts, frameworks, and tools for conducting positioning analysis.

Sustainability analysis can be likened to the determination of the strategic effects of the commitment. It involves an analysis of potential responses to the commitment by competitors and potential entrants in light of the commitments that they have made and the impact of those responses on the evolution of competition. It also involves an analysis of the market imperfections that make the firm's resources scarce and immobile and the conditions that protect the firm's sources of competitive advantage from imitation by competitors. Chapters 11, 14, and 15 develop frameworks and concepts for conducting sustainability analysis.

The culmination of positioning and sustainability analysis, in Ghemawat's view, should be a formal analysis of the net present value of alternative strategic commitments. Positioning analysis provides the basis for determining the revenues and costs associated with each alternative. Sustainability analysis provides the basis for determining the time horizon beyond which the firm's rate of return on incremental investments is no greater than its cost of capital, that is, its economic profits are zero.[30]

Flexibility analysis incorporates uncertainty into positioning and sustainability analysis. As discussed earlier, flexibility is important because it gives the firm option value. Ghemawat points out that a key determinant of option value is the

---

[30]The concept of a time horizon beyond which the firm's investments yield a rate of return no greater than its cost of capital is a standard part of models used by financial analysts to determine the value of firms. In some models, it is called the *forecasting horizon*. G. Bennett Stewart refers to this horizon as "big T." See *The Quest for Value: A Guide for Senior Managers*, New York: HarperBusiness, 1991.

learn-to-burn ratio. This is the ratio of the "learn rate"—the rate at which new information is received by the firm that allows it to adjust its strategic choices, and the "burn rate"—the rate at which the firm is investing in the sunk assets to support the strategy. A high learn-to-burn ratio implies that a strategic choice is characterized by a high degree of flexibility. In this case, the option value of delay is low because the firm can quickly accumulate information about the prospects of its strategic choice before it is too heavily committed. Ghemawat argues that many commitment-intensive choices have the potential for high learn-to-burn ratios, but that the realization of this potential requires careful management. Experimentation and pilot programs are ways that a firm can increase its learn-to-burn ratio and increase the degree of flexibility in making commitment-intensive choices.

The final part of Ghemawat's framework is judgment analysis: taking stock of the organizational and managerial factors that might distort the firm's incentive to choose an optimal strategy. Ghemawat notes that firms can make two types of errors in making commitment-intensive choices: Type I errors—rejecting an investment that is, in fact, good and should have been accepted—and Type II errors—accepting an investment that is, in fact, bad and should have been rejected. Theoretical work by Raaj Kumar Sah and Joseph Stiglitz suggests that the design of decision-making systems inside the organization can influence the likelihood of both types of errors.[31] Specifically, they show that organizations in which the authority to screen and accept investment projects is decentralized will accept a larger proportion of good as well as bad investment opportunities as compared with an organization in which investment decisions are made hierarchically, that is, they are first screened at lower levels and then sent "upstairs" for final approval. This implies that decentralized decision making results in a relatively higher incidence of Type II errors, while hierarchical decision making results in a relatively higher incidence of Type I errors. This analysis suggests that part of the process of making commitment-intensive decisions is a choice of how to make such decisions. In working through the first three parts of this framework, managers must be cognizant of the biases imparted by the incentives of the firm's managers to send accurate information up through the hierarchy, by the structure of the organization, and by its politics and culture. We take up these issues in Chapters 17, 18, and 19.

CHAPTER SUMMARY

◆ Strategic commitments are hard-to-reverse decisions that have long-term impacts. They should be distinguished from tactical decisions that are easy to reverse and whose impact persists only in the short run.

---

[31]Sah, R.K. and J. Stiglitz, "The Architecture of Economic Systems: Hierarchies and Polyarchies," *American Economic Review,* 76, September 1986, pp. 716–727.

◆ Strategic commitments that seemingly limit options may make a firm better off. *Inflexibility can have value.* The reason this is so is that a firm's commitments can alter its competitors' expectations about what it will do, and this, in turn, will lead competitors to make decisions that are advantageous for the firm making the commitment.

◆ The impact of strategic commitments on product market competition depends on the nature of product market competition. The concepts of strategic complements and strategic substitutes are useful for characterizing how commitment affects competition. When reaction functions are upward sloping, actions are strategic complements. When reaction functions are downward sloping, actions are strategic substitutes.

◆ The direct effect of a commitment is its impact on the present value of the firm's profits, assuming that competitors' actions remain unchanged after the firm has made its commitment. The strategic effect of a commitment is the impact of competitive side-effects of the commitment on the firm's profits.

◆ In a two-stage setting, in which a firm makes a commitment and then the firm and its competitors choose tactical actions, the desirability of the commitment depends on whether the actions are strategic substitutes or complements and whether the commitment makes the firm tough or soft. If a commitment makes the firm tough and second-stage tactical actions are strategic substitutes, it may want to undertake the commitment for strategic reasons, even if its direct effect is negative. This is the top-dog strategy. If a commitment makes the firm soft and actions are strategic substitutes, it may want to refrain from the commitment, even if its direct effect is positive. This is known as the lean and hungry look. If a commitment makes the firm tough and the actions are strategic complements, the firm may want to refrain from the commitment, even if its direct effect is positive. This is known as the puppy-dog ploy. Finally, if a commitment makes the firm soft and the actions are strategic complements, the firm may want to make the commitment, even though its direct effects are negative. This is known as the fat-cat effect.

◆ Flexibility is important because it gives the firm option value. A simple example of option value occurs when the firm has the opportunity to delay an investment and await the revelation of new information that bears on its profitability.

◆ Strategic choices are commitment-intensive, in that they involve investments in durable, specialized, and immobile resources and capabilities. Analyzing commitment-intensive choices thus requires careful consideration of the likely sources of competitive advantage (i.e., positioning), the sustainability of the advantage, and the flexibility a firm possesses once it makes a strategic investment. An important determinant of flexibility is the learn-to-burn ratio. Managers must also carefully analyze the biases created by internal organizational factors, such as structure and culture.

QUESTIONS

1. An established firm is considering expanding its capacity to take advantage of a recent growth in demand. It can do so in one of two ways. It can purchase fungible, general purpose assets that can be resold at close to their original value if their use in the industry proves to be unprofitable. Or it can invest in highly specialized assets that, once they are put in place, have no alternative uses and virtually no salvage value. Assuming that each choice results in the same production costs once installed, under what choice is the firm likely to encounter a greater likelihood that its competitors will also expand their capacities?

2. Consider a monopoly producer of a durable good, such as a supercomputer. The good does not depreciate. Once consumers purchase the good from the monopolist, they are free to sell it in the "second hand" market. Often times in markets for new durable goods, one sees the following pricing pattern: the seller starts off charging a high price but then lowers the price over time. Explain why, with a durable good, the monopolist might prefer to commit to keep its selling price constant over time. Can you think of a way that the monopolist might be able to make a credible commitment to do this?

3. Indicate whether the *strategic effects* of the following competitive moves are likely to be positive (beneficial to the firm making them) or negative (harmful to the firm making them).

> **a.** Two horizontally differentiated producers of diesel railroad engines–one located in the U.S. and the other located in Europe–compete in the European market as Bertrand price competitors. The U.S. manufacturer lobbies the U.S. government to give it an export subsidy, the amount of which is directly proportional to the amount of output the firm sells in the European market.
>
> **b.** A Cournot duopolist issues new debt to repurchase shares of its stock. The new debt issue will preclude the firm raising additional debt in the foreseeable future, and is expected to constrain the firm from modernizing existing production facilities.

4. Consider two firms competing in a Cournot industry. One firm–Roomkin Enterprises–is contemplating an investment in a new production technology. This new technology will result in efficiencies that will lower its variable costs of production. Roomkin's competitor, Adams, Co., does not have the resources to undertake a similar investment. Roomkin's corporate financial planning staff has studied the proposed investment and reports that *at current output levels*, the present value of the cost savings from the investment is less than the cost of the project, but just barely so. Now, suppose that Roomkin Enterprises hires you as a consultant. You point out that a complete analysis would take into account the effect of the investment on the market equilibrium between the Roomkin Enterprises and Adams Co. What would this more complete analysis say about the desirability of this investment?

5. The chapter discussed a situation in which a Cournot competitor would refrain from entering a geographically distinct market for its product, even though it would have a monopoly in that market. Under what circumstances would this incentive be reversed?

6. "The more specialized the assets involved in a strategic investment, the greater the option value from delaying the investment." Explain.

THE DYNAMICS OF
PRICING RIVALRY

10

For many years, two companies dominated the morning and afternoon newspaper markets in Sydney, Australia: John Fairfax and Sons, which published the *Sydney Morning Herald* in the morning and the *Sun* in the afternoon; and Rupert Murdoch's News Limited, which published the *Daily Telegraph* in the morning and the *Daily Mirror* in the afternoon.[1] The morning market was clearly segmented; the *Morning Herald* appealed to a more affluent readership than the *Daily Telegraph*. By contrast, the newspapers in the afternoon market competed for the same readers and were close substitutes for one another.

Throughout much of the postwar period, prices in the afternoon market moved in lockstep. Seven price increases occurred between 1941 and January 1974. In four of these cases, the price increase was announced by the *Sun* (acknowledged to be the price leader in the afternoon market) and was matched within days by the *Daily Mirror*. In the three other instances, both papers gave simultaneous notice of the price increase. This pattern of pricing behavior stood in stark contrast to the morning market, where a price increase by one paper would often go unmatched by the other for 9 or 10 months.

But pricing behavior in the afternoon market changed in 1975. In July of that year, Fairfax increased the price of the *Sun* from 10 cents to 12 cents. Breaking with over 30 years of tradition, Murdoch chose instead to keep the price of the *Daily*

---

[1]This example is based on Merrilees, W., "Anatomy of a Price Leadership Challenge: An Evaluation of Pricing Strategies in the Australian Newspaper Industry," *Journal of Industrial Economics*, XXXI, March 1983, pp. 291–311.

Mirror at 10 cents. The price war waged by Murdoch's paper lasted for 3½ years. During this time, the *Daily Mirror's* share of the afternoon market, which had been virtually 50 percent when its price was equal to the *Sun's*, rose to slightly over 53 percent. This allowed the *Daily Mirror* to increase its advertising revenues relative to the *Sun*. William Mirrilees estimates that by underpricing the *Sun*, the *Daily Mirror* increased its annual profit by nearly $1.6 million, while the *Sun's* annual profit fell by approximately $1.3 million.[2] In January 1979, Fairfax finally surrendered, dropping its price back down to 10 cents. Henceforth, Murdoch's *Daily Mirror* would be the price leader in Sydney's afternoon paper market.

This example raises issues about the dynamics of rivalry within a market. What conditions influence the intensity of price competition in a market? Why do firms in some markets seem to be able to coordinate their pricing behavior to avoid costly price wars, while in other markets intense price competition is the norm? What is the value, if any, of policies under which the firm commits to matching the prices charged by its competitors? When should a firm match the price of its rival, and when should it go its own way? These are a few of the questions we take up in this chapter.

This chapter builds on Chapter 8 by introducing a set of models and analytical frameworks that can help us better understand why firms compete as they do. Unlike Chapter 8, much of the discussion here is based on the view that price competition is a dynamic process, that is, one that unfolds over time. Treating rivalry as a dynamic process implies that a firm's decisions made at one point in time affect how competitors, and indeed the firm itself, will behave in the future. For example, the fact that Fairfax did not respond to Murdoch's decision to underprice the *Sun* made Murdoch's decision profitable. However, had Murdoch anticipated that Fairfax would have reverted to the 10 cent price quickly after it became clear that he was not going to increase the price of the *Mirror*, then he might have been better off following Fairfax's lead. This suggests that Fairfax would have benefited from clearly communicating that it was prepared to match whatever price Murdoch's paper charged in the previous week, a policy known as *tit-for-tat* pricing.

Also unlike Chapter 8, this chapter discusses nonprice competition, focusing in particular on competition with respect to product quality. In this part of the chapter we explore how market structure influences a firm's incentives to choose its product quality. It also examines the role that consumer information plays in shaping the nature of competition with respect to quality.

◆ ◆ ◆ ◆ ◆ DYNAMIC PRICING RIVALRY

An obvious but important characteristic of real-world markets is that firms that compete against one another do so over time, again and again. This implies that competitive moves that might have short-run benefits may, in the longer run, be harmful to the firm once its competitors have had time to react and make counter-

---

[2]*Ibid.*, p. 304.

moves of their own. For example, a firm that cuts its price today in an attempt to steal business from rivals may find that they retaliate with price cuts of their own in the future, thus nullifying the business-stealing "benefits" of the original price cut. This section develops a theory of rivalry when firms meet repeatedly over time. The next section then uses these theories to illuminate the link between market structure and the intensity of price competition.

Why the Cournot and Bertrand Models Are Not Dynamic

The reader might wonder whether dynamic elements of competition haven't already been included within the context of the Cournot and Bertrand models. After all, in Chapter 8, we described the process of attaining a Cournot or Bertrand equilibrium as if it came out of a sequence of reactions and counterreactions by each firm to its rivals' decisions. For example, in a simple Cournot industry with two firms, Firm 1 and Firm 2, the process of achieving an equilibrium is described as follows: Firm 2 makes an output decision; Firm 1 then reacts to the quantity chosen by Firm 2 by selecting the quantity along its reaction function that is associated with the quantity chosen by Firm 2 (see Figure 10.1). Firm 2 then reacts to the quantity chosen by Firm 1 by choosing the quantity along its reaction function corresponding to Firm 1's choice. This process continues to unfold until the equilibrium is reached.

FIGURE 10.1
CONVERGENCE TO A COURNOT EQUILIBRIUM.

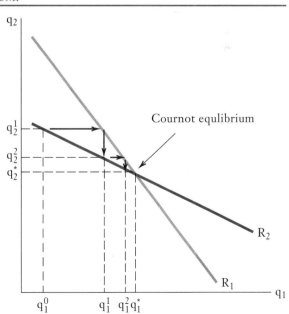

This figure shows the "story" that is sometimes told about how firms reach a Cournot equilibrium. Suppose in an initial period Firm 1 produces q_1^0. Firm 2 then reacts in the next period by producing q_2^1. Firm 1 would then react to this choice by producing q_1^1. Firm 2 would react to this choice by producing q_2^2, which would then induce Firm 1 to produce q_1^2. As the arrows show, this process of reaction and counterreaction will eventually converge to the Cournot equilibrium, q_1^* and q_2^*.

However, this depiction of Cournot competition (and analogous depictions of Bertrand competition) is, strictly speaking, not correct. In truth, both models are *static* models rather than *dynamic*. They are static because in each model all firms simultaneously make once-and-for-all quantity or price choices. The reaction–counterreaction story is nothing more than a convenient fable that helps reinforce the notion that a Cournot (or Bertrand) equilibrium is a point of "stability": No firm has an incentive to deviate from its equilibrium quantity (or price), given that it expects that its rivals will also choose their equilibrium quantities (or prices).

One way to see the inadequacy of the "dynamic" depiction of the Cournot model in Figure 10.1 is to note that each time a firm chooses its quantity, it bases that decision on what its rival did in its *previous* move. Moreover, its "reaction" is the choice that maximizes its *current* (i.e., single-period) profit. But presumably an intelligent firm would take the long view and choose its quantity to maximize the present value of profits over its entire time horizon, and to do this, it must anticipate what its rival will do in the future, not just naively react to what it has done in the past. Figure 10.1 reveals the limitations of naively reacting to the rival firm's previous output choice. Unless the two firms are at the equilibrium point, as Firm 1 reacts to Firm 2 and Firm 2 reacts to Firm 1, what either firm did in the past is an unreliable guide to what each will do in the future.

This discussion should not be taken to imply that the Cournot or Bertrand models are wrong or useless. Both models reduce a complicated phenomenon—industry rivalry—to an analytically convenient form that helps answer such questions as "What impact does the number of firms have on the prevailing level of prices in the market?" or "What would be expected to happen to the level of prices in an oligopolistic market as demand shifts outward?" These models are also useful—as Chapter 9 emphasized—for examining the interplay between strategic commitments of various kinds and tactical maneuvering. However, the Cournot and Bertrand models also have their limitations. Neither can fully explain why in certain highly concentrated oligopolies (e.g., the U.S. steel industry until the late 1960s or the U.S. cigarette industry until the early 1990s), firms can maintain prices above competitive levels without formal collusion and why in other comparably concentrated markets (e.g., regional cement markets), price competition is often fierce. Dynamic models of price competition are more useful for exploring such questions.

Dynamic Pricing Rivalry: Examples and Intuition

Figure 10.2 depicts the demand and cost conditions in a commodity chemical business that consists of two firms. This is a mature business in which demand is stable (i.e., market demand is neither growing nor shrinking) and both firms have access to the same technology, know-how, and factors of production and thus have equal marginal and average costs. For the time being, we ignore issues of capacity constraints and assume that marginal cost is constant at $20 per pound over the entire range of possible output levels. Buyers regard each firm's product as a perfect substitute for the other's, so consumers choose solely on the basis of price.

FIGURE 10.2
MONOPOLY PRICE AND QUANTITY.

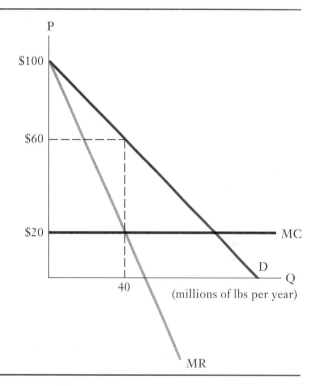

With the market demand curve shown and a constant marginal cost of $20, the monopoly quantity is 40 million pounds per year, and the monopoly price is $60 per pound.

If the two competitors were allowed to collude, they would charge the monopoly price, which as shown in Figure 10.2 is $60 per pound, and together would produce 40 million pounds of the chemical per year. How they divide this market cannot be deduced from monopoly theory, but given that the firms are identical, we can assume that they will split the market 50:50. If so, the monopoly outcome would yield each firm an annual profit of $800 million. By contrast, if the two firms were to compete as Bertrand competitors, they would charge $20 per pound, and their annual profit would be zero.[3] To emphasize that we are not focusing on the issue of formal collusion, we use the term *cooperative pricing* to refer to situations in which firms are able to sustain prices in excess of those that would arise in a non-cooperative single-shot price or quantity-setting game, such as Cournot or Bertrand.

Is cooperative pricing achievable when firms make pricing decisions noncooperatively? The economist Edward Chamberlin argued that it would be. He

---

[3] If the firms competed as Cournot competitors, prices and profits would be $46.67 and $711.11 million, respectively.

suggested that when there are only a few sellers in the market, each would recognize that the profit it gains from cutting price below the monopoly level is likely to be fleeting. The reason is that other firms would retaliate by cutting their prices, and when all is said and done, market shares will not have changed but prices will be lower, leaving the price cutter with lower profits than it had before it cut its price:

> If each seeks his maximum profit rationally and intelligently, he will realize that when there are two or only a few sellers his own move has a considerable effect upon his competitors, and that this makes it idle to suppose that they will accept without retaliation the losses he forces upon them. Since the result of a cut by any one is inevitably to decrease his own profits, no one will cut, and although the sellers are entirely independent, the equilibrium result is the same as though there were a monopolistic agreement between them.[4]

To understand how Chamberlin's argument works in our example, suppose that both firms are currently charging a price somewhere between the Bertrand price of $20 and the collusive price of $60, say $40 per pound. We might imagine that this market has recently been disturbed by a shock, such as an increase in an input price, and that $40 was the price that prevailed before the shock occurred. Firm 1 is considering raising its price to the monopoly level of $60. Firm 1 will profit from this move only if Firm 2 goes along. If Firm 2 keeps its price at $40, it will steal all of Firm 1's customers, and Firm 1's profits will be zero.

One might think that it would be foolish for Firm 1 to raise its price to $60 without having first enlisted Firm 2's agreement that it will follow suit. After all, if Firm 1 raises its price, but Firm 2 does not, Firm 2 will capture 100 percent of the market, and its profits will double from $600 million to $1,200 million per year. Let us suppose that prices can be changed every week, so that if Firm 1 decides to rescind its price increase, it can do so without waiting more than a week. Further, let us suppose that Firm 1 can observe Firm 2's pricing decision right away, so Firm 1 will know immediately whether Firm 2 has followed its price increase.

Under these conditions, a decision by Firm 1 to raise price carries little risk. If Firm 2 refuses to follow, Firm 1 can quickly drop its price back down to $40 after one week. At most, Firm 1 sacrifices one week's profit at current prices (roughly $11.5 million).

Not only is the risk to Firm 1 low from raising its price, but if Firm 1 puts itself in Firm 2's position, it would see that Firm 2 has a compelling motive to follow Firm 1's price increase. To see why, suppose that both firms use a 10 percent annual rate to discount future profits. On a weekly basis, this corresponds roughly to a discount rate of .2 percent (i.e., .002). Firm 1 reasons as follows:

---

[4]Chamberlin, E.H., *Monopolistic Competition*, Cambridge, MA: Harvard University Press, 1933, p. 48.

- *If Firm 2 sticks with the current price of $40, we will learn this quickly, so Firm 2 should anticipate that we will drop our price back down to $40 after the first week. That would mean that by keeping its price at $40, the discounted present value of Firm 2's weekly profit would be*

$$23.08 + \frac{11.54}{(1.002)} + \frac{11.54}{(1.002)^2} + \frac{11.54}{(1.002)^3} + \cdots$$

which equals $5,793 million.[5]

- *If Firm 2 follows us and raises price to $60, we each will earn annual profits of $800 million, which translates into a weekly profit of $15.38 million. By following our price increase, the discounted value of Firm 2's weekly profit is thus*

$$15.38 + \frac{15.38}{(1.002)} + \frac{15.38}{(1.002)^2} + \frac{15.38}{(1.002)^3} + \cdots$$

which equals $7,705 million. Clearly, Firm 2 is better off following our lead, even though for the first week it would be better off if it held back and refused to raise its price to $60.

Because (i) Firm 2 has much to gain by matching Firm 1's price, and (ii) Firm 1 loses little if Firm 2 does not match, it makes sense for Firm 1 to raise its price to $60. If Firm 2 behaves rationally, then it will behave in the way Firm 1 expects it to behave (as described by the above reasoning), and Firm 2 will thus match Firm 1's price increase. The outcome thus corresponds to the monopoly outcome even though neither firm meets nor communicates with each other. A simple calculation reveals that the monopoly price is sustainable as long as Firm 2's *weekly* discount rate is less than 50 percent, which corresponds to an annual discount rate of 2,600 percent.

Firm 1's confidence that Firm 2 would match its price increase would be even stronger if, upon announcing its price increase, Firm 1 also announced or otherwise signaled to Firm 2 that starting next week, its price in any given week would match the price that Firm 2 charged in the preceding week. This is known as the *tit-for-tat strategy*, and is akin to a commitment by Firm 1 to its customers stating that "We will not be undersold." If Firm 1 succeeds in signaling to Firm 2 that it is following a tit-for-tat strategy, and if Firm 2 does not match Firm 1's increase to $60, then Firm 2 knows that Firm 1 will drop its price back down to the original level of $40 after the first week. As it figures out its best reply, Firm 2 will thus go through exactly the same reasoning described above and will find it worthwhile to match Firm 1's price of $60.

By following a policy of tit-for-tat, Fairfax & Sons might have avoided the costly price war described in the introduction to this chapter. Once it became clear

---

[5]This calculation easily follows by using the formula for the present value of an annuity, which is discussed in the appendix to the Economics Primer. Specifically, for any amount C and discount rate i, $\frac{C}{(1+i)} + \frac{C}{(1+i)^2} + \dots = \frac{C}{i}$. Thus, the above calculation simplifies to $23.08 + 11.54/.002 = 5793$.

that Murdoch's *Daily Mirror* was not going to raise its price to 12 cents, Fairfax would have dropped its price back down to 10 cents. Had Murdoch's paper anticipated this behavior by Fairfax, it would have had a powerful incentive to match Fairfax's price.

Dynamic Pricing Rivalry: Theory

To develop further insights about the relationship between market structure and the intensity of pricing rivalry, it is useful to formalize the intuition developed in the example in the previous section. To do so, we consider a market consisting of n firms that produce products that are perfect substitutes for one another. As in the example above, we imagine that the prevailing price in the industry has been p^0, but the industry has just been disturbed by a shock (e.g., an increase in the prices of certain inputs or a change in the price of a substitute product) that has changed the underlying cost or demand conditions. These changes are expected to persist in the foreseeable future.

The new conditions are as follows. Each firm has a constant marginal cost, c. Market demand in each period is given by $D(p)$, and if all firms charge the same price, they split the market evenly. The monopoly price, p^M, is the price that maximizes industry profit, $\Pi(p) = (p - c)D(p)$. We will assume that $p^0 < p^M$, so the firms in the industry are currently charging less than the monopoly price. Let $\Pi^M = (p^M - c)D(p^M)$ denote the maximal level of industry profit, and let Π^0 be the level of industry profit at the prevailing price p^0. Note that $\Pi^0 < \Pi^M$, that is the industry as a whole would be better off at the monopoly price than the prevailing price p^0. However, to make the story interesting, we assume that

$$\frac{\Pi^M}{n} < \Pi^0 \tag{A1}$$

This inequality implies that if all but one firm raises its price to the monopoly level, the firm that holds back (and captures the entire market) would have a higher profit per period than it would if it went along with the price increase. In this sense, the situation we are studying is analogous to the prisoners' dilemma game discussed in the Economics Primer and again in Chapter 8.

Define a period to be the interval during which firms cannot change their prices. A period may be a day, a week, a quarter, or even a year depending on the cost of adjusting prices and announcing changes to consumers. Later on we will explore how the length of the period can affect price competition in this market. At the beginning of each period, the firms simultaneously and noncooperatively set prices. Firms in this market compete over an *infinite horizon*, that is, their relationship has no fixed ending point. To simplify the analysis, we assume that there are no intertemporal demand or cost linkages between the periods. This implies, for example, that the price that a firm sets in a given period affects only its current demand and profits, but does not affect demand in any future period. Similarly, a firm's production volume in a given period affects its costs in that period, but not its future costs (i.e., there are no experience curve effects).

Will the firms in this market be able to raise price to the monopoly price p^M without colluding with each other? The answer depends, in part, on the pricing strategy each firm follows and its expectations about the strategies that its competitors are following. Let us consider a simple strategy: a generalization of the tit-for-tat strategy discussed in the previous section.

> *Starting this period, we will raise our price to p^M. In each subsequent period, our firm will set a price equal to the lowest price that prevailed in the period that immediately preceded it.*

If all firms followed this strategy, each would raise its price from p^0 to p^M and keep it there. Let us imagine that the firms in this industry have somehow managed to signal to one another that they are following the strategy just described and that each intends to move price from the current level to p^M. Of course, resolving this signaling problem is not easy, and we will say more about that later. For now, though, we want to explore whether it would be in a firm's self-interest to follow this strategy. To do so, consider a potential deviator, whom we will call Firm D, who expects that all other firms will follow the tit-for-tat strategy just described. Firm D is contemplating refusing to "cooperate" with the move to the monopoly price and will do so by keeping its price at p^0.[6] Table 10.1 shows the pattern of prices that results when Firm D refuses to cooperate. Table 10.2 shows Firm D's profits if it cooperates and if it does not cooperate. If Firm D does not cooperate, then in the current period, it will be the low-price firm and will capture the entire market demand at price p^0, earning a profit Π^0. In the next period, all other firms will drop their prices back down to p^0, and at that price the firms will split the market evenly. If Firm D does cooperate, all firms will raise price to the monopoly price p^M and will split the monopoly profit Π^M evenly at that price.

TABLE 10.1
EVOLUTION OF PRICES WHEN FIRM D DEVIATES

	Now	*Next Period*	*All Future Periods*
Firm D	p^0	p^0	p^0
Other firms	p^M	p^0	p^0

---

[6]A technical point: Why do we consider this kind of deviation, i.e., one in which Firm D deviates "forever"? Might it be better for the defector to deviate for only a limited period? The answer is that under some circumstances, the optimal cheating policy is to deviate for only a single period and then "apologize," while under other circumstances, it is optimal to cheat "forever." Considering other possible patterns of cheating yields insights similar to those that we will develop below. Focusing on a permanent deviation simplifies the analysis, and in situations in which firms must *raise* their prices to get to the monopoly level, the possibility that some firms might simply refuse to raise theirs seems quite natural.

TABLE 10.2
EVOLUTION OF FIRM D'S PROFITS

	Now	*Next Period*	*All Future Periods*
Firm D deviates	Π^0	Π^0/n	Π^0/n
Firm D cooperates	Π^M/n	Π^M/n	Π^M/n

Using Table 10.2 and letting i denote the per period discount rate, the present value of Firm D's profit if it does not cooperate is

$$\Pi^0 + \frac{\Pi^0/n}{(1+i)} + \frac{\Pi^0/n}{(1+i)^2} + \frac{\Pi^0/n}{(1+i)^3} + \ldots = \Pi^0 + \frac{\Pi^0/n}{i}$$

The present value of Firm D's profit if it cooperates is

$$\Pi^M + \frac{\Pi^M/n}{(1+i)} + \frac{\Pi^M/n}{(1+i)^2} + \ldots = \Pi^M/n + \frac{\Pi^M/n}{i}$$

Straightforward algebra reveals that Firm D is better off raising its price to p^M when

$$\frac{\frac{1}{n}[\Pi^M - \Pi^0]}{\Pi^0 - \frac{1}{n}\Pi^M} \geq i \qquad (10.1)$$

The inequality in (10.1) is a condition for the cooperative outcome to be an equilibrium in a noncooperative game of price setting. Though formidable looking, this inequality has a straightforward interpretation and—as we will discuss below—some powerful implications. The left side of the inequality is a benefit–cost ratio. The numerator of this ratio is the single-period benefit to an individual firm from cooperating; it represents the difference in an individual firm's per-period profit when all firms set the monopoly price p^M as opposed to p^0. The denominator is the extra profit the firm could have earned in the current period if it had refused to cooperate. This forgone profit is the cost of cooperation. The inequality in (10.1) states that cooperative pricing will be sustainable when this benefit–cost ratio exceeds the threshold level on the left side of the inequality. This threshold is equal to the per-period discount rate, i.

The "Folk Theorem"

An immediate implication of the inequality in (10.1) is that if each firm is sufficiently patient—that is, if the discount rate i is close enough to zero—then the cooperative outcome will be sustainable. This result is actually a special case of what game theorists have referred to as the *folk theorem* for repeated games.[7] The folk

---

[7]The term "folk theorem" is used because, much like a folk song, it existed in the oral tradition of economics long before anyone actually got credit for proving it formally.

theorem says that for sufficiently low discount rates, *any price* between the monopoly price p^M and marginal cost c can be sustained as an equilibrium in the infinitely repeated prisoners' dilemma game being studied here.[8] Of course, different outcomes would be attainable through strategies that are different than the tit-for-tat strategy we are focusing on. For example, one equilibrium is for each firm to set a price equal to marginal cost in each period. Given that it expects its competitors to behave this way, a firm can do no better than to behave this way as well.

Coordinating on an Equilibrium

The folk theorem implies that cooperative pricing behavior is a *possible* equilibrium in an oligopolistic industry. It does not, however, guarantee that it *will* be an equilibrium. Achieving a particular equilibrium in a game with many equilibria, some potentially more attractive than others, is a *coordination problem*. For the cooperative outcome to be attainable, firms in the industry must coordinate on a strategy, such as tit-for-tat, which makes it in each firm's self-interest to refrain from aggressive price cutting.

An obvious—and in most economies, illegal—way to solve this coordination problem is through a collusive agreement. Achieving coordination without an agreement or overt communication is far more difficult. Somehow, each firm in the industry must see its way clear to adopting a strategy, such as tit-for-tat, that moves the industry toward cooperative pricing. In short, the cooperation-inducing strategy must be a *focal point*—a strategy that is so compelling that it would be natural for a firm to expect all other firms to adopt it.

Theories of how focal points emerge in economic or social interactions are not well developed.[9] It seems that focal points are highly context- or situation-specific. For example, consider a game called "Divide the Cities" concocted by David Kreps, a professor at the Stanford Graduate School of Business.[10]

> The following is a list of eleven cities in the United States: Atlanta, Boston, Chicago, Dallas, Denver, Houston, Los Angeles, New York, Philadelphia, San Francisco, and Seattle. I have assigned to each city a point value from 1 to 100 according to the city's importance and its "quality of life." You will not be told this scale until the game is over, except that I tell you now that New York has the highest score, 100, and Seattle has the least, 1. I do think you will find my scale is fair. I am going to have you play the following game against a randomly selected student of the Harvard Graduate School of Business. Each of you will be asked to list, simultaneously and without consultation, some subset of these eleven cities. Your list must contain San Francisco and your opponent's must contain Boston. Then, I will give you $100 simply for playing the game. And I will add to/subtract from that amount as follows: For every

---

[8]The multiplicity of potential equilibrium outcomes raises important issues in contexts other than oligopoly pricing. We will study one such application in Chapter 18 when discussing power and culture.

[9]The best work on this subject remains Thomas Schelling's famous book, *The Strategy of Conflict*, Cambridge, MA: Harvard, 1960.

[10]Kreps, D.M., *A Course in Microeconomic Theory*, Princeton, NJ: Princeton University Press, 1990, pp. 392–393.

city that appears on one list but not the other, the person who lists the city will get as many dollars as that city has points on my scale. For every city that appears on both lists, I will take from each of you twice as many dollars as the city has points. Finally, if the two of you manage to partition the cities, I will triple your winnings. Which cities will you list?

This game has a huge number of equilibria (512 to be exact, each corresponding to a partition of the nine cities, other than San Francisco and Boston, which are preassigned). Yet, when the game is played by American students, the outcome is nearly always the same: the Stanford student's list is Dallas, Denver, Houston, Los Angeles, Seattle, and San Francisco. The focal point is an East–West division of the United States, coupled with some elementary equity considerations to deal with the fact that there is an odd number (11) of cities to be divided. (Since Seattle is the lowest valued city, students generally let the western list contain the extra city.) Kreps notes that the focal point of East–West geography becomes less focal when one of the students playing the game is from outside the United States. The U.S. student then often has concerns about the non-U.S. student's knowledge of geography. The game also loses its focal point when the list of cities has a less natural division, for example, if it contained 8 western cities and only 4 eastern ones.

Coordination is likely to be especially difficult in competitive environments that are turbulent and changing rapidly. It can sometimes be facilitated by traditions and conventions that stabilize the competitive environment, that is, by making competitors' moves easier to follow or their intentions easier to interpret. For example, many industries have standard cycles for adjusting prices. Until recently, in the U.S. cigarette industry, June and December were the traditional dates for Philip Morris and RJR to announce changes in prices. The tacit understanding that prices will not be changed except on the traditional dates reduces suspicions that competitors may be cutting prices, making it easier for firms to coordinate on prices at or close to the monopoly level. The practice of quoting prices in terms of standard price points or increments may also create pricing focal points. For example, in the turbine generator industry in the United States in the 1960s, the two sellers, GE and Westinghouse, adopted a practice of employing a single multiplier to determine discounts off the list price. This reduced a complicated pricing decision to a single, easy to understand number.[11]

Why Is Tit-for-Tat so Compelling?

Tit-for-tat is not the only strategy that allows firms to sustain monopoly pricing as a noncooperative equilibrium. Another strategy that, like tit-for-tat, results in the monopoly price for sufficiently low discount rates is the *grim trigger strategy*:

Starting this period, we will charge the monopoly price p^M. In each subsequent period, if any firm ever deviates from p^M, we will drop our price to marginal cost c in the next period and keep it there forever.

---

[11]Various other "facilitating practices," such as price leadership or advance notice of price changes, are discussed below.

The grim trigger strategy relies on the threat of an infinitely long price war to keep firms from undercutting their competitors' prices. In light of other potentially effective strategies, such as grim trigger, why would we necessarily expect firms to adopt a tit-for-tat strategy?[12] One reason is that tit-for-tat is a simple, easy to describe, and easy to understand strategy. Through announcements, such as "We will not be undersold" or "We will match our competitors prices, no matter how low," a firm can easily signal to its rivals that it is following tit-for-tat.

In addition, tit-for-tat is a robust strategy in that a firm that adopts it will probably do well over the long run against a variety of different strategies. A compelling illustration of tit-for-tat's robustness is discussed by Robert Axelrod in his book *The Evolution of Cooperation*.[13] Axelrod conducted a computer tournament in which scholars were invited to submit strategies for playing a (finitely) repeated prisoners' dilemma game. Each of the submitted strategies was pitted against every other, and the winner was the strategy that accumulated the highest overall score of all of its "matches." Even though tit-for-tat can never beat another strategy in one-on-one competition (at best it can tie another strategy), it accumulated the highest overall score across all its matches. It was able to do so, according to Axelrod, because it combines the properties of "niceness," "provocability," and "forgiveness." It is nice in that it is never the first to defect from the cooperative outcome. It is provocable in that it *immediately* punishes a rival who defects from the cooperative outcome by matching the rival's defection in the next period. It is forgiving in that if the rival returns to the cooperative strategy, tit-for-tat will too.

Despite the robustness of tit-for-tat against a wide range of strategies, it is not clear that tit-for-tat is forgiving enough when there is a possibility that firms can misread the pricing moves made by their competitors. Consider what might happen when two firms are playing tit-for-tat, and there is a chance that a cooperative move is misread as an uncooperative one. The firm that misreads the cooperative move as an uncooperative one responds by making an uncooperative move in the next period. That firm's competitor then responds in kind in the period after that. A single misread leads to a pattern whereby firms alternate between cooperative and uncooperative moves over time. If, in the midst of this dynamic, another cooperative move is misread as an uncooperative one, the resulting pattern becomes even worse: Firms become stuck in a cycle of choosing uncooperative moves each period.

Avinash Dixit and Barry Nalebuff have argued that when misreads are possible, pricing strategies that are less provocable and more forgiving than tit-for-tat are desirable.[14] It may be, they argue, desirable to ignore what appears to be an uncooperative move by one's competitor if the competitor then reverts to cooperative behavior in the next period.

---

[12]The following discussion is based on Satterthwaite, M., "Pricing in Oligopolies: The Importance of the Long-Run," Northwestern University unpublished manuscript, 1988.

[13]Axelrod, R., *The Evolution of Cooperation*, New York: Basic Books, 1984.

[14]Dixit, A. and B. Nalebuff, *Thinking Strategically: The Competitive Edge in Business, Politics, and Everyday Life*, New York: Norton, 1991.

◆ ◆

$\mathcal{E}$XAMPLE 10.1

HOW MISUNDERSTANDINGS CAN LEAD TO PRICE WARS[15]

Forgiveness is an especially important property when competitors misread or mis-understand each others' competitive moves. McKinsey consultants Robert Garda and Michael Marn suggest that many real-world price wars are not started by deliberate attempts by one firm to steal business from its competitors; instead they stem from misreads and misunderstandings of competitors' behavior. To illustrate their point, Garda and Marn cite the example of a tire manufacturer that sold a particular tire at an invoice price of $35, but with an end-of-year volume bonus of $2 and a marketing allowance of $1.50, the manufacturer's net price was really $31.50.[16] This company received reports from its regional sales personnel that a rival firm was selling a competing tire at an invoice price of $32. In response, the manufacturer lowered its invoice price by $3, reducing its net price to $28.50. The manufacturer later learned that its competitor was not offering marketing allowances or volume discounts. As a result of its misreading of its competitor's price, the tire manufacturer precipitated a long and vicious price war that ended up damaging the profitability of both firms.

How Market Structure Affects the Sustainability of Cooperative Pricing

Pricing cooperation is harder to achieve under some market structures than others, partly because under certain conditions, firms cannot coordinate on a focal equilibrium, and partly because the benefit–cost ratio in condition (10.1) is systematically influenced by market structure conditions. This section discusses four market structure conditions that may facilitate or complicate the attainment of cooperative pricing and competitive stability.

- Market concentration
- Structural conditions that affect reaction speeds and detection lags
- Asymmetries among firms
- Multimarket contact

---

[15]This example is based on Garda, R.A. and M.V. Marn, "Price Wars," *McKinsey Quarterly*, 3, 1993, pp. 87–100.

[16]A marketing allowance is a discount offered by a manufacturer in return for the retailer's agreement to feature the manufacturer's product in some way. Examples include advertising allowances to compensate for retail advertising or display allowances that are offered in exchange for superior shelf-space for the manufacturer's product or special displays.

Market Concentration and the Sustainability of Cooperative Pricing

The benefit–cost ratio in (10.1) goes up as the number of firms goes down. Thus, the more concentrated the market, the more likely it is that cooperative pricing will be an equilibrium. The insight that market concentration facilitates the sustainability of cooperative pricing has had an important bearing on antitrust policy in the United States and the European Community. For example, in the United States, the Department of Justice and the Federal Trade Commission employ merger guidelines that state that mergers between two competitors are likely to be challenged when the postmerger market concentration exceeds certain thresholds.[17]

The intuition behind the relationship between concentration and the sustainability of cooperative pricing is straightforward. In a concentrated market, a typical firm's market share is larger than it would be in a fragmented market. (In fact, each firm's market share is $\frac{1}{n}$ in the symmetric case we are studying here, and this market share decreases in n.) Thus, a typical firm captures a large fraction of the overall benefit when the industry moves from a lower price, such as p^0 to p^M. Moreover, the single-period profit gain the firm sacrifices from *not* undercutting the rest of the market (i.e., the cost of cooperation) is smaller when the market is more concentrated. This is because a deviator gains from stealing business from rival firms. If the deviator has a large share of the market to begin with, the business it steals is smaller in proportion to the sales it gets if it goes along with the price than it would be if it was in a fragmented market with a small market share. Thus, the more concentrated the market, the larger the benefits from cooperation, and the smaller the costs of cooperation.

There is another sense in which high concentration facilitates cooperative pricing. As we just discussed, for firms to coordinate on tit-for-tat as a focal strategy, competitors must think alike. Although it is difficult to formalize this aspect theoretically, intuitively one expects that coordinating on a particular focal strategy is likely to be more difficult the more firms there are that compete against one another in the market. Established department stores have experienced this firsthand during the past two decades. For nearly a century, until the 1970s, they used simple rule-of-thumb pricing, such as setting prices equal to 200 percent of costs. As a result, they rarely worried about price competition. Entry by newcomers, such as TJ Maxx and Filene's Basement, has disrupted the cooperative pricing equilibrium. These entrants have gained market share by undercutting big department stores, which in turn have been forced to resort to more frequent sales to compete effectively with these newcomers.

Reaction Speed, Detection Lags, and the Sustainability of Cooperative Pricing

The inequality in (10.1) implies that the speed with which firms can react to their rivals' pricing moves affects the sustainability of cooperative pricing. To see why,

---

[17]The thresholds in the 1992 merger guidelines are expressed in terms of changes in the Herfindahl index. See Chapter 8 for a discussion of this measure of market concentration.

imagine that a "period" in the sense we have been using that term corresponds to one month. That is, once a firm sets its price, it must live with it for an entire month before it can change it again. In that case, the profit $\Pi(p)$ is a monthly profit; the discount rate i would be the effective monthly rate of interest, and the inequality in (10.1) would define the relevant threshold.

But how would the inequality change when a period corresponds to a week rather than a month? The weekly discount rate would be one-fourth of the monthly rate, $i/4$, and assuming that sales are distributed uniformly through the month, weekly profit would be $\Pi(p)/4$. Replicating the derivation of (10.1), except now assuming a weekly detection lag, yields an expression nearly identical to (10.1):

$$\frac{\frac{1}{n}[\Pi^M - \Pi^0]}{\Pi^0 - \frac{1}{n}\Pi^M} \geq \frac{i}{4} \tag{10.2}$$

The key difference between (10.1) and (10.2) is that the threshold above which it is optimal for a firm to follow the tit-for-tat strategy and raise its price to the monopoly level is now *smaller*. This suggests that for a given discount rate, the greater the speed of reaction, the greater the likelihood that the cooperative outcome will be sustainable. In the limit, if price cuts can be matched instantly, the effective discount rate goes to zero, and cooperative pricing will always be sustainable.

A firm's ability to react to competitors' price cuts or refusals to match price increases might be delayed because (i) interactions between the firms are infrequent; (ii) there are lags in detecting the prices charged by competitors; (iii) there are ambiguities in identifying which firm among a group of firms in a market is responsible for cutting price; and (iv) it is difficult to distinguish decreases in business volume due to strategic price cutting by rivals from temporary price cuts that are due to unanticipated decreases in market demand. All of these factors reduce the speed with which firms can respond to defections from cooperative pricing and thus also reduce the effectiveness of retaliatory price cuts aimed at punishing price-cutting firms.[18]

Several structural conditions affect the importance of these factors:

- Market concentration
- Lumpiness of orders
- Information about sales transactions
- The number and size of buyers
- Volatility of demand and cost conditions

We will discuss each in turn.

---

[18]Formal models of detection lags and uncertainties in identifying the source and/or causes of price wars are more complicated than the stripped-down theoretical model that was used to derive equation (10.1). Still, these models show that collusion is more difficult to sustain the longer it takes to retaliate against a price cutter.

Market Concentration Deviations from cooperative pricing are easier to detect in concentrated than in fragmented markets. The fewer the number of competitors in a market, the less expensive it is for a firm to monitor its rivals' prices and market shares. But even if firms cannot monitor the prices and market shares of rivals with perfect accuracy, concentration can have an impact. When there is a small number of large firms in an industry, if one firm does defect from the cooperative price, the impact on the sales and profits of nondefecting firms is likely to be more pronounced than it would be if the industry consisted of many small firms. The reason for this is subtle and requires explanation.

Suppose firms in an industry have achieved the cooperative outcome. Even though all firms may be charging the same price, each firm's sales will fluctuate over time because some customers will (for idiosyncratic reasons) switch their patronage from one firm to another. George Stigler demonstrated that for a given rate of switching by customers, market shares will be more volatile when the industry is fragmented than when it is concentrated.[19] It follows that if one firm *does* secretly deviate from the cooperative outcome by cutting price, the impact of this move on its rivals will be more noticeable when they are large. This is because if firms did maintain cooperative pricing, a large firm in a concentrated industry would not expect to experience dramatic declines in its market share, whereas a small firm in an unconcentrated industry would be more likely to see large declines that are entirely due to "bad luck" (random switching by consumers). For example, it might not be unusual for a firm that normally has 2 percent of the market to see its share double to 4 percent and then return to 2 percent purely because of random factors. It would be highly unusual, however, for a firm with a 20 percent share to see its share rise to 40 percent and then later return to 20 percent due to random factors. Thus, given that a competitor has cut price, a large firm is likely to (correctly) attribute the decline in its sales to cheating, while a small firm will find it more difficult to fix the blame for the sales decline on cheating or on "normal" customer switching. Firms in concentrated industries are thus more likely to be "suspicious" when price cutting occurs and are more likely to detect and match the price cuts quickly.

Lumpiness of Orders An important condition reducing the frequency of interaction between firms—and thus intensifying price competition—is "lumpiness" of orders. Orders are lumpy when sales occur relatively infrequently in large batches as opposed to being smoothly distributed in small batches over the course of the year. Lumpiness of orders is an important characteristic in such industries as airframe manufacturing, shipbuilding, and the production of diesel locomotives.

To illustrate the implications of lumpy orders, consider a simple example involving two manufacturers—Gamma and Delta—that are competing to supply a

---

[19]Stigler, G. J., "A Theory of Oligopoly," *Journal of Political Economy*, 72 (1), February 1964, pp. 44–61.

product to a group of large industrial buyers, where the custom in the industry is for buyers to let bids once a year. Suppose Gamma is contemplating raising its price over last year's level. If it does not raise its price, but Delta does, then Delta will not be able to rescind the increase to match Gamma's for an entire year.

If Gamma thinks through the implications of this dynamic in advance, it may conclude that the long response lag makes a one-year cut in price attractive despite the prospects that Delta will retaliate a year from now.[20] Gamma's incentives to keep price low would be even stronger if it had expanded its capacity in anticipation of retaining the business of the large buyers it sold to last year. The loss of this business would then leave Gamma with substantial excess capacity and large fixed costs that would have to covered.

Information About the Sales Transaction: When sales transactions are "public," deviations from cooperative pricing are easier to detect than when prices are normally set in secret. For example, a gasoline station can easily learn that a rival has cut its price because selling prices in this market are publicly posted. By contrast, in many industrial goods markets, prices are privately negotiated between buyers and sellers, so it may be difficult for a firm to learn whether a competitor has cut its price. Because retaliation can occur more quickly when prices are public than when they are secret, price cutting to steal market share from competitors is likely to be less attractive, enhancing the chances that cooperative pricing can be sustained.

Secrecy of transaction terms is a significant problem when transactions involve other dimensions besides a list or an invoice price, as they often do in business-to-business marketing settings. For example, a manufacturer of a consumer product that wants to steal business from competitors can cut its "net price" by increasing trade allowances to retailers or by extending them more favorable trade credit terms. Because it is generally more difficult to monitor trade allowance deals or credit terms than it is to monitor list prices, competitors may find it difficult to detect business-stealing behavior, hindering their ability to retaliate.

Similarly, deviations from cooperative pricing are difficult to detect when product attributes are customized to individual buyers, as in airframe manufacturing or the production of diesel locomotives, for example. When products are tailor-made to individual buyers, a seller may be able to increase its market share by altering the design of the product or by throwing in "extras," such as a supply of spare parts or a service agreement. These are typically more difficult to observe than the list price, complicating the ability of firms to monitor competitors' behavior.

Secret or complex transaction terms can intensify price competition not only because price matching becomes a less effective deterrent to price-cutting behavior, but also because they increase the chance of misreads. Firms are more likely to misinterpret a competitive move, such as a reduction in list prices, as an aggressive attempt to steal business, when they cannot fully observe all the other terms being

---

[20]Of course, as discussed above, Gamma's incentives could go the other way if its discount rate is sufficiently small (meaning that it places nearly as much weight on future as on current profits).

offered by competitors. When this happens, the odds of accidental price wars rise, as we saw in Example 10.1. To the extent that a firm's pricing behavior is forgiving—the effects of misreads may be containable. Still, with secret and complex sales terms, even forgiving strategies may not work in environments where misreads can occur.

The Number of Buyers   When firms normally set prices in secret, detecting deviations from cooperative pricing is easier when each firm sells to many small buyers than when each sells to a few large buyers. The basic reason for this is that buyers have an incentive not to keep secrets. A buyer that receives a price concession from one seller has an incentive to report the price cut to other firms in an attempt to receive even more favorable concessions. The effect of the number of buyers on the likelihood that secret price cuts are detected can be dramatic. Suppose that if a firm cuts its price to a particular customer, there is only a small chance, say .1 percent, that a rival seller will learn of this particular price cut. Suppose that the price-cutting firm has 5,000 customers, each of whom receives the same discount. The probability that a rival will learn about at least one of these price cuts is equal to one minus the probability that a rival will *not* learn of any of the 5,000 price cuts, or $1 - (.999)^{5000} = .993$, a surprisingly large possibility. If we make the probability of detecting a single price cut smaller still, say .01 percent, there is still a $1 - (.9999)^{5000} = .393$ chance that word of at least one of these 5,000 price cuts will find its way back to rival firms. This line of logic implies that firms will have a greater incentive to adhere to cooperative pricing in an industry, such as electronic components distribution, where each firm typically sells to many small buyers, than in an industry, such as jet engines, where the number of buyers is relatively low.

Volatility of Demand Conditions   Price cutting is harder to detect when market demand conditions are volatile. Demand volatility is a particularly thorny problem when a firm can observe only its own price and market share and not those of its rival. If a firm's sales unexpectedly fall, is it because market demand has fallen or one of its competitors has cut price and is taking business from it?

Demand volatility is an especially serious problem when a substantial proportion of a firm's costs are fixed. Then, marginal costs decline rapidly at output levels below capacity, and fluctuations in demand will ordinarily result in substantial swings in the monopoly price. By contrast, when costs are mainly variable, the marginal cost function will be nearly flat, and the monopoly price will not change as demand shifts back and forth. With high fixed costs and variable demand, the problem of coordinating on the monopoly equilibrium is severe since firms are chasing a moving target (the monopoly price). Moreover, at output levels even a little below capacity, marginal costs are likely to be low. Thus, during times of excess capacity, the temptation to cut price to steal business can be high.[21]

---

[21]See Scherer, F.M. and D. Ross, *Industrial Market Structure and Economic Performance*, New York: Houghton Mifflin, 1991 for an excellent graphical exposition of these points.

Firm Asymmetries and the Price Umbrella

The theory on which equations (10.1) and (10.2) are based assumed that firms were identical. When firms are not identical, either because they have different costs or are vertically differentiated, achieving cooperative pricing becomes more difficult.

For one thing, when firms have different marginal costs or have different product qualities, the price that a given firm would charge if it was the monopolist will differ across firms. Figure 10.3 shows this for the special case of two firms with different marginal costs. The firm with the lower marginal cost prefers a lower price than the firm with the higher marginal cost. Unlike the symmetric case where there is a single monopoly price that serves a natural focal point, in the asymmetric case the task of coordinating on a focal price is more difficult.

In addition, differences in costs, capacities, or product qualities create asymmetrical incentives to go along with cooperative pricing even when all firms can agree on what the cooperative price should be. For example, small firms within a given industry often have more incentive to defect from cooperative pricing than larger firms. There are two related reasons for this. First, because industry profit rises when firms move toward the monopoly price and a large firm typically captures a larger share of industry profit than a smaller firm, a larger firm benefits more from the move toward cooperative pricing than a smaller firm does.

FIGURE 10.3
MONOPOLY PRICES WITH ASYMMETRICAL FIRMS.

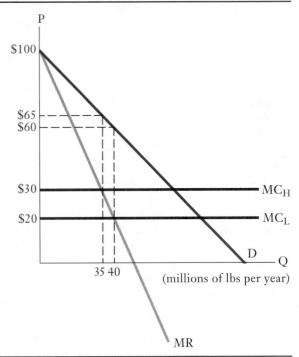

The low-cost firm's marginal cost curve is MC_L, while the high-cost firm's marginal cost curve is MC_H. If the low-cost firm was a monopolist it would set a price of $60. If the high-cost firm was a monopolist it would set a price of $65.

Second, not only do small firms benefit less from cooperative pricing, they may also anticipate that large firms have weak incentives to punish a small firm that undercuts its price. To illustrate this point, consider a small firm that, in the previous period, cut its price 5 percent below the price of a larger competitor. As a result, the smaller firm captures a fraction α of a larger firm's demand.[22] If the larger firm matches the small firm's price cut, it regains its original demand.

Does it pay for the large firm to match? Suppose that the large firm's price is $100, its marginal cost is $50, and its original level of demand is 100 units. If it matches, its profit is

$$(95 - 50)100 = 4{,}500$$

If it does not match, its profit is

$$(100 - 50)100(1 - \alpha) = 5{,}000(1 - \alpha)$$

Not matching is optimal if the second expression is bigger than the first, which occurs if $\alpha < 10$ percent. By allowing the smaller firm to underprice it, the large firm extends a *price umbrella* to the smaller firm. More generally, if β represents the percentage price cut, and $PCM = (p-c)/p$ is the percentage contribution margin of the large firm, then a price umbrella is optimal when

$$\alpha < \frac{\beta}{PCM}$$

This inequality implies that a price umbrella strategy is desirable when

- β is large in comparison to α: The price cut is relatively large, but the price cutter does not steal much market share from the larger firm.

- *PCM* is small: Margins in the industry are relatively small to begin with.

$\mathcal{E}$XAMPLE 10.2

FIRM ASYMMETRIES AND THE 1992 FARE WAR IN THE U.S. AIRLINE INDUSTRY[23]

When firms are different, even the expectation that competitors will instantly match a price cut may not deter certain firms from cutting prices aggressively.

---

[22]Note that unlike the theory in the previous section, the undercutting firm does not steal the entire market of the high-price firm. One reason for this might be that the firms are horizontally differentiated. Another might be that the small firm is capacity constrained.

[23]This discussion is based on Robert Gertner's paper, "The Role of Firm Asymmetries for Tacit Collusion in Markets with Immediate Competitive Responses," working paper, University of Chicago, 1993.

Robert Gertner has argued that low-quality or low-market-share firms may make themselves better off by defecting from collusive prices even though they fully anticipate that their high-quality or high-market-share rivals will match their price cuts right away. To illustrate this argument, Gertner cites the example of Northwest Airlines.

In spring 1992, Northwest Airlines started a fare war that was immediately matched and later escalated by its competitors. The 1992 fare war deepened the already record losses the airline industry was suffering in the wake of the recession that began with the Persian Gulf crisis in 1990. On close examination, it seems curious that Northwest would start a price war. After all, what did it have to gain? Airlines receive information about their competitors' fares instantaneously through a clearinghouse computer system run by the Airline Tariff Publishing Company (ATP). It is implausible that Northwest expected that it could cut fares without eliciting a competitive response. But if it expected that competitors would respond to its price cut, the theory we have just developed suggests that a price cut would be an ineffective way to increase profit: The fare cut would be matched instantly by Northwest's competitors. Relative market shares would not change, and with smaller margin and no increase in share, Northwest would be strictly worse off than it would have been at higher fares. Because reduced margins are especially costly during the summer, when air travel peaks, the timing of Northwest's price cutting seems perplexing.

But these arguments overlook an important point: When firms are asymmetric, they will have different views about how high the price in the industry ought to be. Gertner notes that in the early 1990s, Northwest had a poor route system, an inferior frequent flyer program, and a reputation for poor service. If competitors, such as American and United, charged the monopoly price along a particular route, and Northwest matched, Northwest would probably get less business than these competitors, who had better route structures and better frequent flyer programs. Indeed, in spring 1992, with the industry characterized by excess capacity, Northwest's planes might well have flown nearly empty if all airlines charged prices at the monopoly level.

Under these conditions, Northwest's best hope was probably to move the industry down the market demand curve through deep price cuts. Even though competitors were likely to match these price cuts, the cuts were likely to benefit Northwest for two reasons. First, the price cuts took place during the summer travel season, so much of the additional traffic that they would generate would consist of discretionary vacation travelers. Within this group, Northwest's competitive disadvantages were minimized because differences among airlines in terms of frequent flyer programs or on-time performance are likely to be less important in determining a discretionary traveler's choice of carriers. Second, a disproportionate share of the additional traffic that is generated by the price cut will end up flying the poorer quality airline such as Northwest, simply because at equal prices, seats on the higher-quality carriers will sell out more quickly and cause a "spill" of traffic that only the less desirable carrier can serve. These two points explain why Northwest might have benefited from a price war and why it made sense to launch it during the summer. If Northwest could fill its planes only by stimulating market demand, its incentive was to do so when demand was most price elastic. This occurs during the summer when the mix of travelers is more heavily tilted toward more price elastic leisure travelers.

Example 10.3

Pricing Discipline in the U.S. Tobacco Industry[24]

An interesting example of the role played by a small firm in undermining pricing discipline occurred in the U.S. cigarette industry in the 1980s and 1990s. As shown in Table 8.1, the cigarette industry is one of the most highly concentrated in the American economy, with a four-firm concentration ratio of over 92 percent in 1987 and a Herfindahl index of nearly .25. Throughout the first half of the twentieth century, the cigarette industry displayed a remarkable degree of pricing cooperation. Twice a year (generally in June and December) the dominant firms (which since the 1970s have been Philip Morris or RJR) would announce their intention to raise the list prices of their cigarettes, and within days the other cigarette manufacturers followed with increases of their own. Such pricing discipline helped the industry raise prices by 14 percent per year from 1980 through 1985, a rate far above inflation for the same period. The result was one of the most profitable businesses in the American economy, with operating profit margins (profit before interest and corporate income taxes divided by sales revenues) averaging close to 40 percent throughout the 1980s.

However, Liggett and Myers, the smallest of the six U.S. cigarette companies did not benefit much from the industry's success in keeping prices high. Having misjudged the potential for filter cigarettes in the 1950s, Liggett saw its share of the cigarette market decline from 21 percent in 1947 to just over 2 percent by the late 1970s. As the 1970s ended, Liggett was even contemplating shutting itself down.

As the smallest and least profitable of the big six cigarette producers, Liggett had the least to gain from raising prices in lockstep with its larger rivals, and it had the most to gain by undercutting their prices. Perhaps not surprisingly, then, when the grocery store cooperative Topco approached Liggett in 1980 with a plan to market and sell discount cigarettes at prices 30 percent below branded cigarettes,

---

[24]This example draws from "Strategic Analysis of the Marlboro Friday Price Cuts," a paper prepared by Kellogg Graduate School of Management students Diane Kitiyama, Jon Passman, Todd Reichmann, Craig Safir, and Philip Yau in March 1994. It also draws from "Tobacco Suit Exposes Ways Cigarette Firms Keep the Profits Fat," *Wall Street Journal*, March 5, 1990, pp. A1–A8.

Liggett was receptive. The initial success of the discount cigarettes surprised even Liggett. By 1984, its share of overall cigarette sales had tripled, largely by virtue of its success in the discount cigarette business, which was responsible for 65 percent of Liggett's volume.

Liggett based its launch of discount cigarettes on the theory that the discount market was a niche that its larger competitors would ignore. However, Liggett failed to anticipate the impact that discount cigarettes would have on the demand for premium brands. For example, Brown and Williamson (B&W), the third largest domestic cigarette producer in the 1970s and 1980s, estimated that Liggett's discount cigarettes cost it $50 million in revenues in 1983. In 1984, in a variant on the tit-for-tat strategy, B&W introduced its own line of discount cigarettes called Filter Lights whose packaging was nearly identical to Liggett's Quality Lights. B&W offered their line at the same list price as Liggett's cigarettes, but it effectively undercut Liggett's price by offering trade allowances to wholesalers who stocked the B&W brand. During the mid-1980s, other manufacturers introduced their own discount brands, and by 1989, Liggett's share of the discount cigarette market had fallen from nearly 90 percent to under 15 percent.

Liggett's creation of a discount tier of the cigarette market has profoundly affected the domestic U.S. cigarette business. In the early 1990s, after the decline of its fortunes in the discount segment of the market, Liggett introduced "deep-discount" cigarettes that sell for prices 30 percent below those of the discount brands. Other manufacturers, most notably RJR, also began selling their own deep discount brands, and by 1992 RJR and Philip Morris had over 60 percent of this segment of the market. By 1992, the domestic business could be divided into three clearly defined segments: a premium segment, in which the manufacturers' average price to the wholesale trade was $69 per thousand; a discount tier in which prices averaged $49 per thousand; and the deep-discount tier in which prices were nearly $31 per thousand.

The emergence of a segmented market has complicated pricing coordination. Competitors must now coordinate an entire structure of prices, rather than just one. With declining consumer demand, much of the growth in the discount and deep discount segments has come at the expense of the premium brands, indicating that considerable substitution takes place across segments that a profit-maximizing pricing structure must take into account.

Philip Morris's decision to cut the price of its flagship brand Marlboro on Friday, April 3, 1993 can be understood in light of these considerations. Low prices in the discount and deep-discount segments had eroded Marlboro's market share from 30 percent of the entire cigarette market in 1988 to 21 percent in 1993. Philip Morris found it difficult to induce its other competitors to raise prices in the deep-discount segment where demand was highly price elastic and retailers often absorbed increases in the wholesale price without increasing their own prices so as to keep volumes high. Philip Morris's decision to cut the price of Marlboro by 20 percent in April 1993 was quickly matched by RJR and other competitors, who lowered prices on their premium brands by the same amount.

In the aftermath of "Marlboro Friday," pricing discipline seems to have returned to the cigarette business. Both Philip Morris and RJR were able to lead the rest of the industry to price increases in all segments in 1993, 1994, and 1995. As the great cigarette price war of 1993 drew to a close, prices in the premium segment had fallen by 26 percent, but prices in the discount and deep-discount segments had risen by 8 percent and 48 percent respectively. Marlboro's share of the market, which was 21 percent in April 1993, had climbed to 26 percent by the beginning of 1994 and had risen to 30 percent by mid-1995.

Multimarket Contact

Douglas Bernheim and Michael Whinston have argued that cooperative pricing is easier to maintain when firms compete against one another in more than one market.[25] The simplest intuition for this result is that if one firm cuts price to increase market share in one market, its competitor could threaten to retaliate not only by matching the price in that market, but also by cutting price in the other market. Of course, if the price cutter anticipates a response in the second market, if it does deviate, it too ought to cut price in the second market. The key point about multimarket contact is that the conditions on the discount rate (comparable to [10.1] above) that discourage firms from cutting price in *each market individually* include a smaller range of discount rates than the condition that discourages the firms from cutting price in both markets simultaneously. Thus, when the firms face off in more than one market, the conditions under which cooperative pricing is sustainable through strategies, such as tit-for-tat or grim trigger, are more encompassing than when the firms face each other in a single market.

Market Structure and Cooperative Pricing: Summary

This section has discussed how market structure affects the sustainability of cooperative pricing. Table 10.3 summarizes the impact of the market structure characteristics discussed in this section.

Facilitating Practices

As the discussion in the previous section suggests, market structure can affect firms' ability to sustain cooperative pricing. Firms themselves can also facilitate cooperative pricing by:

---

[25]Bernheim, B.D. and M. Whinston, "Multimarket Contact and Collusive Behavior," *RAND Journal of Economics*, 21, Spring 1990, pp. 1–26. Michael Porter makes a similar, though nontechnical, argument for this point in *Competitive Advantage*, New York: Free Press, 1985, pp. 353–361.

TABLE 10.3
MARKET STRUCTURE CONDITIONS AFFECTING THE SUSTAINABILITY OF
COOPERATIVE PRICING

Condition	How Does it Affect Cooperative Pricing?	Reason
High Market Concentration	Facilitates	•Coordinating on the cooperative equilibrium is easier with fewer firms.
		•Increases benefit–cost ratio from adhering to cooperative pricing.
		•Reduces lag between defection and retaliation by decreasing uncertainty about whether defections have occurred and about identity of defectors.
Firm Asymmetries	Harms	•Disagreement over cooperative price; coordinating on a cooperative price is more difficult.
		•Possible incentive of large firms to extend price umbrella to small firms increases small firms' incentives to cut price.
		•Small firms may prefer to deviate from monopoly prices even if larger firms match.
High Buyer Concentration	Harms	•Reduces the probability that a defector will be discovered.
Lumpy Orders	Harms	•Decreases the frequency of interaction between competitors, increasing the lag between defection and retaliation.
Secret Price Terms	Harms	•Increases detection lags because prices of competitors are more difficult to monitor.
		•Increases possibility of misreads or misunderstandings.
Volatility of Demand and Cost Conditions	Harms	•Increases lag between defection and retaliation (perhaps even precluding retaliation altogether) by increasing uncertainty about whether defections have occurred and about identity of defectors.
Multimarket Contact Between Competitors	Facilitates	•Increases benefit–cost ratio from adhering to cooperative pricing.

- Price leadership
- Advance announcement of price changes
- Most favored customer clauses
- Uniform delivered pricing
- Strategic use of inventories and order backlogs

These practices either facilitate coordination among firms or diminish incentives to cut price. We discuss each in turn.

Price Leadership

In price leadership, one firm in an industry (the price leader) announces its price changes before all other firms, which then match the leader's price. Examples of well-known price leaders include Kellogg in breakfast cereals, Philip Morris in tobacco, and (until the mid-1960s) U.S. Steel in American steel.

Price leadership can be thought of as a way to overcome the problem of coordinating on a focal equilibrium. In price leadership, each firm gives up its pricing autonomy and cedes control over industry pricing to a single firm. Firms thus need not worry that rivals will secretly shade price to steal market share. Of course, as the Sydney newspaper market illustrates, systems of price leadership can break down if the price leader fails to retaliate against defectors. Because of its desire to become the price leader in the afternoon paper market, Rupert Murdoch refused to follow Fairfax's price lead. When Fairfax failed to respond to Murdoch's defection, it found itself in a costly price war that eventually resulted in its being displaced as the leader in the afternoon market.

The kind of oligopolistic price leadership we discuss here should be distinguished from the barometric price leadership that sometimes occurs in competitive markets, such as that for prime rate loans. Under barometric price leadership, the price leader merely acts as a barometer of changes in market conditions by adjusting prices in response to shifts in demand or input prices. Under barometric leadership the identity of the price leader often changes, while under oligopolistic leadership the same firm acts as leader for many years. Recent federal and state antitrust inquiries into the pricing policies of infant formula makers centered on whether the price matching strategies of Abbott Labs and Bristol Myers represented oligopolistic or barometric price leadership. The two firms alternated as price leaders during the 1980s, but the follower always matched the leader as did a third firm, Wyeth. The firms have generally settled these inquiries out of court without admitting wrongdoing.

Advance Announcement of Price Changes

In some markets, firms will publicly announce the prices they intend to charge in the future. For example, in chemicals markets it is not uncommon for firms to announce their intention to raise prices 30 or 60 days before the price change is to take effect. Advance announcements of price changes reduce the uncertainty that firms face about the likelihood that their rivals will undercut them. The practice also allows firms to rescind or roll back proposed price increases that competitors refuse to follow.

To illustrate why advance announcements can facilitate cooperative pricing, consider a simple example in which the industry consists of two identical firms. Each firm chooses its price a month before it goes into effect. The firms can continue to adjust their prices until they are satisfied with them. The equilibrium in this market must be the monopoly price. A firm knows that its rival will always match the price that it announces. Thus each firm's market share is fixed at ½, and each firm's profit is one-half of industry profit no matter what price it charges. As a result, each firm's profit-maximizing price is the monopoly price.

Most Favored Customer Clauses

A most favored customer clause is a provision in a sales contract that promises a buyer that it will pay the lowest price the seller charges. There are two basic types of most favored customer clauses: contemporaneous and retroactive.

To illustrate these, consider a simple example: Xerxes Chemical manufacturers a chemical additive used to enhance the performance of jet fuel. Great Lakes Refining Company, a manufacturer of jet fuel, signs a contract with Xerxes calling for delivery of 100,000 tons of the chemical over the next three months at the "open order" price of $.50 per ton.[26] Under a contemporaneous most favored customer policy, Xerxes agrees that while this contract is in effect, if it sells the chemical at a lower price to any other buyer (perhaps to capture business from one of its competitors), it will also drop the price to this lower level for Great Lakes.[27] Under a retroactive most favored customer clause, Xerxes agrees to pay a rebate to Great Lakes if during a certain period after the contract has expired (e.g., two years), it sells the chemical additive for a lower price than Great Lakes paid. For example, suppose Great Lakes' contract expired on 12/31/95, but its contract contained a two-year retroactive most favored customer clause. If sometime in 1996 Xerxes announces a general reduction in price from $.50 per ton to $.40 per ton, it would have to pay Great Lakes a rebate equal to ($.50 − $.40) × 100,000 or $10,000, the difference between what Great Lakes actually paid and what it would have paid under the new lower price.

Most favored customer clauses appear to benefit buyers. For Great Lakes, the "price protection" offered by the most favored customer clause may help keep its production costs in line with those of competitors. However, most favored customer clauses can inhibit price competition. Retroactive most favored customer clauses make it expensive for Xerxes to cut prices in the future, either selectively or across the board. Contemporaneous most favored customer clauses do not penalize the firm for making across-the-board price reductions (e.g., if Xerxes cuts prices

---

[26]An open order price is simply the price that the manufacturer charges to any buyer who approaches it with an order for the additive.

[27]Hence, the origin of the term "most favored customer clause." Great Lakes is extended the same price terms as the most favored customer of the manufacturer. Thus, if Xerxes offers another refiner a price of $.45, Xerxes will have to drop Great Lakes' price to $.45, too.

to all its customers, it does not have to pay rebates to past customers), but they do discourage firms from using selective price cutting to compete for customers with highly price-elastic demands.

One might wonder whether firms would ever have an incentive to adopt most favored customer policies if their customers do not demand them. After all, it seems as though the ideal situation from a given manufacturer's perspective is when its *competitors* adopt most favored customer policies, thus tying their hands in the competition for customers, but where it itself does not adopt them, leaving it free to selectively or generally price cut. However, Thomas Cooper has shown that because adoption of a retroactive most favored customer clause softens price competition in the future, oligopolists may have an incentive to unilaterally adopt a most favored customer policy, even if rival manufacturers do not.[28]

Uniform Delivered Prices

In many industries, such as cement, steel, or processed soybean products, buyers and sellers are geographically separated, and transportation costs are a significant fraction of the product's total value. In such contexts, the choice of the pricing method can affect the nature of competitive interactions. Broadly speaking, two different kinds of pricing policies can be identified. Under *uniform FOB pricing*, the seller quotes a price for pickup at the seller's loading dock, and the buyer absorbs the freight charges for shipping from the seller's plant to the buyer's plant.[29] Under *uniform delivered pricing*, the firm quotes a single delivered price for all buyers and absorbs any freight charges itself.[30]

---

[28]Cooper, T.E., "Most Favored Customer Clauses and Tacit Collusion," *RAND Journal of Economics*, 17, Autumn 1986, pp. 377–388. David Besanko and Tom Lyons prove a similar result for contemporaneous most favored customer clauses, but show that voluntary adoption is most likely to occur in concentrated industries where a given firm internalizes much of the "competition-softening" effect of most favored customer policies. Both the Cooper model and the Besanko-Lyon model are specific examples of two-stage commitment models, discussed in Chapter 9.

[29]FOB stands for "free on board," so the FOB price is the price the seller quotes for loading the product on the delivery vehicle. If the seller pays the transport charges, the actual delivery charges are added to the buyer's bill, and the net price the seller receives is known as the uniform net mill price.

[30]A third type of pricing is *basing point pricing:* The seller designates one or more base locations and quotes FOB prices from them. The customer chooses a basing point and absorbs the freight costs between the basing point and its plant. For example, if a steel company uses Gary, Indiana as a basing point, and a Chicago customer buys steel from the firm's Birmingham, Alabama plant, it would pay an FOB price plus the freight charges as if the steel had been shipped from Gary to Birmingham. In a sense, basing point pricing represents a kind of intermediate case between FOB pricing and uniform delivered pricing. See Scherer, F.M. and D. Ross, *Industrial Market Structure and Economic Performance*, New York: Houghton Mifflin, 1991 for a thorough discussion of basing point pricing and of antitrust cases in the steel and cement industries that centered on the basing point system.

Uniform delivered pricing facilitates cooperative pricing by allowing firms to make a more "surgical" response to price cutting behavior by rivals. Consider, for example, two brick producers, one located in Bombay and the other in Ahmadabad, India. These firms have been trying to maintain prices at the monopoly level, but the Bombay producer cuts its price to increase its share of the market in Surat, a city between Bombay and Ahmadabad. Under FOB pricing, retaliation requires that the Ahmadabad producer cut its mill price, which effectively reduces its price to all its customers (see Figure 10.4). On the other hand, if the firms were using uniform delivered pricing, the Ahmadabad firm could cut its price selectively; it could cut the delivered price to its customers in Surat, keeping delivered prices of other customers at their original level (see Figure 10.5).[31] By reducing the "cost" that the "victim" incurs by retaliating, retaliation becomes more likely, and the credibility of policies, such as tit-for-tat, that can sustain cooperative pricing is enhanced.

Strategic Use of Inventories and Order Backlogs to Facilitate Pricing Cooperation

Careful adjustment of inventories or order backlogs can facilitate cooperative pricing.[32] Consider an oligopolistic industry in which firms hold inventories (or maintain order backlogs) and demand fluctuates. When market demand drops, the profit-maximizing monopoly price will typically drop as well. The dominant firm may then attempt to lead the industry down to this lower price. If (as expected) its

FIGURE 10.4
FOB PRICING.

When both firms use FOB pricing, the delivered price that a customer actually pays depends on its location. The delivered price schedules are shown by the solid lines in the figure. If the brick producer in Ahmadabad lowers its FOB price to match that of the Bombay producer, then it effectively shifts its delivered price schedule downward. (It now becomes the dashed line.) Even though the intent of the Ahmadabad firm's price cut is to retaliate against the Bombay stealing business in Surat, the Ahmadabad firm ends up reducing its delivered prices to all of its customers.

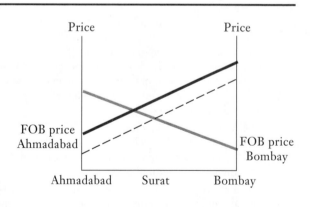

[31]Of course, if the firm does so, it would be using nonuniform delivered pricing rather than uniform delivered pricing.

[32]An order backlog refers to a firm's queue of unfilled orders. Order backlogs are common in businesses, such as airframe manufacturing, in which products are made to order.

FIGURE 10.5
DELIVERED PRICING.

When both firms use delivered pricing, a firm's customer pays the same delivered price, no matter what its location. If the Bombay firm cuts its delivered price to steal business in Surat, the Ahmadabad producer need only cut its delivered price in the vicinity of Surat in order to retaliate.

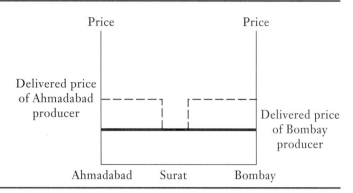

marginal cost is lower than that of its smaller competitors, the move to this lower price might also be accompanied by a shift in market share away from the smaller firms toward the dominant firm.[33] However, the smaller firms may misinterpret this move as an attempt to capture market share from them permanently. To avoid this, the dominant firm may choose instead to absorb the reduced demand by allowing its inventories to build up (or its order backlogs to be drawn down) rather than by cutting its price. By following this strategy—which is known as *buffering*— the dominant firm sacrifices market share (and hence short-run profitability) on current orders by extending a price umbrella to smaller firms. The dominant firm benefits from buffering because it enhances the odds that long-run pricing discipline in the industry will be preserved; when demand picks up, smaller firms will be more likely to raise prices back to the monopoly level.

Ralph Sultan suggests that General Electric may have engaged in buffering in the turbine generator business in the 1950s.[34] In bad times, GE cut its prices less aggressively than its two competitors, Westinghouse and Allis-Chalmers, and during upturns it raised its price less than they did.

Garth Saloner and Julio Rotemberg point out that inventories can facilitate pricing cooperation in a different way. Holding more inventories than it ordinarily would enables a dominant firm to make a credible commitment to retaliate against competitors who deviate from the cooperative pricing outcome by cutting price.[35] Inventories can thus serve as a strategic commitment that a firm

---

[33]Such a shift would be consistent with the conditions for maximization of industry profit when marginal costs are an increasing function of volume.

[34]Sultan, R., *Pricing in the Electrical Equipment Oligopoly, Vol. 2*, Cambridge, MA: Harvard University Press, 1975.

[35]Rotemberg, J.J. and G. Saloner, "Cyclical Behavior of Strategic Inventories," *Quarterly Journal of Economics*, CIV, February 1989, pp. 73–98.

will behave "tough" to induce competitors to act less aggressively. This use of inventories is a specific example of the top-dog strategy discussed in Chapter 9.

♦ ♦ ♦ ♦ ♦ QUALITY COMPETITION

While we have focused our discussion in this chapter on price competition, price is obviously not the only factor that drives consumer decisions and firm strategies. Product attributes, such as performance and durability, also matter, and firms may compete just as fiercely on these dimensions as they do on price.

To simplify the discussion, without substantial loss in insight, we will lump all nonprice attributes into a single dimension called "quality"—quality may be thought of as any product attribute that increases the demand for the product at a fixed price. The next section of this book emphasizes the need for firms to provide a combination of price and quality that offers superior value to that offered by competitors. In this chapter, we focus on how market structure and competition influence the firm's choice of quality.

Quality Choice in Competitive Markets

In a competitive market, either all goods are identical, or they exhibit pure vertical differentiation. Recall from Chapter 8 that when products are vertically differentiated, for any set of prices all consumers will agree as to which products they most prefer. Firms may, therefore, offer different levels of quality at different prices, but the market will force all firms to charge the same price per unit of quality. Firms that charge a price per unit of quality that exceeds the market price will not have any customers, and firms that charge less than the market price will find that they can raise their price a little and still sell as much as they want to. Thus, in equilibrium in a market with vertical differentiation, we may see many levels of quality, but a fixed price per unit of quality. Consumers will be indifferent between shopping from all sellers in the market.

Competition may appear to force all sellers to provide a level of quality commensurate with their price. But this depends on a critical unstated assumption. In particular, consumers must be able to perfectly evaluate the quality of each seller. But what if consumers cannot easily do this? Then, sellers that charge more than the going price per unit of quality may still have customers.

Consider a market in which some consumers have information about product quality and others do not. Suppose that it is costly to be an informed consumer—one must invest time and effort to identify good quality sellers. In this market, uninformed consumers may be able to infer the quality of sellers merely by observing the behavior of informed consumers. For example, a prospective car buyer may be considering the purchase of a recently introduced model. If the buyer finds out that sales of that model are low (for example, the car buyer never sees anyone driving that model), he or she might well question the quality of the automobile even with no direct information about it. If no one else likes the car, it must not be very good.

The car buyer can thus make an informed judgment about the quality of the car without knowing anything about cars except how many people appear to drive different models.

If there are enough well-informed buyers in a market, quality is likely to be adequate for most everyone. For example, Richard Ippolito studied consumer behavior in the market for mutual funds.[36] He found in any given year substantial variation in quality among funds, where quality may be measured in terms of the risk-adjusted return. Quality differences tend to persist for several years, suggesting that fund performance, good and bad, reflects the skills of the fund managers, not just luck. Well-informed investors monitor the performance of different funds and move money into high-quality funds and out of low-quality funds. There are also relatively uninformed investors in this market who do not monitor fund performance and may not even know that their fund is doing poorly. Even so, Ippolito found over time a steady flow of dollars from low-quality to high-quality funds. Many low-quality funds are driven from the market. Ippolito concludes that uninformed investors benefit from the actions of informed investors.

If uninformed consumers cannot gauge quality by observing informed consumers, then a *lemons market* can emerge. The term "lemons market" is derived from the used car market, in which owners are more anxious to sell low-quality cars ("lemons") than high-quality cars.[37] To emerge, a lemons market requires two ingredients: uninformed consumers, and the fact that low-quality products are cheaper to make than high-quality products.

If consumers cannot determine the quality of what they are buying, then sellers will skimp on quality and sell only low-quality products but still charge the going price. Of course, consumers may realize that their ignorance of quality makes them susceptible to the purchase of lemons. They may even insist on paying less for a product, figuring its quality is likely to be low. This poses a problem for sellers of high-quality products, who cannot get their money's worth from suspicious consumers. High-quality sellers may actually refuse to sell their product, figuring that they cannot get a price to cover their opportunity cost. If they want to get a price commensurate with quality, they must rely on money-back guarantees, reviews in independent consumer magazines, and a reputation for quality to convince buyers that their products are not lemons.

An interesting example of the lemons problem is the market for health insurance. Here, buyers know about "quality" and sellers are uninformed. The relevant quality is the state of an individual's health. All else equal, insurers would like to sell to healthy buyers. Unhealthy individuals will need more medical care and can cost insurers tens of thousands of dollars annually. But insurers cannot

---

[36]Ippolito, R., "Consumer Reaction to Measures of Poor Quality: Evidence from the Mutual Fund Industry," *Journal of Law and Economics*, 35, 1992, pp. 45–70.

[37]For a formal treatment of the lemons problem and an interesting discussion of its applications, see Akerlof, G., "The Market for Lemons: Qualitative Uncertainty and the Market Mechanism," *Quarterly Journal of Economics*, 84, 1970, pp. 488–500.

easily determine the health of potential subscribers and fear that enrollees will be "lemons"—in poor health. To solve this problem, insurers sell to groups, such as the employees of large firms. These groups usually contain a representative cross-section of health risks, so insurers worry less about their health. But many insurers also sell to individuals. They naturally suspect that a person seeking insurance is probably less healthy than one who elects to go uninsured. Just as the wary buyer of a used car is willing to pay less when concerned about buying a lemon, the seller of insurance charges more when it is concerned about selling to unhealthy individuals or refuses to sell at all. This explains why employee groups generally get more favorable insurance rates than do individual purchasers. Insurers use other practices to avoid the lemons problem, including refusing to pay for treatment of "preexisting conditions" that the subscriber knew about at the time of purchase, and imposing a waiting period before insurance benefits begin. These practices, though necessary to protect insurers in a competitive marketplace, leave many individuals without insurance coverage and discourage others from changing jobs for fear of losing coverage.

Sanford Grossman and Joseph Stiglitz point out one further problem that may arise in markets where some individuals are well informed and others are not.[38] They consider a market in which consumers of information compete against each other. An example might be the market for corporate control discussed in Chapter 6. Some consumers might spend resources gathering information, but if uninformed consumers can infer what that information is, all may end up on an even footing. As a result, those who gathered the information may be worse off than those who did not, having borne the expense without realizing extra benefits. This implies that there will be underinvestment in information gathering. In the market for corporate control, for example, an investor may devote considerable effort to identifying an underperforming firm. As soon as that investor makes a tender offer for control of the firm, however, other investors will learn the identity of the undervalued firm because tender offers are public information. In the ensuing competition between investors to gain control of the underperforming target, profits may be bid away. In the end, the investor who did the hard work of identifying the target may be worse off than if it did no research at all. This helps explain why takeover artists, such as T. Boone Pickens and Sir James Goldsmith, are extremely secretive in their dealings and why there is a need for speed in effecting takeovers.

Quality Choices of Sellers with Market Power

Sellers with market power view quality as a critical determinant of the demand for their product. Figure 10.6 depicts the demand facing a seller at two levels of quality. We have defined quality to include anything that increases demand, and this is reflected in the figure. When quality is high, demand is higher than when it is low. The vertical difference between the high- and low-quality demand curves repre-

---

[38]Grossman, S. and J. Stiglitz, "On the Impossibility of Informationally Efficient Markets," *American Economic Review*, 70, June 1980, pp. 393–408.

FIGURE 10.6
DEMAND CURVES ASSOCIATED WITH DIFFERENT QUALITY LEVELS.

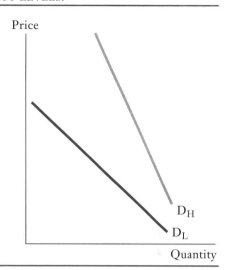

When the firm increases its quality, its demand curve shifts from D_L to D_H. Not only does the firm sell more of the product at any given price when it raises quality, its demand becomes more price inelastic, as indicated by the fact that D_H is steeper than D_L.

sents the additional value of quality. As shown in the figure, the demand curve gets steeper as quality increases. This would occur if consumers who are willing to pay the most for a product are also willing to pay the most to improve quality.

Suppose that a seller with market power had to select a single level of quality for all its products. This could be an appliance maker selecting a level of reliability that will be consistent across its product line, or a car maker selecting a level of safety that will be consistent across its fleet. What level of quality should the seller choose? As with other economic tradeoffs, it should choose quality so that the marginal cost of the quality increase equals the marginal revenue that results when consumers demand more of the product.[39]

The Marginal Cost of Increasing Quality

The idea that it is costly to improve quality contrasts with the literature on continuous quality improvement (CQI).[40] According to the principles of CQI, improvements in the production process can simultaneously reduce costs and increase quality. But once firms come to grips with inefficiencies in production, they must eventually confront tradeoffs between lowering costs and boosting quality. For example, the reliability of an airplane can certainly be improved by assuring that components fit properly. Beyond these assurances of productive efficiency, further improvements can be

[39]To highlight the key tradeoffs, we ignore what in Chapter 9 we called strategic effects. Thus, we focus on the quality choice of a single firm in isolation and do not consider the side effects of its quality choice on the intensity of price competition.

[40]See, for example, Crosby, P.B., *Quality is Free: The Art of Making Quality Certain*, New York: McGraw-Hill, 1979.

achieved by installing costly backup features, such as additional engines and brakes. A similar tradeoff exists for automobile safety. Once car makers have efficiently employed existing technologies, further improvements in safety generally add to production costs. Examples include refinements of the computers governing anti-lock brakes and airbags, reinforcement of body panels, use of fireproof materials, and redesigning cars with "crumple zones" to minimize injuries in collisions. We are concerned here with the tradeoff between boosting quality and holding down costs.

If a firm is producing efficiently, then quality is costly. Moreover, improvements tend to be incrementally more costly as quality nears "perfection." To see why, consider a university that is trying to minimize the chance of losing data in the event of a mainframe computer crash. The university can minimize its losses by running a program to back up the system. Each run of the program is costly, both in terms of manpower and computer downtime. If the university wants to limit losses to a maximum of one week's work, it must run the backup program 52 times annually. Limiting the loss to three days' work requires running the backup program 122 times per year. Limiting the loss to one day's work requires 365 runs. We can thus see that it requires incrementally more and more computer runs to provide incrementally less and less additional protection.

The Marginal Benefit of Improving Quality

When a firm improves the quality of its product, more consumers will want to buy it. How much revenue this brings in depends on two factors:

- The increase in demand brought on by the increase in quality
- The incremental profit earned on each additional unit sold

We discuss each of these factors in turn.

Michael Spence has pointed out that when contemplating an increase in quality, the firm must consider the responsiveness of its "marginal consumers"—consumers who are indifferent as to buying from that firm and buying elsewhere or not buying at all.[41] Since the firm's "inframarginal" customers—those loyal to it—will continue to buy the product after the quantity increases, the financial benefit from an increase in quality stems from new customers.[42] Firms that correctly worry about their marginal consumers may over- or underprovide quality relative to what is best for their average inframarginal consumer. For example, firms will overprovide quality if the marginal consumer is more willing to pay for additional quality than is the inframarginal consumer. The firm adds quality to attract marginal consumers, while raising price to cover the added cost. Marginal consumers with high

---

[41]Spence, A.M., "Monopoly, Quality, and Regulation," *Bell Journal of Economics*, 1975, pp. 417–429.

[42]The reader may wonder why the firm could not benefit from raising its price after boosting quality. This would often be the optimal strategy. But when determining the profitability of increasing quality, it is sufficient to consider the profits realized when price is kept constant. This is another application of the "envelope theorem," discussed in footnote 8 of Chapter 9.

values of quality may be satisfied, but loyal consumers, with lower valuations of quality, are not. Even so, unless the firm grossly miscalculates, it will have more customers and higher price-cost margins than before. In an analogous manner, the firm may underprovide quality to its loyal customers if the marginal customers do not value quality highly.

The purpose of raising quality is to attract more customers. But how can a firm determine how many more customers it will get? An increase in quality will bring in more new customers if (a) there are more marginal customers; and (b) marginal customers can determine with some accuracy that quality has, in fact, increased. David Dranove and Mark Satterthwaite show that these factors are determined, in turn, by (i) the degree of horizontal differentiation in the market, and (ii) the precision with which consumers observe quality.[43] Recall from Chapter 8 that in a horizontally differentiated market, consumers tend to be loyal to sellers who offer a good idiosyncratic match between the product's differentiated attributes and the consumer's tastes and preferences. These loyal consumers may be reluctant to switch to another seller, even one who offers a higher overall level of quality. In a business where location matters, for example, consumers may continue to buy from the nearest seller even though there is a higher-quality seller at the other end of town. This explains why restaurants located in superhighway rest areas can survive despite providing substandard food. These restaurants have little reason to boost quality, since it is unlikely to significantly affect demand. Recently, some states have replaced the independents with national chains, such as Wendy's, who are concerned about brand image and thus generally maintain higher quality than the independents did.

Even if few consumers are loyal to their current sellers, a seller who boosts quality will not necessarily attract new customers. Consumers must be able to determine that quality is higher than it used to be. This is why magazines like *Consumer Reports*, which provide generally unbiased product reviews, are so popular. But consumers cannot get such reviews for many goods and services, for example, many types of furniture, medical and legal services, and home repairs. Consumers would like to know the quality of these goods and services, but may be unable to make such judgments.

When consumers have difficulty judging particular attributes of a product, they may focus on those attributes that they can easily observe and evaluate. Car buyers may kick the tires not because it provides important information about quality, but because they have no better way to evaluate the car.

The fact that consumers focus on measurable attributes helps explain why retailers are so concerned about the external appearance of their shops, and why doctors and lawyers often display their diplomas, especially if they graduated from a prestigious school. Of course, this emphasis on observable attributes may mean that consumers are shortchanged on hard-to-measure attributes that really matter.

---

[43]Dranove, D. and M. Satterthwaite, "Monopolistic Competition When Price and Quality are Not Perfectly Observable," *RAND Journal of Economics*, Winter 1992, pp. 518–534.

Sellers who offer high quality on dimensions that are difficult for consumers to measure will benefit only if they can convince consumers of their superiority. One way to do this is to publicize *objective* quality measures. (Most consumers will discount subjective claims like "We have the best guacamole in town.") There are many examples of this, such as when a film advertisement cites "two thumbs up" or when a car maker boasts of being ranked number one in a J.D. Powers survey. Another way to do this is to allow consumers to sample the product, such as when food makers distribute free samples of new brands in supermarkets. Massive advertising may also help to convince consumers to sample a new product.

Conveying quality information is especially critical for *experience goods*, those whose quality is difficult to evaluate before purchase. Stereophonic equipment, restaurant food, and medical services are all examples of experience goods. These contrast with *search goods*, whose quality is relatively easy to evaluate before purchase. Commodities like grade A wheat or crude oil are examples of search goods. Many consumers goods may also be thought of as search goods, including greeting cards, paper clips, hammers, and branded products like Coca-Cola or Kellogg's Rice Krispies, because their quality is likely to be uniform wherever they are purchased.

Sellers use various techniques to make it easier for consumers to evaluate the quality of experience goods. For example, manufacturers of high-end stereo equipment rely on dealers to demonstrate the quality of their products. Dealers often build special audition rooms, attend seminars on sound technology, and learn exactly which recordings best show off the features of each stereo component. Though costly, these investments are often decisive in convincing consumers to spend thousands of dollars on components.

Dealers are naturally fearful that once they convince a consumer to purchase a high-end product, that consumer will buy it from a discount store. High-end manufacturers also frown on this consumer opportunism. Not only do they want to protect their dealers' investments, they also feel that discount stores cannot properly demonstrate the advantages of their products. If discount stores drive the high-end dealers from the market, then in the long run it will be harder to convince consumers to shell out thousands of dollars for components. Thus, some manufacturers, such as Bang and Olafson, do not distribute through discount stores. To further protect their dealers, many manufacturers grant them *exclusive territories* in which no other store may sell the product. Another technique that manufacturers once used to protect their most reputable dealers from discount houses, thereby encouraging dealers to invest in showing off the manufacturers' goods, is *resale price maintenance* (RPM). RPM allows manufacturers to dictate the retail prices for their products, ensuring that consumers will not learn about a product at one store and then buy it from a discount house. Although many economists believe that RPM protects dealer investments, it is now considered a violation of U.S. antitrust laws.

If two sellers can gain the same increase in sales by increasing quality, who has a stronger incentive to do so? All else being equal, the seller with the higher price-cost margin will make more money from the increase in sales and thus has a stronger incentive to boost quality. Sometimes, market structure will create conflicting incentives to boost quality. A monopolist may have a higher price-cost margin than a competitive firm, but may face few marginal consumers. Every consumer in a competitive market is a marginal consumer to a firm that is about to gain a quality edge over its rivals. Horizontal differentiation has similar off-setting implications for incentives to boost quality. On the one hand, horizontal differentiation creates loyal customers, which allows sellers to boost price-cost margins, raising the gains from attracting more customers by boosting quality. On the other hand, loyal customers are less likely to switch sellers when quality differences are low, implying that each seller faces fewer marginal customers.

Because quality may fall when price-cost margins fall, intense price competition may not always benefit consumers. Dranove and Satterthwaite show that if consumers cannot easily evaluate quality, then reductions in price-cost margins may drive quality down so far that all consumers are worse off. At the least, consumers who value quality highly may be worse off. Price-cost margins may fall for a number of reasons. For example, margins in the airline industry fell in the 1980s as a direct result of deregulation. Before deregulation, price-cost margins in the industry were kept high through restrictions on entry and price regulation, and airlines competed on the basis of service and amenities. When margins fell after deregulation, the ensuing changes in quality were obvious to any frequent traveler: narrower seats, elimination of coach lounges, and deterioration in on-time performance as airlines pressed all their planes into service on new routes, rather than holding some in reserve to minimize delays due to equipment problems.

Price-cost margins may also fall if consumers become increasingly motivated to select a seller on the basis of price. This can occur if an item becomes a relatively significant fraction of a household's total budget, as a college education has become over the past two decades. This can also occur if organizational changes permit consumers to take advantage of better price information and search for the best price, as occurred in hospital markets over the past decade.

$\mathcal{E}$XAMPLE 10.4

THE MEDICAL ARMS RACE

Two decades ago, Congress enacted the National Health Planning and Resources Development Act. A major goal of this legislation was to eliminate the proliferation of high-fixed-cost medical technology, such as open heart surgery suites and computed tomographic (CT) scanning machines. Twenty years later, there is still concern that the United States has too much medical technology. The *Wall Street Journal*, for example, has highlighted Kalamazoo, Michigan, where the two hospitals in town seem to match each other's profligate spending—on open heart surgery suites, linear accelerators, even emergency helicopters. Advocates of controls also point to international comparisons that show that the United States has five to ten times as many open heart surgery suites and CT scans per capita as other developed nations. This technology proliferation has created potential for vast excess capacity, although the hospitals might use the capacity to provide services to patients who have only marginal need for them. Either way, we may be spending far more on medical technology than we need to. Advocates of regulatory controls claim that technology proliferation is the result of excessive quality competition between hospitals. Hospitals believe that they can attract more patients if they have state-of-the-art technology. James Robinson and Harold Luft suggest that the hospitals' most important customers are physicians who must decide where to admit their patients.[44] Robinson and Luft further argue that physicians prefer hospitals with modern technology—this allows them to provide more sophisticated services and charge higher fees. The use of technology to attract physicians has come to be known as the "medical arms race."

Robinson and Luft attempted to show that hospitals in competitive markets had more high-tech services, and higher costs, than monopoly hospitals. For example, they showed that in the late 1970s, hospitals with only one or two neighbors (other hospitals within 15 miles) had lower costs than hospitals with ten or more neighbors. Results like this have led many to conclude that competition in health care does not work because it drives up costs.

This widely publicized work has been criticized on three fronts. One concern is that while the medical arms race may drive up costs, it may also speed diagnosis and treatment. Overall, it is difficult to say that we are worse off as a result. Second, Robinson and Luft's empirical methods may be flawed. In particular, centrally located hospitals (and thus hospitals with more neighbors) may have higher costs not because of competition, but because their central locations make them the most natural places to situate costly new technology. This is the same logic used to explain why the best restaurants and shops are usually located in central business districts. Third, the competitive environment facing hospitals today is considerably different from the 1970s, so that the medical arms race may have ended. Recall that the benefit of raising quality to attract new customers falls as price-cost margins fall. Recall also from Example 8.6 that reorganizing the purchasing of hospital care has significantly lowered price-cost margins in competitive markets. This suggests that hospitals in competitive markets may have less incentive to add high-tech equipment. Jack Zwanziger and Glenn Melnick have documented the decline of the medical arms race in competitive markets.[45] Studying data from California, they show that the positive relationship between competition and costs disappeared by the mid-1980s.

Nowadays, the medical arms race is all but over. In most markets, decisions about what hospital to go to are made more by insurers and employers than physicians.

[44]Robinson, J. and H. Luft, "The Impact of Hospital Market Structure on Patient Volume, Average Length of Stay, and the Cost of Care," *Journal of Health Economics*, 4, 1985, pp. 333–356.

[45]Zwanziger, J. and G. Melnick, "The Effects of Hospital Competition and the Medicare PPS Program on Hospital Cost Behavior in California," *Journal of Health Economics*, 7, 1988, pp. 301–320.

The new decision makers still care about quality, but also about cost. Hospitals with low profit margins no longer feel that new equipment is always a good investment, and can no longer count on attracting more patients just by offering new services. In the past three years, fees for diagnostic imaging have fallen by 10 to 30 percent, and purchases of costly technologies, such as magnetic resonance imaging equipment, have also fallen sharply.

CHAPTER SUMMARY

◆ If firms are sufficiently patient (i.e., they do not discount the future too much), cooperative pricing (i.e., the monopoly price) may be sustainable as an equilibrium outcome, even though firms are making decisions noncooperatively. This is a specific application of the folk theorem from game theory, which says that any outcome between marginal cost and the monopoly price is sustainable as a subgame perfect Nash equilibrium in the infinitely repeated prisoners' dilemma game.

◆ Market structure conditions affect the sustainability of cooperative pricing. High market concentration and multimarket contact facilitate cooperative pricing. Asymmetries among firms, lumpy orders, high buyer concentration, secret sales transactions, and volatile demand conditions make the achievement of pricing cooperation more difficult.

◆ Practices that can facilitate the achievement of cooperative pricing include price leadership, advance announcements of price changes, most favored customer clauses, uniform delivered pricing, and strategic adjustments of inventories or order backlogs.

◆ In competitive markets, firms will provide acceptable quality as long as there is a sufficiently large number of informed consumers. If consumers are generally uninformed, lemons markets can develop in which owners or producers of high-quality goods may refuse to sell altogether.

◆ When sellers have market power, the quality they provide depends on the marginal cost and the marginal benefit of increasing quality. The marginal benefit of increasing quality depends on the increase in demand brought on by the increase in quality and the incremental profit earned on each additional unit sold. This implies that a firm's price-cost margin is an important determinant of its incentives to raise quality.

QUESTIONS

1. Suppose that you were an industry analyst trying to determine if the leading firms in the automobile manufacturing industry are playing a tit-for-tat pricing game. What real world data would you want to examine? What would you consider to be evidence of tit-for-tat pricing?

2. "Pricing cooperation is more likely to emerge in markets where, if one firm raises a price and competitors follow suit, market shares remain unchanged. It is less likely to work well in markets where price matching may not leave market shares constant." Evaluate this statement. Can you think of circumstances under which price matching behavior could alter market shares?

3. A recent article on price wars by two McKinsey consultants makes the following argument.[46]

> That the (tit-for-tat) strategy is fraught with risk cannot be overemphasized. Your competitor may take an inordinately long time to realize that its actions can do it nothing but harm; rivalry across the entire industry may escalate precipitously; and as the "tit-for-tat" game plays itself out, all of a price war's detrimental effects on customers will make themselves felt.

How would you reconcile the views expressed in this quote with the advantages of tit-for-tat claimed in this chapter?

4. Studies of pricing in the airline industry show that carriers that dominate hub airports (Delta in Atlanta, USAir in Pittsburgh, American in Dallas) tend to charge higher fares, on average, for flights in and out of the hub airport than other, non-dominant carriers flying in and out of the hub. What might explain this pattern of prices?

5. It is often argued that price wars may be more likely to occur during low demand periods than during high demand periods. (This chapter makes that argument.) Are there factors that might reverse this implication? That is, can you think of reasons why the attractiveness of deviating from cooperative pricing might actually be greater during booms (high demand) than during busts (low demand)?

6. Consider a duopoly consisting of two firms, Amalgamated Electric (AE) and Carnegie-Manheim (C-M), that sell products that are somewhat differentiated. Each firm sells to customers with different price elasticities of demand, and as a result, occasionally discounts below list price for the most price-elastic customers. Suppose, now, AE adopts a contemporaneous most favored customer policy, but C-M does not. What will happen to AE's average equilibrium price? What will happen to C-M's average equilibrium price?

---

[46]Garda, R.A. and M.V. Marn, "Price Wars," *McKinsey Quarterly*, 3, 1993: 87–100. Quote from pp. 98–99.

ENTRY AND EXIT

11

*I*n the 1970s, Harlequin Enterprises, Ltd. was the leading seller of formula "romance novels" in the United States, with a market share exceeding 90 percent. Harlequin purchased distribution services from publishing giant Simon and Schuster, which sold the books through grocery and drugstores. In 1980, Harlequin dumped Simon and Schuster and elected to handle U.S. distribution itself. Simon and Schuster reacted by entering the romance novel market. Several other firms also entered, and some used Simon and Schuster as their distributor. The number of romance novels reaching the market grew fourfold, and by 1983, sales had grown by 60 percent. Despite industry growth, Harlequin's sales fell by 28 percent, and its market share and profits were cut in half.

In the early 1990s, Microsoft's Windows was the most popular file management environment for the personal computer. Microsoft was founded by Bill Gates, who created the MS-DOS operating system for IBM-compatible personal computers. MS-DOS and Windows were so successful that the market value of Microsoft very nearly equaled that of IBM. IBM tried to increase its share of the operating system market by designing and introducing a feature-laden Windows-like environment for the personal computer that it called OS-2. Microsoft discovered IBM's plans several months before OS-2 was publicly announced. With this lead time, Microsoft was able to design significant improvements into the MS-DOS and Windows environments. When OS-2 was finally introduced, it represented only a marginal improvement over MS-DOS and Windows, and never really caught on.

This chapter is about *entry* and *exit*. Entry is the beginning of production and sales by a new firm in a market, and exit occurs when a firm ceases to produce in a market. The experiences of Harlequin and Microsoft demonstrate that *incumbent* firms—firms that are already in operation—must account for entry in their strategic decision making. *Entrants*—firms that are new to a market—threaten incumbents in two ways. First, *they take market share away from incumbent firms*, in effect reducing an incumbent's share of the "profit pie." In addition, entry of additional firms often *intensifies competition*, when entrants introduce new products, reduce prices, and use other strategies to try to solidify their positions in the market. In this way, entry reduces the size of the "profit pie." Exit has the opposite effect on competitors: Surviving firms increase their share, and competition diminishes.

In this chapter we demonstrate the importance of entry and exit in most markets. We then describe structural factors (i.e., factors beyond the control of the firms in the market) that affect entry and exit decisions. We also address strategies that incumbents may employ to reduce the threat of entry and/or promote exit by rivals. We are especially interested in what antitrust economist Frank Fisher calls *predatory acts*.[1] A predatory act is an entry-deterring strategy by an incumbent that appears to reduce its profits, until one accounts for the additional profits that it earns because the act deters entry or promotes exit by competitors.

◆ ◆ ◆ ◆ ◆ Some Facts about Entry and Exit

Entry is pervasive in many industries. Formally, we say that firm F has entered market M if F introduces a new product or service into M, and (a) F previously did not exist, or (b) was not doing business in M at the time in question. Situation (a) represents entry by a *new firm*, and situation (b) is entry by a *diversifying firm*. Even though one occasionally hears of entry by acquisition, we would not consider F's acquisition of another business to be entry, because this would not involve the production of new products or services. The distinction between new and diversifying firms is often important, such as when we assess the costs of entry, and when we consider strategic responses to it. Recent new entrants in various markets include Boston Market, Starbucks Coffee, and Kiwi Airlines. Recent diversifying entrants include Toyota, which entered the luxury car market under the Lexus nameplate, McDonald's, which opened a chain of indoor playgrounds under the name Leaps and Bounds, and Caremark, a diversified health services company that recently began offering consulting services to health care organizations.

Exit is the reverse of entry—the withdrawal of a product from a market, either by a firm that completely ceases to operate, or by a firm that continues to operate in other markets. In the past few years, GTE exited the long distance communication market, Continental Bank exited consumer banking, and Intel exited the market for DRAM chips.

---

[1]Fisher, F. *Industrial Organization, Economics, and the Law*, Cambridge, MA: MIT Press, 1991.

The best systematic analysis of entry and exit rates across industries is by Timothy Dunne, Marc Roberts, and Larry Samuelson (henceforth DRS).[2] They examined entry and exit in U.S. manufacturing firms between 1963 and 1982. Though dated, their findings present stark evidence of the importance of entry and exit in a wide range of industries, and offer insights about patterns of growth and decline.

Dunne, Roberts, and Samuelson's Evidence on Entry and Exit

DRS examined data from the U.S. Census of Manufacturing for the years 1963, 1967, 1972, 1977, and 1982. The census identifies all manufacturing firms in the United States, as well as individual manufacturing facilities. Each firm reports the products it made in each of its facilities, and then each facility is assigned a primary 2-digit S.I.C. code to indicate its principal industry. Each firm also reports the value of goods shipped from each manufacturing facility. By matching firms across different years of the census, DRS could identify entering and exiting firms, and measure postentry growth and preexit decline. Overall, DRS studied over 250,000 firms in each census year.

To summarize the main findings of DRS, imagine an industry in the year 1996. This hypothetical industry has 100 firms, with combined annual sales of $100 million. Thus, the average incumbent has annual sales of $1 million. If patterns of entry and exit in this industry are representative of all U.S. industries in previous decades, then the following will be true:

1. *Entry and exit will be pervasive.* By the year 2001, between 30 and 40 new firms will have entered. They will have combined annual sales of $12 million to $20 million in 1996 dollars. At the same time, 30 to 40 firms that were operating in 1996 will have left the market. Their 1996 sales would also have been $12–$20 million. In other words, in just five years, the industry will experience a 30 to 40 percent turnover in firms, and the entering and exiting firms will each account for 12 to 20 percent of volume.

    Of the 30 to 40 new entrants, about half will be diversified firms, and half will be new firms. Of the 30 to 40 exiters, 40 percent will be diversified.

2. *Entrants and exiters tend to be smaller than established firms.* A typical entrant will be only one-third the size of a typical incumbent, and will have annual sales of around $350,000. An important exception is entry by diversifying firms that build new physical plants (as opposed to switching an existing plant to making a new product). Though diversifying firms building new physical plants may represent only 5 to 10 percent of all entrants (2 to 4 firms over five years), they tend to be three times the size of other entrants—roughly the same size as the average incumbent.

    Firms that will leave the industry by the year 2001 will, in 1996, be about one-third the size of the average firm. Exit by diversified firms that permanently

---

[2]Dunne, T., M.J. Roberts, and L. Samuelson, "Patterns of Firm Entry and Exit in U.S. Manufacturing Industries," *RAND Journal of Economics*, Winter 1988, pp. 495–515.

close a plant is rare (only about 2 to 3 percent of all exits) but such exit affects facilities roughly twice the size of those of the typical nondiversified exiter.

3. *Most entrants do not survive 10 years, but those that do grow precipitously.* Of the 30 to 40 firms that enter the market between 1996 and 2001, roughly 60 percent will exit by 2006. The survivors will nearly double their size between 2001 and 2006.

4. *Entry and exit rates vary by industry.* Not surprisingly, entry and exit are more common in some industries than in others. Some industries in which entrants are numerous and command substantial market shares include apparel, lumber, furniture, printing, and fabricated metals. Industries with high exit rates include apparel, lumber, furniture, printing, and leather. Industries with little entry include food processing, tobacco, paper, chemicals, and primary metals. Industries with little exit include tobacco, paper, chemicals, petroleum and coal, and primary metals. Clearly, entry and exit are highly related: The conditions that make an industry ripe for entry also foster exit.

The DRS findings have four important implications for strategy:

•   When planning for the future, the manager must account for an unknown competitor—the entrant. Fully one-third of a typical incumbent firm's competition five years hence is not a competitor today.

•   Diversifying competitors who build new plants, though few in number, can threaten incumbents because of their size.

•   Managers should expect most new ventures to fail quickly. At the same time, survival and growth usually go hand in hand, so managers of new firms must be prepared to find the capital necessary to support expansion.

•   Managers should know the entry and exit conditions of their industry. Entry and exit are powerful forces in some industries, but relatively unimportant in others.

◆ ◆ ◆ ◆ ◆   ENTRY AND EXIT DECISIONS: BASIC CONCEPTS

A profit-maximizing, risk-neutral firm should enter a market if the net present value of expected postentry profits exceeds the sunk costs of entry.[3] There are many potential sunk costs involved in entering a market, ranging from the costs of acquiring specialized capital equipment, to obtaining government licenses. Later in this chapter we elaborate on these and other costs of entry.

The firm must assess the nature of *postentry competition* to estimate postentry profits. Postentry competition represents the conduct and performance of firms in

---

[3]A firm or individual is risk-neutral if it is indifferent between a sure thing and a gamble with an equal expected payoff. Individuals are usually risk averse, as evidenced by purchases of auto insurance and health insurance. Shareholders may not want their managers to avoid risk, however, since they can cheaply minimize risk by holding diversified portfolios of debt and equity instruments.

the market after entry has occurred. If postentry competition is expected to be fierce, say because incumbent firms are likely to slash prices to repel the entrant, then postentry profits may be low. The potential entrant may use many different types of information about incumbents, including historical pricing practices, costs, capacity, and other markets that the incumbents operate in, to assess what postentry competition may be like. Even when an entrant believes that postentry competition will be relatively mild, it may not enter if there are significant barriers to entry.

Barriers to Entry

Bain's Typology of Entry Conditions

Barriers to entry are those factors that allow incumbent firms to earn positive economic profits, while making it unprofitable for newcomers to enter the industry.[4] Barriers to entry may be *structural* or *strategic*. Structural entry barriers result when the incumbent has natural cost or marketing advantages, or benefits from favorable regulations. The entrant must overcome these advantages to compete successfully with the incumbent. The incumbent benefits from structural entry barriers even when it ignores the possibility of entry. Strategic entry barriers result when incumbent firms take explicit actions aimed at deterring entry. *Entry-deterring strategies* may include capacity expansion, limit pricing, and predatory pricing, all of which we discuss later in this chapter.

In his seminal work on entry, Joe Bain argued that markets may be characterized according to whether entry barriers are structural or strategic, and whether entry-deterring strategies are desirable.[5] Bain described three entry conditions:

Blockaded entry   Entry is blockaded if the incumbent need not undertake any entry-deterring strategies to deter entry. Blockaded entry may result when there are structural entry barriers, perhaps because production requires significant fixed investments. Blockaded entry may also result if the entrant expects unfavorable postentry competition, perhaps because the entrant's product is undifferentiated from those of the incumbents.

Accommodated entry   Entry is accommodated if structural entry barriers are low, and either (a) entry-deterring strategies will be ineffective; or (b) the cost to the incumbent of trying to deter entry exceeds the benefits it could gain from keeping the entrant out. Accommodated entry is typical in markets with growing demand or rapid technological improvements. Entry is then so attractive that the incumbent should not waste resources trying to prevent it.

---

[4]This definition is a synthesis of the definitions of entry barriers given by Joe Bain in *Barriers to New Competition: Their Character and Consequences in Manufacturing Industries*, Cambridge, MA: Harvard University Press, 1956, and C.C. Von Weizsäcker in *Barriers to Entry: A Theoretical Treatment*, Berlin: Springer-Verlag, 1980.

[5]Bain, J.S., *op. cit.*

Deterred entry   Entry is deterred, if not blockaded, if the incumbent can keep the entrant out by employing an entry-deterring strategy. Moreover, the cost of the entry-deterring strategy is more than offset by the additional profits that the incumbent enjoys in the less competitive environment. Frank Fisher calls such entry-deterring strategies *predatory acts*.[6]

Bain argued that an incumbent firm should analyze the entry conditions in its market and choose an entry-deterring strategy accordingly. If entry is blockaded or accommodated, the firm need do nothing more to deter entry. If entry is deterred, the firm should engage in a predatory act. To assess entry conditions, the firm must understand the magnitude of structural entry barriers, and consider the likely consequences of strategic entry barriers. We discuss the former below, and the latter in the next section.

Structural Entry Barriers

There are three main types of structural entry barriers:

*   Control of essential resources
*   Economies of scale and scope
*   Marketing advantages of incumbency

We discuss each in turn.

Control of Essential Resources   An incumbent is protected from entry if it controls a resource necessary for production. DeBeers in diamonds, Alcoa in aluminum, and Ocean Spray in cranberries all maintained monopolies or cartels by controlling essential inputs. Does this imply that firms should acquire key inputs to gain monopoly status? There are several risks to this approach, some of which we discussed in Chapter 2 in the context of make-or-buy decisions. First, when the firm thinks that it has tied up existing supplies, new input sources may emerge. In each of our examples, new input sources are limited by nature, which helps explain why these monopolies were able to endure. Second, owners of scarce resources may hold out for high prices before selling to the would-be monopolist.

A third risk to attaining monopoly status through acquisition is regulatory. Antitrust laws in many nations forbid incumbents with dominant market shares from preventing competitors from obtaining key inputs. Under what became known as the "essential facilities" doctrine, the U.S. Supreme Court in 1912 ordered the Terminal Railroad Association to permit competing railroads to use a bridge owned by Terminal. As mentioned in Chapter 4, the bridge provided the only access into St. Louis from the east, and the Court feared that Terminal might use its control of the bridge to exclude rival railroads.[7] In 1985, the Supreme Court used similar reasoning to force the Aspen Skiing Company, which controlled three

---

[6]Fisher, F. *Industrial Organization, Economics, and the Law*, Cambridge, MA: MIT Press, 1991.

[7]*United States v. Terminal R.R. Assn.*, 224 U.S. 383 (1912).

of the principle skiing mountains in Aspen, Colorado, to include in its six-day lift ticket access to a fourth facility controlled by another company.[8]

Incumbents can legally erect entry barriers by obtaining a patent to a novel and nonobvious product or production process. Patent laws vary by country, and in some countries, such as China and Brazil, they are nonexistent or extremely weak. An individual or firm that develops a marketable new product or process usually applies for a patent in its home country. In Europe and Japan, the patent rights go to the first person to apply for the patent. In the United States the first person to invent the idea gets the patent. As might be expected, firms seeking U.S. patents often go to considerable expense to document precedence of discovery. Once the patent is approved (it usually takes one to two years, and the invention is protected from imitation during the waiting period), anyone who wishes to use the process or make the product must obtain permission from the patent holder. Patent lives vary by country. In the United States, patent lives are 17 years, but may increase to 20 years as part of an international agreement.

Incumbents may even patent products they have no intention of selling. Such patents are called *sleeping patents*. To understand why a firm would wish to go to the expense of obtaining a sleeping patent, suppose that a firm currently holds the patent on product A. It has recently invented product B, which is slightly inferior to A. The incumbent would gain nothing by marketing B, but if another firm were to independently develop, patent, and market B, the resulting competition could cut into the incumbent's profits. Thus, the incumbent gains by patenting B and withholding it from the market.

Patents are not always effective entry barriers because they can often be "invented around," in part because it is sometimes difficult for a government patent office to distinguish between a new product and an imitation of a protected product. As a result, some innovations, such as Rollerblades and the personal computer, seem to have had no patent protection whatsoever. Conversely, incumbents may file patent infringement lawsuits against entrants whose products are seemingly different from the incumbent's. Some computer industry observers claim that Intel used this strategy to protect its microprocessors from entry by Advanced Micro Devices.

$\mathcal{E}$XAMPLE 11.1

PATENT PROTECTION IN THE PHARMACEUTICAL INDUSTRY

Patent protection is critical to success or failure in the pharmaceutical industry. For example, in the late 1960s, Eli Lilly introduced Keflin, the first of a new class of drugs called cephalosporins (a "magic bullet" antibiotic). Lilly introduced the first "second generation" cephalosporin, Keflex, in 1971. Though belonging to the same chemical class and having similar biological properties, Keflex and Keflin had

---

[8]*Aspen Skiing Co. v. Aspen Highlands Skiing Corp.*, 472 U.S. 585 (1985).

sufficiently different structures to warrant separate patents. These drugs quickly became Lilly's top two sellers—one or both ranked among the top ten selling prescription drugs in the United States every year between 1968 and 1985. The drugs would have sold even better, were it not for the failure of Lilly's patents to provide full protection. Differences in chemical structure enabled several competitors to introduce new cephalosporins by the late 1970s. A few, such as Merck's Mefoxin, also became top sellers.

Patents have proved more enduring in the market for anti-ulcer medications. Tagamet, the first effective medication, was introduced by Smith, Kline, and French (later SmithKline) in 1978. By 1980, it was the top selling prescription drug in the United States. In 1984, Glaxo's anti-ulcer drug Zantac was introduced, and a year later replaced Tagamet as the best selling drug, with Tagamet running second. The substantial profits earned by SmithKline and Glaxo encouraged other companies to develop anti-ulcer drugs. But Glaxo and Tagamet sales held, and are only likely to fall when their patents expire in the mid-1990s. Based on the experiences of other top selling drugs, both brands should experience a 50 percent or greater drop in sales as consumers switch to less costly generic alternatives.

Drug makers can reap handsome returns on their research investments for those handful of drugs, like Tagamet and Zantac, that treat common diseases yet have few substitutes. Those returns rapidly fall when patents expire. Drug makers thus became extremely concerned when the Food and Drug Administration (FDA) required lengthy testing for new drugs before marketing. These tests reduced the *effective patent lives* of new drugs—the time between FDA approval and the expiration of the patent—to as little as three years. In 1984, Congress enacted the Patent Term Restoration Act, which gave new drugs a minimum effective patent life of seven years. The act also simplified the testing requirements for generic manufacturers, thus intensifying postentry competition.

Incumbents may not need patents to protect specialized know-how. Coca-Cola has zealously guarded its cola syrup formula for a century, and no one has learned how to duplicate the sound of a Steinway piano or the beauty of Waterford crystal. Firms may turn to the legally and ethically questionable practice of industrial espionage to steal such information.

Economies of Scale and Scope When economies of scale are significant, established firms operating at or beyond the minimum efficient scale (MES) will have a cost advantage over smaller entrants. The average cost curve in Figure 11.1 illustrates the problem facing a potential entrant in an industry where the MES is 1,000 units, and total industry sales are 10,000 units. An incumbent with a market share of 10 percent or higher is reaching the MES, and has average cost of AC_{MES}. If the entrant only achieves a market share of, say, 2 percent, it will have a much higher average cost of AC_E. The market price would have to be at least as high as AC_E for entry to be profitable.

FIGURE 11.1
ECONOMIES OF SCALE MAY BE A BARRIER TO ENTRY.

The incumbent firm producing at minimum efficient scale of 1,000 units per year has average costs AC_{MES}. If the potential entrant can only hope to produce a volume of output equal to 200 units per year, its average costs will equal AC_E. Market price must be at least this high for the potential entrant to realize profits from entry.

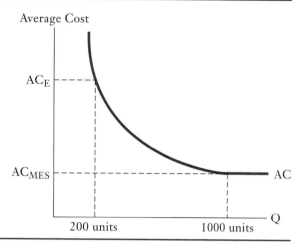

The entrant might try to overcome the incumbent's cost advantage by entering at a large scale in the hope of achieving a large market share. For example, it could spend heavily on advertising before entering the market or invest in the creation of a large sales force. While this strategy may allow the entrant to achieve a market share greater than 2 percent and average production costs below AC_E in Figure 11.1, it involves two important costs. The first is the direct cost of advertising and creating the sales force. Second, if incumbent firms lose market share to the entrant, then their marginal costs will decrease. The result will almost certainly be a reduction in industry price. (The exception would be if the incumbents were colluding on price, and permitted the entrant to join the cartel, either explicitly or implicitly.) The entrant thus faces a dilemma: To overcome its cost disadvantage, it must increase its market share. But if its share increases, price competition is likely to intensify.

Fierce price competition frequently results from large-scale entry into capital-intensive industries. Sometimes, this represents the result of the intensified rivalry that is associated with the increase in the number of firms competing in a market. Sometimes, this represents blatant efforts by incumbents to drive entrants out of business by pricing below marginal costs. This strategy, known as predatory pricing, is described below. An example of intense postentry rivalry is provided by the gunpowder industry. In 1889, eight firms, including the industry leader DuPont, formed a "gunpowder pool" with specific agreements to fix price and output. In the early 1890s, three new firms entered the industry. Their growth challenged the continued success of the pool. DuPont's response to one entrant was to "put the Chattanooga Powder Company out of business by selling at lower prices."[9] In this

_____

[9]Fligstein, N. *The Transformation of Corporate Control*, Cambridge, MA: Harvard University Press, 1990.

way, the gunpowder pool survived until it was broken up by antitrust enforcers. More recently, entry into the airline business by Laker Airlines and People's Express in the early 1980s led to price wars that eventually drove them from the market. The introduction of off-brand cigarettes by the Liggett Group in the early 1980s eventually led to hefty price reductions that significantly eroded the profits of all players in the tobacco industry. The off-price brands survived, perhaps because price-cost margins in the cigarette industry had been extremely high.

Incumbents may also derive a cost advantage from economies of scope. The ready-to-eat breakfast cereal industry provides a good example.[10] For several decades, the industry has been dominated by a few firms, including Kellogg, General Mills, General Foods, and Quaker Oats, and there has been virtually no new entry since the Second World War. There are significant economies of scope in producing and marketing cereal. Economies of scope in production stem from the flexibility in materials handling and scheduling that arise from having multiple production lines within the same plant. Economies of scope in marketing are due to the substantial up-front expenditures on advertising that are needed for a new entrant to establish a minimum acceptable level of brand awareness. It has been estimated that for entry to be worthwhile, a newcomer would need to introduce successfully six to twelve brands.[11] Thus, capital requirements for entry are substantial, making it a risky proposition.

An incumbent launching a new brand would not face the same up-front costs as a new entrant. The incumbent has already established brand name awareness and may be able to use existing facilities to manufacture the new brand. This explains why new product introductions are profitable for incumbent firms but unprofitable for new entrants. Indeed, despite the absence of entry by outsiders, the number of cereals offered for sale has increased dramatically, from 88 in 1980 to 205 in 1990.[12] Newcomers who have successfully entered have chosen niche markets, such as granola-based cereals, in which they may be able to offset their cost disadvantage by charging premium prices.

Economies of scale and scope create barriers to entry because they force potential entrants to enter at a large scale or with a large product variety in order to achieve unit cost parity with incumbent firms. Strictly speaking, though, entering at a large scale or scope is a disadvantage only to the extent that the entrant cannot recover its upfront entry costs if it subsequently decides to exit; that is, only if the up-front entry costs become sunk costs once they are made. An entrant whose upfront entry costs were not sunk could come in at a large scale, undercut incumbent firms' prices, and exit the market and recover its entry costs if the incumbent

[10]For a detailed discussion, see Schmalensee, R., "Entry deterrence in the ready-to-eat breakfast cereal industry," *Bell Journal of Economics*, 9, 2, 1978, pp. 305–327.

[11]Scherer, F.M., "The Breakfast Cereal Industry," in Adams, W. (ed.), *The Structure of American Industry* 7th ed., New York: MacMillan, 1986.

[12]Pine, B.J., *Mass Customization: The New Frontier in Business Competition*, Cambridge, MA: Harvard University Press, 1993, p. 40.

firms retaliate. This strategy, known as "hit-and-run entry," would leave incumbents vulnerable to entry even if economies of scale were so significant in comparison to market demand that the market could support only one firm. For this reason, as Daniel Spulber has pointed out, it is the existence of sunk costs, not economies of scale and scope *per se*, that represents the underlying structural barrier to entry.[13]

Still, in most markets, scale and scope economies in production or marketing can only be achieved by making significant nonrecoverable upfront costs. When Philips contemplated entering the business of pressing compact discs in the early 1980s, for example, it had to confront the fact that a minimum efficient scale pressing plant had no alternative uses. If it subsequently decided to exit the market because of inadequate demand for its compact discs, Philips would only be able to recover the plant's scrap value, which was significantly less than the upfront expenditures needed to build the plant and make it operational.[14]

Because the technological conditions that give rise to economies of scale or scope typically require the firm to incur nonrecoverable upfront costs, the distinction between whether economies of scale represents the entry barrier or sunk costs represents the entry barrier is not that critical. The key insight is that the need to make nonrecoverable commitments in order to become cost competitive with incumbents can make entry an unattractive proposition to potential entrants even though incumbent firms may be profitable.

---

[13]Spulber, D.F., *Regulation and Markets*, Cambridge, MA: MIT Press, 1989.

[14]More generally, it seems unlikely that economies of scale or scope based on input indivisibilities could ever exist without some degree of "sunkness" of costs. This point is developed in Tirole, J., *The Theory of Industrial Organization*, Cambridge, MA: MIT Press, 1988. To illustrate the logic behind this assertion, suppose that there are indivisibilities that force the firm to use a fixed quantity of an input, say capital equipment, no matter how much output the firm produces. Imagine that the fixed costs associated with this equipment are $1 million per year and that the average variable cost of production is $2 per unit. If the firm produces 100,000 units of output during a year, its total cost would be $1.2 million. Suppose, now, that the fixed costs are not sunk; that is, they can be avoided when the equipment is no longer needed. If that were the case, then what the firm should do is to accelerate production so that all output is produced within 6 months, and in so doing, reduce its fixed costs to $500,000 and its total costs to $700,000. But if it can do this, why not accelerate production even more? The more the firm accelerates production, the smaller it can make its fixed costs as a proportion of the total. If the firm has complete flexibility to "hire" capital equipment only when it needs it, it can avoid its fixed costs altogether by accelerating its production so that all production occurs over an infinitesimally small interval! This extreme conclusion does not arise in the real world because the fixed costs of indivisible inputs are always sunk to some degree. Market imperfections often prevent the firms from "hiring" plant and equipment on an as needed basis and disposing of it the instant it is not needed. For example, even if a manufacturer could rent a plant in which it could produce its output, the rental period will typically be over a minimum period of time, and the firm would not be able to reduce its fixed costs by accelerating its rate of production. The rental cost is not only a fixed cost over this period of time, but it is sunk as well.

Marketing Advantages of Incumbency   Chapter 5 discussed umbrella brand-ing, whereby a firm sells different products under the same brand name. This is a special case of economies of scope, but an extremely important one in many con-sumer product markets. An incumbent can exploit the umbrella effect to offset un-certainty about the quality of a new product that it is introducing. Consumers who are satisfied with the incumbent's old products are inclined to believe that its new product will also be satisfactory. The brand umbrella makes the incumbent's sunk cost of introducing a new product less than that of a new entrant because the en-trant must spend additional amounts of money on advertising and product promo-tion to develop credibility in the eyes of consumers, retailers, and distributors.

A brand umbrella will not protect an incumbent if its new product turns out to be unsatisfactory. Would-be repeat purchasers will turn to other sellers' products, and word-of-mouth and poor reviews in consumer magazines may deter first-time purchasers. The incumbent may suffer even further if consumers' dissatisfaction with the new product leads them to doubt the quality of the rest of the incumbent's product line, or if managers of competing firms view the failure of the incumbent in its new venture as a signal that it may be a less formidable competitor than they had previously thought. Thus, while the brand umbrella can give incumbents an advantage over entrants, the exploitation of brand name credibility or reputation is not free of risk.

The umbrella effect may also help the incumbent negotiate the vertical chain. Since the incumbent's other products have sold well in the past, distributors and retailers are more likely to devote scarce warehousing and shelf space to its new products. At the same time, suppliers may be more willing to sell on credit or ex-tend favorable prices. For example, the Columbia/HCA hospital chain obtains pur-chasing discounts for new hospitals it acquires because suppliers trust the chain to make good on its accounts payable.

Incumbents and entrants alike often face high entry barriers when introducing new experience goods. Sellers may choose from a variety of strategies to entice wary consumers to sample their new products. They may set a low introductory price, dispense free samples, or distribute money-saving coupons. They may invest heavily in brand identity. A good example is Coca-Cola's star-studded campaign to launch Diet Coke in the 1980s. Coca-Cola and other companies that rely on mas-sive advertising to introduce new brands believe that consumers are more likely to sample a product that is heavily advertised than one that is quietly introduced. Paul Milgrom and John Roberts offer an explanation for this view.[15] They argue that producers of high-quality experience goods expect to do a lot of repeat business, whereas producers of low-quality goods will soon disappear as consumers discover how bad the products are. It follows that sellers of high-quality products can afford to invest in heavy introductory advertising, since they will recoup their investments in the long run. Sellers of low-quality products do not expect to recoup high up-front advertising expenditures, so do not make them. Milgrom and Roberts hy-

---

[15]Milgrom, P. and J. Roberts, "Price and Advertising Signals of Product Quality," *Journal of Political Economy*, 94, 1986, pp. 796–821.

pothesize that consumers understand these issues, either directly by thinking through the theory or indirectly by drawing on experience. Thus, consumers are more willing to try new products that are extensively advertised, correctly perceiving them to be of higher quality.

$\mathcal{E}$XAMPLE 11.2

ENTRY BARRIERS AND PROFITABILITY IN THE JAPANESE BREWING INDUSTRY[16]

The Japanese brewing industry has enjoyed several decades of financial prosperity. The Japanese market for beer is enormous, with per capita consumption approaching 16 gallons per year. The market is shared by four firms—Kirin, Asahi, Sapporo, and Suntory. These firms have a combined 98 percent market share. The market leader, Kirin, has a nearly 50 percent market share, and its annual sales of $12 billion rival those of Anheuser-Busch, the leading U.S. brewery. The industry aftertax return on assets ranges from 3 to 4 percent, which is good in Japan where inflation is generally very low. Moreover, these firms have been profitable for decades.

Normally, a profitable industry attracts entrants seeking their share of the pie. Even so, Suntory is the only brewery to gain significant market share in Japan in the past 15 years. At that, its market share is less than 6 percent and has dropped since the termination of an agreement to produce Budweiser under a licensing agreement with Anheuser-Busch. The absence of entry usually indicates the presence of entry barriers. In the United States, profitable breweries are protected by strong brand identities. Would-be competitors must invest tens of millions of dollars or more to achieve the brand recognition and strength of image enjoyed by Budweiser and Miller. This deters the market leaders from serious competition from newcomers. Japanese brewers also enjoy brand identity, and brands like Kirin's Ichibanshibori and Sapporo's Black Label have loyal followings. But Japanese brewers also enjoy two entry barriers not shared by U.S. firms. Entry has historically been restricted by the Japanese government, and access to distribution channels is complicated by the dominance of "Ma-and-Pa" retail establishments.

Breweries in Japan must have a license from the Ministry of Finance (MOF). Prior to 1994, the MOF would not issue a license to any brewery producing less than 2 million litres annually. Although this is a relatively small percentage of the total market of 7 billion litres, it represents an imposing hurdle to a startup firm without an established brand name. It is not clear whether the MOF maintained this hurdle to protect the big four breweries, or to reduce the number of firms it

---

[16]Much of the information in this example is drawn from "Only Here for the Biru," *The Economist*, May 14, 1994, pp. 69–70.

needed to tax and regulate. As part of an overall liberalization of marketplace restrictions, the MOF has reduced the license threshold to 60,000 liters. In the wake of this change, existing small brewers formed a Small Brewers Association, and roughly 50 new microbreweries opened.

The growth of microbreweries will undoubtedly put a dent in the sales of the big four, just as it has cut into sales by Bud and Miller in the United States. (Interestingly, the Japanese are studying the production and marketing practices of U.S. microbreweries.) Changes in Japanese retailing practices may pose a greater threat to profits. Half of Japan's beer is sold in bars and restaurants, whose owners appear to be loyal to the big four brewers. Most of the remaining sales are in small Ma-and-Pa liquor stores, which have had little purchasing power and have not aggressively sought to stock low-cost beers. But in recent years, Japanese consumers have begun to turn to new discount liquor stores offering savings of 25 percent or more on the same beers sold at family-run stores. The real threat posed by these discount stores (and, to a lesser extent, by the supermarkets that are slowly replacing neighborhood groceries) is their willingness to sell imported beers. Imports cost two-thirds as much as domestic beers. Entry by imports, facilitated by the growth of new retail channels, will eventually force the big four breweries to lower prices to match the competition, lose market share, or both.

Barriers to Exit

Exit is the opposite of entry. To exit a market, a firm stops production and either redeploys or sells off its assets. A change in ownership that is not accompanied by a cessation of production is not considered to be exit. A risk-neutral, profit-maximizing firm will exit if the value of its assets in their best alternative use exceeds the present value from remaining in the market. However, exit barriers can limit the incentives for the firm to stop producing even when the prevailing conditions are such that the firm, had it known with certainty that these conditions would prevail, would not have entered in the first place.

Figure 11.2 illustrates the effect of exit barriers. The price P_{entry} is the *entry price*—the price at which the firm is just indifferent between entering the industry and staying out. The price P_{exit} is the price below which the firm would either liquidate its assets or redeploy them to another market. Exit barriers drive a wedge between P_{exit} and P_{entry}.[17]

---

[17]Two technical points about Figure 11.2 are in order. First, in many industries there is an intermediate option short of full exit: The firm can "mothball" its production facilities and restart them when demand or cost conditions improve. Second, when there is demand uncertainty, the price that triggers entry will generally increase and the price that triggers entry will generally decrease. This is because firms may defer entry or exit decisions to see how the uncertainty is resolved. See Dixit, A.K. and R.S. Pindyck, *Investment Under Uncertainty*, Princeton, NJ: Princeton University Press, 1994, for a lucid development of the theory of entry, exit, and mothballing under demand uncertainty.

FIGURE 11.2
THE PRICES THAT INDUCE ENTRY AND EXIT MAY DIFFER.

Firms will enter the industry as long as the market price exceeds P_{ENTRY}, the minimum level of average total costs. Firms will exit the industry only if price falls below P_{EXIT}, the minimum level of average variable costs.

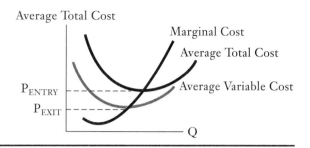

Exit barriers commonly arise when firms have obligations that they must meet whether or not they cease operations. Examples of such obligations include labor agreements and commitments to purchase raw materials. If a firm has to pay off its suppliers even if it stops production, the effective marginal cost of remaining in operation is low, and exit is less attractive. Obligations to input suppliers are a more significant exit barrier for diversified firms contemplating exit from a single market, since the suppliers to a faltering division are assured payment out of the resources of the rest of the firm. Relationship-specific productive assets will have a low resale value, and are thus a second exit barrier.[18] Government restrictions are often a third exit barrier. For example, until recently hospitals required state approval to close.

ENTRY-DETERRING STRATEGIES ◆ ◆ ◆ ◆ ◆

Under what conditions does it pay for an incumbent firm to take actions to raise the barriers to entry into its market? At the most general level, entry-deterring strategies will succeed only if two conditions are met:

1. The incumbent can raise price when it achieves monopoly status.
2. The strategy changes entrants' expectations about the nature of postentry competition. The need for the first condition is obvious—if the incumbent must charge competitive prices at all times, why invest resources to deter entry? The second condition, which we detail below, is necessary because the entrant will ignore any strategy that does not change its expectations about postentry competition, rendering the strategy useless.

It seems as if a monopolist would always be able to raise prices once it has successfully fought off entry. If a monopolist cannot raise price above competitive levels, the market is said to be *perfectly contestable*, a concept developed by William

---

[18]Asset specificity is discussed in length in Chapter 3.

Baumol, John Panzar, and Robert Willig.[19] The key requirement for contestability is "hit-and-run entry," discussed earlier. When a monopolist raises price in a contestable market, a hit-and-run entrant rapidly enters the market, undercuts its price, reaps short-term profits, and exits the market just as rapidly if the incumbent retaliates. The hit-and-run entrant prospers as long as it can set a price high enough, and for a long enough time, to recover its sunk entry costs. If its sunk entry costs are zero, then hit-and-run entry will always be profitable. In that case, the market price can never be higher than average cost, even if there is only one firm currently producing. If the incumbent raised price above average cost, there would be immediate entry, and price would fall. The incumbent has to charge a price that yields zero profits, even when it is an apparent monopolist.

Contestability theory shows how the threat of entry can constrain monopolists from raising prices. However, it has proved difficult to find contestable markets. When the theory was first developed, it was felt that it might apply to the airline industry. Entry into the industry is fairly easy, especially by established carriers entering new routes. A carrier can redeploy aircraft almost overnight, and can secure gates and ground personnel almost as quickly. New carriers can enter almost as fast, by leasing aircraft and gates. Even so, Severin Borenstein showed that airline markets are not perfectly contestable.[20] If they were, then fares should be independent of market concentration. However, Borenstein found that monopoly routes have higher fares than duopoly routes of comparable lengths, although fares on monopoly routes are reduced when another carrier is already operating at one or both ends of the route. If fares on the monopoly route were high enough, such a carrier could quickly redeploy its aircraft there. Borenstein concluded that the threat of potential competition causes the monopolist carrier to moderate its prices, but not to perfectly contestable levels.

It would be surprising if airline markets were perfectly contestable. The hit-and-run entrant must be able to capture business before the incumbent can respond. But with computerized reservation systems linked to computerized tariff clearinghouses, such as the Airline Tariff Publishers, an incumbent airline can adjust its fares instantaneously in response to new entry. Faced with the prospects of duopoly pricing, the potential entrant may feel that the market is not large enough to support two firms, and will not enter. Incumbents in most markets can probably adjust prices rapidly when threatened by entry, so that the applications of the contestability theory are probably limited.[21]

Assuming that an incumbent monopolist's market is not perfectly contestable, it may expect to reap additional profits if it can keep out entrants. We now discuss three ways in which it might do so:

---

[19]Baumol, W., J. Panzar, and R. Willig, *Contestable Markets and the Theory of Industrial Structure*, New York: Harcourt Brace Jovanovich, 1982.

[20]Borenstein, S., "Hubs and High Fares: Dominance and Market Power in the U.S. Airline Industry," *RAND Journal of Economics*, 20, 1989, pp. 344–365.

[21]For a further discussion and critique of contestability, see Tirole, J., *The Theory of Industrial Organization*, Cambridge, MA: MIT Press, 1989.

- Limit pricing
- Predatory pricing
- Capacity expansion

Limit Pricing

Limit pricing refers to the practice whereby an incumbent firm can discourage entry by charging a low price *before entry occurs*.[22] The entrant, observing the low price set by the incumbent, infers that the postentry price would be as low or even lower, and that entry into the market would therefore be unprofitable.

To illustrate how a firm might deter entry by limit pricing, consider a market that will last for two years. Demand in each year is given by $P = 100 - Q$, where P denotes price and Q denotes quantity. The production technology has nonrecoverable fixed costs of $850 per year, and constant marginal costs of $10. In the first year, there is a single firm with the technological know-how to compete in this market. We call this firm N. If there was no danger of entry, N would select the monopoly price of $55 in each period. (This is confirmed by equating the monopolist's marginal revenue to marginal cost.) It would sell 45 units per year and earn $\{(55 - 10) \times 45\} - 850 = \$1{,}175$, for a two-year total of $2,350. (For simplicity, we ignore the effect of discounting second-year profit.)

Firm N is not so fortunate, because another firm, denoted E, has developed the technology necessary to compete in year two. To determine whether entry will be profitable, E must anticipate the nature of postentry competition. Suppose that when E observes N charging $55 in the first year, it concludes that N is not likely to be an aggressive competitor. Specifically, it expects the Cournot equilibrium to prevail in the second year, with both firms sharing the market equally.[23] Based on these expectations, E calculates the profitability of entry. Recall from Chapter 8 that when market demand is $P = 100 - Q$ and marginal costs of both firms equal $10, the Cournot equilibrium price is $40, and each firm sells 30 units. Thus, E expects to earn profits of $\{(40 - 10) \times 30\} - 850 = \$50$ in the second year. If N shares E's belief that competition will be Cournot, then conditional on entry, firm N would also expect to earn $50 in the second year. This would give it a combined two-year profit of $1,225, which is far below its two-year monopoly profit of $2,350.

Firm N may wonder if it can deter entry. In contemplating setting a limit price, it could reason as follows:

If we set a low first-year price, perhaps E will expect the postentry price to also be low. If E expects the postentry price to be sufficiently low, then it will not enter, and we can earn monopoly profits in the second year.

---

[22]Bain, J.S., "A Note on Pricing in Monopoly and Oligopoly," *American Economic Review*, 39, March 1949, pp. 448–464.

[23]Recall from Chapter 8 that in a Cournot equilibrium each firm makes a guess about the other's output, and the guesses prove to be correct.

Following this logic, suppose that firm N selects a first-year price of $30. E may see this price and reason as follows:

> *If firm N charges a price of $30 when it has a monopoly, then surely its price in the face of competition will be even lower. Suppose we enter and, optimistically, the price remains at $30, so that total market demand is 70. If we can achieve a 50 percent market share, we will sell 35 units, and realize profits of {(30 − 10) × 35} − 850 = −$150. If the price is below $30, we will fare even worse. We should not enter.*

If both firms act as described above, then N should set a limit price of $30. By doing so, it would sell to the whole market in the first year, earning {(30 − 10) × 70} − 850 = $550. It would add full monopoly profits of $1,175 in the second year, for total profits of $1,725. (Recall that if N had set the monopoly price of $55 in the first year and shared the market as a Cournot competitor in the second year, it would have earned total profits of $1,225). Firm N earns higher overall profits when it limit prices because it gets the whole market in year one at the limit price, rather than having to share the market in year two at the Cournot price.

The Flawed Logic of Limit Pricing

The previous argument is appealing, but seriously flawed. The first flaw is the artificiality of a two-year model. In a more realistic setting of more than two years, firm N might have to limit price every period in order to constantly deter entry. N would never reap the full monopoly profits that it forsakes when it initially sets the limit price. In this case, limit pricing would be attractive only if the incumbent does not need to lower its price too much to deter entry. This could occur if N enjoys a cost advantage over E and sets its price equal to or just below E's minimum average cost. If E forecasts that the duopoly price will be no higher than N's limit price, E will never enter. By virtue of N's cost advantage, it could reap profits indefinitely. Edwin Blackstone uses this argument in his analysis of Xerox's pricing of plain paper copiers in the 1960s, which we describe in Example 11.3.[24]

ᵗXAMPLE 11.3

LIMIT PRICING BY XEROX

In 1960, Xerox introduced the 914 plain paper copier, the first mass-marketed product to take advantage of the innovative copying technology called xerography. A competing technology being developed at the time, electrofax, had several disadvantages. Electrofax required a paper coating that added $.01 to the cost of each

---

[24]Blackstone, E., "Limit Pricing in the Copying Machine Industry," *Quarterly Review of Economics and Business*, 12, 1972, pp. 57–65.

copy. In addition, the quality of electrofax reproductions was inferior. When electrofax finally reached the market, copying centers had to charge $.005 less per electrofax page to induce customers to use electrofax instead of Xerox. This gave Xerox an effective $.015 advantage per copy. Xerox machines had higher manufacturing costs, however. This translated into a higher retail price, which somewhat offset the lower effective cost per copy.

Xerox usually leased copiers, charging a sliding fee per copy depending on the number of copies made per month. Xerox sought a fee schedule that would deter entry. Edwin Blackstone carefully examined Xerox's prices and costs, as well as the prices and costs of the rival electrofax process to determine if Xerox did, in fact, limit price.

Blackstone estimated that Xerox's monopoly price was about $.10 per page. This was well above the average cost of electrofax copies. If Xerox set this price, electrofax manufacturers might be tempted to enter the market. Blackstone reported that for small customers, who made around 1,000 copies per month, Xerox charged close to the monopoly price. But for medium and large customers, who made over 2,000 copies per month, Xerox charged only about $.05 per page.

Blackstone argued that these prices were consistent with a limit pricing strategy. The 914 had a high manufacturing cost, so that for a small user, the electrofax actually had a smaller effective cost per page. Xerox felt that it was impossible to forestall entry into the small customer segment, and did not artificially reduce its price. As a result, about 25 electrofax firms entered this end of the market by 1968. Xerox had a significant cost advantage among medium and large users, however. It could afford to reduce prices to medium and large customers and still cover average costs. Xerox hoped that this would limit entry. The strategy appeared to be successful: By 1968, only 10 electrofax firms competed in the medium and large customer segments.

Xerox continued to prosper in the plain paper copier market until the government forced it to share its technology (even before its patents expired) in the early 1970s. Many companies, including IBM and Litton, entered the market. By 1978, Xerox's market share of new copiers fell from 100 percent to around 40 percent, and prices fell by 30 percent. The price reductions suggest that Xerox was making substantial profits even when it was limit pricing.

A second flaw in the limit pricing argument is that it relies on an equilibrium that is not *subgame perfect*.[25] In particular, E's expectations about N's postentry pricing are irrational. To see where the logic of limit pricing breaks down, we depict the limit pricing game in game tree form in Figure 11.3. The payoffs to N and E are calculated by using the demand and cost data from the example above.

---

[25]See the Economics Primer for a discussion of the concept of a subgame perfect-equilibrium.

FIGURE 11.3
LIMIT PRICING: EXTENSIVE FORM GAME.

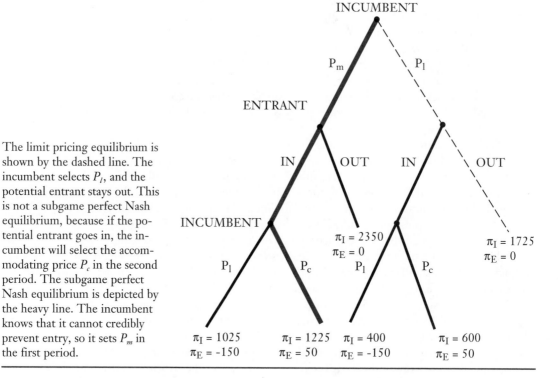

The limit pricing equilibrium is shown by the dashed line. The incumbent selects P_l, and the potential entrant stays out. This is not a subgame perfect Nash equilibrium, because if the potential entrant goes in, the incumbent will select the accommodating price P_c in the second period. The subgame perfect Nash equilibrium is depicted by the heavy line. The incumbent knows that it cannot credibly prevent entry, so it sets P_m in the first period.

INCUMBENT

P_m P_l

ENTRANT

IN   OUT   IN   OUT

INCUMBENT

P_l P_c P_l P_c

$\pi_I = 2350$
$\pi_E = 0$

$\pi_I = 1725$
$\pi_E = 0$

$\pi_I = 1025$
$\pi_E = -150$

$\pi_I = 1225$
$\pi_E = 50$

$\pi_I = 400$
$\pi_E = -150$

$\pi_I = 600$
$\pi_E = 50$

Figure 11.3 shows that in year one, the incumbent's strategic choices are (P_m, P_l), where P_m refers to the monopoly price of $55, and P_l refers to the limit price of $30. The entrant observes N's selection, and then chooses from (In, Out). If E selects "Out," then N selects P_m in year two. If E selects "In," then competition is played out in year two. We suppose that N can control the nature of year-two competition to some extent. In particular, N can maintain the price at $P_l = 30$, or it can "acquiesce" and permit Cournot competition, in which case the price will be $P_c = 40$. Two-year payoffs are reported at the end node for each branch of the game tree.

The limit pricing outcome is shown by the double line in Figure 11.3. Under this outcome, firm N earns total profits of $1,725 and firm E earns $0. This is not a subgame perfect equilibrium, however. To see why not, we must analyze the game using the "fold-back" method.[26] First consider the branch of the game tree

---

[26]See the Economics Primer for a discussion of the use of the fold-back method to determine subgame perfect-equilibria.

in which E ignores the limit price and chooses to enter. According to the limit pricing argument, E stays out because it expects that *after entry has occurred,* N will select P_l. But examination of the game tree shows that it is not rational for N to select P_l. Conditional on entry having already occurred, N should select P_c. N would earn total profits of $600, which exceeds the profits of $400 it earns if it selects P_l. Thus, E's expectations of N's postentry behavior is flawed.

E should anticipate that if it enters, N will select P_c. E should calculate its profits from entry to be $50, which exceeds the profits of 0 that it earns if it stays out. Thus, E will choose to enter, even if N has selected P_l in the first stage of the game. Continuing to work backward, N should anticipate that it cannot prevent entry even if it selects P_l. It should calculate that if it does select P_l, it will earn profits of $600. By selecting P_m in the first stage and P_c in the second stage, N could have earned $1,225.

Our analysis of the game tree is now complete. N will select P_m in the first stage. E will select "In." Second-year competition will be Cournot. This subgame perfect Nash equilibrium is shown by the heavy solid line in Figure 11.3.

This analysis suggests that incumbent firms should not limit price. Potential entrants will recognize that any price reductions prior to entry are artificial, and in no way commit the incumbent to maintain low prices subsequent to entry. Once entry occurs, it would make no sense for the incumbent to continue to suppress price. The lost profit opportunities from having previously set the limit price are sunk. Now that the entrant is already in the market, the incumbent should acquiesce and maximize future profits.

Rescuing Limit Pricing—When Might it Make Sense?

This critique of the logic of limit pricing seems to suggest that no rational firm would ever limit price. Yet there continue to be anecdotal examples, and a few systematic analyses (such as Blackstone's analysis of Xerox) that indicate that limit pricing does occur. One possible explanation is that firms set prices irrationally. If this is correct (and we doubt that it often is), then this analysis should send a message to firms that limit price: Don't do it! Another explanation is that limit pricing is rational, but that the analysis thus far fails to capture important elements of the strategic interaction.

In the past decade, game theorists have identified key conditions under which limit pricing may be profitable. In general, entering firms must be *uncertain* about some characteristic of the incumbent firm or the level of market demand. Reexamination of the extensive form game shows why uncertainty is important. The incumbent wants the entrant to believe that postentry prices will be low. If the entrant is sure about the factors that determine postentry pricing, it can calculate the incumbent's payoffs from all possible postentry pricing scenarios and correctly forecast the postentry price. If the incumbent is best off selecting a high postentry price, the entrant will know this, and will not be deterred from entering.

If the entrant is uncertain about the postentry price, however, then the incumbent's pricing strategy could affect the entrant's expectations. Two types of uncertainty may confound the entrant's forecast. The first is uncertainty about the incumbent's objectives. The analysis of *predatory pricing* discussed in the next section illustrates how this type of uncertainty can promote behaviors that seem irrational in a world of certainty. The second is uncertainty about the incumbent's costs or the level of market demand, which we now discuss.

In a paper that explored the rationality of limit pricing, Paul Milgrom and John Roberts argued that an entrant is likely to know less about the incumbent's costs than the incumbent itself does.[27] If so, by engaging in limit pricing the incumbent may influence the entrant's estimate of its costs, and thus shape its expectations of postentry profitability. To illustrate this argument, suppose that the entrant believes that the incumbent's marginal cost is either $5 or $10. It expects that postentry competition will be Cournot. If it knew for certain that the incumbent's marginal cost is $10, then, as before, the entrant will expect profits of $50 in the second year and would want to enter. If it knew for certain that the incumbent's marginal cost is $5, however, then the entrant would expect profits of −$106 and would not enter.

If the incumbent did not think strategically, it would set its first-year price according to its marginal cost and the demand curve. If its marginal cost was $10, then its first-year price would be $55. If its marginal cost was $5, then its first-year price would be $52.50. If the entrant knew that the incumbent was not thinking strategically, then it could observe the incumbent's first-year price and immediately infer its marginal cost. For example, if the incumbent set a first-year price of $55, the entrant could infer that the incumbent's marginal cost was $10, and therefore that entry would be profitable. If the incumbent thinks strategically, however, then if it has marginal costs of $10, it may reason as follows:

> We should try to convince the entrant that our marginal cost is $5, because it will not want to enter if it thinks we have such low costs. We should set a price of $52.50, which is what the entrant would expect from a low-cost incumbent. Then, the entrant would not know if it was facing a low-cost or high-cost incumbent, and might decide not to enter.

In their analysis, Milgrom and Roberts recognized that because a high-cost incumbent could lower its price to disguise its costs, a low-cost incumbent would try to make sure that the entrant would recognize its cost advantage. To do so, a low-cost incumbent would lower its price by a sufficiently large amount below $52.50 so that the potential entrant is convinced that *only* a low-cost producer would price that low. In effect, a low price becomes a credible *signal* that the incumbent's cost is low. Thus, a low-cost incumbent would price below $52.50. Ironically, though, since the low-cost incumbent charges a price that a rational high-cost incumbent would not charge, the entrant could infer the incumbent's true marginal costs from the first-year price. Limit pricing by the high-cost incumbent would thus not deter entry, and therefore a high-cost incumbent's optimal strategy is to charge its monopoly price and accept entry.

---

[27]Milgrom, P. and J. Roberts, "Limit Pricing and Entry Under Incomplete Information," *Econometrica*, 50, 1982, pp. 443–460.

Garth Saloner has pointed out that for limit pricing to deter entry, the entrant must not be able to perfectly infer the incumbent's cost from its limit price.[28] Saloner supposed that the entrant may be uncertain about the level of demand as well as the incumbent's cost. These two types of uncertainty prove to be sufficient to support an equilibrium in which (a) the incumbent prices below its single-year monopoly price regardless of its cost, and (b) the lower the incumbent's cost, the lower the price that it sets. The low price signals to the entrant that the incumbent's costs may be low and/or market demand may be low. Either signal may be sufficient to deter entry.

Generalizing from Saloner's model, we conclude that the entrant must be uncertain about the nature of postentry competition for limit pricing to be effective. Experienced entrants who have competed in many markets and are well informed about incumbent's costs and the level of market demand are unlikely to be fooled by limit pricing. The limit-pricing incumbent would sacrifice short-term profits without affecting long-term competition.

Predatory Pricing

Predatory pricing refers to the practice of setting a price with the objective of driving new entrants or existing firms out of business. The difference between predatory pricing and limit pricing is that limit pricing is directed at firms that have not yet entered the market, while predatory pricing is aimed at firms that have already entered. Numerous definitions of predatory pricing have been suggested but all of them involve the idea that the preying firm sets its price below cost (e.g., average variable cost or short-run marginal cost) with the expectation that losses incurred by doing so will be recouped once entrants or competitors have been driven from the market and the firm can exercise market power.[29]

The Chain-Store Paradox

It seems intuitive that an incumbent that prices below cost in one market may be able to deter entry in other markets in the future. The intuitive argument, however, is incorrect. To see why, imagine that an incumbent firm operates in 12 markets, and faces entry in each. In January, it faces entry in market 1; in February, it faces entry in market 2, and so forth. Should the incumbent slash prices in January?

We can answer this question by working backward from December, to see how earlier pricing decisions affect later entry. Regardless of the course of action before December, the incumbent will find it optimal not to engage in predatory pricing in

---

[28]Saloner, G., "Dynamic Equilibrium Limit Pricing in an Uncertain Environment," mimeo, Graduate School of Business, Stanford University. See also Matthews, S. and L. Mirman, "Equilibrium Limit Pricing: The Effects of Stochastic Demand," *Econometrica*, 51, 1983, pp. 981–996.

[29]See Martin, S., *Industrial Economics*, New York: MacMillan, 1988, for a good review of the various legal tests for predatory pricing that have been proposed.

market 12. The reason is that there is no further entry to deter. The entrant in the twelfth market knows this, and counting on the rationality of the incumbent, will enter regardless of previous price cuts. But knowing that it cannot deter entry in the twelfth market, the incumbent has no reason to slash prices in November in the eleventh market either. The potential entrant in the eleventh market can anticipate that the incumbent will not slash prices against it, and so enters without fear of retaliation. In October, the incumbent realizes that come November, it will certainly face entry in market 11. Thus, it calculates that there is no deterrent value to slashing prices in market 10. The potential entrant in the tenth market can figure this out too, and so enters. In this way, the problem completely unravels, so that the incumbent realizes that it has nothing to gain from predation in January in the first market! The striking conclusion is this: In a world in which all entrants could accurately predict the future course of pricing, predatory pricing would not deter entry, and therefore would be irrational. R. Mark Isaac and Vernon Smith conducted an experiment in which students played a predation "game." They found that student subjects behaved in accordance with this theory. In their experiment, a student played the role of an incumbent for several periods, setting prices in competition with different students in each period. Students had complete information about payoffs. Isaac and Smith found that "incumbent" students did not slash prices.[30]

This result that predation is seemingly irrational is associated with a puzzle in economics known as the *chain-store paradox*.[31] The paradox is that, despite the conclusion of the model that predatory pricing to deter entry is irrational, many firms are commonly perceived as slashing prices to deter entry. The gunpowder pool cited earlier is one example. General Foods and Standard Oil, described in Examples 11.4 and 11.5, respectively, are two others. The paradox is resolved by considering the role of uncertainty.

What drives the irrationality of predatory pricing in the chain-store paradox is that potential entrants can perfectly predict incumbent behavior in every market and realize that in the "last" market, predatory behavior is irrational, no matter what has happened up to that point. If entrants lack such certainty, then price cutting by an incumbent may affect their expectations of the incumbent's future pricing strategy. For example, suppose that the entrant stands to make profits of π_a if the incumbent is an "easy competitor" and incur losses of π_p if the incumbent is a "tough competitor," where $\pi_a > 0 > \pi_p$. Thus, a tough incumbent's single-period profit maximizing strategy is to set a price at which the entrant would lose money. Suppose also that the entrant believes that the probability that the incumbent is tough is ρ, and the probability that the incumbent is easy is $1 - \rho$. If S equals the

---

[30]Isaac, R.M. and V. Smith, "In Search of Predatory Pricing," *Journal of Political Economy*, 93, 1985, pp. 320–345.

[31]This term was coined by the game theorist Reinhard Selten in his article "The Chain Store Paradox," *Theory and Decision*, 9, 1978, pp. 127–159.

nonrecoverable costs of entry, then entry yields expected profits of $(1-\rho)\pi_a + \rho\pi_p - S$. Before entering, the potential entrant would like to know something about ρ. Suppose that it is certain that the incumbent is easy, that is, $\rho = 0$. Then it will enter as long as $\pi_a > S$, that is, as long as the profits from postentry competition when the incumbent cooperates exceed the sunk cost of entry. However, if the potential entrant believes that there is a good chance the incumbent is tough (i.e., ρ is close to 1), it will forecast that it is unlikely to generate profits to offset the costs of entry, and will stay out.

Obviously, the incumbent wants the entrant to believe that ρ is high. The incumbent could influence the entrant's perceptions by setting a low price in its established markets. Following the logic of the Milgrom-Roberts and Saloner limit pricing analyses, the entrant might infer that an incumbent who sets extremely low prices in its established markets probably has lower costs than it does, and therefore that ρ is big and entry is likely to be unprofitable. If the incumbent instead sets high prices in its established markets, the entrant may feel that ρ is small and that entry is profitable. Thus, predation may deter entry.

Even if the potential entrant is certain of the incumbent's costs, predation may still deter entry. Suppose that the entrant believes that some firms simply dislike competition and will go to great lengths to protect their market share, even if it means sacrificing profits. If a firm can develop a *reputation for toughness*, entrants may be reluctant to challenge it. In an experiment, Yun Joo Jung, John Kagel, and Dan Levin found that when students playing a predation game were unsure about the incumbent's tendencies, incumbents did slash prices to deter entry.[32]

Some well-known firms, including Wal-Mart and American Airlines, enjoy a reputation for toughness earned after fierce price competition led to the demise of some of their rivals. Aggressiveness is also a natural outgrowth of strategies to increase market share. Some firms announce a mission to achieve dominant market shares, such as Black and Decker and McCormick Spices. These announcements may effectively signal to rivals that these firms will do whatever is necessary, even sustain price wars, to secure their share of the market. Along these lines, firms may promote toughness by rewarding workers for aggressiveness in the market. Chaim Fershtman and Kenneth Judd suggest that a firm might reward managers based on market share rather than profits.[33] This will encourage them to price aggressively, thereby enhancing the firm's reputation for toughness, and could ultimately lead to higher profits than if managers were focusing on the bottom line.

[32]Jung, Y.J., J. Kagel, and D. Levin, "On the Existence of Predatory Pricing: An Experimental Study of Reputation and Entry Deterrence in the Chain-store Game," *RAND Journal of Economics*, 25, 1, 1994, pp. 72–93.

[33]Fershtman, C. and K. Judd, "Equilibrium Incentives in Oligopoly," *American Economic Review*, 77, 1984, pp. 927–940.

EXAMPLE 11.4

COFFEE WARS[34]

In 1970, General Foods' Maxwell House was the best selling brand of coffee east of the Mississippi. Procter and Gamble's (P&G's) Folger's brand was the best seller to the West. In 1971, P&G launched an effort to sell Folger's in parts of the Midwest and East where it had not sold before. P&G first introduced Folger's in Cleveland in 1971. P&G followed this with introductions in Pennsylvania in 1973, and Syracuse in 1974, before expanding throughout the East in 1979. To promote Folger's in Cleveland, P&G used a combination of television advertising, retailer's promotions, coupons, and in-pack gifts, and mailed free samples. General Foods responded with mailed and in-pack coupons as well as promotional incentives for retailers to sell Maxwell House. Even so, Folger's claimed 15 percent of the Cleveland market in its first year.

By 1972, executives in General Foods' Maxwell House division were concerned about Folger's "disturbingly successful" entry into Cleveland and feared similar successes throughout the East. At that point, General Foods adopted what came to be known as its "defend now" strategy, which was an attempt to limit Folger's share in the East to 10 percent. A major element of this strategy was heavy price discounting, although General Foods instructed its Maxwell House executives not to sell the coffee below average variable costs. Regardless of these instructions, evidence was presented during the Federal Trade Commission's investigation of this case suggesting that Maxwell House *was* sold below average variable cost in Cleveland (from 1973 to 1974), Pittsburgh (from 1973 to 1975), and Syracuse (from 1974 to 1976). In addition to aggressive price cutting, Maxwell House introduced a so-called "fighting brand" (Horizon) explicitly aimed at disrupting Folger's launch in Philadelphia and Syracuse. The evidence suggests that Horizon was also priced below its average variable cost.

It certainly appears that General Foods was attempting to signal to P&G that it intended to fight aggressively to defend its dominant position in eastern markets. Internal General Foods' documents seem to confirm this. They spoke of a desire to "delay Folger's expansion," "force them to carefully consider the financial wisdom of further eastern expansion," and to engage in "eye for eye" retaliation.[35]

In 1976, the staff of the Federal Trade Commission initiated a complaint against General Foods charging them with attempted monopolization, unfair competition,

---

[34]This example draws on the Federal Trade Commission's opinion in General Food Corp., reprinted in *Antitrust and Trade Regulation Report*, May 3, 1984, pp. 888–905 and Hilke, J. and P. Nelson, "Strategic Behavior and Attempted Monopolization: The Coffee (General Foods) Case," in Kwoka, J. and L.J. White (eds.), *The Antitrust Revolution*, Glenview, IL: Scott Foresman, 1989, pp. 208–40.

[35]Hilke and Nelson, *op. cit.*, pp. 235–236.

and price discrimination in the ground coffee market. In 1984, the full Commission rejected the complaint, exonerating General Foods. The commission reasoned that the relevant coffee market was the United States as a whole (as opposed to individual, geographically based markets) and that within this broader market General Foods did not possess the market power to raise prices above competitive levels should other competitors exit. As a result, the Commission concluded, "Maxwell House did not come dangerously close to gaining monopoly power as a result of any of its challenged conduct in any of the alleged markets. As a result, its actions were output-enhancing and pro-competitive—the kind of conduct the antitrust laws seek to promote."[36]

Excess Capacity

Many firms carry excess capacity. To measure capacity utilization, every year the U.S. Census of Manufacturers asks plant managers to state the levels of current and desired production. The resulting ratio, called *capacity use*, is typically about 80 percent. Firms hold more capacity than they use for several reasons. In some industries, it is economical to add capacity only in large increments. If firms build capacity ahead of demand, then such industries may be characterized by periods in which firms carry excess capacity. Downturns in the general economic business cycle, or a decline in demand facing a single firm can also create excess capacity. Firms in imperfectly competitive industries may be profitable when operating at capacity. Other firms may then enter seeking a share of those profits, creating excess capacity. In these examples, excess capacity results from market forces.

Firms may also choose to hold excess capacity for strategic purposes. Specifically, by holding excess capacity, an incumbent may affect how potential entrants view the nature of postentry competition. Thus, by holding excess capacity, the incumbent may be able to blockade entry.

Sometimes, holding excess capacity may be a signal of the incumbent's willingness to slash prices if entry occurs. The models of predatory pricing and limit pricing may be used to understand how such a signal can deter entry when the entrant is uncertain about the incumbent's intentions. An incumbent who fears that limit pricing or predatory pricing may arouse antitrust concerns may find that excess capacity is an equally effective entry deterrent that is less likely to draw the attention of antitrust enforcers.

Unlike predatory pricing and limit pricing, excess capacity can deter entry even when the entrant possesses full information about the incumbent's costs and strategic direction. When an entrant forecasts the nature of postentry competition, it must estimate the quantity it will be able to sell, and the price it will receive. Models of strategic interaction demonstrate that quantity and price depend, in part, on each firm's costs and capacities. Hence, by holding excess capacity, the incumbent can influence the entrant's forecast of its postentry profitability.

---

[36]Re *General Foods Corp.*, 901.

A Numerical Example of Entry-Deterring Excess Capacity[37]

We illustrate the entry-deterring role of capacity by considering a single market in which the incumbent faces the threat of entry by one firm. We suppose that post-entry competition resembles the Bertrand competition described in Chapter 8, except that each firm has a fixed capacity. With fixed capacity, we need to modify the Bertrand assumptions to compute the equilibrium. We assume the following characterizes postentry competition:

1. Consumers buy from the lowest-price seller,

2. Each firm expects the other to keep its price fixed, even if it is undercut. As in Bertrand competition, this gives each firm an incentive to undercut the other's price until price equals marginal cost.

The equilibrium of this game corresponds to the perfectly competitive outcome in the sense that each firm equates marginal cost to the market price.

We assume that the demand function takes the form:

$$P = 100 - .5(Q_I + Q_E),$$

where Q_I refers to the incumbent's annual output and Q_E refers to the entrant's annual output. Both firms have the same cost function:

$$TC = 100 + 30K + 10Q,$$

where K is the productive capacity of the firm, and Q is the chosen level of output. Q and K are measured in terms of the same units, and K represents an upper bound on how much output the firm can produce in a given year. Thus, $Q \leq K$; that is, the firm cannot exceed its capacity. According to this cost function, there is a fixed cost of production of $100. It also costs the firm $30 for each unit of productive capacity, whether it uses the capacity or not, and an additional $10 for each unit it produces. The sum of the capacity and production costs, $40, is the *long-run marginal cost* of production, and represents marginal cost from the point of view of a firm that has not yet invested in capacity. Once a firm has built capacity, it faces a *short-run marginal cost* of $10.

As an initial step to analyzing the incentives to invest in overcapacity, we consider the incumbent's calculation of the optimal level of capacity to hold if it expects to remain a monopolist and therefore has no strategic incentive to invest in excess capacity. In this case the incumbent will only acquire as much capacity as it plans to utilize. Before investing in capacity, the incumbent has long-run marginal costs of $40. Given the demand curve, $P = 100 - .5Q_I$, marginal revenue is $MR = 100 - Q_I$. Equating marginal revenue and long-run marginal cost, we find that the optimal capacity and output levels are $K_I = Q_I = 60$. At this output, $P = \$70$.

---

[37]The authors would like to thank Mark Satterthwaite for allowing us to use this example from his lecture notes.

TABLE 11.1
MONOPOLY OUTPUT, PRICE, AND PROFIT AS A FUNCTION OF
CAPACITY

Capacity = K_I	50	60	70	80	90	100
Monopolist output = Q_I	50	60	70	80	90	90
Monopolist price = P	$75	$70	$65	$60	$55	$55
Monopolist profit = Π_I	$1650	$1700	$1650	$1500	$1250	$950

Table 11.1 reports the incumbent's monopoly output, price, and profits when it chooses $K_I = Q_I = 60$, as well as for other values of K and Q. For each value of K, the table shows the (short-run) profit-maximizing price and output for the market. As expected, when capacity and output deviate from 60, profits fall. Note that when the incumbent selects $K_I = 100$, its optimal output is $Q_I = 90$. The incumbent prefers to leave some capacity idle because if it increases output beyond 90, it drives marginal revenue below 10, which is the short-run marginal cost of production when capacity is sunk.

Now suppose that the incumbent has selected $K_I = Q_I = 60$. Will the entrant find it profitable to enter? What capacity and output will it choose? When considering entry, the entrant must take into account: (a) the incumbent's sunk investment in capacity K_I; and (b) the expectation that postentry competition will be competitive. As a result, both the entrant and the incumbent will cut prices until each is selling all of its productive capacity.

To illustrate how the entrant evaluates postentry competition, suppose that the incumbent selects $K_I = Q_I = 60$ and P = $70. The entrant contemplates selecting $K_E = Q_E = 80$ and P = $60. At this price, the entrant would control the market—the incumbent would sell nothing. The incumbent, facing this, would undercut the price to P = $59, and sell all of its capacity of 60. Price cuts would continue in this way until both the entrant and incumbent were selling all of their capacity. This would occur at a market price of $30, and a corresponding market demand of 140.

Knowing that the incumbent will produce to its capacity in equilibrium, the entrant faces an "effective" or "residual" demand curve that is found by substituting the incumbent's capacity into the formula for the market demand curve. Thus, if the incumbent selects $K_I = 60$, then the entrant's residual demand curve is: $P = 100 - .5(60 + Q_E)$, or $P = 70 - .5Q_E$. With this demand curve, $MR = 70 - Q_E$. The entrant then equates this to the long-run marginal cost of $40 and should select $K_E = Q_E = 30$. Total production is therefore 90, and the market price is $55. In this case the entrant would make $[(55-40)\times30] - 100 = \$350$.

The first row in Table 11.2 gives different levels of capacity that the incumbent might select. The second row reports the entrant's optimal capacity and output given the incumbent's capacity. For example, we see that if the incumbent selects $K_I = 60$, the entrant selects $K_E = 30$. Note that as the incumbent selects greater capacity, the entrant selects a smaller capacity. This reflects the entrant's expectation that when the incumbent has higher capacity, it will face a lower de-

TABLE 11.2
MARKET EQUILIBRIUM AS A FUNCTION OF INCUMBENT'S CAPACITY

Incumbent's capacity	50	60	70	80	90	100
Entrant's optimal capacity	35	30	25	20	15	10
Market quantity	85	90	95	100	105	110
Market price	57.5	55	52.5	50	47.5	45
Incumbent's profits	775	800	775	700	575	400
Entrant's profits	512.5	350	212.5	100	12.5	−50

mand curve and receive a lower price. The next two rows in Table 11.2 report the market quantity and price. The last two rows report the incumbent's and entrant's profits.

From the last row of Table 11.2 we see that the entrant finds it profitable to enter as long as the incumbent selects capacity of 90 or less. If the incumbent selects capacity of 100, however, the best the entrant can do, if it decides to enter at all, is to earn −$50. It makes negative profits because the market price of $45 is just sufficient to cover long-run marginal costs of $40, but does not provide enough contribution margin to pay off the fixed costs of $100.

If the incumbent felt that entry was inevitable, then it would inspect the next-to-last row of Table 11.2 and determine that the best it can do is to select $K_I = 60$, thereby earning profits of $800. Fortunately, though, entry is not inevitable, because if the incumbent holds sufficient capacity, it may deter entry. In this example, if it selects $K_I = 100$, then the entrant will stay out of the market. Once the incumbent has selected $K_I = 100$, its profit-maximizing output is 90, and it earns profits of $950.

This example shows how investment in additional capacity can deter entry. The additional capacity serves as a *credible commitment* that the incumbent will expand output should entry occur. Here, the amount of capacity necessary to deter entry is so great that the incumbent will keep some of it idle. It is critical that the capacity investment is sunk. If the incumbent could sell its capacity for the full purchase price, then once entry occurred, it would be better off selling off any capacity in excess of 60. The entrant, anticipating this rational response, would enter regardless of how much capacity the incumbent held.

Judo Economics and the Puppy-Dog Ploy

In the preceding example, the incumbent knows that entry leads to lower prices and profits. Thus, it is willing to invest in capacity—even if some eventually remains idle—to deter entry. But suppose that a potential entrant could credibly commit to limiting its output, so that the market price remains high. The incumbent may be willing to accommodate such an entrant, rather than invest in extra capacity to keep it out. The idea that an entrant may be better off committing to staying small so as not to trigger an aggressive response by an incumbent was first described by Judith Gelman and Steven Salop, who dubbed the strategy "judo economics."[38] Drew Fudenberg and Jean Tirole showed that the idea applies to a wide variety of contexts in their discussion of the puppy-dog ploy, which we first described in Chapter 9.[39]

To see how the puppy-dog ploy may help an entrant, suppose that the incumbent in the preceding example has $K_I = Q_I = 60$. We know that in the absence of a commitment by the entrant to stay small, the incumbent will prefer to expand capacity to $K_I = 100$ to deter entry. But what if the entrant can credibly commit to $K_E = Q_E = 10$? If the incumbent does not expand capacity, the market price will be \$65. The incumbent would earn profits (net of capacity costs) of $[(65 - 40) \times 60] - 100 = \$1,400$, and the entrant would make $[(65 - 40) \times 10] - 100 = \$150$. If the incumbent expands capacity to 100, it will keep the entrant out, but only make profits of \$950. Thus, the incumbent is better off not expanding capacity, *as long as it is convinced that the entrant will hold down its production.*

The puppy-dog ploy applies to a wide range of situations in which the incumbent may perform a predatory act. An example is provided by Braniff Airlines. Restaurateur and doll company owner Jeffrey Chodorow and real estate developer Arthur Cohen purchased a struggling Braniff in 1988. Braniff went bankrupt the next year. In settling the Braniff assets, Chodorow and Cohen bought the rights to the Braniff trademark for \$313,000, took over bankrupt Emerald Airlines, and combined the two into a new Braniff. Braniff publicly announced in the spring of 1991 that it intended to limit its flights to Dallas, Los Angeles, New York, Florida, and the Caribbean. Braniff started flying scheduled trips in June 1991. It had some immediate setbacks, including flying a banned Boeing 727 into Los Angeles International Airport (the plane violated local noise pollution ordinances). But Braniff's fate was sealed even before its first scheduled flight took off. In a move that many believe was prompted by Braniff's reentry into its home market of Dallas, American Airlines introduced "value pricing" on May 27, triggering a price war that drove Braniff from the market for good just two months later.

If it had stayed true to its word, Braniff would have carried only 3 percent as many passengers as American. So why did American respond aggressively to Braniff's puppy-dog ploy? Perhaps American feared that other airlines might enter (i.e., American may have set a predatory price to deter later entry). Nor could American be certain that Braniff would not grow. In general, an entrant can do little to assure incumbents that there will not be further entry. Unless resource constraints or patents deter future entrants, the puppy-dog may meet with an aggressive response. If the likelihood of additional entry is small, then there are some ways that the entrant can commit to remaining small to ward off an aggressive response. For example, a restaurateur can renovate a small space next door to established retailers—thereby limiting possibilities for expansion. Or, the restaurateur may select a menu tailored to a very narrow segment of the population.

---

[38]Gelman, J. and S. Salop, "Judo Economics: Capacity Limitation and Coupon Competition," *Bell Journal of Economics*, 14, 1983, pp. 315–325.

[39]Fudenberg, D. and J. Tirole, "The Fat-Cat Effect, The Puppy-Dog Ploy, and the Lean and Hungry Look," *American Economic Review*," 74, 1984, pp. 361–368.

◆◆◆◆◆ EXIT-PROMOTING STRATEGIES

Firms occasionally contend that their rivals are slashing prices just to drive them from the market. The complaining firm argues that consumers should object to low prices, because eventually the price slasher will have monopoly power, raise prices, and more than recoup its losses. As detailed in Example 11.5, oil refiners advanced these arguments when they attempted to break up the Standard Oil Trust a hundred years ago. In 1993, three drugstores in Conway, Arkansas, made a similar claim about the local Wal-Mart store. They successfully sued Wal-Mart under state antitrust statutes, and won a $300,000 award, plus a court order that Wal-Mart increase its drug prices. Complaints about unfairly low prices are often heard during trade disputes. In 1991, the U.S. Department of Commerce ruled that Toyota and Mazda were *dumping* minivans into the U.S. market—by pricing below cost—although the International Trade Commission ruled a year later that U.S. automakers were not harmed by such practices and were not entitled to compensation (begging the question of why Toyota and Mazda would sell below cost in the first place). In 1993, 37 nations accused Chinese firms of dumping products ranging from electronics to textiles, and in 1994, the United States accused the Canadian Wheat Board of dumping wheat. The international General Agreement on Tariffs and Trade (GATT) is frequently renegotiated to deal with complex dumping issues.

◆◆◆

ℰXAMPLE 11.5

HOW STANDARD OIL DROVE OUT ITS COMPETITORS[40]

In 1865, John D. Rockefeller, the senior partner in a Cleveland oil refinery, bought the failing company at auction. Rockefeller's company grew and changed its name to Standard Oil. When the U.S. Supreme Court ordered its breakup in 1911, Standard Oil was the largest business in the world. Rockefeller built his giant by exploiting scale and scope economies in refining, distribution, and purchasing; careful organization of the vertical chain; and a series of shrewd steps to destroy rivals who stood in his way.

Demand for oil boomed following the Civil War, and Rockefeller reinvested all of his profits into expanding Standard Oil's refining capacity. By virtue of its size, Standard could obtain discounts when shipping oil by rail. But Standard did more than obtain discounts. It instituted the practice of "drawbacks," whereby for every barrel sent to New York by a competitor, the rails paid Standard Oil a fee. Naturally, the rail passed this fee along to their other customers, so the net effect of drawbacks was that Standard Oil was subsidized by its competitors.

---

[40]The description of Standard Oil's practices is taken from Yergin, D., *The Prize*, New York: Simon and Schuster, 1991.

Standard soon had near monopsony power in the refining and distribution of oil. As Standard prospered, oil producers were finding rich sources of new supply, so that the price of oil in the 1870s fell precipitously. While Rockefeller felt that enormous profits could be realized in the vertical chain of oil production, he recognized that producers had grown too poor and fragmented to achieve them. He would reap all the profits that oil had to offer by gaining a stranglehold over refining.

It is generally accepted that Standard came to dominate refining through predatory pricing. (It has also been alleged that Standard occasionally blew up competing pipelines.) Rockefeller often initiated dealings with a local refiner by offering to acquire it. When rebuffed, Standard would cut prices, until the refiner was driven from business. Often, it employed "shadow" companies—companies operating under different names, but owned by Standard. Standard thus tried to avoid the bad publicity that had hounded it since the days of drawbacks. By 1879, Standard Oil had succeeded in capturing 90 percent of America's oil refining capacity, and owned all the pipelines of the oil regions. Standard then raised prices to oil producers, squeezing all of the profits out of the vertical chain.

Oil producers, fragmented though they were, responded to Standard's monopsony power by building the first long-distance pipeline, connecting the Pennsylvania oil fields with the Pennsylvania and Reading Railroad. This pipeline—a technological marvel at the time—took Rockefeller by surprise. Standard responded by immediately building long-distance pipelines from the oil regions to all of the major oil refining markets. This foreclosed further forward integration. While oil producers could build competing pipelines, they could not count on each other to avoid using Standard Oil's. This made further pipeline development too risky.

Almost immediately after the construction of the long distance pipelines, oil producers sought to destroy Standard Oil's power by challenging its practices under state anticompetitive statutes. But during the early 1880s, Rockefeller carefully set Standard up as a trust, so Standard did not actually own the companies it had acquired; rather, it held the shares of those companies "in trust" for the shareholders of Standard Oil. This enabled Standard to avoid antitrust problems until it was prosecuted, and eventually broken up in 1911, by federal "trustbusters" using the powers of the Sherman Antitrust Act of 1890.

Not everyone agrees that Standard's pricing policies actually amounted to predation. John McGee observes that Standard eventually acquired almost all of the refiners that it allegedly preyed upon.[41] He argued that it made no sense for Standard Oil to conduct costly price wars if its intention was acquisition. Yamey provided two rebuttals to McGee.[42] First, he pointed out that Standard may have used predation to frighten future opposition as well as to soften up existing competition. Second, Standard may have been able to buy at a more favorable price if

---

[41]McGee, J., "Predatory Pricing Revisited," *Journal of Law and Economics*, 23, 1980, pp. 289–330.

[42]Yamey, B., "Predatory Price Cutting: Notes and Comments," *Journal of Law and Economics*, 15, 1972, pp. 129–142.

its rivals feared an all-out war of attrition. The latter possibility is buttressed by Malcolm Burns, who found that the American Tobacco Trust reduced acquisition costs by preying on its targets.[43]

As discussed, Standard's practices would not have made sense if its rivals could have correctly assessed the future course of competition. McGee argues that many refinery owners were knowledgeable about Standard's cost position, and some were willing to play hardball with Standard. McGee quotes one owner whose response to a "sell or else" offer from Standard was to threaten even deeper price cuts! McGee feels that Standard would not have wasted resources in a costly price war when faced with such tough adversaries. Of course, Standard's deep pockets would have eventually destroyed even the most formidable opponent, if that opponent had been willing to fight it out. If the price war had the desired deterrent effect on other firms, it might have been worth the cost.

McGee's analysis makes the critical point that a successful predation strategy can be extremely costly. Perhaps Standard would have been better off exploiting economies of scale less aggressively. Economists will continue to debate both Standard's strategy and the Supreme Court decision to dissolve it.

Wars of Attrition

Standard Oil, Toyota, and Wal-Mart's rivals accused them of slashing prices below costs to eliminate competition. Rivals claimed that any losses incurred by the incumbent during the bout of price cutting would be more than made up by monopoly profits once they had been forced to exit. This presumes, of course, that the rivals would exit before the incumbent abandoned its strategy. It is not obvious why this should happen. A price war harms all firms in the market regardless of who started it. If, as one might expect, a larger incumbent has a greater capacity to sustain losses than its smaller rivals (e.g., because of more favorable access to lines of credit), then it should be able to outlast them. In this case, the large firm is said to have "deep pockets" from which it can finance the price war. On the other hand, a large firm may also suffer greater losses during the price war, especially if had higher sales, and did not have a cost advantage over smaller rivals. In this case, the large firm may seek to stop the price war to stem its losses.

Price wars are examples of *wars of attrition*. In a war of attrition, two or more parties expend resources battling with each other. Eventually, the survivor claims its reward, while the loser gets nothing and wishes it had never participated in the war. If the war of attrition lasts long enough, even the winner may be worse off than when the war began, because the resources it expended during the war may exceed its ultimate reward.

Many types of interactions fit the description of a war of attrition. The U.S./Soviet nuclear arms buildup between 1945 and the late 1980s is a classic ex-

---

[43]Burns, M., "Predatory Pricing and the Acquisition of Costs of Competitors," *Journal of Political Economy*, 94, 1986, pp. 266–296.

ample. Both countries devoted significant resources to increasing their nuclear arsenals, hoping that the other country would be the first to make concessions at the bargaining table. Eventually, the Soviet Union fell apart, and Russia acknowledged that it could not afford to carry on the buildup.

A price war is a war of attrition. Virtually all firms in an industry are worse off during a prolonged price war. If the price war drives some firms from the market, however, the survivors can increase their market shares and raise prices above the pre–price war levels. If a firm was certain that it would lose a price war, it would prefer to exit the market as soon as the price war began. By exiting immediately, it would avoid the costly battle that it expected to lose anyway.

We should see price wars only when firms are uncertain about whether they can outlast their rivals. The more that a firm believes it can outlast its rivals, the more willing it will be to enter and sustain a price war. Each firm may thus try to convince its rivals that it is better positioned to survive the price war. For example, firms may try to convince rivals that they are actually making money during the price war, or that they care more about winning the war than about making money. Either message may cause a rival to rethink its ability to outlast its opposition, and promote an early exit from the market. (An analogy in the arms race is Ronald Reagan's pronouncement that the United States could survive and win a nuclear war.)

Firms that face exit barriers are also well positioned to win a war of attrition. For example, a firm that is committed to pay its workers and other suppliers regardless of production levels may be indifferent about producing at a loss during the price war or ceasing production altogether. This firm has less to lose during a price war than a firm that can adjust its input costs.

EFFECTS OF DIVERSIFICATION ON ENTRY AND EXIT DECISIONS ◆ ◆ ◆ ◆ ◆

Up to now, we have focused on entry and exit by firms that operate in a single-product market (although the incumbent may be in several geographic markets). But entry and exit decisions may also depend on whether an incumbent or potential entrant is diversified into several product markets. Diversification may affect the costs of entry, postentry profitability, and the nature of postentry competition.

Diversification and Entry Costs

Diversification can affect the costs of entry when products are related through economies of scope. Dunne, Roberts, and Samuelson provided strong evidence that diversification affects entry. They showed that an established firm entering a new market tends to build plants that are, on average, three times larger than those of startup firms entering the same market. Entry by diversified firms is also far more likely to be successful, as evidenced by lower exit rates for diversified firms.

Several factors may reduce the entry costs of diversified firms. Diversified firms tend to be larger, and represent smaller risks to banks than do undiversified firms. This can give them access to lines of credit at low cost. This depends on whether new firms are able to obtain independent investment capital, as may happen when it is difficult for lenders to objectively verify the merits of a new investment. The growth of venture capital specialists in industries such as biotechnology and computer software has reduced the need for entrepreneurs to turn to existing firms to obtain seed capital.

Diversified firms may enjoy economies of scope in production, distribution, or marketing. An unusual but potentially lucrative source of scope economies is to diversify by season. Williams Ski and Patio Shop in Highland Park, Illinois, avoids slack periods in retail sales by completely changing its merchandise every six months. As discussed earlier, umbrella branding may also allow an incumbent to quickly establish a brand identity for new products.

Diversification, Entry, and Coordinated Pricing

A diversified firm entering a new market may choose a different pricing strategy than a new firm, creating further differential gains from entry. To illustrate, consider a natural monopoly market, say the retailing of hamburgers in a small community. The market has "room" only for one hamburger outlet. However, two firms are contemplating whether to enter the market. One, which we call the incumbent, already has a pizza operation in the same community. The other is a startup firm. If the two have the same costs of selling hamburgers, who has the stronger incentive to enter the hamburger market? The answer depends on two general issues associated with entry by diversified firms:

1. Can the incumbent benefit by coordinating the pricing of the two products?
2. Will the incumbent be as willing as the entrant to fight for supremacy in the new market?

The answer to question 1 is yes. The answer to question 2 is no if the products are substitutes, and yes if they are complements. This is true whether the products are substitutes in "product space" (e.g., hamburgers and pizza) or "geographic space" (e.g., the video rental stores along Straight Street discussed in Chapter 8).

The Efficiency Effect

We begin by developing point 1. To do so, we must analyze the prices and profits that the incumbent and entrant will realize in the pizza and hamburger markets. Let the subscript Z denote pizza and the subscript H denote hamburger. Let the weekly market demand for pizza be $Q_Z = 50 - P_Z + .5P_H$ when $P_H < 100$ and $Q_Z = 100 - P_Z$ when $P_H \geq 100$ or hamburger is unavailable. (Price is in cents per slice of pizza, and quantity is in dozens of slices of pizza per week.) With this formulation, pizza is seen to be a demand substitute for hamburger—as the price of hamburgers increases, the demand for pizza increases. The marginal cost of pizza is 40. Let the market demand for hamburger be $Q_H = 100 - P_H$.

When there is no hamburger shop, the incumbent sets P_Z to maximize profits in the pizza market. It is easy to calculate that it should select $P_Z = 70$, thereby earning weekly profits from the sale of pizza of 900. If a new entrant opens a hamburger shop, it will select $P_H = 70$, and earn profits of 900 per week. Thus, the entrant is willing to pay at a rate of 900 per week to enter the hamburger market. With the entrant selling hamburgers at $P_H = 70$, the incumbent pizza seller will prefer to lower its price. It now faces demand of $Q_Z = 85 - P_Z$. It maximizes profits by selecting $P_Z = 62.5$ and earns profits of 506.25.

But notice what happens when the incumbent opens a hamburger shop. It could price in the same way as the entrant, setting $P_H = 70$ and $P_Z = 62.5$, earning profits of 900 and 506.25 in the two markets respectively. Its combined profits of 1,406.25 exceed by 900 the profits it would earn if the entrant were selling hamburgers. Thus, the incumbent, like the entrant, seemingly would be willing to pay 900 to be the sole seller of hamburgers rather than let the entrant in.

But this conclusion is incorrect. The incumbent can do better than select $P_H = 70$ and $P_Z = 62.5$. Realizing that hamburger and pizza are substitutes, the incumbent would want to raise the price of hamburger to avoid *cannibalizing* its pizza business. It turns out that the incumbent maximizes its total profits by selecting $P_H = 77.1$ and $P_Z = 64.3$. Its profits will be 1,437.66, which exceeds by 931.41 the profits it would earn if the entrant were selling hamburgers. Thus, the incumbent would be willing to pay 931.41 to be the sole seller of hamburgers, which is more than the entrant was willing to pay.

The incumbent has more to gain than the entrant from selling hamburgers because the price of hamburger affects its pizza profits. By raising the price of hamburgers from $P_H = 70$ to $P_H = 77.1$, the incumbent loses profits of 53 in the hamburger market, but increases pizza profits by 84. By coordinating pricing—in this case by raising prices in both markets—the incumbent generates greater combined profits from the hamburger and pizza operations than would be possible if the entrant were setting a price to maximize hamburger profits only. The same analysis would apply if the products were demand complements, except that the incumbent would have set lower prices to boost demand across markets. As with this analysis, the incumbent would have more to gain than the entrant from operating in the new market.

This example illustrates what Jean Tirole calls the *efficiency effect*.[44] As Tirole describes it: "Because competition destroys industry profits, an incumbent has more incentive to deter entry than an entrant has to enter." In our example, the incumbent has greater incentive than the entrant to produce hamburgers. More generally, the incumbent has greater incentive to produce demand substitutes or demand complements than does an entrant. In so doing, the incumbent *preempts* entry and maintains its monopoly status.

Is Preemption Credible?

The above analysis omits one critical eventuality: What if the entrant follows the incumbent into the hamburger market? Continuing our example, suppose that the incumbent is the first to enter the market for hamburgers. Now suppose that the

---

[44]Tirole, J., *The Theory of Industrial Organization*, Cambridge, MA: MIT Press, 1989.

entrant also opens a hamburger shop, and as a result a price war erupts, with $P_H = 30$. Both firms are losing money in the hamburger market. In addition, the low price of hamburgers cuts into the incumbent's sale of pizza. The best the incumbent can do in the pizza market is set $P_Z = 52.5$, and earn profits of 156.25, far below the profits of 506.25 it would earn from pizza if $P_Z = 70$. The incumbent has more to lose during the price war than the entrant, and so may be more likely to exit the hamburger market.

Before entering the hamburger market, the incumbent should have recognized that it could not price aggressively in the hamburger market without cannibalizing the pizza market. This would make it vulnerable to an aggressive competitor. It should have considered whether such a turn of events was likely before it sinks money in entering the hamburger market. Of course, if the two products were complements, then a price war would benefit the incumbent in the first market, since the low price in the first market would drive up demand for its complement in the second market. This would permit the incumbent to outlast the entrant.

◆ ◆ ◆ ◆ ◆ EVIDENCE ON ENTRY-DETERRING BEHAVIOR

Although theorists have devoted considerable attention to entry deterrence, there is little systematic evidence regarding whether firms pursue entry-deterring strategies and, if they do, whether those strategies are successful. Most of our evidence comes from antitrust cases, where discovery requirements often provide researchers with detailed cost, market, and strategic information. Pankaj Ghemawat used such evidence to analyze many of the entry-deterring strategies DuPont used in the market for titanium dioxide, which we detail in Example 11.6

XAMPLE 11.6

DUPONT'S USE OF EXCESS CAPACITY TO CONTROL THE MARKET FOR TITANIUM DIOXIDE

Pankaj Ghemawat analyzed DuPont's capacity expansion in the titanium dioxide industry in the 1970s.[45] Titanium dioxide is a whitener used in paints, paper, and plastics. There are a number of ways to make titanium dioxide, all of which involve substantial economies of scale and learning economies. Until the mid-1960s, virtually every firm used the "sulfate process." The lone exception was DuPont, which relied on the "chloride process" that it developed in the 1940s. DuPont's chief raw

---

[45]Ghemawat, P., "Capacity Expansion in the Titanium Dioxide Industry," *Journal of Industrial Economics*, 33, 2, 1984, pp. 145–163.

material in this process was ilmenite. The discovery of low-cost rutile ore—a substitute for ilmenite—gave a decided cost advantage to the chloride process, and all new chloride units, including those built by DuPont, used rutile. Marginal costs for existing sulfate producers (mainly American Cyanamid and Glidden) were still low enough, however, that it was not economical for them to switch processes. In the early 1970s, pollution control legislation rendered the sulfate process unworkable and increased the costs of using rutile ore. The cost of using ilmenite was unaffected.

DuPont recognized that its competitors would soon lose 160,000 tons of sulfate process capacity. DuPont also forecast that demand for titanium dioxide would grow by 377,000 tons in 13 years. Thus, DuPont expected that the industry would need 537,000 tons of additional capacity. In 1972, DuPont elected to "preempt" the market by adding 500,000 tons of capacity. It targeted a market share of 65 percent by 1985. DuPont felt that it could expand faster than its competitors because (a) its competitors had to spend money on cleanup that DuPont, using ilmenite in most of its plants, did not; and (b) it had lower costs of using ilmenite, due to scale and learning economies. Overall, DuPont believed that its costs were about 22 percent lower than its competitors', so that they would be reluctant to compete head to head.

Of course, there is a lag between planning to add capacity and actually having capacity in place. During this lag, DuPont was vulnerable to expansion by competitors. In 1974, Kerr-McGee responded to a shortage of titanium dioxide by starting construction of a 50,000-ton plant. DuPont tried to forestall additional entry. It let its competitors know the magnitude of its planned expansion of existing facilities, and falsely announced that it had begun constructing a new 130,000-ton facility. DuPont also appears to have limit priced—setting prices just under the average total costs of production in the new plants. DuPont's competitors, holding out for higher prices, refused to match. While market forces had historically forced all sellers to charge the same price, this two-tiered pricing structure persisted because DuPont lacked sufficient capacity to handle the whole market. When demand slackened in early 1975, DuPont's competitors lost substantial sales, and were forced to meet DuPont's price.

When demand remained soft through 1975, DuPont reexamined its preemption strategy. It recognized that the costs of adding capacity would be substantial, since it could never hope to ramp up production as originally planned. It also realized that competitors were moving down the learning curve and would be at less of a cost disadvantage. DuPont was prepared to expand capacity as originally planned—on a faster timetable—but only if demand recovered. When demand did not recover in 1976, DuPont scaled back its capacity expansion.

Evidence on entry deterrence from sources other than antitrust cases may be scant for several reasons. First, firms will naturally be reluctant to report that they strategically deter entry, since this may be sensitive competitive information, and might violate state or federal antitrust statutes. Second, many entry-deterring strategies involve pricing below the short-term monopoly price. To assess whether a firm was engaging in such a practice, the researcher would need to know the firm's marginal costs, its demand curve, the degree of industry competition, and the availability of substitutes. Outside of antitrust cases, such information is difficult for researchers to obtain. Last, to measure the success of an entry-deterring strategy, a researcher would need to determine what the rate of entry would have been in the absence of the predatory act. This, too, is a difficult question to answer.

Survey Data on Entry Deterrence

Despite concerns about the willingness of firms to provide responses, Robert Smiley asked major consumer product makers if they pursued a variety of entry-deterring strategies.[46] Smiley surveyed product managers at nearly 300 firms. To encourage the managers to be frank, Smiley promised complete anonymity. Even so, managers may have been reluctant to fully reveal their strategies. Many other possible biases can emerge with survey data (e.g., respondents may want to sound like good strategists, and so overreport their use of various strategies), so the results should be interpreted with caution.

Smiley asked managers about their use of several strategies discussed in this chapter, including:

- Aggressive price reductions to move down the learning curve, giving the firm a cost advantage that later entrants could match only by investing in learning themselves
- Intensive advertising to create brand loyalty
- Acquiring patents for all variants of a product
- Enhancing firm's reputation for predation though announcements or some other vehicle
- Limit pricing
- Holding excess capacity

The first three strategies create high entry costs. The last three strategies change the entrant's expectations regarding postentry competition.

Table 11.3 reports the percentage of product managers who report that their firms frequently, occasionally, or seldom use each of the above strategies for new products and existing products. Note that managers were asked about exploiting the learning curve for new products only.

Over half of all product managers surveyed report frequent use of at least one entry-deterring strategy, and virtually all report occasional use of one or more entry-deterring strategies. Product managers report that they rely much more extensively on strategies that increase entry costs, rather than strategies that affect the entrant's perception about the nature of postentry competition. Perhaps managers

---

[46]Smiley, R., "Empirical Evidence on Strategic Entry Deterrence," *International Journal of Industrial Organization*, 6, 1988, pp. 167–180.

TABLE 11.3
REPORTED USE OF ENTRY-DETERRING STRATEGIES

	Learning Curve	Advertising	R&D/Patents	Reputation	Limit Pricing	Excess Capacity
New Products						
Frequently	26%	62%	56%	27%	8%	22%
Occasionally	29	16	15	27	19	20
Seldom	45	22	29	47	73	48
Existing Products						
Frequently		52%	31%	27%	21%	21%
Occasionally		26	16	22	21	17
Seldom		21	54	52	58	62

do not think about postentry competition. Or perhaps they believe that entrants have strongly held beliefs about the nature of postentry competition that cannot be swayed by predatory acts. Managers also report that they are more likely to pursue entry-deterring strategies for new products than for existing products, especially for strategies that affect entry costs. Smiley reported that product managers often felt that competition among existing products was so intense that no entry-deterring strategies were needed, that is, entry was blockaded.

Other Evidence on Entry Deterrence

A few recent studies complement antitrust studies and survey work by providing evidence on the actual use of entry-deterring strategies by a large sample of firms. Marvin Lieberman examined capacity expansion and entry in 38 chemical products industries.[47] He argued that if incumbents are deterring entry, then they would be willing to add capacity even when the industry is growing slowly or is stagnant. Entrants, on the other hand, would not add capacity unless the industry was growing rapidly. He found no difference between the rates of growth necessary to attract capacity expansion by incumbents and entry by new firms, and concluded that firms were not using capacity expansion to deter entry. Overall, Lieberman found evidence linking excess capacity and entry deterrence in only 3 of 38 industries.

Robert Masson and Joseph Shaanan studied the entry-deterrence effects of limit pricing and excess capacity in 26 industries.[48] They combined information about price-cost margins, scale economies, and capacity utilization, to show that low prices and excess capacity restrict entry. They also found that firms do occasionally limit price to deter entry, but found no evidence that firms deliberately hold excess capacity to deter entry.

---

[47]Lieberman, M., "Excess Capacity as a Barrier to Entry: An Empirical Appraisal," *Journal of Industrial Economics*, 35, 1987, pp. 607–627.

[49]Masson, R. and J. Shaanan, "Excess Capacity and Limit Pricing: An Empirical Test," *Economica*, 53, 1986, pp. 365–378.

CHAPTER SUMMARY

- Entry and exit are pervasive. In a typical industry, one-third of the firms are less than five years old, and one-third of firms in the industry will exit within the next five years.

- A firm will enter a market if the expected postentry profits exceed the sunk costs of entry. Factors that reduce the likelihood of entry are called entry barriers.

- A firm will exit a market if the expected future losses exceed the sunk costs of exit.

- Structural entry barriers result from exogenous market forces. Low-demand, high-capital requirements, and limited access to resources are all examples of structural entry barriers. Exit barriers arise when firms have obligations that they must keep whether they produce or not.

- An incumbent firm can use predatory acts to deter entry or hasten exit by competitors. Limit pricing, predatory pricing, and capacity expansion change entrants' forecasts of the profitability of postentry competition.

- Limit pricing and predatory pricing can succeed only if the entrant is uncertain about the nature of postentry competition. Either of these strategies may convince the entrant that postentry competition will be fierce.

- Firms can engage in predatory practices to promote exit by rivals. Once a firm realizes that it cannot survive the price war, it exits, permitting the survivors to raise price and increase share. A firm may try to convince its rivals that it is more likely to survive the price war, to hasten the rival's exit.

- Diversification both helps and hinders entry. A diversified firm can better coordinate pricing across related products, but may be vulnerable if a price war in one market cuts into its profits in a substitute product market.

- Managers report that they frequently engage in entry-deterring strategies, especially to protect new products. Systematic evidence on the success of entry-deterring strategies, however, is limited.

QUESTIONS

1. Recall the discussion of monopolistic competition in Chapter 8. Suppose that an entrepreneur considered opening a video store along Straight Street in Linesville. Where should the entrepreneur position the store? Does your answer depend on whether additional entry is expected?

2. How a firm behaves toward existing competitors is a major determinant of whether it will face entry by new competitors. Explain.

3. Dunne, Roberts, and Samuelson found that industries with high entry rates tended to also have high exit rates. Can you explain this finding? What does this imply for pricing strategies of incumbent firms?

4. In most models of entry deterrence, the incumbent engages in predatory practices that harm a potential entrant. Can these models be reversed, so that the entrant engages in predatory practices? If so, then what are the practical differences between incumbents and entrants?

5. There has been comparatively little entry into the undergraduate education market, particularly in the niche that also produces academic research. (Indeed, most of the top research universities have been in business for 50 years or more.) Can you explain the low entry rate in this market?

PART THREE

STRATEGIC POSITION AND DYNAMICS

STRATEGIC POSITIONING FOR COMPETITIVE ADVANTAGE[1]

12

*U*ntil the U.S. airline industry was deregulated in 1978, most major domestic airlines competed in the same way. With entry and prices controlled by the Civil Aeronautics Board, airlines battled one another by scheduling more frequent and convenient departures and by enhancing amenities, such as meals and movies. Deregulation of the industry brought with it new entry and new ways of doing business. Consider, for example, the variety of competitive strategies pursued by firms in the industry since deregulation:

- American, the largest trunk carrier, developed a nationwide route structure organized around the hub-and-spoke concept.[2] It built traveler and travel agent loyalty through its frequent-flyer programs and travel agent commission overrides (now on the decline) and attempted to maximize revenue through its sophisticated computerized reservation system, known as SABRE, and its state-of-the-art yield management capabilities.

- USAir was a regionally focused carrier before deregulation. It has tried to avoid head-to-head competition with the major airlines by serving smaller markets that the large carriers exited from following deregulation. As a result, USAir has consistently enjoyed the highest yield (dollars of revenue per passenger-mile). But its smaller planes, lower load factors (percentage of seats filled), and generous labor contracts give it the highest average operating costs in the industry.

---

[1]The authors would like to thank Steve Postrel and Jim Dana for valuable conversations that helped shape some of the ideas in this chapter.

[2]See Chapter 5 for a discussion of the hub-and-spoke concept in the airline industry.

- Continental engaged in bitter and protracted struggles with labor in attempting to cut wages and tighten work rules. Twice bankrupt, it has now positioned itself as a low-price alternative to the big trunk carriers.

- Southwest, an intrastate carrier operating only in Texas before deregulation, expanded incrementally by entering selected cities in the Midwest and southwestern regions of the country, and flying into little-used airports (e.g., Chicago's Midway airport). Eschewing the hub-and-spoke concept, Southwest offers point-to-point service by flying passengers from one city to another in one or two short hops. With less restrictive work rules than other major airlines, a fleet that consists only of Boeing 737s to economize on maintenance and training, and a highly motivated work force, Southwest has enjoyed the lowest average operating costs in the industry. Its flights offer few amenities other than drinks and cheerful flight attendants; rather than attempting to capture traveler loyalty with frequent-flyer programs, Southwest emphasizes low fares and reliable on-time service.

This example illustrates several fundamentally different ways in which firms can position themselves to compete within the same industry. With its extensive route network and its emphasis on loyalty-inducing devices, American attempts to differentiate its services from competitors to insulate itself from the effects of price-cutting by other airlines. Continental, by contrast, has sought to create a cost advantage relative to other airlines in the market. As a result, its pricing has been more aggressive than American. Like American, the cornerstone of USAir's strategy has been to insulate itself from price competition. But USAir has a narrower geographic scope than its larger rivals, and with its smaller, shorter-distance markets, it tends to have more business travelers among its flyers. Southwest's geographic scope is also narrower, and like USAir, it has attempted to serve markets that its larger competitors have bypassed. Unlike USAir, however, the basis of Southwest's success has been a cost advantage that allows it to offer low fares and still make a profit.

Of course, not all of these positions have been equally profitable. Moreover, the profitability of some positions has persisted, while the profitability of others lasted only for a brief time. Southwest has made a profit each year since 1973, while Continental has consistently lost money since the mid-1980s. American and USAir earned positive profits throughout the 1980s, but incurred huge losses during the prolonged industry recession of the early 1990s. This example suggests, then, that at any given time, some strategic positions may be better suited to the industry environment in which a firm operates than others.

The purpose of this chapter is to develop a conceptual framework for characterizing and analyzing a firm's *strategic position* within an industry. This framework employs simple economic concepts to characterize necessary conditions for a strategic position to lead to *competitive advantage* in the market. Chapter 13 then builds on this framework by introducing a number of specific analytical tools for diagnosing the sources of competitive advantage.

This chapter is organized in four main sections. The first section explores the concept of competitive advantage and argues that to achieve it a firm must do a better job than its rivals at creating value. The ability to create value is shaped by how the firm positions itself to compete in an industry. The second section discusses the economic and organizational logic of two broad alternative approaches to positioning: cost advantage and differentiation advantage. The third section covers market segmentation and targeting strategies. The fourth section discusses the concept of *strategic groups*.

COMPETITIVE ADVANTAGE AND VALUE-CREATION: ANALYTICAL TOOLS AND CONCEPTUAL FOUNDATIONS
◆ ◆ ◆ ◆ ◆

A key premise of the Five-Forces framework presented in Chapter 7 is that industry conditions are an important determinant of a firm's profitability. However, some firms—Southwest in airlines, Banc One in banking, Nike in athletic shoes, Merck in pharmaceuticals, Cooper Tire and Rubber in tires, Sainsbury's in grocery retailing in Great Britain—seem to be able to earn rates of profit that exceed the average for their industries. When a firm outperforms its industry, we say it achieves a *competitive advantage*.

This definition of competitive advantage is more precise than the definition found in the traditional strategic management literature.[3] This literature usually defines competitive advantage as the ability of the firm to favorably distinguish itself from competitors in the eyes of consumers, but does not state whether this distinction results from pricing or product design decisions or productive capabilities. Firms gaining an advantage from the former may have a "competitive advantage" in this traditional sense, but at the same time have low rates of profit as compared with the industry average if its price is too low or its costs are too high. We doubt that a firm that does a good job meeting the needs of consumers while sacrificing shareholder value really has much of an advantage over competitors. Moreover, the traditional definition does not consider the possibility of firms that do not *appear* to be distinguishing their products from competitors' because those competitors have reacted to its advantage by cutting their prices.

This chapter develops a framework to explain why some firms achieve competitive advantage and others do not. That framework, summarized in Figure 12.1, says that a firm's profitability is a function not only of industry conditions, but also of the amount of value it creates relative to its competitors. A firm can achieve competitive advantage in the sense we have defined it only if it possesses capabilities that allow it to create more total value than its competitors. A firm that creates more total value can simultaneously earn higher profits and deliver higher net benefits to consumers than its competitors. The amount of value it creates depends on both its cost position and its differentiation position relative to its competitors.

---

[3]See, for example, Christensen, K. and L. Fahey, "Building Distinctive Competencies into Competitive Advantage," *Strategic Planning Management*, February 1984, pp. 113–123.

FIGURE 12.1

FRAMEWORK FOR COMPETITIVE ADVANTAGE.

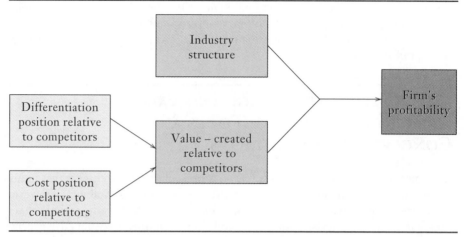

A firm's profitability depends jointly on industry conditions and its success in creating more value than its competitors. The amount of value the firm creates in comparison to competitors depends on its cost and differentiation positions relative to competitors.

The purpose of the next two sections is to present the analytical building blocks that we need to develop this framework more fully. In this section, we define what we mean by *value creation*. To do this, we must introduce the concepts of *perceived benefits* and *consumer surplus*.

Perceived Benefit and Consumer Surplus

A particular computer software package is worth $150 to you. If its market price was $80, you would buy it because (from your perspective) its perceived benefit ($150) exceeds its cost ($80). In making the purchase, you make yourself better off; you have given up $80 to receive something more valuable—a software package whose perceived benefit is worth $150. The extent by which you are better off— $70 in this case ($150 − $80)—is known as consumer surplus.[4]

More formally, if we let B denote the perceived benefit of a product per unit consumed—that is, what a unit of the product is worth to a consumer—and we let P denote the product's monetary price, consumer surplus is the difference $B − P$. The example above suggests a simple model of consumer behavior: A consumer

---

[4]Marketing textbooks often use different terms to describe consumer surplus. One common synonym used in marketing is *delivered value*. See, for example, Kotler, P., *Marketing Management*, 7th ed., Englewood Cliffs, NJ: Prentice-Hall, 1991.

will purchase a product only if its consumer surplus is positive, and given a choice between two or more competing products, the consumer will purchase the one for which consumer surplus, $B - P$ is largest.[5]

The perceived benefit B should be thought of as the *perceived gross benefit* of the product (which depends on attributes, such as performance, reliability, durability, product aesthetics, and image) *minus* (i) the *user cost* of the product: the costs of installing, learning how to use, operating, maintaining, and (eventually) disposing of the product; and (ii) any *purchasing and transactions costs* (excluding the purchase price itself) involved in buying the product, such as the costs of search, transportation, and (if necessary) writing contracts. Consumer surplus is then determined by simply deducting the monetary price from the product's perceived benefit (see Figure 12.2).[6]

The concept of consumer surplus is analogous to the profit of a firm. Indeed, when the consumer *is* a firm, consumer surplus is identical to the increment in profit that the purchase of the good generates. To see this, imagine a firm that is considering purchasing a machine that will reduce production costs by $8,000 per year. In effect, the B of the machine is $8,000. Suppose the firm's discount rate is 5 percent, and the machine costs $100,000. The annualized purchase cost $P = .05*100,000 = $5,000$. "Consumer surplus" is thus $3,000 per year, which corresponds exactly to the increment in the firm's economic profit from purchasing the machine.[7]

---

[5]This is what economists refer to as the "discrete choice" model of consumer behavior. Such a model presumes that the number of units the consumer is contemplating purchasing is fixed (e.g., the consumer is only going to buy a single microwave oven), and the only issues the consumer faces are whether to purchase at all and from whom. The model of consumer choice discussed here and the concept of gross benefit can be extended to the case in which the consumer must not only decide whether and from whom to purchase, but also how many units of the product to purchase. This extension is logically straightforward, but involves introducing additional concepts, such as marginal benefit, that would distract us from the main points we are trying to develop.

[6]Marketing and strategic management textbooks often advocate adding together user costs, purchase and transactions costs, and the monetary price to obtain something that is usually called the *total customer price*. Consumer surplus would then be defined as gross benefit minus the total customer price. While the notion of a total customer price can be useful, we prefer instead to deduct the user and purchase and transactions costs from the *perceived gross benefit* to get what we call B, the *perceived (net benefit)*. We thus distinguish between the monetary price P, which is essentially a transfer of money between consumers and the firm, and the user, purchase, and transactions costs, which entail a real resource sacrifice to society.

[7]Equivalently, we could have expressed everything on a discounted present value basis as opposed to an annualized basis. In that case, $B = $8000/.05 = $160,000$ and $P = $100,000$. Consumer surplus is thus equivalent to the NPV of the project. See the appendix to the Economics Primer for a short introduction to the concept of *net present value*.

FIGURE 12.2

COMPONENTS OF CONSUMER SURPLUS.

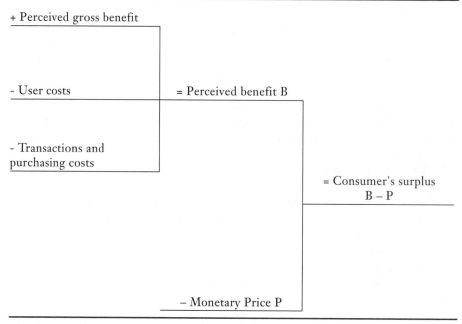

The perceived benefit *B* equals the perceived gross benefit minus user costs and transactions and purchasing costs. Consumer surplus then equals the perceived benefit *B* minus the monetary price *P*.

Whether its customers are firms or individuals, a seller must deliver consumer surplus to compete successfully. The *value map* in Figure 12.3 illustrates the competitive implications of consumer surplus. The horizontal axis represents the level of a key attribute, which (for simplicity) we call quality and denote by *q*. The vertical axis shows the monetary price *P* of the product. Each point in the value map corresponds to a particular price-quality combination. The solid upward-sloping line in Figure 12.3 is called an *indifference curve*. For a given consumer, any price-quality combination along the indifference curve yields the same consumer surplus (i.e., has the same *B − P*). A consumer choosing among products located along the indifference curve would thus be indifferent among the offerings. Products offering price-quality combinations located *below a given indifference curve* yield a consumer surplus that is *higher* than that yielded by products along the indifference curve. From the consumer's perspective, such products provide superior value. Products offering price-quality combinations located *above a given indifference curve* yield a consumer surplus that is *lower* than that yielded by products along the indifference curve. From the consumer's perspective, such products provide inferior value.

FIGURE 12.3
THE VALUE MAP.

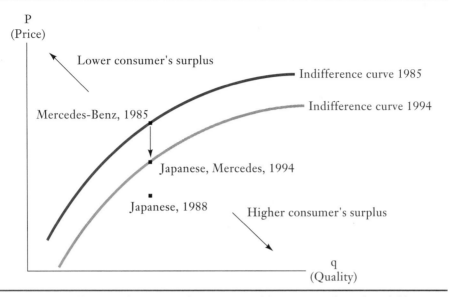

The value map illustrates the price-quality positions of firms in a market. The solid line is an indifference curve. It illustrates price-quality combinations that yield the same consumer surplus. Price-quality positions located below a given indifference curve yield a consumer surplus that is higher than that yielded by positions along the indifference curve. Price-quality positions located above an indifference curve yield consumer surplus that is lower than that yielded by positions along the indifference curve. When some products are positioned on a given indifference curve while others are positioned off the curve, consumers will flock to the firms providing the higher consumer surplus. This was apparently the case in the late 1980s when the Japanese luxury cars, such as Lexus and Infiniti, offered comparable cars at a lower price as compared with established luxury producers, such as Mercedes-Benz.

Competition among firms in a market can be thought of as a process whereby firms, through their prices and product attributes, submit consumer surplus "bids" to consumers. Consumers then choose the firm that offers the greatest amount of consumer surplus. A firm that offers a consumer less surplus than its rivals will lose the fight for that consumer's business. When firms' price-quality positions line up along the same indifference curve—that is, when firms are offering a consumer the same amount of consumer surplus—we say that the firms have achieved *consumer surplus parity*. If firms achieve consumer surplus parity in a market in which consumers have identical preferences (i.e., the same indifference curves), no consumer within that market has an incentive to switch from one seller to another, and market shares will thus be stable. If all firms in the market have the *same* quality, then consumer surplus parity reduces to the simple condition that each firm charge the same price. As discussed in the Economics Primer, a common market price is a necessary (though not sufficient) condition for a perfectly competitive market to be in equilibrium.

When a firm loses consumer surplus parity, its sales will slip and its market share will fall. This happened to Mercedes-Benz in the luxury car market in the 1980s. Figure 12.3 depicts the indifference curve of a representative consumer in this market in 1985 and shows the position of Mercedes-Benz. When the Japanese luxury automobiles, such as Lexus, Infiniti, and Acura, were introduced in the United States in the late 1980s, they offered comparable quality to Mercedes-Benz, but at a lower price. Not surprisingly, they rapidly gained market share. Eventually, the Japanese car makers raised price and Mercedes lowered price, moving all firms to a position of consumer surplus parity on an indifference curve to the southeast of the 1985 indifference curve.

The steepness (i.e., the slope) of an indifference curve indicates the tradeoff between price and quality a consumer is willing to make.[8] Indeed, as shown in Figure 12.4, *the increase in the price along a given indifference curve corresponds exactly to the incremental benefit ΔB caused by an increase Δq in the quality delivered by the product.*[9] A steeply sloped indifference curve indicates that a consumer is willing to pay con-

FIGURE 12.4
INDIFFERENCE CURVES AND THE TRADEOFF BETWEEN PRICE AND QUALITY.

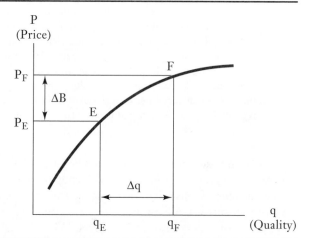

The steepness of an indifference curve indicates the tradeoff between price and quality consumers are willing to make. The increase in price from P_E to P_F along the indifference curve is equal to the change in perceived benefit, ΔB, that results from an increase, Δq, in quality from q_E to q_F.

---

[8]We couch our discussion in terms of the tradeoff between price and quality. More generally, though, the same discussion applies to the tradeoff between price and any benefit-enhancing or cost-reducing attribute.

[9]The logic is straightforward. Each point (E and F in Figure 12.4) yields the same consumer surplus, so $B_E - P_E = B_F - P_F$. Rearranging yields: $\Delta B = B_F - B_E = P_F - P_E$.

siderably extra for additional quality, while a shallow indifference curve indicates that extra quality is not worth much to the customer.

Firms that overestimate the willingness of consumers to trade off price for quality risk overpricing their products and either losing market share to competitors or never becoming a viable competitor in their own right. Such was the fate of *The National*, an all-sports daily newspaper launched with great fanfare in January 1990. Without question, its longer features, color photographs, detailed statistics, and columns and bylines by big-name sportswriters, such as Mike Lupica and John Feinstein, made it superior to the sports coverage provided by local newspapers. However, at a price of 75 cents per issue most potential readers did not find it to be a good value in relation to the available alternatives. *The National's* circulation remained far below projections and the advertising revenue needed to support the highly paid staff of reporters and columnists never materialized. *The National* folded in June 1991.

Firms can also underestimate the willingness of consumers to trade off price and quality. For example, some automakers were relatively slow in introducing airbags and anti-lock braking systems in their vehicles (e.g., Mazda, in the MPV), while others (e.g., Ford, especially the Taurus sedan) were not and gained an advantage.

Value-Created

As goods move along the vertical chain—as raw materials are converted to components, components are assembled into finished goods, and finished goods are distributed to final consumers—value is created. The perceived benefit B represents the value that consumers derive from the finished good. The cost, C, represents the value that is *sacrificed* to convert raw inputs into finished products. *Value-created* is the difference between the value that resides in the finished good and the value that is sacrificed to produce the finished good:

$$\text{Value-created} = \text{Perceived Benefit to Final Customer} - \text{Cost of Inputs}$$
$$= B - C$$

where B and C are expressed per unit of the final product.[10]

The total value-created must be divided between consumers and producers. To see this, consider a product that requires only one step in the vertical chain— the conversion of raw goods into finished goods. As discussed above, consumers do not receive the benefit B for nothing; they must pay a price for it. Consumer surplus, $B - P$, represents the portion of the value-created that the consumer ultimately "captures." The seller keeps a portion of P and uses the rest to pay for the labor, capital, and materials used to convert unfinished components into finished

---

[10]C thus represents the *average cost* of production (as opposed to the total cost), inclusive of all the inputs used in the production and sale of the good. If, for example, the finished good is a barrel of beer, C would be the cost of the labor, capital, and materials used to produce and market the beer, expressed on a per-barrel basis.

products. The producer's profit margin $P - C$ represents the portion of the value-created that it captures. This leads to an important insight. Adding together consumer surplus and the producer's profit gives us the value-created expressed as the sum of consumer surplus and profit:

$$\text{Value-created} = \text{Consumer Surplus} + \text{Producer's Profit}$$
$$= (B - P) + (P - C)$$
$$= B - C$$

Figure 12.5 depicts value-created schematically.[11] The total area of the rectangle is the perceived benefit B. Deducting the unshaded area representing costs C leaves us with the value-created, $B - C$. The price P determines how much of the value-created is captured by sellers as profit and how much is captured by buyers as consumer surplus.

FIGURE 12.5
THE COMPONENTS OF VALUE-CREATED.

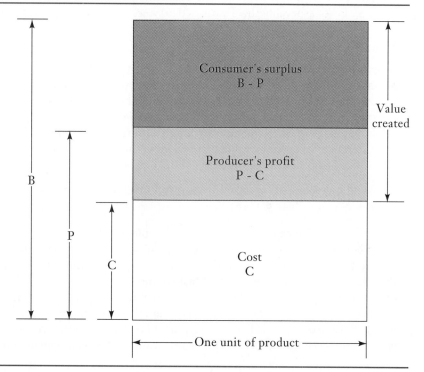

The overall area of the rectangle in the figure equals the perceived benefit B. Deducting the rectangle representing the cost C leaves the shaded region, which is value-created. Value-created can be seen to equal the sum of consumer surplus and producer profit.

[11]This is based on a similar diagram in Chapter 4 of Ghemawat, P., *Commitment: The Dynamic of Strategy*, New York: Free Press, 1991.

◆◆◆

ℰXAMPLE 12.1

THE DIVISION OF THE VALUE-CREATED IN THE SALE OF BEER AT A BASEBALL GAME

In general, filling in numbers for the diagram in Figure 12.5 is difficult because B is hard to measure. But when the product is sold under conditions of monopoly and no reasonable substitutes are available, B can be approximated by making some simplifying assumptions about the nature of the market demand curve. An example of a product sold under these circumstances is beer at a baseball game. Because it is unlikely that a purchaser of beer would regard soft drinks as a close substitute and since patrons are not allowed to bring in their own beer, the stadium concessionaire has as tight a monopoly on the market as one could imagine.

The first step is to estimate B. If we assume that the demand curve for beer is linear, then the relationship between per-unit consumer surplus $B - P$ and the price P is given by

$$B - P = .5P/\eta$$

where η is the price elasticity of demand at price P.[12] The price of a 20 oz cup of beer sold at Cincinnati's Riverfront stadium in 1988 was $2.50.[13] The stadium concessionaire, Cincinnati Sports Service, pays the distributor $.20 per cup for this beer, pays royalties to the City of Cincinnati—$.24 per cup—and the Cincinnati Reds—$.54 per cup—and an excise tax of $.14 per cup. The concessionaire's marginal cost is thus *at least* $1.12 per 20 oz cup of beer. If we assume that $2.50 represents the profit-maximizing monopoly price, then the price elasticity of demand η at $2.50 must be at least 1.8.[14] Using the formula above, this implies that consumer surplus must (on average) be *no greater than* $.69 per 20 oz cup of beer.

---

[12]The derivation of this relationship is not important. However, for interested readers, here goes: Total (as opposed to per-unit) consumer surplus can be shown to equal the area under the demand curve above the price. For a linear demand curve given by the formula $P = a - bQ$ (where Q is total demand), this area is given by $.5bQ^2$. Consumer surplus per unit is thus given by $.5bQ = .5P(bQ/P)$. But the term in parentheses is the reciprocal of the price elasticity of demand; i.e., $\eta = P/bQ$. Thus, per-unit consumer surplus is given by $.5P/\eta$.

[13]This and all subsequent data come from "Sports and Suds: The Beer Business and the Sports World Have Brewed Up a Potent Partnership," *Sports Illustrated*, August 8, 1988, pp. 68–82.

[14]Again, the details of this derivation are not important, but for interested readers here they are: From the Economics Primer, the optimal monopoly price is given by $(P - MC)/P = 1/\eta$. Thus, if $2.50 is the monopoly price, $(2.50 - MC)/2.50 = 1/\eta$. Since $MC \geq \$1.12$, straightforward algebra implies $\eta \geq 1.8$.

Table 12.1 shows the division of value in the sale of the beer using $.69 per cup as our estimate of consumer surplus. It is clear that the brewer captures only a small fraction of the value that is created.[15] By contrast, by controlling the access of the concessionaire to the stadium and to the event, the City of Cincinnati and the Cincinnati Reds are able to capture a significant fraction of the value that is created. Their ability to capture value stems from the fact that prospective concessionaires are willing to compete for the right to monopolize this market. As a result, the city and the Reds can extract a significant portion of the monopoly profit that would otherwise flow to the concessionaire.

TABLE 12.1
DIVISION OF VALUE IN THE SALE OF BEER AT RIVERFRONT STADIUM

Consumer Surplus $.69
Profit to Sports Service ? . . . .$1.38 Sports Service's Costs (labor, materials, insurance, etc.) ?
Profit to Cincinnati Reds $.54
Profit to City of Cincinnati $.20
Taxes $.14
Distributor's Profit ? . . . .$.10 Distributor's Costs (excl. price paid to brewer) ?
Brewer's Profit $.03
Brewer's Costs $.07

---

[15]Without knowing the production costs of Sports Service or the distributor, it is not possible to pin down the actual amount of value that is created through the vertical chain. It should be clear, however, that whatever it is, the brewer captures only a small portion of it.

Value-Creation and Competitive Advantage

No business can exist without creating positive value. If $B - C$ was negative, there would be no price that consumers would be willing to pay for the product that simultaneously covered its production and sales costs. Vacuum tubes, rotary dial telephones, and dedicated word processing units are all examples of products that at one time created positive value, but because of changes in tastes and technology no longer create enough benefits to consumers to justify their production.

To achieve a competitive advantage—to outperform its industry norm—a business must not only create positive value, it must create more value than its competitors, that is, generate a higher $B - C$. This is a simple but powerful insight. The reason it is true follows from our earlier discussion of the competitive implications of consumer surplus. That discussion suggested that competition among firms could be envisioned as a process whereby firms "bid" for consumers on the basis of consumer surplus. The firm whose product characteristics and price offer a particular consumer the greatest amount of consumer surplus will get that consumer's business. Because value-created, $B - C$, is the sum of consumer surplus, $B - P$, and profit, $P - C$, a firm that creates more value than its competitor will be able to match the consumer surplus "bids" of its competitors and end up with a higher profit on the sale. In a market equilibrium in which all firms have attained consumer surplus parity, the firm that creates more value will be more profitable than its rivals.

Understanding why a firm can create value and whether it can continue to do so in the future is a necessary first step in diagnosing a firm's potential for achieving a competitive advantage in the marketplace. Diagnosing the sources of value-creation requires an understanding of why the firm's business exists and what its underlying economics are.[16] This, in turn, involves an understanding of how the firm's products serve consumer needs better than potential substitutes; the technology of production, distribution, and sales; and the underlying structure of the business's costs (e.g., which costs are sensitive to production volume; how costs vary with nonproduction activities, such as sales and marketing; how costs change with cumulative experience).

Projecting the firm's prospects for creating value in the future also involves critically evaluating how the business's fundamental economic foundations are likely to evolve over time. Perhaps the most basic of all is the question of whether changes in market demand or the conditions of technology are likely to threaten how the firm creates value. Although this point seems transparent, it is easily overlooked by firms in the throes of month-to-month battles for market share with their immediate rivals. Evaluating future prospects is also difficult due to the sheer complexity of predicting the future and the risks involved in acting on such predictions.

---

[16]These questions are taken up in greater detail in Chapter 13, which presents a number of frameworks and analytical techniques for diagnosing the sources of competitive advantage.

The common history of an industry may also dull managers to the prospects for change. Threats to a firm's ability to create value often come from outside its immediate group of rivals and may not just threaten the firm, but the whole industry as well. Honda's foray into motorcycles in the early 1960s occurred within segments that the dominant producers at the time—Harley-Davidson and British Triumph—had concluded were unprofitable. IBM's initial dominance in the PC market may well have diverted its attention from the serious threat that the PC and related products, such as work stations, had for its core business of mainframes. The revolution in mass merchandising created by Wal-Mart occurred in out-of-the-way locations that companies like K-Mart and Sears had rejected as viable locations for large discount stores.

◆◆◆

EXAMPLE 12.2

HOW BANC ONE CREATES VALUE

In banking, there are few better examples of superior value creation than Banc One, a "superregional" bank headquartered in Columbus, Ohio.[17] Banc One is the second largest U.S. bank holding company in market value and the eighth largest in total assets. Banc One has consistently outperformed its industry. Boasting an average return on equity of 17 percent, Banc One has been the most profitable of the 25 largest U.S. banks over the decade 1983–93. This strong performance is reflected in the price of Banc One's shares. Between 1977 and 1993, Banc One's stock price (adjusted for stock splits) rose from $3 per share to $36 per share, and the ratio of its market value to book value had risen to nearly 200 percent by the end of 1993.

Banc One has been able to generate persistently high profitability through a threefold strategy implemented under the stewardship of the McCoy family:[18]

[17]The information in this example comes from several public sources, including Banc One annual reports for various years, Hoover handbooks for various years, Morgan Stanley and UBS investment reports, the *Wall Street Journal*, and the "Banc One: 1993," Harvard Business School case 9-394-043.

[18]John H. McCoy began the family reign at the bank in 1935, when he assumed control of what was then called the City National Bank and Trust. John G. McCoy succeeded his father in 1958 and formed the First Banc Group of Ohio in 1967. This group became Banc One in 1979. (The odd spelling of Banc is due to a state law restricting the use of the term "bank" to single-branch operations.) In 1984, John G. McCoy retired and was succeeded by his son John B. McCoy as CEO and President.

[19]Retail banking refers to banking activities (e.g., savings accounts, consumer loans) focused on households. Middle-market banking refers to banking activities focused on medium-sized firms (i.e., firms with sales between roughly $5 million and $150 million per year).

- A focus on retail and middle-market banking[19]
- Consistent investments in new product and technological innovations
- Skill in managing growth through acquisitions, which combines pricing discipline during the acquisition process with cost discipline after acquisition

The first part of Banc One's strategy—the focus on retail and middle-market banking—is built on the development of a network of branch banks in local markets with moderate to low levels of competition. Local branches are frequently run by local managers who are retained after their bank has been acquired by Banc One. Local boards of directors are also retained. Retaining local management and boards guarantees that the knowledge critical for generating profitable business in these markets will be accessible to Banc One. In addition, it preserves relationships with the local business community that the branch has built up over the years. At the corporate level, the bank provides strong centralized financial and credit controls for its branches through an elaborate management information control system, as well as a continuing program of professional training for branch managers.

The second part of Banc One's strategy emphasizes the development of new banking products and technologies. When John G. McCoy assumed control of the bank in 1958, he demanded that 3 percent of profits go toward research, although it was not clear at the time what "research" in banking meant. Since that time, by virtue of its technological innovations, Banc One has developed extensive skills in transactions processing and information management. Banc One has also been innovative and ahead of the rest of the banking industry with products and services, such as bank credit cards, automated teller machines (first to introduce ATMs in 1971), and loans to electronic tax filers in advance of their refunds. The bank has also experimented in banking practices that depart from industry norms, such as the use of extended daily and weekend hours as a convenience to consumers. Finally, due to industrywide changes in the nature of banking, such as deregulation and disintermediation (the growth of financial products and services that do not require the services of traditional banks as intermediaries), Banc One has experimented with products that have not been traditionally offered by banks. In particular, it has growing lines of business in trust administration, securities, and insurance.

The final part of Banc One's strategy is its acquisition program. Since 1968, Banc One has acquired over 100 banks and has developed skills in pricing acquisition targets and integrating acquired banks into its branch network. Banc One's pricing discipline is evident in its willingness to abandon potential acquisitions if they threaten to reduce its stock price. An example of this was the February 1994 decision not to acquire FirsTier Financial, following a slide in Banc One's share price. Banc One's skills in integration are evident in the willingness of potential targets to accept Banc One as an acquirer, even when its price is lower than that of other bidders.

Banc One's strategy creates superior value in numerous ways. For example, it achieves substantial economies of scale and scope in transaction processing and data processing operations. Banc One has sought volume in transactions by expanding its credit card operations, contracting with other banks to process their transactions, and teaming up with Merrill Lynch to process transactions for its cash management accounts. The size of Banc One's branch network is also a source of economies of scale in training and corporate staff functions. In addition, the large number of branches gives corporate headquarters detailed benchmarks against which individual branch managers can be compared. This facilitates monitoring and control of branch operations and sharpens the incentives of local branches to be cost efficient and to seek new business. The branch network also allows for economies of scope in that it can be used to distribute new products to existing customers without an investment in new channels. Along with its cost advantage through scale and scope economies, Banc One's new product innovations allow it to provide superior benefits to consumers. Banc One's strength in generating a stream of new product and service innovations is especially important, since new products in banking can be readily imitated by competitors.

It is also important to note that Banc One's strategy effectively counteracts the Five Forces discussed in Chapter 7. It focuses on areas of banking, such as transactions processing, where competitive pressures are not as severe as they are in traditional banking services, such as lending and deposit-taking. Banc One also has few large corporate clients, which blunts buyer power. For example, until recently Banc One had no loans outstanding greater than $70 million. In addition, the bank has a diversified loan portfolio, with few real estate loans or loans to lesser developed countries, areas which have posed major problems to other large banks. Finally, Banc One's emphasis on acquiring banks in medium to small local markets shields its branches from entry and makes its competitive advantage in these markets more sustainable.

◆ ◆

*E*XAMPLE 12.3

VALUE CREATION AT PROCHNIK[20]

Consistent value creation is hard enough for a firm and its managers to do in the absence of dramatic environmental change. Competition, even under a constant set of technological and regulatory conditions, will keep most firms from earning supranormal returns on a continuing basis. When environmental conditions change dramatically, however, the value-creation problem facing the firm and its managers becomes even more difficult, because the basic ways in which the firm has grown used to creating value become suspect and the firm's skills are no longer valuable. This, in turn, brings the firm's ultimate survival into question.

[20]This example is based on materials from "Prochnik: Privatization of a Polish Clothing Manufacturer," Harvard Business School case 9-394-038.

This situation of radical environmental change was what faced the Polish clothing firm, Prochnik, in 1990, as it became one of the first five state enterprises to be privatized by the Polish government and to be listed in 1991 on the newly formed Polish stock exchange. While Prochnik had been a star performer and a strong exporter to the West under Communism, the post-Communist era was one in which most of the firm's strengths disappeared and its managers were forced to develop new skills and find new market bases for value creation.

Prochnik began operations in 1945 as a supplier of army uniforms to the Polish government. By 1949, the firm's line had expanded to include consumer products. By 1960, Prochnik had come to specialize in producing men's raincoats and had begun exporting them to Western Europe, the United States, and the USSR. By the 1980s, the firm had greatly expanded its productive capacity and exported approximately 70 percent of its output to the United States and European markets and 15 percent of its output to the USSR. In achieving such growth, Prochnik had gained a reputation as Poland's leading producer of men's coats.

Prochnik's past success made it natural that it would be one of the first firms selected for privatization in Poland. Since the success of the past was expected to continue after Communism, the first management team of the newly independent firm was made up of former managers of the firm from the Communist era and was headed by Longin Barski, who had been Prochnik's general director since 1980. Prochnik's initial stock offering sold quickly to domestic and foreign investors.

With the fall of Communism, however, the basis of Prochnik's export success collapsed. The market in the former USSR dried up, while the firm's products lost sales in the West as the Polish government discontinued export subsidies. In addition, Prochnik experienced sharp rises in raw material costs. None of the firm's Communist-era skills seemed to persist into the new era. This change in fortune made investors concerned and led Prochnik's stock price to fall to one fifth of its initial value. It also led to a large management shakeup, which eventually removed Barski and his assistants. Wojciech Kolignan was hired to replace Barski as president of Prochnik's executive committee. Kolignan was a former Prochnik manager, who was well-known and respected in the firm as the manager behind the success of its raincoat business and as somebody who was highly knowledgeable about the Polish fashion industry.

At the urging of prominent investors and with the aid of some consultants, Kolignan and his managers developed a five-part strategy for turning Prochnik around. It targeted high-income customers, focused on the domestic market, located high-paying clients in the West, expanded its product line (possibly to include women's clothes), and attempted to reduce operating costs. The strategy, in part, reflected the necessities of the post-Communism environment in its focus on domestic customers and cost-cutting. The new strategy, however, built on Prochnik's high-quality reputation to foster a differentiation that, if successful, offered the opportunity for persistent profitability in a competitive business.

Prochnik's strategy appears to be working. Costs have come down, while sales per employee have increased substantially. In addition, the price of Prochnik's stock had risen by early 1993 to more than twice its initial offering price. Prochnik's market share has also increased in high-quality product lines, as well as in women's apparel. While Prochnik has been successful, its prospects for future growth are uncertain, due to resource constraints, limits on the size of important domestic market niches, and the likelihood of increased competition from foreign (especially German) rivals if the firm is too successful.

The story of Prochnik shows how much influence knowledgeable and respected managers can have in fostering a value-creation strategy in their firms. Prochnik's flexibility in readjusting its efforts and developing new products can also be attributed to its lack of sunk assets, such as heavy capital goods, which made asset redeployment easier in the face of environmental pressures. In more capital-intensive industries (such as the Gdansk shipyards), such turnarounds were not possible.

Value-Creation and the Value Chain

In Chapter 2, we discussed the *value chain* as a technique for describing the vertical chain of production. The value chain is also a useful device for thinking about how value is created in an organization.[21] The value chain essentially depicts the firm as a collection of value-creating activities, such as production operations, marketing and distribution, and logistics, as shown in Figure 12.6. Each activity in the value chain can potentially add to the benefit B that consumers get from the firm's product and each can add to the cost C that the firm incurs in producing and selling the product. Of course, the forces that influence the benefits created and cost incurred vary significantly across activities.

In practice, it is often difficult to isolate the impact that an activity has on the value that the firm creates. To do so requires estimating the incremental perceived benefit that an activity creates and the incremental cost associated with the activity. However, when different stages produce finished or semifinished goods that can be valued using market prices, it is possible to estimate the incremental value-created by distinctive parts of the value chain. This is called *value-added analysis*. The appendix to this chapter presents a fuller explanation and an example of value-added analysis.

Analyzing competitive advantage involves looking not only at the firm's value chain, but at the entire vertical chain of production, as discussed in Chapters 2 through 4. Those chapters stressed that value can be created through judicious make-or-buy decisions that are sensitive to conditions of technology (e.g., scale economies) and transactions costs (e.g., asset specificity). For example, reducing the risk of the holdup problem through vertical integration can lead to a greater investment in relationship-specific assets, which can often lower overall production costs. An important part of the search for competitive advantage involves reevaluating the organization of the firm's vertical chain to see if past make-or-buy deci-

---

[21]The concept of the value chain was developed by Michael Porter. See Chapter 2 of *Competitive Advantage*, New York: Free Press, 1985.

Figure 12.6
Michael Porter's value chain.

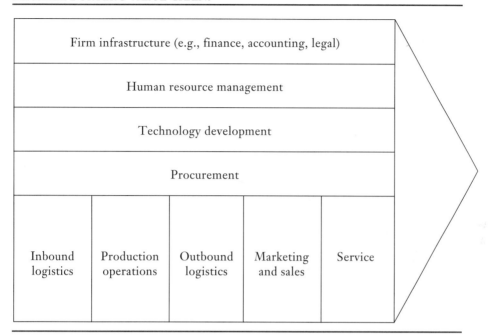

The value chain depicts the firm as a collection of value-creating activities. Porter distinguishes between five primary activities (inbound logistics, production operations, outbound logistics, marketing, and sales and service) and four support activities (firm infrastructure activities, such as finance and accounting, human resources management, technology development, and procurement).

sions are still justified. If vertical integration was initially justified by high transactions costs, it may eventually become inefficient and a source of competitive *disadvantage* if, because of changes in technology, dedicated assets are no longer critical for achieving production efficiency.

Value-Creation, Resources, and Capabilities

The value chain identifies the activities within the firm that create value. But a firm creates *more value* than competitors only by performing some or all of these activities better than they do. This, in turn, requires that the firm possess *resources* and *capabilities* that its competitors do not have; otherwise, any strategy for creating superior value could be immediately copied.[22] *Resources* are firm-specific assets, such as patents and trademarks, brand-name reputation, installed base, organizational

---

[22]This point is developed in greater detail in Chapter 14.

culture, and workers with firm-specific expertise or know-how. Resources differ from nonspecialized assets or factors of production, such as buildings, raw materials, or unskilled labor, in that they cannot be easily duplicated or acquired by other firms in well-functioning markets. Resources can *directly affect* the ability of a firm to create more value than other firms. For example, a large installed base or an established reputation for quality may make the firm's B higher than its rivals. Resources also *indirectly impact* value creation because they serve as the basis of the firm's capabilities.

Capabilities are clusters of activities that a firm does especially well in comparison with other firms.[23] Capabilities might reside within particular business functions (e.g., Procter and Gamble's skills in brand promotion or American Airlines' capabilities in yield management). Alternatively, they may be linked to particular technologies or product designs (e.g., Honda's legendary skill in working with small internal combustion engines and power trains or Canon's proficiencies in optics and precision mechanics).[24] Or they might reside in the firm's ability to manage linkages between elements of the value chain or coordinate activities across it (e.g., an important element in Ford's resurgence in the mid-1980s and its ability to outperform General Motors over the past 10 years was its ability to shorten the time between a product's conception and its introduction, which in turn required proficiency at managing linkages across the design, marketing, engineering, and manufacturing functions of the business).[25]

Whatever their basis, capabilities have several key common characteristics:

1. They are typically valuable across multiple products or markets.

2. They are embedded in what Richard Nelson and Sidney Winter call *organizational routines*—well-honed patterns of performing activities inside an organization.[26] This implies that capabilities can persist even though particular individuals leave the organization.

3. They are tacit; that is, they are difficult to reduce to simple algorithms or procedure guides.

Chapters 2 and 5 discussed the implication of point 1 for the vertical and horizontal boundaries of the firm. Points 2 and 3 have important implications for the sustainability of competitive advantages built upon organizational capabilities and will be developed more fully in Chapter 14.

---

[23]Other terms for this concept include distinctive competences and core competences.

[24]It is this type of capability that C.K. Prahalad and Gary Hamel emphasize in their notion of "core competence." See "The Core Competence of the Corporation," *Harvard Business Review*, May–June 1990, pp. 79–91.

[25]This is what George Stalk, Philip Evans, and Lawrence Shulman emphasize in their notion of "capabilities." See "Competing on Capabilities: The New Rules of Corporate Strategy," *Harvard Business Review*, March–April 1992, pp. 57–69.

[26]Nelson, R.R. and S.G. Winter, *An Evolutionary Theory of Economic Change*, Cambridge, MA: Belknap, 1982.

Resources and capabilities should be distinguished from *key success factors.*[27] Key success factors refer to the skills and assets a firm must possess to achieve profitability in a particular market. Many key success factors involve identifying the appropriate firm boundaries, as detailed in the first section of this text. As such, they should be thought of as market-level characteristics, rather than unique to individual firms. Possessing an industry's key success factors is a *necessary condition* for achieving competitive advantage, but it is not a *sufficient condition*. For example, for a firm to achieve competitive success as a distributor of athletic footwear, it is necessary to have the capability to develop new designs, manage a network of suppliers and distributors, and create marketing campaigns. But simply providing such services is not enough. All of the large footwear firms have product development teams, supply and distribution networks, and large marketing budgets. But only a few firms, such as Nike, excel at these activities to such an extent that they can create more value than their competitors.

Resources, capabilities, and key success factors have in common that they are predictors of a firm's profitability. While the conceptual differences between them are clear, distinguishing one from the others may not be easy in particular situations. For example, a key success factor may be a requirement for success for all firms in an industry, but it may also be a distinctive capability for specific firms.

The manageability of resources, capabilities, and key success factors is also important. Just because some activity or condition can be associated with firm performance does not imply that the managers of a firm can manipulate that factor to its advantage. For example, a central location in an urban area may be the source of a retailer's competitive advantage, but the ability of other firms to duplicate that resource advantage is obviously limited by the scarcity of similarly attractive plots of land. The limits to manageability are often most clear in the case of capabilities. Because capabilities are often tacit, replicating other firms' distinctive capabilities is likely to be very difficult. This point will be developed in more detail in Chapter 14.

$\mathcal{E}$XAMPLE 12.4

MEASURING CAPABILITIES IN THE PHARMACEUTICAL INDUSTRY

Drawing upon detailed quantitative and qualitative data obtained from 10 major firms, Rebecca Henderson and Iain Cockburn attempt to measure resources and capabilities associated with new drug research in the pharmaceutical industry.[28]

---

[27]The concept of key success factors was developed by Hofer, C. and D. Schendel, *Strategy Formulation: Analytical Concepts*, St. Paul, MN: West, 1977.

[28]Henderson, R. and I. Cockburn, "Measuring Core Competence? Evidence from the Pharmaceutical Industry," Massachusetts Institute of Technology, working paper, January 1994.

Though drug discovery is not the only skill that firms must possess in order to compete effectively in the pharmaceutical business, it is an extremely important one. Henderson and Cockburn hypothesize that research productivity (measured as the number of patents obtained per research dollar invested) depends on three classes of factors: the composition of a firm's research portfolio; firm-specific scientific and medical know-how; and the firm's distinctive capabilities. The composition of the research portfolio is important because it is easier to achieve patentable discoveries in some areas than in others. For example, for the past 20 years, investments in cardiovascular drug discovery have been consistently more productive than investments in cancer research. Firm-specific know-how is critical because the conduct of modern drug research requires highly skilled scientists from a variety of disciplines, such as biology, biochemistry, and physiology. Henderson and Cockburn use measures such as the firm's existing stock of patents as proxies for idiosyncratic firm know-how.

Henderson and Cockburn hypothesize that two capabilities are likely to be especially significant in new drug research. The first is skill at encouraging and maintaining an extensive flow of scientific information from the external environment to the inside of the firm. In pharmaceuticals much of the fundamental science that lays the groundwork for new discoveries is created outside the firm. It seems natural that a firm's ability to take advantage of this externally generated information is an important determinant of its success in making new drug discoveries. Henderson and Cockburn measure the extent of this capability through variables such as the firm's reliance on publication records in making promotion decisions; its geographic proximity to major research universities; and the extent of its involvement in joint research projects with major universities.

The second capability they focus on is skill at encouraging and maintaining an extensive flow of information across disciplinary boundaries inside the firm. This is likely to be important because successful new drug discoveries require the integration of knowledge across different scientific disciplines. For example, successful commercial development of HMG CoA reductase inhibitors (drugs that inhibit cholesterol synthesis in the liver) depended on pathbreaking work at Merck on three disciplinary fronts: pharmacology, physiology, and biostatistics. Henderson and Cockburn measure this capability with variables such as the extent to which the research in the firm was coordinated through cross-disciplinary teams and the existence of a single individual with authority to make critical resource allocation decisions in research. The former would be expected to facilitate the flow of information across disciplines, while the latter would be expected to inhibit it.

Henderson and Cockburn's study indicates that differences in firms' capabilities explain a considerable amount of the variability in firms' research productivity. For example, a firm that explicitly rewards research publications is about 40 percent more productive than one that does not. A firm that organizes by cross-disciplinary research teams is about 25 percent more productive than one that does not.

Does this mean that a firm that switches to a team-based research organization will immediately increase its output of patents per dollar by 40 percent? Probably not. This and other measures used by Henderson and Cockburn should be thought of as proxies for deeper resource-creation or integrative capabilities. For example, a firm that rewards publications may have an advantage at recruiting the brightest scientists. A firm that organizes by teams may have a collegial atmosphere that is particularly well suited for team-based organizations to thrive. A team-based organization inside a firm lacking in collegiality may be far less likely to generate increases in research productivity. These observations go back to the point made earlier. It is often far easier to identify distinctive capabilities once they exist than to manage them into existence.

Example 12.5

Time-Based Competition

George Stalk and Thomas Hout have argued that the capability to minimize time in innovation, marketing, production, and logistics is becoming an increasingly important driver of competitive advantage.[29] Time-based competitors, they argue, are able to offer greater varieties of products at lower costs than rivals who take longer to innovate and react to changes in the marketplace.

Drawing from their consulting experiences. Stalk and Hout developed a number of "rules" to characterize the potential benefits that come from being a time-based competitor:

- *The .05 to 5 rule:* Most products and services receive value for only .05 to 5 percent of the time they spend within the value chain. The remainder of time is spent on activities (e.g., order processing, inspection time, and storage time) that do not directly add value.

- *The 3/3 rule:* The amount of time the product spends within the vertical chain is composed more or less equally of

    - The time it takes to process the batch the product is a part of

    - The time it takes to do necessary rework (e.g., fix defects)

    - The time it takes management to decide to send the batch to the next step in the vertical chain (e.g., the time it takes a manufacturer to prepare an order to assemble a finished product from the completed subassemblies)

- *The 1/4–2–20 rule:* For every quartering of the time required to process a product, labor and working capital productivity doubles, resulting in a 20 percent reduction in costs.

---

[29]Stalk, G. and T. Hout, *Competing Against Time: How Time-Based Competition Is Reshaping Global Markets*, New York: Free Press, 1990.

- *The 3 × 2 rule:* Time-based competitors, such as Thomasville in furniture or Atlas in industrial doors, have been able to outgrow their industries by a factor of 3 and increased profit margins by a factor of 2.

The first three rules have to do with the opportunities that exist for creating value by reducing time consumption. The 3 × 2 rule, by contrast, has to do with the competitive implications of time-based competition. It is important to keep this rule in perspective, though. Achieving triple the industry growth rate and twice its profit margin may well be the fruits of a distinctive capability in minimizing cycle times. But to the extent that *all* firms in a market become successful time-based competitors, speed ceases to be a *distinctive* capability, and the growth and profitability advantages that Stalk and Hout emphasize will not materialize.

Value Creation versus Value Redistribution

The idea that competitive advantage requires that a firm create value to outperform competitors contrasts sharply with the view, implicit in much of the corporate diversification activity of the 1970s and 1980s, that a firm can succeed solely through its skills in bargaining with suppliers and buyers or outguessing the market in targeting undervalued firms for acquisition. These skills have much more to do with *redistributing existing value* than *creating new value.* The problem with building strategy around value redistribution, as opposed to value creation, is that the competition to redistribute value is likely to be fierce.[30] Michael Steinhardt, one of the most successful money managers ever, notes how difficult it is to outperform the market in identifying undervalued assets when he says: "Having traded for as long as I have gives me the opportunity to be 51 percent right rather than 50 percent right. Actually, it is more than a 1% edge, but it is not a big advantage like being right 80 percent of the time, or anything approaching that."[31]

Similar logic applies to the redistribution of value through skillful negotiation. Although the capacity to be a tough bargainer is not universal, there are enough tough bargainers out there, so that a firm could rarely be expected to outperform its competitors solely because it does a better job in squeezing its suppliers or its customers. Indeed, it is hard to find examples of firms that have succeeded solely because they have been able to push around their workers, suppliers, or buyers. The same can be said for firms or individuals who attempt to redistribute surplus by taking over other firms and cutting wages or firing workers. Even notorious hardball negotiators, such as Frank Lorenzo (former CEO of Texas Air), find that bargaining skill alone is no guarantee of business success. If, as we would suspect, there are plenty of raiders and turnaround artists who possess skill at renegotiating

---

[30]See Chapter 6 for a fuller discussion of this point.

[31]This quote is taken from Stewart, G. B., *The Quest for Value*, New York: Harper-Business, 1991.

labor contracts and firing workers, then the contest to take over firms to turn them around in this fashion is essentially an auction. In the bidding to win the auction, much of the profit that is available from surplus redistribution is competed away. This would explain the findings, discussed in Chapter 6, that acquiring firms on average do not profit from unrelated acquisitions.

The Role of Industry Structure

The total value created by a firm can be written:

Value-created = Value-created by average firm in industry + differential between firm's value-created and average industry value-created

The percentage of the value-created that a firm retains as profit therefore depends on (a) the percentage of the value retained by an *average firm* in its industry, and (b) the percentage of differential value-created the firm retains. Because each component is important, a firm that greatly outperforms its industry can still earn low profits in an absolute sense. For example, Southwest Airlines outperforms other carriers, but the Five Forces (discussed in Chapter 7) prevent the average carrier from retaining much value. Even a "high flier" like Southwest thus has low profits in comparison to firms in other industries. Conversely, a firm can perform at its industry norm and earn high profits in an absolute sense if industry conditions work to soften rivalry. For example, a favorable industry structure enables cigarette makers to retain a large share of the value-created in their industry, so even an average firm, such as Brown and Williamson, can be very profitable.[32]

The opportunities for retaining value-created will sometimes vary substantially along the vertical chain. This will in part be due to differences in the structure of the industry at each point along the chain. Figure 12.7 illustrates the division of value-created in the production of steel.[33] Producers of scrap, ingot, and billets capture only modest portions of the overall value-created. These industries offer few opportunities for sellers to differentiate themselves. As a result, they are characterized by strong price competition and low profitability. Distributors and component producers, by contrast, capture a relatively larger proportion of value-created. This is also, in part, a consequence of the industry structure in these businesses. For ex-

---

[32]Our analysis has glossed over an important public policy issue. We have spoken of value-created as though firms' activities' created a fixed pie that is divided among consumers and firms. However, the process of competition among firms in and of itself works to create additional value. Competition drives prices down, inducing consumers already in the market to purchase more of the product and enticing new consumers into the market. Competition thus expands the number of transactions in which value is created. This is one reason why competition is valuable for society as a whole even though it may be undesirable for firms whose profits are dissipated as a result and represents an important intellectual justification for antitrust laws designed to prevent firms from colluding to restrict competition.

[33]This figure is reproduced from Exhibit II in Hanna, A. M. and J. T. Lundquist, "Creative Strategies," *The McKinsey Quarterly*, 3, 1990, pp. 56–79.

FIGURE 12.7

DIVISION OF VALUE-CREATED IN THE PRODUCTION OF STEEL.

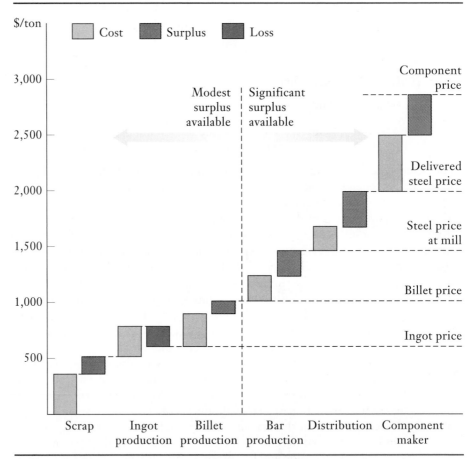

The horizontal axis in the figure shows different stages in the vertical chain for the production of steel. The vertical axis shows the price per ton of various kinds of unfinished and finished steel products. The shaded blocks show the profit (per ton) earned at each stage, while the clear blocks show the costs of production incurred at each stage, over and above the cost of purchasing the input from producers at the previous stage.

Source: Exhibit II in Hanna, A. M. and J. T. Lundquist, "Creative Strategies," *McKinsey Quarterly*, 3, 1990, pp. 56–79.

ample, steel distribution is essentially carried out in regional or local markets. Because the operation of a modern steel service center is characterized by nontrivial economies of scale (a typical service center might take up four city blocks in each direction), barriers to entry into a local or regional market are significant. In addition, through creative management of inventories and outbound logistics, distributors can create significant value that they share with their customers.

STRATEGIC POSITIONING: COST ADVANTAGE AND DIFFERENTIATION ADVANTAGE   ◆ ◆ ◆ ◆ ◆

The search for competitive advantage cannot be reduced to a formula or a simple algorithm. Even if such formulas or algorithms could be concocted, describing them in a textbook like this one would make them valueless because they would be accessible to everyone.

But while there is no single formula for success, it is possible to discern broad commonalities across industries in the different ways that firms position themselves to compete. For example, as discussed in the introduction, American Airlines' strategy in the airline business emphasizes frequent service, a comprehensive route structure, in-flight amenities, such as meals, "air-fones," and movies, and "extras," such as the opportunity to earn frequent flyer mileage. Southwest, by contrast, seeks to exploit its cost advantage (achieved in part, though not exclusively, through no-frills service) by offering low fares. In the delivered pizza business, Pizza Hut's strategy is built on its reputation for a quality pizza and product variety, while Little Caesar has positioned itself as the low-price alternative. In the nonprescription drug industry, Warner-Lambert and American Home Products have well-known branded products (e.g., Listerine mouthwash and Advil pain reliever) whose images are supported through extensive advertising, while Perrigo has succeeded by selling inexpensive imitations of branded products to mass merchandisers, such as K-Mart, Wal-Mart, and Target, who then resell them as house brands.

These examples suggest that it is useful to distinguish between two broad approaches to achieving competitive advantage. The first is to pursue *cost advantage*, seeking to attain a lower C while maintaining a B that is comparable to competitors. The second is to pursue *differentiation advantage*, seeking to offer a higher B, while maintaining a C that is comparable to competitors.[34] In this section, we discuss the economic and organizational logic of cost and differentiation advantage.

The Economic Logic of Cost Advantage

A firm with a cost advantage creates more value than its competitors by offering products that have a lower cost C, with the same, or perhaps lower, perceived benefit B. But even though a firm with a cost advantage may have a lower B than its competitors, its B disadvantage must be less than its C advantage, so that its value-created, $B - C$, is greater than that of its competitors.

There are three qualitatively different ways that this can occur. First, the firm can achieve *benefit parity* by offering the same B as its rivals. This could occur, for example, if a firm exploits economies of scale to lower its average costs relative to rivals who are producing exactly the same good, but at lower volumes. The cost advantage that a large producer of a commodity chemical can achieve over smaller rivals would be an example of this.

---

[34]Whether these approaches are mutually exclusive is taken up in greater detail below.

Second, the firm can achieve *benefit proximity*, which involves offering a B not too much less than competitors. This could occur if the firm automates processes that are better performed by hand, hires less skilled workers, purchases less expensive components, or does not maintain similar standards of quality control. Yamaha's cost advantage over traditional piano producers, such as Steinway, is a good example of this. When there is benefit proximity, the firm must underprice its rivals by more than enough to offset the lower B. Of course, this can be profitable only if the firm's cost advantage is bigger than the price differential between the firm and its competitors. If so, the firm can simultaneously increase consumer surplus and its own profit. Figure 12.8 illustrates this point. The value map depicts an industry in which all firms are initially offering a product with a price-quality

FIGURE 12.8
THE ECONOMIC LOGIC OF COST ADVANTAGE.

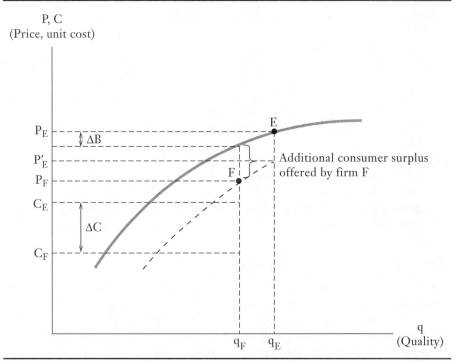

Existing producers in an industry offer a product with quality q_E, price P_E, and unit cost C_E. A new producer, firm F, is able to produce the product at a substantially lower cost, C_F, with only a small sacrifice in quality (q_F versus q_E). Firm F thus creates more value than existing competitors. By setting a price P_F below the solid indifference curve, firm F can share some of the additional value-created in the form of higher consumer surplus. This puts firm F on a lower indifference curve (represented by the dashed curved line). Even if existing competitors respond by lowering their prices to P'_E to restore consumer surplus parity, firm F will still enjoy the highest profit margin in the industry.

position at point E and an average production cost of C_E.[35] Suppose, now, one of these firms, through a combination of automation and cheaper components, can manufacture the product with a lower quality level, q_F but at a substantially lower cost, C_F. By judiciously lowering its price (e.g., to P_F), the low-cost firm can offer more consumer surplus than its competitors and thus increase its share of the market relative to rivals. Even if its competitors restored consumer surplus parity by lowering their prices to P_E', the low-cost firm still has a higher profit margin ($P_F - C_F$ versus $P_E' - C_E$).[36]

Finally, a firm may offer a product that is qualitatively different from its rivals. Firms can sometimes build a competitive advantage by redefining the product in ways that allow for substantial differences in benefits or costs relative to traditional definitions of the product. For example, a formerly high-margin product may be redefined to allow for economies of scale in production and distribution while still providing benefits to consumers. The Timex watch or the 19-cent Bic crystal pen are examples that come to mind. When a product is of much lower cost and quality than competing products, it can theoretically outcompete those products, assuming that the cost differential exceeds the quality differential. This may explain why many people continue to use the U.S. Postal Service rather than private delivery services, such as Federal Express: The cost savings are worth the lower quality.

The Economic Logic of Differentiation Advantage

A firm that creates a competitive advantage based on *differentiation* creates more value than its competitors by offering a product with higher B for the same, or perhaps higher, C. The differentiator can exploit its advantage by setting a price that allows it to offer higher consumer surplus than its rivals, while also achieving a higher profit margin. Figure 12.9 illustrates this point. Firm E sells a moderately priced product that provides a respectable quality, q_E. Its unit cost is C_E. Firm F offers a product with significantly higher quality q_F, and with unit cost C_F, it is only marginally more expensive to produce. From the value map in Figure 12.9, it can be seen that the additional benefit $\Delta B = B_F - B_E$ that consumers perceive from product F outweighs the extra cost of production. $\Delta C = C_F - C_E$, so firm F creates more value than firm E. Because it creates more value, firm F can "share" a portion of the extra value it creates with consumers by setting a price that lies below the solid indifference curve shown in Figure 12.9. Firm F thus offers higher

---

[35]A technical note: To keep the exposition as simple as possible, Figure 12.8 assumes that the market consists of consumers with identical preferences for product quality. Thus, we can represent the strategic position of firms in the market with reference to the indifference curve of a representative consumer in that market. Below, we discuss the implications of strategic positioning in a market where consumers' preferences for product quality differ.

[36]Alternatively, the higher-cost firms might seek their own sources of cost advantage by copying what the cost leader has done. The impediments to copy-cat strategies are discussed in Chapter 14.

FIGURE 12.9
THE ECONOMIC LOGIC OF DIFFERENTIATION ADVANTAGE.

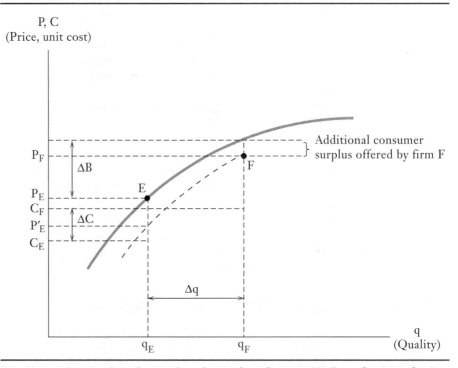

Firm E provides a moderately priced product with quality q_E, price P_E, and unit production cost C_E. Firm F offers a product with significantly higher quality q_F but which costs only a little extra to produce. The additional benefit ΔB provided by firm F more than offsets the additional cost ΔC, so F creates more value than E. By setting a price P_F that is slightly below the solid indifference curve on which firm E's price-quality position is located, firm F can "share" some of the extra value it creates with consumers in the form of higher consumer surplus and, as a result, gain market share at the expense of firm E. Even if firm E responds by cutting price to P'_E to restore consumer surplus parity with E (thus moving to the dashed indifference curve), firm F will still earn a higher profit margin than firm E.

consumer surplus than firm E and will gain market share at E's expense. Even if E responds by cutting its price to restore consumer surplus parity with F (thus, in effect, moving to the dashed indifference curve in Figure 12.9), F's profit margin will still be larger than E's.

As with cost advantage, parity and proximity are also important in differentiation. The differentiating firm's cost disadvantage must be small enough that the firm's value-created, $B - C$, exceeds that of its competitors. A successful differentiator might achieve *cost parity* (same C). A good example is the Japanese auto makers in the 1980s, whose family sedans (e.g., Honda Accord) were no more costly to produce than American-made models, but offered superior performance and reliability. A successful differentiator might instead achieve *cost proximity* (C not too much higher than competitors). Maytag, whose washing machines have much higher reliability and only slightly higher costs than rival brands, is a good example. Finally, a firm could offer substantially higher *B* and *C*, as occurred when Eli Lilly introduced the first cephalosporin, a "magic bullet" antibiotic. Cephalosporins cost much more to produce than available substitutes, such as penicillin, but have fewer side effects and attack a broader spectrum of bacteria.

Extracting Profits from Cost and Differentiation Advantage

Horizontal Differentiation and the Importance of the Price Elasticity of Demand

A seller that creates more value than its competitors would like to keep as much as possible of that value for itself in the form of profits. As we have stressed repeatedly, though, competition limits the firm's ability to capture profits. In the simple model presented in this chapter, competition would take an especially stark form. Because we have assumed that consumers have identical preferences, if a firm provides the highest consumer surplus to one consumer, it provides the highest consumer surplus to all consumers in the market. Competition then would resemble an auction: When a firm increases its consumer surplus "bid" slightly above competitors, it captures the entire market.[37] The auction would end only when no firm is able to submit a profitable consumer surplus "bid" that tops the "bids" submitted by rivals. This leads to two clear recipes for retaining profits for a firm that creates more value than its competitors.

- If a firm achieves a cost advantage (with no reduction in *B*), it can lower its price just below the unit cost of the next most efficient competitor. This makes it unprofitable for competitors to respond with price cuts of their own and thus allows the firm to capture the entire market.

- If a firm achieves a differentiation advantage (with no reduction in *C*), it can raise its price to the point just below unit cost *C plus* the additional benefit ΔB it creates relative to the competitor with the next highest *B*. To top this consumer surplus "bid," a competitor would be forced to cut price below unit cost, which would be unprofitable. At this price, then, the firm with the benefit advantage captures the entire market.

These rather unrealistic recipes result because when consumers have identical preferences, an infinitesimally small decrease in price or increase in quality leads to a large shift in market share. This would not be the case if the market is characterized by *horizontal differentiation* as well as *vertical differentiation*. As discussed in Chapter 8, vertical differentiation refers to situations in which sellers seek advantage by adding or enhancing product attributes that increase *B* for *all* consumers. What we have referred to as differentiation advantage in this chapter refers to ver-

---

[37]This is analogous to the Bertrand model of price competition studied in Chapter 8.

tical differentiation, not horizontal differentiation.[38] Horizontal differentiation arises when products possess attributes that increase B for *some* consumers but *decrease it for others*, and firms differ according to these attributes. For example, a brand's external packaging may make the brand more appealing to some consumers but less appealing to others. A retailer's location may be very convenient for some shoppers, but quite inconvenient for others.[39] Some consumers may have an intense loyalty to one brand of cola that other consumers would never consider purchasing, even at very low prices.

Horizontal differentiation is likely to be strong when there are a great many product attributes that consumers weigh in assessing overall benefit B, and there is substantial disagreement among consumers about the desirability of those attributes. Breakfast cereals, soft drinks, and automobiles are businesses in which horizontal differentiation is significant. Horizontal differentiation is likely to be weak when the product is simple, and there are only a few easily ranked attributes that matter to potential consumers. The production of metals, such as copper, or chemical compounds, such as tetraethyl lead, are businesses characterized by low levels of horizontal differentiation.

In markets where there is some degree of horizontal differentiation, a firm's price elasticity or quality elasticity of demand will no longer be infinite; that is, lowering price or boosting quality will attract some consumers, but others will not switch unless the differential in price or quality is large enough. When there is horizontal differentiation, the price elasticity of demand becomes a key determinant of the ability of sellers to extract profits from value creation and how they should go about doing so. Consider, first, a seller with a cost advantage. If the seller charges the same price as its competitors, it will increase its profits by virtue of having higher price-cost margins on sales to existing customers. This practice is known as *shadow pricing* and is common in health insurance markets, where low-cost Health Maintenance Organizations often set prices that are comparable to more costly forms of insurance. But if the price elasticity of demand is large (but not infinite)— that is, consumers are very price-sensitive because there is little horizontal differentiation among firms—shadow pricing is often not the optimal strategy. The firm will be able to increase profits even more by cutting price below competitors, thereby increasing its market share. This explains why airlines with low costs, such as Southwest or Midway, are not content to shadow price their competitors but instead offer much lower prices.

The Economics Primer points out that there is an inverse relationship between a firm's price elasticity of demand and its optimal price-cost margin—the larger the price elasticity of demand facing the seller, the lower its optimal price-cost margin. We conclude that when a firm competes in a business with low horizontal differentiation, a high price elasticity, and low margins, it should pass along a substantial

---

[38]Indeed, much of the discussion in the traditional strategic management literature implicitly considers the case of vertical differentiation.

[39]The implications of locational differences for price competition between firms are developed in an extended example in Chapter 8.

percentage of any cost advantage it may achieve to consumers, and it should profit from its cost advantage mainly through higher volume. If, by contrast, it competes in a business with high horizontal differentiation, a low price elasticity, and high margins, the firm should profit from its cost advantage mainly through higher margin, rather than higher volume.

The price elasticity of demand is also a key consideration in exploiting a benefit advantage. The extra benefit, whether it is based on superior product performance, better service, or higher reliability, will attract some customers who previously shopped elsewhere. New customers increase the firm's profits to the extent that the price exceeds the marginal cost on each additional sale. A critical determinant of the profitability of the benefit advantage, then, is the price-cost margin the firm earns on each additional customer it attracts because of the improvement, and this, in turn, depends on the price elasticity of demand. When the price elasticity of demand is low, so that price-cost margins are high, the firm obtains large incremental profits from a benefit improvement. We conclude that a strategy of seeking a benefit advantage is likely to be most profitable in businesses with high horizontal differentiation, low price elasticities of demand, and high margins.

Comparing Cost and Differentiation Strategies

Under what circumstances is one source of advantage likely to dominate the other? Though no definitive rules can be formulated, the underlying economics of the firm's product market and the current positions of firms in the industry help shape the relative desirability of one positioning strategy over the other.

Building competitive advantage on the basis of a superior cost position is likely to be relatively more attractive when:

- *Economies of scale and learning economies are potentially significant, but no firm in the market seems to be exploiting them.* Strategies aimed at "growing" market share and accumulating experience will give the firm a cost advantage that its smaller, less experienced rivals cannot match. If the market is growing, however, other firms may soon gain the scale and experience necessary to achieve the same cost position. The personal computer industry is an example where several firms, including IBM, Packard Bell, and Dell, appear to have fully exploited scale economies.

- *Opportunities for enhancing the product's perceived benefit B are limited by the nature of the product.* This might be the case for "commodities" products, such as chemicals and metals. If so, then, more opportunities for creating additional value may come from lowering C rather than from increasing B. Still, it is important to bear in mind that the drivers of differentiation include far more than just the physical attributes of the product and that opportunities may exist for differentiation through better postsale service, superior location, or more rapid delivery than competitors offer.[40]

---

[40]See Chapter 13 for a detailed discussion of benefit drivers.

- *Consumers are relatively price sensitive and are unwilling to pay much of a premium for enhanced product quality, performance, or image.* This would occur when most consumers are much more price sensitive than quality sensitive. Graphically, this corresponds to the case in which consumer indifference curves are relatively flat, indicating that a consumer is unwilling to pay much more for enhanced quality. Opportunities for additional value creation are much more likely to arise through cost reductions than through benefit enhancements. CBIS Federal, a subsidiary of Cincinnati Bell specializing in data processing services for government agencies, failed to understand this point, and thus was an ineffective competitor for government contracts. According to its former chief financial officer, "The government is lower-bidder oriented; they're driven by the lowest price. But CBIS tries to distinguish itself by being the best quality provider—that created overhead that made it difficult to compete (with other vendors)."[41]

- *The product is a search good rather than an experience good.* A *search good* is one whose objective quality attributes the typical buyer can easily access at the time of purchase. Examples include office furniture and (increasingly) personal computers. An *experience good* is a product whose quality can be assessed only after the consumer has used it for a while. Examples include technologically complex products, such as CD players and automobiles. With search goods, the potential for differentiation lies largely in enhancing the product's observable features. But if buyers can discern among different offerings, so can competitors, which raises the risk that the enhancements will be imitated. When this is so, the best opportunity for a firm to create a lasting competitive advantage will come in keeping its costs lower than competitors, while taking care to match their initiatives in product enhancement.

Building a competitive advantage based on superior differentiation is likely to be relatively more attractive when:

- *The typical consumer is willing to pay a significant price premium for attributes that enhance B.* This corresponds to the case in which the typical consumer's indifference curve is relatively steep. In this case, a firm that can differentiate its product by offering even a few additional features may be able to command a significant price premium. Gillette was counting on this effect when it launched its Sensor razor in 1990. It concluded that there was a significant number of men who were willing to pay a relatively high price for blades ($.75 per blade, implying a price premium of 100 percent over disposables, 25 percent over existing cartridge blades, such as Atra, and a 90 percent profit margin) that gave a better shave than disposables or cartridges.[42]

---

[41]"If Cincinnati Bell's So Good, Why's the Stock So Lousy?" *Cincinnati Enquirer*, April 17, 1994, p. H2. Cincinnati Bell sold CBIS Federal in 1993.

[42]"Gillette's Launch of Sensor," Case 9-792-028, Harvard Business School.

- *Economies of scale or learning are significant, and existing firms because of their size or cumulative experience are already exploiting them.* In this case, opportunities for achieving a cost advantage over these larger firms are limited and the best route toward value creation lies through horizontal differentiation—offering a product that is especially well tailored to a particular niche of the market. Microbreweries, such as the Boston Beer Company, have attempted to build a competitive advantage in this way.

- *The product is an experience good rather than a search good.* In this case, differentiation can be based on image, reputation, or credibility, which are more difficult to imitate or neutralize than objective product features or performance characteristics. Bose has made major inroads in stereophonic equipment by exploiting its reputation developed through product innovations that originally appealed to a few stereophiles willing to pay $1,000 or more for high-end speakers.

Implications for Functional Area Strategies

While the approach the firm chooses as a basis for competitive advantage is *guided by* the demand and technological characteristics of the product, it *guides* the operating strategies of the firm's functional areas: marketing, production, engineering, and so forth. Table 12.2 contrasts the characteristics of functional area strategies that typically correspond to the pursuit of cost and differentiation advantage.

Product and marketing strategies in a firm seeking cost advantage will often center on standardized products that can be mass produced and easily serviced. Attaining a differentiation advantage typically requires greater attention to the breadth of product line, the size of the advertising and promotion budget, the best use of warranties, and the amount of resources dedicated to customer service than will an approach emphasizing cost advantage.

In production operations, firms seeking a cost advantage will seek economies of scale in manufacturing and logistics, as well as efficiencies in inventory management. Firms seeking a differentiation advantage, on the other hand, will be more willing to forego such advantages in the hope of greater revenues obtained through higher prices. The need for additional capacity and inventory to allow flexible responses to unpredictable demand may force these firms to organize differently and incur additional costs relative to firms seeking a cost advantage.

A similar distinction is apparent with engineering and design activities. Firms seeking a cost advantage will design products to increase manufacturability or to meet a minimum set of performance standards across several markets (as is the case with so-called "global" firms that produce standardized products for multinational markets). Firms seeking differentiation advantage will design products to meet the needs of important customers or customer segments, even if it makes the product more difficult to manufacture and service.

With research and development activities, the differences between approaches concern both the level and type of activity. Firms pursuing a cost advantage will be

TABLE 12.2

IMPLICATIONS OF COMPETITIVE POSITIONING FOR FUNCTIONAL AREA STRATEGIES

	Competitive Position	
Functional Areas	Cost Advantage	Differentiation Advantage
Product and Marketing Strategies	- standardized products - narrow price-cost margins with prices lower than competition - little or modest product promotion or advertising - modest postsale servicing or maintenance	- customized products - wide price-cost margins, with prices higher than competition - emphasis on building product, image through branding, advertising, and product promotion - extensive postsale service/maintenance - generous warranties
Production Operations Strategies	- large mass-production facilities to exploit economies of scale - capacity added behind demand to ensure full utilization - products made to inventory, with tight controls on inventory levels	- willingness to sacrifice scale in favor of customization and flexible response to unpredictable customer demand - capacity added in anticipation of demand to ensure product availability and minimize chances of stockouts - products made to order
Engineering and Design	- products designed for manufacturability	- products designed to create benefits for customers or lower their costs
Research and Development Strategies	- R&D emphasizes process innovations, rather than new products or basic research	- R&D emphasizes product innovations and basic research more than process
Human Resources/ Organizations and Control Strategies	- "traditional" managerial style, characterized by formal procedure and rigid hierarchy - tough bargaining posture with workers - tight administrative systems emphasizing cost control	- less formal managerial style, fewer formal procedures, less rigid hierarchy to promote innovation and entrepreneurship - higher than average pay to attract skilled workers

more likely to rely on established and routinized technologies and thus will engage in less R&D activity than will firms pursuing a differentiation advantage. When cost-oriented firms engage in R&D, they are also more likely to focus on process innovations, designed to aid manufacturability, than product innovations, which aid product differentiation.

Finally, differences in competitive approaches are often associated with differences in human resource management practices. Pursuing cost advantage rather than differentiation advantage will imply different types of jobs, types of workers, numbers of workers, and pay and benefit issues. Firms pursuing a cost advantage, especially in low-growth industries with stable technologies, will be characterized by more specific and less discretionary jobs, less skilled but larger workforces, and more elaborate controls. The firm pursuing a differentiation advantage, on the other hand, is more likely to delegate decision making to lower-level employees who are closer to the customer, to rely more on employee inputs into decision making, and to have more intensive, albeit less formal, supervision, due to the difficulties these firms have in identifying the process by which jobs are done or the outcomes of good performance.

Of course, the functional area strategies shown in Table 12.2 represent polar cases. The situation of a particular firm is likely to be more complicated, since it may include elements of both cost and differentiation approaches. The notion that functional area strategies are linked to competitive positioning approaches is akin to the attempts of organizational theorists to link organizational configurations with product-market choices. Perhaps the best known work of this kind is by Robert Miles and Charles Snow, who developed a typology of generic strategies consisting of "defenders," "prospectors," and "analyzers."[43] Firms pursuing cost and differentiation advantage correspond to "defenders" and "prospectors" in the Miles and Snow typology, while their "analyzer" type is an intermediate position.

"Stuck in the Middle"

Can a firm successfully pursue both cost advantage and differentiation advantage? Michael Porter has argued that the pursuit of differentiation advantage is usually incompatible with the pursuit of cost advantage. Firms that attempt to pursue both strategies simultaneously, he argues, often become "stuck in the middle," providing less B than firms that have focused on pursuing a differentiation advantage and incurring a higher C than firms that have focused on seeking cost advantage.[44] Porter's argument is based on a simple economic tradeoff: Higher quality or better performing products often cost more to produce. This can occur for a variety of reasons. Producing a higher-quality product may involve more up-front design work, more expensive components, and better trained or more highly skilled labor. To the extent that differentiation is based on doing an especially good job meeting customer needs, it may also require more custom building and thus a less standardized production process. Higher advertising and promotion expenditures may be needed to shape consumer perceptions that the product is special, and greater spending on a sales force may be required if differentiation is created through superior customer service.

---

[43]Miles, R. and C. Snow, *Organizational Strategy, Structure, and Process*, New York: McGraw-Hill, 1978. For a related conceptual framework, see Miller, D. and P. Friesen, *Organizations: A Quantum View*, Englewood Cliffs, NJ: Prentice-Hall, 1984.

[44]See Chapter 2 of Porter, M., *Competitive Strategy*, New York: Free Press, 1980.

In practice, a firm's advantage is rarely based entirely on cost or differentiation. It is possible to cite examples of companies that seem to deliver a higher B than competitors at a lower C: Kellogg in breakfast cereals and Caterpillar in tractors are two examples that come to mind. These examples suggest that the tradeoff between differentiation and cost may not be as strong as the above arguments suggest. The results of empirical studies on the tradeoff between cost and differentiation are also mixed. While almost all studies find visible "footprints" of differentiation-based advantage and cost-based advantage, they also find that these strategies are not incompatible. For example, Danny Miller and Peter Friesen found that in consumer durables industries, firms that appeared to have achieved differentiation advantages in their industries also tended to operate newer plants, had significantly better-than-average capacity utilization, and had direct costs per unit that were significantly lower than the industry average. Firms that appeared to have achieved cost advantages also scored highly on measures of relative differentiation, such as product quality, and advertising and promotion expenses.[45]

From a theoretical perspective, several factors might weaken the observed tradeoff between differentiation and cost positions in an industry.

- *A firm that offers high-quality products increases its market share, which then reduces average cost because of economies of scale or the experience curve.* As a result, a firm might be able to achieve both a high-quality and a low-cost position in the industry. Figure 12.10 illustrates how. By pursuing a differentiation strategy, the firm raises its average cost at *each level of output*, represented by an upward shift in its average costs, from AC_0 to AC_1. But differentiation also shifts the firm's demand curve outward, from D_0 to D_1. Even if the firm raises its price, the movement to the new demand curve coupled with the fact that average cost is a decreasing function of output (reflecting economies of scale) implies that the firm's realized average cost actually goes down, from $AC_0(Q_0)$ to $AC_1(Q_1)$. Charles River Breeding Labs typified this situation in the 1970s with its germ-free technology for raising laboratory animals.[46] The first to adopt germ-free barrier breeding technologies, Charles River Breeders became the quality leader, moved down the experience curve, and established a superior cost position relative to its nearest competitors.

---

[45]Miller, D., and P.H. Friesen, "Porter's (1980) Generic Strategies and Quality: An Empirical Examination with American Data. Part I: Testing Porter," *Organization Studies*, 7, 1986, pp. 37–55. See also Phillips, L.W., D.R. Chang, and R.D. Buzzell, "Product Quality, Cost Position, and Business Performance: A Test of Some Key Hypotheses," *Journal of Marketing*, 47, Spring 1983, pp. 26–43; White, R.E., "Generic Business Strategies, Organizational Context and Performance: An Empirical Investigation," *Strategic Management Journal*, 7, 1986, pp. 217–231; Dess, G.G. and P.S. Davis, "Porter's (1980) Generic Strategies as Determinants of Strategic Group Membership and Organizational Performance," *Academy of Management Review*, 27, 1984, pp. 467–488.

[46]"Charles River Breeding Laboratories," Harvard Business School, Case 9-376-262.

FIGURE 12.10
ACHIEVING DIFFERENTIATION ADVANTAGE AND COST ADVANTAGE SIMULTANEOUSLY.

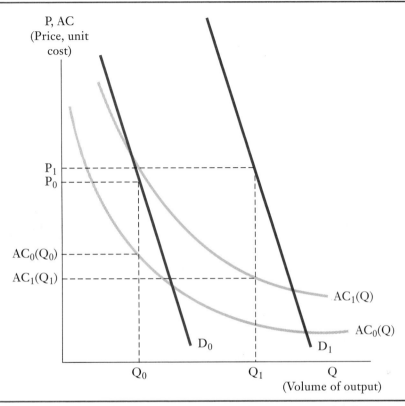

A firm that differentiates itself shifts its demand curve from D_0 to D_1 and shifts its average cost function upward from $AC_0(Q)$ to $AC_1(Q)$. Even if the firm raises its price, the movement to the new demand curve coupled with the fact that unit costs are a decreasing function of output implies that the firm's realized unit cost goes down from $AC_0(Q_0)$ to $AC_1(Q_1)$.

- *The rate at which accumulated experience reduces costs is greater for higher-quality products than for lower-quality products* The reason has to do with the fact that production workers must exercise more care to produce a higher-quality product, which will often lead to the discovery of bugs and defects that might be overlooked for a lower-quality product.[47]

---

[47]Phillips, L., D.R. Chang, and R. Buzzell, "Product Quality and Business Performance: A Test of Some Key Hypotheses," *Journal of Marketing*, 47, Spring 1983, pp. 26–43.

- *Inefficiencies muddy the relationship between cost position and differentiation position.* The argument that high quality is correlated with high costs ignores the possibility that firms may be producing inefficiently, that is, that their C is higher than it needs to be given their B. If so, then at any point in time, in most industries one might observe firms that create less B and have higher C than their more efficient counterparts. Indeed, the entire thrust of the total quality management (TQM) movement is to enable firms to improve production processes to increase B and reduce C.[48]

Figure 12.11 depicts cost and quality positions in the U.S. heavy-duty truck industry in the late 1970s.[49] If all firms were producing as efficiently as possible, but pursuing competitive advantages that emphasized different degrees of cost and differentiation, then firms' positions would line up along the upward-sloping line that we label the *efficiency frontier.* The efficiency frontier shows the lowest level of cost that is attainable to achieve a given level of differentiation, given the available technology and know-how, including TQM techniques to the extent they are successful. Based on arguments given above, one might expect that the efficiency frontier would be upward sloping. Some firms, such as White Motors and International Harvester, however, have operated above the efficiency frontier. These firms delivered less quality and incurred higher costs than competitors, such as Ford and Paccar. Not surprisingly, these firms were consistently less profitable than their more efficient rivals.

⧫⧫⧫

 **XAMPLE 12.6**

"TECHNOPORK"

An interesting example of the interaction of scale economies, differentiation, and market share is occurring in the hog and pork business.[50] Through a combination of new breeding techniques, computerization, and automation, such firms as Premium Standard Farms, Tyson Foods, and Continental Grain Company can produce leaner, more consistent hogs than can small family farmers. The result is pork that is healthier, better tasting, and costs less to produce than the meat that

---

[48]TQM is often associated with the work of W. Edwards Deming. However, Deming never actually used the term. *TQM* was the United States Navy's term for its quality program in the 1980s based on the philosophy and techniques advocated by Deming and summarized in his book *Out of the Crisis*, Cambridge, MA: MIT Press, 1986.

[49]This figure is adapted from Hall, W.K., "Survival Strategies in a Hostile Environment," *Harvard Business Review*, September–October 1980, pp. 75–85.

[50]This example draws from "Power Pork: Corporations Begin to Turn Hog Business into an Assembly Line," *Wall Street Journal*, March 28, 1994, pp. A1 and A5.

FIGURE 12.11

QUALITY AND COST POSITIONS IN THE U.S. HEAVY-DUTY TRUCK MANUFACTURING
INDUSTRY IN THE LATE 1970S.

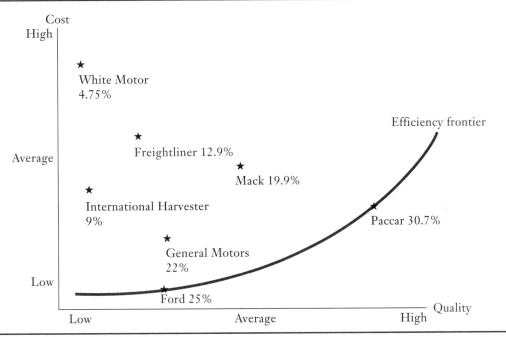

The figure depicts the cost quality positions of various competitors in the heavy truck manufacturing industry
in the United States. The figure also shows each firm's return on assets for the period 1975–1979. If all firms
were producing as efficiently as possible their positions would line up along an upward-sloping efficiency frontier. The efficiency frontier indicates the lowest level of cost that is attainable to achieve a given level of quality, given the available technology and know-how. Firms that are closer to the frontier are generally more
profitable than firms that are farther away.

Source: Figure adapted from Exhibit VII in Hall, W.K., "Survival Strategies in a Hostile Environment,"
Harvard Business Review, September–October 1980, pp. 75–85.

comes from hogs bred using traditional methods. As a result of these new techniques, dubbed "technopork," agricultural economists expect the number of hog
producers to decline by 50 percent in the next 10 years. The producers who will
dominate the industry will probably produce hogs at a lower cost and of a higher
quality than the small producers that have predominated in the industry up to now.

This rise of "technopork" can be explained in terms of Figure 12.10. The investment in land and capital equipment needed to make automated-computerized
pork production pay off can be justified only if a producer can sell at sufficient scale.[51]

---

[51]If this seems like a familiar refrain, it is. This is another example of the "division of
labor determines the extent of the market." See Chapter 2.

Tyson Foods, for example, has set a goal of achieving a 10 percent share of the U.S. hog slaughter by the year 2000, an enormous market share in what historically has been an extremely fragmented industry. Producers like Tyson and Premium Standard may be able to achieve sufficient scale by selling at a lower price, in effect, moving down demand curve D_0 and the average cost curve AC_1. But some of the additional scale may come from the fact that leaner, more consistent hogs may stimulate the demand for pork, thereby shifting the demand curve outward from D_0 to D_1. Pork producers are counting on both effects. Tyson, for example, plans to introduce new pork products, such as breaded, stuffed, and spiced pork with flavors ranging from teriyaki to "Jamaican jerk."

What, then, can we conclude about the notion of "stuck in the middle"? To the extent that it reminds us that the pursuit of differentiation is often not costless (contrary to TQM gurus, quality is often *not* "free") and that a firm's competitive position should relate in an economically sensible way to its resources and distinctive competences, "stuck in the middle" is a useful idea. However, even if there is a tradeoff between B and C, a firm need not provide the highest B or the lowest C to succeed. What matters is the magnitude of value-created, that is, $B − C$, relative to other firms. For example, Breyers Ice Cream is neither the highest nor lowest quality available, but its level of $B − C$ is high enough so that it has been a market leader for many years. Of course, if consumer tastes run to extremes, so that they tend to be either extremely price sensitive or benefit conscious, then products positioned in the middle, such as Breyers, will struggle. It is also possible that in trying to accomplish both cost and benefit objectives simultaneously, the firm may fail to make the investments in developing the resources and capabilities necessary to succeed in either dimension. In these ways, Porter's admonition against getting stuck in the middle may have merit.

Beyond that, however, the conditions under which the pursuit of a differentiation advantage may be consistent with achieving a superior cost position arise frequently enough that it would be incorrect to conclude that differentiation and cost advantage are generally incompatible. In addition, a firm pursuing a differentiation advantage must usually achieve cost parity or cost proximity with its competitors if it is to create more value than they do. In seeking to provide more benefits, management cannot abrogate its responsibility to monitor and control costs or to continuously enhance efficiency. Similarly, since a firm pursuing a cost advantage must usually achieve benefit parity or proximity if it is to create value, it must ensure that the quantity and the quality of its products is not out of line with its competitors. As always, a good grasp of the underlying economic fundamentals is critical. The pursuit of strategic positioning requires a deep understanding of how value is created. This, in turn, involves understanding what drives costs, what attributes create benefits for consumers, and how the drivers of costs and benefits vary across different segments of the market. These subjects are taken up in detail in Chapter 13.

TARGETING AND MARKET SEGMENTATION ◆ ◆ ◆ ◆ ◆

The pursuit of cost advantage and differentiation advantage relates to the broad is-sue of how the firm will create value in its target markets. But the choice of a firm's target markets is itself a key strategic decision, and how a firm selects its target markets often cannot be separated from its approach to value creation.

Segmentation and Targeting Strategies

A market segment refers to a group of consumers within a broader market who possess a common set of characteristics. In consumer goods markets, segmenta-tion characteristics include demographic factors (for example, consumers in the same age group or income class) and geography (for example, consumers located in a particular region of the country). Segmentation in consumer goods markets might also be related to how frequently or intensively consumers use the product (for example, heavy users versus intensive users); their depth of knowledge about the product (consumers who are knowledgeable versus consumers who are less well informed); and their willingness to trade off quality for price. In industrial goods markets, segmentation variables include the buyers' industry; the size of the purchasing firm; the consumer segments the buyer serves; the size of a buyer's or-der; or the buyer's willingness to trade off price for performance, speed of deliv-ery and other dimensions of quality.[52] However segments are defined, the expec-tation is that buyers within segments have similar product requirements and tastes and respond to market mix variables, such as price or advertising, in broadly the same way, while consumers across segments differ in their needs or their market-ing responses.

Targeting refers to the selection of segments that the firm will serve and the development of a product line strategy in light of those segments. Targeting strate-gies can usefully be divided into two broad categories: *focus strategies* and *broad cov-erage* strategies. We discuss each in turn.

Broad Coverage Strategies

A broad coverage strategy is aimed at serving all of the segments in the market by offering a full line of related products. Gillette follows this strategy in shaving products. It offers a full line of razors (both cartridge and disposable) for both men and women, as well as complementary products, such as shaving cream and after-shave lotions. Frito Lay follows this strategy in snack foods, offering a full line of high calorie and "light" salty snack products, such as potato chips, corn chips, tor-tilla chips, and pretzels, as well as condiments, such as salsa, that can be used with those snacks. The economic logic of a broad coverage strategy is the existence of

---

[52]See Chapter 10 of Kotler, P., *Marketing Management*, 7th edition (Englewood Cliffs, NJ) 1991 for a fuller discussion of the dimensions of market segmentation.

economies of scope across product classes. These economies of scope might come from production if the products share common production facilities or components. They might also come from distribution, as is the case with Frito Lay, which has achieved distribution economies due to its product line breadth that other manufacturers of snack foods, such as Eagle or Borden, have been unable to achieve. Or they might come from marketing, as in the case of shaving products where Gillette has attempted to use its brand name to convey a strong image of quality and tradition not only for its razors, but also for its shaving cream and after-shave lotion. This has given Gillette the opportunity to establish the basis for a differentiation advantage in these latter markets at a lower cost than it probably would have had to incur had it not already had an established brand equity position in razor blades.

Both Gillette and Frito Lay illustrate examples of broad coverage strategies that depend on products being tailored to some degree to the needs of different market segments (Gillette sells different razors to men and women; Frito Lay offers both regular and light versions of its popular snack products). However, broad coverage strategies might be either more customized or less customized to the firm's target segments than is the case in these examples. For example, some firms follow a "one-size-fits-all" strategy whereby a common product line is marketed to a variety of different market segments. Microsoft follows this strategy in computer software. Its major software products—Word, Excel, and Powerpoint—appeal to many different kinds of users, but they are not tailor-made to any particular segment. The economic logic of a one-size-fits-all strategy is to exploit economies of scale in production to achieve a cost advantage over one's competitors. The opposite case would be a firm that seeks to appeal to a broad number of different market segments, but attempts to customize its product line to each of its market segments. The economic logic of this variant of a broad based design is to create a differentiation advantage in each of the segments the firm competes in by offering bundles of attributes that best fit the needs of consumers in those segments. The large management consulting companies, such as McKinsey, BCG, and Booz Allen, provide good illustrations of this kind of strategy.

Focus Strategies

Under a focus strategy, a firm concentrates either on offering a single product or serving a single market segment or both. One kind of focus strategy is *product specialization*: the firm concentrates on producing a single type of product for a variety of different market segments. Cray Research follows this strategy in the computer industry. It only sells supercomputers, but the two main segments which it serves (the "classic" segment consisting of universities and research labs, and the industrial segment consisting of firms from such industries as petroleum, automobiles, and pharmaceuticals) differ in the attributes they value and their willingness to trade off price for performance.

Another kind of focus strategy is *geographic specialization*. Here the firm offers a variety of related products within a narrowly defined geographic market. Small local breweries, such as Schoenling in Cincinnati, illustrate this kind of focus. Schoenling offers a full line of beers, including light, premium, and superpremium brands, but it focuses on selling those beers mainly in the Cincinnati market.

A third type of focus is *customer specialization*. Here the focuser offers a variety of related products to a particular class of customers. An example would be a firm that produces industrial process control systems as well as a line of related process control devices, such as valves, flowmeters, and recording instruments, to selected industries, such as petroleum refiners and chemical manufacturers, that utilize related continuous flow processing manufacturing technologies.

A final kind of focus is a *niche strategy*, in which a firm produces a single product for a single market segment. The PBX manufacturer InteCom (now owned by the French telecommunications equipment manufacturer Matra) illustrates a niche strategy; it sells a particular kind of PBX system to big industrial customers, such as Microsoft and General Electric, who need PBXs with over 3,000 lines.

The basic economic logic of a focus strategy is that the firm is sometimes able to achieve deep economies of scale by concentrating on a particular segment or a particular product that it would be unable to exploit if it expanded beyond the segment or product it is concentrating on. In supercomputers, for example, with Cray's established reputation for producing powerful machines that are suitable for a variety of different applications, it makes sense for Cray to market its supercomputers to both classic and industrial users. These users, though different in many ways, share a strong need for powerful computers to solve analyze complex models of physical phenomena. Cray's established reputation for supercomputer performance and its distinctive capabilities in designing supercomputer architecture would not be much help if it chose to expand into, say, mainframes, or software development. Similarly, Schoenling's strong local image ensures that Schoenling will have a large market share in the Cincinnati area, which in turn allows it to benefit from economies of density in distribution.[53] By expanding into markets where its key resource (its strong local brand identity) would have significantly reduced value, Schoenling would find it difficult to achieve the same distribution economies it achieves in its "home" market.

Another economic justification for a focus strategy relates to internal organization and the rewards for innovation. Julio Rotemberg and Garth Saloner point out that by remaining focused on a particular product line, a firm is able to credibly commit not to exploit employees who develop firm-specific innovations that have applicability across the firm's product lines.[54] This is a potential problem when the firm can only reward employees for innovations that are actually implemented. To illustrate, consider a firm that offers products A and B. Employees associated with each product area work at developing innovations that benefit those products and are given a bonus if their innovations are actually implemented. Suppose, too, that the innovations can be substituted across product lines, though perhaps imperfectly. For example, a product enhancement that benefits product A might also be used to enhance product B. A firm that offers products A and B can

---

[53]Chapter 13 contains a discussion of economies of density.

[54]This is a variation of a theme, developed initially in Chapter 2, that it may be more difficult to motivate innovative effort in a large hierarchical firm than in a smaller specialized firm.

take innovations that are successfully developed for, say, product B, and apply them to products A and B. In doing so, the firm avoids paying bonuses to the employees developing innovations in product area A. Of course, if employees anticipate the possibility of this kind of opportunistic behavior, their incentives to exert effort to develop innovations are weakened.[55] For this reason, a firm would like to be able to commit not to behave in this fashion. A narrow focus—offering only product line B, for example—is one way to make such a commitment. An alternative way to make this commitment would be for the multi-product firm to organize the two products as separate businesses, in effect, creating a "Chinese Wall" between them. Rotemberg and Saloner cite Waterford Wedgewood's 1990 decision to separate its crystal and ceramic operations as a reorganization motivated by a desire to stimulate innovative activities in each product line.

Targeting and Pricing

A firm's targeting strategy cannot be viewed in isolation from how it prices its product. This point is illustrated in Figure 12.12, which considers the pricing and targeting problem of a firm that seeks a competitive advantage based on differentiation.

Imagine that the existing firms in an industry are offering a product whose quality and price are described by point E and whose average cost of production is C_E. The potential differentiator offers a product with quality q_F and unit cost C_F. Suppose that there are two clearly defined market segments, which differ according to the price-quality tradeoffs that consumers are willing to make. Consumers in the first segment have steep indifference curves, indicating that they are willing to pay a significant price premium for extra quality. We call this the "premium" segment. Consumers in the second segment have shallower indifference curves; their willingness to pay for extra quality is less than consumers in the premium segment. We call this the "standard" segment.

In this context, what are the implications of different pricing strategies? If the differentiator charges a price like P_F', it will sell only to consumers in the premium segment. This is because the firm's price-quality position lies above the indifference curve of standard consumers, but below the indifference curve of premium consumers. If, by contrast, the differentiator charges a price like P_F'', it will appeal to both segments. Price P_F' provides a high profit margin, but sacrifices volume. Price P_F'' provides a lower profit margin, but captures higher volume. The profit-maximizing position balances the gain in margin against the loss in volume. When the standard segment is large in comparison to the premium segment, the profit-maximizing position will be one that appeals to both groups of consumers because there is a large potential gain in volume from cutting price. If, however, the size of premium segment is sufficiently large, the profit-maximizing position appeals only to the premium segment. Similarly, the smaller the difference in the steepness of the indifference curves of the two segments, the more likely it is that the profit-maximizing position appeals

---

[55]Rotemberg, J. and G. Saloner, "Benefits of Narrow Business Strategies," *American Economic Review*, 84, December 1994, pp. 1330–1349.

FIGURE 12.12
THE ECONOMICS OF MARKET SEGMENTATION.

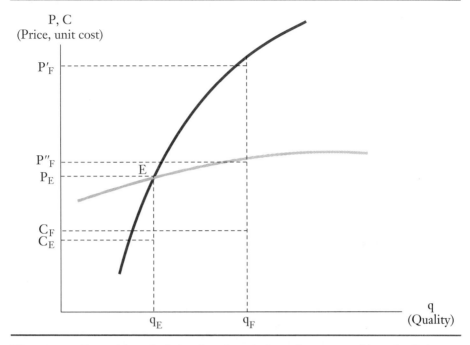

The price-quality position of existing firms in an industry is represented by point E. A new firm, firm F, is able to offer substantially higher quality (q_F versus q_E) with only a small extra cost (C_F versus C_E). It could exploit its advantage by setting a price P'_F, which is just below the (steeply sloped) indifference curve of the premium group. At this price, existing firms would still offer higher consumer surplus to the standard group. Or it could exploit its advantage by setting a price P''_F, which would lure away both premium and standard customers from existing firms. The first strategy achieves a high margin but sacrifices volume; the second sacrifices margin for volume.

to both segments. This is because the potential price premium from appealing only to premium consumers is not very large. But when the indifference curve of premium consumers is significantly steeper than that of standard consumers, however, the firm can achieve high margins if it prices so that it appeals only to premium consumers. This is likely to be the profit-maximizing outcome.

A potential differentiator that charges a price such as P''_F to appeal to both the premium and the standard segments can be viewed as pursuing a "one size fits all" strategy. But notice that this strategy makes the firm potentially vulnerable to entry by a focused competitor who seeks only to serve the premium segment. If a focused entrant offers a level of quality aimed at stealing the premium customers away from the firm, the incumbent firm faces a dilemma. If it responds by cutting price in an attempt to hold on to its customers in the premium customers, it sacrifices margin on sales in the standard segment, and it may be reluctant to do this. In the language of Chapter 9, a "one size fits all" strategy should be thought of as a "soft" commitment, which will work to the firm's disadvantage if it faces the possibility of entry by focused competitors. By contrast, a broad coverage strategy in which the firm tailors its product qualities and prices to the individual segments it serves (that is, a strategy in which the firm offers different versions of its product with distinct $[q,P]$ combinations) would put the firm in a position where it could respond more aggressively to entry by focused competitors who seek to steal its business in the premium segment. The reason is that the firm may now be able to cut the price in the premium segment without affecting margins in the standard segment and may therefore be more willing to cut the price in the premium segment if entry were to occur there. In this sense, a broad coverage strategy in which products are customized to individual segments can be viewed as a "tough" commitment.

Of course, if the firm does offer a distinct quality-price combination for each segment, it will have to confront the issue of cannibalization. That is, it will have to choose the qualities and prices in such a way that the version of the product that is targeted at the standard segment does not have such a price advantage over the product targeted for the premium segment that it attracts customers in both segments. Philip Morris had to confront this issue in the early 1990s when its flagship brand Marlboro experienced losses in market share that were due in part to the price-value cigarettes that Philip Morris itself was selling.[56] One effect of the reduction in prices of premium brands that occurred in the wake of "Marlboro Friday" in April 1993 was to reduce the appeal of price-value cigarettes to customers who might otherwise have purchased branded cigarettes.[57]

The basic economic factors that come into play in determining the optimal pricing of a product line are similar to those just discussed. The optimal differences in price and quality depend on, among other things, the relative sizes of the targeted market segments and the differences between the price-quality tradeoff that each group is willing to accept.[58]

Segmentation and Competition

When selecting market segments to serve, a firm must not only consider potential cost economies and demand, but also the potential for competition within the segment. A firm may be far more profitable as the only seller in a low-demand

---

[56]Price-value cigarettes are cigarettes that sell at prices below the premium brands, such as Marlboro or Winston, and are targeted at lower income consumers whose demand for cigarettes is likely to be more price-sensitive than consumers of branded cigarettes. The rise of the price-value segment is discussed in Example 10.3 in Chapter 10.

[57]This point is discussed in more detail in Example 10.3.

[58]See Besanko, D., S. Donnenfeld, and L. White, "Monopoly and Quality Distortion: Effects and Remedies," *Quarterly Journal of Economics*, November 1987, pp. 743–767 for a formal analysis and an intuitive discussion of the key issues.

segment than as one of several competitors in a high-demand segment. Firms such as Wal-Mart, Southwest Airlines, and Columbia/HCA (a for-profit hospital chain) have all prospered by establishing monopoly positions in small markets, while their competitive counterparts in larger markets have been less profitable.

To illustrate how demand and competition interact in the choice of market segments, consider firms choosing between two types of technologies for producing a product. Technology T1 requires a sunk investment of $5,000 and can produce products with a quality level $q = 30$ and marginal cost (MC) equal to $10 per unit of product sold. Technology T2 also requires a sunk investment of $5,000, and can produce products with quality level $q = 18$ and $MC = 2 per unit of product sold. If all consumers had the same preferences, then all firms would select the same technology. For example, if all consumers evaluate quality so that the perceived benefit B was determined by the formula $B = q$, all firms would select T1. The reason is that T1 offers a higher $B - C$ than T2. Specifically, T1 offers $B_1 - C_1 = 30 - 10 = 20 per unit, whereas T2 offers $B_2 - C_2 = 18 - 2 = 16 per unit. (The subscripts refer to the particular technologies under consideration.) On the other hand, suppose that all consumers evaluated benefits so that $B = .5q$. (We might think of these customers as being less quality conscious than the consumers for whom $B = q$.) T2 would dominate this market, for it would offer $B_2 - C_2 = 7 per unit, versus $B_1 - C_1 = 5 per unit for T1. (Since both technologies have identical sunk costs, we can ignore them for purposes of comparing the technologies.)

Now suppose that the market can be segmented into two groups of customers for a particular product. All customers will buy exactly one unit of the product in question. There are 15,000 type H customers, all of whom evaluate quality so that $B = q$. There are only 2,000 type L customers, all of whom evaluate quality so that $B = .5q$. As discussed in the previous section, we might expect consumers to self-select so that type H customers purchase products made with T1, and type L customers purchase products made with T2. Which market promises to be more profitable?

To determine the profitability of each segment, we need to anticipate pricing behavior and the possibilities for entry. We suppose that prices are set as follows:

1. Firms with a given technology take the price charged by firms with the other technology as given.

2. If only one firm has selected a given technology, it selects the price that maximizes its profits, given the price charged by firms that have selected the other technology.

3. If two or more firms choose the same technology, they set price so that $P = (1 + 1/N) \times MC$, where N is the number of firms. In other words, if there are three firms that select T1, they will set $P = (1 + 1/3)$10 = 13.33. This pricing rule resembles pricing in a Cournot model (discussed in Chapter 8), in the sense that prices approach marginal cost as the number of firms increases.

4. If firms select price according to (3) and end up with no customers (i.e., all customers choose products made by the other technology), then they reduce price

until they do have customers. This will generate a self-selection equilibrium, in which firms with T1 sell to type H customers, and firms with T2 sell to type L customers.

We also need to consider entry possibilities. We suppose that the investment of $5,000 in either technology is sunk and irreversible. We also suppose that any number of firms can access either technology if they are willing to bear the sunk cost.

With these assumptions, we can determine the equilibrium prices and the number of firms with each technology. We begin by determining how many firms with T1 can profitably serve the 15,000 type H customers. Suppose 5 firms invest in technology T1. Their price will be $P = (1+1/5)10 = \$12$. Assuming that they split the market equally, each firm will have sales of 3,000 units, total revenue of $36,000, and total cost of $35,000 ($30,000 in variable costs and $5,000 in fixed costs). Thus, the profits of each firm choosing T1 will be $1,000. Note that there will be no additional entry. If a sixth firm enters with T1, the price would be $11.67. Each firm will have sales of 2,500 units, total revenue of $29,175, and total costs of $30,000. Anticipating that costs will exceed revenues, the sixth firm will not invest in T1.

If five firms have invested in T1, will any firms invest in T2? A firm that invests in T2 could not compete in the type H market. Even if it charged a price of $P_2 = MC_2 = 2$, type H consumers would derive $B_1 - P_1 = \$18$ from sellers with T1 and only $B_2 - P_2 = \$16$ from the seller with T2. Thus, any firm employing T2 would need to focus on type L customers. Note that the consumer surplus of a type L consumer that purchases from a firm that has invested in T1 is $B_1 - P_1 = .5q_1 - P_1 = 15 - 12 = \$3$. A firm with T2 must offer at least this level of consumer surplus to attract type L customers, or it will have no sales. This implies that a firm with T2 can charge a price no higher than $6. At this price, $B_2 - P_2 = .5q_2 - P_2 = 3$, which leaves type L consumers indifferent between T1 and T2.

If just one firm selects T2 and sets a price equal to $6, it will have sales of 2,000 units, revenues of $12,000 and total costs of $9,000 (variable costs of $4,000 and fixed costs of $5,000), for total profit of $3,000. Will a second firm enter the market segment? Were a second firm to enter, price would fall to $(1+\frac{1}{2})2^* = \$3$. If the two firms split the demand equally, each would have sales of 1,000 units, total revenues of $3,000, and total costs of $7,000. Anticipating a loss of $4,000, the second firm will stay out.

To summarize the equilibrium, there will be five firms with T1, selecting $P_1 = \$12$, and earning profits of $1,000 each. There will be a single firm with T2, selecting $P_2 = \$6$, and earning profits of $3,000. In this example, the single firm serving the niche market of type L customers earns more than half of all of the firms serving type H customers combined!

Segmentation by Monopolists

Suppose that entry into the type H market segment was not so easy. For example, suppose that T1 and T2 are each protected by patents. What would equilibrium prices look like if there was just one firm with each technology? In equilibrium, the T1 firm would just serve type H customers, and the T2 firm would just serve type

L customers. To see why, suppose that prices were such that all customers preferred T1. For this to be the case, it must be that $B - P$ for both types is higher with T1. This would occur if $B_1 - P_1 > B_2 - P_2$ for each type of customer. This is satisfied if $30 - P_1 > 18 - P_2$ and $15 - P_1 > 9 - P_2$. This implies $P_1 - P_2 < \$6$. But if this were the case, then for any price charged by the firm with T1, the firm with T2 could profitably steal away the type L customers by lowering price. For example, if $P_1 = \$12$ and $P_2 = \$7$, then the firm with T2 will have no customers. By lowering price to $P_2 = \$5$, the firm with T2 will steal all the type L customers from the firm with T1, and still be charging a price that exceeds marginal cost. A similar analysis can be used to show why the T2 firm could not hold on to both type L and type H customers.

An equilibrium in which the firm with T1 sells to type H customers and the firm with T2 sells to type L customers must have the following characteristics:

1. The firm with T2 will not select $P_2 > \$9$. At any higher price, type L customers will not buy their product.

2. The firm with T1 will select $P_1 = P_2 + \$12$. If it were to select a higher price, it would lose its type H customers to the firm with T2. By the same token, it would not gain any customers by setting a slightly lower price.

3. If $P_1 < \$15$, then the firm with T2 will select $P_2 = P_1 - \$6$. If it were to select a higher price, it would lose its type L customers to the firm with T1. By the same token, it would not gain any customers by lowering price slightly below this level.

The only pair of prices that satisfies all three conditions is $P_1 = \$21$ and $P_2 = \$9$. To see why other price combinations would not be equilibria, note that conditions 2 and 3 cannot be simultaneously satisfied. Thus P_1 must be greater than \$15. This implies that P_2 must equal \$9, for this is the highest price that type L customers are willing to pay for T2. This further implies that $P_1 = \$21$, the highest price that T1 firms can charge without losing customers to T2 firms. At these prices, the firm with T1 sells 15,000 units for total revenue of \$315,000, total cost of \$155,000, and profit of \$160,000. The firm with T2 sells 2,000 units for revenue of \$18,000, total cost of \$9,000, and profit of \$9,000. Comparing this equilibrium to the one derived in the previous section, we see what a difference entry can make.

STRATEGIC GROUPS ◆ ◆ ◆ ◆ ◆

Different firms within the same industry often seem to pursue different strategies. For example, firms may differ according to their degree of forward and backward integration, the age and quality of their physical assets, or the attributes of their products. A *strategic group* is a set of firms within an industry that are similar to one another and different from firms outside the group on one or more key dimensions of their strategy.[59]

---

[59]See Porter, M., "The Structure Within Industries and Companies' Performance," *Review of Economics and Statistics*, May 1979, pp. 214–227 and Porter, M., *Competitive Strategy*, New York: Free Press, 1980.

By identifying strategic groups, a firm can more readily find its close and distant competitors, as well as analyze the likely competitive implications of changes in firm strategy. In a classic application of these ideas, Michael Porter identified several strategic groups in the U.S. chain saw industry in the 1970s.[60] One group included Beaird Poulan and targeted price-conscious casual users, such as homeowners, with less powerful saws. A second group included recognized quality leader Stihl and targeted professional users, such as loggers and construction workers, with powerful, feature-laden saws. A third group included leading sellers Homelite and McCullough and produced a wide variety of models that were sold to all consumer segments through chain saw dealers as well as mass merchandisers. Due to an increase in demand by casual users, Homelite contemplated increasing its business in the casual-user segment. By identifying the strategic group already targeting that segment and considering the likely competitive responses of firms in that group, Homelite foresaw the fierce price rivalry that might result from such a move and elected not to change its strategy.

Identification and Analysis of Strategic Groups

How does one identify strategic groups? An unambiguous approach to the problem is elusive. While firms may differ in myriad ways, not all differences among them will generate meaningful strategic groups. Strategic dimensions used to identify groups include:

- *Organization variables*: scale and scope, distribution channels, vertical integration, diversification, relationship to parent, relationship to government
- *Marketing and product characteristics*: price, quality, image, technological leadership, service
- *Financial variables*: cost, debt position (leverage)

To identify strategic groups, one usually selects two or more of these dimensions, and maps the location of each firm in the industry. How does one select the dimensions? One should avoid dimensions along which all firms pursue the same strategy. For example, few if any restaurants could be considered R&D leaders, and few airlines have diversified into other goods and services (United being the exception during part of the 1980s). At the same time, many strategic dimensions will be related, so that how firms measure up on each dimension is correlated. Using both dimensions provides no more information than using a single dimension. For example, pharmaceutical firms that are R&D leaders historically market their products directly through physicians (by informing them of product attributes), whereas "copycat" firms tend to compete on price. An analysis that uses "R&D" and "marketing strategy" is no more informative than one that uses only one of

---

[60]Chapter 7 of Porter, M., *Competitive Strategy*, New York: Free Press, 1980, pp. 153–154 and "The Chain Saw Industry in 1974," Case 11 in Porter, M., *Cases in Competitive Strategy*, New York: Free Press, 1983, pp. 189–207.

these dimensions. A further consideration when selecting dimensions is the presence of mobility barriers, which are discussed below.

Strategic Maps

One can summarize alternative strategic paths in an industry by identifying strategic groups on a *strategic map*. Begin by identifying two strategic dimensions that most clearly distinguish the firms. In airlines, these might be the extent of routes (e.g., global versus niche markets) or pricing strategy. In pharmaceuticals, these might be R&D intensity and product market scope. Next, draw a "map" placing each dimension along one axis. The dimensions need not be ordinal (i.e., with scores arrayed from lowest to highest). For example, a map of the pharmaceutical industry could include a dimension called "product type" with a scale that includes "generic," "branded," and "both." Conclude by locating each firm on the map. This is often subjective, but can sometimes be supported by data.

Firms with similar strategies will cluster together on the strategic map. One can employ nonparametric statistical techniques (available with many statistical software packages) to cluster firms. The resulting strategic groupings identify subsets of competitors. Alternatively, one can just eyeball the clusters. Success within a group will depend on some combination of the same factors that produce success within an industry, such as having a cost or differentiation advantage. The weights identified for these factors, however, will differ across strategic groups.

Figure 12.13 illustrates a strategic group analysis for the downtown Chicago restaurant business in about 1980. The dimensions of the map are type of dining (business versus casual) and the quality of the food. The circles on the map represent clusters of restaurants pursuing similar strategies. Three groups emerge. The first, which included Eli's and Morton's (two revered steak houses), offered high-quality food in a conservative, business setting. The second, which included many local coffee shops, offered adequate-quality food in a no-nonsense setting, ideal for the fast business lunch. The third, which included the "Rock and Roll" McDonald's (so called for its 1950s memorabilia) and the Billy Goat Tavern (immortalized on television's *Saturday Night Live*) sold adequate-quality food in a lively setting.

There are obvious entry opportunities that become clear from this strategic map. The first is to compete in group #3 by offering adequate-quality, high-fun dining. Ed Debevic's Short Order Deluxe, Hard Rock Cafe, and Planet Hollywood are examples of entrants that have positioned themselves in that way. A second opportunity is for high-quality, casual dining to fill the empty lower-right quadrant of the map. Entrants here include Hat Dance, Scoozi, Bistro 110, and Oprah Winfrey's Eccentric.

Groups, Scarce Resources, and Mobility Barriers

Strategic groups are subject to the same competitive forces as industries. In particular, a strategic group can outperform its industry only if it is immune from entry by firms in other strategic groups. The reason is that the underperforming firms would wish to mimic the strategies of the firms in the successful strategic group.

FIGURE 12.13

STRATEGIC MAP OF CHICAGO RESTAURANTS IN 1980.

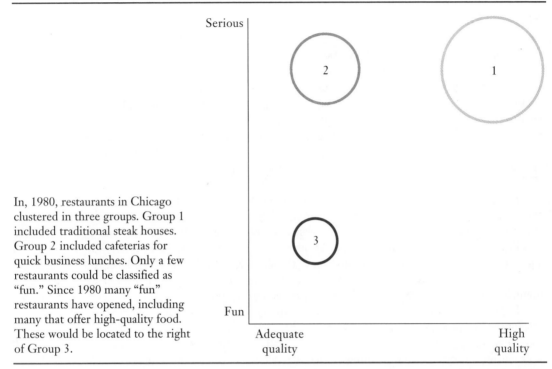

In, 1980, restaurants in Chicago clustered in three groups. Group 1 included traditional steak houses. Group 2 included cafeterias for quick business lunches. Only a few restaurants could be classified as "fun." Since 1980 many "fun" restaurants have opened, including many that offer high-quality food. These would be located to the right of Group 3.

Factors that prevent firms from changing strategic groups are called *mobility barriers*.[61] In the absence of mobility barriers, a strategic group cannot earn abnormally high returns for long.

Where do mobility barriers come from? To some extent, they arise from the same sources as entry barriers. Patents, scale economies, and strategic deterrence may all contribute to mobility barriers. Karel Cool and Dan Schendel argue that mobility barriers may result if firms make resource and scope commitments.[62] Following this logic, David Dranove, Margaret Peteraf, and Mark Shanley argue that the resources and capabilities that form the basis for strategic group identification should be *scarce*.[63] They argue that scarcity creates mobility barriers. If resources are not scarce, then a group could not be profitable for long, because

[61]Caves, R. and M. Porter, "From Entry Barriers to Mobility Barriers," *Quarterly Journal of Economics*, May 1977, pp. 241–261.

[62]Cool, K.O. and D.E. Schendel, "Quality Differences Among Strategic Group Members," *Strategic Management Journal*, 9, 1988, pp. 207–223.

[63]Dranove, D., M. Peteraf, and M. Shanley, "The Economic Foundations of Strategic Group Theory," General Motors Research Center Discussion Paper 93-59, Northwestern University, 1994.

other firms would see how profitable the group is, obtain the same resources and capabilities, and enter the group. Entry into the group by new firms would erode its profits, just as entry into an industry erodes industry profits. This has certainly been the experience of restaurants in Chicago. Rapid entry (and evolving tastes) have made it difficult to make profits in any strategic group for very long.

If a group is protected by mobility barriers, then the profits of that group will depend on the structure and conduct of its members. As detailed in Chapter 8, firms that are otherwise protected from competition may still be unprofitable if there are many of them, if they are horizontally undifferentiated, or if they have excess capacity.

CHAPTER SUMMARY

◆   A firm achieves a competitive advantage if it can achieve higher rates of profitability than rival firms. A firm's profitability depends jointly on industry conditions and the amount of value the firm can create relative to its rivals.

◆   Consumer surplus is the difference between the perceived benefit B of a product and its monetary price P. A consumer will purchase a product only if its consumer surplus is positive. A consumer will purchase the product from a particular seller only if that seller offers a higher consumer surplus than rival sellers offer.

◆   A value map is a tool for illustrating the competitive implications of consumer surplus. An indifference curve shows the price-quality combinations that yield the same level of consumer surplus.

◆   Value-created is the difference between the perceived benefit B and the unit cost C of the product. Equivalently, it is equal to the sum of consumer surplus and economic profit.

◆   To achieve a competitive advantage, a firm must not only create positive value, it must create more value than rival firms. If it does so, it can outcompete other firms by offering a higher consumer surplus than rivals. Even if rivals respond (e.g., by cutting price) and restore consumer surplus parity, the firm will still earn a higher rate of profit than rivals.

◆   The bases of competitive advantage are superior resources and organizational capabilities. Resources are firm-specific assets that other firms cannot easily acquire. Organizational capabilities refer to clusters of activities that the firm does especially well in comparison to rivals.

◆   Creating more value than rivals does not imply that the firm's profitability will be high in an absolute sense. Industry structure is critical in determining the share of value-created that firms capture as profit.

◆   There are two broad routes to achieving competitive advantage. The first is for the firm to achieve a cost advantage over its rivals by offering a product with a lower C for the same, or perhaps lower, B. A firm exploits its cost advantage by selling at a price discount relative to other firms. If this discount is less than the firm's C advantage but is greater than its B disadvantage (if any), the firm will offer greater consumer surplus than rivals and will increase its share in the target market.

◆ The other broad route to competitive advantage is to achieve a differentiation advantage over its rivals by offering products with a higher B for the same, or perhaps higher C. A firm exploits its differentiation advantage by charging a price premium. If this premium is less than the firm's B advantage but greater than its C advantage (if any), the firm will increase its share of the target market.

◆ When firms are horizontally differentiated, the price elasticity of demand plays a critical role in how a firm profits from either a cost advantage or a benefit advantage. When the price elasticity of demand is high, a firm with a cost advantage will pass along much of the advantage to consumers through lower prices and will profit from its advantage through higher volume. When the price elasticity of demand is low, the firm best profits from its cost advantage through higher margins, rather than through higher volume.

◆ The price elasticity of demand also is key in determining the profitability of a benefit advantage. If the price elasticity of demand is high, so that price-cost margins are low, the extra demand created by the benefit advantage will not add much to profit. A benefit advantage is thus most valuable in industries with high horizontal differentiation and thus high price-cost margins.

◆ Whether a value-creation advantage should be exploited in a narrow market segment or a broader one depends on the relative size of the segments and differences between segments in the willingness of consumers to trade off quality and price.

◆ Building a competitive advantage based on superior cost position is likely to be attractive when: there are unexploited opportunities for achieving scale, scope, or learning economies; opportunities for enhancing the product's perceived benefit are limited by the product's nature; consumers are relatively price sensitive and are unwilling to pay a premium for enhanced quality or performance; and the product is a search good rather than an experience good.

◆ Building a competitive advantage based on differentiation position is likely to be attractive when: the typical consumer is willing to pay a significant price premium for attributes that enhance B; economies of scale or learning are significant and existing firms are already exploiting them; and the product is an experience good rather than a search good.

◆ A firm is said to be "stuck in the middle" if it simultaneously pursues both a cost advantage and a differentiation advantage, but succeeds in achieving neither. Some firms do achieve both, perhaps because a firm that increases its market share due to a superior-quality position benefits from economies of scale or learning. The benefits of learning may also accumulate more rapidly for higher-quality products. Finally, a firm may have both a cost advantage and a differentiation advantage if it faces inefficient competitors.

◆ Targeting refers to the selection of market segments that the firm will serve and the development of a product line strategy in light of those segments. Targeting strategies can usefully be divided into two broad categories: focus strategies, in which a firm concentrates either on offering a single product or serving a single market segment or both and broad coverage strategies, in which the firm serves most or all segments of the market by offering a full line of related products.

◆ When selecting a market segment to serve, the firm should consider the potential for competition in the niche. If the segment is small, the firm may face little competition and earn substantial returns.

◆ Strategic groups are sets of firms within an industry that are similar to one another and different from firms outside the group on one or more key dimensions of strategy. A strategic group map illustrates strategic group membership.

◆ Factors that prevent firms from changing strategic groups are called mobility barriers. They arise from the same sources as entry barriers and result from the scarcity of key resources and capabilities.

QUESTIONS

1. Why would the role of the marketing department in capital-intensive industries (e.g. steel) differ from that in labor-intensive industries (e.g. athletic footwear)? How does this relate to positioning?

2. "Firms that seek a cost advantage should adopt a learning curve strategy; firms that seek to differentiate their products should not." Comment on both of these statements.

3. Consider a market in which consumer indifference curves are relatively steep. Firms in the industry are pursuing two positioning strategies: some firms are producing a "basic" product that provides satisfactory performance; others are producing an enhanced product that provides performance that is superior to that of the basic product. Consumer surplus parity currently exists in the industry. Are the prices of the basic and the enhanced product likely to be significantly different or about the same? Why? How would the answer change if consumer indifference curves were relatively flat?

4. Two firms, Alpha and Beta, are competing in a market in which consumer preferences are identical. Alpha offers a product whose benefit B is equal to $100 per unit. Beta offers a product whose benefit B is equal to $75 per unit. Alpha's average cost C is equal to $60 per unit, while Beta's average cost C is equal to $50 per unit.

    a) Which firm's product provides the greatest value created?

    b) In an industry equilibrium in which the firms achieve consumer surplus parity, by what dollar amount will the profit margin, $P–C$, of the firm that creates the greatest amount of value exceed the profit margin of the firm that creates the smaller amount of value? Compare this amount to the difference between the value created of each firm. What explains the relationship between the difference in profit margins and the difference in value-created between the two firms?

5. Industry 1 consists of four firms that sell a product that is identical in every respect except for production cost and price. Firm A's unit production costs are 10 percent less than the others, and it charges a price that is 1 percent less than the others. Industry 2 consists of four firms that sell a product that is identical in every respect except for production cost and price. Firm X's unit production costs are 10 percent less than the others, and it charges a price that is 8 percent less than the others. Both industries are characterized by stable demand and comparable entry barriers.

The above situations have prevailed for years. The managers of the above firms are very smart and are surely acting in the best interest of their owners, whose only goal is to maximize profits. Based on this information only, can you determine which industry has the higher price-cost margin (i.e., [price-unit production cost] as a percentage of price) and why?

◆ ◆ ◆ ◆ ◆ APPENDIX: VALUE-ADDED ANALYSIS

We illustrate value-added analysis with the example of a firm that produces blue jeans. The firm sells its product to three different types of customers. It sells *unlabeled jeans* to manufacturers who attach their own labels to jeans and sell them as house brands. It also sells jeans under its own brand name label (which is supported through extensive advertising and product promotion) to independent wholesalers, who then distribute them to retailers. Finally, using in-house distribution capabilities, it sells and distributes its labeled blue jeans directly to retailers. For simplicity, then, we can think of the firm's value chain as consisting of three major activities: manufacturing; brand management, which includes the marketing undertaken to support the brand; and distribution. Manufacturing creates value by transforming raw materials into finished jeans. Brand management creates value by transforming what would otherwise be no-name jeans into branded jeans with a superior image. Distribution creates value by distributing jeans that would otherwise be sold to wholesalers. Value-added analysis determines the incremental profit created by each of these activities.

Consider the information shown in Table A12.1:

TABLE A12.1
VOLUMES, PRICES, AND COSTS FOR A BLUE JEANS FIRM

Total quantity of blue jeans manufactured	110,000 pairs per year
Unlabeled jeans sold to private labelers	25,000 pairs per year
Labeled jeans sold to wholesalers	70,000 pairs per year
Labeled jeans, self-distributed	15,000 pairs per year
Selling price, unlabeled jeans	$4.00 per pair
Selling price, labeled jeans sold to wholesalers	$14.00 per pair
Selling price, labeled jeans, self-distributed	$18.00 per pair
Production cost per unit, unlabeled jeans	$2.50 per pair
Production cost per unit, labeled jeans	$2.55 per pair
Distribution cost per unit	$1.80 per pair
Total brand promotion and advertising expenses	$800,000 per year

Note that the profit contribution is

$$25,000 \times (4 - 2.50) + 70,000 \times (14 - 2.55) + 15,000(18 - 2.55 - 1.80)$$
$$- 800,000 = \$243,750.$$

The value-added analysis proceeds as follows:

- *Value added in manufacturing* = profit that would have been made if all jeans are sold unlabeled:

$$= 110,000 \times (4 - 2.50) = \$165,000 \text{ or } \$1.50 \text{ per pair.}$$

- *Value added in brand management* = incremental profit made by selling labeled jeans to wholesalers as opposed to selling unlabeled jeans:

$$= 85,000 \times [(14 - 2.55) - (4 - 2.50)] - \$800,000 = \$45,750,$$

or $.54 per pair.

- *Value added in distribution* = incremental profit made by selling labeled jeans to retailers as opposed to selling them to wholesalers:

$$= 15,000 \times [(18 - 2.55 - 1.80) - (14 - 2.55)] = \$33,000,$$
or $2.20 per pair.

Note that the sum of the value added across the three activities is equal to the total profit contribution. This is not coincidental. It happens because value-added analysis carefully counts only the incremental profit generated by an activity. Perhaps surprisingly, the analysis reveals that the highest total value added comes from manufacturing, not from branding the jeans, and the highest value added per unit comes from distribution. While branding the product and supporting it with advertising and promotion are certainly important activities in this company, this analysis reveals that they do not contribute much to profit because they are costly in comparison to the benefits they generate.

ANALYZING COST AND DIFFERENTIATION POSITION

13

*W*hen the Douglas Aircraft Company of Los Angeles introduced its DC-9 jet in 1965, it appeared as though it would be Douglas's greatest success since its legendary DC-3 twin-engine propeller plane was introduced in the late 1930s. The DC-9 was the first jet that could be handled by a flight crew of only two pilots. It promised to be inexpensive to fly and easy to maintain (its engines could be changed in 28 minutes, as opposed to 4 hours for the DC-8). The DC-9 hit the market during a boom in the airline industry when the airlines were preparing to replace their aging fleets of propeller and turbo-prop planes used for short-distance flights. And Douglas had a two-year head start over archrival Boeing, whose short-range offering, the 737, was not scheduled to be ready for airline service until 1967.

Yet by late 1966, the DC-9 program had turned into a fiasco that threatened the viability of the company. Expecting to break even after it sold the 20th plane, Douglas found that it was losing nearly $200,000 per plane even after the 50th one was sold. Needing to borrow $330 million to operate in 1967, Douglas approached its bankers for a line of credit. But its bankers balked and suggested instead that the Douglas family sell their company to get the needed cash. After entertaining offers from General Dynamics, Martin Marietta, North American Aviation, and Signal Oil and Gas, the Douglas family agreed to sell the company to the St. Louis-based defense contractor, McDonnell Company, in January 1967.

Douglas's problems stemmed largely from a failure to anticipate production costs, rather than a failure to procure orders for its jets. (Orders for the DC-9 in 1966 actually exceeded projections.) In pricing its planes, Douglas counted on

499

learning economies that never materialized. This was partly due to circumstances beyond Douglas's control: A tight labor market in Los Angeles in 1966 resulted in far more labor turnover than Douglas expected, which slowed the rate of learning-by-doing among its workforce. But Douglas also failed to anticipate factors that were within its control. For example, to match Boeing's product line in jets, Douglas decided to produce several different versions of the DC-9. This complicated the production environment and slowed the rate of learning, making costs higher than expected.

Chapter 12 discussed two broad routes to competitive advantage: superior cost position (lower C than competitors for the same or perhaps lower B) and superior differentiation position (higher B than competitors for the same or perhaps higher C). To access the potential for achieving an advantage based on either lower costs or superior differentiation, one needs to be able to analyze the behavior of costs and the sources of differentiation advantage. The Douglas aircraft example illustrates the importance of understanding the factors that drive costs. Example 13.4, "The MicroChannel Bus," presented later in this chapter, illustrates the importance of understanding the drivers of differentiation.

The purpose of this chapter, then, is to present a set of tools, techniques, and approaches for analyzing a firm's cost and differentiation positions relative to its competitors and for empirically estimating the economic factors that drive C and B. The chapter has three main parts. The first part discusses the measurement of costs and the analysis of cost drivers. The second presents a number of approaches for estimating and characterizing the importance of two significant cost drivers: economies of scale and the learning curve. The third discusses the analysis of differentiation and the estimation of benefit drivers.

◆ ◆ ◆ ◆ ◆ EVALUATING A FIRM'S COST POSITION

Why do some firms have a cost advantage over their competitors? What activities or what parts of these firms account for their advantage? This section introduces concepts and tools for addressing these questions. The evaluation of a firm's cost position proceeds in two steps. The first step is to disaggregate costs into economically significant categories. The second is to identity *cost drivers*, the basic economic forces that cause costs to vary across different organizations.

Disaggregating Costs

Costs can be disaggregated in three principal ways: by behavior; by classes of inputs; and by activities. We can disaggregate costs *behaviorally* by distinguishing between variable, fixed, and semifixed costs, as discussed in the Economics Primer. Breaking down costs in this fashion is especially useful for analyzing pricing and output and capacity expansion decisions of individual firms, as well as for analyzing the dynamics of rivalry and entry and exit decisions, discussed in Chapters 8 through 11.

Costs can also be broken down according to *classes of inputs*. Traditional cost accounting systems distinguish *manufacturing costs* from *nonmanufacturing costs*. Nonmanufacturing costs include selling, advertising, and promotion expenses, as well as expenses associated with the management of the company. They would also include the expenses incurred in conducting research and development. Nonmanufacturing expenses are typically reported as a separate line item in a firm's income statement, often labeled "selling and general administrative expenses" (SGA).

Manufacturing costs include all of the costs associated with producing the product.[1] Conventionally, these are broken down into three main categories:

- *Direct materials costs*: This includes the costs of all materials and components that can be physically traced to the finished good. For a manufacturer of personal computers, the sheet metal used for the outer casing would be included in direct materials.

- *Direct labor costs*: This includes the costs of labor that are physically traceable to the production of the finished goods. The salaries of assembly line workers or machine workers would be included in direct labor costs.

- *Manufacturing overhead* (or indirect manufacturing costs): This includes all the costs associated with manufacturing other than direct labor and direct materials. Indirect manufacturing costs typically are broken down as follows:

    i. *Indirect labor costs*—salaries of production workers whose efforts usually are not directly traceable to the finished good, including maintenance personnel, quality-control workers, and inspectors.

    ii. *Materials overhead*—includes the costs of indirect materials (supplies, such as glue or solder, that are used in small quantities in many products). It also includes the costs related to the procurement and movement of materials, such as the salaries of purchasing, receiving, and stockroom personnel.

    iii. *General factory administrative expenses*—salaries of plant managers, security personnel, personnel administrators, cost accountants, and supervisors.

    iv. *Facilities and equipment costs*—includes largely variable expenses, such as electricity and water, as well as fixed expenses, such as depreciation of plant and equipment, rent, and property taxes.

    v. *Engineering costs*—salaries of industrial and operations engineers and drafters whose work pertains to the design of the production process.

---

[1]Manufacturing costs are closely related to, but not the same as, the category "cost of goods sold" (CGS), which is reported on the firm's income statement. With accrual accounting, CGS includes the cost of the goods that had previously been in the firm's finished goods and work-in-process inventories. The specific relationship between CGS in a given period and the manufacturing costs incurred in that period is:

CGS = Mfg. Cost + beginning of period work-in-process inventory − end of period work-in-process inventory + beginning of period finished goods inventory − end of period finished goods inventory.

The sum of direct labor and direct materials costs is often referred to as *prime cost*. Direct labor plus manufacturing overhead is often called *conversion cost*.

Disaggregating costs on the basis of input classes has traditionally been most useful for decisions concerning the operating efficiency of the firm. In recent years, however, the cost structure of the typical manufacturing firm has undergone significant changes. Table 13.1 illustrates these changes.[2] Greater automation has led to a decline in the importance of direct labor costs. More sophisticated inventory control, coupled with an overall decision in the levels of inventories, has reduced spoilage and defects, resulting in lower direct materials expenses. The movement in many firms toward more flexible, customized production has increased setup costs (generally a part of manufacturing overhead), and increases in the level of automation have increased depreciation expenses (also included in manufacturing overhead).

Activity-Cost Analysis

Another way to disaggregate costs is through *activity-cost analysis*. This approach views the firm as a set of value-creating activities and assigns costs accordingly. Templates, such as Michael Porter's value chain (discussed in Chapters 2 and 12) or the McKinsey Business System framework, which divides the firm into six distinct activities (technology, product design, manufacturing, marketing, distribution, and service), can be used to identify relevant activities for this analysis. Broader or narrower categories of activities can also be used, though, as data permit.

Table 13.2 illustrates a simple example of activity-cost analysis for two firms in the trucking industry, Roadway Express and ABF Freight Systems in 1983. Roadway

TABLE 13.1

COMPONENTS OF COST FOR A TYPICAL MANUFACTURING FIRM: 1960s VERSUS 1990s

	% of Manufacturing Costs		% of Total Cost	
	1960s	*1990s*	*1960s*	*1990s*
Direct labor	40%	10%	36%	7%
Direct materials	35%	35%	32%	25%
Manufacturing overhead	25%	55%	23%	39%
Manufacturing costs	100%	100%	90%	70%
SGA			10%	30%
Total costs			100%	100%

---

[2]Data for Table 13.1 were provided by Professor Bala Balachandran, Department of Accounting, Kellogg Graduate School of Management, Northwestern University.

TABLE 13.2
ACTIVITY-COST ANALYSIS OF TWO TRUCKING FIRMS IN 1983

	Roadway Express TOTAL	$/ton-mile	ABF Freight Systems TOTAL	$/ton-mile
Production Operations				
Line haul (drivers, fuel, rentals, purchased transport)	$427,057	$0.079	$146,533	$0.073
Pickup & delivery	$231,591	$0.043	$66,874	$0.033
Platform (loading & unloading)	$246,810	$0.046	$56,562	$0.028
Terminal (consolidation & sorting)	$76,007	$0.014	$19,404	$0.010
TOTAL	$981,465	$0.182	$289,373	$0.144
Maintenance	$26,777	$0.005	$4,792	$0.002
Insurance & safety	$14,688	$0.003	$2,877	$0.001
Traffic & sales (sales, promotion, advertising, rate negotiation)	$41,249	$0.008	$20,072	$0.010
Billing & collecting	$21,886	$0.004	$17,891	$0.009
General & administrative	$42,322	$0.008	$8,627	$0.004
TOTAL operating expenses	$1,128,387	$0.209	$343,632	$0.171
Total ton-miles (000)	5,392,839		2,013,723	
Tons of revenue freight (000)	5,037		2,064	
truck-load (percent)	32.04%		56.44%	
less-than-truck load (percent)	67.96%		43.56%	

Source: Trinc's Blue Book of the Trucking Industry: 1984, McLean, VA: Trinc Transportation Consultants, 1984.

was (and still is) one of the largest nationwide carriers specializing in less-than-truckload (LTL) shipments. ABF was (and still is) considerably smaller than Roadway. In 1983 ABF had an advantage over Roadway in overall operating costs (1.71 cents per ton-mile versus 2.09 cents per ton-mile). Though this difference may seem small, it is significant in an industry where prices rarely exceed unit costs by more than 5 percent. ABF's advantage over Roadway in 1983 was largely due to lower costs of production operations (1.44 cents per ton-mile versus 1.82 cents per ton-mile). This can be attributed to several factors. In 1983, ABF handled a considerably larger portion of full truckload (TL) shipments than Roadway. This saves on terminal-related expenses. ABF also has been widely regarded as leader in the development of efficiencies in terminal operations. These efficiencies allowed ABF to reduce the number of consolidation facilities required per ton of freight and to cut the amount of handling required for its LTL freight.[3]

Dividing the firm's costs according to activities can be difficult and data intensive: Most internal accounting systems do not subdivide costs along the lines suggested by either the McKinsey framework or Porter's value chain. However, cost analysis of this sort can be extremely valuable because the drivers of costs within different activities are typically different. This approach is also consistent with the development of modern frameworks in managerial accounting, such as activity-based costing.[4]

Cost Drivers

Cost drivers explain why costs would vary across firms. We discuss cost drivers in terms of average costs, rather than total costs, because a larger firm's total costs would be higher than a smaller firm's simply because of their size difference.[5] We find it useful to classify cost drivers into four broad categories, each of which has several subcategories:

---

[3]Since 1983 industry observers have credited Roadway with achieving significant operating efficiencies of its own. By the early 1990s, Roadway had become one of the industry's most aggressive discounters, while maintaining one of the highest price-cost margins.

[4]See Cooper, R. and R. S. Kaplan, *The Design of Cost Management Systems*, Englewood Cliffs, NJ: Prentice Hall, or Shank, J. K. and V. J. Govindarajan, *Strategic Cost Analysis: The Evolution from Managerial to Strategic Accounting*, Homewood, IL: Irwin; 1989.

[5]One way to control for the effects of size in analyzing cost difference among different size firms is to express total costs as a percentage of sales revenue. Accountants call this *common-size analysis*. Common-size analysis can be useful, but it contains a potential source of confusion. To illustrate, we can write the ratio of total costs to sales revenue as $AC^*Q/P^*Q = AC/P$, where Q denotes the volume of output per period. This expression implies that one firm's total cost-to-sales ratio might be lower than another's either because its average costs are lower or its price is higher (or both). Common-size analysis of cost advantage should account for differences in prices among firms. Such differences might be due to product quality, product mix, or geographical point of sales.

- Cost drivers related to *firm size or scope*
    - economies of scale
    - economies of scope
    - capacity utilization
- Cost drivers related to *cumulative experience*
    - learning curve
- Cost drivers *independent of firm size, scope, or cumulative experience*
    - input prices
    - location
    - economies of density
    - complexity/focus
    - process efficiency
    - discretionary policies
    - government policies
- Cost drivers related to the *organization of transactions*
    - organization of the vertical chain
    - agency efficiency.

We will discuss each cost driver in turn.

Cost Drivers Related to Firm Size, Scope, and Cumulative Experience

Chapter 5 contains an extensive discussion of economies of scale, scope, and cumulative experience, so here we will just review the key results. *Economies of scale* exist when average costs go down as the scale of operation increases. *Economies of scope* exist when average costs go down as the firm produces a greater variety of goods. A paramount source of economies of scale and scope is indivisible inputs. Indivisible inputs cannot be scaled down below a certain minimum size and thus give rise to fixed costs. As the volume or variety of output increases, these fixed costs get spread out, leading to lower per-unit costs of production. In the short run, the spreading of fixed costs often arises because of greater *capacity utilization*. In the long run, the spreading of fixed costs arises when it becomes economical for a firm to substitute a technology with high fixed costs but low variable costs for one with low fixed costs but high variable costs. Other important sources of economies of scale are: (i) economies of scale due to the physical properties of processing units (i.e., the cube-square rule); (ii) increases in the productivity of variable inputs as volume increases (e.g., because of greater specialization of labor); (iii) economies of inventory management.

Cumulative experience can reduce average costs as firms move down the *learning curve*. Learning economies should not, however, be confused with economies of scale that arise when the firm spreads out *nonrecurring fixed costs* over the volume of output it produces over time. To illustrate this distinction, consider a small producer of a specialty valve. The up front costs of designing the valve are incurred only once. The dies and jigs used to fabricate the valve can be reused from one year to the next, so these costs are nonrecurring as well. Even though the firm's annual rate of production may be small, its average cost per unit might still be low because it has produced the same model year after year.[6] The spreading of nonrecurring fixed costs will cause unit production costs to decrease with volume, even if the firm does not become more proficient in manufacturing the good as it accumulates experience.

Cost Drivers Independent of Firm Size, Scope, or Cumulative Experience

These factors make one firm's unit costs different from a competitor's even if their sizes and cumulative experience are the same. Conceptually, these cost drivers shift the firm's average cost curve, as opposed to moving the firm along it (see Figure 13.1).

FIGURE 13.1
COST DRIVERS INDEPENDENT OF SCALE AND THE AVERAGE COST FUNCTION.

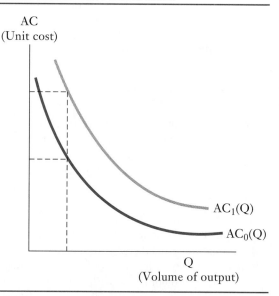

Cost drivers independent of scale shift a firm's average cost function upward or downward (e.g., from $AC_0(Q)$ to $AC_1(Q)$).

AC (Unit cost)

$AC_1(Q)$
$AC_0(Q)$

Q (Volume of output)

---

[6]Spreading nonrecurring fixed costs over time is sometimes referred to as economies of model volume. For further discussion of economies of model volume, see McGee, J., "Efficiency and Economies of Size," in Goldschmidt, H. J., M. H. Mann, and F. J. Weston (eds.) *Industrial Concentration: The New Learning*, Boston: Little, Brown, 1974, pp. 55–96.

An important cost driver independent of scale is *input prices*, for example, wage rates, energy prices, and prices of components and raw materials. When firms in the same industry purchase their inputs in national markets, their input prices will be the same. But firms in the same industry often pay different prices for inputs. Differences in wage rates may be due to differences in the degree of unionization (e.g., large trunk airlines, such as United and American, are unionized, but many new entrants, such as Kiwi, are not). Differences in wages, the price of energy, or the price of delivered materials can also be attributed to location differences among firms.

Location can influence costs in other ways besides accounting for differences in input prices. For example, because of weak local infrastructure and coordination problems that arose due to the distance between corporate headquarters and its production facility, the Lionel Corporation found it more expensive to produce toy trains in Tijuana, Mexico than Michigan, despite the large wage-rate advantage of the Mexican location.[7]

Economies of density (which were discussed in Example 5.1 in the context of airline hub-and-spoke operations) refer to cost savings that arise with greater geographic density of customers. Economies of density can arise when a transportation network within a given geographic territory is utilized more intensively (e.g., when an airline's unit costs decline as more passengers are flown over a given route). They also arise when a geographically smaller territory generates the same volume of business as a geographically larger territory (e.g., when a beer distributor that operates in a densely populated urban area has lower unit costs than a distributor selling the same amount of beer in more sparsely populated suburbs). In both cases, the cost savings are due to an increase in density (e.g., passengers per mile, customers per square mile) rather than an increase in scope (e.g., number of routes served) or scale (e.g., volume of beer sold).

One firm may achieve lower average costs than its competitors because its production environment is less *complex* or more *focused*. A firm that uses the same factory to produce a large number of different products may incur large costs associated with changing over machines and production lines to produce batches of the different products. It may also incur high administrative costs to track different work orders. A good example of the impact of complexity on production costs can be found in the railroad industry. Historically, the Pennsylvania and New York Central railroads had some of the highest costs in the railroad business because they carried a much higher proportion of less-than-carload freight than railroads such as the Norfolk and Western and the Southern.[8] The Pennsylvania and the

---

[7]"U.S. Companies are Coming Home: Costs, Quality Concerns Spell End for Offshore Operations," *Chicago Tribune*, November 22, 1987, p. F10.

[8]Less-than-carload shipments are those that take up less than a full railroad car, and thus necessitate greater handling. The Pennsylvania and New York Central's disadvantage in this regard was related to location. The Norfolk and Western and the Southern had lines through Appalachian coal country and were able to operate far more unit coal trains than the Pennsylvania and New York Central could.

New York Central needed more classification yards, more freight terminals, and greater manpower per ton of freight than their more focused counterparts who specialized in bulk traffic, such as coal and lumber. After the two roads merged to form the Penn Central in 1968, they were spending 15 cents for every dollar of sales revenue on yard expenses, as compared with an average of less than 10 cents per dollar of sales for all other railroads.[9]

A firm may have lower average costs than its rivals because it has been able to realize production *process efficiencies* that its rivals have been unable to achieve, that is, the firm uses fewer inputs than its competitors to produce a given amount of output or it employs a production technology that uses lower-priced inputs than those utilized by rivals. For example, in the early 1990s, Ford was using 25 percent less labor than General Motors to produce a typical vehicle. This effect is often difficult to disentangle from the learning curve, since the achievement of process efficiencies through learning-by-doing is at the heart of the learning curve. An example of a process efficiency not based on experience is the Chicago and Northwestern Railroad's (CNW) decision in the mid-1980s to reduce the crew size on its freight trains from 4 to 3 by eliminating one of the brakemen. This move has allowed the CNW to become one of the lowest-cost competitors in the railroad business.

One firm may also have lower average costs than its competitors because it has deliberately chosen to avoid expenses that its rivals are incurring. Its costs are lower because of *discretionary factors* that, at least to some extent, are within the firm's control. For example, in the tire business Cooper Tire and Rubber generally refrains from national advertising. This results in selling and administrative expenses that are significantly lower than its competitors (e.g., in the early 1990s, Cooper's selling and general administrative expenses were about 5 percent of sales, while Goodyear's were roughly 16 percent of sales). Similarly, in mainframe computers, Amdahl keeps costs low by being an R&D "follower" rather than a pioneer of new innovations.

Finally, a firm may have lower average costs than its rivals because of the effects of *government policies*. For obvious reasons, this factor plays an important role in international markets. For example, Japanese truck producers have long been at a disadvantage in selling trucks in the United States because of the steep import duty levied on Japanese trucks by the U.S. government.

Cost Drivers Related to the Organization of the Transaction

Chapters 2, 3, and 4 discussed how the *organization of the vertical chain* can influence the level of production costs. For transactions in which the threat of holdup is significant, in which leakage of private information is a concern, or coordination is complicated, a firm that organizes the exchange through the market may have

---

[9]Daughen, J. R. and P. Binzen, *The Wreck of the Penn Central*, Boston: Little Brown, 1971, pp. 210–212.

higher administrative and production expenses than a firm in which the same exchange is vertically integrated. In the production of men's underwear, for example, vertical integration of sewing and textile conversion operations in the same plant reduces coordination costs by improving scheduling of production runs.

One firm's costs may be higher than another because of differential degrees of *agency efficiency*. A firm's internal administrative systems, organizational structure, or compensation system may make it more vulnerable to agency or influence costs than its competitors. Paul Carroll's account of IBM's struggles in the 1980s and 1990s is full of examples of delays in decision making and excessive costs that arose from IBM's "contention system" that allowed executives within one business or functional area to critique ideas that came from outside their primary areas of responsibility.[10]

Agency costs often increase as the firm grows larger and gains more activities to coordinate internally or grows more diverse and thus creates greater conflicts in achieving coordination. The firm's agency efficiency relative to other firms can also deteriorate as its competitors adopt new and innovative ways of internally organizing that solve the same coordination problems at lower cost.

Cost Drivers, Activity-Cost Analysis, and Cost Advantage

In general, the cost of each activity in the firm's vertical chain may be influenced by a different set of cost drivers. For example, in the production of men's underwear, cumulative experience is an important cost driver in sewing but not in the more capital-intensive processes of yarn production and textile conversion. Economies of scale, by contrast, is an important cost driver in yarn production and textile conversion, but not in sewing.

Viewing firms as a collection of activities, each influenced by its own set of cost drivers, suggests that there are two major routes to achieving a cost advantage. The first is to do a better job than competitors in exploiting or controlling the key cost drivers within various activities. The second is to fundamentally alter the configuration of activities in the vertical chain. Changes in the vertical chain may be necessary due to changes in technology, which will alter the tradeoffs between outsourcing activities or performing them internally. They may also stem from changes in market conditions, which alter the prevailing costs of using the market rather than internal organization for coordinating transactions. The notion of altering the activities in the vertical chain is at the heart of what has come to be known as "process reengineering," a management philosophy that advocates that firms should not take the existing configuration of activities and processes for granted, but rather should start from scratch and redesign the chain of activities to maximize the value that can be delivered.[11] Classic examples of this include

---

[10]Carroll, P., *Big Blues: The Unmaking of IBM*, New York: Crown Publishers, 1993.

[11]See Hammer, M. and Champy, J., *Reengineering the Corporation*, New York: Harper Business, 1993.

Federal Express, which dramatically changed the economics of small-package delivery in the 1970s by using the hub-and-spoke network; Dell, which ignored conventional wisdom in the computer business by selling personal computers directly to consumers, thereby avoiding sales force and distribution expenses; and Wal-Mart, which pioneered the use of electronic computerized inventory control systems and hub-and-spoke-based logistics systems, fundamentally changing the economics of mass-merchandising.

◆ ◆ ◆ ◆ ◆ ESTIMATING AND CHARACTERIZING THE IMPACT OF COST DRIVERS

Cost drivers are an important tool for explaining why costs vary across activities and firms. But how would one assess the importance of different cost drivers in practice? For example, when firms merge with other firms or invest for growth, they often tout the cost reductions they will realize through scale economies or learning. These claims may or may not be based on a serious estimate of the magnitude of the cost savings that the firms expect to achieve. Given the inevitable costs associated with mergers and growth, such estimates are clearly desirable.

This section discusses two broad approaches for estimating the impact of cost drivers: analyses that rely on managerial accounting data and analyses based on statistical techniques, such as *regression analysis* and *frontier analysis*. These estimation approaches differ in the comparison group used for analysis. An approach using accounting data focuses on the behavior of a limited group of firms for which detailed information is available. Costs in the future are projected on the basis of past costs of the same firm. Regression and frontier analysis, on the other hand, emphasize comparisons across a broader sample of firms, using data that are comparable across the sample.

Our discussion of both accounting and statistical approaches is framed in terms of two key cost drivers, economies of scale and the learning curve, but many of the main ideas (especially regression analysis) can also easily be adapted to estimate the impact of other cost drivers. This section concludes with a discussion of the concept of *slope*, a tool for summarizing the relative importance of different cost drivers.

Using Accounting Data to Estimate the Magnitude of Scale Economies

Accounting data includes the data from balance sheets and income statements, which are generated for external reporting purposes (e.g., to allow investors and analysts to assess the overall financial health of an enterprise). It also includes managerial accounting data, such as the internal costing of departments, that allow firms to identify the fixed and variable costs of operations. Accounting data are often used to assess the magnitude of scale economies when firms contemplate mergers because the ability to achieve synergies not available to the firms individually is often a principal justification for a merger. The firms often identify and estimate the magnitude of synergies as a component of a *due diligence* examination by lenders. A due diligence is a detailed analysis of the financial and managerial consequences of a merger and relies primarily on accounting data provided by the merging firms.

Managerial accounting data can be especially useful for projecting the results of future firm operations under mergers or other conditions. For example, if the partners in a merger anticipated that they could consolidate their purchasing functions, they could estimate the reductions in staff, order-processing costs, space, and so forth and use cost accounting data to put a dollar value on these savings.

A good example in which accounting data were used to estimate the benefits of a merger is the 1991 merger between Chemical Bank and Manufacturers Hanover.[12] At the time of the merger, Chemical CEO Joseph Sponholz announced that savings of $650 million annually were "both a floor and in the bag." Savings were anticipated to come from several areas. The partners forecast laying off 6,200 workers, for an annual savings of $350 million. Additional savings would come from closing 70 bank branches, eliminating Chemical's credit card processing center, and consolidating executive offices. Many industry analysts and economists agreed that these savings estimates were realistic and that further consolidation was inevitable, as other banks sought similar economies. Indeed, bank consolidation has continued through the 1990s.

Managerial accounting data can also serve as the cornerstone of activity-cost analyses of scale economies. Consider a specific activity, such as marketing. By estimating the increase in labor, advertising time, promotional effort, and so forth needed to achieve a given increase in sales and using internal accounting data to determine the incremental costs of these inputs, the firm can determine whether marketing activity is characterized by economies of scale. If the incremental marketing costs are less than average marketing costs, then scale economies in marketing are present, and larger firms will have a cost advantage in this activity. If, instead, the incremental marketing costs equal or exceed average marketing costs, then scale economies in marketing are not present, and a small firm will not be at a disadvantage in this activity.

Using Regression Analysis to Estimate the Shapes of Cost Curves

Consider the following cost and output data for three chain saw manufacturing plants:

Plant	Annual Output	Average Cost
1	10,000	$50
2	20,000	$47
3	30,000	$45

---

[12]See "2 Banks See Big Savings in Merger," *New York Times*, November 17, 1991, p. D1 and "The Bank Merger: For New York, A Loss of Jobs and Revenue," *New York Times*, July 16, 1991, p. A1.

Average costs apparently fall as output increases. It would be natural to conclude from this pattern that there are economies of scale in chain saw production. We can even estimate the magnitude of the economies—it appears that a plant producing 30,000 saws annually has average costs that are $5 lower than those at a plant producing 10,000 saws annually.

Just how confident should we be about the presence and magnitude of scale economies in this instance? The differences in costs at the three plants might have nothing to do with scale economies. For example, plant 1 may be located in a region where labor costs are unusually high. Increasing production at that plant, or building a larger plant, may not affect labor costs (or may even drive them up), and therefore may not improve plant 1's cost position. To take another example, the supplier of steel to plant 2 may have been crippled by a strike, forcing that plant to pay more for its steel from another supplier. As was the case with plant 1, increasing the scale of operation might not affect costs. To be confident that the cost/output relationship truly reflect scale economies, these alternative explanations need to be ruled out.

These are the ideas underlying *regression analysis* of *cost functions*. Regression analysis is a statistical technique for estimating how one or more factors affect some variable of interest. For cost functions, the variable of interest is average cost, and the factors may include output, wage rates, and other input prices.

To illustrate, suppose that we suspect that the average cost function is a quadratic function of the volume of output:

$$AC = \beta_0 + \beta_1 Q + \beta_2 Q^2 + \beta_3 w + noise$$

where Q denotes production volume (e.g., number of standard-size chain saws produced per year), w denotes the local wage rate, and *noise* represents all of the other factors that affect the level of cost that cannot be measured and which are not explicitly included in the analysis.

We can interpret the cost function as follows: The average cost at any particular plant is equal to some function of plant output, plus a function of wage rates, plus "noise." We expect β_3 to be positive as higher wages contribute to higher costs. We expect β_1 to be negative, suggesting that as output rises, average costs fall. We expect β_2 to be small and positive. Thus, at large levels of output (and therefore at very large levels of output ^{2}), average costs may start to level off or even increase, as the positive effect of $\beta_2 Q^2$ offsets or dominates the negative effect of $\beta_1 Q$. It is the combination of β_1 whose negative slope indicates economies of scale and β_3 whose positive slope indicates diseconomies of scale, that produces the characteristic parabolic or U shape of the average cost function.

Finally, the noise term represents variation in costs due to factors other than size and wage rates. If we had good information about sources of that variation, we could directly include additional variables in the cost function. Otherwise, we are forced to accept that our cost function is necessarily imprecise. Regression analysis "fits" the cost function to actual cost/output data. In other words, regression provides estimates of the parameters β_1, β_2, and β_3. Regression analysis then infers from the magnitude of the noise just how confident we should be about the accuracy of the parameter estimates.

FIGURE 13.2
"PRECISELY"-FIT COST FUNCTION.

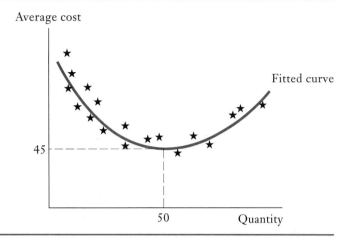

Average cost

Fitted curve

45

The cost/quantity pairs for each firm generally lie close to the curve that best fits the data.

50   Quantity

FIGURE 13.3
"IMPRECISELY"-FIT COST FUNCTION.

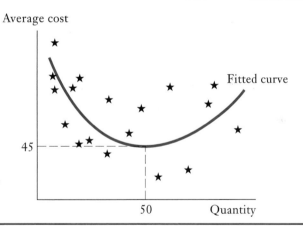

Average cost

Fitted curve

45

The cost/quantity pairs for each firm generally lie far from the curve that best fits the data.

50   Quantity

Figures 13.2 and 13.3 illustrate these ideas. These figures plot average costs and output pairs at several plants in two hypothetical industries. Suppose that local wage rates are the same at all plants, so that the only sources of variation in costs are output and noise. We can use regression analysis to fit cost functions of the following form:

$$AC = \beta_0 + \beta_1 Q + \beta_2 Q^2 + noise$$

to each set of data (yielding two different average cost curves). If, as expected, β_1 is negative and β_2 is positive, the average costs curve will be U-shaped, and the output at which average cost is minimized will equal $-\beta_1/2\beta_2$.[13] The regression finds the values of β_0, β_1, and β_2 that best fit the actual data. The best fit is achieved when the sum of the squared distances between the actual cost values and the values on the fitted parabola is minimized. Best-fitting parabolas are drawn through the scatterplots in Figures 13.2 and 13.3.

Given the cost/output pairs that we chose, the best-fitting parabolas are identical. In both cases $\beta_0 = 70$, $\beta_1 = -1$, and $\beta_2 = .01$. Thus, minimum average cost is achieved at output 50, with average cost = 45. In both figures this output is near the upper end of the range of outputs, suggesting that most firms still have unexploited economies of scale. An important difference between Figures 13.2 and 13.3 is that the parabola in Figure 13.2 appears to come much closer to fitting the data than the parabola in Figure 13.3. In other words, actual costs depart significantly from the fitted curve much more often in Figure 13.3. Even though regressions report the same parameter estimates for both figures, they will report much lower confidence levels for the parameter estimates for Figure 13.3.[14] In fact, the poor fit of the curve in Figure 13.3 might make it difficult to statistically determine whether a parabolic or linear average cost function best fits the data.

$\mathcal{E}$XAMPLE 13.1

A QUADRATIC COST FUNCTION FOR THE SAVINGS AND LOAN INDUSTRY

J. Holton Wilson's study of scale economies in the savings and loan (S&L) industry provides a good example of the quadratic specification of average cost described in this section.[15] Wilson collected data for 86 S&Ls located in western states in the United States for the years 1975 and 1976. The measure of size that Wilson used was the S&L's total assets. During this period, larger S&L's were generally more profitable than smaller S&L's, suggesting the possibility of economies of scale. This conclusion was confirmed by Wilson's estimates. For 1975, he estimated the average cost function for the S&L industry to be given by:

$$AC = 2.38 - .615A + 0.54A^2$$

---

[13]This can be derived by differentiating AC with respect to Q, and solving for the value of Q that makes this resulting derivative equal to 0.

[14]A confidence level states the probability with which a true parameter value lies within a particular range.

[15]Wilson, J. H., "A Note on Scale Economies in the Savings and Loan Industry," *Business Economics*, January 1981, pp. 45–49.

where AC denotes long-run average cost, and A denotes the dollar value of assets. As discussed above, this curve is a U-shaped parabola. In this case, the long-run average cost function reaches a minimum at \$569 million in assets. This lies at the upper end of the range of sizes of the S&Ls in Wilson's study, which suggests that most of these S&Ls had not fully exhausted the available scale economies.

There is a large literature on the estimation of cost functions. Cost functions have been estimated for various industries, including airlines, telecommunications, electric utilities, trucking, railroads, and hospitals.[16] Most of these studies estimate functional forms for the average cost function that are more complicated than the simple quadratic functions discussed here. Nevertheless, the basic ideas underlying these more sophisticated analyses are those described here, and these studies can be used to derive estimates of minimum efficient scale. Michael Long et al., summarize minimum efficient scale estimates from a dozen studies of one industry—hospitals.[17] Their work points out that many issues need to be resolved before a particular cost function estimate for an industry can be accepted. They find that estimates of the minimum efficient size hospital vary tremendously from one study to another—estimate ranges from 160 beds to 2,580 beds—leaving them to question the ability to ever determine the true optimal hospital size.

$\mathcal{E}$XAMPLE 13.2

ECONOMIES OF SCALE IN THE RAILROAD INDUSTRY[18]

During the last 15 years, the U.S. railroad industry has undergone a dramatic restructuring. The number of so-called Class I railroads (those with annual revenues greater than \$10 million) shrank from 56 in 1974 to 21 in 1986. Much of this shrinkage was due to consolidations or mergers, such as the merger between the Norfolk and Western and Southern railroads and the acquisition of the Missouri

---

[16]John Panzar's article "Determinants of Firm and Industry Structure," in Schmalensee, R. and R. D. Willig, (eds), *Handbook of Industrial Organization*, Amsterdam: North Holland, 1989, pp. 3–59, reviews some of the work on estimation of cost functions and provides many references to the literature.

[17]Long, M. J., R. P. Ament, J. L. Dreachslin, and E. J. Kobrinski, "A Reconsideration of Economies of Scale in the Health Care Field," *Health Policy*, 1984, 25–44.

[18]This example draws heavily from Vellturo, C. A., E. R. Berndt, A. F. Friedlaender, J. S. W. Chiang, and M. H. Showalter, "Deregulation Mergers, and Cost Savings in Class I U.S. Railroads, 1974–1986, *Journal of Economics and Management Strategy*, 1, Summer 1992, pp. 339–369.

Pacific and Western Pacific railroads by the Union Pacific. Nearly all of the mergers that have taken place since the late 1970s have been justified on the basis of operating efficiencies due to economies of scale.

The data in Table 13.3, which show average variable cost and traffic volume for selected U.S. Class I railroads, seem to support the argument that there are economies of scale. The two largest railroads in terms of traffic volume in 1986, Burlington Northern and Union Pacific, also had the lowest average variable costs. However, as we cautioned above, it is dangerous to draw conclusions about economies of scale simply on the basis of observed differences in average costs and firm sizes. Other factors may also influence the average cost. And indeed the data in Table 13.3 are hardly conclusive. The third and fourth lowest railroads in terms of average variable costs are two small systems, the Chicago Northwestern and the Kansas City Southern.

To test more carefully the hypothesis that railroading is characterized by economies of scale, Christopher Vellturo, Ernie Berndt, Ann Friedlaender, Judy Chiang, and Mark Showalter estimated cost functions for each of the Class I railroads for selected years, including 1986. Their estimates can be used to determine the elasticity of average variable cost with respect to various cost drivers, such as traffic volume, capital stock, average haul length, and route mileage. A cost elasticity indicates the percentage change in average variable cost caused by a 1 percent

TABLE 13.3
TRAFFIC VOLUME AND AVERAGE VARIABLE COST AMONG U.S. CLASS I RAILROADS, 1986

Railroad	1986 Traffic Volume (millions of ton-miles of freight)	1986 Average Variable Cost ($ per ton-mile)*
Burlington Northern	190,000	.0054
Union Pacific	140,000	.0087
CSX	130,000	.0122
Norfolk Southern	91,414	.0143
Santa Fe	67,141	.0112
Chicago Northwestern	26,576	.0090
ICG	19,992	.0170
Soo	19,502	.0105
Kansas City Southern	11,187	.0089
Missouri-Kansas-Texas	8,102	.0131

*Variable costs include: labor, rolling stock, fuel, materials, and supplies.

Source: Table calculated from information in Table II of Vellturo, C. A., E. R. Berndt, A. F. Friedlaender, J. S. W. Chiang, and M. H. Showalter, "Deregulation, Mergers, and Cost Savings in Class I U.S. Railroads, 1974–1986," *Journal of Economics and Management Strategy*, 1, Summer 1992, pp. 339–369.

change in the level of the cost driver, holding the levels of all other cost drivers fixed. If the elasticity of average variable cost with respect to traffic volume is negative, that would be evidence of scale economies in railroading, because it would indicate that average variable costs fall as traffic volume increases.

Table 13.4 shows the cost elasticities that are implied by the cost functions estimated by Vellturo et al. The elasticity of average variable cost with respect to traffic volume is indeed negative, confirming the presence of economies of scale. The estimates also suggest that average variable costs decline as average length of haul increases. Since most of the railroad mergers of the late 1970s and 1980s increased average haul length, this finding supports the view that these mergers enhanced cost efficiency. Note that Table 13.4 indicates positive cost elasticities for route mileage, which implies that average variable costs rise as a railroad's route mileage increases. This may seem to contradict the conclusion that scale economies exist. But remember that the cost elasticity of a cost driver tells us what happens when that driver is increased, but all other cost drivers remain constant. An increase in a railroad's route mileage, without a corresponding increase in traffic, is akin to decreasing a railroad's capacity utilization. Since lower capacity utilization is often associated with less efficient usage of variable inputs and thus higher average variable costs, it should not be surprising the cost elasticities for route mileage are positive.

TABLE 13.4
ESTIMATED COST ELASTICITIES FOR U.S. CLASS I RAILROADS, 1986

| | Elasticity of average variable cost with respect to: | | | |
Railroad	Traffic volume	Amount of way and structure capital	Route mileage	Average haul length
Burlington Northern	−.574	−.109	.293	−.341
Union Pacific	−.579	−.123	.403	−.435
CSX	−.523	−.171	.508	−.814
Norfolk Southern	−.532	−.209	.550	−.770
Conrail	−.356	−.192	.166	−.669
Missouri-Kansas-Texas	−.697	−.352	.081	−.300
Santa Fe	−.455	−.171	.151	−.351
Soo	−.867	−.214	.563	−.327
ICG	−.372	−.125	.101	−.830

Source: Table calculated from information in Table III of Vellturo, C. A., E. R. Berndt, A. F. Friedlaender, J. S. W. Chiang, and M. H. Showalter, "Deregulation, Mergers, and Cost Savings in Class I U.S. Railroads, 1974–1986," *Journal of Economics and Management Strategy*, 1, Summer 1992, pp. 339–369.

Frontier Analysis

Regression techniques for determining the shape of the cost curve are based on fitting a curve roughly through the middle of a range of cost/quantity pairs achieved by different firms at different times. As Figures 13.3 and 13.4 show, some firms' cost and quantity pairs will be above the fitted curve and others will be below it. If we interpret the fitted curve as representing the expected production cost for various levels of output, then a natural interpretation of the variation of cost/quantity pairs above and below the fitted curve is that some firms are more efficient than others. Using this interpretation, firms whose cost/quantity pairs are below the fitted curve are more efficient than average because their costs are less than expected for a firm producing that level of output. Similarly, firms whose cost/quantity pairs are above the fitted curve are less efficient than average.

Frontier analysis is based on this interpretation of regression analysis. The intuition behind frontier analysis is simple. Instead of fitting a curve that passes through the middle of a distribution of cost/quantity pairs, imagine fitting a curve that just touches the lowest cost/quantity pair. This curve, which is depicted in Figure 13.4, is the *efficiency frontier*, a concept introduced in Chapter 12. Except for firms right on the frontier, all other firms are "less efficient" because their costs exceed the theoretically achievable frontier cost levels. The further away from the frontier a firm finds itself, the less efficient it is. A firm inside the frontier might conclude that it is not operating at maximum efficiency, and therefore it should be able to lower its costs and maintain or even increase its quantity. This is closely related to the concept of *total quality management* (TQM), which teaches that firms can lower their costs and maintain or increase *quality* by improving the efficiency of their production processes.

FIGURE 13.4
THE EFFICIENCY FRONTIER.

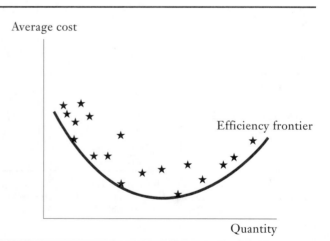

The efficiency frontier fits a curve to the lowest cost/quantity pair. Firms whose cost/quantity pairs are above the frontier are "less efficient" because their costs exceed the theoretically achievable frontier cost levels.

Most frontier analyses use data on productive inputs and outputs, rather than costs and outputs. They also use sophisticated empirical techniques that account for complicated production technologies, as well as the effects of random chance on production levels. Richard Caves and David Barton present an excellent overview of frontier analysis techniques for the interested reader.[19]

Some economists challenge the argument that firms that lie above the frontier are not fully efficient. The apparent inefficiency may stem as much from the failure of the economist to correctly model the firm as from actual inefficiencies in the firm's operations. For example, the allegedly inefficient firm may be producing a good that is slightly differentiated from those produced by its competitors, necessitating higher costs. Or the firm may use a different mix of inputs not adequately handled by the economist's model relating inputs and costs to output.

However, these challenges do not negate the value of the frontier analysis approach. Just as in the survivor principle approach, frontier analysis requires that firms compare themselves to their competitors. A firm identified as lying inside the frontier may eventually explain its alleged inefficiencies. But in the process it will be forced to reexamine its production techniques and will often find that its production is less efficient than its competitors'.

Estimating Learning Curves and Slopes

Learning curves can also be estimated using multiple regression techniques. To do this, it is often convenient to estimate an equation with the following functional form:

$$logAC = \alpha + \epsilon \, logE + \gamma_1 \, logX_1 + ... + \gamma_N \, logX_N + noise$$

where "log" represents the natural logarithm, E denotes cumulative production volume, $X_1, ..., X_n$ denote the levels of cost drivers other than cumulative production volume that affect average cost (e.g., scale, capacity utilization, input prices, complexity, and so forth), and *noise* denotes the impact of factors that cannot be measured and are thus not included in the analysis. These other cost drivers are included in the equation to distinguish between cost reductions that are due to learning and cost reductions that are due to economies of scale or favorable positions on other cost drivers. The parameters ϵ and γ are the cost elasticities, comparable to those discussed in Example 13.2 and depicted in Table 13.4: ϵ is the percentage change in average cost per 1 percent change in cumulative experience, and γ_1 is the percentage change in average cost per 1 percent change in cost driver, X_1. Logarithms are used in the above equation, so that the estimated coefficients really are elasticities.

---

[19]Caves, R. and D. Barton, *Efficiency in U.S. Manufacturing Industries*, Cambridge, MA: MIT Press, 1990.

Marvin Lieberman uses a functional form similar to the one above to estimate the learning curve for a set of 37 chemical processing industries.[20] To control for the effects of economies of scale, he includes annual production volume and average plant scale in the analysis. His estimates of the cost elasticity of cumulative experience range between $-.28$ and $-.47$.

Once the above equation is estimated, a tool that is often used to characterize the magnitude of a cost driver's impact on average cost is *slope*. We encountered this concept in the discussion of the learning curve in Chapter 5.[21] Slope indicates the level to which average cost declines (as a percentage of a baseline level) when the cost driver doubles. If, for example, the slope of the learning curve is 86 percent, then doubling cumulative experience reduces average costs to 86 percent of their previous level. Formally, if X represents the level of a particular cost driver (e.g., production volume, cumulative experience, capacity utilization) and $AC(X)$ is the level of average costs when the level of the driver is at X, the slope S of driver X is given by

$$S = AC(2X)/AC(X)$$

When the slope is close to 1, $AC(2X)$ will be close to $AC(X)$ and the driver has a rather small impact on costs. The farther the slope is away from 1, the greater the impact of the driver on costs. In the turbine generator industry, it was thought that the slope of the experience curve was .93 and that the slope of unit size was .68. A doubling of cumulative experience reduced a firm's unit costs to 93 percent of what they were previously. A doubling of unit size reduced a firm's costs to 68 percent of what they were previously.[22]

How does one calculate the slope of a cost driver? It can be shown that the slope of cost driver X_i is given by

$$S_i = 2^{\gamma_i}$$

where γ_i is the cost elasticity of cost driver i. If, for example, the cost elasticity for scale is $-.50$, the slope of scale is $2^{-.50} = .71$, indicating that doubling scale reduces average costs to 71 percent of their initial level.

---

[20]Lieberman, M. B., "The Learning Curve and Pricing in the Chemical Processing Industries," *RAND Journal of Economics*, Summer 1984, pp. 213–228. Rather than using average cost as the dependent variable, Lieberman used price because of the difficulties in obtaining proprietary cost data from firms. Price is often used as a surrogate for average cost in learning curve studies. While not perfect, this approach will yield plausible estimates of the effects of learning if price-average cost margins remain constant over the analysis.

[21]In the context of the learning curve, slope is synonymous with progress ratio.

[22]These data are taken from "General Electric versus Westinghouse in Large Turbine Generators," in Porter, M., *Cases in Competitive Strategy*, New York: Free Press, 1983, pp. 102–118.

$\mathcal{E}$XAMPLE 13.3

COST DRIVERS AND COST ADVANTAGE IN THE TITANIUM DIOXIDE INDUSTRY

Pankaj Ghemawat's study of DuPont's capacity expansion in Titanium Dioxide (TiO$_2$) industry in the 1970s, already discussed in Example 11.6 in Chapter 11, contains data that help to illustrate how slope can be used to diagnose the sources of magnitude of cost advantage.[23] Recall that TiO$_2$ is a whitener used in the production of paint, paper, and plastics. There are two distinct technologies for producing it: the sulfate process and the chloride process. By the early 1970s, U.S. waste disposal regulations had made the sulfate process extremely expensive. All of the new plants built after that time employed the chloride process. DuPont was the only firm that had mastered the use of ilmenite ore in the chloride process. By 1973 this was a source of cost advantage because the price of rutile ore had increased relative to ilmenite ore (influenced in part by environmental policies in Australia, the largest source of both rutile and ilmenite).

Using DuPont and industry data, Ghemawat estimated an average cost function for the production of titanium dioxide. His estimate is as follows:

$$log\ AC = 6.499 - .329\ log\ EXP - .243\ log\ CAP - .304\ log\ CU$$

where:

   EXP = cumulative production of TiO$_2$ production at all DuPont's plants.

   CAP = average capacity of DuPont's TiO$_2$ plants.

   CU = average capacity utilization at DuPont's TiO$_2$ plants.

From this cost function, one can use the formula presented above to calculate that the slope of the learning curve is 79.6 percent, the slope of average capacity size (a proxy for economies of scale) is 84.5 percent, and the slope of capacity utilization is 81 percent. Ghemawat also estimates that a 50,000-ton rutile plant operating at full capacity would produce TiO$_2$ at a cost of 18 cents/lb, while a 50,000-ton ilmenite chloride plant run by a firm with comparable experience would produce TiO$_2$ at a cost of 17.6 cents/lb. (See Table 13.5.) DuPont's average plant scale was nearly 100,000 tons, and its cumulative output using the chloride process was at least twice as great as its next most experienced competitor. Based on this information and the estimated slopes of the cost drivers, one could then estimate the magnitude of DuPont's cost advantage over smaller and less experienced competitors who were relying on the rutile chloride process.

---

[23]Ghemawat, P., "Capacity Expansion in the Titanium Dioxide Industry," *Journal of Industrial Economics*, 32, December 1984, pp. 143–163.

TABLE 13.5
COSTS OF PRODUCTION FOR TiO$_2$ IN 1972 (CENTS/LB): 50,000-TON-PER-YEAR PLANT, OPERATING AT CAPACITY

	Chloride-ilmenite	Chloride-rutile	Sulfate
Ore	2.5	3.5	2.5
Other ingredients	3.9	2.9	3.7
Energy	1.5	1.5	2.9
Labor	1.9	2.9	3.7
Miscellaneous	4.6	4.6	4.1
Depreciation	3.0	2.5	4.0
Waste disposal	0.2	0.1	0.3
TOTAL	17.6	18.0	21.2

Source: Ghemawat, P., "Capacity Expansion in the Titanium Dioxide Industry," *Journal of Industrial Economics*, 33, December 1984; 153.

◆ ◆ ◆ ◆ ◆ ANALYZING THE SOURCES OF DIFFERENTIATION ADVANTAGE

This section introduces the concept of benefit drivers and presents a variety of analytical techniques for estimating them.

Benefit Drivers

A firm creates a differentiation advantage by offering a product that delivers larger perceived benefits to prospective buyers than competitors' products, that is, by offering a higher *B*. The perceived benefit, in turn, depends on the attributes that consumers value, as well as those that lower the user and the transactions costs associated with the product. These attributes, or what we call benefit drivers, form the basis on which a firm can differentiate itself.[24] Benefit drivers can include many things and developing an analysis of them in any particular case obviously involves understanding who the firm's prospective buyers are, how they might use the firm's product or service, and which of their needs the firm's product satisfies.

Broadly speaking, benefit drivers can be classified along five dimensions:

• *Physical characteristics of the product itself*: These drivers relate to the product itself and include factors such as product performance, quality, features, aesthetics, durability, and ease of installation and operation.

---

[24]This idea forms the basis of "Lancasterian" demand theory in economics. See Lancaster, K., *Consumer Demand*, New York: Columbia University Press, 1971.

- *The quantity and characteristics of the services or complementary goods the firm or its dealers offer for sale*: Key drivers here include postsale services, such as customer training or consulting services, complementary products (e.g., spare parts) that the seller bundles with the product, product warranties or maintenance contracts, and the quality of repair or service capabilities.

- *Characteristics associated with the sale or delivery of the good*: Specific benefit drivers include speed and timeliness of delivery, availability of credit and favorability of credit terms, location of the seller, and the quality of presale technical advice.

- *Characteristics that shape consumer's perceptions or expectations of the product's performance or its cost in use.*[25] Specific drivers include the product's reputation for performance, the seller's perceived staying power or financial stability (this would be important for industrial transactions in which the buyer anticipates an ongoing relationship with the seller), and the product's installed base (i.e., the number of consumers currently using the product; a large installed base would lead to the expectation that the costs of developing product know-how are likely to be low).

- *The subjective image of the product:* Image is a convenient way of referring to the constellation of psychological rewards that the consumer receives from purchasing, owning, and consuming the product. Image is driven by the impact of advertising messages, packaging, or labeling, and by the prestige of the distributors or outlets that carry the products.

A useful geometric representation of how benefit drivers differ across sellers is with a *perceptual map*. A perceptual map is similar to the concept of a value map introduced in Chapter 12 except that instead of depicting firms' positions in terms of price and a benefit driver (e.g., product performance or quality) as the value map does, the perceptual map depicts firms' positions in terms of two different benefit drivers. Figure 13.5 depicts a perceptual map for the U.S. domestic airline industry. The two dimensions depicted are service quality (which embraces on-time performance and low levels of customer complaints) and the scope of the airline's domestic and international route structure. This is an important consideration for consumers who are accumulating frequent-flyer mileage on an airline. Southwest Airlines consistently ranks above all other airlines on the standard measures of service quality, but it has a small and unexciting route structure. By contrast, United Airlines has an impressive international and domestic route structure, but ranks poorly in terms of service quality. Finally, some airlines, such as TWA and Northwest, rank poorly in both dimensions. In markets where they compete head-to-head with airlines with better route structures or stronger reputations for quality, these airline have little choice but to compete on the basis of low price.

---

[25]Michael Porter refers to these as *signaling criteria*. See *Competitive Advantage*, New York: Free Press, 1985, pp. 142–146.

FIGURE 13.5
PERCEPTUAL MAP OF THE U.S. AIRLINE INDUSTRY.

The horizontal axis in the figure represents the scope of the airline's route network (domestic and international). This is an important benefit driver for flyers who are accumulating frequent-flyer mileage. The vertical axis depicts service quality, reflecting factors such as on-time performance and amenities.

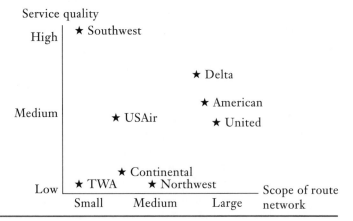

♦ ♦

EXAMPLE 13.4

IBM AND THE MICROCHANNEL BUS

Although the point may seem obvious, benefit drivers must be viewed from the consumer's perspective, not the firm's. Differentiation is meaningful only when it enhances the benefits as perceived by consumers. Firms often engage in false differentiation by building in attributes that appeal to the designer's sense of technical virtuosity, but that do not enhance the product's value from the consumer's perspective. IBM's heavy promotion in 1987 of the MicroChannel bus in its PS-2 personal computer is a classic example of meaningless differentiation.[26] IBM figured that the bus (a series of circuits for carrying data from one part of the computer to another) would distinguish the PS-2 from the clones made by Compaq and others, who were also getting ready to launch machines based on the 386 chip. To signal how serious it was about the MicroChannel, IBM decided to stop producing the AT, the largest selling personal computer up to that time, because the AT used a different kind of bus. IBM did not want to let consumers choose between the old standard and the new standard. Unfortunately, as Paul Carroll wryly notes, "selling a computer based on the bus is like selling a house based on its plumbing. . . " and "MicroChannel was IBM's version of Colgate's MFP, a mystery ingredient that no one understood but was supposed to be magic." In the end, most personal

---

[26]This example is drawn from Carroll, P., *Big Blues: The Unmaking of IBM*, New York: Crown, 1993.

computer buyers could not have cared less that IBM's 386 machine had a MicroChannel bus and the clones did not. The clones sold anyway because of their much lower prices. When given the opportunity to adopt MicroChannel through a licensing agreement, most clone makers declined.

Methods for Estimating and Characterizing Perceived Benefits

Unlike a firm's costs, which (at least in principle) can be tracked through its accounting system or estimated with statistical techniques, a product's perceived benefit is more difficult to estimate. Any approach for estimating and characterizing benefits has four components. First, an overall measure of the benefits provided to the consumer must be obtained. Second, the relevant benefit drivers must be identified. Third, the magnitude of the benefit must be estimated. Fourth, the willingness of consumers to trade off one driver for another needs to be identified. A full analysis of the techniques for estimating benefits falls within the domain of demand estimation in economics and marketing research. Here we briefly mention four approaches that might be used to estimate a firm's benefit position relative to its competitors and the importance of benefit drivers.

- Reservation price method
- Attribute rating method
- Conjoint analysis
- Hedonic pricing analysis

Reservation Price Method

Because a consumer purchases a product if and only if $B - P > 0$, it follows that the perceived benefit B represents a consumer's *reservation price*—the maximum monetary price the consumer is willing to pay for a unit of the product or service. Since such an overall measure of consumer benefit is rarely available, it must be estimated from survey data or else imputed from database information on consumer choices. One approach to estimating B, then, is simply to ask consumers the highest price they would be willing to pay. Marketing survey research that precedes the introduction of new products often includes a question along these lines. Once reservation prices have been identified, the analysis of benefit drivers can follow using the techniques discussed below.

Attribute-Rating Method

Attribute rating is a technique for estimating benefit drivers directly from survey responses and then calculating overall benefits on the basis of attribute scores. Under this approach, target consumers are asked to rate a set of products in terms of a list of attributes. For example, for each attribute consumers might be given a fixed number of points to allocate among each product. Each attribute is then assigned an "importance weight," and relative perceived benefits are determined by calculating the weighted average of the product ratings.

To illustrate, consider three hypothetical makers of washing machines and an average set of ratings by a group of representative consumers.

| | | Brand | | |
Importance Weight	Attribute	I	II	III
40%	Performance (washing ability)	40	40	20
30%	Water-use efficiency	35	35	30
20%	Ease of use	30	30	40
10%	Noise level	50	20	30
100%	Weighted Score	37.5	34.5	28

Brand I's weighted score is 8.6 percent higher than brand II's and 33.9 percent higher than brand III's. This method would then conclude that the reservation price of brand I exceeds the reservation prices of brands II and III by 8.6 and 33.9 percent respectively.

Weighted scores can be divided by costs to construct "B/C ratios." Recall that a firm's strategic position is determined by the amount of $B-C$ it generates versus its competitors. As long as products have cost and or benefit proximity, the ranking of B/C ratios across firms will be similar (though not necessarily equal) to the rankings of $B-C$ differences. Thus, products with high B/C ratios will generally enjoy a superior strategic position than their lower B/C rivals.

Comparing B/C is quite common in public policy, where it is called "cost efficiency analysis." For example, some Canadian provinces use survey methods to develop "scores" that measure the benefits of different health care treatments. They divide these scores by the costs of treatment to construct benefit-to-cost ratios, and allocate health care resources to those treatments with the highest ratios. Pharmaceutical manufacturers are using similar methods in the United States to promote the advantages of new products that they claim have high benefit-to-cost ratios.

One problem with this approach is that benefits are usually not expressed in dollars. When benefits and costs are not measured on the same scale, it is impossible to compute meaningful measures of $B-C$. Several sophisticated statistical procedures have been introduced to try to measure benefits, in dollars, of specific product attributes. These include conjoint analysis and hedonic pricing, which we describe below.

Conjoint Analysis

Conjoint analysis refers to a set of statistical tools used by market researchers to estimate the relative benefits of different products attributes.[27] Its principal value is

---

[27]For a review of conjoint analysis and its applications in marketing, see Green, P. E. and V. Srinivasan, "Conjoint Analysis in Marketing Research: New Developments and Directions," *Journal of Marketing*, 54, October 1990, pp. 3–19.

in estimating the magnitude of different benefit drivers and the tradeoffs that consumers are willing to make among them. Although conjoint analysis can take several different forms, consumers are usually asked to rank a product with different features at different prices. For example, they might be asked to rank the following four "bundles": (i) a CD player without a shuffle-play feature at a price of $500; (ii) the same CD player without a shuffle-play feature at a price of $600; (iii) the same CD player, but with a shuffle-play feature, at a price of $500; and the CD player with a shuffle-play feature at a price of $600. Consumers would almost certainly rank (i) over (ii) and (iii) over (iv). However, the choice between (i) and (iv) is less clear. The proportion of consumers that ranks (iv) over (i) provides information about consumers' willingness to pay for a shuffle-play feature. In a typical conjoint analysis, consumers are asked to rank many different bundles, and researchers then use regression analysis to estimate the impact of price and product features on consumers rankings. This analysis, in turn, can be used to estimate how much consumers are willing to pay for additional features or product enhancements.

Hedonic Pricing

The logic of hedonic pricing analysis is similar to that of conjoint analysis. However, unlike conjoint analysis, hedonic pricing makes use of data about actual consumer purchases to determine the value of particular product attributes. For example, consumers purchase automobiles according to a variety of attributes, including horsepower, interior room, and braking capabilities. By examining how automobile prices vary with different combinations of features, analysts can determine how much consumers are willing to pay for each individual attribute. Hedonic pricing has been used to identify the value of innovations in computerized axial tomography, the value of spreadsheet compatibility (see Example 13.5), and the benefits of improving job safety (see Example 13.6).[28] The term "hedonic" comes from "hedonism" and is meant to convey the idea that the pleasure or happiness a consumer derives from a good depends on the attributes that the good embodies.

The basic technique in hedonic pricing is to use multiple regression analysis to estimate an equation of the form:

$$log\, P = \alpha_0 + \alpha_1 log\, X_1 + \alpha_2 log X_2 + \ldots + \alpha_N log X_N + noise$$

where P denotes the product's price and X_i denotes the level of particular attribute i. The estimated coefficient α_i represents the elasticity of the market price of the product with respect to the ith attribute. If, for example, X_i represents the length of an automobile, and $\alpha_i = 1.5$, then the analysis indicates that a 1 percent increase in length translates into a 1.5 percent increase in price. If the average price of a

---

[28]Zvi Griliches pioneered the development of modern hedonic price analysis. See "Hedonic Price Indexes for Automobiles: An Econometric Analysis of Quality Change," in *The Price Statistics of the Federal Government*, New York: National Bureau of Economic Research, 1961, pp. 173–196. See Trajtenberg, M., "A Penny for Your Thoughts: Patent Citations and the Value of Innovations," *RAND Journal of Economics*, 21, Spring 1990; 172–187 for an application of this technique to computerized axial tomography scanners.

175-inch car is $15,000, this analysis suggests that consumers would be willing to pay an extra $2,250 for an extra 17.5 inches in length, all else equal. This analysis thus generates implicit "prices" for attributes. These prices are sometimes referred to as hedonic prices.

Hedonic pricing can be an extremely powerful tool in evaluating the economic tradeoffs involved in enhancing a product. In effect, this analysis can help a firm determine the slope of the consumer indifference curves that were discussed in Chapter 12. A firm considering adding additional features to a basic product or enhancing its performance would compare the hedonic price of the enhancement to its incremental cost. If, in the target market, the hedonic price exceeds the incremental cost, the enhancement would be worthwhile.

By including firm-specific "dummy variables" (variables that take on a value of "1" if the product is sold by a given firm and "0" if it is not) in the multiple regression analysis above, hedonic pricing analysis can also be used to assess the extent to which consumers are willing to pay more for one firm's product than for those of competitors, independent of differences in observable attributes. That is, the analysis can gauge the power of a brand name or reputation. Table 13.6 shows the result of a hedonic pricing analysis of the personal computer industry by Joanna Stavins.[29] In addition to showing the extent to which product attributes, such as size of the hard drive and the amount of RAM, affect consumers' willingness to pay for personal computers, the analysis also shows that the Apple and Compaq brand names had significantly positive impacts on price, while Commodore and Atari brand names had a negative effect on prices.

◆ ◆

EXAMPLE 13.5

HEDONIC PRICING ANALYSIS OF NETWORK EXTERNALITIES IN THE MARKET FOR SPREADSHEETS

For some products, such as computer hardware, computer software, and consumer electronics, the benefit that a consumer anticipates receiving from purchasing a product increases according to the number of consumers that currently use the product or are expected to use the product in the future. Economists refer to this phenomenon as *network externalities*, because when additional consumers join the "network" of current consumers, they have a beneficial "external" impact on the consumers who are already part of the network. Network externalities explain why (as discussed earlier) installed base might be an important driver of benefits for some products and also explains why product *compatibility* is often desirable. If, for

---

[29]Stavins, J., "Estimating Demand Elasticities in a Differentiated Product Industry: The Personal Computer Market," working paper, October 1992.

TABLE 13.6
HEDONIC PRICING ANALYSIS OF PERSONAL COMPUTERS

Dependent variable: log Price

Independent variables	*Coefficient*	t-*statistic* [a]
log hard drive size	0.164	19.64
log RAM	0.339	18.10
log Mhz	0.213	5.82
log number of floppy drives	0.367	7.98
log number of slots	0.085	4.38
Black & white monitor dummy	0.068	2.53
Color monitor dummy	0.134	1.93
Discount market dummy	−0.274	−9.86
Extra equipment dummy	0.224	2.68
Portable dummy	0.218	5.66
16-bit processor dummy	0.252	7.24
32-bit processor dummy	0.587	9.59
Model age	0.055	3.95
Apple dummy	0.157	2.67
Atari dummy	−0.574	−7.66
Commodore dummy	−0.413	−6.23
Compaq dummy	0.339	6.51
IBM dummy	0.032	0.75
NEC dummy	0.137	2.25
Radio Shack dummy	−0.023	−0.45
Zenith dummy	0.242	3.78
Wyse technology	0.040	0.54
Epson dummy	−0.119	−1.53
Kaypro dummy	0.093	1.18
NCR dummy	0.318	4.04
Northgate dummy	0.185	1.94
Intercept	6.167	66.78

Source: Stavins, J., "Estimating Demand Elasticities in a Differentiated Product Industry: The Personal Computer Market," unpublished manuscript, October 1992, p. 26.

[a]The "t-statistic" is a measure that can be used to determine if a coefficient is "meaningfully" different from zero (that is for reasons other than pure chance). A t-statistic less than −2 or greater than 2 usually indicates a meaningful difference from zero.

example, two word processing packages are compatible (i.e., files created in one package can be read by the other), then not only can more consumers share files among themselves, but there may also be a critical mass of users that makes the offering of complementary products economical. For example, a larger network of compatible word processing packages increases the odds that a developer of a graphics add-in package or a grammar-checking package will find a profitable market for its product.

Neil Gandal has applied hedonic pricing analysis to an investigation of network externalities in the market for computer spreadsheets.[30] During 1986–1991, Lotus 1-2-3 was the best-selling spreadsheet in the market and (at that time) was considered to be the industry standard. Many, but not all, spreadsheet packages sold during this period were compatible with Lotus 1-2-3. If consumers were willing to pay a price premium for Lotus-compatible spreadsheets, that would be evidence of the existence of network externalities in the market for spreadsheets. Using data on spreadsheet prices and product features from 1986 through 1991, Gandal estimates a hedonic pricing equation to determine what, if any, price consumers were willing to pay for Lotus compatibility.

Gandal's hedonic pricing analysis reveals strong evidence of network externalities. The analysis implies that if two spreadsheet packages were comparable in terms of product features, such as sorting, recalculation, ability to link with external databases, and graphics capabilities, the one that was Lotus compatible commanded a significantly higher price. To illustrate the strength of this effect, Gandal's estimates imply that Lotus compatibility will increase the *log of price* of an average-priced spreadsheet by about 12 percent. This corresponds to roughly a threefold increase in terms of *actual price*. Thus, Gandal's analysis implies that a Lotus-incompatible spreadsheet selling for $100 would have sold for nearly $300 had it been Lotus compatible, with no changes in any of its other features.

$\mathcal{E}$XAMPLE 13.6

USING HEDONIC PRICING TO VALUE IMPROVEMENTS IN WORKPLACE SAFETY

Hedonic pricing models are not limited to consumer goods. An interesting and important application is to estimate the value of improving workplace safety. Employers offer their workers a bundle of job attributes, including effort required (physical and mental), quality of the work site, friendliness of coworkers and management, opportunities for advancement, and safety. The wage that the worker receives reflects these attributes. For example, many individuals will accept relatively lower wages than they could earn elsewhere if they enjoy the work, or if the job offers opportunities for advancement.

There is no doubt that wages also reflect job safety. Examples may be found throughout history. Shakespeare may have written that the English nobility risked

---

[30]Gandal, N., "Hedonic Price Indexes for Spreadsheets: An Empirical Test for Network Externalities," *RAND Journal of Economics*, 1, Spring 1994, pp. 160–170.

their lives supporting Henry V's invasion of northern France for the glory of England, but it is more likely that they were enticed by the prospect of capturing and ransoming French knights. A young Napoleon recruited volunteer armies by promising a share of any spoils of battle. Employers today recognize the need to compensate workers for risk. Construction workers are paid more to work on bridges than on other, less dangerous settings, for example.

The theory of competitive labor markets states that employers with dangerous job sites must pay workers enough to compensate them for risking their health. Conversely, employers with safe job sites can pay workers less—workers take their compensation in the form of improved job safety, rather than wages. This suggests that the different wages paid to workers at jobs with different levels of risk are a measure of how much workers value job safety. Given a precise measure of the value of job safety, employers could determine whether it was worthwhile to invest in improving workplace safety.

Many researchers have obtained data about workplace safety and wages to estimate the value of job safety.[31] Michael Moore and Kip Viscusi use a detailed data set to provide one of the most reliable estimates to date.[32] Their data report work-site fatality rates and wage rates by occupation and state. They found that workers were paid $250 to $700 per year extra to assume an additional risk of dying on the job of 1/10,000. This implies that employers should be willing to spend as much as $7,000,000 ($700 divided by 1/10,000) to improve worksite safety if it is expected to save at least one life.

Kip Viscusi, Wesley Magat, and Joel Huber use an approach related to hedonic pricing analysis to demonstrate that the value that consumers place on changes in product attributes may depend on changes that make the product safer.[33] The authors asked shoppers to state how much they would be willing to pay to reduce the chances of minor injuries associated with the use of insecticides and toilet bowl cleaners. Consumers stated that they were willing to pay an average of roughly $3 to reduce the risk of inhalation and skin poisoning from 15/10,000 per use to zero. The authors then asked how much the product would have to be discounted for consumers to be willing to increase the risk of poisoning from 15/10,000 to 16/10,000. Most consumers stated they would not be willing to use the product at any price! It appears that consumers are much less willing to accept health risks above the status quo than they are willing to pay for reductions in health risk.

---

[31]For a comprehensive survey of this literature, see Viscusi, W. K. "The Values of Risk to Life and Health," *Journal of Economic Literature*, 31, 1993, pp. 1912–46.

[32]Moore, M. and W. K. Viscusi, "Doubling the Estimated Value of Life," *Journal of Policy Analysis and Management*, 7, 1988, pp. 476–90.

[33]Viscusi, W. K., W. Magat, and J. Huber, "An Investigation of the Rationality of Consumer Valuations of Multiple Health Risks," *RAND Journal of Economics*, 18, Winter 1987, pp. 465–79.

CHAPTER SUMMARY

◆ Diagnosing the sources of cost advantage involves disaggregating costs into economically meaningful categories and identifying the relevant cost drivers—the forces that cause costs to vary across organizations.

◆ Costs can be disaggregated behaviorally (e.g., fixed versus variable), by type or class of input (e.g., direct labor, direct material, etc.), or by activity. Templates, such as Michael Porter's value chain or the McKinsey Business System framework, can be used to classify activities for this analysis.

◆ Cost drivers include those related to firm size, scope, and cumulative experience, as discussed in Chapter 5. But there are other cost drivers independent of firm size, scope, or experience, such as location, economies of density, complexity, process efficiency, discretionary policies, government policies, the organization of the vertical chain, and agency efficiency.

◆ There are a number of techniques to quantify the magnitude of scale economies, including analysis of accounting data that sorts out fixed and variable costs, and regression analysis that compares costs and outputs of firms of varying sizes.

◆ Slope is a way of characterizing the relative importance of cost drivers. Slope indicates the level to which average costs decline (as a percentage of a baseline level) when the cost driver doubles.

◆ The attributes that determine the perceived benefit B are called benefit drivers. Benefit drivers may be related to the physical characteristics of the product (e.g., performance, features, or product aesthetics); the quantity and characteristics of the services or complementary good the firm offers for sale; characteristics associated with the sale or delivery of the good (e.g., speed and timeliness of delivery); characteristics that shape consumer's perceptions or expectations of the product's performance (e.g., the seller's reputation, size of installed base); and the subjective image of the product.

◆ Methods for estimating the relative importance of different benefit drivers include assessing consumer reservation prices through survey techniques; attribute weighting by panels of consumers; conjoint analysis, and hedonic pricing analysis.

QUESTIONS

1. Example 13.3 presents information on cost drivers in the Titanium Dioxide industry. Based on the information provided in the example, calculate the magnitude of the cost advantage that DuPont would have over a competitor who operates a 50,000 ton rutile chloride plant. Assume that both DuPont and its competitor achieve the same level of capacity utilization.

2. Table 13.4 shows estimated cost elasticities for different Class I U.S. railroads. For each railroad, use these elasticities to calculate slopes with respect to traffic volume; route mileage; average haul length; and the amount of way and structure capital.

3. Consider the following data

	Firm A	Firm B
Cummulative experience	150,000 units	56,000 units
Average plant capacity	20,000 units/year	15,000 units/year
Complexity index*	30	52
Index of unit size	1.00	.87

*number of production setups required per year

slopes

Experience	.91
Capacity	.85
Complexity	.69
Unit size	.85

Assuming that the only relevant differences between Firm A and Firm B's unit costs are due to the cost drivers shown above, based on the above information what is Firm A's cost advantage over Firm B (in percentage terms)?

4. In his estimate of slopes of learning curves in various chemical industries, Marvin Lieberman used price data rather than data on unit costs. Under what circumstances would the time path of prices be expected to track the time path of unit costs reasonably closely? Which do you think is likely to decline more rapidly? Does your answer depend on whether firms are explicitly setting prices to exploit the learning curve for profit?

5. In the newspaper business, key categories of cost include production costs, distribution costs, and editorial costs. Here are some key stylized facts about newspapers and their costs:[34]

- Newspaper production is highly labor intensive, so production costs are mainly variable and rise in nearly direct proportion to both circulation (number of newspapers sold) and copy size (number of pages per newspaper).

- As a typical newspaper publisher distributes its newspapers further and further away from its printing site, sales of newspapers per square mile decline.

---

[34]This is based on information in the case *The USA Today Decision: Making Headlines Across the Nation (A)*, Harvard Business School case 9-792-030.

- Editorial costs are the costs of the editorial staff—reporters and editors. Papers with larger copy sizes generally have larger editorial staffs than papers with smaller copy sizes. Editorial staffs often increase in size as newspaper's circulation increases.

Based on this information . . .

a) Are distribution costs per newspaper likely to go up, go down, or stay the same as circulation goes up, holding copy size fixed?

b) Are editorial costs per newspaper likely to go up, go down, or stay the same as circulation goes up, holding copy size fixed?

c) Are production costs per newspaper likely to go up, go down, or stay the same as circulation goes up, holding copy size fixed?

d) Are production costs per newspaper likely to go up, go down, or stay the same as copy size goes up, holding circulation fixed?

6. A researcher estimates a hedonic pricing equation for a particular product with the following form

$$log\ P = 10.56 + .56\ log\ q$$

where P denotes price and q is a measure of product performance. A firm that produces this product has the opportunity to implement a product enhancement that increases the product's performance by 10 percent. Reliable engineering estimates suggest that average variable production costs will rise by 7 percent if this enhancement is implemented. Should the firm implement this enhancement?

SUSTAINING COMPETITIVE ADVANTAGE

14

$\mathcal{T}$he mid-1980s were prosperous times for Domino's Pizza. Between 1982 and 1988, while industry sales grew 10 percent per year, Domino's sales increased nearly 40 percent per year, and the number of its stores increased from less than 500 to over 5,000 worldwide. Domino's was, by far, the most profitable firm in the fast-food pizza business, and its success allowed Domino's founder, Tom Monaghan, to accumulate a net worth in excess of $400 million.

Domino's strategy was straightforward and simple: It offered a limited menu (two pizza sizes and ten toppings) to keep costs down. Focusing entirely on delivery (it offered no carry-out or eat-in pizza), Domino's guaranteed that a pizza would be delivered within 30 minutes or else the customer would get it free. This strategy drew widespread attention and praise. "Back in '85 and '86," said one pizza industry executive, "Domino's was like Superman." George Stalk and Thomas Hout, in their book *Competing Against Time*, cited Domino's (along with companies such as Sony, NEC, Matsushita, Benneton, and Federal Express) as an excellent example of a time-based competitor.

But by the early 1990s, Domino's competitive position had significantly weakened. Starting in 1989, its revenues and profits began to decline. In 1991, the company lost money for the first time since the 1970s. (See Figure 14.1.[1]) Domino's share of the delivered pizza market, once over 90 percent, fell to 46 percent by 1991. Once seen as one of the hottest growth companies around, Domino's attracted no serious interest when Monaghan put it up for sale in the early 1990s.

---

[1]The data in Figure 14.1 are taken from Sympson, R., "Can Monaghan Deliver?, *Restaurant Business*, April 10, 1992, pp. 78–88.

FIGURE 14.1

DOMINO'S PIZZA SALES REVENUES AND NET INCOME, 1988–1991.

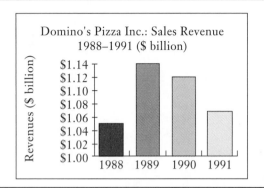
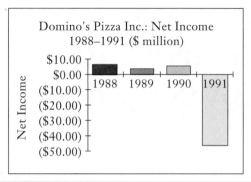

Between 1989 and 1991, Domino's sales revenues fell, and in 1991 it had its first loss since the 1970s.

Emblematic of Domino's decline was Monaghan's decision to sell the Detroit Tigers baseball club to his archrival Michael Illyich, owner of Little Caesar's Pizza.

A number of events contributed to Domino's decline. In 1986, backed with the financial resources and marketing savvy of PepsiCo, Pizza Hut had entered the delivered pizza business. Through a combination of massive spending on advertising and promotion, a reputation for superior pizza, and operating innovations, Pizza Hut increased its share of the delivered pizza market to nearly 25 percent by 1994. In 1989, Little Caesar's, which traditionally focused on the carry-out pizza market, launched a two-for-one campaign in which it essentially cut the price of a carry-out pizza to half of what Domino's charged. And in late 1993, a St. Louis jury ordered Domino's to pay $78 million to a woman who was injured in a traffic accident involving a Domino's delivery van. Within a week of this judgment, Domino's ran ads in newspapers throughout the United States announcing the end of its famous 30-minute guarantee.

What happened to Domino's has happened to many other companies: Competitive advantages that have taken years to build up are suddenly and quickly eroded by imitators who copy or improve the firm's formula for success or by innovators who neutralize the firm's advantage through new technologies, products, or ways of doing business. All this, combined with a dose of bad luck, can spell the end of even the top firms. Yet, while competitive advantages for many firms are fleeting, other firms seem to sustain competitive advantages year after year. For example, Wal-Mart has achieved returns on equity in excess of the industry average in mass merchandising for nearly 25 years, and Banc One has been first among the largest 25 banks in return on assets and return on equity since 1983.

Chapters 12 and 13 asked: Why do some firms outperform their industries? This chapter extends that inquiry by asking: Why do some firms persistently outperform their competitors, despite the efforts of other firms to imitate or neutralize the sources of their advantage? What, in short, makes a competitive advantage sustainable, and why?

HOW HARD IS IT TO SUSTAIN PROFITS?   ◆ ◆ ◆ ◆ ◆

Regardless of the competitive environment the firm is in, it is often very difficult to sustain profits. Some enemies of sustainability, such as imitability and entry, are threats in all market structures. Others, such as price competition, may be greater threats in competitive markets.

Threats to Sustainability in Competitive Markets

The theory of perfect competition is a logical starting point for our discussion of sustainability of competitive advantage. That theory—discussed in detail in the Economics Primer—has a fundamentally important implication: Opportunities for earning profit based on favorable market conditions will quickly evaporate as new entrants flow into the market, increase the supply of output, and drive price down to average cost. But just how relevant is this theory? After all, it seems to be cast in the context of an extremely special industry structure: Firms produce a homogeneous good, face identical technologies and input costs, and are so small relative to the size of the market that they act as price takers. Few industries outside of agriculture and fishing seem to be characterized by these stark conditions.

But the dynamic of perfect competition can operate under seemingly more complex conditions than those assumed in the standard theory. Even in industries

FIGURE 14.2
THE PERFECTLY COMPETITIVE DYNAMIC.

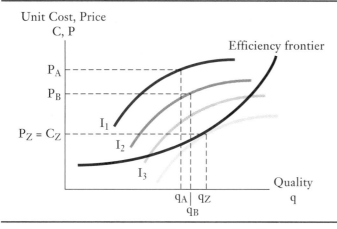

This figure depicts a market in which consumers have identical tastes, which are reflected by indifference curves, such as I_1, I_2, and I_3. The upward sloping line is the efficiency frontier for this market. A price-quality position, such as (P_A, q_A) could not be sustained when there is free entry and costless imitation. An entrant could offer a lower price and higher quality (e.g., P_B, q_B) and steal the market from incumbent firms. The perfectly competitive equilibrium occurs at price-quality combination (P_z, q_z). At this point, economic profits are zero, and there is no other price-quality position that simultaneously results in greater consumer surplus and higher profit.

where firms can vary the attributes of their products, potential profits can be dissipated through entry and imitation. Figure 14.2 depicts a market in which consumer benefits B are driven by a single attribute, which we call quality (denoted by q). In this market, we assume that all consumers have identical price-quality tradeoffs, that, as in Chapter 12, can be represented by upward sloping indifference curves, such as I_1, I_2, and I_3. (Recall from Chapter 12, that price-quality combinations along a given indifference curve yield the same level of consumer surplus for a consumer in the target market.) Figure 14.2 also shows the efficiency frontier in this market. As discussed in Chapter 12, the efficiency frontier shows the most efficient cost-quality positions that are potentially available to firms in this market. The efficiency frontier, in effect, represents a theoretical barrier that no firm can cross.

Suppose that this market is characterized by costless imitation and free entry. Because imitation is costless, existing firms and potential entrants can achieve any cost-quality position along the efficiency frontier. That is, no firm would be able to achieve higher quality at the same or lower cost as its competitors because its formula for efficiency would be instantly copied. Because of free entry, a situation in which firms offer products with quality q_A at price P_A would not persist because a new entrant could come into the market, offering the same or higher quality (e.g., q_B), undercut the price P_A (e.g., P_B), and steal the entire market from incumbent firms. Costless imitation and free entry thus imply that competitive advantage in this market cannot be sustained.

The perfectly competitive equilibrium in this market occurs at point Z, where the efficiency frontier is tangent to an indifference curve. At this equilibrium, each firm offers quality q_Z, incurs cost C_Z, charges price $P_Z = C_Z$, and earns zero economic profit. At point Z, all profitable opportunities for price-cutting, cost reduction, and quality enhancement are exhausted. Cutting price, while maintaining quality Q_Z and cost C_Z, is clearly unprofitable. Moreover, profitability cannot be increased by cutting costs or enhancing quality because the alternative *cost-quality positions* available to a firm at Z are those along the efficiency frontier. That is, raising quality can be done only at a higher cost, while costs can be reduced only by sacrificing quality. To make a profit while operating at any cost-quality position other than Z, a firm's price P would have to exceed cost, that is, its *price-quality position* would have to lie above the efficiency frontier. Except for point Z, however, all such positions would lie above the consumer indifference curve through Z, which means that each would yield less consumer surplus than consumers receive at Z. Once firms reach Z, no other competitive position in this market is viable, and a competitor in this business can earn no more than zero economic profit.

Threats to Sustainability in Monopolistically Competitive Markets

In the simple market described in the previous section, firms could differentiate themselves vertically—that is, by quality. But this did not shield the firms from the rigors of price competition. Because all consumers were assumed to have the same preferences, a firm that offers a price-quality combination (such as A) that is inferior to one offered by competitors (such as B) would make no sales. A monopolistically competitive market, however, is different from the one depicted in Figure 14.2 in that sellers are usually horizontally differentiated in distinct niches (i.e., they cater to consumers with different preferences over key product attributes).[2] A seller can thus raise its price without fear of losing all its customers—the demand curve facing each seller is downward sloping. As pointed out in the Economics Primer, when a seller faces a downward-sloping demand curve, it is optimal for it to set a price above marginal cost.

But even though a monopolistically competitive seller sets price above marginal cost, there is no guarantee that it will earn profits. The seller may be covering incremental costs, but it must also have sufficient sales volume to cover its fixed costs as well. However, if incumbent sellers are making profits, and there is free entry into the market, new firms will enter. By slightly differentiating themselves from incumbents, these entrants will find their own niches, but will inevitably take some business from incumbents. As discussed in Chapter 8, entry will continue in this way until incremental profits just cover fixed costs. The pizza delivery market is a good example in which entry by differentiated sellers led to the decline of the successful incumbent. Other examples include personal computing, luxury cars, and mass market retailing. Successful incumbents in monopolistically competitive markets can do little to preserve profits unless they can deter entry, strategies for which are discussed in Chapter 11.

Threats to Sustainability Under All Market Structures

Even in oligopolistic or monopolistic markets, where entry might be blockaded or deterred, a successful incumbent may not stay that way for long. One reason is that success may be due to factors that the incumbent cannot control, such as the weather or general business conditions. A March snowstorm in Colorado that delays shipments of Coors beer to the West Coast will hurt Coors sales for the month, and will help sales of competing brands, such as Budweiser and Miller. But one would not expect Coors' April sales to stay down, nor would one expect Budweiser and Miller to sustain the one-month sales increase. If, as expected, April sales revert to historical levels, we would say that profits showed *regression to the mean*. The general point about regression to the mean is this: Whenever a firm does exceedingly well, one must consider the possibility that it was the beneficiary of unusually good luck. Conversely, an underperforming firm might have been the victim of bad luck. Since good luck is unlikely to repeat itself (or otherwise it would not have been luck), one might expect that the successful firm will be less successful and that the underperforming firm will show some improvement. The possibility of regression toward the mean means that one should not expect firms to repeat extreme performances, whether good or bad, for very long.

Extremely good performance may not always be the result of good luck. As we discuss later in this chapter, there are a number of ways in which firms may develop

---

[2]The difference between horizontal and vertical differentiation is discussed in detail in Chapters 8 and 12.

genuine advantages that are difficult for others to duplicate. Even this does not guarantee a sustainable flow of profits, however. While the advantage may be inimitable, so that the firm is protected from the forces of rivalry and entry, the firm may not be protected from powerful buyers and suppliers. Powerful buyers and suppliers can threaten firms in any market structure, but they are most likely to emerge in oligopolistic or monopolistic markets, where successful firms can earn large profits.

A good example of where supplier power has threatened sustainability is major league baseball in the United States. Thanks in part to economies of scale and in part to an exemption from the U.S. antitrust laws, major league baseball has enjoyed uninterrupted monopoly status throughout the twentieth century. Even so, many owners are unable to turn a profit. One reason is the powerful Major League Baseball Player's Association, which through litigation and a series of successful job actions in the 1970s and 1980s was able to elevate the average salary to over $1 million a year. Fearful that they could no longer sustain profits in the face of ever-escalating salaries, the owners took a tough bargaining stance in 1994, which eventually led to a players' strike and the cancellation of the 1994 World Series. Many observers felt that the owners were so concerned about long-term profitability that they were willing to suspend play for the entire 1995 season to obtain concessions from the players. Indeed, a new rule requiring 75 percent of the owners to agree to any new contract with the players' union was evidence of the owners' resolve.

Evidence: The Persistence of Profitability

If the forces threatening sustainability are pervasive, economic profits in most industries should quickly converge to zero. Entry, imitation, price cutting, and other forces would drive a firm's rate of return toward its *cost of capital*—the rate of return just sufficient to induce investors to provide financial capital to the firm. This, in turn, implies that profit persistence should be weak: No matter how profitable a firm is today, its profit will converge toward the perfectly competitive level. By contrast, if there are impediments to the operation of the competitive dynamic (e.g., entry barriers as discussed in Chapter 11, mobility barriers as discussed in Chapter 12, or barriers to imitation as will be discussed later in this chapter), then we should expect to see profits persist: Firms that earn above-average profits today should continue to do so in the future; low-profit firms today should continue to be low-profit firms in the future.

What pattern of profit persistence do we actually observe? The most comprehensive study of profit persistence has been carried out by the economist Dennis Mueller.[3] Working with a sample of 600 U.S. manufacturing firms for the years 1950–1972, Mueller used statistical techniques to measure profit persistence. Perhaps the easiest way to summarize Mueller's results is to imagine two groups of U.S. manufacturing firms. One group (the "high-profit" group) has an aftertax accounting return on assets (ROA) that is, on average, 100 percent greater than the

---

[3]Mueller, D. C., "The Persistence of Profits Above the Norm," *Economica*, 44, 1977, pp. 369–380. See also Mueller, D. C., *Profits in the Long Run*, Cambridge: Cambridge University Press, 1986.

accounting ROA of the typical manufacturing firm. The other group (the "low-profit" group) has an average ROA that is, on average, 100 percent less than that of the typical manufacturing firm. If the typical manufacturing firm has an ROA of 6 percent in 1995 (which is roughly the average ROA for U.S. manufacturing firms over the last 20 years), the average ROA of the high-profit group would be 12 percent, while the average ROA of the low-profit group would be 0 percent. If profit persistence follows the pattern in Mueller's sample, by 1998 the high-profit group's average ROA would be about 8.6 percent, and by 2010, the group's average ROA would stabilize at about 7.8 percent, a level 30 percent greater than that of the average manufacturing firm. Similarly, by 1998 the low-profit group's average ROA would be about 4.4 percent, and by 2010 the group's average ROA would stabilize at about 4.9 percent or about 19 percent less than the average manufacturing firm. These patterns are shown in Figure 14.3.[4]

FIGURE 14.3
THE PERSISTENCE OF PROFITABILITY IN MUELLER'S SAMPLE.

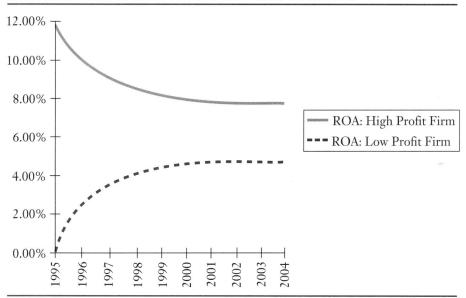

The high-profit group's average ROA starts out at 12% in 1995, and decreases over time, converging to rate slightly less than 8%. The low-profit group's average ROA starts at 0% in 1995, and increases over time, converging to a rate slightly greater than 4%. The profits of the two groups get closer over time, but do not converge toward a common mean, as would be predicted by the theory of perfect competition.

---

[4]Our characterization of these patterns of profit persistence is based on the results in Table 2.2 in Mueller's book. We should point out that Mueller's study is far more elaborate than we have described here. He uses regression to estimate equations that give persistence patterns for each of the 600 firms in his sample. Our grouping of firms into two groups is done to illustrate the character of the main results.

Mueller's results suggest that firms with abnormally high levels of profitability tend, on average, to experience decreases in profitability over time, while firms with abnormally low levels of profitability tend, on average, to experience increases in profitability over time. However, as Figure 14.3 illustrates, the profit rates of these two groups of firms *do not* converge to a common mean. Firms that start out with high profits converge, in the long run, to rates of profitability that are higher than the rates of profitability of firms that start out with low profits.

A possible explanation for this lack of convergence is that the risk characteristics of the two groups are different. Perhaps firms in the high-profit group are riskier on average than the firms in the low-profit group, and the capital markets require a higher rate of return from them. The high-profit group may have an average risk-adjusted cost of capital of 7.8 percent, and the low-profit group may have an average rate of 4.9 percent. By the year 2010, both groups are earning zero *economic profits* because their respective nominal rates of return equal their costs of capital.

In his study, Mueller tests whether there is a systematic relationship between the riskiness of firms and the level to which their profits converge in the long run. Using a variety of measures of risk, Mueller concludes that differences in risk among the firms in his sample *do not* account for the lack of convergence to a common mean. This suggests that the lack of convergence to a common mean indicates long-run differences in economic profitability among firms, rather than differences in risk.

In summary, Mueller's analysis reveals that differences in profitability diminish over time, but are not entirely eliminated. This work implies that, while the forces pushing markets toward the perfectly competitive outcome are not entirely absent, other forces impede the competitive dynamic. Michael Porter's Five Forces, summarized in Chapter 7, represent an important class of such forces. Many factors, such as high entry barriers or other structural conditions that soften price competition, protect the profitability of an *entire industry*. These factors were described in Section II and summarized in the Chapter 7 discussion of the Five Forces framework. In this chapter, though, we are concerned with a different class of forces: those that protect the competitive advantage of an *individual firm* and allow that firm to persistently outperform its industry. These forces are, at least in principle, distinct from Porter's Five Forces. A firm may operate in an industry with intense pricing rivalry and low entry barriers, but the sources of its competitive advantage may be so difficult to understand or to imitate that its advantage over its competitors is secure for a long time. By contrast, structural conditions in an industry may serve to facilitate pricing coordination among firms in that industry, allowing higher-than-competitive returns, but the barriers to imitation in the industry may be so low that no firm can be more profitable than any other.

◆ ◆ ◆ ◆ ◆ SUSTAINABLE COMPETITIVE ADVANTAGE

This section discusses the economic foundations of sustainable competitive advantage. It begins by linking sustainable advantage to the concepts of resources and capabilities in Chapter 12. It then introduces the concept of an isolating mechanism and discusses its importance for sustainable advantage.

The Resource-Based Theory of the Firm

Chapter 12 defined *competitive advantage* as the ability of a firm to outperform its industry, that is, to earn a higher rate of profit than the industry norm. A competitive advantage is *sustainable* when the advantage persists despite efforts by competitors or potential entrants to duplicate or neutralize it.[5]

As argued in Chapter 12, for a firm to achieve a competitive advantage, it must create more value than its competitors. A firm's ability to create superior value, in turn, depends on its stock of resources (i.e., firm-specific assets and factors of production, such as patents, brand-name reputation, installed base, and human assets) and its distinctive capabilities (i.e., activities that the firm does especially well in comparison to competitors) that arise from its experience in using those resources.

The link between value creation and resources and capabilities implies that for a competitive advantage to be sustainable, the market must be characterized by persistent asymmetries in terms of firms' resources and capabilities. Firms must differ from each other, and these differences must persist over time. Resource heterogeneity is the cornerstone of an important framework in strategy: the *resource-based theory of the firm.*[6] That theory points out that if all firms in a market have the same stock of resources and capabilities, no strategy for value creation is available to one firm that would not also be available to all other firms in the market. Any strategy that confers advantage could be immediately replicated by any other firm. It thus follows that to be sustainable, a competitive advantage must be underpinned by resources and capabilities that are *scarce* and *imperfectly mobile*, which means that well-functioning markets for the resources and capabilities do not or cannot exist.

That a resource must be scarce to sustain a competitive advantage is clear. Imperfect mobility is perhaps less obvious. Its necessity can be understood by imagining a situation in which critical resources can be bought and sold on the open market. If so, then any strategy for superior value creation could potentially be implemented by any firm through the purchase of the appropriate resources. When value-creating resources are scarce, we would expect firms to bid against one another to acquire them. The additional economic profit (or, equivalently, rent) that would have resulted from the competitive advantage would then be transferred to the owner of the resources. For example, where key resources are

---

[5]This definition is adapted from Barney, J., "Firm Resources and Sustained Competitive Advantage," *Journal of Management*, 17, 1991, pp. 99–120.

[6]Presentations of this theory can be found in Barney, J., "Firm Resources and Sustained Competitive Advantage," *Journal of Management*, 17, 1991, pp. 99–120; Peteraf, M. A., "The Cornerstones of Competitive Advantage: A Resource-Based View," *Strategic Management Journal*, 14, 1993, 179–191; Dierickx, I. and K. Cool, "Asset Stock Accumulation and Sustainability of Competitive Advantage," *Management Science*, 35, 1989, pp. 1504–1511; Grant, R. M., "The Resource-Based Theory of Competitive Advantage: Implications for Strategy Formulation," *California Management Review*, Spring 1991, pp. 119–145; Wernerfelt, B., "A Resource-Based View of the Firm," *Strategic Management Journal*, 5, 1984, pp. 171–180. The pioneering work underlying the resource-based theory is Penrose, E. T., *The Theory of the Growth of the Firm*, Oxford: Blackwell, 1959.

talented employees, such as superstars in creating specialized financial derivatives, the extra-value-created would be captured by the superstar employees as higher salaries, rather than by the firm as higher profit. Moreover, in the race to acquire the value-creating resources, firms could squander the rents that the resources create in the first place. An example of this would be where the key resource is a potentially valuable location that can support only one retail outlet. If a retailer waited to purchase the land until the time was "just right"—the profit potential was at its height—it would probably be too late. A more forward-looking retailer would prematurely build a store before the location is ready to yield its maximal profit to preempt potential competitors from acquiring the location. In this way, the profitability of the location would be dissipated.

Why Are Resources Immobile?

There are several reasons why resources might be imperfectly mobile. Many valuable resources, such as the know-how an organization has acquired through cumulative experience, or a firm's reputation for "toughness," cannot be packaged in any meaningful way and sold in an outside market. Such assets are effectively nontradeable. Other assets may be tradeable, but because they are relationship-specific, they may be far more valuable inside one organization than another. This limits the incentive for parties outside the organization to bid them away. A related point is that some assets may be *cospecialized*—that is, they are more valuable when used together than when separated. For example, USAir's gates and landing slots at Pittsburgh airport are probably far more valuable to USAir than they are to a potential bidder for those slots because of the strong "brand identification" USAir has in Pittsburgh and because prospective flyers out of Pittsburgh have built up large stocks of frequent-flyer miles on USAir.

EXAMPLE 14.1

AMERICAN VERSUS NORTHWEST IN YIELD MANAGEMENT

An interesting example of resource mobility arose in a recent lawsuit involving American Airlines and Northwest Airlines.[7] The case centered on an allegation that Northwest airlines stole valuable information related to American's yield management capabilities.

Yield management refers to a set of practices designed to maximize an airline's yield—the dollars of revenue it collects per seat mile it flies. Yield management techniques combine mathematical optimization models with forecasting techniques

---

[7]This example is based on the article, "Fare Game: Did Northwest Steal American' Systems? The Court Will Decide," *Wall Street Journal*, July 7, 1994, pp. A1, A8.

to help an airline determine fares, fix the number of seats it should sell in various fare categories, and adjust its inventory of seats in response to the changes in demand conditions over time. American Airlines is widely acknowledged to have the most sophisticated yield management capabilities in the airline industry. In the early 1990s, its system was thought to have added $300 million to American's annual revenues.

By contrast, Northwest's yield management capabilities were below average. In the late 1980s, it hired a consultant to devise a mathematical model to underpin a new system. But management soon became skeptical of the consultant's efforts. The system the consultant devised was estimated to cost $30 million, but its success was far from certain. In 1990, Northwest fired the consultant.

Northwest then tried to purchase a yield management system from American. However, in return for the system, American demanded Northwest's operating right to fly between Chicago and Tokyo, a route whose market value was estimated at between $300 to $500 million. Northwest refused to trade.

Instead, in the fall of 1990, Northwest hired John Garel, the chief of the yield management department at American. Garel then identified American's best yield managers, and tried to hire them at Northwest as well. Out of the 38 new yield management employees hired by Northwest in 1990, 17 came from American, often with generous raises of 50 to 100 percent.

Along with hiring many of American's yield managers, Northwest also managed to acquire a diskette containing American's "spill" tables, which are a key ingredient in mathematical models used to plan the acquisition of new aircraft. Northwest had tried to purchase the spill tables along with American's yield management system in 1990. American alleged that the diskette was copied by one of its former employees recruited by Northwest. Northwest also obtained internal American documents on how to improve a yield management system. One of the documents was entitled "Seminar on Demand Forecasting," which was used by Northwest to vastly improve its system called AIMS. American alleges that its system contains five critical techniques, all of which were copied by Northwest. One Northwest yield manager characterized the revision as "a heart transplant of the AIMS system."

In 1993 American sued Northwest in federal court. It sought to bar Northwest from using its revised yield management system and sought $50 million in damages. American has also brought a suit against KLM, the Dutch airline that is Northwest's international marketing partner. According to American, Northwest passed along the internal American documents to KLM. This litigation is ongoing.

This example illustrates that the resources that are the basis of competitive advantage can be highly mobile. This is especially so when those resources are talented individuals, but is also true when the resource is information, a technique, or formula that can be written down or stored on a computer diskette. It is also interesting that Northwest was unable to capture all of the extra value that it hoped to obtain by hiring the American yield managers. Some of it had to be shared with these individuals in the form of higher salaries. This highlights a general point about competitive markets. When a scarce resource is fully mobile and as valuable to one firm as to another, all of the extra profit that the firms can earn as a result of the resource will be competed away as they bid against one another to acquire the resource.

Isolating Mechanisms

Scarcity and immobility of critical resources and capabilities are necessary conditions for a competitive advantage to be sustainable, but they are not sufficient. A firm that has built a competitive advantage on the basis of a set of scarce and immobile resources may find that advantage undermined if other firms can develop their own stocks of resources and capabilities that duplicate or neutralize the source of the firm's advantage. For example, Xerox's advantage in the plain paper copier market in the 1970s was built, in part, on superior servicing capabilities backed by an extensive network of dealers who provided on-site service calls. Canon successfully challenged Xerox in the small copier market by building highly reliable machines that rarely broke down and did not have to be serviced as often as Xerox's. Canon's superior product design neutralized Xerox's advantage and reduced the value of Xerox's servicing capabilities and its dealer network.

Richard Rumelt coined the term *isolating mechanisms* to refer to the economic forces that limit the extent to which a competitive advantage can be duplicated or neutralized through the resource creation activities of other firms.[8] Isolating mechanisms thus protect the competitive advantages of firms that are lucky enough or foresightful enough to have acquired them. Isolating mechanisms are to a firm what an entry barrier is to an industry: Just as an entry barrier impedes new entrants from coming into an industry and competing away profits from incumbent firms, isolating mechanisms prevent other firms from competing away the extra profit that a firm earns as a result of its competitive advantage.

There are different kinds of isolating mechanisms, and different authors classify them in different ways.[9] We find it useful to put them into two distinct groups:

- *Impediments to imitation*: These are isolating mechanisms that impede existing firms and potential entrants from duplicating the resources and capabilities that form the basis of the firm's advantage. For example, many firms are attempting to compete in the market for 3-D computer graphics, but none has been able to match the distinctive capabilities that Silicon Graphics Inc. (SGI) has developed in this field. Clearly, there are impediments that prevent competitors from copying the actions of this very successful firm.

---

[8]Rumelt, R. P., "Towards a Strategic Theory of the Firm," in R. Lamb (ed.). *Competitive Strategic Management*, Englewood Cliffs, N.J.: Prentice Hall, 1984, pp. 556–570.

[9] See, for example, Chapter 5 of Ghemawat, P., *Commitment: The Dynamic of Strategy*, New York: Free Press, 1991 or Yao, D., "Beyond the Reach of the Invisible Hand," *Strategic Management Journal*, 9, 1988, pp. 59–70.

- *Early-mover advantages*: These are isolating mechanisms that, once a firm acquires a competitive advantage, set in motion a dynamic that increases the magnitude of that advantage relative to competitors and potential entrants over time. For example, the fact that SGI has developed a large installed base of users for its workstations makes it more attractive for software developers to write applications using SGI's special graphics capabilities, which in turn increases the attractiveness of SGI's workstations to prospective buyers.

Figure 14.4 illustrates the distinction between these two classes of isolating mechanisms. In Figure 14.4*a*, all firms begin by occupying the same strategic position. A "shock" then occurs that propels firm G into a position of competitive

FIGURE 14.4
IMPEDIMENTS TO IMITATION AND EARLY-MOVER ADVANTAGES.

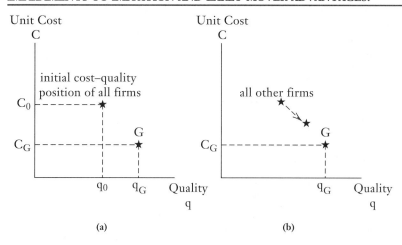

(a)   (b)

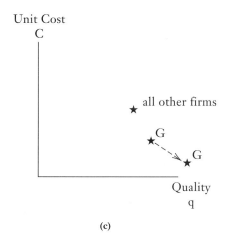

(c)

(a) The initial-cost quality position of all firms in the market is (C_0, q_0). Following a shock, firm G achieves a competitive advantage based on higher quality and lower cost. (b) Impediments to imitation: As time passes, G's competitors may be able to reduce costs and increase quality, but they are unable to duplicate G's superior cost-quality position. (c) The dynamics of an early-mover advantage: As time passes, G's cost and quality advantage over competing firms grows more pronounced.

advantage relative to other firms in the market. We use the term "shock" broadly to refer to fundamental changes that lead to major shifts of competitive positions in a market. Examples of shocks are process or product innovations, discoveries of new sources of consumer value or market segments, shifts in demand or tastes, or changes in regulatory policy that create opportunities for firms to significantly shift their strategic position in a business. Isolating mechanisms that impede imitation prevent other firms from fully replicating G's advantage. This is shown in Figure 14.4*b* as the inability of other firms to match G's competitive position as time passes. Early-mover advantages work somewhat differently. The fact that G was the first firm to benefit from a shock implies that as time passes it is able to widen its competitive advantage relative to other firms in the market. This is shown in Figure 14.4*c*.

If shocks occur infrequently and isolating mechanisms are powerful, then a firm's competitive advantage will be long-lived. Firms whose competitive advantages are protected by isolating mechanisms, Rumelt argues, may be able to take their strategies as given for long periods of time, while nevertheless earning higher returns than existing competitors (or new entrants that might come into the business). The companion insight is that consistently high profitability does not necessarily mean that a firm is well managed. As Rumelt notes, "even fools can churn out good results (for a while)."

The next two sections discuss impediments to imitation and early-mover advantages in greater detail.

Impediments to Imitation

In this section, we discuss four impediments to imitation:

* Legal restrictions on imitation
* Superior access to inputs or customers
* Market size and scale economies
* Intangible barriers to imitating a firm's distinctive capabilities: causal ambiguity, dependence on historical circumstances, and social complexity.

Legal Restrictions on Imitation

Legal restrictions, such as patents, copyrights, and trademarks, as well as governmental control over entry into markets, through licensing, certification, or quotas on operating rights, can be powerful impediments to imitation.[10] Jeffrey Williams points out that between 1985 and 1990, patent-protected products as a group yielded higher returns on investment than any single industry in the United States.[11]

---

[10]Patents, copyrights, and trademarks are discussed more fully in Chapter 11.

[11]Williams, J., "How Sustainable is Your Advantage?" *California Management Review*, 34, 1992, pp. 1–23.

It is important to note that patents, copyrights, trademarks, and operating rights can be bought and sold. For example, Ted Turner has been successful at buying the copyrights to old movies, such as *Gone With the Wind*, and showing them on his network of television stations. Thus, while scarce, these resources may also be highly mobile. This mobility implies that a firm that tries to secure a competitive advantage through the purchase of a patent or an operating right may well find that it must pay a competitive price to get it. If so, the purchase of the asset will be a breakeven proposition unless the buyer can deploy it in ways that are unavailable to other prospective purchasers. This requires superior information about how to best utilize the asset or the possession of complementary resources that enhance the value of the patent or the operating right relative to other firms.

We encountered this issue in Chapter 6 in the context of our discussion of acquisition programs by diversifying firms. The evidence showing that unrelated acquisitions were generally unprofitable is consistent with the idea that buyers cannot profit from acquisitions unless they can deploy the asset in superior ways. Another implication of asset mobility is that the owner of the patent or operating right may be better off selling it to another firm. For example, many universities have offices that sell the patents obtained by members of their faculties. Universities realize that it makes much more sense for other firms to develop marketable products. This illustrates the key point about patents and other operating rights: Once a patent or operating right is secured, it has sustainable value by virtue of its exclusivity. Whoever holds the asset holds that value. But maximizing that value is ultimately a make-or-buy decision, whose resolution rests on the principles developed in Part I of this book.

Superior Access to Inputs or to Customers

A firm that can obtain high-quality or high-productivity inputs, such as raw materials or information, on more favorable terms than its competitors will be able to sustain cost and quality advantages that competitors cannot imitate. Favorable access to inputs is often achieved by controlling the sources of supply through ownership or long-term exclusive contracts. For example, International Nickel dominated the nickel industry for three-quarters of a century through its control of the highest grade deposits of nickel, which were concentrated in western Canada. Topps monopolized the market for baseball cards in the United States by signing every professional baseball player to a long-term contract giving Topps the exclusive right to market the player's picture on baseball cards sold with gum or other confectionery products. This network of long-term contracts, which was eventually declared illegal in the early 1980s, effectively blocked access to an essential input in card production—the player's picture.

The flip side of superior access to inputs is superior access to customers. A firm that secures access to the best distribution channels or the most productive retail locations will have an advantage competing for customers over rivals. A manufacturer could prevent access to retail distribution channels by insisting on *exclusive dealing* clauses, whereby a retailer agrees to sell only the products made by that manufacturer. Prior to World War II, most American automobile producers had exclusive dealing arrangements with their franchised dealers, and according to

Lawrence White, this raised the barriers to entering the automobile business.[12] Most of these clauses were dropped voluntarily in the early 1950s, following a set of antitrust decisions that seemed to threaten the Big Three's ability to maintain their exclusive dealing arrangements. Some observers speculate that the termination of these exclusive dealing requirements made it easier for Japanese manufacturers to penetrate the American market in the 1970s and 1980s.[13]

Superior access to inputs and customers may be vulnerable to changes in technologies or tastes, or the opening up of new input or product markets. For example, International Nickel's dominance of the world nickel market ended when new high-quality nickel deposits were discovered elsewhere in the 1970s. Moreover, just as patents and trademarks can be bought and sold, so can scarce locations or contracts giving the firm control of scarce inputs or distribution channels. Thus, superior access to inputs or customers can confer sustained competitive advantage only if the firm is able to secure access at "below-market" prices. If, for example, it is widely known that a certain site contained a high-quality supply of uranium, the price of that land would be bid up until the economic profits were transferred to the original owner, and the profitability of the firm that purchases the land would be no higher than the profitability of the losing bidders. Similarly, baseball teams, recognizing the extra revenues that result from signing a superstar, such as Ken Griffey, Jr. or Frank Thomas, will compete against one another to acquire these players, so that the original owners (Griffey Jr. or Thomas) capture the economic profit associated with their extremely rare and valuable skills. The corollary of this logic is that control of scarce inputs or distribution channels allows a firm to earn economic profits in excess of its competitors only if it acquired control of the input supply when other firms or individuals failed to recognize its value or could not exploit it.

Market Size and Scale Economies

Imitation may also be deterred when minimum efficient scale is large relative to market demand, and a firm has secured a large share of the market. We have already discussed this situation in Chapters 5 and 11 in connection with the idea that economies of scale can limit the number of firms that can "fit" in a market and thus represent a barrier to entry. Scale economies can also discourage a smaller firm already in the market from seeking to grow larger to replicate the scale-based cost advantage of a firm that has obtained a large market share.

The logic of this isolating mechanism is illustrated in Figure 14.5. Two firms, one large and one small, produce a homogeneous product, and face the same long-run average cost function. The large firm's volume exceeds minimum efficient scale (MES), which is 4,000 units per year in the figure; the small firm's volume—1000 units per year—is less than MES. If the small firm invested in additional capacity and expanded output to MES in an attempt to lower its average cost, the market

---

[12]White, L., "The Automobile Industry," in Adams, W. (ed.), *The Structure of American Industry*, 6th ed., New York: Macmillan, 1982.

[13]See, for example, Scherer, F.M. and D. Ross, *Industrial Market Structure and Economic Performance*, 3rd ed., Boston, MA: Houghton Mifflin, 1990, pp. 563–564.

FIGURE 14.5
ECONOMIES OF SCALE AND MARKET SIZE AS AN IMPEDIMENT TO
IMITATION.

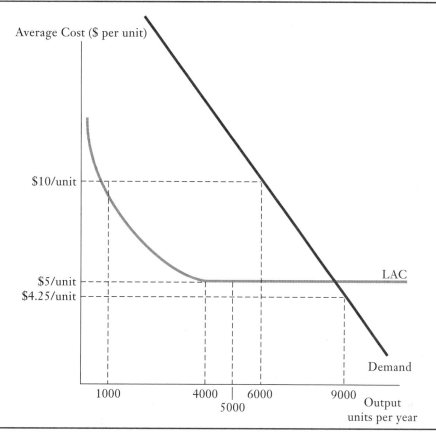

A large firm and a small firm are currently competing in a market in which the product cannot be effectively differentiated. The downward sloping straight line is the market demand
curve. Production technology is characterized by economies of scale, with the long-run average cost function, LAC, declining until the minimum efficient scale of 4,000 units per year is
reached. The large firm currently has a capacity of 5,000 units per year, while the small firm
has a capacity of 1,000 per year. If the small firm attempted to expand capacity to 4,000 units,
and both firms produced at full capacity, the market price would fall to $4.25, and at this price
the small firm would be unable to cover the costs of its investment in new plant. Thus, while
it is theoretically possible for the small firm to imitate the source of the large firm's cost advantage, it is undesirable for it to do so.

price would fall below the minimum of long-run average cost ($5 in the figure).
The small firm would thus be unable to earn an adequate rate of return on its investment in its new plant. This illustrates that while a small firm may theoretically
imitate the source of a larger firm's competitive advantage, it may nevertheless be
unprofitable for it to do so.

Scale-based barriers to imitation and entry are likely to be especially powerful in markets for specialized products or services where demand is just enough to support one large firm. This has been the case, for example, in the market for hot sauce, which has been monopolized by McIlhenny (producer of Tabasco sauce) for over a century. But a scale-based advantage can be sustainable only if demand does not grow too large; otherwise, the growth in demand will attract additional entry or induce smaller competitors to increase their size, allowing them to benefit from economies of scale. This happened in the market for table wines, as Sutter Home expanded in a growing market and virtually matched the cost advantages held by industry leaders Gallo and Taylor.

Intangible Barriers to Imitation

Legal restrictions, superior access to customers or scarce inputs, and scale economies are tangible barriers to imitation. But barriers to imitation may also be intangible, especially when the basis of the firm's advantage is distinctive organizational capabilities. Several conceptually distinct intangible barriers to imitation can be identified:

- causal ambiguity
- dependence on historical circumstances
- social complexity

Causal Ambiguity   Richard Rumelt uses the term *causal ambiguity* to refer to situations in which the causes of a firm's ability to create more value than its competitors are obscure and only imperfectly understood.[14] Causal ambiguity is a consequence of the fact that a firm's distinctive capabilities typically involve *tacit knowledge*. That is, capabilities are difficult to articulate as an algorithm, formula, or set of rules. Swinging a golf club in a way so that the ball is hit with long-range accuracy is an example of a tacit knowledge: It is conceivable that with enough practice one can learn how to do it, but it would be difficult to describe in words what someone else would have to do to replicate that skill. Much of the know-how and collective wisdom inside an organization is of this sort. Tacit capabilities are typically developed through a process of trial and error and refined through practice and experience. Rarely are they written down or codified in procedures manuals. As a result, the firm's managers may not even be able to describe persuasively what they do better than their rivals.[15] For this reason, causal ambiguity not only may be a powerful impediment to imitation by other firms, but it may also be an important source of diseconomies of scale. For example, David Teece has pointed

---

[14]Rumelt, R. P., "Towards a Strategic Theory of the Firm," in R. Lamb (ed.), *Competitive Strategic Management*, Englewood Cliffs, N.J.: Prentice Hall, 1984, pp. 556–570. See also Reed, R. and R. J. DeFillipi, "Causal Ambiguity, Barriers to Imitation and Sustainable Competitive Advantage," *Academy of Management Review*, 15, 1990, pp. 88–102.

[15]This point has been made by Polanyi, M., *The Tacit Dimension*, Garden City, NY: Anchor, 1967, and by Nelson, R. and S. Winter, *An Evolutionary Theory of Economic Change*, Cambridge, MA: Harvard University Press, 1982.

out that causal ambiguity might prevent the firm from translating the operational success it achieves in one of its plants to another.[16]

The tacit nature of causal ambiguity poses an additional threat. Just as superior firms may be unable to identify what they do especially well, ordinary firms may mistakenly believe that they have superior skills. Their inability to articulate their strengths may be chalked up to causal ambiguity. Absent evidence of superior skills (e.g., cost data, market research, competitive benchmarks relative to other firms, financial measures, or comments of knowledgeable observers, such as securities analysts), it is dangerous for managers to assume that their capabilities dominate those of competitors.

Dependence on Historical Circumstances Another reason why competitors might not be able to replicate the distinctive capabilities underlying a firm's competitive advantage is because their distinctiveness is partly bound up in the history of the firm. A firm's history of strategic action comprises its unique experiences in adapting to the business environment. These experiences can make the firm uniquely capable of pursuing its own strategy and at the same time quite incapable of imitating the strategies of competitors. For example, in the 1960s and 1970s, Southwest Airlines was constrained by U.S. regulatory policy to operate out of secondary airports in the unregulated (and thus highly price competitive) intrastate market in Texas. The operational efficiencies and the pattern of labor relations it developed in response to these conditions may be difficult for airlines, such as American and United, to imitate. Neither of these large carriers would be comfortable with Southwest's smaller scale of operation and historically constrained route structure.

The historical dependence of a firm's capabilities also limit its opportunities for growth. If Southwest Airlines attempted to expand much beyond its current structure, it would need to develop skills in hub-and-spoke operations and yield management that characterize large national carriers and that Southwest has little experience with. Absent distinctive capabilities for operating on a national scale, it is difficult to see how Southwest could outperform American, United, or Delta. The fate of Midway Airlines is instructive on this point. Midway succeeded as long as it kept within its limited route structure out of Chicago's Midway airport. When it expanded its activities by opening a hub in Philadelphia, it soon found itself at a competitive disadvantage versus other carriers and shortly afterward went bankrupt.

Historical dependence also implies that a firm's strategy may be viable only for a limited period of time. To use another example from the airline industry, People's Express prospered in the period immediately following deregulation through a low-price strategy based on lower labor costs. This strategy was viable, however, only to the extent that the major carriers were burdened by high labor

---

[16]Teece, D., "Applying Concepts of Economic Analysis to Strategic Management," in Harold Pennings and Associates (eds.), *Organizational Strategy and Change*, San Francisco: Jossey-Bass, 1985.

costs from their union contracts. With the passage of time, these costs were reduced as more labor contracts were renegotiated. This, in turn, limited the prospects of People's Express for sustaining its advantage.

Social Complexity Jay Barney has pointed out that a firm's advantage may also be imperfectly imitable because the processes that underlie the advantage are socially complex. Socially complex phenomena include the interpersonal relations of managers in a firm, and the relationship between the firm's managers and those of its suppliers and customers. Social complexity is distinct from causal ambiguity. For example, every one of Toyota's competitors may understand that an important ingredient of that firm's success is the high level of trust that exists between it and its component suppliers. But systematically managing a process that creates such trust, while perhaps highly desirable, is extremely difficult to do.

The dependence of competitive advantage on causal ambiguity, history, and social complexity implies that major organizational change runs the risk of neglecting these factors and thus actually harming the firm's position. If the sources of advantage are complex and difficult to articulate, they will also be hard to consciously redesign. Perhaps this is why organizational change efforts, such as reengineering, are often more successful in new or "greenfield" plants than in existing ones.

Early-Mover Advantages

This section discusses four distinctive isolating mechanisms that fall under the heading of early-mover advantages:

- Learning curve
- Network externalities
- Reputation and buyer uncertainty
- Buyer switching costs

Learning Curve

The economies of the learning curve are discussed at length in Chapters 5 and 13. A firm that has sold higher volumes of output than its competitors in earlier periods will move further down the learning curve and achieve lower unit costs than its rivals. Firms with the greatest cumulative experience can thus profitably "underbid" rivals for business, thus further increasing their cumulative volume and enhancing their cost advantage.

Network Externalities

For some products, such as computer software or consumer electronics, a consumer's benefit from purchasing the product is greater the more consumers currently use the product or are expected to use it in the near future. For example, the more consumers who use a particular spreadsheet, such as Microsoft's Excel, the more likely it is that books will be published giving tips about how to use it more efficiently and the greater is the chance that the user can find a friend or co-worker who can help solve specific problems that arise in using the product. Economists refer to this phenomenon as a *network externality*: When additional consumers join the "network" of users, they create a positive "external" benefit for consumers who are already part of the network.[17] When a network externality exists, a firm that has made more sales than its competitors in early periods and has thus developed a large installed base has an advantage when competing against firms with smaller installed bases. This further increases the firm's installed base relative to its competitors, increasing its advantage even more.

Network externalities can influence rivalry not only between individual firms, but also between different technologies, as illustrated by the battle between the VHS and Beta formats in video cassette recorders (VCRs). Beta-format technology was pioneered by a consortium of Japanese firms led by Sony. When Sony introduced its machines ahead of schedule, Victor Corporation of Japan (JVC) reacted by introducing a VHS format VCR. Though Beta-format is superior to VHS on most dimensions, Sony's high prices allowed VHS makers to capture a large share of the U.S. market.

As the installed base of VHS users grew throughout the 1980s, its advantage over the Beta format became ever larger as more and more producers of videos made titles available under VHS but not under Beta. Eventually, sales of the Beta-format VCRs fell to near zero in the United States, and Beta-format tapes are no longer produced. The existence of network externalities explains why some seemingly inferior technologies flourish, despite the availability of superior technologies. Example 14.2 discusses a classic example of this: the persistence of the QWERTY keyboard.

EXAMPLE 14.2

QWERTY[18]

You have probably noticed that the first six keys in the top row of letters on the keyboard of your personal computer are Q, W, E, R, T, and Y. This corresponds to how keys have been arranged on typewriters for over a century. However, the standard typewriter keyboard (or QWERTY) is not the optimum arrangement of letters for promoting speed and accuracy of typing. Most of the world's records for

---

[17]Example 13.5 in Chapter 13 discusses the use of hedonic pricing analysis to determine the economic impact of network externalities in the market for computer spreadsheets.

[18]This example is based on David, P., "Clio and the Economics of QWERTY," *American Economic Review*, 75, May 1985, pp. 332–337.

speed typing have been set on typewriters that use the Dvorak Simplified Keyboard (DSK), patented in 1932 by August Dvorak and W.L. Dealey. For example, during the 1940s, the U.S. Navy conducted experiments that revealed that the cost of teaching a group of experienced typists to use DSK would have a payback period of 10 days due to their increased speed. Despite the demonstrated superiority of the DSK and occasional attempts to generate interest in it (e.g., in the 1980s, Apple equipped its Apple IIC computers with a switch that converted its keyboard from QWERTY to DSK), the QWERTY arrangement remains the industry standard.

Why is this so? Dvorak attributed the persistence of the QWERTY keyboard to a conspiracy among members of the typewriter oligopoly to suppress an innovation that would, by increasing typing efficiency, decrease the demand for typists and, ultimately, typewriters. Yet, this would not explain why modern producers of computer keyboards continue to stick to the QWERTY standard. A more plausible explanation has to do with network externalities. This is the explanation given by the economic historian Paul David in his entertaining analysis of "QWERTY-nomics."

David begins by noting that early typewriters had a serious design limitation: The printing point was located underneath the paper carriage. As a result, what was typed was invisible to the typist unless he or she raised the carriage to remove the paper. When an operator was typing fast, the typebars would sometimes jam, and when this happened, each succeeding stroke typed the same letter onto the paper. This would be discovered only after the typist removed the paper from the carriage to see what had been printed, occasioning much frustration on the part of early users. The QWERTY keyboard was invented in 1873 by a Milwaukee printer named Christopher Latham Scholes, who after much experimentation, found that this arrangement minimized typebar clashes. Within a year of its discovery by Scholes, Remington's mechanics had perfected the QWERTY keyboard. For Remington, a pleasing side benefit of the QWERTY arrangement was that the first row of the keyboard contained all of the letters a salesman would need to type out the Remington brand name, TYPEWRITER.

The next two decades witnessed tremendous technological progress in the design of typewriters. Not only were machines developed with visible printing points, but some designs did away with typebars altogether and relied on cylinders or balls for typing (anticipating the development of the typing balls on IBM Selectrics). Much of this progress undermined the original rationale for the QWERTY keyboard.

Yet the QWERTY keyboard persisted. An important reason, David notes, was the development of "touch typing" in the late 1880s. Touch typing was originally taught on QWERTY keyboards. This created a powerful network externality that made it increasingly likely that a business would purchase a typewriter with a QWERTY keyboard, rather than one with some other arrangement. But if the savings from using alternative systems, such as DSK, were so large, why didn't businesses purchase typewriters with other keyboards and retrain their workers to use them? The answer lies in the separation of the ownership of the "hardware" (i.e., the typewriter, which was owned by the business) and the "software" (i.e., the touch typing skill, which was "owned" by the individual worker). Few businesses would have found it worthwhile to provide their workers with a generalized skill that could have been taken elsewhere. Few individuals would have found it worthwhile to invest in developing these skills because at the turn of the century there was virtually no market for "at-home" typewriters. With weak incentives for businesses and individuals to alter their skills, manufacturers of non-QWERTY machines found that the most profitable course of action was to become QWERTY-compatible. The development of the touch typing know-how was thus reinforced by an increase in the installed base of QWERTY machines. By the early twentieth century, QWERTY has become the entrenched standard and has remained so ever since, even though its original rationale has disappeared.

Reputation and Buyer Uncertainty

In the sale of experience goods—goods whose quality cannot be assessed before they are purchased and used—the reputation for quality that a firm establishes can be a significant early-mover advantage.[19] Consumers who have had a positive experience with a firm's brand will be reluctant to switch to competing brands if there is a chance that the competing products will not work. Buyer uncertainty coupled with reputational effects can make a firm's brand name a powerful isolating mechanism. Once the firm's reputation has been created, it will have an advantage competing for new customers, increasing the number of customers who have had successful trials, and thus further strengthening its reputation.

The nature of a later mover's disadvantage can be illustrated with a simple example.[20] Consider a newly introduced brand of analgesic that is competing with the brand that pioneered the product category. The pioneer entered the market at a price of $2.50, and at that price, a certain number of consumers tried its product. Suppose that the pioneer's product works, that is, it treats sinus headaches more effectively and with fewer side effects than aspirin. What price should the new brand charge? It turns out that if it is offered at the same price as the pioneering brand ($2.50) its sales will be zero. Why? Consider, first, consumers who thought about purchasing the analgesic from the pioneer but chose not to. Because these consumers were unwilling to purchase the product at $2.50 from the pioneer, they will presumably be unwilling to purchase it at the same price from the new entrant. Consider, next, consumers who purchased the analgesic from the pioneer and used it successfully. These customers know that if they purchase from the pioneer, they will receive a product that works, but if they purchase from the new entrant, there

---

[19]Chapter 12 discusses the distinction between experience goods and search goods and the implications of that distinction for competitive positioning.

[20]The analysis in this section is based on Richard Schmalensee's paper, "Product Differentiation Advantages of Pioneering Brands," *American Economic Review*, 72, June 1982, pp. 349–365.

is a risk the product will not work. If the entrant does not offer a lower price than the pioneer, these customers will not try its product. Finally, consider consumers who are new to the market, that is, had not previously considered purchasing an analgesic at all. For these consumers, the established reputation of the pioneering brand will tilt the balance in favor of that brand over the new entrant's brand, so if these consumers purchase at all, they will purchase from the pioneer. It follows, then, that at a price of $2.50, an entrant would make no sales even though its product might be indistinguishable from the pioneering brand. The later mover can penetrate the market only by selling at a price below the pioneer's. If later movers fail to penetrate the market, the reputation of the early mover becomes stronger over time, as more and more consumers purchase the brand and are satisfied with it.

IBM's competitive advantage in the market for mainframes was, for many years, sustained by considerations such as those just described. The old saying, "You'll never get fired for buying an IBM," captures this point. In the 1970s, one industry expert was quoted as saying that it would take at least a 30 percent difference in the price-performance ratio to induce a customer to choose a competing brand over IBM.[21] IBM's reputational advantage also extended to peripheral equipment, such as tape drives. For example, Gerald Brock reports the results of an internal IBM study that revealed that 46 percent of IBM's customers would pass up a 20 percent discount from a competitor and continue to purchase equipment from IBM.[22]

Of course, the new entrant could try to overcome a pioneering brand's reputational advantage by launching an advertising campaign to persuade consumers that its product's benefits are superior to those of the early mover. However, this is easier said than done. The consumer behavior literature in marketing suggests that pioneering brands have a profound impact on the formation of consumer preferences.[23] If a pioneer can persuade enough consumers to try the product, its attributes will be considered by consumers to be the ideal configuration for that type of product. For consumers to be persuaded to switch to a new brand, the new brand cannot be perceived as being just a little better than the pioneer, it must be perceived as significantly better. A good example of the perceptual advantage enjoyed by a pioneering brand is Chrysler's position in the minivan market. Chrysler introduced the first minivan in 1983. Despite the fact that Chrysler's minivans are not significantly superior or lower priced than those of Ford or GM, in the mid-1990s nearly two out of every three American minivans were made by Chrysler. The resilience of the Tylenol brand against competitors following the 1984 product tampering crisis is another example of the advantage enjoyed by pioneering brands.

---

[21]This comes from Greer, D.F., *Industrial Organization and Public Policy*, 3rd ed., New York: Macmillan, 1992, p. 141.

[22]Brock, G.W., *The U.S. Computer Industry: A Study of Market Power*, Cambridge, MA: Ballinger, 1975.

[23]See, for example, Carpenter, G. S. and K. Nakamoto, "Consumer Preference Formation and Pioneering Advantage, *Journal of Marketing Research*, August 1989, pp. 285–298.

XAMPLE 14.3

THE DEMISE OF THE BRAND?

The early 1990s were difficult for many established brands. In the ready-to-eat cereal industry, the market share of private-label brands (i.e., brands of cereal sold under a supermarket's label) more than doubled between 1986 and 1992. In the cigarette industry, Philip Morris's stock price dropped by nearly 25 percent when it reduced the price of its flagship brand Marlboro in response to competitive incursions by discount cigarettes (some of the most popular of which were sold by Philip Morris!). More generally, research by the advertising agency BBDO suggests that nearly two-thirds of consumers around the world believe that there are "no relevant or discernable differences" among competing brands for many products.[24] Other studies have found relatively low levels of brand loyalties for such products as canned vegetables, garbage bags, blue jeans, and batteries.[25]

These examples remind us that early-mover advantages based on brand name reputation may not last forever. This is true for several reasons. First, the benefits from reputation can be overexploited. For example, managers may misjudge the relevant price elasticity of demand and price the brand too high. This happened to brands such as Kraft Singles cheeses and Pillsbury cake mixes in the early 1990s, allowing private-label brands to make inroads and undermining the perceptual advantages enjoyed by the established brand name. At the same time, grocers established their own "brand names." A notable example of this is the British grocer Sainsbury's, whose store brands in products ranging from detergents to chocolates enjoy images and command prices comparable to the leading worldwide brands.

Second, reputation benefits may not be defensible against the efforts of buyers to appropriate them. For example, advances in information technology have increased the savvy with which supermarket chains and mass merchandisers allocate scarce shelf space. In the 1980s and 1990s, many consumer goods manufacturers responded to this increase in buyer power by reducing the relative proportion of marketing budgets that went to advertising and increasing the proportion that went to promotions, such as shelf space allowances (discounts in the wholesale price in return for a promise of prominent shelf space), aimed at persuading retailers to carry their products.

Third, changes in tastes, demographics, or even macroeconomic conditions can also undermine the power of an established brand name reputation. For example, marketing research suggests that higher-income people are more brand-loyal and less price-sensitive than lower-income people. The recession of the early 1990s

---

[24]This survey is reported in "Shoot Out at the Check Out," *The Economist*, June 5, 1993, pp. 69–70.

[25]See, for example, the data reported in "Brand Loyalty Is Rarely Blind Loyalty," *Wall Street Journal*, October 19, 1989, pp. B1, B8.

may have weakened the power of established brands as consumer incomes declined and a relatively larger proportion of consumers were tempted to shop on the basis of price, rather than established reputations.

Finally, technology can weaken the advantages of established brands. Technological advances in manufacturing have raised the quality of many consumer packaged goods and have made it easier for manufacturers to extend established product lines. A third more new products were introduced in the United States in 1992 as compared with five years earlier. This product proliferation may blur distinctions among competing brands, altering consumer perceptions of the differences among competing brands, and increasing an established brand's price elasticity of demand.

Buyer Switching Costs

For some products, buyers incur substantial costs when they switch to another supplier. Switching costs can arise when buyers develop brand-specific know-how that is not fully transferable to substitute brands. For example, a consumer who develops extensive knowledge in using Word Perfect would have to reinvest in the development of new know-how if he or she switched to Ami-Pro. Switching costs also arise when the seller develops specific know-how about the buyer that other sellers cannot quickly replicate or provides customized aftersale services to buyers. For example, a client of a commercial bank whose managers have developed extensive knowledge of the client's business would face a switching cost if it changed banks. Finally, through coupons or "frequent-customer" points, firms can create switching costs by tying discounts to the completion of a series of transactions with customers. For example, some law firms, such as Dombroff & Gillmore of Washington, D.C., have begun to use "frequent-client" programs in pricing legal services. Customers whose billings exceed a certain level within a given period of time receive a pool of credits that can be used to reduce future legal fees. The stock of these credits that a customer builds up is valuable only to the extent that the customer continues to use the services of Dombruff & Gillmore.

Switching costs can be a powerful advantage to an early mover. To illustrate how, suppose that an established firm with a large customer base faces the threat of competition from a potential entrant whose product provides the same level of quality as the early mover's. However, the product requires time to learn how to use, so a customer purchasing from the entrant faces a cost of S dollars (per unit output) of learning to use its brand. To take business away from the early mover, then, the new entrant must charge a price that is at least S dollars less than the price set by the established brand. This is because (for these customers) consumer surplus when purchasing from the established firm is $B - P_{EM}$, while the consumer surplus when purchasing from the entrant is $B - P_N - S$, where P_{EM} and P_N are the prices of the early mover and entrant, respectively. Consumer surplus is higher for the new brand only if $P_N < P_{EM} - S$. In principle, then, the early mover could set price a shade less than $C + S$ (where C is unit cost), and at this price, the established firm would make a profit, but the entrant would not.

However, this argument is incomplete. The new entrant is at a disadvantage in competing for the customers who have already purchased from the established firm, but it is not at a disadvantage in competing for new customers entering the market for the first time. Ignoring (for a moment) the possibility of network externalities or reputation effects, these customers incur a learning cost whether they purchase from the entrant or the established firm. Indeed, as Paul Klemperer has shown, the established firm is less willing to compete on price to win these new customers.[26] This is because if the established firm cuts price to attract these new customers, it reduces the profit margin on sales to its loyal customers. The new entrant, who has no loyal customers, incurs no such sacrifice. Thus, the gain in profit to an entrant from a given cut in price is greater than the gain in profit to the established firm from the same price cut. The incumbent firm's installed base of loyal customers acts like a "soft" commitment, of the kind discussed in Chapter 9, which makes it compete less aggressively on price than the entrant does.

Joseph Farrell and Carl Shapiro point out that when the market is growing through the addition of new customers, the presence of switching costs will deter entry only if economies of scale are significant or there are network externalities that enhance the benefit to a consumer of purchasing from the established firm rather than the entrant.[27] Farrell and Shapiro's analysis shows that in the absence of scale economies or network externalities, the existence of switching costs in a growing market will actually encourage more entry than otherwise would have occurred in the absence of switching costs! This is because the entrant counts on the reluctance of the established firm to sacrifice margins on its installed base by setting a price that is low enough to capture the business of the new customers. By ceding the new customers to the entrant, the incumbent firm makes it profitable for the entrant to come into the market. Farrell and Shapiro conjecture that markets with high switching costs, but low scale economies or network externalities, would be characterized by *stabilizing inertia*: A firm that gains a lead in market share in earlier periods would, in later periods, set higher prices and let its share erode over time. This may explain the tremendous growth of statistical software packages such as STATA, which sell for less and enjoy higher growth than industry leaders such as SAS and SPSS.

[26]Klemperer, P., "Markets with Consumer Switching Costs," *Quarterly Journal of Economics*, 102, 1987, pp. 375–394.

[27]Farrell, J. and C. Shapiro, "Dynamic Competition with Switching Costs," *RAND Journal of Economics*, 19, Spring 1988, pp. 123–137.

◆ ◆

Example 14.4

Sustainability at Intel

Rapid technological change can bring down longtime industrial giants like IBM (see Example 14.5). But it can also produce new success stories that must also struggle to stay on top. In the personal computer industry, the software maker Microsoft has been highly profitable for a decade or longer. Intel, which makes the microprocessors that are the "engines" of most personal computers, has also had a decade of profitability. The sustained success of Microsoft is readily explained by the theory of network externalities. For example, the initial dominance of Microsoft's MS-DOS operating system led software makers to develop programs that run in a DOS environment. This further built up the demand for DOS-based computers, which then fed back into the software development market. More recently, Microsoft's development of Windows has created new opportunities for network externalities that have further extended Microsoft's competitive advantage.

Intel's success is only partly due to network externalities. The company has been highly profitable since 1987. It currently earns close to $1 billion annually in net profits, representing a 17 percent return on sales. Intel's success was assured when, in 1980, IBM chose the company's 8088 microprocessor chip to be the engine of its personal computers. With the large installed base of 8088 machines and their successors, Intel benefits from a network externality—any new chip must be compatible with the DOS environment that has developed around Intel chips. Even so, many firms have sought to develop competing chips, and a number of would-be competitors have emerged in the past decade. Intel claims that its continued success is evidence of the superiority of its chips. Its competitors argue instead that Intel relies on illegal acts to sustain its success. Indeed, the battle for control of the microprocessor industry is being waged as much in the courtroom as it is in the marketplace.

Through the years, Intel has been accused of excessive zealousness in suing any firm that tried to introduce a competitor for its 80X86 line of processors, which are the mainstay of DOS-based personal computers. In each case, Intel claims that the competitor has infringed on Intel's patents. For example, in the mid-1980s Intel sued NEC, charging that NEC copied Intel's "microcode"—the instructions that govern how a microprocessor reacts to electronic signals. In defending its penchant for litigation, CEO Andrew Grove explained, "[Property protection] is very important to us. We're basically a technology-based company. The fruits of our research and development are highly coveted." Intel's competitors took a different view of Intel's litigious nature. Most felt that Intel filed groundless lawsuits simply to scare away competitors. Fighting lawsuits is very costly, and could deter startup firms. One potential competitor, Advanced Micro Devices (AMD), has spent over $100 million fighting Intel lawsuits (again concentrating on the use of Intel microcode).[28] In addition, the possibility of a damage award against AMD has limited

---

[28]Slater, M., "AMD Wins Key Microcode Court Case," *Microprocessor Report*, 8, 1994, p. 10.

its ability to borrow money for other business expenses. AMD chairman Jerry Sanders has described Intel as the "Saddam Hussein of the semiconductor industry." Other firms that have been embroiled in patent infringement suits with Intel include Hyundai Electronics, General Instrument, Atmel, Cyrix, and NEC.

In 1994, Intel lost two key court decisions that could clear the way for more robust competition in the microprocessor marketplace, and eventually spell the end of Intel's sustained success. The first decision by a San Jose jury held that Intel could not prevent AMD from using Intel microcode. The deciding factor in the case was a 1976 agreement between the two companies that allowed AMD to copy Intel microcode in "microcomputers."[29] Intel has appealed the decision, and the decision does not apply to other competitors. The second setback to Intel was delivered by the U.S. Supreme Court, which refused to examine several lower court rulings regarding licensing arrangements with foundries (chip manufacturing plants). During the 1980s, major chip purchasers such as IBM insisted that Intel license out production of chips to independent foundries to protect them against holdup by Intel. These foundries, in turn, have sold the chips to competing semiconductor makers, such as Cyrix. The court decision means that once the chips are sold, patent rights are exhausted. Firms such as Cyrix are now free to manufacture clones of Intel chips.

On the heels of these court decisions, several firms are chipping away at Intel's dominance. AMD and Cyrix are fighting to become the number-two chip seller, with both anticipating sales of one million chips in 1995. Intel continues to fight the AMD ruling in the courts, but is exploring other strategies to hold onto its 90 percent plus market share. Intel continues to enjoy a strong brand image and even budget computer makers like Dell are reluctant to switch brands, even when price differences between Intel chips and competing chips were 30 percent or higher. In the fall of 1994, Intel launched an unprecedented advertising campaign to further bolster its image. It also slashed prices by as much as 40 percent on some chips, including some Pentium chips. With its patent protection stripped away, however, Intel's ability to continue its sustained profitability is very much in question. It must now rely on new strategies, with an emphasis on marketing, to stay ahead of the crowd. The negative publicity Intel suffered in late 1994 over flaws in its Pentium chip illustrates the challenges associated with this new strategic direction.

Early-Mover Advantages and Competition for Market Share

The prospect of securing an early-mover advantage often makes it valuable for a firm to capture a large market share in a growing market. This suggests that although early-mover advantages may suppress competition once they are acquired, there may be intense competition for market share by firms seeking to acquire an early-mover advantage. Does the prospect of achieving early-mover advantages

---

[29]*Ibid.*

stimulate or suppress competition? The answer seems to be ambiguous and depends in subtle ways on the specific early-mover advantage and the specific industry context. For example, Michael Katz and Carl Shapiro show that when network externalities exist, firms who have entered in the early stage of an industry's life cycle may be willing to set price below average variable cost to build up market share, so that they can benefit from network externalities later on.[30] On the other hand, Paul Klemperer points out that in markets with switching costs, if consumers are savvy, they will anticipate that a high-market-share firm will exploit them later on.[31] Small cuts in price today designed to attract customers who later become "captive" due to switching costs will thus not attract many consumers. As a result, each firm's demand curve early in the market will be relatively price inelastic, and firms end up setting higher prices than they would have in the absence of switching costs. The presence of switching costs may suppress competition early, as well as later, in the industry life cycle.

Early Mover Disadvantages

Some firms pioneer a new technology or product, but fail to become the market leader. Royal Crown in diet cola and EMI with computerized axial tomography (the CAT scanner) are notable examples. This suggests that it is not inevitable that early movers will achieve sustainable competitive advantage in their industries.

Early movers may fail to achieve a competitive advantage because they lack the *complementary assets* that are needed to commercialize the product.[32] This was the case with EMI Ltd., a British music and electronics company perhaps best known for signing the Beatles to a record contract in the early 1960s. EMI lacked the production and marketing know-how to successfully commercialize the CAT scanner developed in its R&D laboratory, and it eventually sold this business to GE in the late 1970s. The importance of complementary assets goes back to our discussion of the evolution of the hierarchical firm in Chapter 1. In the nineteenth century, firms that became successful early movers in their industries, such as Swift, International Harvester, and BASF, not only invested in the physical assets needed to produce their products, but also developed organizational capabilities and administrative hierarchies needed to market the product and coordinate the flow of product through the vertical chain.

Early movers may also eventually fail to establish a competitive advantage because they make "bets" on what turn out to be the wrong technologies or products. An example would be Wang Laboratories' bet that the "office of the future" would be organized around networks of dedicated word processors. Given the uncertainty about demand or technology that exists when an early mover enters a market, these bets may be good ones: that is, the expected present value of profits exceeds the cost

[30]Katz, M. L., and C. Shapiro, "Technology Adoption in the Presence of Network Externalities," *Journal of Political Economy*, 94, 1986, pp. 822–841.

[31]Klemperer, *op. cit.*

[32]Teece, D., "Profiting from Technological Innovation: Implications for Integration, Collaboration, Licensing, and Public Policy, *Research Policy*, 15, 1986, pp. 285–305.

of entering the market. But an inherent property of decision making under uncertainty is that good decisions do not always translate into good outcomes. In the 1970s, Wang could not have known that the popularity of the personal computer would destroy the market for dedicated word processors. Of course, early movers can sometimes influence how the uncertainty is resolved, as when the early mover is able to successfully establish a technology standard when there are network externalities. If so, being a pioneer can be attractive, even in the face of considerable uncertainty.

But even when network externalities or learning effects are present, the importance of luck or trivial circumstances cannot be fully excluded. Often which technology or product design becomes the industry standard is determined by factors unrelated to the relative superiority of competing designs. For example, in the 1950s, when nuclear reactors were beginning to be built in the United States, a number of alternative technologies seemed feasible: reactors cooled by light water, heavy water, gas, and liquid sodium.[33] But following the Russian's launch of the Sputnik in 1957, the priority for the U.S. government was not technological virtuosity, but quick construction of a large number of land-based reactors to preserve the U.S. lead over the Soviets in nonmilitary applications of nuclear power. Because the Navy had been using light water designs in their nuclear submarines, light water reactors became the early favorites as the government encouraged private utilities to embark on crash programs to construct reactors. Once development began, firms moved down the learning curve for this particular technology, and by the 1960s, it had become the industry standard. This was so despite research that suggested that gas-cooled reactors might have been technologically superior.

* *

€XAMPLE 14.5

SUSTAINABILITY AT IBM[34]

Few firms provide a better example of both the possibilities for sustained profitability and the depths to which a firm can fall if advantage is not sustained than IBM. As late as 1986, IBM was the dominant firm in the computer industry, and the firms that had competed strongly with IBM in the 1950s, firms such as Burroughs, Control Data, and Honeywell, became known collectively as the "Bunch." IBM was also one of the most admired firms in the country. For example, in each of the first

---

[33]This example comes from Arthur, W.B., "Positive Feedbacks in the Economy," *Scientific American*, 262, February 1990, pp. 92–99.

[34]The material in this example is adapted from Carroll, P., *Big Blues: The Unmaking of IBM*, New York: Crown, 1993; DeLamarter, R., *Big Blue: IBM's Use and Abuse of Power*, New York: Dodd, Mead, 1986; and Ferguson, C. H., and C.R. Morris, *Computer Wars: The Fall of IBM and the Future of Global Technology*, New York: Times Books, 1994.

four years of *Fortune*'s corporate reputation rankings (1982–86), IBM was ranked the most respected firm in America by competitors, directors, and security analysts.

By 1994, IBM's stock price had plunged by half (losing more than $75 billion in total market value in the process), its share in traditional markets was drastically reduced, and its personal computer business, a business it had helped create, was plagued with difficulties. The corporate workforce had fallen from 407,000 in 1986 to 207,000 in 1993, with future cuts likely. In addition, the reputation of the firm for managerial excellence was severely tarnished, with its managers increasingly viewed as outcasts by others in the computer industry. What had happened at IBM?

IBM built its strong position in computers on the basis of product quality and new product development, coupled with a strong sales force and almost legendary customer service. From a dominant position in punch card and tabulating machines, the firm gained a strong position in electronic computing on the basis of its ability to transfer the skills gained from large defense computer contracts into models of business computers that effectively met user needs. IBM sales grew from $40 million prior to World War II to over $1 billion dollars by 1957.

The height of the firm's dominance was perhaps reached in the two decades following the introduction of the 360/370 series in the mid-1960s. This line of products embodied a vision of comprehensive product performance, along with the idea of software compatibility, to meet all reasonable customer needs with one set of products and to ensure that the previous investments of customers in learning how to use a particular generation of products would not be rendered obsolete by subsequent new product introductions.

The 360/370 product strategy succeeded, providing IBM with a dominant market position. This position was strong enough to engender an antitrust suit from the U.S. Justice Department that took 13 years to litigate. It was also highly sustainable, since customers had substantial product loyalty to IBM and substantial switching costs in considering other products. In its heyday, IBM was indeed the computer brand you would not get fired for purchasing. The dominant position of the firm by 1983 in its core and related businesses is apparent in the following market share figures.

	Rank	IBM Share
Mainframes	1	72%
Mass storage	1	70%
Software	1	30%
PBX	2	21%
Terminals	1	40%
Small business/microcomputers	2	17%
Personal computers	1	28%
Word processors	1	25%
Semiconductors (Intel)	3	18%

In 1980, IBM had more than a tenfold lead in the value of its installed base in mainframes over the next largest competitor, Sperry Rand ($37.6 versus $3.5 billion). By 1984, in the world market for mainframes, IBM had a 76.8 percent share, far ahead of the second-place Burroughs, which had a 5.6 percent share.

IBM's decline stemmed from the failure of its managers to understand how a product it had pioneered, the personal computer (PC), would radically transform the entire computer business and alter the basis of its sustained high performance. In particular, it did not anticipate the growth in power of personal computers, and with it, the increasing ability of these machines to substitute for the larger mainframes and minicomputers upon which IBM advantage had traditionally rested.

IBM managers apparently also did not recognize until it was too late that the PC would become a standardized product whose value would not depend on reputation and service. The customer service capabilities that served IBM so well with mainframes were of limited value with PCs. To get needed information, customers could consult with other users or with the numerous popular PC magazines that have developed. Rather than worry about long-term commitments, the ability to upgrade, and servicing arrangements, customers can increasingly just buy another machine in a year or two.

When PCs are commodities, value accrues to the owners of the two critical components of the machine: the microprocessors and the operating system. IBM's decisions in the early 1980s led to its loss of control over these two components and left it in a highly competitive PC business without a sustainable basis of competitive advantage. Control over the operating system fell to Bill Gates and Microsoft, who acquired rights to the DOS operating system for $75,000 and built a company that had a market value of $27 billion in 1993. Control over microprocessor technology fell to the Intel Corporation, which developed the successful 386 and 486 series of processors, along with its new Pentium series. IBM instead bet that its 286 microprocessor would be sufficient, a bet that it lost.

IBM's loss of leadership was not due to technological change. The firm had and continues to possess more than sufficient technological prowess to compete. The failure of IBM to sustain its advantage stems from managerial decisions that failed to anticipate the path of product changes and allowed competitors to obtain dominant market positions on the basis of market share and network externalities. While it is easy, *ex post*, to discuss managerial mistakes, it is not clear that all of these decisions were faulty *ex ante*. For example, IBM also failed to capitalize on its initial work in developing computer architectures based on the RISC (Reduced Instruction Set Computing) technology and instead supported the architecture in use in the 370 series mainframes. This failure stemmed in part from the bureaucratic decision-making processes that had come to characterize the firm. It also, however, stemmed from legitimate disagreements about the value of competing approaches. Decisions may be reasonable at the time, even though they later turn out to be incorrect.

IMPERFECT IMITABILITY AND INDUSTRY EQUILIBRIUM ◆ ◆ ◆ ◆ ◆

The previous section argued that imperfect imitation and early-mover advantages prevent the perfectly competitive dynamic from running full course. But how, specifically, would an industry equilibrium depart from the perfectly competitive model when these isolating mechanisms are at work?

Richard Rumelt and Steven Lippman make the important point that when there is imperfect imitability, firms in an otherwise perfectly competitive market may be able to sustain positive economic profits over long periods, but an average firm will earn below-average profits, and indeed may appear to be making negative economic profits.[35] These arguments can be illustrated with the example in Figure 14.6. The figure depicts an industry in which firms produce undifferentiated products but have different costs of production. Average variable cost (AVC) and marginal cost (MC) are constant up to a capacity of 1,000,000 units per year. We assume that this level of capacity is small relative to the overall size of the market, so the industry will be able to accommodate many firms producing at capacity. The most efficient firms in this industry can achieve an AVC of $1 per unit. There are many potential entrants into this market, but because imitation is imperfect, not all of them will be able to emulate the practices of those that achieve the low-cost position in the market.

The problem that each entrant faces is that prior to entry, it does not know what its costs will be. Accordingly, prior to entering the market, a prospective competitor believes that there is a 20 percent probability that its AVC will take on each of five values shown in the figure: $1, $3, $5, $7, $9. A potential entrant thus realizes that while it may be able to successfully imitate the most efficient firms, its costs may also be higher than theirs. Suppose, finally, a firm must incur the cost of building a factory if it comes into the industry. This factory costs $36,000,000 to build and (for simplicity) never depreciates. Investors expect a return of 5 percent on their investment, so the annualized cost of the factory is .05 × $36,000,000 = $1,800,000 or $1.8 per unit of capacity. If we suppose further that the factory represents specialized capital that can be used only in this industry, and therefore has zero scrap value, the $1.8 represents the per-unit cost of entry.

What will the equilibrium price be? Because there are many potential entrants, entry will occur as long as expected economic profit is positive, or equivalently, as long as the firm's expected operating profit (i.e., revenues minus variable costs) exceeds the costs of entry. In equilibrium, price will fall to the level at which entry is no longer attractive. Thus, at the equilibrium price, a firm's expected operating profit just equals the cost of entry. This seems straightforward, but there is one complication: Not all entrants will survive. Some will find that their AVC is greater than the price and will drop out of the market. The expected profit calculation must take this possibility into account.

In this example, the price that makes a prospective entrant just indifferent between entering and not entering is $6.[36] Why? At that price, firms that learn that

---

[35]Lippman, S. A. and R. P. Rumelt, "Uncertain Imitability: An Analysis of Interfirm Differences in Efficiency Under Competition," *Bell Journal of Economics*, 13, Autumn 1982, pp. 418–438.

[36]The equilibrium price was calculated through trial and error. A systematic method exists for calculating the equilibrium price in this market, but its discussion would add little to the economic insights that are generated by this example.

FIGURE 14.6

AVERAGE VARIABLE AND MARGINAL COST FUNCTIONS WITH
IMPERFECT IMITABILITY.

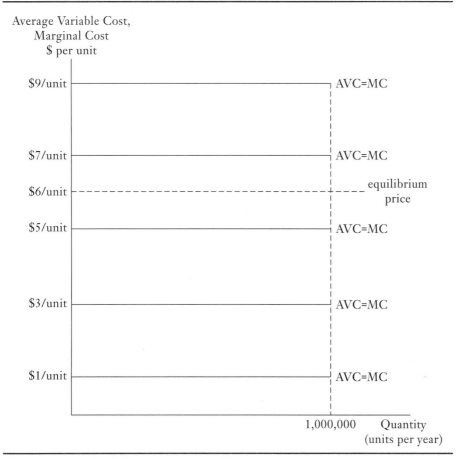

The figure shows the different average variable cost functions (AVC) that a firm might
have if it enters this market. Since AVC cost is constant up to the capacity of 1,000,000
units per year, the AVC function coincides with the marginal cost (MC) function. The
firm's AVC can take on one of five values, $1, $3, $5, $7, or $9, each with equal (i.e., 20
percent) probability. The equilibrium price in this market is $6 per unit. At this price,
each firm's expected economic profit is zero.

their AVC is $7 or $9 exit the industry because they would lose money on each unit
of output they produce. These firms, in effect, earn zero operating profits, but because they have incurred the up-front entry cost, they end up net losers. A firm
with an AVC of $1, $3, or $5 will produce up to its capacity, and at a price of $6,
will earn a per unit operating profits of $5, $3, and $1, respectively. A potential en-

trant's expected operating profit per unit of capacity, when the price is $6 is thus:

$$.2\times5 + .2\times3{:}+ .2\times1 + .2\times0 + .2\times0 = \$1.8$$

Since this expected operating profit equals the entry costs of $1.8 per unit, a price of $6 leaves potential entrants just indifferent between entering or not. Put another way, at a price of $6, each firm's *expected* rate of return on its investment is equal to its cost of capital of 5 percent. This is illustrated in Table 14.1.

This example illustrates Lippman and Rumelt's points. Some firms in the industry (those with AVC of $1 or $3) earn positive economic profits, that is, their return on investment exceeds their cost of capital. Other firms (those with AVC of $5) fail to recover their entry cost; their return on investment is less than their cost of capital. No firm can, with certainty, match the positive economic profits of the most efficient firms. And a firm with AVC of $5 is better off remaining in the industry and earning a positive operating profit even if it does not fully cover the entry cost because the entry cost cannot be recovered if it were to exit.[37] Note also that the profit of an "average" entrant—one with AVC of $5—is less than the average profit of those firms that are active in the market.

While the numerical example is special, the insights are robust. The most efficient firms earn positive economic profits because no firm can be certain that it can imitate their competitive advantage. Average entrants earn subpar returns relative to active firms because the least efficient firms simply will not survive. As price

TABLE 14.1
SUMMARY STATISTICS FOR IMPERFECT IMITABILITY EXAMPLE

AVC	Probability	Annual Revenue @ $6/unit	Annual Total Variable Costs	Annual Operating Profit	ROI (annual operating profit/$36 million)
$1/unit	.2	$6,000,000	$1,000,000	$5,000,000	13.89%
$3/unit	.2	$6,000,000	$3,000,000	$3,000,000	8.33%
$5/unit	.2	$6,000,000	$5,000,000	$1,000,000	2.78%
$7/unit	.2	$0	$0	$0	0%
$9/unit	.2	$0	$0	$0	0%
				Expected ROI	5%

[37]Of course, if the firm's capital depreciated over time, then once it wears out, it would not reinvest if it knew that its AVC would continue to be $5. However, if reinvesting in capital gives the firm a new "draw" from the distribution of average variable costs, then at a market price of $6, the firm would be just indifferent between reinvesting and not reinvesting.

declines toward the equilibrium level, these firms will drop out of the industry. If an average entrant survives, it will now be at the bottom end of the distribution of remaining firms.[38]

The example also illustrates the distinction between *ex ante* and *ex post* economic profitability. Before entering (i.e., *ex ante*), each firm's expected economic profit is zero, that is, each firm expects to earn its 5 percent cost of capital (see Table 14.1). After entering (i.e., *ex post*), a firm's economic profit may be positive or negative, that is, a firm may earn more or less than the competitive return of 5 percent. This yields an insight of fundamental importance: To assess the profit opportunities available in a particular business, managers should not just focus on the performance of the most successful firms. For example, the fact that some biotechnology firms earn annual returns on investment in excess of 50 or 60 percent does not mean a typical entrant can expect to earn this return. In addition, the average return of *active firms* can also be a misleading statistic of expected *ex ante* profitability. In the example above, the average ROI of active producers is (13.89 + 8.33 + 2.78)/3 = 8.33 percent, which overstates *ex ante* profitability. The reason for this is that a simple average of the profitability of active firms does not take into account unsuccessful firms that have lost money and exited the industry. Existing biotechnology firms may have average rates of return of 30 percent, but the *ex ante* expected ROI is likely to be less than 30 percent because many entrants in this business have already exited, posting substantial losses during their brief lives.

CHAPTER SUMMARY

◆ If the dynamic of perfect competition operates, no competitive advantage will be sustainable, and the persistence of profitability over time should be weak, as most firm's profits should converge to the competitive level.

◆ Evidence on profit persistence suggests that the profits of high-profit firms decline over time, while those of low-profit firms rise over time. However, the profits of these groups do not converge to a common mean. This lack of convergence cannot be ascribed to differences in risk between high-profit and low-profit firms. More likely, it reflects impediments to the operation of the dynamic of perfect competition.

---

[38]This insight can be restated by drawing an analogy with a professional golf tournament. A tournament (which almost always involves four rounds of golf) typically has a "cut" after the first two rounds in which golfers with scores that place them in the bottom half of the field are not allowed to finish the tournament. Typically, golfers who achieve the average score in a tournament's first rounds will just make the cut. Barring a miracle, these golfers will usually end up with scores after four rounds that are at the bottom of the group of golfers who survive the "cut" and finish the tournament.

◆   The resource-based theory of the firm emphasizes asymmetries in the resources and capabilities of firms in the same business as the basis for sustainable competitive advantage. Resources and capabilities must be scarce and immobile—not tradeable on well-functioning markets—to serve as the basis of sustainable advantage.

◆   Competitive advantages must also be protected by isolating mechanisms in order to be sustainable. An isolating mechanism prevents competitors from duplicating or neutralizing the source of the firm's competitive advantage. Isolating mechanisms fall into two broad classes: barriers to imitation and early-mover advantages.

◆   Specific barriers to imitation are: legal restrictions, such as patents or copyrights, that impede imitation; superior access to scarce inputs or customers; economies of scale coupled with limited market size; and intangible barriers to imitation, including causal ambiguity, dependence on historical circumstances, and social complexity.

◆   Sources of early-mover advantages include: the learning curve, network externalities, brand name reputation when buyers are uncertain about product quality, and consumer switching costs.

◆   When there are barriers to imitation, an equilibrium in a competitive market occurs at a price at which *ex ante* expected economic profits are zero. However, some firms may earn *ex post* positive economic profits. These profits are protected because of the conjunction of sunk costs and uncertainty. No firm can be certain that it can imitate the most successful firms in the market, but a firm must incur nonrecoverable entry costs before it can learn just how close it is likely to come to the efficiency of the best firms in the market.

QUESTIONS

1.   Which of the following circumstances are likely to create first-mover advantages:

   a. Maxwell House introduces the first freeze-dried coffee.

   b. A consortium of U.S. firms introduce the first high-definition television.

   c. Smith Kline introduces Tagamet, the first effective medical treatment for ulcers.

   d. Wal-Mart opens a store in Nome, Alaska.

2.   Each of the following parts describes a firm that was an early mover in its market. In light of the information provided indicate whether the firm's position as an early mover is likely to be the basis of a sustainable competitive advantage.

   a. An early mover has the greatest cumulative experience in a business in which the slope of the learning curve is 1.

   b. A bank has issued the largest number of automated teller machine cards in a large urban area. Banks view their ability to offer ATM cards as an important part of their battle for depositors, and a customer's ATM card for one bank does not work on the ATM systems of competing banks.

c. A firm has a 60 percent share of T3MP, a commodity chemical used to make industrial solvents. Minimum efficient scale is thought to be 50 percent of current market demand. Recently, a change in environmental regulation has dramatically raised the price of a substitute chemical that indirectly competes with T3MP. This change undermines the market for the substitute, which is about twice the size of the market for T3MP.

3. Coke and Pepsi have sustained their market dominance for nearly a century. General Motors and Ford have recently been hard hit by competition. What is the difference between the product/market situations in these two cases that affects sustainability?

4. "Often times, the achievement of a sustainable competitive advantage requires an investment and should be evaluated as such. In some cases, the benefits from the investment may not be worth the cost. Rather than trying to build a sustainable position, the firm should "cash out," for example, by exiting the industry, selling the assets business to another firm, or refraining from investing additional capital in the business for future growth."

Evaluate this statement keeping a focus on two questions: (a) In light of the factors that help a firm sustain a competitive advantage, explain in what sense achieving a sustainable advantage requires an "investment." (b) Can you envision circumstances under such an investment that would not be beneficial to the shareholders of the firm?

THE ORIGINS OF
COMPETITIVE ADVANTAGE:
INNOVATION, EVOLUTION,
AND THE ENVIRONMENT

15

*P*erhaps no product so epitomizes the emergence of Japanese technological and marketing muscle on a global scale as the video cassette recorder (VCR), the world's largest selling consumer electronics product. Chapter 14 recounts the battle that took place in the 1980s between the Beta format (pushed by Sony) and the VHS format (pushed by Victor Corporation of Japan [JVC][1]). However, the battle to shape the future of the video recording industry began nearly 25 earlier when the American-based Ampex Corporation invented video tape and a video recording and playback machine. Ampex translated its innovative success into a dominant position in the market for high-performance video recording systems for commercial users. Throughout the 1960s Ampex pursued the development of a cartridge-based video player and an associated video camera for the household market, and in 1970 it introduced a system known as Instavision. But Instavision was a commercial flop: It cost over $1,500 for a cumbersome-looking video player and $500 for the camera. Two years later, Ampex abandoned the project, concentrating instead on commercially oriented applications of video-recording technology. Two other American entrants into the VCR-race, Cartridge Television Inc. (CTI) and RCA also failed. CTI developed a video recording and playback machine that was included as a feature on high-end television sets manufactured by Admiral and Packard Bell. However, the product was plagued by technological glitches, and de-

---

[1]In the early 1950s, Matsushita purchased a 50 percent ownership stake in then-financially-troubled JVC. However, JVC has generally been independently managed and has often competed with Matsushita in the markets they both serve.

spite an agreement with Columbia and United Artists to provide films on video-tape, there were not enough films to maintain consumer interest.[2] RCA, the pioneer of the color television set, sought to develop a commercially viable VCR throughout the early 1970s. But in 1977 it too abandoned its efforts, in part because it was unable to develop an economical process for manufacturing its VCR designs and in part because it believed that the videodisc technology would leapfrog the VCR and become the commercially preferred design for playing back recorded images.

While American efforts were falling short, the efforts of several foreign firms were more successful. By the mid-1970s, JVC, Matsushita, Sony of Japan, and Philips of the Netherlands had all mastered the daunting technological challenges involved in manufacturing video recorders for a commercial market (e.g., figuring out how to compress 2 to 4 hours of video tape into a cartridge the size of a small paperback). Sony's Betamax system got an early hard start after Matsushita decided to delay the production of its system, which it believed was technologically inferior to the Video Home System (VHS) being developed by JVC. Betamax developed an especially strong following in the high-end professional market. However, JVC set the stage for overtaking Sony in the far larger household market when it introduced a VHS machine that could record for two hours, as compared with just one hour for the Sony machines. Soon after, JVC and Matsushita convinced other consumer electronics firms, such as Thorn-EMI in the U.K., Thompson in France, and AEG-Telefunken in West Germany, to adopt the VHS model in the design of their machines, giving VHS an important advantage in the race to become the technology standard. Philips, whose V2000 format was incompatible with both Sony and JVC, introduced its product a year and a half after JVC introduced VHS. Although it had managed to keep pace with its Japanese rivals in the race to develop the technology, Philips' late introduction put it at a disadvantage in the competition to accumulate an installed base of users. Eventually, Philips also began to manufacture VCRs in the VHS format.

This example shows that the origins of a firm's current marketplace success often stretch far back in time. JVC-Matsushita's success in the VCR business was shaped by decisions and commitments that those firms made 15 to 20 years before VCRs became commercially viable. This suggests that developing a competitive advantage involves taking a deep look into the future to anticipate unmet or even unarticulated consumer needs, placing bets on alternative technologies, investing in the development of new products and new capabilities to produce and deliver those products to market, and then being the first to introduce those products in the marketplace in order to benefit from the various early-mover advantages, such as network externalities or the learning curve, discussed in Chapter 14.

This chapter studies the origins of competitive advantage. Chapter 14 argued that competitive advantage comes out of the ability of a firm to exploit market shocks and opportunities, and that the firm's advantage is then protected by early-mover advantages and various barriers to imitation by other firms. But we did not

---

[2]CTI eventually went bankrupt.

discuss why some firms are better or luckier than others at exploiting shocks or taking advantage of opportunities. Why, for example, was it Ted Turner, and not the established networks who seized the opportunity to develop a television network devoted entirely to news? Why was Honda, and not Harley Davidson or Triumph, able to tap into what turned out to be a large U.S. market for light and middle-weight motorcycles? Why did JVC succeed where Ampex failed in the market for VCRs?

This chapter is divided into seven main parts. The first part discusses the role of innovation and entrepreneurship in a market economy, emphasizing economist Joseph Schumpeter's notion of creative destruction and highlighting its importance for business strategy. The next two parts examine the impact of firm size, market position, and market structure on firms' incentives to innovate. The fourth part explores innovation from the perspective of evolutionary economics. It focuses on how a firm's history and internal resources and capabilities affect its ability to innovate and develop new capabilities. The fifth part examines the relationship between the firm's local environment and its ability to gain competitive advantage. This section is particularly concerned with how demand and factor market conditions, as well as the economic infrastructure in the firm's domestic market, determine competitive advantage. The sixth section examines the evidence on what determines innovativeness within firms and markets. The final section discusses the process of managing innovation inside the firm.

CREATIVE DESTRUCTION ◆ ◆ ◆ ◆ ◆

A short answer to the question, "What are the origins of competitive advantage?" is that some firms exploit opportunities for creating profitable competitive positions that other firms either ignore or are unable to exploit. Seizing such opportunities is the essence of entrepreneurship. Entrepreneurship is often seen as synonymous with discovery and innovation. But an equally important part of entrepreneurship, according to economist Joseph Schumpeter, is the ability to act on the opportunity that innovations and discoveries create:

> To undertake such new things is difficult and constitutes a distinct economic function, first, because they lie outside the routine tasks which everybody understands and secondly because the environment resists in many ways that vary, according to social conditions, from simple refusal either to finance or to buy a new thing, to physical attack on the man who tries to produce it. To act with confidence beyond the range of familiar beacons and to overcome that resistance requires aptitudes that are present in only a small fraction of the population and define the entrepreneurial type as well as the entrepreneurial function. This function does not essentially consist in either inventing anything or otherwise creating the conditions which the enterprise exploits. It consists in getting things done.[3]

---

[3]Schumpeter, J., *Capitalism, Socialism, and Democracy*, New York: Harper & Row, 1942, p. 132.

Schumpeter considered capitalism to be an evolutionary process that unfolded in a characteristic pattern. In any market, there are periods of comparative quiet, during which firms that have developed superior products, technologies, or organizational capabilities earn positive economic profits. These quiet periods are punctuated by fundamental "shocks" or "discontinuities" when old sources of advantage are destroyed and replaced with new ones. The entrepreneurs who exploit the opportunities these shocks create go on to achieve positive profits during the next period of comparative quiet. Schumpeter called this evolutionary process *creative destruction.*

For Schumpeter, the process of creative destruction had two important implications. First, static efficiency—the optimal allocation of society's resources at a given point in time—is less important than dynamic efficiency—the achievement of long-term growth and technological improvement:

> A system—any system, economic or other—that at every given point of time fully utilizes its possibilities to the best advantage may yet in the long run be inferior to a system that does so at no given point of time, because the latter's failure to do so may be a condition for the level or speed of long-run performance.[4]

Second, business strategy and market outcomes can be evaluated only in the context of the process of creative destruction. Schumpeter was critical of economists who focused exclusively on the outcomes of price competition when judging the social benefits of firms' performance in a market. For Schumpeter, what really counted was not price competition at a given point in time, which he dismissed as mere tactical maneuvering, but rather competition from new products, new technologies, and new sources of organization:

> This kind of competition is as much more effective than the other as a bombardment is in comparison with forcing a door, and so much more important that it becomes a matter of comparative indifference whether [price] competition in the ordinary sense functions more or less properly; the powerful lever that in the long run expands output and brings down prices is in any case made of other stuff.[5]

Schumpeter's ideas are important for business strategy because they emphasize that the isolating mechanisms discussed in Chapter 14 are never permanent. Competitive advantages based on inimitable resources or capabilities or early-mover advantages can eventually become obsolete as new technologies arise, tastes change, or government policy evolves. This process is depicted in Figure 15.1, which shows the hypothetical time path for profits for a firm that has achieved a sustainable advantage.

Recently, scholars have used Schumpeter's notion of creative destruction to develop frameworks that can guide managers in thinking about strategic decision making. For example, Richard D'Aveni argues that in industries ranging from consumer electronics to airlines and computer software to snack goods, the sources of

---

[4]*Ibid.*, p. 83.

[5]*Ibid.*, pp. 84–85.

FIGURE 15.1
HYPERCOMPETITION AND COMPETITIVE ADVANTAGE.

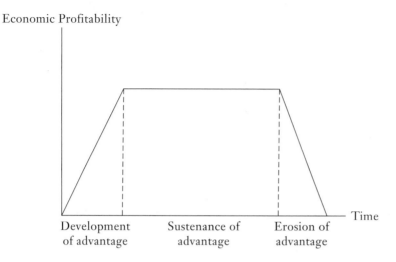

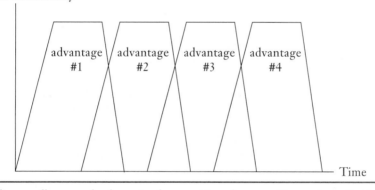

The upper diagram illustrates the dynamic of competitive advantage. Economic profits rise as the advantage is developed. They then plateau during the period in which the advantage is sustainable. Eventually the advantage is eroded, and economic profitability declines. Richard D'Aveni argues that in many markets, the period during which advantages are sustainable is shrinking. In such environments, a firm can sustain positive economic profits over time only by continually developing new sources of advantage, as shown in the bottom diagram.

Source: These figures are based on Figures 1-1 and 1-2 in D'Aveni, R.A., *Hypercompetition: Managing the Dynamics of Strategic Maneuvering,* New York: Free Press, 1994, pp. 8, 12.

competitive advantage are being created and eroded at an increasingly rapid rate.[6] In effect, he argues that the length of the plateau in Figure 15.1 is shrinking. D'Aveni calls this phenomenon *hypercompetition* and argues that in hypercompeti-

---

[6]D'Aveni, R., *Hypercompetition: Managing the Dynamics of Strategic Maneuvering,* New York: Free Press, 1994.

tive environments a preoccupation with sustaining competitive advantage can often be fatal. Instead, he believes that a firm's chief strategic goal should be to disrupt existing sources of advantage in its industry (including its own) and create new ones. The route to long-term success in hypercompetitive environments lies not in trying to sustain a long-term advantage, but rather (as illustrated in Figure 15.1) in seeking to achieve a sequence of temporary advantages that keep the firm one step ahead of the rest of the industry. D'Aveni cites Gillette as an example of a successful hypercompetitive firm. After the launch of the highly successful Sensor razor in 1989, Gillette continued its efforts to design an even better razor and eventually introduced a superior version of Sensor in Europe and a highly successful Sensor for women in the United States. From the experiences of Gillette and other successful hypercompetitive firms, such as Microsoft and American Airlines, D'Aveni develops what he calls a "new 7-S" framework to help guide strategy formulation in hypercompetitive environments.[7]

Gary Hamel and C.K. Prahalad promote related ideas.[8] They argue that companies, such as CNN, Honda, NEC, and Sony, succeeded because of their sustained obsession with achieving global dominance in their industries. Prahalad and Hamel call this obsession *strategic intent*. The strategic intent of these companies was out of proportion to their existing resources and capabilities. Prahalad and Hamel refer to this gap between ambition and resources as *strategic stretch*. These companies had to expand and adapt their current stock of resources and create new ones. They were more concerned with "leveraging" resources than with achieving "strategic fit" between their current resources and their environment.

The ideas of D'Aveni and Prahalad and Hamel remind us that in environments characterized by rapid technological development and fickle tastes, a firm that rests on its laurels, seeking only to harvest existing sources of advantage, can be quickly displaced by more innovative rivals. Moreover, firms may be able to create their own shocks, rather than waiting for the environment to change or for other firms to disrupt existing sources of advantage in the industry. However, managers must also keep this advice in perspective. The *sunk cost effect* and the *replacement effect* discussed in the next section show that it may not always pay for an established firm to match the innovative activity of its competitors. D'Aveni's emphasis on destroying existing sources of advantage and Prahalad and Hamel's emphasis on "stretch" may thus be more pertinent for smaller firms in a market or for firms seeking to expand into new markets than for industry leaders. As always, though, general advice can never be applied without considering the specific context in which the firm operates and the underlying economics of competitive advantage.

---

[7]The intended comparison is with the original McKinsey 7-S framework that Tom Peters and Robert Waterman popularized in their book, *In Search of Excellence*, New York: Warner Books, 1982.

[8]Hamel, G. and C.K. Prahalad, *Competing for the Future*, Cambridge, MA: Harvard Business School Press, 1994. See also Hamel, G., and C.K. Prahalad, "Strategic Intent," *Harvard Business Review*, May–June 1989, pp. 63–76 and "Strategy as Stretch and Leverage," *Harvard Business Review*, March–April 1993, pp. 75–84.

THE INCENTIVE TO INNOVATE   ◆ ◆ ◆ ◆ ◆

Business history contains many instances of companies with a wealth of assets—innovative products, strong reputations, deep financial resources, and powerful distribution channels—whose market position was eroded or overtaken by companies with seemingly much smaller resource bases. Xerox versus Canon in copiers, Sony versus RCA in television, and CNN versus the networks in news programming are a few examples that come to mind. A frequent explanation for this is that small firms are more "nimble" and less bureaucratic than large firms, and thus are more willing to innovate and break with established practices. This explanation is often expressed in familiar cliches contrasting large and small companies. Large companies become "fat and happy," or they "fall asleep" and ignore firms that come out of nowhere to challenge their dominance. Small companies are "hungry" or are "lean and mean" and have the courage and incentives to pursue innovative approaches that their larger rivals lack.

Though superficially appealing, these arguments are not profound. They fail to answer a fundamental question: Why would established firms be *systematically* less able to innovate or break with established practice than new entrants or marginal firms in an industry? Implicit in the familiar cliches seems to be a model of nonmaximizing behavior: Dominant firms work less hard at innovating, identifying new markets, and developing new capabilities than their smaller rivals. But why should this be? It may be that the agency problems discussed in Chapter 2 are more severe in bigger firms than in smaller ones. Agency problems may also be greater in firms that are less threatened with product market competition. Or managers in large firms may be systematically more risk averse than those in smaller firms.

While these ideas have merit, there is another explanation. The unwillingness of a firm to innovate may be not the result of managerial myopia or a reluctance to take risks, but rather a profit-maximizing response to the circumstances the firm faces. This section examines two forces that may make it rational for firms to refrain from innovating: (1) the sunk cost effect; and (2) the replacement effect. It also discusses a force called the efficiency effect (which we introduced in Chapter 11) that offsets the sunk cost and replacement effects and strengthens an established firm's incentive to innovate. We discuss each effect in detail below.

The Sunk Cost Effect

The *sunk cost effect* has to do with the asymmetry between a firm that has *already* made a commitment to a particular technology or product concept and one that is *planning* such a commitment. It is the phenomenon whereby a profit-maximizing firm sticks with its current technology or product concept even though the profit-maximizing decision for a firm starting from scratch would be to choose a *different* technology or product concept. The sunk cost effect arises because a firm that has already committed to a particular technology has made investments in resources and organizational capabilities that are likely to be specific to that technology and are thus less valuable if it switches to another technology. For an established firm, the costs associated with these investments are sunk and thus should be ignored when the firm considers the decision to switch to a new technology. Ignoring these sunk costs creates an inertia that favors sticking with the current technology. By contrast, a firm that has not yet committed to a technology compares the costs of all of the alternative technologies under consideration and is thus not biased in favor of one technology over another.

To illustrate the economics of the sunk cost effect, consider the problems of an established firm and a new entrant who are both contemplating whether to adopt a newly developed technology (denoted by a subscript N) or an established technology (denoted by a subscript O). The new technology reduces operating costs as compared with the old technology, but it entails a larger up front investment in physical assets and know-how. For simplicity, assume that a firm's revenues are not affected by which technology it adopts. A new entrant adopts the new technology if the present value of operating costs (denoted by VC) plus up-front investment costs (denoted by I) are less than the present value of operating costs plus up-front investment costs from adopting the established technology. That is, it should adopt the new technology if

$$VC_N + I_N < VC_O + I_O$$

We can rearrange this equation as follows:

$$I_N - I_O < VC_O - VC_N$$

$$\Delta I < \Delta VC \tag{15.1}$$

where $\Delta I = I_N - I_O$, and $\Delta VC = VC_O - VC_N$. This condition says that the firm will adopt the new technology if the present value of the savings in operating costs, ΔVC, from using the new technology instead of the old technology exceeds the additional investment cost, ΔI, required by the new technology. Let us assume that this condition, which we denote by (15.1), holds.

Consider, now, the problem of an established firm that has already made the investment I_O in the established technology. This investment is sunk and should be ignored in making the decision about whether to adopt the new technology. Suppose, further, that the established firm has benefited from accumulated experience, so its operating cost with the established technology is a fraction, αV_O (where $\alpha < 1$), of what a new entrant would hope to achieve under the established technology. The established firm goes through the same analysis as the new entrant, but gets a different condition for when adoption of the new technology is optimal:

$$VC_N + I_N < \alpha VC_O$$

Performing some straightforward algebraic transformations, we can express this as

$$I_N - I_O < VC_O - VC_N - (1 - \alpha)VC_O - I_O$$

or

$$\Delta I < \Delta VC - [(1 - \alpha)VC_O + I_O] \tag{15.2}$$

The condition under which it pays for an established firm to adopt the new technology (denoted by [15.2]) establishes a more severe hurdle for the new technology than is the case for a new entrant. The established firm will adopt the new technology only if the additional investment cost is less than savings in operating costs *less* an additional amount, $[(1 - \alpha)VC_O + I_O]$, that depends on the established firm's experience advantage and the sunk costs it has already incurred. It is possible that even though condition (15.1) holds, and a new entrant adopts the new technology, condition (15.2) would not hold, and an established firm would stick with the established technology. This is the sunk cost effect.

$\mathcal{E}$XAMPLE 15.1

THE SUNK COST EFFECT IN STEEL: THE ADOPTION OF THE BASIC OXYGEN FURNACE

In the early 1950s, a new steelmaking technology became commercially viable: the basic oxygen furnace (BOF). Perfected by an Austrian steel firm, Linz-Donawitz, the BOF reduced milling time to 40 minutes as compared with the 6 to 8 hours in the open hearth (OH) technology that had been the industry standard since World War I. Despite the apparent superiority of BOF, few American steelmakers adopted it. Throughout the 1950s, U.S. steelmakers added nearly 50 million additional tons of OH capacity; but they did not begin to replace their OH furnaces with BOFs until the late 1960s. Meanwhile, steelmakers in the rest of the world were building new plants incorporating state-of-the-art BOF technology. The cost advantage afforded by this new technology was a key reason why Japanese and Korean steelmakers were able to penetrate the American domestic market.

Why did American steelmakers continue to invest in a seemingly inefficient technology? The standard explanation has been bad management. For example, two knowledgeable observers of the steel industry, Walter Adams and Hans Mueller, wrote:

> The most likely explanation of the hesitant adoption of the Austrian converter [i.e., the BOF] by the large American firms is that their managements were still imbued with Andrew Carnegie's motto "invention don't pay." Let others first assume the cost and risk of research and development, and of breaking in a new process, then we'll decide. The result was that during the 1950s, the American steel industry installed 40 million tons of melting capacity which, as *Fortune* observed, "was obsolete when it was built."[9]

Without denying the possibility of managerial myopia, there is, however, another explanation. American steel firms throughout the first half of the twentieth century had developed a considerable amount of specific know-how related to the OH technology. Their investment in this know-how was sunk: It could not be

---

[9]Adams, W. and H. Mueller, "The Steel Industry," in Adams, W. (ed.), *The Structure of American Industry*, 7th ed., New York: Macmillan, 1986, p. 102.

recovered if they switched to the BOF technology. This sunk investment created an asymmetry between established American firms and new Japanese firms that made it cost effective for American firms to stick with the older OH technology.

The findings of Sharon Oster's study of technology adoption in the steel industry are broadly consistent with the hypothesis that American steel firms chose between alternative technologies based on profit-maximization criteria.[10] For example, because the BOF technology used relatively more pig iron, as opposed to scrap iron, than the OH technology, a steel plant that was located closer to sources of pig iron would save more operating costs by adopting the BOF technology. Oster finds that firms that produced their own pig iron were more likely to adopt BOF than were firms that had to buy it from outside suppliers. More generally, Oster found that the magnitude of the savings in operating costs, ΔVC, from adopting the BOF varied considerably among firms and that firms with larger cost savings were more likely to adopt BOF.

The point of this discussion is not to argue that there was not poor management in the steel industry. There almost certainly was, at least in some firms. However, we cannot attribute the lack of innovation in this industry entirely to poor management. Large sunk investments in know-how and capabilities are hard for a firm to ignore when choosing a technology. The presence of these sunk investments distinguished American producers from producers in Japan, Korea, and elsewhere who were investing in "greenfield" plants (i.e., new steelmaking facilities). Unfortunately, these differences may have planted the seeds for the competitive decline of the U.S. integrated steel sector in the 1970s and 1980s.

The Replacement Effect

Does a profit-maximizing monopolist have a stronger or weaker incentive to innovate than a new entrant? The Nobel Prize economist Kenneth Arrow pondered this question over 30 years ago.[11] He considered the incentives for adoption of a process innovation that will lower the average variable costs of production. The innovation is drastic: Once it is adopted, producers using the older technology will not be viable competitors. Arrow compared two different scenarios: (i) the opportunity to develop the innovation is available to a firm that currently monopolizes the market using the old technology; (ii) the opportunity to develop the innovation is available to a potential entrant who, if it adopts the innovation, will become the monopolist. Under which scenario, Arrow asked, is the willingness to pay to develop the innovation greatest?

---

[10]Oster, S., "The Diffusion of Innovation Among Steel Firms: The Basic Oxygen Furnace," *Bell Journal of Economics*, 13, Spring 1982, pp. 45–68.

[11]Arrow, K., "Economic Welfare and the Allocation of Resources for Inventions," in Nelson, R. (ed.), *The Rate and Director of Inventive Activity*, Princeton, NJ: Princeton University Press, 1962.

Arrow concluded that assuming equal innovative capabilities, an entrant would be willing to spend more than the monopolist to develop the innovation. The intuition behind Arrow's insight is this: A successful innovation for a new entrant leads to monopoly; a successful innovation by the established firm also leads to a monopoly, but since it already had a monopoly, the gain from innovation is less than it would be for the potential entrant. Through innovation an entrant can replace the monopolist, but the monopolist can only replace itself. For this reason, this phenomenon is called the *replacement effect*.[12]

Arrow's insight explains why an established firm would be less willing to "stretch" itself to innovate or develop new sources of advantage than a potential entrant or a marginal firm in an industry. His logic applies not only to process innovations, but to new product innovations as well.[13] Arrow's argument also shows that established firms may be overtaken by innovative entrants, not because the established firms are poorly managed or suffer disproportionately from agency costs, but because of a natural market dynamic. An established firm's success can sow the seeds of its (potential) destruction. This is not to deny that poor management, myopia, excessive risk aversion, or agency problems can hasten a dominant firm's decline. But they may not be telling the entire story. Arrow's analysis is another useful reminder that the quality of strategies formulated under considerable uncertainty cannot be judged solely by *ex post* outcomes.

The Efficiency Effect

Arrow's analysis pertains to the "pure" incentive to innovate. That is, it has to do with a firm's willingness to innovate, when the innovation opportunity is not available to competitors or potential entrants. If an incumbent monopolist anticipates that potential entrants may also have an opportunity to develop the innovation, then the strategic considerations that we emphasized in Chapters 9 and 11 become relevant. In particular, the *efficiency effect* discussed in Chapter 11 comes into play. The efficiency effect has to do with the fact that the benefit to a firm from being a monopolist as compared with being one of two competitors in a duopoly is greater than the benefit to a firm from being a duopolist as compared with not being in the industry at all (and thus earning no profit).[14] The efficiency effect makes an incumbent monopolist's incentive to innovate stronger than that of a potential

---

[12]This term has been coined by Jean Tirole. Tirole discusses the replacement effect at length in his book *The Theory of Industrial Organization*, Cambridge, MA: MIT Press, 1988.

[13]See, for example, Ghemawat, P., "Market Incumbency and Technological Inertia," *Marketing Science*, 10, Spring 1991, pp. 161–171.

[14]The efficiency effect arises because competition destroys industry profitability. Thus, total industry profit if the monopolist develops the innovation will exceed total industry profit under the duopoly competition that results if the entrant develops the innovation.

entrant. The reason is that the incumbent can lose its monopoly if it does not innovate, whereas the entrant will become (at best) a duopolist if it successfully innovates.[15]

In the competition between established firms and potential entrants to develop new innovations, the replacement effect, the efficiency effect, and the sunk cost effect will operate simultaneously. Which effect dominates depends on the specific conditions of the innovation competition.[16] For example, the replacement effect and sunk cost effects may dominate if the chance that smaller competitors or potential entrants will develop the innovation is low. In that case, the main effect of the innovation for the established firm will be to cannibalize current profits and to reduce the value of established resources and organizational capabilities associated with the current technology. By contrast, the efficiency effect may dominate when the monopolist's failure to develop the innovation means that new entrants almost certainly will. In this case, a key benefit of the innovation to the established firm is to stave off the deterioration of profit that comes from additional competition from firms that may develop a cost advantage or a benefit advantage over it if they successfully innovate.

◆ ◆

$\mathcal{E}$XAMPLE 15.2

INNOVATION IN THE PBX MARKET[17]

Private branch exchanges (PBXs) are dedicated switching centers that route calls from a customer's telephone to the telephone company's central exchange. Pankaj Ghemawat's study of innovation in the PBX industry illustrates a case in which the replacement and sunk cost effects played a dominant role in shaping the incentives to innovate.

From the time PBXs were developed around the turn of the century through the late 1980s, there have been four distinct generations of PBX technology: electromechanical voice-only PBXs, electronic voice-only PBXs, voice-and-data PBXs, and voice-data-and-video PBXs. The dominant supplier of voice-only PBXs well into the 1980s was AT&T. In 1980, for example, it held 58 percent of the industry's installed base and made 46 percent of new shipments. AT&T only sold old-fashioned

---

[15]This assumes that the innovation is not so drastic as to make the established firm's competitive position nonviable if the entrant develops the innovation but the competitor does not. In a race to develop a drastic innovation that makes the current technology or product concept nonviable, an entrant's incentive to develop the innovation would be equally as strong as an incumbent's.

[16]Innovation competition is discussed in further detail in the next section.

[17]This example is based on Ghemawat, P., "Market Incumbency and Technological Inertia," *Marketing Science*, 10, Spring 1991, pp. 161–171.

electromechanical PBXs, and its manufacturing costs were among the highest in the industry. Nevertheless, it was one of the most profitable producers of PBXs because its position was protected by powerful isolating mechanisms. PBXs are expensive systems meant to last for 10 to 15 years, and buyers value reliability highly. (Even a temporary failure of a PBX can be disastrous to a business.) Over the years, AT&T had developed a reputation for building PBXs that performed as promised, and this helped it secure both repeat and new business. In addition, AT&T owned the wiring in its PBX installations and would not sell it to competitors. Thus, if a customer switched suppliers, the new supplier would have to rewire the customer's place of business, and such rewiring could represent about 40 percent of the cost of the new PBX. AT&T also benefited from an important experience-based advantage: It had dealt with so many customers over the years that it could draw from an extensive information base in forecasting that buyers would need to replace existing PBX systems. The smaller, less-experienced competitors in the voice-only market could not match AT&T's extensive customer knowledge and thus could not target their sales efforts as effectively as AT&T could. Finally, AT&T owned the most effective channel for distributing PBXs to final customers: the local Bell operating companies.

AT&T showed little interest in developing second generation voice-only PBXs based on digital electronics. The leading suppliers of second-generation voice-only PBXs were Rolm, which made 10 percent of new PBX shipments in the United States in 1980, and Northern Telecom, whose 1980 share of new shipments was 8 percent. Neither these firms nor AT&T attempted to develop third-generation PBXs that integrated voice and data transmission. For example, in the early 1980s, Rolm decreased its R&D spending as a percentage of sales and concentrated instead on building an in-house sales network for selling voice-only PBXs. The firms that had pioneered voice-and-data PBXs were marginal players in the industry or new entrants. The one that succeeded in developing a commercially successful voice-and-data PBX was a company called InteCom, which was founded in 1978 and went public in 1982.

InteCom soon found itself in a highly competitive business with few apparent isolating mechanisms. Design engineers were regularly raided by competing firms seeking to improve their PBX designs, although InteCom's turnover was somewhat lower than that of many other small firms due to its promise of rapid promotion and liberal use of stock options for its employees. Moreover, patent protection was unavailable. In 1982, InteCom held no patents and had no applications pending. Its managers estimated that any competitor would be able to copy all relevant aspects of its voice-and-data PBX design within 12 to 18 months. Yet, despite this, InteCom did not invest heavily in developing the fourth generation of PBXs: those capable of carrying not only voice and data but also video images. Instead, its strategy was to capture as much profit as it could as the first-mover in the voice-and-data segment of the PBX market and take advantage of growth opportunities that existed in this segment. This inertia was aided by the uncertain prospects for voice-data-image PBXs. InteCom's strategy was successful, at least from the perspective of its founders. By the time it went public in 1982, InteCom's initial capital of $1.5 million had grown to over $400 million of shareholder value, of which $100 million belonged to its founders.

While the behaviors of the firms in this example are consistent with sunk cost and replacement effects, they are also consistent with other explanations of the sources and diffusion of innovations. These alternative explanations do not exclude the one we have already discussed.

The failure to develop a new generation of PBXs could stem from organizational inertia. Innovation may not be in the interest of those involved in producing the current generation, and they may use their discretion within the firm to impede innovative efforts by top managers. Internal resistance to change and the need for "championing" innovations are common issues in the management of innovation, which we will discuss later in this chapter.

A reluctance to innovate could also stem from the perception that the market would not be receptive to the innovation, even though it was technically superior and feasible to produce. A common distinction in the innovation literature is between "technology push" and "demand pull" explanations.[18] In a technology push explanation, the source (or "locus") of innovation is in the firm and its product designers. In a demand pull explanation, the locus of innovation is the set of users outside of the firm, who communicate their needs to product designers. In the case of PBXs, the technological development of new generations made the product increasingly complex and forced users to bear more risks of failure and product obsolescence. These costs to users eventually increased the commercial viability of less sophisticated systems, such as Centrex. These systems used telephone company equipment and thus placed more of the risks of failure and obsolescence on the provider rather than the user of the product.

◆ ◆ ◆ ◆ ◆ INNOVATION COMPETITION

Chapters 9 and 10 emphasize the importance of thinking about how competitors will respond when a firm develops products and chooses prices for them. It is equally critical to anticipate rivals' responses when selecting a level of investment in R&D. Even if a firm thoughtfully takes into account the R&D expenses necessary to produce a marketable product, the size of the target market, and the fit between the project under consideration and other projects that the firm is working on, its innovative efforts may fail if it fails to anticipate the possibility that other firms may innovate first.

When several firms are competing to develop the same product, the firm that succeeds in doing so first can gain significant advantage. The most obvious advantage is that the first innovator may be able to protect its ideas with patents and trademarks. Consider, for example, the race between Thomas Edison and Alexander Graham Bell to develop the modern telephone. Bell developed it first

---

[18]Kamien, M.I. and N.L. Schwartz, *Market Structure and Innovation.* Cambridge, UK: Cambridge University Press, 1982; Scherer, F.M., *Innovation and Growth: Schumpeterian Perspectives*, Cambridge, MA: MIT Press, 1984.

and claimed patent rights. Edison developed a similar prototype a short time later. Bell's patent claim withstood court challenges from Edison. By virtue of the network externality that developed around the Bell telephone system, the patent has proved to be worth hundreds of billions of dollars.[19]

Even without the legal protection of patents and trademarks, the first innovator may gain significant early mover advantages.[20] For example, if there are network externalities, the first innovator may gain an important head start in the race to become the technology standard. The first innovator may also benefit from the effect that its product has on consumer perceptions by being the first to market. As discussed in Chapter 14, research in marketing reveals that consumers view the attributes of pioneering brands as embodying the ideal configuration against which all other brands are benchmarked.

Still, being the first to develop a product may not be sufficient unless the firm can acquire the capabilities needed to manufacture the product and to market it. For example, biotechnology companies race each other to patent both products and the processes for making them. The California biotech firm Celtrix holds valuable patents on a cell-regulating protein that may prove useful in healing damaged cells. Though successful in the race to *develop* the protein, Celtrix lost to Genentech in the race to patent the *process for producing* the protein. Celtrix has been forced to enter a joint venture arrangement with terms favorable to Genentech in exchange for the rights to use the patented process.

Patent Races

The term *patent race* has been used to characterize the battle between firms to innovate first. To develop a better understanding of the forces that drive innovation, economists have studied a number of different models of patent races. In these models, the first firm to successfully complete the project "wins" the patent race and obtains exclusive rights to develop and market the product. The losing firms get nothing. While this is a rather extreme characterization, it does highlight the often critical advantage that goes to the first innovator, and it gives insight into how the magnitude of that advantage affects the incentives to innovate. These models also emphasize an important strategic point: Firms in a patent race must anticipate the R&D investments of competitors. Failure to do so can be costly.

Deterministic Patent Races

A simple patent race model illustrates why it is important for a firm to anticipate competitors' investment decisions. Suppose that several firms are trying to develop the same product. The first to succeed obtains a patent and monopoly rights to the product, while the other firms get nothing. To highlight key issues in patent races,

---

[19]Smith, G.S., *The Anatomy of a Business Strategy: Bell, Western Electric, and the Origins of the American Telephone Industry.* Baltimore, MD: Johns Hopkins, 1985, pp. 35–38, 99.

[20]Chapter 14 discusses early-mover advantages in detail.

imagine that R&D is completely "deterministic." In other words, the amount spent on R&D is precisely related to the time required to develop the project, make it commercially viable, patent it, and bring it to market. The more the firm spends on R&D, the sooner the project is completed. Finally, suppose that all firms have the same research capabilities: If two firms spend the same amount on R&D, they will complete the project at the same time. The firm that spends the most will thus win the race.

We will use the concept of a Nash equilibrium from game theory to characterize the results of this patent race.[21] In a Nash equilibrium, each firm makes an optimal R&D investment decision, given the decisions of the other firms. In the Nash equilibrium of this patent race, only one firm spends money on R&D. To see why this is so, suppose instead that two or more firms spend money on R&D. If they spend different amounts, then the firm being outspent will lose the race for sure. Spending any positive amount of money that is less than the amount spent by the highest spending firm is not a good decision, because the firm can do better by spending nothing. If two or more firms spend the same amount, then they have equal chances of winning the race. Neither firm is then satisfied with its decision because each believes that if it increases spending by just a penny, it will win the race for sure. Given that no firm will spend less on R&D than its rival is spending and that firms will not spend the same amount, the only possibility is that only one firm invests in R&D and the other firms spend nothing. How much will the firm doing R&D spend? It must spend exactly the same amount that it expects to earn after it receives the patent. If it spent any less, another firm could outspend it and still make a positive profit.

Although the deterministic model trivializes the true nature of R&D, it does point out two fundamental principals of patent races. First, the value of one firm's R&D investment depends on how much other firms are spending on R&D. An investment is valuable only if it could enable a firm to leapfrog the development timetable of the firm that is leading the race. Second, firms in a patent race may end up spending so much that they collectively earn no profits. Otherwise, additional firms will enter the race. In the simple model, this principle is reflected by the single R&D firm spending so much money on R&D that it expects to earn zero profits. This principle, of course, reconfirms a point made in Chapter 14: Unfettered competition to acquire the scarce resources that can serve as a foundation for a competitive advantage—patents, superior locations, or market position in a market characterized by scale economies—will destroy profitability. Sustaining a competitive advantage not only involves acquiring the scarce resource but also capturing its scarcity value as profit. For this to happen, there must be imperfections in the market for the scarce resource, which impede the perfectly competitive dynamic.

---

[21]Game theory is reviewed in the Economics Primer. The concept of a Nash equilibrium is applied in various ways in Chapters 8, 9, 10, and 11.

Probabilistic Patent Races

It is more realistic to suppose that spending the most on R&D does not guarantee that a firm will win the patent race. Instead, suppose that the time it takes to complete the project is a *probabilistic* function of the amount spent on R&D, and (as before) the firm that completes the project first gets the patent. Suppose further that a firm can accelerate the expected completion date by increasing its R&D expenditures. However, no amount of R&D spending can guarantee that a firm will win the race.

A convenient concept in modeling probabilistic patent races so that they have the characteristics just described is the *exponential distribution*. To illustrate it, suppose that x denotes the firm's rate of spending on R&D. If R&D follows an exponential process, the point in time at which the firm successfully completes the project is *random*, but the *expected time of completion* is $1/\tau(x)$, where $\tau(x)$ is an increasing function of x. The function $\tau(x)$ can be thought of as the effectiveness of a firm's research efforts. Thus, the greater a firm's rate of spending on R&D, the greater the effectiveness of its R&D efforts, and the shorter the expected duration until the innovation is successfully completed. (For convenience, we will think of the completion time in terms of years.) Since innovation is probabilistic, the actual duration may be earlier or later than this, however.

Several key conclusions emerge when patent races are modeled using the exponential distribution:

- If N firms are in the race, and each invests x dollars, then the average time before the first successful innovation is $1/(N\tau(x))$, and each firm has an equal chance of being the first to innovate. When there are more firms investing, the expected time to completion decreases. This assumes that firms pursue independent research projects. If there are spillovers—if one firm's progress benefits other firms (e.g., because of mobility of researchers across firms)—the expected completion time will be somewhere between $1/(N\tau(x))$ and $1/\tau(x)$.

- Suppose that firm i spends x_i dollars on R&D, and all other firms spend x. Then the probability that it will innovate first is $\tau(x_i)/[\tau(x_i) + (N - 1)\tau(x)]$ where the summation is taken over all the $N-1$ other firms in the market. This implies that the chances of a firm being the first to innovate depend on its own innovative effort $\tau(x_i)$ and the sum of the productivity of its rivals' efforts, $(N-1)\tau(x)$.

The numerical example in Table 15.1 illustrates some of the issues a firm faces when considering an increase in R&D outlays. Let the effectiveness of R&D be given by $\tau(x) = \sqrt{x}$, where x is millions of dollars in R&D. This function demonstrates *diminishing marginal returns to R&D*—each incremental expenditure produces a smaller and smaller increase in $\tau(x)$. Although there is little hard evidence on whether marginal returns to R&D are increasing or decreasing, it is clear that all processes must *eventually* show diminishing marginal returns. As the probability of immediate success approaches 1, so that R&D is completely successful, additional outlays cannot produce further meaningful gains in R&D productivity.

TABLE 15.1

RELATIONSHIP BETWEEN A FIRM'S R&D OUTLAYS AND ITS CHANCES OF WINNING THE PATENT RACE

Firm i's R&D Outlay	R&D Outlays of Other Firms	Total Number of Firms	Total Industry R&D Outlays	Expected Time to First Innovation	Probability that Firm i is First
$1 million	$1 million	4	$4 million	3 months	.25
$2 million	$1 million	4	$5 million	2.72 months	.32
$2 million	$1.5 million	4	$6.5 million	2.36 months	.28
$9 million	$9 million	4	$36 million	1 month	.25
$10 million	$9 million	4	$37 million	.99 months	.26
$500,000	$500,000	8	$4 million	2.1 months	.125
$1.5 million	$500,000	8	$5 million	1.9 months	.198

Suppose that four firms are each spending $1 million on R&D, for a total of $4 million in industry R&D. The expected length of time until the first innovation is $1/(4\sqrt{1}) = 1/4$ years, or three months. Each firm believes that it has a .25 chance of being the first to innovate. Now suppose that one firm is contemplating increasing its R&D outlays by $1 million, to a total of $2 million. That firm calculates that if all other firms keep their R&D outlays fixed at $1 million, its chances of winning the patent race will increase to $\sqrt{2}/(\sqrt{2} + 3) = .32$. Suppose instead that the firm expects other firms to increase their R&D budgets to $1.5 million each. Then its chances of being first to innovate will be only $\sqrt{2}/(\sqrt{2} + 3\sqrt{1.5}) = .28$.

If the four firms each spend $9 million on R&D, then the expected length of time until the first innovation is $1/(4\sqrt{9}) = 1/12$ years, or one month. Each firm still believes that it has a .25 chance of being the first to innovate. A firm that increases its R&D outlays by $1 million to a total of $10 million calculates that if the other firms keep their R&D budgets fixed, its chances of being the first to innovate will be .26. The increase in the probability of success is small because the $1 million addition to R&D spending is small in percentage terms, and the firm experiences diminishing marginal returns to R&D. The firm would have to increase its R&D outlays to $18 million to boost its chances of being the first innovator to .32.

Contrast the previous situation with one in which eight firms are each spending $500,000 on R&D. Total industry R&D is again $4 million, yet the expected time until the first innovation is now $1/(8\sqrt{.5}) = .177$ years, or about two months. Each firm believes it has a .125 chance of being the first to innovate. If one firm increases its investment in R&D from $500,000 to $1.5 million, its chances of being the first to innovate increase to $\sqrt{1.5}/(\sqrt{1.5} + 7\sqrt{.5}) = .198$. The increase in probability of success is large because the $1 million increase is large in percentage terms, and the firm has not yet reached the region where marginal returns diminish sharply.

These results suggest that when a firm is determining whether to increase its investment in innovation, it must account for the following factors:

- By how much does the investment increase its R&D productivity and thereby also increase its chances of winning the patent race? If there are diminishing returns to productivity, then increasing R&D outlays may not greatly improve the firm's chances of winning the race. If there are increasing returns, additional expenditures are usually warranted, unless they provoke competitors to increase their expenditures.

- Will other firms increase their R&D expenditures in response, thereby decreasing the firm's chances of winning the patent race? This competitive response will reduce the profitability of R&D regardless of whether it demonstrates increasing or decreasing returns.

- How many competitors are there? If there are diminishing returns to R&D, then several small R&D firms may be a bigger threat to successful innovation than a single competitor that spends the same total amount of money as do all the small firms put together. If there are increasing returns, then one large firm conducting extensive R&D may be a more formidable competitor. In this case, large investments in R&D by a single firm may crowd out investments by other firms.

Choosing the Technology

The patent race model that we just discussed assumes that firms have a single R&D methodology, and may choose only how much to spend on it. In reality, however, firms may be able to select from a variety of methodologies. For example, while some supercomputer makers pursued vector technology that emphasized improvements in hardware, others pursued massively parallel processing that utilized improvements in software. When choosing a research methodology, firms must consider the methods being pursued by their rivals. Two dimensions of interest when choosing a methodology are (1) the riskiness of the methodology; and (2) the degree to which the success of one methodology is correlated with the success of another.

Riskiness of R&D

Research methodologies may have different completion dates. When one methodology is demonstrably faster than another, the choice is clear. But what if two methods have the same expected completion date, but the date for one is less certain than for the other? To see how competition affects the choice of methods, consider a firm choosing between two approaches to developing a new product. If either approach succeeds, and the firm is the first to develop the product, it can obtain a patent or achieve some other early-mover advantage. Approach A follows time honored methods for R&D and is certain to be successful within two or three years. In contrast, the time frame for Approach B is relatively unproved. While it is sure eventually to bear fruit, success may come within one to four years. For both approaches, the time to innovation is distributed *uniformly*, meaning that it is equally likely to be any time in the interval.

A monopolist will generally be indifferent between the two approaches, because they have identical expected times to development. If several firms are competing to develop the same product, however, each will wish to choose Approach B. To see why, suppose that there are four firms, and each chooses Approach A. Each firm has a .25 chance of being the first to innovate. Now suppose that one firm switches to Approach B. It has a .33 chance of innovating in less than two years, in which case it is sure to be the first. Even if it innovates after two years, it still has a chance of being the first to innovate. Thus, its chances of being first are greater than .33. Since this is greater than its chances of being first when all firms chose Approach A, it will prefer Approach B. A similar argument may be used to show that all firms will prefer Approach B, no matter what their competitors are doing.[22]

Correlated Research Strategies

The previous example assumed that Approaches A and B were independent of each other, implying that the success or failure of one approach was unrelated to the success or failure of the other. In fact, research methods may be correlated, so that if one is successful, the other is also more likely to be successful. In general, society benefits more when firms pursue uncorrelated approaches than when they pursue correlated approaches, even when some of the uncorrelated approaches have a low probability of success. The reason is that when firms take uncorrelated approaches, the probability that at least one approach is successful increases. But will a firm be willing to undertake research strategy with low success probabilities? If there are many firms performing research, the answer is yes. If all the firms pursue the same strategy, then each firm has an equal chance of success. The more firms there are, the lower the chance that any particular firm will win the patent race. A firm that pursues a strategy that is uncorrelated with the one pursued by everyone else stands to win the race if the popular approach is unsuccessful. Thus, a "niche" R&D strategy can be profitable even if the strategy has a low probability of producing an innovation, so long as the outcome is uncorrelated with the outcomes of the other firms.

◆ ◆ ◆ ◆ ◆ EVOLUTIONARY ECONOMICS AND DYNAMIC CAPABILITIES

The theories of innovation discussed in the previous section are rooted in the tradition of neoclassical microeconomics. In these theories, firms are seen as choosing the level of innovative activity to maximize profits. These theories help sharpen our intuition about the conditions that shape a firm's incentive to innovate. They also provide insights about relationships between R&D activity and such conditions as the number and size distribution of firms competing in an industry.

Evolutionary economics, most commonly identified with Richard Nelson and Sidney Winer, offers a perspective on innovative activity that differs from micro-

---

[22]It can be shown that firms will generally prefer the risky approach even if there are only two competitors, with the gains from this choice becoming more transparent as the number of firms increases. See Tirole, J., *The Theory of Industrial Organization*, Cambridge, MA: MIT Press, 1988.

economic perspective.[23] Evolutionary economics lends itself to studying the impact of the firm's resources, capabilities, and history on its incentives to innovate, factors that are not prominent in the theories discussed above. Instead of viewing a firm's decisions as determined by profit maximization, evolutionary economics sees the firm decisions as determined by *routines:* well-practiced patterns of activity inside the firm. A firm's routines include methods for producing things, procedures for hiring new workers, and policies for determining the levels of advertising expenditures. They can be arrayed from lower-order routines (e.g., procedures for processing customer orders) to higher-order ones (e.g., rules of thumb the firm uses to allocate capital to competing uses inside the organization). As discussed in Chapter 12, at any given time, the routines of an organization determine its distinctive capabilities—what it can do better than other firms.

Firms do not change their routines very often because getting members of an organization to alter what has worked well in the past is an "unnatural" act, and it is therefore costly for the management of a firm to change the organization's routines. Thus, firms do not adapt their routines in response to relatively minor changes in their external environment or market conditions. However, as Schumpeter stressed, firms that stick to producing a given set of products in a particular way may not survive. Thus, a firm typically needs to engage in a continuous search for ways to improve its existing routines. The ability of a firm to maintain and adapt the capabilities that are the basis of its competitive advantage is what David Teece, Gary Pisano, and Amy Shuen have referred to as its *dynamic capabilities.*[24] Firms with limited dynamic capabilities fail to nurture and adapt the sources of their advantage over time and eventually are supplanted by other firms. Firms with strong dynamic capabilities are able to adapt their resources and capabilities over time and take advantage of new market opportunities to create new sources of competitive advantage.

For several reasons, a firm's dynamic capabilities are inherently limited. First, learning is typically incremental rather than pathbreaking. That is, when a firm searches for ways to improve its operations, it is nearly impossible to ignore what it has done in the past, and it is difficult to conceptualize new routines that are fundamentally different from its old ones. Thus, the search for new sources of competitive advantage is *path dependent*—it depends on the route the firm has taken in the past to get to where it is now. But even small path dependencies can have important competitive consequences. A firm that has developed significant commitments to a particular way of doing business may find it hard to adapt to seemingly

---

[23]Nelson, R.R. and S.G. Winter, *An Evolutionary Theory of Economic Change*, Cambridge, MA: Belknap Press, 1982.

[24]Teece, D.J., G. Pisano, and A. Shuen, "Dynamic Capabilities and Strategic Management," University of California at Berkeley, working paper, 1992. See also Teece, D.J., R. Rumelt, G. Dosi, and S. Winter, "Understanding Corporate Coherence: Theory and Evidence," *Journal of Economic Behavior and Organization*, 23, 1994, pp. 1–30 for related ideas.

minor changes in technology. This is underscored in Rebecca Henderson and Kim Clark's study of the photolithographic alignment equipment industry described in Example 15.3.

◆◆◆

$\mathcal{E}$XAMPLE 15.3

ORGANIZATIONAL ADAPTATION IN THE PHOTOLITHOGRAPHIC ALIGNMENT EQUIPMENT INDUSTRY[25]

Photolithographic aligners are an important input in the production of solid-state semiconductor devices. To produce a semiconductor, small intricate patterns must be transferred to a thin wafer of material, such as silicon. This process of transfer is known as lithography. The pattern that is transferred is drawn onto a mask, which is used to block light as it falls onto a light-sensitive chemical coating placed on the wafer. A constant stream of seemingly incremental innovations in the industry has dramatically improved the performance of aligners. The industry has moved from so-called contact aligners to proximity aligners and from scanning projection to what are called "steppers." In nearly every case, an established firm that had invested in state-of-the-art equipment and know-how was displaced when the technology changed.

Kasper Instruments illustrates this dynamic. It was founded in 1968, and by 1973 had emerged as the leading supplier of contact aligners. But in the mid-1970s, the proximity alignment technique was pioneered. Unlike in contact aligning, in proximity aligning the mask and the wafer are separated during exposure. Although this distinction seems relatively minor, in fact the two techniques involved subtle differences in design. In particular, successful design of a proximity aligner requires acquisition of new know-how related to the design and production of the gap-setting mechanism—the mechanism that determines how far apart the mask and the wafer are held during the lithography process. Incorporating the gap-setting mechanism necessitated subtle changes in the integration of all the other components of the aligner. Moving from contact aligners to proximity aligners thus entailed a significant shift in product design and production know-how.

Kasper failed to develop successful proximity aligners, mainly because of its previous success in designing contact aligners. Kasper conceived of the proximity aligner as a modified contact aligner, and saw the move into contact aligners as a routine extension of its product line. A gap-setting mechanism that had been used in its contact aligners was slightly modified for use in its proximity aligners. But Kasper's proximity aligner did not work well because the gap-setting mechanism

[25]This example is based on Henderson, R. and Clark, K.B., "Architectural Innovation: The Reconfiguration of Existing Product Technologies and the Failure of Established Firms," *Administrative Science Quarterly*, 35, March 1990, pp. 9–30.

was not accurate enough to ensure adequate performance. In response to customer complaints about its product, Kasper attributed many of the problems to customers' own errors, which was the main source of malfunctions with its successful contact aligners. When Canon introduced a highly successful proximity aligner in the mid-1970s, Kasper failed to understand why it worked so well and dismissed it as a mere copy of the Kasper aligner. The Kasper engineers did not consider the redesigned gap mechanism that made the Canon aligner such a significant advance to be particularly important. From 1974 on, Kasper aligners were rarely used in proximity mode, and by 1981, the company had left the industry.

A second limitation on a firm's dynamic capabilities is *complementary assets*. These are firm-specific assets that are valuable only in connection with a particular product, technology, or way of doing business. The development of new products or capabilities or the opening of new markets can either enhance or destroy the value of complementary assets. Microsoft's installed base in DOS was a valuable complementary asset when it developed Windows in the late 1980s. By contrast, as discussed in Example 15.1, the development of the basic oxygen furnace in the steel industry reduced the value of American steel firms' existing capabilities in the open hearth process. A proposed change in an organizational routine that undermines the value of a complementary asset can give rise to the sunk cost effect discussed earlier, thereby reducing the likelihood that a firm will adopt the change.

Finally, the existence of "windows of opportunity" can also impede the development of dynamic capabilities. In the early stages of a product's development, its design is typically fluid, manufacturing routines have not been developed, and capital is generally non-product specific. Firms can still experiment on competing product designs or ways of organizing production. However, as time passes, a narrow set of designs or product specifications often emerge as dominant. At this point, network externalities and learning curve effects take over, and it no longer becomes attractive for firms to compete with established market leaders. This implies that firms that do not seize opportunities for adapting their existing capabilities or committing themselves to new markets when these uncertain windows of opportunity exist may find themselves eventually locked out from the market or having to compete at a significant disadvantage relative to early movers.

THE ENVIRONMENT ◆ ◆ ◆ ◆ ◆

Michael Porter argues that competitive advantage originates in the local environment in which the firm is based. This conclusion is based on the detailed case studies of numerous industries that appeared in his book *The Competitive Advantage of Nations*. Porter was intrigued by the fact that despite the ability of modern firms to transcend local markets, competitive advantage in particular industries was often strongly concentrated in one or two locations: The world's most successful producers of high-voltage electrical distribution equipment are in Sweden; the best producers of equipment for tunneling are Swiss; the most successful producers of large diesel trucks are American; and the leading firms in microwaves are from Japan.

Like Schumpeter and Nelson and Winter, Porter views competition as part of an evolutionary process. Firms initially gain competitive advantages by altering the basis of competition. They do so not just by recognizing the existence of new markets or technologies but by moving aggressively to exploit these opportunities. They sustain their advantages by investing to improve existing sources of advantage and to create new ones. A firm's home nation plays a critical role in shaping managers' perceptions about the opportunities that can be exploited; in supporting the accumulation of valuable resources and capabilities; and in creating pressures on the firm to innovate, invest, and improve over time.

Porter identifies four attributes in a firm's home market, which he collectively refers to as the "diamond," that promote or impede its ability to achieve competitive advantage in global markets (see Figure 15.2):

- Factors conditions
- Demand conditions
- Related supplier or support industries
- Strategy, structure, and rivalry

Factor Conditions   Factor conditions refer to a nation's position with regard to factors of production (e.g., human resources, infrastructure) that are necessary to compete in a particular industry. Because general-purpose factors of production are often available locally or can be purchased in global markets, the most important factors of production are those that are highly specialized to the needs of particular industries. For example, since the 1950s, Japan has had one of the highest numbers of engineering graduates per capita. This, according to Porter, has had much more to do with its success in industries, such as automobiles and consumer electronics, than the low wages of its production workers.

Demand Conditions   The second determinant of the firm's prospects for achieving competitive advantage is the condition of local demand, which includes the size, growth, and character of home demand for the firm's product. The character of the firm's buyers and the nature of their demand are particularly important. Sophisticated home customers or unique local conditions stimulate firms to enhance the quality of their products and to innovate. For example, in air conditioners, Japanese firms, such as Panasonic, are known for producing small, quiet, energy-efficient window units. These product characteristics are critical in a country where air conditioning is important (summers are hot and humid), but large, noisy units would be unacceptable because houses are small and packed closely together and electricity costs are high.

Related and Supporting Industries   Firms that operate in a home market that has a strong base of internationally competitive supplier or support industries will be favorably positioned to achieve competitive advantage in global markets. While

FIGURE 15.2
THE ENVIRONMENT AND THE ORIGINS OF COMPETITIVE ADVANTAGE.

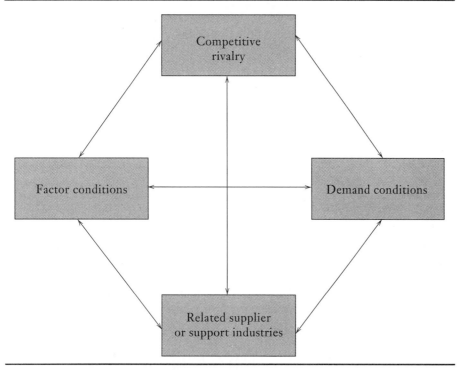

Michael Porter argues that the ability of a firm to develop a competitive advantage depends on demand and factor conditions within the firm's home market, the presence of related supplier or support industries, and the degree of competitive rivalry within the home market.
Source: This diagram is based on Figure 3.1 in Porter, M., *The Competitive Advantage of Nations*, New York: Free Press, 1990, p. 72.

many inputs are mobile, and thus firms do not need geographical proximity to make exchanges, exchanging key inputs, such as scarce production know-how, does require geographical proximity. Companies with skillful home-based suppliers can be early beneficiaries of newly-generated production know-how and may be able to shape the direction of innovation in supplying firms. For example, Italian shoe manufacturers have established close working relationships with producers of leather that allow them to learn quickly about new textures and colors. Leather producers, in turn, learn about emerging fashion trends from the shoe manufacturers, which helps the former plan new products.

Strategy, Structure, and Rivalry   The final environmental determinant of competitive advantage, according to Porter, is the context for competition in the firm's home market. This includes local management practices, organizational structure, corporate governance, and the nature of local capital markets. For example, in

Germany and Switzerland, most shares in publicly-traded firms are held by institutional investors who do not trade frequently, and capital gains are exempt from taxation. As a result, day-to-day movements in share price are not seen as significant, which, according to Porter, creates a stronger propensity for companies in these industries to invest in research and innovation than is true of their counterparts in the United States and Britain.

Rivalry in the home market is another important part of the competitive context. According to Porter, local rivalry affects the rate of innovation in a market far more than foreign rivalry does. Although local rivalry may hold down profitability in local markets, firms that survive vigorous local competition are often more efficient and innovative than are international rivals who emerge from softer local conditions. The airline industry is a good example of this. The U.S. domestic airline industry is far more price competitive than the international industry, where entry is restricted and flag carriers may still receive state subsidies. Coming out of the intensely competitive U.S. industry, U.S. airlines, such as American and United, that fly international routes are far more cost efficient and often provide better service than many of the international airlines they compete with.

As Porter points out, the role of the local environment for competitive advantage does not eliminate the need for the industry, positioning, and sustainability analyses discussed in Chapters 7 through 14. Instead, it highlights considerations that are usually ignored in strategy formulation, such as the role of local competition in forging competitive strength in markets outside the firm's home country. Nor are Porter's ideas at odds with those of Nelson and Winter, who emphasize the role of organizational factors in innovation. Many firms in favorable environments do not achieve competitive advantage, indicating that the firm's local environment is not determinative. However, Porter's framework emphasizes that firms located in unfavorable local environments face extra challenges beyond the organizational inertia and path dependence that are emphasized by evolutionary economics.

◆ ◆ ◆ ◆ ◆ THE DETERMINANTS OF INNOVATIVENESS: WHAT DOES THE EVIDENCE SHOW?

This chapter has emphasized two fundamental reasons why rates of innovation differ among firms. First, some firms may have greater *incentive* to innovate, so that they devote more resources to innovation. This may allow them to develop more new products than other firms even if they are not particularly efficient innovators. Second, some firms may possess a greater *ability* to innovate. They possess skills and resources that allow them to develop new products and services at relatively low cost, or they are situated in more favorable local environments. Unfortunately, empirical research is only beginning to investigate the importance of these sources of innovation, and we need to learn much more about how firms improve their innovativeness.

Firm Size, Market Structure, and Innovativeness

Much of the research on innovativeness follows the tradition of that on market structure and performance discussed in Chapter 8. The main question is whether innovation varies according to firm size and market structure.

Measuring Innovativeness

To determine the effects of firm size and market structure on innovation, we must measure innovation. We can use the value-creation framework introduced in Chapter 12 to develop a conceptual definition of innovation: An innovation is a new product or process that increases value-created, $B - C$ (consumer benefits less production costs). Minor advances raise $B - C$ by a small amount; major innovations raise $B - C$ substantially. Several recent studies have directly measured the increase in $B - C$ from innovation. One is the study of personal computers by Joanna Stavins that we described in Chapter 13. Another is a study of CT scanners by Manuel Trajtenberg. Trajtenberg showed that innovations in CT scanner technology in a single year (1974) increased aggregate value-created by over $10 billion (in 1994 dollars).[26] The methods used by Stavins and Trajtenberg to measure $B - C$ require extensive data on individual purchases and modern analytical techniques, such as the hedonic pricing method described in Chapter 13. For these reasons, most studies of innovation do not directly measure $B - C$.

A commonly used measure of innovativeness is the rate of introduction of new products, sometimes by their market shares. Firms that introduce more products or garner greater market shares are considered to be more innovative than those that introduce few products and have low shares. This measure raises obvious problems: Are all new products of equal benefit? Can a new product offer a minor improvement over existing products yet garner huge market shares? Even so, this measure is often easy to obtain and can sometimes raise critical issues for policy and strategy. For example, research on new drugs has shown the number of new prescription drugs introduced in the United States fell in the mid-to-late 1960s, after the passage of legislation in 1962 intended to improve drug safety (in the wake of the Thalidomide tragedy). Many concluded that the legislation had the unanticipated drawback of reducing innovative output. Later research showed that larger drug firms, especially those in the United States, were responsible for disproportionate numbers of new drugs and top-selling drugs. According to some researchers, the onerous testing requirements of the Food and Drug Administration (FDA) created economies of scale in drug development, and forced U.S. firms to develop capabilities in creating major drug breakthroughs that were more likely to win FDA approval.

Patents are another readily available measure of innovativeness. Government patent offices issue patents for novel and useful products and processes. As with new products, the increase in $B - C$ afforded by any given patent may vary from

---

[26]Trajtenberg, M., *Economic Analysis of Product Innovation–The Case of CT Scanners*, Cambridge, MA: Harvard University Press, 1990.

zero (many patents are never commercially exploited) to billions of dollars (such as for some medical breakthroughs). Researchers have tried a variety of means to distinguish among patents in terms of their importance. Some researchers interview industry experts to identify significant innovations. Others study how the stock market reacts to announcements of patent grants—a sharp increase in the share price of the patent holder may indicate a high value for the patent. On the other hand, a small increase could indicate that the patent is not valuable, or that the market had anticipated the granting of the patent and already bid up the share price prior to the announcement date. Another approach is to determine whether a patent affected later innovations. This might show up in later patent applications that cite the patent in question. Manuel Trajtenberg provides evidence that this measure is correlated with the benefits of innovation in the CT scanner industry.

There are other problems with using patent counts to measure innovation. Many innovations are not patented, as firms sometimes prefer to keep their ideas secret rather than rely on patent laws for protection. (Many patents may be "invented around" by firms that discover new approaches to old problems by reviewing the patents of other firms.) In addition, many innovations, including computer software, are protected by copyright, rather than patent. Some, such as improvements in integrated circuit design, may not be protected at all. Despite these problems, researchers continue to use patent counts because they believe such counts are correlated with underlying levels of innovativeness, and because patents are easy to count.

Many studies examine measures of innovative *effort*, rather than innovation output. Such measures are helpful for testing hypotheses regarding the incentives of firms to perform R&D, as opposed to their ability to innovate. Effort is usually measured by expenditures on R&D or by the number of personnel engaged in R&D. Neither kind of data is consistently reported across firms or industries, however, due to differences in accounting rules, job classifications, and difficulties in determining how to depreciate accumulated stocks of knowledge. (The latter is necessary to distinguish between the innovative efforts of current workers and the accumulated wisdom of workers in the past.)

Effects of Firm Size and Market Structure on Innovation

Earlier in this chapter, we contrasted a large established firm's incentives to innovate to a new entrant's incentives. We concluded that there were forces (sunk cost effect, replacement effect) that weakened the established firm's incentives and those that strengthened its incentives (the efficiency effect). Later, by examining the economics of patent races, we concluded that the incentive to innovate also depends on market structure. But what does the evidence show? Are large established dominant firms less likely to innovate than entrants or small marginal firms, or are they more likely to innovate? Does innovative activity tend to vary systematically with market structure? By and large, the evidence on these questions is mixed.

Wesley Cohen and Richard Levin reviewed dozens of empirical studies of innovation, including studies that look at the importance of firm size and market structure.[27] Most of the studies they reviewed measured *R&D effort*, as measured by the ratio of R&D expenditures to sales, as opposed to *R&D output*, as measured by patent counts or numbers of new products. Studies undertaken in the 1960s generally found that innovative effort increased only slightly with firm size. Studies undertaken in the 1970s and 1980s found a stronger positive relationship between effort and firm size. Studies undertaken in the 1970s and 1980s found a stronger positive relationship between effort and firm size. The most recent studies using detailed data at the level of business units within firms, find that what drives R&D effort is the size of the business unit, not of the corporate parent. Even then, the relationship between size and effort is rather weak. The weak relationship between size and R&D effort is paralleled by studies that attempt to measure R&D output. These studies show that the share of innovations accounted for by large firms is roughly proportional to their share of employment.

Cohen and Levin report similarly mixed findings in studies of diversification and innovation. One might think that a diversified firm would have more incentive to innovate than an undiversified firm since many innovations have unpredictable benefits and a diversified firm would have greater opportunities to exploit them. But most studies find no systematic relationship between diversification and innovative effort. Some old case studies by Jewkes, Sawers, and Stillerman and a recent systematic study by Long and Ravenscraft suggest that different *patterns* of diversification may lead to different levels of R&D.[28] For example, big firms often purchase small firms that specialize in R&D, and then exploit economies of scale in development and marketing to bring their innovations to the market. On the other hand, corporate raiders may believe that their acquisitions have overinvested in R&D, and cut it back accordingly.

The evidence linking market structure to innovation is also inconclusive. Although most papers reviewed by Cohen and Levin find a positive relationship between market concentration and innovative effort, a few find a negative relationship, and one finds an "inverted-U" relationship—effort falls, then increases, as concentration increases. There is a "chicken or egg" problem with most of these studies—does concentration lead to more innovative effort, or does more innovative effort lead to concentration? As with other questions about innovation, empirical research yields no clear solution. As Cohen and Levin conclude, the empirical results concerning how firm size and market structure relate to innovation are fragile.

---

[27]Cohen, W. and R. Levin, "Innovation and Market Structure," in R. Schmalensee and R. Willig (eds.), *Handbook of Industrial Organization*, Amsterdam: North Holland, 1989.

[28]Jewkes, J., D. Sawers, and R. Stillerman, *The Sources of Inventions*, London: Macmillan, 1958; Long, W. and D. Ravenscraft, "LBOs, Debt, and R&D Intensity," *Strategic Management Journal*, 14, 1993, pp. 119–135.

Innovation and Access to Information

In *The Double Helix*, biologist James Watson describes the many increments in knowledge that enabled him and James Crick to discover the structure of DNA.[29] Their experience is a paradigm for many innovations: Knowledge is gained sequentially by a research community that shares its findings until research goals are met. The sequence of research in many fields may be conveniently divided into two phases: basic research and applied research. Basic research includes theoretical models and preliminary studies designed to further understanding of scientific principles rather than to facilitate design or development of a specific product. Applied research applies principles from basic research to specific products with the goal of bringing a product to the market. The boundaries between basic and applied research are often fuzzy. Sometimes basic research leads directly to new products, such as when Alexander Fleming accidentally discovered that mold on oranges inhibited the growth of bacteria. This led directly to the development of penicillin. At other times, applied research leads to fundamental contributions to general knowledge, such as the contributions of biotechnology firms to basic genetic science.

Despite these ambiguities, there is a general consensus that basic research is the proper domain of academic and government scientists because the results do not immediately translate into marketable products, whereas applied research is the domain of corporate researchers. For example, the U.S. National Institutes of Health (NIH) fund roughly $10 billion in biomedical research every year, nearly all of which is basic research. Private pharmaceutical companies in the United States spend a comparable amount on research, but over 80 percent is applied research.

In their study of biomedical research, Michael Ward and David Dranove showed that NIH-funded basic research leads to industry-funded applied research, after a lag of five to ten years.[30] This finding suggests that there are important channels of communication between basic and applied researchers. Firms may act to improve these channels. Drug manufacturers, for example, hire academic researchers as consultants and sponsor conferences. Firms may also locate near basic researchers, thereby increasing opportunities for casual and formal interactions. Adam Jaffe examined the flow of information from basic to applied researchers in four industries (drugs, chemicals, electronics, and mechanical).[31] He found local "markets" for research and development. Information developed by

---

[29]Watson, J.P., *The Double Helix: A Personal Account of the Discovery of the Structure of DNA*. London: Weidenfeld and Nicolson, 1981.

[30]Ward, M. and D. Dranove, "The Vertical Chain of Research and Development in the Pharmaceutical Industry," *Economic Inquiry*, forthcoming.

[31]Jaffe, A. "Technological Opportunity, and Spillovers of R&D: Evidence for Firms, Patents, Profits and Market Value," *American Economic Review*, 76, December 1986, pp. 984–1001.

basic researchers at universities tends to be disseminated most rapidly among local applied research firms. This gives firms located near leading research institutions a competitive advantage in new product development.

In general, an applied or basic researcher will benefit from frequent interactions with other researchers. This suggests that a "community" of researchers may benefit from synergistic interactions that make them more productive than if each worked in isolation. At the same time, a single community of researchers may take a common approach to problem solving, thereby limiting creativity. Sometimes firms set up competing research groups as a way of simultaneously developing research teams while fostering competition and creativity. A good example is the U.S. Department of Energy's management of independent nuclear research facilities at Lawrence Livermore Labs in California and Los Alamos Labs in New Mexico.

Research and Capabilities

As discussed above, strategy researchers have focused attention in recent years on the role of firm-level capabilities in influencing innovation and the origins of competitive advantage; however, there is little empirical research demonstrating the role of capabilities in research and development. Rebecca Henderson and Kim Clark's research on innovation in photolithographic aligner business, described in Example 15.3, shows the importance of path dependence in shaping firms' ability to exploit new technological opportunities. Similar findings emerge from a series of case studies by Dorothy Leonard-Brown. She finds that core capabilities contribute to R&D effectiveness in a firm's traditional areas of strength.[32] But she also finds that in a rapidly changing market, core capabilities breed core "rigidities" that arise when skills and managerial systems that served the firm well in the past prove to be unproductive. Workers and managers resist change because it renders their skills less valuable. Leonard-Brown showed that these rigidities hampered firms like Ford, Chaparral Steel, and Hewlett-Packard as they expanded into new product markets. Deborah Dougherty has documented similar resistance to change by firms with well-established capabilities.[33] These findings are broadly consistent with the idea, discussed above, that when new opportunities reduce the value of complimentary assets, firms may be hindered in their attempt to pursue these new opportunities.

Connie Helfat has tested David Teece's idea that complementarities in knowhow create economies of scope in R&D.[34] Helfat reviews research showing that firms often diversify by acquiring other firms with similar research needs. She then

---

[32]Leonard-Brown, D., "Core Capabilities and Core Rigidities: A Paradox in Managing New Product Development," *Strategic Management Journal*, 13, Summer 1992: 111–126.

[33]Dougherty, D., "Interpretive Barriers to Successful Product Innovation in Large Firms," *Organization Science*, 1992, 3, pp. 179–202.

[34]Helfat, C., "Know-how Complementarities and Knowledge Transfer Within Firms: The Case of R&D," Wharton School, working paper, 1994.

examines R&D expenditures on a variety of projects by petroleum firms. The nature of the underlying technology suggests that there are few scope economies for many of the projects. But two areas of research, coal gasification and coal liquification, rely on similar refining technologies and do display scope economies. Helfat finds that firms that invest heavily in coal gasification research also invest heavily in coal liquification research, suggesting that firms recognize the scope economies and pursue the two research directions simultaneously.

◆ ◆ ◆ ◆ ◆ MANAGING INNOVATION

Since large firms are complex organizations whose singleminded actions cannot be taken for granted, we must consider them as vehicles for innovation and not just as inventors and users of innovations. How innovation occurs within firms is often as important as innovation outcomes in understanding how firms create value for their customers. As Rosabeth Kanter argues, this involves seeing innovation as the process of bringing any new problem-solving idea into use.[35] This idea of organizational innovation is also developed in research on innovative cultures and internal or corporate entrepreneurship.

Corporate research and development programs have often been inflexible and unresponsive to market opportunities. This has prompted some firms to consider alternative ways of managing their innovative processes. For example, the creation of corporate venture departments in the past two decades reflects the growing sensitivity of larger corporations to their need for mechanisms to identify and exploit opportunities for innovation beyond current products, processes, and services. Innovation outside of formal organizational mechanisms has also received attention in recent years. This work has focused on corporate entrepreneurs who push new projects forward in the face of bureaucratic obstacles.[36]

The innovation strategies of large firms need not focus solely on internal development, however. Other approaches, such as spinoffs, joint ventures, and strategic alliances, can also facilitate entry into new business areas or the development of new capabilities. One example of an interorganizational alternative to firm-based research and development is the public-private research consortium.[37] In these

---

[35]Kanter, R.M., *The Change Masters*, New York: Simon and Schuster, 1983.

[36]Burgelman, R.A., "A Process Model of Internal Corporate Venturing in the Diversified Major Firm," *Administrative Science Quarterly*, 28, 1983, pp. 223–244; Peterson, R.A., "Entrepreneurship and Organization," in Nystrom, P.C. and W.R. Starbuck (eds.), *Handbook of Organizational Design*, Vol. I, New York: Oxford University Press, 1981, pp. 65–83.

[37]Gibson, D.V. and E.M. Rodgers, *R & D Collaboration on Trial*, Cambridge, MA: Harvard Business School Press, 1994; Browning, L.D., J.M. Beyer, and J.C. Shetler, "Building Cooperation in a Competitive Industry: SEMATECH and the Semiconductor Industry," *Academy of Management Journal*, 38, 1995, pp. 113–151.

formal alliances, member firms pool their resources and coordinate their research activities with those of academic institutions in explicit collaboration in large-scale high-tech projects. Governments also fund these ventures as well as exempt their activities from antitrust prohibitions against collaboration among competitors. While the Japanese pioneered these consortia in computer technology in the 1970s, American and European counterparts developed in the early 1980s. Perhaps the best known American consortium, MCC (Microelectronics and Computer Technology Corporation), was founded in 1982 by 16 computer and semiconductor firms. By 1993, MCC included over 100 member firms.

In general, a firm faces a dilemma in managing its innovative activities. On the one hand, formal structure and controls are necessary to coordinate innovative activities. On the other hand, looseness and flexibility may be needed to foster innovativeness, creativity, and adaptiveness to changing circumstances. These competing requirements create ongoing tensions for managing innovation activities.

CHAPTER SUMMARY

- Creative destruction refers to the process whereby old sources of competitive advantage are destroyed and replaced with new ones. According to economist Joseph Schumpeter, the essence of entrepreneurship is the exploitation of the "shocks" or "discontinuities" that destroy existing sources of advantage.

- A dominant established firm's incentive to innovate may be weaker than that of a smaller firm or a potential entrant. The sunk cost effect and the replacement effect weaken the established firm's incentive to innovate. The efficiency effect, by contrast, strengthens the dominant firm's incentive to innovate as compared with a potential entrant.

- The sunk cost effect has to do with the asymmetry between a firm that has *already* made a commitment to a particular technology or product concept and one that is planning such a commitment. It is the phenomenon whereby a profit-maximizing firm sticks with its current technology or product concept even though the profit-maximizing decision for a firm starting from scratch would be to choose a *different* technology or product concept.

- When an innovation offers the prospect of the adopter becoming a monopolist, a potential entrant has a stronger incentive to develop the innovation than an incumbent monopolist. Because it already has a monopoly, the gain to the monopolist from the innovation is less than it is for the potential entrant. Through innovation an entrant can replace the monopolist, but the monopolist can only replace itself. For this reason, this phenomenon is called the replacement effect.

- The efficiency effect has to do with the fact that the benefit to a firm from being a monopolist as compared with being one of two competitors in duopoly is greater than the benefit to a firm from being a duopolist as compared with not being in the industry at all (and thus earning no profit). The efficiency effect makes an incumbent monopolist's incentive to innovate stronger than that of a potential entrant. The reason is that the incumbent can lose its monopoly if it does not innovate, whereas the entrant will become (at best) a duopolist if it successfully innovates.

- The term patent race has been used to characterize the battle between firms to innovate first. Models of patent races highlight the often critical advantage that goes to the first innovator, and give insight into how the magnitude of that advantage affects the incentives to innovate. Patent race models also emphasize an important strategic point: Firms in a patent race must anticipate the R&D investments of competitors. Failure to do so can be costly.

- Patent race models imply that when a firm is determining whether to increase its investment in innovation, it must account for the following factors: (i) By how much must the investment increase its R&D productivity and thereby also increase its chances of winning the patent race? (ii) Will other firms increase their R&D expenditures in response, thereby decreasing the firm's chances of winning the patent race? (iii) How many competitors are there?

- Evolutionary economics sees the firm decisions as determined by routines—well-practiced patterns of activity inside the firm—rather than profit maximization. At any given time, the routines of an organization determine its distinctive capabilities—which it can do better than other firms. Firms do not change their routines very often because getting members of an organization to alter what has worked well in the past is an "unnatural" act. But firms that stick to producing a given set of products in a particular way may not survive. Thus, a firm typically needs to engage in a continuous search for ways to improve its existing routines. The firm's dynamic capabilities refer to its ability to maintain the bases of its competitive advantage over time.

- Michael Porter argues that competitive advantage originates in the local environment in which the firm is based. Porter identifies four attributes in a firm's home market that promote or impede its ability to achieve competitive advantage in global markets: factors conditions; demand conditions; related supplier or support industries; and strategy, structure, and rivalry.

- Empirical studies find mixed evidence on the relationship between innovative effort and firm size. The evidence linking market structure to innovation is also inconclusive. Although many studies have found a positive relationship between market concentration and innovative effort, a few find a negative relationship, and one finds an "inverted-U" relationship—effort falls, then increases, as concentration increases.

- In general, a firm faces a dilemma in managing its innovative activities. On the one hand, formal structure and controls are necessary to coordinate innovative activities. On the other hand, looseness and flexibility may be needed to foster innovativeness, creativity, and adaptiveness to changing circumstances. These competing requirements create ongoing tensions for managing innovation activities.

QUESTIONS

1. IQ Inc. currently monopolizes the market for a certain type of microprocessor, the 666. The present value of the stream of monopoly profits from this design is thought to be $500 million. Enginola (which is currently in a completely different segment of the microprocessor market from this one) and IQ are contemplating spending money to develop a superior design that will make the 666 completely obsolete. Whoever develops the design first gets the entire market. The present value of the stream of monopoly profit from the superior design is expected to be $150 million greater than the present value of the profit from the 666.

Success in developing the design is not certain, but the probability of a firm's success is directly linked to the amount of money it spends on the project (more money, greater probability of success). Moreover, the productivity of Enginola's spending on this project and IQ's spending is exactly the same: Starting from any given level of spending, an additional $1 spent by Enginola has exactly the same impact on its probability of winning as an additional $1 spent by IQ has on its probability of winning. The table below illustrates this. It shows the probability of winning the race if each firm's spending equals 0, $100 million, and $200 million. The first number represents Enginola's probability of winning the race, the second is IQ's probability of winning, and the third is the probability that neither succeeds. Note: *this is not a payoff table.*

			IQ's Spending	
Enginola's Spending		*0*	*$100 million*	*$200 million*
	0	(0,0,1)	(0,.6,.4)	(0,.8,.2)
	$100 million	(6,0,.4)	(4,.4,.2)	(3,.6,.1)
	$200 million	(8,0,.2)	(6,.3,.1)	(5,.5,0)

Assuming that

(i) each firm makes its spending decision simultaneously and non-cooperatively;

(ii) each seeks to maximize its expected profit;

(iii) neither firm faces any financial constraints,

which company, if any, has the greater incentive to spend money to win this "R&D race"? Of the effects discussed in the chapter (sunk cost effect, replacement effect, efficiency effect) which are shaping the incentives to innovate in this example.

2. In their article "Strategy as Stretch and Leverage," Gary Hamel and C.K. Prahalad argue that industry newcomers have a stronger incentive to supplant established firms from their leadership positions than established firms have to maintain their leadership positions. The reason, they argue, is that a greater gap exists between a newcomer's resources and aspirations as compared to a market leader.[38] Is Hamel and Prahalad's argument consistent with profit-maximizing behavior by both the leader and the newcomer? Is their argument consistent with ideas from evolutionary economics?

3. Consider the Nash equilibrium in a probabilistic R&D race involving identical firms. How is the number of competitors likely to affect (i) a firm's incentive in R&D; (ii) the time it takes for the R&D race to be won?

4. "Industrial or antitrust policies that result in the creation of domestic monopolies rarely result in global competitive advantage." Explain.

---

[38]Hamel, G. and C.K. Prahalad, "Strategy as Stretch and Leverage," *Harvard Business Review* (March–April 1993), 75–84.

PART FOUR

INTERNAL

ORGANIZATION

INCENTIVES AND
AGENCY

16

*I*n 1993, Chicago Bears president Michael McCaskey negotiated new contracts for the team's leading offensive and defensive players, quarterback Jim Harbaugh and defensive end Richard Dent. Harbaugh was an average quarterback whom fans admired for his tenacity, if not his profiency throwing the ball. Dent was one of the best at his position, but many fans complained that Dent frequently gave less than 100 percent effort. McCaskey offered Harbaugh a long-term contract that paid $5 million for the 1993 season, and nearly $3 million per season thereafter. McCaskey originally gave Dent a multiyear contract that paid nearly $1.2 million per year. McCaskey and Dent agreed to add a clause to that contract enabling Dent to become a free agent at the end of the season.

Jim Harbaugh's 1993 season was not successful. The Bears' offense was one of the worst in the league, Harbaugh's play received much criticism from fans and press alike, and he was released. Richard Dent, on the other hand, had an outstanding season culminating in a selection to the Pro Bowl, the league's all-star game. Many Bears fans believe that the disparate performances of Harbaugh and Dent were the direct result of their contracts. Harbaugh's salary was high, even by professional sports standards. He earned enough money in 1993 to retire on and, in spite of a poor year, signed with the Indianapolis Colts for $900,000 per year in 1994–1995. These factors may have limited his financial incentive to perform well. Dent, on the other hand, believed that a strong performance would attract huge financial offers from other teams, allowing him to realize a substantial increase in income in 1994. This motivated him to work harder than he had in the past.[1]

The owners of sports teams are using the lessons learned from the Harbaugh and Dent situations, and others like them, to rethink how to motivate their star athletes. Eddie DeBartolo, the owner of the San Franscisco 49ers football team, heavily emphasized incentives based on individual and team performance. Many sports analysts feel that the enormous bonuses offered to defensive players such as Ken Norton and Deion Sanders contributed to their outstanding play and, ultimately, the 1995 Super Bowl championship. In the wake of the 49ers' success, we expect other owners to increase their use of incentives.

Agency theory examines the use of financial incentives to motivate workers, as exemplified by the variety of contracting issues that emerge in professional sports. In many situations, one individual or organization, known as the *principal*, delegates responsibility to another, known as the *agent*, to act on its behalf. Examples of agency relationships abound. The owners of a firm may delegate managerial responsibility to a chief executive officer. The vice president of procurement may delegate purchasing decisions to a purchasing manager. Parents may delegate responsibility for curriculum development to a teacher. In all these situations, the principal hopes that the agent's interests are aligned with its own. But agents are often selfish. Without explicit contractual obligations, the agent may act in his or her own interest rather than further the interests of the principal.

The pursuit of self-interest by agents may undermine agency relationships. A CEO may aim for job security rather than maximizing shareholder wealth. A purchasing manager may prefer to obtain supplies of imputs from long-time acquaintances rather than searching for the lowest–cost supplier. Teachers may shun new methods and materials to reduce preparation time.

This chapter examines the agency relationship. We will discuss why principals use agents, the opportunities for solving agency problems through contracting, the characteristics of an efficient contract for solving agency problems, and the conditions that lead to inefficiencies even when the best possible contracts are used. These conditions are common, so that contracts alone may be insufficient for resolving many agency problems. Chapter 18 discusses a powerful alternative to contracts—"culture."

◆ ◆ ◆ ◆ ◆   THE AGENCY RELATIONSHIP

Individuals often hire others to work on their behalf. The workers do not always do as the employer would like. Agency theory describes the opportunities and pitfalls that arise in efforts to align their interests.

---

[1]As it turned out, the league implemented a cap on the total salaries that may be paid by each team. Team owners noted that many big salary players, including Harbaugh, did not perform up to expectations. Only a handful of top players now receive the kinds of contracts that Harbaugh received in 1993. Owners also are reluctant to offer guaranteed contracts that pay in future years regardless of current performance.

What Is an Agency Relationship?

An agency relationship exists when one individual, called the agent, acts on behalf of another, called the principal.[2] Usually, the principal possesses an asset and employs an agent to increase its value. For example, the management of General Motors' Saturn division may employ an advertising agency to increase the demand for Saturn automobiles. "Buy" decisions, such as this, constitute an important class of agency relationships. Others include expert/client relationships, such as the doctor/patient relationship, and employer/employee relationships.

Some of the reasons why the principal uses an agent can be drawn directly from the discussion of the make-or-buy decision in Chapter 2. Consider a principal who possesses an asset that is a significant component of a value chain. For example, the principal may be General Motors, whose assets include tools, dies, and an assembly line. But the principal may lack the expertise or scale to efficiently perform all of the tasks in the value chain. In this case, the principal may employ an independent agent, such as an engineering or marketing firm, to perform one or more of those tasks, while retaining ownership of the finished product.[3]

It may be possible for the principal and agent to switch roles. For example, General Motors could manufacture cars for the marketing firm, which would then become the retailer. This is not too far-fetched—firms such as Benetton and Nike are essentially marketing firms that obtain their products from contracting manufacturers. In these cases, the marketing firm is the principal, for it holds the finished good and must bear the risk if it fails to sell. The manufacturing firm is the agent.

The notion that the principal owns a productive asset and the agent possesses expertise that may be used in conjunction with that asset extends to expert/client relationships. Patients "own" their own bodies and employ physician/agents to "add value." In some cases, no obvious asset is involved, such as when an accused criminal/principal retains a lawyer/agent.

The Agency Contract

The terms of the agency relationship are spelled out by a *contract*. The contract specifies the payments to be made by the principal to the agent, contingent on the agent taking specific actions and/or the principal observing certain outcomes. The contract may be explicit; the terms are written down and legally enforced. An example is the contract between General Motors and workers in its Saturn division. This contract specifies bonuses to be paid out contingent on profits reported in audited accounting returns. The contract may be implicit; the terms are understood

---

[2]One of the first and most influential papers to describe the agency relationship in these terms is Ross, S., "The Economic Theory of Agency: The Principal's Problem," *American Economic Review*, 63, 1973, pp. 134–9.

[3]The relationship between asset ownership and the make-or-buy decision is detailed in Grossman, S. and O. Hart, "The Costs and Benefits of Ownership: A Theory of Lateral and Vertical Integration," *Journal of Political Economy*, 94, August 1986, pp. 691–719. Chapter 4 presents a summary of their ideas.

by all participants and are enforced through reputation effects and the desire to maintain long-term relationships. An example is the tenure system used in academia. Faculty understand that tenure is attainable if their research and teaching are well regarded by their peers and their students. However, there are usually no rules specifying what constitutes tenurable performance, and the courts have allowed academic institutions great leeway in using their judgment, rather than rules spelled out in advance, as the basis for tenure decisions.

At a minimum, the contract that the principal offers the agent must satisfy two types of conditions. First, the agent must be willing to accept the contract; the contract must offer the agent the opportunity to achieve a wage at least as great as the agent's next best alternative, or *threshhold wage*. If the contract does not offer the threshhold wage, the agent will prefer to work for someone else under other terms. During the 1980s, opportunities expanded for nurses to earn high incomes in relatively low-stress positions outside hospitals, such as in home health care. This raised the threshold wage necessary to employ nurses in hospitals, thereby driving up the wages of hospital nurses.

Conditional on accepting the contract, the agent must be willing to comply with its terms. In other words, the actions that the principal expects the agent to undertake must be compatible with the incentives spelled out in the contract. This is called the *incentive compatibility constraint*. If the contract does not satisfy the incentive compatibility constraint, then the principal will be unhappy with the actions taken by the agent, and may have been better off not employing the agent at all. We say that if an agent does not act in the principal's best interest, the agent is *shirking*. The actions of the chief of operations at the Chicago post office in 1993–1994 appear to give new meaning to the term shirking. As part of her job, she was responsible for assigning craftsmen to repair and renovation projects. She used her authority to have her office remodeled. The project included a private bathroom and kitchen, and cost around $200,000. Her contract prevented her supervisors from taking any legal action, although she was not permitted to move into the office. The postal service (and, ultimately, postal service customers) had to bear the cost.

The First-Best Efficient Contract

Thus far, we have discussed a variety of conditions under which agency relationships appear to break down and agents have an opportunity to shirk. The principal's goal is a contract under which the agent will not shirk. What would be the features of such a contract? Suppose that a principal seeks to devise a contract that maximizes his or her wealth. One desirable characteristic of such a contract is that the agent's actions should be economically *efficient*, that is, the agent's actions should optimally trade off costs and benefits. For example, suppose that Ford wishes to make customers in the 18 to 25 age bracket aware of its redesigned Mustang, and hires a marketing firm to place its advertisements. It would be inefficient for the marketer to advertise in the *New York Times* or *Wall Street Journal*, because ads in *Rolling Stone* or *Sports Illustrated* would reach the target audience at a lower cost.

There are often many possible contracts that would encourage the agent to act efficiently. The one that makes the principal as well off as possible is the one that pays the agent's threshold wage. (The principal could not offer less than the threshold wage, for the agent would not agree to the contract.) A contract that leads the agent to take the efficient action and accept the threshold wage is *first-best efficient* for the principal.

To understand the problems that arise in agency relationships, it is helpful to consider some situations in which agents usually act efficiently even without elaborate contracts. There are many such situations. The owners of an airline usually expect their pilots to fly at the appropriate speed and in the right direction. Purchasers of eyeglasses can expect opticians to grind their lenses according to prescription. Purchasers of clothing expect that alterations will improve the fit. Three factors contribute to efficiency in these cases:

1. Agents do not possess hidden information. Principals know what constitutes efficient action and what outcome to expect.

2. Principals have full information about actions and/or outcomes.

3. The agents are at little risk. They know that if they do not shirk, they can expect to be rewarded.

Under these three conditions, opportunism by the agent is impossible. Principals know what to expect, can determine if actions and/or outcomes meet expectations, and can fairly reward agents who act efficiently. At the same time, agents know that if they act efficiently, they will be rewarded.

To summarize, first-best efficient contracts are possible, but only when certain features are present: no hidden information, observable actions and/or outcomes, and absence of risk considerations. The next section details how agency problems may arise and how they can be resolved if any of these features are absent.

PROBLEMS IN AGENCY RELATIONSHIPS ◆ ◆ ◆ ◆ ◆

Agents do not always do what principals would like them to. Problems can arise due to moral hazard and imperfect observability. Contracts must be structured to overcome these problems.

Moral Hazard

Problems arise in agency relationships because the agent does not always prefer to take the action that the principal most prefers.[4] We might expect this to happen as a matter of course. After all, agents and principals usually have different objectives.

---

[4]Donald Parsons points out that agency problems were less severe in the 19th century because most workers were self-employed, that is, the principal and the agent were the same person and therefore had the same objectives. Family-run businesses had diminished agency problems, since the interests of family members were probably closely aligned. Parson, D., "The Employment Relationship: Job Attachment, Work Effort, and the Nature of Contracts," in Ashenfelter, O. and R. Layard (eds.), *The Handbook of Labor Economics*, Amsterdam: North Holland, 1986.

For example, the owner of a business may want to maximize profits, but workers may seek to minimize the chances that they will lose their jobs. In this case, workers may take fewer risks than the owner might prefer. Or, workers may seek to minimize effort, thereby working less hard than the owner would prefer. The principal and agent could address such problems by agreeing to a contract that binds the agent to act in the principal's interests. But contracts are inevitably incomplete. As a result, there are opportunities for shirking, or what is often referred to as *moral hazard*.[5]

Hidden Action and Hidden Information

Moral hazard describes selfish behavior that cannot be prevented by contract. The term is frequently used to describe how insurance changes behavior. For example, individuals with auto theft insurance may be less likely to lock their cars than if such insurance were not available. To take another example, individuals with insurance for prescription drugs may not seek out low-cost generics. Moral hazard usually has a negative connotation—the gains from moral hazard behavior usually come at the expense of others.

Moral hazard is closely related to the concepts of hidden action and hidden information described in Chapter 3. Recall that a hidden action cannot be observed and/or verified. If an agent's actions are hidden—if the principal cannot detect that the agent is shirking—then the principal might not be able to use a contract to rule out undesirable actions. For example, suppose that a pharmaceutical company would like an independent clinical research organization (CRO) to validate the clinical research on a new drug that the CRO did for the pharmaceutical company. The pharmaceutical company could require the CRO to produce evidence of validation. But validation requires substantial physical and mental effort that the pharmaceutical company cannot easily observe. Thus, validation is a hidden action and so is not contractible. Consequently, the CRO could shirk on validation without substantial risk of punishment.

An effort to control hidden action may help explain Domino's "30-minute delivery guarantee" described in Chapter 14. Recall that Domino's announced, through national ads, that it would offer a $3 discount on any pizza delivered in more than 30 minutes. Fast delivery was a key element of Domino's success. Domino's could have tried to promote fast delivery through internal monitoring— say by fining franchise owners with poor on-time performance. But Domino's could not easily verify pizza delivery times, and could not expect franchise owners to report truthfully their on-time performance to top management. But consumers could easily verify delivery times, and with the help of the guarantee, had an incentive to report late deliveries. By offering the guarantee, Domino's used consumer monitoring where internal monitoring would not suffice.

---

[5]For a rigorous mathematical treatment of the roles of moral hazard and attitudes toward risk in agency relationships, see Holmstrom, B., "Moral Hazard and Observability," *Bell Journal of Economics*, 10, Spring 1979, pp. 74–91.

Moral hazard may also result when the agent possesses hidden information—knowledge about the conditions of demand, technology, or cost that the principal does not have. This information is often critical for determining the agent's best course of action. By keeping some information hidden, the agent may be able to shirk without fear of punishment. The agent simply uses his or her informational edge to persuade the principal that the chosen action was, in fact, appropriate.

Hidden information helps explain why promoting research and development is an especially difficult agency problem. As discussed in Chapter 2, innovative ideas are hard to evaluate. Firms must assess both the scientific and commercial viability of the ideas. Innovators often have private information about the scientific merits of their ideas, and thus may know better than anyone else whether they are on the verge of a significant breakthrough. But if seed money is allowed to only the most promising projects, researchers would have an incentive to be overly optimistic about their ideas. This makes it difficult for employers or other investors to determine which projects to fund.

Firms also have difficulty measuring innovative effort. One consequence is that firms often have a hard time identifying the most promising innovators. If innovators are not rewarded, they might seek employment elsewhere. At the same time, other would-be innovators might be reluctant to invest the necessary time and energy. Another consequence is that firms that fund research usually put the researcher at financial risk for the outcome. Firms such as Cray Research have successfully launched new businesses by giving innovative employees an ownership stake in spinoff companies, such as Circuit Tools. In this way, researchers end up becoming significant risk takers.

The combination of hidden information about innovative ideas and imperfect observability of innovative effort helps explain the preponderance of small R&D firms in the biotechnology industry, as described in Example 16.1.

$\mathcal{E}$XAMPLE 16.1

FROM GIANTS TO DWARVES: THE EVOLUTION OF BIOMEDICAL RESEARCH AND DEVELOPMENT[6]

During the 1960s, 1970s, and 1980s, a few large pharmaceutical firms were responsible for developing most new ethical drugs. Some firms, such as Merck, Eli Lilly, Abbott, Glaxo, Hoechst, and Rhone-Poulenc, routinely ranked in the *Fortune* Global 500. Today, many of the most promising new medical treatments come from new firms specializing in biotechnology. Unlike the giant drug houses,

---

[6]Many of the facts in this example come from Bylinsky, G., "Genetics: The Money Rush Is On," *Fortune*, May 30, 1994, p. 94.

biotech firms are small. The largest and best-known biotech firms, Amgen and Genentech, have less than one-tenth the sales of Merck and Abbott. The typical biotech firm is much smaller, with a few dozen employees, and is likely to be owned by its researcher/founder in partnership with a venture capitalist. The transition from large hierarchical firm to small entrepreneurial firm is the direct result of the changing nature of research technology, and the associated changes in the agency relationship between investor and researcher.

Conventional medical R&D, that is, the style of research that dominated until the 1980s and is still prevalent today, relies a good deal on trial and error. Researchers concoct new compounds and test them for therapeutic effects. Until recently, scientists had limited ability to predict the actions of new compounds, and would conduct thousands of tests per compound to determine what biological effects, if any, they had. Testing, or "screening," involved standard tasks in isolation, purification, compounding, and measurement. Big firms held two advantages over small firms in this process. First, firms with large biochemical "libraries" could screen new compounds more efficiently. Second, once a product was identified, large firms enjoyed economies of scale in development, distribution, and sales. Agency considerations in the research process were minimal. The standardized nature of the R&D process meant that individual researchers possessed little hidden information.

Beginning in the 1970s, biomedical researchers pioneered the use of theoretical models as the basis for constructing new molecules. Armed with knowledge of how biological and chemical substances interact with organ systems, scientists can now predict the actions of new molecules before testing. As a result, the massive screens for biological effect have given way to research protocols that are tailored to individual products. Firms now depend on the scientific creativity of individual researchers to identify new products. Indeed, there is little agreement as to the best methods for developing new gene therapies, and biotech firms are pursuing several different development strategies.

While the current direction of biomedical research puts a premium on innovative development and applications of theory, researchers with innovative ideas face problems when they seek funding. J. Craig Venter, one of the pioneers of genetic research, experienced the headaches common to the field. Venter championed the use of computers and biotech instruments to isolate and decode gene fragments. This technique could lead to cures for many diseases, and Venter sought funds to expand his lab. He applied to the Human Genome Project, an international consortium of government research programs, but was met with skepticism. Finally, Venter turned to HealthCare Management Investment Corp. This venture capital firm helped Venter start Human Genome Sciences (HGS), promised to fund up to $85 million in HGS research, and gave Venter a significant ownership stake in HGS.

Venter's frustration in dealing with the Human Genome Project is similar to that experienced by researchers seeking funds from other large organizations. Researchers face a difficult problem. They possess hidden information about how to do research that, if correct, could be worth a fortune. How does the researcher convince an organization to fund research without giving away the hidden information?

One obvious solution is for the researcher to self-fund the R&D. However, R&D is so costly that self-funding is impractical for most scientists. Even so, a prerequisite for obtaining venture capital funds is for a researcher to put up a lot of his or her own money (as well as money from friends and family members). Another solution emerged in the 1980s, when specialized venture capital firms, such as HealthCare Management Investment Corp., emerged. These firms possess two critical assets. First, they are skillful at evaluating researchers and their projects. Many of these firms employ leading researchers to evaluate proposals. Second, they are not potential competitors of the researchers. The venture capitalists sign agreements not to use information obtained from researchers seeking funds. Even so, researchers are often reluctant to disclose all their methods, and the course of knowledge in biotechnology changes so rapidly that a proposal can rapidly become obsolete. For these reasons, venture capitalists often evaluate the researcher as much as or more than the research itself, and favor researchers who are confident enough in their own abilities to risk their own savings.

Large pharmaceutical firms have recently increased their involvement in biotech. For example, SmithKline Beecham paid $125 million for the rights to any products produced by HGS, and Hoffman LaRoche paid $70 million for the rights to develop products initiated by the biotech firm Millenium. This division of labor makes sense. Researchers retain an ownership stake, creating incentives for them to pursue the most promising research directions. Large drug makers can then exploit their economies of production, distribution, and marketing to bring the products to market.

Observability

One key to preventing shirking is *observability*.[7] If the principal has the potential to observe actions and outcomes, and the desired actions can be spelled out in a contract and observed in a manner that can be verified in court, then the principal can solve the agency problem. The principal contractually requires agents to take the correct actions, and punishes them if they fail to do so. Some desirable actions are easy to observe and contract on. For example, people who sell their houses often require their sales agents to publish advertisements, host open houses, and show the house to a specified number of qualified buyers. Other actions may be harder to observe. In real estate selling, the seller cannot easily observe the sales "pitch" and other efforts used by the sales agent. For this reason, contracts are more likely to stipulate pay based on observable outcomes. Continuing the example, the owner probably has agreed to pay the agent a commission contingent on the desired outcome—the timely sale of the house.

---

[7]The seminal work on the value of information in agency relationships is Holmstrom, B., "Moral Hazard and Observability," *Bell Journal of Economics*, 10, Spring 1979, pp. 74–91. One of Holmstrom's findings is that the principal is always better off with information about the agent's performance, no matter how noisy, than with no information at all.

The outcome of interest to a house seller—the closing of the sale—is easy to observe and measure. In many other agency relationships, the desired actions and outcomes are more difficult to observe and measure. If the principal cannot adequately measure the action or outcome of greatest interest, it may instead measure another action or outcome as a *proxy*. But the proxy measure must be *highly correlated* with the desired measure. Two measures are correlated when they tend to move together. High correlation is essential for a good proxy, for two reasons. First, if the proxy is not correlated with the measure of interest, then the score on the proxy will be irrelevant to the scores on the preferred measure. Second, since agents seek to maximize their performance according to whatever measure they are being judged on, if the measures are uncorrelated, then agents will try to maximize performance on the proxy measure without necessarily improving their performance on the preferred measure.

Law enforcement provides a number of examples in which the principal (i.e., taxpayers) must substitute easily measured outcomes for desired outcomes. Taxpayers would like the police to maintain safe and efficient roadways. But this is a highly subjective measure, since (a) it is difficult to know just how safe and efficient the roads would be without police, and (b) any measure of road safety and efficiency is multidimensional, combining accidents of varying severity, traffic tie-ups, and so on. This measure would also introduce unwanted risk (see below) to the pay of police, since their ability to control safety is limited. Rather than pay police based on some composite measure of roadway safety and efficiency, taxpayers have implicitly supported a system in which police are rewarded based on easily quantified measures, such as the number of speeding tickets written. Of course, this leads police to concentrate efforts on catching speeders. While the frequency of speeding is certainly correlated with roadway safety, focusing on this particular measure may not be the best way to promote safety and efficiency. Similar issues arise in efforts to promote public safety. Example 16.2 discusses the development of performance measures in health care, and Example 16.3 illustrates problems in the agency relationship in social work, a situation where the desired outcome is nearly impossible to measure.

EXAMPLE 16.2

MEASURING PERFORMANCE OF HEALTH CARE ORGANIZATIONS

There is an ongoing information revolution in health care. The revolution is the result of two factors. Health care purchasers increasingly seek to spend their dollars more wisely, and reductions in computer costs lower the costs of accessing and analyzing large data sets. Purchasers use health care data to assess the performance of providers and steer patients to those providers that they believe offer the best combination of cost and quality.

To be cost-effective, purchasers must be able to measure quality. But what are the features of good-quality health care? Quality is clearly multidimensional, but most would agree that living longer and without pain are two desirable outcomes of any treatment. Until 1984, payers had no systematic information about any dimensions related to these outcomes. One of the most widely used indicators of hospital quality, accreditation by the Joint Commission on Accreditation of Hospitals, was based on such factors as the number of fire extinguishers and the size of hallways. Patients were forced to choose their providers on the basis of this measure, as well as other easily obtainable measures, such as location and the quality of the food. In 1984, the Health Care Finance Administration started reporting hospital "inpatient mortality" rates. These give the probability that a patient with a given illness would die during the hospital stay. This is a better measure of quality, but it is still imperfect because patients may die after discharge. For example, a hospital may transfer dying patients to other hospitals or to their homes, but would appear to have a low inpatient mortality rate. Despite this and other problems, purchasers used mortality data because they believed it was correlated with their preferred quality measures.

As health care data grow increasingly accessible, payers are using more sophisticated quality measures. The Pennsylvania Corporate Hospital Quality Rating Project represents an effort by the University of Pennsylvania and local business and industry to develop a more thorough measure of hospital quality. Their measures include inpatient mortality, postoperative length of stay, and infection rates, all of which are believed to be correlated with "living longer and without pain." Purchasers in Pennsylvania use this information to identify the best hospitals to send their enrollees to. Hospitals are using similar information to evaluate their own performance. Hospitals that score poorly may spend a little time questioning the measures, but spend far more time seeking out ways to score better the next time. Similar measures are being developed for physicians, and many observers believe that physicians in the future will have to provide evidence of quality to obtain staff privileges at hospitals, win contracts from Health Maintenance Organizations, and command high wages.

$\mathcal{E}$XAMPLE 16.3

INCENTIVES IN A SOCIAL SERVICE AGENCY

Some organizations do not confront market pressures. Organizations, such as public agencies, for example, are often mandated by law and continue to exist and grow without regard to their efficiency or effectiveness. However, even when an organization does not face competitive market pressures, individuals within the organization still respond to the incentives that the organization offers. The incentives offered by nonmarket organizations are not the market-based incentives (such as shares of stock or performance-based pay) common in for-profit firms, but they affect behavior nonetheless. Incentives in nonmarket organizations can be long-term economic rewards (such as promotions based on performance), or they can be social rewards, such as praise or the avoidance of punishment. In general, social rewards may be used more often because of the relatively strict seniority rules in many public bureaucracies.

The Illinois Department of Children and Family Services (DCFS), the state child services agency, is a good example of the power of incentives in nonmarket organizations. There are two main types of jobs in DCFS: investigators (people who investigate reports of child abuse, and determine whether the child should be removed from the home), and caseworkers (people who manage the therapy offered to the child and family once abuse has been identified). The main decision to be made by investigators is whether to remove a child from the home. The main decision to be made by caseworkers is whether to return a child to the home.

This agency lives in the public spotlight, and legislative officials can prosper or suffer at the polls according to public perception of the agency's performance. The agency receives bad press when something harmful happens to a child. On the other hand, the media tend not to report cases where children are removed from their homes with insufficient justification. Media reports influence the budget the agency receives from the state legislature. Naturally, the legislature encourages the agency to prevent child abuse, while it is less concerned about keeping children in their homes. Primarily through punishments and reprimands (or negative social reinforcement, in the language of behavioral psychology), the agency passes this conservative bias along to the investigators and caseworkers.

For investigators, the conservative bias means that the easiest decision for them to make is to remove a child from the home if there is a suspicion of abuse and make the child a ward of the state. Finding that a claim of abuse is unfounded is risky: If something were to later happen to that child due to abuse or neglect, the media eye would turn to the agency, and the investigator would be reprimanded. Removing a child from a healthy family environment may occasionally result in a lawsuit for the agency, but such lawsuits tend not to receive much media attention, and therefore rarely result in a reprimand for the investigator.

For caseworkers, the conservative bias means that the easiest decision for them to make is to keep a child in the system (in a foster home, for example). If a child is released from the system and is later abused again in the home, the agency will receive public scrutiny, and the censure will trickle down to the caseworker responsible. In cases where the decision to release a child is the correct one, the family does not reenter the system, and the media do not give attention to the "success stories."

We can conceptualize the judgments of the investigators and caseworkers using the following analysis. There are two possible judgments an investigator may make: Either the child is being abused (calling for removal from the home environment) or the child is not (which means that the child will be left in the home environment). Because of the agency's conservative bias, the investigators have incentives to make one type of error (False Positives) over another (Misses). It is safer for them to remove the child from the home than to risk having a Miss. Caseworkers have a slightly different decision to make: Is it safe to return the child to the home? Their incentives lead them to errors in the direction of Misses, rather than False Positives. That is, even when it may actually be safe to return a child to the home, they will err on the side of caution.

These two incentive systems together mean that the agency takes in far more children than it discharges: The investigators tend to let too many into the system, and the caseworkers are reluctant to let the children back out of the system. Over the years, this has resulted in a huge increase in agency case-loads (from 25,000 children in 1991 to almost 41,000 in 1994), to the point where the agency is beginning to receive media attention for failing to discharge children quickly enough. The investigators and caseworkers are each responding to the incentives offered to them by the agency, and their behavior is rational when judged within the boundaries of their jobs. However, perhaps in part because the agency does not face the discipline of a market environment, it offers its workers incentives to perform behaviors that would have dysfunctional consequences for the system as a whole.

For public bureaucracies, the media may sometimes partially correct for the lack of market competition, although this correction tends to be far from perfect. Perhaps now that the agency is receiving a different kind of attention from the media, it will change the incentives offered to investigators and caseworkers, thereby also changing their willingness to make one type of error over another. It is the incentives offered by the system, rather than abiding personal traits of workers, that are the main influence on the behavior of the agency's workers.

Teams and Observability

In many agency situations, the principal hires a team of agents to work on a common problem. The decision to organize workers into teams is analyzed in Chapter 17. A critical issue of interest here is how to reward individual team members when it is only possible to measure the output of the team as a whole. One approach is to treat the team as a single agent and pay the team a single fee. The team then determines how to split the fee. This approach works only to the extent that the team implements a reward scheme that prevents shirking. But instead, the team may elect to share any fee equally. Individual team members may then choose to shirk, feeling that this will minimally affect the overall team product. Team members can prevent shirking by exerting peer pressure or by refusing to work with shirking workers on future projects. Armen Alchian and Harold Demsetz offer another solution: Assign one team member the job of monitoring and rewarding or punishing the other workers.[8] They also suggest that the monitor keep any profits that are

---

[8]Alchian, A. and H. Demsetz, "Production, Information Costs, and Economic Organization," *American Economic Review*, 62, 1972, pp. 777–797.

left over after paying the other team members, that is, the monitor becomes the owner of the team. This gives the monitor incentives to be a vigilant monitor and to offer fair contracts that encourage hard work while attracting good workers.

Piece Rate Contracts

One of the most common contracts in which pay is based on an easily observed outcome is the *piece rate* contract. A piece rate contract pays a fee for each unit of output. For example, suppose that the owner of a shoe assembly plant wants workers to produce as many shoes as they can. The owner could offer a piece rate contract that pays workers a fee for each fully assembled shoe. This would encourage them to work rapidly, even when the owner does not directly observe their effort.

The appeal of using piece rates to motivate workers is based on a simple behavioral rule:

> When agents are paid a fixed "fee per X," where X may stand for a period of time such as a day, or a unit of output such as pages in a report, and so on, and the fee exceeds the opportunity wage, then agents will work hard to provide X.

Thus, if the shoemaker offers a simple fee-per-shoe contract, workers will work hard to produce as many shoes as possible (until the fee no longer compensates for the time and energy required to work that hard). This may be exactly what the shoemaker desires. On the other hand, the consequences of single-minded dedication to increasing output may be undesirable. For example, if workers work too fast, quality may suffer, driving down demand and possibly increasing costs due to the need to rework defective shoes. In this case, the owner might want to structure the contract to pay on the basis of quality and quantity. For example, the owner could specify that defective shoes would not be paid for. If the owner can identify defects at relatively low cost, this type of contract could be an effective motivator. However, it might be difficult for the shoemaker to verify quality, since it might not be known after the shoe has been worn for a while. If so, compensating workers based on quality would not be feasible. The incentive to skimp on quality that arises under a piece rate is a moral hazard problem that results from hidden actions (the principal cannot verify that the agents are shirking on quality) and imperfect observability (quality is difficult to measure).

The quantity/quality problem associated with piece-rate contracts is related to the situation where the agent is producing two or more goods or services. The agent will allocate time to those goods and services for which the compensation per unit of time is highest. This is easily seen in professional basketball, where players seem to devote more time to perfecting dazzling "slam dunks" than productive, but rather mundane "bounce passes." A comparison of the endorsement opportunities for the leading slam dunkers like Shaquille O'Neill with those for top playmakers like Kevin Johnson helps to explain this allocation of time.

The piece rate may encourage hard work, but it will not generally guarantee the efficient amount of effort. Consider once again the shoe assembly plant. Suppose that the owner makes a profit of $6 for each assembled shoe. Suppose further that if a worker exerts effort e, the number of shoes produced per day equals

$.5e$. It follows that the *marginal contribution* of each additional unit of effort to profit is $.5 \times \$6$ or $\$3$. However, effort is costly—all else equal, most people prefer to work less hard. Specifically, suppose that the cost of effort is $e + .01e^2$. This implies that the marginal cost of effort is $1 + .02e$. The efficient level of effort would equate the marginal contribution of $\$3$ with the marginal cost. This occurs at $e = 100$, with corresponding output of 50 shoes per day. But suppose that the owner pays a piece rate of $\$4$ per shoe. From the worker's perspective, the marginal contribution of effort is $\$2$ per unit of effort. Equating this to marginal cost yields an effort $e = 50$, with corresponding output of 25 shoes per day. The worker's effort is inefficiently low because any piece rate that would leave the owner with a profit does not pay the worker the full benefit of his or her output. Alternate schemes might pay a fixed amount if the worker reaches a production goal (e.g., $\$500$ if the worker produces 100 shoes), or penalize the worker if output is too low. These schemes have problems of their own associated with risk that we discuss later on in this chapter.

Many other problems may arise with "fee per X" contracts, especially when the principal does not know what the optimum output should be. For example, stockbrokers are occasionally charged with "churning"—placing excessive buy and sell orders for their clients to increase their commissions. In a well–known case, prior to 1989, Dun & Bradstreet paid commissions to salespeople whose clients increased their purchases. In 1989, disgruntled clients filed lawsuits alleging that salespeople used deceptive practices to place large orders.[9] To take another example, car owners are normally suspicious of mechanics who recommend major repairs. In another well–known case, Sears auto service centers in California were found to have prescribed unnecessary repairs. One apparent culprit was Sears' reward system—Sears paid service center managers on the basis of total volume of business.

What If the Principal Does Not Know How Much Output to Expect?

The output that a hard-working agent can be expected to produce is called the *performance standard*. Thus far, we have assumed that the principal knows enough to set an appropriate performance standard. But what if the principal knows little about the production process or the conditions under which the agents are working? If the principal relies on the agent to help construct the standard, the agent may use hidden information to convince the principal to set a standard that is too easy to achieve. How then should the principal set the standard when it does not know how much the agents can be expected to produce?

A common performance standard is past productivity. One problem with this standard is that of "regression to the mean." Managers who do exceedingly well today may credit some of their success to good luck. But good luck is unlikely to hold for very long (or it wouldn't be luck), and future performance may continue to be

---

[9]Roberts, J.L., "Credit Squeeze: Dun & Bradstreet Firm Faces Flap Over How It Sells Reports on Businesses," *Wall Street Journal*, March 2, 1989, p. A1.

strong in absolute terms, yet fail to exceed past performance. In light of this, it may be unfair to hold productive workers to standards based on their own past performance. Conversely, poor performers usually suffer from at least a small measure of bad luck. Assuming that their bad luck does not hold, they might be expected to perform better the next year even if they do not work any harder, and a standard based on past performance may be too easy to meet.

Another problem with standards based on past performance is that clever agents can manipulate them. They realize that the harder they work this year, the higher will be next year's standard, a phenomenon known as the "ratchet effect."[10] Anticipation of the ratchet effect gives an agent an incentive to cut back on current effort to make future goals more reachable. For example, American auto manufacturers were accused of dragging their feet in complying with fuel emissions standards in the early 1980s. One explanation is that they feared that early compliance with the standards would lead Congress to "ratchet" the standards upward later on.[11]

Agents may also manipulate the recording of expenses and revenues to give the appearance of steadily improving performance. This occurred at food giant H. J. Heinz during the 1970s.[12] Managers were paid bonuses under a management incentive plan. They received points for achieving personal goals, and were expected to exceed their past year's accomplishments. Some managers manipulated payments to vendors to make it appear that their divisions had maintained growth, enabling them to receive their bonuses.

When more than one agent is performing the same task, the principal might set a relative standard, that is, evaluate agents relative to each other. This is often associated with what are known as *tournaments*, and is described in detail later in this chapter. Rather than evaluate agents relative to the past or to each other, the principal could employ engineering studies (for example, time and motion studies) to objectively determine an appropriate standard.

◆ ◆ ◆ ◆ ◆ ATTITUDES TOWARD RISK AND PERFORMANCE-BASED CONTRACTS

Whether or not the principal can perfectly measure outcomes, its ability to implement a first-best efficient contract may depend on the agent's willingness to assume risk. Often, the productivity of an agent depends on forces that it cannot completely

---

[10]The ratchet effect has been studied by a number of scholars, including Weitzman, M., "The Ratchet Principle and Performance Incentives," *Bell Journal of Economics*, Autumn 1980: 302–308 and Freixas, X., R. Guesnerie, and J. Tirole, "Planning Under Incomplete Information and the Ratchet Effect," *Review of Economic Studies*, 52, 1985: 173–192.

[11]See Yao, D., "Strategic Responses to Automobile Emissions Control: A Game Theoretic Analysis," *Journal of Environmental Management and Policy*, 15, 1988: 419–438.

[12]See H.J. Heinz, "The Administration of Policy (A)," Harvard Business School, Case 9-382-034.

control. Farm workers cannot completely control the size of harvests because they do not control the weather. Medical researchers cannot completely control the rate of discovery of new drugs because they cannot predict whether they will have to deal with side effects. The principal may have a hard time determining if low output is due to shirking or bad luck. Contracts that pay according to measured output may therefore expose agents to unwanted risk, since they may end up receiving low pay for hard work. The cost of forcing the agents to bear risk depends on how *risk averse* they are.

Risk Aversion

We say that an agent is *risk neutral* if he or she is indifferent between a sure thing and a gamble of equal expected value. For example, a risk-neutral individual would be indifferent between a "safe" asset that provided a certain return of $1,000 and a "risky" asset that provided a return of $2,000 with probability .5 and $0 with a probability .5. An agent is *risk averse* if he or she prefers the sure thing (e.g. the "safe" asset in the previous example) to a gamble of equal expected value. An agent is *risk loving* if he or she prefers the gamble. Most individuals are risk averse, as evidenced by purchases of health insurance, auto insurance, and other protections against financial loss.[13] This implies that all else equal, they prefer jobs where their income is assured to jobs where they have the same expected income but their income is at risk.

When agents are risk neutral, we can rank the desirability of risky outcomes by calculating their expected values. However, when they are risk averse, we must use the *expected utility* criterion to rank outcomes. As will be shown below, this involves calculating the utility associated with various monetary outcomes and taking the expected value of these utility numbers to determine an expected utility.

To see how the principal is affected by his or her agent's attitudes toward risk, consider the problem facing the producer of a perishable good employing a Great Lakes shipper to deliver the good across the lakes to market. We will assume that this shipment represents a small portion of the shipper's income, so that the shipper cares about the expected profits from the shipment without regard to risk (i.e., the shipper is risk neutral). If the good can reach the market in just one day, the shipper can sell it for a profit of $20,000. However, because the good is perishable, the producer stands to lose $3,000 per day for each additional day en route. The shipment can be delayed for a variety of factors. Some are directly related to the effort put out by the shipper. These include the attention that the shipper pays to currents and weather conditions, and the speed and care with which goods are transferred to and from the ship. Other factors are beyond the shipper's control. These include the currents, weather, and delays at ports of call caused by other boat traffic. We suppose that all of these factors are unobservable to the producer, who can only observe when the goods reach market.

---

[13]This does imply that individuals will not gamble. Many people enjoy gambling for its own sake, such as casino gambling or playing the lottery, but risk aversion suggests that most would not risk substantial portions of their income in such endeavors.

TABLE 16.1
TIME AND COST OF SHIPPING PERISHABLE GOODS

Days	Probability of Completion: Shipper Works Hard	Cost: Shipper Works Hard	Probability of Completion: Shipper Works Slowly	Cost: Shipper Works Slowly
1	.3	6,000	.1	4,500
2	.5	8,000	.2	6,000
3	.1	10,000	.5	7,500
4	.1	12,000	.2	9,000

Performance-Based Contracts

The producer and shipper both know that the trip can take anywhere from one to four days, with the time depending on the shipper's effort and random chance. Table 16.1 gives the probability of trips of different durations, as well as the shipping costs. In calculating costs, we assume that the shipper's opportunity cost if it gives maximum effort (i.e., "works hard") includes a fixed component of $4,000 and a variable component of $2,000 per day. If the shipper works less hard (i.e., "works slowly"), its opportunity costs are only $3,000 plus $1,500 per day. For example, there is a 30 percent chance that a hard-working shipper would require one day to complete the trip, with costs of $6,000. If the shipper works hard, its *expected* arrival time is two days, and its *expected* costs are $8,000. If the shipper works slowly, its expected total costs will be $7,200, spread out over an average of 2.8 days.

Is it economically efficient for the shipper to work hard? The answer is yes. To see why, it is necessary to compare the value and cost of hard work. Hard work reduces the expected shipping time by .8 days. Recall that each day is worth $3,000 to the producer. Thus, hard work is worth $2,400 (in expected value) to the producer. Given an expected total shipping time of two days, the additional cost of hard work is $1,000 (the difference between the fixed cost of hard work and slow work) plus $1,000 (two times the difference in the daily cost of hard work and slow work), for a total of $2,000. Thus, maximum effort is efficient. Henceforth, we will refer to hard work as efficient, and slow work as shirking.

How can the principal encourage the shipper to work efficiently? Suppose that the principal offered a fee-per-day contract that just covers the shipper's costs: $4,000 plus $2,000 per day. Facing this contract, if the shipper worked efficiently it would make zero economic profits. But the shipper can do better if it chooses to work slowly. By shirking, it would receive a fixed payment of $4,000, which exceeds its fixed costs by $1,000. It would also receive a payment of $2,000 for each day at sea, which exceeds its variable costs by $500 per day. Since the trip is expected to take 2.8 days, the shipper that shirks has an expected payment of $9,600 and expected costs of $7,200, for an expected economic profit of $2,400.

This fee-per-day contract is similar to *cost-based contracts* that are common in public sector procurement, such as in the military and in health care.[14] Under cost-based contracts, the agent is reimbursed for the costs deemed appropriate for producing the desired outcome, plus some prenegotiated profit margin. This provides the agent with several opportunities for shirking. When the agent can take hidden actions, it may make less of an effort to control costs. It might also disguise inputs or manipulate accounting records to make it appear that it has incurred greater costs than it actually has.[15] The federal government uses several techniques to fight these practices. In military procurement, the government maintains "second sources" that can produce the desired product if the principal contractor reports cost overruns. In health care, the government sets a performance standard for hospital costs based on average costs incurred by hospitals across the entire country. Thus, if one hospital increases its costs, it will not receive a commensurate increase in reimbursements.

Continuing with our example, it is obvious that the producer of the perishable good would like to offer a contract that rewards the shipper for arriving as soon as possible (or, punishes the shipper for arriving late). Such a *performance-based contract* makes payment contingent on the agent meeting some prespecified performance objectives. For example, the producer could offer to pay the shipper $10,250 if the shipment arrives in one or two days, and $0 if the shipment takes three days or more. Should the shipper take this contract? If it did, would it take the efficient action?

We can first determine that a risk-neutral shipper would not take this contract if it intended to shirk. Upon shirking, it would have only a 30 percent chance of getting the $10,250 payment, for an expected revenue of $3,075. But its expected costs would be $7,200, and so it would expect to lose money. Thus, this contract has one nice feature from the producer's standpoint—it knows that if the shipper accepts the contract, it will not shirk. But would the shipper take the contract?

---

[14]For a summary of research on defense procurement, see Anton, J. and D. Yao, "Measuring the Effectiveness of Competition in Defense Procurement: A Survey of the Empirical Literature," *Journal of Policy Analysis and Management*, 9, 1990, pp. 60–79.

[15]On the other hand, if an agent has hidden information about its expected production costs, the principal might actually prefer a cost-based contract. The reason is as follows: By making the agent's payment equal to its realized cost plus a fixed fee, the agent's net profit will be independent of its realized production cost. This removes the agent's incentives to misreport information about expected costs, which allows the principal to make better decisions about which products to purchase. When both hidden information and hidden action problems exist, there is a tension between the good information properties and the poor motivation properties of cost-based contracts. The optimal contract under these circumstances often involves partial cost-reimbursement; that is, the agent's payment equals a fixed fee plus a fraction (e.g. 75 percent) of its realized production costs. See Laffont, J. J. and J. Tirole, "Using Cost Observation to Regulate Firms," *Journal of Political Economy*, 94, June 1986, pp. 614–641, or Besanko, D. and D. Baron, "Monitoring, Moral Hazard, and Risk Sharing in Procurement Contracting," *RAND Journal of Economics*, 18, Fall 1987, pp. 509–532.

The contract would appear to be acceptable to the shipper. If it works hard, it has an 80 percent chance of receiving $10,250. This implies an expected payment of $8,200, which exceeds the expected cost of $8,000. A risk-neutral shipper would thus accept the contract and would take the efficient action under it. This contract is very nearly first-best efficient. The shipper takes the efficient action, and expects to receive $200 more than its opportunity cost. (A contract that paid $10,000 for a one- or two-day arrival would be first-best efficient.)

The shipper may not like this contract if it is risk-averse. A risk-averse individual prefers sure things to gambles of equal expected value. Although this contract offers an expected payment of $8,200, the actual payment is a bit of a gamble:

- A 30 percent chance of making $4,250 (i.e., the shipment arrives in 1 day)

- A 50 percent chance of making $2,250 (i.e., the shipment arrives in 2 days)

- A 10 percent chance of losing $10,000 (i.e., the shipment takes 3 days)

- A 10 percent chance of losing $12,000 (i.e., the shipment takes 4 days)

A well-known result in decision theory is that a risk-averse individual will not accept a gamble unless offered a premium above and beyond the expected payment. The producer must offer an expected payment exceeding $8,200 to get a risk-averse shipper to agree to the contract. This additional payment is called the *risk premium*. In Appendix A we work out numerical examples in which the producer must offer a risk premium of $2,000, $4,800, or more. The magnitude of the risk premium depends on the agent's degree of risk aversion. If, for example, the necessary risk premium is $2,000, the producer would have to pay $12,250 in the event of a timely delivery, and $2,000 in the event of a late delivery, compared with $10,250 and $0 when risk was not an issue.

These calculations show that when the principal cannot distinguish poor performance due to shirking from poor performance due to bad luck, a performance-based contract must necessarily impose an element of risk on the agent. To implement this contract, the principal must pay a risk premium above and beyond the payment required to implement the first-best efficient contract. Although the examples in Appendix A rely on utility functions to compute the risk premium, the costs of risk bearing may manifest themselves in other ways. For example, agents may incur influence costs attempting to demonstrate that poor performance resulted from bad luck. Another problem arises when agents grow accustomed to meeting performance criteria, but then fail due to reasons that they believe are unrelated to effort. Conflicts arise when management attempts to enforce the contract. This occurred at DuPont in the early 1990s, when the firm's fibers division failed to meet its growth targets, due in part to the recession, and management withheld bonuses. Workers at the fiber division grew so disgruntled that DuPont raised salaries to compensate for the lost bonuses.

The "Second-Best" Contract

We have seen that the combination of hidden information, hidden actions, and risk aversion can make it impossible for the producer to offer a first-best efficient contract. In the example above, the contract between the shipper and the producer must balance two incompatible elements:

1. A cost-based contract provides the shipper with an incentive to shirk, exposing the producer to unwanted delays.

2. A performance-based contract imposes unwanted risk on the shipper, forcing the producer to pay a risk premium in excess of expected shipping costs.

Fortunately, the producer can avoid this undesirable either-or choice by offering a *risk-sharing* contract that guarantees the shipper some income, but provides enough incentive so that it does not shirk.

The *second-best* contract—so-called because the first-best contract that promotes efficiency without paying a risk premium is unattainable—is the risk-sharing contract that offers the best balancing act from the principal's perspective. Specifically, the second-best contract is the one that maximizes the principal's expected profit subject to the constraints that (1) the contract makes the agent's utility at least as high as it would be if the agent instead pursued its best alternative opportunity; and (2) the contract induces the agent to provide the level of effort the principal most prefers, given the need to compensate the agent to provide that effort. Because it may be costly to motivate the agent to provide effort, the principal may be content to choose a second-best contract that elicits less than the first-best efficient effort level. When this is so, the second-best contract cannot fully eliminate the agency costs associated with hidden actions.

A simple way to represent the second-best contract is as follows:

$$W = A + BX$$

where W is the agent's compensation and X is measured performance (e.g., profit, total output, or quality). The variable A represents the fixed component of the agent's compensation; it is received no matter what the performance measure. The variable B represents the extent to which compensation is tied to performance. The larger is B, the more sensitive the agent's compensation is to performance. If one contract has a higher B than another, we say that the first provides higher-power performance incentives than the second.

The optimal value of B in the second-best contract depends on four factors already encountered, and is summarized in Table 16.2 (for a mathematical derivation of these results, see Appendix B to this chapter):

1. *The agent's risk aversion:* A high-power incentive contract will be very expensive when the agent is highly risk averse because the agent will have to be given a large risk premium to compensate for the risk it bears under an incentive contract that is sensitive to performance. *In general, the more risk averse the agent, the lower the optimal value of B in the second-best contract.*

Table 16.2
Factors Affecting Use of High-Powered Performance Incentives

Factors Favoring High-Powered Performance Incentives	Factors Favoring Low-Powered Performance Incentives
Low Risk Aversion	High Risk Aversion
Low Effort Aversion	High Effort Aversion
High Marginal Contribution of Effort	Low Marginal Contribution of Effort
Relatively Noise-Free Performance Measures	Relatively Noisy Performance Measures

2. *The agent's effort aversion:* An agent is effort averse if its marginal cost of effort is an increasing function of the amount of effort it provides. This does not mean that the agent always wishes not to work, but that the agent's cost of working is rapidly increasing. This would be true, for example, as workers work extra hours to finish a project. The extra time cuts into limited leisure time, and may be highly valued by the agents. If the agent is highly effort averse, it takes a very high-powered incentive contract (i.e., high B) to induce even a little extra effort. Even if the principal makes an offsetting reduction in A, the increase in B is costly, since it raises the required risk premium. This cost is higher for more risk-averse agents. *In general, the more effort averse the agent, the lower the optimal value of B in the second-best contract.*

3. *The marginal contribution of effort to profitability:* If additional effort does not increase the principal's profit much, then it will not be worth introducing high-powered incentives that will only serve to increase the agent's risk. *In general, the lower the marginal contribution of effort to performance, the lower the optimal value of B in the second-best contract.*

4. *The noisiness of the performance measure:* If the performance measure is "noisy"—it does a poor job of tracking the outcome that the principal really cares about—then high-powered performance incentives will impose unwanted risk, necessitating a higher risk premium. *In general, the noisier the performance measure, the lower the optimal value of B in the second-best contract.*

Knowledge of these factors enables the principal to better tailor contracts for different workers under specific conditions. Here are some examples:

1. The profitability of local supermarkets strongly depends on store managers' staffing and pricing decisions (high marginal contribution of effort). Profits are easy to measure at the store level (relatively noise-free performance measure). These features of supermarkets help explain why it makes sense for Stop and Shop and other chains to pay their local store managers on the basis of store profits and losses. By contrast, managers of shifts at fast-food outlets have little control over demand, pricing, and other factors that affect profits. (These are much more affected by national-level policies governing advertising and menu composition.) Although it is possible to measure the profitability of a shift, the

absence of a strong link between effort and profits leads most store owners to pay their shift managers a salary.

2. The total value of the shares of publicly traded firms reflects their expected long-run profitability. Share value is not only a good measure of performance, it is also easily measured. Not surprisingly, chief executive officers and other top executives whose decisions are of critical importance to long-run profitability receive large portions of their incomes in the form of stocks and stock options. In this way, their personal wealth is a direct function of the performance of their firms.

Improving the Principal's Chances: Increasing Observability

If noisy observation of actions and outcomes impedes efficiency, then the principal ought to gain by improving the precision of its observations. Milton Harris and Arthur Raviv have considered how the optimal contract should vary with the precision of monitoring and conclude that less-noisy performance measures lead to higher-powered incentives.[16] They analyze contracts of the form: Pay a high wage (i.e., a wage that exceeds the agent's opportunity cost) if the observed performance exceeds a threshold; dismiss the agent if it does not. They show that when monitoring grows more precise, agents are more willing to tolerate hard-edged contracts, they work harder, fewer are dismissed, and those that are retained accept a lower wage. All of these properties result from the interplay between worker risk aversion and the risk imposed by imperfect monitoring. Harris and Raviv's findings may be summarized as follows:

1. By using precise measures, the principal can reduce the risk premium that must be paid to get agents to accept the contract. This leaves the principal with a higher share of the total output produced by the agent.

2. By using precise measures, the principal can rely on performance-based incentives without exposing the agent to additional income risk. This increases the agent's output.

But even precise performance measures are sometimes insufficient to ensure good outcomes under performance-based incentive contracts. George Baker, Robert Gibbons, and Kevin J. Murphy suggest that objectively verifiable performance measures should be supplemented by subjective measures.[17] They argue that objective measures can be "gamed," that is, workers may devote too much time to improving their performance on these measures, to the detriment of their overall contributions to the firm. Subjective measures of performance may be a useful complement to objective measures to prevent such gamesmanship.

---

[16]Harris, M. and A. Raviv, "Optimal Incentive Contracts with Imperfect Information," *Journal of Economic Theory*, 20, 1979, pp. 231–259.

[17]Baker, G., R. Gibbons, and K. J. Murphy, "Subjective Performance Measures in Optimal Incentive Contracts," Harvard Business School, working paper, 1992.

◆ ◆ ◆ ◆ ◆ LIMITED LIABILITY

Often, the only way to prevent shirking is to impose penalties for poor performance. But this may be difficult when agents have limited liability that restricts the maximum penalty that can be imposed. When this occurs, the principal may have to pay a premium for good performance instead of punishing bad performance. In this way, the agent's limited liability works to the principal's disadvantage.

Using Penalties to Punish Shirking

In the shipping example, the first-best efficient contract is not feasible if the agent is risk averse, but it can be implemented if the agent is risk neutral. That contract would take the following form: The shipper receives a substantial payment if it delivers the produce in only one or two days, but is penalized if the shipment takes longer. The form of this contract—the agent expects to earn more if its performance is above average than if its performance is below average—characterizes a first-best efficient contract in which pay is based on performance. This is so for two reasons. First, the agent must get paid more for good outcomes than bad, or else it will shirk. Second, the agent must lose money (relative to its opportunity cost) in the event of poor performance, or else the expected payment by the principal exceeds the agent's opportunity cost.

If the agent is risk neutral, then the principal can use penalties to implement the first-best efficient contract. A rule of thumb regarding the use of penalties is as follows: If shirking increases the probability of an undesirable outcome, then a contract that severely penalizes that outcome will provide a disincentive for shirking. Continuing the shipping example, the principal could pay the agent $20,000 in the event of a delivery in three days or less, and impose a penalty of $100,000 in the event of a four-day delivery. If the shipper took the contract, it would not work slowly, for this would give it a 20 percent chance of paying the penalty and a negative overall expected profit. If it takes the contract and works hard, it gets an expected payment of $8,000, which just equals its opportunity cost. Since the payment just equals the opportunity cost, and the agent takes the efficient action, the contract is first-best efficient.

But what if the shipper lacks the wealth to pay such a large penalty? We say that an agent who is unable to pay large penalties has *limited liability*. Limited liability is a key feature of corporate law.[18] Stockholders of a firm are not liable for more than they invest in a firm. If, for example, a shareholder buys $100 worth of stock in a firm, the shareholder puts that $100 at risk, but no more. The shareholder would not be forced to pay out of its personal wealth if the corporation defaults on its debts or is assessed a large penalty for violating the law or breaching a contract.

---

[18]See Easterbrook, F. and D. Fischel, *The Economic Structure of Corporate Law*, Cambridge, MA: Harvard University Press, 1991, for a discussion of this point.

One way a company can attempt to limit its liability is by declaring bankruptcy. Texaco followed this course in 1987 when faced with the prospect of paying $10 billion in damages to Pennzoil. Pennzoil had lost to Texaco in a battle to acquire Getty Oil in 1984, after reaching what it believed was a binding agreement with the directors of Getty to sell the company to Pennzoil. As part of the deal with Getty, Texaco agreed to indemnify Getty's directors against any lawsuits stemming from the sale, so when Pennzoil sued Getty for breach of contract, Texaco became liable for damages. The jury's decision to award $10 billion in actual and punitive damages was widely criticized in the press, but following numerous appeals to both Texas and federal courts, the award was upheld. After Texaco entered bankruptcy in 1987, Pennzoil and Texaco commenced negotiations to limit the size of the penalty, and in December 1987, reached agreement for Texaco to pay only $3 billion to Pennzoil.

When the penalty necessary to deter shirking exceeds the amount that the agent can pay, the principal may not be able to implement the first-best efficient contract. To see why, we will reconsider the shipping example, using somewhat different costs and arrival times. Suppose the costs and arrival times are as reported in Table 16.3. Suppose further that each day that the shipment remains at sea costs the producer $25,000. This implies that it is efficient for the shipper to work hard to assure a one-day delivery.

If the agent has unlimited liability, then the following contract is first-best efficient: The producer pays the shipper $10,000 if the shipment takes one day, but if the shipment takes two days, the shipper must pay a $10,000 penalty. The shipper is sure to recover its opportunity costs if it works hard. But if it shirks, then half of the time the shipment will arrive in one day, and it will receive revenue of $10,000 less costs of $1,000, for a profit of $9,000. The other half of the time the shipment will arrive in two days, and it will pay a penalty of $10,000 as well as incur costs of $1,000, for a loss of $11,000. This implies an expected loss of $1,000. Thus, even if the shipper is risk neutral, it will prefer to work hard. If it is risk averse, it will be even less inclined to work slowly.

In this example, the penalty is the key to achieving first-best efficiency. To get the shipper to take the efficient action—to prevent shirking—the producer must make the shipper willing to bear the higher costs of hard work. To see how strong these incentives must be, let P represent the probability that a shirking shipper will complete the shipment in two days. (One can think of P as the probability that the

TABLE 16.3
TIME AND COST OF SHIPPING PERISHABLE GOODS

Days	Probability of Completion: Shipper Works Hard	Cost: Shipper Works Hard	Probability of Completion: Shipper Works Slowly	Cost: Shipper Works Slowly
1	1.0	10,000	.5	1,000
2	0	—	.5	1,000

producer will find out that the shipper is shirking, because if the shipment takes two days, the producer knows for sure that the shipper has shirked.) Let C be the additional cost to the shipper of working hard. To assure that the shipper does not shirk, the producer must pay at least C/P more for a one-day shipment than for a two-day shipment. In our example, $P = .50$ and $C = \$9,000$, so the producer must pay the shipper at least $18,000 more for a one-day delivery than for a two-day delivery. There are many ways to do this: for example, the shipper could pay $40,000 for a one-day delivery and $22,000 for a two-day delivery. By paying the shipper exactly the $10,000 opportunity cost of working hard, and extracting an $8,000 or higher penalty for shirking, the producer pays the minimum necessary to achieve the efficient outcome, thereby achieving first-best efficiency.

Efficiency Wages

The producer cannot implement the first-best efficient contract unless it can force the shipper to pay the penalty if the shipment takes two days. Otherwise, the shipper will ignore the threat of the penalty and conclude that it is better off shirking. The most that the producer can collect in the event of a two-day shipment is the shipper's net worth. For example, if the shipper's net worth is $3,000, then this is the largest penalty that the producer can hope to collect. To assure that the shipper works hard, the producer will need to pay $18,000 − $3,000 = $15,000 in the event of a one-day delivery, and collect a penalty of $3,000 in the event of a two-day delivery. This implies that the producer will pay a hard-working shipper $15,000 for sure, which exceeds the shipper's opportunity cost by $5,000.

This example shows that when the agent has limited liability, the principal may have to pay the agent more than its opportunity cost to prevent shirking. This payment is called an *efficiency wage*. Curt Eaton and William D. White, and Carl Shapiro and Joseph Stiglitz proposed the idea of efficiency wages to help explain why employers do not lower wages of their employees, even when there are many qualified job applicants willing to work for less.[19] As in the shipping example, Shapiro and Stiglitz suppose that agents can either choose to work hard or shirk. Agents have an opportunity wage W^* that they can earn in their next-best employment opportunity, and they cannot be forced to pay a penalty to the principal. In a perfectly competitive labor market with no agency considerations, the principal would pay no more than W^* to its workers. Now suppose a worker shirks. The principal could fire the worker, but if work can quickly be obtained elsewhere, the worker will have lost no wages and will have benefited from not having worked too hard. The principal could try to make the worker pay a fine, but many agents have limited ability to pay fines, and contracts that extract fines from fired workers are illegal. (If penalties were allowed, employers could fire workers arbitrarily, or

---

[19]Eaton, B. C. and W. D. White, "Agent Compensation and the Limits of Bonding," *Economic Inquiry*, 20, July 1982, pp. 330–343. Shapiro, C. and J. Stiglitz, "Equilibrium Unemployment as a Worker Disciplining Device," *American Economic Review*, 74, June 1984, pp. 433–444.

manipulate evaluations, just to extract the fine.) The remaining option for the principal is to make the worker want to keep the job. The principal can do this by paying a wage $W > W^*$, that is, the principal pays an efficiency wage W that exceeds the opportunity wage. By paying an efficiency wage, the principal "punishes" the worker who is caught shirking. Even if employment is found at the opportunity wage, the worker still loses $W - W^*$.

If we let P represent the probability that the principal catches a shirking worker, and C the additional cost to the worker of working hard, then the principal can prevent shirking by setting $W > W^* + C/P$.[20] It might be more realistic to suppose that a fired worker would have a hard time finding another job. The fired worker who cannot find employment at wage W^* might instead have to settle for unemployment compensation $W' < W^*$. Suppose that the probability of finding another job is Q. To prevent shirking, the principal must pay a wage W that is at least as large as $W' + Q(W^* - W') + C/P$.[21] According to this inequality, the efficiency wage is larger: (1) the lower the probability P of detecting shirking, (2) the higher the cost C to the agent of working hard, (3) the higher the wage W^* that the agent can get from another job, (4) the higher the probability Q that the fired agent can find another job, and (5) the higher the unemployment compensation W'.

The principal can take several steps to reduce the wage it must pay to assure hard work. The principal can invest in accounting and other monitoring practices to increase its chances of detecting shirking. It can carefully document instances of shirking, so that when a prospective new employer of the shirking agent calls for references, it can make a convincing case that the agent was, in fact, shirking. Finally, it can reduce the costs of working hard, for example, by offering catered dinners to employees who work late. All of these efforts to eliminate shirking can be costly. Chapter 18 introduces what many strategists believe is a less costly means of assuring hard work—establishing a consistent and supportive corporate culture.

Sorting

Thus far, we have said little about the characteristics of the agent that works for the principal. In our discussion and examples, there is a single agent, and the principal uses a contract to motivate that agent to work hard. In reality, the principal may

---

[20]To see that this is correct, suppose that $C = 10$. Thus, the worker always gains 10 by shirking. But if caught, it stands to lose $W - W^*$. If $P = 1$, then the worker is always caught. The firm must pay 10 more than the opportunity wage to convince the worker not to shirk. If $P = .5$, then the shirking worker stands to lose $W - W^*$ only half the time. Thus, $W - W^*$ must equal 20 for the worker to be indifferent between shirking and working hard. As P decreases, the chances of getting caught fall, and $W - W^*$ must increase further to discourage shirking.

[21]The worker receives unemployment compensation W' with probability Q, and wage W^* with probability $1 - Q$. Thus, the worker receives expected compensation $QW' + (1 - Q)W^*$. This can be rearranged to $W' + Q(W^* - W')$. In addition, the worker must receive C/P to discourage shirking.

have many agents to choose from, who may possess different abilities and motives. Some may have more skills; others may have stronger work ethics. Depending on the nature of the contract, the principal may attract different types of agents, but would obviously like to attract hard-working, highly skilled agents. When the level of wages or structure of the incentive contract systematically influences the characteristics of the agents a principal can hire, we say that *sorting* occurs.

Job sorting is a common phenomenon. Sometimes workers sort themselves according to their values. For example, Myron Roomkin and Burt Weisbrod argue that some individuals are willing to accept lower pay to work at charitable institutions, and this allows many nonprofit organizations to attract top talent without paying top salaries.[22] Workers sort themselves by skill as well. Firms like Microsoft, Cray Research, and 3M are well known for attracting the brightest talent. Some of this is due to idiosyncratic factors that are hard to duplicate; for example, computer hardware designers wanted to work with the eccentric Seymour Cray, and software designers wanted to work with Bill Gates and his staff. But the explicit and implicit reward structure of the firm can also attract the right kinds of workers.

How does the type of contract affect sorting? The following rules of thumb are useful:

- More able workers and risk takers prefer pay-for-performance contracts.
- Workers with low mobility are more tolerant of schemes that link pay to job tenure. As discussed in the next section, this could affect internal labor markets.
- Agents (firms or workers) with limited liability are more willing to accept contracts that provide larger rewards for success and large penalties for failure.

Clearly, managers must account for sorting when designing agency contracts. For example, universities know that tenure policies focusing exclusively on research will not only encourage existing faculty to spend most of their time doing research, but will also tend to attract new faculty who perceive themselves to be skilled researchers.

◆ ◆ ◆ ◆ ◆ INTERNAL LABOR MARKETS

All workers within a firm, from top management on down, may pursue objectives that are incompatible with maximizing the firm's profits. However, agency problems may be more severe for some kinds of workers than for others. Employers can easily observe the performance of some workers, such as copy-room workers and janitors, and can easily replace them if they shirk too much. Peter Doeringer and Michael Piore described these workers as being in the *secondary sector* of the economy.[23] Agency concerns in the secondary sector are minimal. Firms use short-term contracts to govern these employment relationships. Wages are fully deter-

---

[22]Roomkin, M. and B. Weisbrod, "Managerial Compensation in For-profit and Nonprofit Hospitals: Is There a Difference?" Northwestern University, working paper 1994.

mined by market forces, with few if any pay-for-performance provisions. Employers find it more challenging to evaluate workers in the *primary sector*, including most skilled workers and professionals. These workers tend to stay in a single firm for many years. Their contributions to firm profits are significant, but their individual outputs are more difficult to measure. Comparisons with workers at other firms for purposes of setting wages are difficult due to the specialized nature of their work and their firm-specific knowledge.

Firms frequently rely on *internal labor markets* to solve agency problems for managers and professionals in the primary sector. The internal labor market consists of an employer and a group of employees organized around a functional area (e.g., accounting), geographic area, or product. In an internal labor market, the employer relies heavily on *implicit contracts* to solve agency problems. Rather than specify output-based rewards, such as a fixed fee for producing a strategic plan, the employer lets its employees know that those who add value will be rewarded with opportunities for higher wages, promotion, and end-of-year bonuses.

Ideally, the firm would wish to pay its workers according to the value they create. This would motivate workers to add value, while reducing payment to those workers who add little value (and whose jobs may be unnecessary as a result). Firms do this explicitly for some workers, for example, salespeople in many industries are paid commissions. There are several problems with paying other types of workers according to value added, however. First, it is often difficult for firms to determine value added. Second, some workers, such as those on assembly lines, may have jobs that are easy to describe but would be costly to consistently monitor. Finally, it is sometimes difficult to precisely measure the output of workers, especially managers and professionals. For example, how does one determine the value added of a strategic plan or of a new engineering design?

Backloading Compensation

We say that compensation is *backloaded* if wages are below productivity early on, but exceed productivity with seniority. Backloaded compensation is exemplified by the *wage/tenure profile*.

The Wage/Tenure Profile

One of the most distinctive features of internal labor markets is the sharply rising "wage/tenure" profile, as depicted in Figure 16.1.[24] At most firms, wages increase with job tenure. A simple explanation is provided by *human capital* theory. Human capital is the knowledge and skills (physical and intellectual) that an individual

---

[23]Doeringer, P. and M. Piore, *Internal Labor Markets and Manpower Analysis*, Lexington, MA: D.C. Heath, 1971.

[24]For a review of research on the wage/tenure profile, see Hutchens, R., "Seniority, Wages, and Productivity: A Turbulent Decade," *Journal of Economic Perspectives*, 3, 1989, pp. 49–64, and Carmichael, H. L., "Self-enforcing Contracts, Shirking, and Life-cycle Effects," *Journal of Economic Perspectives*, 3, 1989, pp. 65–84.

possesses that make that individual a productive worker. The increasing wage/tenure profile could simply represent an increase in productivity over time. Gary Becker has suggested that workers might accept very low wages early in their careers if they receive on-the-job training that enhances their productivity and job opportunities later on.[25] This story is consistent with the relatively low wages earned by medical residents, law clerks, and bank trainees, for example.

Certainly, increases in human capital help explain part of the wage/tenure profile. But this fails to explain three other important features of internal labor markets. First, until recent federal legislation made them largely illegal, many U.S. firms had mandatory retirement policies. Second, many pension plans offer a higher rate of return to employees who retire early. These two facts imply that firms appear to prefer younger workers to older workers, a preference that is incompatible with the view that older workers are more productive. Finally, James Medoff and Katherine Abraham have shown that wages increase with job tenure even if performance does not.[26] This is shown in Figure 16.2. In other words, wages are *backloaded*, so that workers are paid less than what they are worth to the firm early in their tenure and more than what they are worth late in their tenure. This helps explain why firms may prefer younger workers to older workers—the firm is overpaying older workers relative to their productivity. But why do firms backload wages? The answer may be found in agency theory.

Figure 16.1
The wage-tenure profile.

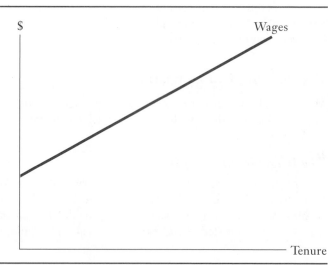

Wages tend to increase with job tenure. This may reflect increased productivity of older workers, or it may be tied to incentives.

[25]Becker, G., "Investment in Human Capital: A Theoretical Analysis," *Journal of Political Economy*, 70, 1962, pp. 9–49.

[26]Medoff, J. and K. Abraham, "Experience, Performance, and Earnings," *Quarterly Journal of Economics*, 95, 1980, pp. 703–736.

FIGURE 16.2
BACKLOADED COMPENSATION.

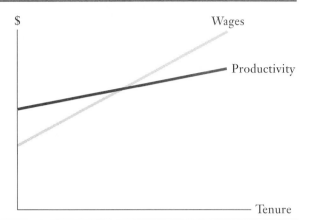

Wages tend to increase faster than productivity. For many workers, wages do not exceed productivity until they have been on the job for several years. Backloaded compensation may be useful for preventing shirking by younger workers.

Agency Explanations for Backloaded Wages

Gary Becker, George Stigler, and Edward Lazear have argued that firms may not be able to sufficiently punish workers to prevent them from shirking.[27] At most, firms can fire workers, who may then collect unemployment compensation or find another job. To prevent shirking, firms offer deferred compensation as a kind of performance guarantee, or "bond." To receive the bond, workers must avoid getting laid off, and thus do not shirk. This explanation is closely related to efficiency wage theory, in which agents have limited liability, so the promise of above-market wages in their present job deters shirking. Here, the promise of above-market wages in future years deters shirking.

A steep wage/tenure profile may also facilitate the development of firm-specific assets. Many firms train workers to perform specialized tasks—training that has little or no value should the workers leave. This training is costly to firms. In addition, the firm must tolerate low productivity by new workers until they move down the learning curve. Firms that make such investments would naturally like their workers to remain with the firm for a long time. A steep profile encourages such loyalty.

Robert Hutchens points out that workers who make firm-specific investments may be reluctant to accept a steep profile.[28] The firm could lay off the workers and thereby avoid paying wages in excess of productivity. The workers, whose skills are firm-specific, might have a difficult time finding other employment. H. Lorne

[27]Becker, G. and G. Stigler, "Law Enforcement and Compensation of Enforcers," *Journal of Legal Studies*, 3, 1974, pp. 1–18; Lazear, E., "Why is There Mandatory Retirement?" *Journal of Political Economy*, 87, 1979, pp. 1261–1284.

[28]Hutchens, R., "Seniority, Wages, and Productivity: A Turbulent Decade," *Journal of Economic Perspectives*, 3, 1989, pp. 49–64.

Carmichael argues that firms must rely on implicit contracts and long-term relationships to convince employees to accept specific training.[29] These ideas are closely tied to the concepts developed in Chapter 18 on organizational culture.

If the wage/tenure profile serves as a carrot to reward hard work and investments in training, then increased labor market turnover may have a pernicious effect on effort. We have already discussed in Chapters 3 and 6 how these ideas have shaped thinking about the implications of corporate takeovers for the relationship between firms and workers. Recall from Example 3.3 Andrei Shleifer and Lawrence Summers' argument that an outside raider can abrogate implicit wage agreements. This would allow the raider to reduce the wages paid to employees with longer tenure. Since these employees' skills are firm specific, they may have to accept the lower wages. Corporate restructurings and downsizing in the absence of takeovers may have the same effect with alarming consequences for long-term productivity. Workers with little tenure may perceive that they are unlikely to keep their jobs long enough to climb up the wage/tenure profile. This may reduce incentives to work hard and make firm-specific investments.

Bonuses, Promotions, and Tournaments

Most workers receive some kind of annual performance evaluation, depending on which they may receive a wage increase of varying size. The increase is generally small, however, and the difference between what the best performers and average performers receive can be very small. Table 16.4 summarizes compensation information compiled by the HayGroup.[30] The table reports average pay increases between 1993–1994 based on end-of-year evaluation scores in leading U.S. industrial firms. Top performers received wage hikes of just 7 percent. More significantly, the difference in wage hikes between top performers and satisfactory performers was just 3 percent.

TABLE 16.4
AVERAGE ACTUAL MERIT INCREASES

Performance Level	Percentage Increase in Wages: 1993–1994
Highest	7.0%
Next to highest	5.0%
Fully satisfactory	4.0%
Lowest with Increase Permitted	2.0%

[29]Carmichael, H. L., "Self-enforcing Contracts, Shirking, and Life Cycle Effects," *Journal of Economic Perspectives*, 3, 1989, pp. 65–84.

[30]*The Hay Report: Compensation and Benefits Strategies for 1995 and Beyond*, HayGroup, 1995.

While the data in Table 16.3 suggest that firms use pay-for-performance methods, the modest 3 percent differential between top and average workers does not seem like a large enough incentive for hard work. Many firms rely on two additional techniques to motivate workers: bonuses and promotion.

Bonuses

In 1993, *Fortune* magazine ran an article that cited a Hewitt Associates survey of 2,000 U.S. companies showing that the percentage of salaried workers eligible to receive bonuses increased from 47 percent in 1988 to 68 percent in 1993.[31] During that time, the average bonus increased from 3.9 percent of base salary to 5.9 percent. The HayGroup reports even higher percentages—bonuses represent 7 percent of base salary for entry-level professionals and 14 to 23 percent of base salary for middle and advanced managers.

Bonuses increase the degree to which pay is tied to performance. As we have discussed, this increases the incentives to work hard. However, when a buyer fraction of an employee's compensation is accounted for by bonuses, the employee faces greater income risk. Why have bonuses gained in popularity in recent years? One possibility is that workers are growing less risk averse. This could be occurring because more and more workers have spouses who also work, so that the amount of the bonus as a percentage of household income may be relatively unchanged from years ago, even as the size of the bonus is increasing in nominal terms.

A second explanation is that firms are growing more sophisticated at measuring performance, therefore reducing the risk that a hard worker will be punished. Bonus pay is usually linked to one of three measures: firm performance, business unit performance, or individual performance. Ideally, the firm would like to base the bonus on individual performance, but this is often difficult to measure. Business unit performance is also a useful measure, especially for those workers who have responsibility for their unit's decision making. Improvements in activity-based accounting facilitate the measurement of individual and business unit performance, enhancing the effectiveness of pay-for-performance schemes.

In recent years, firms have linked bonuses to the development of individual skills, as exemplified by the completion of graduate education or attendance at training programs. These relatively risk-free compensation schemes may promote worker productivity, or could be a useful sorting mechanism (workers willing to pursue a graduate degree may have more innate ability than workers reluctant to do so). Some schemes reward less quantifiable skills, such as "flexibility" and "consumer-service orientation." While these can be important, they are also difficult to measure and may introduce unwanted subjectivity.

For bonus schemes to be fully effective, firms must avoid the temptation to renege on them. The difficulty of precisely measuring individual worker performance enables firms to falsely lower their performance evaluations across the board to avoid paying bonuses. However, the firm that is perceived as lying about per-

---

[31]Tully, S., "Your Paycheck Gets Exciting," *Fortune*, November 1, 1993, pp. 84.

formance evaluations today may be unable to use them to motivate workers in the future. Use of verifiable measures, such as firm-level performance, reduces the possibility that firms will misrepresent performance, but minimize the link between bonus and individual performance.

Promotions

James Emshoff, an expert on corporate restructuring, observes that the hierarchical firm offers opportunities for promotion unavailable in "flat firms" with few layers of hierarchy.[32] The possibility of promotion serves as another carrot to motivate workers. There are many job levels in a typical hierarchical firm. Federal government workers progress through a series of 16 "GS" ranks, where promotion is based on job responsibility, performance evaluation, and educational attainment. Private firms may have as many as eight job levels or more. Within each level may be several salary grades. The number of positions at each successively higher job level usually declines as one goes up the corporate ladder. George Baker, Michael Gibbs, and Bengt Holmstrom (BGH) examined the hierarchy at one firm with nearly 5,000 employees.[33] They found that there were eight levels, but that only 116 (2 percent) of the workers were in one of the top four levels.

"Promotions" usually involve movement through higher salary grades and levels. The Hay Group reports that for 1992–1993, the average wage increase for workers in industrial firms who receive a promotion to a higher salary grade was around 10 percent.[34] This exceeds the wage differential between the top performers and bottom performers who remain in the same level. The possibility of promotion and the attendant salary increases undoubtedly help motivate workers. In the firm that they examined, BGH confirmed that wage differences across levels served to reward ability; in other words, more highly skilled workers were rewarded through promotions up the corporate hierarchy.

Like the one studied by BGH, most firms have fewer and fewer positions as one moves up the hierarchy.[35] This implies that not all workers at any given level will be promoted to the next level. The notion of promoting the hardest-working and most able workers has been likened to athletic *tournaments*, in which individu-

---

[32]Emshoff, J., "Is It Time to Create a New Theory of the Firm?" *Journal of Economics and Management Strategy*, 2, 1993, pp. 3–14.

[33] Baker, G., M. Gibbs, and B. Holmstrom, "The Wage Policy of a Firm," Harvard Business School, working paper, 1993.

[34]*The Hay Group Compensation and Benefits Strategies for 1994 and Beyond* (HayGroup, 1994).

[35]An interesting exception is academics. At many schools, including Northwestern, there are comparable numbers of tenured and untenured professors. The untenured professors are generally not in a tournament. If all the untenured professors under review exceed a historically determined standard, then all may receive tenure. Conversely, if none are performing well enough, none may receive tenure. Tenure may be viewed as a kind of "pay-for-performance" system.

als and teams are ranked relative to other competitors.[36] Promotion tournaments work in much the same way—a worker earns rewards by outperforming coworkers and moving up the hierarchy. Tournaments can be effective at reducing shirking and in attracting highly skilled workers seeking rewards for their talents.

If firms could accurately evaluate individual worker performance, there would be no need for tournaments. Firms would simply follow the contracting principals laid out earlier in this chapter. Tournaments are useful when relative performance is easier to measure than absolute performance. In a well-known application of this idea, the fictional real estate salesmen in the play *Glengarry Glen Ross* competed to see who would be among the top three in sales. The rest would be fired. This scheme rewards hard work and ability (although it does not promote teamwork!). More importantly, it is easier to design and implement than a scheme that rewarded each worker based on absolute performance. Such a scheme would require that the owner of the firm know how much each salesperson could be expected to sell, and then compare actual and expected sales. Actual sales is a function of effort, but also of the overall economy, of the product being sold, and of other factors beyond the control of any individual salesperson. Thus, this scheme introduces much risk. A tournament eliminates much of this risk. Firmwide fluctuations in sales affect all salespersons equally. Their relative performance remains largely a function of their own effort and ability and is therefore a less noisy measure.

H. Lorne Carmichael points out that tournaments may be useful even when firms can measure absolute performance.[37] Suppose that a firm offers a bonus or a chance for promotion to its best-performing workers (and offers baseline wages below opportunity costs to hold down total compensation). If the bonus is high enough, all workers will work hard even if only some receive it. An interesting feature of this scheme is that, unlike pay-for-performance schemes based on absolute performance, the firm has no incentive to lie about its performance measures, since it will pay the bonus no matter what. Carmichael points out that with such a tournament the firm need not have an established career ladder to promote hard work—the tournament promotes hard work by contract. This allows even young and relatively unprofitable firms without a proven reputation for rewarding older workers to create incentives for hard work.

Though widespread in business, tournaments do have potential drawbacks. They are subject to influence costs, as workers try to convince their bosses that they deserve a high relative ranking. Workers may collude to reduce output, without any reduction in overall compensation. Even worse, they may deliberately sabotage the efforts of others. This was a frequent allegation made against premed students in the 1970s who perceived admission to medical school to be a tournament.

---

[36]For further discussion of labor market tournaments, see Edward Lazear and Sherwin Rosen, "Rank Order Tournaments as Optimal Labor Contracts," *Journal of Political Economy*, 89, 1981, pp. 841–864.

[37]Carmichael H. L., "Self-enforcing Contracts, Shirking, and Life Cycle Incentives," *Journal of Economic Perspectives*, 3, 1989, pp. 65–84.

✦ ✦

$\mathcal{E}$XAMPLE 16.4

MOTIVATING SECONDARY SECTOR WORKERS WITH PROMOTIONS: SERVICEMASTER

ServiceMaster Industries contracts with health care providers, schools, and industry to manage their housekeeping, foodservice, laundry, and other relatively unskilled employees. With annual revenues well in excess of $2 billion, and an annual growth rate of 10 to 20 percent, it is regarded as a remarkable and wholly unexpected success story. An important part of ServiceMaster's success is its human resources management policy.

In the 1950s, ServiceMaster recognized that hospital administrators preferred to "buy" rather than "make" management functions pertaining to low-level activities such as housekeeping. ServiceMaster provided on-site management support and promised to boost productivity. Although ServiceMaster developed new products and techniques (including novel techniques for mopping floors), it considered its employees its greatest asset, and used a number of techniques to motivate them. Employees were treated like family, and it was not unusual for top management to devote personal attention to the personal problems of lower-level workers. The company also used financial incentives, including bonuses and generous pay hikes. In addition, roughly three-fourths of the firm's associates held stock in the company.

But the greatest motivational tool at ServiceMaster is its promotional ladder. Most of ServiceMaster's managers began their careers in the secondary economy, as foodservice workers, housekeepers, and so on. Workers (known as "field managers") can advance up a career path with eight levels, from "employee" to "division manager." Promotion opportunities begin even earlier—nearly 20 percent of management trainees are hired from the ranks of support staff that ServiceMaster is contracted to supervise. The company's sustained growth had made the promotional ladder an effective motivating tool—workers at all levels, including those still employed by ServiceMaster's clients, correctly perceived that there were significant opportunities for promotion as long as they work hard. ServiceMaster further rewards top workers with support for educational programs ranging from literacy training to college education. The hard work of ServiceMaster employees has made the company a huge success.

A promotional ladder can motivate workers only if they believe that the opportunities for promotion are genuine. With this in mind, ServiceMaster faces two problems as it strives to sustain its success. First, it must continue to grow to assure ever more opportunities for promotion. To maintain its growth strategy, it has acquired a lawn care business and expanded overseas. But as viable growth opportunities dry up, the company will be unable to maintain its historic rate of promotion. Second, the promotional ladder ends at division manager. Workers moved up this ladder are usually unable to advance to the central office, whose employees are often recruited from business schools. ServiceMaster has been reluctant to expand the responsibilities of managers promoted through the ranks, but must still find a way to motivate them. Both of these problems may reduce the motivating force of the promotional ladder in years to come.

Executive Compensation

Ice cream maker Ben and Jerry's is well known for its executive compensation policy— the higher paid executives make no more than five times the salary of the lowest paid employees. Ben and Jerry's is an exception, however, and top executives at most American companies can make salaries that are nearly one hundred times those of their lowest paid employees. While some criticize these seemingly bloated salaries, others point out that such high salaries are necessary for motivational purposes. One reason for high salaries is the promotional tournament—high executive compensation motivates middle managers seeking to advance up the corporate ladder. As a worker moves up the ladder, opportunities for further promotion diminish, and the increment in wages between successive promotions increases. For example, Table 16.5 reports the number of positions for which salaries were reported and average salary in the eight management job levels of the firm studied by Baker, Gibbs, and Holmstrom.

As the table shows, there are few positions at the top of the ladder. Of 3,300 management positions, only 74 (2.2 percent) were in levels 5 or higher. At the same firm, pay increments jumped as workers moved to higher levels. Level 2 workers earn an average of $7,000 more than level 1 workers (a 21 percent pay hike to a level 1 worker). In contrast, the differential between levels 4 and 5 is $46,000 (a 67 percent pay hike to a level 4 worker). Salary differences increase even more dramatically at the top of the hierarchy. If the firm uses the corporate ladder to motivate workers, then such huge salary increments are essential. When opportunities for promotion are small (as they are at this firm), owners must promise workers significant financial rewards from promotion or else workers will not feel that the effort to get promoted is worthwhile. (The alternative is to continue to promote lots of workers, leading to a top-heavy organization.)

TABLE 16.5
SALARY INCREASES UP THE PROMOTIONAL LADDER

Job Level	Positions	Average Salary
8	1	$502,000
7	3	$328,000
6	14	$165,000
5	56	$115,000
4	574	$69,000
3	819	$49,000
2	889	$40,000
1	944	$33,000

This tells only part of the executive compensation story. In addition to the lure of moving up the ladder and the associated substantial pay raises, executives also receive bonuses. According to the HayGroup, in large companies (companies with annual revenue of $2 billion or more), the chief executive officer's (CEO's) bonus may be as large as 50 to 70 percent of his or her base salary.

Perhaps the most important component of executive compensation comes in the form of stocks and stock options. Stock options enable the holder to buy stock in a company at a predetermined price. If, say, you hold an option to buy Microsoft's stock at a price of $60 per share, and the current price of the stock is $50 per share, you would have no reason to exercise the option. But suppose the price of the stock increases to $70. Then you could purchase those shares for $60 each and resell them immediately for $70.

Suppose, now, you own a company whose market value is currently $50 per share, and you hire a manager to help increase the value of the company. You could give the manager shares in the company, and this would certainly provide some motivation for the manager to work hard to increase the value of the company. But if value does not increase, the manager can still sell the shares. If instead you give the manager options to buy stock at $60 a share, then not only is the manager motivated to increase value, but the options are worthless if value does not increase. Thus, the stock options put the manager at greater risk for failing to increase value. Many people believe that this makes stock options a powerful motivator. The HayGroup reports that in the largest firms, stock options and similar long-term incentives are comparable in size to base salary.

If salaries, bonuses, and stock options truly motivate performance, then executive compensation should increase when firms do better, and decrease when firms do poorly. Michael Jensen and Kevin J. Murphy measured the relationship between executive compensation and firm performance.[38] They examined salaries, bonuses, and stock options of CEOs as reported in *Forbes'* "Executive Compensation Surveys" from 1974 to 1986. They found that at the typical firm, the CEO's salary and bonus were not very responsive to firm performance. Specifically, they found that a CEO whose shareholders lost $400 million in a single year would earn an average of $800,000 in salary and bonus, whereas a CEO whose shareholders gained $400 million would earn $1,040,000 in salary and bonus. Thus, an $800 million swing in firm performance was associated with a $204,000 swing in salary. Jensen and Murphy question whether such an income differential can provide proper motivation. On the other hand, they found that stocks and stock options do provide some motivation. The same $800 million swing in performance was associated with a $1.2 million swing in the value of stocks and options. Finally, Jensen and Murphy found that CEOs are dismissed so infrequently that the threat of dismissal is not an important motivator.

---

[38]Jensen, M. and K. J. Murphy, "Performance Pay and Top Management Incentives," *Journal of Political Economy*, 98, 1990, pp. 225–264.

Jensen and Murphy's findings have prompted much debate about the appropriate level of executive compensation in the United States. Some feel that CEOs are vastly overpaid relative to their employees, and that fairness dictates that they get paid less. Others feel that CEOs are underpaid because they have too little money at personal stake relative to the sizes of their companies. Using Jensen and Murphy's findings, the variability in a CEO's income is only 2 percent as large as the variability in the company's income. Many believe that if the CEO is largely responsible for company performance, he or she should have a bigger personal stake in the company's gains and losses. In an era of golden parachutes (large cash buyouts of CEOs who are replaced before the end of their contracts), CEOs may indeed face inadequate incentives to maximize shareholder value.

Recently, Richard Ippolito and others have shown that the relationship between performance and compensation may be more complex than previously thought.[39] These researchers study the flow of funds into mutual funds, but their findings are relevant for executive compensation. They find that funds do not attract new investors unless they significantly outperform the market, and they do not lose current investors unless they significantly underperform the market. Figure 16.3 shows this "flow-performance relationship." Now consider the manager of a fund that is at point A, with performance P_A and a flow of funds F_A. Suppose this manager makes a risky investment. The upside gain in the event of a successful investment would be to move the fund to B. The fund would gain $F_B - F_A$ customers. On the other hand, if the fund failed, the fund would move to point C. By the nature of the fund performance relationship in Figure 16.3, the fund would not lose any investors. Because the upside gain exceeds the downside loss, the risky investment is desirable from the point of view of the fund manager. By the same token, the manager of a fund at point D may prefer a safe investment to a risky one that could further deteriorate performance if it failed. Judy Chevalier and Glen Ellison present evidence to support the hypothesis that fund managers choose the riskiness of investments as a response to the flow-performance relationship depicted in Figure 16.3.[40]

How do these findings relate to executive compensation? CEOs or division managers often face nonlinear compensation profiles that resemble the flow-performance relationship in Figure 16.3. The division manager may be fired, for example, if the division does very poorly, but may not receive significant rewards unless the division does extremely well. This would encourage the manager of a weak, but not disastrous division, to avoid taking risks. At the same time, the manager of a solid, but not outstanding division, may assume additional risks to increase the odds of a significant reward, such as a promotion.

---

[39]Ippolito, R., "Consumer Reaction to Measures of Poor Quality: Evidence from the Mutual Fund Industry," *Journal of Law and Economics*, 35, 1992, pp. 45–70.

[40]Chevalier, J. and G. Ellison, "Risk Taking by Mutual Funds as a Response to Incentives," working paper, 1995.

FIGURE 16.3
RELATIONSHIP BETWEEN PERFORMANCE AND FLOW OF FUNDS.

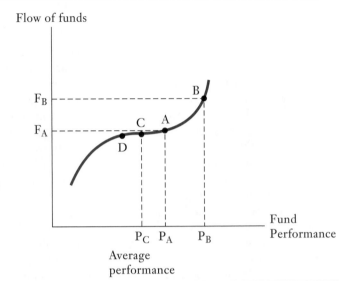

Funds flow out of the very worst funds and into the very best funds. If fund A improves its performance from P_A to P_B, it will attract funds. If its performance falls to P_C, however, the losses in funds will be minimal. Thus, the manager of fund A has an incentive to take on risk. By contrast, the manager of fund D will play it safe.

◆◆◆

$\mathcal{E}$XAMPLE 16.5

EXECUTIVE COMPENSATION AT GENERAL DYNAMICS[41]

Shortly after former Apollo astronaut William Anders took the helm at General Dynamics (GD) in 1989, he realized that the company was in trouble. Though ranked 50th on the Standard and Poor's 500, the tank and fighter plane manufacturer was ranked only 497th in performance. With the cold war winding down, the future did not look bright. Anders realized that it was necessary to motivate GD's top managers to develop and implement new business strategies.

Anders relied on a controversial compensation scheme to help achieve his objectives. Anders himself received over 30,000 shares of GD stock and over 100,000 stock options when he took over. He believed that other GD executives and managers should also be rewarded on the basis of corporate performance as measured by share value (as opposed to accounting-based bonuses that GD previously used). He implemented a new compensation scheme in which 150 top executives received stock and option packages, 1,150 executives and managers exchanged stock options at unattainably high prices for more reasonably priced options, and lower-

---

[41]Information for this example comes from "Compensation and Strategy at General Dynamics," Harvard Business School, Case 9-494-048.

level employees were encouraged to hold GD stock. In addition, he established a Compensation Committee that disbursed annual bonuses in the form of cash and stocks. Bonuses were awarded to executives on the basis of corporate and operating unit performance. The most controversial element of the bonus scheme was the Gain/Sharing Plan. Top executives could see bonuses equal to or exceeding their base salary if the GD share price rose $10 or more.

In 1991, GD took a number of steps to improve profits. It cut back capital spending and research and development, reduced inventories and working capital, laid off workers, and wrote-off $1 billion in bad risks. In the same year, GD landed a big Air Force contract and won permission to delay repayment of debts owed to the federal government from another project. From a low of $21 a share in January, GD's share price soared to over $50 in December. GD continued to refocus its strategies, and in 1992 it sold off all but its core defense businesses. By October 1993, GD shareholder wealth had increased by $4.7 billion.

In spite of GD's apparent success, Anders' compensation strategy drew much criticism. The Gain/Sharing Plan alone allowed top executives to triple their base salary in 1991, and earn millions of dollars more in stock options. Critics claimed that GD executives had sought short-term profits to boost their incomes at the expense of GD's long-term success. If we accept the standard view in modern finance that share price values represents the market's assessment of the long-run value of a firm, then the sharp rise in share prices suggests that these criticisms are off base. To the extent that the compensation system triggered the variety of strategies that brought GD back from the dead, it stands as powerful evidence of the use of financial incentives based on corporate objectives to promote corporate performance.

CHAPTER SUMMARY

◆ Agency theory examines the use of financial incentives to motivate workers. In an agency relationship, one individual, known as the *principal*, delegates responsibility to another, known as the *agent*, to act on his or her behalf.

◆ The principal and the agent are likely to have divergent goals. The principal would like the agent to take the most efficient action, while paying the agent a threshold wage. A contract that accomplishes this is first-best efficient. An agent who does not take the efficient action is said to be shirking.

◆ First-best efficiency is achievable if the principal can costlessly monitor the actions and/or outcomes of the agent, and the agent is not exposed to income risk.

◆ When the agent possesses hidden information or can take hidden actions, the principal must offer incentives that prevent the agent from shirking. One technique is to base rewards on easily observed outcomes that are correlated with the desired outcomes. The principal must also be concerned that the agent may manipulate information used for setting standards and evaluating performance.

◆ Piece-rate contracts are an example of a simple fee-for-X reward scheme based on easily observed outcomes. But these schemes may discourage workers from paying attention to other important outcomes that are less closely scrutinized.

◆ When the principal cannot perfectly determine effort from output, then output-based reward schemes introduce risk to the agent, who may work hard but receive a relatively low payment if luck is bad. The principal may need to increase the agent's base compensation to get a risk-averse agent to accept the risk.

◆ The second-best contract balances hard-edged incentives against the costs of exposing the agent to risk. Sometimes the principal can greatly improve performance by improving observability, rather than by altering contracts on the margin.

◆ Contracts that rely on punishments for motivation are problematic when agents have limited liability. The principal may need to increase the wage paid in the event of favorable outcome—that is, pay an efficiency wage—to compensate for the inability to collect from the agent in the event of an unfavorable outcome.

◆ The principal may use contracts to get workers to sort themselves by ability. More able workers are more likely to accept contracts that tie wages to performance.

◆ Firms use raises, bonuses, and promotions to motivate workers in the internal labor market. Bonuses and promotions are likely to provide stronger motivation, since raises tend to be only marginally related to performance.

◆ Wages tend to be backloaded, both to encourage loyalty and to motivate younger workers. Increases in labor market volatility may reduce the effectiveness of backloading.

◆ The incentive effects of promotions are similar to those in athletic tournaments. As workers climb the corporate ladder, opportunities for promotion diminish, but the rewards increase. Top management is further motivated by stock options whose value can exceed base salary.

QUESTIONS

1. In the United States, lawyers in negligence cases are usually paid a contingency fee equal to roughly 30 percent of the total award. Lawyers in other types of cases are often paid on a hourly basis. Use agency theory to assess the merits and drawbacks of each type of fee arrangement from the client's (i.e., the principal's) perspective. Be sure to discuss incentive and sorting effects.

2. Suppose that a principal desires a worker to perform two tasks, but can observe performance on only one task. Under what conditions should the principal closely tie pay to performance on the first task?

3. How can firms maintain the incentive benefits of the internal labor market in an era where employee turnover is rapidly increasing?

4. The credit card market has grown increasingly competitive. To maintain customer satisfaction, banks that issue credit cards usually provide an "800" number service center in which telephone operators handle customer inquiries, complaints, and requests for service. Some banks evaluate operators on the basis of the number of calls handled per day, while occasionally monitoring calls for courtesy and accuracy. (Banks have already determined that it is not cost effective to do more monitoring.) Evaluate this monitoring system. What would you do differently? Consider the benefits and costs of any change you recommend.

APPENDIX A: COMPUTING RISK PREMIA IN THE SHIPPING EXAMPLE   ◆ ◆ ◆ ◆ ◆

This appendix uses decision theory to compute the risk premium that would have to be paid to get a risk-averse shipper to accept the pay-for-performance contract described in this chapter. Suppose the shipper's utility function has the form: $U = \sqrt{(12,000 + Y)}$ where Y is the payment from shipping the perishable goods. If the shipper refuses the contract, it will have utility $U = \sqrt{12,000} = 109.5$. If it accepts the contract, it will have expected utility of only 102.4.[42] Thus, it prefers not to take the contract. The shipper would have to receive \$12,500 for a one- or two-day delivery to have expected utility of 109.5. This means that the producer would expect to pay the shipper .8 (\$12,500) = \$10,000, which represents a \$2,000 risk premium in excess of expected shipping costs. The risk premium represents the expected payment in excess of costs that the shipper insists on receiving if it is to accept this risky contract.

Had the shipper been even more risk averse, the premium would have to be even higher. We can see this by altering its utility function. The utility function $U = \sqrt{(12,000 + Y)}$ is a special case of a class of functions known as power functions. These functions take the form $U = BX^{\alpha}/\alpha$. For the utility function that we have examined, $B = .5$, $X = 12,000 + Y$, and $\alpha = .5$. As α decreases, the utility function demonstrates increased risk aversion. For example, if $\alpha = .3$, the shipper's utility if it refuses the contract would be $.67 \times 12,000^{.3} = 11.21$. If it accepts the contract, its expected utility would be 10.25. The producer would have to guarantee the shipper roughly \$16,000 for a one- or two-day delivery to overcome risk aversion. The expected payment of $.8 \times (\$16,000) = \$12,800$ represents a \$4,800 risk premium.

APPENDIX B: THE OPTIMAL SECOND-BEST CONTRACT   ◆ ◆ ◆ ◆ ◆

This appendix develops the mathematics of the optimal second-best contract to illustrate how that contract depends on the four factors discussed in the text: the agent's risk aversion, the agent's effort aversion, the marginal contribution of effort, and the precision of the performance measure.

---

[42]This equals $(.30 \sqrt{16,250}) + (.50 \sqrt{14,250}) + (.10 \sqrt{2,000})$.

We consider a setting in which an agent produces output for a principal, who then resells the output in the open market. The agent is risk averse, and its expected utility is assumed to depend on its expected payment, the variance of that payment, and the amount of effort it provides:

$$EU = E(W) - .5r\text{Var}(W) - .5ce^2$$

where: e denotes effort; $.5ce^2$ is the cost to the agent of providing effort level e; W denotes the agent's compensation; $E(W)$ is the expected value of that compensation; $\text{Var}(W)$ is the variance of that compensation; and r is a parameter reflecting the agent's risk aversion. The larger is r, the more risk averse the agent, that is, the greater the negative impact of income variability (as measured by $\text{Var}(W)$) on the agent's utility. Note that the parameter c is a measure of the agent's effort aversion. The marginal cost of effort is ce, so higher value of c implies a more effort-averse agent.

The quantity of output X is assumed to be a simple linear function of the agent's effort plus "noise," n, which embodies factors that are beyond the agent's control. Thus, $X = me + n$, where m is the marginal contribution of effort. We assume that the expected value of the noise term is 0, and its variance is denoted by v; that is, $E(n) = 0$, and $\text{Var}(n) = v$. Note that the performance measure X can be high either because the agent's effort is high or because of factors beyond the agent's control that have a favorable impact on n. The larger is the variance v, the less noisy is the performance measure X.

The agent's compensation is given by a contract of the form $W = A + BX$. Given this contract, the agent's expected utility can be written:

$$EU = E(A + B(e + n)) - .5r\text{Var}(A + B(e + n)) - .5ce^2$$

which, given the statistical properties of expected value and variance, can be written:

$$EU = A + Be - .5ce^2 - .5vrB^2$$

Note that B can have a negative impact on the agent's expected utility through the term $.5vrB^2$. This reflects the fact that basing compensation on a noisy performance measure is undesirable to a risk-averse agent. The degree to which it is undesirable depends on the agent's risk aversion, r, and the noisiness of the performance measure, v.

We assume that the principal is risk neutral. Its revenue is, for simplicity, equal to the market price times the amount of output the agent produces. For simplicity, assume that this market price is $1 per unit. This implies that the principal's expected profit is given by $E(X) - E(W) = me - Be - A$.

Suppose that the principal desires the agent to chose a particular level of effort e_0 and wishes to make the agent's expected utility equal to what it would get in its best outside opportunity, which we assume is zero. What must the incentive contract look like?

First, the contract must be such that at e_0, the marginal benefit of effort to the agent equals marginal cost. This implies:

$$B = ce_0 \tag{1}$$

Second, the contract must yield an expected utility of 0. This means that the fixed component A must be such that:

$$A = -Be_0 + .5ce_0^2 + .5vrB^2 \tag{2}$$

The optimal second-best contract maximizes the principal's expected utility, subject to providing the agent with the expected utility it gets in its next best opportunity (constraint ([2])) and that the contract induces the agent to choose the desired level of effort (constraint ([1])). Substituting equations (1) and (2) into the expression for the principal's profit, the principal's expected profit can be written as:

$$me_0 - .5ce_0^2 - .5vrc^2e_0^2$$

The principal's most preferred effort level maximizes this expression. Straightforward calculus establishes that the optimal effort, e^* is given by:[43]

$$e^* = m/c[1 + rvc]$$

Using expression (1), this, in turn, implies that the optimal value of B is given by:

$$B^* = m/[1 + rvc]$$

Note that B^* depends on the four factors discussed in the text:

- B^* decreases in r—the more risk averse the agent, the lower is the power of the incentives in the second-best contract.

- B^* decreases in c—the more effort averse the agent, the lower is the power of the incentives in the second-best contract.

- B^* increases in m—the higher is the marginal contribution of effort, the higher the power of the incentives in the second-best contract.

- B^* decreases in v—the noisier the performance measure, the lower the power of the incentives in the second-best contract.

---

[43]Differentiating the expression for the principal's profit with respect to e_0 and setting it equal to 0 yields

$$m - ce_0 - vrc^2e_0 = 0$$

Solving this for e_0 yields:

$$e_0 = \frac{m}{c[1 + rvc]}$$

STRATEGY AND STRUCTURE

17

$\mathcal{U}$ntil the early 1980s, the Pepsi-Cola Company was composed of three divisions that reported to corporate headquarters.[1] The Pepsi USA division was largely responsible for creating marketing campaigns—the famous "Pepsi Challenge" was its brainchild. The Pepsi Bottling Group (PBG) bottled and distributed the product in local markets in which Pepsi had opted not to use independent bottlers. PBG was also responsible for local marketing campaigns, such as promotional giveaways. The Fountain Beverage Division (FBD) sold to fast-food outlets, restaurants, bars, and stadiums.

Pepsi experienced several problems with this structure. It grew difficult for Pepsi to negotiate with regional and national retailers, such as Piggly Wiggly and Wal-Mart. Pepsi USA and PBG often ran competing (and sometimes conflicting) promotional campaigns. Workers in PBG and FBD also resented the high salaries and high profiles of the Pepsi USA employees. To deal with these problems, Pepsi reorganized its beverage operations in 1988. Pepsi USA, PBG, and FBD ceased to exist. Sales and account management responsibilities were decentralized among four geographic regions. Decisions about national marketing campaigns, finance, human resources, and corporate operations, including trucking and company-owned bottlers, were centralized at headquarters and handled nationally.

But this reorganization did not solve Pepsi's coordination problems for long. Negotiations with national accounts often had to pass through several layers of

---

[1]Some material in the example is drawn from Pepsi-Cola U.S. Beverages (A), Harvard Business School Case 9-390-034.

management before a final decision could be reached, resulting in the loss of important accounts, most notably Burger King. Conflicts between national and local promotional campaigns continued to arise. So in 1992, Pepsi reorganized again. This time, marketing and sales campaigns were further centralized, and responsibility for a given retail outlet was delegated to a single salesperson.

Throughout these two reorganizations, Pepsi enjoyed extremely popular products and a comparatively benign competitive environment. Even so, the firm's top managers believed that these favorable factors were not sufficient to guarantee continued success, and that to remain profitable, Pepsi needed to reorganize.

Ample general evidence supports Pepsi's view that technology, product mix, and market position do not fully account for a firm's performance. Harvey Leibenstein found that differences in firm performance were systematically related to the costs firms incurred carrying out similar sets of activities. For example, he reports on a study of two oil refineries in Egypt located within a mile of each other. The labor productivity of one was nearly double that of the other for several years. This changed when under new management the inefficient refinery began making strong productivity gains with the same labor force.[2] Daniel Garvin studied 18 manufacturing plants for air conditioners and found that performance was not related to capital investment or automation, but was instead explained by organizational routines that helped or hindered coordination and information flow.[3] After reviewing dozens of such studies, Richard Caves and David Barton found that it is common for firms in the same industry, with similar technologies and labor forces, to have substantially different levels of productivity.[4]

Similar firms could achieve different results for many reasons. Some are idiosyncratic to the firm, such as the role of Bill Gates in attracting talent to Microsoft. Others reflect the implementation of total quality management programs and other productivity-enhancing practices that reduce costs and boost quality at firms like Motorola. Still others concern information failures and management errors, such as the apparently systematic overbidding by some oil companies for offshore oil rights during the 1970s.[5] While important, these factors are difficult to generalize about.

---

[2]Leibenstein, H., *Beyond Economic Man*, Cambridge, MA: Harvard University Press, 1980, pp. 34–47. Leibenstein calls these efficiencies *nonallocative* or '*x-efficiencies*'. These efficiencies differ from allocative economies, which concern the optimal use of resources vis-a-vis alternatives and have been the concern of traditional economic approaches.

[3]Garvin, D., *Managing Quality*, New York: Free Press, 1988.

[4]Caves, R. and D. Barton, *Efficiency in U.S. Manufacturing Industries*, Cambridge, MA: MIT Press, 1990, pp. 1–3.

[5]Capen, E. C., R. B. Clapp, and W. M. Campbell, "Competitive Bidding in High Risk Situations," *Journal of Petroleum Technology*, 23, June 1971, pp. 641–653; Hendricks, K. and R. H. Porter, "An Empirical Study of an Auction with Asymmetric Information," *American Economic Review*, 78, December 1988, pp. 865–883.

Some factors, however, appear to be generally applicable to the study of inter-firm differences in behavior and performance. These include innovation, motivation, and culture, which we discuss elsewhere in this text. In this chapter, we consider organizational structure, by which we mean the general and persistent patterns by which the firm organizes its tasks, how its staff perform tasks, and the means by which it facilitates information flows.

If a firm's strategy is to be carried out, or *implemented*, effectively, individuals working within the firm must be aware of the strategy and its operational details. Workers' activities must also be coordinated by management. Uncoordinated or uninformed employees may delay the implementation of the strategy or even obstruct it. The problem of informing and coordinating employees to carry out the directives of a strategy is a daunting one, especially in large firms with tens (or even hundreds) of thousands of employees. A firm's structure reflects how it regularly solves problems of information and coordination.

Strategy implementation, however, is not just a problem of information and coordination. Individuals may also work at cross-purposes with the firm because its information and control system permits opportunistic behavior. If we add the problems of incentives and controls that were discussed in Chapter 16 to the problem of coordinating cooperative agents, the difficulty in organizing the firm to carry out its strategy is compounded. It is this problem that we consider in this chapter. In his classic set of case studies, *Strategy and Structure*, Alfred Chandler arued that the top managers of large industrial firms organized their firms to best allow them to pursue their chosen business strategy—or, simply put, that *structure follows strategy*.[6] This theme, which we believe is applicable to firms of all sizes, is the focus of our discussion.

While the appropriate bases for organization structure and strategy implementation are receiving increased attention by economists, many of the ideas we consider in this chapter have been developed largely in noneconomic terms. Decisions about choosing a structure, however, are economic decisions, since they concern how best to reduce the firm's coordination and transactions costs. While we know less about the economic basis of organization structure, issues of structure can and should be analyzed by the principles that we have developed in earlier chapters.

AN INTRODUCTION TO STRUCTURE ◆ ◆ ◆ ◆ ◆

The topic of organizational structure requires the introduction of many new terms and concepts. Before demonstrating the link between strategy and structure, we must review some basic concepts and describe the major kinds of organizational forms.

---

[6]Chandler, A. D., *Strategy and Structure*, Cambridge, MA: MIT Press, 1962.

Individuals, Teams, and Hierarchies

Our discussion of firm structure begins by considering how to organize simple tasks performed by a small group of people. Such tasks can be structured in several ways:

- *Individually:* In this arrangement, the members of the work group are treated as if they were independent—they receive incentives based on individual actions and outcomes. In this situation, the collection of individuals performing tasks is at best a nominal group, in which individuals may share a work space (such as a workshop used by several independent artisans).

- *Self-managed teams:* A self-managed team is a collection of individuals, each member of which works with others to set and pursue some common set of objectives. Individuals are then rewarded, in part, based on team performance. Organizing as a team makes sense when individual actions must be coordinated, or when team production exceeds the sum of the individual work output. This may occur, for example, when team production permits the use of specialization among group members.

- *Hierarchy of authority:* In this arrangement, one member of the group specializes in monitoring and coordinating the work of the other members.

We have separated these three approaches to organizing a work group for simplicity. Most firms combine them in some way. An employee may do some tasks individually and others in a team. While most firms employ some form of hierarchy, the strength of formal authority varies widely among firms, with some resembling a collection of independent workers rather than a hierarchy, a common situation in professional service firms. A work group may have some activities organized around individuals and others around the group, while a supervisor may monitor the activities and outputs of the group as a whole as well as those of individuals.

For many tasks, any of these three approaches may be a workable way for a group to organize. Each of them, however, will be relatively more appropriate than the others in different circumstances. Major differences between the three structures are found in the degree of interaction among the workers and the costs of coordinating them. Treating the workers as self-managing individuals is most appropriate when their tasks do not require coordination. When coordination is necessary, say because the work involves design attributes or relationship-specific investments, then either a team or hierarchy is more appropriate. Coordination among members of even fairly small teams can be a problem, however, as illustrated by the organizational structures in Figure 17.1.

The first structure in Figure 17.1 illustrates channels of authority and communication when members of a three-person group act as a self-managing team. Each individual must interact with every other, for a total of six interactions. In the second structure, three workers receive instructions from "supervisor" S, for a total of three interactions. In general, the number of potential interactions among n independent individuals is $n(n - 1)/2$, whereas the number of interactions among n individuals, one of whom supervises the others, is $n - 1$. Hence, as n increases, the hierarchy of authority economizes on the number of interactions. This may reduce sharing of information and development of team culture, but it also reduces associated coordination problems. As the number of relations coordinated increases, however, individual supervisors can exhaust their coordinative abilities and go beyond their optimal *span of control*, by which we mean the number of subordinates directly reporting to a supervisor. If this occurs, a further specialization of management and the addition of more supervisors will be needed. This is depicted in the third structure in Figure 17.1.[7]

Group self-management is more appropriate than a hierarchy would be when the work outcomes benefit from frequent group interaction and group incentives (such as from sharing information among group members or from the motivational value of group support), and when the costs of group coordination do not detract from group outcomes. Organizing by groups, however, makes it difficult to monitor and control individual outputs. Beyond a certain size, group self-management becomes too costly to coordinate. In addition, when it is part of a larger organization, the group's objectives may conflict with those of the parent. The parent must introduce some form of hierarchy to maintain and evaluate the group and thereby eliminate agency problems.

FIGURE 17.1
COORDINATIVE RELATIONSHIPS WITH AND WITHOUT SUPERVISORS.

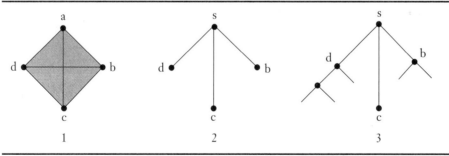

Source: Adapted from Jacquemin, 1991.

---

[7]For a discussion, see Jacquemin, A., *The New Industrial Organization*, Cambridge, MA: MIT Press, 1991. The issue of the optimal span of control for firms is a longstanding one in administrative research, and there is no consensus apart from the influence of such factors as the firm's size and technology, the qualifications of subordinates, or the characteristics of the market being served.

◆ ◆

$\mathcal{E}$XAMPLE 17.1

THE DIVISION OF LABOR AMONG SEAMEN: 1700–1750

In his study of the organization of work for Anglo-American seamen just before the American Revolution, Marcus Rediker provides detailed examples of how the three basic approaches to task organization that we have been discussing—individual, group, and hierarchy—interacted in the daily routines of merchant ships.[8] Merchant-shipping was a large and visible industry that employed upwards of 40,000 seamen at any given time during the first half of the eighteenth century. These seamen were grouped into crews of between twelve and eighteen men, depending on the size of the ship and the route and purpose of the voyage. The management of crews was typically made up of the captain and his (first) mate. Larger crews had a second mate. The crew also included craftsmen, such as a carpenter, boatswain, gunner, or quartermaster (the cook was not considered a skilled worker). The rest of the crew were seamen (or "common tars").

Many of the ship's basic tasks were subject to a specialized individual division of labor. A crew of 12 was usually divided into five or six different ranks and an equal number of pay stations, and a man's position in that status ordering depended on his skills and experience. Even the level of seaman had two ranks—able and common—that were based on experience. The wages seamen received depended on their place within this ordering of skill and experience.

Along with this individual division of labor, several core tasks required collective organization. For example, in loading or unloading heavy objects, such as cannon, from the ship, a collective effort was necessary to operate the various tackle and lever arrangements (such as the capstan or parbuckle) that were needed to lift heavy items. Substantial collective efforts and high levels of team coordination were also needed to operate the riggings, especially during storms. Not only was collective effort in these tasks necessary for a voyage to succeed, but the failure to coordinate could seriously injure crew members and could also damage the ship's cargo. The need for precise timing of group efforts was behind the songs and chants so often associated with life on merchant ships.

Hierarchy was also important. The captain, or master, was the direct representative of the owners of the ship (and often a partial owner himself). He had nearly complete authority on board and was responsible for navigation, securing provisions, and transacting business in port. He was also responsible for discipline and settling disputes. The mate, who was second in command, was responsible for the daily operations of the ship, but had far less power than the captain. The primary unit of social organization through which hierarchy operated was the watch.

---

[8]Rediker, M., "The Anglo-American Seaman as Collective Worker: 1700–1750," in Innes, S. (ed.), *Work and Labor in Early America*, Chapel Hill, NC: University of North Carolina Press, 1988, pp. 252–286.

The crew was divided into two watches, called "starboard" and "larboard," one commanded by the captain and the other by the mate. These two units alternated around the clock in manning four-hour shifts that provided the basic cycle around which the continuity of ship operations was organized and maintained.

$\mathcal{E}$XAMPLE 17.2

TEAM OR INDIVIDUAL ORGANIZATION AMONG TELEPHONE OPERATORS: 1889–1929

The switchboard was a significant factor in the development of viable telephone service in the United States. Without switching capabilities, telephones were merely sophisticated intercoms. After the Bell Company merged with Western Electric in 1882, switchboard development proceeded rapidly, and widespread automated switching systems were introduced immediately after World War I ended in 1918. Historians of the Bell System have seen the growth of switchboard technology as an important step in the growth of a national and worldwide telephone network.[9]

As the technology of the switchboard developed, so did the method by which switching was organized. The initial multiple switchboards were in use in telephone companies by 1879 and required considerable coordination among several operators. Incoming calls to one board requesting connections on another board were "trunked through" from the first operator to the second. The second operator was alerted to the incoming call by a special annunciator on each board. A central supervisor, who sat at a centrally located table in the switching room, coordinated the work of the operators. The supervisor also handled nontelephonic messages coming in and out of the office. This system required carefully organized work plans. The larger the volume of calls, the more complex were the coordination problems of this system. In the terms that we have been discussing, this organization of work combined team organization and simple hierarchy (via the supervisor). The team basis of this work is apparent in Figure 17.2A, which shows a switchboard circa 1889.

As switchboard technology developed, banks of individual operators, who could perform their tasks independently of each other, replaced the team orientation. The work became much more routine and was eventually automated. The individual basis of later switchboard work is apparent in Figure 17.2B, which shows a bank of operators circa 1928.

---

[9]This discussion is based on Garnet, R. W., *The Telephone Enterprise*, Baltimore, MD: Johns Hopkins University Press, 1985; Smith, G. D., *The Anatomy of a Business Strategy: Bell, Western Electric, and the Origins of the American Telephone Industry*, Baltimore, MD: Johns Hopkins University Press, 1985; Vallas, S. P., *Power in the Workplace: The Politics of Production at AT&T*, Albany, NY: State University of New York Press, 1993, chaps. 1–3.

FIGURE 17.2A
AN EARLY SWITCHBOARD, WITH MALE OPERATORS, IN 1879.

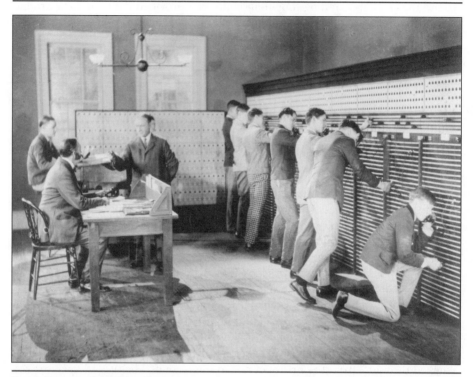

Source: Courtesy of AT&T archives.

Observers will note another difference between Figures 17.2A and 17.2B: Female employees replaced males in switchboard activities throughout the Bell System during this period. This shift is associated with the paternalistic strategy of the Bell Company that frustrated unionization efforts and earned the company the name "Ma Bell." These women also received lower wages than did men. An intentionally gender-based scheme of work such as this would not be tolerated today. Bell system managers, however, had a straightforward justification. They claimed that young women as operators performed better than young men. For example, one manager wrote:

> Our experience has been [most satisfactory] with young ladies' help; the service is very superior to that of boys and men. They are steadier, do not drink beer and are always on hand.[10]

[10]Quoted in Vallas, S. P., *Power in the Workplace: The Politics of Production at AT&T*, Albany, NY: State University of New York Press, 1993, p. 42.

FIGURE 17.2B   667
A CENTRAL OFFICE ON CANAL STREET, MANHATTAN, IN 1928.

Source: Courtesy of AT&T archives.

Most individuals work at firms that are much bigger than the work units discussed in Examples 17.1 and 17.2. This raises the issue of how to organize groups of work units within a larger organization. This is the problem of *complex hierarchy*, which we consider next.

Complex Hierarchy

Large firms often require *complex hierarchies*. By this we mean that the structure of the firm involves multiple groups and multiple levels of groupings. Complex hierarchy arises from the need not just to organize individuals into groups, but to organize groups into larger groups. Grouping in large firms quickly becomes complicated and includes two related problems:

* Departmentalization
* Coordination of activities within and between subgroups to attain the firm's objectives

Most attempts at organization design combine solutions to departmentalization and coordination problems under the specific conditions a firm faces.[11] We discuss each of these problems in turn.

Departmentalization

Departmentalization involves the division of the organization into formal groupings. These groups may be organized along a number of dimensions: common tasks or functions, inputs, outputs, geographic location, and time of work. Examples of departments organized around common tasks or functions include accounting, marketing, and production. Examples of input and output-based groupings include the Pepsi Bottling Group and Fountain Beverage Division that we discussed at the beginning of the chapter. Examples of departments organized around location include regional sales offices or service centers. An example of time-based groupings would be multiple shifts within a manufacturing firm.

While theories of organization design are often presented in noneconomic terms, choices of which structure to use have potentially important consequences for the firm and thus need to be evaluated on the basis of their relative costs and benefits. Choosing the dimensions on which to organize departments almost always involves nontrivial economic tradeoffs. For example, organizing on the basis of task may lead to greater consistency in a firm's purchasing, manufacturing, and sales operations, but organizing geographically might help the firm respond more efficiently to customer demands in different locations. Which of these options to choose should depend on their relative economic consequences for the firm.

In general, when selecting dimensions along which to organize departments, the firm should consider economies of scale and scope, transactions costs, and agency costs. A firm should combine workers or teams into a department when there are economies of scale or scope in the activities they perform. For example, if a multiproduct firm can achieve significant scale economies in research and development,

---

[11]The classic statement of these two problems is in March, J. and H. Simon, *Organizations*, New York: Wiley, 1958, pp. 22–27. For a review of research on these problems, see McCann, J. and J. R. Galbraith, "Interdepartmental Relations," in Nystrom, P. C. and W. H. Starbuck (eds.), *Handbook of Organizational Design*, vol. 2, New York: Oxford University Press, 1981, pp. 60–84.

then an organizational structure that included a companywide research department would be more efficient than dispersing R&D personnel throughout a number of independent product groups. Workers and teams should also be organized into departments when they share significant relationship-specific assets.

Eric Miller provides an example of this logic in his study of a small task group organization.[12] He takes a weaving mill and shows how there are several ways in which the tasks associated with producing its product can be grouped. Not all ways of grouping are equally efficient, however. Specifically, it is necessary to group tasks that involve treating the product with chemicals, such as bleaching and dyeing, since these require care in how they are performed and linked with other tasks. On this basis, they were grouped into one department, separate from those tasks, such as warping, sizing, or weaving, that did not involve chemical treatments. This grouping scheme is illustrated in Figure 17.3, along with an example of an inappropriate, or what Miller terms unnatural, grouping.

FIGURE 17.3 ORGANIZING TASKS IN A WEAVING MILL

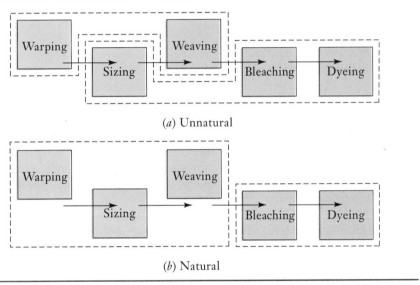

(a) Unnatural

(b) Natural

The figure shows two ways to organize tasks in a weaving mill. The first (a) is deemed "unnatural" by Miller because the task sequence necessitates the unnecessary effort of shifting product back and forth between steps involving chemical treatment and steps not requiring such treatment. The process shown in (b) is more "natural" because it places tasks requiring chemical processing together, which avoids the need to shift product back and forth.

Source: Adapted from Miller, 1959, 257.

---

[12]Miller, E. J., "Technology, Territory, and Task: The Internal Differentiation of Complex Production Systems," *Human Relations*, 12, 1959, pp. 243–272.

Finally, the choice of an organizing dimension should consider the implications for agency costs in the firm, such as we have already examined in Chapter 16. For example, as we discuss below, measuring the performance of functional departments, such as finance and purchasing, can be difficult. This makes it hard to evaluate and appropriately reward the performance of managers of functional departments, which could increase agency costs inside the firm. These agency costs are likely to increase as the firm grows in size and complexity.

Departmentalization is rarely straightforward. Each individual worker performs a particular function involving one or more input or output markets in a particular location at a particular time. If workers are organized solely according to function, then decision-making authority can be ambiguous when problems arise that are not aligned with issues associated with that function. For example, there may be problems when an accounting department questions purchasing practices associated with a particular region or output market. Conversely, if workers are organized solely according to region or output markets, then authority with regard to accounting issues may be unclear. Designers of a complex hierarchy must assign decision-making authority to different groups, and determine how to resolve conflicts when issues emerge that cut across the departmentalization.

Coordination and Control

Once groups have been identified and organized, the interrelated problems of coordination and control arise. *Coordination* involves the flow of information within an organization to facilitate subunit decisions that are consistent with each other and with organizational objectives. *Control* involves the location of decision-making rights and rule-making authority within the hierarchy. Coordination and control involve issues of technical and agency efficiency discussed in Chapter 4. They affect technical efficiency because decision makers need access to critical information at the lowest cost, while assuring that the firm takes full advantage of economies of scale and scope in production. Poor coordination between the Pepsi Bottling Group and Pepsi USA resulted in technical inefficiencies when the two divisions failed to economize on marketing and sales efforts. Coordination and control also affect agency efficiency because organization structures may differ in the opportunities they offer to decision makers within the firm to pursue personal or unit objectives (e.g., maximizing perquisite consumption) that are inconsistent with the objectives of the firm.

There are two alternative approaches for developing coordination within firms.[13] The first emphasizes *autonomy* or *self-containment* of work units, while the second emphasizes the importance of strong *lateral relations* across work groups. With autonomous work units, unit managers control information about operating

---

[13]This distinction is taken from information-processing approaches to organization design. For a review, see McCann and Galbraith, 1981, *op. cit.* A similar distinction between informational decentralization and informational consolidation is sometimes made in economic analyses of organization structure. See Baron, D. and D. Besanko, "Information, Control, and Organizational Structure," *Journal of Economics & Management Strategy*, 1, Summer 1992, pp. 237–276.

decisions, and the flow of information between units is minimal. Unit managers provide summary financial and accounting data, including profit data when available, to headquarters. Operating information remains within the units, however. Self-containment allows managers to focus their efforts on coordination within units, while allowing headquarters to use market-oriented incentives that tie managerial rewards to overall unit performance.

A common example of self-containment is when a firm organizes into separate product groups, each of which contains the basic business functions of manufacturing and sales and would be capable of existing by itself in the marketplace. Managers in these groups, which are often called *profit centers*, are controlled on the basis of a target profit goal and are rewarded for meeting or exceeding the goal and punished for failing to achieve it. They have limited interactions with the other groups. Profit centers are commonly used in diversified firms, such as Proctor and Gamble and Johnson and Johnson. When self-contained groups focus on other performance measures besides profit, such as cost, revenue, or investment goals, they are called *responsibility centers*. Research programs at pharmaceutical companies are examples of responsibility centers.

The alternative to self-contained or autonomous groupings is to emphasize strong lateral relations across work groups. Building strong lateral relations makes sense when the realization of economies of scale or scope requires close coordination of the activities of work groups. Lateral relations can be informal, such as with *ad hoc* or temporary teams or liaisons, or they can be formalized through the firm's organizational structure. An example of a formal attempt to foster lateral relations is the *matrix organization*, in which employees are subject to two or more sets of managers at once, such as when an engineer reports both to a research and development department and to a project office within a firm, or when a salesperson reports to the head of sales for a particular product and to a regional manager who represents the entire firm. We describe the matrix organization in more detail in the next section. While lateral relations may bolster coordination between units, they may also increase agency problems by weakening the relationship between managerial compensation and unit performance.

The allocation of authority within the firm is typically considered in terms of *centralization* versus *decentralization*. As some decisions come to be made at higher levels—that is, by more senior managers—the firm is said to be more centralized regarding those decisions. Conversely, as certain decisions are made at lower levels, the firm can be said to be more decentralized regarding those decisions. Centralization and decentralization are frequently considered alternatives for a firm—a firm is either one or the other. The situation in real firms is more complicated, however. Most firms are centralized for some decisions and decentralized for others and characterizing a firm as centralized or decentralized is at best a matter of degree.

Types of Organizational Structures

While the organizing problems firms face, as well as the details of firms' organizational structures, may differ greatly, the structures of large organizations generally fit one of four categories:

- The unitary *functional* structure (often called the U-form)
- The *multidivisional* structure (often called the M-form)
- The *matrix* structure
- The *network* structure

Traditional discussions of organizational structure have focused on the first three structures, which are the most widely used ones in practice. The network structure, which we briefly described in Chapter 4, represents a recent development that emphasizes contracting rather than internal organization. We describe each of the four types of structures below and depict each by a sample organization chart.

Functional Structure (U-form)

Figure 17.4 represents the unitary functional structure or U-form. The term "unitary functional" refers to the fact that there is a single department responsible for each of the basic business functions (e.g., finance, marketing, production, purchasing) within the firm. In effect, this structure is characterized by a division of labor that allows for specialization of the basic tasks the business performs. An example of a firm organized largely along functional lines is Cray Research, which has companywide departments of finance, marketing and sales, hardware research and development, and software research and development. The component groups or units in the functional structure are called *departments*. Each department depends on direction from central headquarters and probably could not exist autonomously outside of the firm except as contract vendors to a firm that independently secures the other functions.

The functional structure was motivated by the division of labor that characterized economic growth in the nineteenth century. It made sense to organize firms around the specialists that emerged in accounting, finance, sales, and production.

FIGURE 17.4

SAMPLE CHART OF A FUNCTIONAL ORGANIZATIONAL STRUCTURE.

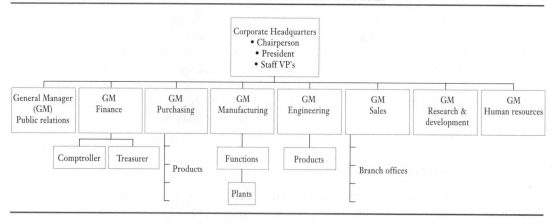

Even so, large firms were slow to adopt the functional structure. The early growth of large firms that was discussed in Chapter 1 was characterized by loose combinations of formerly independent firms, often still run by their founders. These combinations failed to coordinate leadership, and generally did not combine work groups performing similar tasks into companywide departments. Rather, they looked more like alliances or associations of equals. U.S. Steel looked this way when it became the first billion-dollar firm in 1901. Functional organization developed when managers realized that firms that rationalized their activities along functional lines outperformed those competitors that did not. The widespread adoption of the functional structure among large firms occurred during the first merger wave that occurred after 1895, although Standard Oil had been rationalizing its structure along functional lines for several years.[14]

A similar process of rationalization is taking place in Europe today in anticipation of greater European economic integration. Such firms as Asea Brown Boveri (ABB) and Electrolux are growing large as they merge with competitors in other countries. These larger firms are finding that increased economies will be demanded from the larger European market than were required for success in national markets. These demands are forcing these firms to rationalize their structures and reduce their workforce levels more than they anticipated. While the structures of these firms are more complex than those of large industrial firms around 1895, they continue to include a functional dimension as an important aspect of their corporate organization.[15]

Multidivisional Structure (M-form)

Figure 17.5 shows the divisional (or multidivisional) structure. It is composed of a set of autonomous divisions led by a corporate headquarters office, assisted by a corporate staff that provides information about the internal and external business environment. Rather than organizing by function or by task, a multidivisional structure organizes by product line, related business units, region, or customer type (e.g., industrial versus consumer versus government products). *Divisions* are groupings of interrelated subunits. The subunits that comprise a division can be functional departments or even other divisions that in turn are composed of departments.

The multidivisional structure was a response to problems with the functional structure in large, diversified firms. As firms diversify across geographic or product markets, it becomes important to coordinate different functional areas within each market. For example, geographically diversified firms, such as McCaw Cellular Communications or Waste Management, run what amount to autonomous businesses in distinct geographic markets. A divisional structure organized along geo-

---

[14]Fligstein, N., *The Transformation of Corporate Control*, Cambridge, MA: Harvard University Press, 1990, chaps. 2 and 3.

[15]Taylor, W., "The Logic of Global Business: An Interview with ABB's Percy Barnevik," in Kanter, R., B. Stein, and T. Jick (eds.), *The Challenge of Organizational Change*, New York: Free Press, 1992, pp. 289–301.

FIGURE 17.5

SAMPLE CHART OF A MULTIDIVISIONAL STRUCTURE.

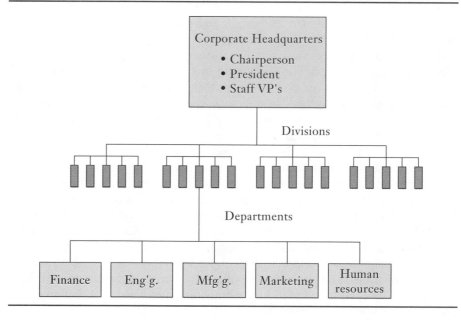

graphic lines allows these firms to coordinate production, distribution, and sales functions within their different markets, each of which may have unique competitive conditions.

The divisional structure also solves another problem of large organizations: the desire to reduce agency costs by closely linking individual pay to performance.[16] A simple example of this occurs in retailing. In a chain of retailers, such as Piggly Wiggly or Macy's Department Stores, each store is, in effect, its own division, with profits calculated on a store-by-store basis. This provides top management with a simple measure of store performance, which they can then use to evaluate individual store managers and reward good performance. As discussed in Chapter 16, the lower the "white noise" or measurement error in the performance measure used in pay-for-performance schemes and the less susceptible it is to covert manipulation by managers, the more effective the pay-for-performance scheme will be in motivating managerial effort and reducing agency costs. The divisional structure generates a clear measure of the extent to which divisional performance contributes to overall corporate success: divisional profits and losses. Equally clear and nonmanipulable measures of the contribution of functional department performance to overall corporate success are often not available. This could change, however, with the development of modern activity-based accounting

---

[16]Chapter 16 discusses pay-for-performance in greater detail.

systems that enable top managers to evaluate middle managers in complex environments. If so, the justification for a divisional structure based on agency costs may be weakening.

Divisions are often divided into functional areas. For example, each of the regional divisions of Waste Management has marketing, service, and finance departments. Conversely, a functional organization can be organized along divisional lines. For example, IBM recently reorganized its sales organization from a geographic to an industry-focused structure. The rationales for these subdivisions are exactly as stated above—to take advantage of economies of scope, monitoring, and evaluation, at lower, albeit more appropriate, levels of organization.

Matrix Structure

Figure 17.6 illustrates the matrix structure: The firm is simultaneously organized along multiple dimensions (usually two). Any particular combination of dimensions might be used. For example, matrix structures can include product groups and functional departments or two different types of divisions (such as geographic and client divisions). The individuals working at the intersections of the matrix, usually middle managers, such as those in Figure 17.6, report information to two hierarchies and have two bosses. For example, the Pepsi matrix that was created in the late 1980s was organized along geographic and functional lines. Area manufacturing managers simultaneously reported to regional general managers (geographic-based divisions) and a national senior vice president for operations (functional-based divisions). While the matrix may extend throughout the entire firm, some levels within the firm may be outside the matrix. Pepsi again provides an example, as its national marketing group has remained autonomous from the matrix.

A matrix structure is valuable when economies of scale or scope or agency considerations provide a compelling rationale for organizing along more than one dimension. For example, Pepsi believed that national coordination of manufacturing helped achieve scale economies in production, justifying organization along functional lines, while regional coordination increased Pepsi's effectiveness in negotiating with large purchasers, justifying organization along geographic lines.

A matrix structure also allows the organization to economize on scarce human resources. For example, a producer of industrial controls for continuous-flow manufacturing environments (e.g., oil refining, chemical processing, flour milling) may find that it maximizes the effectiveness of its product development, marketing, and servicing efforts by organizing into product groups based on customer type, for example, an oil industry group, a chemical industry group, and so forth. To develop new applications for existing products and designs for new products, the firm relies on chemical and electrical engineers who must develop a considerable amount of firm-specific, product-specific, and customer-specific know-how to be most productive. Because recruiting and training good engineers is costly and because the engineers benefit from interaction and collaboration with one another, it may neither be possible nor desirable for the firm to maintain a separate engineering department within each product group. For this firm, a matrix structure in which engineers are part of a companywide engineering department but also report to individual product groups may allow the firm to economize on scarce human resources while also encouraging its engineers to develop product-specific and customer-specific know-how.

A disadvantage of a matrix structure is that employees can find themselves torn between two lines of authority. For example, if a conflict develops in a matrix between the demands of an area manager and a product manager over a salesman's obligations toward a major client, the hierarchy does not dictate which manager would prevail, since they share the same level within the firm. This would not happen in functional or divisional organizations, where managers at some level will have the authority to settle such disputes by fiat. In a matrix, however, a conflict such as this must be settled through discussion and negotiation between affected individuals on the merits of each case.

FIGURE 17.6

A MATRIX ORGANIZATION STRUCTURE WITH PROJECT AND FUNCTION DIMENSIONS.

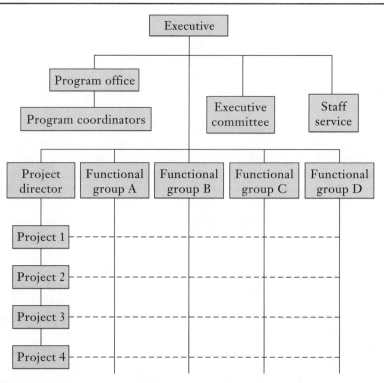

Source: Adapted from McCann and Galbraith, 1980.

Network Structure

Figure 17.7 represents the network structure. Work groups in a network may be organized by function, geography, or customer base, but relationships between work groups in a network are governed more by the often-changing implicit and explicit requirements of common tasks than by the formal lines of authority that characterize other structures.[17] As suggested in Chapters 2 through 4, a network is attractive, compared to market specialists, when the often substantial coordination costs of employing it are less than the gains obtained from it in technical efficiency. The Japanese *keiretsu* structure that was discussed in Chapter 4 is a variety of the network structure in which informal ties between member firms facilitate coordination and reduce agency problems. The fluid relationships among firms in the biotechnology industry provide an example of network structures that facilitate information flows among high-technology companies. Such flows are necessary because the technologies of these firms can have broad applications that include such

FIGURE 17.7
THE SPIDER'S WEB ORGANIZATION—AN EXAMPLE OF A NETWORK.

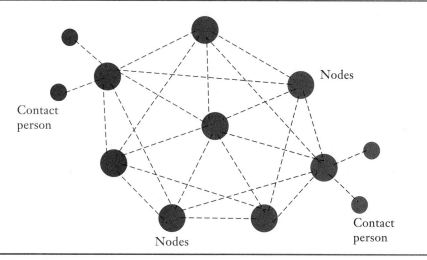

The figure shows a network organization structure based on communications patterns.
Source: Adapted from J. B. Quinn, *Intelligent Enterprise,* 1992, pp. 120–129.

---

[17]For an extended discussion of the network organization, see Baker, W. E., "The Network Organization in Theory and Practice," in Nohria, N. and R. G. Eccles (eds.), *Networks and Organizations,* Boston: Harvard Business School Press, 1992, pp. 397–429. For an application of network ideas to service organizations, especially those dependent on professional knowledge, see Quinn, J. B., *Intelligent Enterprise,* New York: Free Press, 1992, chaps. 4 and 5.

diverse areas as pharmaceuticals, seeds, and beer. Several observers have seen these interfirm networks as a principal reason for the historically high levels of new product development in this industry.[18]

◆ ◆ ◆ ◆ ◆ CONTINGENCY THEORY

We have argued that the appropriate organizational structure balances tradeoffs between scale and scope economies, transactions costs, agency costs, and information flows. This suggests that the best organizational structure for a particular firm depends on the specific circumstances it faces. For example, a functional structure may work well for a manufacturer of supercomputers, such as Cray Research, but would probably work poorly for a large superregional bank, such as Banc One.

The idea that there is no uniformly "best" organizational structure for all firms in all circumstances is known as *contingency theory*. Contingency theory has focused on three factors that may affect the relative efficiency of different structures:

- Technology and task interdependence
- Information flows
- The tension between differentiation and integration

Technology and Task Interdependence

Technology refers to the processes by which the firm's outputs are produced. Contingency theory states that as the characteristics of the firm's technology change, the firm's structure will also change to accommodate new coordination needs. For example, as a firm's technology changes to permit increased production volume and more routine handling of raw materials, structure would need to change to accommodate the increased volume of activities and the increased number of decisions. This might require the creation of a new division with responsibilities in purchasing.

James Thompson points out that technology determines the degree of *task interdependence*, which is the extent to which two or more positions depend on each other to do their own work.[19] Task interdependence largely determines how much coordination among different positions is needed and thus helps determine how positions or subgroups should be linked to one another within an organization. Thompson defines three modes of task interdependence: reciprocal, sequential,

---

[18]For recent studies of interfirm networks that focus on Japanese and biotechnology examples, see Nohria, N. and R. G. Eccles (eds.), *Networks and Organizations*, Boston: Harvard Business School Press, 1992, pp. 309–394. Also see Mizruchi, M. and Schwartz, M. (eds.), *Intercorporate Relations*, Cambridge, UK: Cambridge University Press, 1987. For a general approach to network analysis that includes relations within and between firms, see Burt, R. S., *Structural Holes*, Cambridge, MA: Harvard University Press, 1992.

[19]Thompson, J. D., *Organizations in Action*, New York: McGraw-Hill, 1967.

and pooled. *Reciprocal interdependence* exists when two or more workers or work groups depend on each other to do their work. An example would be a team of individuals, each of whom is responsible for writing part of the computer code for a personal computer operating system. The contribution of any one worker is practically worthless without the contribution of the other members of the team. *Sequential interdependence* exists between two or more positions when one depends on the outcomes of the others, but not vice versa. For example, the assembly of an automobile cannot go forward without the production of the components that go into the automobile. But because the components could, in principle, be sold in the open market, component production is not dependent on the assembly function. Finally, *pooled interdependence* exists when two or more positions are not directly dependent on each other to do their work, but are associated only through their independent contributions to the success of the firm.

Organization design, according to Thompson, can be understood as a successive grouping of positions to facilitate the coordination of activities and the use of shared resources. Without effective coordination, economies of scale and scope may not be realized. In addition, poor coordination will impair the firm's ability to respond to changes in market demand or customer needs. The need to achieve coordination implies that positions that are reciprocally interdependent should be grouped together. Positions that are sequentially dependent may be grouped together in a separate unit or in formalized relationships, depending on how interdependent they are, while positions characterized by pooled interdependence need only be linked through their affiliation with the firm.

As technology changes, so will the nature of task interdependence, thus also changing the appropriate structure of the firm. The rise of network organizations is a good example of this. Advances in computer and telecommunications technologies have weakened reciprocal and sequential interdependence among many positions and have significantly reduced the costs of coordinating activities among individuals and groups. For example, using faxes, personal computers, and "groupware" computer software, engineers and product specialists located on different continents can coordinate the design of a new product without ever meeting face to face. Such coordination would not have been possible 15 years ago. Not only does the reduction in the costs of coordination reduce the need for members of a team to be part of the same formal organization within a firm, as discussed in Chapter 2, it also may eliminate the need for them to be part of the same firm.

Improving Information Processing

Jay Galbraith presents a contingency-based argument for organization design based on considerations of information processing.[20] Galbraith argues that work groups can normally operate independently and can manage themselves, according to work rules that become routine over time. Administrative hierarchy (i.e., bosses,

---

[20]Galbraith, J. R. and R. K. Kazanjian, *Strategy Implementation: The Role of Structure and Process*, 2nd ed., St. Paul, MN: West Publishing, 1986.

supervisors, and so forth) develops, according to Galbraith, to handle "exceptions": decisions that cannot easily be made by applying standard organizational routines. Successively higher levels of organization are needed to handle more difficult exceptions. Decisions that reach the top of an organization are presumably the more difficult and least routine of all the decisions the firm faces—that is, strategic decisions.

An implication of Galbraith's argument is that changes in organizational structure come about in response to changes in the amount, complexity, or speed of information processing that a firm must undertake to make decisions. As work groups are forced to process more information or act more quickly, existing organizational routines become increasingly strained. For example, marketing decisions that may have been fairly routine in an industry characterized by stable demand, high entry barriers, and a few well-known domestic competitors may become less routine as the market becomes more globalized or as changes in technology destroy entry barriers. Making effective pricing and promotion decisions may now require keeping track of unfamiliar foreign competitors and monitoring demand conditions in an increasingly segmented market. This might easily overwhelm standard operating procedures that were developed in a simpler, more stable era. As this happens, exceptions become more frequent, and top management may be asked to play a more significant role in making decisions that heretofore had been made by subordinate departments.

The reorganization of Pepsi in 1988 provides a good illustration of how demands for faster information processing that are driven by changes in a firm's external business environment can overwhelm its existing hierarchy. For Pepsi, a key change was the emergence of large regional supermarket chains. These chains often operated in territories that encompassed several different regional offices within the Pepsi Bottling Group. But Pepsi's existing structure gave no one regionwide authority over pricing decisions. When faced with requests for promotions or special pricing deals by a large supermarket chain, executives at Pepsi Bottling Group often disagreed about the appropriate strategy to follow. Their disputes were then funneled up the hierarchy to Roger Enrico, then the head of Pepsi USA, who was forced to become involved in region-level pricing and promotion decisions. Not surprisingly, this impaired Pepsi's ability to respond and put it at a competitive disadvantage in a market that demands nimble marketing responses to fast-changing circumstances. Part of the reason Pepsi chose a geographically oriented structure when it reorganized was to clarify the lines of authority in pricing and promotions. The new structure created the position of area general manager, who was given final authority for operational decisions (including pricing and promotions) within areas that were roughly the size of the territories of large supermarket chains.

Instead of changing its formal organizational structure, a firm can respond to demands for more complex or faster information processing through more informal changes, such as developing positions with responsibilities that cut across the established hierarchy or creating cross-functional teams, that is, teams whose objectives require the coordination of different functions and whose members are drawn from and knowledgeable about these functions. Incorporating cross-cutting positions or teams into a structure increases the amount of information flowing to individuals throughout the organization, which adds a lateral dimension to organization structure.

A lateral organization will be valuable when decision making is ideally decentralized or when the firm lacks top managers capable of making final decisions for several different functional or divisional areas.[21] For example, the firm could face demands for both standardized products and customized products that appeal to consumer tastes that vary substantially across local markets. If neither set of demands can be subordinated to the other, and these demands have contradictory implications for the firm's production operations or marketing and sales, then a cross-cutting approach to organization is likely to be beneficial. Creating a team with control over the relevant product dimensions and overall responsibility for the final product will place operational responsibility on the most knowledgeable individuals and give them the incentives to balance competing demands so as to arrive at the best outcome for the firm.

Galbraith's arguments highlight the role of organizational structure in promoting more effective *information processing* and *decision making*. Arthur Stinchcombe emphasizes the role of organizational structure in promoting more efficient retrieval of information.[22] Stinchcombe observes that firms process information from their environments to reduce uncertainty about the future conditions in which they will operate. The sources of information are often idiosyncratic to the firm or its industry. In some industries, certain customers will be the principal source of information, while in others, the most critical information could come from suppliers or from professional meetings. Stinchcombe argues that the firm should structure itself to facilitate the efficient retrieval of information. For example, a pharmaceutical firm might want an independent R&D department capable of rapid interaction with medical school faculty, an important source of ideas for new product development. Different levels of a firm's structure can deal with different informational needs. For example, if responsibility for controlling labor costs is given to local work groups, they will have the proper incentives to gather information about local labor market conditions. Dealing with federal regulations, however, should be the responsibility of a broader work group.

Stinchcombe also believes that firms should internalize activities (rather than rely on market coordination) when information from them is critical. It is important for firms to be "where the news breaks, whenever it breaks," since rapid information

---

[21]For details on lateral organizations, see Galbraith, J. R., E. E. Lawler, and Associates, *Organizing for the Future: The New Logic for Managing Complex Organizations*, San Francisco, CA: Jossey-Bass, 1993.

[22]Stinchcombe, A. L., *Information and Organizations*, Berkeley, CA: University of California Press, 1990. This discussion is taken from the overall framework of the book, which is presented in chapter 1 (pages 1–20). The framework is applied throughout the book to a variety of topics in economic sociology, manufacturing information systems (chapter 3), divisionalization (chapter 4), and innovation (chapter 5).

processing facilitates effective adjustments.[23] This is related to Kenneth Arrow's argument (discussed in Chapter 4) that firms may integrate upstream to obtain better information about input availability and prices.[24] Of course, as innovations in computer technologies, telecommunications, and financial markets reduce the costs to firms of information gathering, this has become less important in choosing an organizational structure.

Balancing Differentiation and Integration

Paul Lawrence and Jay Lorsch, in their study of the plastics, food, and container industries, discovered a tension between the benefits from creating independent specialized work groups that perform distinct tasks or serve unique markets, a phenomenon they refer to as *differentiation*, and the need to integrate disparate groups into a corporate whole.[25] In designing a structure, managers must balance differentiation and integration. Organizational structures may fail to sufficiently differentiate the activities of their firms. An example would be a firm that groups products facing different market conditions in the same division and motivates managers in different groups by the same incentive scheme. A uniform (undifferentiated) incentive compensation system will not be appropriate when business units face different levels of market maturity. Units facing mature markets may be capable of managing their production and distribution activities to meet moderate but not high performance objectives. Units facing new or high-growth markets, on the other hand, may be less able to match unit activities to outcomes on a regular basis. However, the average performance may be much higher for these units. To attempt to motivate managers in both types of units with the same incentive scheme will lead to a situation in which managers in one or both units are not motivated to attain their best performance levels. In addition, managers will be apt to see the scheme as unfair.

It is also possible to differentiate too much. For example, when several groups in a firm are given responsibility for marketing decisions, as was the case in Pepsi's organizational structure before it reorganized in 1988, the result could be intergroup conflicts over the appropriate marketing strategy or duplicative expenditures on activities, such as advertising or product promotion. (This happened at Pepsi.) Differentiation should be deemphasized when the distribution of resources and information between work groups is not distinct, so that planning, decision making, and control are necessary to help the managers of the firm act in a unified manner so that they speak with one voice to the extent possible and do not allow their pursuit of individual goals to detract from the firm's overall performance.

---

[23]Stinchcombe, A. L., *Information and Organization*, pp. 3–4.

[24]Arrow, K., "Vertical Integration and Communication," *Bell Journal of Economics*, 6, Spring 1975, pp. 173–182.

[25]Lawrence, P. R. and J. W. Lorsch, *Organization and Environment*, Boston: Harvard Business School Press, 1986.

◆ ◆

$\mathcal{E}$XAMPLE 17.3

ORGANIZATIONAL STRUCTURE AT AT&T

To illustrate contingency theory, we return to the emerging telephone system and AT&T, which we discussed in Example 17.2. Robert Garnet examined the growth of the Bell System between 1876 and 1909, during the early years of the firm when neither its monopoly status nor even its corporate survival could be taken for granted.[26] Garnet's study illustrates the relationship between a firm's structure and contingency factors, such as size and market turbulence.

One conclusion of contingency theory is that as the volume of its activities increases, a firm will have to reorganize. AT&T found itself in this situation during these years. Figures 17.8a and 17.8e show the tremendous increase in the volume of services provided by AT&T, as it built its national system from the web of licensing arrangements and informal relationships that prevailed until 1880. Figures 17.8b through 17.8d show how AT&T grew during this period, in terms of miles of wire laid and number of offices and employees. This increased volume of operations and the parallel increase in firm size suggest the need for a substantial reorganization.

Another conclusion of contingency theory is that as the environment becomes more volatile, for example, because of increased competition, a firm will need to reorganize to promote rapid processing of information. AT&T did face such increased competition during this period. Its initial patents expired in 1894, after which many new competitors entered local telephone markets. This new competition continued until 1913, when AT&T reached an agreement (called the Kingsbury Commitment) with the U.S. Department of Justice, in which antitrust complaints were dropped in exchange for assurances of access to AT&T lines by competitors and promises to notify the government prior to further growth. This agreement reestablished a near-monopoly status for AT&T and made its business environment more predictable. According to a contingency view, the increased competition after 1894 would put pressures on AT&T to reorganize to increase efficiency and flexibility and thus better respond to environmental demands.

The changes made by AT&T in its organization structure are consistent with contingency explanations. When the firm was first consolidated around 1880, it was a loose affiliation of Bell Company interests and licensees, held together not by formal structure, but by the terms of licenses and by partial equity ownership of licensees by the Bell Company. By 1884, this structure had become inefficient, and attempts were made to tighten the leases, improve accounting controls, and consolidate the firm. Company performance during this time is shown in Figure 17.9. By 1890, the first significant change in organization structure was proposed, based

---

[26]Garnet, R. W., *The Telephone Enterprise: The Evolution of the Bell System's Horizontal Structure, 1876–1909*, Baltimore, MD: Johns Hopkins University Press, 1985.

FIGURE 17.8

GROWTH OF BELL SYSTEM AS REFLECTED BY PLANT AND OPERATING
STATISTICS AT FIVE-YEAR INTERVALS.

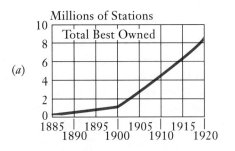

(a)

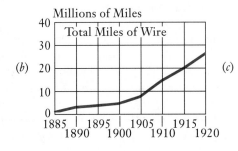

(b)

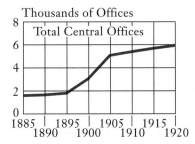

(c)

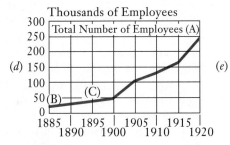

(d)

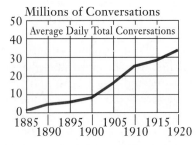

(e)

(A) Does not include the Employees of Western Electric Co., Inc.
(B) Does not include Long Lines Employees
(C) Published Figure, 14,517

Source: FCC, Telephone Investigation, p. 42.

on the territorial structure of the Metropolitan Telephone and Telegraph
Company of New York. (See Figure 17.10.) In addition, revisions were made in
corporate accounting procedures in 1891. The AT&T managers made these
changes in anticipation of the challenges that would arise after 1894.

Another major reorganization occurred at AT&T in 1909, this time focusing
on operating companies that were organized on state lines and that were subject to

FIGURE 17.9
PER-STATION STATISTICS: BELL TELEPHONE SYSTEM.

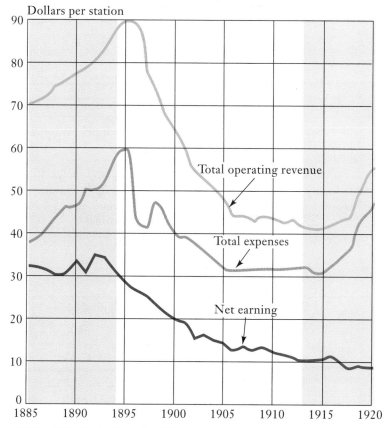

1885 – 1894 Early Period of Monopoly
1894 – 1913 Period of Competition
1913 – 1920 Period of "The Kingsbury Commitment"

Source: FCC, Telephone Investigation, p. 135.

overall control by AT&T corporate headquarters.[27] Each operating company was internally organized along functional lines. This reorganization occurred, coincidentally, at the lowest ebb of corporate performance before the Kingsbury Commitment. Figure 17.11 shows this reorganization of the Bell Companies. AT&T corporate headquarters was also reorganized on functional lines in 1912.

---

[27]A state basis for defining operating companies rather than some other geographic criterion was necessary because state governments were regulating telephone companies. Management responses that differed from one state to another were needed.

FIGURE 17.10

TERRITORIAL ORGANIZATION—1890: METROPOLITAN TELEPHONE AND TELEGRAPH CO.

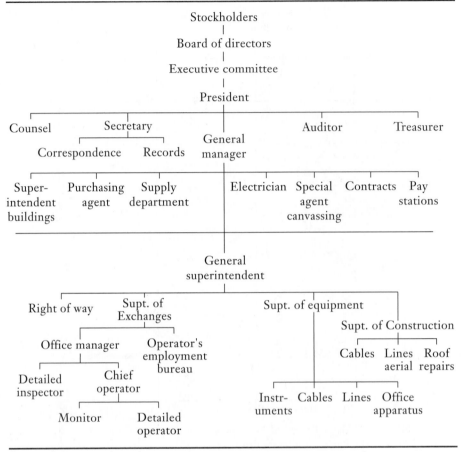

Source: AT&T Historical Archive.

These changes are also consistent with a contingency view. The functional structure improved the operating companies' ability to handle the increased volume of operations that developed during this period. The new headquarters structure fostered a division of labor between operating companies and headquarters and allowed the firm to expand as the Bell system grew.

◆ ◆ ◆ ◆ ◆ STRUCTURE FOLLOWS STRATEGY

Understanding the relationship between structure and contingency factors, such as technology and external demands for information processing, is necessary for explaining how a firm organizes. Contingency factors are not sufficient, however, be-

FIGURE 17.11
FUNCTIONAL ORGANIZATION—BELL TELEPHONE COMPANIES.

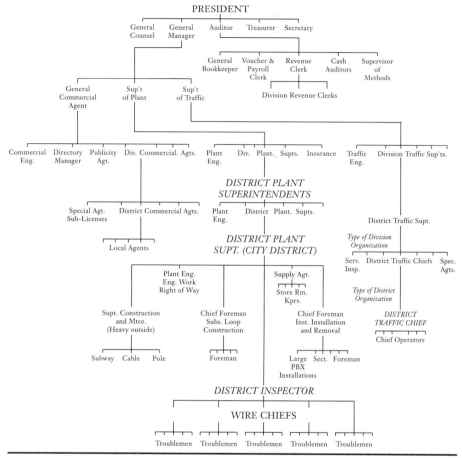

Source: AT&T, Historical Archives, *Application of Some General Principles of Organization* (New York, 1909).

cause many plausible factors may affect a firm in a given situation. The appropriate organizational structure depends on the context of the firm's strategy. The importance of strategic choices in understanding organizational structure was first articulated by Alfred Chandler in his classic work, *Strategy and Structure*.[28]

Strategy and Structure presents case studies of the evolution of organizational structure at DuPont, General Motors, Standard Oil of New Jersey (which later became Exxon), and Sears. Based on these case studies and others he conducted, Chandler concluded that the organizational structures of large vertically and hori-

---

[28]Chandler, A. D., *Strategy and Structure*, Cambridge, MA: MIT Press, 1962.

zontally integrated firms developed in response to the strategic choices their managers made. These choices, in turn, developed as the firm's managers responded to changes in its market and technological environment. In effect, Chandler found that changes in organization structure were driven by changes in strategy, which, in turn, were associated with changes in the external conditions firms faced. Put succinctly, Chandler's thesis is that *structure follows strategy*.

Chandler's basic argument runs as follows. In the late nineteenth century, developments in the technological and market infrastructures (which we describe in detail in Chapter 1) created opportunities for achieving unprecedented economies of scale and scope in various industries, such as tobacco, chemicals, light and heavy machinery, and meatpacking. Firms such as American Tobacco, DuPont, McCormick Harvesting Machine Company (which became International Harvester), and Swift responded to these opportunities by investing in large-scale production facilities and internalizing activities, such as sales and distribution, that had previously been performed for them by independent companies. They also developed managerial hierarchies. For example, within five years after investing in the Bonsack machine, an automated device for rolling cigarettes, American Tobacco Company had hired enough middle managers to fill an entire building on New York's Fifth Avenue. The first organizational structure typically employed by these early hierarchical firms was the functional structure, or U-form. This structure allowed firms to achieve a specialization of labor that facilitated the achievement of economies of scale in manufacturing, marketing, and distribution.

The firms that were the first in their industries to invest in large-scale production facilities and develop managerial hierarchies expanded rapidly and were often able to dominate their industries. But most of the early growth of these firms was within a single line of business or occurred within a single market. For example, as late as 1913, only 3 percent of DuPont's sales came from outside its core business of gunpowder, and nearly all of its gunpowder was sold in the United States.[29] But shortly after 1900, the strategies of many of these large hierarchical firms began to change. To continue to exploit economies of scale and scope, they moved away from a focus on a single line of business or a single market. Some firms, such as Singer and International Harvester, aggressively expanded overseas. Indeed, by 1914, the largest commercial enterprises in imperial Russia were Singer and International Harvester.[30] Other firms, such as DuPont and Proctor and Gamble, expanded primarily by diversifying their product lines. By 1920, for example, DuPont had expanded into paint and varnish, dyestuffs, celluloid, and rayon.

This shift in strategy—from a focus on a single business or market to product line diversification—revealed serious shortcomings in the U-form. These drawbacks are related to the issue of performance evaluation discussed earlier. Measuring the

---

[29]Chandler, A. D., *Strategy and Structure*, p. 78.

[30]Chandler, A. D., *Scale and Scope: The Dynamics of Industrial Capitalism*, Cambridge, MA: Harvard University Press, 1990, p. 200.

extent to which a functional department, such as sales, purchasing, or finance, contributes to firm profitability is difficult. This makes it hard to reward or punish managers of functional departments based on measurable indicators of how their departments perform. Without such measures, however, the firm's top management must monitor departmental managers directly to evaluate the quality of their effort. This may be possible in a firm with a simple line of business operating in a single geographic market. But in a firm that has diversified its product line or expanded overseas, the activities of functional departments are much more difficult to monitor. According to Chandler, the attempt by the top management of the newly diversified firms to monitor functional departments led to administrative overload and searches for alternative organizational structures. Nowhere is this more vividly illustrated than in the case of DuPont, where in 1921 the breakdown of the functional structure led to a massive reorganization along multidivisional lines. Chandler quotes a letter from a DuPont manager written at a time when DuPont seemed to be losing money on all of its products but explosives. This letter was highly critical of DuPont's executive committee—the body responsible for overall control of the company's affairs:

> The Executive Committee has failed and will continue to fail because, although it is held responsible for results, it is not properly constituted and it lacks authority. . . . It has never been found practicable for this Committee to discuss and control the affairs of any one department. Furthermore, it is unreasonable to expect that a majority of the members will be able to subject their own Departments to such self-examination and criticism so that the Company as a whole will operate efficiently. The various Departments of the Company lack an adequate directing and coordinating force at the present time, without which success is impossible.[31]

The multidivisional structure, or M-form, that emerged in the United States after 1920 was an organizational response to the limitations of the functional organization in diversified firms. The M-form created a division of labor between top managers and division managers that removed top managers from involvement in the operational details of functional departments, allowing them to specialize in strategic decisions and long-range planning. Division managers in this division of labor would monitor the operational activities of the functional departments that reported to them and would be rewarded on the basis of divisional performance. As we have discussed, divisional contributions to overall corporate success are easier to measure than functional-area contributions. Thus, running divisions as profit centers and basing rewards for division managers on divisional profit-and-loss statements are effective ways to motivate divisional managers.

While corporate structures have evolved since the days of the M-form, the principle that structure follows strategy still applies. The network structure of the well-known clothing manufacturer Benetton provides a clear example. Benetton's generic strategy is to differentiate itself from its competitors based on unique color

---

[31]Chandler, A. D., *Strategy and Structure*, p. 105.

combinations and bold designs. It has a formal structure that is functional, although many of its traditional functions are performed outside of Benetton by contractors (or *outsourced*). The organization operates not just through internal coordination, but through active external coordination of a network of suppliers and distributors, with whom Benetton maintains longstanding ties. The critical functional areas of product design and dyeing are performed in-house. Top management maintains direct lines of communication with store owners to facilitate exchange of information about customer demands. Benetton also works with several suppliers who can rapidly fill orders for undyed wool and cotton sweaters. Benetton's network structure built around functional areas enables it to rapidly tailor its product line to meet ever-changing consumer tastes.

$\mathcal{E}$XAMPLE 17.4

STRATEGY, STRUCTURE, AND THE ATTEMPTED MERGER BETWEEN THE UNIVERSITY OF CHICAGO HOSPITAL AND MICHAEL REESE HOSPITAL

The idea that strategy follows structure has important implications for mergers between firms that had pursued different strategies before they merged. In attempting to meld together two organizations following different strategies, issues relating to the control of assets and resources frequently arise. As we saw in Chapter 4, the allocation of rights of control of assets is a key determinant of how efficiently a vertical chain or a partnership of two organizations performs. Inside an organization, structure determines the basic rights to control the firm's assets. Thus, organizational structure can critically affect the success of a merger.

The attempted merger between the University of Chicago Hospital and the Michael Reese Hospital provides an example in which control of assets and resources was a key issue in the attempted integration of the two organizations. The University of Chicago Hospital is on the campus of a leading research university. This relationship led the hospital to pursue a strategy based on a reputation for providing state of the art medicine. Indeed, advertisements for the hospital described the research accomplishments of its medical staff. Consistent with this strategy, most physicians had faculty appointments in the university's medical school and were evaluated on the basis of research accomplishments. Physician salaries were based more on their academic standing than on the patient revenues they brought to the hospital.

The University of Chicago Hospital's nearest competitor on the city's south side was the Michael Reese Hospital. This hospital also had a long history of quality care, with special emphases on community service and on close relationships between medical staff and patients. The medical staff was organized according to a traditional scheme for a hospital—they were identified by clinical areas, but billed patients for their services independently of the hospital's billings. In other words, physicians were rewarded exclusively for providing patient care.

The two hospitals sought to merge in 1985. The merger would allow the hospitals to consolidate some services, reallocate others, and possibly avoid price and nonprice competition in the markets they both served. Anticipating the potential for conflict as two previously autonomous medical staffs sought to control complex resources and set policy for the merged unit, the two hospitals attempted to negotiate an organizational structure before they merged. As it turned out, the two hospitals could not develop an agreeable structure to manage their surgical departments as a single integrated unit. University physicians refused to be evaluated on the basis of clinical care, while Reese physicians refused to be thought of as research faculty. Unable to coordinate this vital area and fearful that economies of scale would not be realized, the hospitals called off the merger.

Evidence on Strategy and Structure

As business conditions change, a firm's strategy will also change in response to new opportunities and threats from the environment. If, as Chandler argues, structure follows strategy, the firm may also have to reorganize if it is to implement its new strategies successfully. The behavior of firms facing a common environment during periods of strategic change allows us to test the validity of this argument. We report on two tests of the structure-follows-strategy thesis: one that compared the performance of firms with different organizational structures in the same industry (petroleum) and the other comparing the performance of firms following the same strategy (diversification) but with different organizational structures.

Evidence from the Petroleum Industry

Henry Armour and David Teece conducted a test of the structure-follows-strategy hypothesis by examining reorganizations in the petroleum industry.[32] They studied 28 of the 32 petroleum firms in the *Fortune* 500 in 1975 for each year between 1950 and 1975. Firms were characterized according to their structural types: U-form, M-form, and intermediate types. Changes in structure from year to year were noted for each firm. The performance of firms, in terms of their return on equity, was also assessed. The study then examined the association between performance and structural type.

---

[32]Armour, H. O. and D. J. Teece, "Organizational Structure and Economic Performance: A Test of the Multidivisional Hypothesis," *Bell Journal of Economics*, 9, Spring 1978, pp. 106–122.

Armour and Teece found a strong association between a firm's early adoption of the M-form structure and profitability. However, this association did not persist once the M-form structure had been largely adopted throughout the industry (by 1969–1975). Their results suggest that the M-form provided a relative advantage to firms facing similar competitive conditions but that it did not provide a lasting advantage to the firms that initially adopted the structure. The study broadly supports the structure-follows-strategy thesis.

Evidence from Diversified Firms

The structure-follows-strategy argument of Chandler has a natural application to diversified firms. In particular, the M-form structure is likely to be associated with a product-market strategy emphasizing related diversification. The reason for this is clear: A strategy based on managing a portfolio of diverse businesses would seem to presume an organizational structure of somewhat autonomous divisions that can be bought, sold, or spun off as separate business units. If they pursued a diversification strategy, firms that did not initially reorganize their activities into divisions would be expected to encounter administrative and coordination problems among component businesses that would eventually lead to divisionalization.

Richard Rumelt considered this issue in his study of diversification strategy (recall the discussion of his work in Chapter 6). Among the firms he studied, Rumelt found that an M-form structure was associated with the pursuit of a diversification strategy in the years between 1949 and 1959 in ways that supported the Chandler hypothesis. Specifically, the shift to a multidivisional structure seemed to occur as a response to the administrative problems brought about by diversification. Between 1959 and 1969, the association between diversification and the adaptation of organization structure was less clear. Reorganization in this period was more an effort to change the content of business portfolios than to adjust to the organizational needs of a newly chosen diversification strategy. The idea that the initial adoption of the M-form was due to shifts in strategy, while later reorganizations were due to other considerations is supported by Michael Russo, who studied the diffusion of the M-form in the electric utility business.[33]

---

[33]Russo, M., "The Multidivisional Structure as an Enabling Device: A Longitudinal Study of Discretionary Cash as a Strategic Resource," *Academy of Management Journal*, 34, 1991: 718–733. Russo also found the adoption of the M-form to be associated with increases in a firm's levels of discretionary cash, a result consistent with managerial explanations for diversification, such as the free cash flow theory of Michael Jensen that was discussed in Chapter 6.

[34]For examples of these applications, see Stopford, J. and L. Wells, *Managing the Multinational Enterprise*, London: Longmans, 1972; Yoshihara, H., "Towards a Comprehensive Concept of Strategic Adaptive Behavior of Firms," in Ansoff, H. I., R. P. Declerck, and R. L. Hayes (eds.), *From Strategic Planning to Strategic Management*, New York: Wiley, 1976, pp. 103–124; and Galbraith, J. R. and R. K. Kazanjian, *Strategy Implementation*, 2nd ed., St. Paul, MN: West, 1986, pp. 128–144.

Strategy, Structure, and the Multinational Firm

From its initial development, Chandler's thesis that structure follows strategy has been applied to the organization of firms that compete internationally.[34] As multi-divisional firms became larger and more important, they were more likely to expand their operations overseas. These firms initially created "international divisions" to manage their activities in foreign countries. As foreign business grew, however, this structure was increasingly ineffective at coordinating foreign operations that, in effect, duplicated the activities of the domestic firm in multiple national markets. This problem led to reorganization into multinational firms, which are characterized by separate divisions for different countries (or regions, if national markets were sufficiently similar or if the volume of business in a particular area was small).

As the overseas business of multinationals continued to grow, they faced further pressures for coordination across countries as well as specialization within countries, especially for firms with technologies that permit the realization of substantial scale and scope economies. This led to the development of global strategies that viewed the entire world as the firm's market of interest. In turn, firms that pursued this strategy reorganized to promote scale economies in global production and distribution. The final step in the development of these firms in the international arena occurred when headquarters discovered that it needed to balance responsiveness to local conditions with centralization to achieve global economies. This transnational strategy is becoming associated with flexible organizations that combine matrix and network structures.

But are multinationals really different from any other multidivisional firm? To justify the view that multinationals are different, one needs to identify the conditions firms in the international arena face that are different from those that domestic firms face. There are several possibilities.[35] First, international markets may offer more opportunities for scale and scope economies than national markets. For example, one way in which Japanese firms like Canon and Ricoh were able to compete with American firms in the production and sales of copiers from their initial product base in cameras was by increasing share in regional markets above what would have been available domestically.[36] This gave them previously unattainable scale economies. Second, competition in multiple national markets may make a firm less dependent on regulatory conditions in any single country, allowing it to face less risk from government interference than domestic firms would have to deal with. The diversity of values faced by firms in multiple national markets could also prompt more innovation than a purely domestic market would. Finally, the variety of business and financial conditions that multinational

---

[35]Kim, W. C., Hwang, P. and W. P. Burgers, "Multinationals' Diversification and the Risk-Return Trade-Off," *Strategic Management Journal*, 14, 1993, pp. 275–286.

[36]Porter, M. E., *The Competitive Advantage of Nations*, New York: Free Press, 1990, pp. 407, 577.

firms face in an international environment provides them with increased opportunities for financially driven diversification strategies, foreign exchange transactions, and related activities.

◆ ◆

ℰXAMPLE 17.5

TRANSNATIONAL STRATEGY AND ORGANIZATION STRUCTURE AT SMITHKLINE-BEECHAM[37]

SmithKline-Beecham, a transnational pharmaceutical firm that was created in 1989 by the merger of the American firm SmithKline-Beckman and the British firm Beecham, illustrates the interaction of strategy and structure in global markets. A merger with Beecham was attractive to SmithKline for several reasons. SmithKline depended on a few products (primarily the anti-ulcer drug Tagamet) for much of its sales. It was vulnerable to losing market share to generic drugs, and was open to a takeover because it had overdiversified. Moreover, SmithKline-Beckman and Beecham had several complementary product lines. Beecham was strong in consumer health products and self-medications, while SmithKline was stronger in prescription drugs. The two firms also had potential synergies in their scientific competences and new product development schedules. Merging them resulted in a firm with a combined annual research and development budget of over $750 million. Finally, the firms had complementary geographic markets: Beecham was strong in Europe, and SmithKline in the United States and Japan.

In principle, SmithKline might have been able to expand into new products and markets and develop additional scientific competences either through internal development or through hybrid organizational arrangements, such as strategic alliances and joint ventures.[38] But SmithKline felt that internal product development and market expansion would have occurred too slowly to be of much practical value in the increasingly competitive global pharmaceuticals market. And while it did experiment with strategic alliances and joint ventures, SmithKline often found them to be inadequate. Alliances proved to be too loose to provide incentives for the allied firms to cooperate with each other, and the autonomous standing that the partners retained under joint ventures led to governance and incentive problems in securing cooperation.

Given the complex synergies that motivated the merger, determining an organizational structure for the combined firm was a significant issue associated with the implementation of the merger. Henry Wendt, the CEO after the merger,

---

[37]This example is based on material in Wendt, H., *Global Embrace*, New York: Harper Business, 1993, chaps. 2 and 6.

[38]Strategic alliances and joint ventures are discussed in Chapter 4.

summed up the organization problem in the following way: "Neither form of organization structure (product or geography) simultaneously captures the kinds of global-local synergies of skills, scale, and scope now considered necessary by aggressive transnational companies." SmithKline-Beecham eventually adopted a "flexible matrix" structure made up of "modified matrix-based multifunctional teams." This structure combines centralized functional decision structures with local decision-making autonomy. The flexible matrix emphasized strong local management teams, with responsibility for customer-focused functions, including sales, marketing, and product design. In addition to local decision-making autonomy, the structure allows global efficiencies to be pursued at the corporate level by functional groups, such as manufacturing, information technologies, and research and development.

$\mathcal{E}$XAMPLE 17.6

SAMSUNG: REINVENTING A CORPORATION[39]

Often, major environmental shifts force corporations to reassess strategies and restructure their organizations to adapt to changed circumstances. The Samsung business group provides an excellent example of how to reinvent a corporation when faced with the hostile market forces that Asian firms must increasingly endure.

Samsung was founded in 1938 as a general trading store, exporting fruit and dried fish to Japanese-occupied Manchuria. It has since grown to become the largest South Korean business group, or *chaebol*, at $54 billion in sales. Samsung operates in such diverse industries as aerospace, chemicals, and finance, but is best known as the world's largest maker of leading-edge computer memory chips.

Samsung's rise to prominence, however, has been based on strong central government support, an inexpensive labor force, and authoritarian culture. As a result, Samsung's strategy from the 1960s until the mid-1980s has been based on using cheap labor to produce lower-quality products at low prices. By also producing large volumes, Samsung reaped economies of scale and thus captured comfortable margins, which also enabled it to enter a variety of businesses with great success.

In the late 1980s, however, a combination of factors negatively impacted Samsung's historical sources of competitive advantage and caused it to reevaluate the strategies that had brought the company such unparalleled success for over two

[39]This example is based on materials from four sources: "Samsung's Radical Shakeup," *Business Week*, February 28, 1994, pp. 74–76; "Samsung: Korea's Great Hope for High Tech," *Business Week*, February 3, 1992, pp. 44–45; "Good to be Big, Better to be Good," *The Economist*, August 18, 1990, pp. 7–10; "Samsung: South Korea Marches to its own Drummer," *Forbes*, May 16, 1988, pp. 84–89.

decades. Samsung does not have unions because it pays high wages, but the general labor climate has become less friendly. The value of the South Korean currency, the won, has also appreciated, making South Korean exports more expensive. In addition, increased global competition has further eroded Samsung's competitive positioning.

In response, Chairman Lee Kun-Hee has launched a sweeping remake of Samsung's culture, including a restructuring of operations. Lee has radically decentralized managerial decision making and encouraged individuality in a company that was known for its rigid hierarchy and subservience to authority. Managers who are not able to assume such decision responsibility are fired. To encourage individuality, Lee has initiated training programs and other innovative techniques. For instance, each year Samsung sends 400 managers abroad, fully subsidized, for 12 months to do whatever they want. The only requirement is that when they return, they must show proficiency in the host country's language and culture.

In addition to reinventing the culture at Samsung, Lee has also consolidated groups with related businesses and has decided to specialize in more capital- and technology-intensive industries. Samsung has also initiated a major quality campaign to shift from a low-quality, low-cost producer to high quality. Lee wants to continue to pursue high-quality, high-tech markets and compete on an equal basis with leading American, Japanese, and European firms.

However, this dramatic shift in culture and operations also requires being at the leading edge in innovation and productivity. Samsung has traditionally adopted technology from more advanced firms, but Lee recently instituted a massive R&D spending program to make Samsung more self-sufficient. Further, Lee has spent a lot of money automating plants and even moving some plants to Mexico to achieve labor savings. Samsung has truly transformed itself in response to major changes in global markets as well as in South Korea. One sign that Lee's programs are working is that Samsung has recently won IBM's seal of approval as a supplier, clearing up many doubts about the ability of Samsung to provide quality products.

Does Structure Follow Strategy?

It is reasonable to think that how a firm organizes will depend on the strategy it pursues. If structure is a tool for coordination, then the purposes to which the tool is put—the firm's strategy—should be identified before designing a structure. While the structure-follows-strategy argument provides a foundation for the intentional development and reorganization of firms, there are limits to our ability to redesign organizations, and other factors besides managerial intentions are needed to understand how structures develop. These may include the history or broader environmental context of the firm, as well as trends in how other firms are organizing.

While structure and strategy are no doubt linked, the mechanism by which they are linked is often unclear. Sociologists, such as Charles Perrow and Jeffrey Pfeffer, have argued that structure is more determined by the power of the various groups within a firm to select a structure favorable to their interests and unfavorable to the interests of opponents.[40] While managers can reorganize to solve their coordination and control problems, these problems can often be solved in several ways and do not require the adoption of a particular organizational form. Arthur Stinchcombe provides a detailed analysis of Sears that parallels the ideas of efficient information processing and reduction of transactions costs that we discussed above.[41] While he agrees that changes in large firms are prompted by executives' problems in coordination, he argues that firms do not have to adopt the multidivisional form to solve them. He also shows how the problems faced by large firms are not all of the same type, nor is their solution necessarily consistent with the superiority of the multidivisional structure. For example, he demonstrates the importance for Sears of a centralized purchasing office (presuming a functional basis of organizing) even when the firm had supposedly adopted a multidivisional structure.

This section discusses several ways in which structure and strategy might be linked other than through the purposeful design of organizational structure to achieve the successful implementation of strategy. We focus on two possible linkages.

- Structure influences strategy through its effect on information flows and decision-making biases in the organization.

- Structure and strategy represent a complex set of behavior patterns, or routines, that evolve over the history of the firm in response to changes in its external environment.

Structure, Strategy, and Decision Making

Thomas Hammond argues that structure influences strategy because critical knowledge and decision-making capabilities in large firms are dispersed throughout the firm rather than concentrated in top managers.[42] If this is true, then a firm's

---

[40]For a classic argument on the structure of the business firm as being influenced by a "dominant coalition" of top managers, see March, J., "The Business Firm as a Political Coalition," *Journal of Politics*, 24, 1962, pp. 662–678. For a view of reorganizations as being determined by shifts in resource dependencies, see Pfeffer, J., *Managing with Power: Power and Influence in Organizations*, Boston: Harvard Business School Press, 1992; For Perrow's arguments on structure as a source of power for managers, see the exchange between Chandler, Williamson, and Charles Perrow concerning power versus efficiency explanations for organization structure in Van de Ven, A. H. and W. F. Joyce (eds.), *Perspectives on Organization Design and Behavior*, New York: Wiley, 1981.

[41]Stinchcombe, A. L., *Information and Organizations*, Berkeley, CA: University of California Press, 1990, pp. 126–131.

[42]Hammond, T. H., "Structure, Strategy, and the Agenda of the Firm," in Rumelt, R., D. E. Schendel, and D. J. Teece (eds.), *Fundamental Issues in Strategy*, Boston: Harvard Business School Press, 1994, pp. 97–154.

structure determines how and in what order lower-level decision makers come together to contribute their information to corporate decisions—it sets the agenda for top managers in making strategic decisions. Because it sets the agenda for the firm, structure determines which options are considered for a decision, which options are to be compared, and in what order comparisons are to be made.

A related point is that organizational structure can bias the information that flows up through the hierarchy to the decision makers at the top. The perspectives of lower-level decision makers may be systematically biased according to the requirements of their positions within the firm's structure. For example, manufacturing, sales, and research personnel often differ in their time frames (e.g., short-run versus long-run orientations) and their responsibilities to the organization.[43] This means that top managers bear the additional burden of compensating for lower-level biases.

Hammond also argues that organizational structure determines which decision options are considered and the criteria by which they are evaluated. The options that managers consider must be based in part on the current activities of the firm and on information about current product market conditions. For most firms, this information comes from lower-level individuals in the firm by way of the firm's structure. Different structures present different sets of options to executives. For example, it will be difficult to develop a strategy emphasizing mergers and acquisitions in a firm that has not organized its product lines into separate units that can be bought and sold.

Structure also influences how strategies are implemented by providing rules for resolving disputes. These may be consistent or inconsistent with the requirements of the firm's strategy. For example, if a strategy requires that employees perform their tasks and represent themselves to customers consistently, then disputes among employees should be referred up the hierarchy, so that a consistent approach to problems can be developed. A structure that provides incentives to employees to use the hierarchy for dispute resolution would be consistent with this strategy. On the other hand, if a strategy required the timely use of localized knowledge by employees, then dispute resolution approaches that consistently referred problems up the hierarchy to superiors would be inconsistent with the strategy and would probably increase the costs of implementation for the firm.

A firm's structure also influences what information reaches top managers about strategy implementation. If top managers delegate much of their decision making to lower-level individuals, then they will learn about implementation primarily from the conflicts that are referred upward for resolution. If the firm's structure is biased to prevent certain types or amounts of conflicts from being referred upward, the information that top managers receive will be similarly biased.

---

[43]This point about position-based bias is well established in organizational analysis. For example, see Barnard, C., *The Functions of the Executive*, Cambridge, MA: Harvard, 1938; Cyert, R. and J. March, *A Behavioral Theory of the Firm*, Englewood Cliffs, NJ: Prentice-Hall, 1963; Lawrence, P. and J. Lorsch, *Organization and Environment*, Cambridge, MA: Harvard Business School Press, 1986.

The overall message is that structure can bias in various ways the information or set of decisions that reach top managers. Gary Miller takes this point further and argues that an exclusive reliance on formal hierarchy, administrative controls, or incentive systems is likely to be self-defeating. An optimal piece-rate system, for example, will always tempt managers to cheat and raise performance standards to obtain more from employees. An optimal group incentive system will likewise generate temptations for members to take advantage of the efforts of others. While formal hierarchy may improve on transactions costs in the marketplace (as discussed in Chapter 3), it generates its own set of intractable problems, or dilemmas, for managers. Miller suggests that formal hierarchy and administrative controls need to be supplemented by less formal devices, such as leadership and culture, for achieving the cooperation of managers and subordinates.[44]

Structure as Routine and Heuristic

Richard Nelson and Sidney Winter, the proponents of "evolutionary economics," view the actions of firms (e.g., what they produce; how they market their products; how much they invest in research and development; whom they hire and fire) as the result of a complex set of behavior patterns, or *routines*.[45] These routines evolve over the history of the firm in response to changes in the firm's external environment. They simplify the complexity of the information a firm receives from its environment and constitute its "learning by doing." As a firm encounters problems, it experiments with variations from current routines until it obtains a satisfactory result. When that occurs, the organization "remembers" the solution by continuing to perform the routine in the future. In this sense, an organization's routines form the basis of its competences—what it does particularly well. A firm's routines can also concern conflict resolution and governance. As the firm develops, it also encounters problems with conflict, incentives and motivation, and control. Satisfactory solutions to these problems are retained in routines, while unsatisfactory activities are eventually changed. Thus routines represent "truces" among contending parties within the firm.

Nelson and Winter offer two views of the strategy-structure relationship, both of which differ from Chandler. The first is a bottom-up view of strategy and structure, in which both evolve from a series of local interactions of the firm with its environment rather than from the formulation and implementation of a comprehensive reorganization decision by top managers. The relationship of the firm to its environment, as well as the current patterns of interpersonal relationships generally referred to as the firm's "structure," are the cumulative result of a long series of adaptations to environmental stimuli.

---

[44]Miller, G. J., *Managerial Dilemmas*, Cambridge, UK: Cambridge University Press, 1992, chaps. 10 and 11.

[45]Nelson, R. R. and S. G. Winter, *An Evolutionary Theory of Economic Change*, Cambridge, MA: Belknap, 1982.

Nelson and Winter also present a view of the strategy-structure relationship that considers how managers make decisions. Seen this way, strategy and structure are high-level *heuristics*, or principles for decision making that reduce the average time that decision makers must spend in searching for solutions to difficult nonroutine problems. Strategy is a set of principles for solving the firm's problems of survival and profitability. Structure, analogously, is a set of principles for coordinating actors within the firm in a manner consistent with the firm's activities in the environment. A heuristic view of strategy and structure is inconsistent with a comprehensive optimizing view of top-management decision making, however. In their strategic decisions, managers will be bound by routines and will tend either to maintain prior decisions or to incrementally modify them. Large-scale strategic change by firms will be rare, as will comprehensive reorganizations. Current decisions about strategy and structure will be heavily constrained by past decisions.

CHAPTER SUMMARY

◆ Organizational structure refers to the general and persistent patterns by which firms organize tasks, people in tasks, and information flows.

◆ If a firm's strategy is to be carried out, or *implemented*, effectively, individuals working within the firm must know about the strategy and its operational details. A firm's structure reflects the ways in which the firm solves problems of information and coordination on a regular basis.

◆ Problems of incentives and controls complicate the problem of coordinating cooperative agents to carry out the firm's strategy.

◆ Simple tasks, performed by small work groups, can be structured in three ways: (1) *Individually:* where members of the work group are treated as if they were independent and receive incentives based on individual actions and outcomes; (2) *Self-managed teams:* where a collection of individuals is treated as interdependent and where each member works with others to set and pursue some common set of objectives, with individuals rewarded, in part, for group performance; and (3) *Hierarchy of authority:* where one member of the group specializes in monitoring and coordinating the work of the other members.

◆ Large firms often require *complex hierarchies*, by which is meant a structure that involves multiple groups and multiple levels of groupings. Complex hierarchy arises when there is a need to organize simple work groups together into larger groups.

◆ Complex hierarchy involves two related problems: (1) *departmentalization* and (2) *coordination of activities within and between subgroups.*

◆ Departmentalization involves the identification of formal groupings within the organization. These groups may be organized along a number of different dimensions: common tasks or functions, inputs, outputs, geographic location, and time frame of work.

◆ Once groups have been identified and organized, problems of coordination and control arise. *Coordination* involves the flow of information to facilitate subunit decisions that are consistent with each other and with organizational objectives. *Control* involves the location of decision-making rights and rulemaking authority within the hierarchy.

◆ There are two alternative approaches for developing coordination within firms. The first emphasizes *autonomy* or *self-containment* of work units, while the second emphasizes the importance of strong *lateral relations* across work groups.

◆ The allocation of authority within the firm is typically considered in terms of *centralization* versus *decentralization*. As decisions are made at higher levels—that is, by senior managers—the firm is said to be more centralized regarding those decisions. Conversely, as certain decisions are made at lower levels, the firm can be said to be decentralized regarding those decisions.

◆ Four basic types of structure for large organizations can be identified: (1) the unitary *functional* structure (often called the U-form); (2) the *multidivisional* structure (often called the M-form); (3) the *matrix* structure; and (4) the *network* structure.

◆ The best organizational structure for a particular firm depends on the specific circumstances it faces. The notion that there is no uniformly "best" organizational structure for all firms in all circumstances is known as *contingency theory*.

◆ Contingency theory has focused on three factors that affect the relative efficiency of different structures: (1) technology and task interdependence; (2) information flows; and (3) the tension between differentiation and integration.

◆ Contingency factors are not sufficient for understanding a firm's structure, however, since many plausible contingencies may affect a firm in a given situation. Determination of the appropriate organizational structure must be considered in the context of the firm's strategy.

◆ The first structure typically employed by large firms was the functional structure, or U-form. This structure allowed a specialization of labor to facilitate economies of scale in manufacturing, marketing, and distribution.

◆ The multidivisional structure, or M-form, which emerged in the United States after 1920, is an organizational response to the limitations of the functional organization in diversified firms. This structure creates a division of labor between top managers and division managers that removes top managers from involvement in the operational details of functional departments and allows them to specialize in strategic decisions and long-range planning. Division managers in the M-form firm monitor the operational activities of the functional departments that report to them and are rewarded on the basis of divisional performance.

◆ While corporate structures have evolved since the days of the M-form, the principle that structure follows strategy still applies for more complex structures, such as matrices or networks.

◆ The thesis that structure follows strategy has been applied to firms that compete internationally. As multidivisional firms became larger, they were more likely to expand their operations overseas and initially created "international divisions" to manage their activities in foreign countries. This structure grew ineffective at co-ordinating foreign operations, which led firms to reorganize in multinational struc-tures, characterized by separate divisions for different countries.

◆ As their overseas business grew further, multinationals faced further pressures for coordination across countries as well as specialization within countries. This led to the development of global strategies that viewed the entire world as the firm's market of interest. Firms that pursued global strategies reorganized to promote scale economies in global production and distribution.

◆ Recently, multinationals have discovered the need to balance responsiveness to local conditions with centralization to achieve global economies. This is the transnational strategy, and it is becoming associated with flexible organizations that combine matrix and network structures.

◆ While the structure-follows-strategy argument provides a foundation for the intentional development of organization of firms, there are limits to our ability to redesign organizations, and other factors besides managerial intentions are needed to understand structures. These include the history and the broader environmen-tal context of the firm, as well as trends in how other firms are organizing.

Questions

1. A team of eight individuals must fold, stuff, seal, and stamp 250 preaddressed envelopes. Offer some suggestions for organizing this team. Would your sugges-tions differ if, instead of envelopes, the team was responsible for assembling 250 personal computers? Why?

2. Matrix organizations first sprang up in businesses that worked on scientific and engineering projects for narrow customer groups. Examples include Fluor, which built oil refineries in Saudi Arabia, and TRW, which supplied aerospace equipment to NASA. What do you suppose the dimensions of the matrix would be in such firms? Why would these companies develop such a complex structure?

3. Consider a firm whose competitive advantage is built almost entirely on its ability to achieve economies of scale in producing small electric motors that are used by the firm to make hair dryers, fans, vacuum cleaners, and food processors. Should this firm be organized on a multidivisional basis by product (hair dryer division, food processor division, etc.) or should it be organized functionally (marketing, manufacturing, finance, etc.)?

4. What types of structures would a firm consider if it was greatly expanding in global operations?

5. In the 1980s, Sears acquired several financial services firms, including Allstate Insurance and Dean Witter Brokerage Services. Sears kept these businesses as largely autonomous divisions. By 1995, the strategy had failed and Sears had di-vested all of its financial services holdings. Bearing in mind the dictum that struc-ture follows strategy, identify the strategy that Sears had in mind when it acquired these businesses, and recommend a structure that might have led to better results.

6. It is sometimes argued that a matrix organization can serve as a mechanism for achieving *strategic fit*—the achievement of synergies across related business units resulting in a combined performance that is greater than the units could achieve if they operated independently. Explain how a matrix organization could result in the achievement of strategic fit.

POWER AND CULTURE

18

*M*ichael Eisner, the chairman and CEO of the Walt Disney Company, is justly credited with its turnaround and resurgence, which began with his ascendence to the top job in 1984 and continued into the 1990s.[1] Growth under Eisner has truly been astonishing. Disney's share price rose 1,400 percent over 10 years, from a value of $3 in December 1983 to $42 in December 1993. Sales have grown at an annual rate of over 21 percent, from $1.3 billion in 1983 to $7.5 billion in 1992, while net income increased at an annual rate of 27 percent over the same period, from $93 million to $817 million. In a decade of restructurings and layoffs, total Disney employees rose from 30,000 in 1983 to 58,000 in 1992. This growth and profitability are based on a major strategic reorientation of the Disney businesses that has included a reemphasis on theme parks, enhanced video marketing effort for the Disney film library, and a rebirth of animated feature films, with such successes as *The Little Mermaid*, *Beauty and the Beast*, *Aladdin*, and *The Lion King*. Eisner's strategy also included new ventures in cable television, TV production, the retailing of Disney merchandise, and even sports teams (the Anaheim Mighty Ducks hockey team). There is little doubt that Michael Eisner is the ruler of the Magic Kingdom, and he helps represent the firm to investors and the public.

However, 1994 did not prove to be an entertaining year for Eisner and Disney. Part of Eisner's troubles certainly stem from the continuing poor performance of Euro Disney, which lost nearly a billion dollars in 1993 and for which Disney took

---

[1]The information and quotations used in this example were obtained from the Bloomberg wire service.

a $350 million charge. The difficulties that were most noteworthy in 1994, however, appeared to center on Eisner himself and on conflicts within his management team over succession and power. To start with, Disney's president and chief operating officer, Frank Wells, died unexpectedly in a helicopter crash. Then, the continuing poor performance of Disney's nonanimated features led Eisner to fire Ricardo Mestres, head of Disney's Hollywood pictures unit. Following that, Eisner aroused uncertainty among Disney observers when he had to have emergency coronary bypass surgery. Finally, investors were unsure about Disney's intentions concerning possible ventures into telecommunications. Eisner had opposed such ventures earlier in the year, but then had increasingly voiced support for them. The future direction of Disney was unclear, even with continuing high earnings.

It was in this context that Eisner announced the resignation of Jeffrey Katzenberg, the chairman of the Walt Disney Studios, who had come to Disney along with Eisner from Paramount in 1984 and whose unit had been responsible for much of Disney's profits during the decade, on the basis of its highly successful animated feature films. According to multiple news reports, the resignation reflected Katzenberg's dissatisfaction at not being appointed to the number two position at Disney, which had been vacant since the death of Frank Wells. Katzenberg's intention to leave if passed over for promotion was signaled in September 1993, when he waived substantial Disney stock options ($100 million), so that he could leave the studio within the year if he wished, well in advance of his contract terms.

Rather than fill the number two position with someone other than Katzenberg, Eisner announced a sweeping reorganization of Disney's filmed entertainment businesses into two groups. The first would deal with television and telecommunications services and would be headed by Richard Frank, who had been president of the Walt Disney studios since 1985. The second group would concentrate on the production and distribution of motion pictures and would be headed by Joe Roth, the head of Caravan Pictures, a Disney Studios unit.

Observers uniformly took Katzenberg's resignation as indicating that Eisner did not want to share decision-making power at the top of Disney, even if it meant the loss of Katzenberg. One Disney insider was quoted as saying, "I guess Eisner has to be a one-man show." Katzenberg, on the other hand, felt he had earned the right to more participation in the direction of Disney and was resolved to leave if he could not obtain that participation. It is also claimed that he sought a more independent relationship with his longtime mentor Eisner.

The reaction of observers to these top management changes was mixed. Some felt that Katzenberg's exit cast doubt on the vitality of Disney's film business, especially its profitable animated feature films, at a time when problems persisted with Euro Disney and when future directions were unclear. Others saw the reorganization as a tangible commitment toward improving weak business lines (such as nonanimated feature films) and resolving uncertainty regarding Disney's direction in providing programming and other services to telecommunications firms. As one analyst said, "Because of the actions he (Eisner) has taken, he has shown that he is taking charge." Analysts were also mixed in their recommendations regarding Disney stock, whose performance fluctuated during this period.

It is unclear how these changes will affect Disney's competitive strategy. For example, Katzenberg had been a strong proponent of the acquisition by Disney of CBS and the prospects for the merger are less certain since his resignation. There is also speculation that Katzenberg will eventually end up at a competitor of Disney, such as Sony. This seemed very likely in late 1994, when Katzenberg announced the formation of DreamWorks SKG, a joint venture with Hollywood moguls Steven Spielberg and David Geffen.

These events raise issues about the nature of power and culture within large firms. What is power? How do CEOs, such as Eisner, gain it? How does a strong reputation for success enhance one's power? How much do executives value and use their power and what types of tradeoffs do they make among power over organizational decision making, compensation, and corporate performance? Power is also tied up with the culture of a firm. A firm's culture, if it is strong, can both constrain its manager's strategic activities and help them maintain their stature and perceived performance in the firm. What was the nature of the corporate culture at Disney under Eisner? How did Eisner build that culture? To what extent is he limited in his strategic options because of the Disney tradition? These are some of the issues of interest to us in this chapter, which considers the topics of power and corporate culture. As was the case with organization structure, power and culture have been considered by scholars largely in noneconomic terms. Our focus is on their economic importance for firms in enabling action in the absence of the ability of parties within the firm to cost-effectively contract for needed services.

POWER AND CULTURE IN COMPLEX ORGANIZATIONS ◆ ◆ ◆ ◆ ◆

As we have discussed throughout this book, the modern firm represents a complex division of labor across several dimensions of activity. Within each business unit, the firm embodies a variety of activities linked together both horizontally and on the vertical chain. Each business unit can be composed of a variety of divisions, departments, and subunits within departments. These groupings *within* business units are complicated by groupings *among* business units, which range from larger divisions to more complex matrix relationships. Furthermore, individuals within the firm maintain extensive relationships with outsiders, including buyers, suppliers, competitors, media, and regulators.

The complexity of firms gives rise to a similarly complex array of goals and subgoals by which individuals can link their individual activities and rewards to those of the groups and subunits to which they belong and ultimately to the performance of the firm. The overall performance of the firm is thus determined by the aggregation and integration of the performance of individual employees and managers. The complexity of the firm's goal and reward structures, however, raises the strong likelihood of conflicts among individuals over what goals to pursue as well as how and when to pursue them. An individual may be tempted to pursue his or her own goals, even to the detriment of the firm, provided the incentive is sufficiently strong. One would like to think that, at least in principle, a control system could be designed to integrate individual behaviors into unified organizational action, but that seems impossible. The conditions that give rise to market failures (and thus prompt the choice of internal organization in the first place) also work to frustrate hierarchical control, through problems of hidden action and hidden information (discussed in Chapter 16) that provide ample room for opportunistic behavior by employees. The informational limitations of hierarchies, coupled with the often conflicting requirements of incentive compatibility and technical efficiency, imply that conflicts among employees over which tasks to perform and how to perform them are unlikely to be resolved through formal controls alone.

Organization structure represents the formal and contractual allocation of decision-making rights within firms, while organization controls are made up of those explicit and contractible incentive arrangements that firms can make with their employees. Yet there is much within organizations that must occur outside the scope of contractible arrangements. It is in this context of incomplete contractual arrangements and chronic goal conflict within firms that power and culture are important.

While organization structure and controls provide the general pattern of arrangements within which a firm functions, power and culture produce unified action in conditions in which governance problems would frustrate such action, although they do so in different ways. Power and politics produce action, in the absence of contracts, through the subordination of individual interests to those of the dominant individuals in the firm. Politically powerful actors use the self-interest of others, both inside the firm, and in key external stakeholders, to secure concerted action. Culture, on the other hand, is a set of collectively held values, beliefs, and norms of behavior that modifies individual employee preferences, so that collective action is possible and guides employees toward firm goals. As David Kreps explains, "culture . . . gives hierarchical inferiors an idea *ex ante* how the firm will 'react' to circumstances as they arise—in a very strong sense, it gives identity to the organization."[2] While power and culture are interrelated, we discuss them separately in the remainder of the chapter.

◆ ◆ ◆ ◆ ◆ POWER

Because power and related terms are so widely used by both academics and business practitioners, the meanings associated with them are many and potentially

---

[2]Kreps, D. M., "Corporate Culture and Economic Theory," in Alt, J. and K. Shepsle (eds.), *Perspectives on Positive Political Economy*, Cambridge, U.K.: Cambridge University Press, 1990.

confusing.[3] We take power to be an individual's ability to accomplish his or her goals by means of resources obtained through *noncontractual exchange relationships* with other actors. This is not the same as authority, which stems from the explicit contractual decision-making rights granted an individual by a firm. A powerful manager may exercise his or her power by redirecting the activities of other actors away from their immediate goals and toward the accomplishment of his or her own goals. In this sense, power is the ability to get things done. Influence, a related term that is often used interchangeably with power, concerns the exercise or use of power in a given situation by an individual rather than the individual's overall power or his or her general ability to get things done.

Power exists at many levels in a firm.[4] At the level of individuals, for example, particular managers may be powerful relative to their peers in the management team. Visible examples of the exercise of individual power occur in the top management ranks of a firm, where the power of the CEO relative to the board of directors is critical to allocating key resources. It is also common to discuss power at the level of departments or groups. In universities, for example, academic departments continually vie for budgetary resources and view their success in obtaining such resources as tangible evidence of their power, which may stem from their popularity with students, from the research productivity of their faculty, or from success in securing government and foundation grants. Finally, firms can exercise power in their product markets, in other factor markets (such as with raw material or labor suppliers), or in relations with other environmental stakeholders. A powerful firm like Disney, for example, may obtain more favorable distribution of a new animated film than a rival movie studio would. It would also have power in negotiations with toy manufacturers seeking to develop products based on Disney characters.

The Sources of Power

Power is often exerted in an economic market, as when a firm with a patent for a new drug uses its market power to set a high price-cost margin. Our interest here is in power that cannot be exerted in the market, that is, power that cannot be easily priced. Individuals attain this power when they possess resources that are of value to others but are not bought or sold in a market. Examples include Michael Eisner's power to veto a new film project, or an academic dean's power over new

---

[3]For social science applications of power, see March, J. G., "The Power of Power," in Easton, D. (ed.), *Varieties of Political Theory*, New York: Prentice-Hall, 1966. For definitional issues, see Kipnis, D., *The Powerholders*, Chicago: University of Chicago Press, 1976, pp. 8–14; Pfeffer, J., *Power in Organizations*, Marshfield, MA: Pitman, 1981, chap. 1; and Lukes, S., *Power: A Radical View*, London, U.K.: Macmillan, 1974.

[4]Perrow, C., *Complex Organizations: A Critical Essay*, 2nd ed., New York: Random House, 1986, p. 262.

course offerings. What are the sources of such power? Answering this involves two separate questions. First, what types of resources can provide power to actors? Second, under what conditions does the possession of a resource give its holder power?

John French and Bertram Raven identified five general bases of power: legitimate power, reward power, coercive power, expert power, and referent power.[5] *Legitimate (or formal) power* is based on the formal authority one receives by occupying a high-ranking position. By legitimate, we mean that an individual, by virtue of his or her position, has a right to expect compliance from others and that others in the firm will generally defer to that individual when making certain specified decisions—this area of deference on the part of employees is what Chester Barnard referred to as the "zone of indifference."[6]

Along with formal authority, French and Raven argue that power can be based on the control of rewards or punishments. *Reward power and coercive (or punishment) power* are similar, in that they concern particular situations and not longer-term relationships. They differ in their implications for the strength of the relationship between actors and those they attempt to influence, with coercion implying hostility between parties and a reduced expectation of longer-term cooperation as compared with reward power, which is more positive and can develop into a long-term relationship. Using rewards may not always lead to long-term cooperation, however, in the absence of other bases of power, since a discontinuation of rewards means an end to incentives to cooperate just as a removal of punishments means an end of incentives to comply.

French and Raven propose two other bases of power: expert and referent power. Both of these are generally more effective than rewards and punishments alone in influencing others. *Expert power* stems from the possession of specialized knowledge that is valued by some other actor or by the organization as a whole. This type of power accrues to those who are perceived to possess specialized knowledge that can solve the problems of others. Expert power may also be seen as the deference that is often granted to experts in a given situation, irrespective of the particular value that their knowledge may have for that situation. *Referent power* accrues to those who have earned the admiration of others, in the capacity of a role model or a charismatic leader, or on some other personal or symbolic basis that secures compliance by means of the target of influence wanting to comply in order to please or identify with the holder of referent power.

The limits to power based on formal authority in organizations are well known, and for a manager's power to persist, it will need to be based on more than just position or formal rank within the organization. Managers need to be seen as

---

[5]French, J. R. P., Jr. and B. Raven, "The Bases of Social Power," in Cartwright, D. (ed.), *Studies in Social Power*, Ann Arbor: University of Michigan, Institute for Social Research, 1959.

[6]Barnard, C., *The Functions of the Executive*, Cambridge, MA: Harvard University Press, 1938, pp. 167–171.

legitimate by those whom they expect to comply with their orders. This legitimacy must rest on more than formal rank. Even if the possession of decision-making rights through formal authority gives managers added influence over their subordinates, two factors can minimize the power that goes with formal authority. First, the division of labor within the firm means that managers must of necessity delegate authority for the details of the firm's activities to subordinates, who exercise discretion in performing them. Second, there are physical limits to the ability of managers to oversee subordinates. Given these limitations, any compliance obtained primarily on the basis of formal authority alone may not last long, once the manager moves on to other tasks and stops directly observing subordinates. Despite their formal authority, managers thus depend on subordinates, even while subordinates depend on managers.[7] John Kotter, who bases his work in part on that of French and Raven, argues that successful managers need to build several bases of power, especially referent and expert power, whose effects are more persistent than formal authority, reward power, or coercive power.[8]

Power is also based on image or reputation. For example, an individual with a well-known history of getting their way in conflicts will have a reputation for power that may lead potential adversaries to comply with his or her demands without a struggle. Similarly, judgments of expertise or other types of power will often be based on prior accomplishments. This makes sense if past successes were due to individual abilities and if the situation at hand is similar to those in the past. Otherwise, there is no reason to expect an individual to repeat past successes and therefore no reason to defer (or delegate power) to that person. Power stemming from a long string of successes may be put at risk by a significant or poorly timed failure. In the example at the beginning of this chapter, the coincidence of poor results from Euro Disney, the death of Frank Wells, and Michael Eisner's heart surgery in a short period of time made several analysts ambivalent about Disney's future and the strength of its management team in the long run.

Power is not only rooted in individuals, however. It also stems from the interactions of individuals within and between firms, and from the control of information and resources in these interactions. In particular, power stems from such relational characteristics as: (1) the relative dependence of an actor on others in a set of interrelated jobs and tasks (for example, when one actor depends on the work produced by another, but not vice versa); (2) the centrality of an actor within an organization's communication network; (3) the degree to which the individual is substitutable within a relationship; and (4) the dependence of a firm, or a unit within a firm, on the ability of key individuals to cope with uncertainties that affect performance. We develop these points in more detail in the next section, where we consider the roots of power in social exchange.

---

[7]Mechanic, D., "Source of Power of Lower Participants in Organizations," *Administrative Science Quarterly*, 7, 1962, pp. 349–364.

[8]Kotter, J., "Power, Dependence, and Effective Management," *Harvard Business Review*, July–August 1977, pp. 125–136.

◆ ◆

$\mathcal{E}$XAMPLE 18.1

THE SOURCES OF PRESIDENTIAL POWER

One of the most famous studies of the bases of power was *Presidential Power*, Richard Neustadt's 1960 analysis of how Franklin Roosevelt, Harry Truman, and Dwight Eisenhower dealt with issues of power and influence during their administrations. The book was widely read during the Kennedy administration and has remained important to sitting presidents, their staffs, and policy analysts.[9]

Neustadt is most interested in the conflict between the image of the president as powerful and the reality of the presidency as institutionally weak. Presidential power does not consist of the president taking direct action, such as Truman's recall of MacArthur or his seizure of the steel mills in 1952, or Eisenhower's decision to send troops to Little Rock, Arkansas in 1957, to assist in desegregation. These command decisions were exceptions rather than typical uses of power. In addition, in each instance they did not solve the president's policy problems. Rather, they used up scarce presidential power and, at best, allowed the president and other actors involved in a situation more time to search for lasting solutions to the problems. Neustadt suggests that instances of command or fiat are more likely to be evidence of a lack of power than of its effective use. In a given situation, however, there may have been no other choice than to command. For example, whatever problems Truman encountered in recalling MacArthur, the cost of not recalling him would probably have been higher.

Presidential power is the ability to influence the people who make and implement government policies. It has three sources. The first consists of the bargaining advantages that come with the office that enable the president to persuade others to work in his interest—the formal powers and authority of the president. The second source of presidential power is professional reputation, which consists of the expectations of professional politicians, bureaucrats, and others in the political community regarding the president's power and his willingness to use it. This is related to the president's ability to control the votes of Congress on key issues. Once the president loses control of a majority in Congress, he cannot guarantee that his programs will be enacted, and he loses power. A third source of Presidential power is his prestige among the public, specifically how the political community assesses his support among different constituencies and the consequences to politicians of failure to support the president.

Although the global political situation facing the president of the United States is different from those facing firms, Neustadt's three sources are consistent with those that we discussed above. The formal powers of the job, whether stemming from the Constitution, laws, or customs, along with the institutional routines that have grown up around them, provide a basis for power for any incumbent, a basis

---

[9]The material for this example is taken from Neustadt's 1990 revision. See Neustadt, R. E., *Presidential Power and the Modern Presidents*, New York: Free Press, 1990.

that can be used well or poorly. Professional reputation in the setting of a firm refers to the common expectations among observers of how the powerholder will act in a given situation, based on accumulated experience with the powerholder. Finally, prestige for politicians is analogous to the control over resources that are critical to any organization. For the president and professional politicians, that resource is public sentiment that translates into votes at election time.

Looking back on his initial work in 1990, in light of the six presidents who had served since *Presidential Power* was first published, Neustadt maintained his fundamental conclusions, but better developed their details. For example, the experience of Nixon and Watergate, on the one hand, and Johnson and Vietnam, on the other, showed the importance of credibility and perceived legitimacy for both public prestige and professional reputation. Similarly, while Neustadt still emphasizes the importance of political skills for the president, the experiences of Johnson and Nixon also emphasize the relevance of individual temperament for success in office. The president needs to be patient enough to tolerate a complex political system that rarely allows him to successfully implement major policy initiatives immediately, but rather over the course of several years.

Neustadt still sees political skills and experience as crucial for success in office. (The presidency is no place for amateurs.) Political skills and experience, however, while necessary to success in the presidency, are not sufficient. Both Nixon and Johnson were highly experienced in elective office and possessed formidable political skills, yet their sense of power led each of them to support policies that ultimately dissipated their power and impaired their effectiveness.

SOCIAL EXCHANGE AND RESOURCE DEPENDENCE

◆ ◆ ◆ ◆ ◆

The most common view of power in organizations is based on the idea of *social exchange*. By social exchange, we mean a transfer between two or more parties of resources, or rights to control resources, that occurs outside the terms of a market context.[10] Power arises from persistent inequalities in the terms of repetitive social exchanges between a pair of individuals.

To illustrate how power arises in social exchanges, suppose that A and B are exchange partners. If an acceptable exchange occurs between them, the transaction is complete. Suppose, however, that they cannot complete an exchange (or series of exchanges) acceptably, and that, as a result, A provides more of value to B than B can provide to A in return. B, in effect, "owes" A the deficit of the exchange.

[10]For the principles of social exchange, see Coleman, J. S., *Foundations of Social Theory*, Cambridge, MA: Belknap, 1990, chap. 2. For sociological treatments of exchange theory, see Emerson, R. M., "Power-Defense Relations," *American Sociological Review*, 27, 1962, pp. 31–41; and Blau, P. M., *Exchange and Power in Social Life*, New York: Wiley, 1964. For a social psychological perspective, see Thibaut, J. W. and H. H. Kelley, *The Social Psychology of Groups*, New York: Wiley, 1959.

Note that this is not a formal debt, and A cannot sue B to recover the deficit. Over time, this deficit may be made up in other exchanges, the nature of which is not specified in advance. As B's deficit to A increases, B is said to be increasingly *dependent* on A. A is said to have power over B to the extent that B is dependent on A, that is, A has the opportunity to obtain B's resources at his discretion to satisfy his objectives. The dependence of B upon A is mitigated to the extent that A depends upon B for some other matter or in some other set of exchanges. If there was such an interdependence, then neither A nor B would be dependent on the other, since the exchange deficits of one would cancel out those of the other. These two aspects of an exchange view of power—power and dependence—can be summed up as follows. The power of A over B (P_{AB} is equal to B's dependence on A (D_{BA}). The net power of A over B is given by ($P_{AB} - P_{BA} = D_{BA} - D_{AB}$).

How does this view of social exchanges differ from the economic exchanges with which we have been concerned in other chapters? If both parties agree to participate, why are power relationships any different from other exchanges? In voluntary exchanges, why would an actor like B choose to become dependent on another actor like A and presumably commit future resources to A's discretion? Why would A provide resources in the present for the uncertain future obligations of B? After all, despite B's "debt," A cannot use formal means, such as the courts, to force compensation from B.

One way to address these questions has been to argue that dependence relations are entered into because better alternatives are not available. That is, the resources controlled by the other party are important to the future of the firm, clear substitutes for these resources are lacking, alternative sources for them are unavailable, and contracting for the exchange is unnecessarily costly. This is the *resource dependence* view of power, expressed by Jeffrey Pfeffer.[11] In this view, individuals and firms seek to gain power by reducing their dependence on other actors, while increasing the dependence of other actors on them. This is analogous to the efforts by firms to avoid supplier power by securing multiple supply channels and to achieve market power by selling to customers with few alternatives. Pfeffer also suggests that firms avoid dependence on suppliers of critical inputs through long-term contracting or vertical integration. Absent coordination or transactions costs, however, this is not a viable solution as the supplier will insist on a premium price for relinquishing its power to the integrated firm.

The resource dependence view helps explain why firms benefit from asymmetric social exchange, but does not explain why individuals are willing to give up resources today in exchange for an uncertain exercise of power in the future. One explanation is that, on the merits of the exchange itself, it is beneficial to the actor providing resources to trust that the other party will reciprocate. The expectation

[11]Pfeffer, J., *Managing with Power: Politics and Influence in Organizations*, Boston, MA: Harvard Business School Press, 1992; Pfeffer, J., *Power in Organizations*, Marshfield, MA: Pitman, 1981; Pfeffer, J. and Salancik, G., *The External Control of Organizations: A Resource Dependence Perspective*, New York: Harper and Row, 1978.

of nonreciprocity may be low, since the other actor needs what is provided on a continuing basis. Conversely, the value expected from the other actor may be sufficiently high that some nontrivial chance of nonreciprocity is tolerable. The willingness of an actor to provide resources in exchange for unspecified future consideration may also be based on more general societal or cultural norms of reciprocity or trustworthiness.[12]

Along with the idea that actors will work to reduce their dependency on other actors, the resource dependence view also has implications for which individuals within a firm are likely to attain power. Specifically, individuals who control critical resources will accumulate power. In particular, those individuals who can help the firm cope with special problems that pose major threats to the firm and its activities will come to exercise the most power within the firm. Examples of this can be seen in firms where members of a critical occupational or professional group gain control (petroleum engineers in oil companies), where individuals with links to key regulators or stakeholders gain control (lawyers in regulated businesses, such as public utilities), or where individuals who possess unique skills gain control (surgeons in some teaching hospitals).[13]

Measuring Power

To analyze power and use it in decisions, one must first be able to identify it (or its absence). The task of measuring power, however, has several problems attached to it.[14] Identifying the relevant actors involved in an exchange is often difficult. Assessing the relative power of actors is also difficult, because such assessments are often based on self-reports, and individuals with power may want to understate their positions, while individuals without power may want to overstate their positions. It is also unlikely that all individuals contacted will be equally knowledgeable about the actual power distribution in the firm. There are also difficulties about how to interpret observed asymmetric relationships.

Can one use the resource dependence view of power to identify actual power relationships among individuals or firms? The answer is generally no. The fact that one party provides resources but apparently receives nothing immediate in return does not imply that party either has power or is dependent. The actor providing resources while receiving nothing in return may already be powerful and thus will benefit from the dependence of the other party. The actor could also be dependent,

---

[12]Kahneman, D., J. L. Knetsch, and R. H. Thaler, "Fairness and the Assumptions of Economics," *Journal of Business*, 59, October, 1986, pp. S285–S300; Coleman, J. S., *Foundations of Social Theory*, Cambridge, MA: Belknap, 1990, pp. 177–180.

[13]This variant of the resource dependence approach is the "strategic contingencies" view of power. See Hickson, D. J., C. R. Hinings, C. A. Lee, R. E. Schneck, and J. M. Pennings, "A Strategic Contingencies Theory of Intraorganizational Power," *Administrative Science Quarterly*, 16, 1971, pp. 216–229.

[14]For a discussion of technical issues in assessing power, see Pfeffer, J., *Power in Organizations*, chap. 1.

however, and is providing resources to a more powerful actor while receiving much less in return. Finally, there may simply be no power relationship between the actors, indicating that they do not expect to be dependent on each other or to be compensated in power terms for the exchange of resources.

Edward Laumann and David Knoke developed what they term *resource deployment* and *resource mobilization* perspectives on power to clarify the ambivalence of an observed uneven exchange.[15] A resource deployment strategy (RDS) looks at power from the standpoint of the actor providing resources, while the resource mobilization strategy (RMS) looks at power from the standpoint of the recipient of resources. RDS considers that power comes from getting others to employ your resources on your behalf—that you control their behavior. RMS, on the other hand, considers power as the ability to obtain resources from other actors that you can employ while pursuing your goals—you control their resources and not their behavior. A thorough analysis of resource-dependence relationships in a situation requires a comparison of the results of both models over the set of situations of interest to identify which model provides the best explanation for different situations.

Power and Transactions Costs

Recall from Chapters 3 and 4 that transactions costs are the costs of using the firm or the market as a mode of economic coordination. As market-related transactions costs increase, it becomes more desirable to use the firm rather than the market. Conversely, as bureaucratic dysfunctions and influence costs increase within firms, it becomes increasingly reasonable to either reorganize the firm or else use the market more. The conditions that give rise to high transactions costs in the marketplace are precisely those situations in which power relations associated with resource dependencies will most likely be observed. The reason is simple. Transactions costs arise in complex situations that are not easily governed by contract. In these situations, the development and exercise of power are most important.

To see the relationship between power and transactions-cost arguments, consider the holdup problem discussed in Chapter 3. There, asset specificity prevents the owner of an asset from redeploying it to other uses. Inefficiencies arise due to underinvestment in relationship-specific assets. When it is costly to craft contingent claims contracts to govern exchanges, the solution to the holdup problem may be to vertically integrate or otherwise reorganize to reduce dependence on a given seller.

Vertical integration does not automatically solve the holdup problem by eliminating asset specificity, however. Instead, it relies on powerful managers to craft governance mechanisms that assure parties to an exchange within the integrated firm that they will be compensated for their investments. In this way, powerful managers provide the assurances to individuals that market contracts cannot provide. How power is exercised is critical, because of the persistence of bureaucratic rigidities and their associated influence costs. Formal control and budgetary systems are likely to be incomplete in practice and thus will not remedy problems of hidden in-

---

[15]Laumann, E. and D. Knoke, *The Organizational State*, Madison, WI: University of Wisconsin Press, 1987.

formation and hidden action within firms. This means that many of the dependency problems experienced in imperfect market exchanges may also be experienced inside the firm. For example, holdup may occur within firms if the effective control of sunk assets depends on the cooperation of interdependent employees that are not linked together by a common source of authority. An upstream unit in a firm that provides a critical component (for example, a microprocessor with several applications) to another unit may also provide that same unit to other branches of the firm or to outside buyers. If one of the downstream units depends on it critically and does not have ready access to alternate sources, the upstream unit may be in a position to hold it up, even though they are in the same firm, due to the discretion of the supplier and the vulnerability of the buyer. Clearly, a powerful manager who can punish holdup activities by subordinates can improve intrafirm efficiency.[16] But hidden information and hidden action may allow the upstream unit to disguise its holdup activities, thereby limiting the power of the manager.

If resource dependence and transactions-cost explanations of firms are related in their implications, as we suggest they are, then we would expect to see an association between the degree of resource dependence between industries that buy or sell from each other and the extent of merger and acquisition activity between those industries. We would expect to see more mergers in a situation where firms in one industry were relatively dependent on the sales to or purchases from firms in the other than in a situation of mutual interdependence across a pair of industries. In the former situation, a powerful manager may be needed to assure effective exchanges, given market imperfections. In the latter situation, however, mutual interdependence would assure effective exchanges in the market. Menachem Brenner and Zur Shapira investigated this question, making use of input-output data from the U.S. Federal Trade Commission.[17] Even though they made use of highly aggregated industry definitions (two-digit SIC codes), their results were largely consistent with a resource-dependence explanation.[18] Mutual interdepen-

---

[16]Oliver Williamson implies this same linkage between transactions-cost analysis and power analysis when he critiques the theories of work organization offered by several radical economists and shows how transactions-cost analysis can address the same phenomena more effectively. He criticizes the power approach not for its content, but rather for its overly broad definitions and its inattention to microanalytic detail. See Williamson, O., *The Economic Institutions of Capitalism*, New York: Free Press, 1985, pp. 206–239.

[17]Brenner, M. and Z. Shapira, "Environmental Uncertainty as Determining Merger Activity," chap. 3, in W. Goldberg (ed.), *Mergers*, New York: Nichols Publishing, 1983, 51–65.

[18]SIC refers to the *Standard Industrial Classification* scheme that is maintained by the U.S. Office of Management and Budget and that underlies all establishment-based federal economic statistics classified by industry. In it, each business unit receives a seven-digit SIC code number that classifies the unit first into general categories and then into progressively finer categories representing detailed distinctions of product lines. The broader SIC classifications are more frequently used for strategic analysis. In particular, the four-digit SIC code is commonly used to represent the industry level, while the two-digit code referred to here is used to represent broader multiple-industry groups, such as metal mining, food stores, chemicals and allied products, and insurance.

dence across industries was inversely related to the proportion of vertical mergers involving those industries, while dependence was positively related. Their results were evident for both upstream and downstream relations between industries, but were stronger for downstream relations. Vertical mergers appeared to be motivated by the need to reduce environmental uncertainty through the control of critical resource relationships.

Michel Crozier provides another example of power gained by control over key information in his well-known case study of a French cigarette firm.[19] The firm was a government-controlled monopoly, facing a stable competitive environment and stable demand for the product. As a result, the only contingency that the managers of the firm faced in meeting its production schedules was in keeping their machines operating and avoiding breakdowns in production. The maintenance workers in the firm had come to control access to knowledge of how to keep the machines operating with minimal breakdown through their tradition of training new engineers verbally, rather than with standardized documentation. Over the years, the original documentation for the machines had disappeared. These workers thus gained considerable power relative to management and other workers, such as machine operators. The power of the maintenance workers and technical engineers in the factory was not unlimited, however. Plant managers could recommend that the plant be retooled. If this retooling happened, then new machines would replace the old ones, and full documentation about the machines would be available to managers. Thus both sources of power of the maintenance engineers would be eliminated. This situation resulted in a rough power equilibrium within the plant. At the conclusion of Crozier's study, however, that equilibrium was fragile, and the organization was entering a period of crisis.

Structural Views of Power

Although power ultimately stems from control of scarce resources, it may be embodied in the structure of a firm. Occupying particular locations within a structure provides more power to the occupants. For example, Jeffrey Katzenberg's position as head of the Walt Disney Studios most likely gave him more power within the Disney organization than the heads of other business units possessed. Several types of structure can provide power to well-situated members. Often the most powerful individuals in a firm will occupy key positions in multiple structures. For example, Michael Eisner probably has more power at Disney by virtue of his being chairman and CEO than he would have if he occupied only one of the two positions.

Within the formal structure of authority that characterizes most firms, designated leaders or managers will have authority over others by virtue of their position. Perhaps the most common example of this is the military, where uniformed individuals salute superior officers irrespective of whether they are one's own or not. Individuals in positions of authority can expect designated followers to comply with

---

[19]Crozier, M., *The Bureaucratic Phenomenon*, Chicago: University of Chicago Press, 1964, pp. 61–142.

their directives, within a generally defined sphere of action. In effect, employees agree to acknowledge the decision-making authority of superiors on matters within their organizational jurisdiction. This acknowledgment is Chester Barnard's "zone of indifference," discussed earlier. The willingness of employees to give a manager some benefit of doubt regarding their decision rights is the basis of the manager's formal or "position power" within the firm. This position power is received by virtue of the manager's location in the structure and the legitimacy of the structure for firm members.

Structure can also mean the information network operating within a firm or the informal social relationships that develop among the firm's employees, customers, suppliers, and other stakeholders during their interactions. If information on key developments, such as in the marketplace or with regulators, is critical for firm performance and a particular individual is in a position to regulate that flow of information from the market into the firm, that individual will control a critical resource for the firm and will accrue power from that control. For example, Thomas Whisler studied decisions in insurance companies about the introduction of computers and the adoption of management information systems. He found considerable conflict over issues of where in the organization the computers would be located, whose budget would be charged, and who would control their use. He attributed this conflict to the recognition by managers of the power that would accrue to those who gained control over the information system of the firm.[20] Similarly, acceptance by a given constituency, such as sales representatives, may be important for the success of some firm initiatives. In such a case, a prominent position within the relevant social networks will be a critical resource that gives the incumbent power within the firm.

As we have mentioned for other types of power, the information provided by a key individual must be both important to the firm and difficult to replace before control of that information leads to power. The individual must be indispensable. If the firm has other means to obtain the needed information or can find other means of gaining access to key constituencies, then the location of an individual in an informational or social network will not influence his or her power.

Ronald Burt provides a general version of structural power in his theory of structural holes.[21] A *structural hole* is a relationship in a social network in which one actor is the critical link between individuals or entire groups. To associate with each other, these individuals or groups must go through the actor occupying (or spanning) the structural hole. The presence of a structural hole allows the individual who can span the hole to use the control of information or resource flows to his or her own advantage—that is, as a source of power. The elimination of a structural hole, such as when representatives of the two previously separate groups begin interacting on their own, would eliminate the dependence of the two groups

[20]Whisler, T., *Information Technology and Organizational Change*, Belmont, CA: Wadsworth, 1970.

[21]Burt, R. S., *Structural Holes: The Social Structure of Competition*, Cambridge, MA: Harvard University Press, 1992.

on the focal individual and thus also eliminate his or her power. Structural holes are generic features of networks, whether the networks are composed of individuals or organizations. The potential for power from spanning a structural hole is applicable to most types of networks, including market networks, formally defined networks within a firm, or informal networks that span the formal boundaries of firms, voluntary organizations, or government agencies.

Providing a valued relationship between two otherwise unconnected parties (either actors or groups of actors) forms a basis of power for those individuals employing what Burt calls a *tertius gaudens* (happy third) strategy. The tertius is the "third who benefits," and the strategy involves the actor who spans the structural hole bargaining with the parties on either side of the hole for the most favorable terms. There are two kinds of tertius strategies. The first occurs by being the third between two parties in the same relationship, such as being the broker in a buyer-seller relationship. The second is to be the third between two parties in two or more relations with conflicting demands. An example of this would be parties working on different projects who have to compete for scarce time with their common manager. Following a tertius strategy creates power for an actor through his or her control of the movement of information between contacts on either side of the relationship, making this strategy a general example of a resource-dependence logic as applied to social networks.

Roberto Fernandez and Roger Gould apply ideas of structural holes in their study of the influence of brokerage positions in decision making on national health policy.[22] Brokers span structural holes in that they permit communication between actors who do not regularly communicate with each other. In the domain of national health policy, brokers add value, and thus potentially accrue power, in two ways. First, the sheer number of actors involved in health policy formation makes it unlikely that any actor will be able to regularly maintain contacts with all other actors. Brokers can provide established channels for communications. Second, particular policy issues may present temporary opportunities for coordination to a given pair of actors who might otherwise never communicate with each other. Brokers can recognize and bring about such opportunities for productive contact.

Fernandez and Gould examine whether and under what conditions the occupancy of different types of brokerage positions provides an actor with influence. They found that occupancy of brokerage positions was generally associated with a reputation for having influence. To gain this influence, however, actors also had to be perceived as neutral in the decision-making process. Given the contentiousness of health policy debates and the expectation among interest groups of government neutrality on political matters, this is a reasonable result. Exceptions to this general finding occurred for situations in which it was reasonable for the government to take a stand, for example, when the government is contracting with outside vendors seeking its business. Overall, these results imply a paradox of power that is based

---

[22]Fernandez, R. M. and R. V. Gould, "A Dilemma of State Power: Brokerage and Influence in the National Health Policy Domain," *American Journal of Sociology*, 99, May 1994, pp. 1455–1491.

on spanning gaps in social networks—spanning structural holes appears to augment power, so long as no overt attempts are made to pursue one's interests on the basis of that power. It is less clear how these results apply in nongovernmental domains, where there are few explicit expectations regarding the neutrality of actors spanning structural holes.

Do Successful Organizations Need Powerful Managers?

It is tempting to claim that an organization must have powerful managers to succeed. After all, power represents the means to get things done in a firm. Unless employee relationships can be completely governed by incentive contracts, a manager must have some power if he or she expects to be successful. The implications of power for firm performance are not unambiguously good, however. A manager might use power for personal interests that significantly diverge from those of the firm. The results may be counterproductive for the manager and harmful for the firm.[23]

Even the most powerful manager in a firm is someone else's agent. At the top of the firm, the CEO is the agent of the shareholders, by way of the board of directors. In the presence of agency costs arising from hidden actions, hidden information, and related problems, a powerful manager may divert information and resources toward personal goals. For example, a powerful financial management team within a firm may push for a merger to increase their team's influence on corporate policy, rather than for the underlying business fundamentals of the deal, such as whether it offers opportunities for increased scale or scope economies. The effects of this abuse of power can be especially critical for a firm in a changing business environment. The financial management team may have risen to power at a time when restructuring was vital to the firm's success and the team provided the skills needed to implement restructuring effectively. If R&D is now more important to the firm than financial prowess, then the financial management team may trade on its status and organizational position to divert resources away from R&D and toward mergers, merely to hold on to power.

Clearly, power is a two-edged sword, whose effects for firms can be positive or negative. We expect that the accumulation of power will be helpful or harmful according to the following conditions:

Accumulation of power is helpful when

1. There are high agency costs between managers and lower-level workers.
2. The firm's environment is relatively stable.

Accumulation of power is harmful when

1. There are high agency costs between levels of upper management.
2. The firm's environment is relatively unstable.

---

[23]Coleman, J. S., "Legitimate and Illegitimate Use of Power," in Coleman, J. S. (ed.), *Individual Interests and Collective Action*, Cambridge, U.K.: Cambridge University Press, 1986, pp. 247–266.

A good example of the dangers of power is provided by the Chernobyl nuclear power plant accident in 1986.[24] P.S. Neporozhny, the Soviet Minister of Energy and Electrification until 1985, wielded great power in overseeing the entire nuclear power program. This power grew not from his scientific knowledge or engineering expertise (he was decidedly ill-informed about the intricacies of nuclear reactors and their differences from other sources of power), but rather from his position in the Soviet government and, presumably, his bureaucratic achievements in the Soviet political system. While the position of energy minister was initially unimportant, it became more significant with the growth of nuclear power. Neporozhny used his power to institute a policy of secrecy that prevented higher officials (i.e., his principals) from learning about accidents and other deficiencies in the nuclear program. By doing so, the incentives of government managers to expend resources on reactor safety were lessened, which made the safety problem in the Soviet nuclear power program even worse.

This policy of secrecy was continued by Neporozhny's successor and was in full force when the Chernobyl reactor exploded. Not only did this policy prevent Soviet leaders from reevaluating the program, it also led to deadly delays in responding effectively to the accident. From this example, we see that high agency costs at the upper levels of management, combined with rapidly changing technology, allowed individuals to attain power who were not sufficiently informed to effectively oversee the nuclear energy program. The subsequent abuse of power by these individuals led to the worst nuclear accident ever. Apparently little changed after Chernobyl in the Soviet government regarding the abuses of power that can occur under conditions of secrecy. Less than three months after the accident, new government instructions forbade any public discussions of Chernobyl by government officials with representatives of the press, radio, or television.

◆ ◆

XAMPLE 18.2

POWER AND POOR PERFORMANCE: THE CASE OF THE 1957 MERCURY

While power may be useful in getting things done, it can also be dysfunctional if it helps the wrong programs to be accomplished—that is, if it is used to circumvent the checks and balances that are necessary to evaluate the market feasibility and cost effectiveness of any effort. An example of this occurred with the development of the 1957 Mercury. Called the "Turnpike Cruiser" by Ford managers and a "steel cartoon" by its critics, the model was introduced to great fanfare, but failed to make

---

[24]The information in this example comes from Medvedev, G., *The Truth About Chernobyl*, New York: Basic Books, 1991. Medvedev was the senior government investigator of Chernobyl, and his book summarizes the findings of the investigation.

good on its high costs and lofty sales projections. Overall, Ford lost an estimated $369 on every 1957 Mercury it sold, and the car proved a harbinger of even greater problems that came with the now-infamous Edsel. In his group history of the careers of the "Whiz Kids" at Ford, John Byrne provides an example of the functions and dysfunctions of power in the career of one of the Whiz Kids responsible for the new Mercury, Francis "Jack" Reith.[25]

Reith had a number of power bases from which to push the development of the new Mercury. First, he was a dynamic and almost charismatic leader, who drove his subordinates, but inspired considerable admiration in the process. He was also highly intelligent and very effective at persuading others to follow his direction. Reith also possessed a considerable track record since he joined Ford in 1946. Most recently, he had received credit for the successful turnaround and sale of Ford's subsidiary in France. On the basis of this success, Reith enjoyed the support of his superiors, Lewis Crusoe and Henry Ford II. He also gained standing from his association with the Whiz Kids, who had nearly all distinguished themselves at Ford and who were clearly recognized as a group as well as individually. Finally, Reith had position power, in that he was promoted to the head of the Mercury division, once his 1957 plan had been approved.

Reith saw the 1957 Mercury as part of a larger plan by which Ford could seriously contend with General Motors for leadership in automobiles through a major expansion of an existing make (Mercury) and the introduction of an entirely new one (the Edsel). Reith's boss, Lewis Crusoe, promised him his support (and the top job) at Mercury, if the plan could be approved by the board of directors. In preparing for that board meeting, Reith used all of his bases of power effectively.

He was perhaps too effective. There were doubts about the initiative in several quarters. The plan promised too much (a 54% sales increase). It required a larger expansion of the dealer network than had ever been anticipated by the firm before. The projected expenses of the project were staggering and, in effect, required a large increase in market share if the project was to be justifiable. As one executive remembered, "the numbers were totally unrealistic. They had to be. It was the only way to justify the plan" (Byrne, p. 225). The estimated price for the project was equal to the company's total profit before taxes the previous year ($485 million).

These doubts were not raised, however, because Reith's colleagues, whose job it was to ask difficult questions about projects, failed to do so in this case, out of deference to their friend. When questions were raised, Reith and Crusoe jointly overpowered the opposition. Much of this persuasion was based on fear, intimidation, and concern over the career consequences of resistance. In the process, the rational analysis that the Whiz Kids introduced to Ford was forgotten.

---

[25]Byrne, J. A., *The Whiz Kids*, New York: Currency Doubleday, 1993. The Whiz Kids were a group of academics and operations analysts, including Reith, Charles Thorton, Robert McNamara, and Arjay Miller, who distinguished themselves in operations analysis for the Army Air Force in World War II and later joined the management of Ford as a group in early 1946. Most rose to senior positions within Ford and two, McNamara and Miller, rose to its presidency.

The failure of the car, which ended Reith's career at Ford, was due in part to the flawed decision processes described above that allowed Reith to push through his initiative at the expense of critical analysis. Reith and his managers, however, also failed to pay attention to market research, which indicated increased consumer interest in safety and decreased interest in the stylistic flourishes that characterized the car. Instead, the 1957 Mercury was based on managerial intuitions about consumer preferences for stylish cars rather than on data. The car also suffered from numerous quality and safety problems. In making this error, however, Reith was not alone. The year 1957 was a strong one for the Volkswagen, a small, simple car that focused on fuel economy. It was also the first year in which consumer's interest in automobile safety and quality increased. Many managers in Detroit missed this shift in the market, which would lead to further problems for the industry in the 1960s and 1970s.

EXAMPLE 18.3

POWER SHIFTS IN THE NEWSPAPER BUSINESS

Power conflicts are often sharpest during periods of pronounced environmental change, which shifts the control over the key contingencies facing firms from one group to another, without altering formal power, as expressed by the organizational structure of the firm. New groups come to claim more decision-making rights as a result of the influence they wield in the future of the firm. Established groups, however, can resist claims for influence by new groups through their control over the firm's formal authority structure.

The newspaper business has seen increased conflicts in the past two decades between the marketing and related functions of the business, on the one hand, and the editorial function, on the other. Newspapers have always gained revenues through subscription and newsstand sales, along with the sale of advertising, and incur significant costs in paper and supplies, editorial expenses, printing, and distribution. There is also a traditionally strong role for an independent editorial function in newspapers that relies on constitutional guarantees of freedom of the press, stresses the public interest, and is characterized by a critical and at times adversarial role versus business, government, or other large interests. While there has long been tension between a newspaper's editorial and business functions, the tradition in large newspapers is to balance the two, while preserving the independence of the editorial function. This was known in the industry as "the separation of church and state," as is perhaps best typified by the *Chicago Tribune*, which, until the 1980s, maintained separate elevators in its headquarters for editorial and noneditorial staff.[26]

---

[26]Squires, J. D., *Read All About It! The Corporate Takeover of America's Newspapers*, New York: Times Books, 1994, pp. 72–73.

This balance has been disrupted because several factors have greatly increased the competitiveness of the business environment for newspapers. Advances in satellite, cable, and data-processing technologies have changed what used to be separate industries, such as newspapers, magazines, television, radio, movies, and computers into a much larger and less defined information-processing sector. Newspapers are no longer the only, or even the principal source of news for readers. They are also no longer the only, or the most appropriate medium for their traditional advertisers, who can now choose among online services, cable television, broadcast television and radio, and direct mail as alternative media for their advertising expenditures. In their traditional functions of providing printed information and advertising to readers, newspapers have never had a more competitive environment.

At the same time, the ownership of newspapers has increasingly come under control of concentrated investor groups that are strongly motivated to maximize profitability. The traditional owner-publishers who controlled large urban daily newspapers in the twentieth century, with names like Hearst, Pulitizer, Bingham, and McCormick, have increasingly given up their control to newspaper groups (also called chains), such as Gannett or Knight-Ridder. The number of newspaper groups grew from 13 in 1910 to 155 in 1980, while during that period, the percentage of newspapers owned by the groups grew from 3 percent to 65 percent. This concentration of ownership has continued through the 1980s, and today few major newspapers remain independent. The largest of these corporate groups have diversified beyond newspapers and are now multimedia corporations that manage a wide range of broadcast and information businesses, from books and magazines on the one hand, to cable television, satellite operations, network programming, radio, and interactive media on the other.[27]

While newspapers have generally been profitable businesses, these new corporate owners have been more strongly motivated to maximize their profitability than previous owner-publishers were. As a result, the balance of power between business and editorial functions within papers has shifted, with business functions coming to hold more power. This is apparent in conflicts between business and editorial staff on issues where the professional interests of the two diverge.

One area where such conflicts emerge is investigative journalism, where the interests of good business and good journalism may conflict if key community advertisers are targets of inquiry. Andrew Krieg details an example of this in his book on the effects of the acquisition in 1979 of the *Hartford Courant* by the Times-Mirror group.[28] In 1983, the paper mounted an exploratory investigation of workplace hazards and illnesses, as well as the processes by which these hazards were

---

[27]For more details on newspaper groups, see Krieg, A., *Spiked: How Chain Management Corrupted America's Oldest Newspaper*, Old Saybrook, CT: Peregrine Press, 1987, chap. 3; Mayer, M., *Making News*, Boston, MA: Harvard Business School Press, chap. 5; Squires, J. D., *Read All About It! The Corporate Takeover of America's Newspapers*, New York: Times Books, 1994.

[28]Krieg, A., *Spiked: How Chain Management Corrupted America's Oldest Newspaper*, chap. 11.

regulated and how workers were treated after they became ill and filed workers' compensation claims. The investigation reached a number of disturbing conclusions about workplace hazards and how insurance companies handled claims. The problem with this story was that Hartford is known as "the insurance city," in part because 14 major insurers are headquartered there. In addition, one of Connecticut's largest private employers, United Technologies, was also headquartered in Hartford and was criticized in the story.

After a year of preparation, the story was canceled (or "spiked") by a new editor appointed by the *Times-Mirror* chain. He claimed that the story was boring and poorly written and would not interest readers. Subsequently, a greatly reduced "human interest" version of the story, one that omitted critical references to insurers and United Technologies, was run in a night edition. Krieg's response to the alleged flaws in the story is to note that much of the story was subsequently published elsewhere, to wide acclaim. The clear interpretation that Krieg gives to the cancellation and subsequent dilution of the story is that it was due to the perceived threat posed by the story to the insurance companies and the business community, upon whose advertising the paper depended for three-quarters of its revenues.

The Decision to Allocate Formal Power to Individuals

Thus far, our discussion of power has skirted a critical managerial issue: Why should the firm grant formal authority to individuals who already wield great power by virtue of their control over key resources? When should power not be allocated to such individuals? To begin to answer these questions, we should recall the transactions-cost rationales for why firms exist that were discussed in Chapters 3 and 4. The choice of internalizing decisions within a hierarchy is made in part because transactions costs make dispute resolution in markets too costly. Firms internalize decisions because of the opportunity to use administrative discretion and fiat to resolve decision-making disputes more efficiently. That a firm has the opportunity to reduce transactions costs by administrative discretion in decision making does not shed light on who should be allowed to exercise that discretion on behalf of the firm. This is precisely the question of who should receive formal power in the firm.

A first part of the answer is that *knowledgeable* individuals should receive power. It is reasonable to assume that if formal power is to be used effectively, then its holders should be informed about the policies they will need to approve and the disputes they will have to resolve. The importance of knowledge as a basis for position authority and power has been recognized since the earliest writings on bureaucratic organizations. For example, knowledge, in terms of both technical expertise and about the organization, was a critical aspect of Max Weber's theory of bureaucracy, which was essential for the development of modern organization theory.[29]

---

[29]Weber, M., *Economy and Society*, Vol. 1, Berkeley, CA: University of California Press, 1978, pp. 212–226.

It may be argued that the holder of formal power on an issue need not be the most knowledgeable individual in the firm on that issue. Indeed, in some settings (research laboratories, for example), it would be inefficient to make the best scientist the manager, since that individual would be most useful to the firm as a generator of knowledge rather than a resolver of disputes. Even so, it is important for that scientist's manager to possess sufficient knowledge to evaluate performance and allocate resources.

A second basis for allocating formal authority concerns the motivations and interests of the managers who would receive power. A manager must not only be knowledgeable. The manager must also have the same interests as the firm. Otherwise, the firm will become vulnerable to holdup by the very person whose responsibility was to reduce transactions-cost problems through internal decision making. Holdup would be likely to occur when the firm makes relationship-specific investments with managers whose interests are likely to diverge from the firm if noncontractible contingencies arise, as suggested by the Grossman-Hart argument, discussed in Chapter 4. The ownership of the specialized human capital that managers provide to the firm in such situations cannot be fully transferred, which would leave managers with the opportunity to hold up the firm. This is less of a problem when the interests of managers are tied to those of the firm, such as through substantial bonuses that are linked to firm performance.

If the wielders of power in the firm control critical resources, then the firm is also vulnerable to their exit, especially if they join the competition. This implies that power should go to individuals who are relatively likely to stay with the firm. Excessive turnover of key decision makers not only takes critical knowledge out of the firm, but also paralyzes its strategic decision making. Julio Rotemberg argues that firms actually prefer to give decision makers power rather than higher wages as a way of reducing turnover. Power may be thought of as a firm-specific asset—the worker may get better pay elsewhere, but might not achieve comparable levels of power and influence.[30]

It is essential that the firm solve the problem of allocating formal power to individual managers. The best match of individuals and formal powers is likely to be a matter of balancing, in response to changes in the firm's environment and changes in the people holding power. This may be why the management shuffles at Disney that were mentioned at the beginning of this chapter received such attention. The allocation of power to managers is a fundamental task of management and is intimately connected with the direction that the firm takes and how successful it is.

CULTURE ◆ ◆ ◆ ◆ ◆

According to many students of business strategy, the profitability of firms is only partly linked to issues of technical and agency efficiency, competitive strategy, and positioning. It is also a function of the firm's *culture*. Concepts related to culture

---

[30]Rotemberg, J. J., "Power in Profit-Maximizing Organizations," *Journal of Economics and Management Strategy*, 2, 1993, pp. 165–198.

are frequently employed to explain such anomalies as the persistent high performance of some firms versus their competitors or apparent performance differentials between otherwise comparable firms in different countries or geographic regions. Although the basis of corporate culture research stems from some classic case studies of firms and public sector organizations, the more recent popularity of such books as *In Search of Excellence*, by Tom Peters and Robert Waterman and *Theory Z*, by William Ouchi has also sparked interest in corporate cultures, especially as traditionally successful large U.S. firms showed weakness relative to foreign (and especially Japanese) competition.[31]

What Is Corporate Culture?

By *corporate culture*, we mean a set of collectively held values, beliefs, and norms of behavior among members of a firm that influences individual employee preferences and behaviors. Culture also refers to the material products that provide evidence of collective values and norms, such as symbols, art, ritual practices, or other social constructions, and that are made use of by members of the firm.[32] The underlying values, beliefs, and norms that are the basis of culture are difficult to observe and measure, however. A more operational view, which also suits our interest in culture's economic implications, is that culture represents the behavioral guideposts in a firm that are not spelled out by contract but which nonetheless constrain and inform the firm's managers and employees.

There is great disagreement regarding the definition and scope of culture.[33] Moreover, different departments within a firm may have different cultures. In addition, a firm's culture may appear to be diverse, reflecting the culture of the various countries in which its product divisions are located. While there may be such a thing as a firm culture, distinguishing its effect from those of other cultures may be difficult. What appears to be a firm's culture in a given situation may actually be

---

[31]For a thorough review of early studies of organizational culture, see Trice, H. M. and J. M. Beyer, *The Cultures of Work Organizations*, Englewood Cliffs, NJ: Prentice-Hall, 1993. Also see Peters, T. and R. Waterman, *In Search of Excellence*, New York: Harper and Row, 1982; Ouchi, W., *Theory Z: How American Business Can Meet the Japanese Challenge*, Reading, MA: Addison-Wesley, 1981; Deal, T. and A. A. Kennedy, *Corporate Cultures: The Rites and Rituals of Corporate Life*, Reading, MA: Addison-Wesley, 1982; Pascale, R. T. and A. G. Athos, *The Art of Japanese Management*, New York: Simon and Schuster, 1981; and Lincoln, J. R. and A. L. Kalleberg, *Culture, Control, and Commitment*, Cambridge, UK: Cambridge University Press, 1990.

[32]Kotter, J. P. and J. L. Heskett, *Corporate Culture and Performance*, New York: Free Press, 1992; Barney, J. B., "Organizational Culture: Can It Be a Source of Competitive Advantage?" *Academy of Management Journal*, 11, 1986, pp. 656–665; Trice, H. M. and J. M. Beyer, *The Cultures of Work Organizations*, Englewood Cliffs, NJ: Prentice-Hall, 1993.

[33]Geertz, C., *The Interpretation of Cultures*, New York: Basic Books, 1973, chap. 1; Smircich, L., "Concepts of Culture and Organizational Analysis," *Administrative Science Quarterly*, 28, 1983, pp. 339–358; Trice, H. M. and J. M. Beyer, *The Cultures of Work Organizations*, Englewood Cliffs, NJ: Prentice-Hall, 1993.

the result of an overlapping of national culture, local culture, firm culture, subunit culture, and group culture. While culture may be broad in scope, we are interested in those aspects of it that can potentially influence a firm's economic performance. In addition, while it may be difficult in a large firm to identify a single culture that embraces all members, we are interested in that culture (or subcultures) that is most prevalent among the firm's decision makers, since it will have the most economic significance. Such a culture or subculture need not include all of the firm's employees.

Culture and Performance

An obvious concern for general managers is whether an organization's culture affects its performance. It turns out that it is difficult to directly link the two. Culture may be associated with high performance without necessarily causing that performance. For example, IBM, until it experienced problems in the late 1980s, was seen as having a strong culture, combining customer service, employee development, and professional standards, that contributed to its success.[34] However, IBM's persistently high earnings, as well as its competitive practices, may have provided an environment in which a strong culture could develop and persist. It is unclear whether the culture caused the firm's high performance or vice versa.

Jay Barney identifies the conditions under which culture can be a source of sustained competitive advantage.[35] First, the culture must be valuable for the firm. This is critical and is elaborated upon below. To be a source of sustained competitive advantage, corporate culture must also be specific to the firm. If the culture is common to most firms in the market, so that it reflects the influence of the national or regional culture or a set of industry norms, then it is unlikely to lead to a relative competitive advantage, since most firms in the industry or sector will share the same cultural attributes. Finally, culture must be inimitable. If a firm's culture is easy to imitate, then other firms will begin to emulate it, once the firm has been successful. This will soon nullify the advantage that culture gave the firm.

That organizational cultures can be described by researchers does not render them imitable. The influence of the culture on the firm is likely to rest on tacit factors that are not easily described and that represent the accumulated history of the firm much better than does a simple description. The complexity that would make it difficult for others to imitate a culture will also make it difficult for managers to internally modify the culture of their firms to significantly improve performance. Barney even suggests a tradeoff between the degree to which a culture is manipulable and the amount of sustained value that can be obtained from it. A culture that is manipulable is not likely to be linked to the fundamental resource

---

[34]Kotter and Heskett, *Corporate Culture and Performance*, p. 17.

[35]Barney, J. B., "Organizational Culture: Can It Be a Source of Sustained Competitive Advantage?" *Academy of Management Review*, 11, 1986, pp. 656–665; for the general criteria, see Porter, M., *Competitive Strategy*, New York: Free Press, 1980.

commitments of the firm, which form the basis for sustained competitive advantage. Rather, it is more likely to be common to several firms and imitable and hence less valuable.

To the extent that culture creates value for firms, it does so in three ways. First, culture reduces information-processing demands on individuals within the firm, allowing them to better focus on their regular tasks. Second, it complements formal control systems and thus reduces the costs of monitoring individuals within the firm. Third, culture shapes the preferences of individuals within a firm toward a common set of goals. It thus reduces the negotiation and bargaining costs of individuals within the firm and permits more cooperative activities to develop. We discuss these value-creating properties of culture in more detail below.

Culture Simplifies Information Processing

A culture's values, norms of activity, and accompanying signals can focus the activities of employees on a limited set of arrangements. This frees them from the need to continually negotiate what their tasks will be within the firm. A strong culture may thus reduce the costs of decision making and permit a specialization of effort.[36] It allows individuals who work together to share a set of expectations about their work and thus reduces uncertainty. This affects both the content of actions (certain product definitions over others, certain levels of riskiness in advertising and new product development versus others) and the forms of interactions among employees, customers, and stakeholders, including appropriate language, rules for transactions, and other matters. By focusing activities, culture can thus increase a firm's technical efficiency.

An example of how culture can help reduce uncertainty and focus activities is the case of Cray Research.[37] Founded by Seymour Cray in 1976, Cray became well known for its innovations in the development of supercomputers. The culture of the firm was an important part of its reputation. This culture stressed innovation and strong employee commitment, using the accomplishments and activities of Cray himself as focal points and examples. In the critical years following 1978, however, Cray grew at a phenomenal rate. Had the culture of the firm not been strong, it could probably not have absorbed this growth and remained prosperous. Without a strong culture, the coordination costs of the workforce alone might have overwhelmed the ability of Cray managers to adapt to change. The number of Cray employees, for example, grew five times between 1978 and 1983, from 321 to 1,551. During that same period, total revenue grew from $17 million to nearly $170 million. While this growth occurred, however, the structure of the firm remained fairly simple, and decision making remained decentralized in small work groups. Had there been no central focus for managers and employees, the complexity of managing such an enterprise in such an unstructured manner would have posed major problems for Cray executives of the type discussed in Chapter 17.

---

[36]Trice, H. M. and J. M. Beyer, *The Cultures of Work Organizations*, Englewood Cliffs, NJ: Prentice-Hall, 1993, pp. 2–22.

[37]Information in this example comes from *Cray Research, Inc.*, Harvard Business School Case 9-385-011.

Culture Complements Formal Controls

Culture, as a set of collective values and behavioral norms can serve a control function within organizations. Culture controls the activities of employees on the basis of their attachment to the firm rather than on the basis of incentives and monitoring. Individuals who value attachment to the culture will align their individual goals and behaviors to those of the firm. If culture serves this function in a firm, then individual activities will be controlled more efficiently than they will be through formal control systems, since individuals will control themselves and monitoring costs will be reduced. If a firm's culture is strong, by which we mean it is intensely held by most employees, it may be more effective at controlling employees than a formal control system would be. The combination of motivated self-control, informal monitoring by coworkers, and the lack of specificity of organizational norms means that individuals are more likely to be compliant than they would be if controlled by formal systems which, by their incompleteness, allow for more opportunistic behaviors.

William Ouchi has written extensively on culture as an alternative control system to bureaucratic or market models of control.[38] Ouchi introduces the idea of *clan control*, by which he means control through a system of organizational norms and values. This model of control forms the basis for Ouchi's analysis of the differences between Western and Japanese firms.[39] Clan control is characterized by moderate to low specialization of organizational roles and tasks, long-term employment in the organization, individual self-motivation and responsibility, and collective decision making. This type of control is distinguished from *bureaucratic control*, which is characterized by much greater specialization of organizational roles and tasks, short-term employment, individual responsibility, and individual decision making. Both are distinguished from *market control*, which is control on the basis of price in a market.

Ouchi's framework is useful in distinguishing how culture, as a means of control, is different from rules and regulations in an authority system on the one hand, and from market prices on the other. In this sense, the framework provides a set of *ideal types*. However, Japanese firms may not be as different from Western firms as Ouchi suggests, and clan control may be too diffuse, unless it is supplemented by other controls. James Lincoln and Arne Kalleberg suggest that the supposed clan control of Japanese firms is better explained by the skill of these firms' managers at fostering consent and loyalty from individual workers through job guarantees, worker participation in decisions, welfare services, and needs-based compensation than by the power of the overarching cultural values within which Japanese firms operate. While culture may affect organizational practices, management practices, such as those of Japanese firms, also influence the dominant values of the firm.[40]

---

[38]Ouchi, W. G., "Markets, Bureaucracies, and Clans," *Administrative Science Quarterly*, 25, 1980, pp. 129–140; Ouchi, W. G. and J. B. Johnson, "Types of Organizational Control and their Relationship to Emotional Well Being," *Administrative Science Quarterly*, 23, 1978, pp. 293–317; Ouchi, W. G., *Theory Z*, Reading, MA: Addison-Wesley, 1981.

[39]Ouchi, W. G., *Theory Z*, Reading, MA: Addison-Wesley, 1981.

[40]Lincoln, J. R. and A. L. Kalleberg, *Culture, Control, and Commitment*, Cambridge, UK: Cambridge University Press, 1990, chap. 1.

Most firms, however, will make use of some combination of the control techniques that Ouchi describes. Very competitive marketplaces, like the Chicago Board of Trade, will also be governed by an extensive set of rules, as well as by a long history and set of traditions. Bureaucratic organizations may use market-based controls within their structures, such as a profit-center system (explained in Chapter 17), but can also be governed by strong cultural norms. It is difficult to envision a clan organization for a firm that would not involve some formal organization and controls and that would exempt the firm from the demands of the product markets in which it competed. High-performing firms are likely to have all three types. For example, Banc One (see the example in Chapter 12) has a strong culture and an extensive control system. It does not ignore marketplace demands either. Banc One maintains a strong competitive position, based on both cost and differentiation advantages, and as a result, it possesses a strong market share in the states where it maintains most of its operations.

Culture Facilitates Cooperation and Reduces Bargaining Costs

Gary Miller has examined the complex relationship between culture and organizations, in which culture mitigates the detrimental effects of power dynamics within firms by creating "mutually reinforcing" norms within the organization that permit mutually beneficial cooperative activities to emerge that would not be likely among self-interested actors outside the organization. Miller builds on the work of David Kreps, who examines the problems of securing cooperative outcomes in repeated games. Both Miller and Kreps are interested in the implications of a result called the *folk theorem*.[41]

The folk theorem concerns the possibilities for achieving an equilibrium result in repeated play of games, such as the prisoner's dilemma (discussed in Chapter 10 in the context of price competition in an oligopoly). Its general result is that many Nash equilibria are possible in infinitely repeated games. Not only are many equilibria possible, but these solutions do not need to be cooperative. Indeed, some can be conflictual, combining expectations of opportunistic behavior with threats of strong retaliation if the other player responds inappropriately.

The implications of this result for cooperation within organizations are important, once it is realized that attempting to arrive at a cooperative organizational arrangement by means of contracts, incentives, and monitoring is directly analogous to solving a complicated repeated game situation. The result of the folk theorem implies that it may not be possible to arrive with certainty at a cooperative organizational arrangement—cooperation is only one of many possible arrangements. In addition, even if cooperation was possible, the costs of reaching it, in terms of the haggling costs involved in choosing one arrangement over other possible ones, are likely to be high.

Miller takes this point and argues that any attempt to solve organization problems through contracts, incentives, and formal controls is likely to entail large influence

---

[41]Miller, G. J., *The Political Economy of Hierarchy*, Cambridge, UK: Cambridge University Press, 1992, chap. 10; Kreps, D. M., *A Course in Microeconomic Theory*, Princeton, NJ: Princeton University Press, 1990, chap. 14.

costs, due to hidden action, hidden information, and related problems that we discussed in Chapter 16. The problem with hierarchical organization is that, while it mitigates transactions costs associated with market coordination of economic activity, it creates dilemmas of its own. These dilemmas cannot be resolved by recourse to formal governance mechanisms or by increased controls over employees. Building on ideas of Kreps, Bengt Holmstrom, and others, Miller argues that any hierarchical organization will have serious principal-agent problems built into its structure. A "machine" model of organization is likely to self-destruct.

Most real organizations appear to arrive at some acceptable organizational arrangements, despite these bargaining problems. To account for this, Kreps suggests that norms and social conventions may provide a focus for actors around which a consensus can form. This set of norms and conventions on behavior is the organization's culture. Kreps defines corporate culture as "the means by which a principle [of group decision making] is communicated to hierarchical inferiors. . . ." It says "how things are done and how they are meant to be done" in the firm.[42]

Miller argues that a firm's culture can resolve these problems if its norms stress cooperation and not conflict. A cooperative culture can modify individual expectations and preferences and allow actors to expect cooperation from others in the organization. If the content of the culture is noncooperative, however, it will not serve this function. The ability to have this set of mutually reinforcing overarching values and norms is what allows firms to fashion solutions to agency problems that would not be possible in a market.

Miller is ambiguous about the ability of management to intentionally influence a firm's culture. On the one hand, he argues that managers can exercise leadership that fosters cooperation rather than conflict among employees. On the other hand, a cooperative firm culture is also likely to be fragile, so that attempts to modify it to gain managerial advantage could backfire and result in employees becoming noncooperative.

EXAMPLE 18.4

CORPORATE CULTURE AT 3M[43]

The 3M corporation has become known for a nearly endless array of useful products that builds on the firm's strength in adhesive chemistry—*Scotch tape* and *Post-it* note pads are just two of the best-known 3M products, which have ranged from health

---

[42]Kreps, D. M., "Corporate Culture and Economic Theory," in Alt, J. and K. Shepsle (eds.), *Perspectives on Positive Political Economy*, Cambridge, UK: Cambridge University Press, 1990.

[43]The materials for this example came from stories in *Minneapolis/St. Paul* magazine, July 1992; and *Corporate Report Minnesota*, June 1990.

care products, such as the bioelectronic ear, to copy machines. In developing these products, 3M also became known for its innovative culture and was featured in such books as *In Search of Excellence.*

The innovative culture is not just an accident or a byproduct of prior successes and a strong technological base. It appears to stem from activities taken by 3M managers, from the top of the firm down to the smallest venture teams, to encourage innovative activities and protect risk-takers.

Innovation has been a consistent priority of 3M's top management. Louis Lehr, who was chairman of the board and CEO of 3M from 1980 to 1986, provides a good example of this emphasis. During his tenure as CEO, while the firm basked in its reputation for innovativeness, Lehr commissioned an internal survey to identify the actual levels of innovativeness in the firm. He found that, while many employees believed and took pride in the firm's reputation, others in the finance, warehousing, and sales/marketing departments did not feel very innovative, but believed that innovation and entrepreneurship at 3M were largely confined to the laboratory areas. In response to the survey, Lehr established a task force to let employees know that everyone in the firm could be entrepreneurial and to establish such innovative practices as quality circles throughout the firm. Lehr saw that resting on the appearance of being entrepreneurial was not sufficient. Employees throughout the firm needed to know that they were expected to think and behave differently and that 3M would support them in doing so.

Innovation is also built into the 3M corporate planning and control systems. A standard goal in long-term plans of business unit managers, for example, is that after five years, 25 percent of a unit's sales must come from new products. The results of these programs are apparent in the 2,500 new products that the firm introduces each year.

The stimulation of innovative and risk-taking activities has also been part of the general management style at 3M. In evaluations, risk-takers are favored over non-risk-takers. Successful individuals and teams receive firmwide recognition, as well as opportunities to work on new projects. Dual personnel tracks allow technical specialists to progress in their project careers without necessarily having to move into management. Managers are urged to "smooth the way" for innovators, by providing resources and rewards, removing organizational obstacles to projects, and protecting innovators from the usual penalties for failure. This is summed up in the idea of project sponsorship by senior managers.

Innovation not only comes from internal management, but from contacts with product users. Innovative firms keep in active contact with users and avoid the NIH (not invented here) syndrome that can impede innovation at other firms. At 3M, managers are pushed to incorporate market-based strategic analyses into their project planning. One of 3M's core product groups, Scotchlite Brand Reflective Materials, developed in this way over 50 years ago, when feedback from government customers identified a need for increasing the visibility of highway signs after dark.

It is not clear how much of 3M's success is caused by its innovative culture. Many of the firm's products, such as *Scotch tape* and *Scotchguard*, were developed from accidental discoveries. However, the 3M culture does seem to try to increase the firm's ability both to generate trials, from which such discoveries might come, and to ensure that 3M can develop and commercialize those discoveries that do occur.

Culture, Inertia, and Poor Performance

Culture is also important for how it can impair firm performance. Examples of an apparent negative association between culture and performance are nearly as common as those that indicate a positive association. In fact, sometimes the same firm can provide examples of both. As was discussed in Chapter 14, IBM was seen as recently as 1986 as a powerful exemplar firm that was widely admired for its management depth and corporate culture. Yet, less than ten years later, IBM was being criticized for its inertial culture.

If culture is truly related to firm performance, it is because the fundamental alignment of the firm and its environment is a positive one, in that the firm has made investments and oriented its business toward a set of technological, competitive, and regulatory conditions that exist and affect the firm's operations in the ways that the firm's managers anticipated. Another way to say this is to adopt the contingency logic discussed in Chapter 17. When the firm's strategy fits with the demands of its environment, then culture can support the direction of the firm and make it even more efficient.

The negative influence of culture on performance becomes important when the environmental situation faced by a firm changes and makes significant demands on it to adapt to survive. Then, the conditions making culture a source of sustained advantage that were raised earlier in this chapter by Barney will make culture a source of persistent poor performance. In an unfavorable business environment, in particular, the unmanageability of culture will become a source of inertia or a barrier to change. It will also become apparent in maladaptive decisions by managers that seek to forestall change instead of addressing environmental problems. This inertia may occur for several reasons. Executives with long tenure in the firm may have learned their jobs during prosperous times and may be poorly equipped to handle change. The power bases within a firm may allow threatened parties in the firm to block change. The terms of managers and board members, the rules by which they are chosen, and the procedures by which they operate may be designed with a conservative bias that frustrates change. This could occur, for example, as a result of staggered and lengthy terms for the board.

EXAMPLE 18.5

CORPORATE CULTURE AND INERTIA AT ICI

Andrew Pettigrew provides an example of how cultural inertia can stymie organizational adaptation in his case studies of Imperial Chemical Industries (ICI), the leading British chemical manufacturer.[44] In 1973, ICI was the largest manufacturing firm in Great Britain. It possessed a strong and homogeneous management culture that had spanned its nearly 50 years of existence. Sales growth in 1972 was strong in chemicals, at twice the national growth rate for manufacturing. ICI had also been successful at new product development, with half of its 1972 sales coming from products that had not been on the market in 1957.

Strong threats to ICI's continued success developed in its business environment in the 1970s. These threats included overcapacity in its core businesses, threats of both inflation and recession in the British domestic economy, and import threats from Europe and North America. These pressures substantially affected ICI's profitability in 1980, when its profit totals and profitability ratios were halved. Several years of consistently poor performance followed. In the five years between 1977 and 1982, ICI cut its domestic workforce by nearly one third.

Individuals within top management had been recommending changes in the structure and governance system of ICI to allow it to better adapt to changed economic and political conditions since at least 1967, when the need for change was raised by a single individual during a board election and ignored. A board committee on the need for reorganization had been set up in 1973 and issued a report calling for extensive organizational changes within ICI. The report encountered extreme political opposition from the start and, in the words of an executive director, "sank at the first shot." These calls for reorganization and strategic change were not adopted by ICI until 1983, by which time the firm had already experienced several years of poor performance.

Pettigrew's analysis of this history highlights the culture of conservatism and "smoothing" of problems that dominated ICI during this time. These aspects of its culture were functional during prosperous and stable times, but were dysfunctional during periods of environmental shifts. Individuals who had benefited from the prior success of the firm were able to block initiatives, while external stimuli that could move management to action, such as poor performance, were not forthcoming until 1980. As management and board members changed during the 1970s, however, the culture also changed, so that management became more receptive to change. Despite the best efforts of the individuals who saw the need for change, however, the culture constrained the firm and kept its managers from deciding upon change until conditions were present. The culture of ICI, which had benefited the firm during its first 50 years, kept it from adapting in the late 1970s.

---

[44]Pettigrew, A. M., *The Awakening Giant: Continuity and Change at ICI*, Oxford, UK: Blackwell, 1985, chap. 10, pp. 376–437; Pettigrew, A. M., "Examining Change in the Long-Term Context of Culture and Politics," chap. 11 in Johannes M. Pennings and Associates, *Organizational Strategy and Change*, San Francisco: Jossey-Bass, 1985, pp. 269–318.

Culture and Power

We have considered culture and power as two important aspects of firm behavior that are not governed by contract. Power concerns the ability to get things done by controlling critical resources, while culture involves the ability of the firm's general normative orientation to direct the behaviors of its employees and keep their activities within generally accepted bounds. While we have discussed them separately, several issues remain about how they might interact in a firm. How might culture and political relationships interact on a given issue? Does culture enhance the influence of powerful individuals or limit it? Can culture, or at least its consequences, be managed or shaped by individuals in the firm? Researchers have offered different answers to these questions. Jeffrey Pfeffer argues that power and culture are alternate means of getting things done in organizations. Of the two he sees power as the more useful, since it is less costly to maintain and less fragile than culture. Andrew Pettigrew views power and culture as complementary sources of influence. Managers can control the symbolic resources of the organization and thus can influence how the values of the firm can be used to support their personal interests. Gary Miller also links power and culture, but more as alternatives, with managerial leadership and culture as possible substitutes for organizational processes based on conflictual power relationships.

◆ ◆

XAMPLE 18.6

POLITICS, CULTURE, AND CORPORATE GOVERNANCE

Analyses of laws governing corporate governance in such areas as the board of directors, executive pay, and tender offers, have emphasized how given practices contribute to the efficiency of firms by attenuating principal-agent problems in the firm and thus reducing the costs of such problems for owners. Stemming from this economic explanation, corporate law has been seen as the set of governance principles that has evolved over years of corporate trials and that constitutes the starting point in determining how firms govern themselves.[45] Gerald Davis and Tracy Thompson argue that economic explanations are incomplete and neglect the influence of actors in the political and cultural environment of the firm on governance changes.[46] The political environment is important because the laws

---

[45]See Easterbrook, F. H. and D. R. Fischel, *The Economic Structure of Corporate Law*, Cambridge, MA: Harvard University Press, 1991, for the most forceful statement of this position.

[46]Davis, G. F. and T. A. Thompson, "A Social Movement Perspective on Corporate Control," *Administrative Science Quarterly* (forthcoming).

and regulations governing corporate activities, while of economic significance, are the products of political bodies, such as legislatures and regulatory agencies. The cultural environment is important because the attitudes and values of the general public on a given issue will be a source of legitimacy for political actors and will thus influence how they go about regulating firms.

Davis and Thompson provide an example of the importance of explanations incorporating power and culture in their discussion of the controversy in the early 1990s over "runaway executive pay." On its economic merits alone, it appeared that shareholders had at best weak incentives to pursue the issue. While the average U.S. CEO made 85 times the pay of a typical factory worker (versus 17 times in Japan), the dollar amounts that were paid to these executives were so small, relative to the overall value of the firm, that they had little or no effect on corporate performance (and would still have had no effect if overpaid executives had given back their entire salaries to their firms). While it was plausible that linking executive pay to corporate performance would help the firm's share price, it was far from clear that this actually happened. Regardless of its economic merits, however, the issue of CEO pay took on national political significance, in that it received extensive media coverage, many politicians raised the issue, and several pieces of legislation limiting executive pay were introduced in Congress.

Shareholder activist groups and institutional investors were more interested in changing the proxy rules of firms—the mechanisms by which shareholders vote on the management of the firm—than in fighting over CEO pay. They had been stymied at reforming proxy rules, however, because these had traditionally been the province of state governments, where pro-business interests were better organized and defeated reform proposals. In fact, 40 states had passed significant antitakeover legislation in the 1980s, including Delaware, where most major firms were incorporated.

Shareholder activist groups and large institutional investors seized upon the political attention given to the CEO pay issue at the national level (that of the SEC), where they were relatively better organized and prepared to lobby, to pursue proxy reform indirectly, through a focus on excessive CEO pay as but one instance of a broad failure of management accountability. The apparent affront to national values and sensitivities caused by excessive CEO pay gave activists the opportunity to move proxy reform from the state government level, where they had little power, to the SEC, where they enjoyed greater power. This allowed the SEC to take up proxy reform at a national level. By the end of 1992, this campaign had succeeded in expanding the power of large shareholders, as evidenced by their greater participation and influence in corporate governance. This influence extended down from the national political domain to individual firms. Negative publicity and pressure on such large firms as ITT, W.R. Grace, and Ryder led to changes in executive compensation systems that more tightly linked pay to corporate performance.

Changes in a firm's larger political and cultural context also affect the incentives that top managers employ. As the incentives and compensation of top managers are better aligned to firm performance, follow-up changes in the rest of the firm may involve substantial reorganization, decentralization of decision making, and the increased use of market-based performance incentives. These changes, in turn, will prompt changes in norms and values, leading the firm to develop a culture aligned to shareholder value. Michael Useem provides a detailed description of how these changes affected the cultures inside firms and how managers in firms that realigned themselves toward shareholder value used their control over organizational architecture, symbols, and vocabulary to support realignment.[47]

Some firms resist reorganization, and a near-crisis atmosphere develops among employees. In these situations, culture is inertial rather than supportive of change. Other firms react much more positively. The 1990 reorganization of Hewlett-Packard both maintained the firm's culture and improved shareholder value. While the reorganization required the elimination of thousands of positions in a firm that had prided itself on not laying off employees, the aggressive management approach of CEO John Young managed to retain the firm's innovative culture and to significantly increase performance.[48]

Chapter Summary

◆ *Power* is an individual's ability to accomplish his or her goals by means of resources obtained through *noncontractual exchange relationships* with other actors.

◆ There are five general bases of power: legitimate power, reward power, coercive power, expert power, and referent power. Power can also be based on image or reputation.

◆ The most common view of power in organizations is based on the idea of *social exchange*—a transfer between two or more parties of resources, or rights to control resources, that occurs outside of a market context.

◆ In the *resource-dependence* view of power, individuals and firms seek to gain power by reducing their dependence on other actors, while building the dependence of other actors on them through the control of critical resources.

◆ The conditions that give rise to high transactions costs in the marketplace are the same as those that give rise to power relations associated with resource dependencies.

◆ Power is also embodied in the structure of a firm. Particular positions give their holders more power than others have.

---

[47]Useem, M., *Executive Defense: Shareholder Power and Corporate Reorganization*, Cambridge, MA: Harvard University Press, 1993, chap. 3.

[48]Yoder, S. K., "A 1990 Reorganization at Hewlett-Packard Is Already Paying Off," *Wall Street Journal*, July 22, 1992, pp. A-1; A-10.

◆ Power can help or hurt a firm's performance. Power is helpful when there are high agency costs between managers and lower-level workers and when the firm's business environment is stable. Power is harmful when there are high agency costs between levels of upper management and when the firm's environment is relatively unstable.

◆ Formal power should be allocated to individual managers on the basis of the value they create for the firm, the costs of replacing them, and the likelihood that they will tend to act in a manner consistent with the firm's objectives rather than in conflict with those objectives.

◆ *Culture* is a set of collectively held values, beliefs, and norms of behavior among members of a firm that influences individual employee preferences and behaviors on the job.

◆ To help in sustaining a firm's competitive advantage, culture must be valuable, rare, and inimitable by competitors.

◆ A culture's values, norms of activity, and accompanying signals can focus the activities of employees on a limited set of task and governance arrangements. This frees employees from the need to continually renegotiate their tasks within the firm, which reduces the costs of making decisions and permits a better specialization of effort.

◆ Culture, as a set of collective values and behavioral norms, can serve a control function within firms by controlling the activities of employees on the basis of their attachment to the firm, rather than on the basis of individual incentives and monitoring.

◆ Culture mitigates the detrimental effects of power dynamics within firms by creating "mutually reinforcing" norms that permit the emergence of mutually beneficial cooperative activities that would not be likely among self-interested individuals in the marketplace.

◆ When a firm's strategy "fits" with the demands of its environment, then its culture can support the direction of the firm and make it even more efficient. When the environment changes, however, and requires firms to adapt to changes, culture is more likely to be inertial and lead to maladaptive firm behavior.

QUESTIONS

1. How does the resource-dependence view of power differ from the perspective of transactions-cost economics? In what situations would their predictions about economic transactions be similar; in which situations would they be different?

2. If agents are risk neutral and have unlimited liability, and the principal can find an objective measure that is correlated with performance, then a principal can write first-best efficient contracts. Does this imply that the principal can ignore culture and power?

3. How does the exercise of power and culture within an organization expose agents to risk? Which method, incentives, power, or culture, do you think is most effective at motivating risk-averse workers?

4. Is formal authority different from other sources of power?

5. How might a favorable location within the interpersonal networks of a firm help an individual acquire and maintain additional bases of power?

6. Social-exchange views of power tend to emphasize individual abilities to make decisions and prevail in conflicts. How might power also be associated with an individual's ability to not make decisions and to avoid conflict?

7. Discuss structural holes in the context of value creation and value extraction. Use these ideas to identify some of the skills necessary to be a financially successful general manager.

8. How can there be several different cultures with the same firm? If this situation occurs, what are its implications for the relationship between culture and performance?

9. Why is culture generally inertial in its effects on firms? Why is a firm's culture difficult to engineer or change?

STRATEGY AND THE GENERAL MANAGER

19

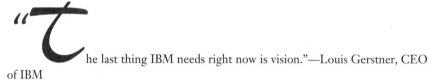

"The last thing IBM needs right now is vision."—Louis Gerstner, CEO of IBM

"It's an accountant's answer, not a leader's."—Robert Galbreath of Philip Crosby Associates, commenting on Gerstner's statement.

"Being a visionary is trivial. Being a CEO is hard. All you have to do to be a visionary is to give the old 'MIPS to the moon' speech. That's different from being the CEO of a company and seeing where the profits are."—Bill Gates, CEO of Microsoft[1]

These quotes all refer to the job of the most senior general manager within a firm, the chief executive officer (CEO). While the job of the CEO is not identical to those of other managers, it is analogous to other general management jobs in its basic roles and responsibilities. What is the role of the chief executive officer (CEO)—a problem solver or a visionary? We believe that a successful manager must be both. Managers must skillfully carry out a firm's internal and external relations, but must also establish a profitable and defensible position in often fierce markets. Bill Gates has skillfully managed vertical relations, market competition, and the innovative process within Microsoft. But he also had the vision from the beginning to understand that a large installed base of DOS-based personal computers would create a network externality permitting DOS to become the industry standard and Gates to become a multibillionaire (although we doubt he used the term *network externality*). While most general managers will not realize the same financial rewards as Gates, they will face similar short- and long-term strategic problems. This chapter describes the many

[1]Miller, M. and L. Hays, "Gerstner's Nonvision for IBM Raises a Management Issue," *Wall Street Journal*, July 29, 1993, p. 131.

problems and tasks confronting the general manager and the roles that the manager must bring to the job in response to these demands.

The general manager (GM) has comprehensive decision-making responsibilities for a unit at some level within the firm. CEOs and presidents are GMs, as are those in charge of divisions or product groups. GMs may also be located at lower levels, such as at a plant or a local sales office. For example, John Kotter found seven types of general management positions in his comparative case studies, ranging from corporate CEOs to division managers to operations and product market managers in profit centers.[2] It is often misleading to discuss GM tasks in terms of individual managers, however. While the GM is frequently a single individual, responsibility for decision making is often exercised by management teams. For a firm's strategic decisions, the top management team is increasingly important.[3]

The GM position has interested business observers ever since the development of the first large firms. Alfred Chandler noted that the first references to managers appeared in the early journals of railroad engineers, reflecting the role of the railroads in fostering modern models of firms. As large firms developed around 1900, the general manager became a critical asset that substituted administrative expertise for the risks of marketplace decisions. Managers became the "visible hand" that replaced the "invisible hand" of the market in making important decisions.[4]

As managers became more important within firms, interest in them grew among observers, students, and even critics of business. General management classes in leadership and business policy have had an important part in MBA curricula since the first programs developed shortly after 1900. Classic essays and prescriptions about the general manager, by such authors as Chester Barnard, Philip Selznick, and Alfred Sloan, remain in print today.[5] Even critics of large corporations, in a tradition that began with the work of Adolphe Berle and Gardiner Means, have focused on the increasing power and importance of managers, coupled with their lack of accountability to shareholders, as threats to social and economic stability.[6] The link between the general manager and the firm's strategy has persisted in current research, partly because of the enormous influence of the Business Policy group at the Harvard Business School, which developed the concept of strategy as a "simple practitioner's theory" of general management activities—that is, strategy is synonymous with what GMs do.[7]

---

[2]Kotter, J., *The General Managers*, New York: Free Press, 1982, pp. 22–27.

[3]Donaldson, G. and J. W. Lorsch, *Decision Making at the Top: The Shaping of Strategic Decisions*, New York: Basic Books, 1983, pp. 12–14.

[4]Chandler, A., *The Visible Hand*, Cambridge, MA: Belknap, 1977.

[5]Barnard, C., *The Functions of the Executive*, Cambridge, MA: Belknap, 1938; Selznick, P., *Leadership and Administration*, Berkeley, University of California Press, 1957; Sloan, A., *My Years with General Motors*, Garden City, NY: Doubleday, 1964.

[6]Berle, A. and G. Means, *The Modern Corporation and Private Property*, New York: MacMillan, 1932.

[7]See Bower, J., C. Bartlett, C. Christensen, A. Pearson, and K. Andrews, *Business Policy: Text and Cases*, 7th ed., Homewood, IL: Irwin, 1991, p. ix.

Despite the attention to and interest in them, we still know little about GMs, how they manage, how they lead, and related issues. Theories of management have been superficial and prescriptive, while evidence about managerial behaviors has been both sparse and difficult to interpret, due to the lack of developed theory. For example, Warren Bennis, in reviewing research on strategy and leadership concludes that "never have so many labored so long to say so little."[8] Only recently have researchers chosen to obtain sufficient data on managerial behaviors and produce rigorous studies rather than offer prescriptions or general surveys of managerial attitudes.

What Do General Managers Do?   ◆ ◆ ◆ ◆ ◆

At the conclusion of a book on the economic principles that underlie strategic decisions, it is reasonable to ask if we have any principles to offer regarding the tasks and roles of those who make strategic decisions—the general managers of a firm and its business units. If the GM's tasks could be simply mapped onto the economic decisions required by the firm, then understanding the position would not be difficult. There would also be little to say above and beyond what we have already discussed in earlier chapters. Problems with the GM position arise because a manager must make whole sets of behaviors simultaneously. This fact greatly complicates our view of the position and motivates our search for managerial roles. In the remainder of this chapter, we discuss the general manager's tasks and roles. We then consider the many tensions among these roles that make the GM position so difficult. We conclude by noting that, just as the definition of the firm has changed in response to social and business conditions, the definition of the GM has also evolved and is different from one era to the next.

Case Studies of General Managers

Henry Mintzberg's case studies of managerial roles were among the first to show how the actual behavior of managers differed from both common perceptions and widely accepted prescriptions. He found that, rather than being reflective and systematic planners, managers actually acted on the basis of short, discontinuous interactions, and were rarely reflective at all. Similarly, rather than favoring written, aggregated, and well-analyzed quantitative information, managers strongly favored informal, disaggregated, and largely verbal media for communicating and obtaining information. While much of a manager's work is routine, it tends not to be written down or standardized. Rather, managers organize their work according to more informal roles and rely on intuition and judgment to make their decisions. Managerial roles include: interpersonal roles, such as being a leader; informational roles, such as being the spokesman for the firm or one of its units; and decisional roles, such as being a negotiator or someone who handles disturbances. Mintzberg

---

[8]Bennis, W. and B. Nanus, *Leaders: The Strategies for Taking Charge*, New York: Harper and Row, 1985, p. 4.

was one of the first observers to separate description from prescription and show that management was more a craft than a science.[9]

John Kotter's case studies of GMs have developed this line of research in more detail, showing the variety of ways in which individual general managers adjust to the highly fluid surroundings in which they must accomplish their tasks. He comes to two general conclusions. First, effective managers build agendas for their businesses and then work to accomplish them. This is a more fluid process than the common stereotype of managerial goal-setting implies. Second, effective GMs build extensive interpersonal networks to get the information they need and to accomplish their agendas. Kotter also emphasizes the firm-specific nature of the assets that GMs accumulate makes it unlikely that they can easily move from one industry to another and be successful or that their firms will be successful in recruiting GMs from outside the firm and the industry.[10] This view of GMs as builders of relationship networks has been further developed by John Gabarro, who examines how GMs develop in their jobs, and Hermine Ibarra, who considers the characteristics of successful GM networking strategies.[11] It is also consistent with the structural hole argument of Ron Burt (discussed in Chapter 18) that managers gain power by virtue of their occupying critical network positions.

The Roles of the General Manager

In addition to the fluid view of managerial tasks developed by Mintzberg, Kotter, and others, we can also ascribe some more substantive roles to the GM. These roles are interrelated and stem from the basic decisions that GMs and their teams make. The GM is an *entrepreneur and value creator*, in that it is managers who make and change the fundamental position of the firm in its product market, as well as the resource commitments necessary to create value in a given position. The GM is also an *organizer/implementer*, who establishes a division of labor in the firm and coordinates the allocation of decision-making rights with the requirements of the firm's strategy. Related to this role, the GM is a *contractor*, who balances inducements and contributions in formal agreements with employees, buyers, suppliers, and other key contributors to firm action. Since there are limits to the possibilities for contracting within the firm, the GM is also a *facilitator*, who uses interpersonal skills and power to build relationships and secure agreement even in the absence of formal contracts. Along with coordinating action within the firm, the GM also has

---

[9]Mintzberg, H., *The Nature of Managerial Work*, New York: Harper and Row, 1973. For a shorter summary, see Mintzberg, H., "The Manager's Job: Folklore and Fact," *Harvard Business Review*, July–August 1975, pp. 49–61.

[10]Kotter, J., *The General Managers*, New York: Free Press, 1982, pp. 60–79.

[11]Gabarro, J. J., "When a New Manager Takes Charge," *Harvard Business Review*, May–June 1985, pp. 110–123; Ibarra, H., "Structural Alignments, Individual Strategies, and Managerial Action: Elements Toward a Network Theory of Getting Things Done," in Nohria, N. and R. G. Eccles (eds.), *Networks and Organizations: Structure, Form, and Action*, Boston: Harvard Business School Press, 1992, chap. 6.

the role of a *competitor*, who adapts the firm's activities to those of other firms in the industry. Finally, the GM performs the role of a *reevaluator and change agent*, who readjusts the firm's assets and commitments in response to significant changes in basic business conditions that affect the firm and threaten the basis of its profitability. We discuss these managerial roles in detail below.

The General Manager as Value Creator/Entrepreneur

Many managerial decisions follow from the long-lasting choices of the firm regarding how best to use its resources to create and sustain economic value. The managerial role of defining the firm and how it creates and sustains value is analogous to the entrepreneurial function of management that Alfred Chandler, Henry Mintzberg, and others considered the central creative task that managers perform. Just as entrepreneurs make choices about where to commit the capital of their investors and how best to manage those investments, so GMs make choices regarding how best to commit the capital of owners and position the firm in its product markets to create value on a sustained basis. The sheer size of large firms ensures that GMs will need to make many of these important decisions that define the boundaries of the firm and its value-creation opportunities. The large amount of fixed strategy-specific assets required by these decisions ensures that the decisions that GMs make in this role will commit the firm to a strategic position and be long lasting in their implications for firm performance.

While the value-creator/entrepreneur role is critical for the firm, many GMs find at the time they assume their positions that they and their firms are already committed to an extensive set of value-creation opportunities, by virtue of their firm's history, sunk investments, and long-term relationships. Large manufacturing plants, once built, often cannot be readily adjusted to meet new market demands. Long-term labor agreements can constrain the human resource flexibility of firms for years. In stable, regulated environments, this is not a problem. If conditions change unexpectedly, however, firms may be vulnerable to competitors who are not constrained by prior investments and commitments. This suggests that GMs may face serious constraints in defining how their firm creates value.

While these constraints may limit a manager's freedom to create new strategies, however, they do not render the value-creation function altogether moot. Rather, the constraints that managers face increase the pressures on them to identify and exploit opportunities for value creation within their firms and within their existing market relationships. Perhaps the greatest opportunities for contemporary managers lie in these marginal opportunities for value creation. Observers of GMs, such as James Brian Quinn, Charles Lindblom, H. Edward Wrapp, and others argue that opportunities for value creation tend to be incremental rather than broad and that GMs tend to spend little time on broad policy decisions.[12]

---

[12]Quinn, J. B., *Strategies for Change: Logical Incrementalism*, Homewood, IL: Irwin, 1980; Lindblom, C., "The Science of Muddling Through," *Public Administration Review*, Spring 1959, 79–88; Wrapp, H. E., "Good Managers Don't Make Policy Decisions," *Harvard Business Review*, September/October 1967, pp. 91–99.

The General Manager as Organizer/Implementor

GMs also organize their firms and implement their strategic choices. Chandler's dictum that structure follows strategy (discussed in Chapter 17) implies this role. This is also the intuition behind approaches to "generic strategies," in which the implementation decisions of managers in different functional activities of the firm should be consistent with the strategic choices of the firm's GMs (discussed in Chapter 12).

The organizer/implementor role involves several generic managerial decisions. The first is how to best coordinate information and resource flows within the firm around the strategy. This is akin to Galbraith's idea of organizational design on the basis of efficient information processing (discussed in Chapter 17). This role also involves decisions on which organizing dimensions are most important, which types of activities need the most coordination, the priority according to which coordination should occur, and the ways in which conflicts over coordination should be resolved. Another important aspect of this role is delegation, specifically in deciding who should have decision-making rights over which of the firm's decisions.

Decisions concerning organization and implementation are not just derivative from the firm's strategy, however. Implementation decisions often require information that is not available until after strategic decisions have been made. This information can involve highly contingent matchings of people and organizational resources that force managers to link the content of a strategy with specific situational conditions and requirements. The failure to make these decisions well may imply more than suboptimizing by the firm for a given strategy. Implementation mistakes could threaten the entire value of the strategy. For example, this could occur when a strategy predicated on specialized human capital in the firm is implemented in ways that alienate key individuals and even drive them away from the firm. Poorly thought out changes in incentive systems could produce this result.

The choices that managers make in implementing their strategies are also important when they commit the firm to courses of action that are difficult to alter, either by large investments in sunk assets or through the development of critical relationships that impede the firm's flexibility and responsiveness to environmental changes. Implementation choices can thus constrain the GM's future decisions, such that the firm's future strategic choices will be determined in part from its current implementation activities.

The General Manager as Contractor

Managers are contractors, both inside and outside of the firm. Contracting was the starting point for our discussion of the vertical boundaries of the firm from a transactions-cost perspective in Chapters 2 and 3. As the transactions costs of securing activities through the market increase, it becomes increasingly worthwhile to internalize these activities inside the firm, because of asset specificity and market imperfections. Based on our consideration of incentives and controls in Chapter 16, we can conclude that, to the extent that it is possible, managers should act as contractors and try to accomplish their ends both within and outside of the firm on the basis of contingent claims contracts. In dealing with employees and other stakeholders in the firm, a contracting perspective is also relevant, even if most employees do not have an explicit employment contract. This is because interactions akin to contract negotiation can occur in a wide range of relationships. When they do occur, the manager's role is the same—to get the best deal and spell out the terms as completely as possible.

While the contracting role of GMs is clearly important to the firm in its external dealings with other firms and organizations, the management literature has underemphasized the importance of contracting within the firm. Indeed, as we discuss below, the other means by which managers accomplish their objectives within firms, such as the use of power, culture, and leadership, make sense largely as options to use when contracts cannot be fashioned at all or only with excessive costs. Chester Barnard, in his classic, *The Functions of the Executive*, used the GM's contracting role in his inducements/contributions framework for understanding executive action.[13] Gordon Donaldson and Jay Lorsch also implicate the contractor role in their analysis of how top managers balance the demands of stakeholders from product, capital, and labor markets in order to maintain the independence of the management team.[14]

The General Manager as Powerholder

As we discussed in Chapter 18, a wide range of activities occur within the firm that cannot be fully specified and for which cost-effective contracts cannot be easily developed. These activities can nonetheless be important to the firm. In these situations, power can be understood as the ability of individuals to mobilize resources to accomplish their goals through noncontractual asymmetric relationships. In pursuing their objectives for the firm and/or their units, managers also need to develop new bases of power and to use them skillfully to complement their formal authority and their contracting activities and to secure the cooperation of all the parties necessary for an activity to succeed.

While power is important for the job performance and career growth of managers, the costs to the firm of using power also need to be considered. The goals of managers will only rarely be fully aligned with the firm's, and conflicts will often arise among managers who implement different aspects of a firm's strategy. In such situations, the successful use of power by a manager may hinder firm performance by impeding the achievement of other managers, even while it aids firm performance through the activities of the powerful manager. Even if the achievement of others' goals is not impeded by power, the exercise of influence itself will be costly. In addition, GMs are not immune from the temptation to pursue some personal goals, even at the expense of the firm's goals. In such circumstances, power will detract from firm performance. The overall costs of using power and its net effect on firm performance will be clear only in regard to specific decision situations.

---

[13]Barnard, C., *The Functions of the Executive*, Cambridge, MA, 1938, pp. 91–95.

[14]Donaldson, G. and J. Lorsch, *Decision Making at the Top*, New York: Harper, 1983, pp. 32–48, 160.

The General Manager as Facilitator

In many situations, GMs need the cooperation of others, yet cannot either contract for that cooperation or bring their power and influence to bear on the other party. One example of this would be when a manager needs the cooperation of a manager with comparable authority in the firm. Another example would occur when the success of an activity depends on effort by crucial employees, but where the manager cannot monitor what the employees actually do, where the employees can legitimately refuse to provide such effort, and where the manager cannot provide sufficient tangible incentives. In these situations, the GM's role is to persuade and shape the impressions and preferences of others to increase the chances of cooperation. These managerial activities are often associated with the building on an organization culture.

Managers can facilitate cooperation by building relationships with key individuals inside their firms and within their larger business environments. If a manager is embedded within a persistent network of valued relationships, then it will be easier for disputes over particular transactions to be resolved, since the parties will most likely value the maintenance of the long-term relationship more than the particular gains to be obtained from a particular transaction. John Kotter sees relationship-building as a central activity of general managers. In emerging or newly deregulated markets, relationships may be especially crucial for strategic success, since the legal and institutional infrastructure may not have developed sufficiently to permit the cost-effective governance of particular transactions. In Eastern European countries, such as Poland, Hungary, and the Czech Republic, for example, concepts of contract and fiduciary obligation are still underdeveloped. Western firms entering these markets need to do so on the basis of longstanding relationships with governmental and business leaders rather than on specific guarantees that may not be maintained in the event of a contracting dispute. This means that the firms that are first to enter these markets have the potential for building first-mover advantages through relationships with key actors.[15]

Gary Miller advances this culture- and relationship-building view of how managers facilitate cooperation as a complement to how they use incentives, controls, and formal structure.[16] By engaging in these nonpecuniary motivational activities, managers shape employee expectations of how activities within the firm will be conducted, how managers will work with employees, how disputes will be resolved, and other issues. In shaping these expectations, managers limit the range of activities open to employees and reduce the chances for noncooperative norms to develop within the firm.

Robert Eccles and Nitin Nohria take this role of shaping expectations within the firm further by arguing that a fundamental managerial task is to craft a rhetoric

---

[15]For more detail on these issues, see Buckley, P. J. and P. N. Ghauri (eds.), *The Economics of Change in East and Central Europe*, London, UK: Academic Press, 1994.

[16]Miller, G. J., "Managerial Dilemmas: Political Leadership in Hierarchies," in Cook, K. S. and M. Levi (eds.), *The Limits of Rationality*, Chicago: University of Chicago Press, 1990.

that directs and motivates individuals in the firm to take action.[17] To them, it is part of the manager's job to fashion a language system within the firm that encourages individuals to engage in productive cooperative activity. This occurs from building individual and collective identities, rationalizing action in terms of identities, and defining performance in terms that best explain past results and motivate future behaviors. This perspective is consistent with studies of managerial behavior, such as Kotter's, that show that managers spend most of their day talking. This view of the GM's role in crafting rhetoric can be taken to extremes in situations in which firms face strongly contradictory demands from various environmental stakeholders or when demands to rationalize activities conflict with the activities that firms need to pursue in order to be efficient. Nils Brunsson provides case examples of how conflicting political demands on firms can cause GMs to promote systematic hypocrisy, in an attempt to rationalize irreconcilable demands.[18]

The General Manager as Competitor

As the manager of a business unit that competes in a market, the GM must also adjust the activities of his or her unit to the activities of competitors who are trying to gain a competitive advantage. At a minimum, this role requires that GMs understand the nature of competition in their markets. They must also gather and analyze information about competitors, anticipate their reactions to proposed moves, and make judgments about how and to what extent to communicate with them and about how best to modify their unit's strategic activities on the basis of these judgments. The types of firm activities influenced by this role range from pricing and discretionary expenditures relating to advertising and product positioning on the one hand and to longer commitments of sunk assets on the other. Interactions with competitors can be direct or indirect and can be as limited as an evaluation of their observed activities without any explicit, implicit, or even tacit collusion. The activities associated with this role may occur during product market interactions, but could also involve other areas of firm or unit action, such as at trade association meetings.

The General Manager as Adapter

Managers' decisions are often time, condition, and strategy specific. What appears to be a reasonable set of investments at one time may prove to be less desirable as conditions change. Significant environmental change may even lead GMs to reassess their basic decisions regarding the horizontal and vertical boundaries of the firm. For example, this could occur as managers in basic metals industries, such as steel and aluminum, discover that the market conditions that made extensive vertical integration reasonable during the early history of these industries now make

---

[17]Eccles, R. G. and N. Nohria, *Beyond the Hype: Rediscovering the Essence of Management*, Boston: Harvard Business School Press, 1992.

[18]Brunsson, N., *The Organization of Hypocrisy: Talk, Decisions, and Actions in Organizations*, Chichester, UK: Wiley, 1989.

vertically integrated firms inertial and nonresponsive to conditions in world markets that have become more competitive.

If conditions have changed fundamentally, then the firm needs to change itself significantly in order to survive in its new situation. Sometimes, change can occur by redirecting discretionary resources. More likely, however, major change requires making new and risky sunk investments along with costly changes of relationships and assets to which the firm may be committed on the basis of past investments. Such fundamental reorientation may be possible (the example of Disney comes to mind), but it is also likely to be painful, as whole categories of assets and employees that were valuable under one set of conditions are now no longer valued and must be let go. Those workers who remain after their firm restructures will often find that their position in the firm has been greatly altered. Workers who are now critical to the value-creation activities of the firm may find their positions enhanced. Other workers, however, will find themselves increasingly relegated to a peripheral and tenuous role in the firm and will see themselves as increasingly vulnerable to future cutbacks. These situations have consistently occurred as firms have restructured.[19]

The Tensions of Managerial Work

Some of the managerial roles discussed above need to be part of the behaviors of a firm's management team at any given time, in order for the firm to accomplish its tasks. There are inherent tensions among many of these roles, however, which may pose different problems for managers in a given situation. While they can be managed, these tensions can probably never be effectively eliminated.

A first tension concerns the degree of routine between different parts of a manager's tasks. Some parts of the firm can be managed routinely, with clear goals, tasks, and outcomes, an effective incentive system, and ample information flows. The job of the GM for these parts of the firm is to administer clearly defined systems. For other decisions that a manager makes within the firm, however, the task is less easy. For example, it may be difficult to integrate disparate functions at the firm level because of the different tasks associated with each function, the different goals that each function pursues, the different time span for results for each function, and even the different language each function employs.

The problem of managing individuals from manufacturing, sales, and research and development under a single set of policies and procedures provides a classic example of this tension.[20] While each function may be manageable and possess char-

---

[19]Donaldson, G., *Corporate Restructuring: Managing the Change Process From Within*, Boston: Harvard University Press, 1994; Harrison, B., *Lean and Mean: The Changing Landscape of Corporate Power in the Age of Flexibility*, New York: Basic Books, 1994; Useem, M., *Executive Defense: Shareholder Power and Corporate Reorganization*, Cambridge, MA: Harvard University Press, 1993.

[20]For a classic study of this type of managerial tension, see Lawrence, P. R. and J. Lorsch, *Organization and Environment: Managing Differentiation and Integration*, Homewood, IL: Irwin, 1969.

acteristics with sufficient routines to allow the development of administrative procedures, the functions will differ in which of their characteristics are manageable and what values to attach to a given set of results. While manufacturing will have a well-defined set of tasks, a short-term time frame, and unambiguous results, research and development (R&D) will have less defined tasks, a long-term time frame, and more ambiguous (although potentially more valuable) results. The sales function will differ from both manufacturing and R&D on these dimensions. It will have a longer time frame than manufacturing but a shorter one than R&D. It will have less ambiguous results than R&D, but will be less clear on the most efficient means than manufacturing. To be effective, the GM must both administer each function and integrate the functions so that the firm can coordinate how its product reaches its customers and how new products are developed. This integration function is often less routinized and more sporadic, reactive, and unpredictable than the administrative tasks associated with each function. Yet the GM must perform both types of tasks.

In addition to routine and nonroutine internal tasks, the GM also faces a market at some level and thus must respond to unpredictable market demands, just as would any other market participant, along with performing his or her internal tasks. Marketplace demands become further complicated if the GM has to jump additional internal hurdles set through the firm's capital budgeting and planning systems. The policy instituted by General Electric under Jack Welch, that business units be number one or two in their respective markets or risk being sold off, is an example of how corporate management can attempt to intensify the market pressures that GMs face and thus motivate managers to greater effort.

Corporate-level GMs face their own variant of this tension in their dealings with subsidiary managers. On the one hand, if they fail to intervene with divisional management, they risk being shown to be unnecessary and ineffective. If divisions do not need corporate monitoring and guidance, then what purpose does corporate management serve? On the other hand, intervening in the activities of division risks harming corporate performance by hurting the responsiveness of divisions to market pressures. Corporate GMs also face their own integration problems in getting corporate staff units to work together for the benefit of the firm rather than to justify particular projects or groups.[21]

However much order one can find in some of the GM's tasks, the overall demands of the job make it appear disorganized and reactive. Nowhere is this tension for GMs between routine and disorder more apparent than in formal strategic planning processes, such as those popularized by General Electric, that attempt to make strategic decision making routine and to control the most nonroutine aspects of the business environment that firms face. This tension is emphasized by Henry Mintzberg in his critique of strategic planning systems.[22]

---

[21]Goold, M., A. Campbell, and M. Alexander, *Corporate-Level Strategy: Creating Value in the Multibusiness Company*, New York: Wiley, 1994, chaps. 5–8.

[22]Mintzberg, H., *The Rise and Fall of Strategic Planning*, New York: Free Press, 1994, pp. 380–396.

A second tension that the GM faces stems from the need to adopt different (and potentially conflicting) perspectives, according to the particular managerial role that he or she is playing. For example, relative to the board of directors and the shareholders, the GM is an agent whose ultimate objective is to maximize shareholder value. However, the GM can also act like a principal in relationships with employees and in contractual relationships with actors outside the firm.

This tension in the GM's role relative to owners and other stakeholders is well recognized in writings about top managers. Gordon Donaldson and Jay Lorsch, in their study of top management decisions, show how the GM can come to perceive owners as but one of the many stakeholder constituencies that must be accommodated when managing the firm.[23] Chester Barnard's inducement-contribution framework also suggests that owners, as suppliers of capital, are among the stakeholders of the firm and that the firm's success depends on balancing the demands of many different stakeholders.[24] David Hickson and his colleagues document how strategic decisions are characterized by the involvement of numerous parties inside and outside firms. The more parties involved, the greater the likelihood that there will be serious conflicts of interest among them.[25]

A third tension is between the general manager's implementor and adaptor roles. As discussed in Chapter 9, implementing a firm's strategy often requires investments in sunk strategic assets that commit the firm to a given course of action for a long time. Commitment, however, presumes some stability in the firm's strategic environment, so that the firm can persist in its strategic activities long enough to recoup its investments. Managers are all too aware, however, that the business environment can change and that their firms need to be flexible enough to respond to these changes. The commitment of resources required to pursue a firm's strategy often conflicts with the need to respond to environmental pressures and uncertainties.

This tension between commitment and flexibility is apparent in the work of Gary Hamel and C.K. Prahalad.[26] On the one hand, Hamel and Prahalad focus on the need to build a *strategic intent*, by which they mean a fundamental focus of a firm's strategy that commits it well beyond its current resource profile. On the other hand, a firm can become inflexible and overfocused on a particular strategy. Firms need to achieve what Hamel and Prahalad describe as *strategic stretch*, which involves a view of strategy that combines commitment to the firm's ambitions with the flexibility to change with circumstances.

An example of this tension between commitment and flexibility would be the situation faced by Western capital-intensive firms seeking to develop their businesses in emerging markets. On the one hand, these firms would work hard to commit resources to a new market, in order to gain first-mover advantages and a

---

[23]Donaldson, G. and J. Lorsch, *Decision Making at the Top*, New York: Harper, 1983.

[24]Barnard, C., *The Functions of the Executive*, Cambridge, MA: Belknap, 1938.

[25]Hickson, D. J., R. J. Butler, D. Cray, G. R. Mallory, and D. C. Wilson, *Top Decisions: Strategic Decision-Making in Organizations*, San Francisco, CA: Jossey-Bass, 1986, pp. 42–54.

[26]Hamel, G. and C. K. Prahalad, *Competing for the Future*, Boston: Harvard School, 1994.

position that will allow the firm to continually prosper once the market develops. On the other hand, the political and economic instability of emerging markets will make firms hesitate before commiting their resources. Firms that handle this tension well, as the telecommunications firm Ameritech has in its investments in Eastern Europe, do so by combining sunk investments in physical capital with risk pooling of capital providers, careful contracting with host nations, and the creation of options for future investments to hedge against current commitments.

For general managers in charge of subunits within the firm, a further tension exists between firm and subunit objectives. A division of labor inside the firm that creates subunits runs the risk that managers will try to maximize subunit performance at the expense of overall firm profitability. For multidivisional firms, the problem is compounded by the delegation of operational authority to divisional managers. This means that for product market decisions, the divisional GM is independent, while still remaining just one component of corporate profit objectives. These tensions can become particularly acute when, as in corporate portfolio strategies, division managers may be called upon to limit the expansion of their own divisions to cross-subsidize the activities of other divisions.[27]

Changing Definitions of Managerial Work

While in many important ways, we think that managers act according to general principles that remain applicable over time, they make decisions in a changing context that we discussed in Chapter 1. Their decisions regarding the definition of the firm and its strategic choices so change the firm and how it operates that the nature of managerial work itself changes. The nature of managerial work is defined by the nature of the firms in which managers work.[28] Since the nature of the firm has changed greatly over the past century, the nature of the GM's job has also changed, no doubt frustrating the efforts of observers who seek to neatly characterize it. Writings about GMs have frequently emphasized the changing nature of managerial work, to the point where the rhetoric of change has become part of a manager's tasks, even when a manager is working in a period of relative stability rather than one of dramatic change.[29]

When managers first became prominent, large vertically and horizontally integrated firms were new and had developed in response to the inability of existing markets to handle the requirements of firms that had to produce and distribute large volume production to a mass market. Under these conditions, the manager was seen as a visible hand that substituted for the market and whose job required much more administration than market coordination.

As firms grew larger and more diverse, however, they became more difficult to administer. Firms responded by introducing the M-form, whose structure included

---

[27]Hrebiniak, L. and W. Joyce, *Implementing Strategy*, New York: MacMillan, 1984.

[28]Leavy, B. and D. Wilson, *Strategy and Leadership*, London, UK: Routledge, 1994.

[29]Eccles, R. and N. Nohria, *Beyond the Hype: Rediscovering the Essence of Management*, Boston: Harvard Business School Press, 1992, chap. 1.

a decentralization of decision making, the introduction of profit-based controls of business unit managers, and a division of labor in decision-making between corporate and divisional managers. These changes made the already difficult problems of coordination across business units and among corporate GMs more salient and introduced market-based decision-making criteria into managers' behavior.

As conditions have changed again in the 1990s, with the global expansion of firms, the general increase in rivalry in many industries, and changes in telecommunications and data processing that have made it possible to communicate more quickly with more people, the tasks of managers have changed further. Christopher Bartlett and Sumantra Ghoshal see these changes in terms of a shift from corporate strategy to corporate purpose.[30] By corporate purpose, Bartlett and Ghoshal mean that managers must increasingly integrate strategy and operations at much lower levels within the firm than had previously been the case. This approach combines managerial roles of value creation, implementation, and facilitation in ways that were less common in the strategy-structure approach to managing the multidivisional firm. Instilling a corporate purpose ensures that lower-level managers, who increasingly work in diverse markets around the globe, can effectively address local market issues and remain linked to corporate objectives. By internalizing corporate purpose in its employees, firms can achieve a degree of integration that would not be possible under more formalized integration approaches.

Changes in business conditions that require adaptation by managers are often limited to particular sectors or geographic areas. In deregulated industries, managers are being forced to obtain market-related skills, as traditional restrictions on entry are eliminated and new rivals emerge. In different geographic areas, political changes are forcing similar adjustments by managers. Changes in Eastern Europe, following the fall of Communism in 1989, provide a good example of this. In these countries, business and governmental infrastructures were obsolete and unsuitable for current economic conditions. This has prompted large-scale experimentation throughout the region, both in the governmental sphere, where formerly state-owned enterprises are being privatized and a commercial and legal infrastructure is being developed, and in the new private sector, where new forms of organization in manufacturing, distribution, and human resources are developing. While there may be aspects of culture and history that affect managerial needs in these emerging markets, such as the bureaucratic culture developed under fifty years of Communism, the problems of management development in these areas are similar in many ways to the general managerial challenges facing Western firms today.

General management roles are also being shaped by the changing demographic profile of the workforce in industrialized nations. The aging of the Baby Boom generation, the increased entry of women into the workforce, and related factors have made it more difficult for firms to employ the incentives and controls that had been effective with managers after World War II. Good managers are

---

[30]Bartlett, C. A. and S. Ghoshal, "Changing the Role of Top Management: Beyond Strategy to Purpose," *Harvard Business Review*, November–December 1994, pp. 79–88.

often turning down promotions, transfers, and increased responsibilities in an effort to balance work and family issues. Work and family issues are requiring firms to get increasingly involved in providing child care and related services if they hope to retain talented managers.[31]

CHAPTER SUMMARY

◆ The general manager (GM) is both a problem solver and a visionary. As a problem solver, the GM defines and manages the boundaries of the firm, sets a competitive strategy, and oversees the firm's internal incentives, culture, and structure. As a visionary, the GM identifies a sustainable position for long-term success.

◆ GMs use both formal and informal means to accomplish objectives. While relying on qualitative analyses as much or more than quantitative analyses, they also rely on formal agendas and information networks.

◆ The GM may play one or all of several roles: entrepreneur, organizer/implementer, contractor, facilitator, competitor, and reevaluator/changer. Tensions arise when these roles require conflicting actions.

◆ GMs have had to change their roles in response to changing technological, regulatory, and competitive conditions.

---

[31]For an excellent discussion of these issues, see Bailyn, L., *Breaking the Mold: Women, Men, and Time in the New Corporate World*, New York: Free Press, 1993.

INDEX